3ds Max® Modeling: Bots, Mechs, and Droids

Jon Weimer

3ds Max® Modeling: Bots, Mechs, and Droids

Jon Weimer

Wordware Publishing, Inc.

Library of Congress Cataloging-in-Publication Data

Weimer, Jon
3ds Max modeling : bots, mechs, and droids / by Jon Weimer.
p. cm.
Includes index.
ISBN 10: 1-59822-044-6
ISBN 13: 978-1-59822-044-5 (pbk., companion DVD)
1. Computer animation. 2. Computer graphics. 3. 3ds max (Computer file).
I. Title.
TR897.7.W4485 2008
006.6'96--dc22

2008002682

1100 Summit Avenue, Suite 102
Plano, Texas 75074

Printed in the United States of America

ISBN 10: 1-59822-044-6
ISBN 13: 978-1-59822-044-5
10 9 8 7 6 5 4 3 2 1
0803

All inquiries for volume purchases of this book should be addressed to Wordware Publishing, Inc., at the above address. Telephone inquiries may be made by calling:

(972) 423-0090

Contents

Preface

Who Should Buy This Book?

Have you wanted to learn how to create 3D models, but were concerned that you lacked the artistic skills or were daunted by looking at a computer interface with hundreds of controls? Perhaps you wanted to learn to model, but were put off by having to wade through a 500-page discussion of the UI before getting down to business. If so, this is the book for you.

From the very first page (well, the first page of the Introduction, anyway), you'll start modeling something you can show your friends. We'll pick up anything you need to know about the UI *when* you need to know it. This book will get you up to speed modeling faster than you ever thought possible! And without having to spend years studying artistic techniques.

Okay, I can see you don't believe me. I have absolutely no artistic skills. None. Fortunately, you don't need them to model in 3D. That's right, I said it out loud! I told you 3D's dirty little secret. All those things you need to know to draw a lifelike image of your Aunt Sally — perspective, balance, shading, etc. — are done *for* you by the program. You don't even need to be able to draw a straight line. Modeling in 3D is more like building something with LEGO bricks than painting, sketching, or modeling with clay. You start with building blocks, called *primitives*, which are a lot like LEGO pieces, and combine them to make your model. If you can build something with LEGOs, you can model in 3D. It really is that simple.

What Can You Expect?

As I said, this is a book designed to take you from not knowing anything about modeling to building a sophisticated model in a short amount of time. This book will not teach you to design the coolest robots ever. If that's what you're looking for, might I suggest two excellent Gnomon Workshop DVDs by LucasFilm's Feng Zhu:

http://www.thegnomonworkshop.com/dvds/fzh01.html
http://www.thegnomonworkshop.com/dvds/fzh02.html

If you're interested in learning more about lighting in Max, I'd suggest Wordware's *3ds Max Lighting* by Nicholas Boughen (1-55622-401-X).

Who Should Not Buy This Book?

If you're the type of person who buys *3ds Max for Dummies*, and then complains on Amazon.com that it didn't have enough advanced modeling techniques, this is *not* the book for you. This book is designed for beginners. Does that mean there's nothing in here for intermediate modelers? No. I try to touch on as many tools as I can. So while you may be an intermediate modeler, you may never have had the need to use a Hose primitive or Soft Selection and you can learn to do that here.

If you are interested in more advanced techniques, here is a list of excellent resources you may find valuable:

Books:

3ds max Lighting by Nicholas Boughen, Wordware Publishing (1-55622-401-X)

Modeling a Character in 3ds max: Second Edition by Paul Steed, Wordware Publishing (1-55622-088-X).

Essential CG Lighting Techniques with 3ds Max by Darren Brooker, Focal Press (978-024052022)

Rendering with mental ray & 3ds Max by Joep van der Steen, Focal Press (978-0240808932)

DVD Training:

Global Illumination: Exteriors by Chris Nichols (www.thegnomonworkshop.com/dvds/cni01.html)

Global Illumination: Interiors by Chris Nichols (www.thegnomonworkshop.com/dvds/cni02.html)

Environment Creation for Production by Tim Jones
(www.thegnomonworkshop.com/dvds/tjo01.html)

Environment Lighting for Production by Tim Jones
(www.thegnomonworkshop.com/dvds/tjo02.html)

Character Modeling for Production by Ian Joyner
(www.thegnomonworkshop.com/dvds/ijo01.html)

Character Texturing for Production by Ian Joyner
(www.thegnomonworkshop.com/dvds/ijo02.html)

Creature Modeling for Production by Laurent Pierlot
(www.thegnomonworkshop.com/dvds/lpi01.html)

Creature Detailing for Production by Laurent Pierlot
(www.thegnomonworkshop.com/dvds/lpi02.html)

Creature Texturing and Rendering for Production by Laurent Pierlot
(www.thegnomonworkshop.com/dvds/lpi03.html)

Matte Painting Production Techniques by Chris Stoski
(www.thegnomonworkshop.com/dvds/cst01.html)

3D Matte Painting and Camera Mapping by Chris Stoski
(www.thegnomonworkshop.com/dvds/cst02.html)

Set Extension and Lighting Effects by Chris Stoski
(www.thegnomonworkshop.com/dvds/cst03.html)

Using This Book

From the very first page, you'll hit the ground running by building your first model. We are not going to spend a lot of time explaining what every button and drop-down list does. As we go along, I will explain how to use each of the relevant controls. I'll also provide you with the exact values that I'm using so you will get results similar, if not exactly the same, to mine.

While this book may seem dauntingly long, it's because I'm taking pains not to skip any steps. When I was learning 3D, I became very frustrated by books and videos that either skipped steps or made model modifications between lessons. This does not happen here at the risk of going a bit long. To help with the length, I've broken the modeling down by days. You are not limited to this. If you want to sit down and do an entire model in one sitting, by all means go ahead.

I've also provided some unique tips and notes boxes to help you learn.

Don't Forget: The Don't Forget box reminds you of things you need to remember to do.

Fire Drill: Fire Drills guide you to avoid making common mistakes.

FYI: FYI boxes give you essential background information in as concise a way as possible. In many instances, FYI boxes explain why we're doing certain things when it's not obvious.

Message: Message boxes, though rare, provide you additional resources and information you might find valuable or to help you to improve your skills.

Urgent: Urgent boxes apprise you of important steps that you should not skip! Otherwise, you may make a serious mistake or damage your model.

What's on the DVD?

And finally, the companion DVD contains includes all the images in the book in full color, a PDF version of a chapter on creating an android, and video tutorials totaling 10 hours. The files are organized in the following folders:

- Chapter 4 — A PDF of Chapter 4, "Maxi the Android," and reference images used to create the android
- Images — Full-color versions of all the images in the book, compressed and organized by chapter
- Materials — Three videos showing how to create and work with materials, along with support files
- MATRIX — A tutorial from 3-d Palace demonstrating the modeling and animation of the devastating sentinel bots from the film *The Matrix*
- max script — A MAXScript file used in Chapter 3 to paint rivets on armor

The author may be contacted at agentprovo@everestkc.net.

What's Different in 3ds Max 2008?

If I were buying this book, the first thing I would want to know, after how much it costs, is whether or not it is up-to-date with the latest version. The answer is yes. You can use this book to learn modeling using 3ds Max 6 through 2008. What follows is a description of what is new in modeling* in 3ds Max 2008 and how that affects this book. Fortunately, there were only minor changes in the modeling tools between versions 8 and 2008.

Preview of SubObject Selection

This new feature is a switch contained in a new rollout in the Selection panel. This allows you to preview a selection at the subobject level. When SubObject is turned on, the preview selection highlights whatever subobject the cursor is over. This makes 3ds Max selection work like Cinema 4D's. Also, like Cinema 4D's Live Selection, you can "paint" a selection while holding down the Control key. While this is a huge benefit over previous versions of Max, it is just a selection aid and will not change any of the techniques shown in this book.

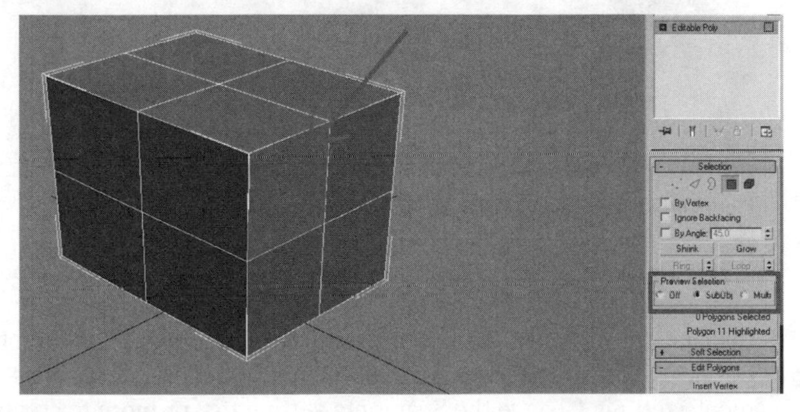

Figure N-1

* This material is taken from the New Features section of 3ds Max 2008's Reference.

Press/Release Shortcut

This allows you to "hot swap" between two editing functions. For example, suppose you are using the Bevel tool. To switch to Extrude, you would press the Shift+E keyboard shortcut. You will be able to extrude as long as you press and hold Shift+E. Once you release the keys, you return to the Bevel tool. While some may find this a time-saver, and while it can be used with the techniques shown in this book, it will not be used in the text.

Chamfer Edge Segments

Chamfering is a term from woodworking that refers to beveling an edge. Specifically, if two surfaces are at right angles, chamfering will flatten the edge to 45 degrees. In contrast, *filleting* rounds corners.

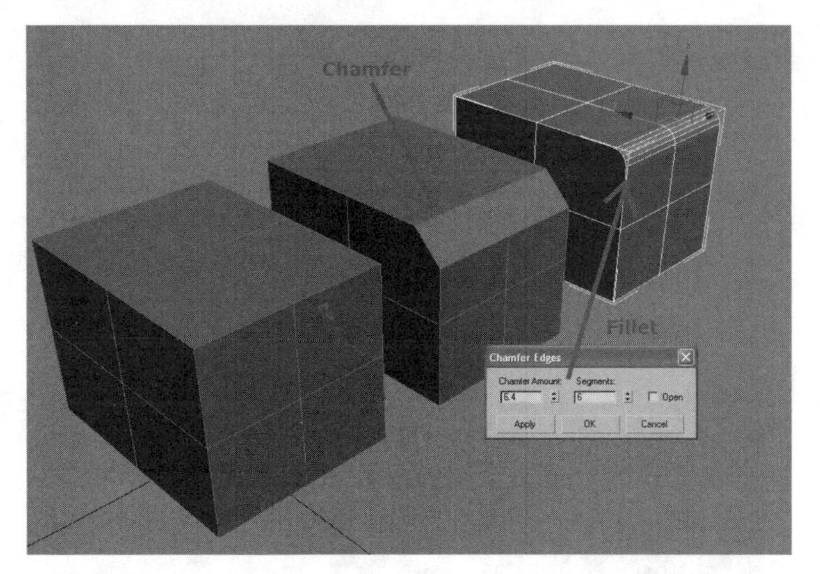

Figure N-2

When you used the Chamfer tool in previous versions of Max, you could only adjust the Chamfer Amount setting, which affected the severity of the chamfering angle. If you wanted to round an edge (fillet), you had to perform successive chamfers. In 2008, the Chamfer tool now has a Segments setting. Change the Segments setting to 2 or more to create a fillet; the more segments you add, the smoother the rounding.

Since we do a fair amount of chamfering in this book, this will be the most significant difference. The way this impacts you, the reader, is when we get to a section in which we're rounding edges using a series of chamfers, you can use this approach instead. However, adding segments using Chamfer Edges creates segments that are equally spaced. Often, when we do a successive chamfer in the book, we'll be using differing chamfer amounts each time, so if you want your model to look *exactly* like the examples, you won't be able to make use of this Segments setting anyway, since my model will *not* have equally spaced segments.

SubObject Normal Constraint

SubObject Normal Constraint has been added to the Edit Geometry rollout. This is similar to Edge Constraint. Edge Constraint limits a subobject's (e.g., vertex, polygon, edge) transformations (e.g., move, scale, rotate) to the boundaries of a particular edge. SubObject Normal limits each subobject's transformations to its normal, or the average of its normals. In most cases, this causes subobjects to move perpendicular to the surface. I do not use Edge Constraint or Face Constraint in this book, so this change is not relevant.

Working Pivot

Use Working Pivot allows you to use a working pivot to make quick transforms without having to change the main pivot. Although this is a very useful addition to Max and greatly accelerates the workflow for *advanced* users, it does not significantly impact the content of this book.

Acknowledgments

No book of any size is the creation of just one person, just as it takes hundreds of dedicated people to build a car or an airplane. I would like to thank the following people for their contributions, whether direct or indirect, in the completion of this book.

- Thanks to Cris Robson of 3D Palace and Jon Bell for teaching me everything I know about 3ds Max modeling.
- Thanks to the best publishing team an author could ask for: Beth Kohler, Alan McCuller, Martha McCuller, and Tim McEvoy.
- Thanks to my wife, Anna, for her love and support.

Last, but definitely not least, thanks to Steve McPherson, my partner in crime and the best illustrator and LightWave artist I know.

This is the bot we create in this chapter, complete with texture and lighting.

Introduction to Max

Welcome to the wonderful world of modeling in Max. This book teaches you modeling; we won't be touching on animation, materials, or lighting. If you want a more well-rounded treatment, I suggest you pick up a copy of *Essential 3ds Max 2008* by Sean McBride (ISBN 1-59822-050-0), available from Wordware.

In this book, I'm going to teach you to model the best way you can: by modeling. We're not going to spend any time explaining the intimate details of the user interface; we'll learn what we need when we need it. One of the biggest challenges when learning a 3D package is to not be overwhelmed by the huge number of functions and features.

That said, there are just a few things that you will need to know to start working. That's what this chapter is for. If you already know the basics, like what a primitive is and how to navigate the user interface, you're welcome to skip ahead to Chapter 1. However, we will be building a cool bot in this chapter and you might miss something special. You never know. When you're done with this chapter, you'll know every tool you need to model anything. All those other tools and widgets, once you learn them, are time-savers and icing on the cake.

FYI: The product we now know as 3ds Max by Autodesk, Inc. has gone through a number of release versions and name changes over the years, and has also been titled 3D Studio MAX and 3ds max. The current release is 3ds Max 2008.

Primitives and Extended Primitives

Open 3ds Max. If you're using the default UI setup, your screen should look like this:

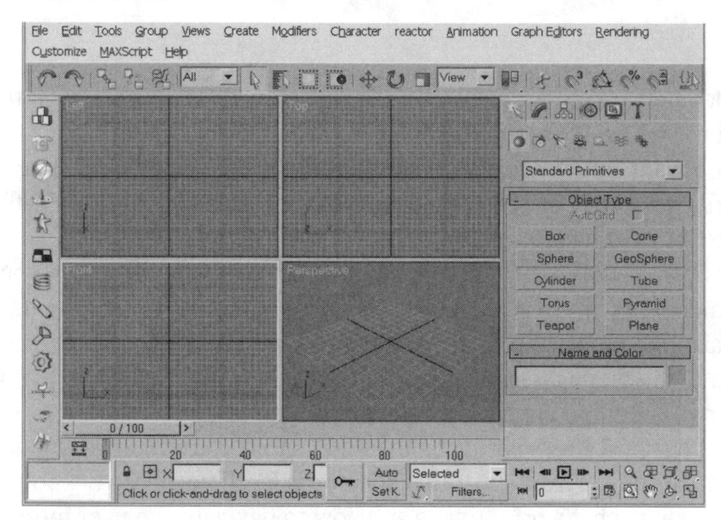

Figure I-1: Default UI layout

FYI: Depending on your screen resolution settings, the toolbars and other UI controls may be located slightly differently.

Don't worry if you have additional toolbars showing. The only features you *need* for the exercises in this chapter are the main toolbar and the command panel (as shown in Figure I-1). If your UI does not show the command panel or the main toolbar, not to worry. Pull down the **Customize** menu, select **Show UI**, and then check both **Show Command Panel** and **Show Main Toolbar**, as shown in Figure I-2.

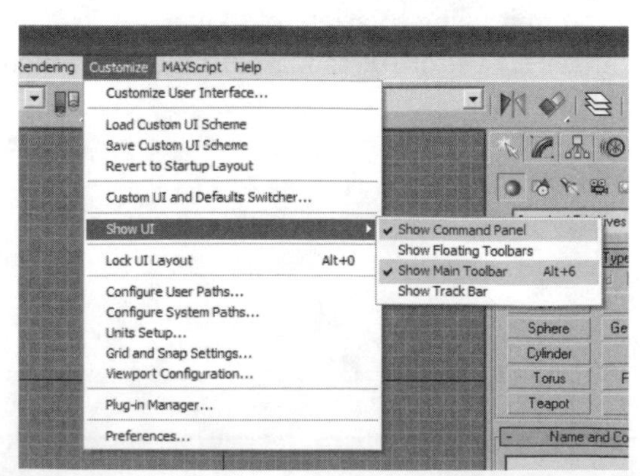

Figure I-2: Configuring your UI layout

Click on the Perspective viewport and hit the Maximize Viewport toggle button, which is the bottommost icon on the right side of your screen. Alternatively, you can press Alt+W to toggle between maximizing your view and displaying the four orthogonal views.

Figure I-3: Maximize Viewport toggle

Standard Primitives

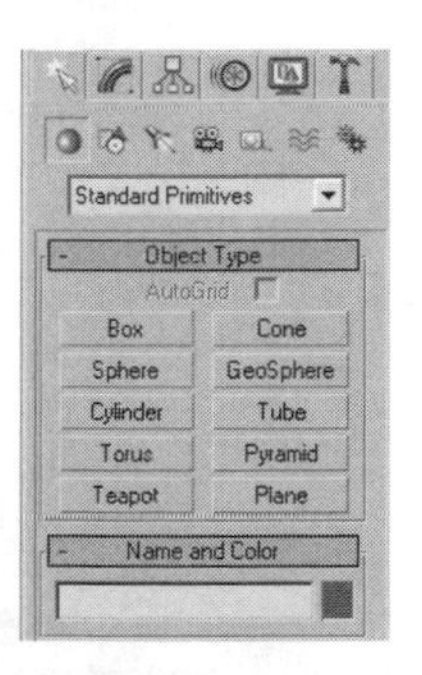

Figure I-4: The Create panel

Look on the right side of the screen. This is the command panel. We'll be spending a lot of time here. The command panel is composed of subpanels, which are accessible by clicking the tabs at the top of the panel. The default tab (a white arrow pointing to a white asterisk) is the one at the upper left. This is the Create panel, and this is where all projects start.

At the top of the Create panel is a drop-down list that displays the words Standard Primitives. *Primitives* are basic 3D computer graphics (CG) forms. CG modeling in 3D is more akin to sculpture than drawing or sketching. Just as a sculptor starts with a block of stone or clay and sculpts a form from it, 3D modeling starts with a primitive and the modeler sculpts an object from it using a variety of tools.

Max provides you with a list of 10 standard primitives, which are listed in the rollout labeled Object Type. Ninety-nine percent of the time, you will only use four of these primitives: box, sphere, cylinder, and torus.

Left-click* on the **Box** button. Click and hold the left mouse button while dragging anywhere in the Perspective view. When you have a

* From here on out, I will use the term "click" to mean clicking the left mouse button. When I want you to use the right or middle mouse buttons, I will specifically say so.

rectangle shape and size you like, release the mouse button and drag up to finish creating a 3D box. Left-click again to release the tool. Voilà! You've created your first 3D object.

Do the same thing for each of the primitives. Click on a button and drag in the viewport to create the primitive. Play around a little. I'll wait.

Your screen should now be a cluttered mess like this:

Figure 1-5: Standard primitives

FYI: You may find that your primitives are all different colors. Max automatically assigns colors to primitives unless you specifically tell it not to.

To disable automatic color generation, or to change the color of a particular primitive, click the color swatch in the rollout labeled Name and Color on the Create panel. This opens the Object Color palette. To change an object's color, either click one of the swatches and click OK or click the Add Custom Colors button to open a standard color picker. To avoid having Max assign random colors, uncheck Assign Random Colors and all primitives drawn will be the color shown in the current color swatch. I personally like a lot of color because it allows me to distinguish the different parts of my model, so I leave Assign Random Colors selected.

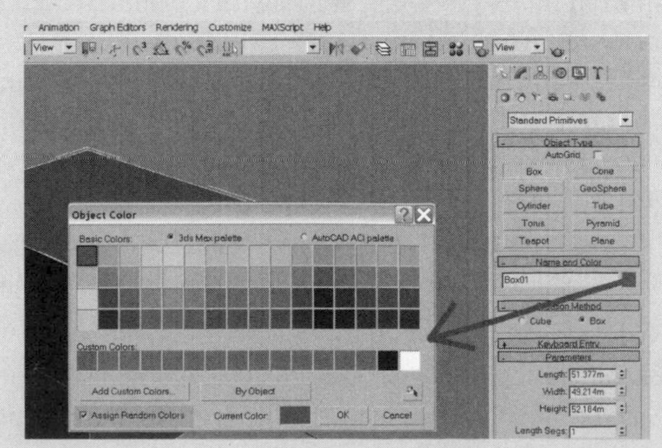

Figure 1-6

Let's clean up a bit. Click the **Select Object** tool, which is the white arrow on the main toolbar (alternatively, you can select this tool by hitting the **Q** key). Click every object except the box to select them and press the **Delete** key. That should leave you with just the box. Now click the box (*do not* hit Delete).

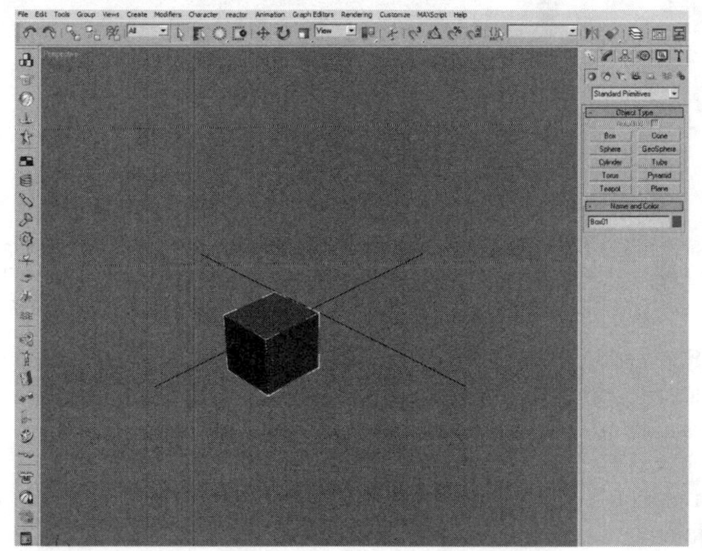

Figure I-7

That box looks far away. Press the **Z** key. That will zoom and frame the box in the current view.

Figure I-8: Zoomed and framed

Notice the white lines at each corner. This shows you a box primitive is made up of six faces (three you can see and three that you can't). The **F3** key toggles your view between shaded and wireframe modes. Click on the **Arc Rotate** button at the bottom-right corner of the screen so you can move the mouse to rotate around the object and verify that the box is indeed composed of six faces.

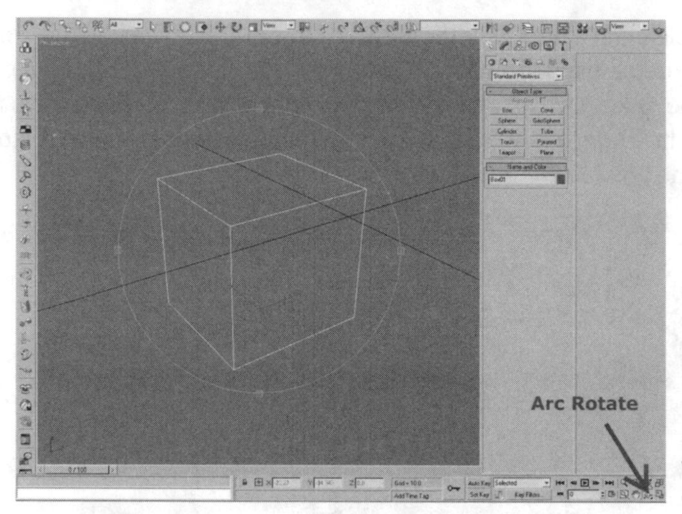

Figure I-9: Wireframe mode and Arc Rotate

Hit **F3** to return to shaded mode. Toggling between wireframe and shaded modes is something that you'll be doing frequently.

Look at the tabs on the command panel. The second tab's icon looks like a blue rainbow surrounded by dotted lines. This is the Modify panel and the icon, I guess, is supposed to represent a primitive that has been modified using a Bend modifier (we'll talk about that in a later chapter). Click on the Modify panel tab.

Figure I-10: Modify panel

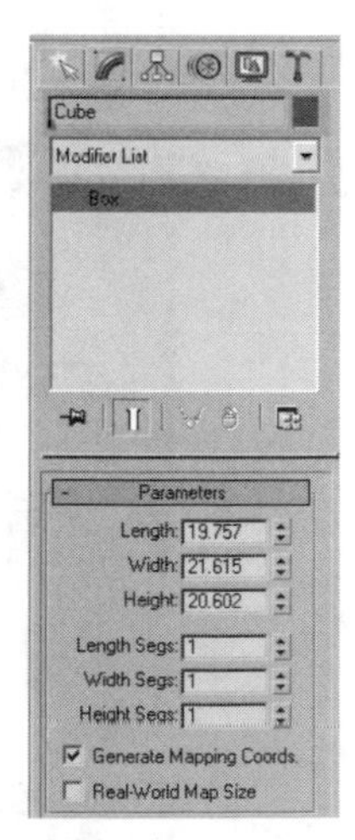

Figure I-11: Changing an object's name

The Modify panel is where you can very accurately adjust various aspects of an object, such as its name, dimensions, and how many faces it has. To change the object's name, click in the field containing the name (Box01), highlight **Box01** (or whatever Max has called yours), and type **Cube**. It's as easy as that! Now change it back to **Box01**; we don't actually need to change its name right now.

In the rollout labeled Parameters, you will see three fields representing the dimensions of the cube. Notice that they have up and down arrow buttons next to them. These are called *spinners*, meaning you can press the up arrow to increase the value in the field or press the down arrow to decrease the value. Personally, I prefer to type in my own values, which you can do as well. Click in the Length, Width, and Height fields and change them to match the values in Figure I-12.

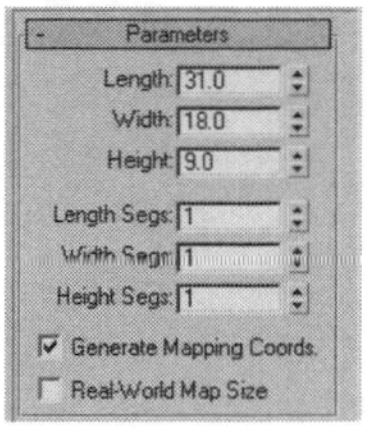

Figure I-12

Throughout this book, I'll give you the exact values I'm using, so you can get results close to mine. If you're a free spirit, or simply have problems with authority, that's fine too; enter whatever values you like. But, if you're like me, when you're learning a new skill you want to stick as close to the examples as possible.

Look below the object dimensions and you'll see three more fields: Length Segs, Width Segs, and Height Segs. Think of a segment as a line or edge. Adding segments will add faces to your cube. Currently, your cube has six faces. Just as an experiment, change the segment settings to match Figure I-13.

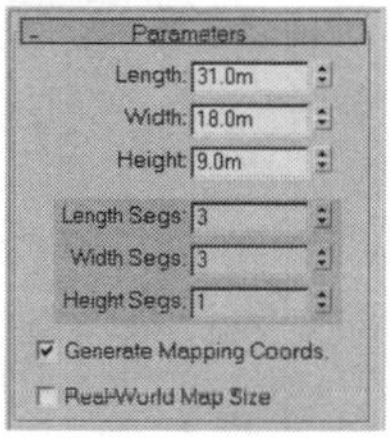

Figure I-13

What the -- ? Nothing happened! If your cube didn't appear to change, trust me ... It did. In order to see the change, you have to have edged faces mode turned on. Hit **F4**.

Figure I-14: Edged faces mode

You should now see the new faces. If you saw the faces, and now you don't, just hit F4 again. Most "F" keys in Max work as toggles.

FYI: Like in most other programs, the function keys in Max allow you to quickly access commands. The most frequently used keys are F3 to toggle wireframe and shaded modes, F4 to show edges, and F9 to do a quick render of your object.

As you can see from Figure I-14, adding segments in the Modify panel subdivided our original six faces. Again, this is something we will be doing a lot of.

Editable Polygons

Primitives are aptly named because you can't do anything with them other than add segments and change their dimensions. In order to proceed further in the modeling process, you have to convert the primitive into a form that can be edited: an *Editable Polygon*.

To convert an object to an Editable Polygon, right-click on the object, choose **Convert To**, and select **Convert to Editable Poly**.

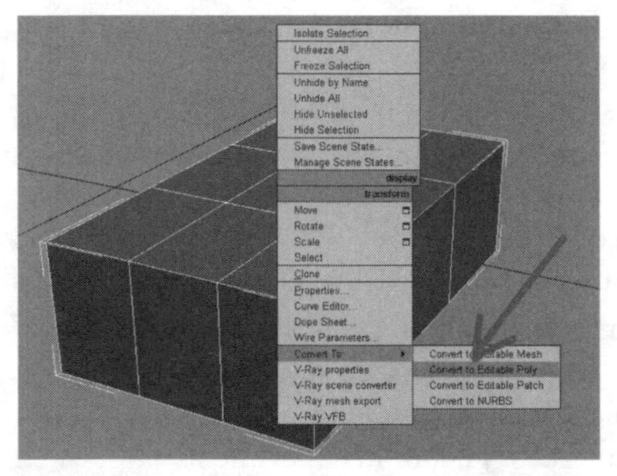

Figure I-15: Convert to an Editable Polygon

Nothing much seems to have changed, but if you look to the right you'll see that the controls on the Modify panel have changed. Not only is there a brand new set of selection tools available to you, but you now have a set of editing or modeling tools you can use to sculpt the object.

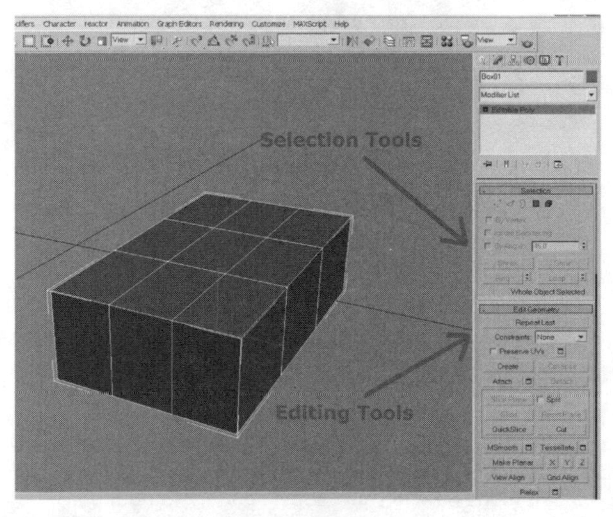

Figure I-16: The Modify panel has more tools when an Editable Polygon is selected.

Once you convert an object to an Editable Polygon, the faces of the object are composed of four *vertices* (or points). Two vertices, when connected, create an *edge*. Four connected edges create a *face*. Editable objects are created by faces.

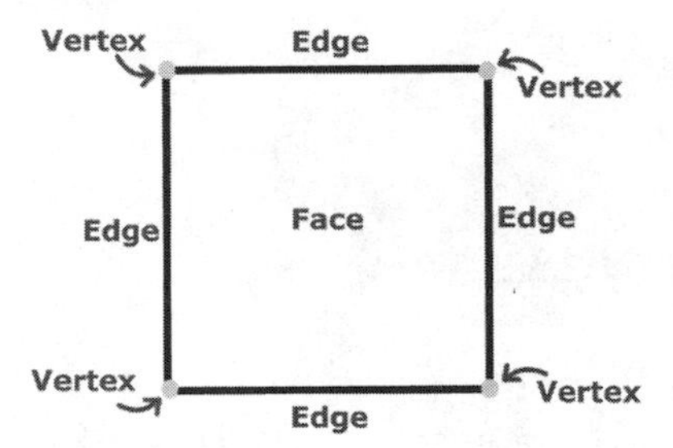

Figure I-17: Editable Polygon structure

3D modeling is nothing more than moving edges, faces, and vertices to form new shapes.

Day 1: Building a Simple Bot

Okay, using the same box we've been practicing on, we're now going to create a bot similar to the B9 from the old TV show *Lost in Space*. To make it easy to follow along, I'm dividing the material into discrete steps (so you can stop to take a break when necessary or grab a frosty beverage of your choice :-)).

1. In the Selection rollout of the Modify panel, click the **Edge** selection mode button, then hit the **F3** key to switch to wireframe mode (to better see what you're doing). Now hold down the **Ctrl** key and click on the top three edges on the front and back of the object.

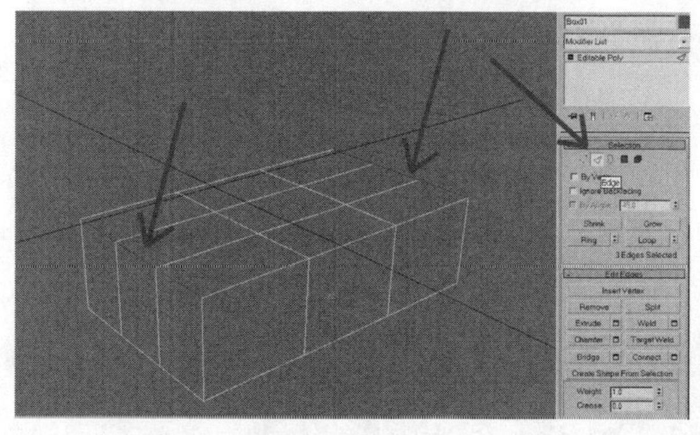

Figure I-18: Select edges

2. In the Edit Edges rollout, click the **Chamfer Settings** button (the square button to the right of the Chamfer button). Enter **5.0** for the Chamfer Amount and then click **OK**.

FYI: Chamfer, like Loft and Lathe, is a function that takes its name from woodworking. To chamfer means to cut off a corner or edge to create a bevel. In Max, you can chamfer vertices, polygons, and edges.

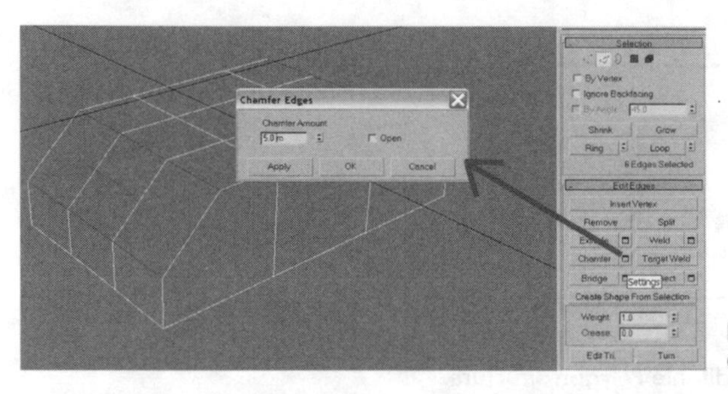

Figure I-19: Chamfer settings

2008 Version! To the frustration of modelers, nearly all the changes in the 2008 version of Max are changes in workflow compatibility with other Autodesk products. There are very few changes to the actual modeling tools, and those changes are just tweaks. Chamfer is a good example. In the 2008 version, the Chamfer function now has a spinner that allows you to enter multiple edges and saves you from having to do multiple chamfers to round an edge.

FYI: There are two ways to use a given tool. You can either click the tool button or click the Settings button to its right. If you click the tool button, you then click and hold the left mouse button while dragging the mouse to use the tool, making changes by eye. Clicking the Settings button opens a dialog box where you can enter an exact value. Many modelers who are artists prefer to click the tool button and use the mouse to manually sculpt the object. I prefer entering exact values with the Settings button. For the purposes of this book, I'll use the Settings button so you can more easily follow along.

FYI: A word about polygons. An ideal polygon has four edges, created by four linked vertices. Sometimes, as happened when we chamfered, you can end up with a polygon that has more than four sides. This can cause you trouble later, such as when you try to use smoothing. It's good practice to turn polygons with more or less than four sides into four-sided polygons.

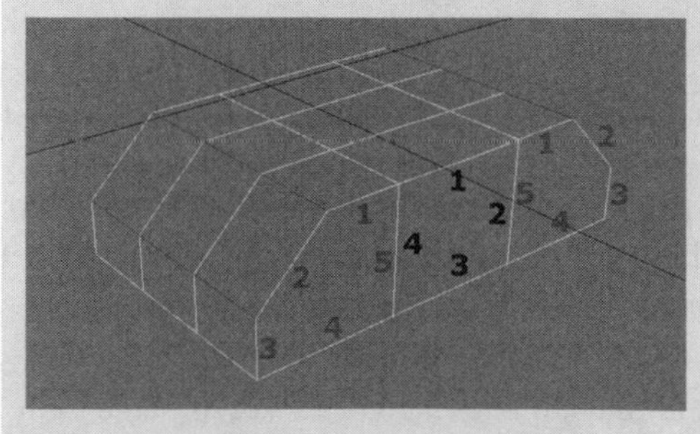

Figure I-20: Four-sided vs. five-sided polygons

3. Hit the **L** key to switch to the Left viewport, hit the **Z** key to zoom and frame the object, and then click the **Edge** selection mode button to turn off the tool.

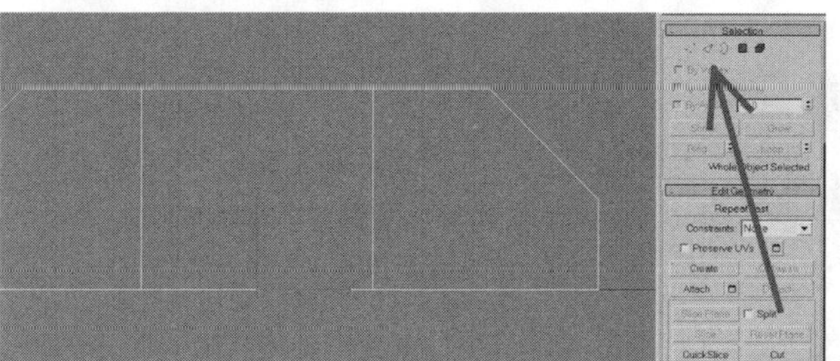

Figure I-21: Turn off edge selection

4. Click the **Polygon** selection mode button and then hold down the left mouse button and marquee-select the front faces of the model.

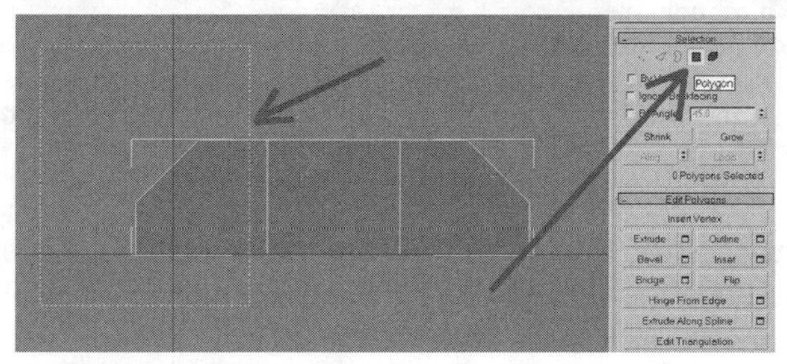

Figure I-22: Select the front faces

5. The polygons turn red to indicate they've been selected. In the Edit Geometry rollout, click the **Slice Plane** button. The slice plane appears on the screen as a yellow line. Currently, however, it is facing the wrong direction. Rather than being horizontal, it should be vertical.

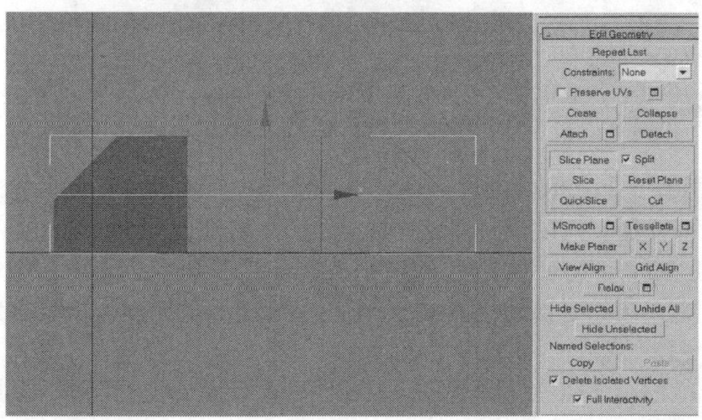

Figure I-23: Using Slice Plane

FYI: The Slice Plane tool uses a plane (a two-dimensional rectangle) to create a perfectly straight cut through all the faces it intersects. We'll be using it to fix the five-sided polygon problem.

6. Hit the **E** key to activate the Select and Rotate tool (the gizmo shows as multicolored concentric circles that appear at the pivot point of an object or tool).

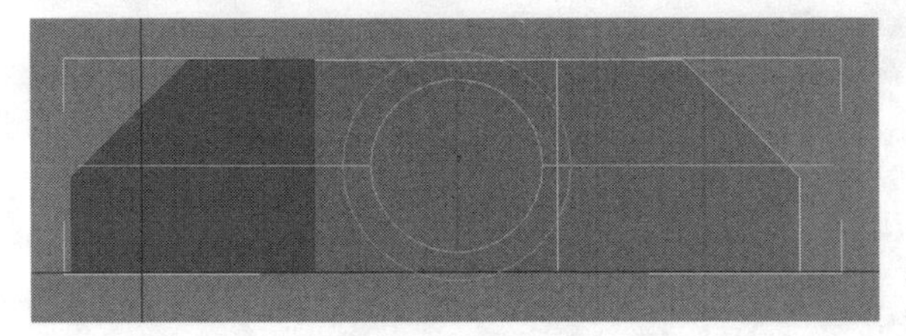

Figure I-24: Select and Rotate tool

FYI: Gizmo? Yeah, it's a pretty dumb name. Gizmo is Max's generic term for a manipulator. The gizmo's shape tells you what type of manipulation it does. Circles mean rotate, crossed arrows mean move, and arrows connected by a triangle mean scale (i.e., resize).

The manipulate tools (select, scale, and rotate) have two modes like the modeling tools. You can select them and then click and hold the left mouse key while moving the mouse. Or you can right-click on the button on the main toolbar to open a dialog box for entering exact values.

7. Right-click the **Select and Rotate** tool to open the dialog box and enter **90** in the Offset Screen Z field to rotate the slice plane 90 degrees on the Z axis.

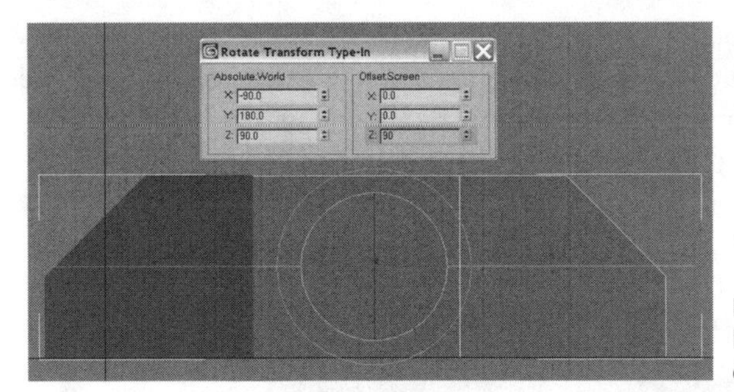

Figure I-25: Rotate Transform dialog box

8. Hit the **W** key to activate the Select and Move tool (hereafter referred to as the Move tool). Click and drag the mouse to move the red X axis arrow to the left (to move the slice plane in the X axis only), until the slice plane is positioned as shown in the following figure.

Figure I-26

9. As you might guess from looking at Figure I-26, strategically placing a cut here will resolve our five-edged polygon problem. Well… at least in the front. Click the **Slice** button to slice the polygons beneath the slice plane.

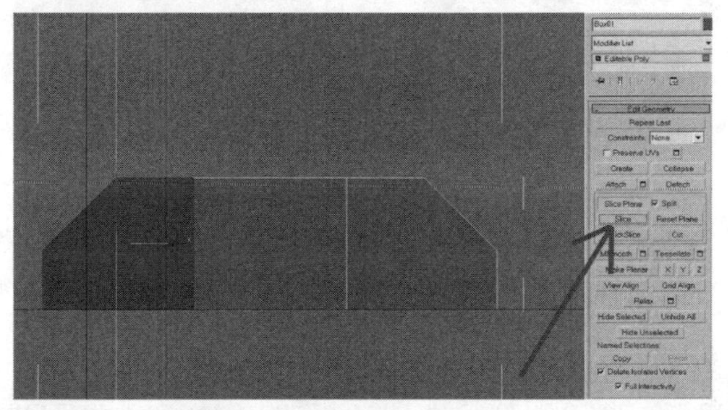

Figure I-27

10. Click the **Slice Plane** button again to turn it off and then marquee-select the matching polygons in the rear. Note that the front faces have been cut, turning the five-sided and four-sided polygons into two four-sided polygons.

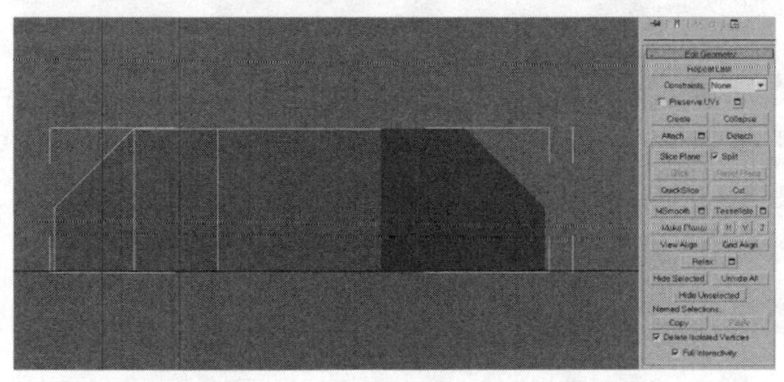

Figure I-28

11. Click the **Slice Plane** button to reactivate it, hit the **W** key to activate the Move tool, drag it in the X axis to position it as shown in Figure I-29, then click the **Slice** button. Click the **Slice Plane** button again to turn it off.

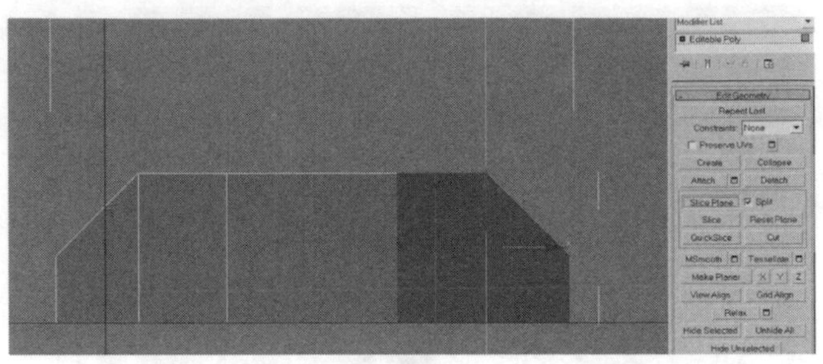
Figure I-29

12. Hit the **Q** key to activate the Selection tool. Click anywhere in the gray area, except on the object, to deselect the polygons.

Figure I-30

Fire Drill: You may have solved the five-edged polygon, but possibly created another problem for yourself. Unless the slice plane is *exactly* positioned over the top vertices, the slice may create a row of polygons very close to the top row. So close it's hard to see. This extra row will create a sixth face. So it's good practice when doing this sort of operation to use the Weld tool to weld any errant vertices together. If there are no errant vertices, the Weld tool won't do anything. However, if you have accidentally made some extra vertices, the Weld tool will fix it.

13. Marquee-select the top-left vertices.

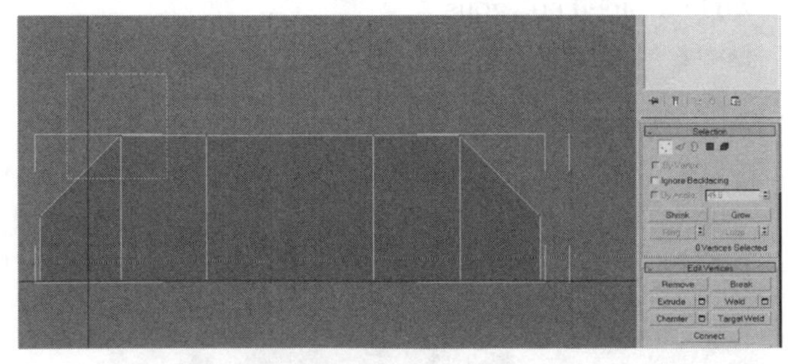
Figure I-31

14. Hold down the **Ctrl** key and marquee-select the top-right vertices.

Figure I-32

15. Click the **Weld Settings** button and set the Weld Threshold to **0.01**. If there aren't any overlapping vertices, the Before and After numbers will be equal. Since there should be three edges on the front (six vertices) and three edges on the back (six vertices), if the slice plane has created new vertices that number should be double, or 12. This means the After value should be 12 less than the Before value (meaning that 12 vertices will be welded together).

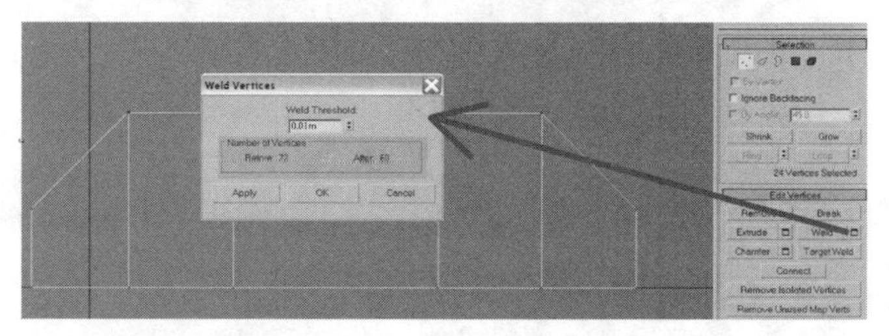

Figure I-33: Weld vertices

16. Click **OK** to weld the vertices. You've solved the five-edged polygon problem.

17. Hit the **F** key to go to the Front view and hit the **F3** key to toggle from wireframe to shaded. If the edges aren't showing, hit the **F4** key to show the edges.

18. Click the **Polygon** selection mode button and marquee-select the leftmost polygons. Then, holding down the **Ctrl** key, marquee-select the rightmost polygons.

Figure I-34

Figure I-35

19. Hit the **P** key to switch to Perspective view. Click the **Arc Subobject Rotate** tool, then click and hold the mouse and move the mouse to orbit the view around the model until you get an approximation of the view shown in Figure I-36.

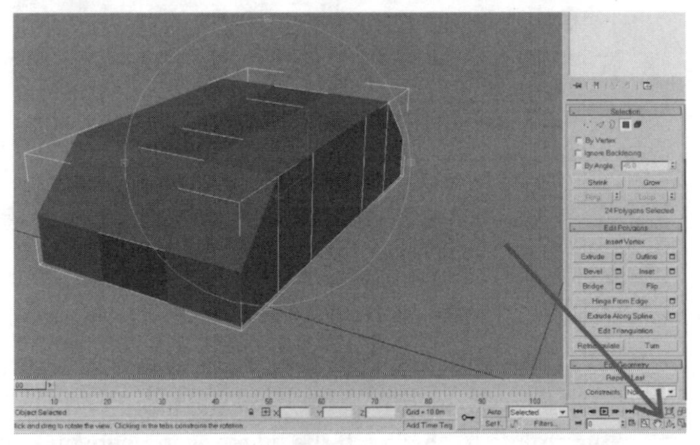

Figure I-36

FYI: There are three flavors to the Arc Rotate tool: Arc Rotate (top), Arc Rotate Selected (middle), and Arc Subobject Rotate (bottom). Arc Rotate rotates the view around an imaginary center of *all* the objects in the scene. Arc Rotate Selected, as its name implies, rotates around the selected object. Arc Subobject Rotate, the method we'll use most often, rotates the view around the selected subobject (vertex, edge, polygon).

FYI: Introducing: Bevel, the wonder tool! The Inset tool takes existing faces and creates a smaller set of faces within them. The Extrude tool takes existing faces and grows them either outward or inward, depending on the Height value. Bevel combines both tools into one, making Inset and Extrude all but unnecessary. It has three settings: Type, Height, and Outline. Setting the Height and the Outline allows you to inset (or outset) and extrude simultaneously. Only want to extrude? No problem! Set the Outline amount to 0, then set the Height, and it works like Extrude. Only want to inset (or outset)? Set Height to 0 and enter a positive number for Outline amount to outset, or a negative number to inset.

20. Click the **Bevel Settings** button and enter the values you see in the following tables:

Type	Height	Outline	Apply/OK
Group	0	–1	Apply

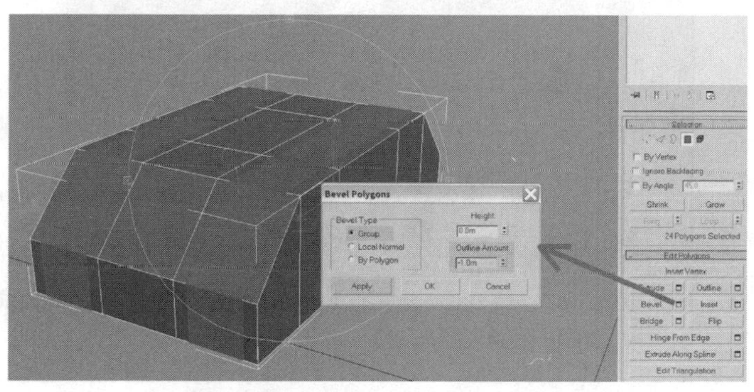

Figure I-37

Type	Height	Outline	Apply/OK
Local Normal	–0.6	0	OK

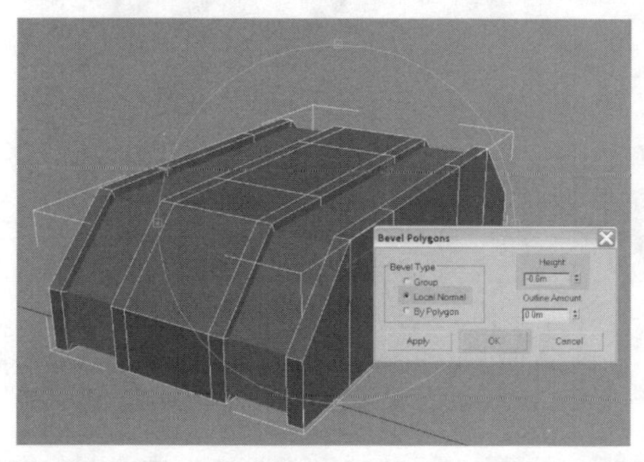

Figure I-38

FYI: Why switch Bevel Type from Group to Local Normal? Local Normal refers to the direction a face is pointing. When Group is used, all the polygons are moved or scaled in the same direction. When Local Normal is used, each polygon is moved in the direction it's facing.

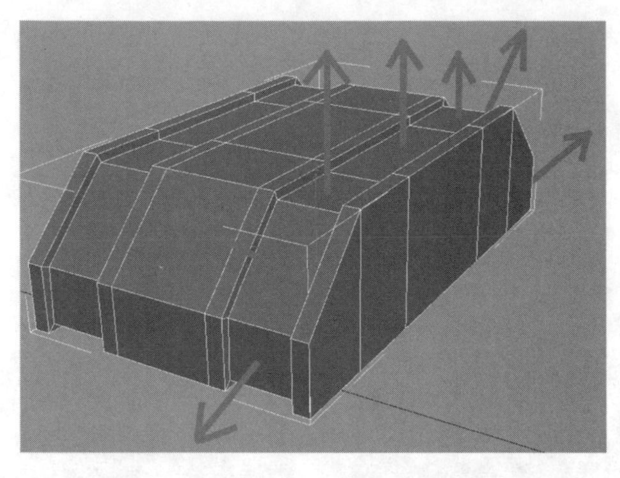

Figure I-39: Local normals

21. Open the Create panel, select **Box**, check **AutoGrid**, and create a box with these settings:

Length	Width	Height	Length/Width/Height Segs
1.4	3.7	0.5	7/7/1

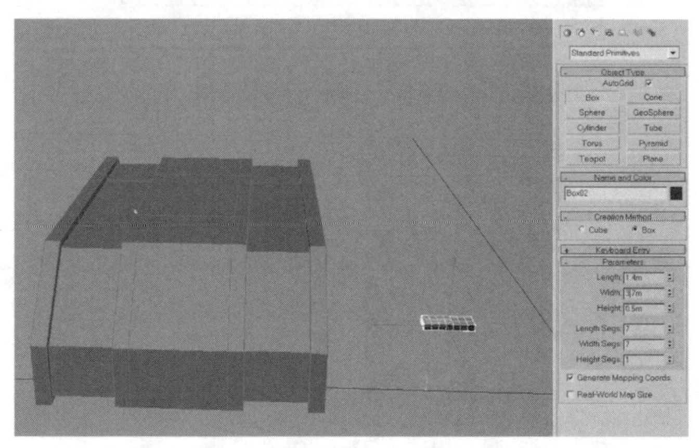

Figure I-40

22. Let's make some tracks! Hit the **Z** key to zoom and frame the box you made, then right-click and choose **Convert To > Convert to Editable Poly**.

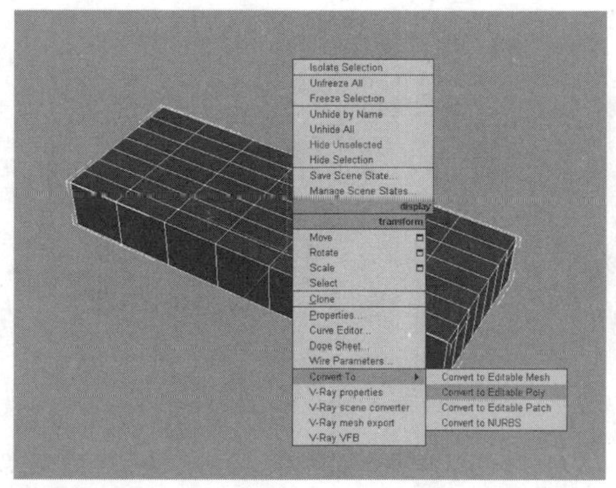

Figure I-41

23. Select the four polygons shown below and then click the **Bevel Settings** button. Apply these settings:

Type	Height	Outline	Apply/OK
Group	0.65	–0.2	OK

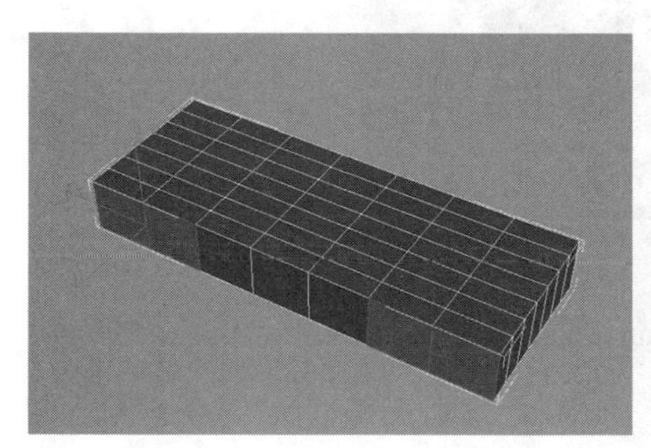

Figure I-42

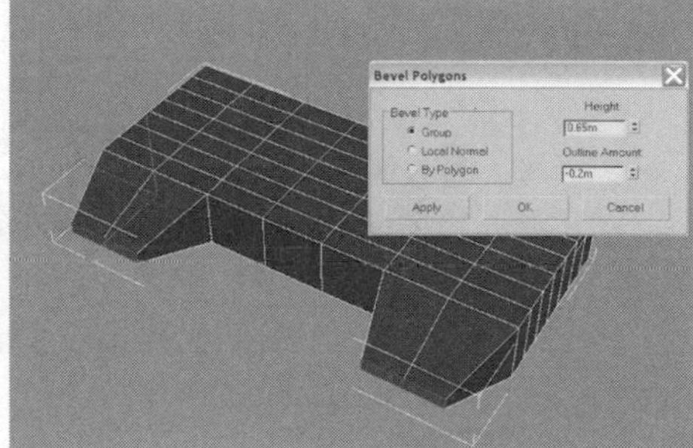

Figure I-43

24. Click the **Arc Subobject Rotate** tool (bottom right) and rotate around the back of the box. Select the three polygons shown in Figure I-44, and apply these settings:

Type	Height	Outline	Apply/OK
Group	0.65	–0.2	OK

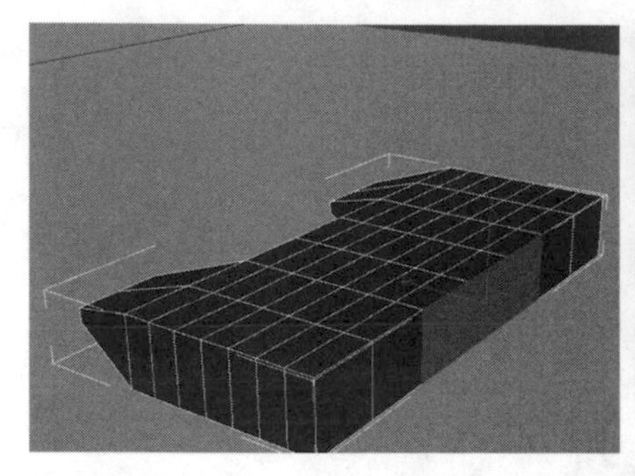

Figure I-44

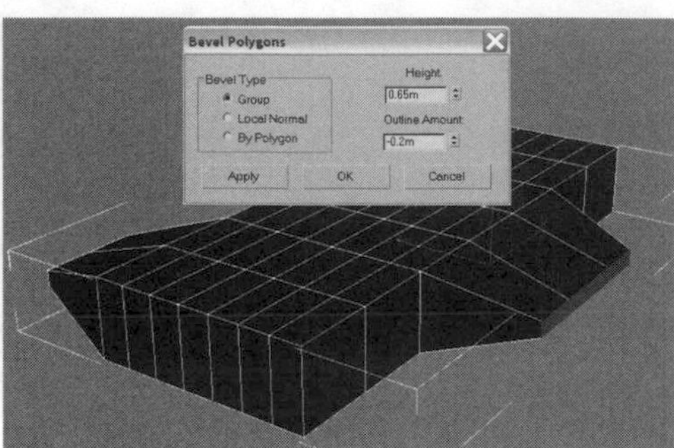

Figure I-45

25. To make the tread on the track segment, select the polygons shown highlighted below on the top of the track segment (nothing special about the pattern, so feel free to use your own).

Figure I-46

26. Click the **Bevel Settings** button and do two bevels with the following settings:

Type	Height	Outline	Apply/OK
Group	0.0	–0.04	Apply
Group	0.05	–0.02	OK

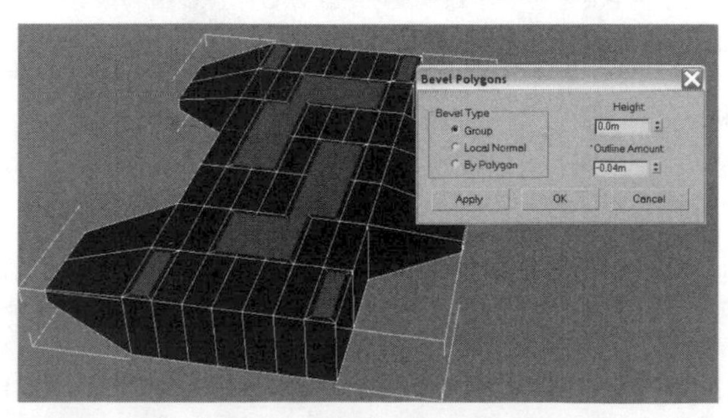

Figure I-47

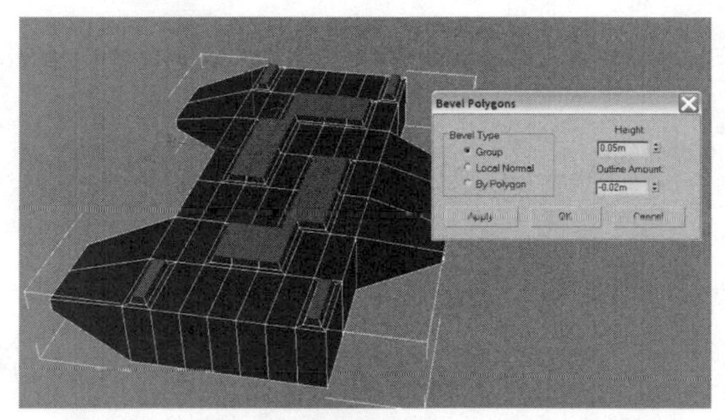

Figure I-48

27. Click the **Polygon** selection mode button again to turn it off, select the body, click the **Edge** selection mode button, select one of the edges inside the recessed area, and then click the **Loop** button. (Note: This is easier to do if you toggle wireframe (**F3**).)

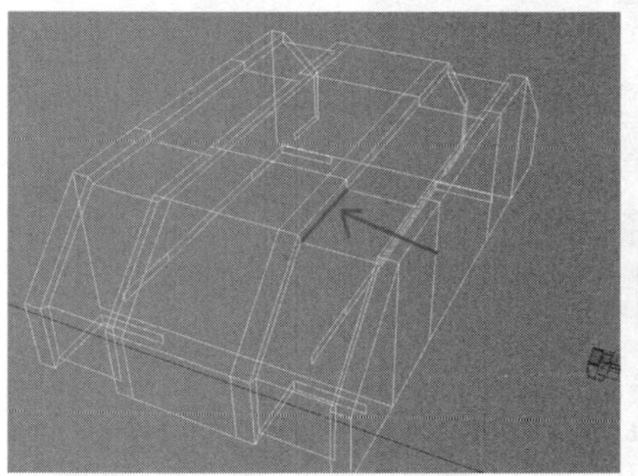

Figure I-49

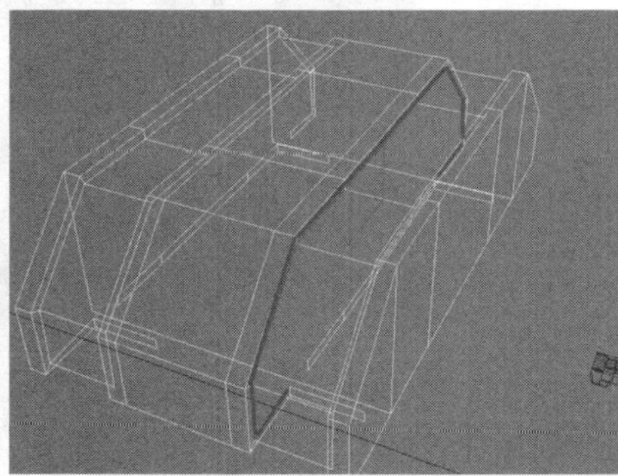

Figure I-50

28. In the Edit Edges rollout, click the **Create Shape From Selection** button, type **track** for the object's Name, click **Linear**, and then click **OK**.

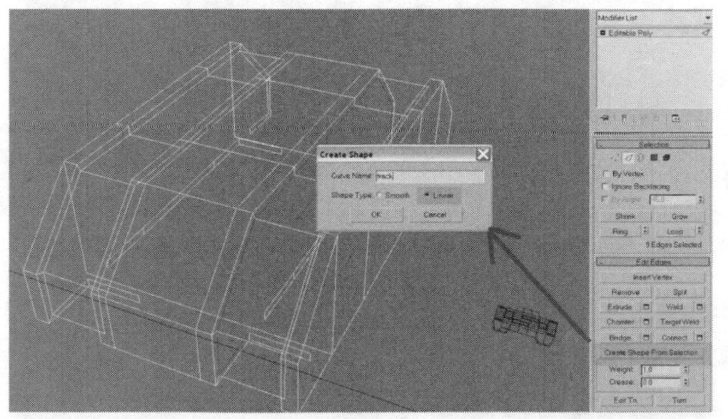

Figure I-51

FYI: Create Shape From Selection is one of the most deceptively powerful tools in your Max arsenal. It will take any selection and turn it into a spline, or path. The spline itself is not renderable (unless you specifically tell Max to render it, which we'll do in a later chapter). But it can be very handy in creating a path for other geometry to follow. In this case, the spline will form the basis for our tank track.

29. If you haven't done so yet, select the track object you made in steps 22-26, and rename it **tread** by typing in the field at the top of the command panel, as shown in Figure I-52.

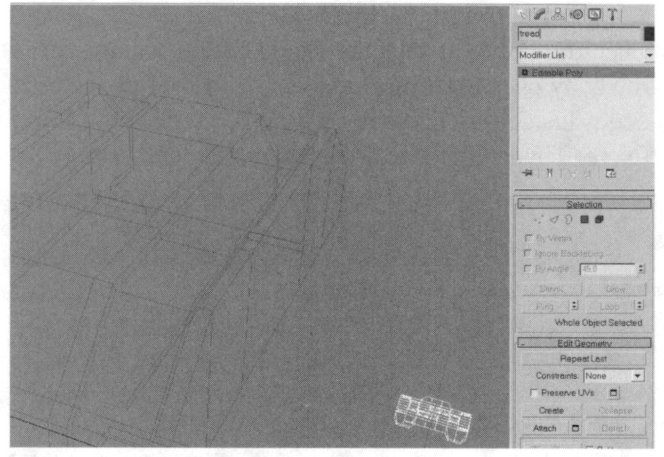

Figure I-52

30. Hit the **H** key and select **track** from the list, right-click on the **Scale** tool, and scale the path to between 105% and 115%, or until the path is above and below the edges of the body. Make sure the track is not touching or intersecting the base and is about equidistant from the base on both the top and bottom (use the Move tool if necessary).

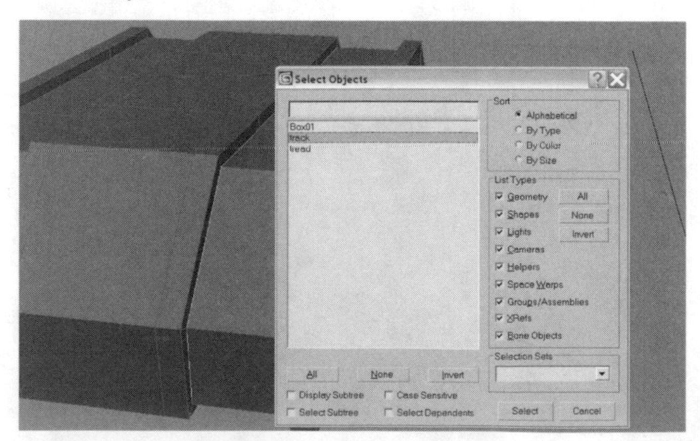

Figure I-53

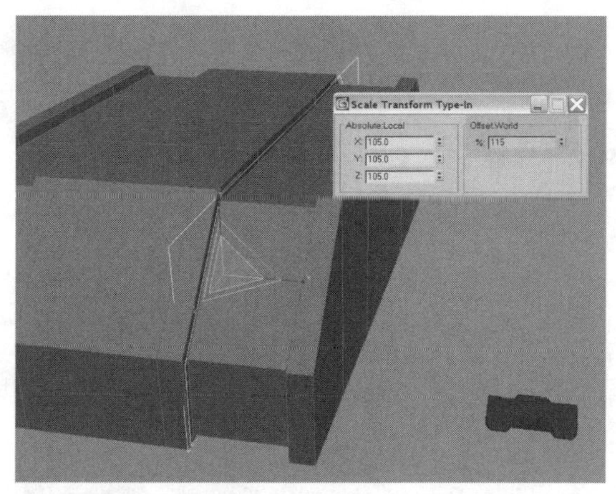

Figure I-54

Fire Drill: This is one of those things that's hard to get right the first time out. It really does take a couple of attempts. In the steps that follow, we'll be using the shape as a guide for arranging clones of the tread into a tank tread. However, once the clones are made, their arrangement can be altered by altering the size and shape of the path. So generally, you take your best guess, generate, and arrange the clones. If their arrangement doesn't suit you, edit the path (e.g., scale the shape) and the clone arrangement will automatically be adjusted. So... once you've made your clones, don't delete the shape until you're certain you're done with it.

31. Hit the **W** key and center the track in the groove, then select the **tread** object.

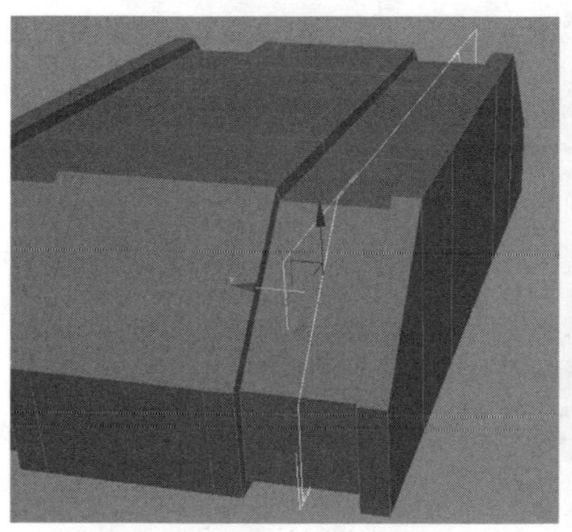

Figure I-55

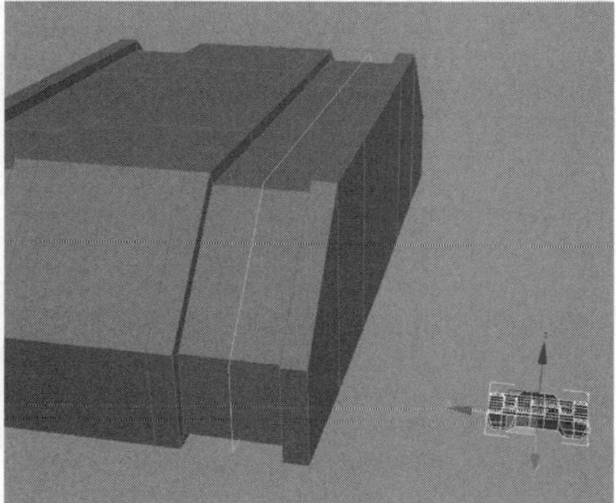

Figure I-56

32. From the main toolbar, select the **Tools** menu, then select **Spacing Tool.** When the Spacing Tool dialog box opens, click the **Pick Path** button, hit the **H** key, select **track**, and then click **Pick.**

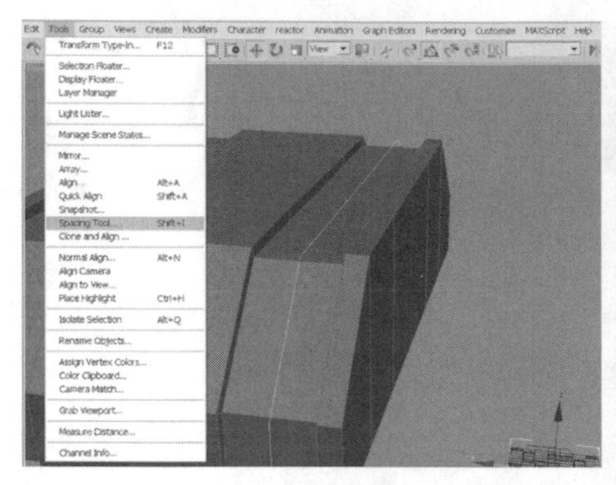

Figure I-57

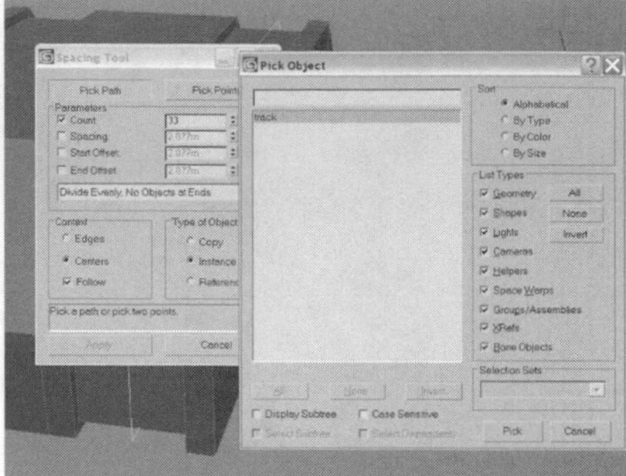

Figure I-58

33. In the Spacing Tool dialog box, click **Count** and type **34** for the number of clones. In the drop-down list in the middle of the dialog box, select **Divide Evenly, No Objects at Ends**, set the context to **Centers** and enable **Follow**, select the type of object to be **Instance**, and click **Apply**. Then close the dialog box. You've just made 34 tread objects we'll call "links."

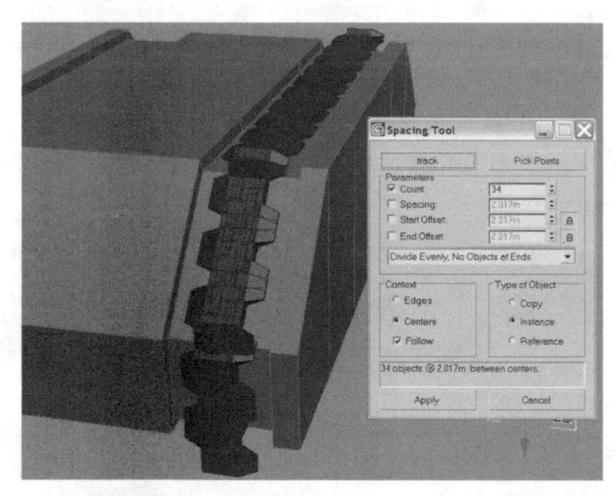

Figure I-59

FYI: The settings relate to how the objects (tread links) will be arranged. Count specifies the number of tread links on our track. The drop-down list tells Max to evenly space each link. Think about a tank track. Are the treads not evenly spaced? As for that No Objects at Ends bit... that means the last link will be left off so you won't have any overlapping. Context tells Max how to space them (from the center of each link).

Urgent: While the track looks cool, it's not really what I had in mind. The single extrusion is meant to slide between the dual extrusions, so we'll have to fix that by rotating the orientation of the tread link.

34. Press **Ctrl+Z** to undo the last step, then select the tread link, right-click the **Rotation** tool on the main toolbar, and enter **90** for the Absolute World Z axis. Repeat steps 32 and 33 to recreate the track.

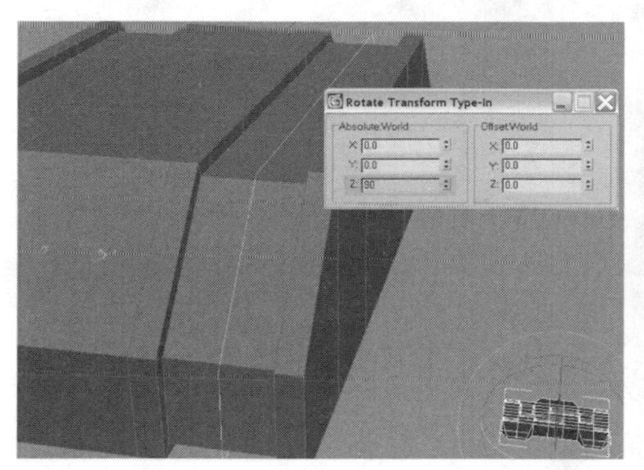

Figure I-60

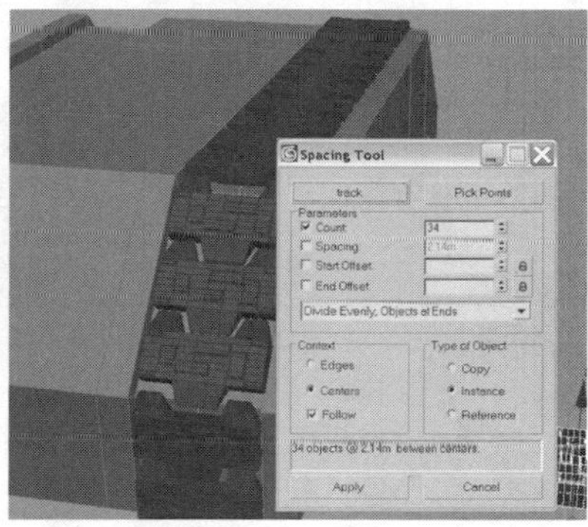

Figure I-61

Fire Drill: Now the tread is arranged the way it's supposed to be. However, you'll still have to tweak some of the links manually. The Spacing tool is not a perfect solution. It saves you a lot of heavy lifting, but expect to do some tweaking to get the look you want.

35. Select the tread link, right-click, and select **Hide Selection** to hide the tread. Then hit the **H** key and select all 34 tread objects.

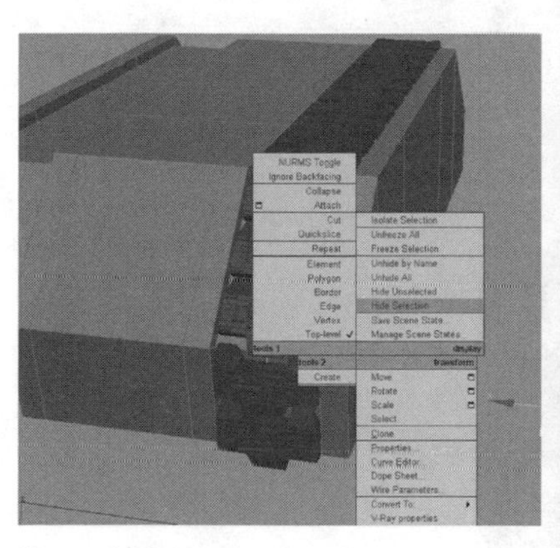

Figure I-62

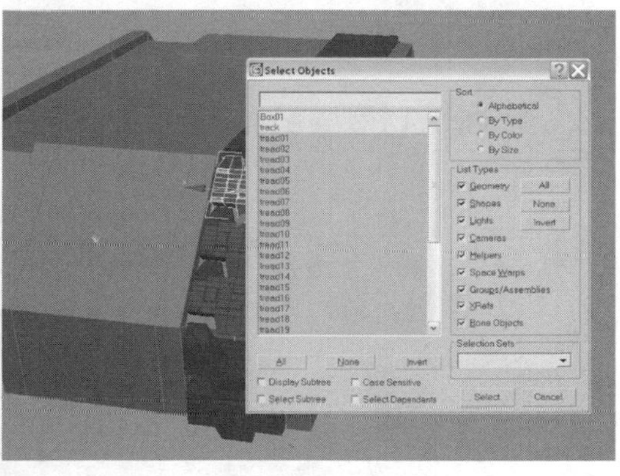

Figure I-63

36. Hit the **W** key to select the Move tool, then hold down the **Shift** key and drag in the X axis (left). When the Clone Options dialog opens, click **Instance** to create an Instance clone of the track in the left groove. Hit the **H** key and select **Box01**.

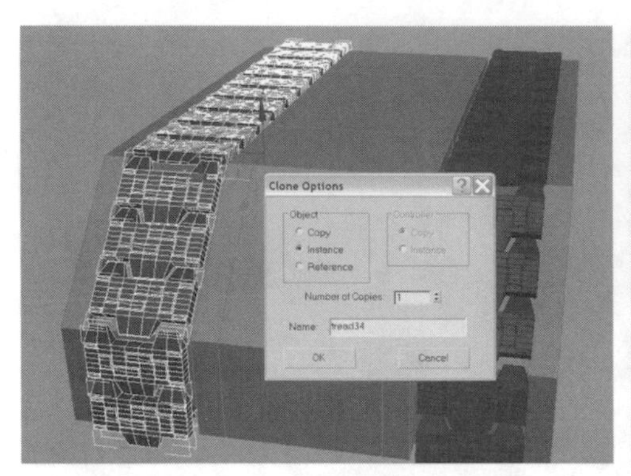

Figure I-64

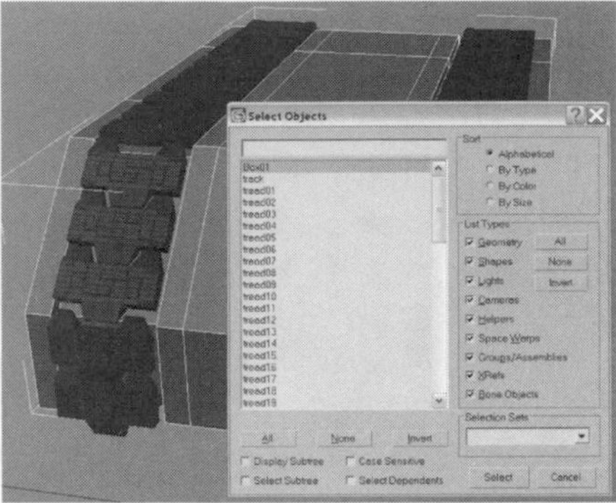

Figure I-65

37. Rename Box01 to **base**, click the **Attach List** button (the box to the right of the Attach button), select all the tread objects, and click the **Attach** button.

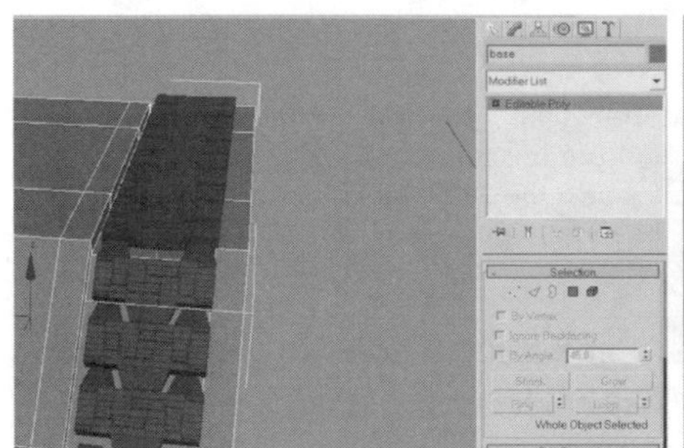

Figure I-66

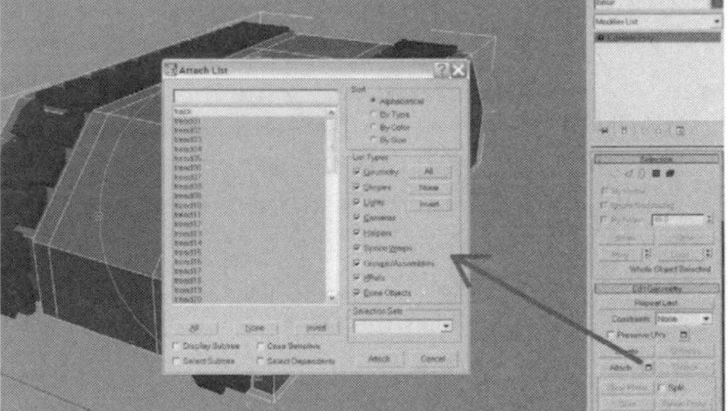

Figure I-67

38. Hit **F9** to do a test render.

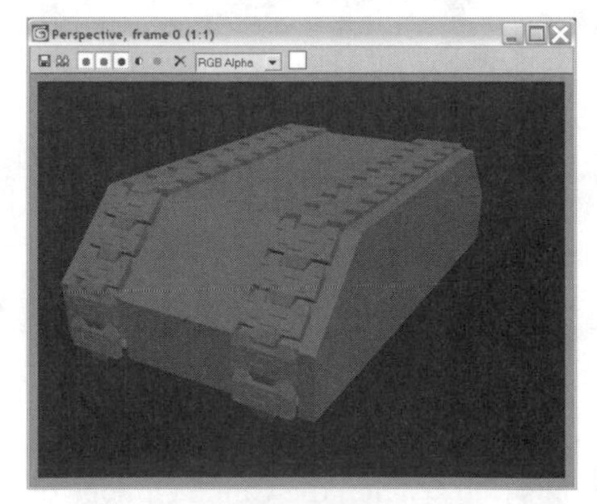

Figure I-68

39. Select the polygon in the middle of the base and then click **Bevel Settings**. Enter the following values for the bevel:

Type	Height	Outline	Apply/OK
Local Normal	1.0	0	Apply

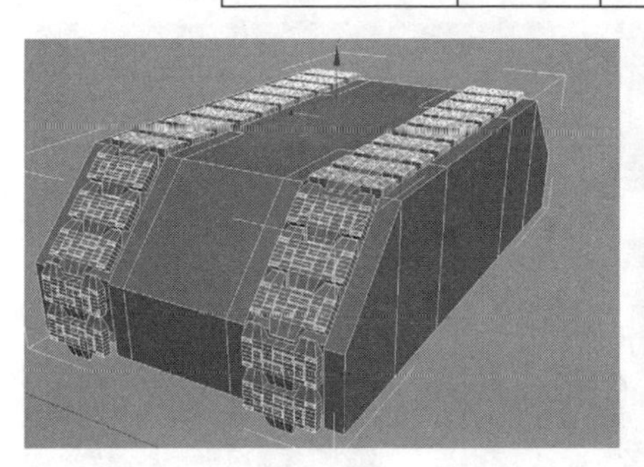

Figure I-69

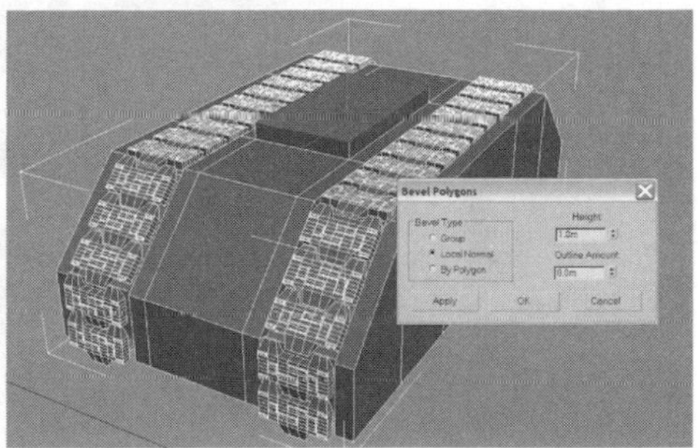

Figure I-70

Type	Height	Outline	Apply/OK
Local Normal	0	5	Apply
Local Normal	2	0	Apply

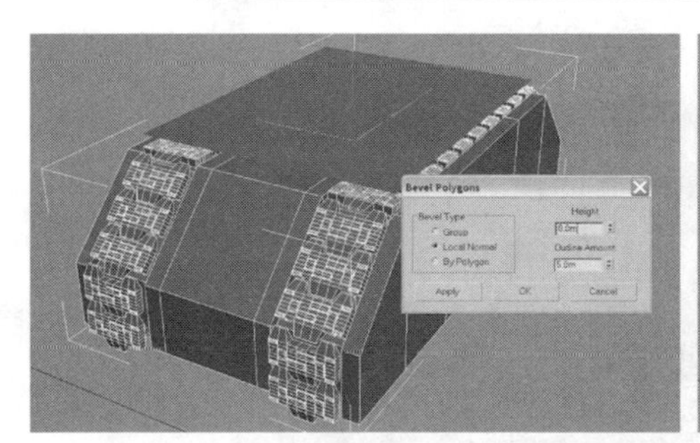

Figure I-71

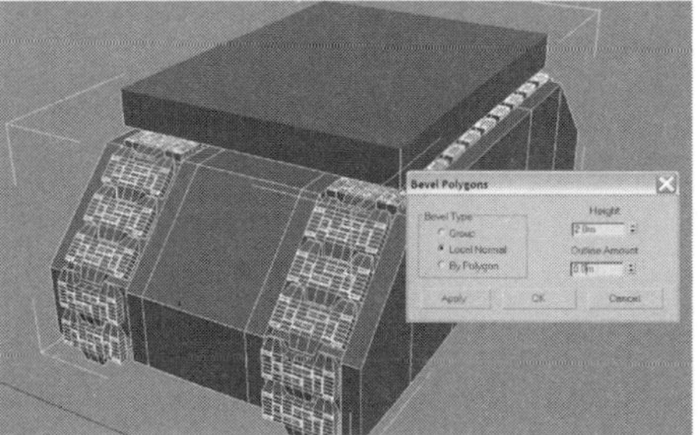

Figure I-72

Type	Height	Outline	Apply/OK
Local Normal	0.6	–1	Apply
Local Normal	0	–1	OK

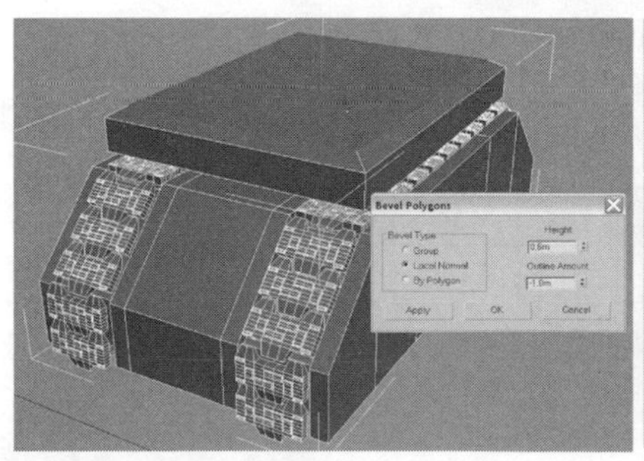

Figure I-73

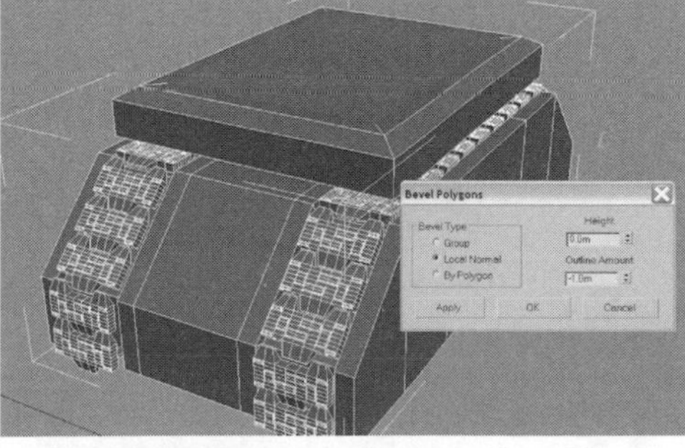

Figure I-74

40. Select the polygon, right-click the **Scale** tool, select **Non-uniform Scale** (the middle icon), and type **70** for the Offset World Y axis.

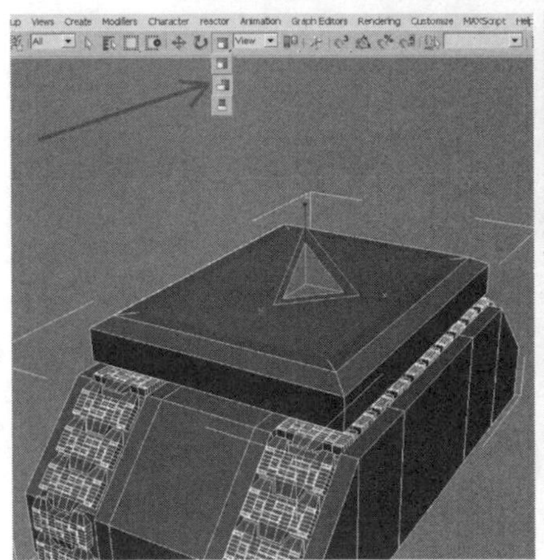

Figure I-75

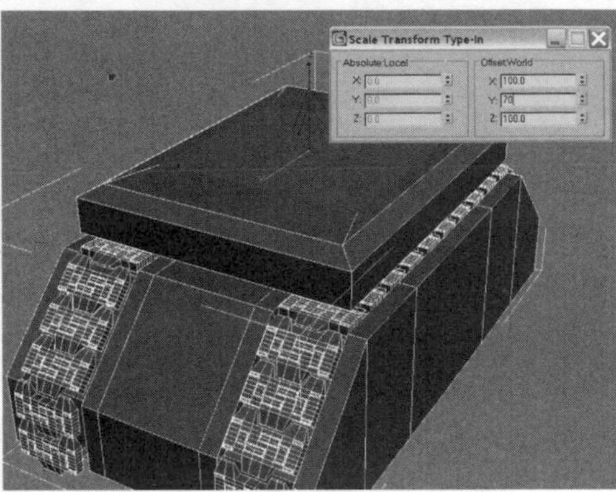

Figure I-76

41. Extrude the polygon **–1.0**.

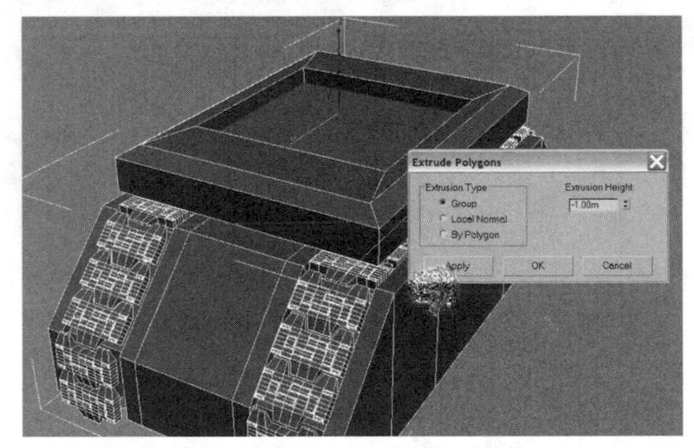

Figure I-77

42. Hit the **T** key to switch to the Top viewport, choose **AutoGrid**, and create a Cylinder in the indentation you just created with the extrusion. Then right-click and select **Convert to Editable Poly**. Use the following values for the cylinder:

Radius	Height	Height/Cap Segs	Sides	Smooth
3	2	1/1	24	Checked

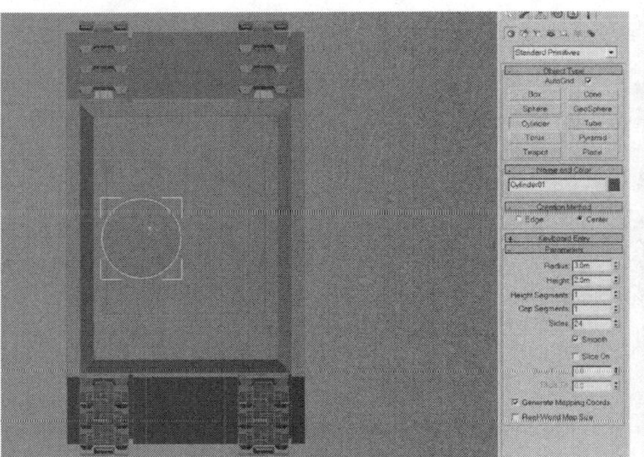

Figure I-78

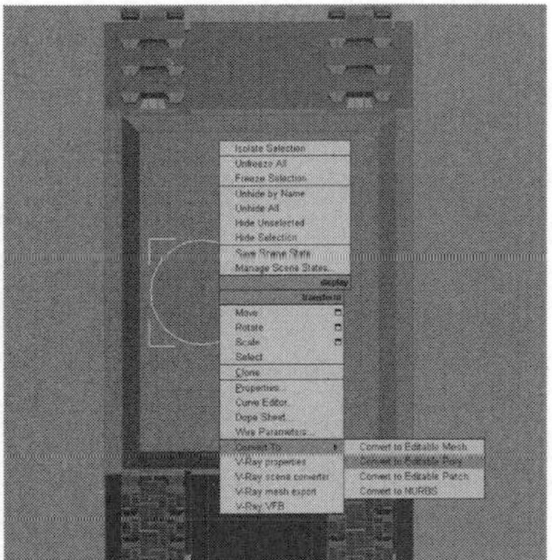

Figure I-79

43. Shift-drag to create an Instance clone and position it as shown.

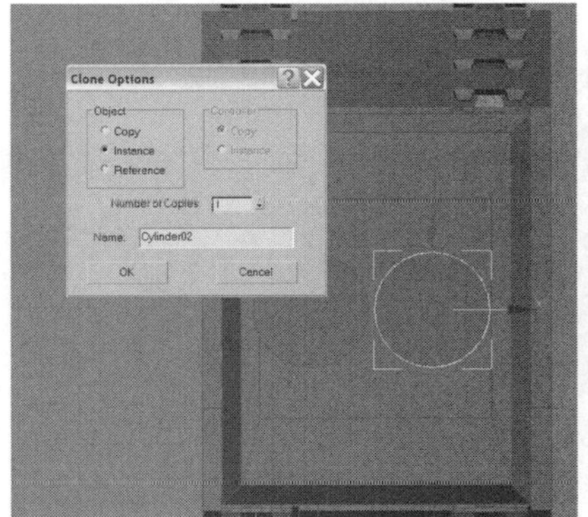

Figure I-80

Figure I-81

44. Click **Attach List** and attach the second cylinder to the first. Then select the six middle facing polygons on each cylinder and delete them.

Figure I-82

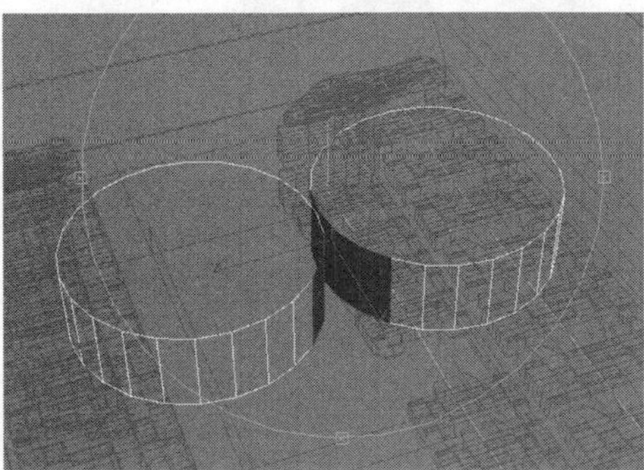

Figure I-83

45. Click the **Border** selection mode button and then click the borders created by the deletion of the polygon. Under Edit Borders, click the **Bridge Settings** button to bridge the gap and create new geometry.

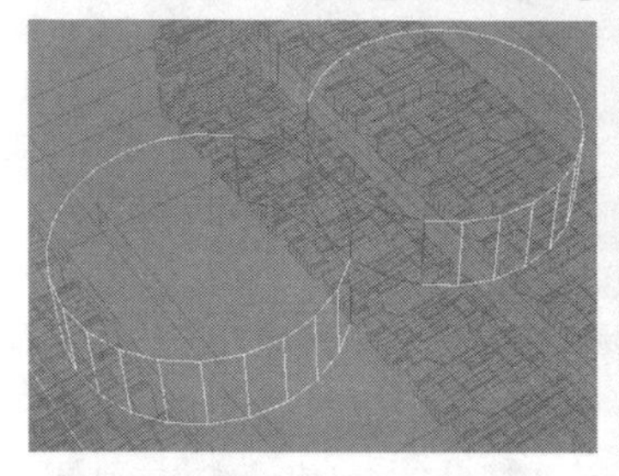

Figure I-84

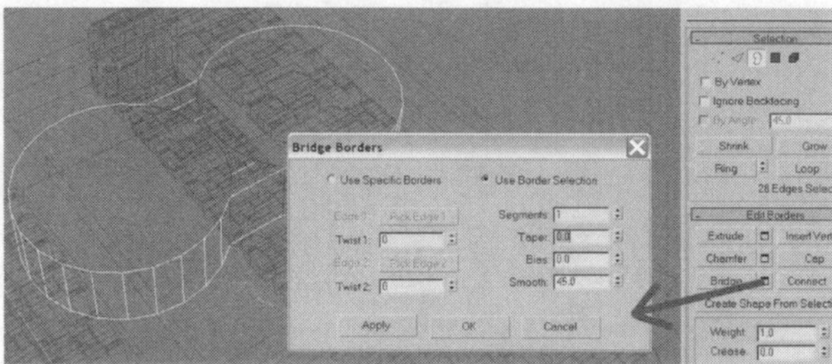

Figure I-85

46. Click the **Polygon** selection mode button, then polygon-select all the polygons on top, delete them, and border-select the resulting border.

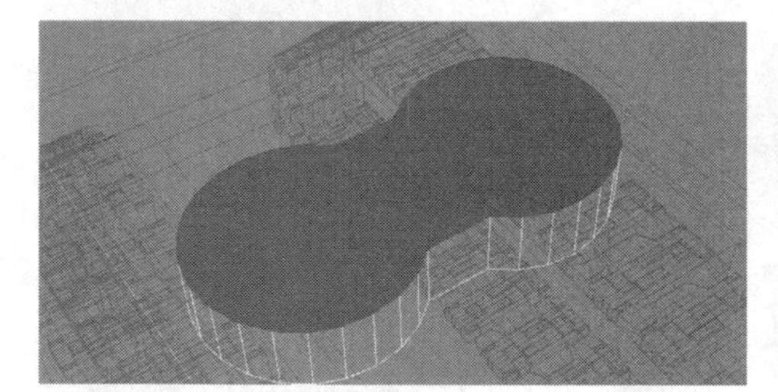

Figure I-86

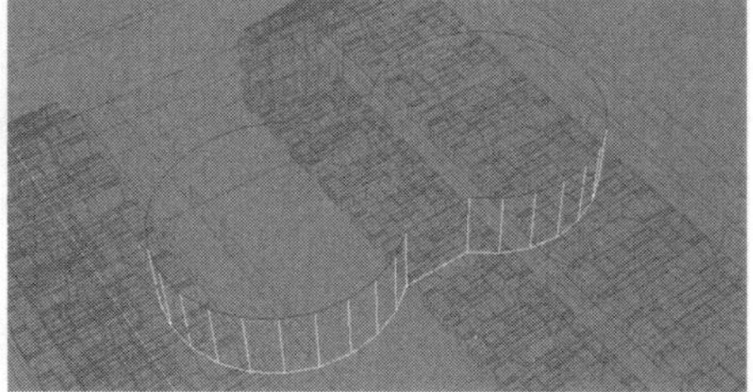

Figure I-87

47. Press the **Cap** button to cap the border. Select an edge on the top and bottom and then click **Loop** to select the top and bottom edges.

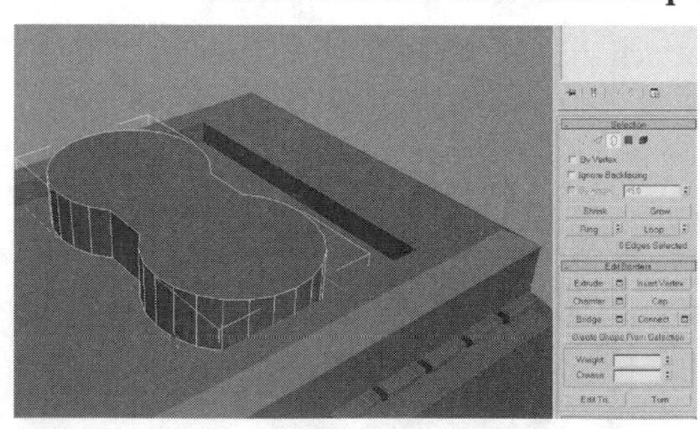

Figure I-88

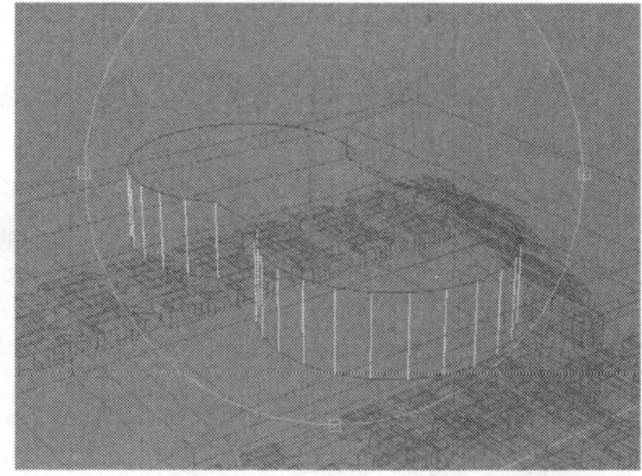

Figure I-89

48. Click the **Chamfer Settings** button, chamfer the edges by **0.12**, and then click **Apply**. Chamfer the edges again by **0.04** and click the **Apply** button.

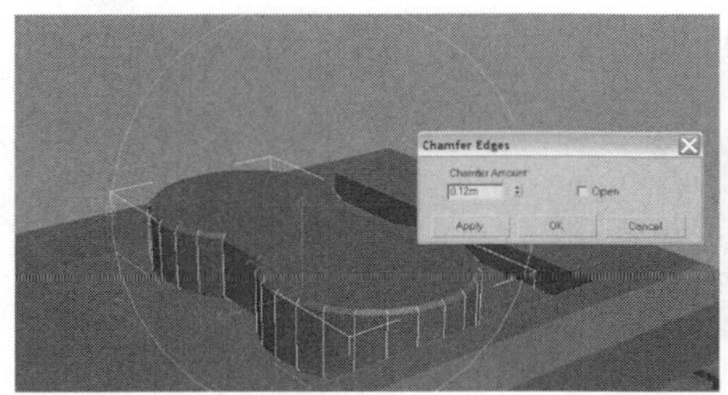

Figure I-90

Figure I-91

49. Chamfer the edges one more time, by **0.02**, and click **OK.** Now select the top.

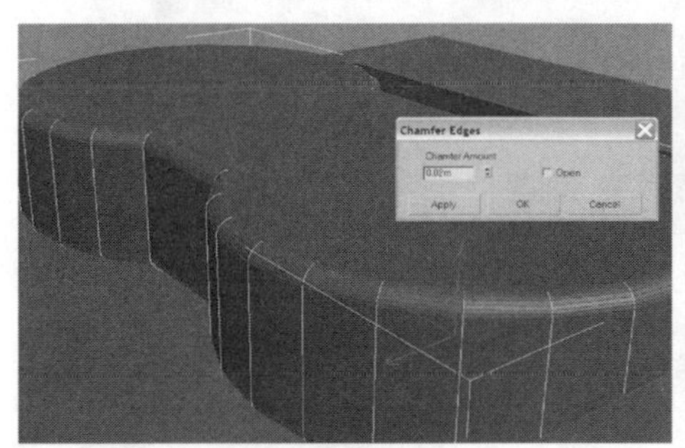

Figure I-92

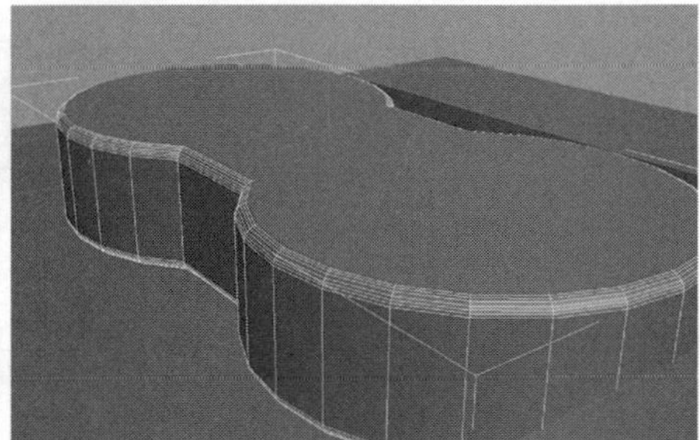

Figure I-93

50. Click the **Bevel Settings** button and enter these values:

Type	Height	Outline	Apply/OK
Group	0	–0.2	Apply
Group	0.2	0	OK

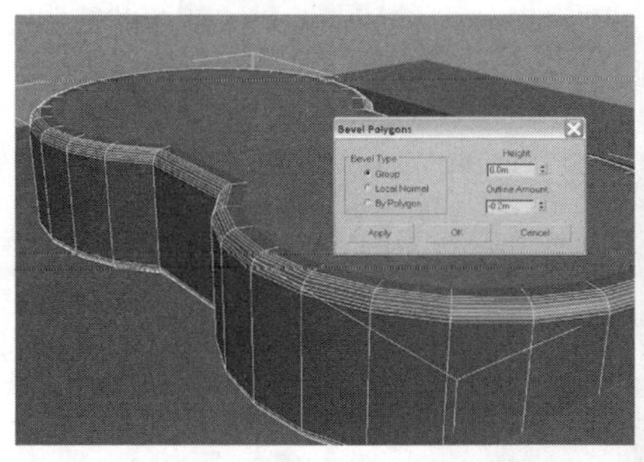

Figure I-94

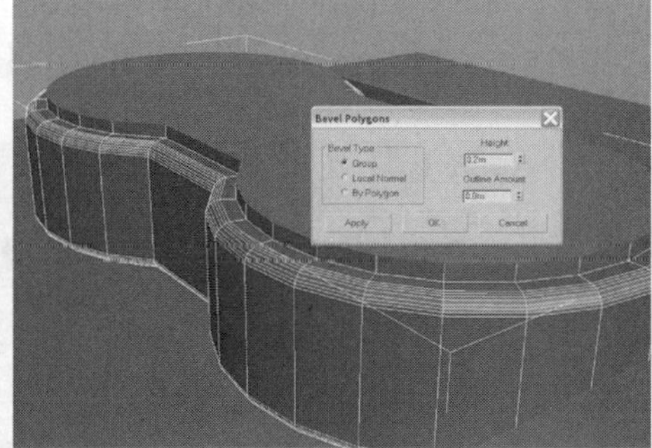

Figure I-95

51. Select and delete the top polygon.

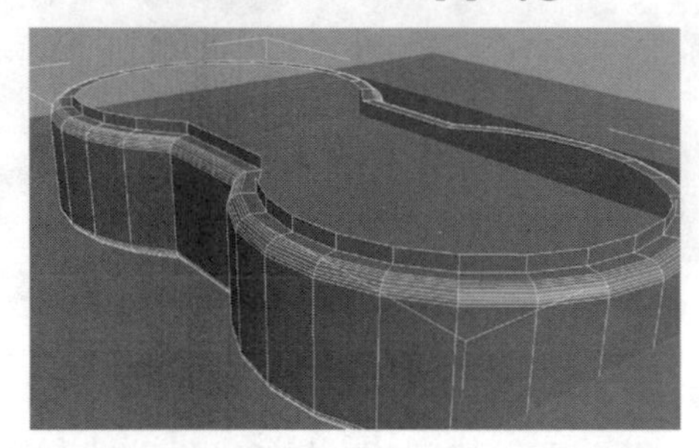

Figure I-96

52. Select the object you've been working on, rename it **torso**, and then select the bottom polygon.

53. Click the **Bevel Settings** button to bevel the bottom polygon and then delete it.

Type	Height	Outline	Apply/OK
Group	0	–0.2	OK

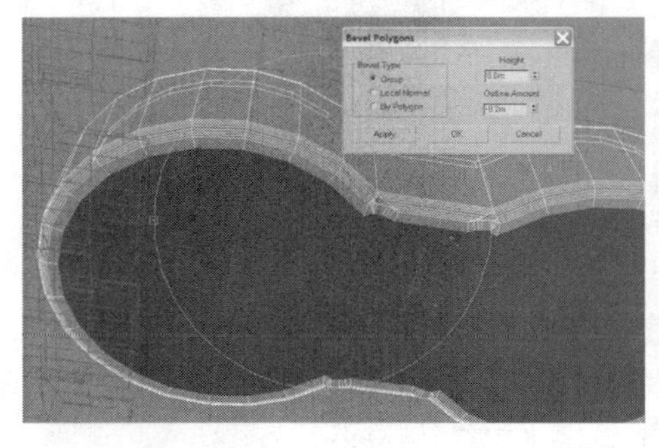

Figure I-97

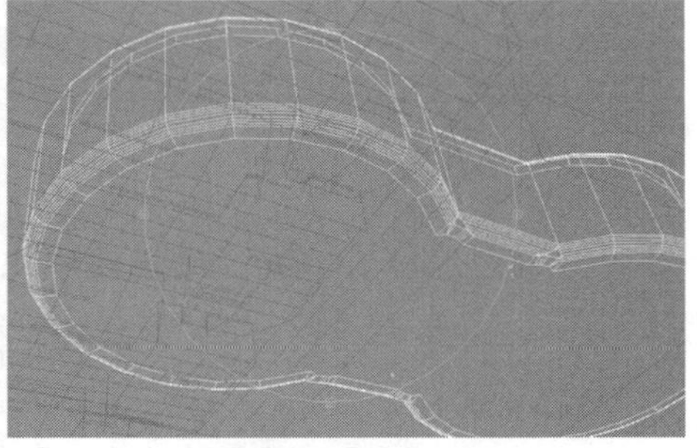

Figure I-98

54. Click the **Polygon** selection mode button to turn it off and select the object you've been working on. Hit **W** to select the Move tool, and Shift-drag the object up, around **2** in the Z axis.

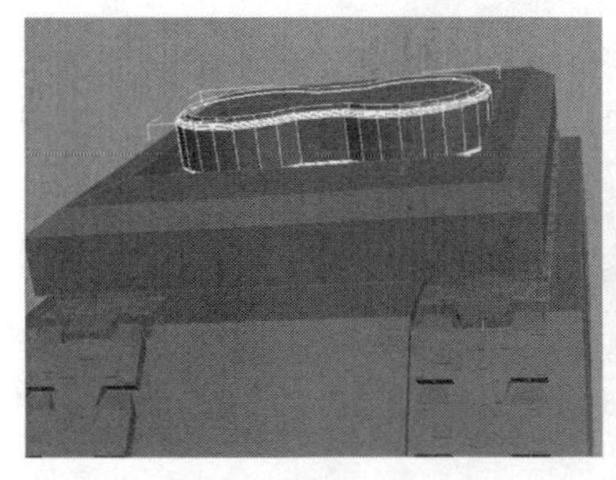

Figure I-99

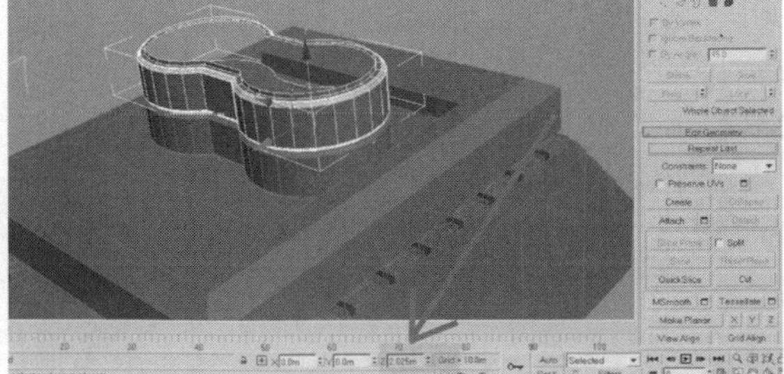

Figure I-100

55. Create four clones and then select the base, click the **Attach List** button, select the clones, and click **Attach.**

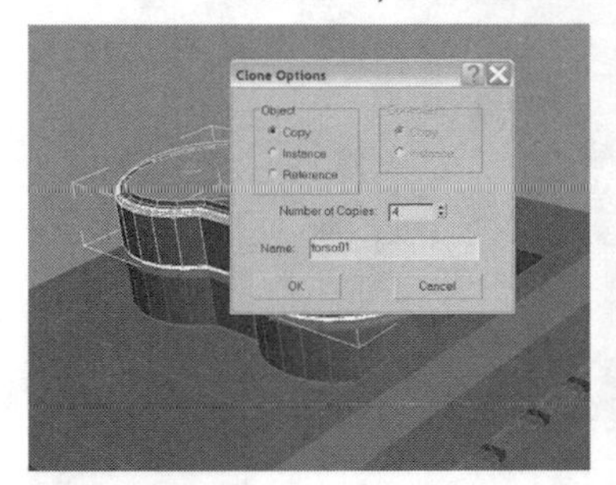

Figure I-101

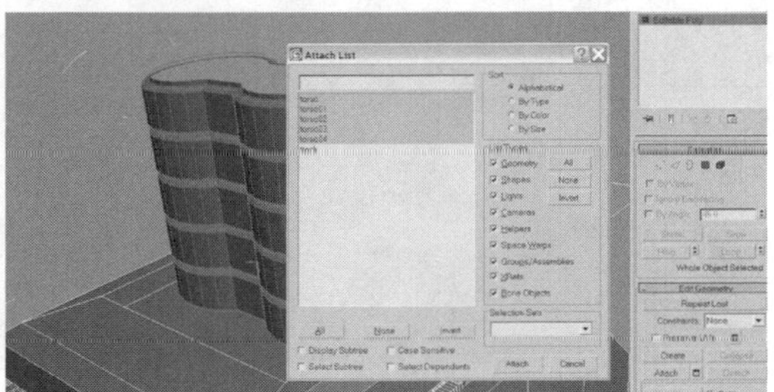

Figure I-102

56. Click the **Element** selection mode button and click the legs you made from clones. Right-click on the **Scale** tool, select **Non-uniform Scale**, and scale the legs **150** in the Offset World Y axis (or more if you want thicker legs).

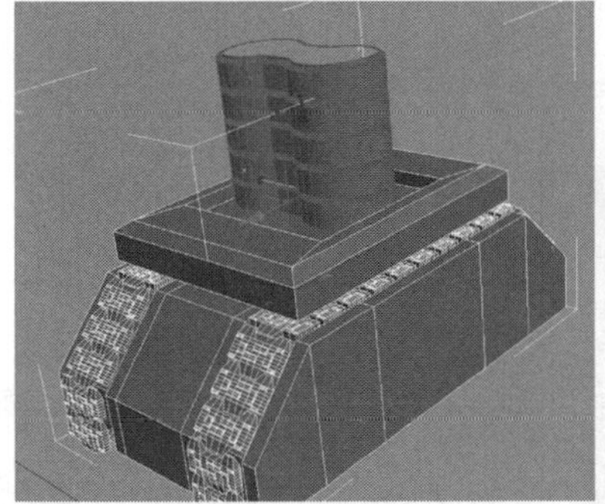

Figure I-103

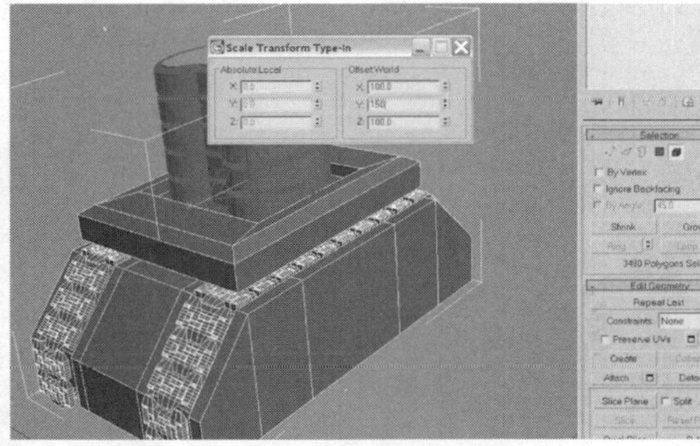

Figure I-104

57. A quick render (hitting **F9**) shows the legs look good but are a little rough. If you like this look, skip the next step. Otherwise, close the render window, click the **Modifier** drop-down list, and add a **Smooth** modifier to the stack to smooth the model.

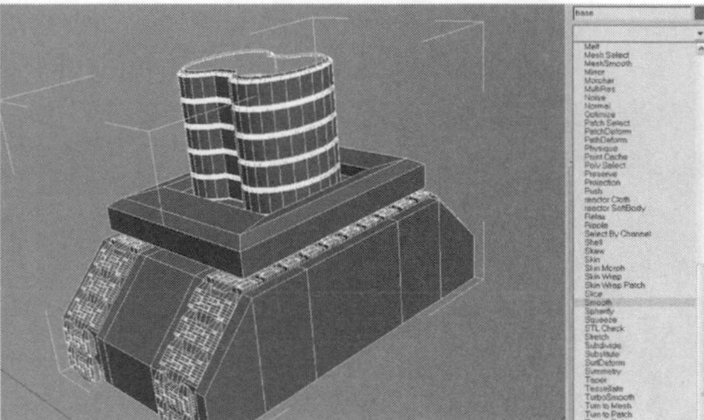

Figure I-105 Figure I-106

FYI: It's called "the stack" because you can stack modifiers on top of each other to achieve special effects. The order in which the modifiers appear in the stack (top to bottom) will change the effect on the model. Using the stack, like nesting materials, can give you some very sophisticated effects, but can be challenging. For that reason, we won't be adding more than a couple modifiers to the stack at a time. Collapsing the stack makes a permanent change (which you can undo) to the model. Until that point, you can add, remove, and move modifiers within the stack.

58. Click the **Auto Smooth** check box, right-click the **Smooth** modifier, and select **Collapse To** to collapse the stack.

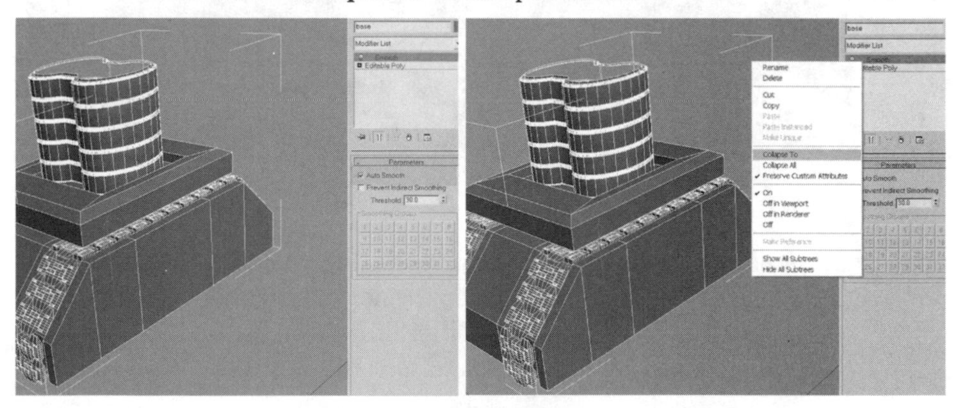

Figure I-107 Figure I-108

59. Hit **F9** to do a quick render and see the effect of the smoothing.

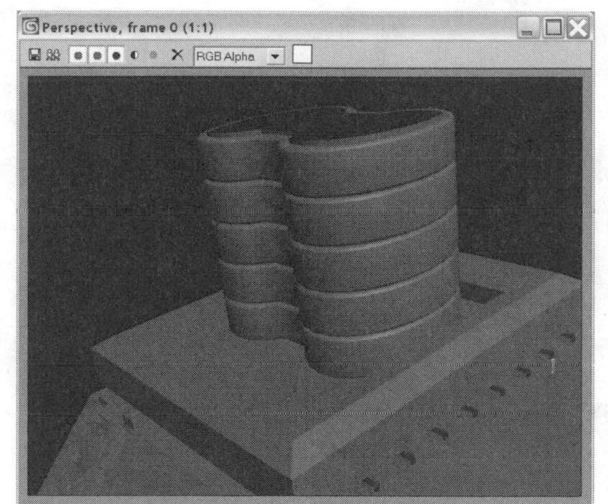

Figure I-109

Day 2: Finishing the Bot

1. Switch to the Top viewport. In the Create panel's drop-down list, select **Extended Primitives**, then click the **Capsule** button. Use these values for the Capsule:

Radius	Height	Sides	Height Segs	Smooth
10	30	24	1	Checked

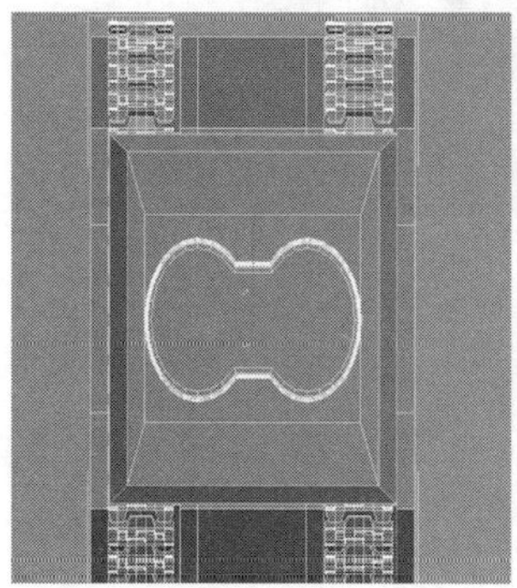

Figure I-110

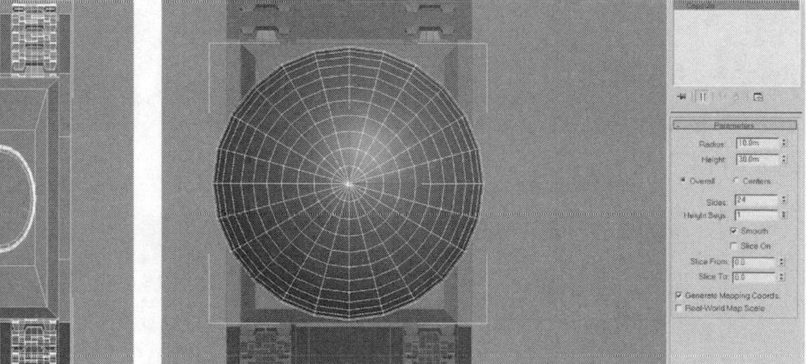

Figure I-111

2. Right-click the capsule and choose **Convert to Editable Poly.** Right-click the **Scale** tool, switch to **Non-uniform Scale**, and type **75** for the Offset World Z axis.

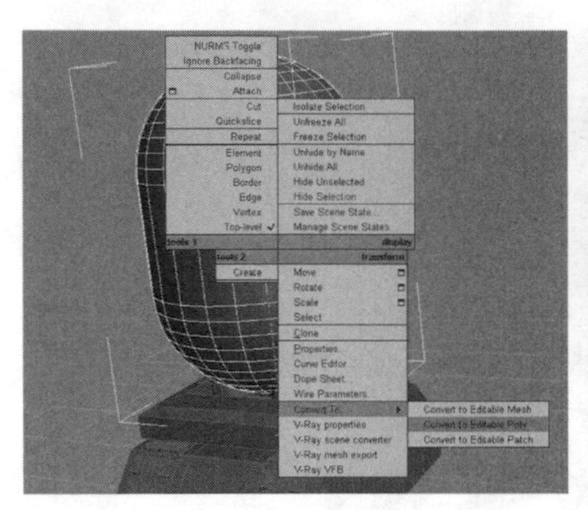

Figure I-112

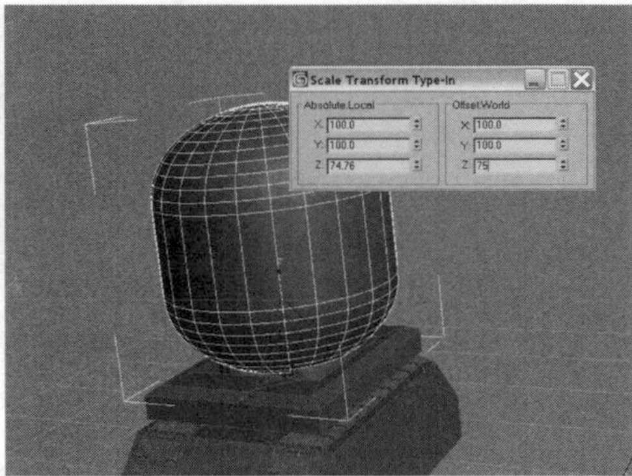

Figure I-113

3. Hit **W** to activate the Move tool and move the capsule up in the Z axis until it is just covering the top of the legs. Toggle to wireframe mode (**F3**), then click the **Arc Subobject Rotate** tool and rotate until you can see the bottom of the capsule. Then select a polygon at the center of the tip and click **Grow** until six rings of polygons have been selected.

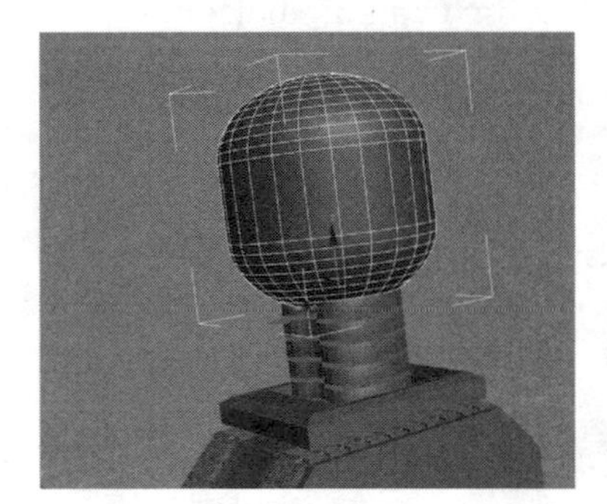

Figure I-114

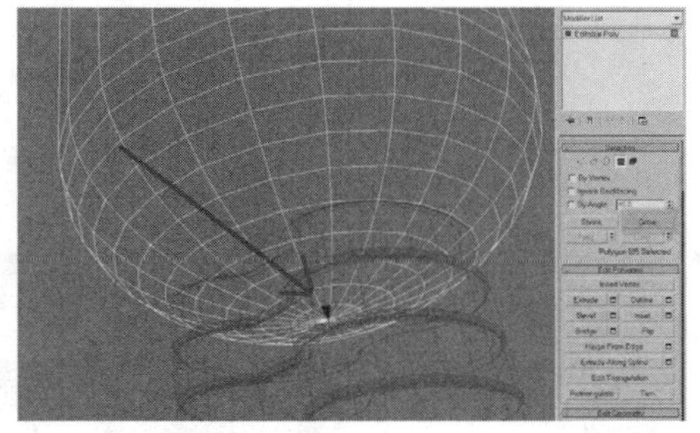

Figure I-115

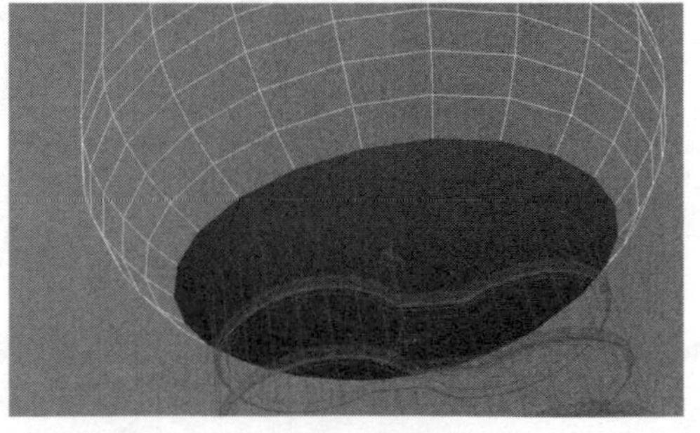

Figure I-116

4. Delete the selected polygons, border-select the hole, and then Cap it.

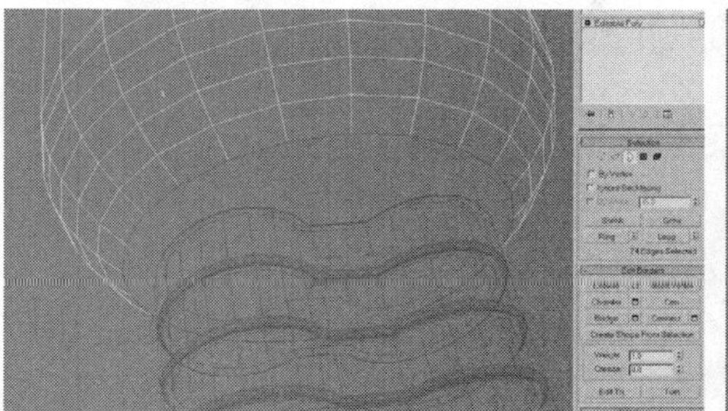
Figure I-117

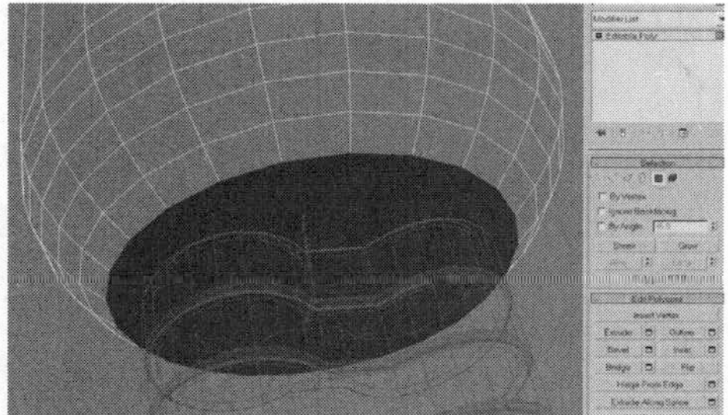
Figure I-118

5. Click **Bevel Settings**, bevel the cap, click the **Polygon** selection mode button to turn it off, select the **base**, click **Attach List**, and attach the capsule to the base.

Type	Height	Outline	Apply/OK
Group	0	–0.6	Apply
Group	–7	0	OK

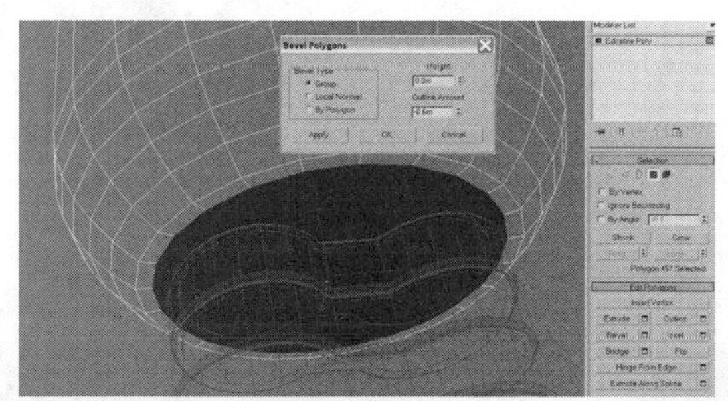

Figure I-119

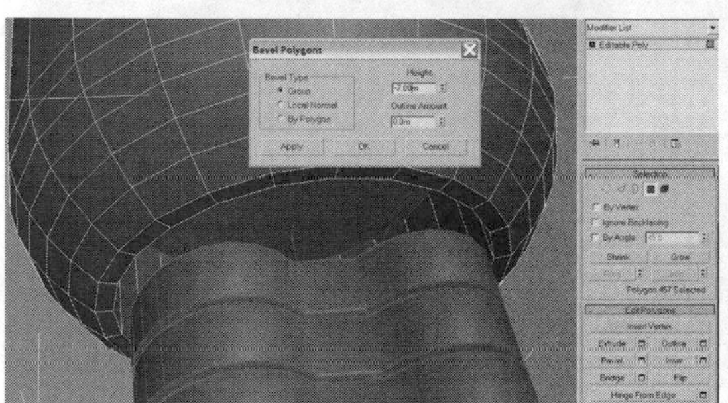

Figure I-120

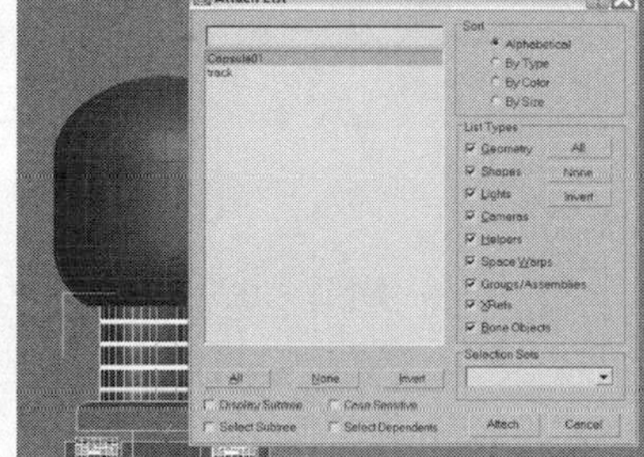

Figure I-121

6. [Optional Step] Since this is a static model and I don't intend to animate it, I'm going to attach the track. So... select the **base**, click **Attach List**, select **track**, and click **Attach**. However, if you wish to animate this track, you'll have to link it to the base so it will move

along with the base as well as on its own. If desired, select the track and on the main toolbar click the **Select and Link** tool (third button from the left). Click the **base** to make it the track's parent. Then hit the **Q** key to turn off the tool and reactivate the main selection tool.

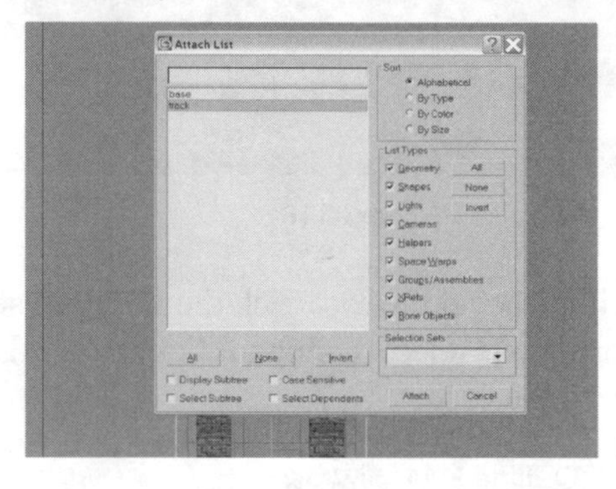

Figure I-122

7. Click the **Polygon** selection mode button, then hold down the **Ctrl** key and select the polygons you see in Figure I-123. Click **Bevel Settings**:

Type	Height	Outline	Apply/OK
Group	–0.45	–0.4	OK

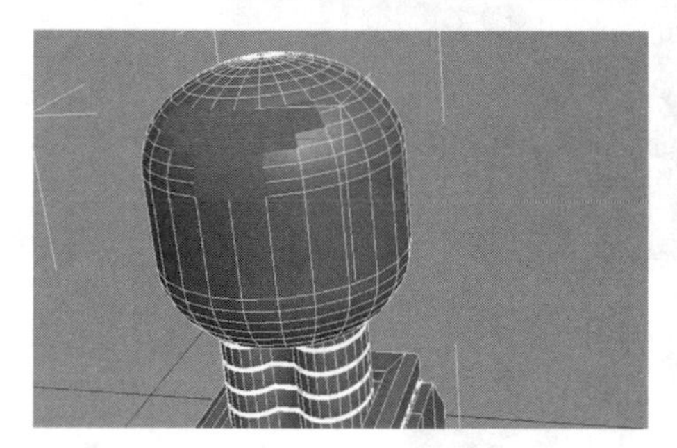

Figure I-123

Figure I-124

8. [Optional Step] If you prefer an illuminated bezel to a radiator, skip step 9, click **Detach**, detach as object, and name the object **bezel.** Select and Link the bezel to the body. Now you can add a translucent material to the bezel and place a light beneath it to achieve a really cool effect.

9. With the same polygons selected, under the Edit Geometry rollout click the **Tessellate Settings** button and click **Apply** twice, then click **OK**. Click **Bevel Settings**:

Type	Height	Outline	Apply/OK
By Polygon	–0.2	–0.05	OK

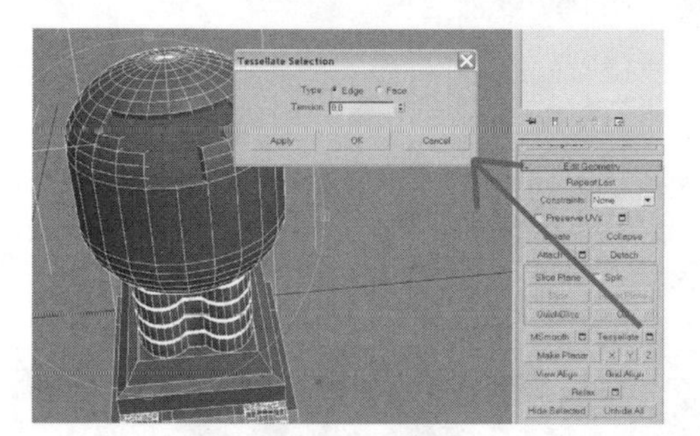

Figure I-125

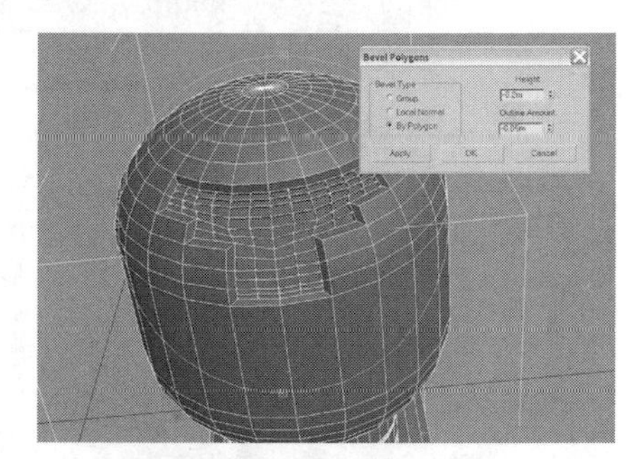

Figure I-126

Fire Drill: For the "obsessives" in the audience, I'm aware that the tessellated polygons are not straight or evenly sized. This is intentional. Ever take a close look at a car radiator? With age, the little aluminum blades get nicked and dented, and sometimes badly caved in. That's the effect I was going for. If this bugs you (and I know it will bug some of you), feel free to select the individual vertices and move them using the Move tool to straighten the grating and right this outrageous wrong. I won't think any less of you. In the meantime, the rest of us are going to pop a Corona and put on a Jimmy Buffett CD while we wait.

10. Select the two front polygons and Bevel them:

Type	Height	Outline	Apply/OK
Group	0	–0.45	Apply

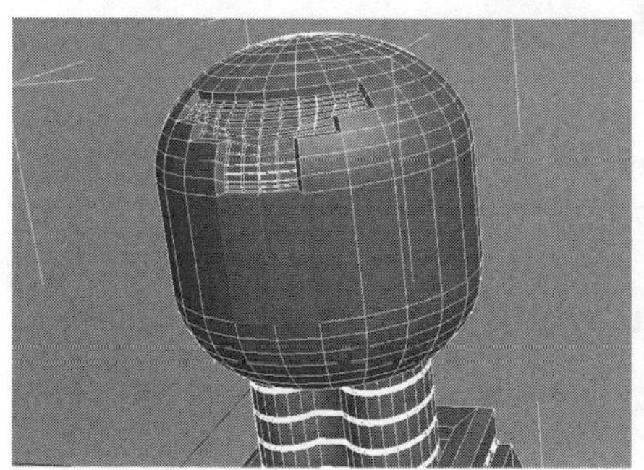

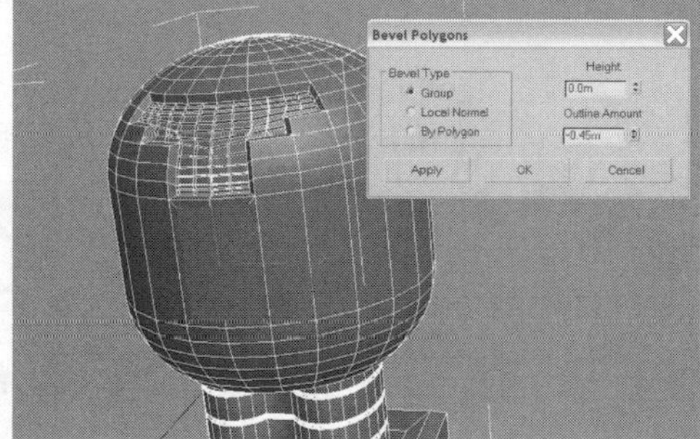

Figure I-127

Figure I-128

11. Bevel the two front polygons twice more:

Type	Height	Outline	Apply/OK
Group	0	–0.2	Apply
Group	–0.4	0	OK

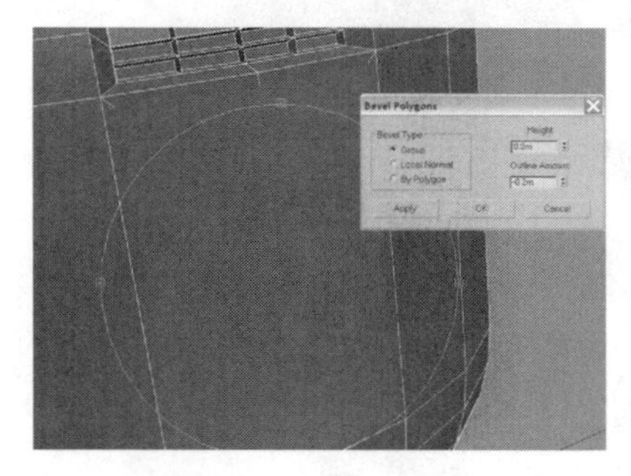

Figure I-129

Figure I-130

12. Edge-select the inner three edges, click the **Connect** button, enter **2** in the Segments field, and click **OK**.

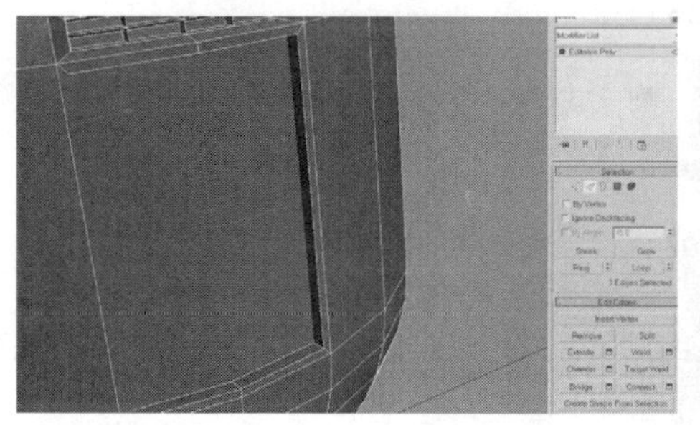

Figure I-131

Figure I-132

13. Polygon-select the inner, middle two polygons, and then Inset them by **0.1**.

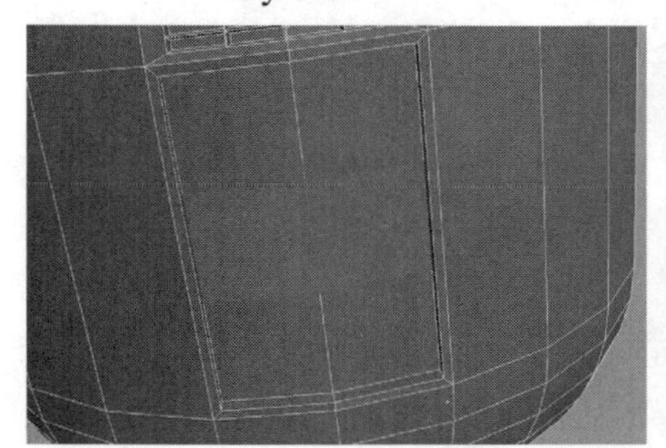

Figure I-133

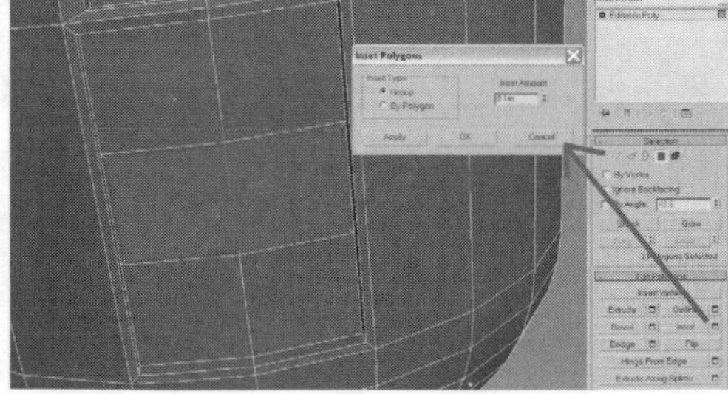

Figure I-134

14. Tessellate twice and then click the **Bevel Settings** button. Use the values in the following tables:

Type	Height	Outline	Apply/OK
By Polygon	0	–0.04	Apply

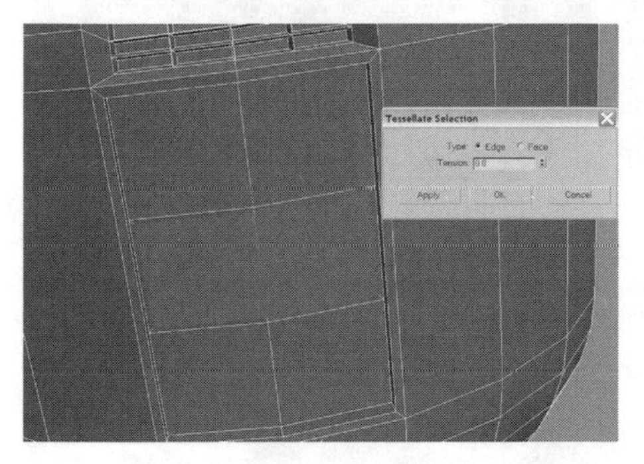

Figure I-135

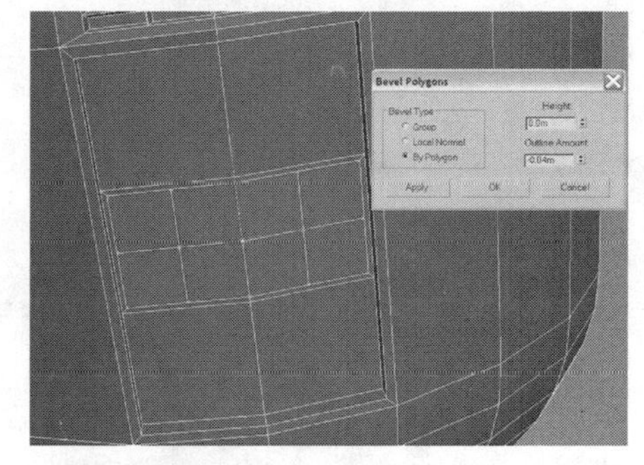

Figure I-136

Type	Height	Outline	Apply/OK
By Polygon	0.2	0	OK

Figure 1-137

15. Select the bottom two polygons and Tessellate them twice, then Bevel them by polygon twice:

Type	Height	Outline	Apply/OK
By Polygon	0	–0.05	Apply

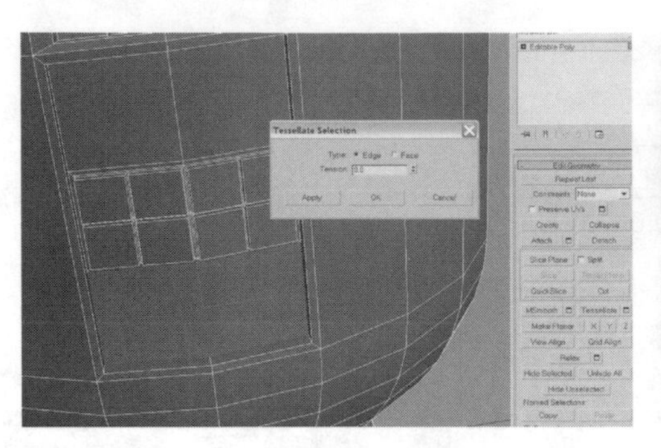

Figure I-138

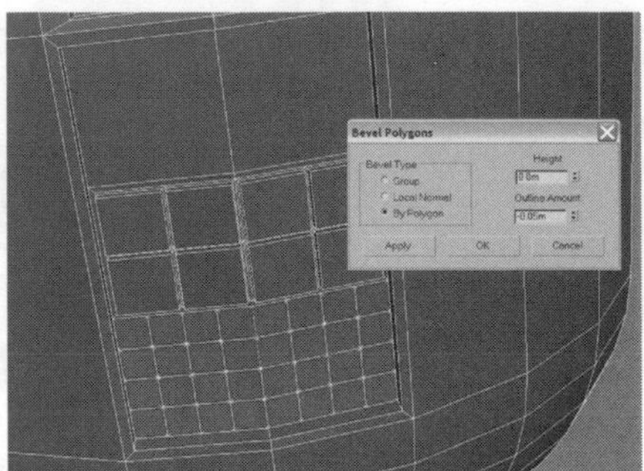

Figure I-139

Type	Height	Outline	Apply/OK
By Polygon	–0.01	0	OK

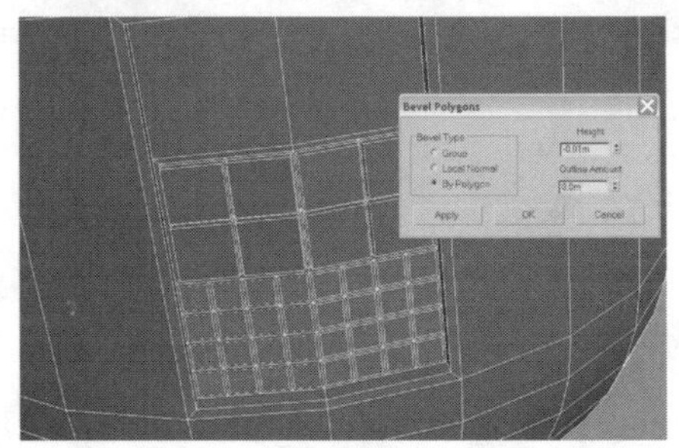

Figure I-140

FYI: MSmooth can be used to make a round object from a rectangular one. First, make the object as square as possible. Then make a small inward extrusion (usually 0.01).

16. Click **MSmooth** and then click the **Grow** button.

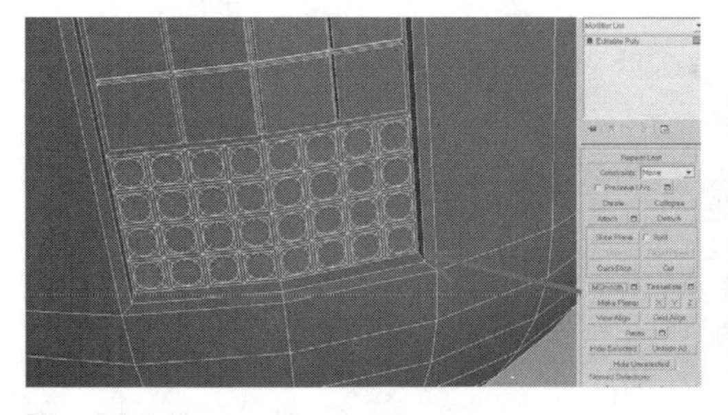

Figure I-141

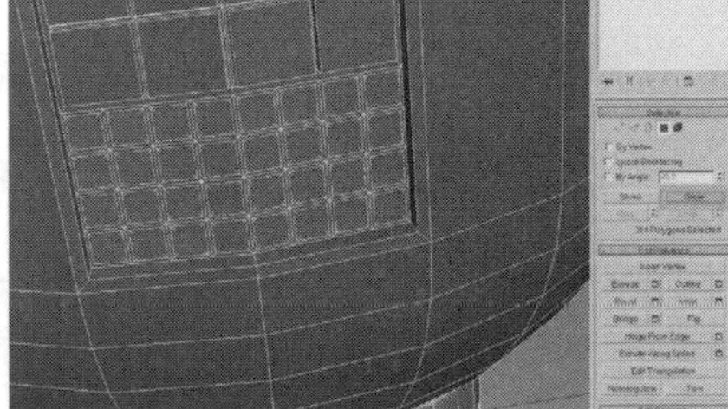

Figure I-142

17. Extrude by **0.02** and then click the **Shrink** button.

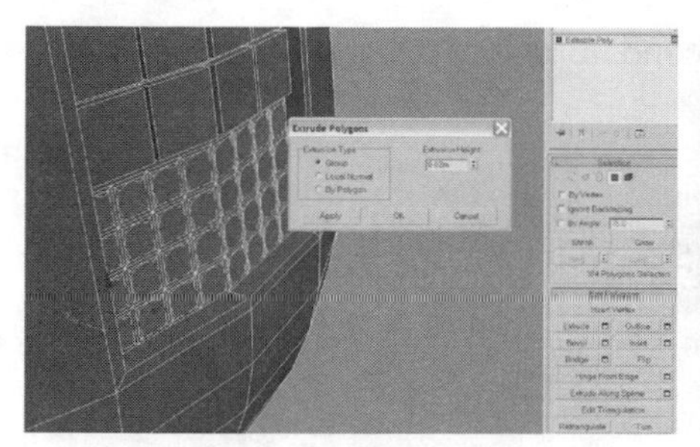

Figure I-143

Figure I-144

18. Bevel the polygons. Then select 10 polygons on the bottom edge of the body, as shown in Figure I-146.

Type	Height	Outline	Apply/OK
Group	0.04	–0.08	OK

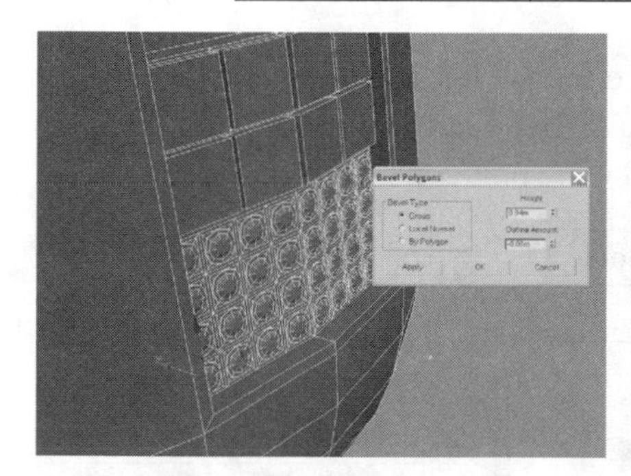

Figure I-145

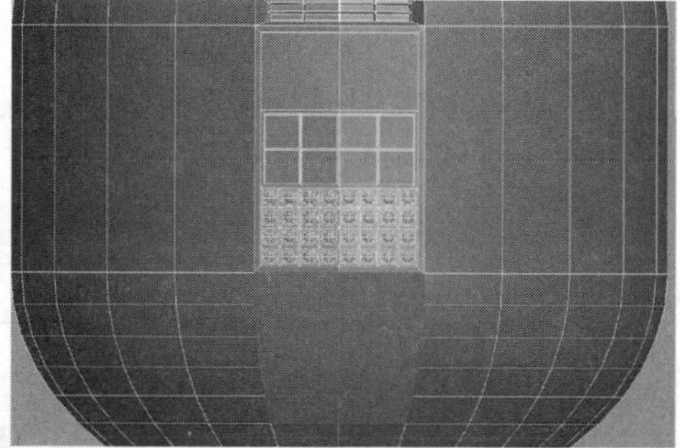

Figure I-146

19. Bevel the same polygons twice more:

Type	Height	Outline	Apply/OK
Group	0	–0.2	Apply
Local Normal	–0.25	0	OK

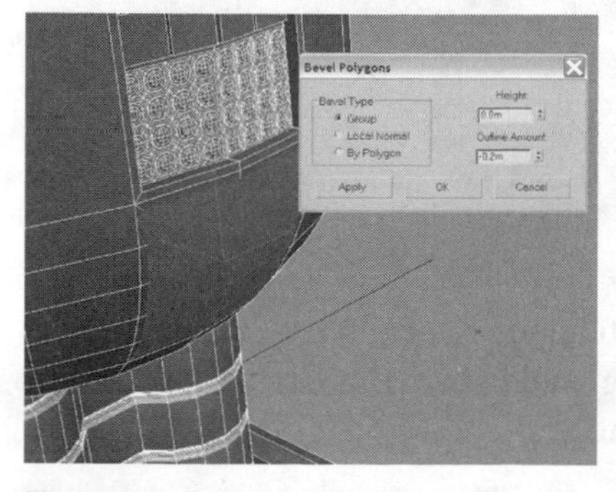

Figure I-147

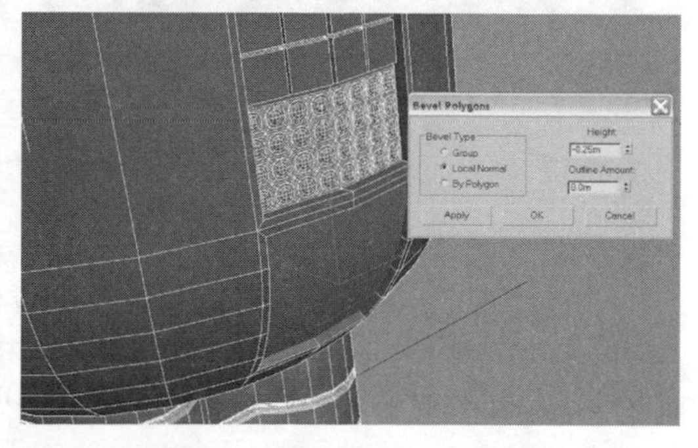

Figure I-148

20. Select the polygons on the second, fourth, sixth, eighth, and tenth rows. Bevel the polygons:

Type	Height	Outline	Apply/OK
Local Normal	–0.54	–0.15	OK

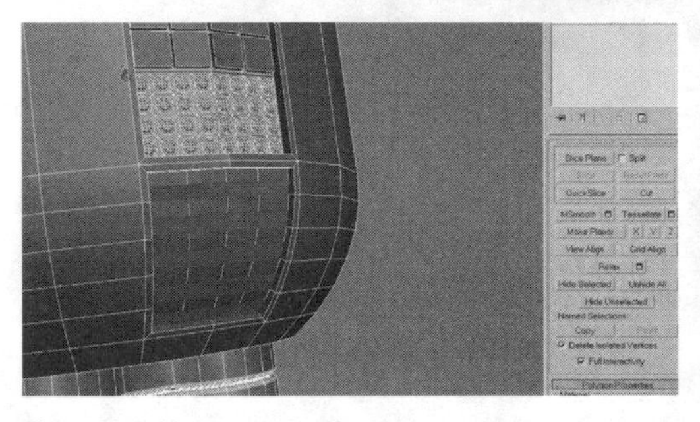

Figure I-149

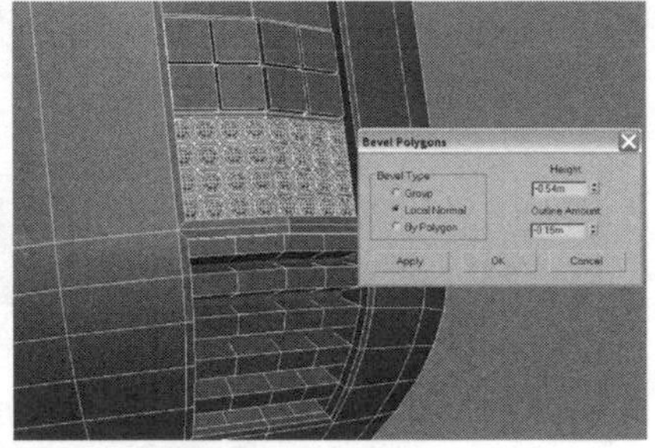

Figure I-150

21. Using AutoGrid, create a Sphere for the left eye. Convert the sphere to an Editable Polygon, Arc Subobject Rotate around the back, and delete the backward-facing polygons.

Radius	Segments	Hemisphere
0.95	24	0.50

Figure I-151

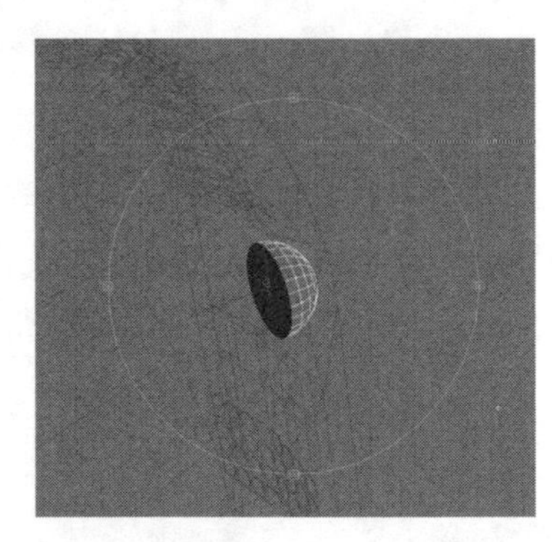

Figure I-152

FYI: To make a hemisphere, create a sphere and then set Hemisphere to 0.50.

22. Using the **Move** tool, Shift-drag to clone the right eye. Select the body, click the **Attach List** button, hold down the **Ctrl** key, and click the two spheres. Then click **Attach.**

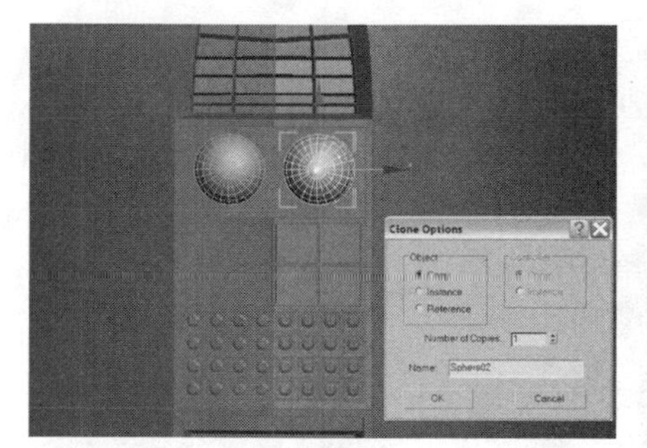

Figure I-153

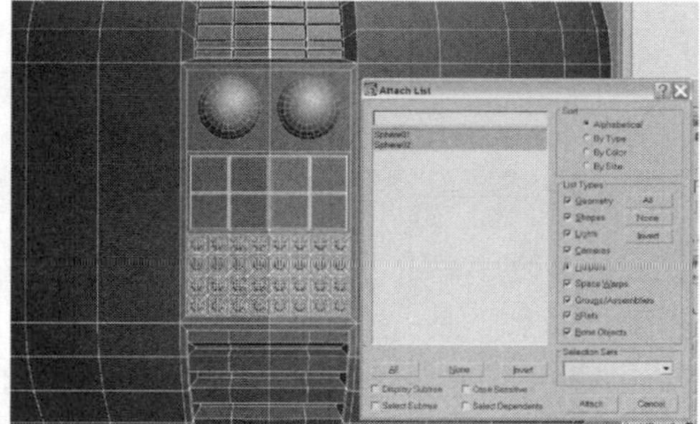

Figure I-154

23. Switch to the Top viewport (**T**), use AutoGrid to create a Torus (a doughnut) on top of the body, and then choose **Convert to Editable Poly.**

Radius 1	Radius2	Rotation	Twist	Segments	Sides
4	1.7	0	0	36	24

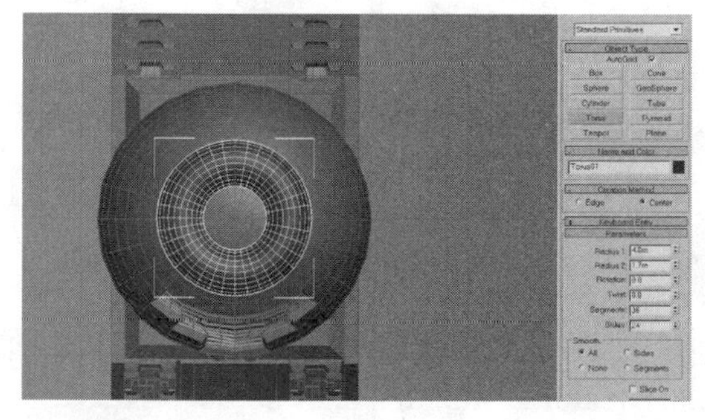

Figure I-155

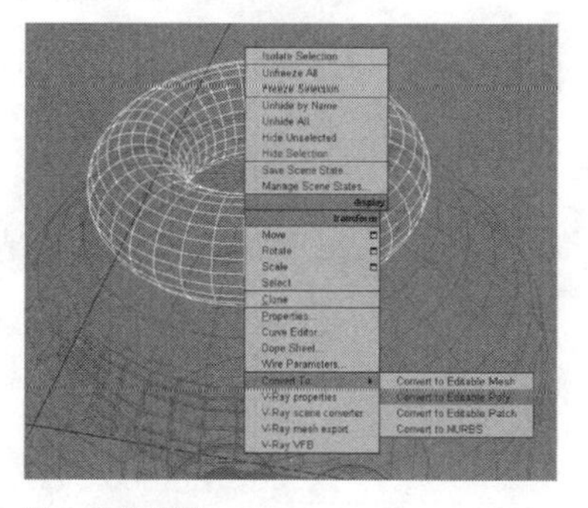

Figure I-156

24. Toggle to wireframe (**F3**), select a vertical edge, and then, under the Selection rollout, click the **Ring** button.

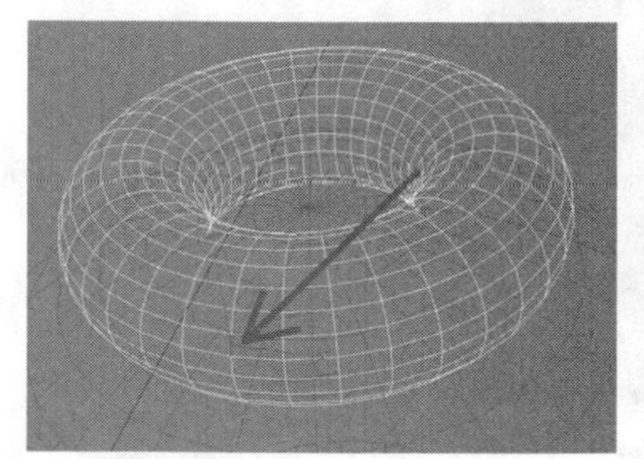

Figure I-157

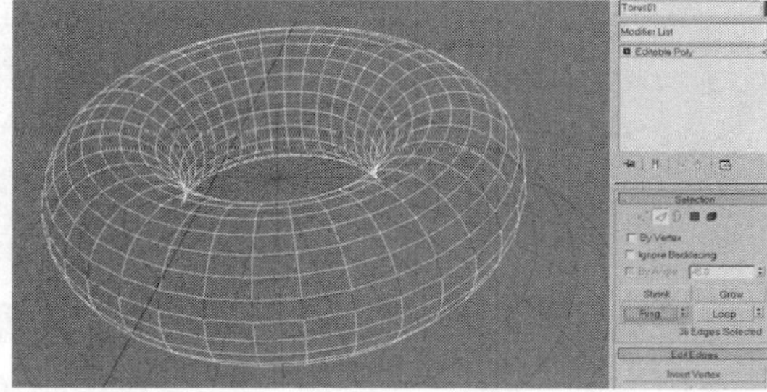

Figure I-158

25. Under the Selection rollout, click the **Loop** button, and then Extrude the edges to an Extrusion Height of **0.8** with an Extrusion Base Width of **0.5**.

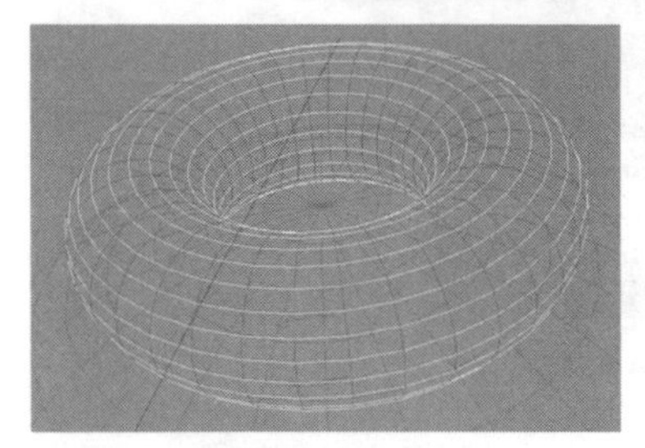

Figure I-159

Figure I-160

26. Uniform Scale the torus by typing **85** in the Offset World field. Switch to the Front view (**F**), right-click on the **Scale** tool, select **Non-uniform Scale**, and type **60** for the Offset Screen Y axis.

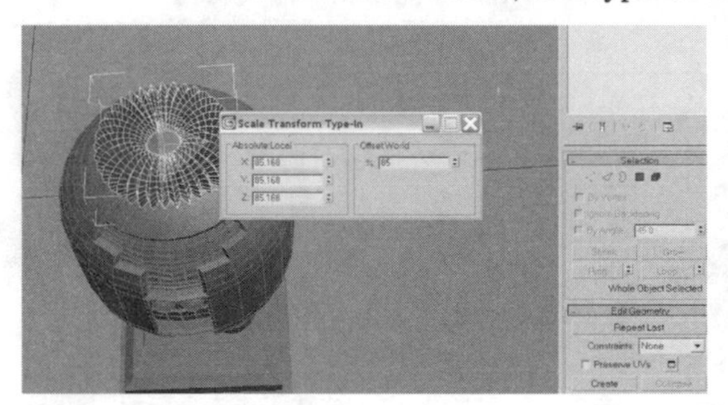

Figure I-161

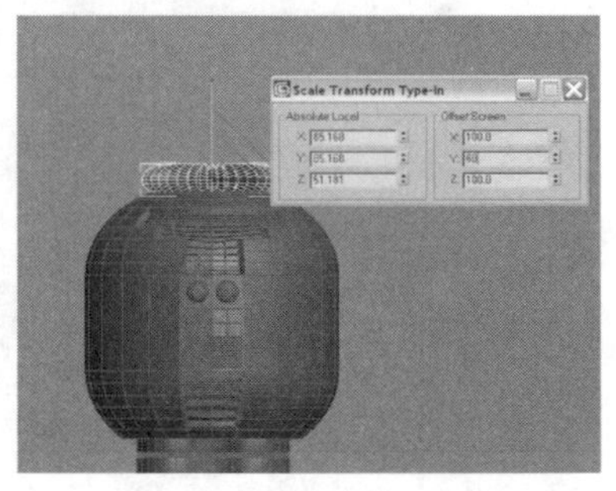

Figure I-162

27. Select the body, click the **Attach List** button and choose **Torus01**. Switch to the Top view and select the 24 polygons on the top of the body that are visible through the torus' hole.

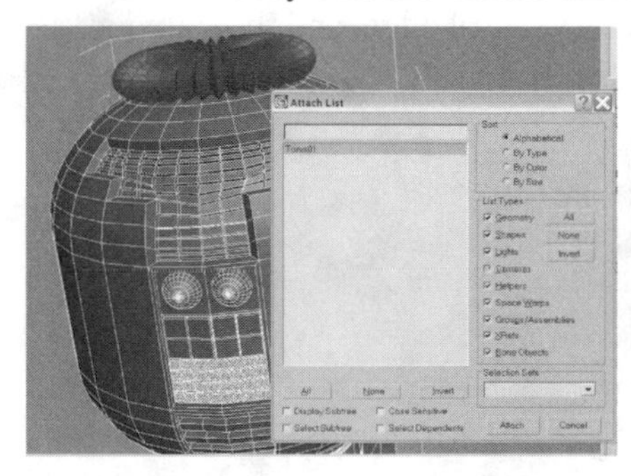

Figure I-163

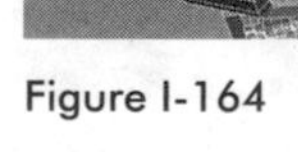

Figure I-164

28. Bevel the polygons seven times by Local Normal with the values in the following tables:

Type	Height	Outline	Apply/OK
Local Normal	1.7	0	Apply
Local Normal	0	–0.3	Apply

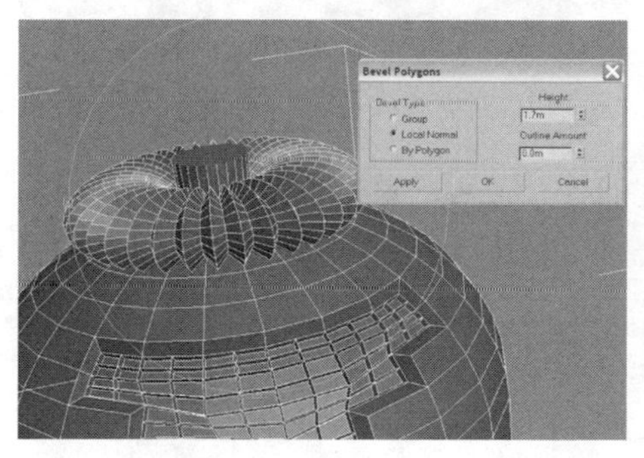

Figure I-165

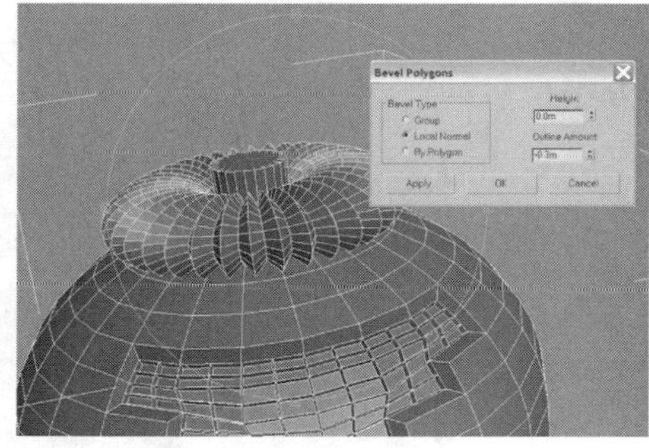

Figure I-166

Type	Height	Outline	Apply/OK
Local Normal	0.9	–0.3	Apply
Local Normal	0	–0.1	Apply

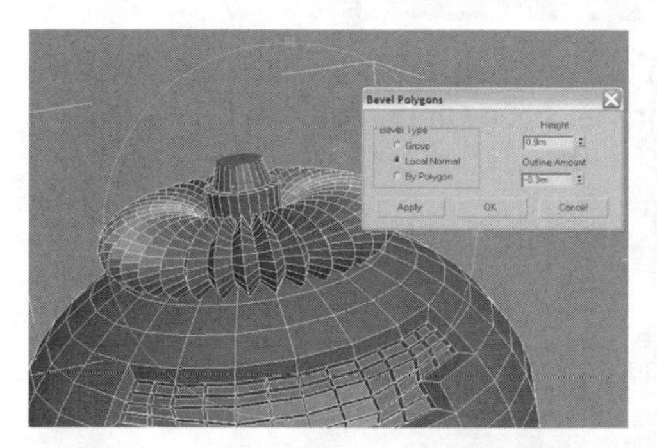

Figure I-167

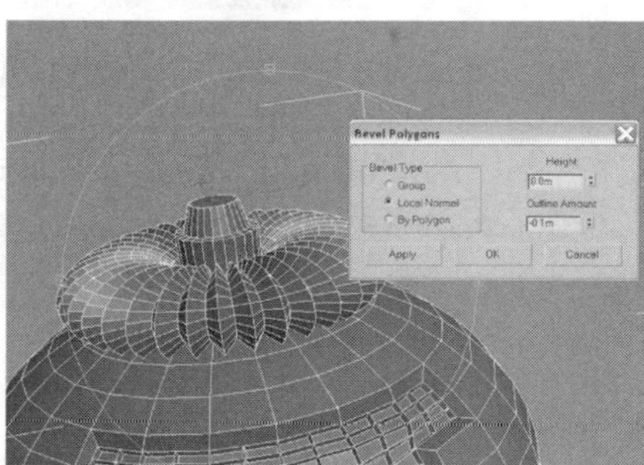

Figure I-168

Type	Height	Outline	Apply/OK
Local Normal	1	–0.23	Apply
Local Normal	1	–0.23	Apply

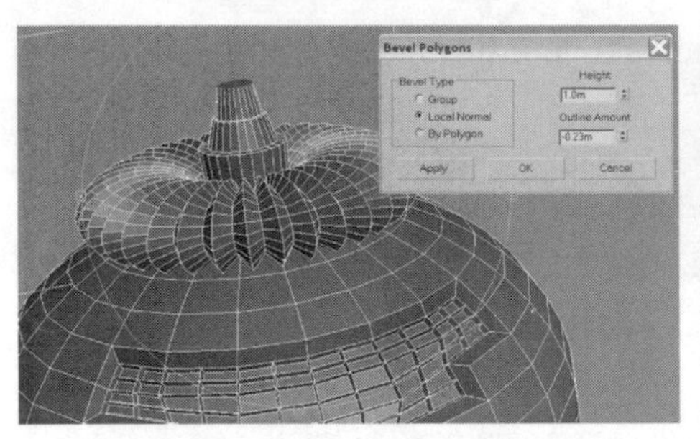

Figure I-169

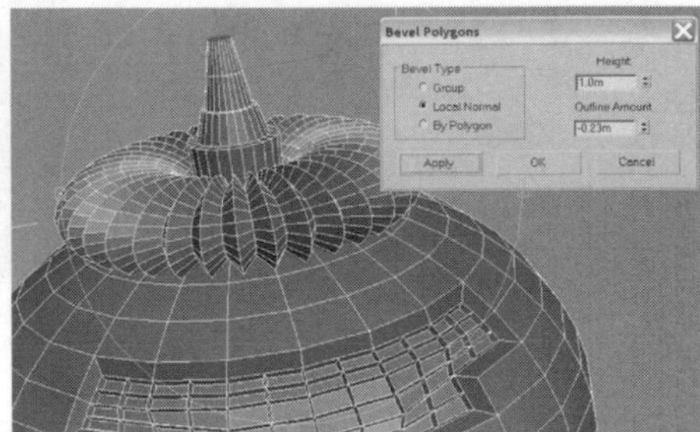

Figure I-170

Type	Height	Outline	Apply/OK
Local Normal	2	0	OK

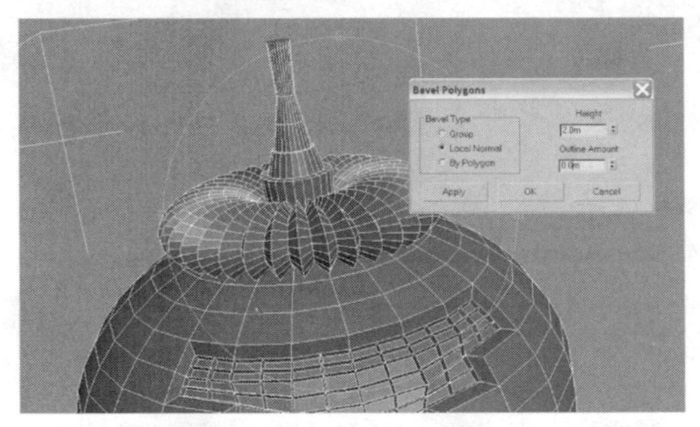

Figure I-171

29. Switch to the Top view. On the Create panel, use the drop-down list to select **Extended Primitives**, click **Chamfer Cylinder**, and use AutoGrid to create a Chamfer Cylinder on top of the body. Enter these values for the object:

Radius	Height	Fillet	Height/Fillet/Cap Segs	Sides	Smooth
6	3	0.8	1/12/2	32	Checked

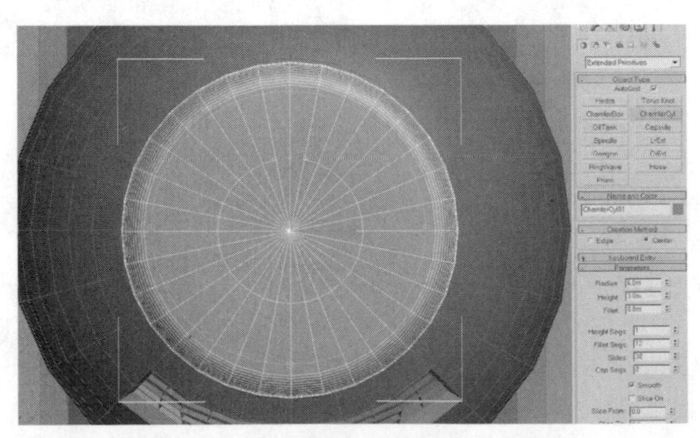

Figure I-172

30. Convert the chamfer cylinder to an Editable Polygon, then select the top 64 polygons (up to the start of the fillet) and use the Move tool to raise them around **0.1** in the Z axis.

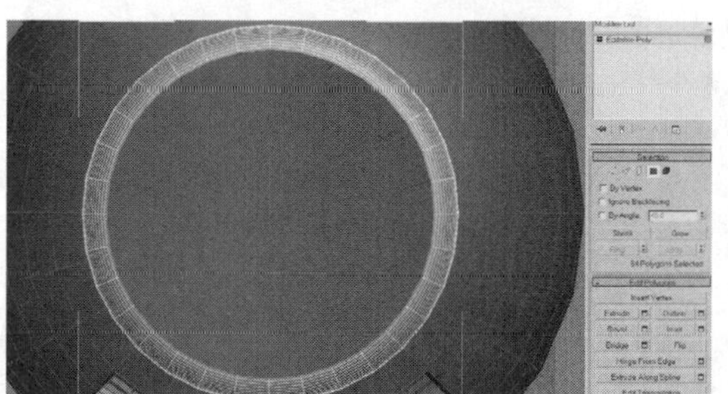

Figure I-173

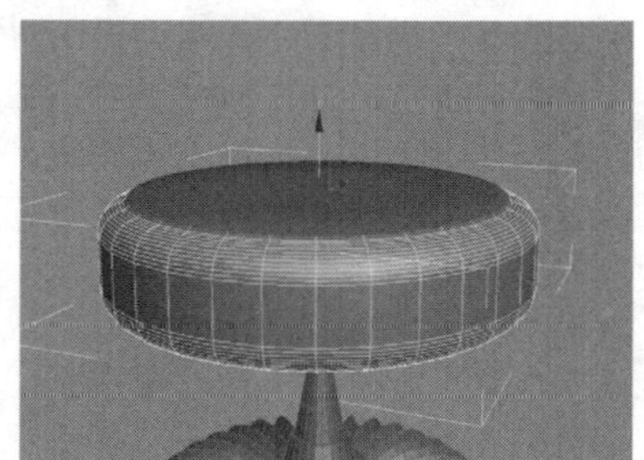

Figure I-174

31. Click the **Shrink** button to shrink the selection, and raise the remaining polygons around **0.6** in the Z axis. Open the Modifier list and add a **MeshSmooth** modifier to the stack.

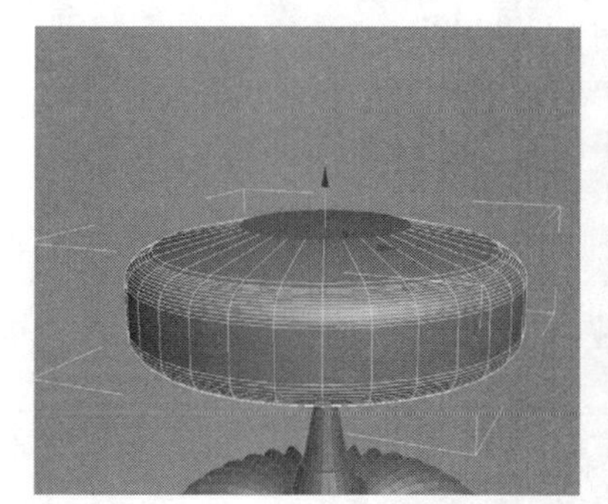

Figure I-175

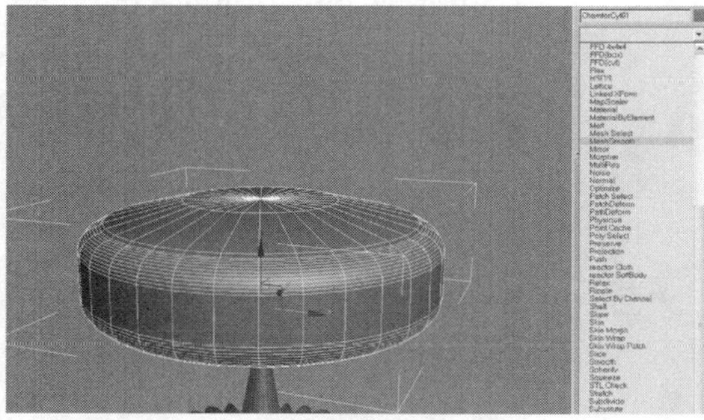

Figure I-176

32. Under Subdivision Method, make sure **NURMS** is shown in the drop-down list, and that **Apply To Whole Mesh** is selected. Then enter **2** in the Iterations field, **1** in the Smoothness field, and make sure Render Values Smoothness is checked and set to **1**.

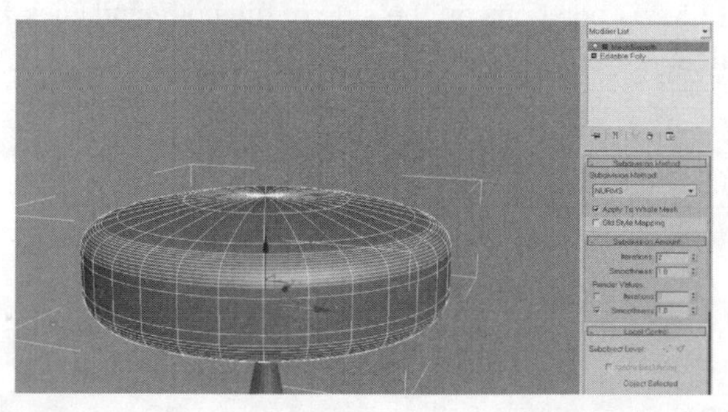

Figure I-177

33. Right-click on the **MeshSmooth** modifier and choose **Collapse All** to make the modifier permanent. Switch to the Front view (**F**) and use the Move tool (**W**) to lower the cap in the Y axis until the antenna enters the cap about halfway.

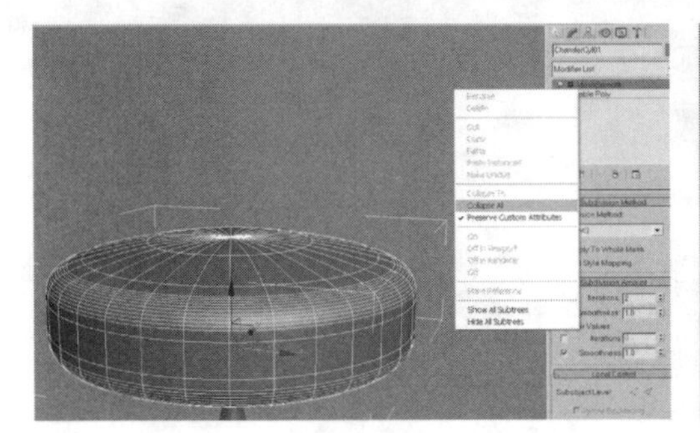

Figure I-178

Figure I-179

34. Select the body, click the **Attach List** button, and choose **ChamferCyl01** to attach the chamfer cylinder.

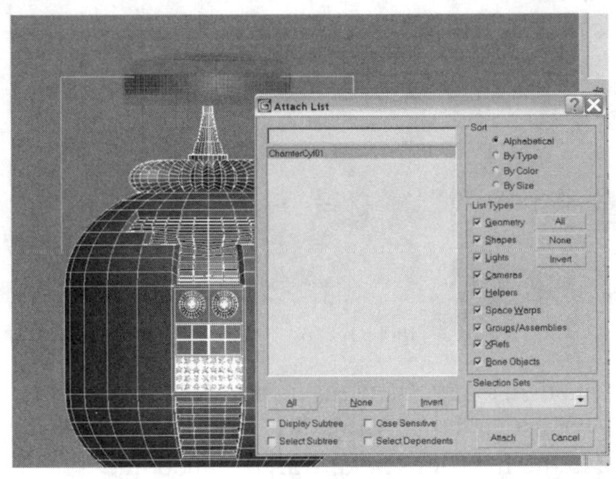

Figure I-180

35. Select the six polygons on the side of the body and click **Bevel Settings**:

Type	Height	Outline	Apply/OK
Local Normal	0	–0.7	OK

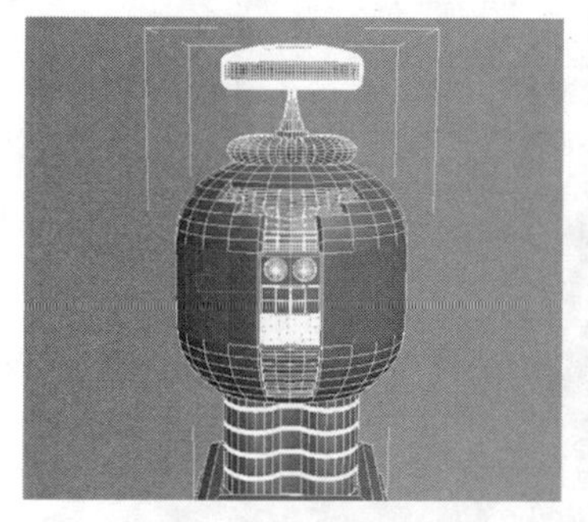

Figure I-181

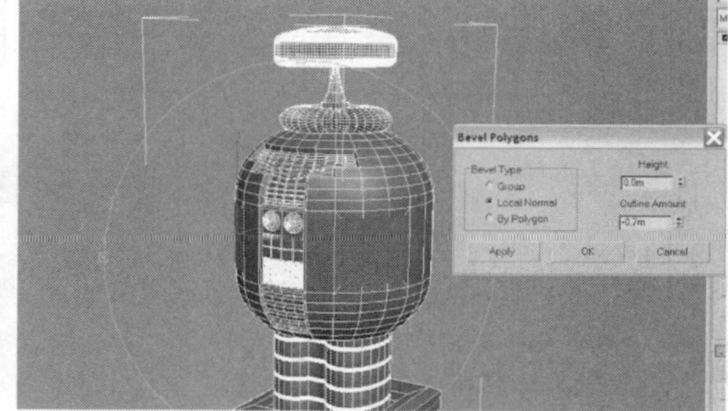

Figure I-182

36. Select the new faces made by the bevel on the right side. Click **Hinge From Edge**, enter **–30** for the Angle and **10** for the Segments, click the **Pick Hinge** button, and click the leftmost edge.

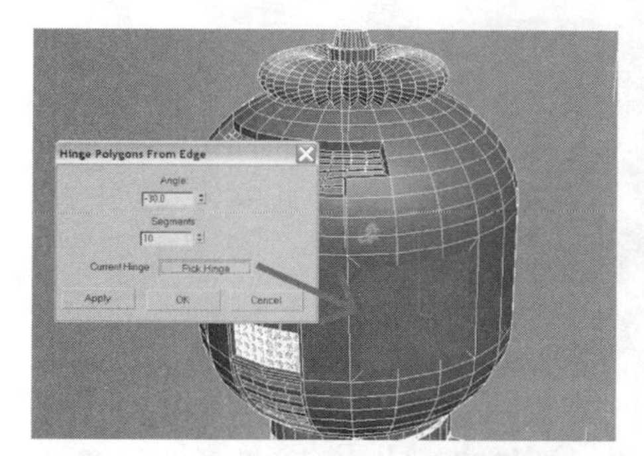

Figure I-183

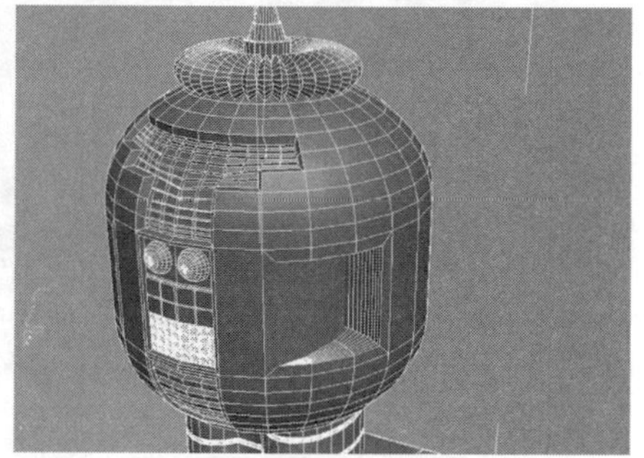

Figure I-184

37. Repeat the Hinge From Edge procedure for the other side:

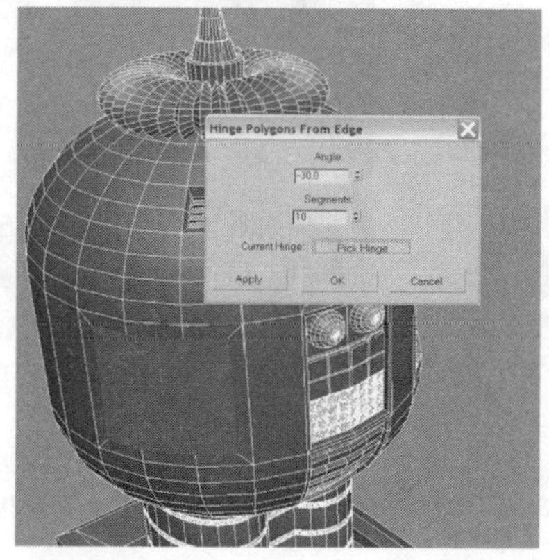

Figure I-185

38. Using AutoGrid, create a Cylinder inside the armhole on the right side, and then apply a Bend modifier to its stack.

Radius	Height	Height/Cap Segs	Sides	Smooth
2.56	10	10/1	24	Checked

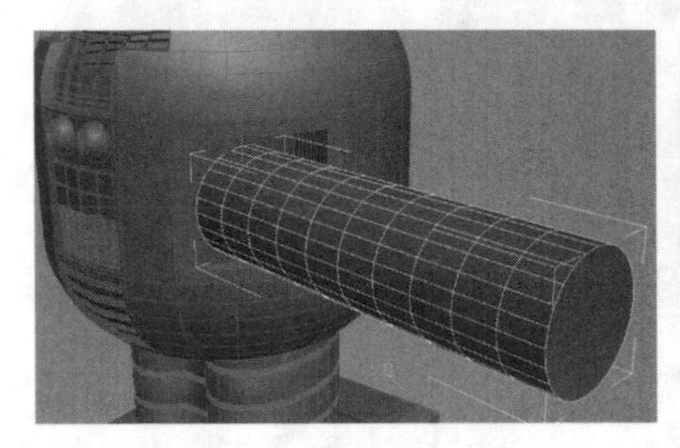

Figure I-186

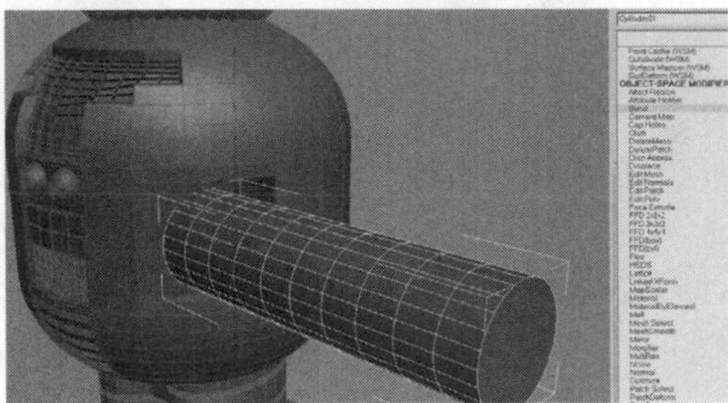

Figure I-187

39. Set the Bend Angle to **–100** and the Bend Axis to **Z**.

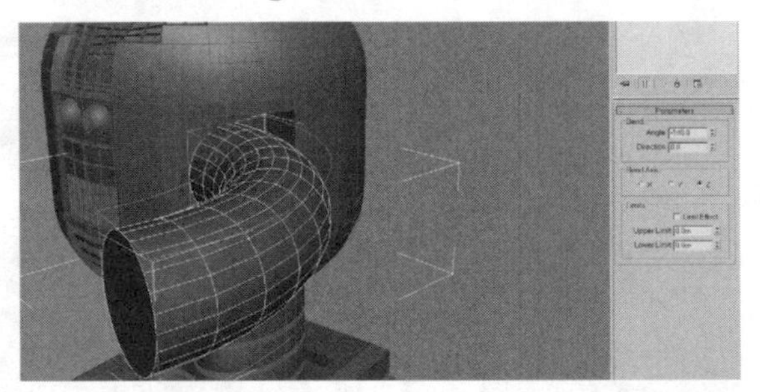

Figure I-188

40. Right-click the stack and choose **Collapse All**. Polygon-select the front of the arm.

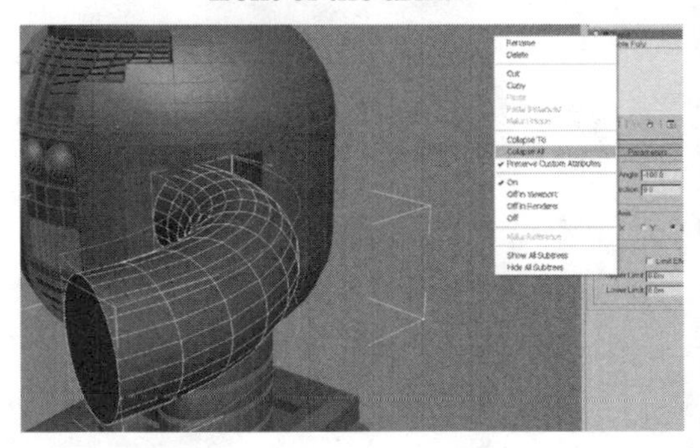

Figure I-189

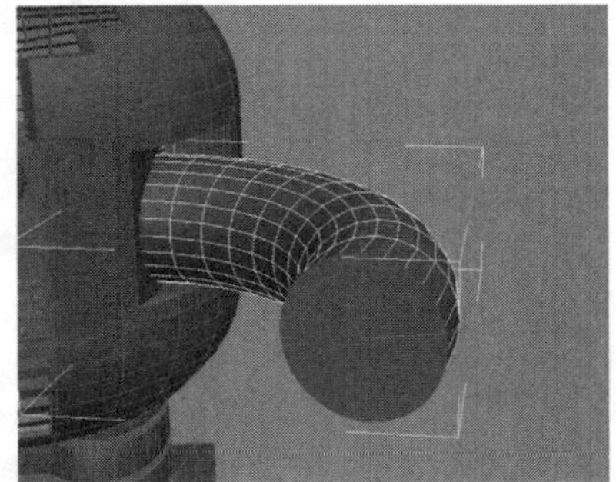

Figure I-190

41. Click **Bevel Settings** and bevel four times with the values in the following tables:

Type	Height	Outline	Apply/OK
Group	0	–0.5	Apply
Group	1.38	–0.2	Apply

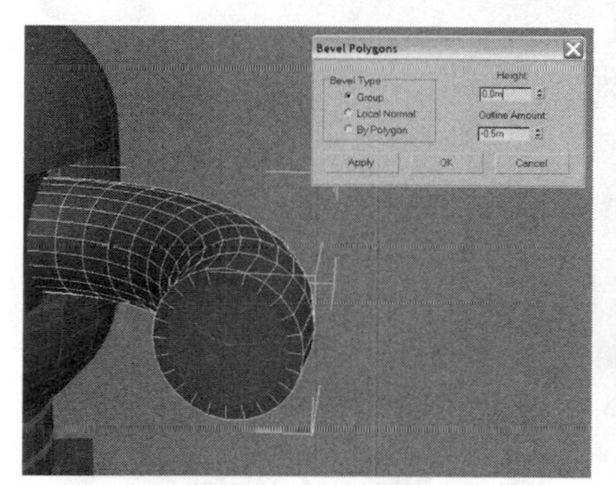

Figure I-191

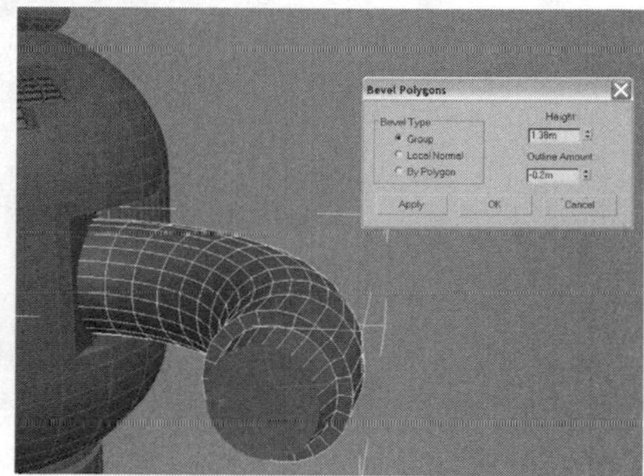

Figure I-192

Type	Height	Outline	Apply/OK
Group	0	–0.9	Apply
Group	–0.6	0	OK

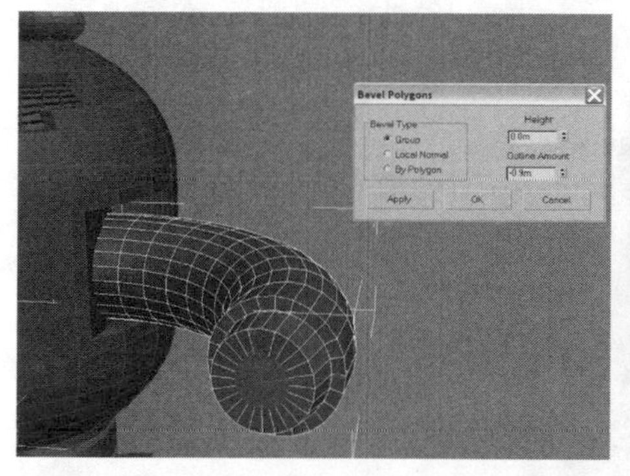

Figure I-193

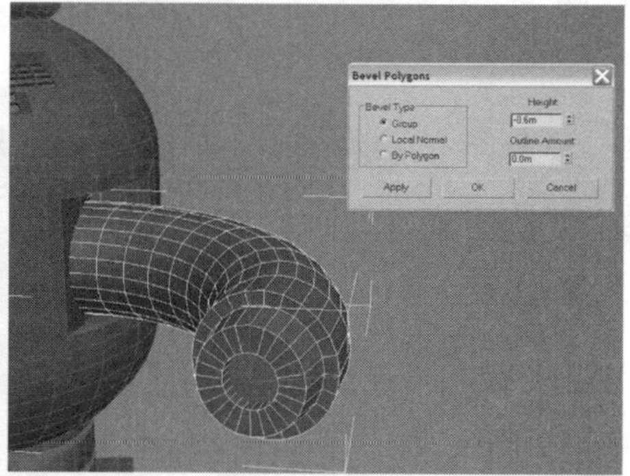

Figure I-194

42. Now let's create a claw. Switch to the Right viewport and, using AutoGrid, create a Tube with these settings:

Radius 1	Radius 2	Height	Height/Cap Segs	Sides	Smooth	Slice On/ From/To
2.173	1.597	0.429	1/1	24	Checked	Checked/100/–77

Figure I-195

43. Switch to the Top viewport and rotate **–27** on the Z axis (the inner yellow circle control rotates an object in Z).

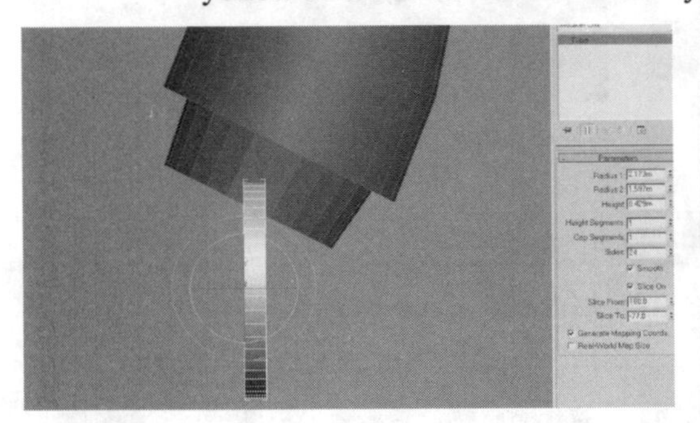

Figure I-196

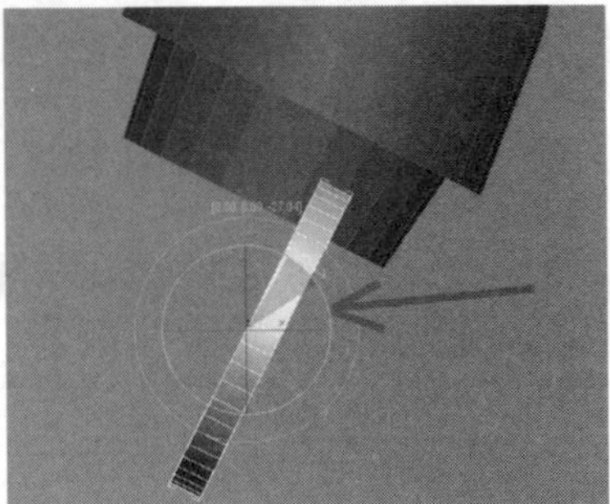

Figure I-197

44. Switch to the **Move** tool. There is a yellow square between the X and Y axes. Dragging on the square allows you to move in both axes simultaneously. Move the claw in the X/Y to center it on the front of the arm.

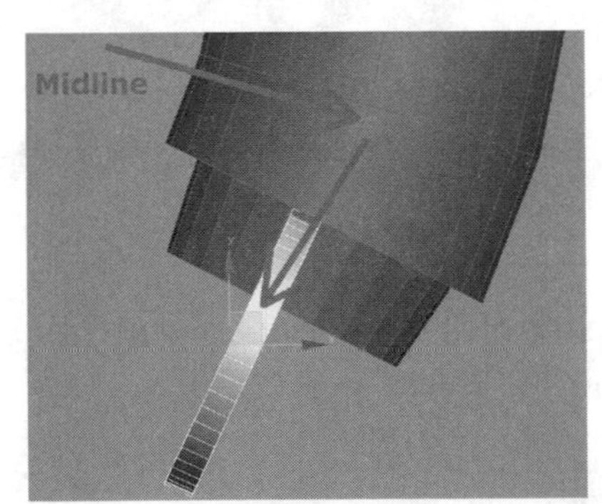

Figure I-198

45. Increase the Height of the claw to around **0.96**, and then switch to the **Move** tool. Notice the Move gizmo's axes are pointing in directions that are not very useful.

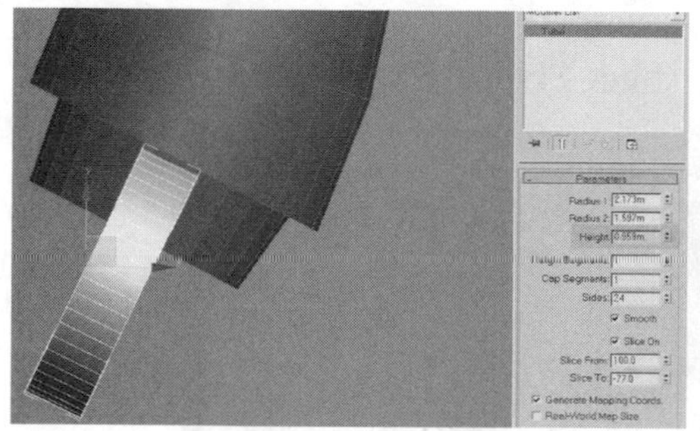

Figure I-199

Figure I-200

46. Change the Reference Coordinate System from View to **Local** and notice that the gizmo realigns itself to be oriented to the claw. Move the claw in the X axis to center it on the front of the arm.

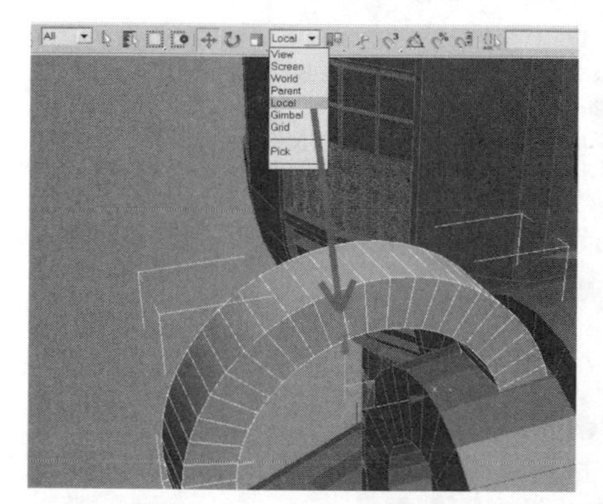

Figure I-201

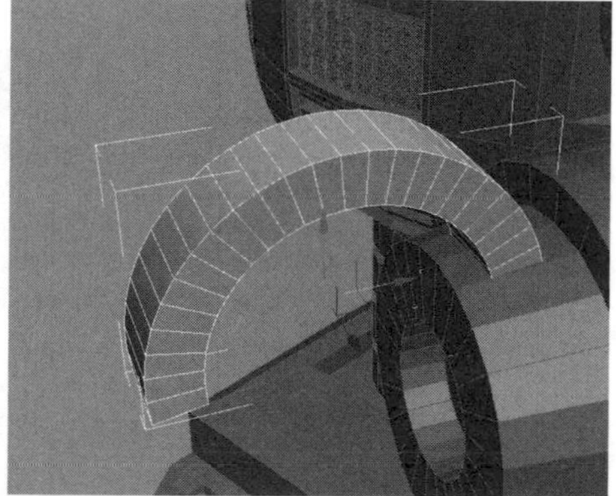

Figure I-202

47. Convert the claw to an Editable Polygon and switch to the Front view.

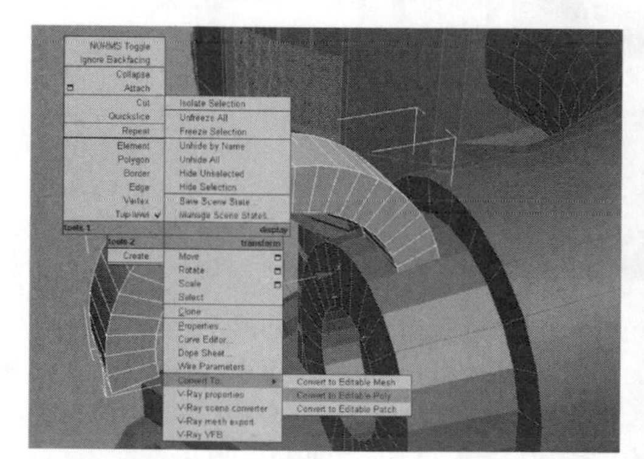

Figure I-203

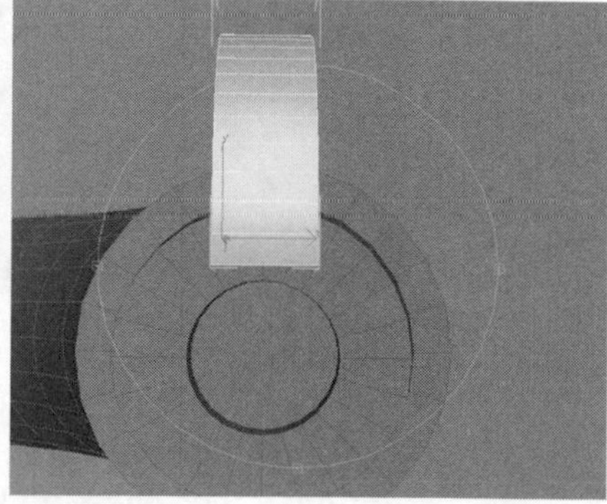

Figure I-204

48. Select the Hierarchy tab, click the **Pivot** button, and under the Adjust Pivot rollout, click **Affect Pivot Only**. Note the position of the Pivot gizmo.

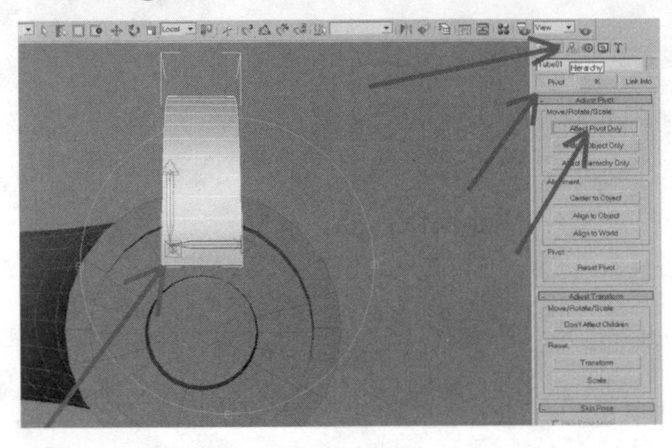

Figure I-205

FYI: An object's pivot starts out centered. In the case of a tube, it starts out in the center of the tube. You can create a clone by holding down the Shift key and using the Rotation tool. Objects rotate around their pivots, so when you make clones using the Rotation tools, the clones are made around the pivot of the original.

Affect Pivot Only moves the pivot point while leaving the original object in the same position.

49. Move the pivot down in the X axis and center it in front of the hole in the front of the arm.

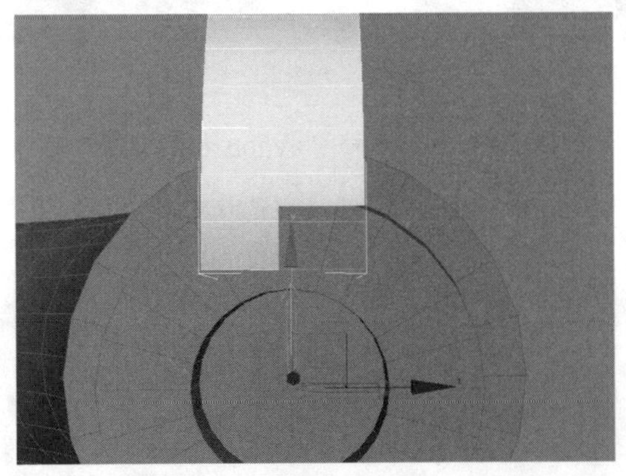

Figure I-206

50. Click the Create panel icon to turn off Affect Pivot Only. Click the **Angle Snap Toggle** button on the main toolbar (this limits rotation to 5 degree increments). Change the Reference Coordinate System to **Local**, then click the **Rotation** tool on the main toolbar.

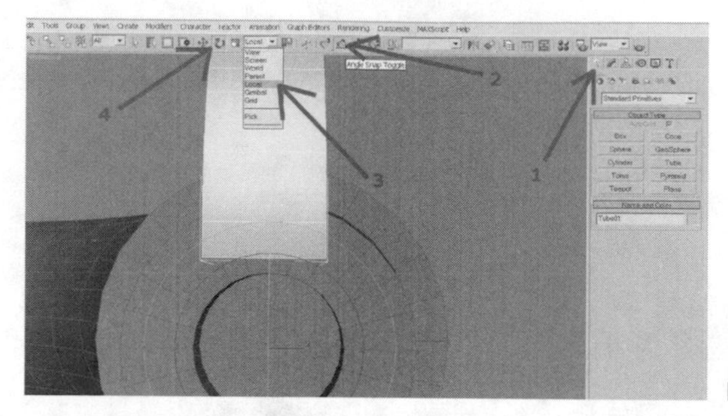

Figure I-207

51. Hold down the **Shift** key and rotate the middle, yellow ring until the X axis reads **90** degrees. Switch the Object type to **Instance**, set the Number of Copies to **3**, and set the Name to **claw.**

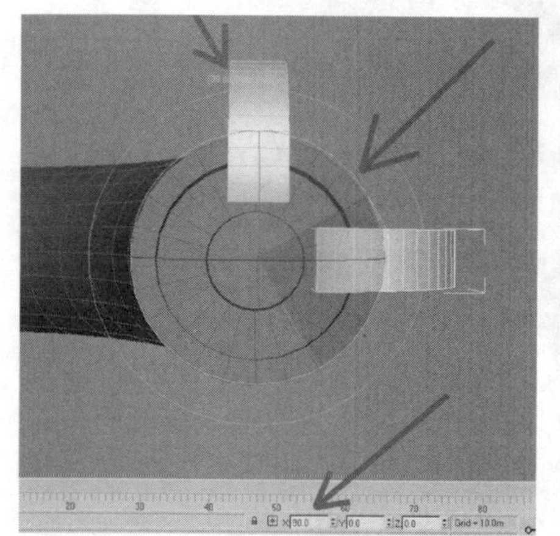

Figure I-208

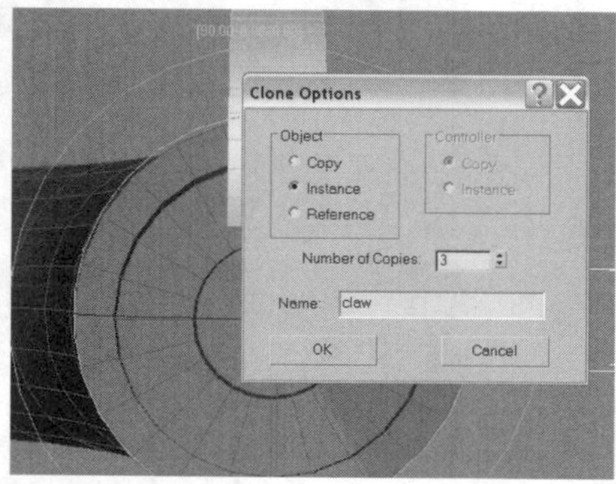

Figure I-209

52. Select the arm, click the **Attach List** button, hold down the **Ctrl** key, click the claws, and click the **Attach** button. Click **Affect Pivot Only**, then move the pivot to the center of the body.

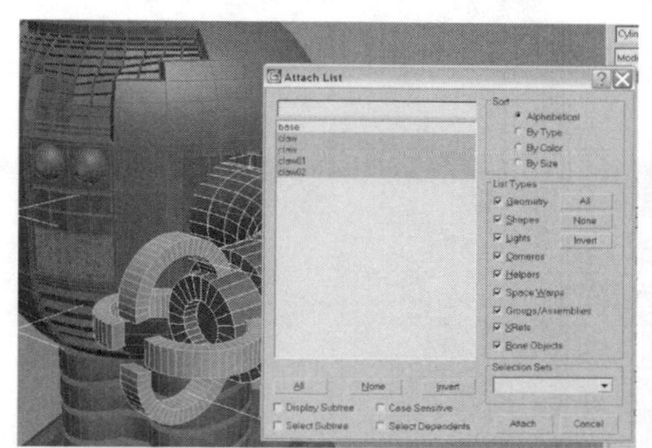

Figure I-210

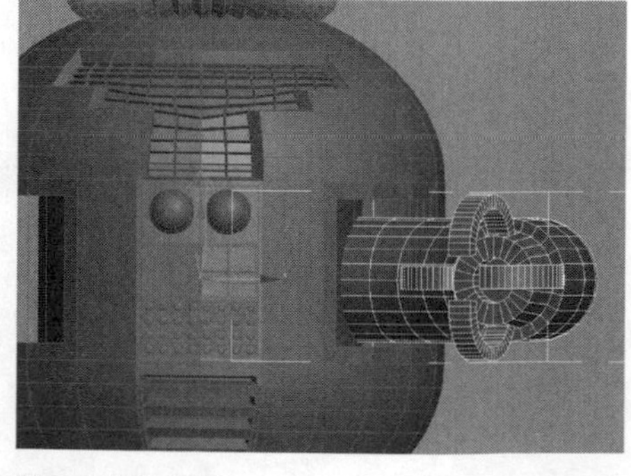

Figure I-211

53. Switch to the Front view. Click the **Mirror** button on the main toolbar, select **XY** as the Mirror Axis and **Instance** under Clone Selection, and then click **OK.**

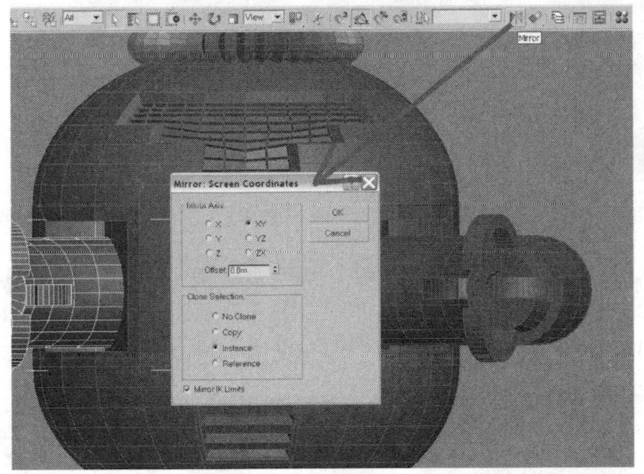

Figure I-212

54. Select the body, click **Attach List**, hold down the **Ctrl** key, select **Cylinder01** and **Cylinder02** (the arms), and click **Attach.**

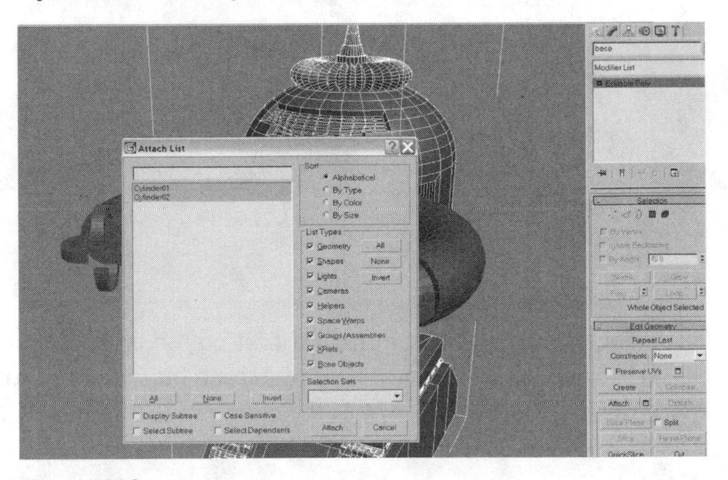

Figure I-213

55. Switch to the Top view and create a Cylinder using AutoGrid with these settings:

Radius	Height	Height/Cap Segs	Sides	Smooth
3.6	0.6	1/1	36	Checked

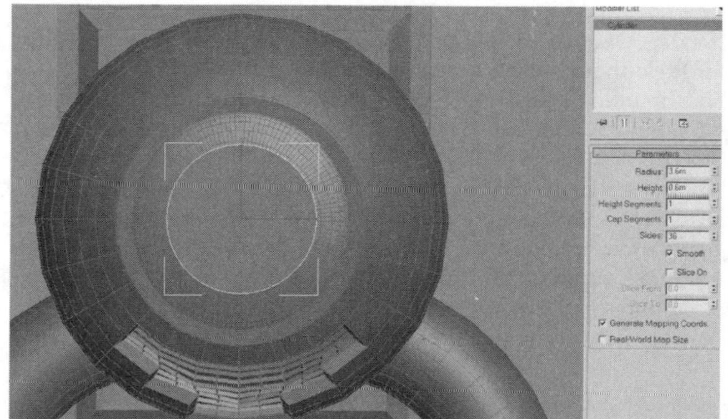

Figure I-214

56. Switch to the Front view and move the cylinder down until it rests atop the antenna. Select the body and attach the cylinder.

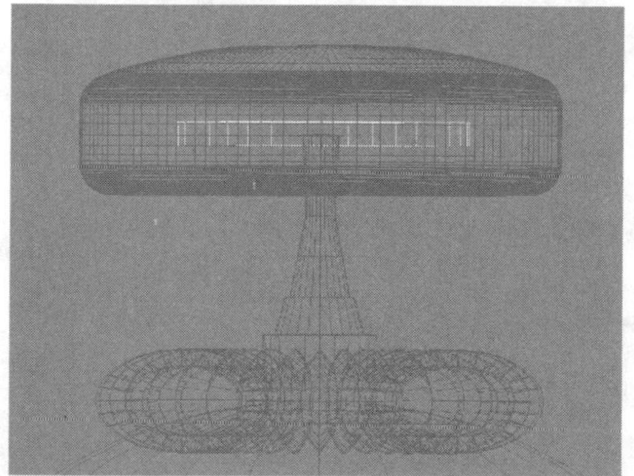

Figure I-215

57. Switch to the Perspective view and hit **F9** to do a quick render.

Figure I-216

Fire Drill: Okay ... so why does the image at the beginning of the chapter look photorealistic and your finished model looks ... well ... like this. For the uninitiated, a 3D model is *always* going to look like this. Sorry to burst your bubble. What makes your model look real is the textures you apply and the renderer you use. Texturing and rendering are so complex in their own right that entire books are dedicated to just these topics. To get you off to a good start with lighting, check out Nicholas Boughen's excellent book, *3ds Max Lighting* (Wordware, 1-55622-401-X). To learn more about rendering using Max's excellent built-in mental ray rendering engine, check out Joep van der Steen's excellent *Rendering with mental ray & 3ds Max* (Focal Press, 978-0240808932).

Here's the spider bot we create in Chapter 1.

Chapter 1
Spider Bot

In this chapter, you'll learn to make a small surveillance bot like the one in the video game *Deus Ex: The Invisible War*. Let's face it: A spider bot isn't as sexy as, say, a heavily armored mech. But though they look complicated, spider bots are generally easy and quick to build.

Day 1: Building the Body

1. Go to the Create panel and create a Box using these settings:

Length	Width	Height	Length/Width/Height Segs
100	100	100	4/2/3

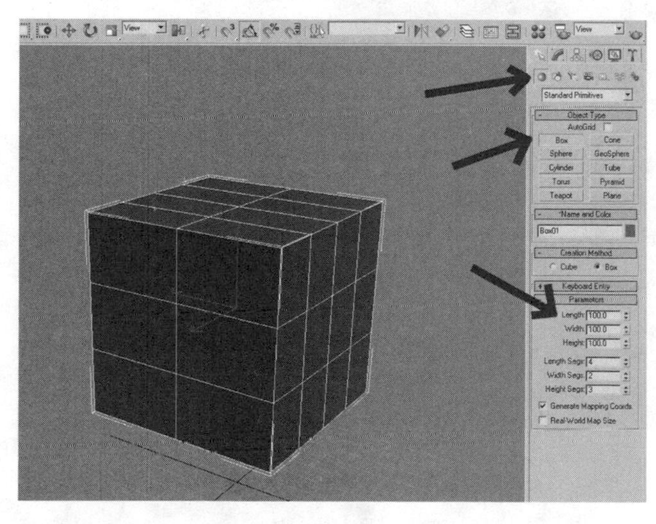

Figure 1-1

2. Right-click the box and select **Convert To > Convert to Editable Poly.**

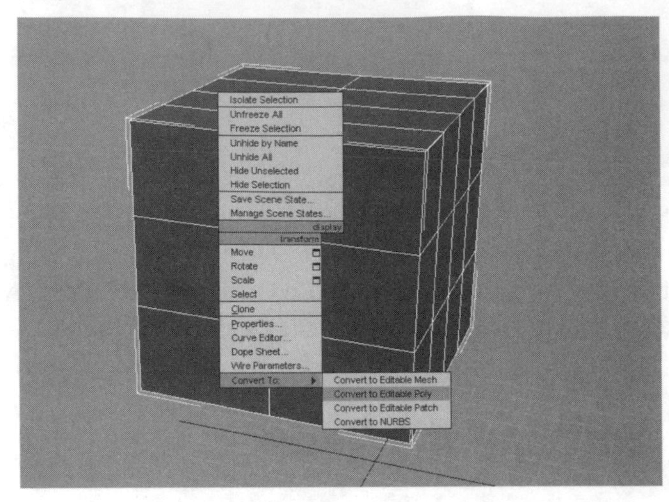

Figure 1-2

3. Under Selection, click the **Polygon** selection mode icon and then select the left half of the box.

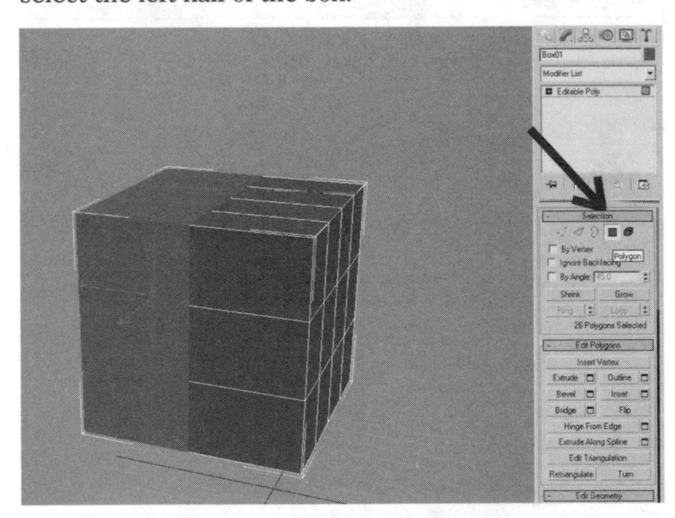

Figure 1-3

4. Delete the selected polygons. Click the down arrow next to the Modifier List, select the **Symmetry** modifier to add it to the stack, and under Mirror Axis select **X** and check **Flip.**

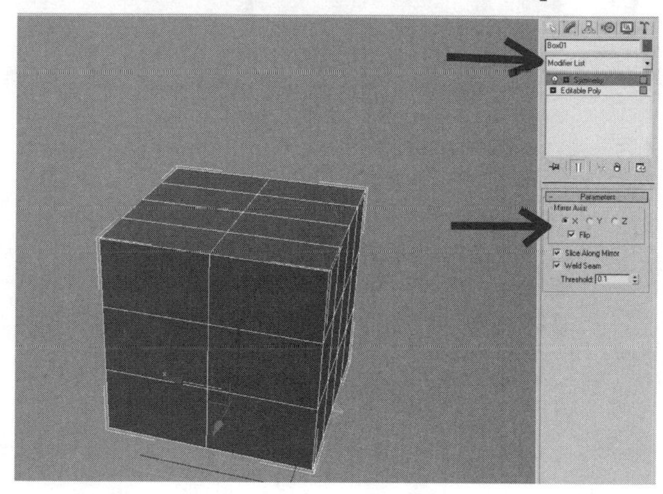

Figure 1-4

FYI: A Symmetry modifier mirrors any changes you make to the original object. This modifier is especially handy when building objects with two identical sides, like a human head, because you only have to make changes to one side.

You can toggle modifiers on and off in the viewports. There's an icon at the bottom of the stack that looks like a test tube. When it's pressed, the effects of the modifier will be shown in the viewport. When it's unselected, the modifier's effect will be turned off.

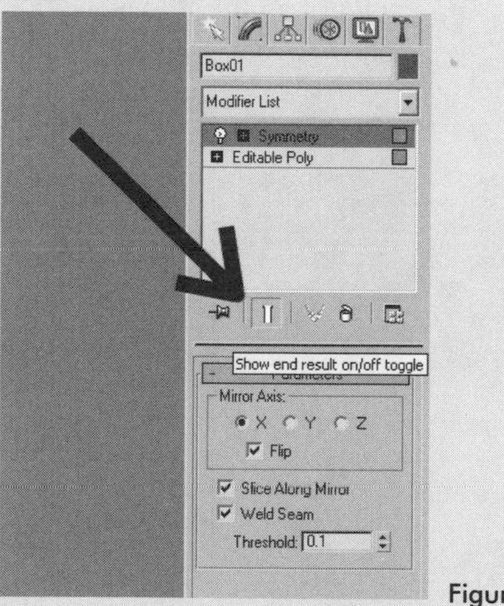

Figure 1-5

5. Click the plus sign next to Editable Poly in the stack and it will give you a list of selection options. Click **Polygon**.

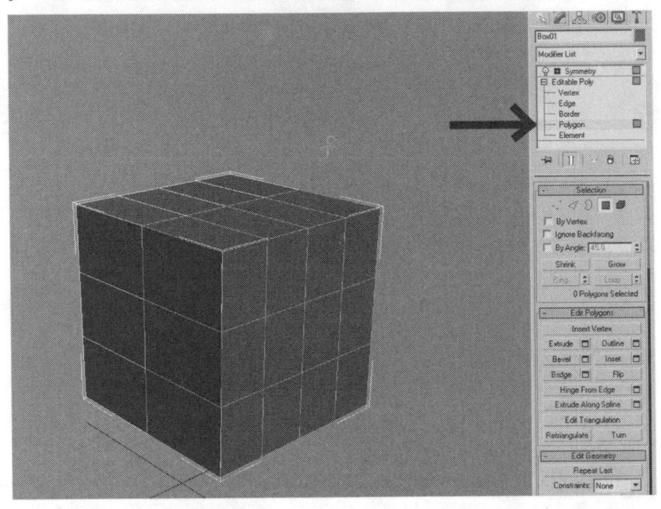

Figure 1-6

6. Select one of the polygons and use the Move tool (**W**) to pull the polygon in the X axis. Notice how the other side automatically follows:

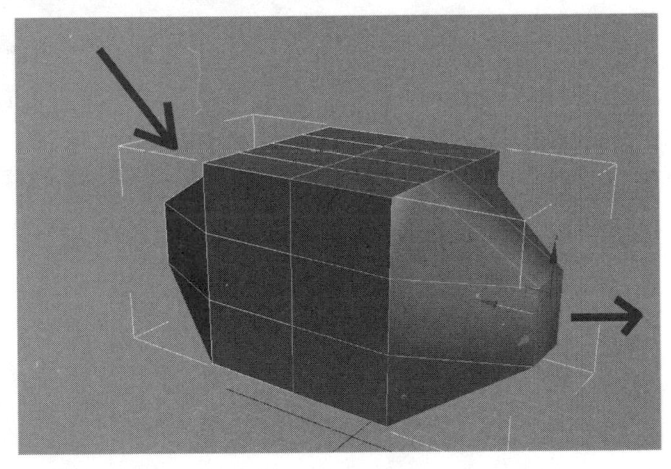

Figure 1-7

7. Undo (**Ctrl+Z**).

FYI: The most popular methods of 3D modeling are polygonal (sub-D) and NURBs. Polygonal modeling, which is what we'll do in this chapter, is the easier of the two and lends itself to making hard-edged, inorganic models, like robots. The downside is that it's hard to make smooth surfaces with just polygonal modeling. NURBs are great for making smooth surfaces, but they're a bit harder to work with and are harder to use to make hard-edged surfaces.

In order to have the modeling ease of polygons but achieve a smooth, injection-molded look, we'll use a MeshSmooth modifier. When added to the stack, a MeshSmooth modifier takes the underlying polygon model and adds additional geometry to smooth it out.

8. Add a **MeshSmooth** modifier to the stack using the default values.

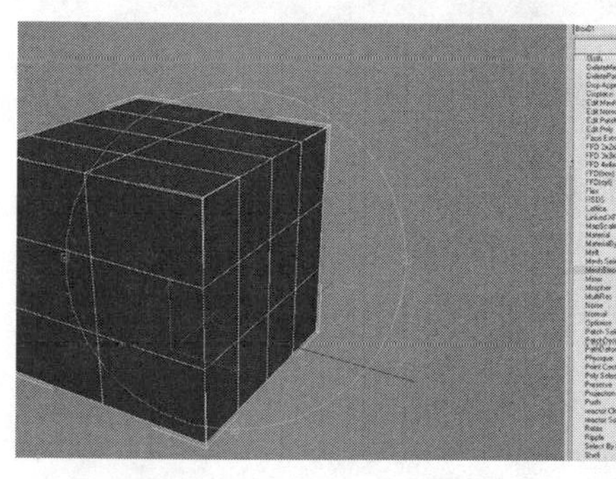

Figure 1-8

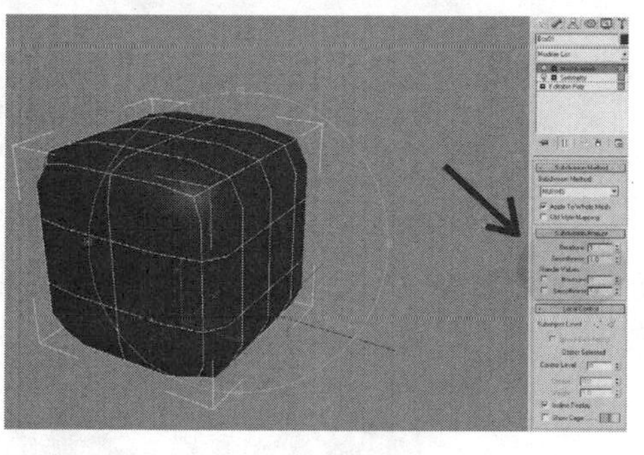

Figure 1-9

FYI: In most modeling situations, you only need to worry about the controls under the Subdivision Amount rollout. The more iterations you add, the smoother your model will be, but... each iteration adds more geometry, which means a bigger hit on your system resources. In most instances, you don't need more than around three iterations. Also, you want to set your render iterations higher than your viewport iterations. That way, you can "rough out" your model with a minimal resource hit and use the higher iterations for final rendering.

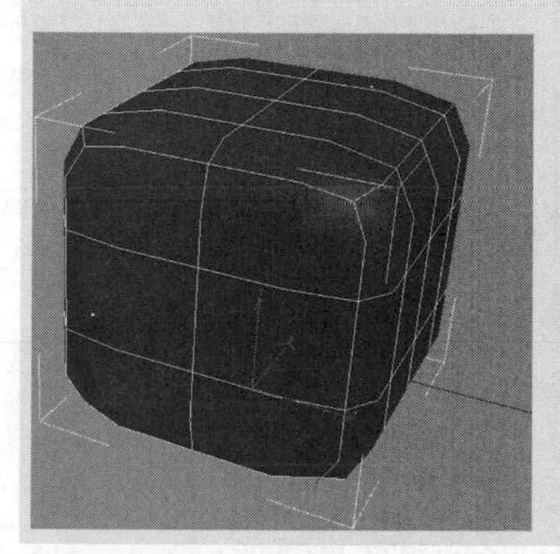

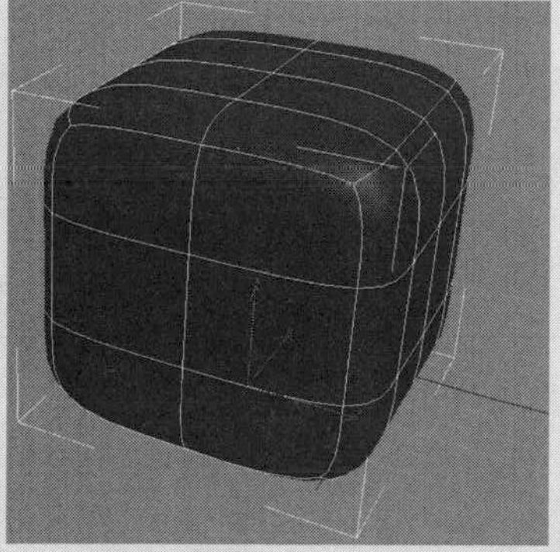

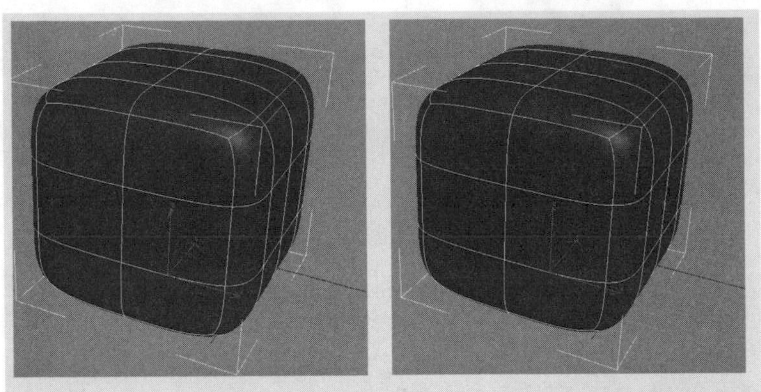

Figures 1-10 to 1-13: One iteration through four iterations

As you can see, after three iterations you reach a point of diminishing returns. The surface continues to get smoother, but the changes are so small they're hard to detect. Generally, you want to model at iteration 1 or 2 and use a setting of 3 or 4 for your rendering. You can best understand how this smoothing process works by switching to wireframe and unchecking Isoline Display under Local Control.

Notice what's happening. Each iteration subdivides the object into smaller and smaller polygons. This is why it's called subdivision surfacing or sub-D.

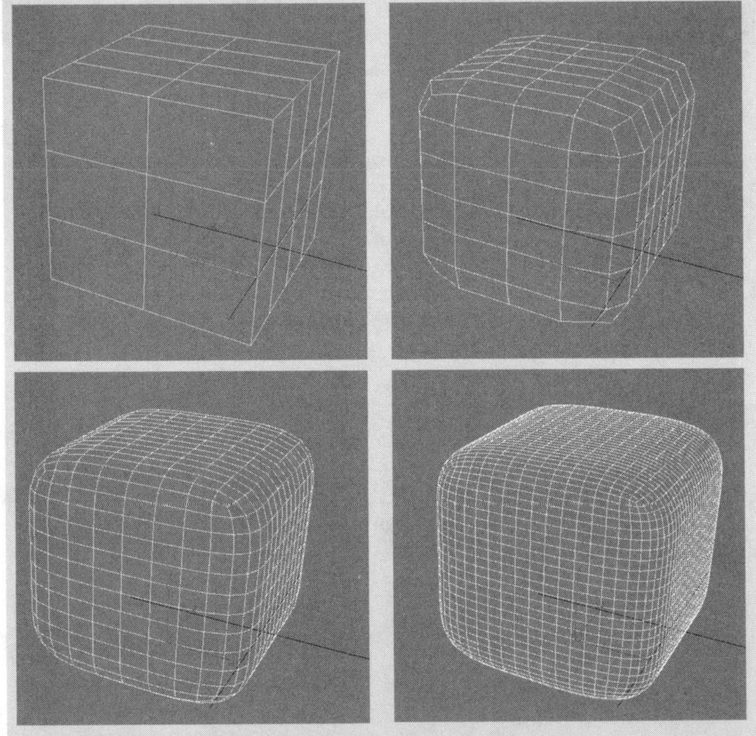

Figures 1-14 to 1-17: Zero iteration through three iterations

9. Set Iterations to **2**, select the same polygon you did in step 6, and pull out it out the same way.

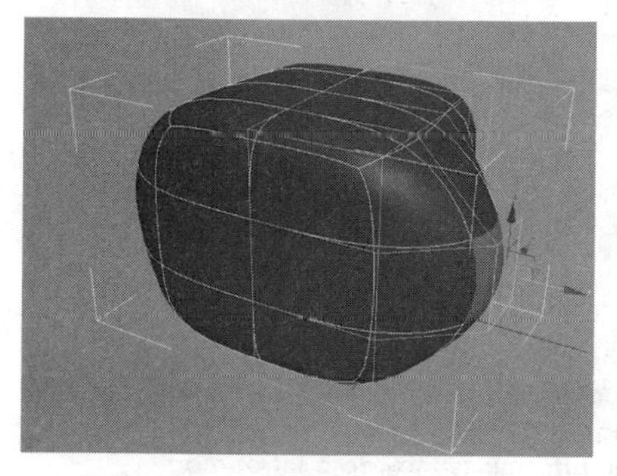
Figure 1-18

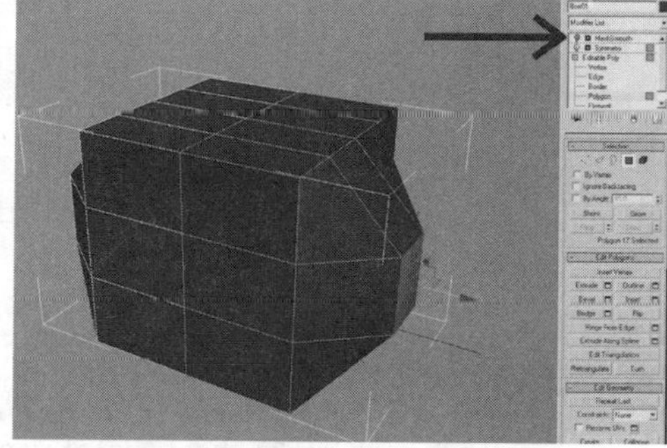
Figure 1-19

FYI: Note the differences between step 6 and step 9. If you click the light bulb icon to the left of the MeshSmooth modifier, it will toggle the modifier on and off. If you toggle it off, you'll see that nothing has changed from a modeling point of view; the modifier simply refines the underlying model.

10. Undo the move you made in the last step, and select the middle row of four polygons.

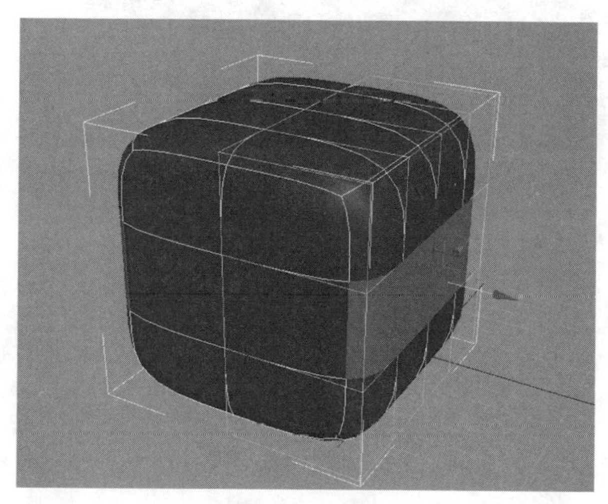
Figure 1-20

11. Under the Edit Polygons rollout, click the **Extrude Settings** button.

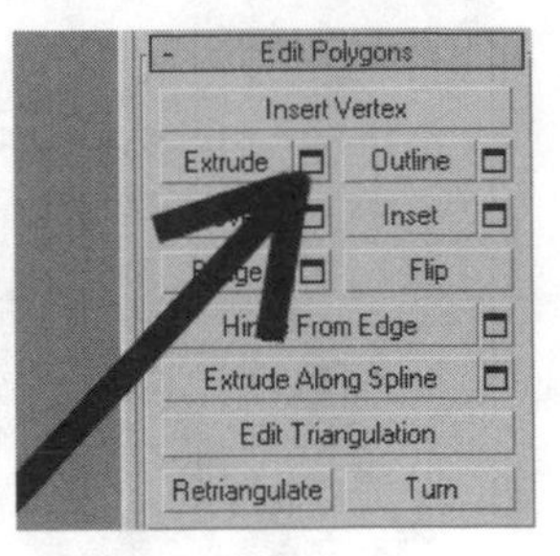

Figure 1-21

FYI: Throughout Max, you're given a choice, as you are here, of clicking a button and using a gizmo to perform actions (e.g., extrusions) by hand and eye, or clicking to open a settings box and typing exact values. One of the things I dislike about a lot of video tutorials is they do a lot of modeling using the gizmo technique, which makes it hard to achieve the same results. This can be very frustrating when you're just learning. Perhaps it's because I'm an engineer and not an artist that I prefer to enter exact values.

12. When the settings box opens, select **By Polygon** as the Extrusion Type and set the Extrusion Height to **0.1**. Click **Apply.***

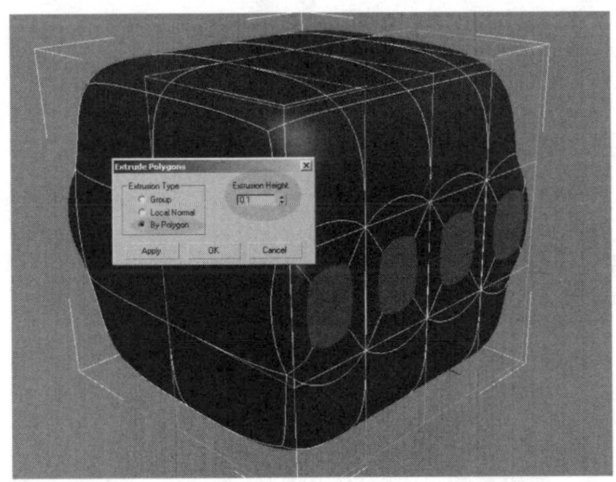

Figure 1-22

* Thanks to Matt J. Bell for teaching me the sub-D process. His four-legged spider bot, which appeared in Issue 40 of *3D World*, was the first 3D model I ever made, and his tutorial was the first training I had in 3D modeling.

13. Perform another extrusion by changing the Extrusion Height to **2.0** and clicking **Apply**.

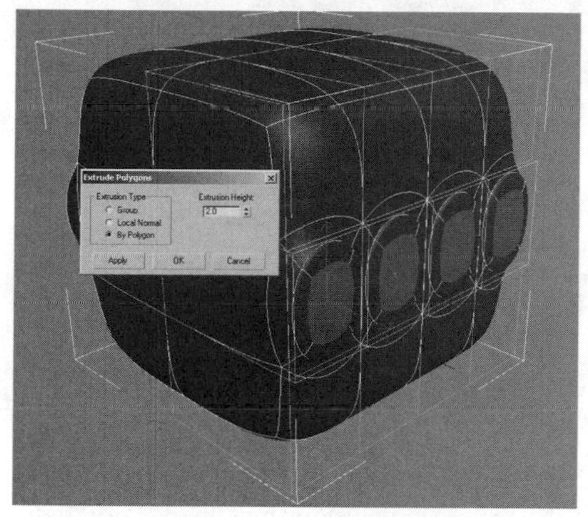

Figure 1-23

14. Extrude again with the Extrusion Height set to **1.0** and click **OK** (*not* Apply) to complete the extrusion and close the dialog box.

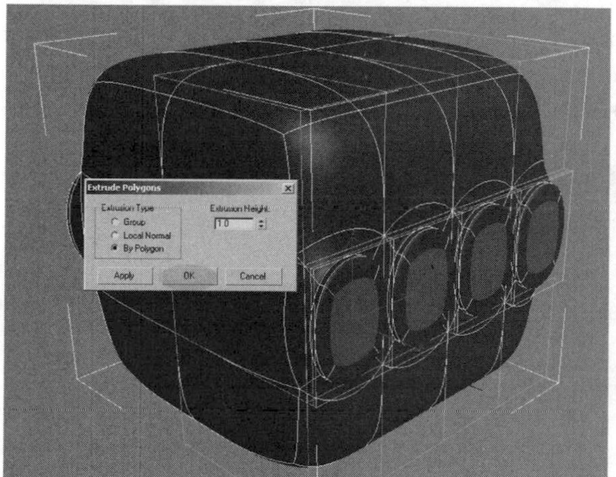

Figure 1-24

FYI: What's with the small extrusions? When you are using NURMS or MeshSmooth, the closer together the edges, the sharper the edges of the end product. Consider the three identical boxes in the top row in Figure 1-25. The only difference between them is the number of edges and how close those edges are. Compare their NURMS versions in the row below, and see how close edges serve to straighten the edges. This process of placing edges close together to make sharper corners when using NURMS is called "increasing the tension," because adding edges close together is somewhat like stretching the skin of a drum.

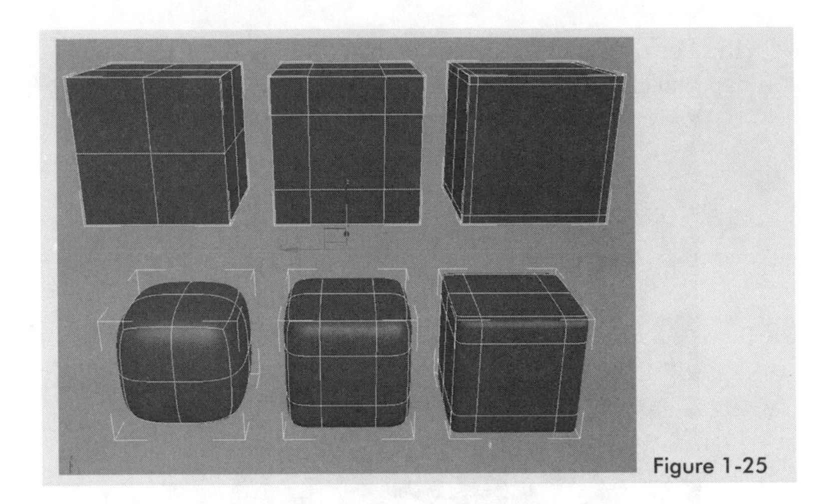

Figure 1-25

15. Right-click on the **Select and Uniform Scale** button on the toolbar to open the dialog box, type **70** in the Offset World field, and click the close (X) button.

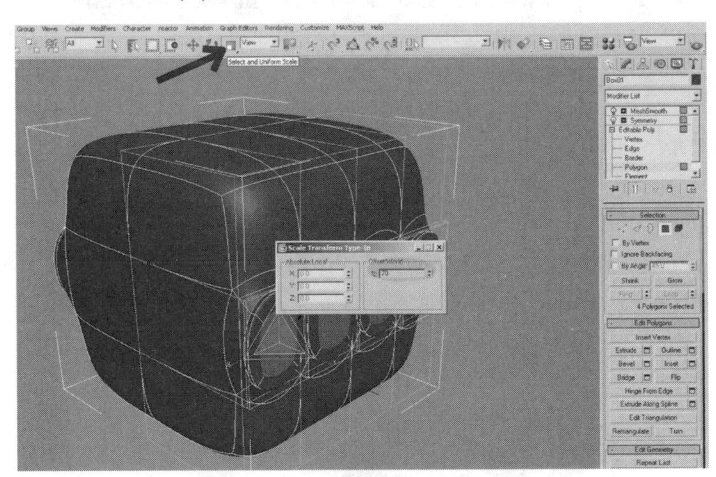

Figure 1-26

16. Extrude the polygons with a Height of **–5.0**.

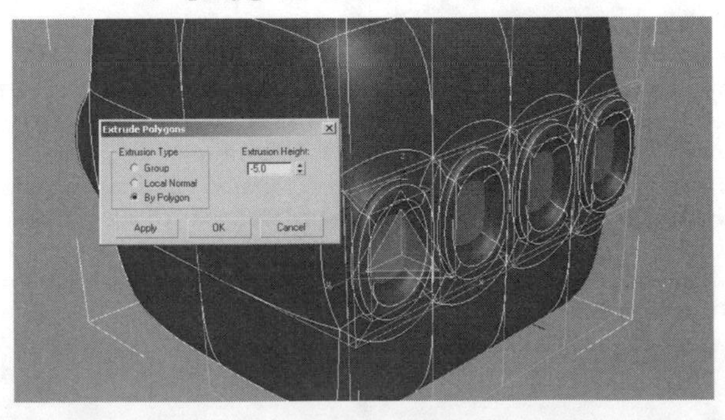

Figure 1-27

17. Select the front three polygons and Move (**W**) them **–20** units in the Offset World Y axis.

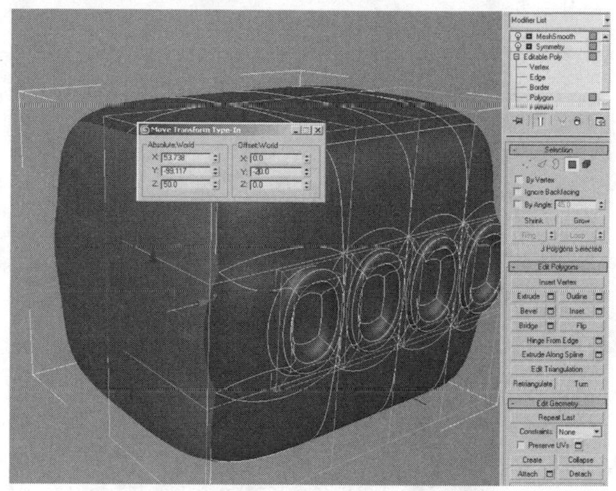

Figure 1-28

18. Select the **Symmetry** modifier, then right-click and select **Collapse To** to make the Symmetry modifier permanent.

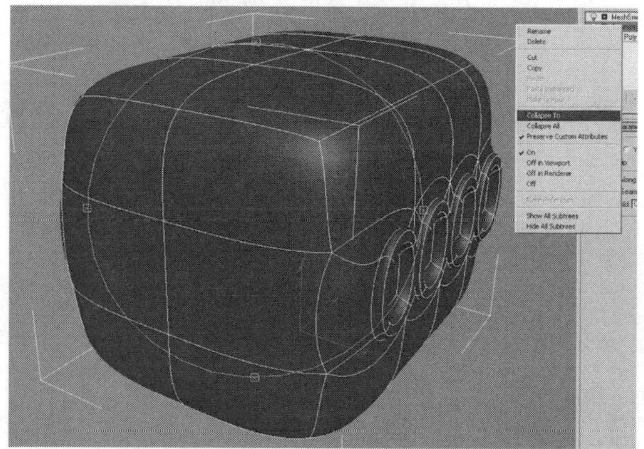

Figure 1-29

FYI: Converting to an Editable Polygon collapses *all* the modifiers and makes them permanent. On the other hand, Collapse To collapses only the selected modifier down one level. For now we want to keep MeshSmooth, but we're done with the Symmetry modifier.

19. Select the front four polygons, right-click the **Scale** tool, and type **80** in the Offset World field to scale the polygons down by 80 percent in all axes.

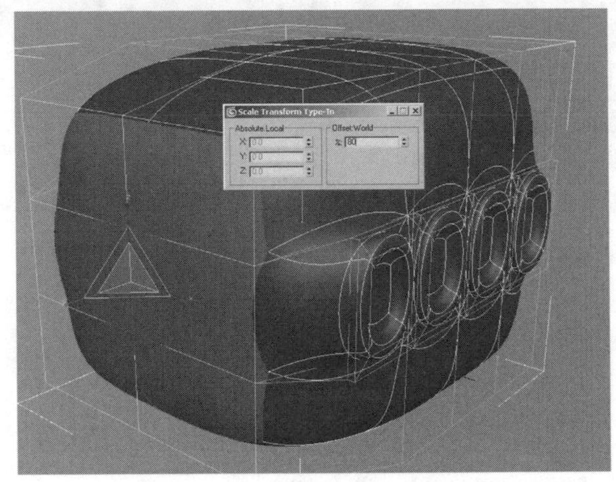

Figure 1-30

20. Switch to the Front view and, using AutoGrid, create a Tube and center it in the middle of the front surface of the bot using these settings:

Radius 1	Radius 2	Height	Height Segs	Cap Segs	Sides	Smooth
14	12	6	1	1	18	Checked

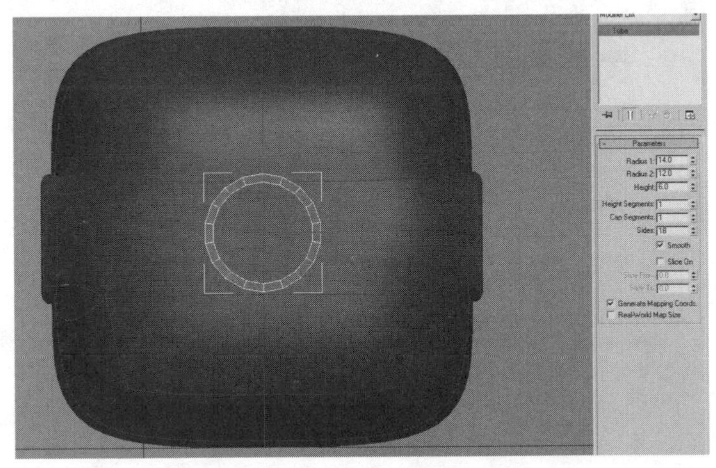

Figure 1-31

21. Right-click and choose **Convert to Editable Poly**, switch to wireframe (**F3**) to get a better view, Arc Rotate so you can see the back of the tube, and delete the back-facing polygons. (Back-facing polygons are those that face toward geometry that no one will see.)

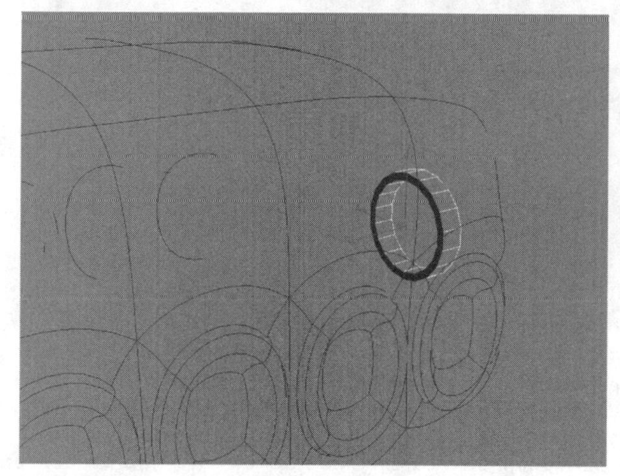

Figure 1-32

Don't Forget: It's good practice to delete polygons that no one is ever going to see. The more polygons you have, the longer it takes to render. While we won't specifically focus on building low-polygon models in this book, the ability to build low-polygon models is a skill valued by the game industry.

22. Next, delete the polygons inside the tube, since this will be a socket for an eye and nobody will see these polys either.

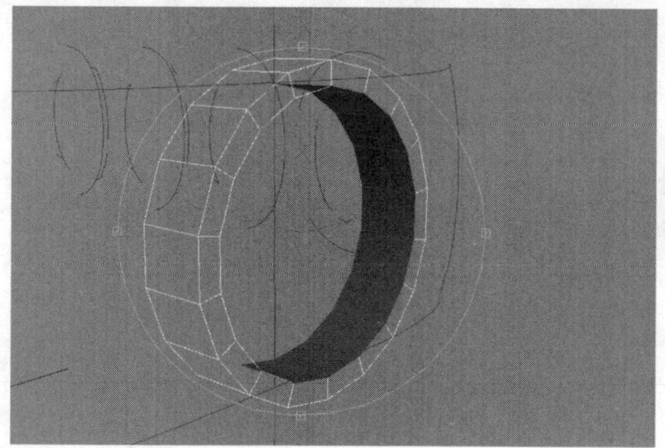

Figure 1-33

23. Under Subdivision Surface, click **Use NURMS Subdivision**. Set the Display Iterations to **2** and the Render Iterations to **3**.

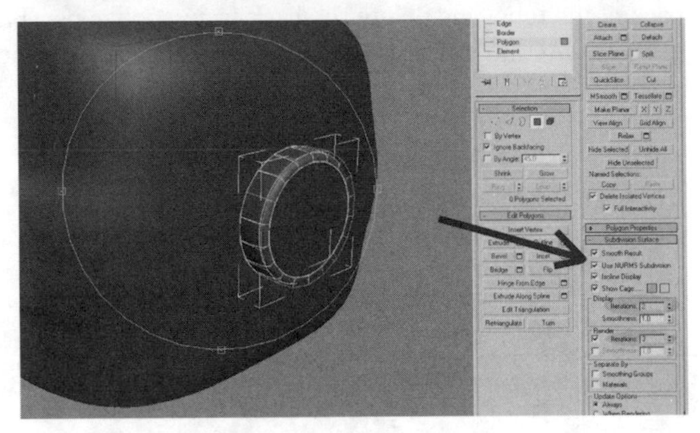

Figure 1-34

FYI: So why didn't I use a MeshSmooth modifier here? Generally, I use a MeshSmooth modifier either when I want the option of making the smoothing permanent by collapsing the stack or when I want it to interact with one or more other modifiers. Use NURMS Subdivision does the same thing, but you can toggle it on and off.

24. Switch to Border selection mode and select the border of the tube that touches the bot's body; again, this is easier to do in wireframe (**F3**).

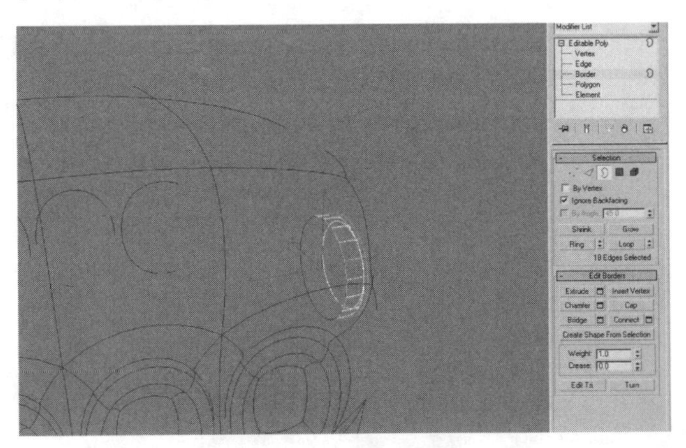

Figure 1-35

25. Switch back to shaded mode (**F3**), click **Create Shape From Selection**, and name the shape **seal.**

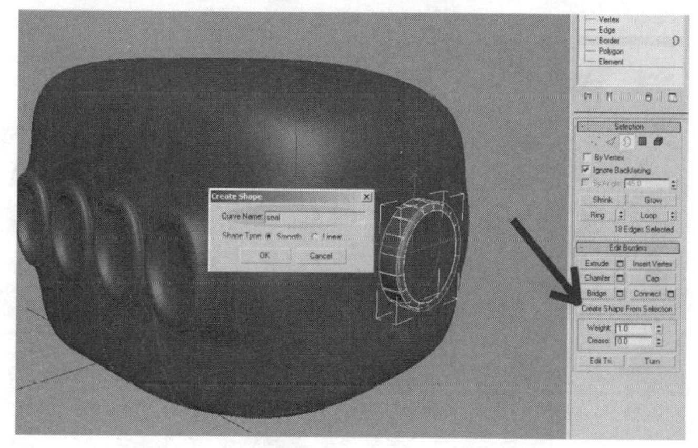

Figure 1-36

FYI: This technique is really slick for creating great-looking "seals" on mechanical models. Create Shape From Selection takes the selection and creates a spline object; in this case, a ring. You then select the shape and, under its settings, make it renderable. After you're satisified with the size and shape, you convert it to an Editable Polygon.

26. Hit the **H** key and select **seal** from the list.

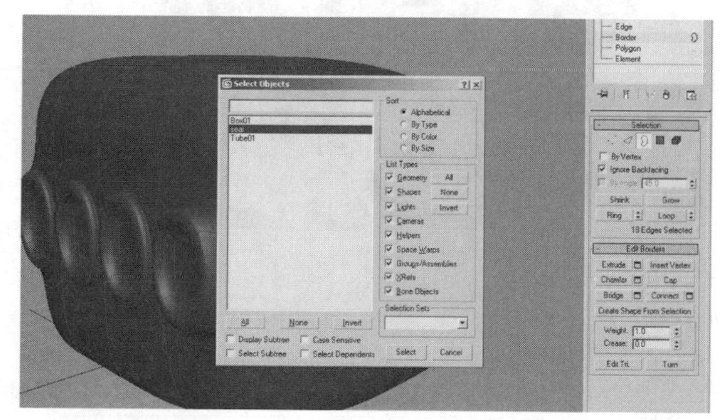

Figure 1-37

27. Under Rendering, check **Enable In Renderer** and **Enable In Viewport.**

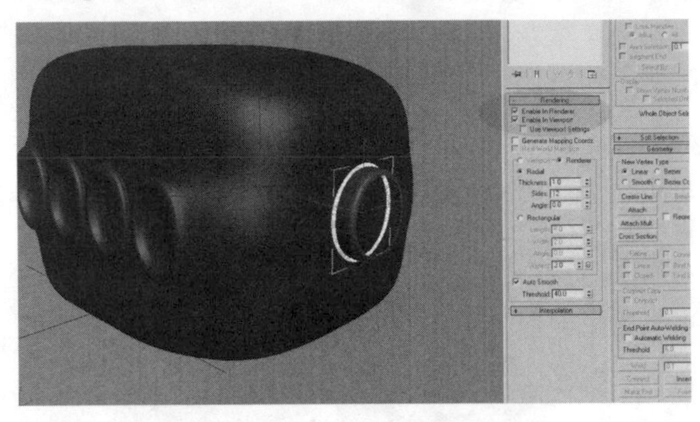

Figure 1-38

28. Right-click and choose **Convert to Editable Poly.**

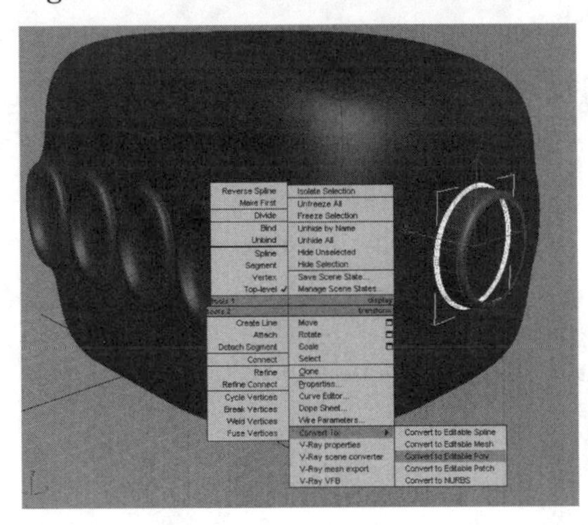

Figure 1-39

29. Select the tube. Under Edit Geometry, click **Attach List**, select **seal** from the list, and click **Attach** to attach the seal to the tube.

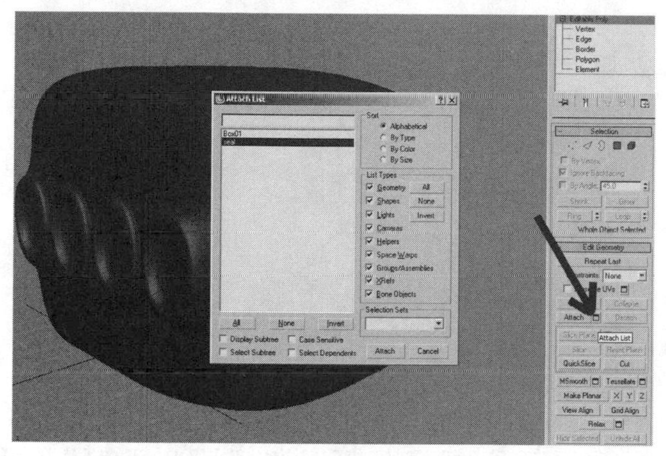

Figure 1-40

30. Rename the tube to **eye_socket**, click the **Select and Link** button on the toolbar, and drag the eye_socket onto the body.

Figure 1-41

FYI: So why use Select and Link? Why not use Attach? Attach does more than "attach" one object to another; it makes the selected object a part of the other object. Using Select and Link, the objects maintain their own identity but are linked, in a parent-child relationship, for the purpose of animation. Specifically, when the parent is moved, the child object follows. How do you know which is which? When you use Select and Link, the selected object is the child and the object you drag it onto is the parent. In our case, the body is the parent and the eye_socket is the child. So whenever we move the body, the eye_socket will follow as if it were glued to the body. However, Select and Link does not affect your ability to animate the child separately from the parent.

31. Switch to AutoGrid and create a Sphere with a Radius of **12.55** in the center of the tube.

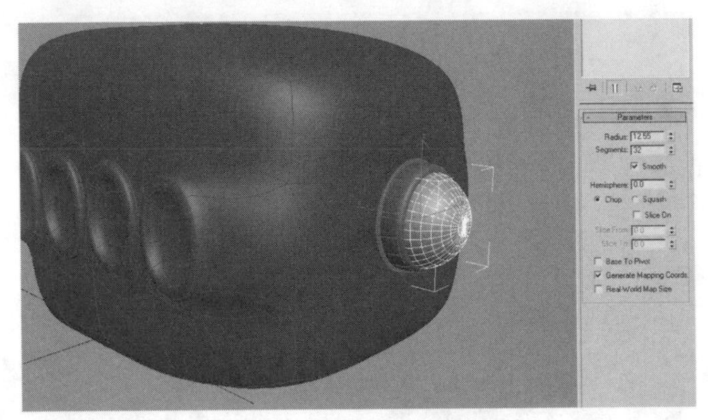

Figure 1-42

32. Convert the sphere to an Editable Polygon, select a segment of the third ring, and click the **Loop** button to select the entire ring.

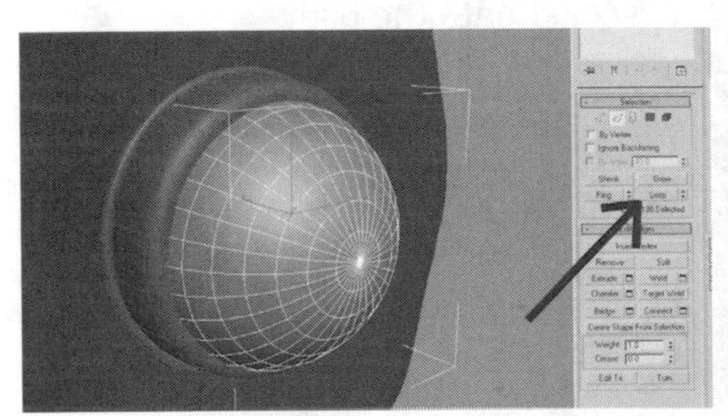

Figure 1-43

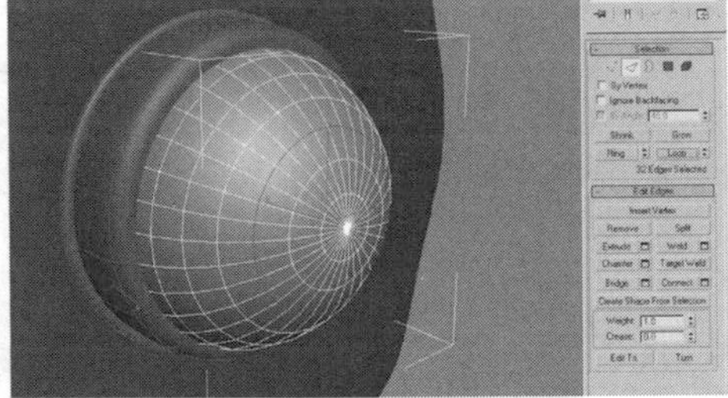

Figure 1-44

33. Click the **Extrude Settings** button and enter an Extrusion Height of **–0.8** and an Extrusion Base Width of **0.04**.

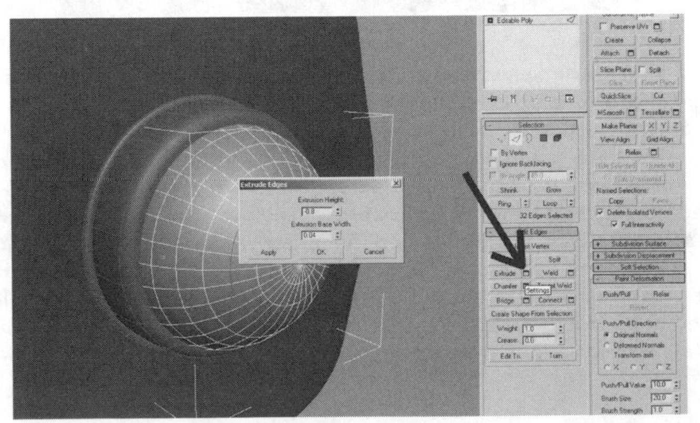

Figure 1-45

FYI: This extrusion pulls the selected edges inward, creating a groove that visually separates the iris from the rest of the eye.

34. Rename the sphere to **eye** and the box to **body.**

35. Select and Link the eye to the eye_socket, and click the **Schematic View** button on the main toolbar.

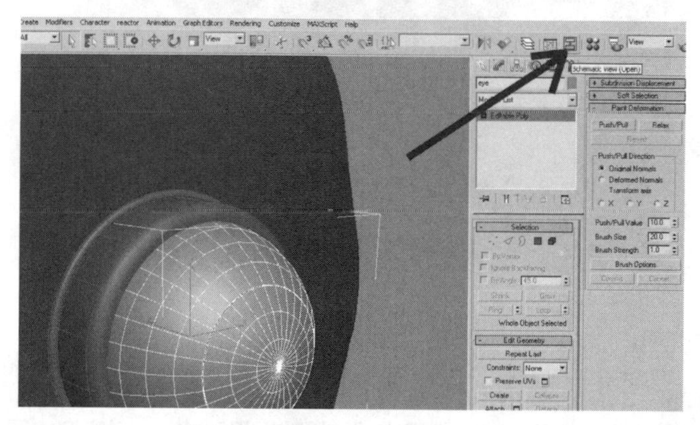

Figure 1-46

FYI: Schematic view is handy because it graphically shows all the linkages between objects. Admittedly, it's not particularly useful yet, but it does show that the eye is parented to the eye_socket and the eye_socket is parented to the body. Schematic view becomes more powerful when your scene contains multiple objects with large numbers of interlinked pieces (see Chapter 2, "Hunter-Killer").

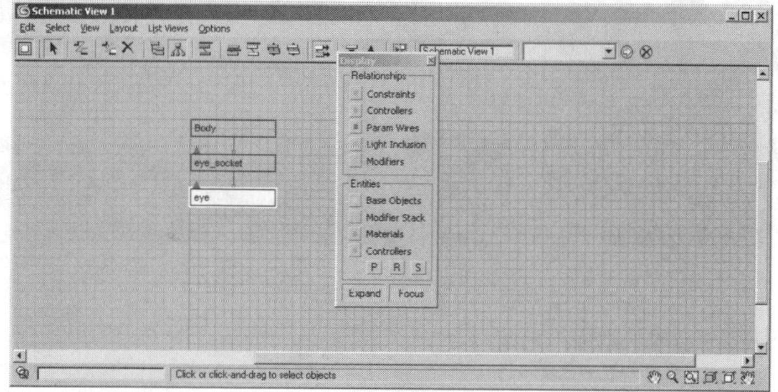

Figure 1-47

36. Select the **eye** and the **eye_socket**. Select **Group** from the Group menu, type **eye_assembly** in the name field, and then click **OK**.

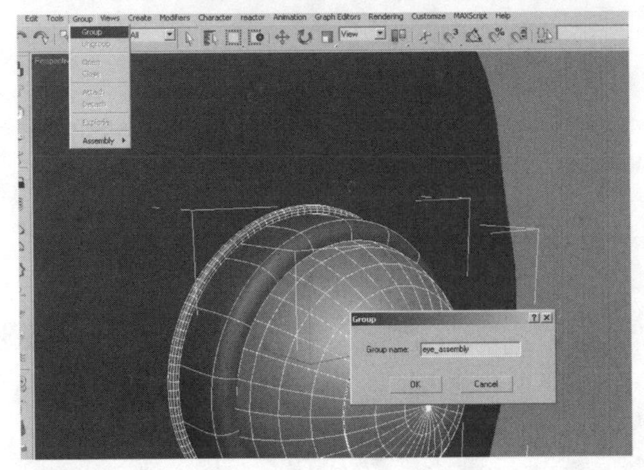

Figure 1-48

Fire Drill: Contrary to what you may think, grouping objects does *not* link them together for the purposes of animation, nor does it attach them together. So why do it? Using Group allows us to easily select a collection of elements we want to perform an operation on; in this instance, cloning.

37. Select the **eye_assembly**, select the Move tool (**W**), hold down the **Shift** key, and click and drag in the X axis to create a clone.

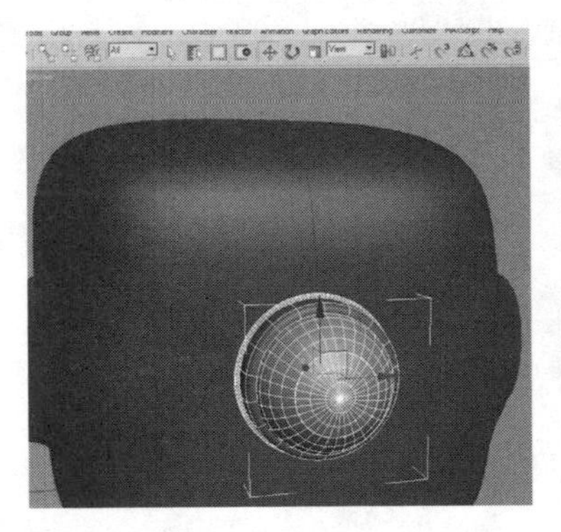

Figure 1-49

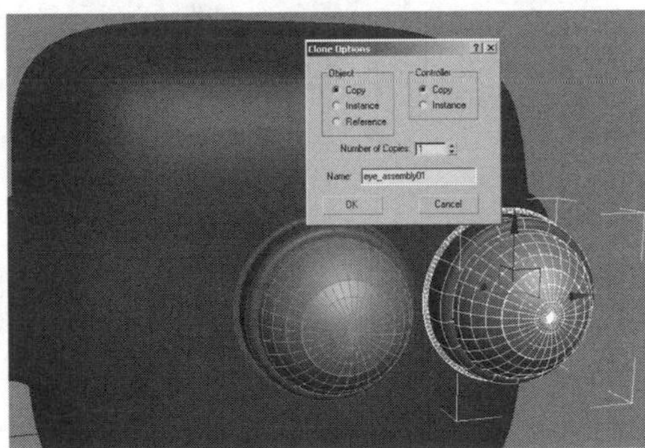

Figure 1-50

38. Right-click on the **Scale** tool and type **50** in the Offset World field.

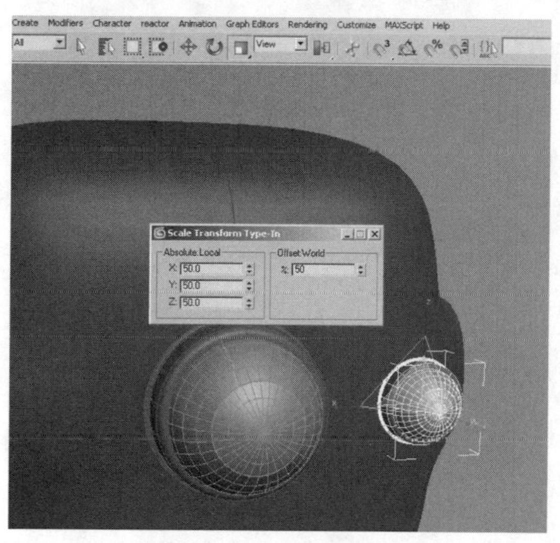

Figure 1-51

39. Move the smaller eye in the X axis until its position is as shown in Figure 1-52.

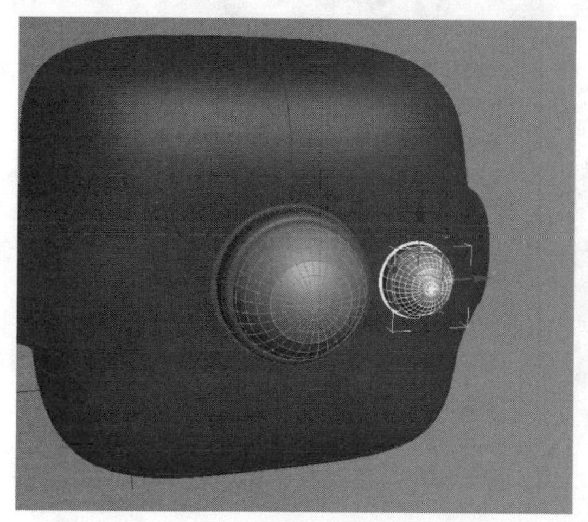

Figure 1-52

40. Shift-move the smaller eye in the Z axis and create two clones.

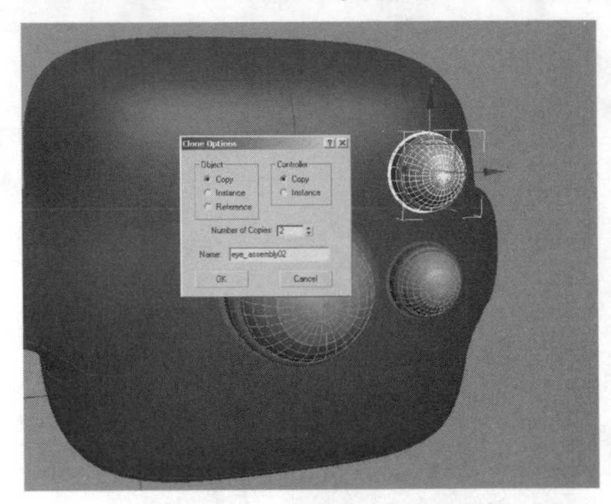

Figure 1-53

41. Move the eyes in the X and Z axes until they are positioned like this:

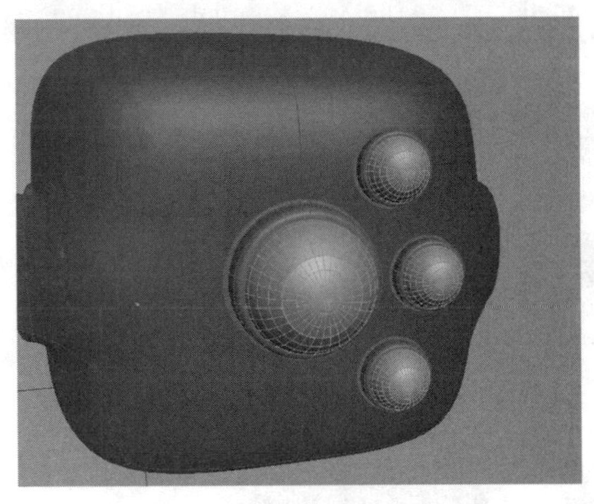

Figure 1-54

42. Select the three smaller eyes, click **Mirror**, mirror them in the X axis, and use an Offset of **–38.454** to position them.

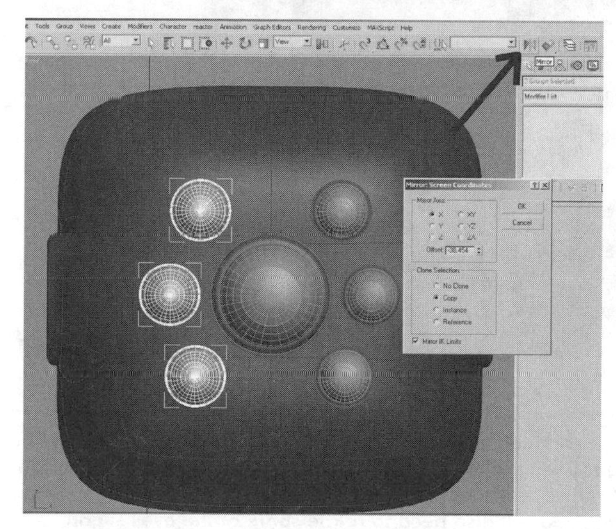

Figure 1-55

43. Select and Link the six smaller eyes to the body.
44. Arc Rotate in the Perspective view until you are happy with the angle you're viewing the bot from, and hit **F9** to do a quick render.

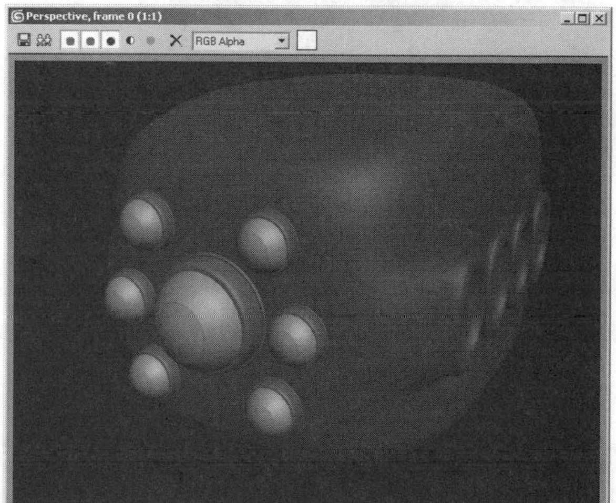

Figure 1-56

Message: Don't worry if the default colors make your render look "cartoonish." Take a look at the three materials videos on the companion DVD to see how the use of materials can make the bot look more menacing.

Figure 1-57

Urgent: If you look at Figure 1-57, you'll see that the smaller eyes are protruding too far. We need to select them and move them back into the body, so that the seals are flush with the body. Since the body is irregularly shaped, you will also need to rotate some of the eyes slightly so they are snugly placed against the body.

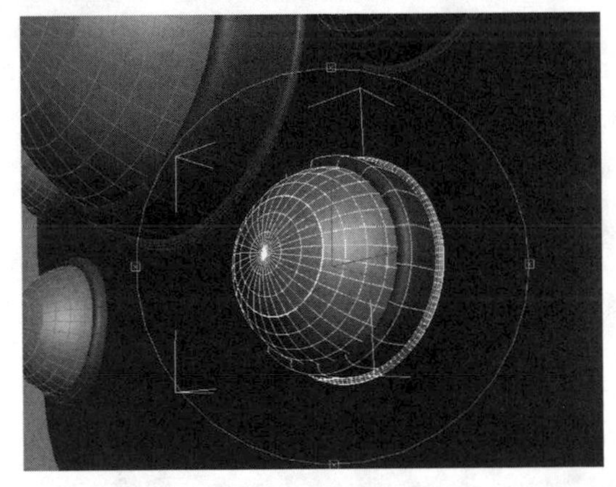

Figure 1-58

FYI: When building a model with a large number of parts, it's sometimes easier to separate parts (e.g., the eyes) into separate layers, which you can turn on or off or freeze to prevent you from accidentally selecting them. So why would you want to turn "off" a layer? Sometimes, when you have a lot of parts, some parts can get in the way of your viewing or modeling. Also, when you have a high number of polygons, your system can start to drag. Turning off a layer with a high number of polygons, such as the eyes in this model, will free your computer from having to compute all those polys while you're modeling a different part.

45. Click the **Layer Manager** button on the main toolbar to open the Layer Manager.

Figure 1-59

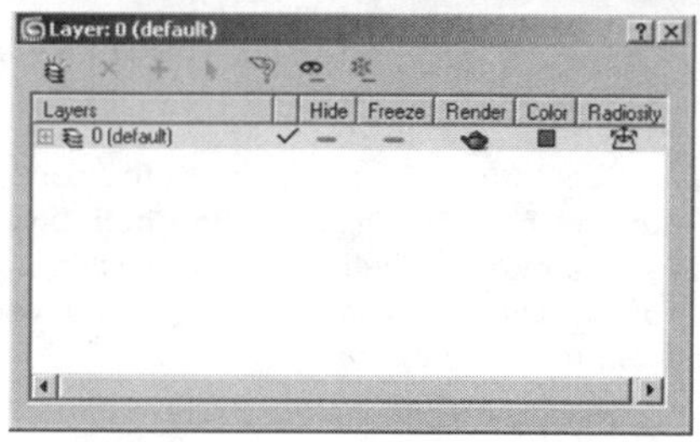

Figure 1-60

46. Hit the **H** key and select the eye_assembly objects.

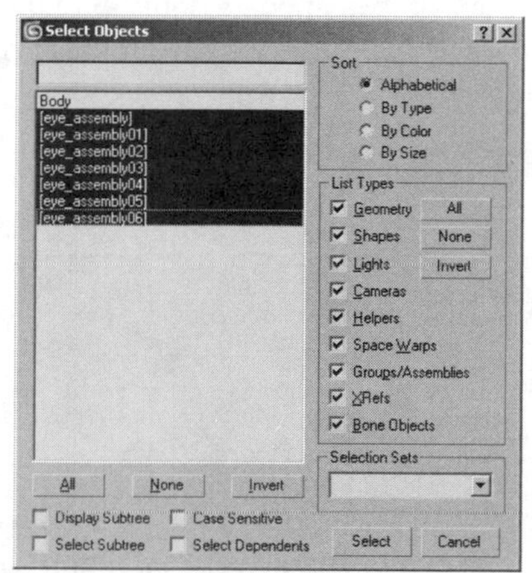

Figure 1-61

47. In the Layer Manager, click the **Create New Layer** button.

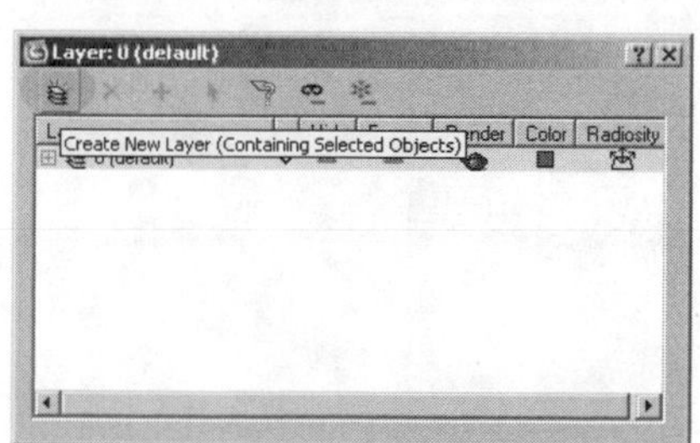

Figure 1-62

48. A new layer (Layer01) appears. Click the + to the left of Layer01 to show that all the selected objects have been added to that layer.

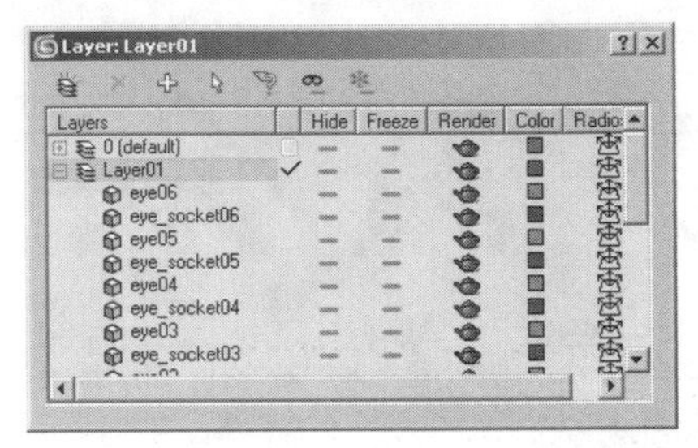

Figure 1-63

FYI: Long-time Adobe users will be intimately familiar with the concept of layering. If you are not in that group, suffice it to say that nothing much has really changed other than your objects have been separated into layers that can be turned on and off for convenience. In this case, the eyes have been put on a layer separate from the body.

49. Click **Layer01**, rename it **eyes**, and click on the dash in the Hide column. A little burglar mask icon appears, indicating that the layer has been hidden. To show it again, all you have to do is click the burglar mask to toggle the layer.

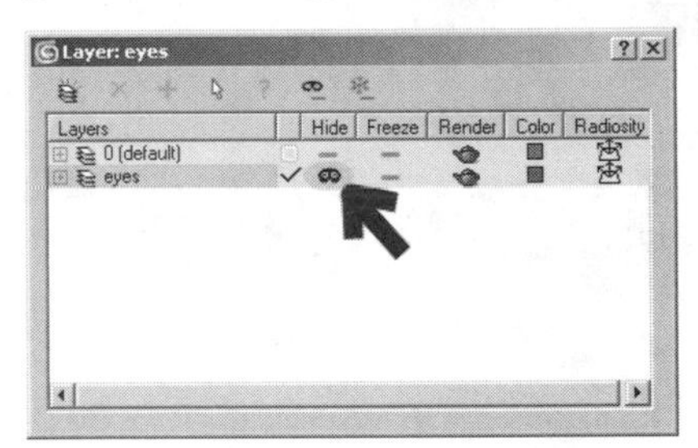

Figure 1-64

50. Make sure a check mark is shown next to the default layer (which is the layer the body is on) and not the eyes layer. If not, click in the box beside the default layer as shown in Figure 1-65.

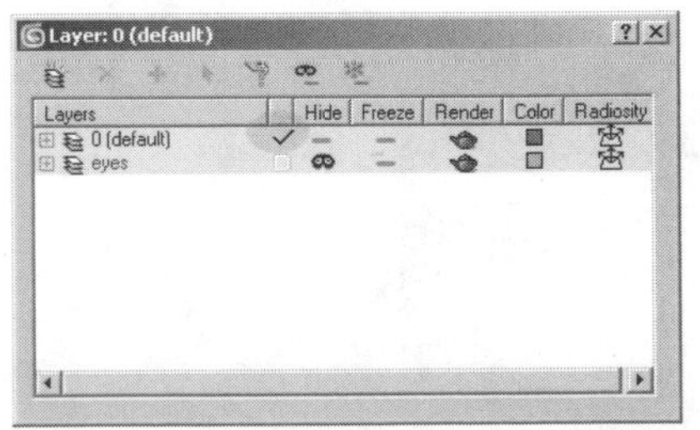

Figure 1-65

Fire Drill: The check mark indicates the layer on which new objects will be created. If you're trying to create objects and Max seems to be making them but they're not appearing, chances are you're looking at one layer but creating on a hidden layer. For example, if we had left the check mark next to the eyes layer (which is invisible), any objects we created would've been invisible because they were being created on an invisible layer.

Day 2: Building the Legs

Spiders have eight legs, so that requires a lot of work to model. Rather than reinventing the wheel eight times, we'll simply make one leg and then clone it seven times.

1. Switch to the Perspective view, click the **Polygon** selection mode icon in the Selection rollout, and marquee-select the left half of the model.

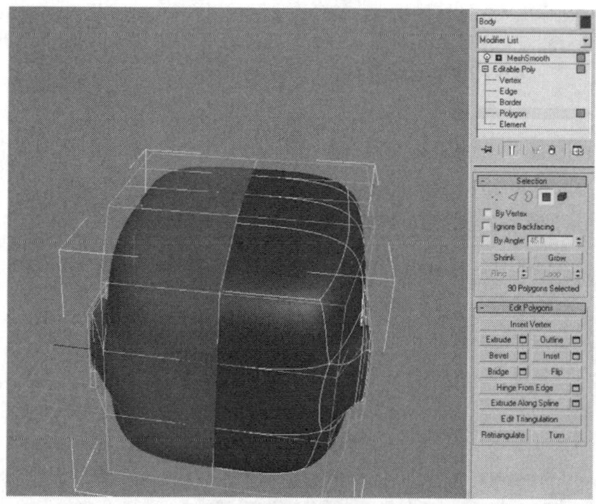

Figure 1-66

2. Delete the selected polygons, select **Editable Poly** in the stack, and add a **Symmetry** modifier between MeshSmooth and Editable Poly.

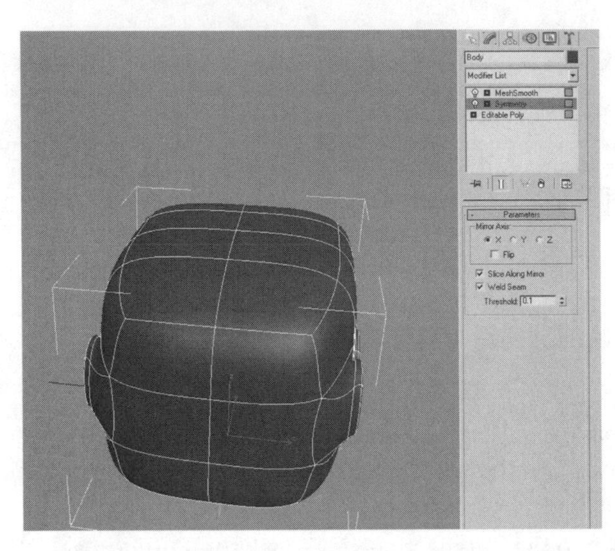

Figure 1-67

FYI: At this point, you might ask why we went to all the trouble of collapsing the stack to *remove* the Symmetry modifier (see step 18 on page 71) only to add it back in this step. Collapsing the first modifier was necessary for correctly scaling the bot's nose, which we'll see is a necessary component in an upcoming step.

3. Click the **light bulb** icon next to the MeshSmooth modifier to turn it off. Then, under Editable Poly, select **Polygon** and select the four inner polygons on the sockets on the right side.

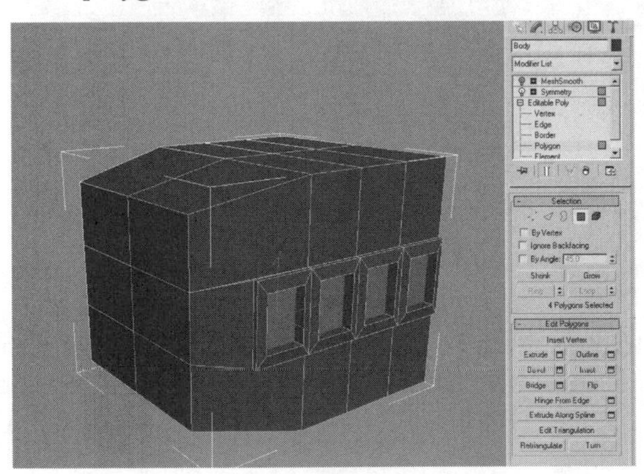

Figure 1-68

Don't Forget: If you're only seeing half of the model, when you click Polygon under Editable Poly, click the little test tube icon at the bottom of the stack to show the effects of the modifiers. The MeshSmooth effect will not show, however, because you temporarily turned it off with the light bulb icon.

4. Switch to the Front view, switch to wireframe mode, switch to the Move tool, and move the polygons **–8.196** on the X axis or until the first edge coincides with the front edge of the nose.

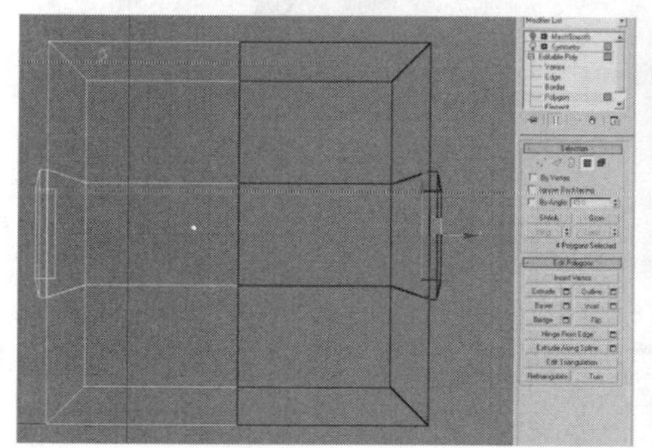

Figure 1-69

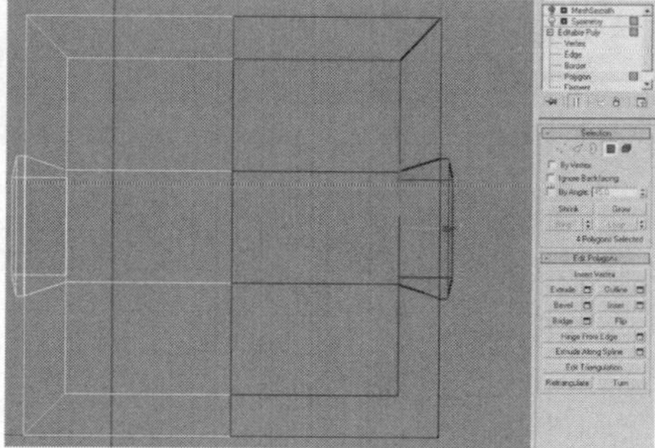

Figure 1-70

5. Toggle MeshSmooth back on, switch to the Front viewport, and create a Sphere with a radius of **8.5** in the socket, using AutoGrid.

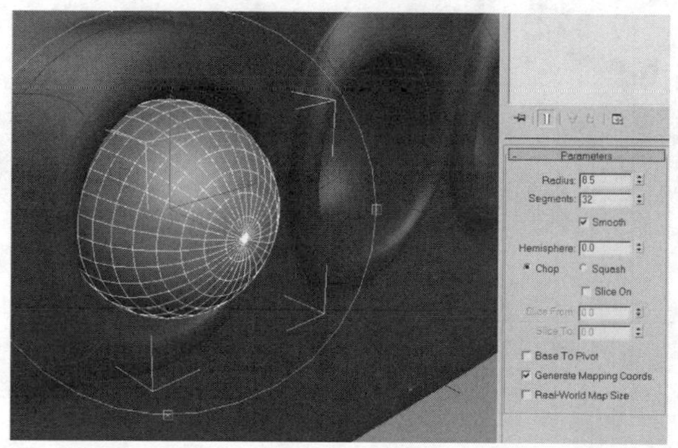

Figure 1-71

6. Convert the sphere to an Editable Polygon, select and delete the top three rows of polygons, and Cap the hole.

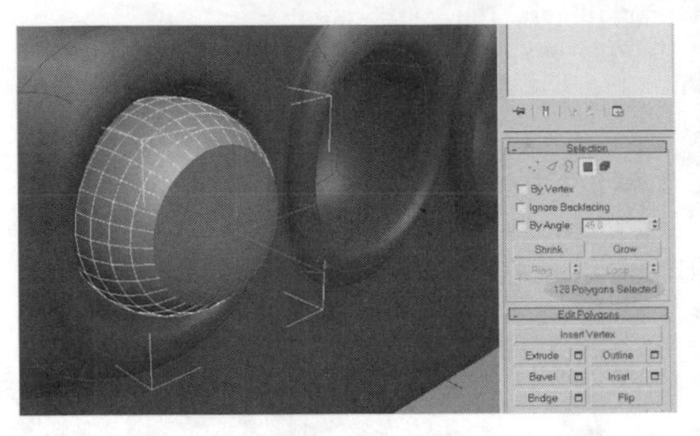

Figure 1-72

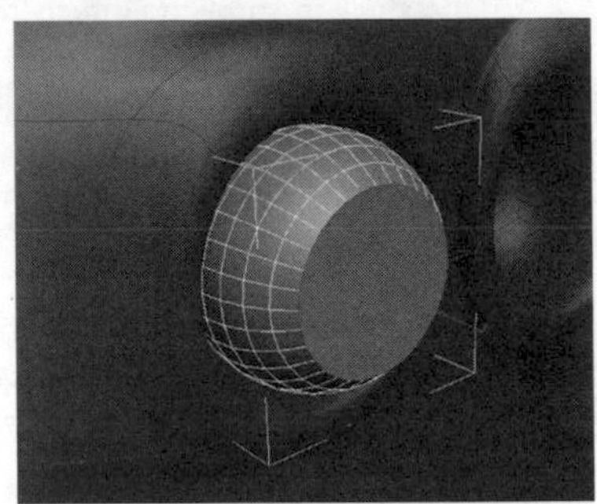

Figure 1-73

7. Polygon-select the cap, click **Bevel Settings**, and enter the values in the following tables:

Type	Height	Outline	Apply/OK
Group	0	–0.8	Apply

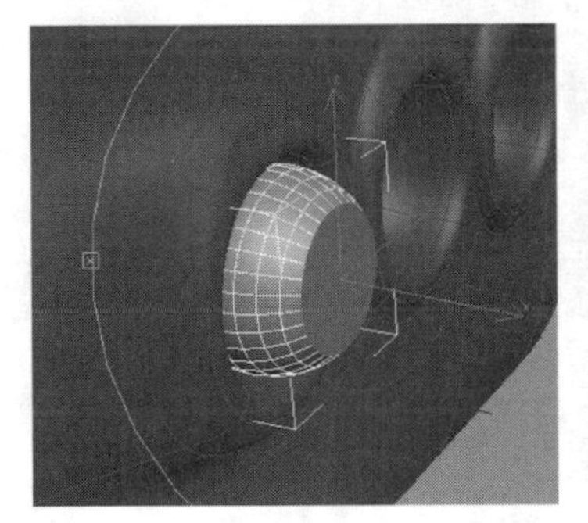

Figure 1-74

Figure 1-75

Type	Height	Outline	Apply/OK
Group	0.03	0	Apply
Group	0	0.8	Apply

Day 2: Building the Legs

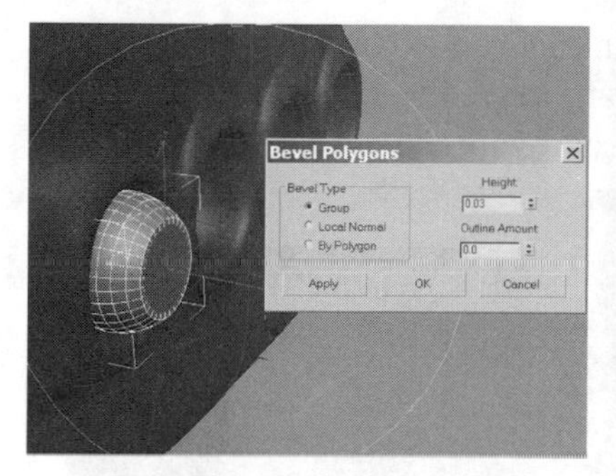

Figure 1-76

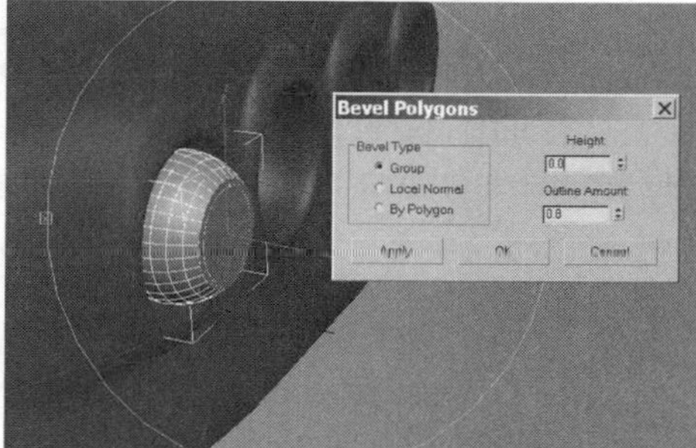

Figure 1-77

Type	Height	Outline	Apply/OK
Group	40	0	OK

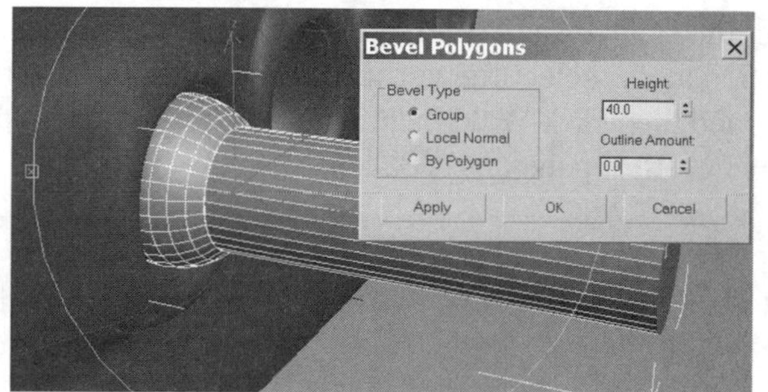

Figure 1-78

8. In the Right view, create a Sphere with a Radius of **8.5**, using AutoGrid, over the shaft you just made:

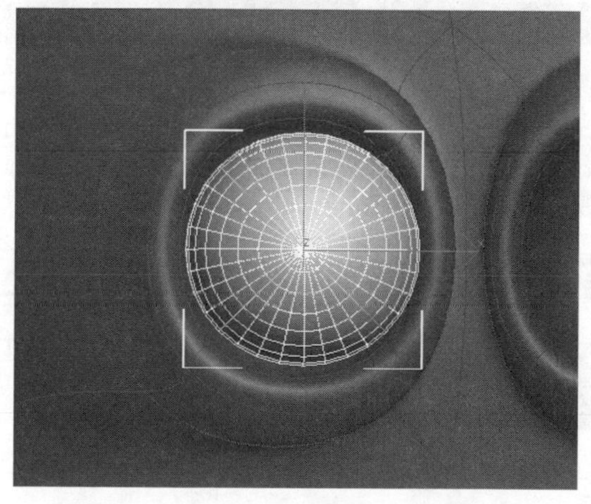

Figure 1-79

9. Delete the 128 polygons shown in Figure 1-80 from the sphere, delete the end polygon on the shaft, move the sphere against the shaft, and align the edges of the shaft with the edges on the sphere as shown in Figure 1-81.

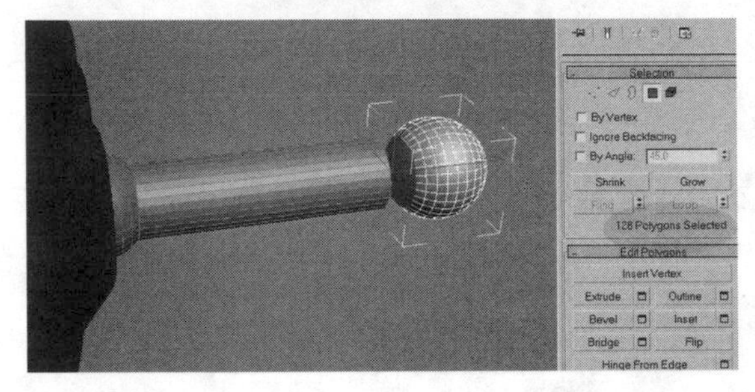

Figure 1-80

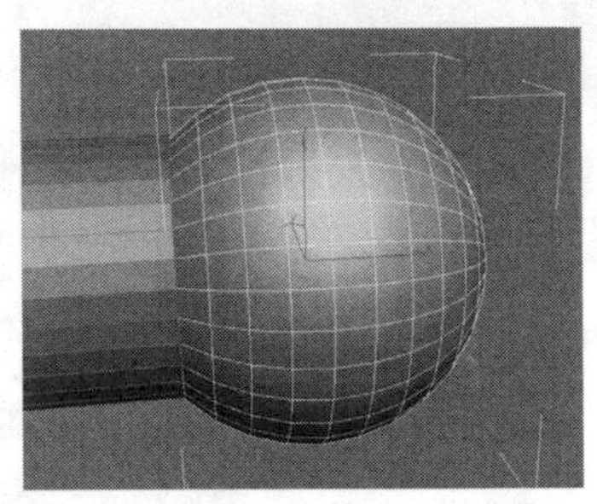

Figure 1-81

10. Select the shaft, click **Attach**, attach the sphere, switch to Vertex selection mode, select the vertices where the shaft and the sphere meet, and then click **Weld** (adjusting the Weld Threshold until the number of After polygons is 32 less than the Before).

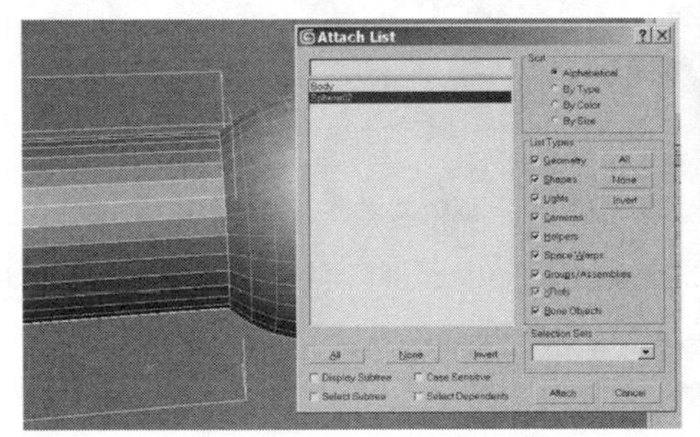

Figure 1-82

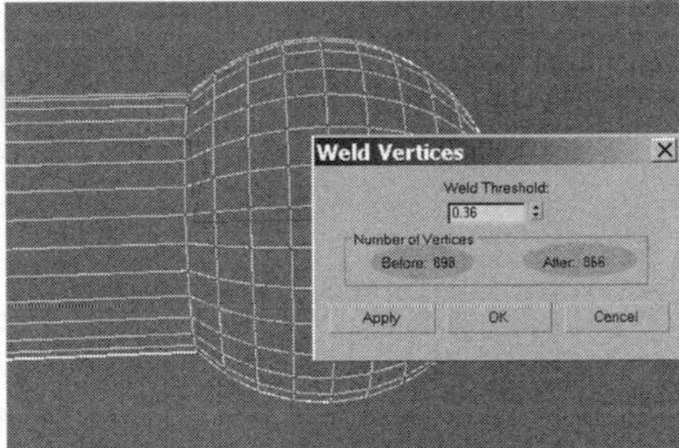

Figure 1-83

11. Using AutoGrid, create a Tube on top of the ball joint you just made. Then switch to the Front view, and center the tube on the ball joint. Use these settings for the Tube:

Radius 1	Radius 2	Height	Height/Cap Segs	Sides	Smooth
10.303	9.207	4	5/1	18	Checked

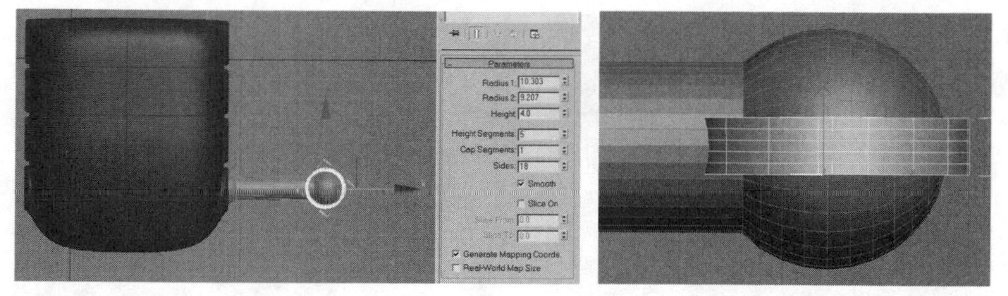

Figure 1-84

Figure 1-85

12. Change Radius 2 to **8.667**, Height Segments to **1**, Sides to **32**, and Height to **12**, then use the Move tool to center the tube vertically on the ball joint.

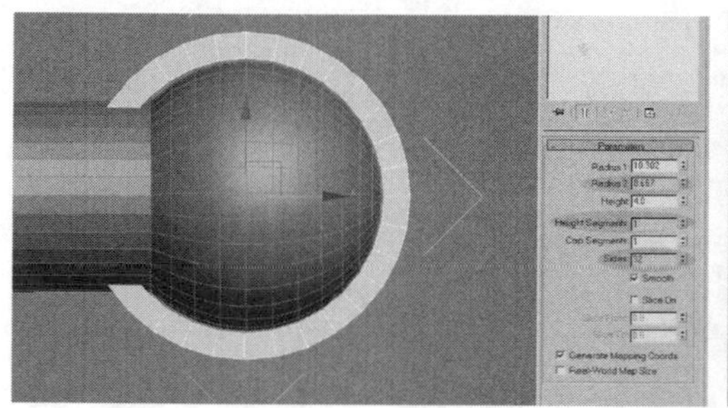

Figure 1-86

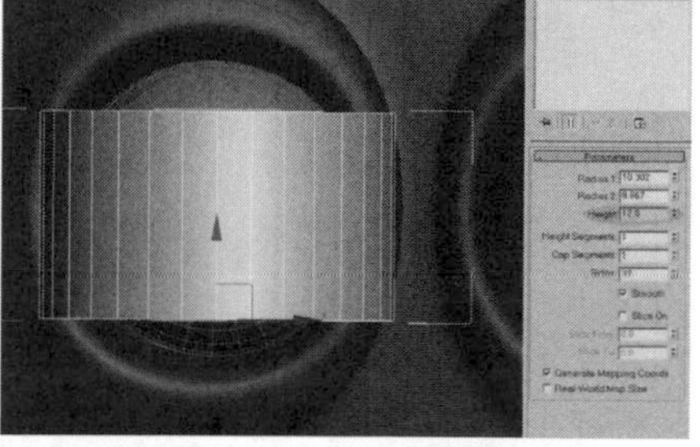

Figure 1-87

13. Arc Rotate around the tube to make sure it is evenly positioned on the ball joint and then click the **Slice On** check box. Set the Slice From to **–100** and the Slice To to **13.0** to create a crescent.

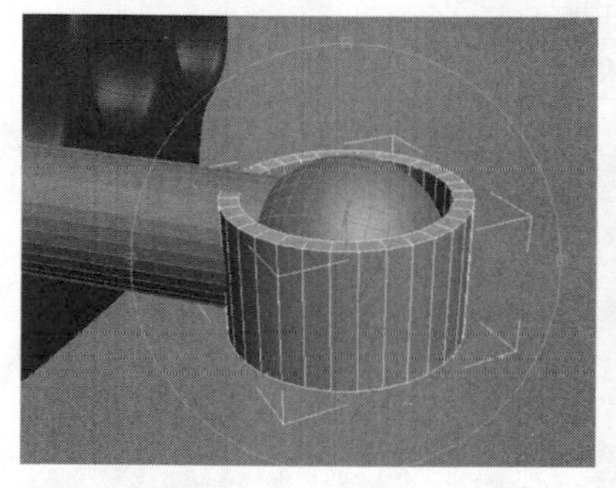

Figure 1-88

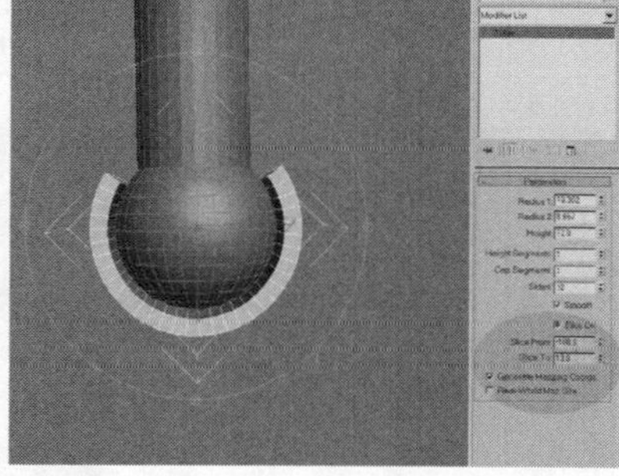

Figure 1-89

14. Switch to the Right viewport, choose **Convert to Editable Poly**, and select the 10 polygons on the outer surface. Then Extrude by **5** as a group.

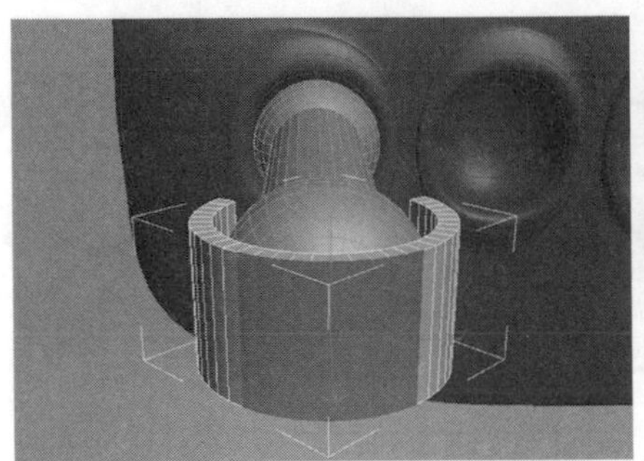

Figure 1-90

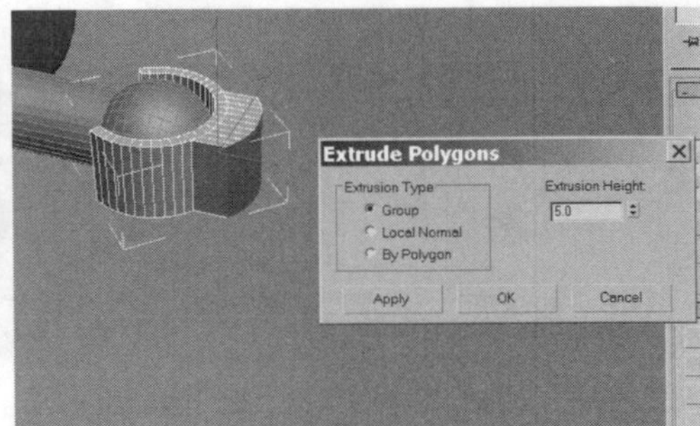

Figure 1-91

15. Switch to the Front view and use the Non-uniform Scale tool to scale the polygons down to **0** in the Offset Screen X axis. Then click **Bevel Settings** and enter the values in the following table.

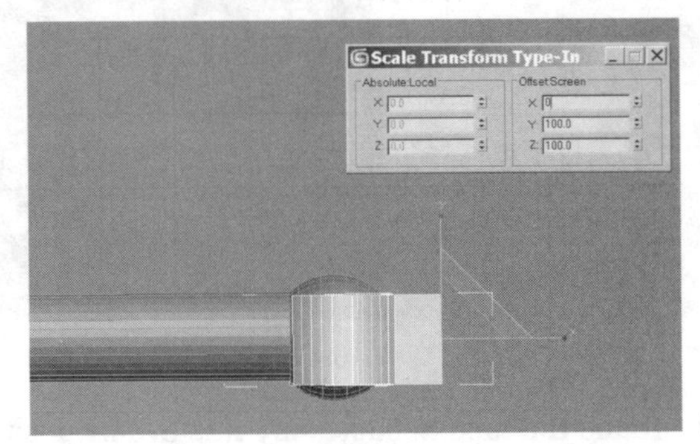

Figure 1-92

Type	Height	Outline	Apply/OK
Group	0	2	Apply
Group	40	0	OK

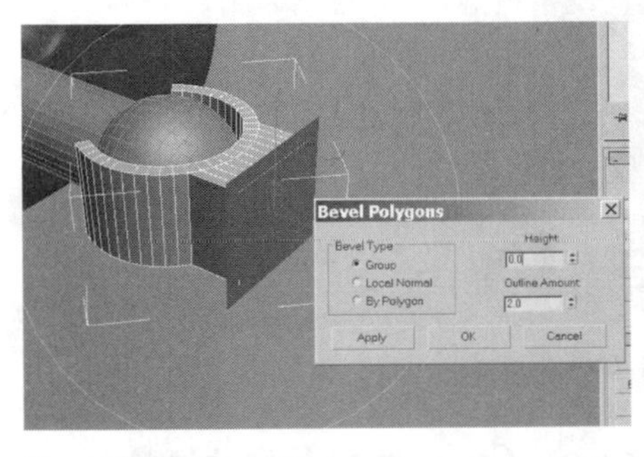

Figure 1-93

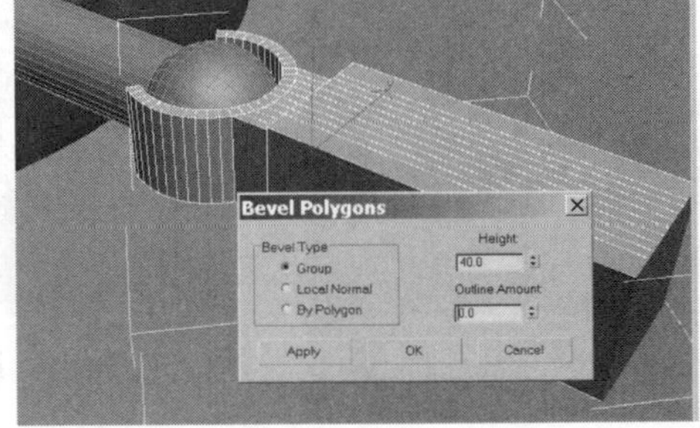

Figure 1-94

16. Extrude the end polygons by **4.0** and hit **Apply** nine times, then click **OK.**

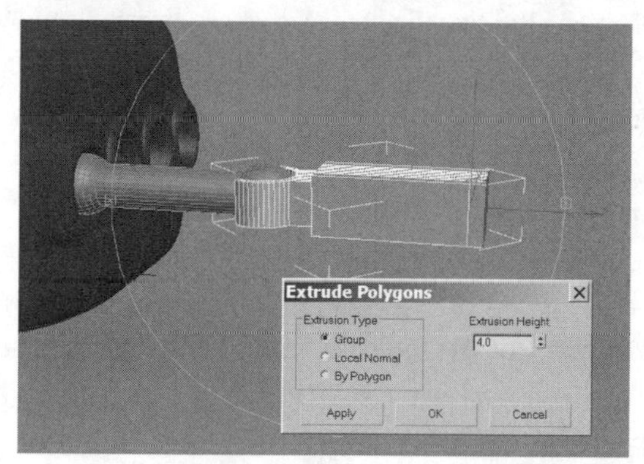

Figure 1-95

17. Switch to the Top view and click **Grow 11** times until the extrusion extends back to the joint. Then right-click the **Non-uniform Scale** tool and scale the polygons down to **60** in the Y axis.

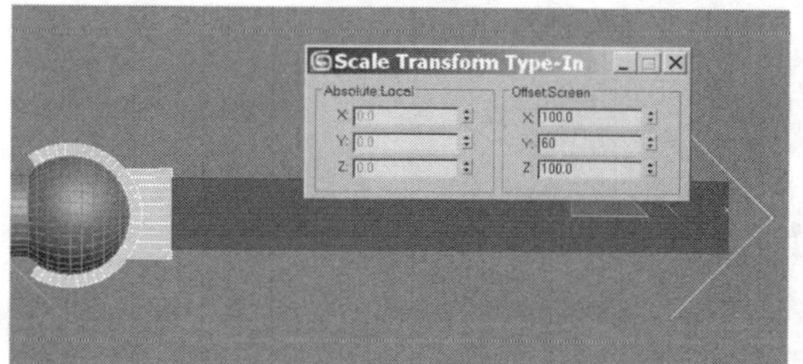

Figure 1-96

18. Click **Shrink** once to shrink the selection to only include the extruded tip and then add a Bend modifier to the stack.

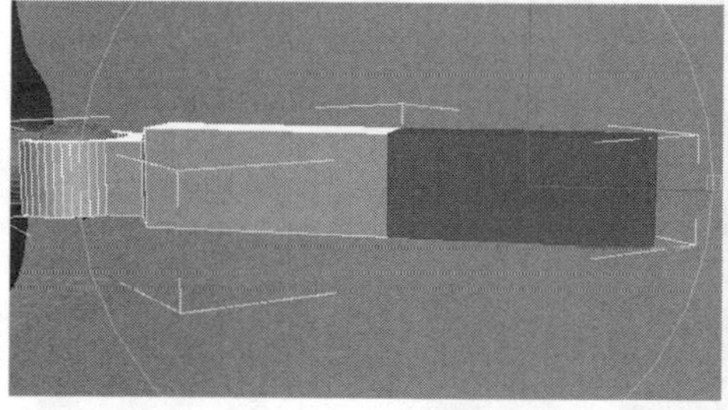

Figure 1-97

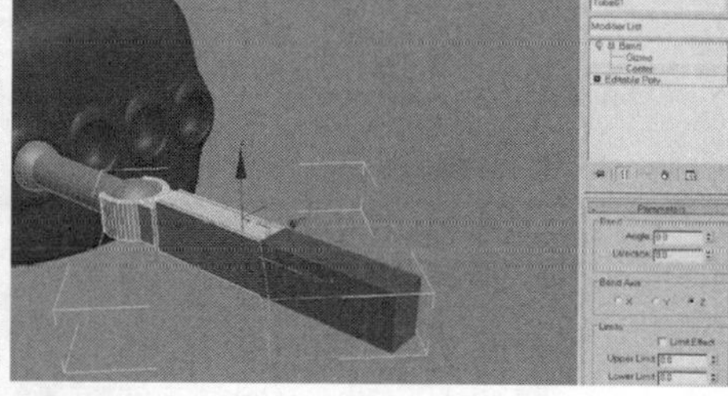

Figure 1-98

Urgent: Notice that the Bend gizmo (orange box) is turned the wrong way. Specifically, it's turned on its side. Why? Look at the bounding box (if you have Show Bounding Box turned on) for the whole object. It's turned 90 degrees too. What is going on? We used a Tube primitive to create the leg, and, if you recall, we created it so it was oriented vertically (i.e., rotated 90 degrees). That wouldn't normally be a problem, but in this case, it screws up the orientation of our Bend modifier. Fortunately, like most problems we encounter, this one is easy to fix. You just need to change the orientation of the gizmo. Oh. Is that all?

19. Click the + to the left of the Bend modifier, select the gizmo, right-click on the **Rotate** tool, and input **–45** for the Offset World Z axis.

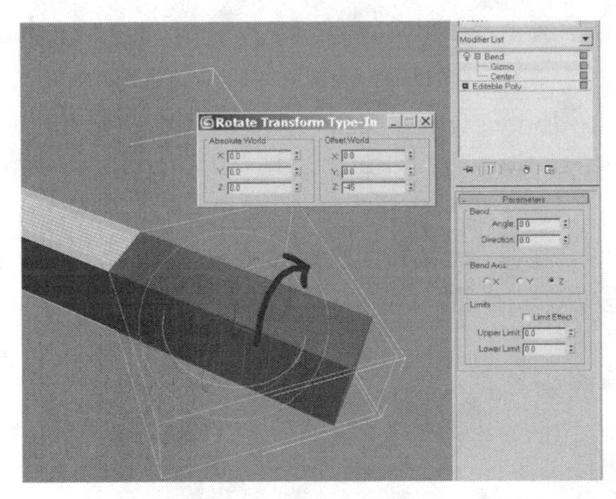

Figure 1-99

20. Input **–90** for the Offset World X axis to rotate the gizmo and then close the Rotate dialog box.

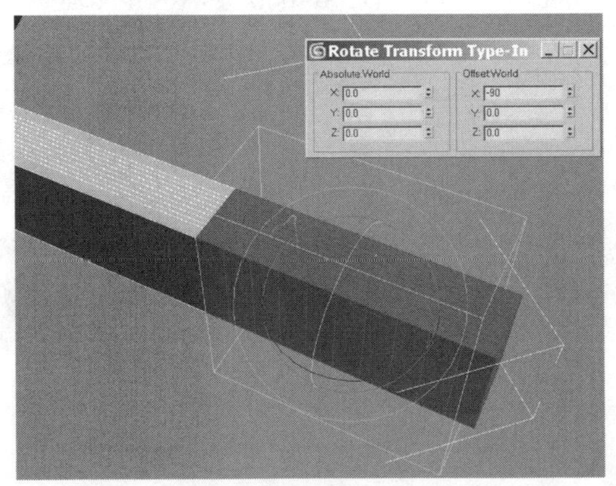

Figure 1-100

21. With the Bend gizmo still selected, right-click on the **Non-uniform Scale** tool, input **110** for the Offset World X axis to stretch the gizmo to enclose the extruded tip, and close the dialog box.

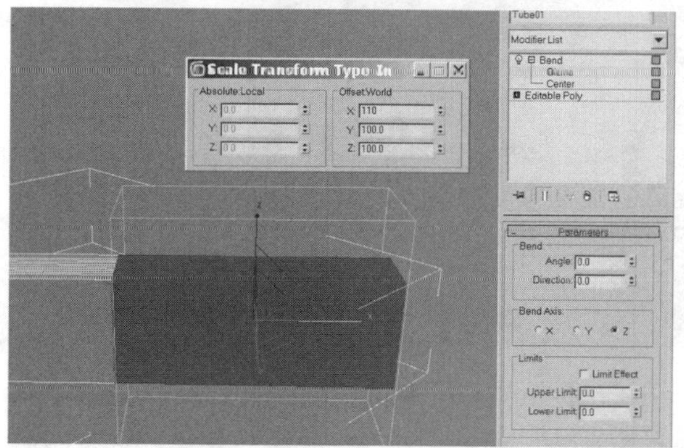

Figure 1-101

22. Select **Bend Center** from the stack and use the Move tool to move the center in the X axis until it's flush with the left edge of the Bend gizmo.

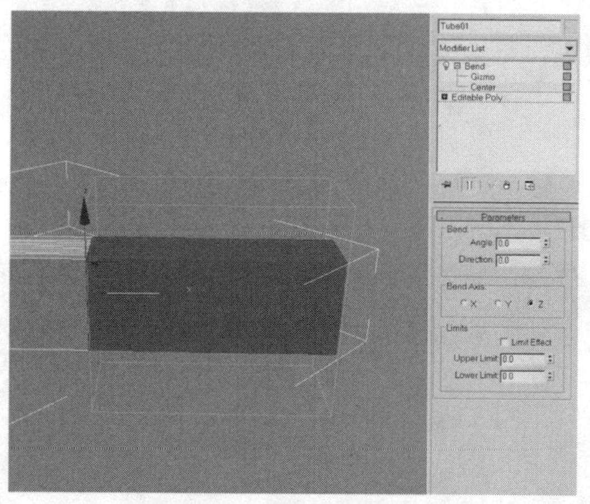

Figure 1-102

23. Set the Bend Angle to **30** and the Bend Axis to **Y**, check **Limit Effect**, and set the Lower Limit to **–30**. Collapse the stack.

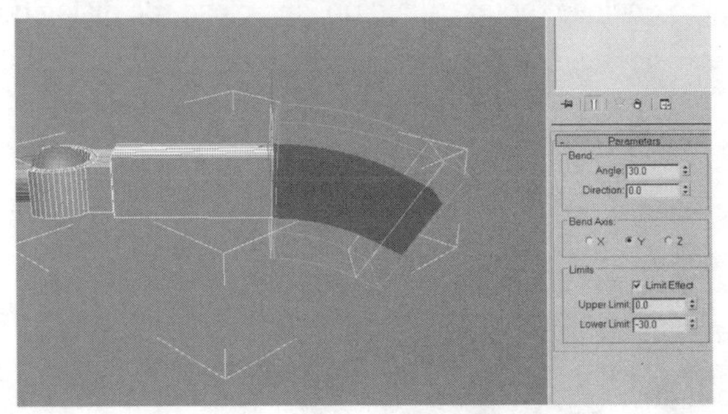

Figure 1-103

24. Select the polygon at the end of the extrusion and Extrude it by **20**.

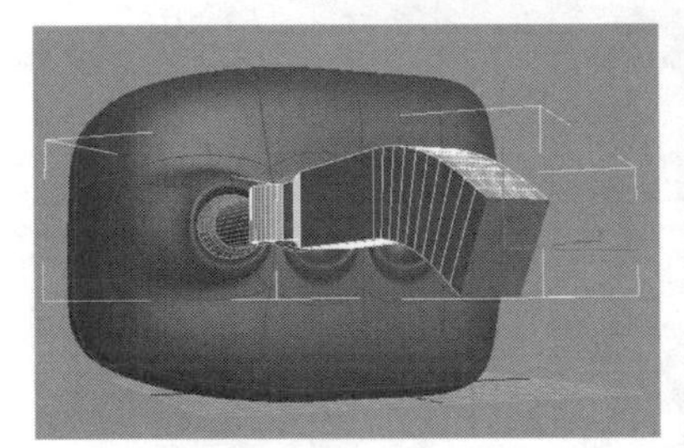

Figure 1-104

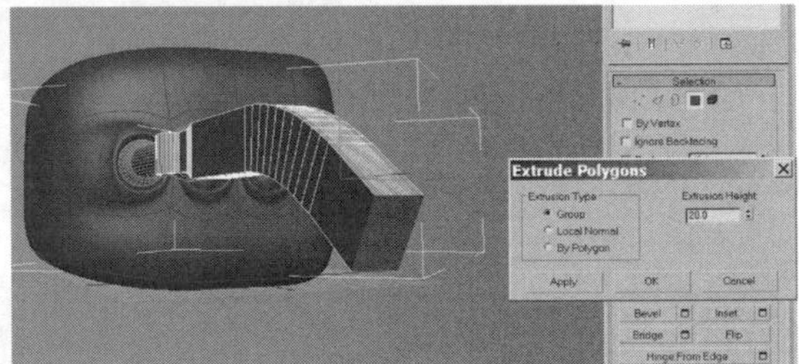

Figure 1-105

25. Select the 11 segments on the tip of the extrusion, click **Connect**, and click **OK**.

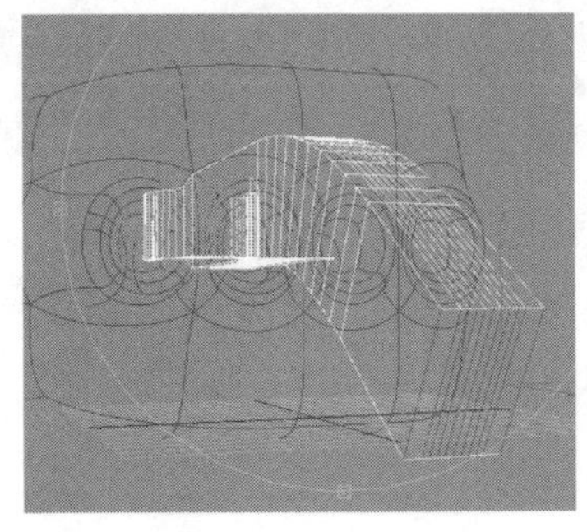

Figure 1-106

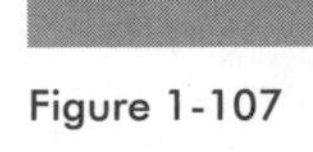

Figure 1-107

26. Select the bottom polygons and delete them.

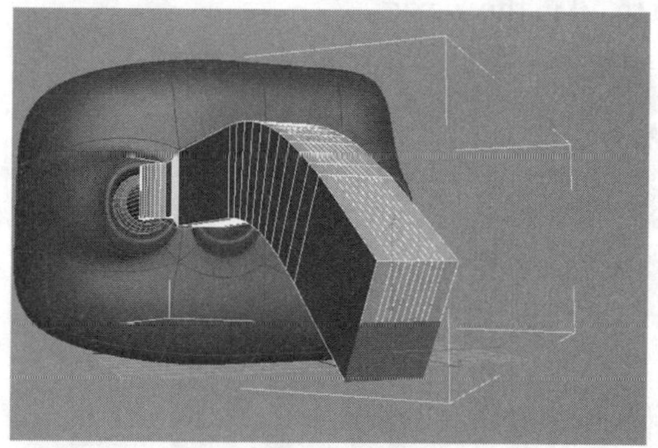

Figure 1-108

27. Select the top polygons and click **Hinge From Edge**. Set the Angle to **180** and the number of Segments to **10**, click the **Pick Hinge** button, and click the edge at the bottom of the selected polygons.

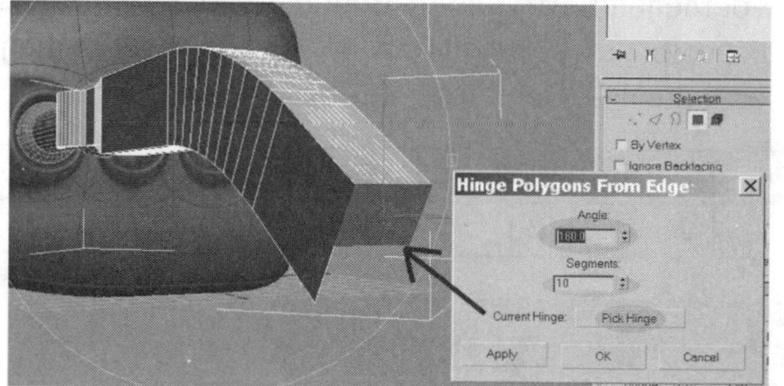

Figure 1-109

28. Delete the backward-facing polygons, select the 22 overlapping vertices as shown, click **Weld Settings**, lower the Weld Threshold until the number of After vertices is 11 less (i.e., half of 22) than the Before, and then click **OK** to weld the overlapping vertices.

Figure 1-110

29. Select the polygons you just made with Hinge From Edge and Scale them down to **40** in the Y axis.

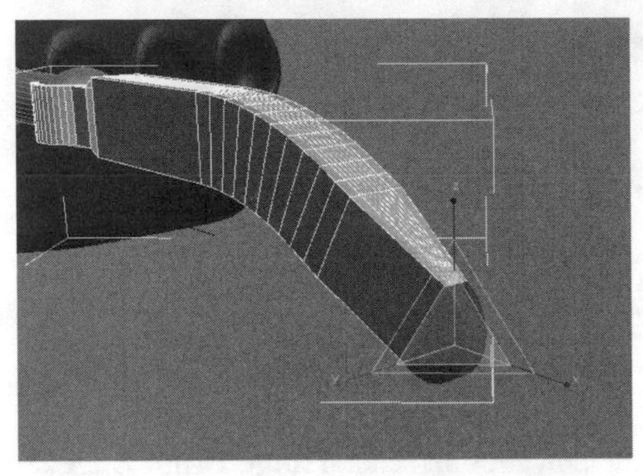

Figure 1-111

30. Switch to the Front view. Using AutoGrid, create a Cylinder in the center of the joint. Arc Rotate around the joint to make sure the cylinder is positioned equally between the two parts of the joint and intersects the ball. Use these settings for the cylinder:

Radius	Height	Height/Cap Segs	Sides	Smooth
2	21	1/1	32	Checked

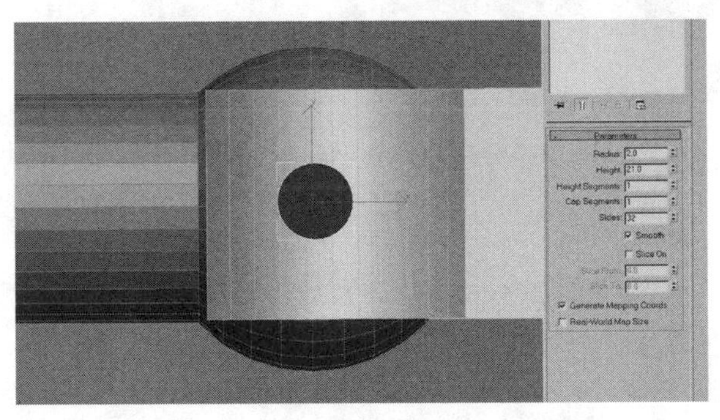

Figure 1-112

31. Select and Link the upper leg to the body, Select and Link the cylinder you just made to the upper leg, and Select and Link the middle leg to the cylinder.

32. Hide the upper and middle legs and the cylinder.

Day 3: Detailing the Body

The first thing we're going to want to do is to create a plane beneath the body to act as a floor, and then add some seams. Bots are assembled, meaning there would be seams. Even if the body were injection molded, there'd have to be some way of taking it apart to insert the internal components.

1. Create a Plane object and position it beneath the body, then select the body, right-click the stack, and select **Collapse All** to collapse the stack.

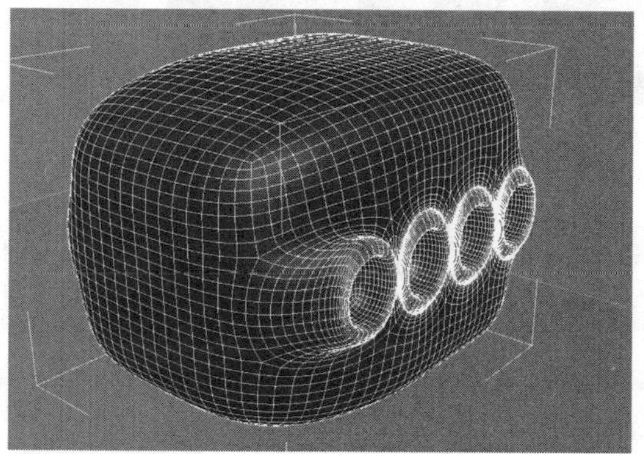

Figure 1-113

2. In the Front view, select a horizontal edge in the center of the model (just look at the model and follow the edges until you find a horizontal one that crosses through the center of the front leg socket) and click **Loop**.

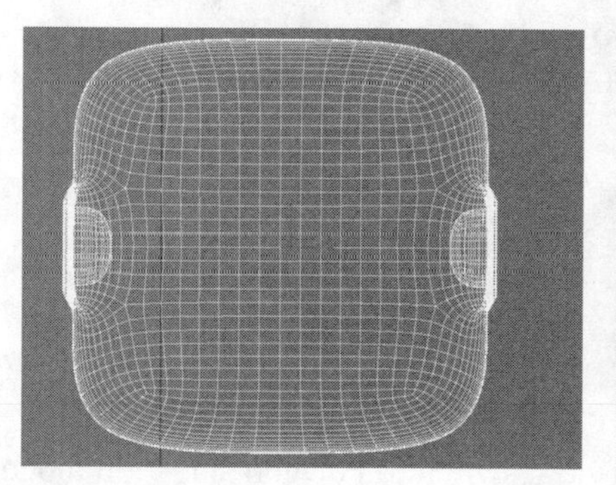

Figure 1-114

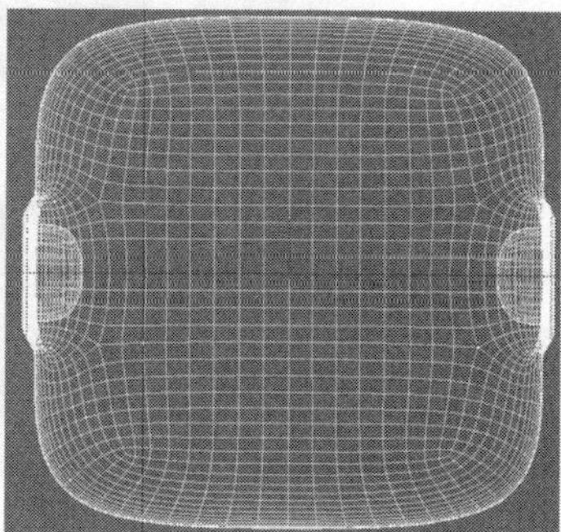

Figure 1-115

3. With the edges selected, click the **Extrude Settings** button and set the Height to **–2** (so the edge will be pushed inward) and the Base Width to **0.08**.

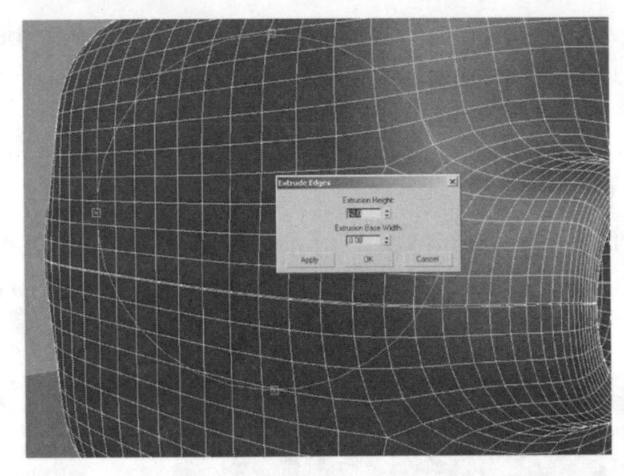

Figure 1-116

FYI: So why these numbers? We want a channel deep enough so it reads when you render, but not so deep that it looks cavernous. Look at objects around you. Most seams are fairly shallow. Likewise, Base Width needs to be wide enough to read, but not so wide it jacks up your model or looks weird. There's nothing magical about my numbers. I used trial and error until I got something that looked good to me. Praise Undo! If you don't like the seam created by my numbers, experiment with your own. Part of the fun of 3D is trying new things!

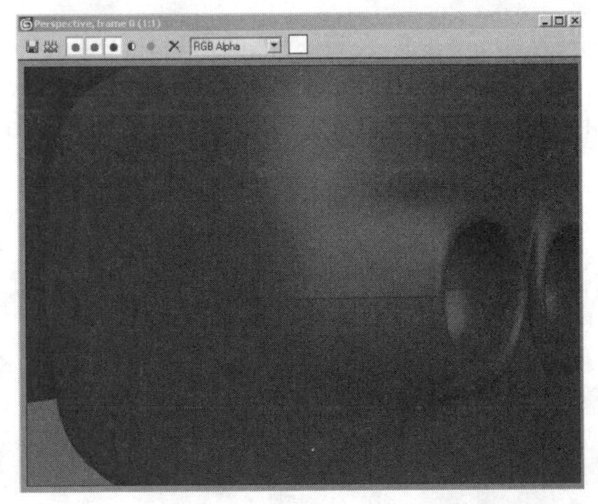

Figure 1-117

4. Switch to the Top view, switch to Polygon selection mode, select and delete the left half of the model, and add a Symmetry modifier to the stack.

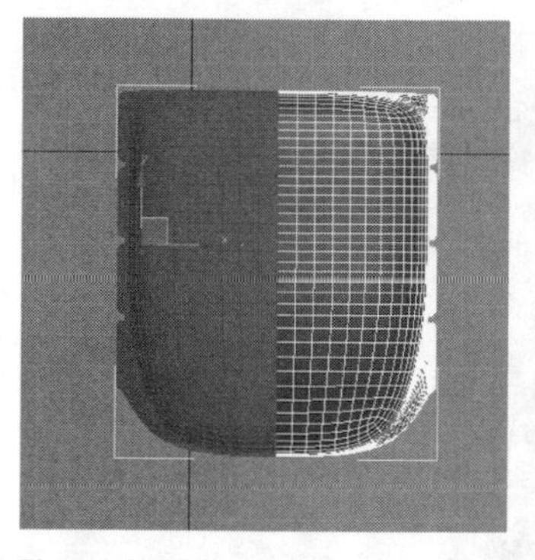

Figure 1-118

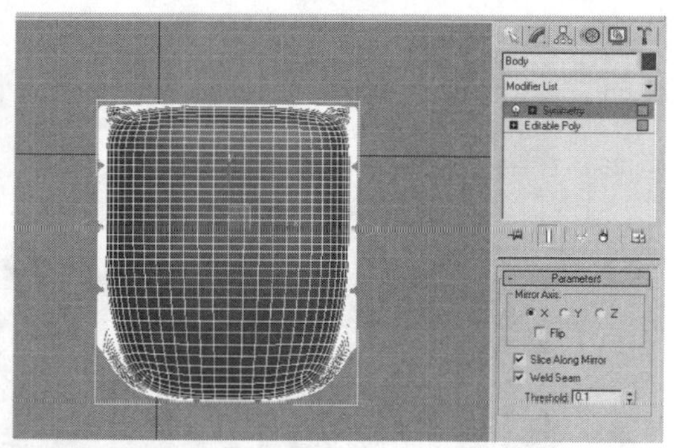

Figure 1-119

5. Switch to the Perspective view, select the **Edge** selection mode tool, and select the edges shown (just above the socket of the first leg). Note: Make sure the edges are selected *inside* the socket until they reach the middle seam.

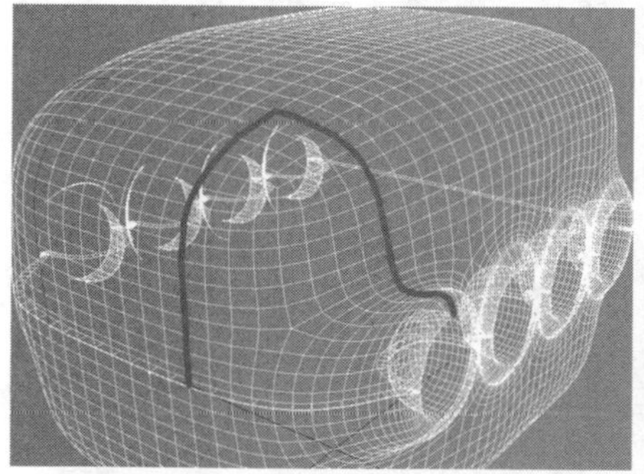

Figure 1-120

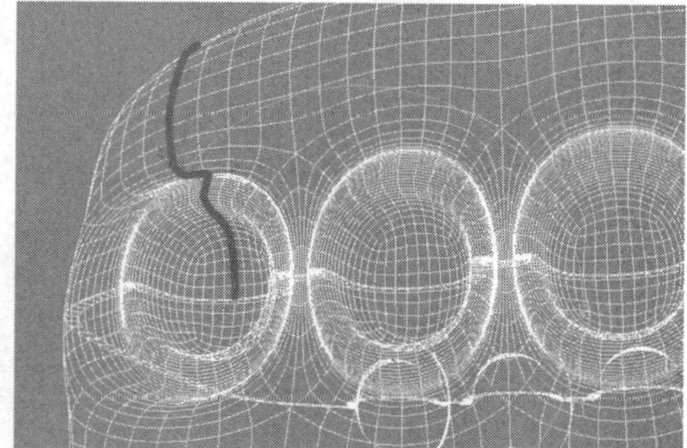

Figure 1-121

Message: The above edges have been exaggerated with a heavy outline to make them easier to see.

6. Extrude the edge **–2** with a Base Width of **0.02**.

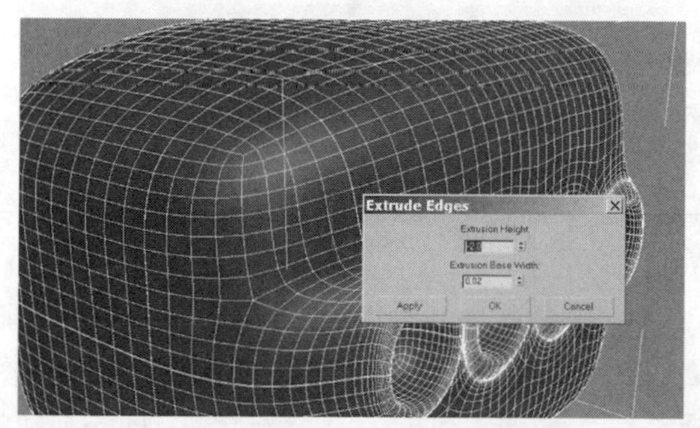

Figure 1-122

FYI: Doesn't look like much has happened, but we want a subtle seam and not a canyon. And since we have Symmetry applied, Max has made a matching seam on the left side. To really see the seams, do a test render.

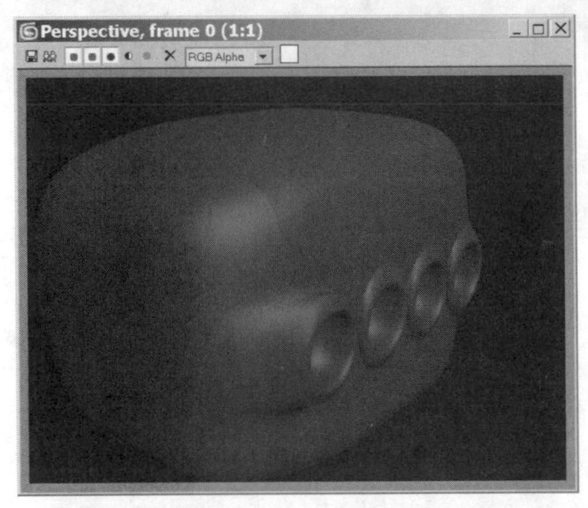

Figure 1-123

7. Switch to the Perspective view, select the **Edge** selection mode tool, and select the edges. Note: Make sure the edges are selected *inside* the socket until they reach the middle seam.

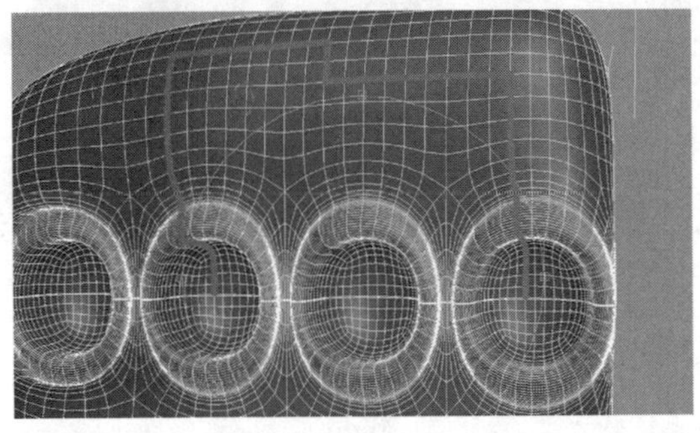

Figure 1-124

8. Extrude the selected edges with a Height of **–2** and a Base Width of **0.02**.

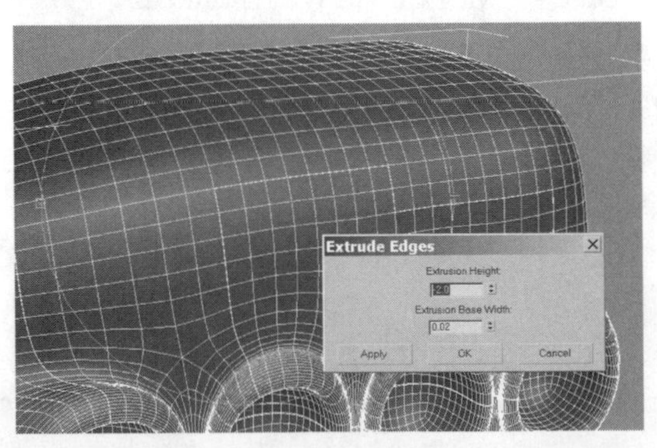

Figure 1-125

9. Select the 56 polygons shown, delete them, select the border, and Cap the hole.

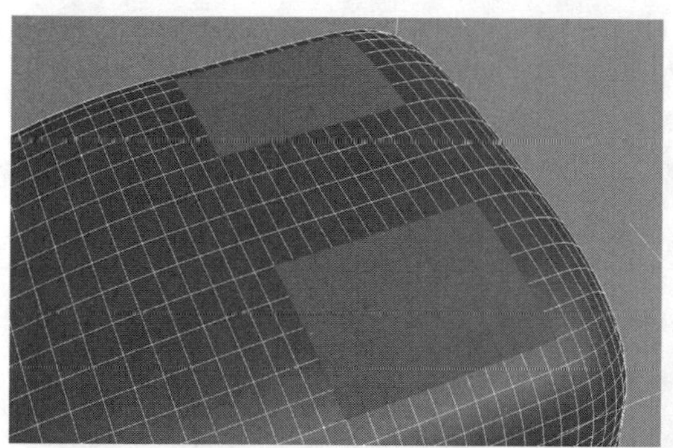

Figure 1-126

10. Click **Bevel Settings** and enter the values in the following table:

Type	Height	Outline	Apply/OK
Group	0	–1.0	Apply
Group	0.1	0	Apply
Group	0	1.0	Apply
Group	1.1	0	OK

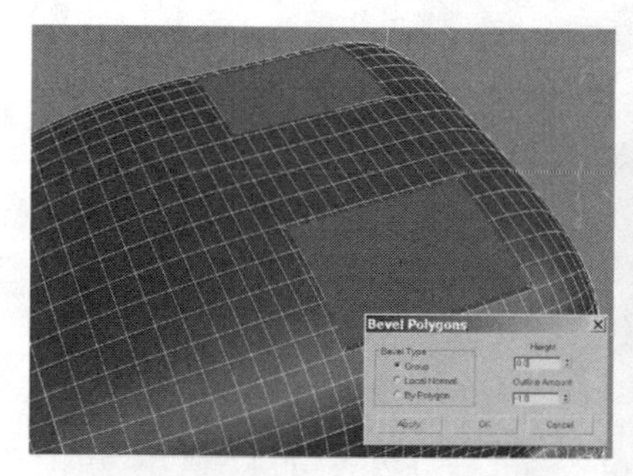

Figure 1-127

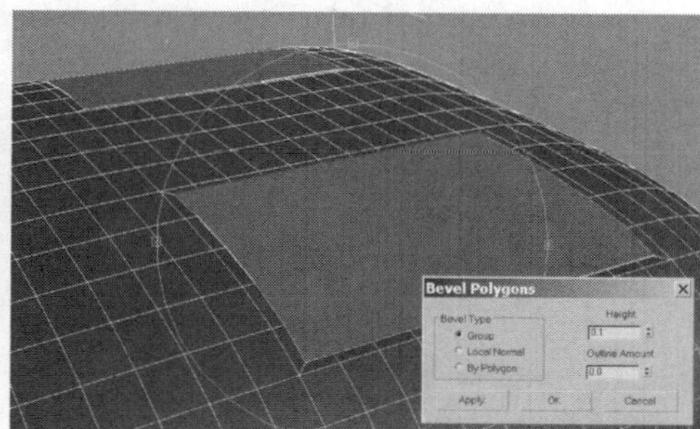

Figure 1-128

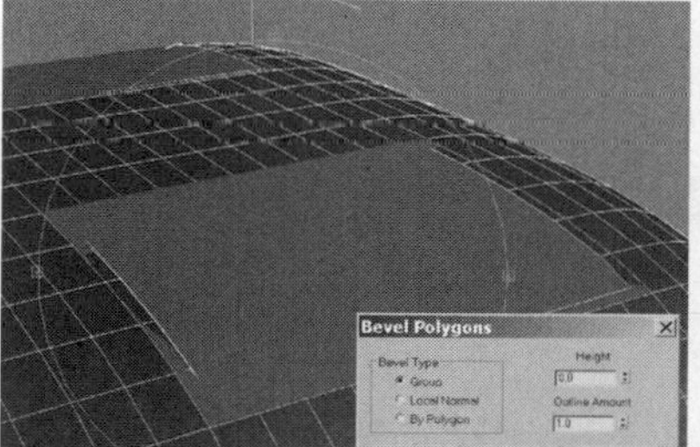
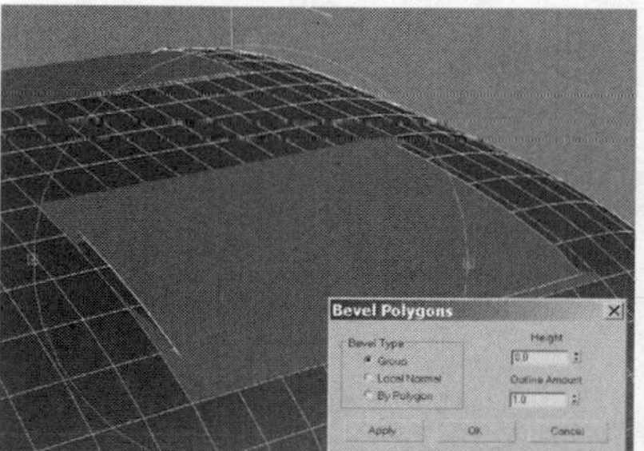

Figure 1-129

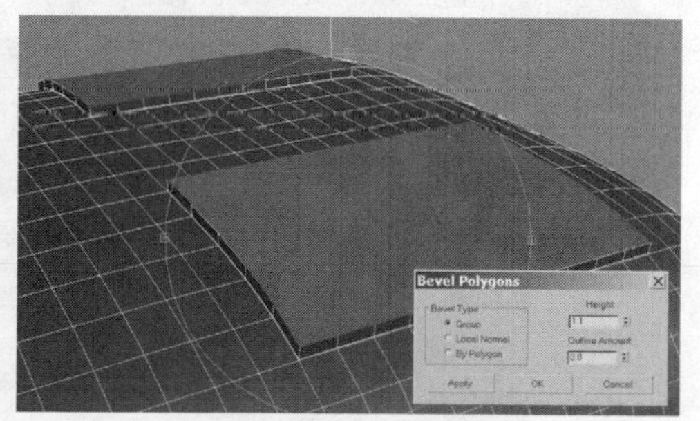

Figure 1-130

11. In Figure 1-131, the edges of the front panel have been accentuated to help you see them better. Notice the intersection highlighted with the circle. This is where we will place our first screw for mounting the panel. Find that intersection.

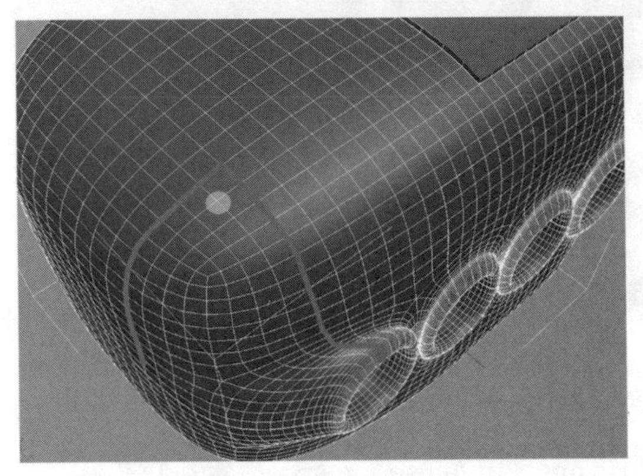

Figure 1-131

12. At that intersection, using AutoGrid, create a Sphere with a Radius of **0.9**, **32** Segments, and a Hemisphere of **0.5**.

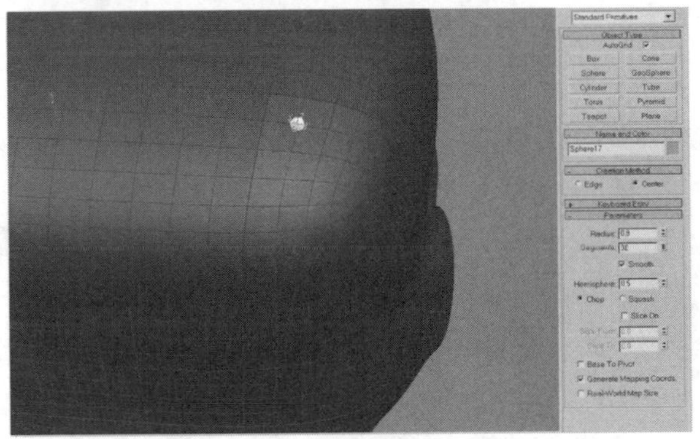

Figure 1-132

13. Zoom in tight on the sphere and make sure it is evenly seated against the surface of the plate.

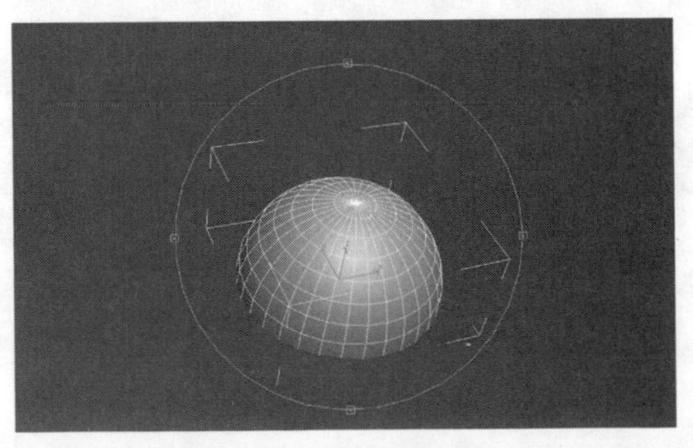

Figure 1-133

14. Convert the sphere to an Editable Polygon, rename it **screw**, and delete the backward-facing polygons.

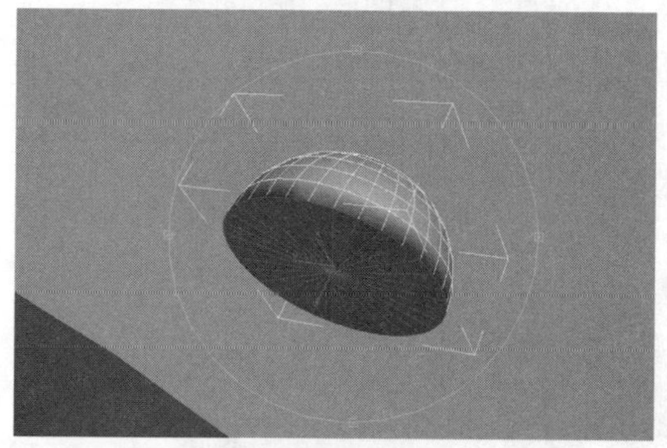

Figure 1-134

15. Select the 64 polygons shown:

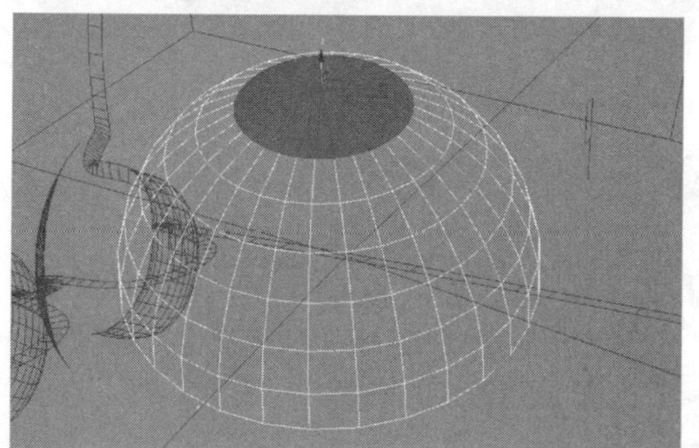

Figure 1-135

16. Click **Bevel Settings** and enter the values in the following table, then switch to the Move tool (**W**) and move the polygons **–0.15** in the Z axis:

Type	Height	Outline	Apply/OK
Local Normal	–0.05	–0.05	OK

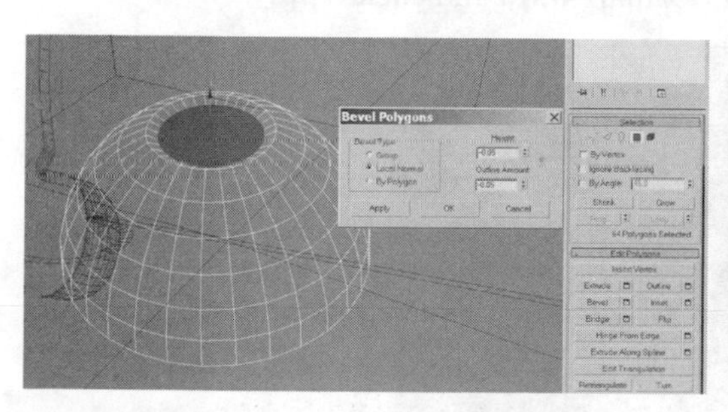

Figure 1-136

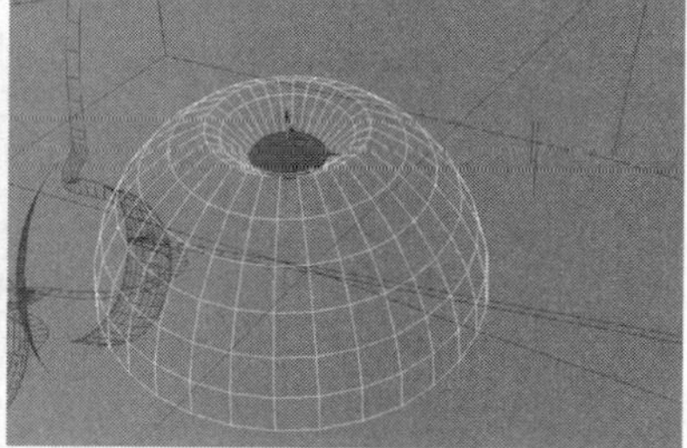

Figure 1-137

17. Click **Shrink** and then click **Bevel Settings:**

Type	Height	Outline	Apply/OK
Local Normal	–0.05	–0.05	OK

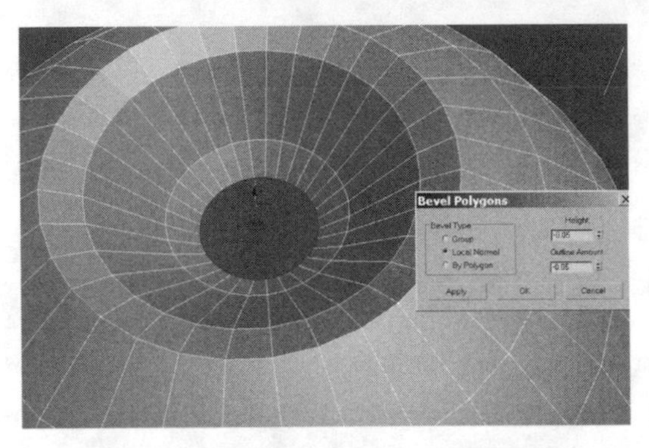

Figure 1-138

18. Select the polygons shown in Figure 1-139.

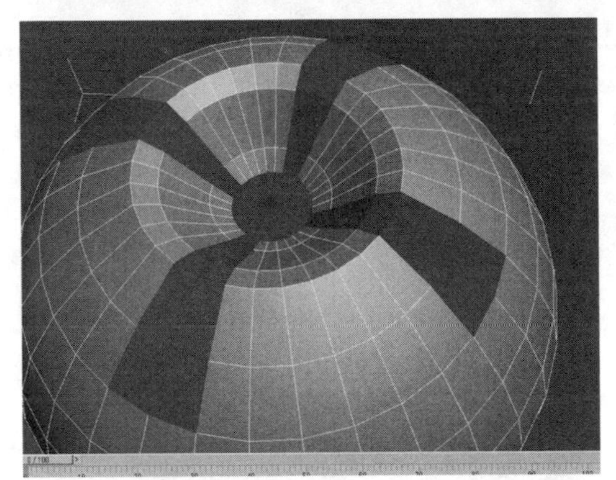

Figure 1-139

19. Extrude them by Local Normal **–0.06** and click **Apply.**

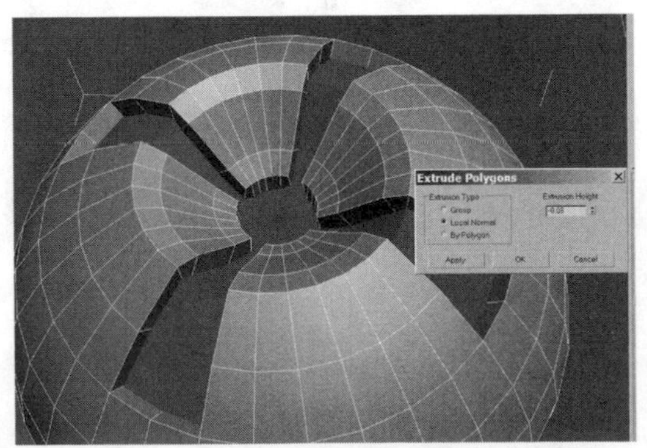

Figure 1-140

20. Extrude them by Group **–0.25** and then click **OK**.

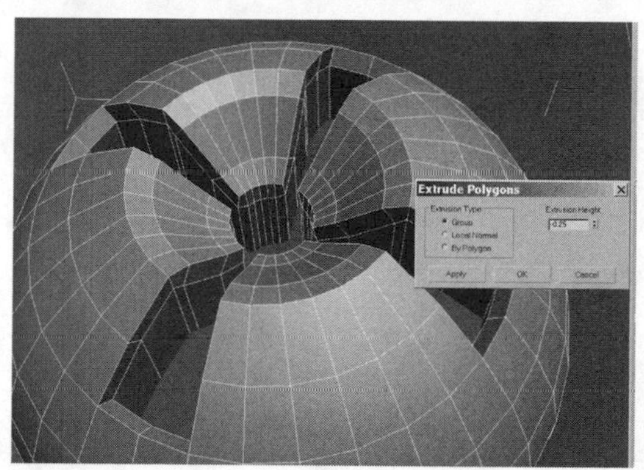

Figure 1-141

21. Click **Use NURMS Subdivision** and set the iterations to **0** for Display and **2** for Rendering.

Figure 1-142

22. Object-select the screw, Shift-drag to make two clones, and position them on the access panel as shown:

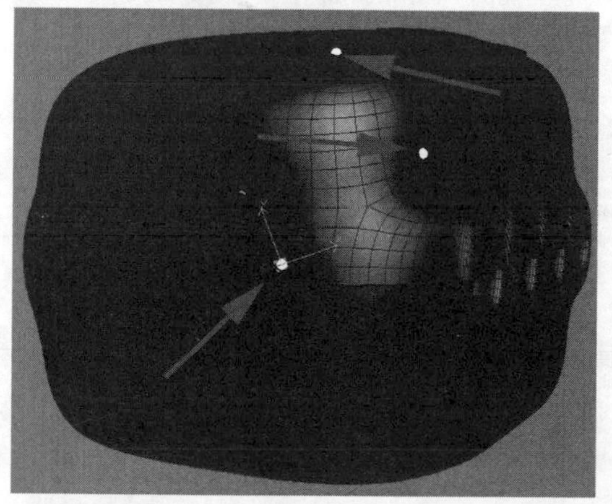

Figure 1-143

23. Object-select the screw, make six clones, and position them on the side access panel as shown:

Figure 1-144

24. Object-select the body, click the **Attach List** button, and attach all the screws to the body.

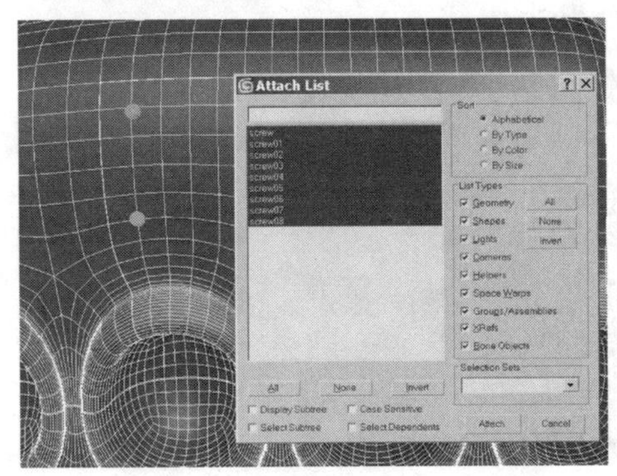

Figure 1-145

Urgent: Notice that we have some weirdness going on with some polygons poking through the top of our model. To fix it we merely need to raise the top polygon in the Z axis.

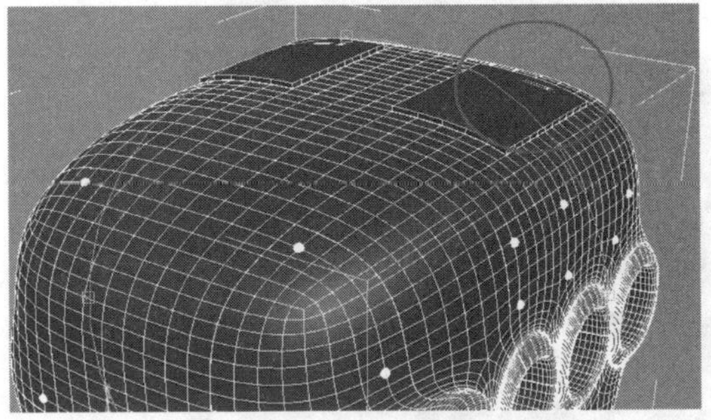

Figure 1-146

31. Chamfer the edge by **0.03** and click **OK**.

Figure 1-163

32. Convert the body to an Editable Polygon (to collapse the stack), select the polygons shown, and Extrude them by **1.5**.

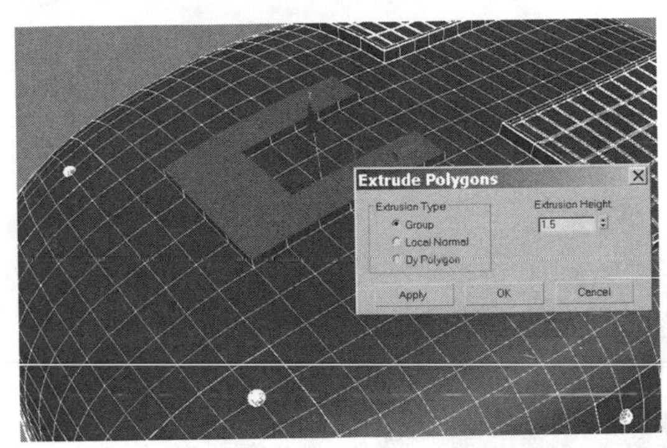

Figure 1-164

33. Switch to the Front view, select **Extended Primitives** under the Create panel, and click on **Capsule**. Create a capsule above the cradle you made in the previous step, and use the Move and Rotate tools to position it in the cradle.

Radius	Height	Sides	Height Segs	Smooth
8	35	32	1	Checked

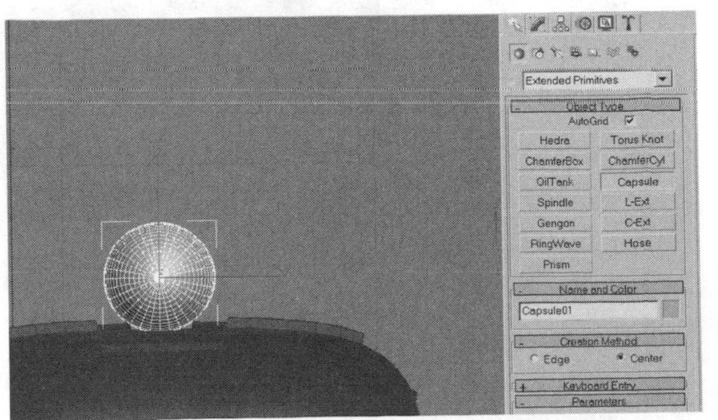

Figure 1-165

25. Highlight the cap and move it **1.0** in the Z axis.

Figure 1-147

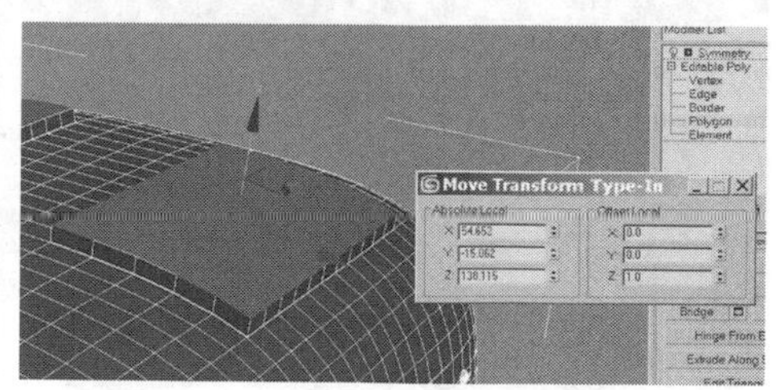

Figure 1-148

26. Select the vertices shown and then click the **Connect** button to connect them with an edge.

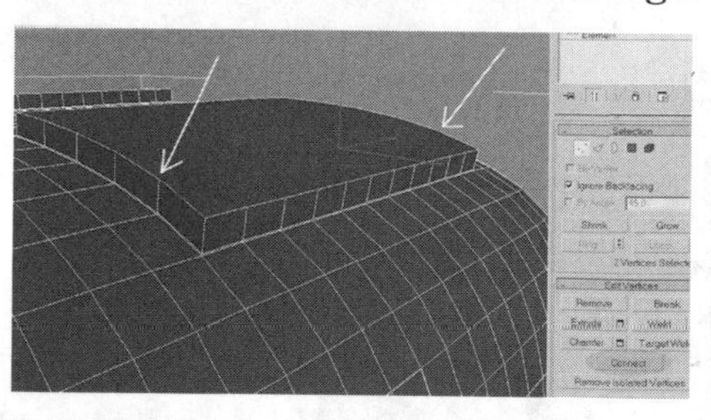

Figure 1-149

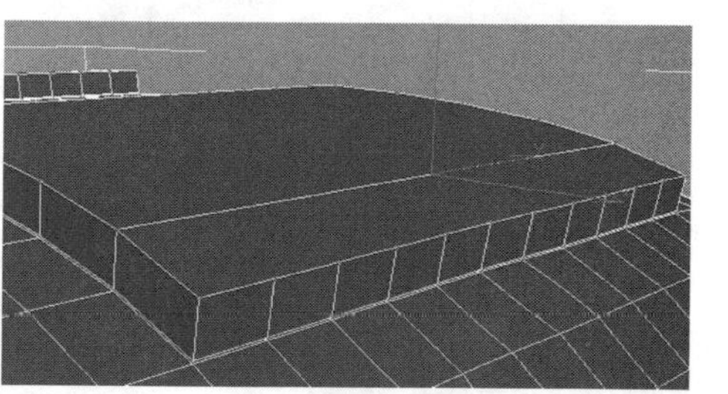

Figure 1-150

27. Repeat the last step until all the vertices (eight total) have been connected.

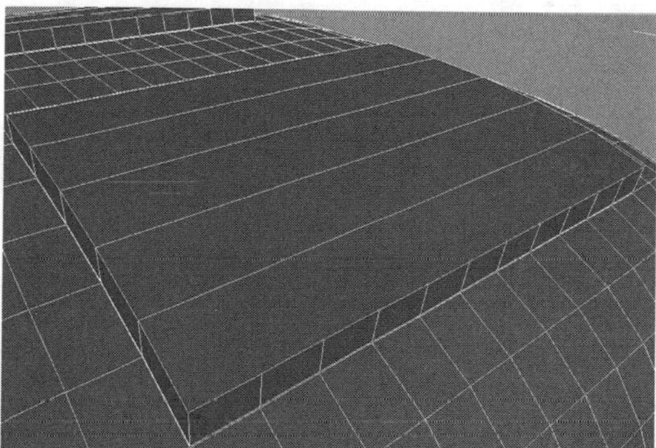

Figure 1-151

28. Use the Cut tool to split the edges in the opposite direction, and then repeat it until all the vertices have been connected.

Figure 1-152

Figure 1-153

29. Select the top polygons and click **Bevel Settings**:

Type	Height	Outline	Apply/OK
Group	0	–0.75	Apply

Figure 1-154

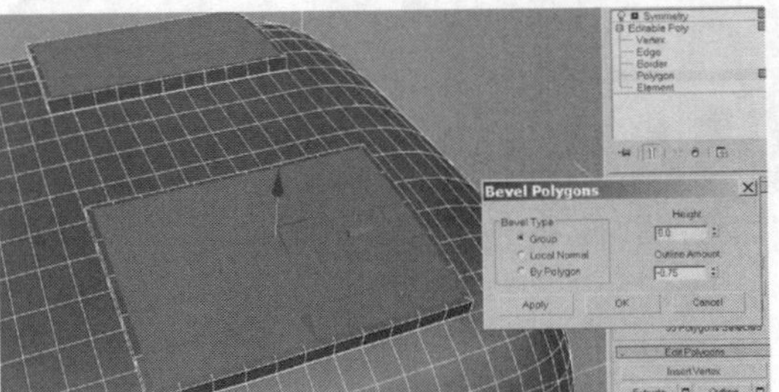

Figure 1-155

Type	Height	Outline	Apply/OK
Group	–1	0	Apply
Group	0	–0.05	Apply

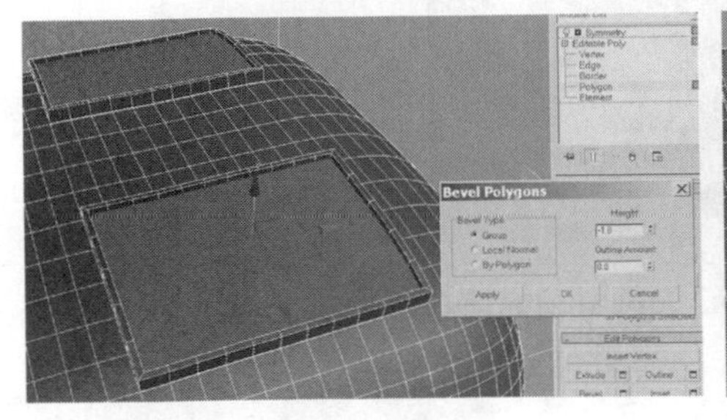

Figure 1-156

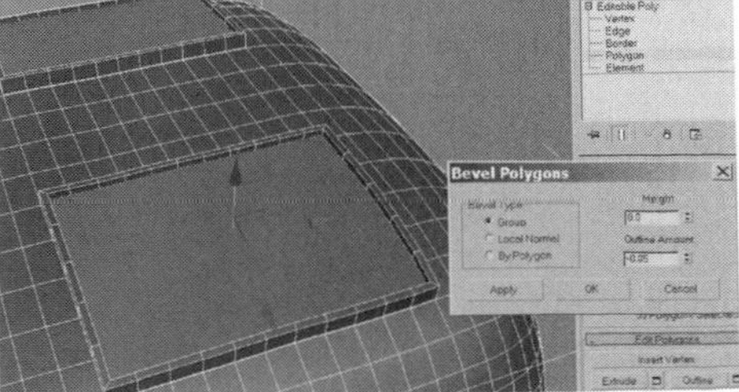

Figure 1-157

Type	Height	Outline	Apply/OK
Group	0.5	0	Apply
By Polygon	0	–0.2	Apply

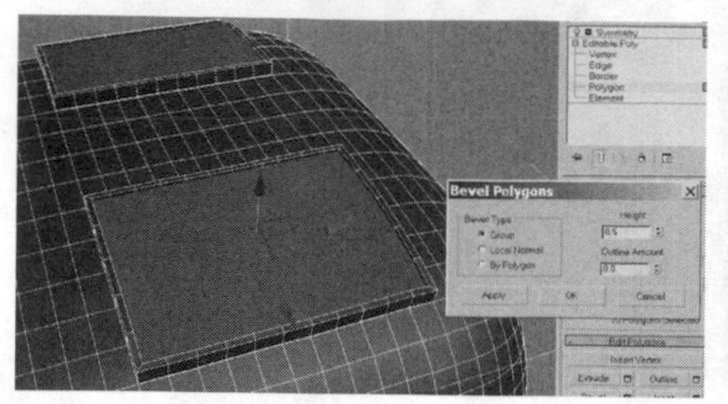

Figure 1-158

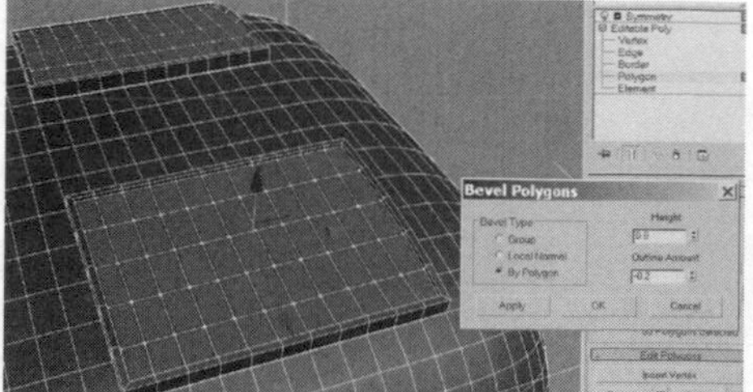

Figure 1-159

Type	Height	Outline	Apply/OK
By Polygon	0.02	0	OK

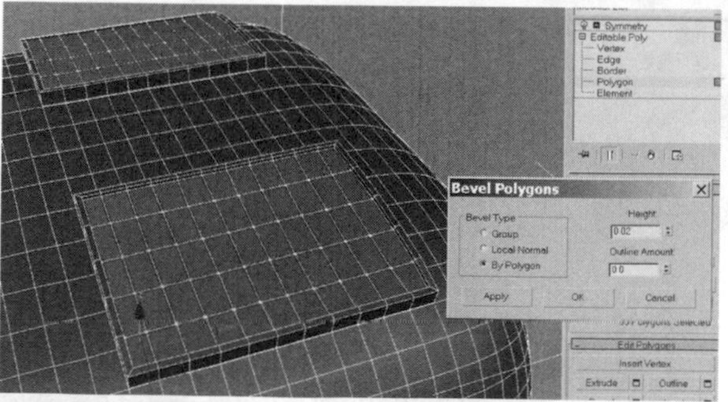

Figure 1-160

30. Select one of the outer edges, click **Loop**, Chamfer the edge by **0.08**, and click **Apply**.

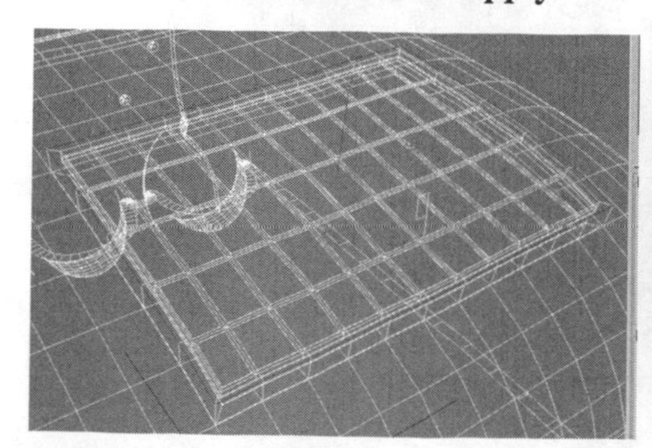

Figure 1-161

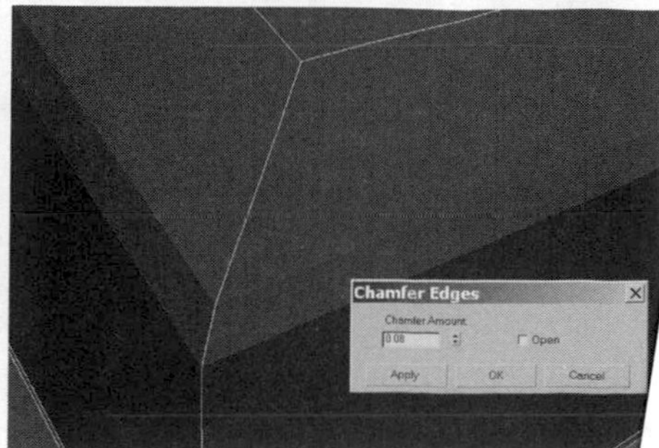

Figure 1-162

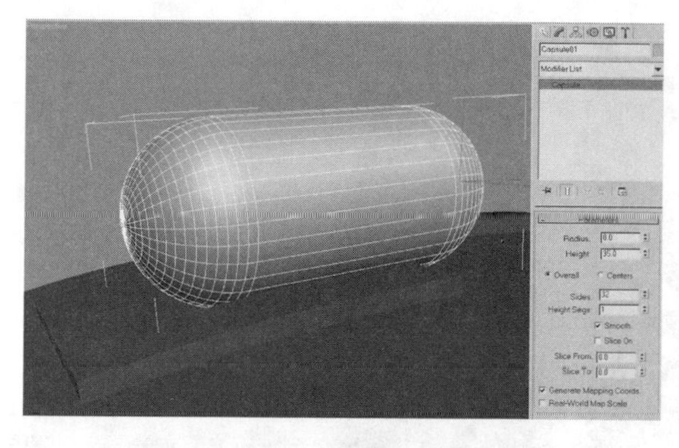

Figure 1-166

34. Convert it to an Editable Polygon, rename it **tank**, and Select and Link it to the body.

35. Switch to the Front view, use AutoGrid to create a Tube to surround the tank, and call it **Magnet**.

Radius 1	Radius 2	Height	Height Segs	Cap Segs	Sides
8	13	3.3	1	1	32

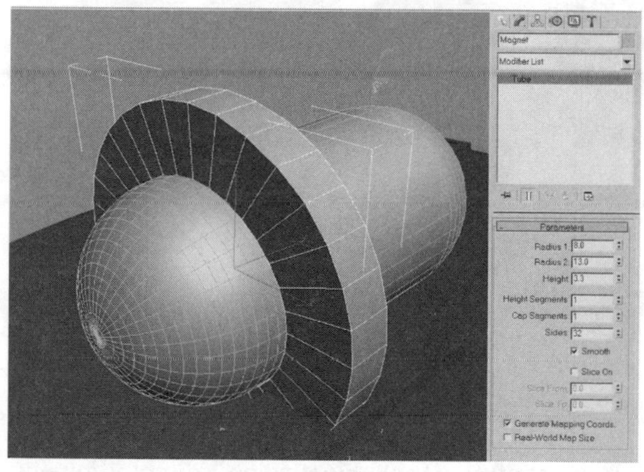

Figure 1-167

36. Shift-move the magnet in the Z axis to make a clone and position it as shown in Figure 1-168.

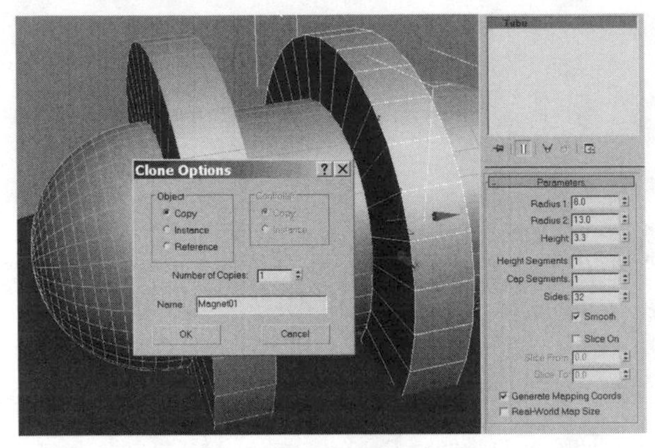

Figure 1-168

37. Use AutoGrid to create a Box on the front surface of the front magnet and rename it **control_panel**.

Length	Width	Height	Length/Width/Height Segs
1.799	2.4	0.6	1/2/1

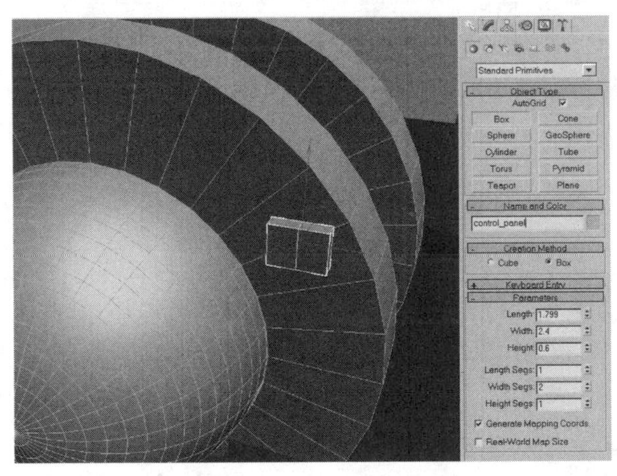

Figure 1-169

38. Convert the control_panel object to an Editable Polygon, delete the backward-facing polygons, and attach it to the magnet.

39. Using AutoGrid, create a Cylinder on the top right of the control_panel object.

Radius	Height	Height/Cap Segs	Sides	Smooth
0.2	0.15	1/2	32	Checked

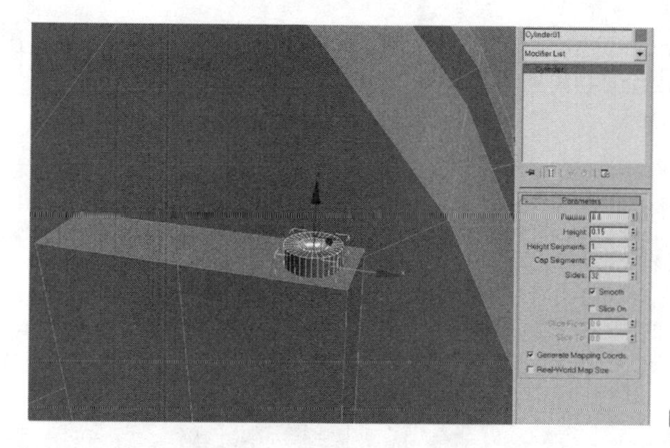

Figure 1-170

40. Convert the cylinder to an Editable Polygon and delete the bottom-facing polygons.

41. Using Edge selection mode, select and Loop the center cap segments, then right-click the **Scale** tool and scale them up by **160** percent.

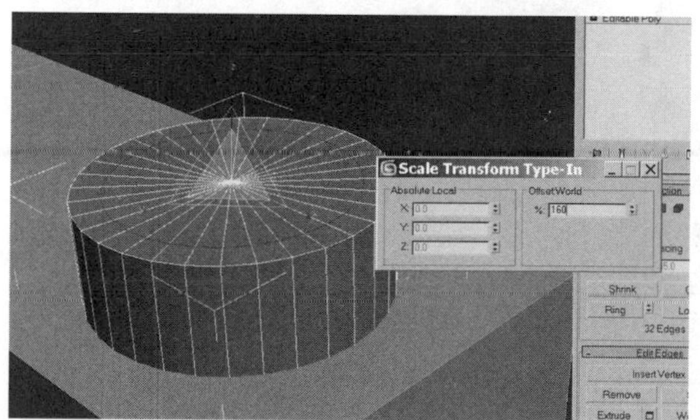

Figure 1-171

42. Select the top polygons, Extrude them by Local Normal to **1.4**, and click **Apply.**

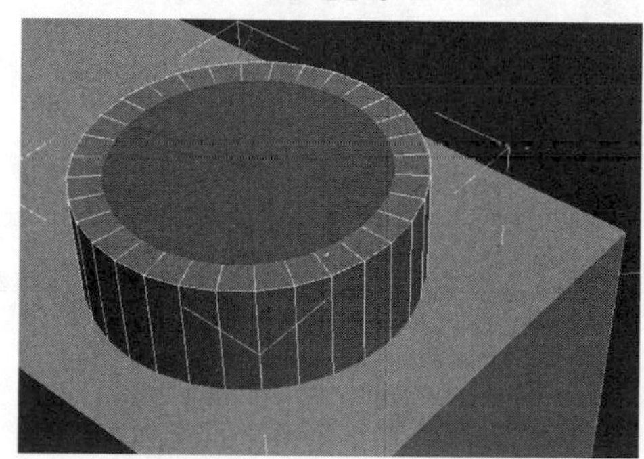

Figure 1-172

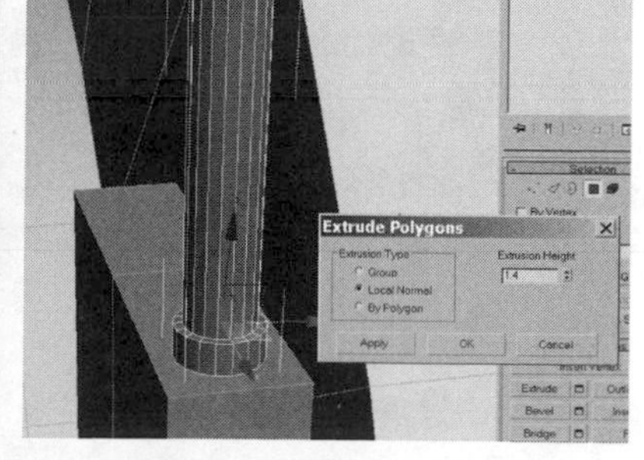

Figure 1-173

43. Change the Extrusion Height to **0.05**, click **Apply** eight times, and then click **OK.**

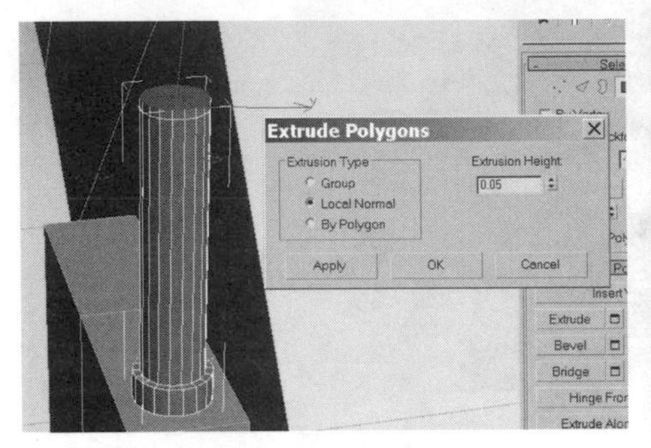

Figure 1-174

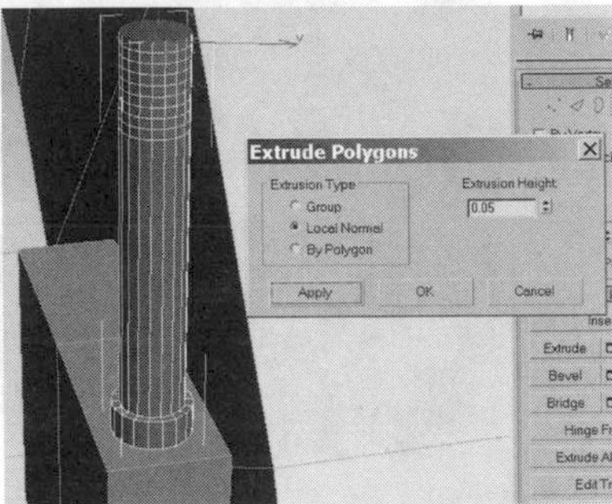

Figure 1-175

44. Click the **Grow** button nine times or until the top segments have all been selected.

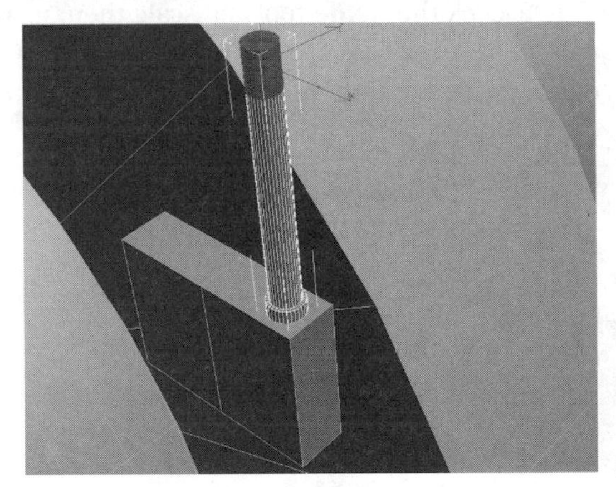

Figure 1-176

45. Add a Bend modifier to the stack, click the rollout, select the Bend modifier's Center, and move it down in the Z axis until it is aligned with the bottom segment of the selected area.

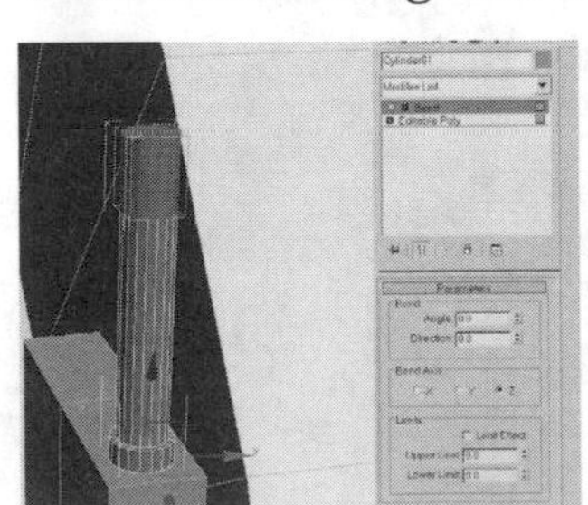

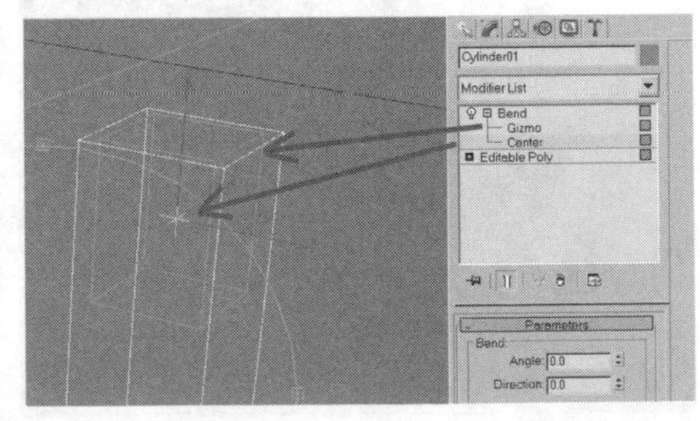

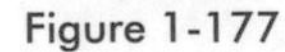

Figure 1-177

Figure 1-178

FYI: Unfortunately, the gizmo is obscured by the selection highlighting, even if you're in wireframe mode. However, highlighting is disabled when you use the Arc Rotate tool, and you can see an orange box (the gizmo), representing the area affected by the Bend modifier. The Bend modifier affects the selected area, which in this case is the top nine segments and not the whole object. The Bend modifier bends the geometry from the center of the gizmo; the Center is represented by yellow crosshairs. By default, it's centered (duh), which means the selected area will bend from the center of the selection. This is not what we want. We want the bend to start from the bottommost segment (which corresponds to the bottom of the orange box) and we want its effect to extend over the entire selection area. So ... we have to move the Center down to the bottom of the gizmo so the bend will start there, which corresponds to the first segment.

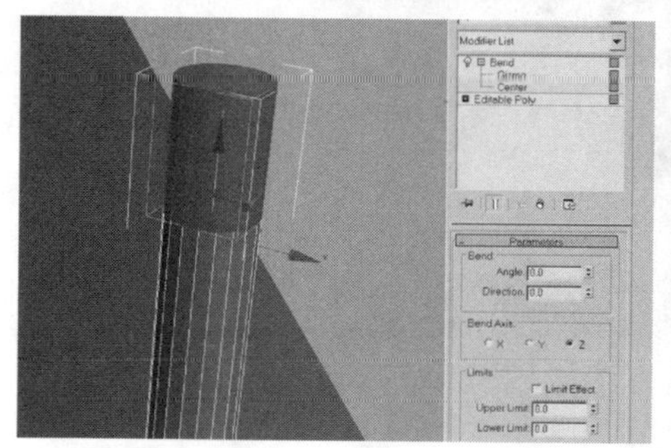

Figure 1-179

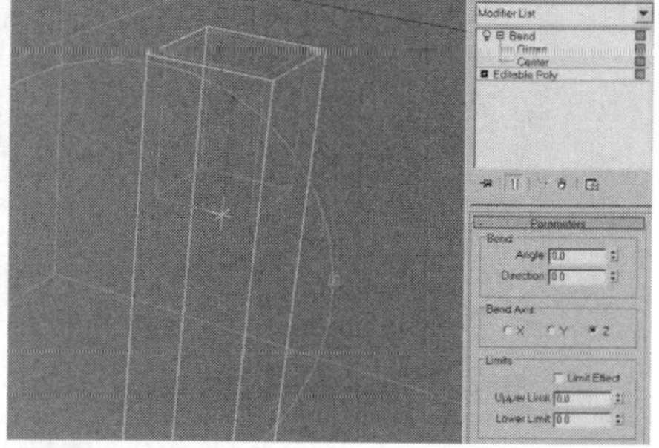

Figure 1-180

46. Under Parameters, set the Bend Angle to **77** degrees, the Direction to **–90**, and the Bend Axis to **Z**.

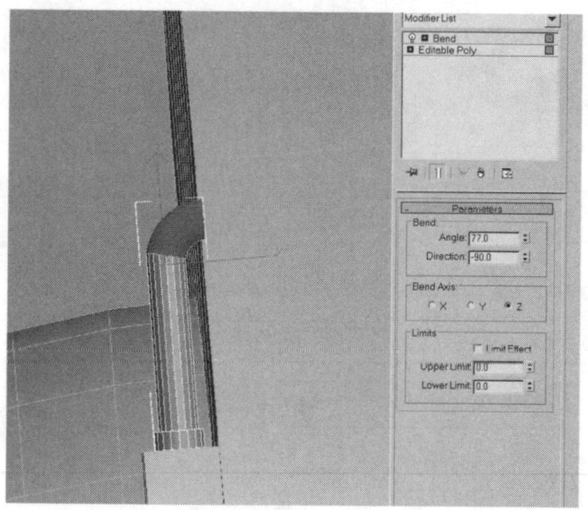

Figure 1-181

FYI: The reason the angle is 77 and not 90 is because the top of the bot is sloped and the magnets are actually tilted slightly forward, making the pipe angled slightly forward.

47. Right-click on the Bend modifier and select **Collapse All** to make the bend permanent; we'll be needing to make another bend momentarily so we want a clean object.

48. Click the **Shrink** button until only the 18 polygons on the tip of the pipe are selected.

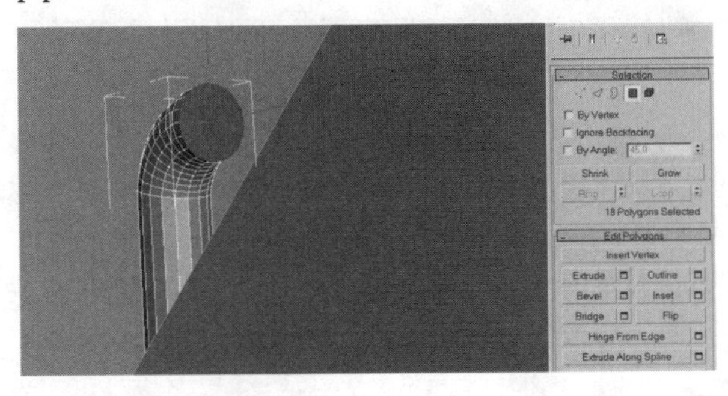

Figure 1-182

49. Click **Bevel Settings:**

Type	Height	Outline	Apply
Group	0	0.04	Apply
Group	0.04	0	Apply

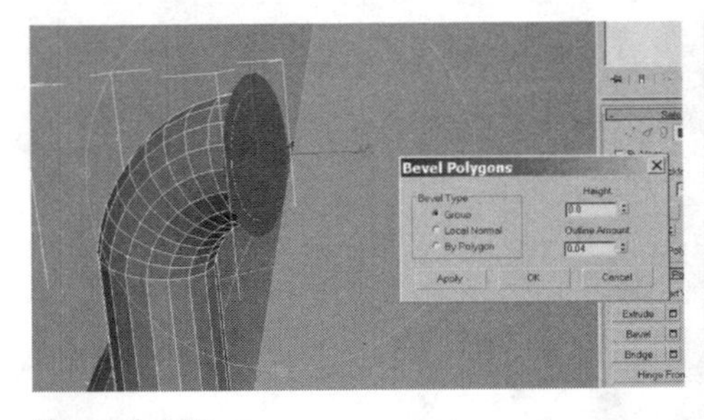

Figure 1-183

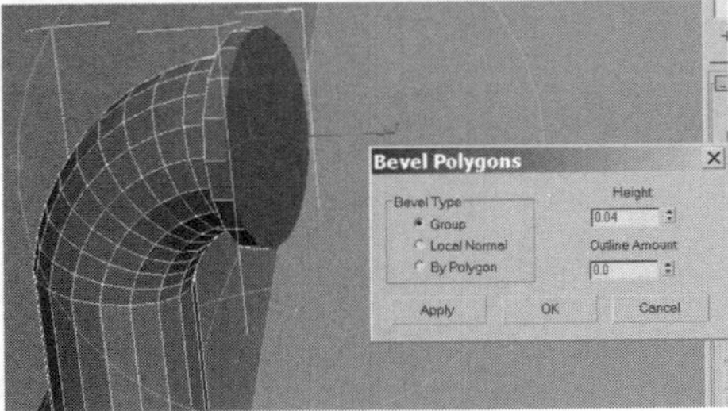

Figure 1-184

Type	Height	Outline	Apply/OK
Group	0	–0.02	Apply
Group	0.01	0	Apply

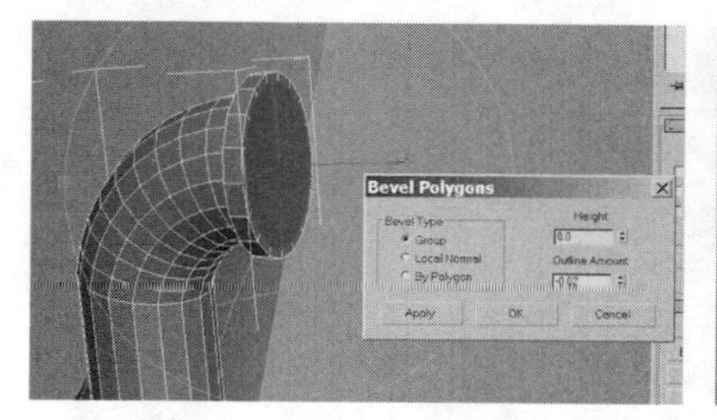

Figure 1-185

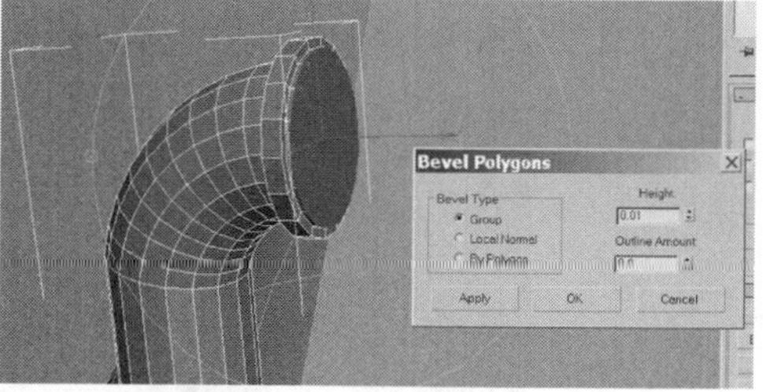

Figure 1-186

Type	Height	Outline	Apply/OK
Group	0	0.02	Apply
Group	0.04	0	Apply

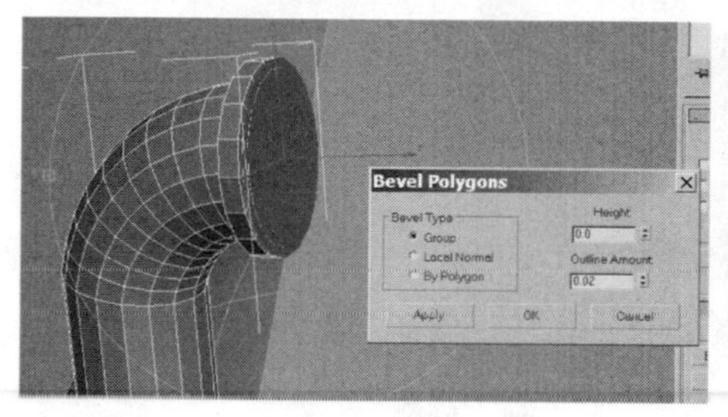

Figure 1-187

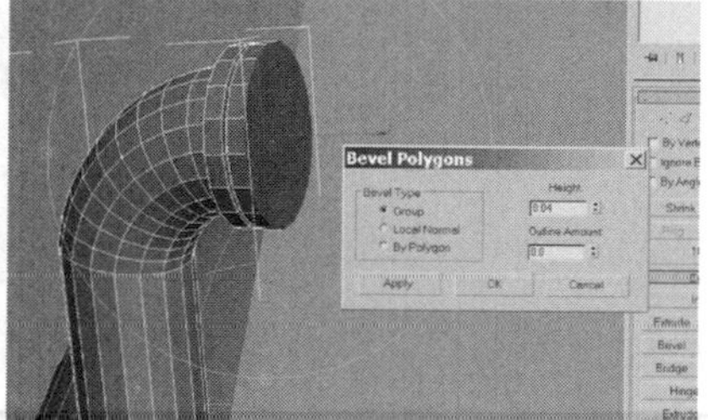

Figure 1-188

Type	Height	Outline	Apply/OK
Group	0	0.02	Apply
Group	0.04	0	Apply

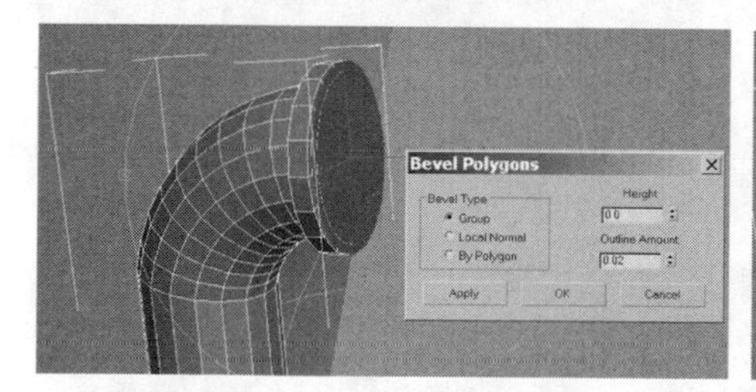

Figure 1-189

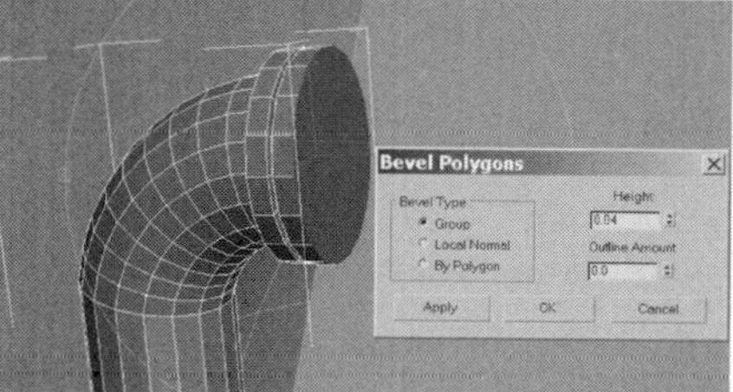

Figure 1-190

Type	Height	Outline	Apply/OK
Group	0	–0.04	OK

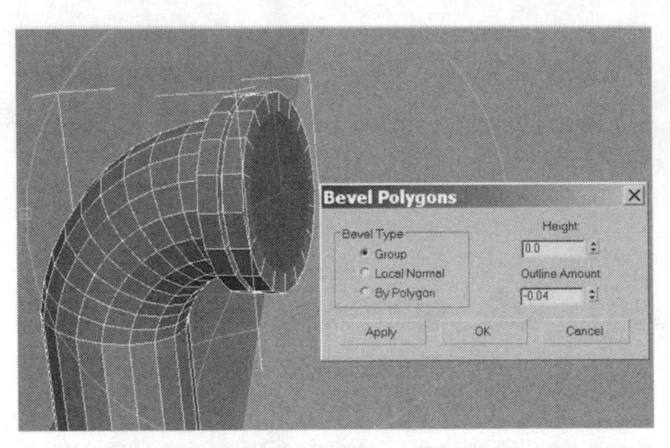

Figure 1-191

50. Extrude the polygons **12.5** or until the pipe is just shy of the midpoint of the second magnet and then hit **Apply** (*not* OK).

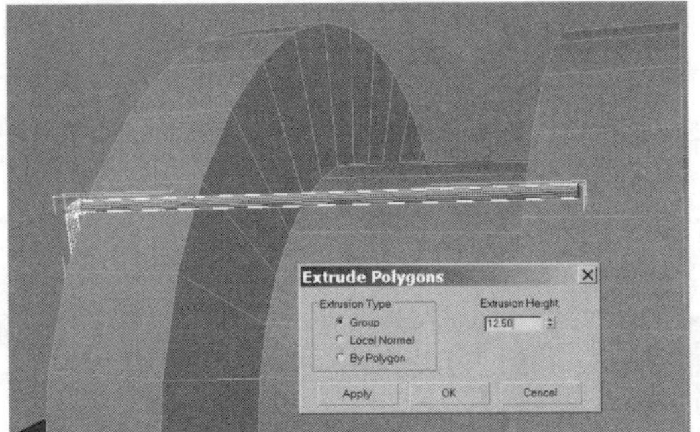

Figure 1-192

51. Extrude the polygons **0.05**, hit **Apply** eight times, and then hit **OK**.

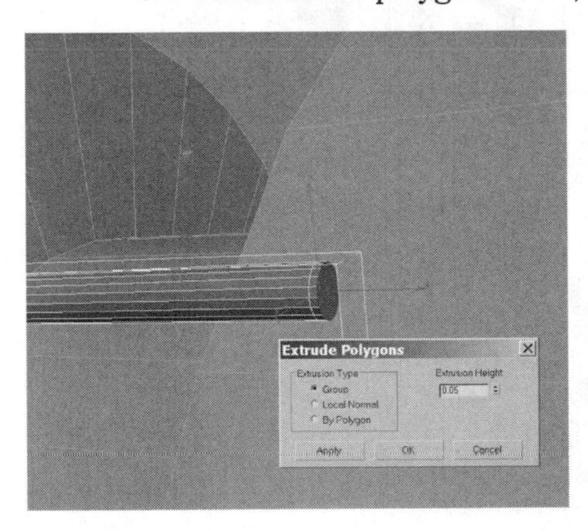

Figure 1-193

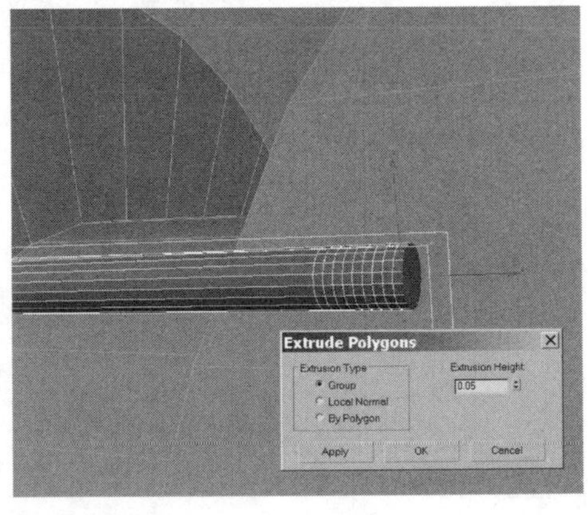

Figure 1-194

52. Click **Grow** nine times until the end is selected, and then add a Bend modifier to the stack.

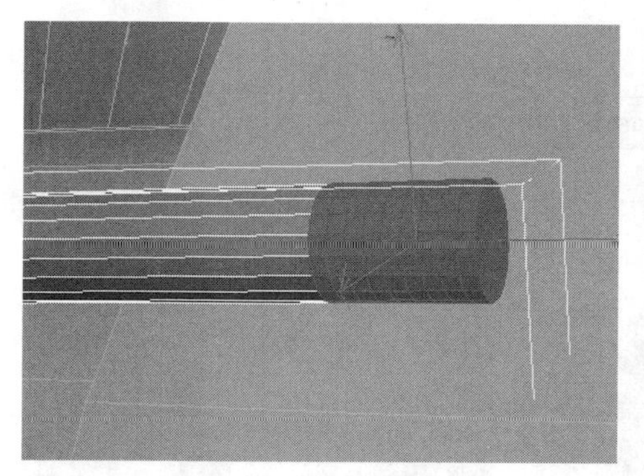
Figure 1-195

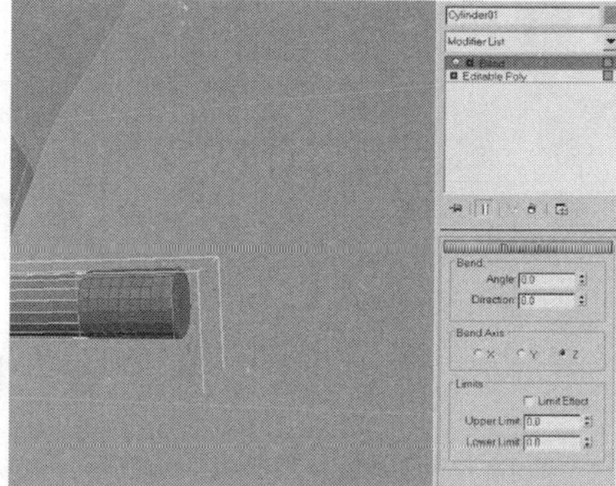

Figure 1-196

53. Move the Bend modifier's Center to the end of the Bend modifier the way you did with the previous bend and set the Parameters to Angle **–90** and Direction **–26**.

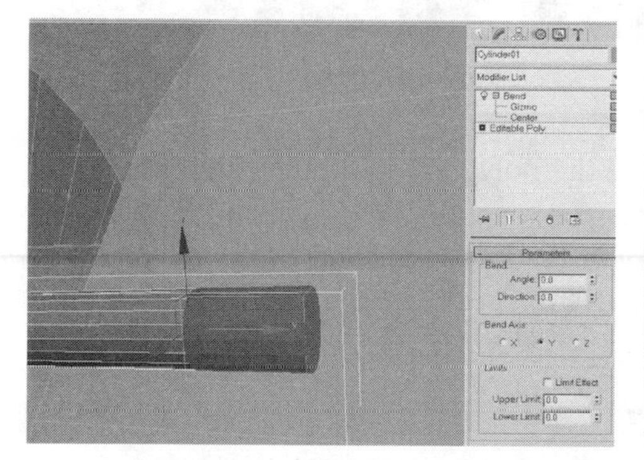

Figure 1-197

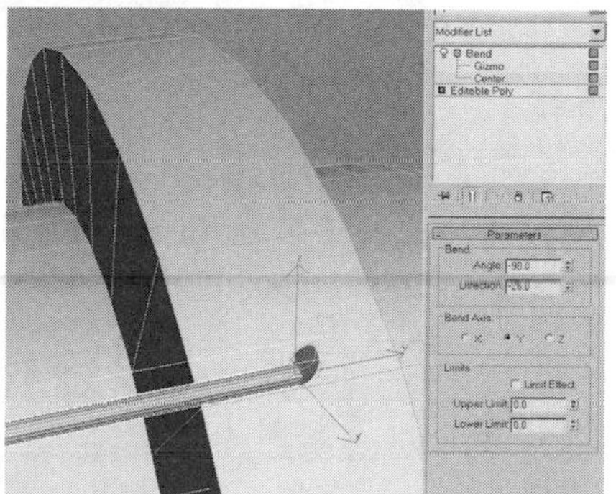

Figure 1-198

54. Click **Shrink** nine times, or until only the polygons at the tip of the pipe are selected, and then Extrude them **2**.

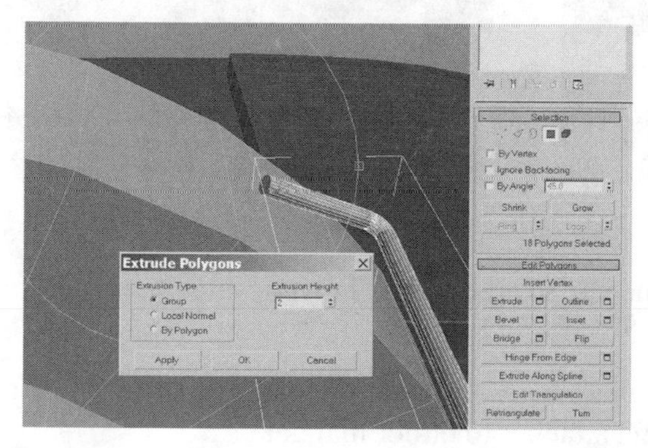

Figure 1-199

55. Click **Bevel Settings:**

Type	Height	Outline	Apply/OK
Group	0	0.1	Apply
Group	0.1	0	OK

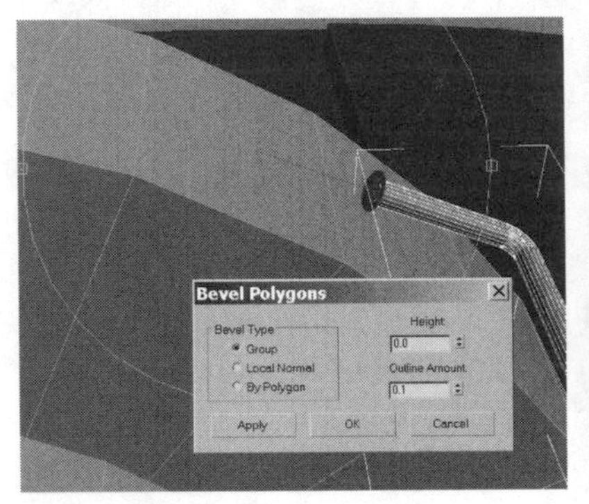

Figure 1-200

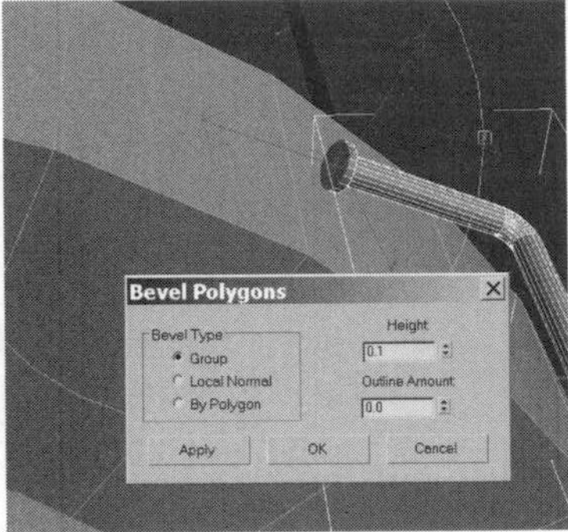

Figure 1-201

56. Hit the **Delete** key to delete the polygons and then, using AutoGrid, create a Box (just above the pipe) and use the Move and Rotation tools to position it as shown in Figures 1-202 and 1-203:

Length	Width	Height	Length/Width/Height Segs
1	1.9	0.8	2/2/1

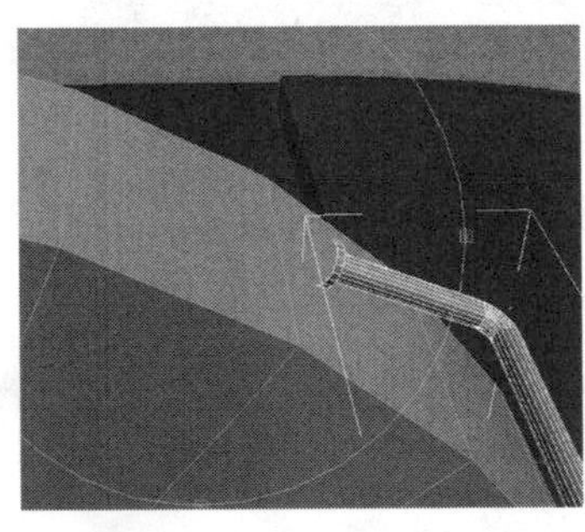

Figure 1-202

Figure 1-203

57. Convert the box to an Editable Polygon and rename it **control_panel02**.

58. Select the rear magnet, attach the box to it, and then object-select the pipe and attach it to either magnet.

59. Select the magnet, use Polygon Selection mode to select the upper-right quarter of control_panel02, and click **Bevel Settings:**

Type	Height	Outline	Apply/OK
Group	0	–0.04	Apply
Group	0.05	0	Apply

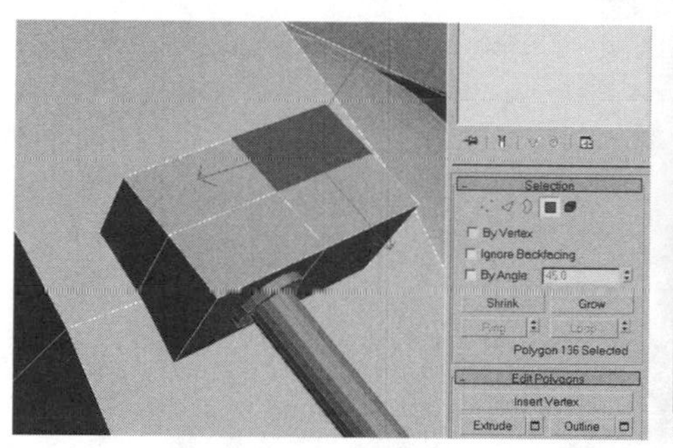

Figure 1-204

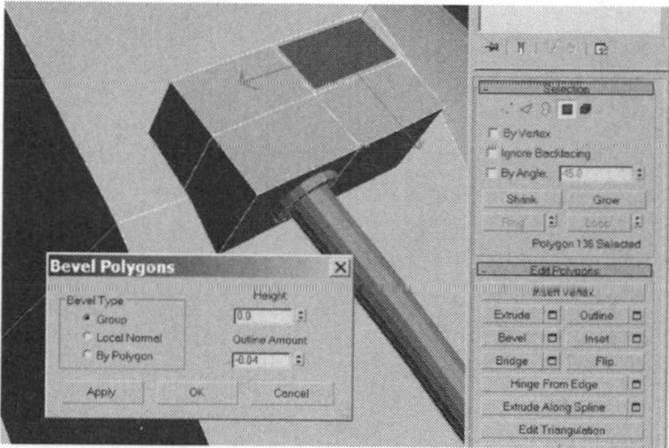

Figure 1-205

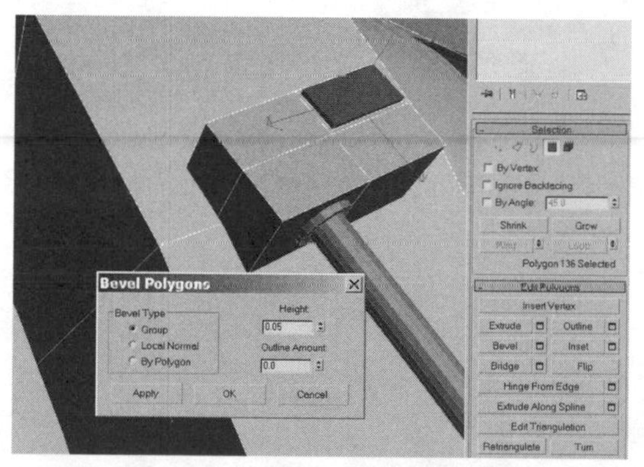

Figure 1-206

60. Under Edit Geometry, click **Tessellate** and then select the polygons in an L shape.

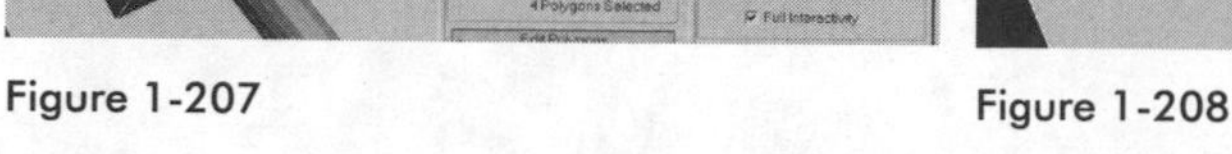

Figure 1-207

Figure 1-208

FYI: Tessellate subdivides the selected geometry each time you click the button. In this case, each time you hit the button it will subdivide each rectangular polygon into four polygons.

61. Click **Bevel Settings:**

Type	Height	Outline	Apply/OK
Group	0	–0.03	Apply
By Polygon	0.05	–0.02	OK

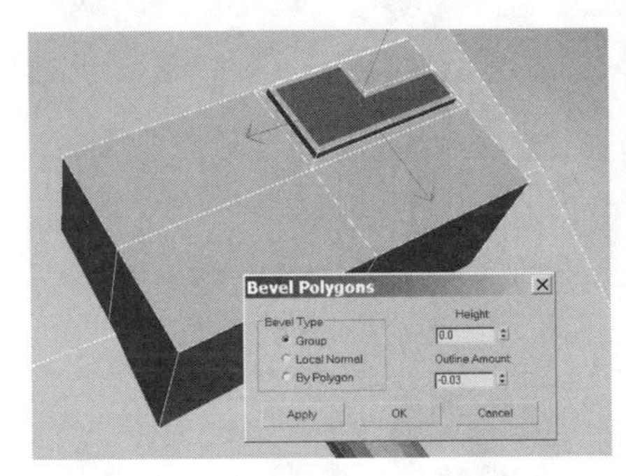

Figure 1-209

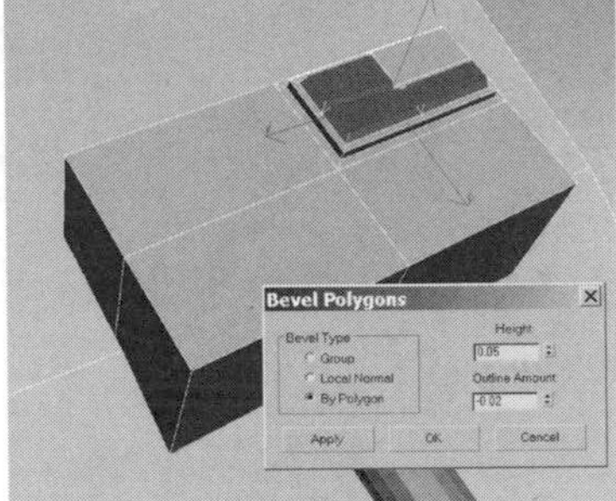

Figure 1-210

62. Select the two polygons on the left of the box and click **Bevel Settings:**

Type	Height	Outline	Apply/OK
By Polygon	0.05	–0.02	OK

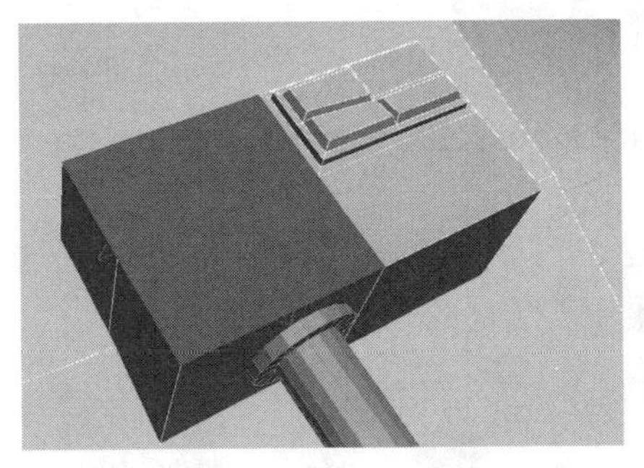

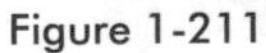
Figure 1-211

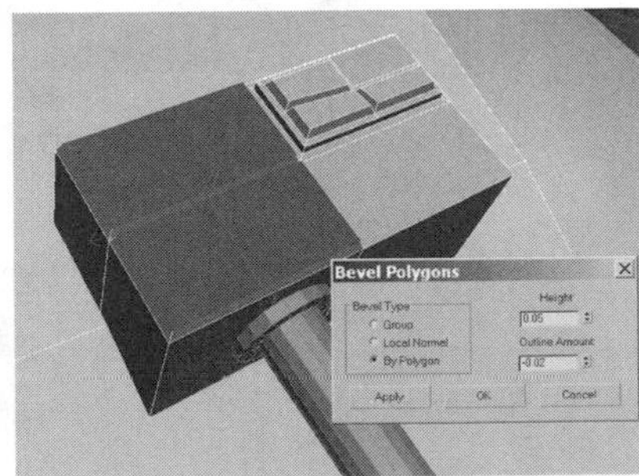

Figure 1-212

63. Switch to the front control panel, select the front two polygons, hit the **Tessellate** button, and then select the two polygons in the upper-right of the panel.

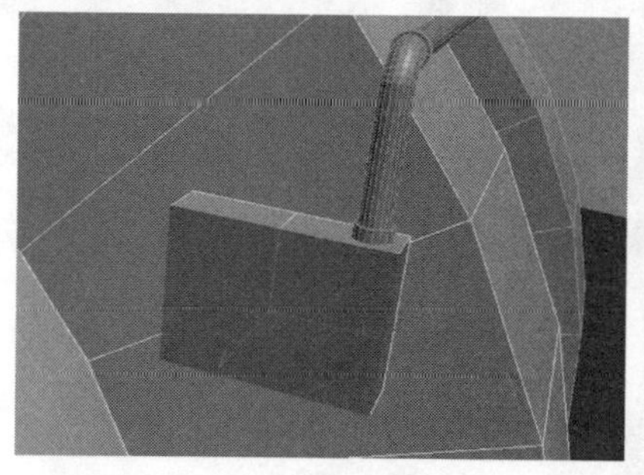

Figure 1-213

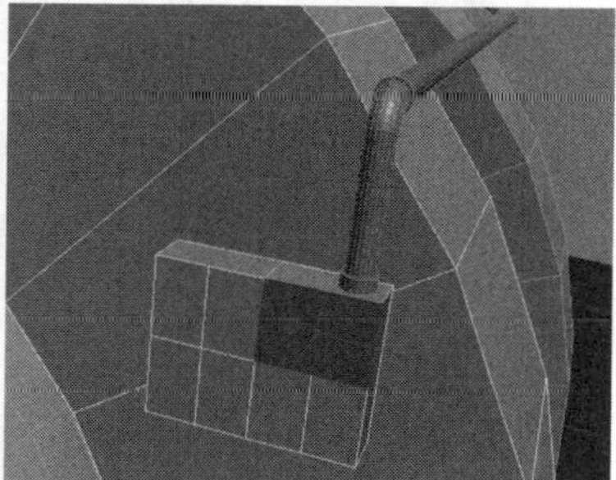

Figure 1-214

64. Click **Bevel Settings:**

Type	Height	Outline	Apply/OK
Group	0	–0.03	Apply
Group	0.02	–0.03	OK

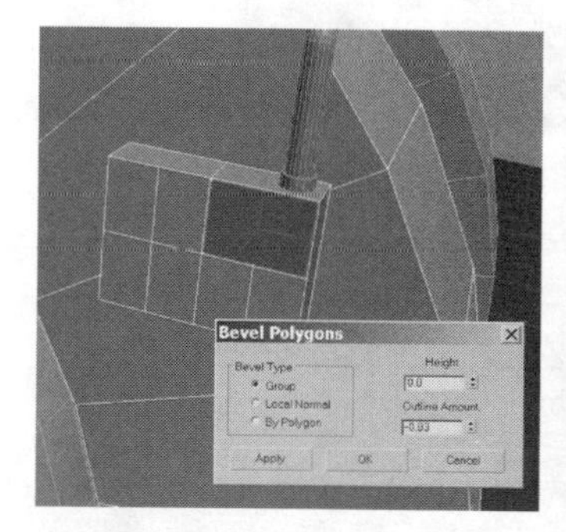

Figure 1-215

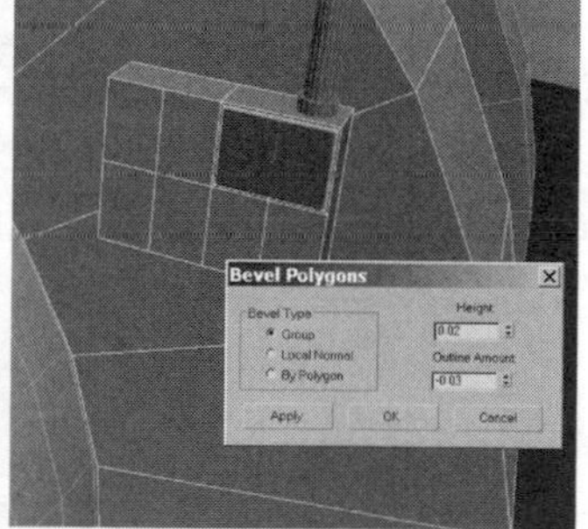

Figure 1-216

65. Select the lower-right two polygons and click **Bevel Settings:**

Type	Height	Outline	Apply/OK
Group	0	–0.1	Apply
Group	0.04	0	OK

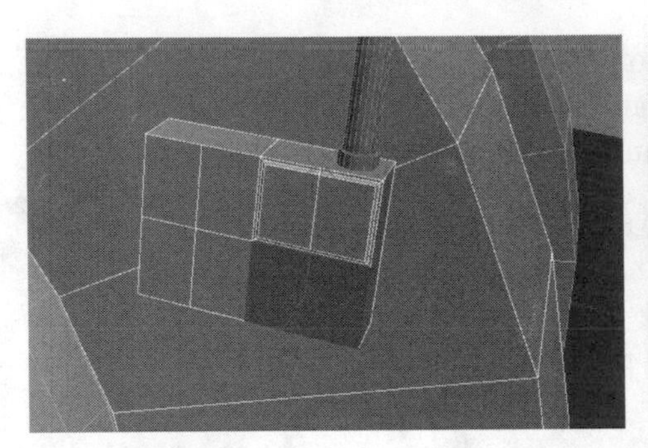

Figure 1-217

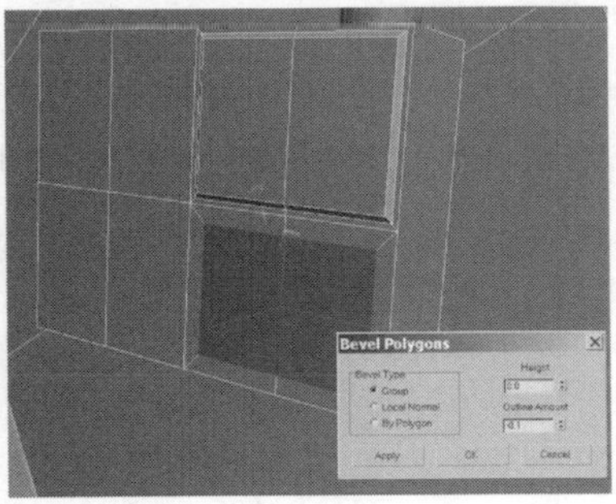

Figure 1-218

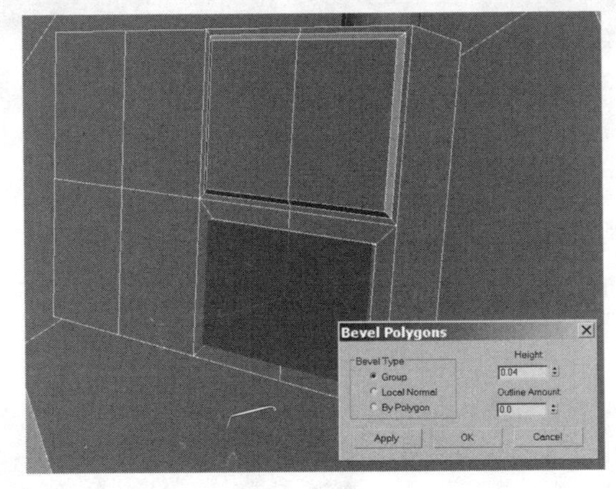

Figure 1-219

66. Hit the **Tessellate** button four times and click **Bevel Settings**:

Type	Height	Outline	Apply/OK
By Polygon	0.02	–0.01	OK

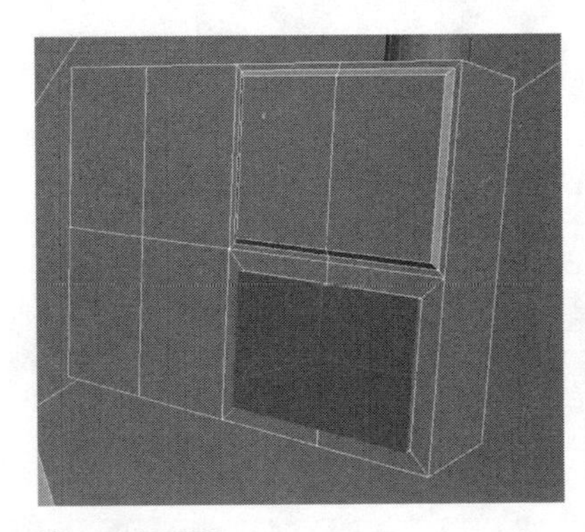

Figure 1-220

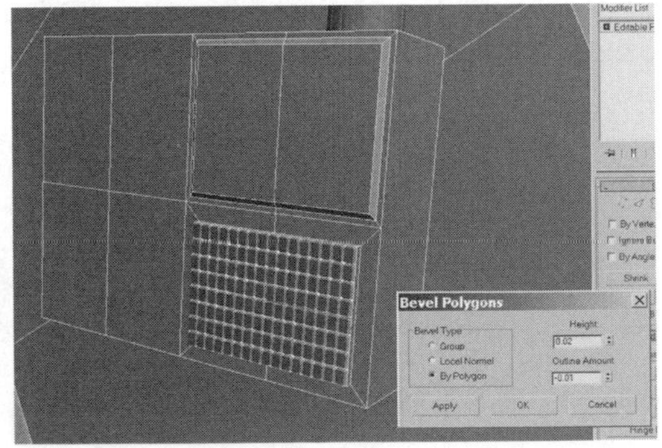

Figure 1-221

67. Select the left four polygons and click **Bevel Settings**:

Type	Height	Outline	Apply/OK
Group	0.02	–0.01	OK

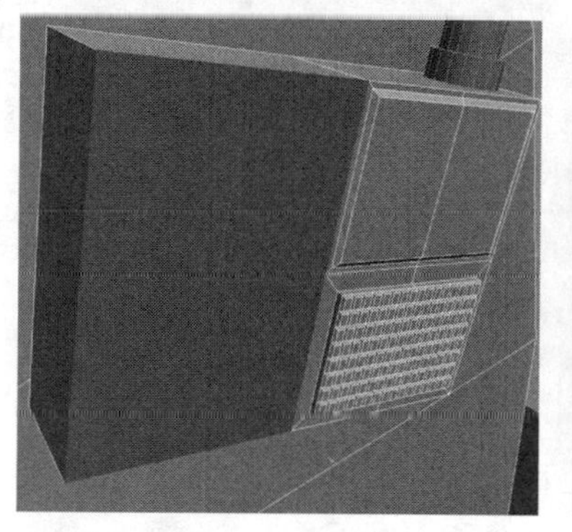

Figure 1-222

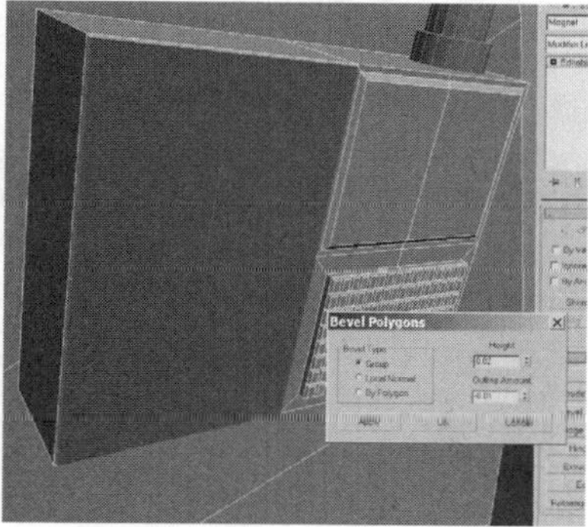

Figure 1-223

68. Select the left three polygons as shown (in a reverse L shape) and click **Bevel Settings:**

Type	Height	Outline	Apply/OK
By Polygon	0.02	–0.1	Apply

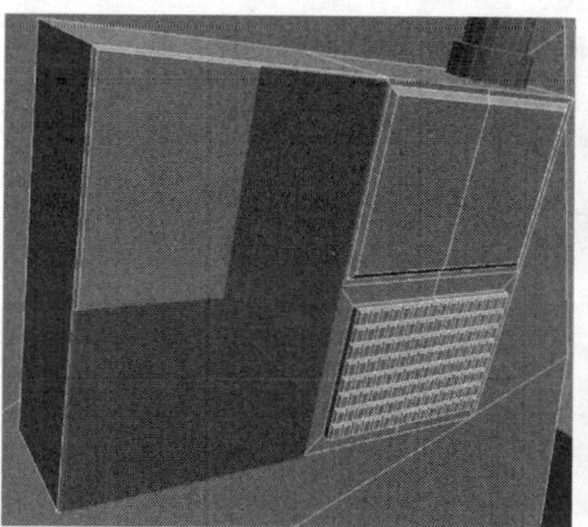

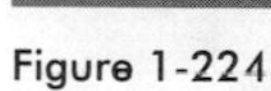

Figure 1-224

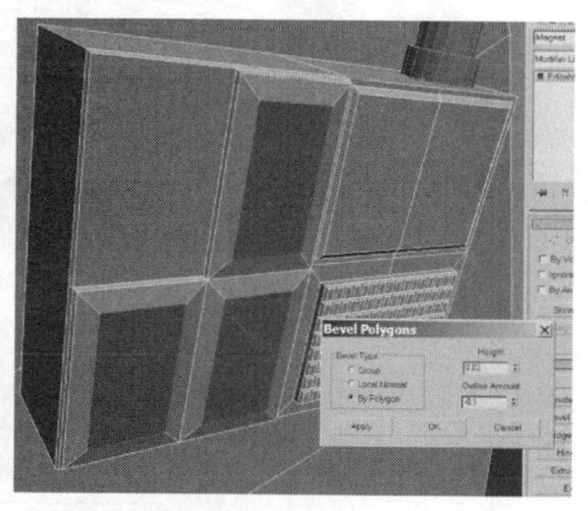

Figure 1-225

Type	Height	Outline	Apply/OK
By Polygon	0.0	–0.01	Apply
By Polygon	–0.02	–0.01	OK

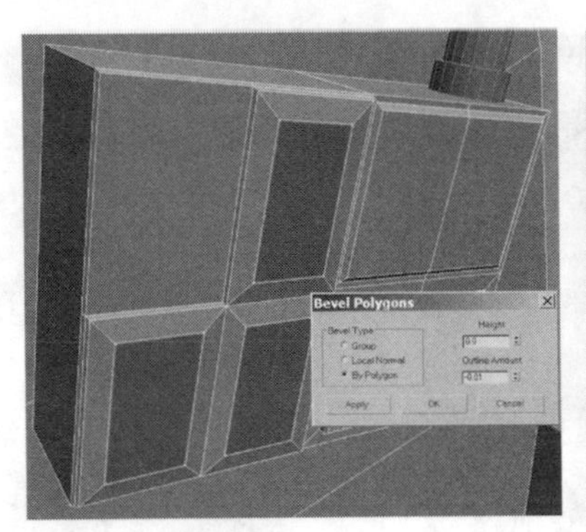

Figure 1-226

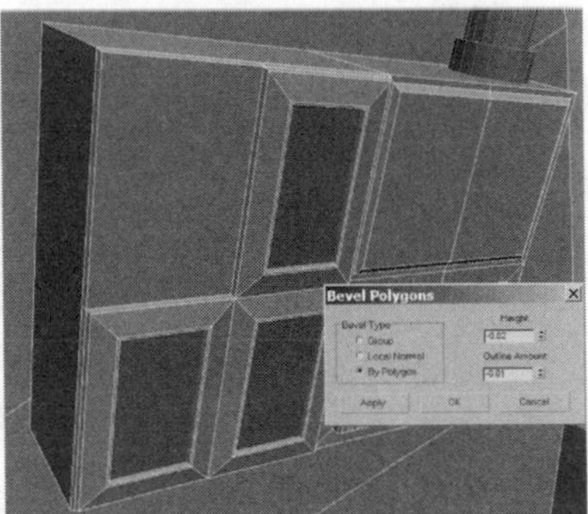

Figure 1-227

69. Hit the **Tessellate** button four times and then click **Bevel Settings**:

Type	Height	Outline	Apply/OK
By Polygon	–0.02	–0.02	OK

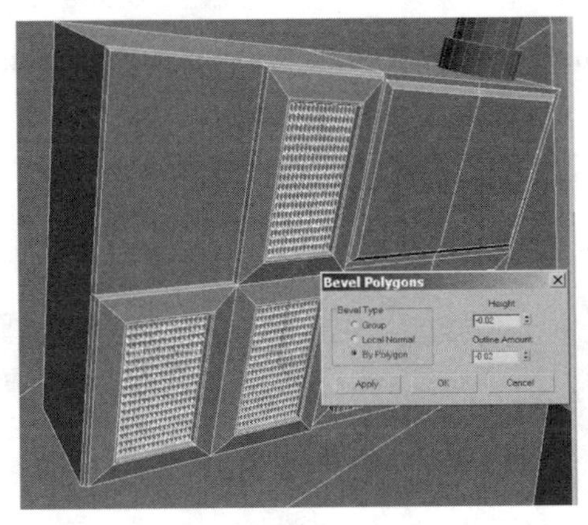

Figure 1-228

70. Select the upper-left polygon and then click **Bevel Settings**:

Type	Height	Outline	Apply/OK
By Polygon	–0.02	–0.02	Apply
By Polygon	0	–0.1	OK

Figure 1-229

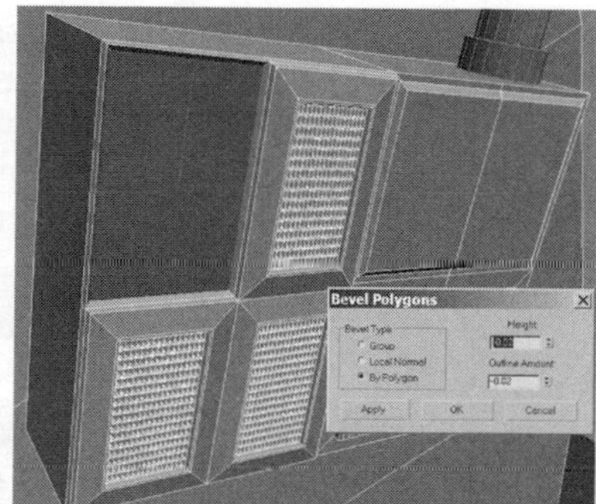

Figure 1-230

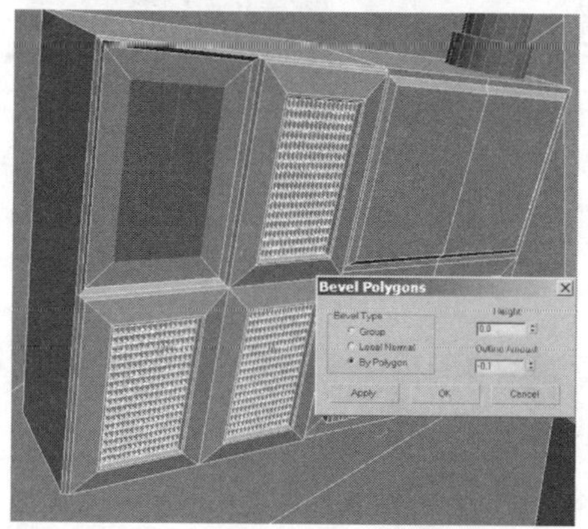

Figure 1-231

71. Scale the polygons in the Z axis, right-click the **Move** tool, and Offset the Local Z by **0.4**.

Figure 1-232

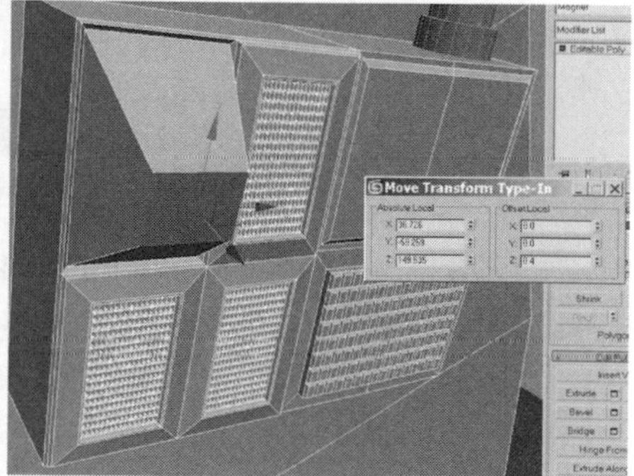

Figure 1-233

72. Click **Bevel Settings:**

Type	Height	Outline	Apply/OK
By Polygon	–0.02	–0.02	Apply
By Polygon	–0.02	–0.02	Apply
By Polygon	–0.3	0	OK

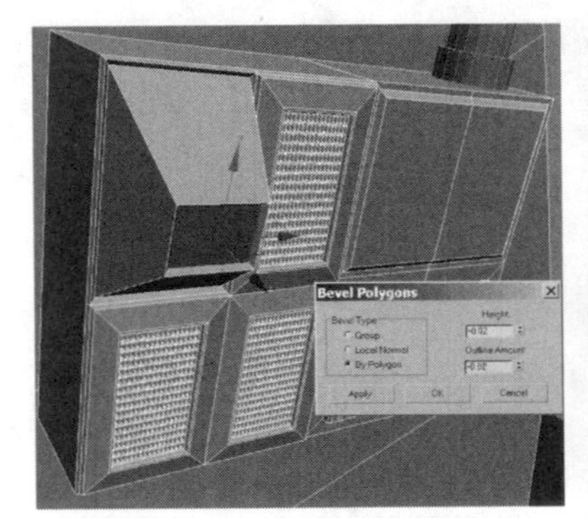

Figure 1-234

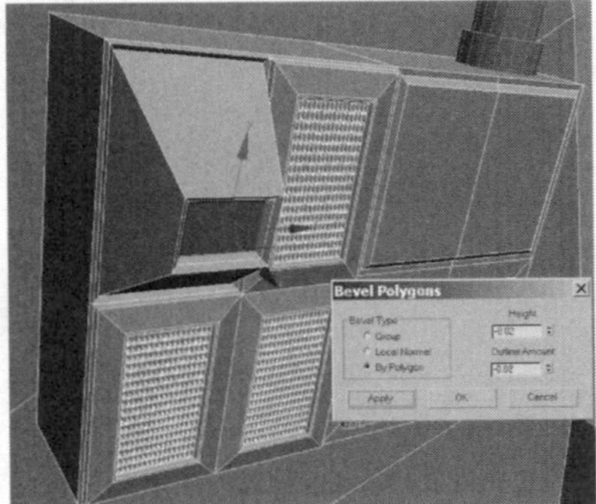

Figure 1-235

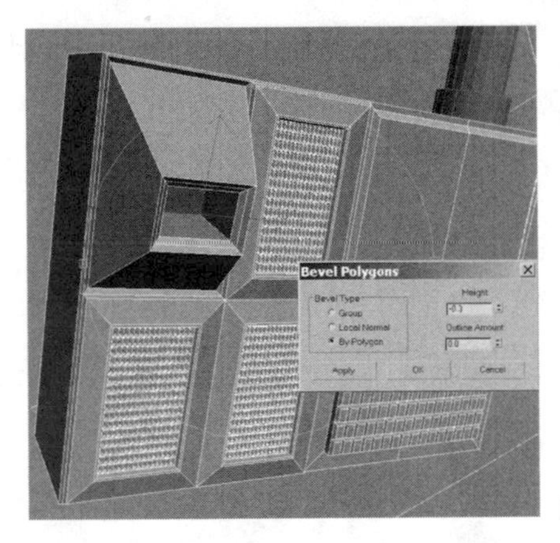

Figure 1-236

73. Under Edit Polygons, click the **Hinge From Edge Settings** button, and enter **–90** for the Angle and **9** for Segments. Click the **Current Hinge** button and select the edge shown in Figure 1-238 (the edge is exaggerated to make it easier to see).

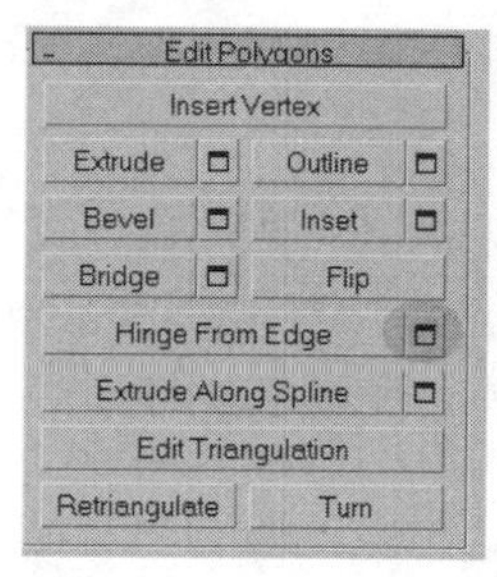

Figure 1-237

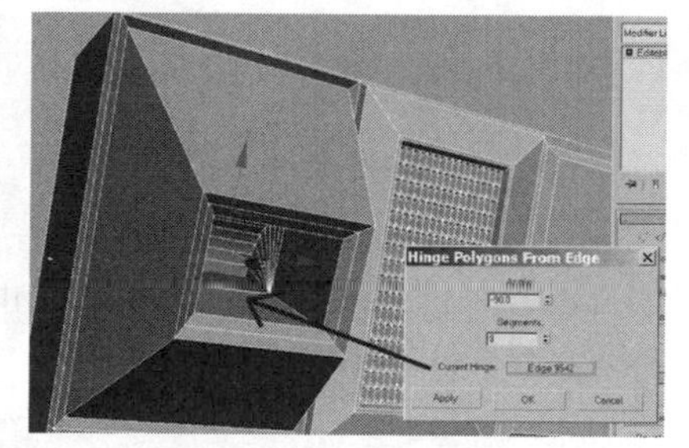

Figure 1-238

FYI: Hinge From Edge creates new polygons from the edge you select at the angle you specify. The number of segments you enter determines how many polygons are created by the hinge. The more segments you enter, the more curve the final geometry will have. In our case, we wanted to create an air intake that curved *back* into the geometry, so we used a negative angle. Since that angle was 90 degrees, I used nine segments, which means new geometry would be created at 10-degree increments, creating a nice curve.

74. Extrude the polygon **–0.065** and then delete the polygon since you can't see it (it's inside the model).

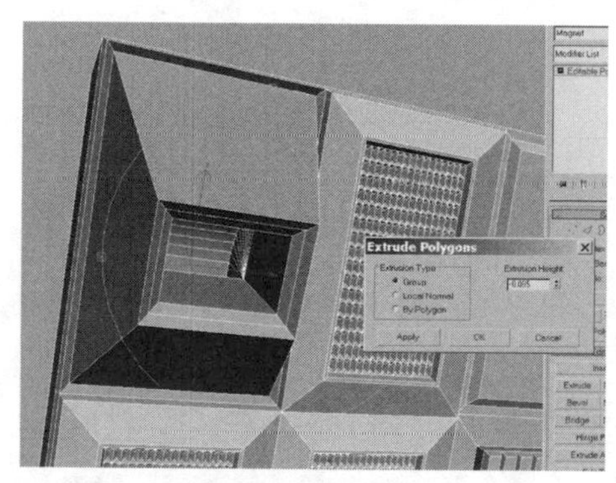

Figure 1-239

Day 4: Wiring the Eyes

1. Arc Rotate around the front, select the centermost polygons (96 total) on the front center of the tank, and Extrude them by **33.** Then click **Bevel Settings:**

Type	Height	Outline	Apply/OK
Group	0	–0.2	Apply

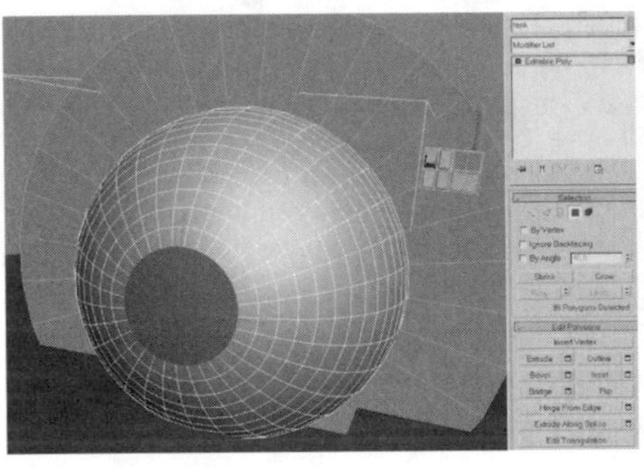

Figure 1-240

Figure 1-241

Type	Height	Outline	Apply/OK
Group	–0.2	0	Apply
Group	0	–0.1	Apply

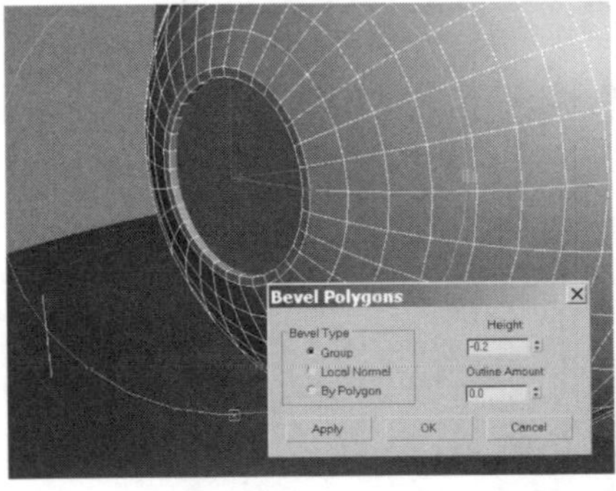

Figure 1-242

Figure 1-243

Type	Height	Outline	Apply/OK
Group	0.1	0	OK

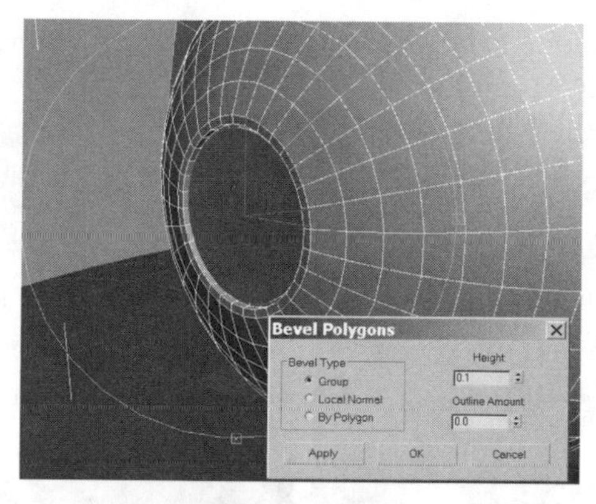

Figure 1-244

2. Using AutoGrid, create a Tube in the center of the sphere.

Radius 1	Radius 2	Height	Height/Cap Segs	Sides	Smooth
0.65	0.5	0.3	1/1	32	Checked

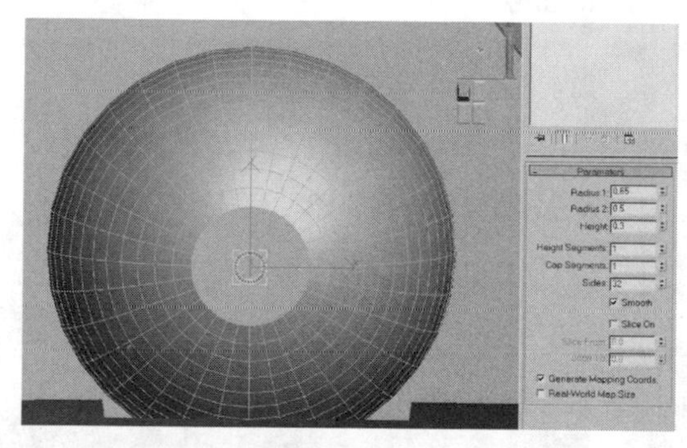

Figure 1-245

3. Convert the tube to an Editable Polygon, name it **socket**, and delete the backward-facing polygons.

4. Hold down the **Shift** key and drag in the X axis to create a clone.

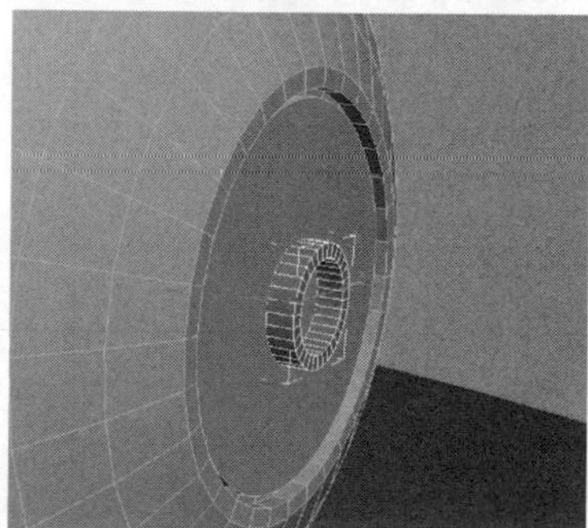

Figure 1-246

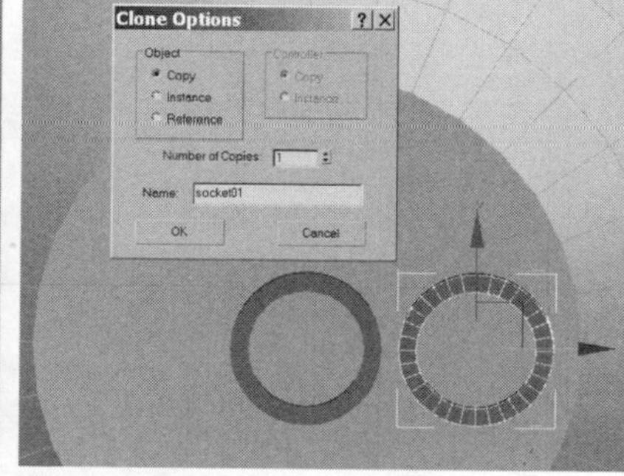

Figure 1-247

5. Scale down the clone to between 20 and 30 percent of the original (pick a size *you* like) and then create a clone of it to the left of the original and set the Number of Copies to **5**.

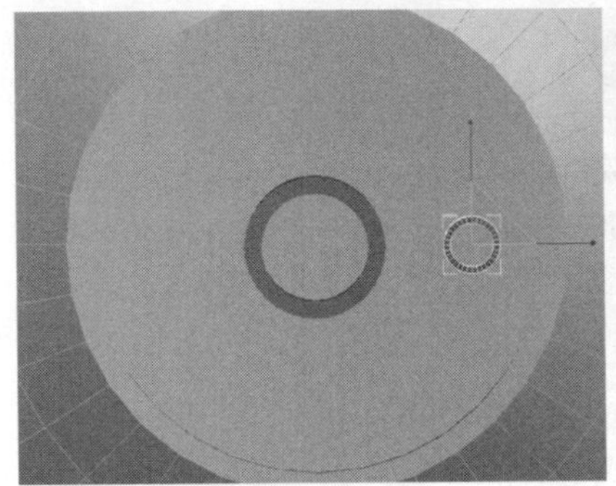

Figure 1-248

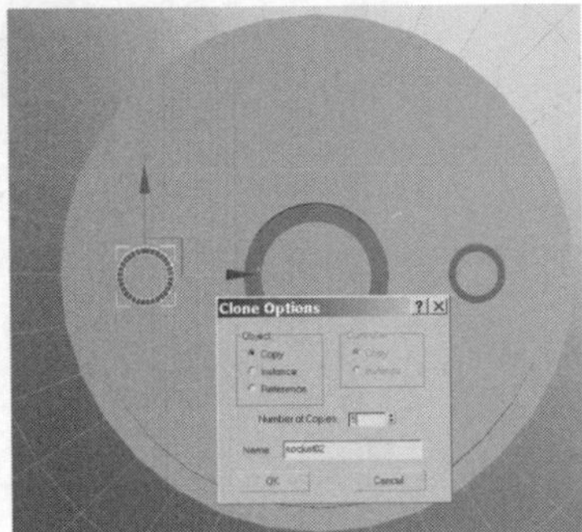

Figure 1-249

6. Position the clones as shown, select them, then use Select and Link to link them to the tank.

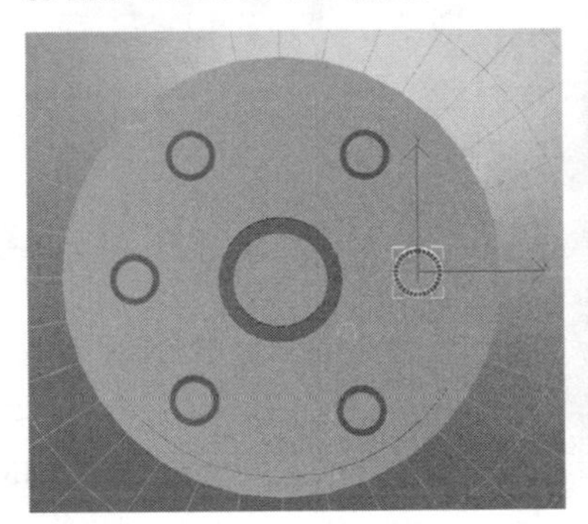

Figure 1-250

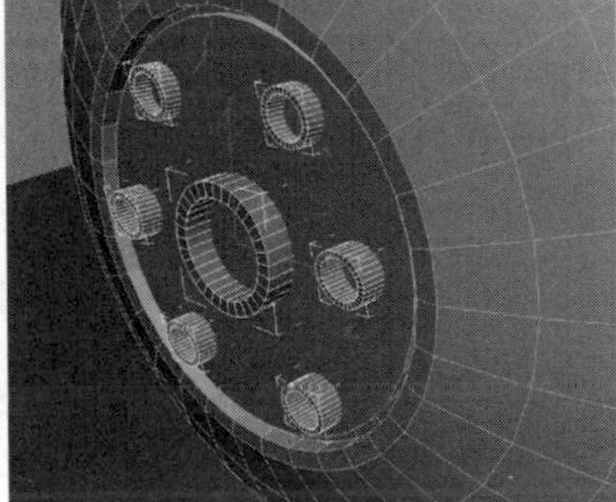

Figure 1-251

7. Unhide the eye assemblies, select the large middle one, click the **Group** menu item, and select **Open** (to allow you to edit the individual components).

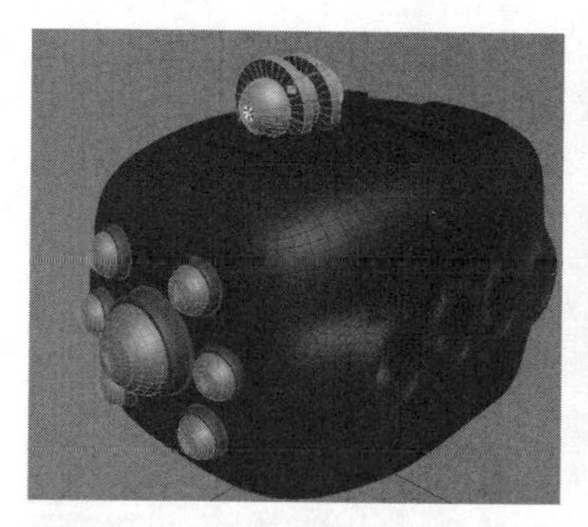

Figure 1-252

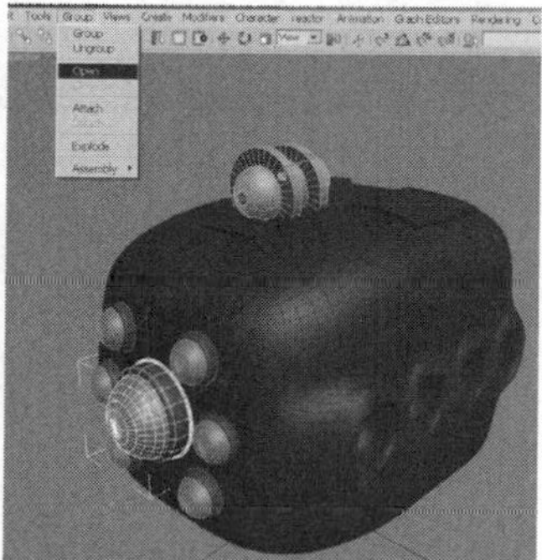

Figure 1-253

8. Under the Create panel, select **Extended Primitives**, click the **Hose** button, and draw out a hose in the Perspective viewport (don't worry about the dimensions — they're irrelevant in this case).

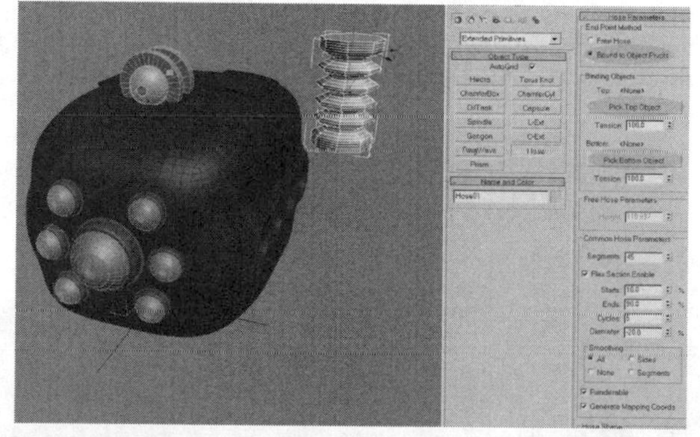

Figure 1-254

FYI: Take a breath. I know there are a lot of controls for Hose, but like the million or so gauges on a 767, most of them you'll never use. The "master" control, so to speak, is the End Point Method. What you select will determine which of the other controls you'll use. You can either make a free hose (meaning you can move it wherever you like), or you can make a hose that is bound to objects. Think of a bound hose as being the type of hose that's under the hood of your car. Both ends are attached to something. When you select the bound type, you'll pick two objects that the hose will connect (i.e., bind to) with (i.e., binding objects): the top object and the bottom object. Top and bottom are a bit misleading, since the objects can actually be side by side or front to back. Once you select the objects the hose will be bound to, you'll then adjust the tension on each end, which will determine the overall shape of your hose. Is it tightly wrapped like a rubber band, or is it loose and flexible like a garden hose? The greater the tension, the closer the hose will be pulled toward the binding object. Now ... that wasn't so bad, was it?

9. Select **Bound to Object Pivots** as the End Point Method. Under Binding Objects, click the **Pick Top Object** button, hit the **H** key to open the selection list, pick **socket** from the list, and then click **OK.**

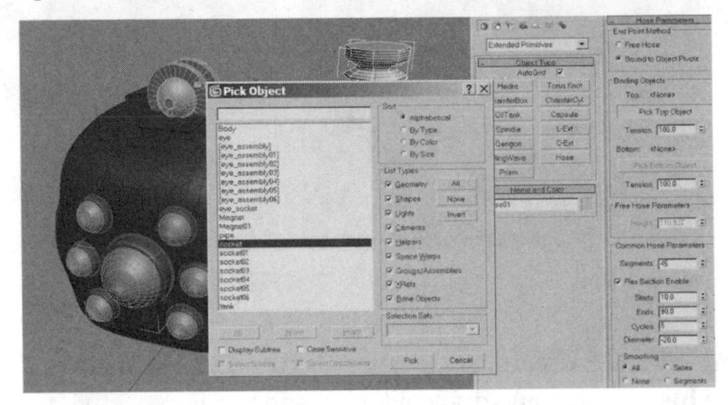

Figure 1-255

Fire Drill: Nothing happened! What gives? Nothing will happen until you select the bottom binding object. At that point, the hose will jump to the connections, and then the fun really begins.

10. Click the **Pick Bottom Object** button, hit the **H** key to open the selection list, pick **eye_socket** from the list, and then click **OK.**

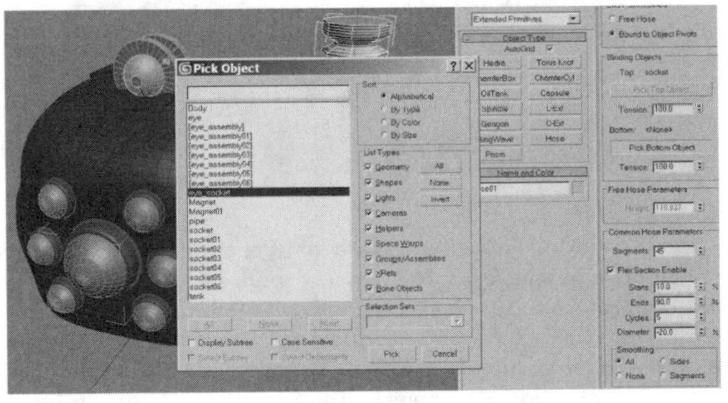

Figure 1-256

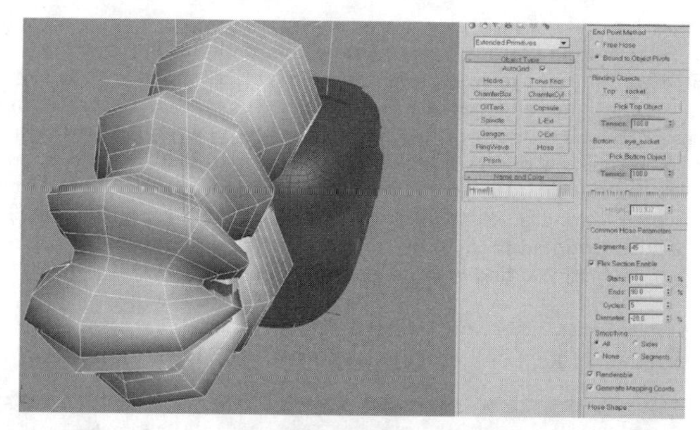

Figure 1-257

Fire Drill Oh ... that looks much better. Thanks for nothing! The reason the hose looks like a mess is because 1) its diameter is too big for the model and it needs to be resized, and 2) we haven't adjusted the tension yet. No worries, mate.

11. Set the Top Tension to **48** and the Bottom Tension to **2.0**; this disparity will make the hose flexible enough to curve around the front of the bot. Next, under Common Hose Parameters, set the Segments to **34**, check the **Flex Section Enable** box, set the Starts to **30**, set the Ends to **66**, set Cycles to **24**, and set the Diameter to **94**. Finally, under Hose Shape choose **Round Hose** with a Diameter of **0.93** and **16** Sides.

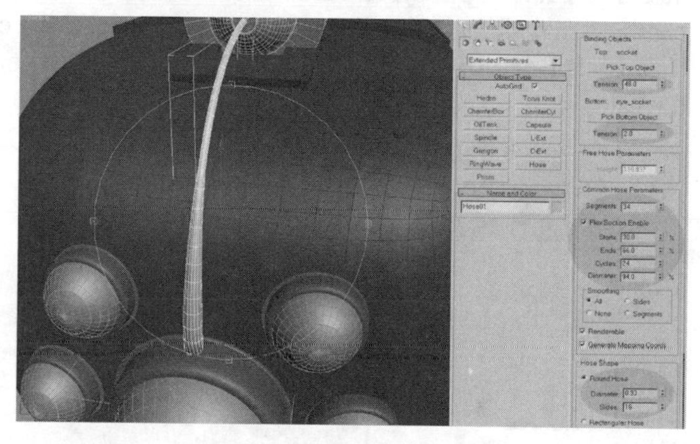

Figure 1-258

FYI: Even though there is a Hose Shape setting, the Common Hose Parameters settings are what determine the hose's "shape." It's really hard to explain the effect of any given control, as the interactions of the controls determines the overall shape. Changing any given control can give you a radically different looking hose. The best way to learn is to fiddle with the controls. The values I used were the result of trying different values until I found a set I liked. I wanted my hoses to represent wires, and as such I wanted them to be smoothish. Play around with the different controls until you find a shape that you like. Go ahead. I'll wait.

12. Hit the **H** key, select **eye_assembly02**, and open the group.

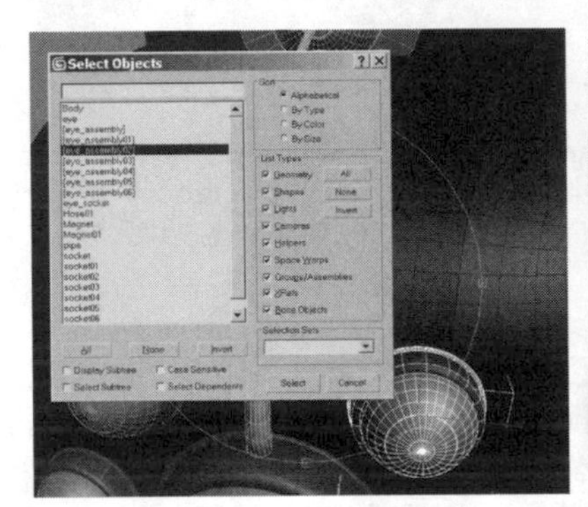

Figure 1-259

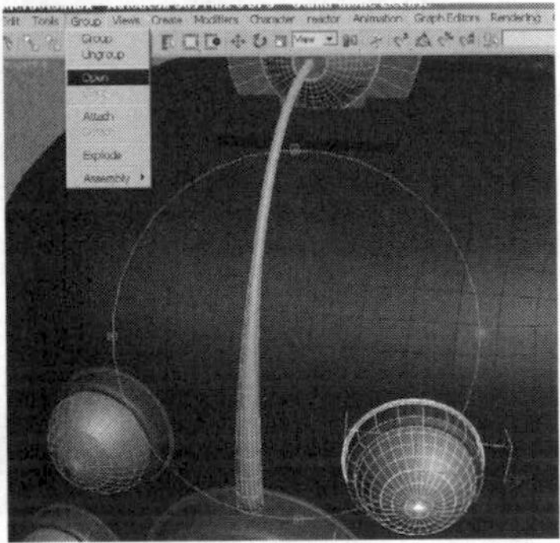

Figure 1-260

13. Create a hose, set the End Point Method to **Bound to Object Pivots**, click **Pick Top Object**, hit **H**, select **socket04** (your actual numbers may differ depending on how you arranged the clones), click **Pick Bottom Object**, hit **H**, and select **eye_socket02** from the list.

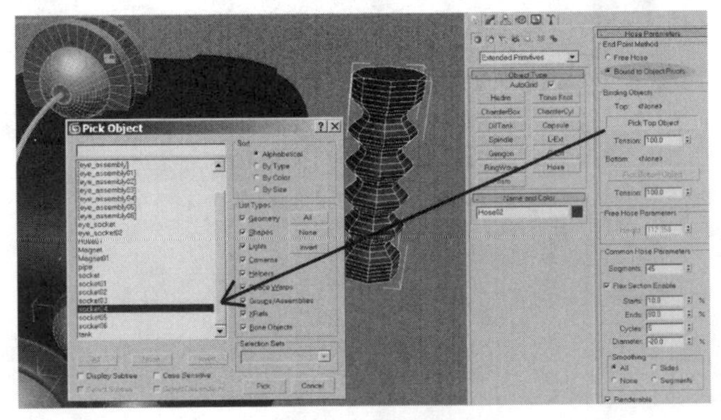

Figure 1-261

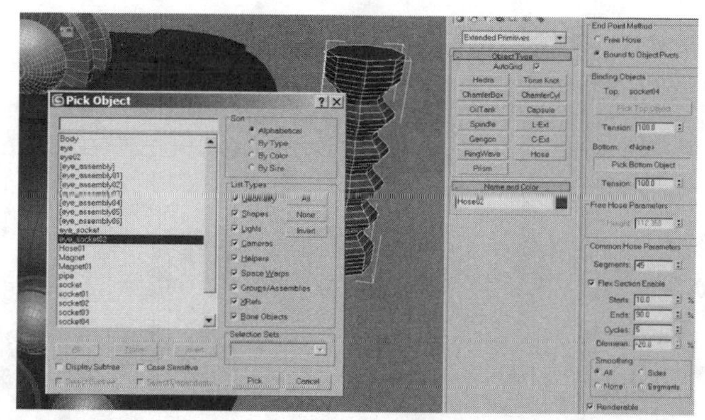

Figure 1-262

14. Set the Tensions, Common Hose Parameters, and Hose Shape settings the way you did in step 11. You might consider using different shapes for each eye. I chose to make narrower hoses for the smaller eyes, but feel free to go crazy.

15. Wire the eye at the three o'clock position the same way you wired the last two eyes.

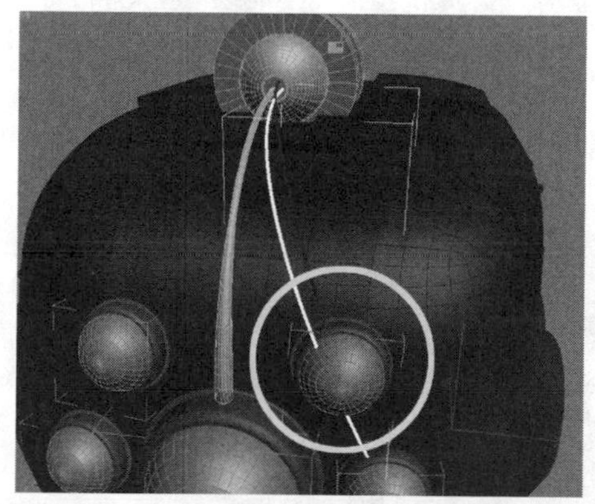

Figure 1-263

Fire Drill: Whoops! What just happened? Why is my three o'clock eye going through my one o'clock eye? If you look closely at the End Point Method setting, you'll see that it actually says Bind to Object Pivots. The hose is not really bound to the object at all, but rather to its pivot points. Since an object's pivots start out centered to the object, the hose will attach there. Unfortunately for us, the arrangement of our eyes ensures that the hoses for the lower eyes will cross through the centers of the eyes above them. Fortunately, since the eyes will not be moving, moving their pivots won't affect anything other than the curvature of the hose.

16. Select the **eye_socket**, click the **Hierarchy** tab, click **Affect Pivot Only**, and use the **Move** tool to reposition the pivot until the hose no longer penetrates the eye above it. (I found moving the pivot to the left side of the eye socket fixed the problem and ended up looking really cool.)

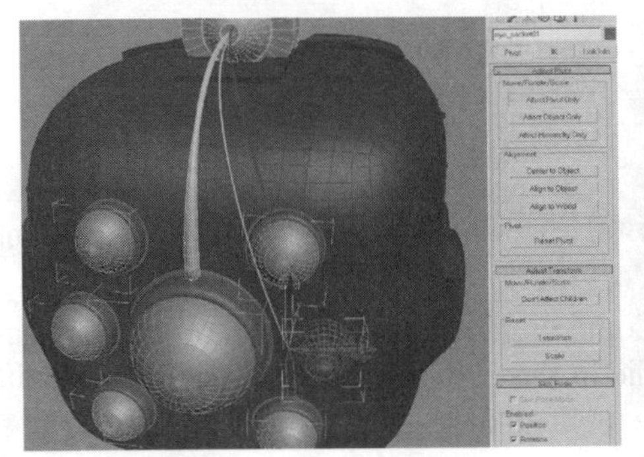

Figure 1-264

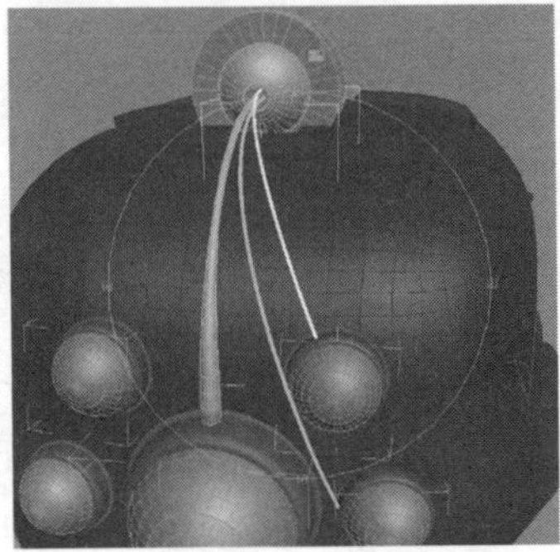

Figure 1-265

Fire Drill: When you move the pivot point of one or both binding objects, you'll probably need to reset your hose's tension settings.

17. Wire the remaining eyes the same way, and then hit **F9** to do a test render.

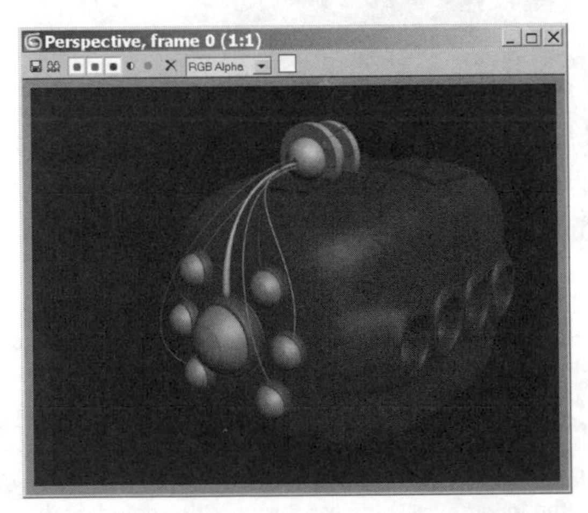

Figure 1-266

Day 5: Refining the Middle Leg and Adding the Hydraulic Pump

1. Unhide the leg.

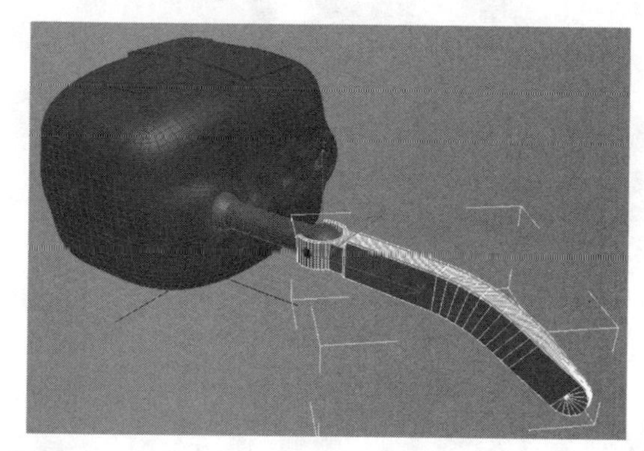
Figure 1-267

2. Select the vertices making up the tip of the leg and scale them to **80%** of their size.

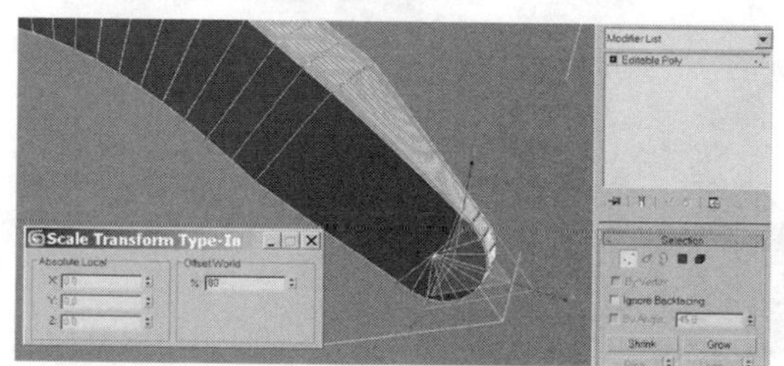

Figure 1-268

3. Select the next row of vertices.

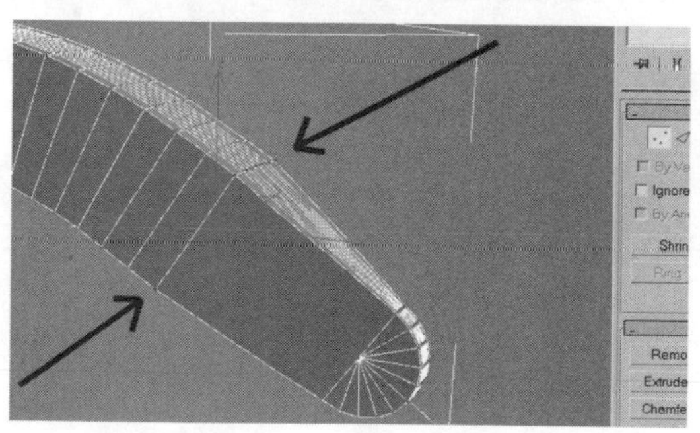

Figure 1-269

4. Right-click the **Scale** tool, select **Non-uniform Scale**, and enter **90** into Offset World Y axis.

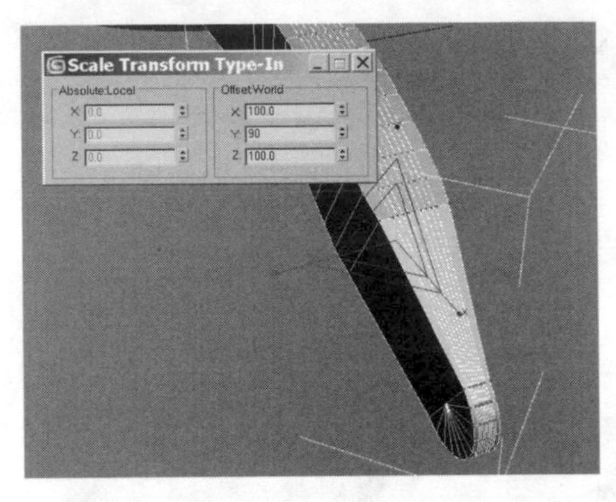

Figure 1-270

5. Select the next row up and Non-uniform Scale them to **95** in the Y axis.

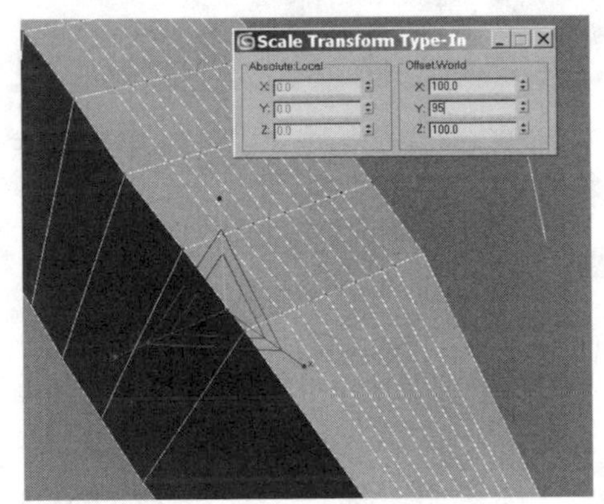

Figure 1-271

6. Select the outer edges of the leg.

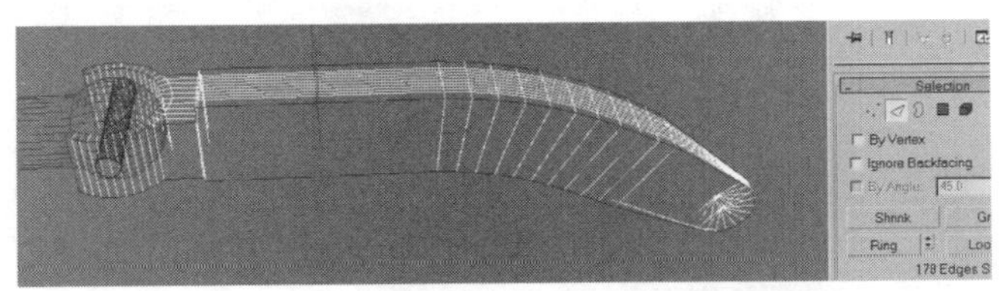

Figure 1-272

7. Chamfer the edges by **0.2** to create a more refined edge.

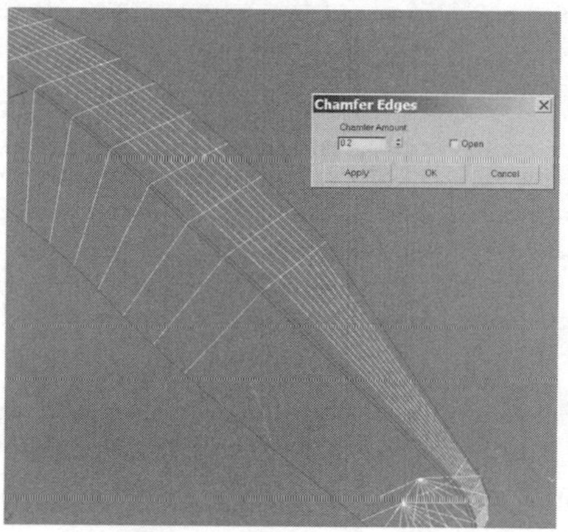

Figure 1-273

8. Select the four polygons shown in Figure 1-274 and Extrude them by **6.**

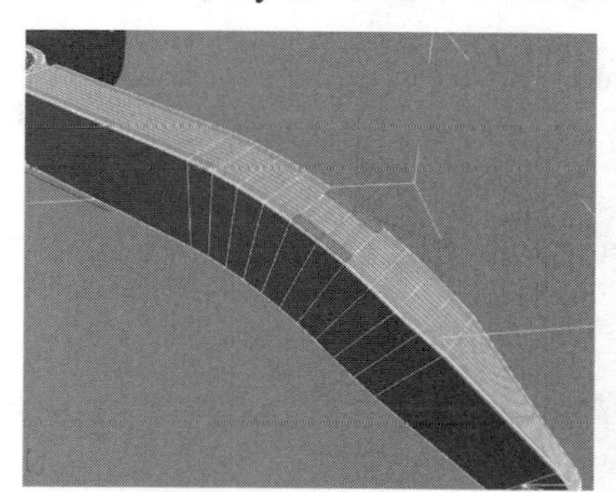

Figure 1-274

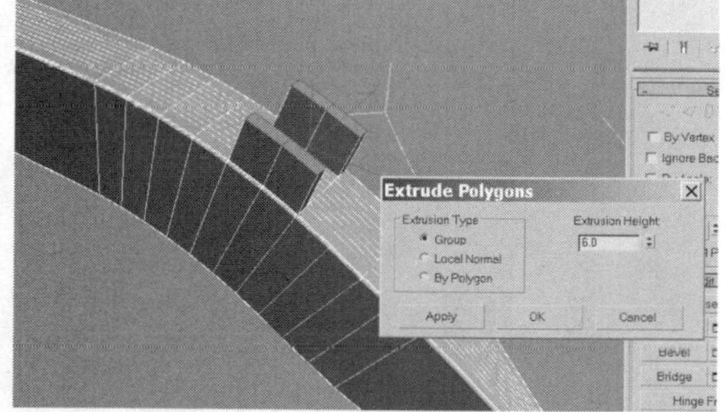

Figure 1-275

9. Select and delete the two polygons shown and Extrude them by **6.**

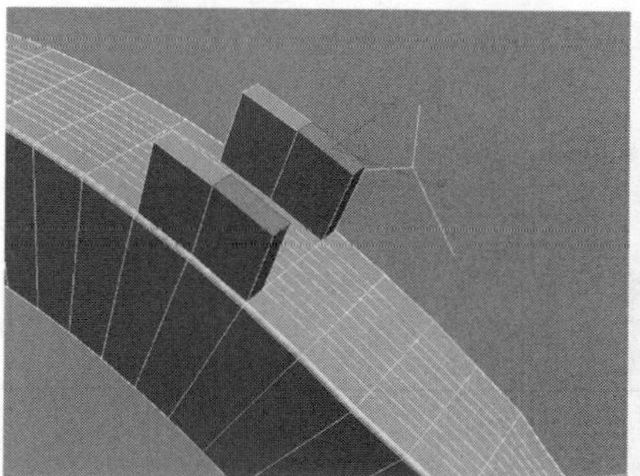

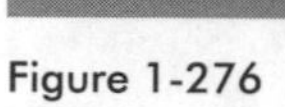

Figure 1-276

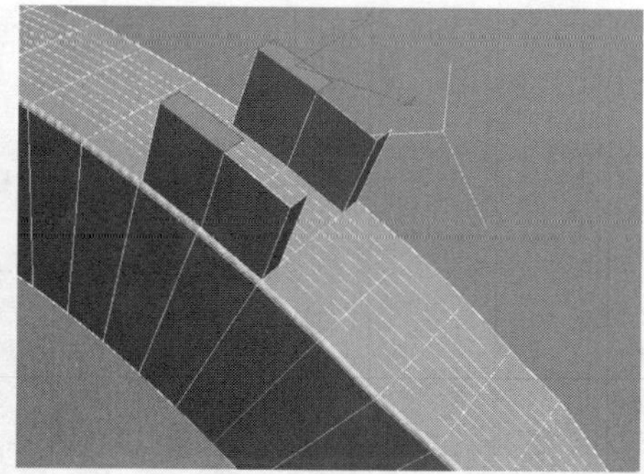

Figure 1-277

10. Select one of the remaining upper polygons, click **Hinge From Edge**, set the Angle to **183.5**, set the Segments to **10**, click **Pick Hinge**, click the poly's bottom edge, and then delete the backward-facing polygon. Repeat on the other side and then weld the vertices.

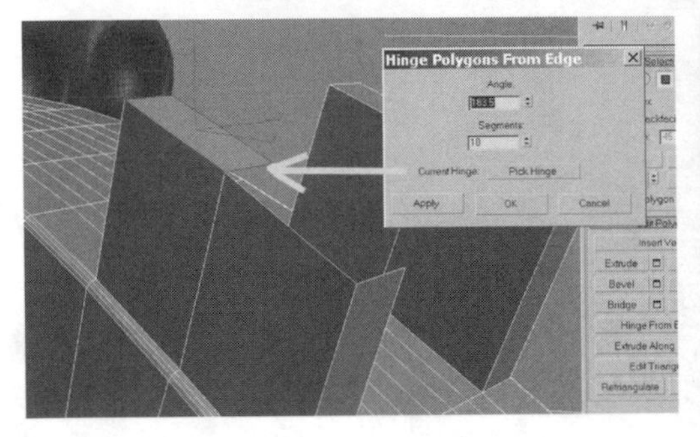

Figure 1-278

Figure 1-279

11. Using AutoGrid, create a Tube around the middle of the upper leg.

Radius 1	Radius 2	Height	Height/Cap Segs	Sides	Smooth
6.2	6.8	16	5/1	32	Checked

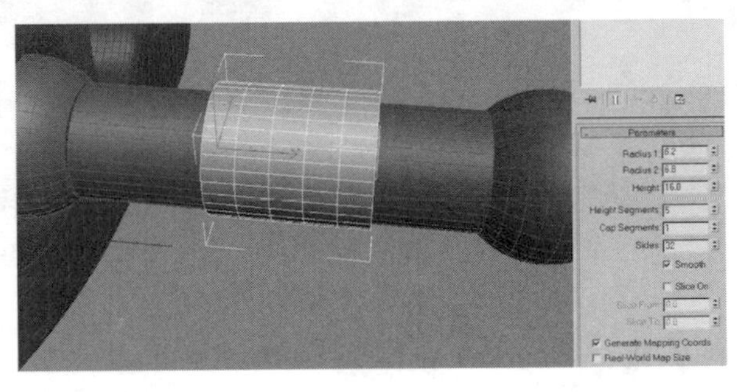

Figure 1-280

12. Convert the tube to an Editable Polygon, select the top 24 polygons, and Extrude them by **15**.

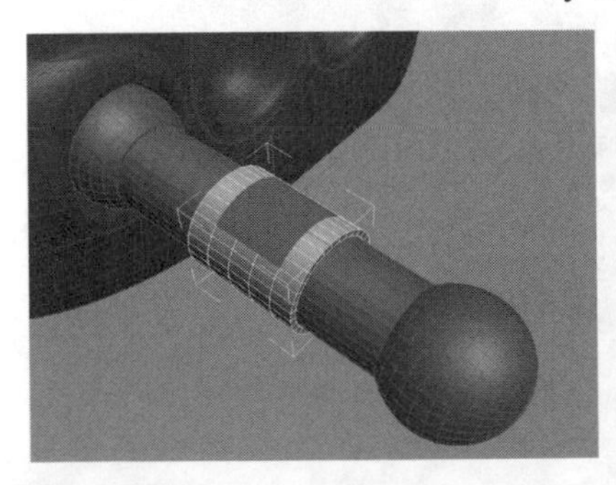

Figure 1-281

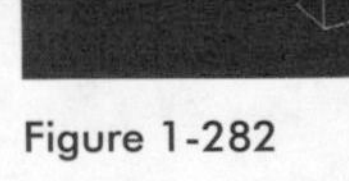

Figure 1-282

13. Non-uniform Scale the top polygons down to **0** in the Z axis, and then Extrude them by **5** three times.

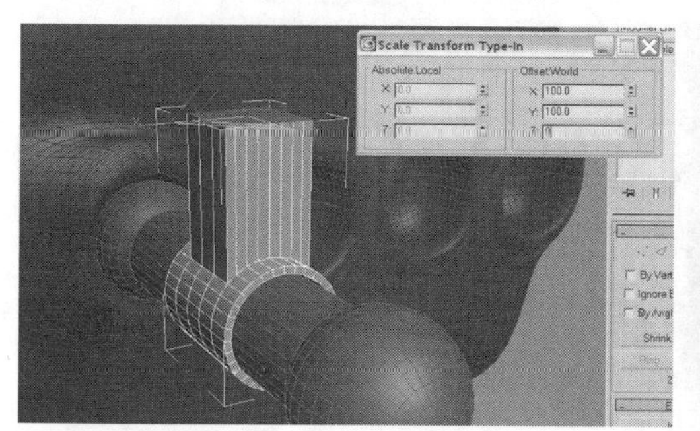

Figure 1-283

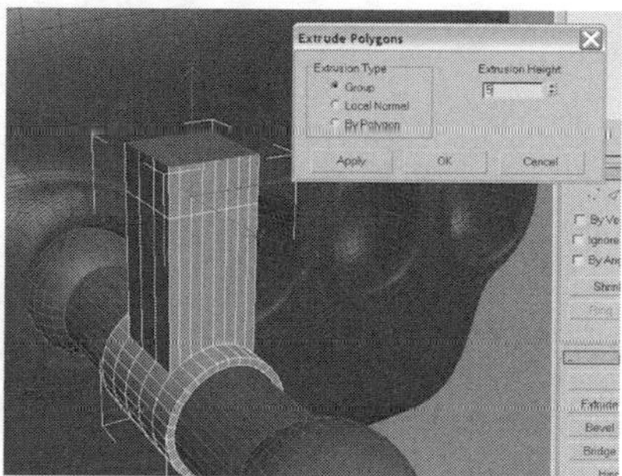

Figure 1-284

14. Select the four polygons shown and Extrude them by **5**.

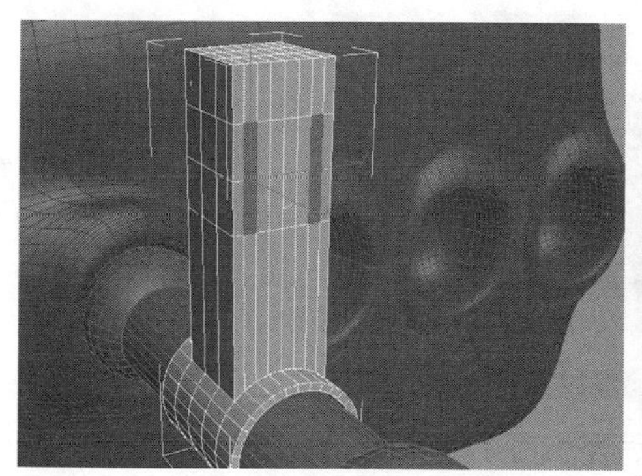

Figure 1-285

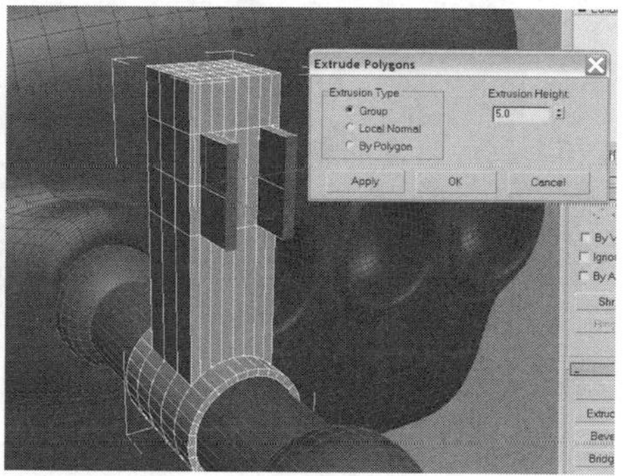

Figure 1-286

15. Select the bottom two polygons and delete them. Select the top polygon, Hinge From Edge **180** degrees with **10** segments, and delete the backward-facing polygon. Repeat for the other side.

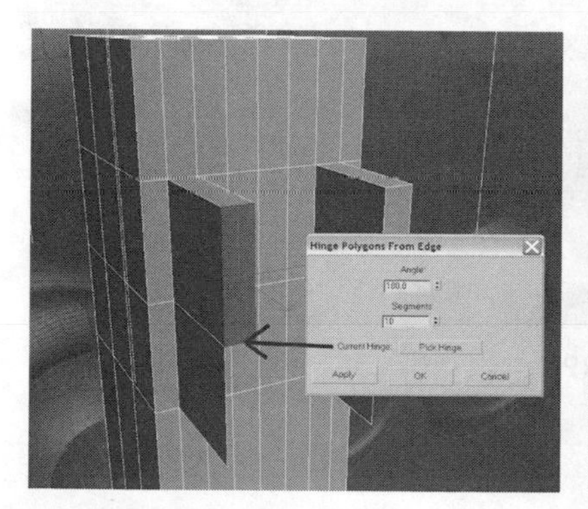

Figure 1-287

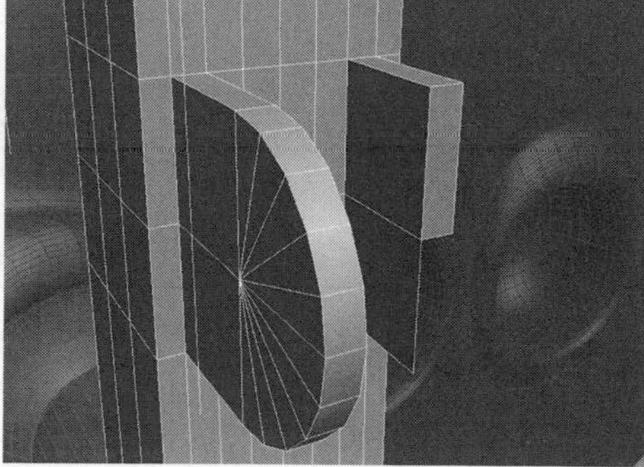

Figure 1-288

16. Select the vertices and Weld them. Then select the 27 top edges shown in Figure 1-290.

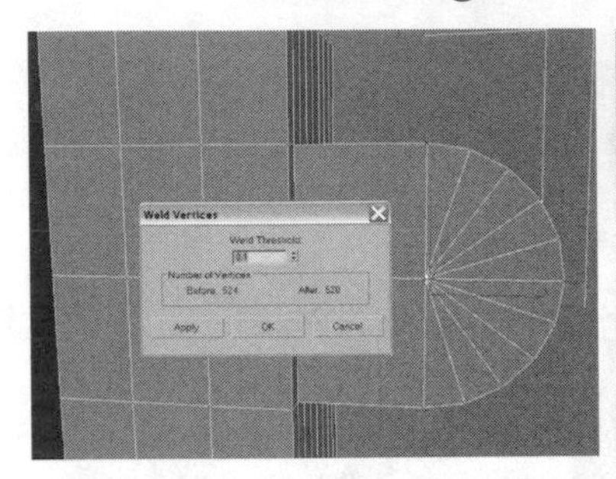

Figure 1-289

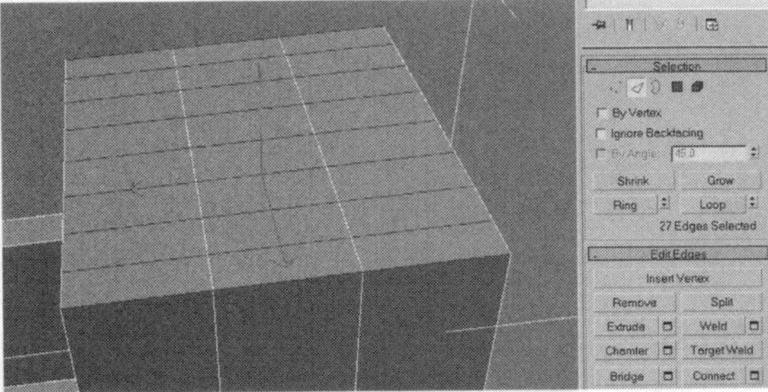

Figure 1-290

17. Click **Connect**, switch to the Top view, and select the middle 16 polygons on the top.

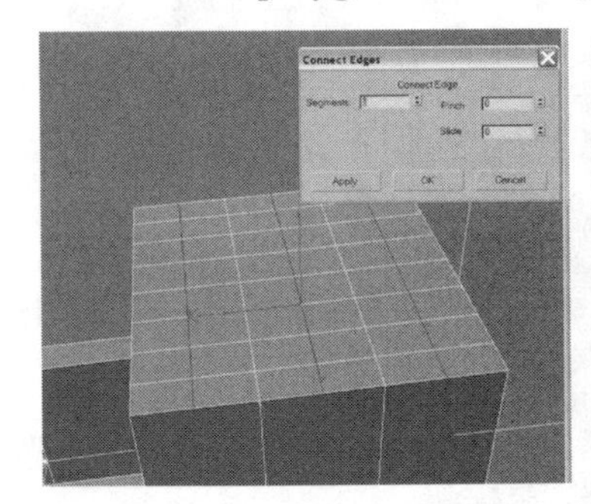

Figure 1-291

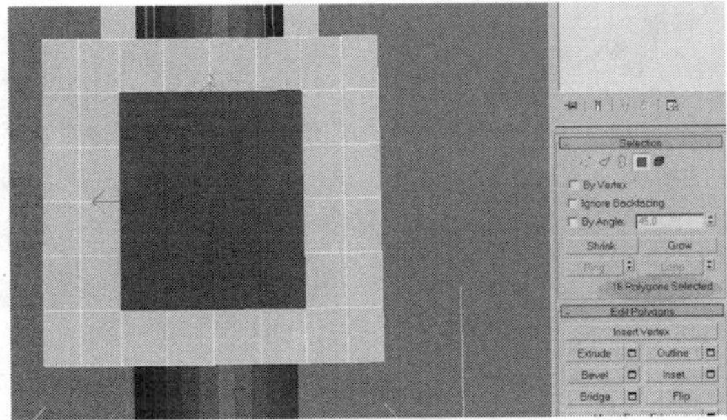

Figure 1-292

18. Scale the polygons until they form a square, delete them, and border-select the hole.

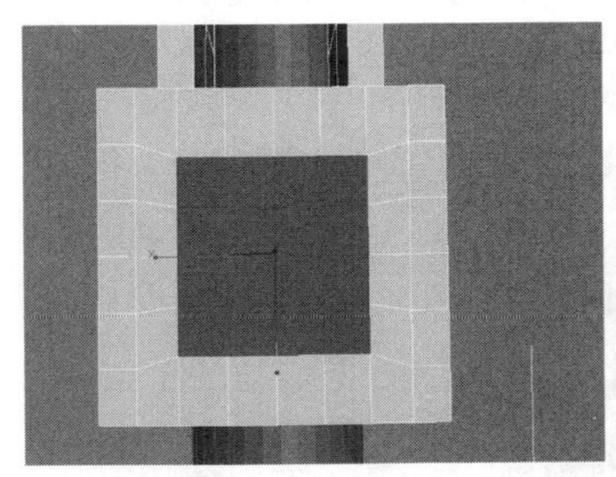

Figure 1-293

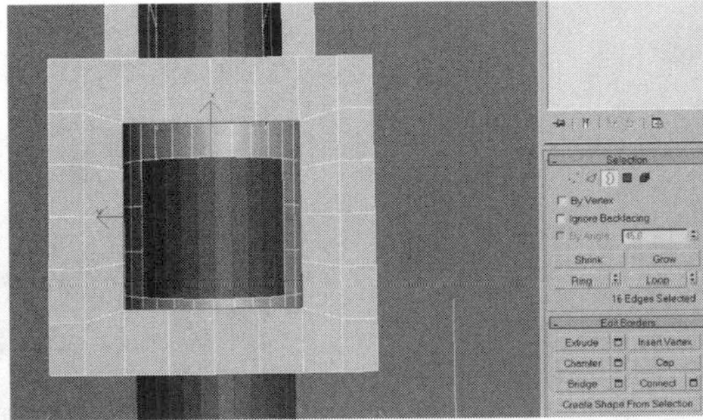

Figure 1-294

19. Press **Cap** to fill the hole with a single polygon, select the polygon, click the **Tessellate** button to tessellate the polygon, switch to Vertex selection mode, and select the middle vertex.

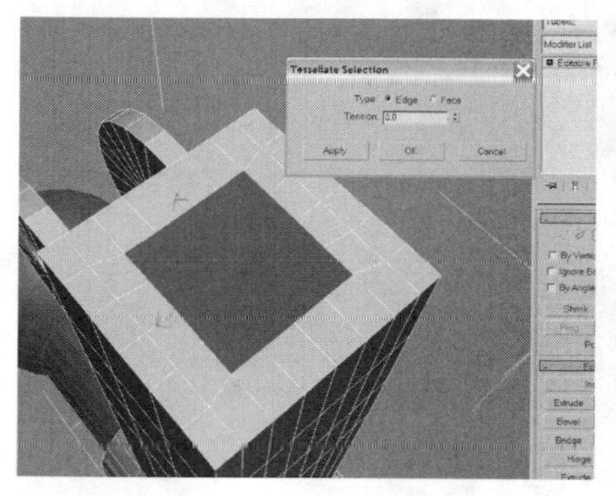

Figure 1-295

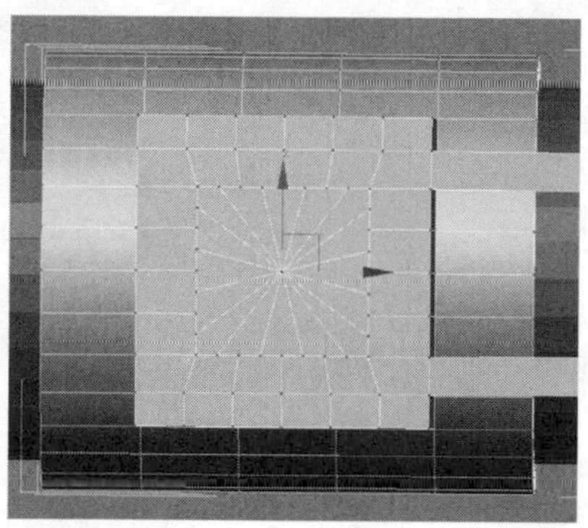

Figure 1-296

20. Chamfer the vertex by **2.25** to create a circular polygon from the square. Select the circular polygon.

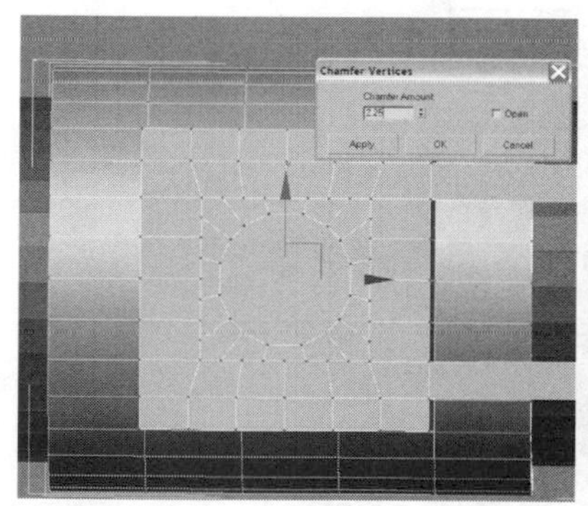

Figure 1-297

Figure 1-298

21. Click **Bevel Settings:**

Type	Height	Outline	Apply/OK
Group	0.2	–0.15	Apply
Group	0.2	–0.15	Apply
Group	10	0	Apply
Group	1	0	Apply

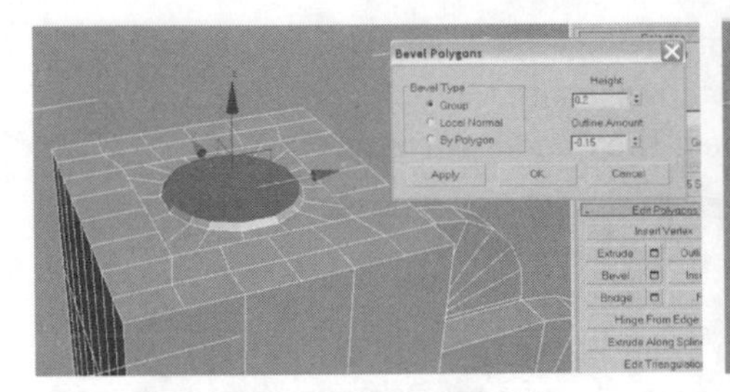

Figure 1-299

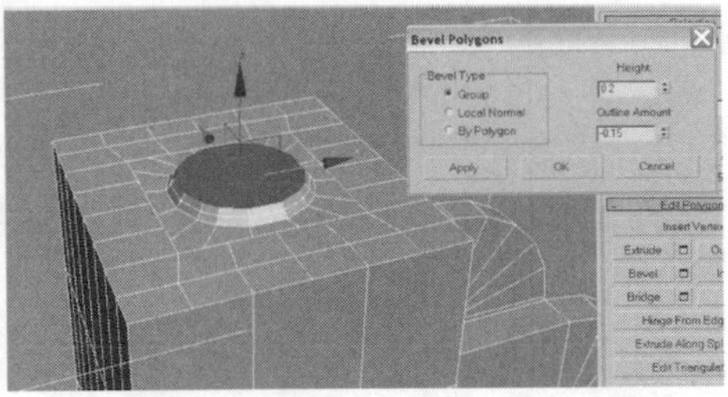

Figure 1-300

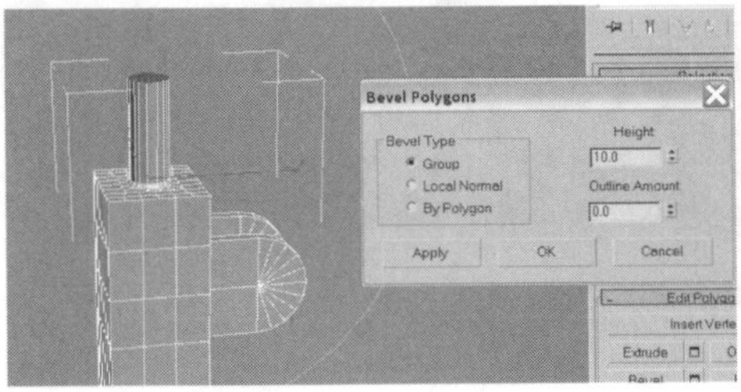

Figure 1-301

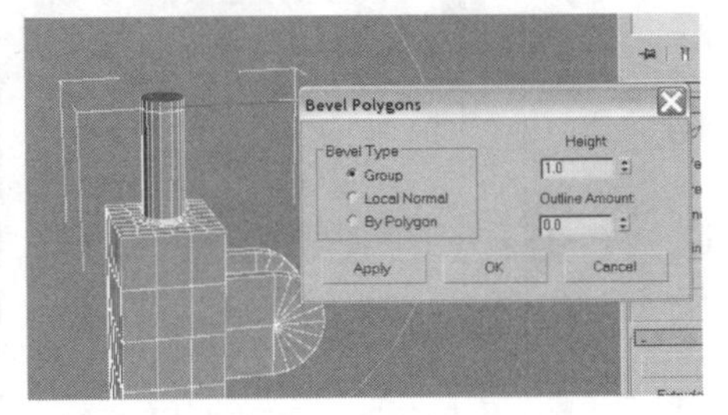

Figure 1-302

Type	Height	Outline	Apply/OK
Group	0	3	Apply
Group	0.5	0	Apply

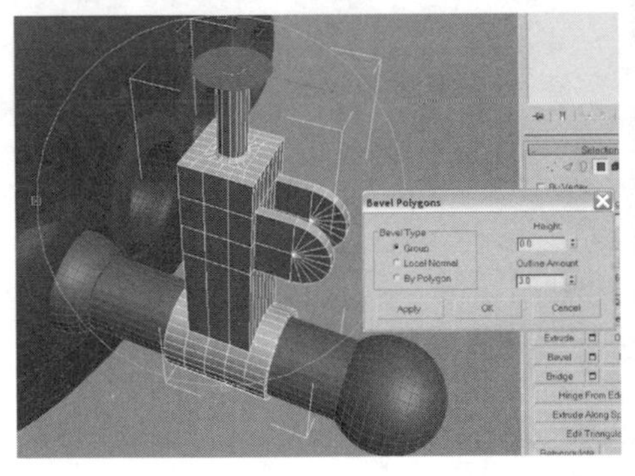

Figure 1-303

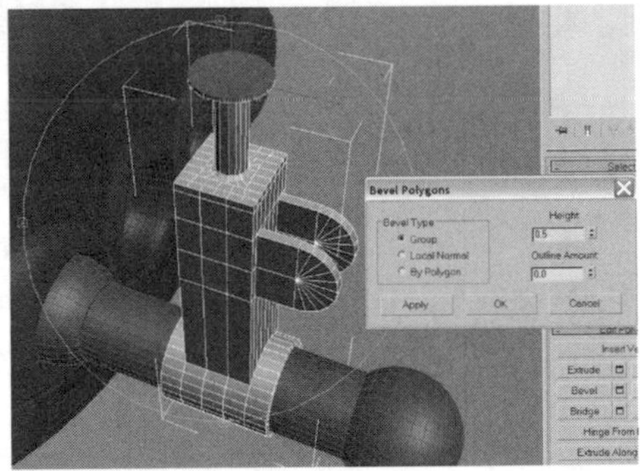

Figure 1-304

Type	Height	Outline	Apply/OK
Group	2.5	0	Apply
Group	0.5	0	Apply

Day 5: Refining the Middle Leg and Adding the Hydraulic Pump

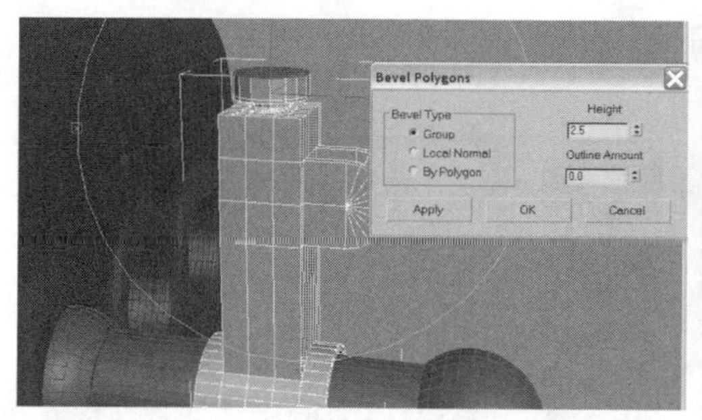

Figure 1-305

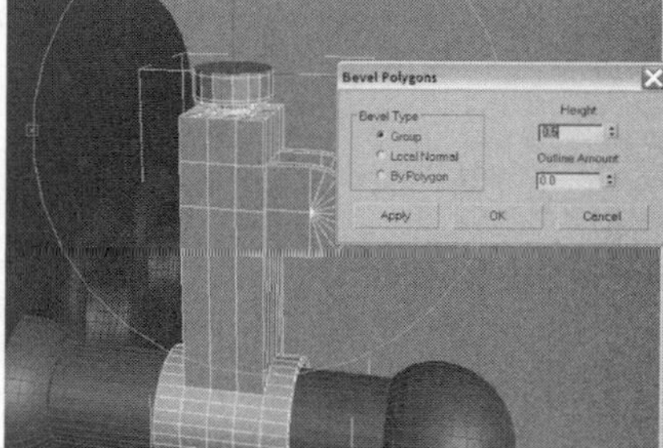

Figure 1-306

Type	Height	Outline	Apply/OK
Group	0	–1	Apply
Group	–1.75	0	Apply

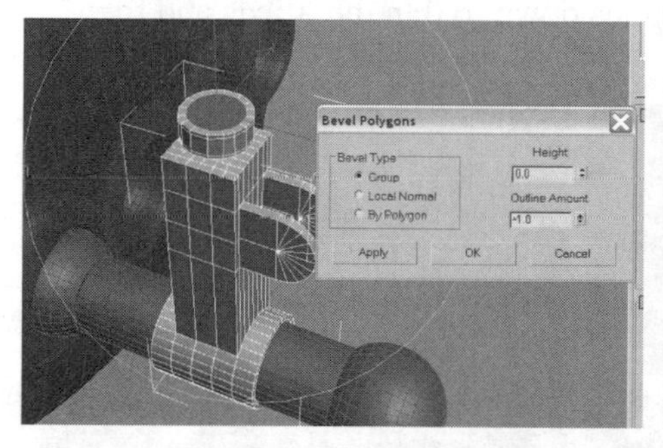

Figure 1-307

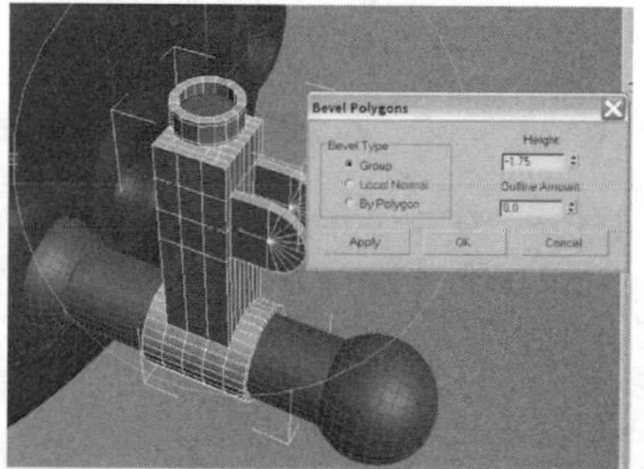

Figure 1-308

Type	Height	Outline	Apply/OK
Group	0	–0.4	OK

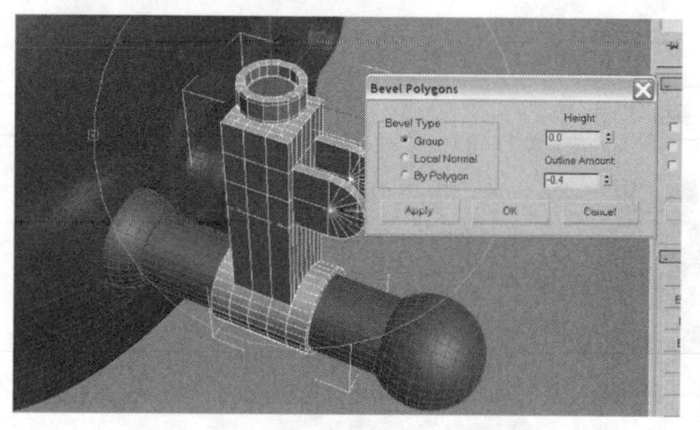

Figure 1-309

22. Select the five middle polygons facing back toward the body and Extrude them **5**.

Figure 1-310

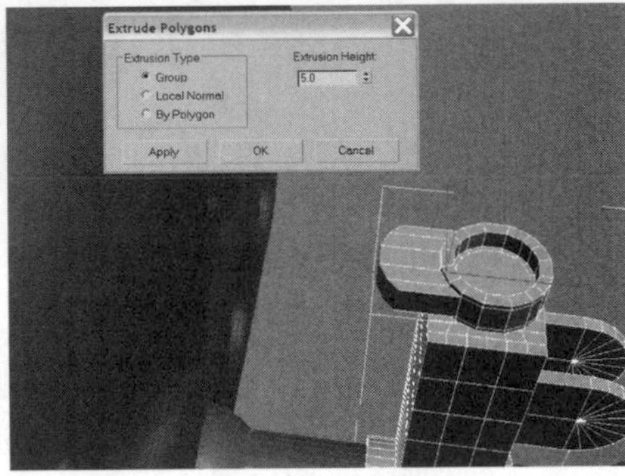

Figure 1-311

23. Non-uniform Scale the polygons down to **0** in the X axis and then delete them.

Figure 1-312

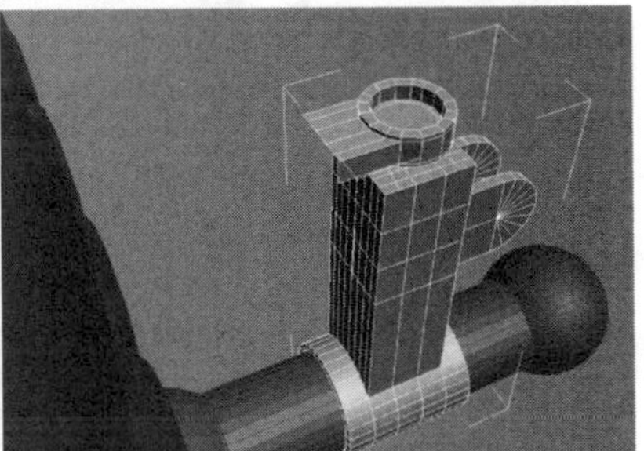

Figure 1-313

24. Create a Cylinder to the left of the extrusion:

Radius	Height	Height/Cap Segs	Sides	Smooth
4.5	–4.053	2/1	16	Checked

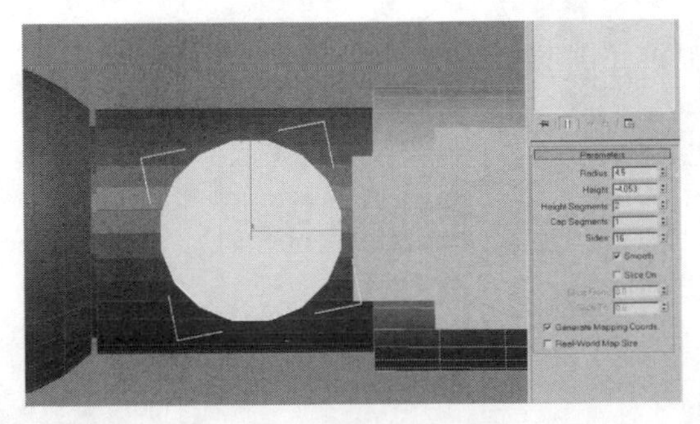

Figure 1-314

25. Select the middle edge and Chamfer it by **1.3**.

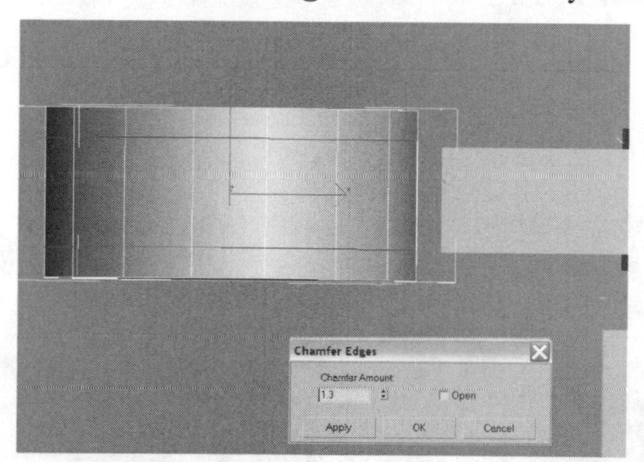

Figure 1-315

26. Select the middle five polygons that face the hydraulic system and Extrude them by **3.2**.

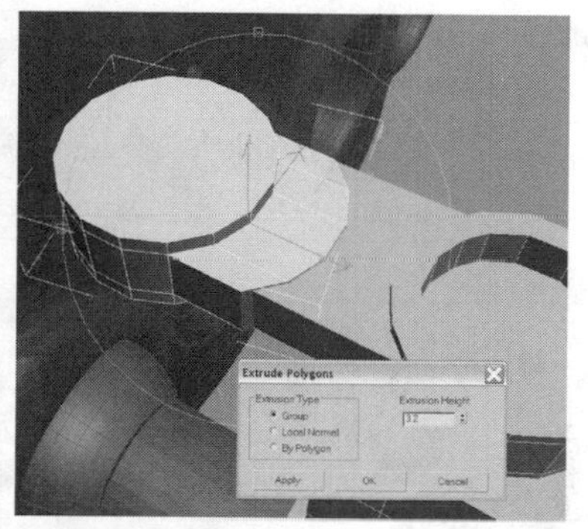

Figure 1-316

Figure 1-317

27. Use the Non-uniform Scale tool to flatten the polygons by scaling them down to **0** in the X axis.

28. Select the hydraulic system, click **Attach List**, and select **Cylinder01** to attach it. Then Weld the vertices together along the seam.

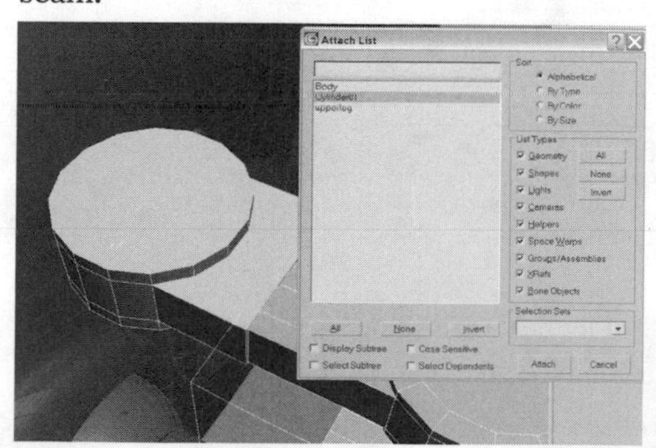

Figure 1-318

29. Select the top polygon shown in Figure 1-319 and then click **Bevel Settings:**

Type	Height	Outline	Apply/OK
Group	0	–0.8	Apply

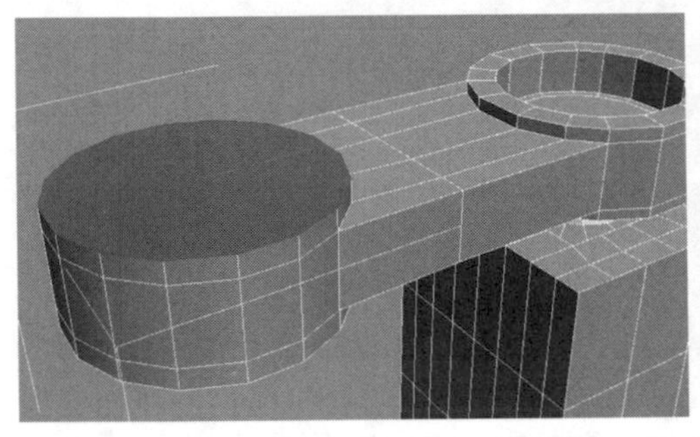

Figure 1-319

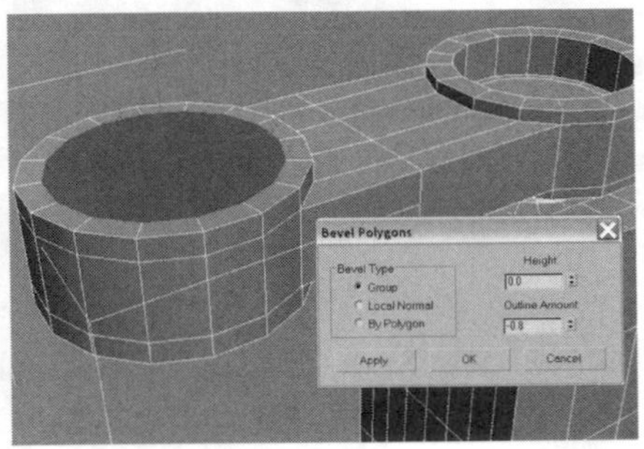

Figure 1-320

Type	Height	Outline	Apply/OK
Group	–0.5	0	Apply
Group	0.0	–0.8	Apply

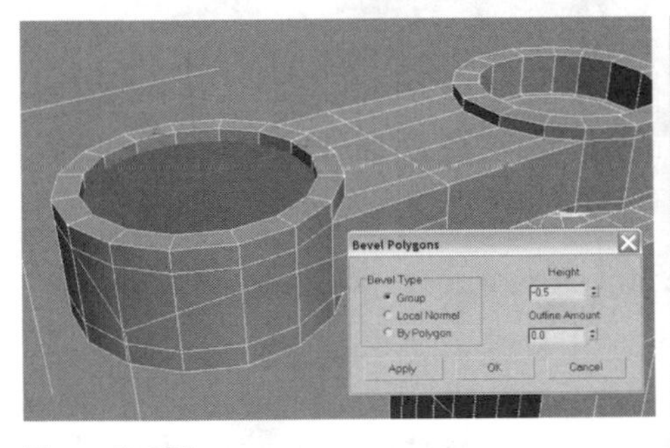

Figure 1-321

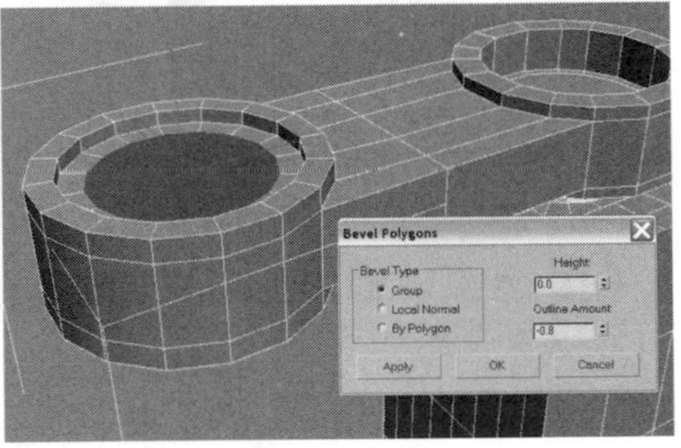

Figure 1-322

Type	Height	Outline	Apply/OK
Group	0.3	0	Apply
Group	0.0	–0.4	Apply

Day 5: Refining the Middle Leg and Adding the Hydraulic Pump

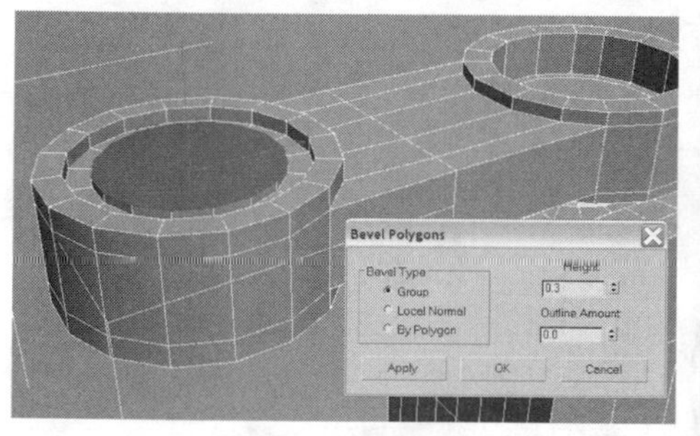

Figure 1-323

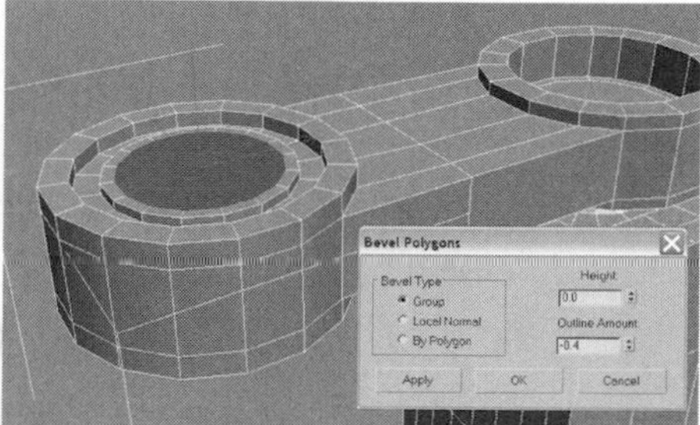

Figure 1-324

Type	Height	Outline	Apply/OK
Group	–0.4	0	OK

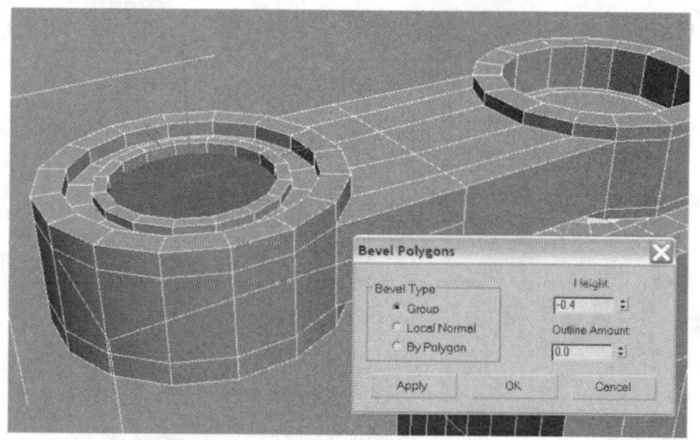

Figure 1-325

30. Using AutoGrid, create a Cylinder in the indentation you just made.

Radius	Height	Height/Cap Segs	Sides	Smooth
1.8	1	1/1	16	Checked

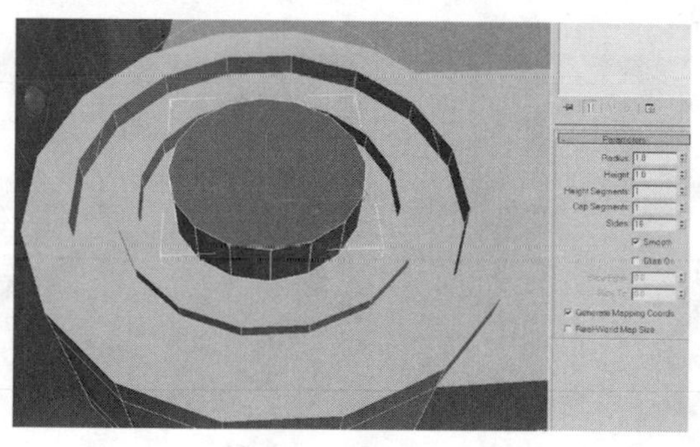

Figure 1-326

31. Convert the cylinder to an Editable Polygon, delete the back-facing polygon, and use the Cut tool to make the cuts shown.

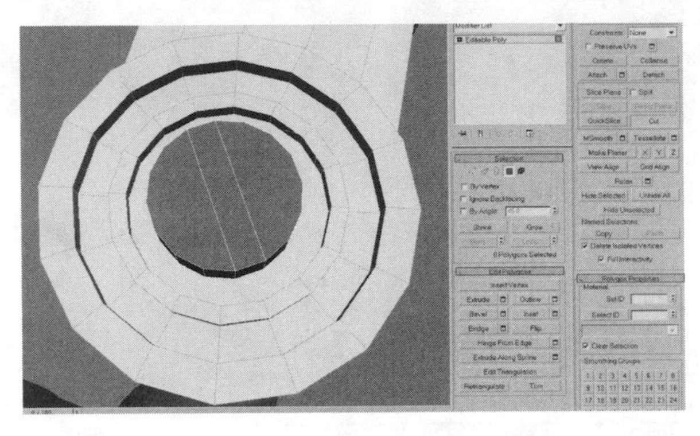

Figure 1-327

32. Select the two outer polygons and Extrude them **0.4** to create a screw.

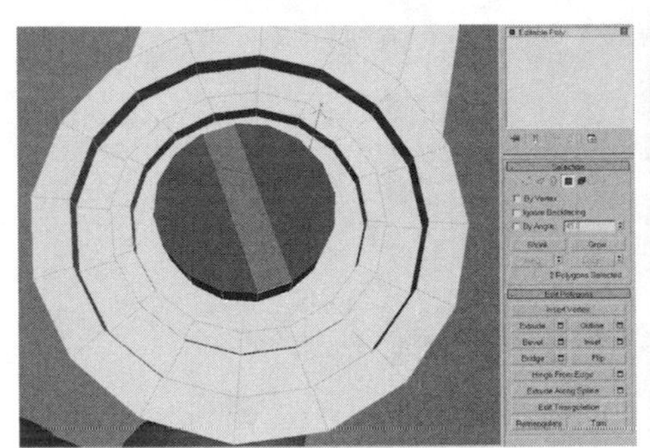

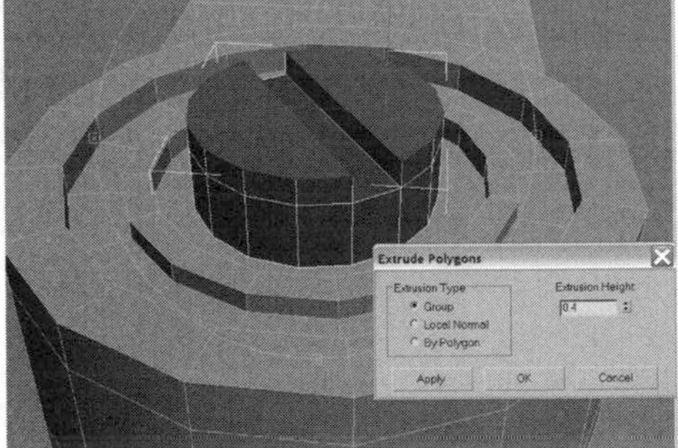

Figure 1-328

Figure 1-329

33. Select the outer edges of the screw, Chamfer the edges by **0.07**, and click **Apply**.

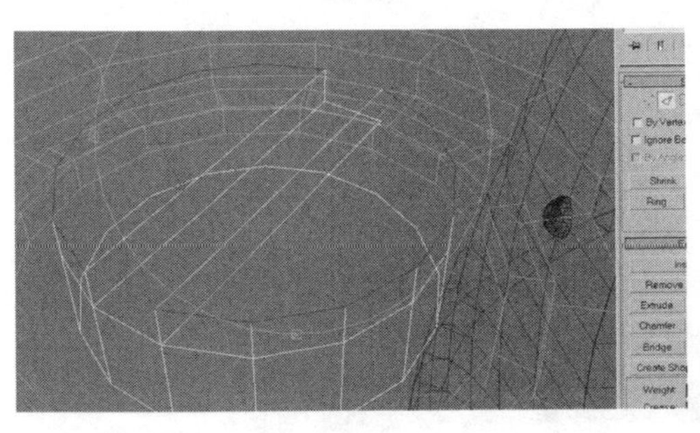

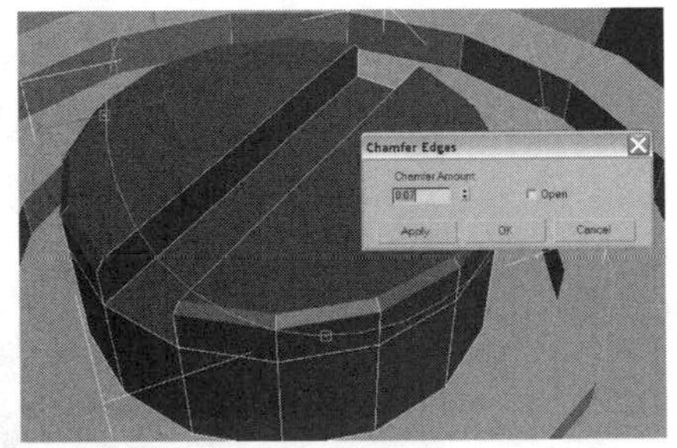

Figure 1-330

Figure 1-331

34. Chamfer the edge by **0.03** and then click **OK**.

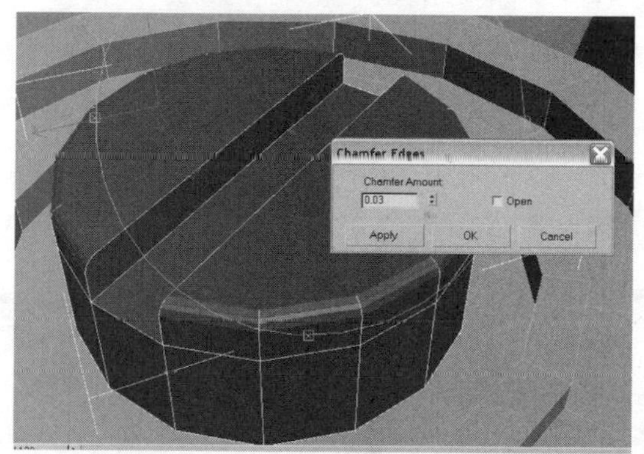

Figure 1-332

35. Add a Smooth modifier to the screw's stack, click **Auto Smooth**, collapse the stack, and Select and Link the screw to the hydraulic pump.

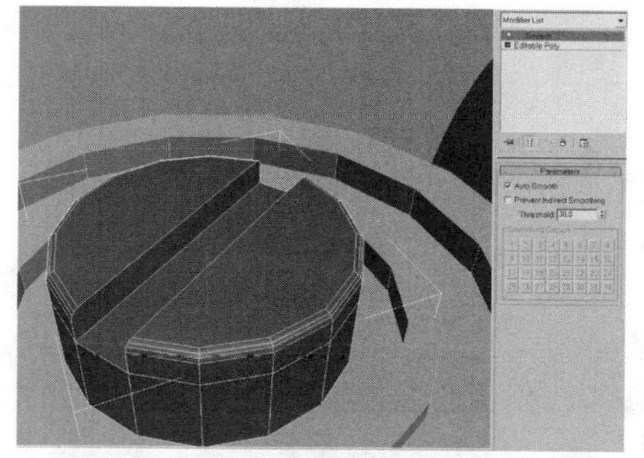

Figure 1-333

36. Select the polygon on the underside of the cylinder.

Figure 1-334

37. Click **Bevel Settings:**

Type	Height	Outline	Apply/OK
Group	0	–0.8	Apply
Group	–0.3	0	Apply

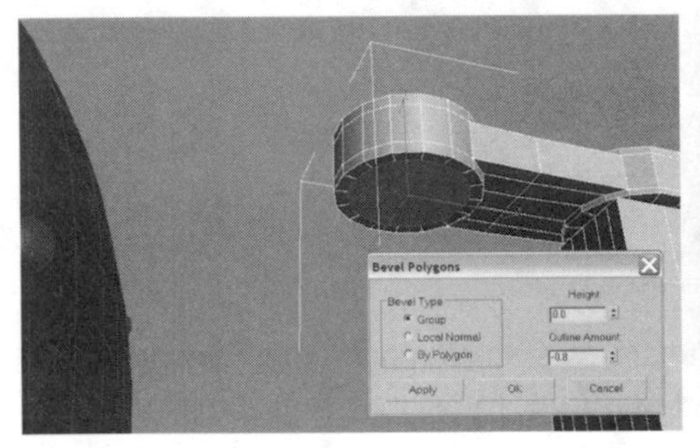

Figure 1-335

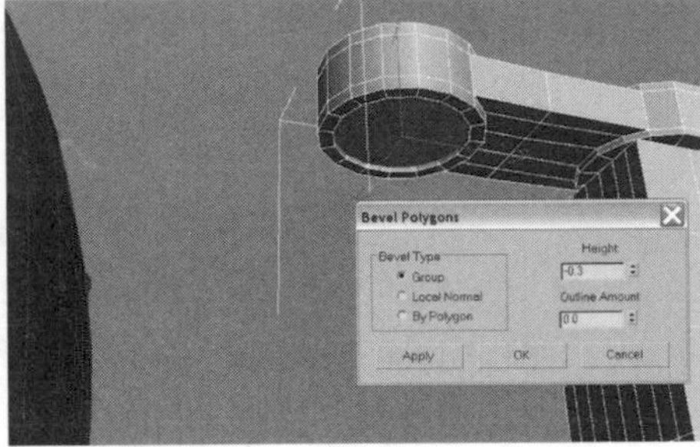

Figure 1-336

Type	Height	Outline	Apply/OK
Group	0	–0.6	Apply
Group	0.8	0	Apply

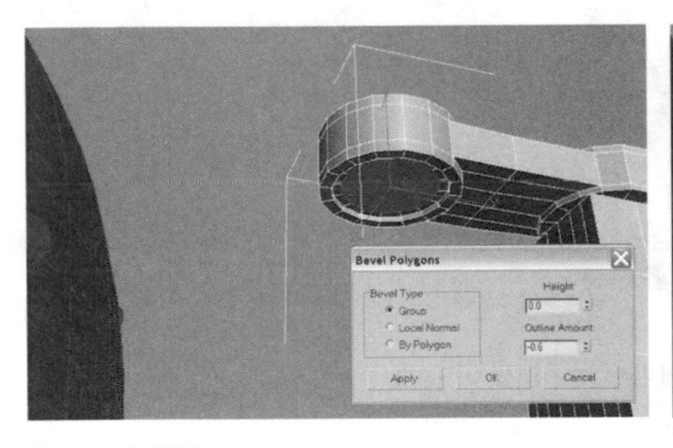

Figure 1-337

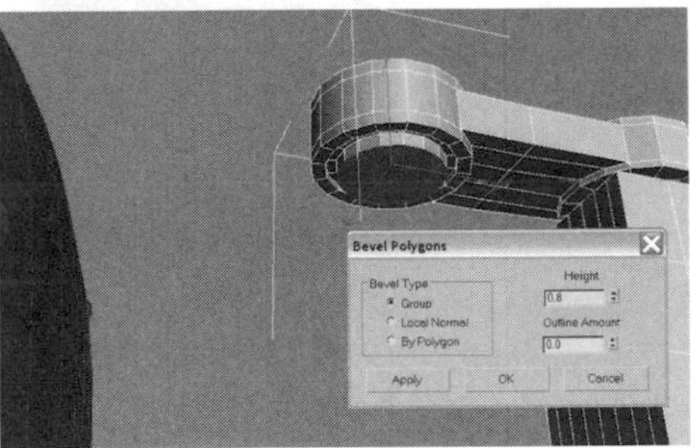

Figure 1-338

Type	Height	Outline	Apply/OK
Group	0	1	Apply
Group	0.4	0	Apply

Day 5: Refining the Middle Leg and Adding the Hydraulic Pump

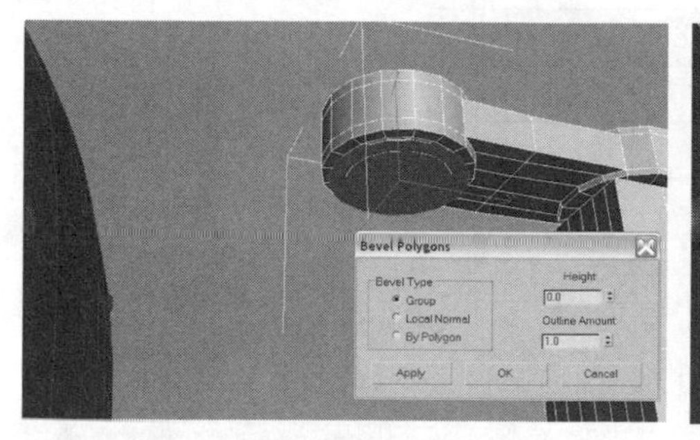

Figure 1-339

Figure 1-340

Type	Height	Outline	Apply/OK
Group	2.25	0	Apply
Group	0.6	0	Apply

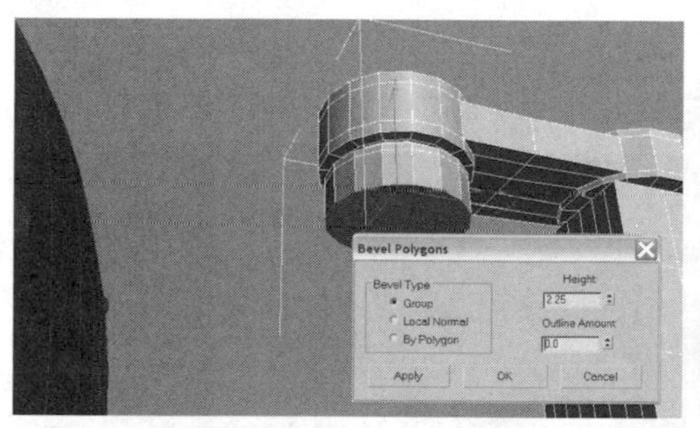

Figure 1-341

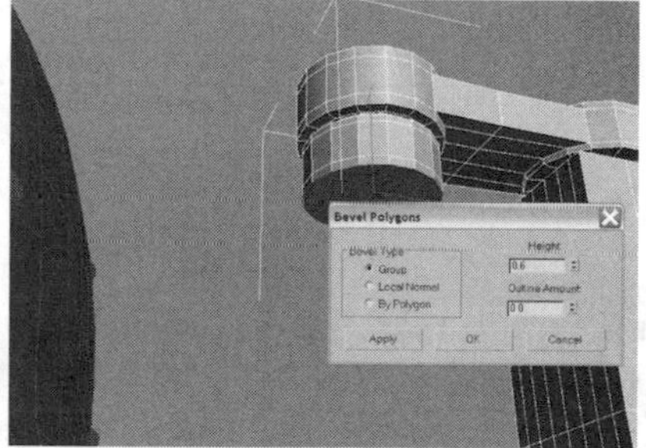

Figure 1-342

Type	Height	Outline	Apply/OK
Group	0	–0.9	Apply
Group	–0.5	0	Apply

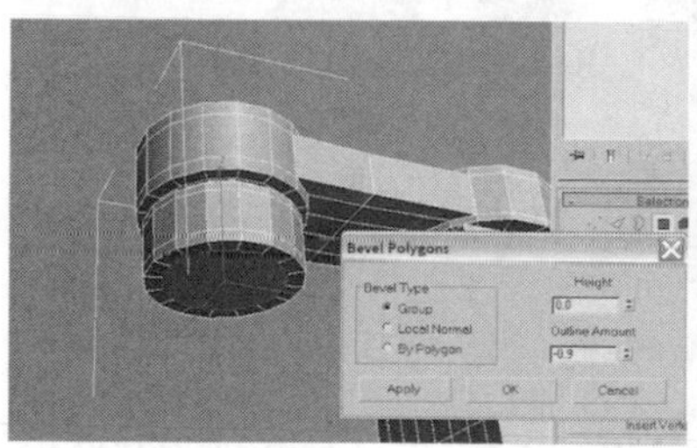

Figure 1-343

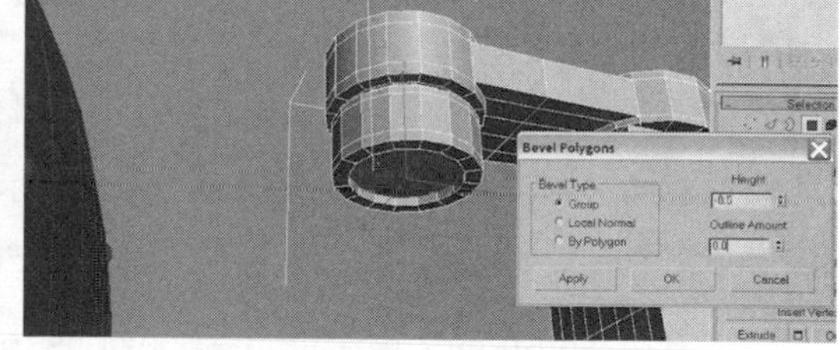

Figure 1-344

Type	Height	Outline	Apply/OK
Group	0	–0.7	Apply
Group	0.06	0	Apply

Figure 1-345

Figure 1-346

Type	Height	Outline	Apply/OK
Group	0.2	–0.6	Apply
Group	0.2	–0.6	Apply

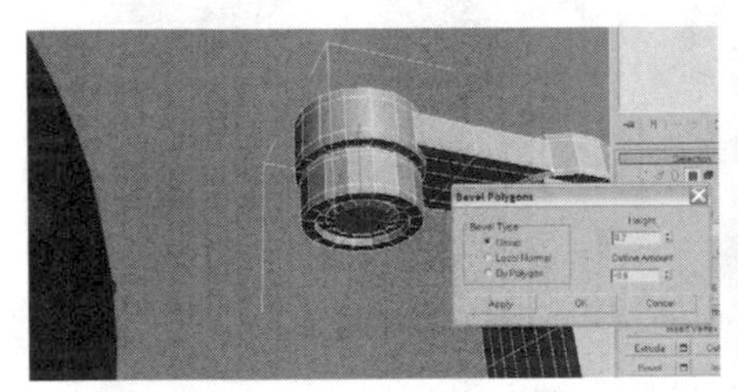

Figure 1-347

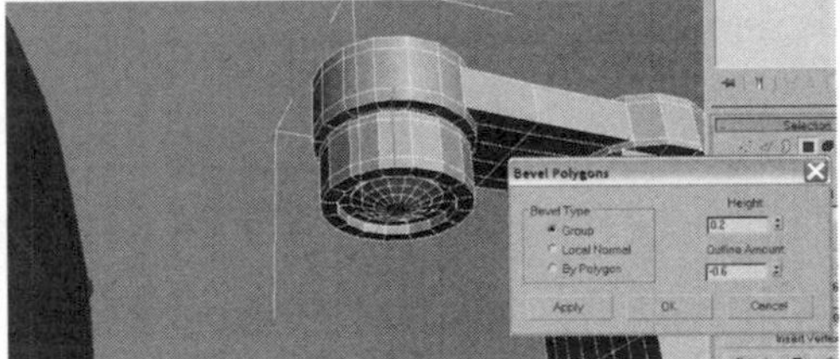

Figure 1-348

38. Select the three polygons shown and Extrude them by **11**.

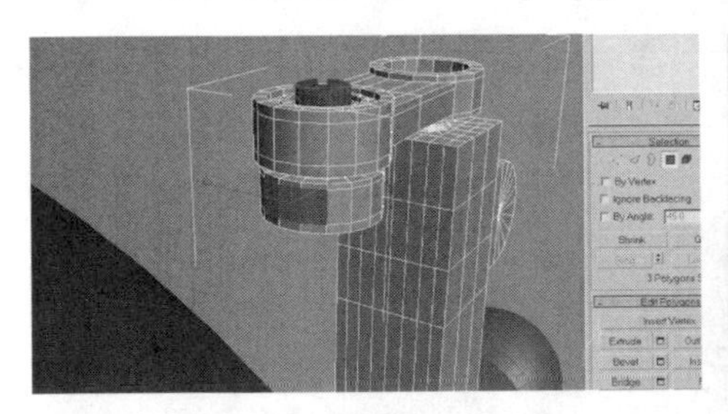

Figure 1-349

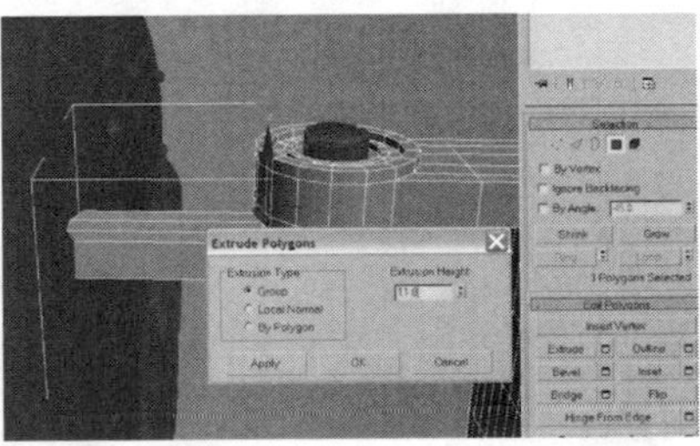

Figure 1-350

39. Non-uniform Scale the polygons to **0** in the X axis, delete the polygons, border-select the resulting hole, and use the Move tool to move the border in the X axis until it is flush with the body.

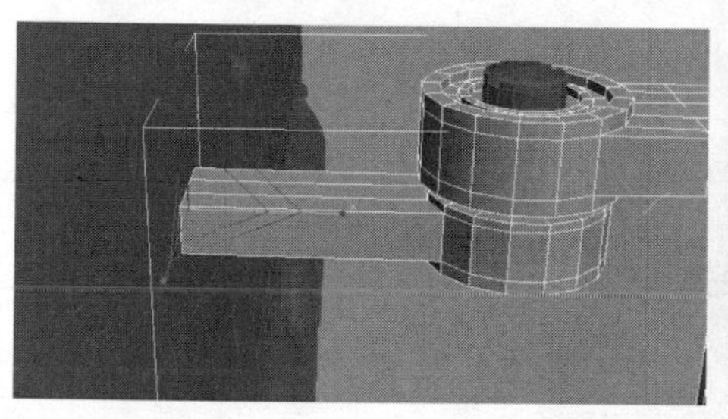

Figure 1-351

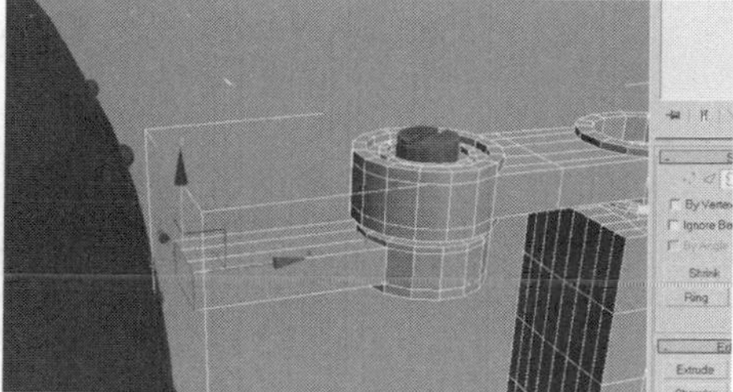

Figure 1-352

40. Use the Rotate tool to adjust the border until it is evenly flush against the surface of the body, click the **Create Shape From Selection** button, and name the resulting shape **leg_seal**:

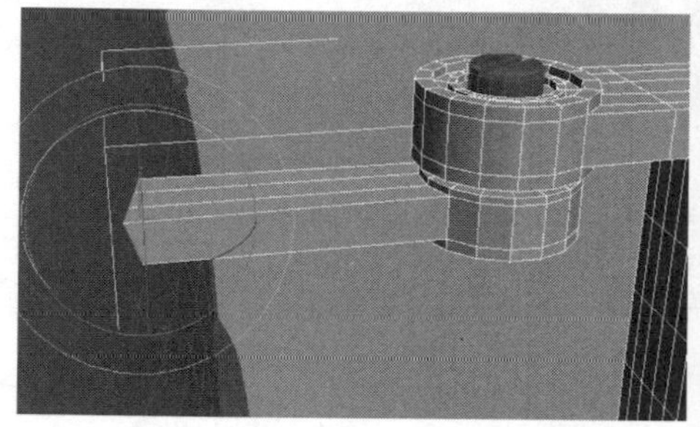

Figure 1-353

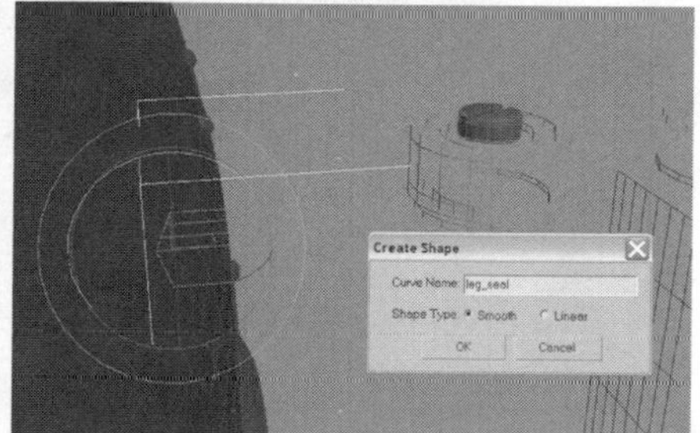

Figure 1-354

41. Hit the **H** key and select **leg_seal** from the list. Under Rendering, click **Enable In Renderer**, **Enable In Viewport**, **Generate Mapping Coords**, and **Radial.** Set Thickness to **2**, Sides to **12**, and Angle to **0.**

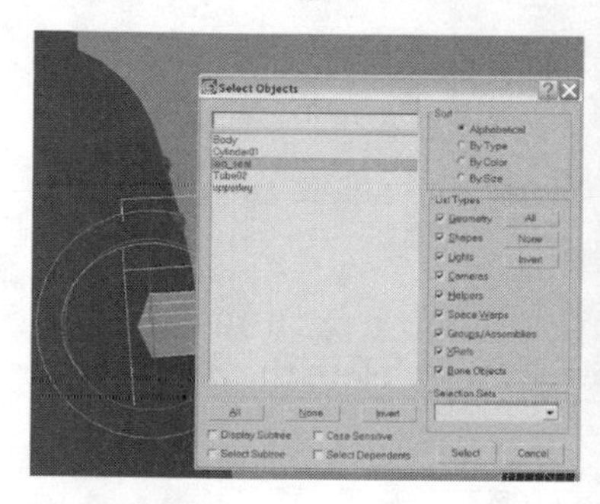

Figure 1-355

Figure 1-356

42. Select and Link the seal to the body and hit **F9** to do a test render of the hydraulic system.

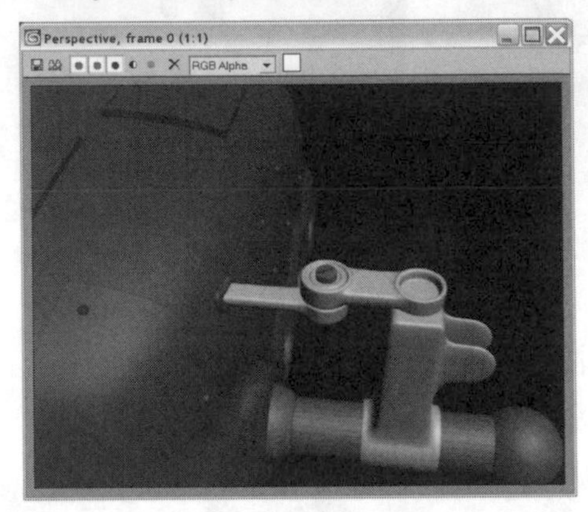

Figure 1-357

43. Use AutoGrid to create a Gengon on top of the hydraulic system.

Sides	Radius	Fillet	Height	Side/Height/Fillet Segs	Smooth
6	2.2	0.1	3.2	1/1/3	Unchecked

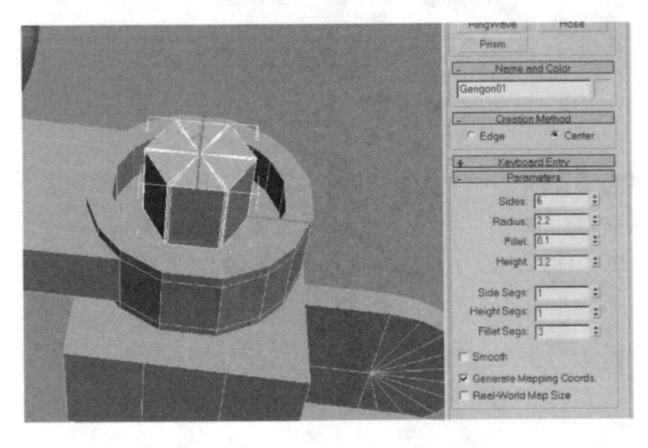

Figure 1-358

44. Convert the gengon to an Editable Polygon and delete the downward-facing polygon.

45. Using AutoGrid, create a Cylinder on top of the gengon you just created. Convert it to an Editable Polygon and delete the downward-facing polygon.

Radius	Height	Height/Cap Segs	Sides	Smooth
1.3	1.3	1/1	8	Checked

Figure 1-359

46. Hit the **H** key, select the gengon and the cylinder from the list, and then use Select and Link to link them to the hydraulic system.

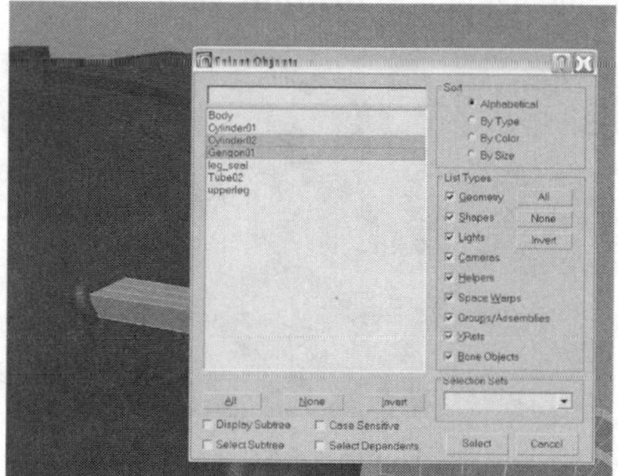

Figure 1-360

47. With the gengon and cylinder still selected, hold down the **Shift** key and use the Move tool to create four clones on top of the body.

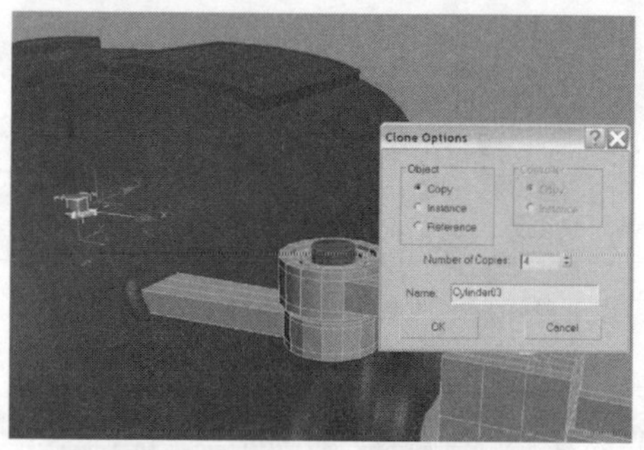

Figure 1-361

48. Arrange the four clones on top of the body as shown, with the surface just beneath the body's surface, then use Select and Link to attach them to the body.

Figure 1-362

49. Border-select the bottom border of the gengon, click **Create Shape From Selection**, and name it **hydraulic_seal**.

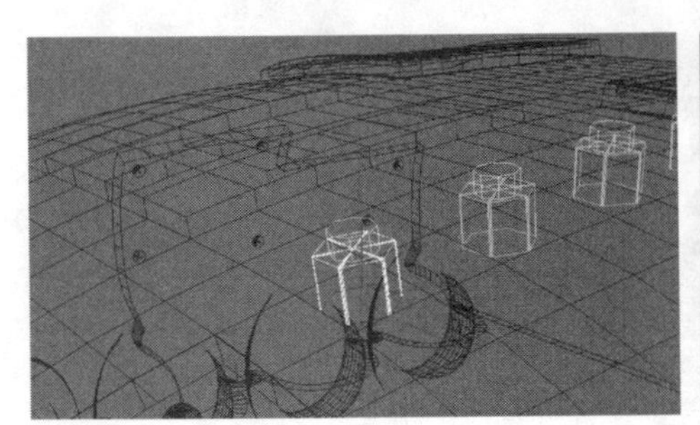

Figure 1-363

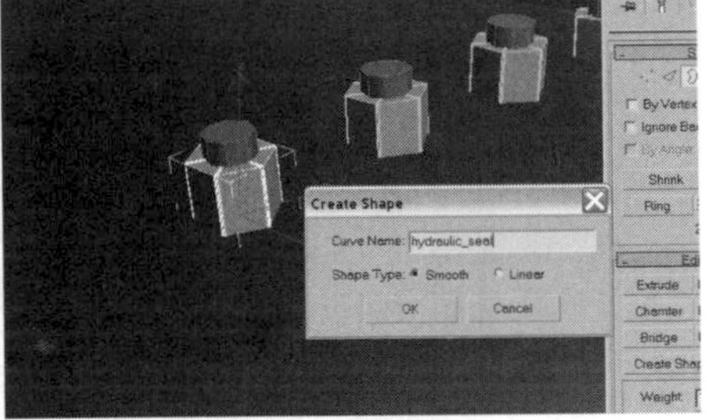

Figure 1-364

50. Hit the **H** key, select **hydraulic _seal**, and enable the shapes in the renderer and the viewport. Set Thickness to **0.8**, Sides to **12**, and Angle to **0**.

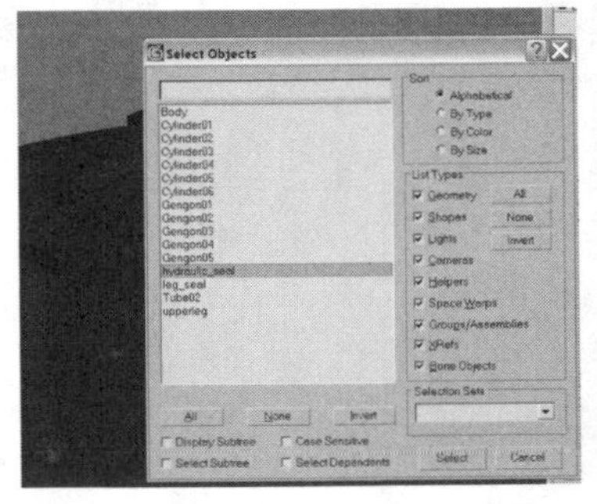

Figure 1-365

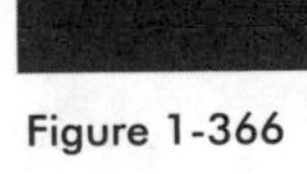

Figure 1-366

51. Use the Rotation and Move tools so that the seals are evenly flush against the body. Hit **H** to select the 12 objects that make up the four hydraulic connections.

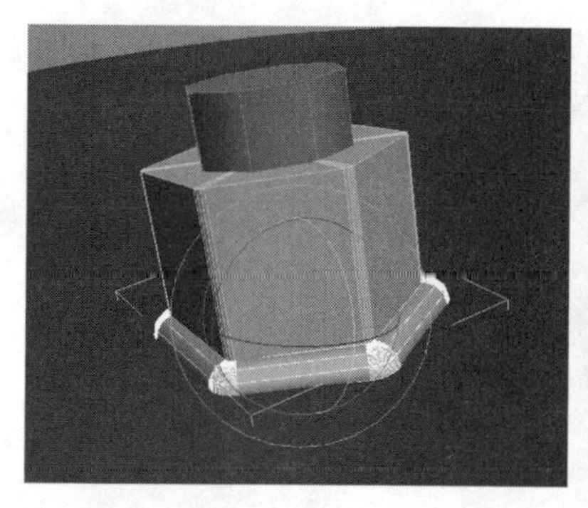

Figure 1-367

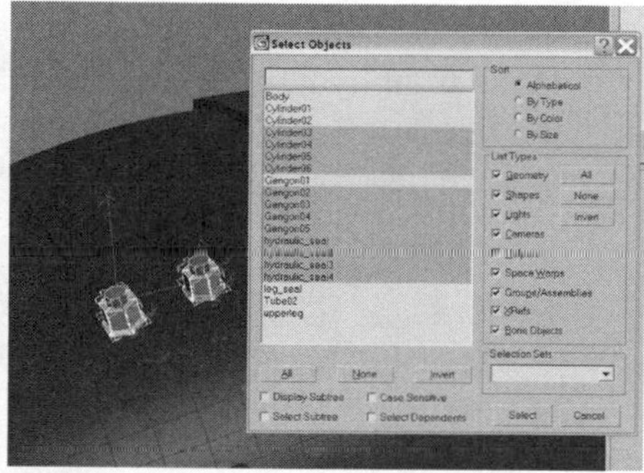

Figure 1-368

52. Use the Mirror tool to create clones on the left side of the body (you'll need to use an offset of around –52.6), then hit the **H** key, select all the hydraulic connections, and Link them to the body.

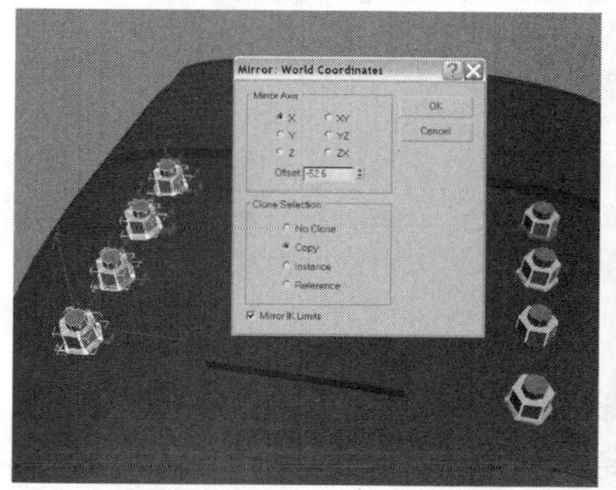

Figure 1-369

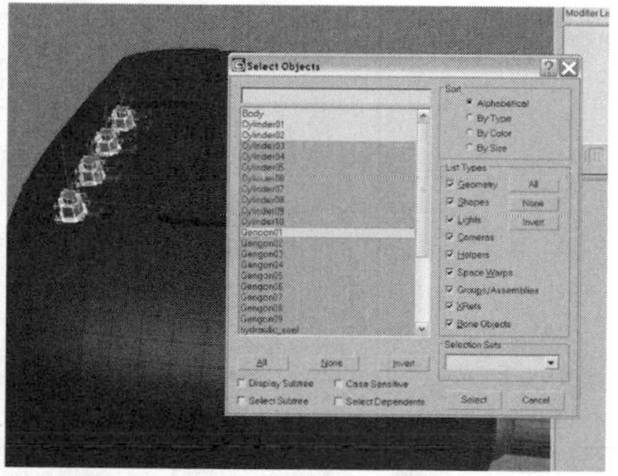

Figure 1-370

53. Create a Hose with the end points set to **Bound to Object Pivots.**

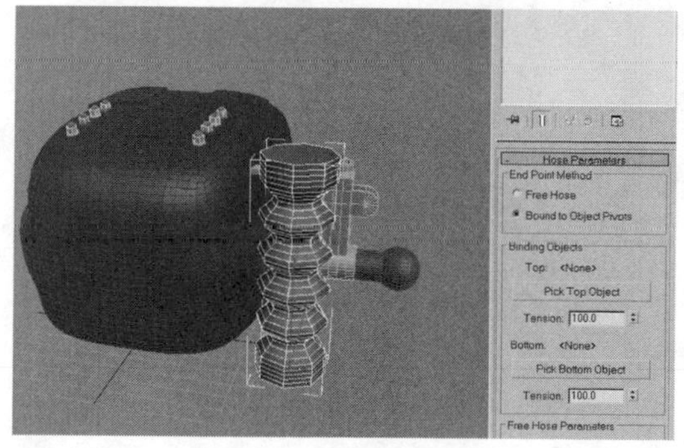

Figure 1-371

54. Click **Pick Top Object**, hit the **H** key, and click the cylinder on top of the front hydraulic connection. Next, click the **Pick Bottom Object** button, hit **H**, and then pick the cylinder that is on top of the gengon that is atop the hydraulic cylinder.

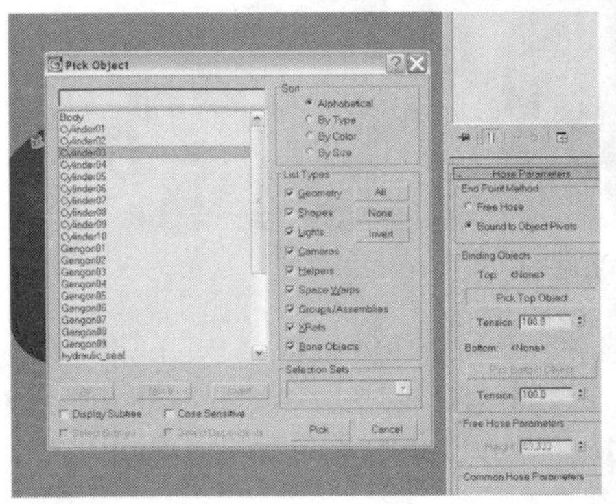

Figure 1-372

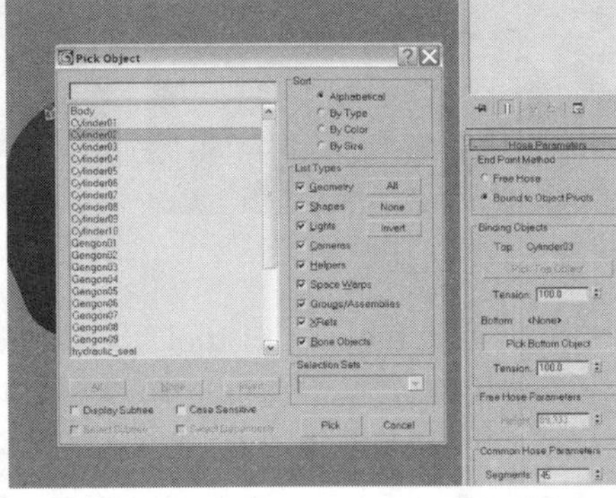

Figure 1-373

55. Set the Top Tension to **60**, the Bottom Tension to **40**, and the Segments to **91**, and choose **Flex Section Enable**. Set the Starts to **2**, the Ends to **99**, the Cycles to **26**, and the Diameter to **70**. Under Hose Shape, click **Round Hose**, and set Diameter to **3** and Sides to **16**.

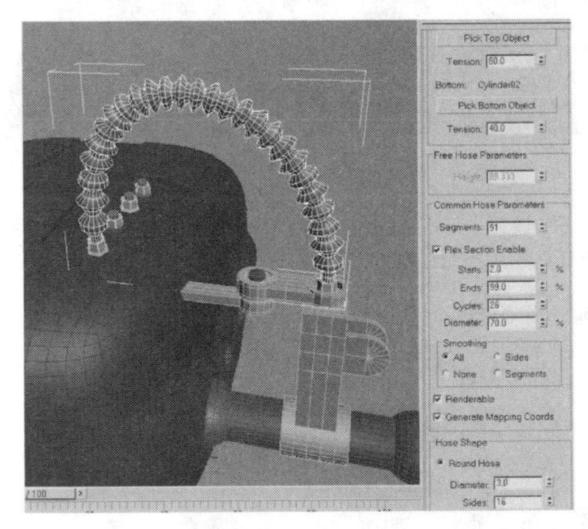

Figure 1-374

56. Press **F9** to do a test render.

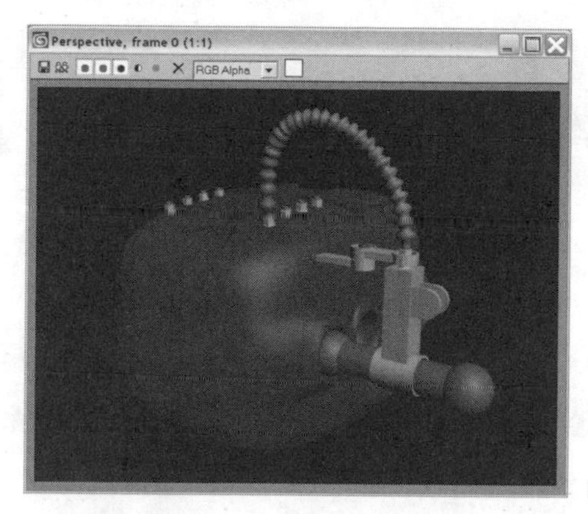

Figure 1-375

57. Select the two polygons on the front of the hydraulic pump as shown in Figure 1-376.

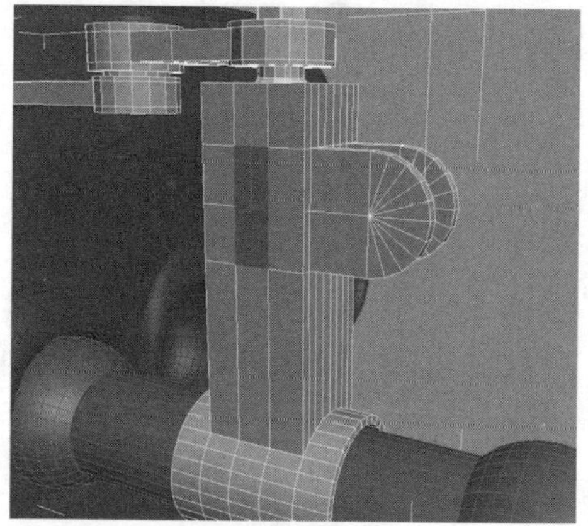

Figure 1-376

58. Click **Bevel Settings:**

Type	Height	Outline	Apply/OK
By Polygon	0	–0.2	Apply
By Polygon	–0.7	–0.2	OK

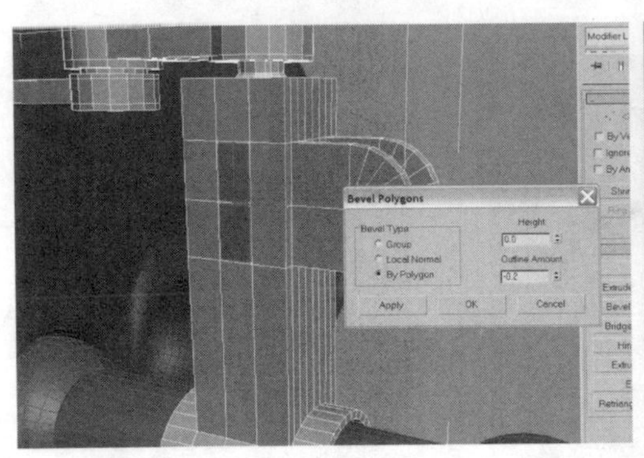

Figure 1-377

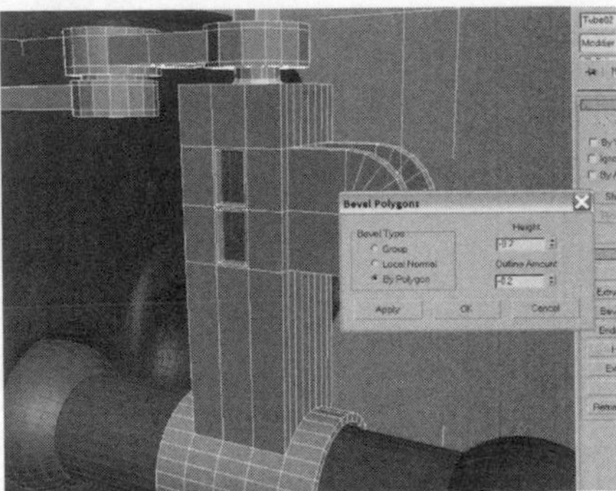

Figure 1-378

59. Turn on **Use NURMS Subdivision.** Click **MSmooth**, accept the default settings, and click **OK.**

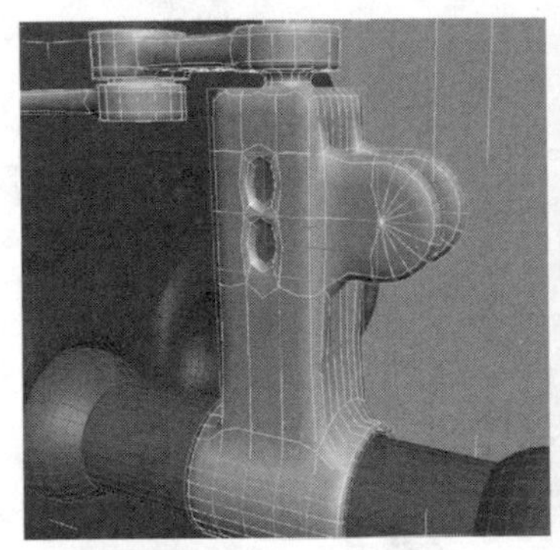
Figure 1-379

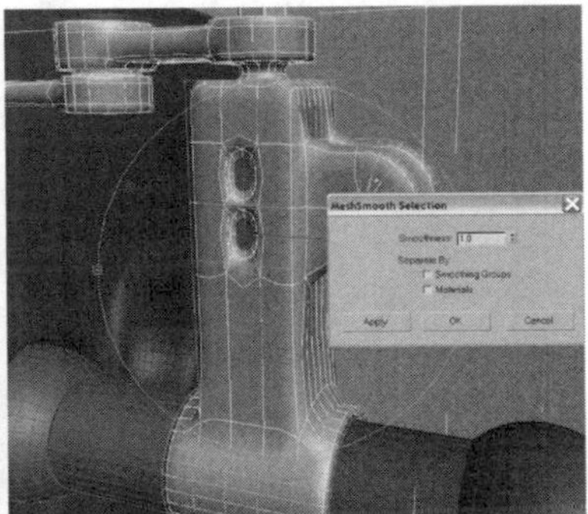
Figure 1-380

60. Click **Grow** to increase the selection.

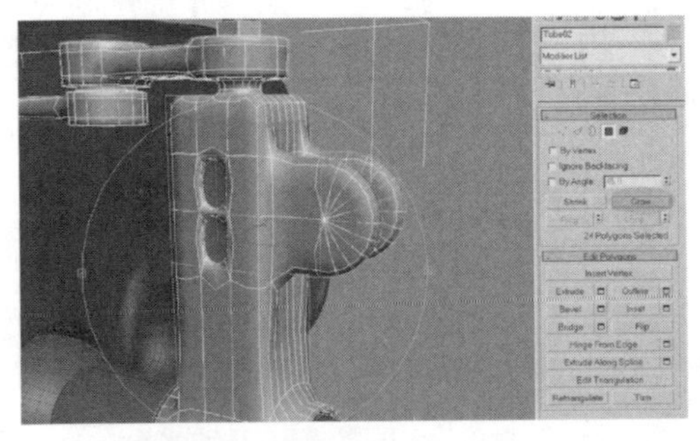
Figure 1-381

61. Click **Bevel Settings:**

Type	Height	Outline	Apply/OK
Group	3.6	–0.3	OK

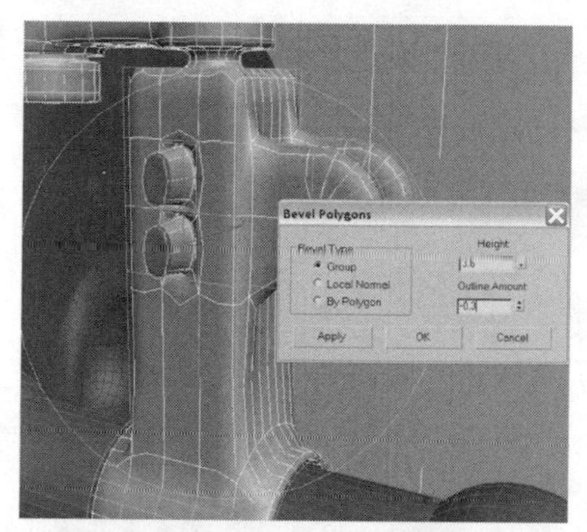

Figure 1-382

62. Click the **Shrink** button to choke the selection.

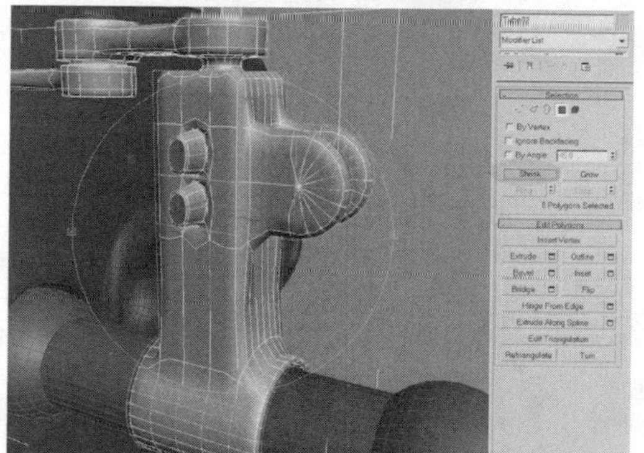

Figure 1-383

63. Click **Bevel Settings:**

Type	Height	Outline	Apply/OK
Group	0	–0.15	Apply
Group	0	–0.15	Apply

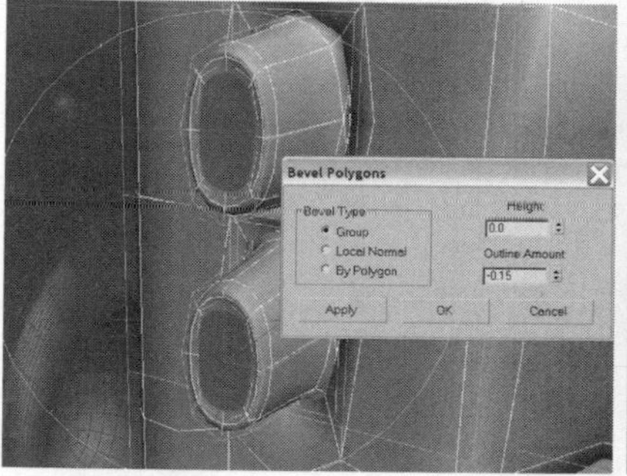

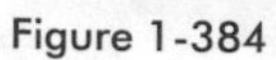

Figure 1-384

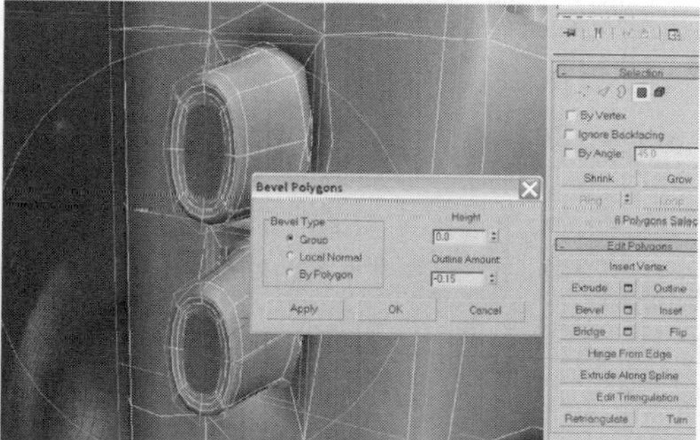

Figure 1-385

Type	Height	Outline	Apply/OK
Group	–2.6	0	OK

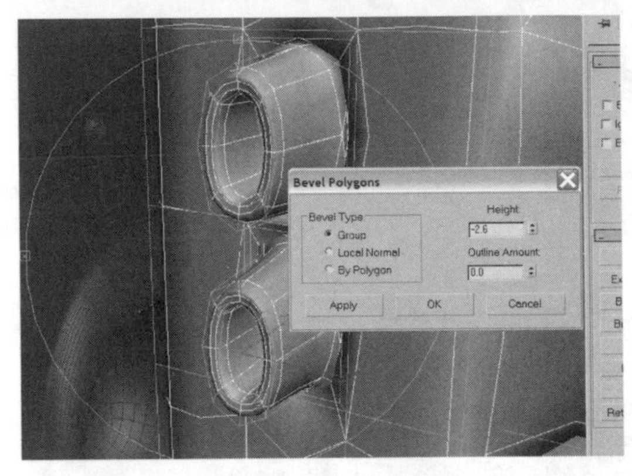

Figure 1-386

64. Delete the polygons, border-select the holes, and click **Cap**.

Figure 1-387

Figure 1-388

65. Click **Detach**, rename the objects **hydraulic_anchor** and **hydraulic_anchor2**, and then use Select and Link to link them to the hydraulic pump.

FYI: Okay. Why did we do step 64 if we're going to just turn around and undo it in step 65? Well ... strictly speaking, we didn't. We needed the internal polygons to be separate objects for a later step when we create the hydraulic hoses. These polygons will be the upper objects we'll link the hoses to the leg with.

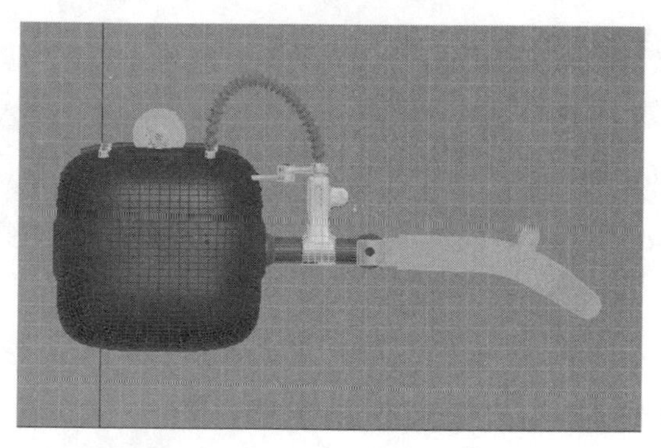

Figure 1-389

Day 6: Creating the Claw and Connecting the Hydraulics to the Legs

1. Create a Cylinder inside the tip of the middle leg.

Radius	Height	Height/Cap Segs	Sides	Smooth
5.0	8.0	5/1	32	Checked

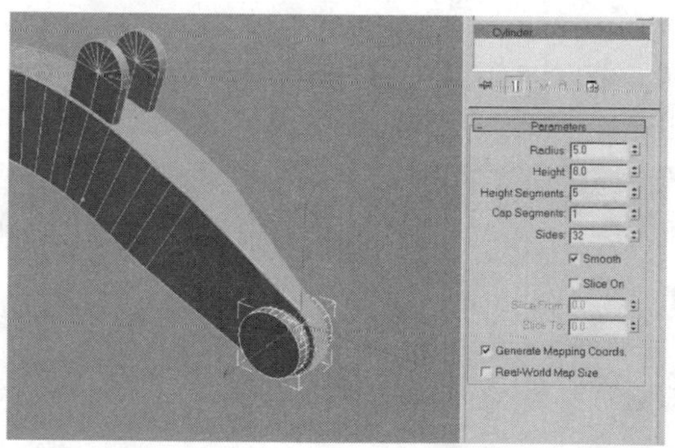

Figure 1-390

2. Convert the cylinder to an Editable Polygon, select the 12 polygons facing away from the tip of the leg on both sides of the cylinder, and Extrude them by **5**.

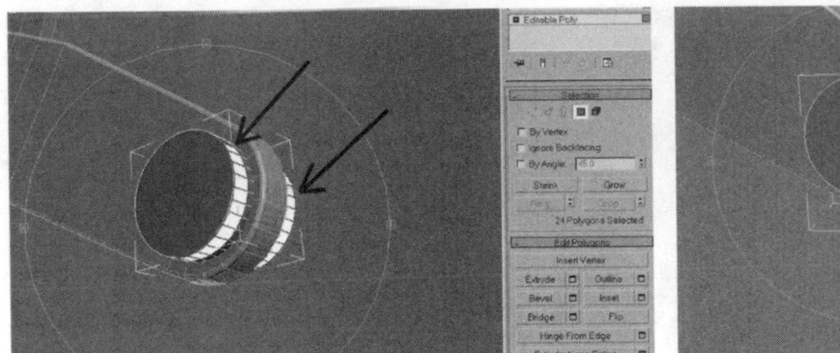

Figure 1-391

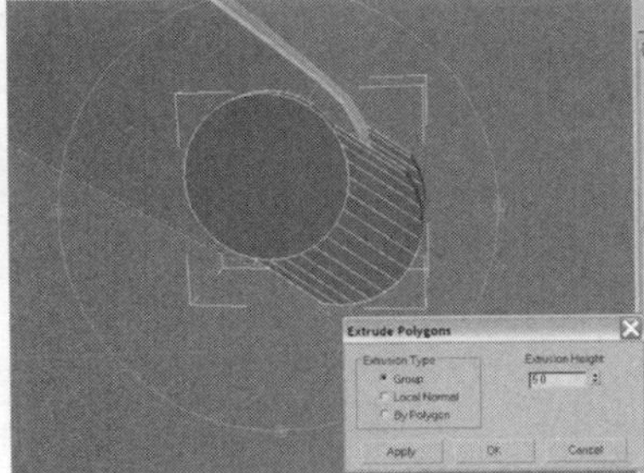

Figure 1-392

3. Use the Scale tool to scale the polygons down to **0** in the Local Z axis and select the 12 inner polygons on both sides.

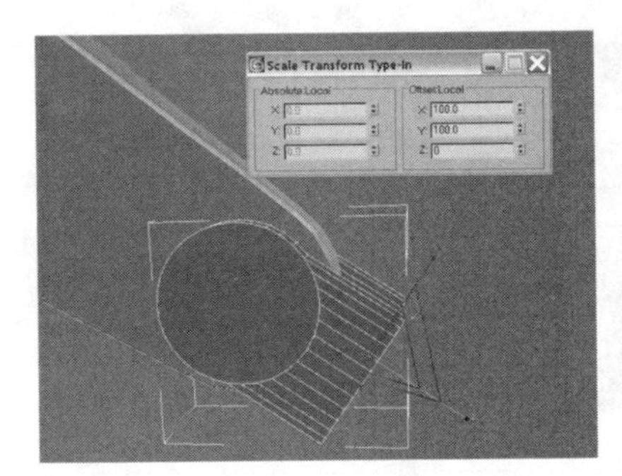

Figure 1-393

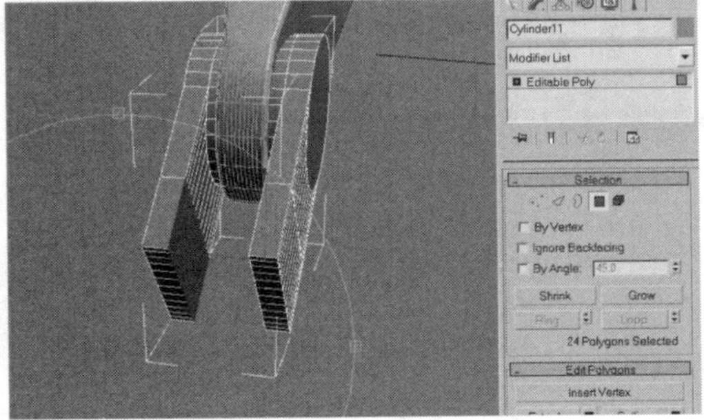

Figure 1-394

4. Extrude the polygons by **2.4**, delete the polygons, and Weld the vertices together.

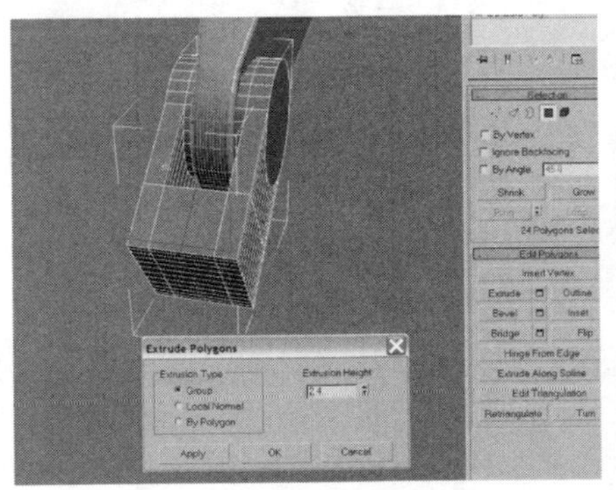

Figure 1-395

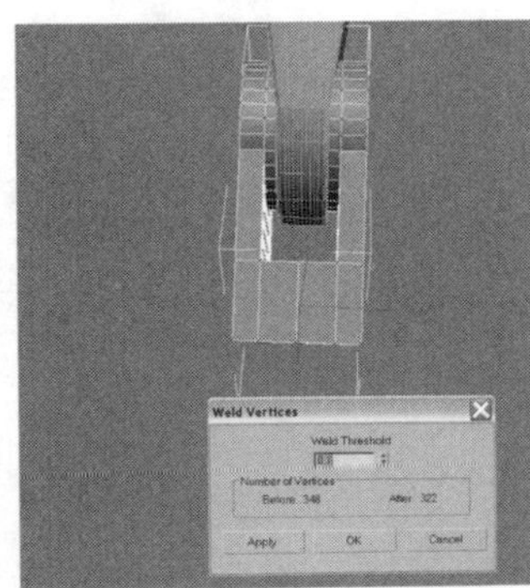

Figure 1-396

5. Edge-select the seam and then Chamfer the edge by **1**.

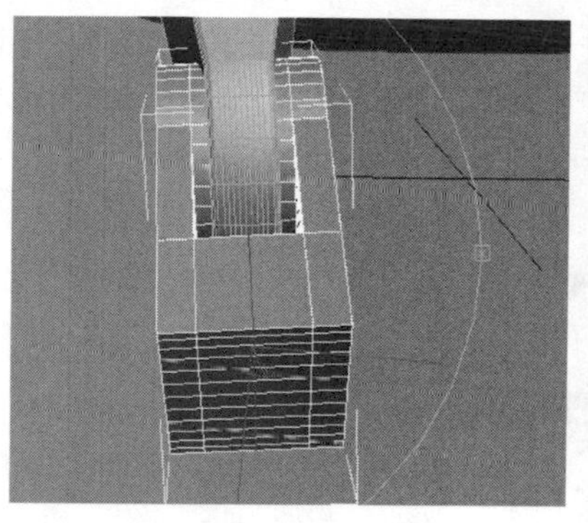

Figure 1-397

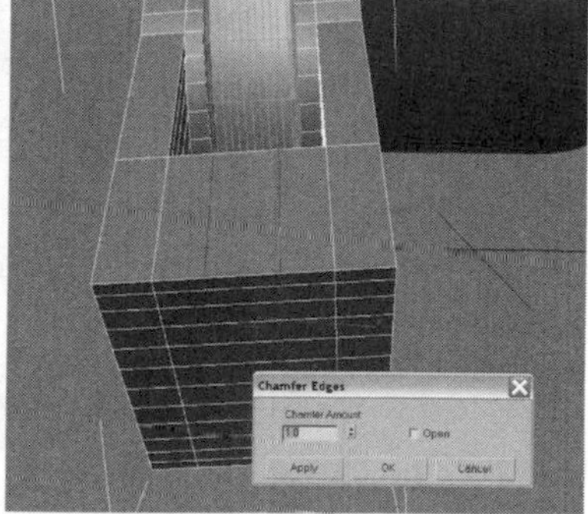

Figure 1-398

6. Select the two edges shown in Figure 1-399 and click **Connect**, and then do the same thing for the other side. Select the four polygons shown in Figure 1-400.

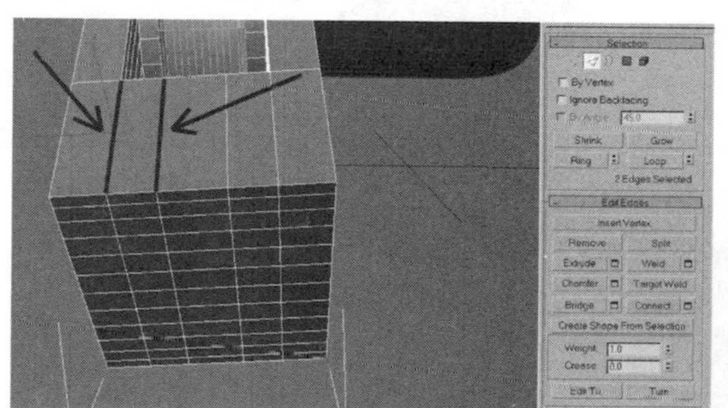

Figure 1-399

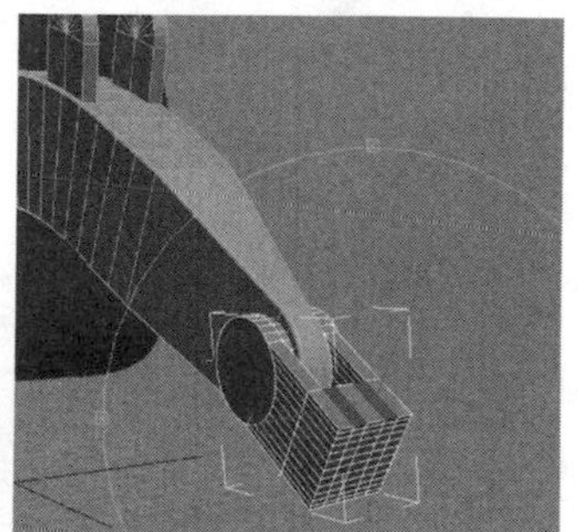

Figure 1-400

7. Extrude the polygons by **5** and then delete the bottom two polygons.

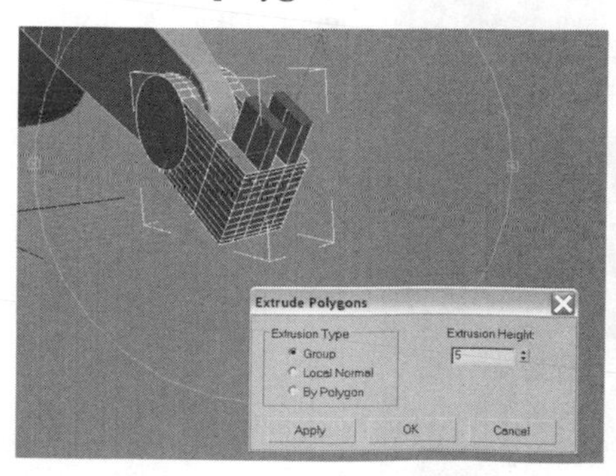

Figure 1-401

Figure 1-402

8. Click the top polygon and choose **Hinge From Edge** with Angle set to **180** degrees and Segments set to **10**. Delete the backward-facing polygon and Weld the resulting vertices together. Then repeat it for the other side.

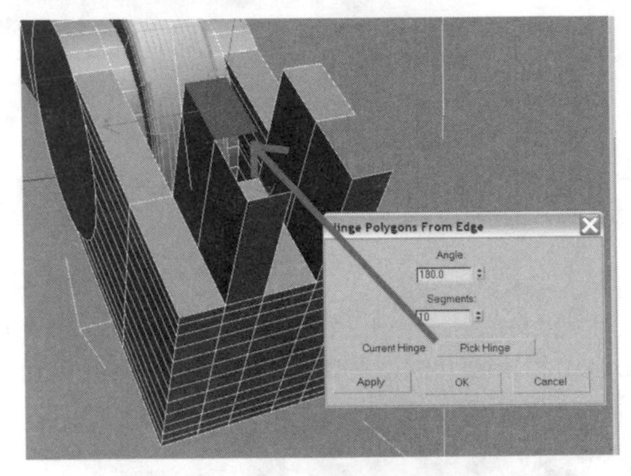

Figure 1-403

9. Click the 24 polygons on the front edge, Extrude them by **3**, and hit **Apply** (*not* OK).

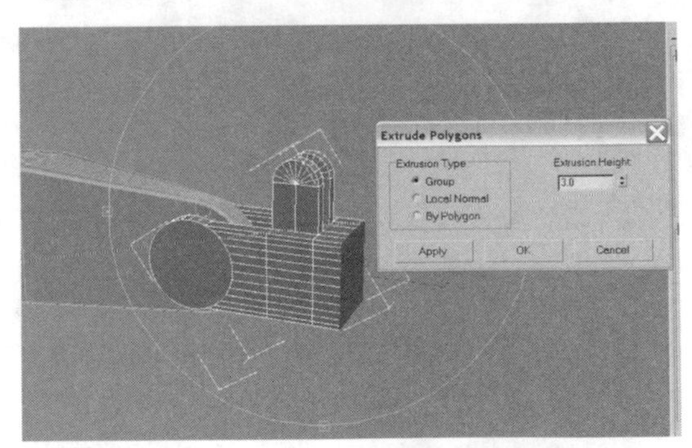

Figure 1-404

10. Click **Apply** 11 more times and then click **OK**.

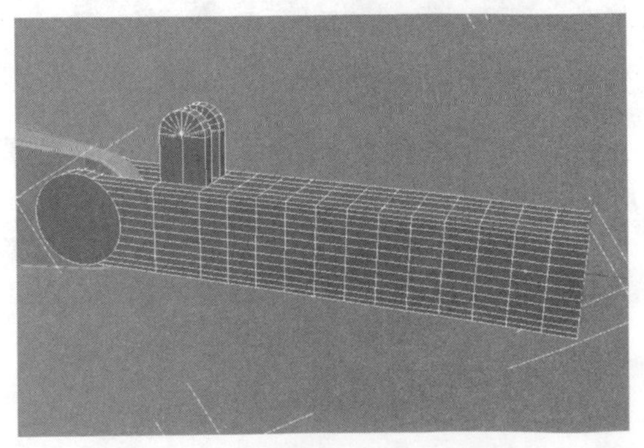

Figure 1-405

11. Click **Grow** 10 times, add a Taper modifier to the stack, then select **Gizmo.**

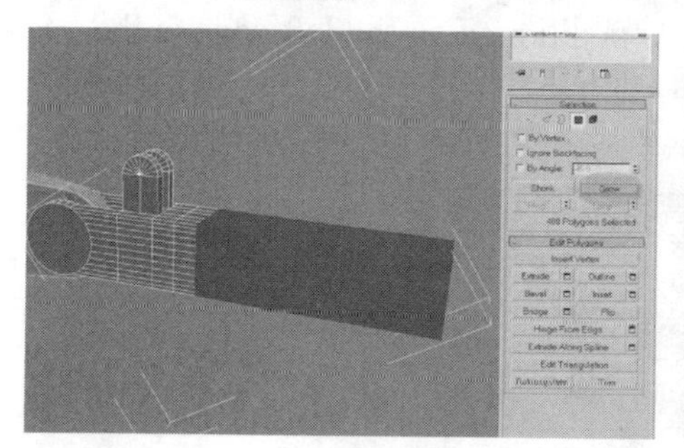

Figure 1-406

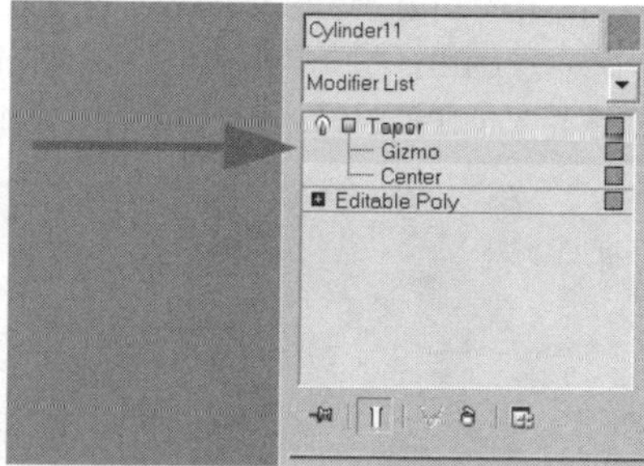

Figure 1-407

12. Use the Rotate gizmo to make the Z axis face backward and the X axis face away from the body. Scale the gizmo to be the same size as the selected area, and set the Taper Amount to **–1.8**, the Taper Axis Primary to **X**, and the Taper Axis Effect to **ZY**. Then collapse the stack.

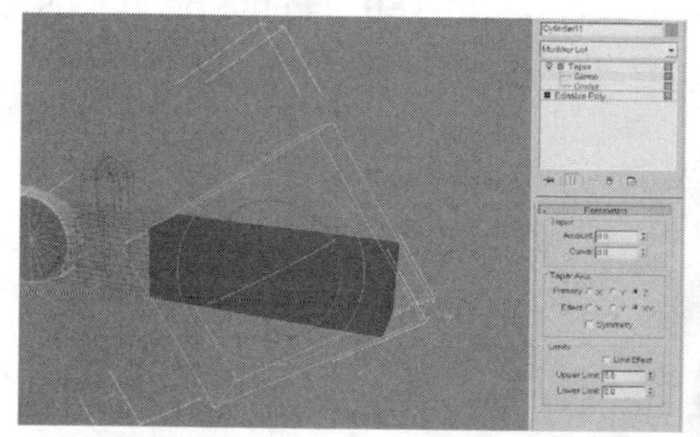

Figure 1-408

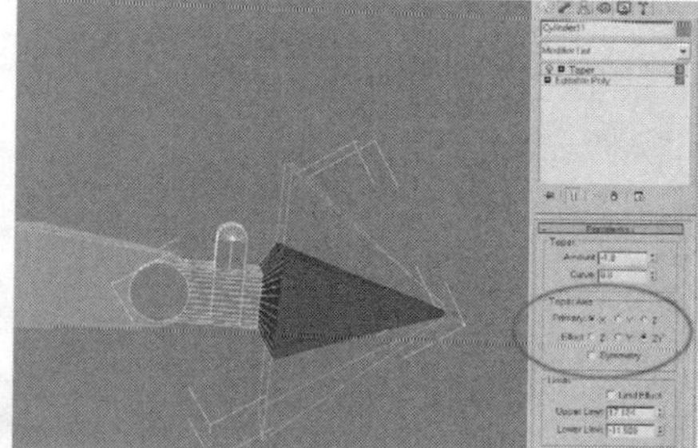

Figure 1-409

13. Click **Grow** until the selected polygons form an arrowhead as shown. Click **Detach** to detach it as an object.

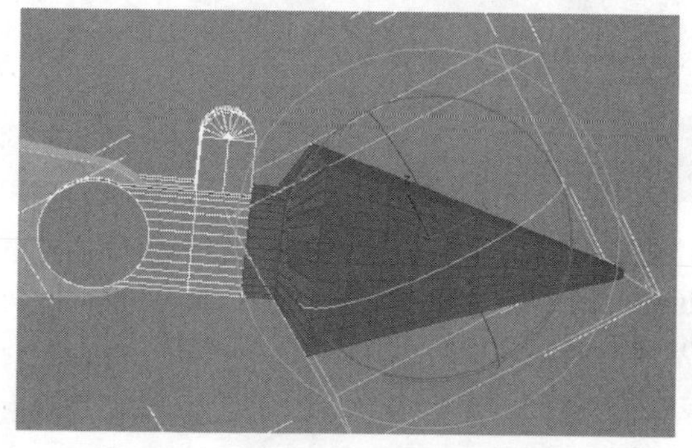

Figure 1-410

14. Add a Bend modifier to the object's stack. Position and scale the gizmo so it encompasses only the triangular portion. Click the center and move it so the center is positioned on the left edge of the gizmo. Also, be sure the axes are positioned as you see them in Figure 1-411. If not, use the Rotate tool to align them as shown.

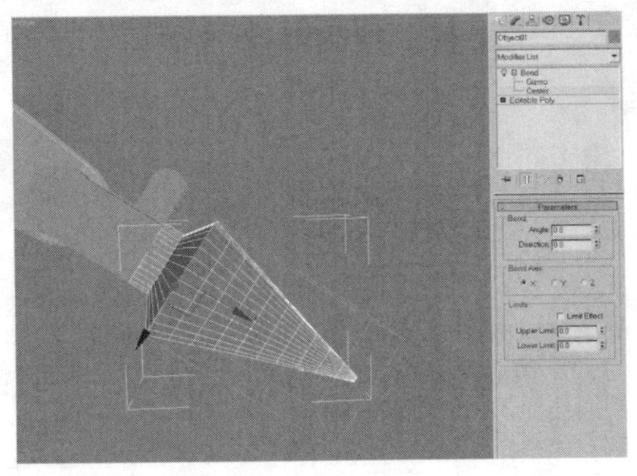

Figure 1-411

15. Set the Bend Angle to **90**, the Direction to **–180**, and the Bend Axis to **X**. Click **Limit Effect** and set the Upper Limit to **45**. Collapse the stack.

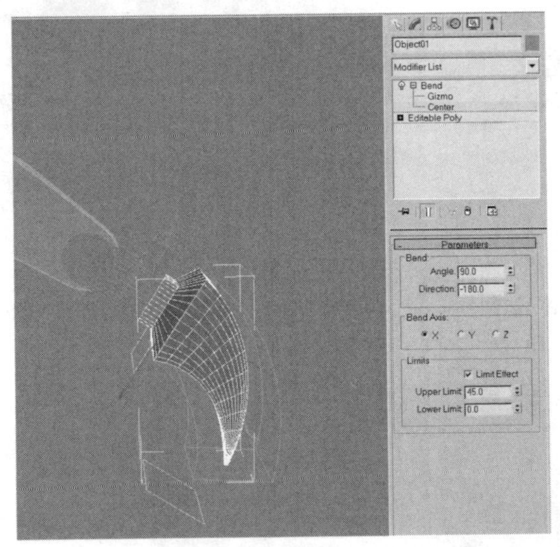

Figure 1-412

16. Select the joint part of the claw, which you detached from, hit the **Attach List** button, and select **Object01** (or whatever you called the part you detached and bent). Click **Attach**.

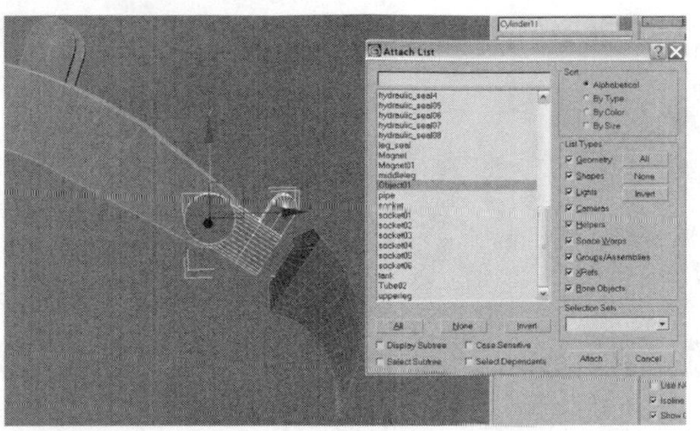

Figure 1-413

17. Vertex-select the vertices along the seam and Weld them.

Figure 1-414

Figure 1-415

18. Select the polygons on the front and rear of the joint.

Figure 1-416

19. Click **Bevel Settings:**

Type	Height	Outline	Apply/OK
Group	0	–0.6	Apply
Group	–0.8	0	Apply

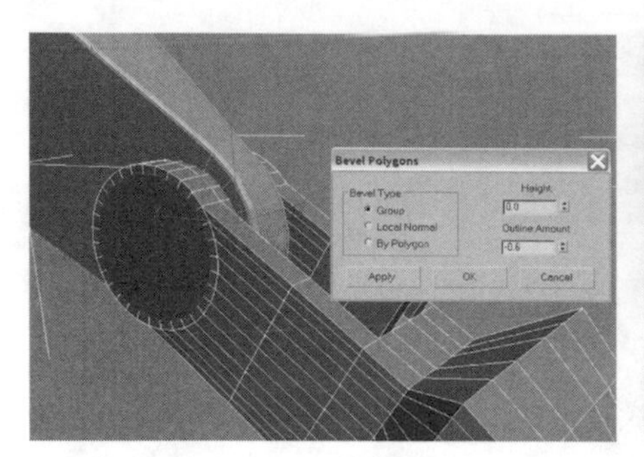

Figure 1-417

Figure 1-418

Type	Height	Outline	Apply/OK
Group	0	–0.5	Apply
Group	0.6	–0.5	Apply

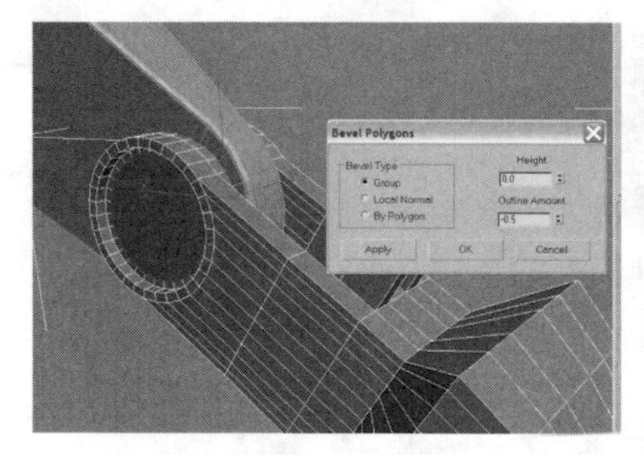

Figure 1-419

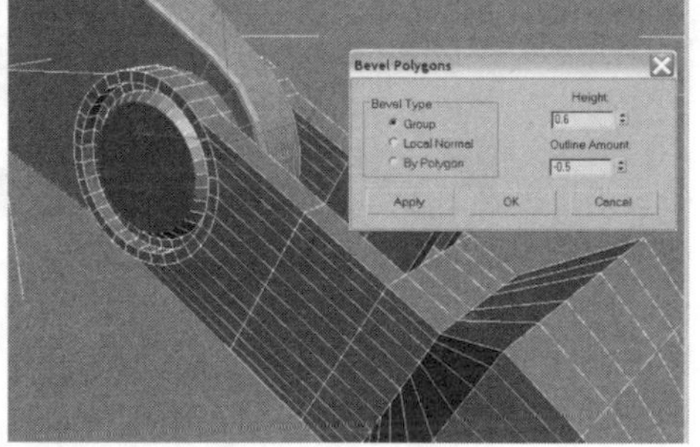

Figure 1-420

Type	Height	Outline	Apply/OK
Group	0.6	–0.5	Apply
Group	0	–0.5	Apply

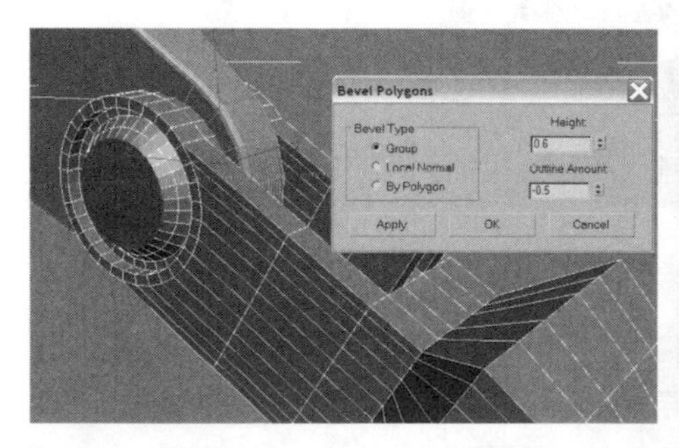

Figure 1-421

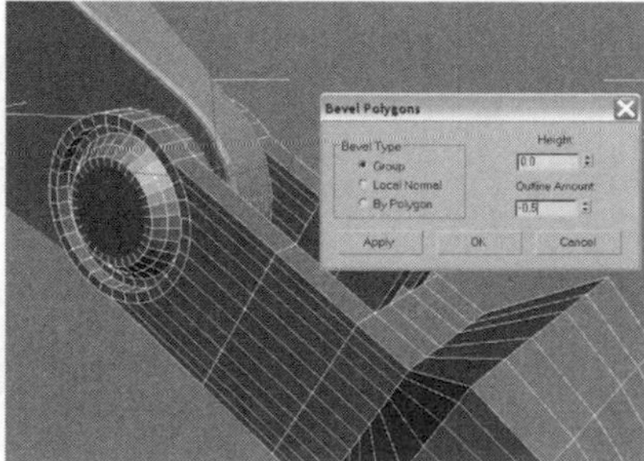

Figure 1-422

Type	Height	Outline	Apply/OK
Group	–0.3	–0.9	OK

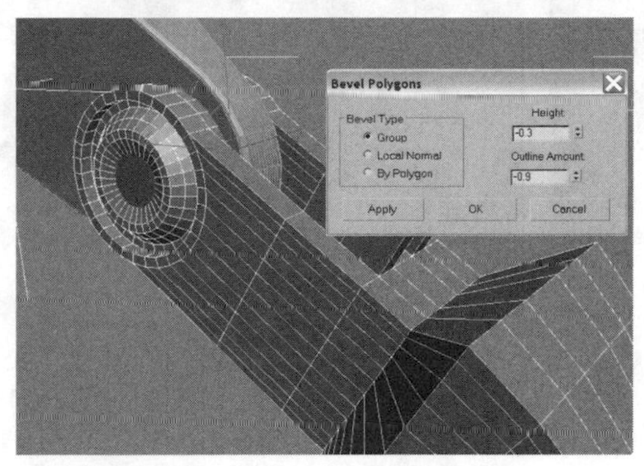

Figure 1-423

20. Create a Cylinder using AutoGrid on top of the joint of the hydraulic pump and then convert it to an Editable Polygon. Move it into position inside the joint.

Radius	Height	Height/Cap Segs	Sides	Smooth
3.14	5.361	5/1	32	Checked

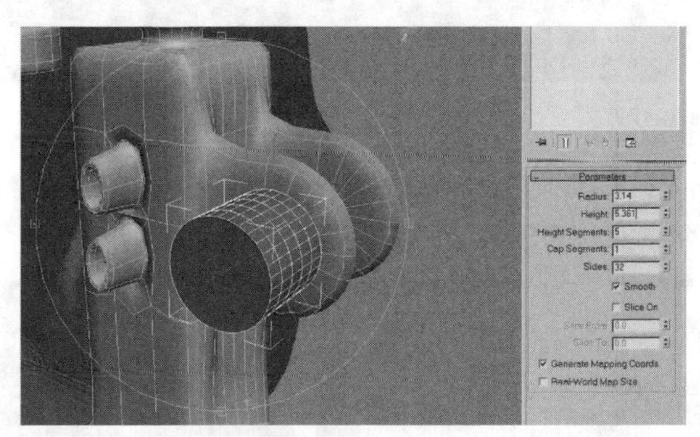

Figure 1-424

21. Select the middle 15 polygons shown in Figure 1-425, delete them, border-select the hole, and Cap it.

Figure 1-425

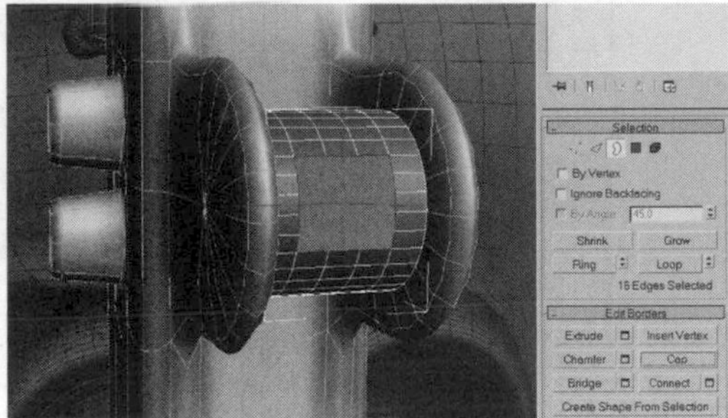

Figure 1-426

22. Select the cap, click the **Tessellate Settings** button, click **Face**, and then click **OK**. Switch to Vertex selection mode and click the middle vertex.

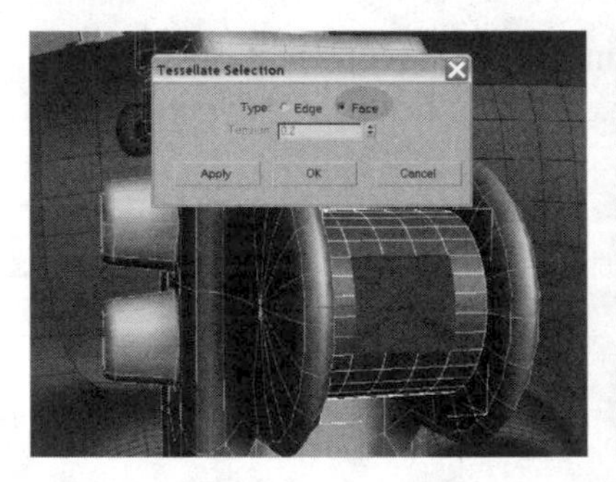

Figure 1-427

Figure 1-428

23. Chamfer the vertices by **1.39**, select the same polygons, and Scale the polygons down to **0** in the Z axis.

Figure 1-429

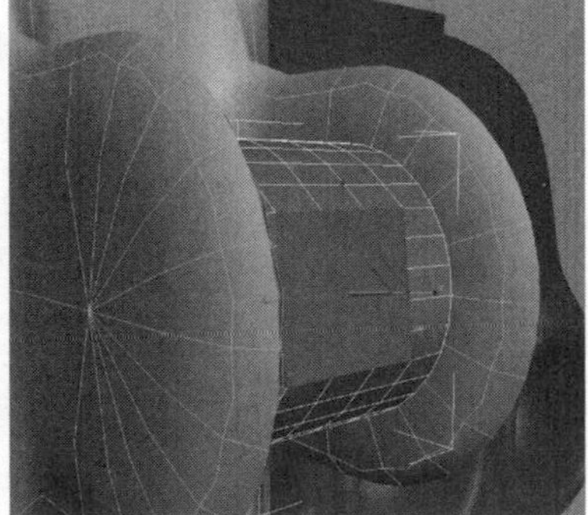

Figure 1-430

24. Click **Shrink** so that only the round polygon is selected, and click **Bevel Settings:**

Type	Height	Outline	Apply/OK
Group	1.4	1.0	OK

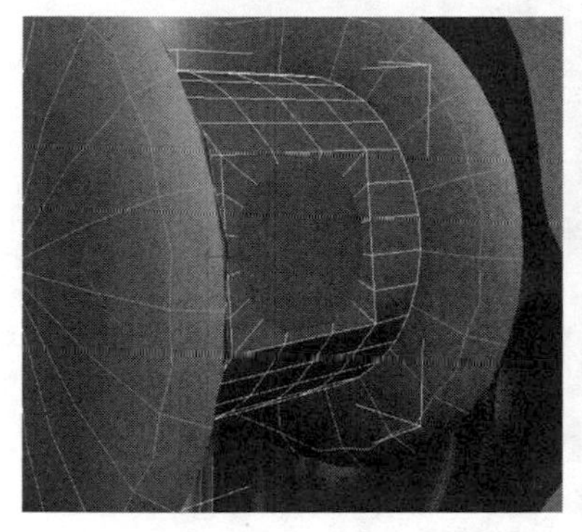

Figure 1-431

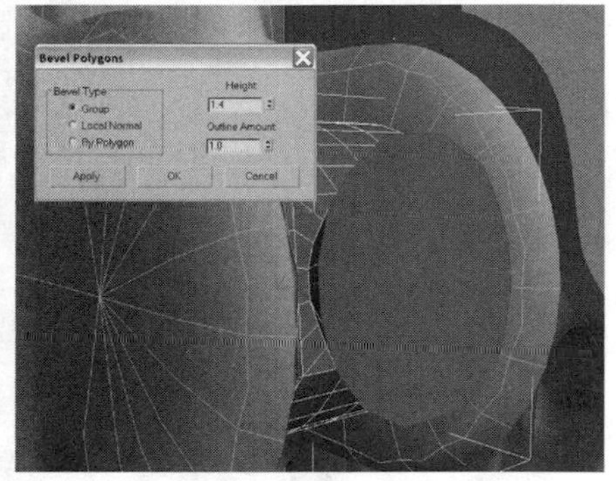

Figure 1-432

25. Delete the polygon.

26. Create a Cylinder as shown, convert it to an Editable Polygon, and delete the backward-facing polygon.

Radius	Height	Height/Cap Segs	Sides	Smooth
2.39	0.9	1/1	16	Checked

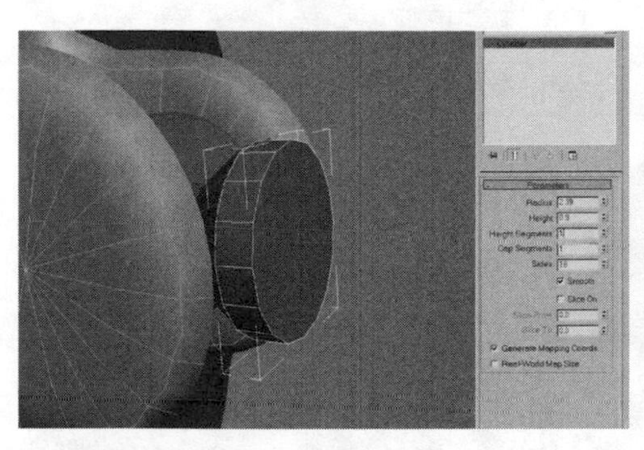

Figure 1-433

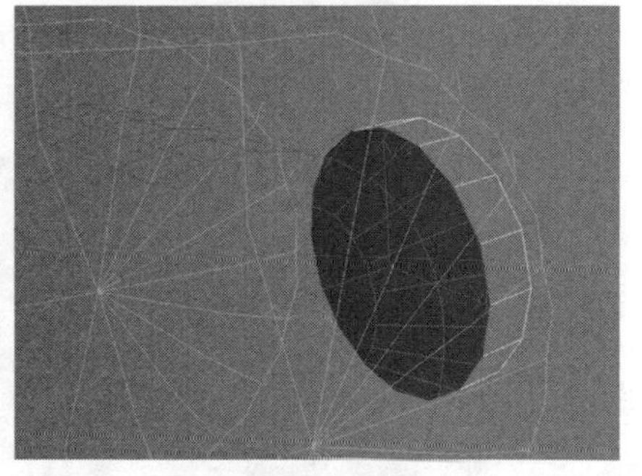

Figure 1-434

27. Click the axle, click **Attach List**, attach the cylinder, and turn on **Use NURMS Subdivision**, then set the Display Iterations to **1** and the Render Iterations to **3**.

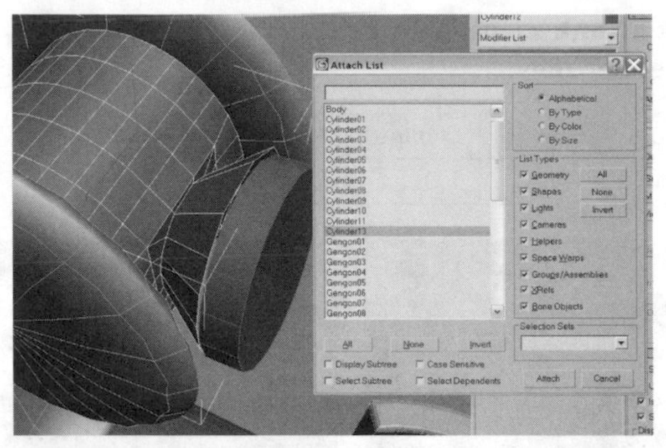

Figure 1-435

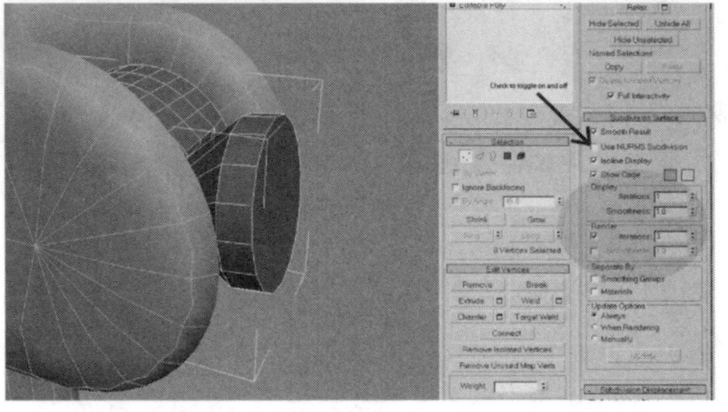

Figure 1-436

28. Click **Bevel Settings:**

Type	Height	Outline	Apply/OK
Group	0	0.6	Apply
Group	50	0	Apply

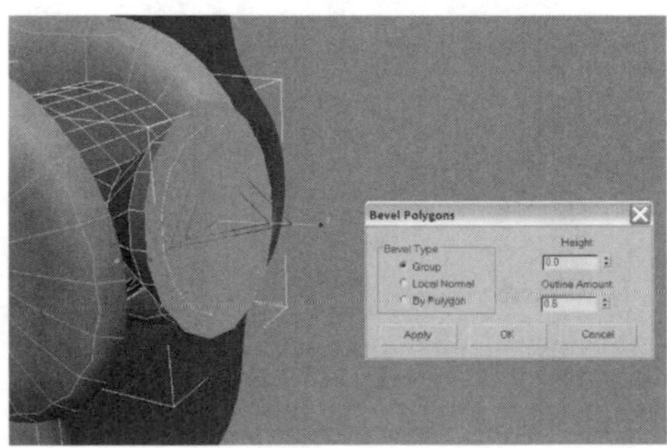

Figure 1-437

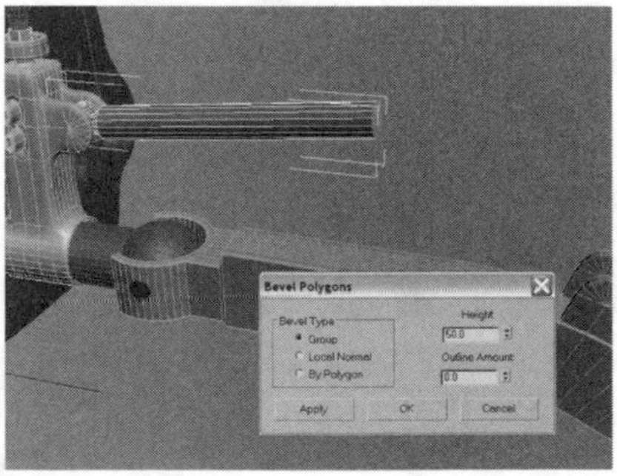

Figure 1-438

Type	Height	Outline	Apply/OK
Group	0	–0.3	Apply
Group	0	–0.1	Apply

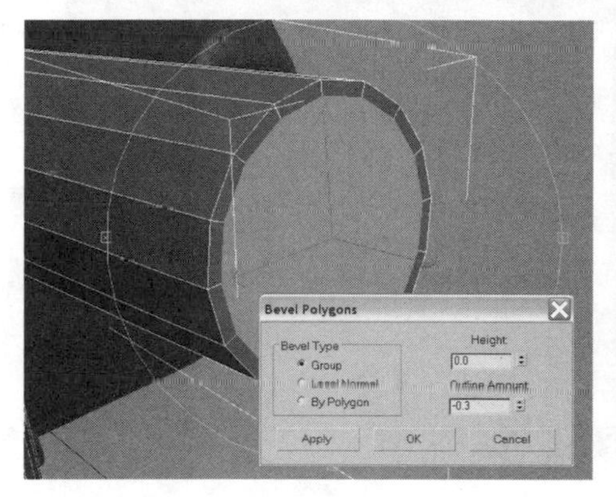

Figure 1-439

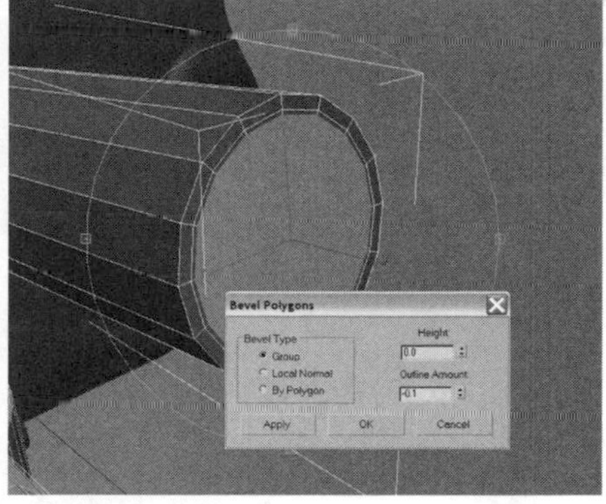

Figure 1-440

Type	Height	Outline	Apply/OK
Group	0	–0.3	Apply
Group	–34.99	0	OK

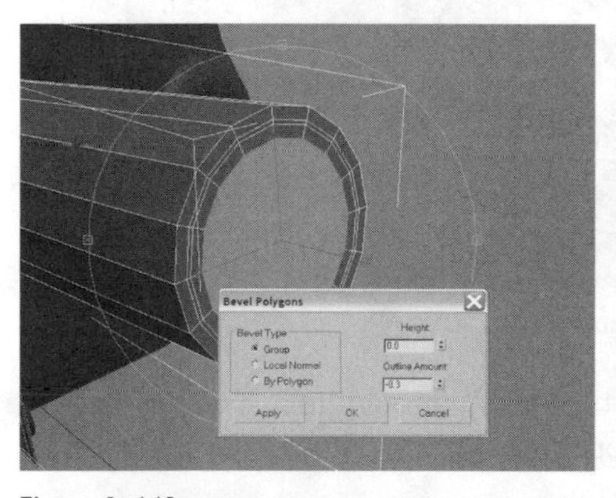

Figure 1-441

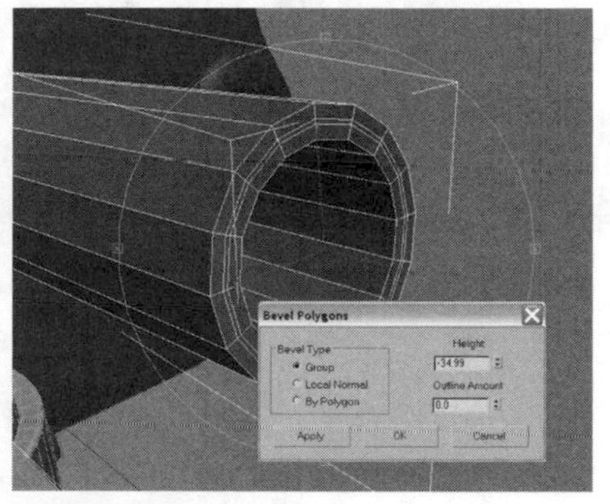

Figure 1-442

29. Detach the polygon, rename it **shaft**, and then use the Move tool to move it in the Z axis into position above the joint stanchions of the middle leg.

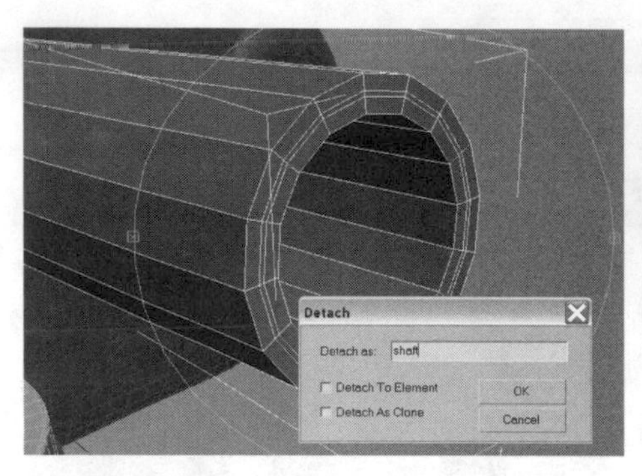

Figure 1-443

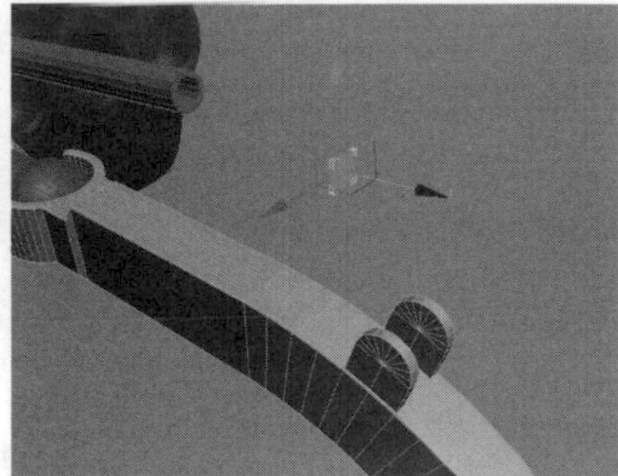

Figure 1-444

30. Click **Bevel Settings:**

Type	Height	Outline	Apply/OK
Group	0	–1.0	Apply
Group	1.0	0.6	OK

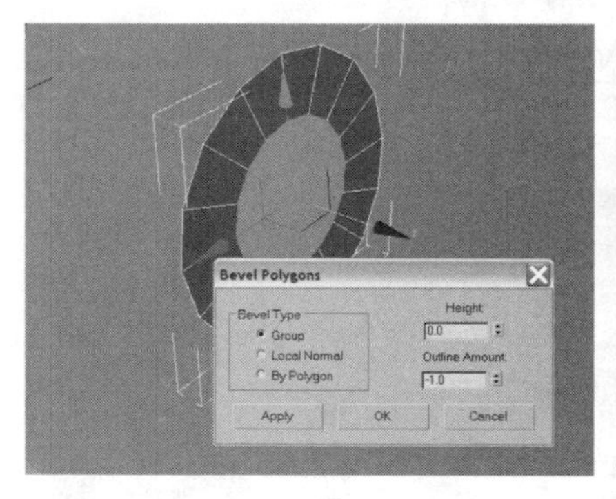

Figure 1-445

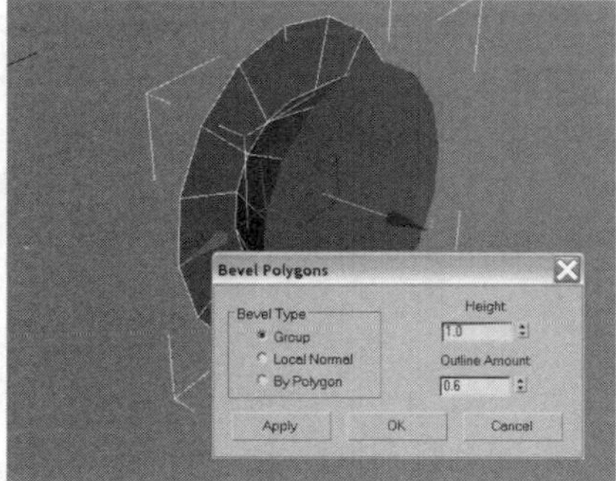

Figure 1-446

31. Create a Cylinder between the stanchions on the middle leg, convert it to an Editable Polygon, then Shift-drag to create a clone on the other side of the stanchion.

Radius	Height	Height/Cap Segs	Sides	Smooth
1.3	–6.675	5/1	32	Checked

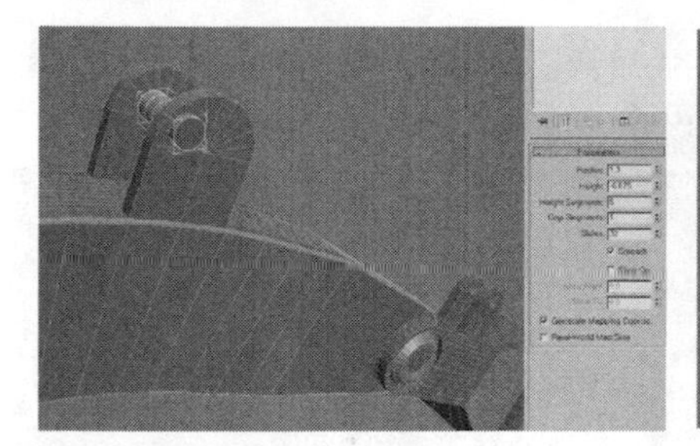

Figure 1-447

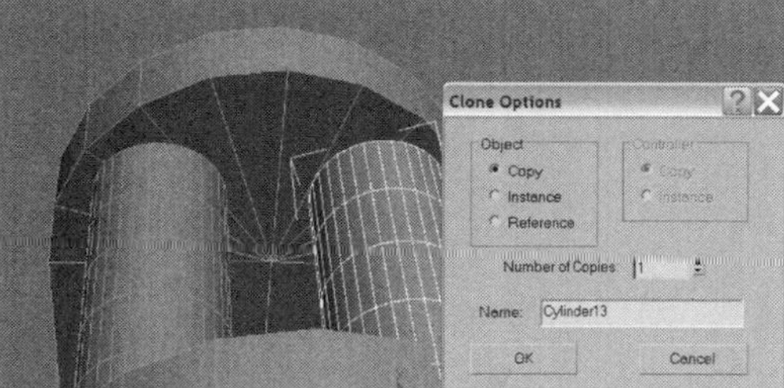

Figure 1-448

32. With both cylinders selected, open the Hierarchy tab, click **Affect Pivot Only** and **Center to Object** to center the pivots. Select the 15 polygons shown on the body side of the cylinder.

Figure 1-449

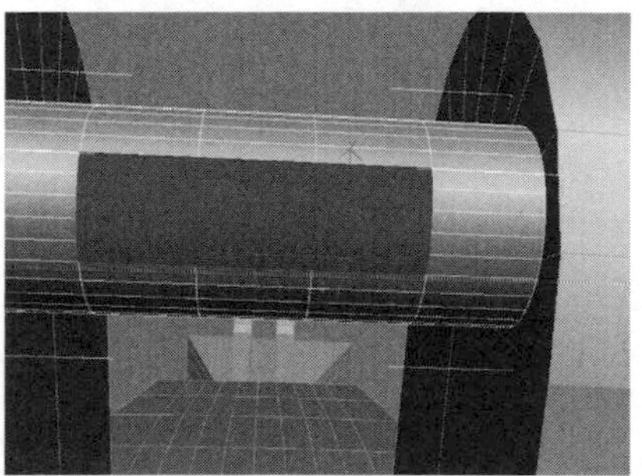

Figure 1-450

33. Delete the polygons and Cap the border. Then, using the Non-uniform Scale tool, scale the cap in the X and Y axes until you get a selection that is roughly square.

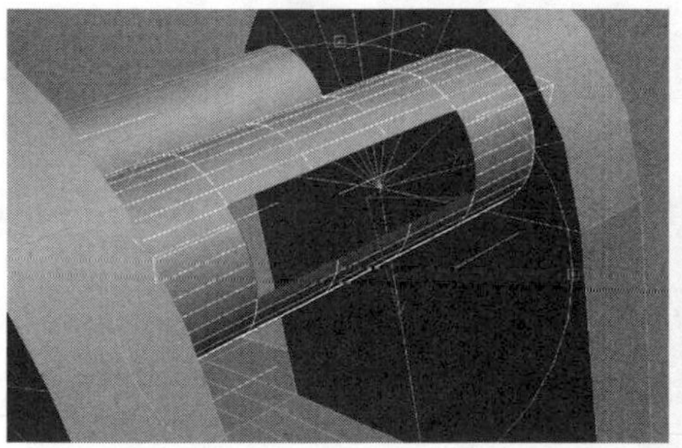

Figure 1-451

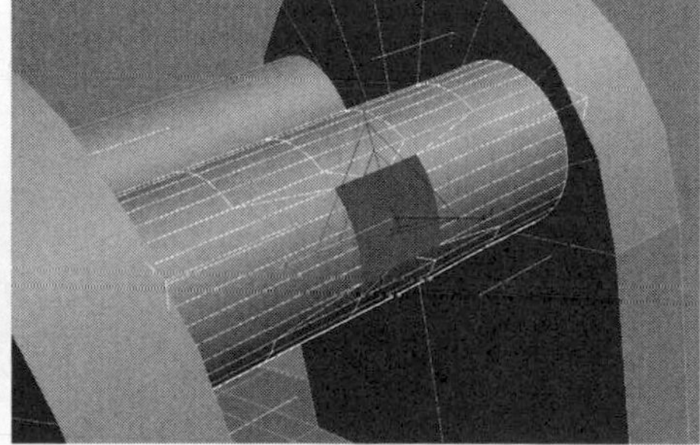

Figure 1-452

34. Tessellate the cap, choosing **Face** as the Type, and then Non-uniform Scale it down to **0** in the Z axis.

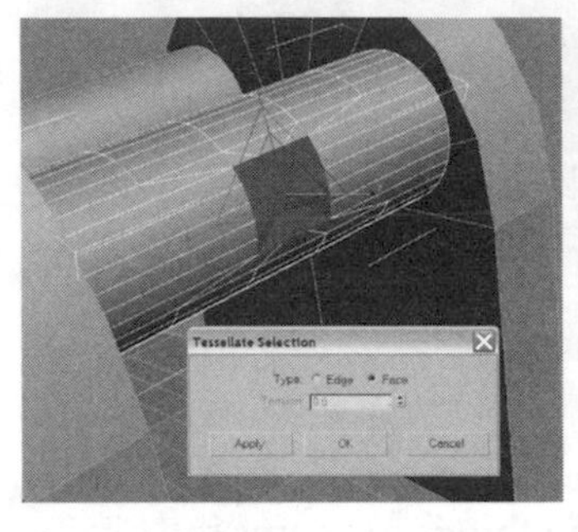

Figure 1-453

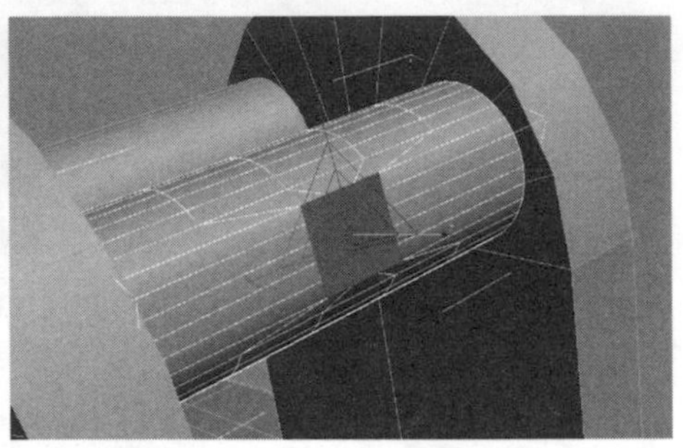

Figure 1-454

35. Vertex-select the middle vertex and Chamfer the vertices by **0.58.** Select the polygon.

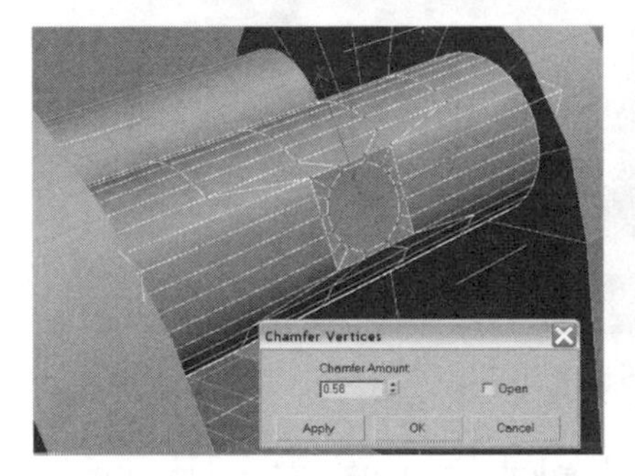

Figure 1-455

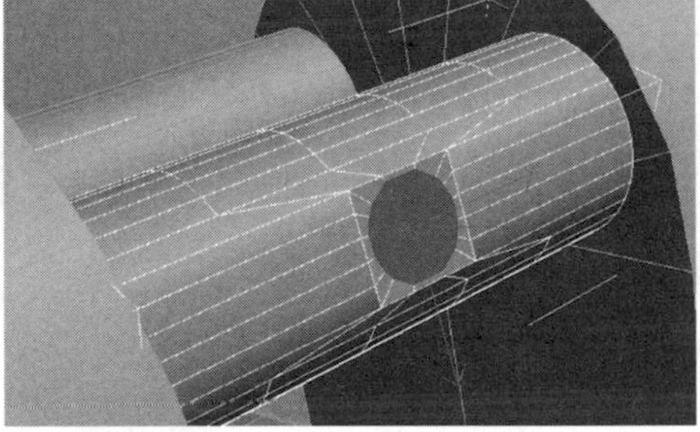

Figure 1-456

36. Click **Bevel Settings** and then delete the resulting polygon:

Type	Height	Outline	Apply/OK
Group	0.5	0.4	OK

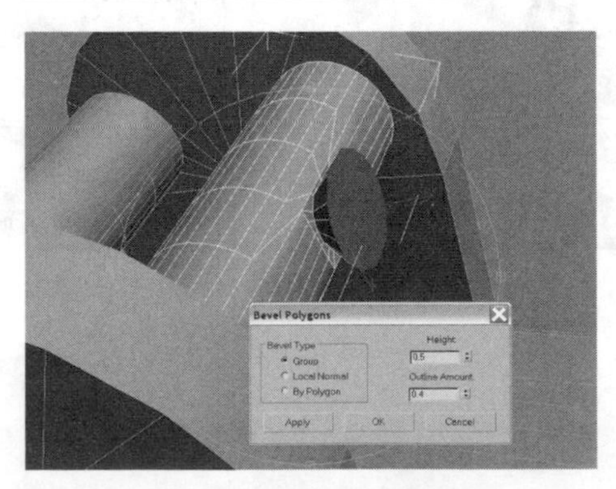

Figure 1-457

37. Using AutoGrid, create a Cylinder, convert it to an Editable Polygon, and delete the back-facing polygon.

Radius	Height	Height/Cap Segs	Sides	Smooth
1	0.3	1/1	16	Checked

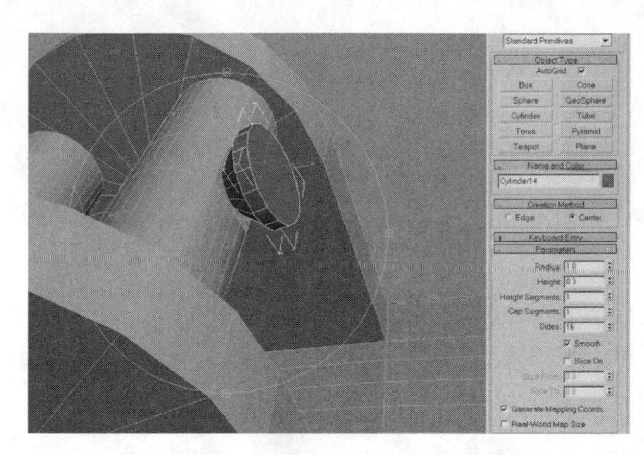

Figure 1-458

38. Attach the cylinder and Weld the vertices, then select the top polygon and delete it.

Figure 1-459

39. Select the shaft and center its pivot, then move it down to meet the axle on the middle leg.

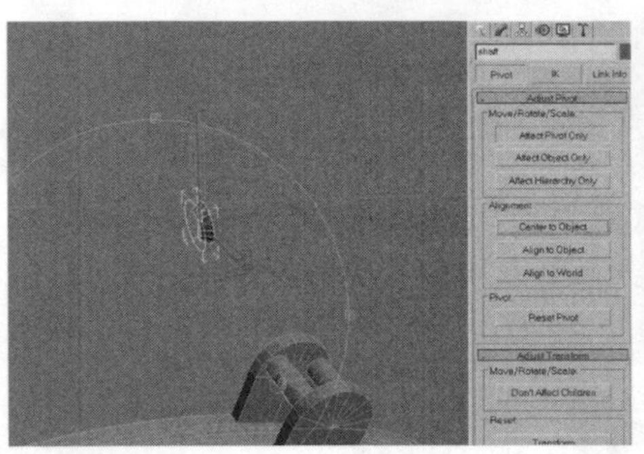

Figure 1-460

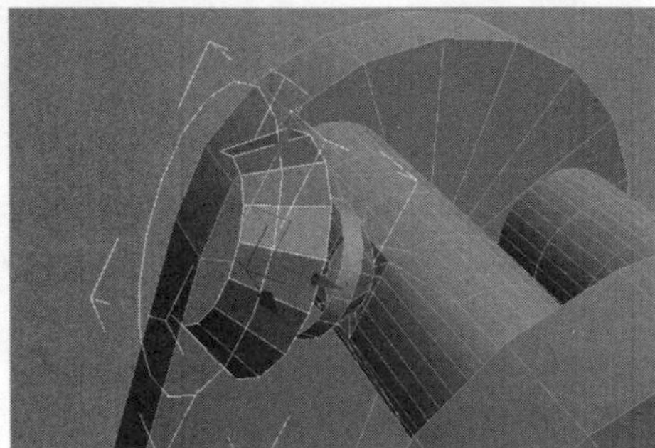

Figure 1-461

40. Border-select the open part on the axle on the middle leg. Scale it and the open part of the shaft until they fit. Attach the shaft to the axle.

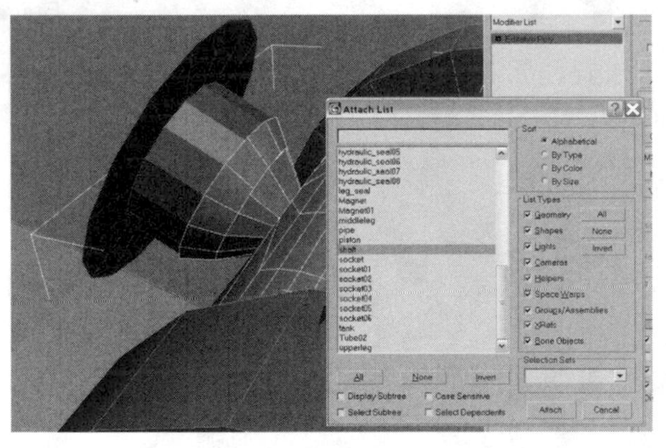

Figure 1-462

41. Border-select the open part on the shaft/axle that faces the body and Extrude it about **40** to **50**. (At this point the extrusion just has to be long enough to fit around halfway into the piston attached to the hydraulic system; you can size it to fit later.)

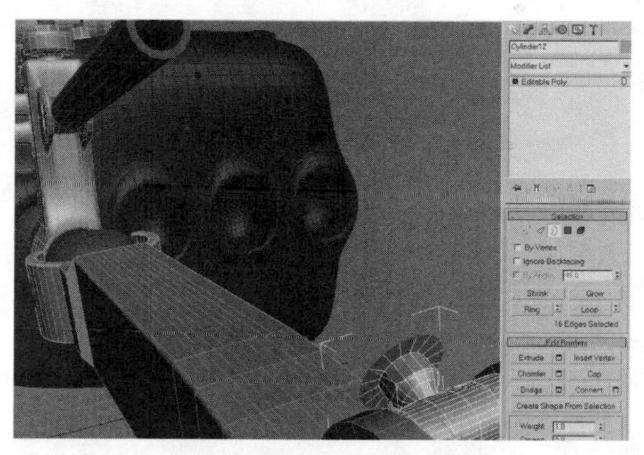

Figure 1-463

42. Set the pivots for the piston and the shaft so they are centered as shown, with their X axes facing each other.

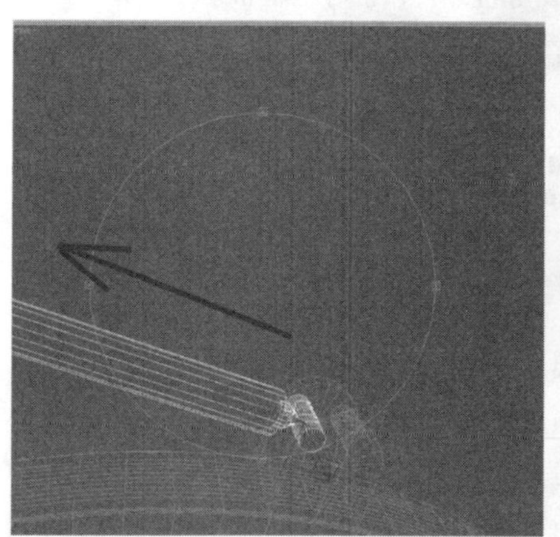

Figure 1-464

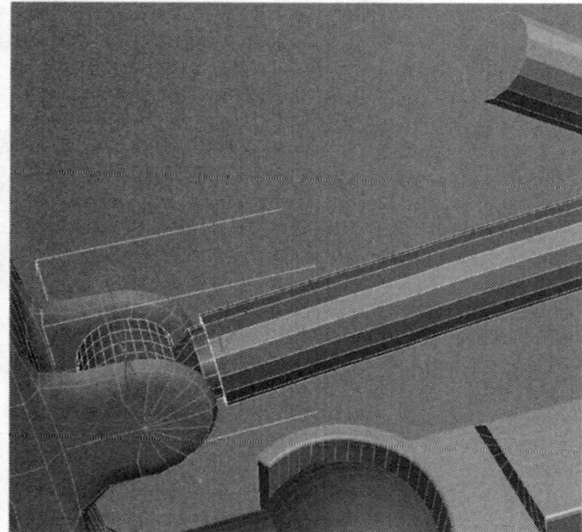

Figure 1-465

Urgent: This is a crucial step. In order for the hydraulics to work right, the pivots for the piston and the shaft have to be aligned.

43. Select the piston. On the Create panel, click the **Motion** icon (it looks like a wheel). Click the plus sign next to Assign Controller, select **Rotation: Euler XYZ**, and then click the **Assign Controller** button (which has a question mark for an icon).

Figure 1-466

FYI: Animation in Max is handled by *controllers*. Controllers store and interpolate animation values. For our purposes, we'll be using a "LookAt" controller. A LookAt controller makes sure that whatever is assigned to it is always aligned with (looking at) a target. For example, the most common use of a LookAt controller is to make sure an animated character's eyes are looking at a target object. For each eye, you would assign a LookAt controller and link it to a target object the eyes are supposed to follow. In our case, we'll assign a LookAt controller to the piston and link it to the shaft's pivot point. That way, when the shaft moves, the piston will follow.

44. Select **LookAt Constraint** from the Assign Rotation Controller list. In the LookAt Constraint rollout, click the **Add LookAt Target** button and then pick **shaft** from the Pick Object list.

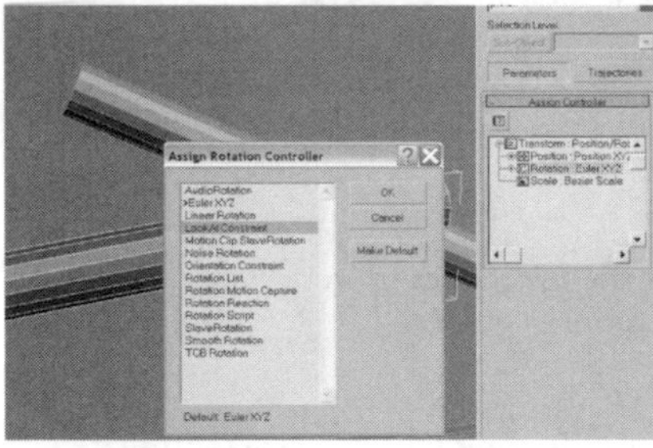

Figure 1-467

Figure 1-468

45. Under Select LookAt Axis, select **X;** this will be the axis that the piston will align to and is the reason I had you make sure the pivots for the piston and the shaft were facing each other.

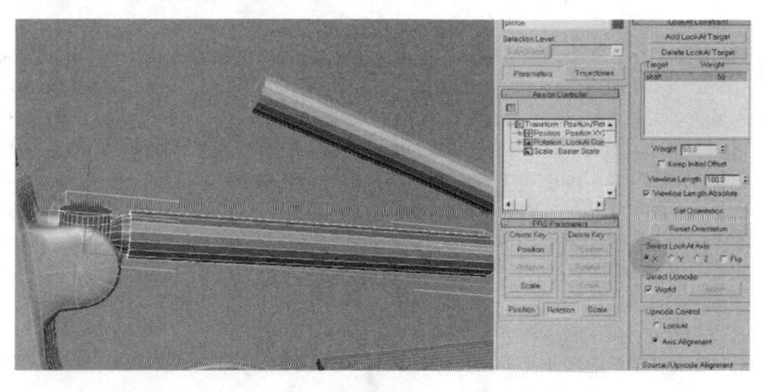

Figure 1-469

Fire Drill: So why is the piston turned? I deliberately did not tell you to make sure that not only the X pivots were facing each other, but that the Z axes had to be aligned in the same direction. Look back at Figures 1-464 and 1-465 and examine them closely. In 1-464, the shaft's pivot Y axis is pointing down, while its Z axis is pointing toward the front. In 1-465, however, the piston's pivot Z axis is pointing down and the Y axis is pointing back. This explains why, once we add the LookAt constraint, the piston rotates 90 degrees. The LookAt constraint is working perfectly, ensuring that the X axes are aligned. But to do so required Max to rotate the shaft. Fortunately, this is easily fixed by rotating the piston's pivot to align its Z axis with that of the shaft's pivot.

46. Select **Affect Pivot Only** and use the Rotate tool to rotate the piston's pivot until it is aligned.

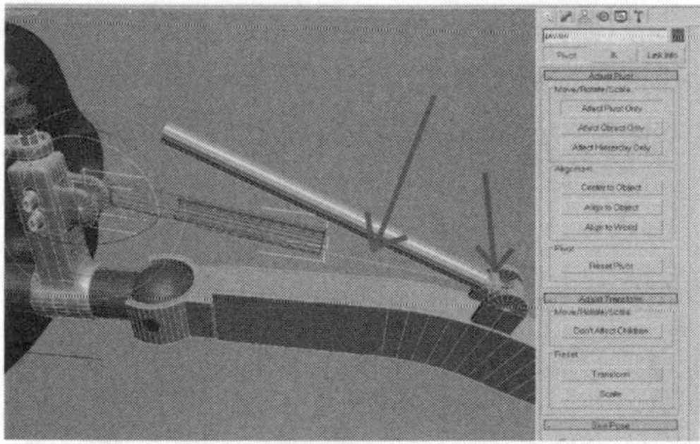

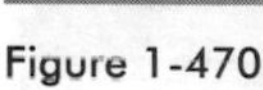

Figure 1-470

Figure 1-471

FYI: Notice a thin blue line in Figure 1-470. That indicates the linkage of the LookAt controller to its target.

Fire Drill: At this point, we're going to run into some difficulty when we try to assign a LookAt controller to the shaft, with the piston's pivot as a target. Because we've already constrained the piston's pivot to "look at" the shaft's pivot, Max won't let us use the piston's pivot as a target for a LookAt constraint assigned to the shaft. To get around this, we'll use a dummy, linked to the shaft, as a target.

A *dummy* is a non-rendering object that is designed for situations just like this. It's simply a non-rendering object.

47. Under the Create panel, click the **Helper** button (looks like a tape measure), click the **Dummy** button, and create a Dummy object between the stanchions on the hydraulic pump. Select and Link the dummy to the piston and Link the piston to the hydraulic pump.

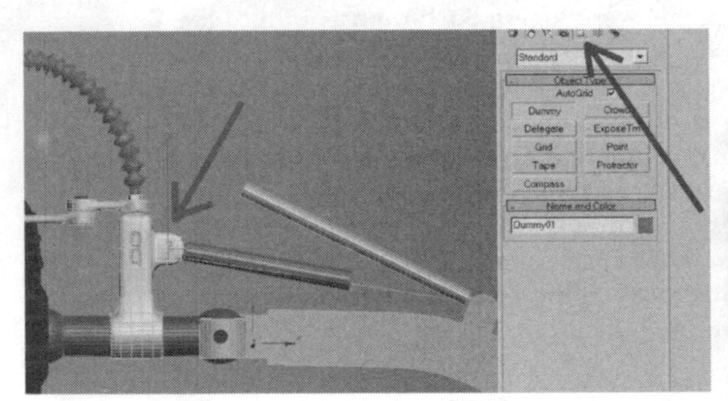

Figure 1-472

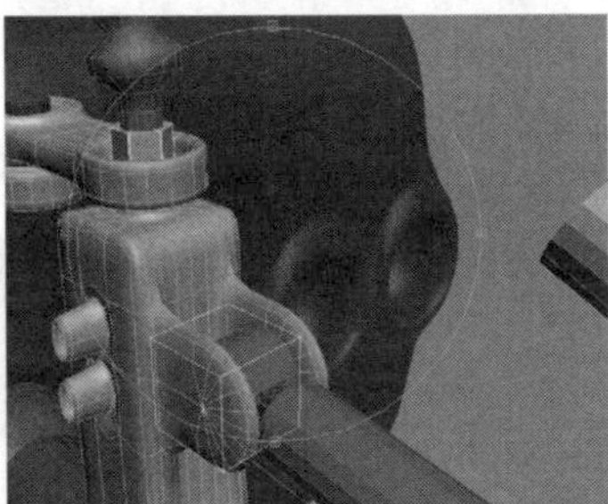

Figure 1-473

48. Select and Link the shaft to the middle leg (not shown). Select the shaft and click the **Motion** tab (the fourth tab on the Create panel). In the Assign Controller rollout, select **Rotation: Euler XYZ** and click the **Assign** button (it has a question mark icon). A bunch of new rollouts will appear. Click **Add LookAt Target** and pick **Dummy01** from the list.

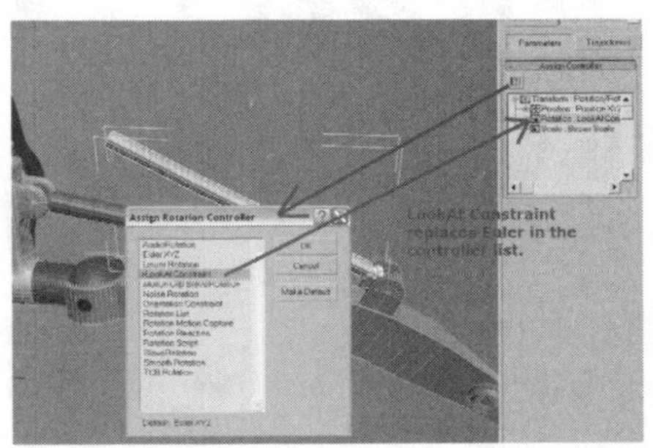

Figure 1-474

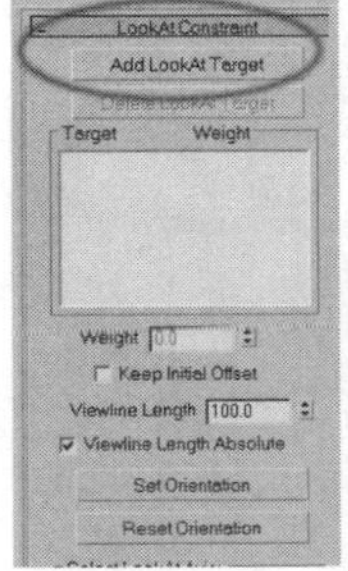

Figure 1-475

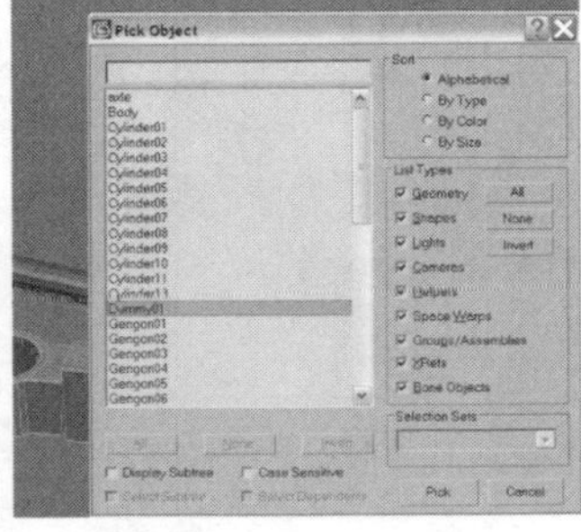

Figure 1-476

49. Align the dummy's pivots to coincide with the shaft's (the blue line from this constraint should converge with that of the previous

constraint). Then select the tip of the shaft and scale it to comfortably fit within the piston.

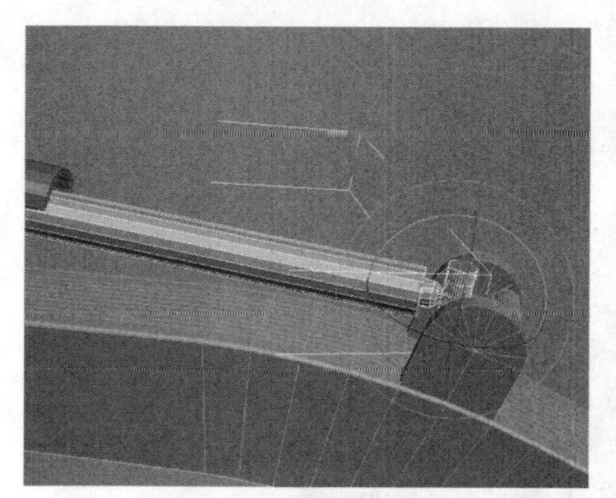
Figure 1-477

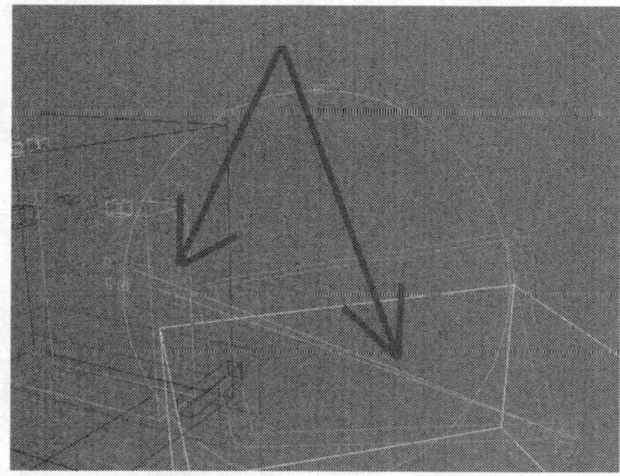
Figure 1-478

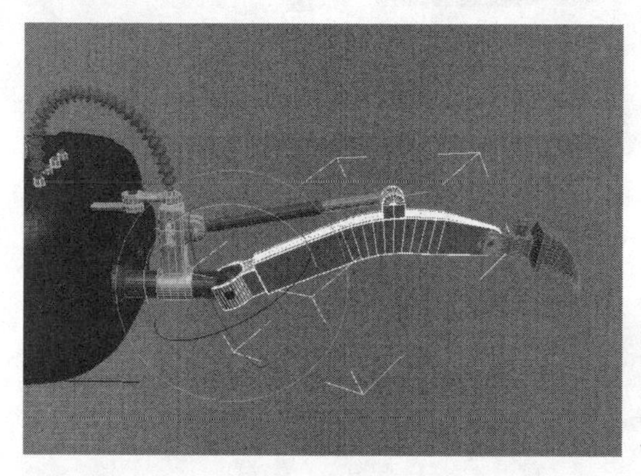
Figure 1-479: Now, when you move the middle leg, the shaft will move in and out of the piston the way a normal piston would work.

50. Repeat steps 20-30 and 32-49 to attach the claw to the middle leg stanchion.

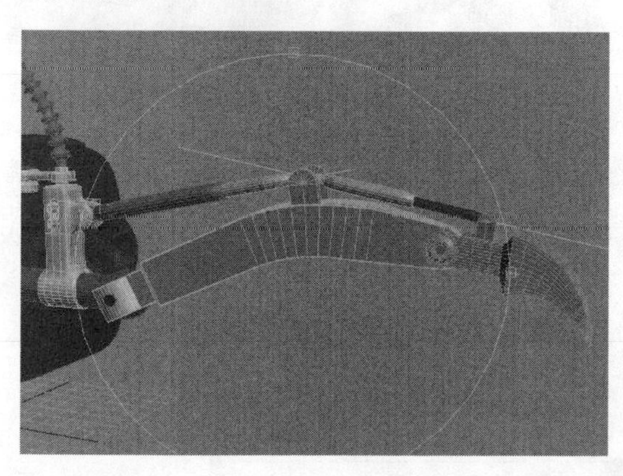
Figure 1-480: Now, when you move the middle leg, both pistons should work.

51. Create a Cylinder on top of the first piston (the one attached to the hydraulic pump), about three-fourths of the way down the shaft. Convert it to an Editable Polygon and delete the bottom-facing polygon.

Radius	Height	Height/Cap Segs	Sides	Smooth
1.5	2.6	1/1	32	Checked

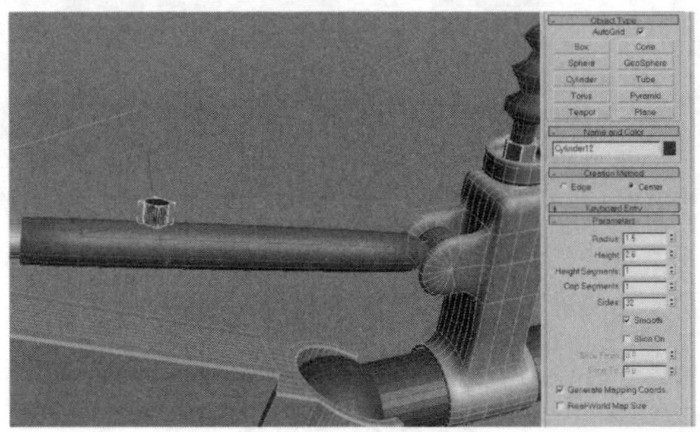

Figure 1-481

52. Select the piston, click **Attach List**, and attach the cylinder you just created.

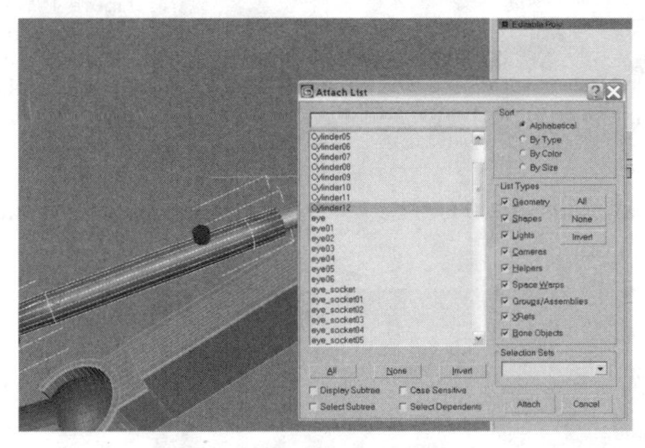

Figure 1-482

53. Select the polygon on top of the cylinder you just attached, and click **Bevel Settings:**

Type	Height	Outline	Apply/OK
Group	0	–0.1	Apply
Group	0	–0.25	Apply

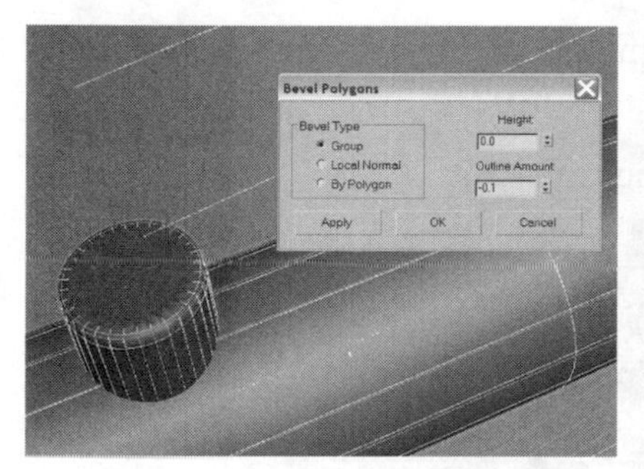

Figure 1-483

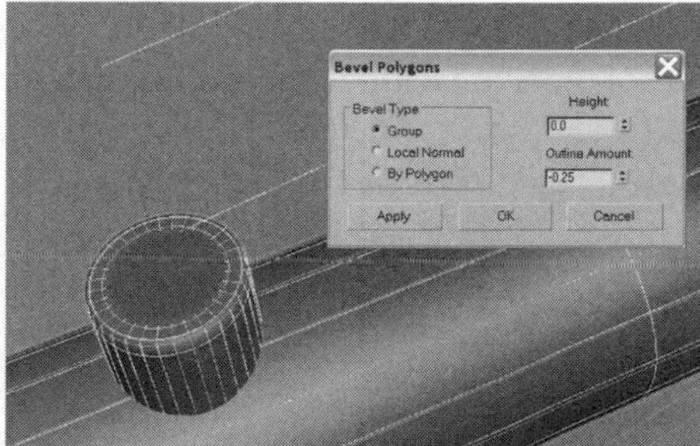

Figure 1-484

Type	Height	Outline	Apply/OK
Group	–0.4	0	OK

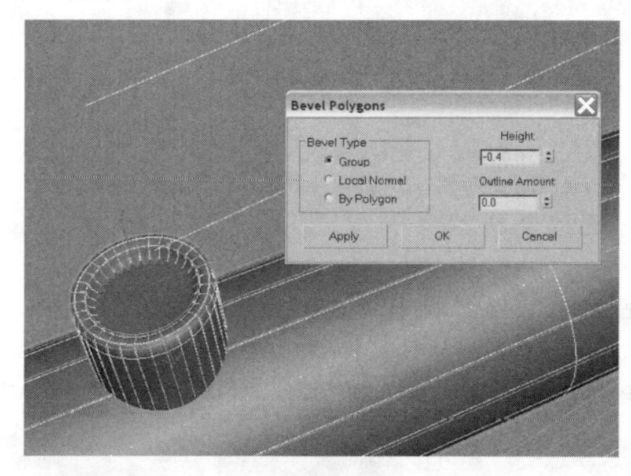

Figure 1-485

54. Click **Detach** and change the label to **piston_mount**, then Select and Link it to the piston.

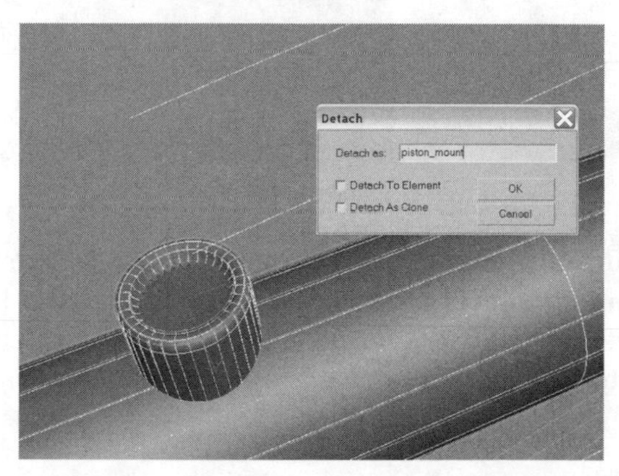

Figure 1-486

55. Repeat steps 51-54 to create a mount on the claw piston, on the outside facing front. Call it **piston_mount02**.

56. Create a Hose like the one in Figure 1-487.

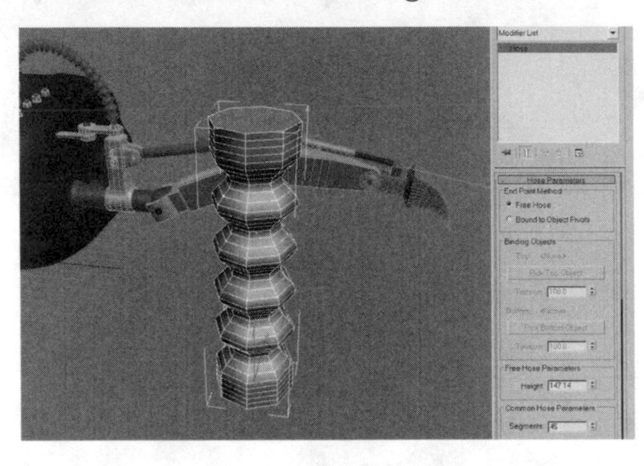

Figure 1-487

Don't Forget: I promised you in the FYI box at the end of the last section that we would use the polygons we detached from the hydraulic pump and called hydraulic_anchor. Well ... that time is now.

57. Switch the hose from Free to **Bound to Object Pivots**. Click **Pick Top Object**, hit **H**, and select **hydraulic_anchor** from the list. Then click **Pick Bottom Object**, hit **H**, and select **piston_mount**.

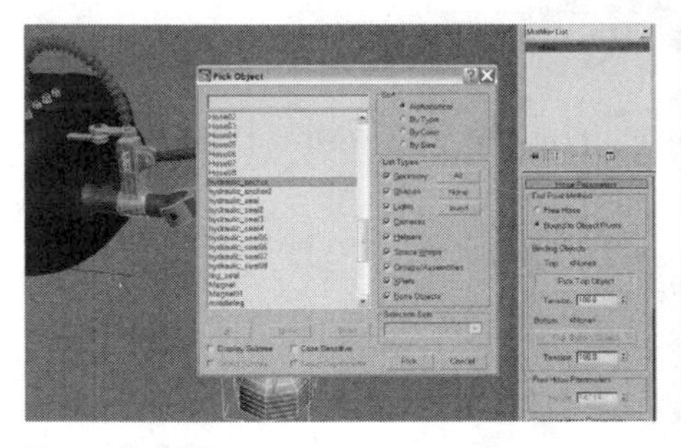

Figure 1-488

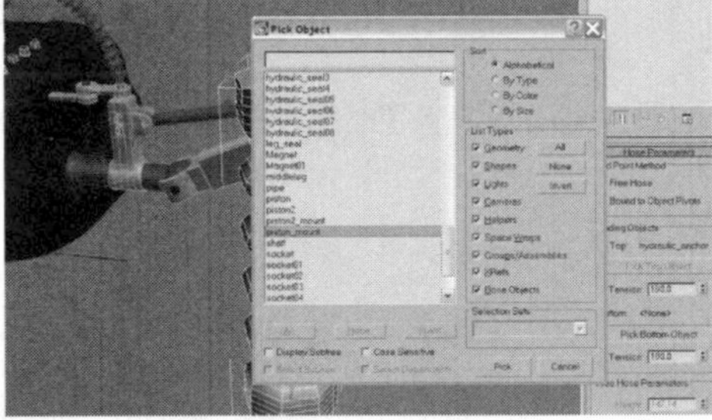

Figure 1-489

58. Select **hydraulic_anchor** and **piston_mount** and center their pivots by choosing **Center to Object**. Set the Top Tension to **83**, the Bottom Tension to **20**, the Segments to **70**, the Diameter to **1.5**, and the Sides to **16**.

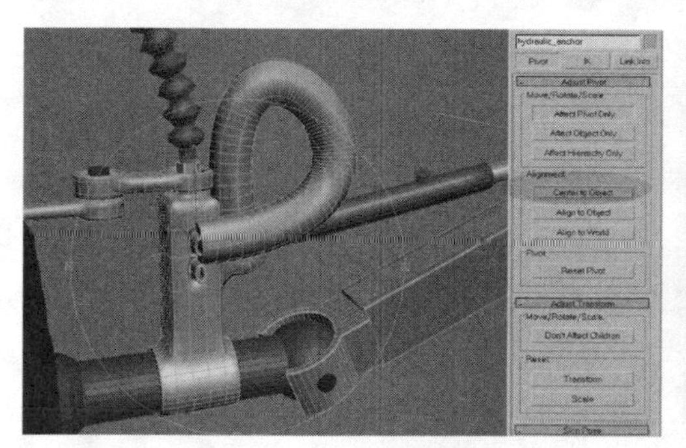
Figure 1-490

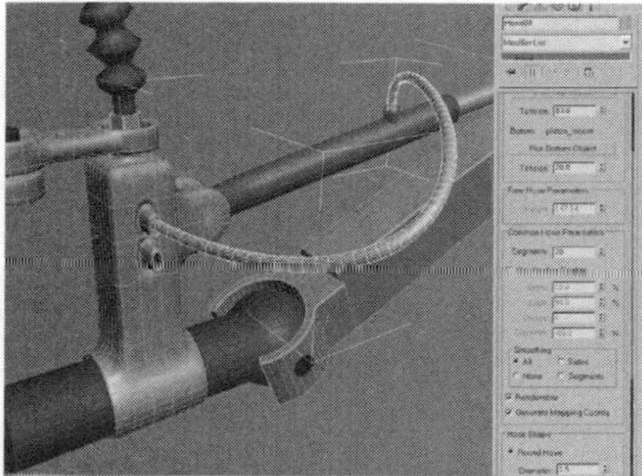
Figure 1-491

59. Repeat steps 56-58 to create a hose connecting hydraulic_anchor02 to piston_mount02.

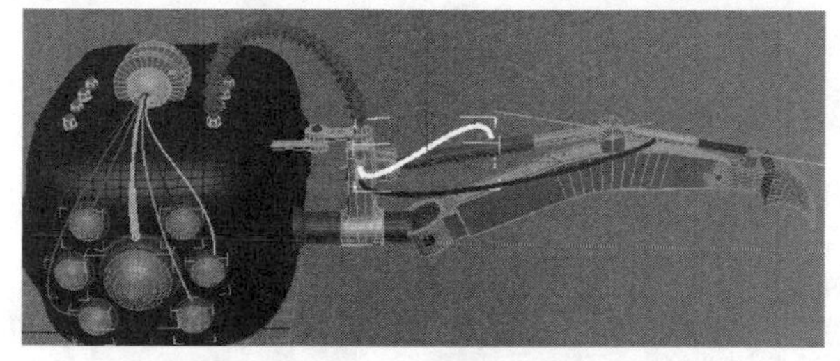
Figure 1-492

60. Select the polygons shown in Figure 1-493.

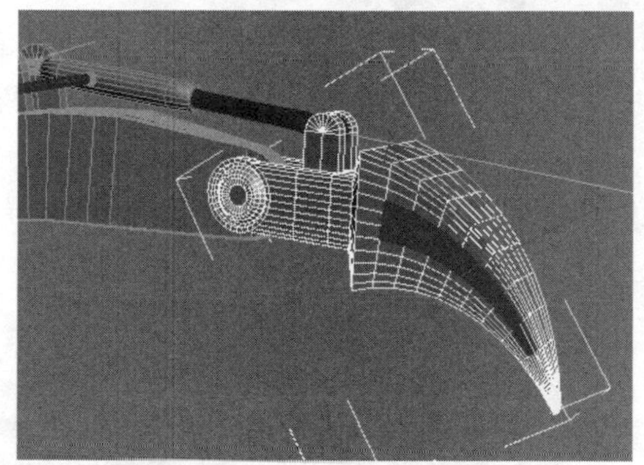
Figure 1-493

61. Click **Bevel Settings:**

Type	Height	Outline	Apply/OK
Group	–1.0	–1.0	OK

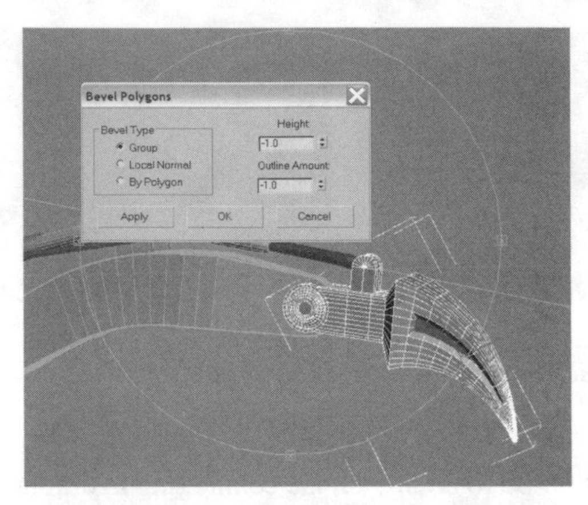

Figure 1-494

62. Select the polygons on the top of the claw as shown in Figure 1-495.

Figure 1-495

63. Click **Bevel Settings** and then add a Smooth modifier to the stack. Collapse the stack.

Type	Height	Outline	Apply/OK
Group	1.0	–0.3	OK

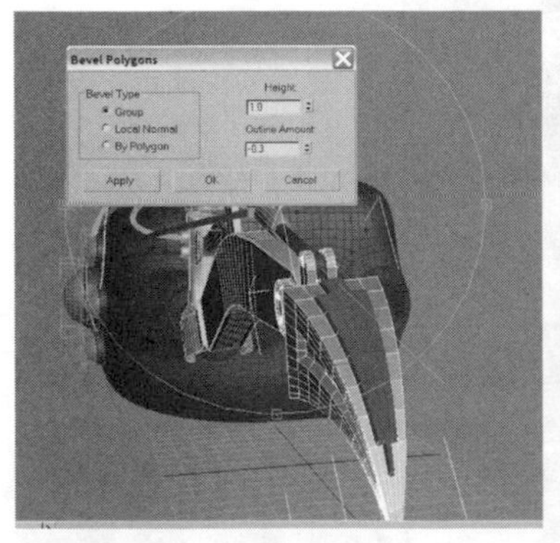

Figure 1-496

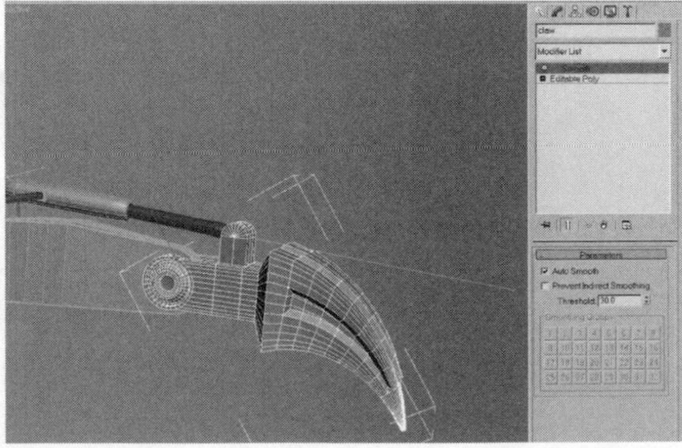

Figure 1-497

64. Select the 11 polygons shown in Figure 1-498 on both the front and back sides of the middle leg.

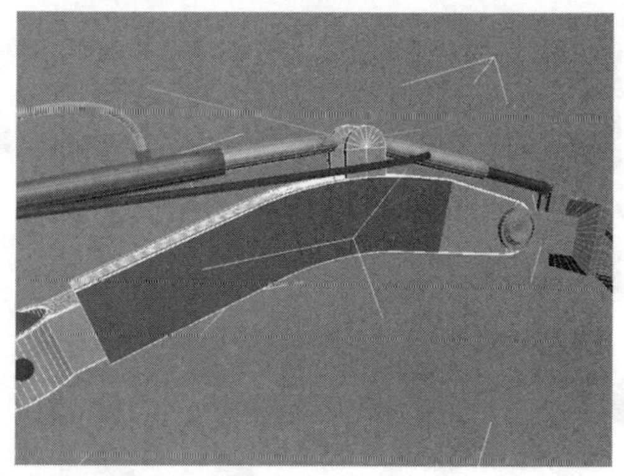

Figure 1-498

65. Click **Bevel Settings:**

Type	Height	Outline	Apply/OK
By Polygon	0.1	–1.2	OK

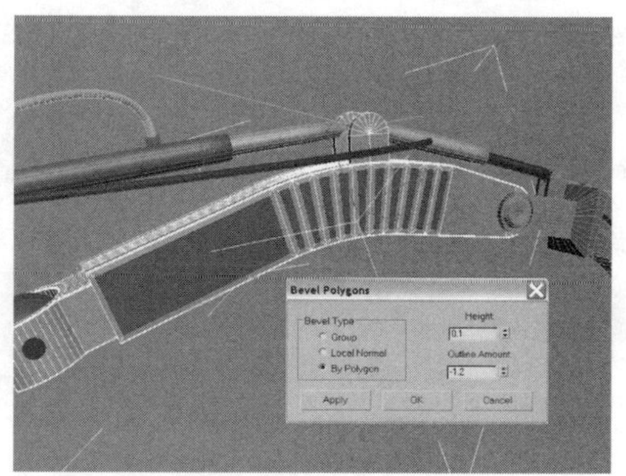

Figure 1-499

66. Add a Smooth modifier to the stack and then collapse the stack.

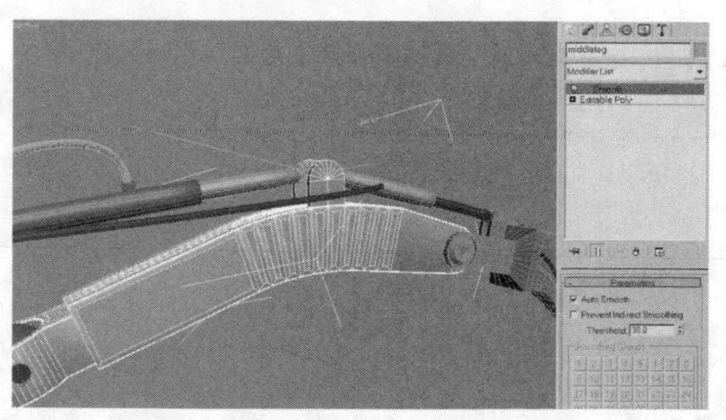

Figure 1-500

67. Add a Smooth modifier to the upper leg's stack and then collapse the stack.

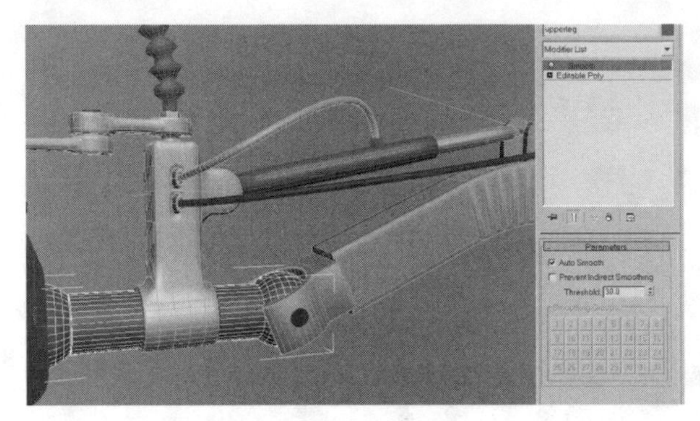

Figure 1-501

Day 7: Creating the Remaining Legs

1. Select the components making up the leg as shown below.

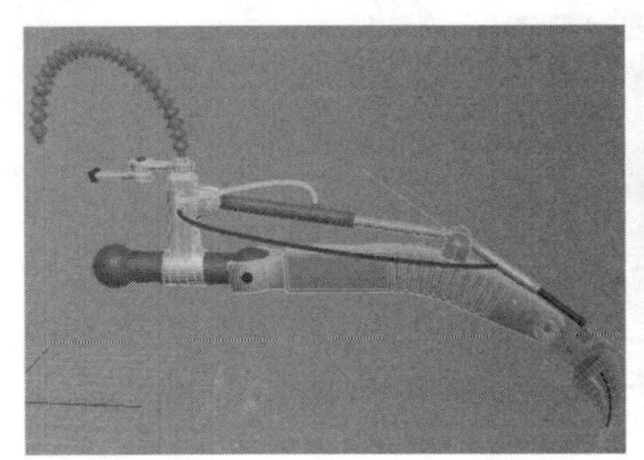

Figure 1-502

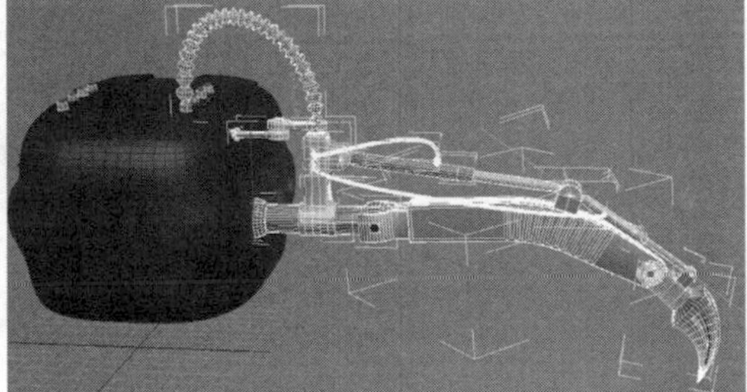

Figure 1-503

2. Shift-drag in the Y axis to create a clone; be sure it is aligned with the socket.

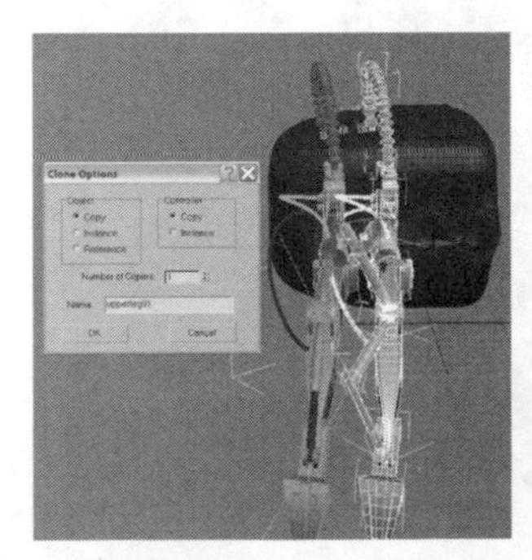

Figure 1-504

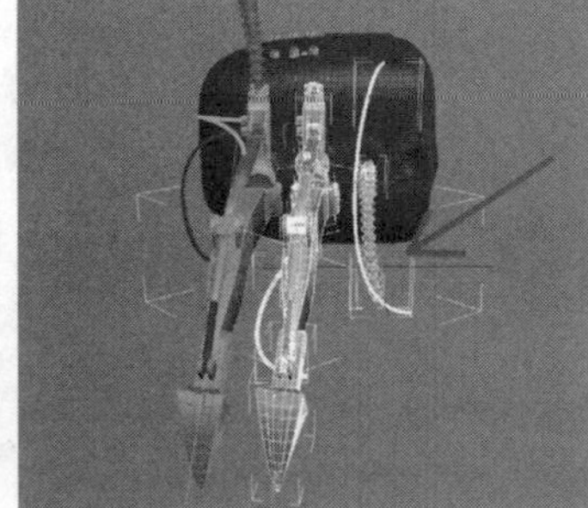

Figure 1-505

Fire Drill: You can see from Figure 1-505 that constrained objects get — what's the technical term? — seriously jacked up when you clone them. Max does not automatically update constraints when you create a clone. So ... you have to select each constrained clone and update its constraint target to the new target.

3. Select a cloned hose, open the Modify panel, and assign its binding object to cloned versions.

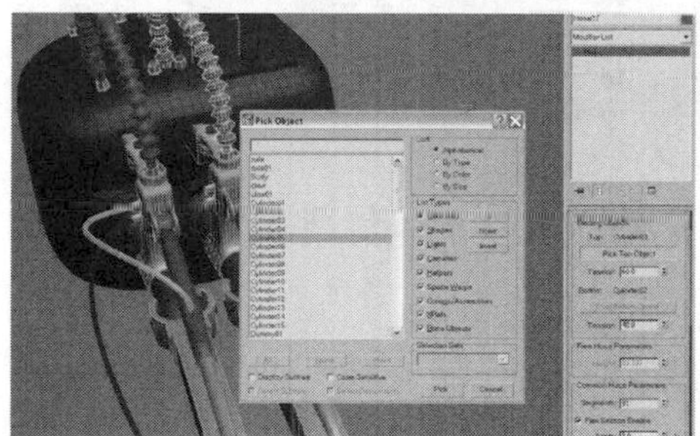

Figure 1-506

Figure 1-507

4. Reattach the hoses to their cloned binding objects and check that the pistons' and shafts' LookAt constraints are attached to the right objects. Make sure the legs and claw are still linked together.

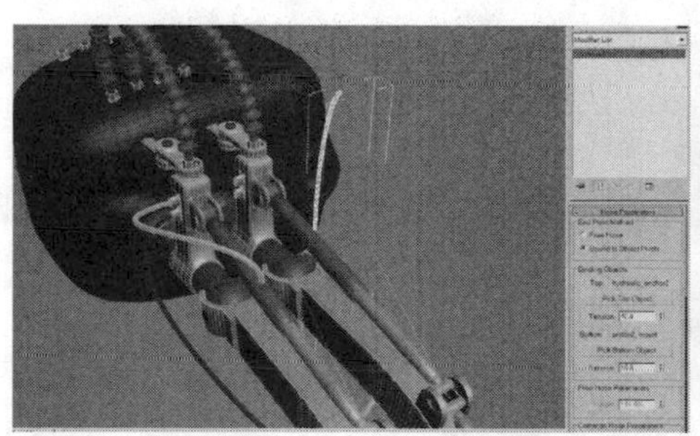

Figure 1-508

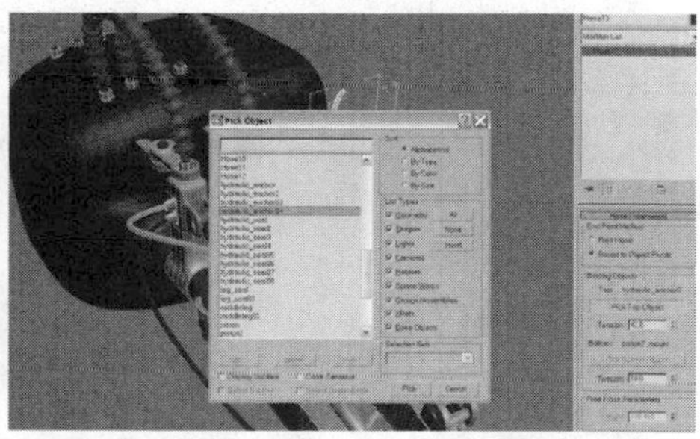

Figure 1-509

5. Select all the leg clements again and clone them into the next socket. Reconnect all the bindings and constraints, and then clone a leg into the last socket.

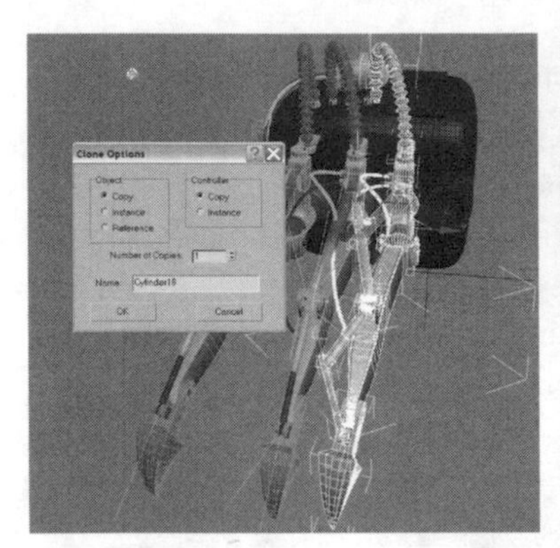

Figure 1-510

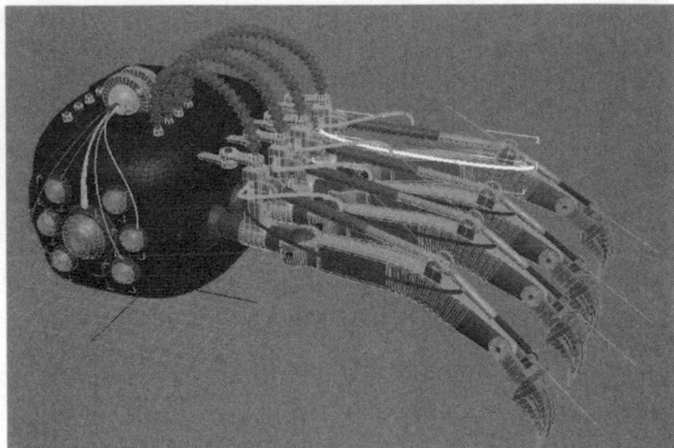

Figure 1-511

FYI: At this point, we'd normally mirror clone the objects and be done. However, Max has other ideas. Not only do you get the same problem with linkages, but the hoses inexplicably get turned inside out. Rather than fixing them, it's easier just to make new ones.

6. Select all the front leg's elements, *except the hoses*, and clone them into the first socket on the left side. Reconnect all the bindings and constraints, and then create new hoses. Select the front left leg and clone it to create the remaining left legs.

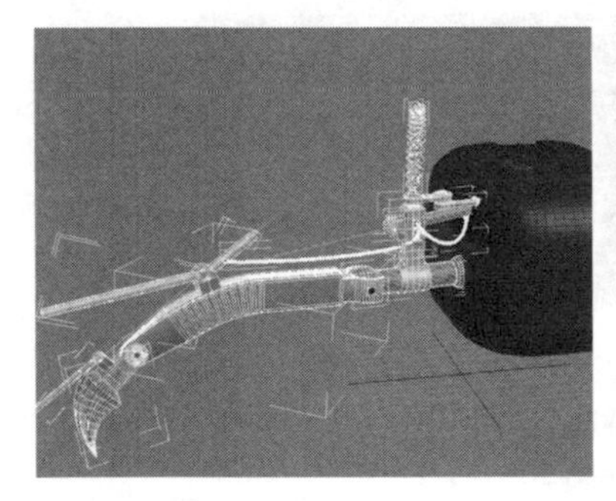

Figure 1-512

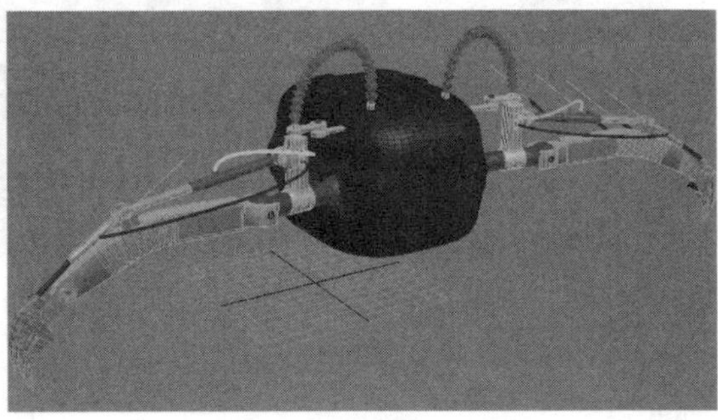

Figure 1-513

7. When you've added all the legs, hit **F9** to do a render and you're done!

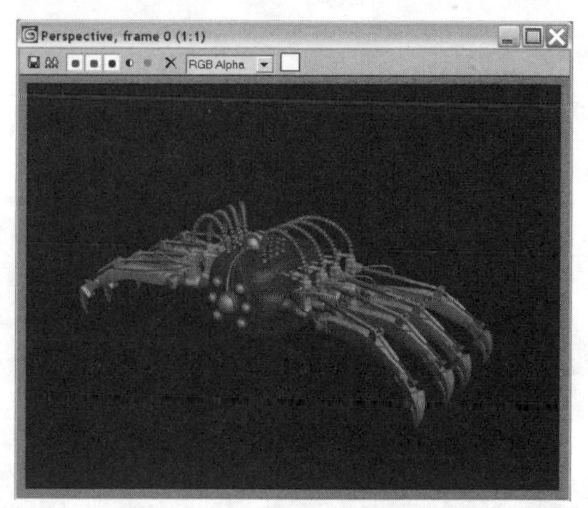

Figure 1-514

Why Doesn't My Model Look Real?

One of the first things you need to understand about 3D modeling — guess I should've mentioned this first, huh? — is that your finished product, no matter how good the model, is going to look like crap. Or ... in this case, a child's toy rather than a menacing purveyor of carnage. The reason? Materials.

You ever see a 1970 Hemi 'Cuda without its paint job? Pretty unimpressive. Okay, a 1970 Hemi 'Cuda is pretty impressive with or without paint. But you see my point: Materials make all the difference in the world. If you want to learn how to slap a nifty paint job on your spider bot, check out the three materials videos on the companion DVD.

This is the hunter-killer bot we create in Chapter 2, complete with texture and lighting.

Chapter 2
Hunter-Killer

Unlike the lowly maintenance bot, the hunter-killer has become a staple in nearly every science fiction video game and film. Less intellectually sophisticated than a droid and not as heavily armored as a mech, hunter-killers are antipersonnel bots designed for maximum agility over any terrain.

While most people credit James Cameron for the creation of the hunter-killer in *Terminator II: Judgment Day*, I would argue that the first hunter-killer I ever saw was in 1979. I speak of Don Coscarelli's dreaded chrome ball from the movie *Phantasm*. Like most hunter-killers, the chrome ball was capable of hovering and fast pursuit, and had a limited form of artificial intelligence as well as the single purpose of killing people.

While I still find the prospect of a chrome ball hooking itself into my flesh and drilling a hole into my brain to be chilling, it's just not that interesting to model. So … we are going to go the route of the HKs from *Terminator II* and *Deus Ex II*.

Urgent: This is a very high-polygon model, meaning you'll need a fast machine and a lot of memory. So why include it? Well … there are a lot of interesting things to build and learn in this chapter (e.g., making working pistons). If you don't feel your computer can handle the whole thing, just do the parts that interest you (e.g., the engines). I actually prefer to build high-poly models because I love their intricacies and the way they look when they're done.

Day 1: Building the Eye-Pod

1. Create a Sphere with a Radius of **30** and **32** Segments.

Figure 2-1

2. Switch to the Front view, turn on **Angle Snap**, and Rotate **90** degrees in the Y axis so that the poles are now on the right and left sides instead of the top and bottom.

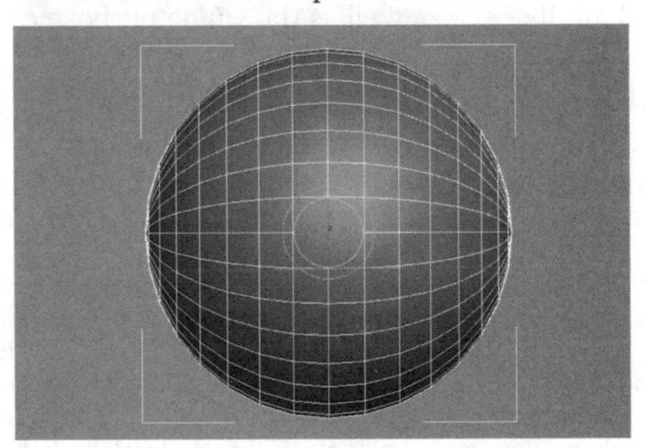

Figure 2-2

3. Convert it to an Editable Polygon and select the 320 large polygons that make up the middle of the sphere.

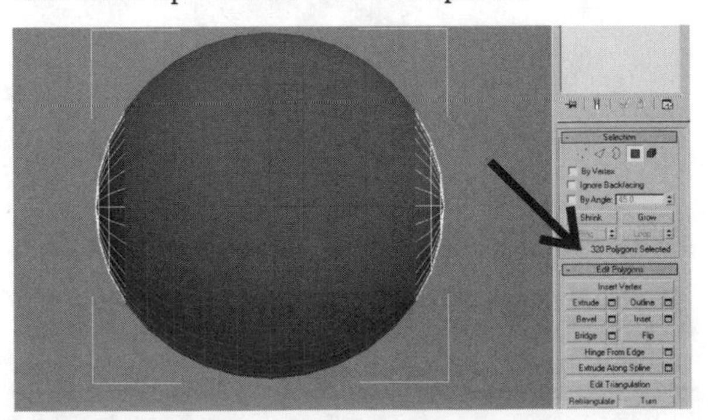

Figure 2-3

Don't Forget: It helps to switch back and forth between wireframe and shaded mode (F3) when selecting polygons, especially in tricky objects like tubes.

4. Click **Detach** and label the object **eye_pod.**

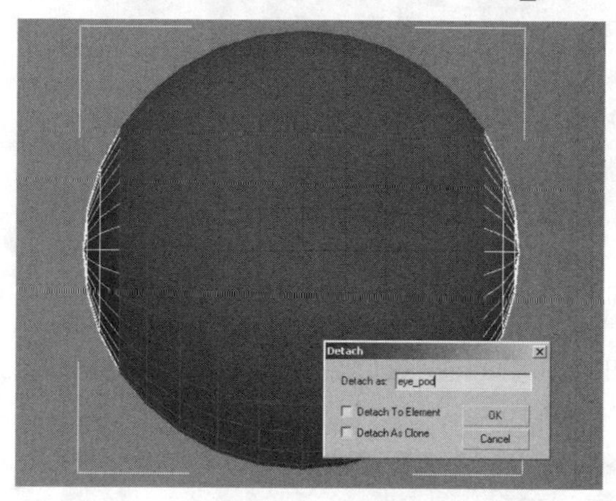

Figure 2-4

5. Rename the remaining two sides **eye_brace** and hide them.

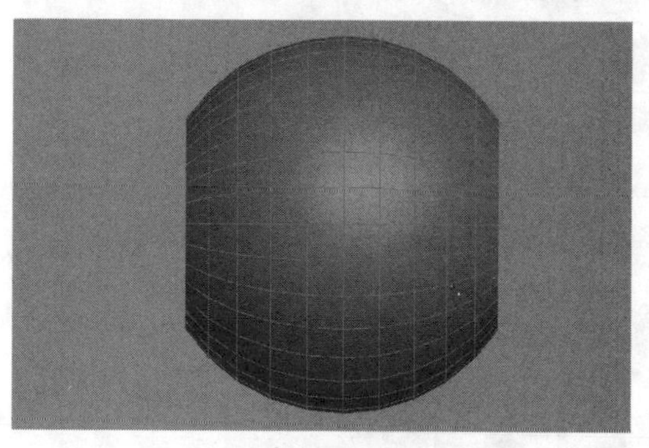

Figure 2-5

6. Using AutoGrid, create a Tube that is roughly the size of the smallest polygon on the eye_pod's surface.

Radius 1	Radius 2	Height	Height/Cap Segs	Sides	Smooth
1.6	1.8	0.64	1/1	32	Checked

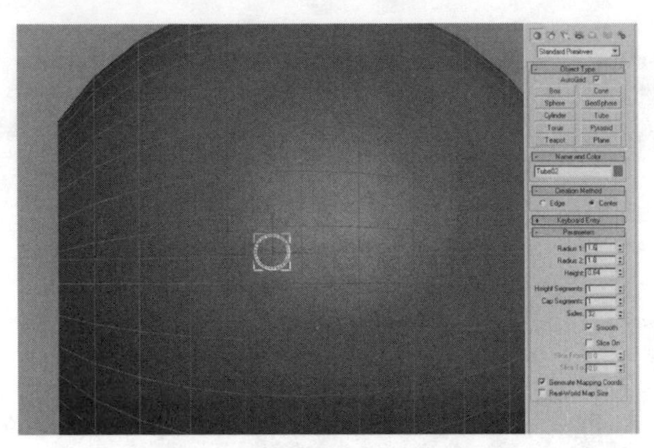

Figure 2-6

7. Convert the tube to an Editable Polygon, rename it **eye_socket**, and delete the back-facing polygons (i.e., the ones facing the sphere that no one will see). Then select the polygons inside the eye_socket and delete them too.

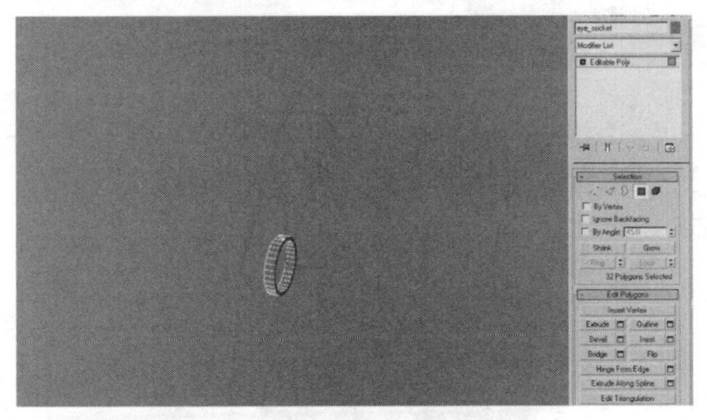

Figure 2-7

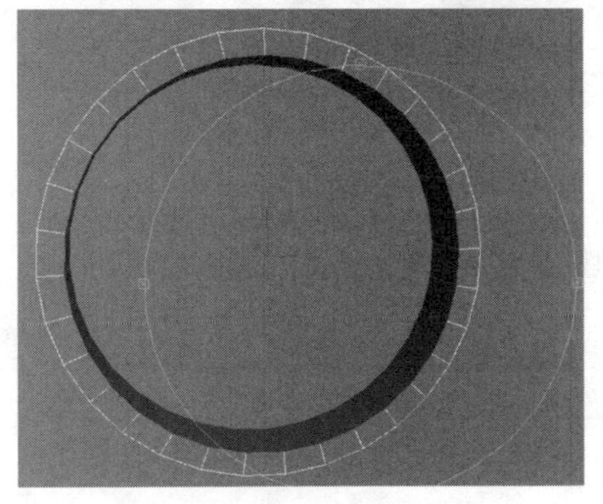

Figure 2-8

8. Select the outer and inner edges of the tube and Chamfer them, first by **0.03** and then by **0.01**.

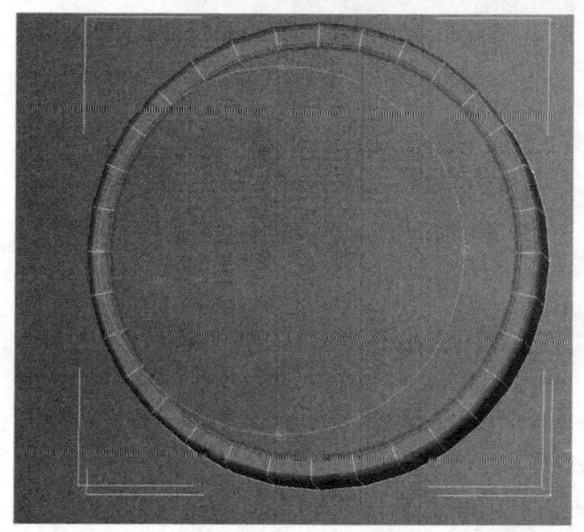

Figure 2-9

Don't Forget: You don't need to Chamfer the edge facing the eye_pod because it'll be beneath the surface and not visible.

9. Using AutoGrid, create a Sphere in the center of the eye_socket with a Radius of **1.616**, **32** Segments, and **0.5** for the Hemisphere setting. Use the Move tool to raise the sphere to the lip of the socket.

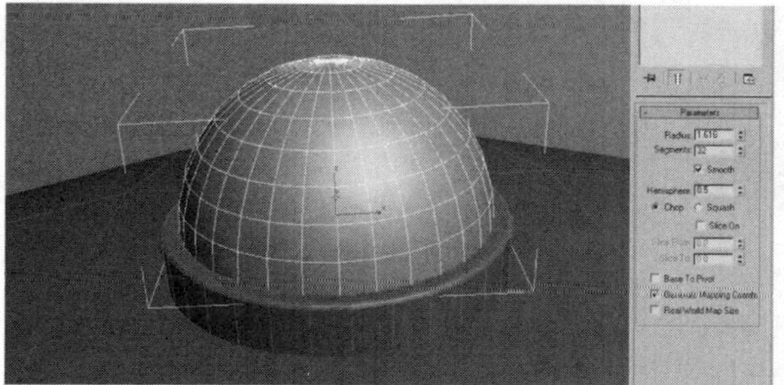

Figure 2-10

10. Convert the sphere to an Editable Polygon, rename it **eye_ball**, and delete the back-facing polygons (those facing the eye_pod); this is easier to do in wireframe.

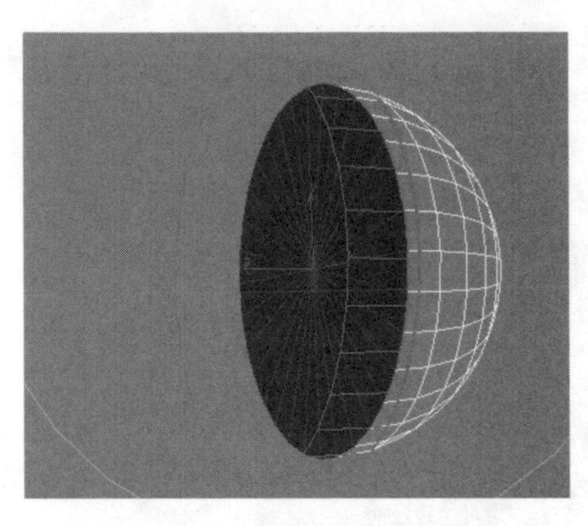

Figure 2-11

11. Select the **eye_socket** panel, attach the **eye_ball**, then switch to Vertex selection mode, select all the vertices on the eye_socket and the eye_ball, and click **Weld** (using a threshold of **0.01**) to weld them together into a single object (vertices should drop from 577 to 542). Rename the merged object **eye.**
12. Select the **eye_pod** and the **eye** and hide them.
13. Unhide the **eye_brace** and delete one side (we'll Mirror it later).
14. Switch to the Right view and zoom in on the eye_brace. Create a Sphere using AutoGrid with a Radius of **0.75**, **32** Segments, and **0.5** for the Hemisphere setting and name it **rivet.**

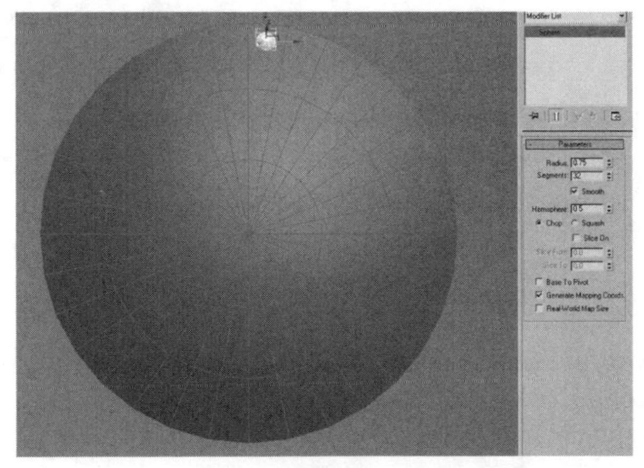

Figure 2-12

15. Convert it to an Editable Polygon, then switch to Perspective view, select the back-facing polygons, and delete them.

Figure 2-13

16. Switch to the Right view (if you switched the view in the previous step), click the Hierarchy tab, and click **Affect Pivot Only.**

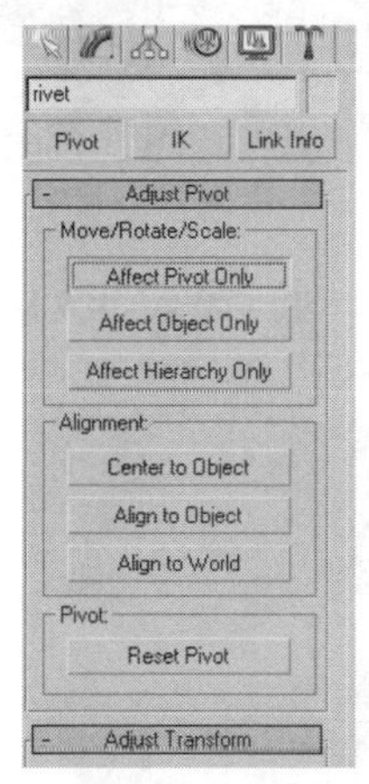

Figure 2-14

17. Use the Move tool to move the rivet's pivot point to the center of the brace. Turn off **Affect Pivot Only.**

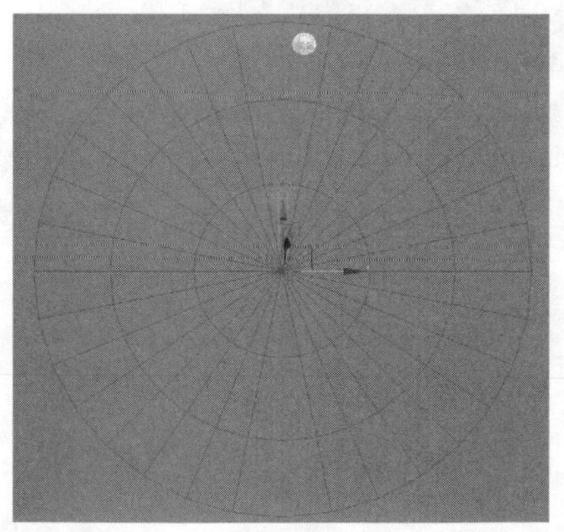

Figure 2-15

18. Select the **Rotate** tool, hold down the **Shift** key, and rotate **–11.23** degrees in the Z axis. Then select **Copy** and type **31** for Number of Copies. Click **OK**.

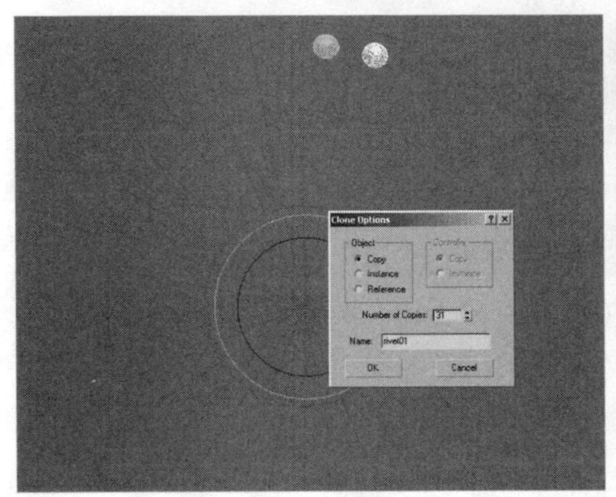

Figure 2-16

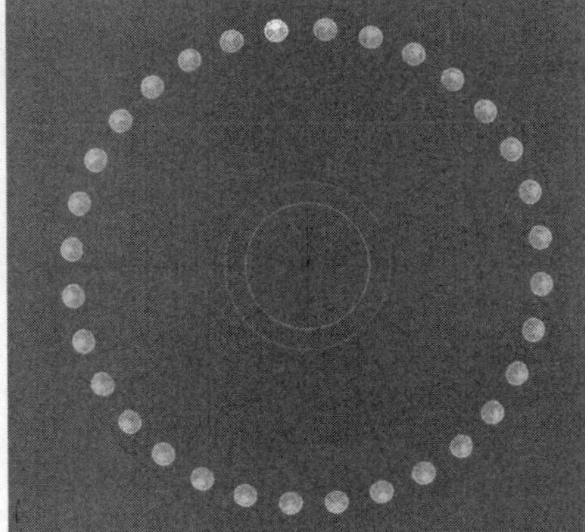

Figure 2-17

19. Arc Rotate around the bracket in the Perspective view to make sure all the clones are penetrating the brace.

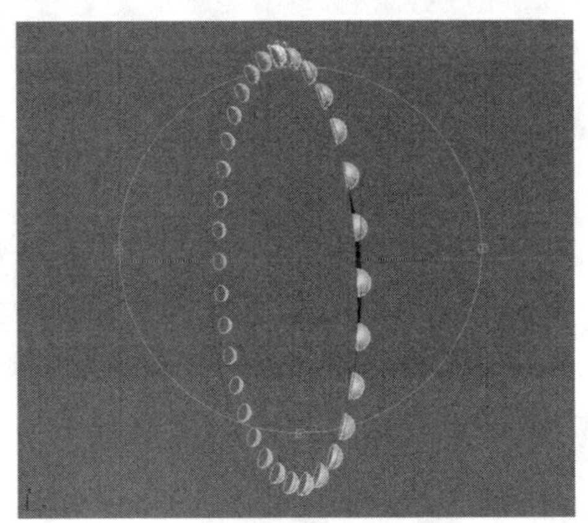

Figure 2-18

20. Select the **bracket**, click **Attach List**, and attach all the rivets.

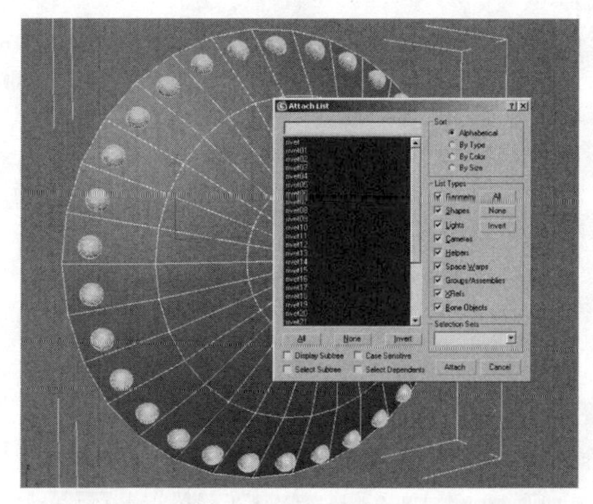

Figure 2-19

21. Unhide the **eye_pod.**

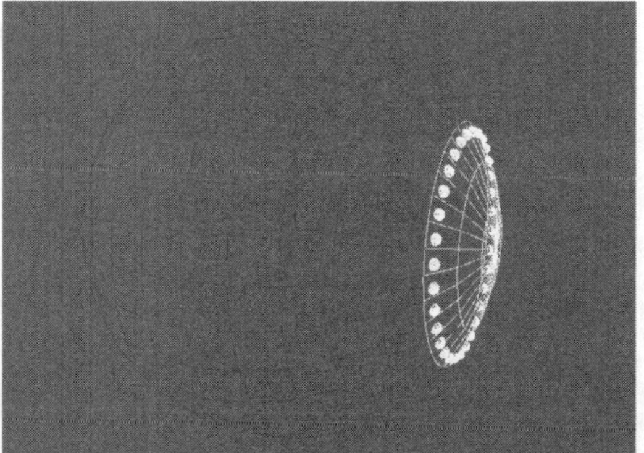

Figure 2-20

22. Mirror the brace in the X axis.

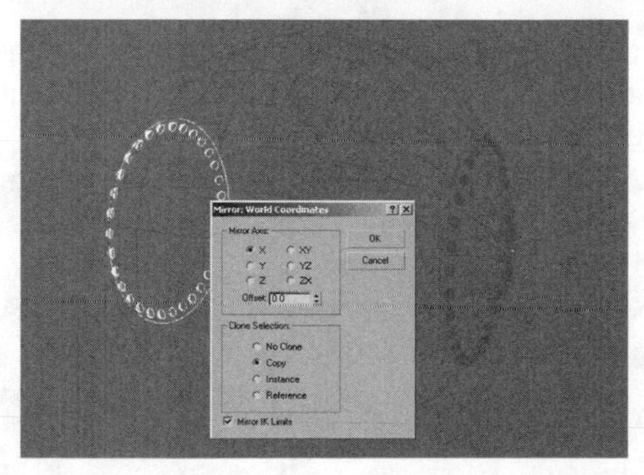

Figure 2-21

23. Select the **eye_pod**, click **Attach List**, and attach the braces to the eye_pod.

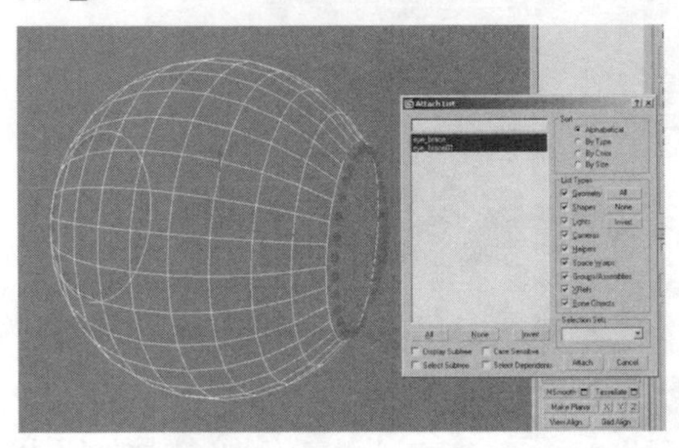

Figure 2-22

24. Select the center 32 polygons on both braces, delete them, and then Cap the borders.

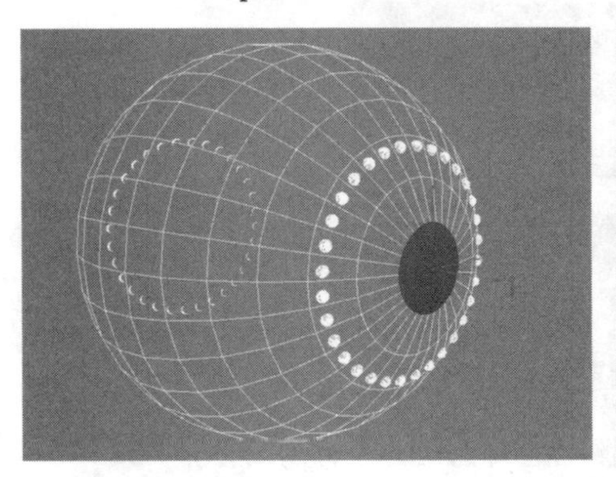

Figure 2-23

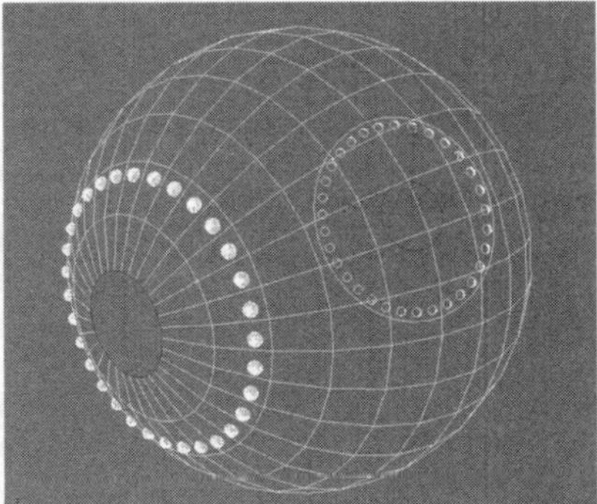

Figure 2-24

25. Switch to the Front view, select the caps, and Extrude the polygons **–29.316** or until they intersect in the center. Delete them, select the vertices, and then Weld them.

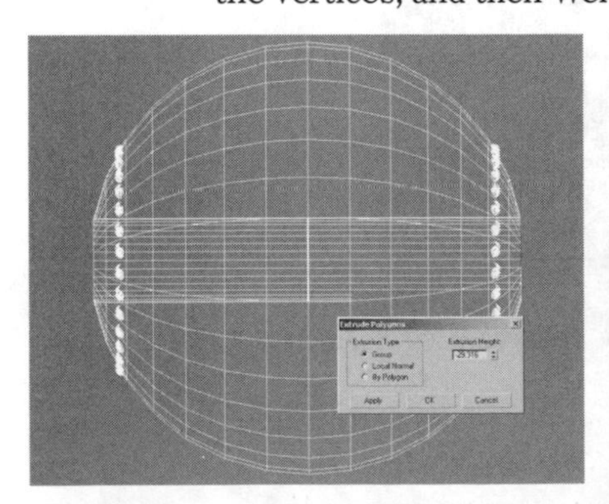

Figure 2-25

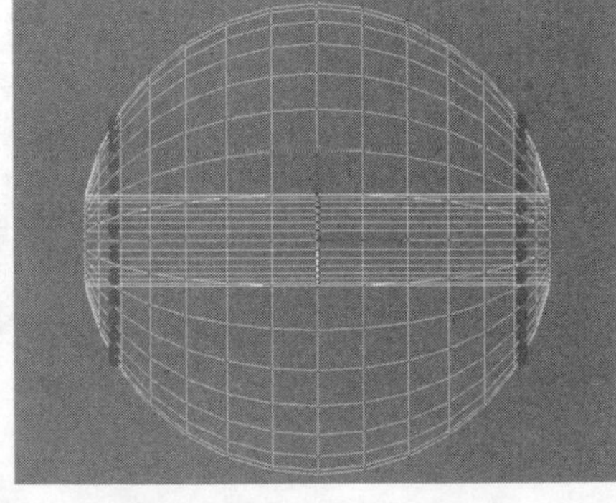

Figure 2-26

26. Select the borders of the tube you made, and Chamfer by **1** and then by **0.3**.

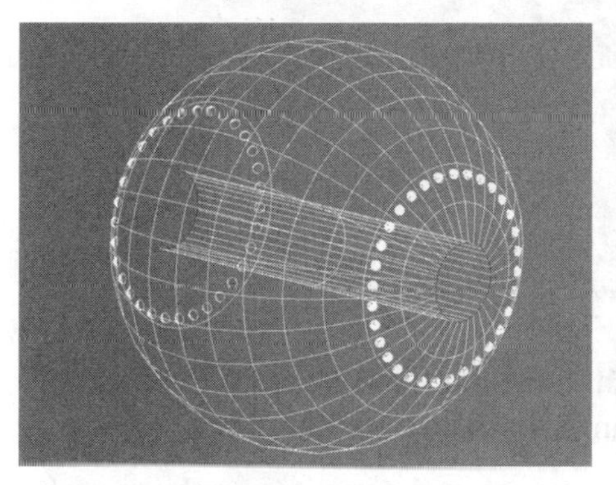

Figure 2-27

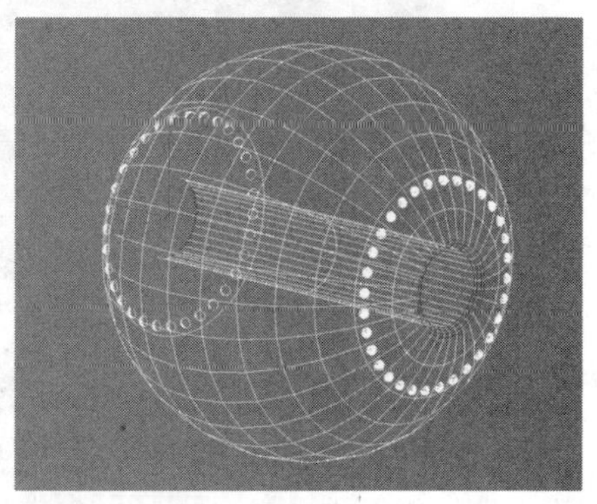

Figure 2-28

27. Add a Smooth modifier to the stack, click **Auto Smooth**, and then convert it to an Editable Polygon to collapse the stack.

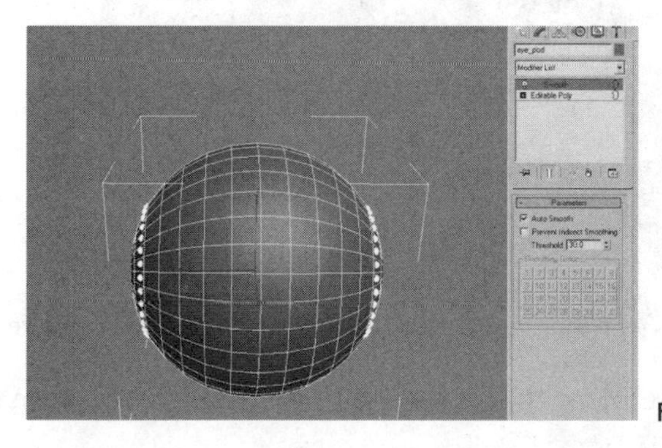

Figure 2-29

Day 2: Building the Engine Nacelles I

1. Switch back to the Front view.
2. Create a Tube with the following settings:

Radius 1	Radius 2	Height	Height/Cap Segs	Sides	Smooth
15	12	50	5/1	18	Checked

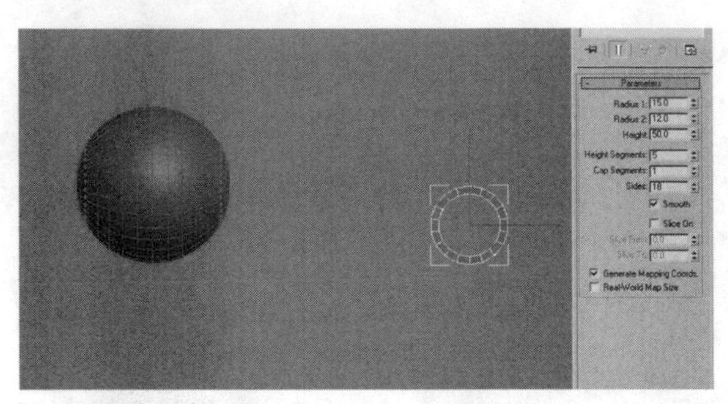

Figure 2-30

3. Hide the eye_pod and switch to the Left view. Convert the tube to an Editable Polygon and change its name to **L_nacelle**.
4. Switch to Vertex selection mode, select the vertices on the rear of the tube, and scale them down to **70%** in all three axes to make an exhaust nozzle.

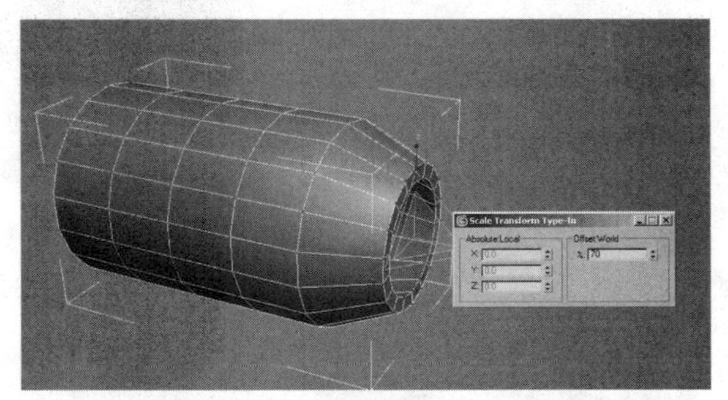

Figure 2-31

5. Repeat step 4 for the front vertices, but scale them down to **90%** in all three axes.
6. Switch to the Left view and select the nine polygons in the middle of the nacelle shown in Figure 2-32, and then Extrude them as a group **–2.0** (to recess them).

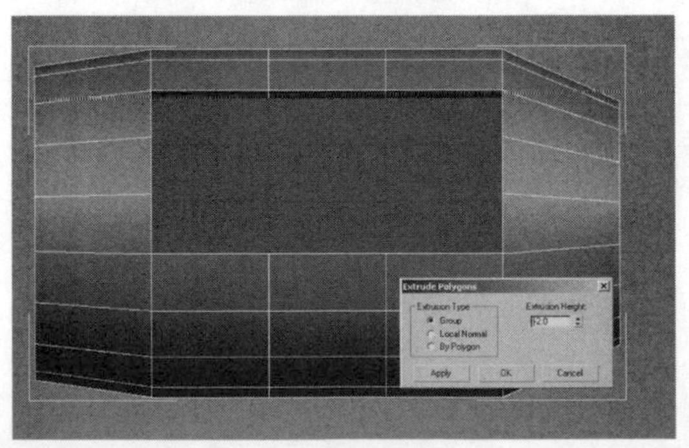

Figure 2-32

7. Select the top left and right polygons in the area you just recessed and under Edit Geometry, click the **Tessellate** button.

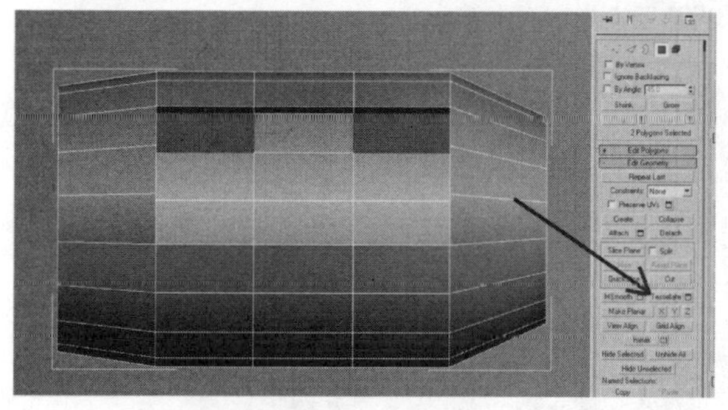

Figure 2-33

FYI: Tessellate subdivides an object (in this case dividing the selected polygon into four polygons). We are creating jacks for a wiring harness.

8. Select the top-left polygon and bottom-right polygon created by the tessellation.

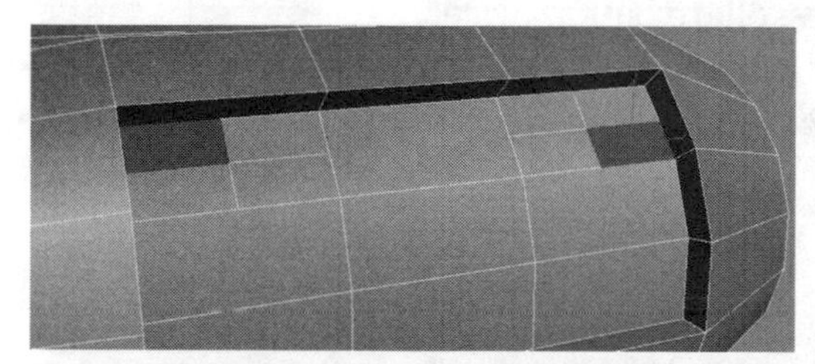

Figure 2-34

9. Click **Inset** and type **0.5** for the Inset Amount.

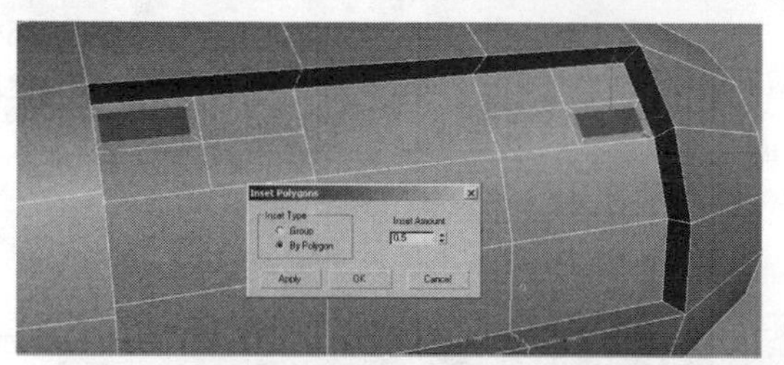

Figure 2-35

10. In the Perspective view, scale the polygons to **60** in the Y axis.

Figure 2-36

11. Set the Reference Coordinate system to **Local**, right-click the **Move** tool, and type **1.0** in the Offset Local Z axis (to raise the polys and form a crude pyramid).

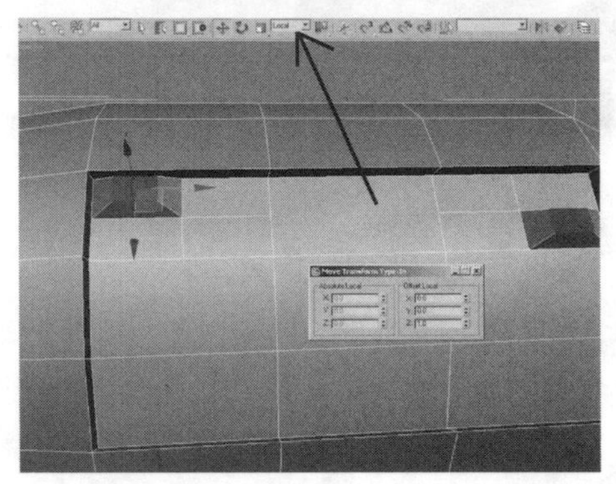

Figure 2-37

Urgent: Step 11 is an important step. Do not skip it! Otherwise, when you move the polygons they'll be at an off angle.

12. Hit the **Tessellate** button twice.

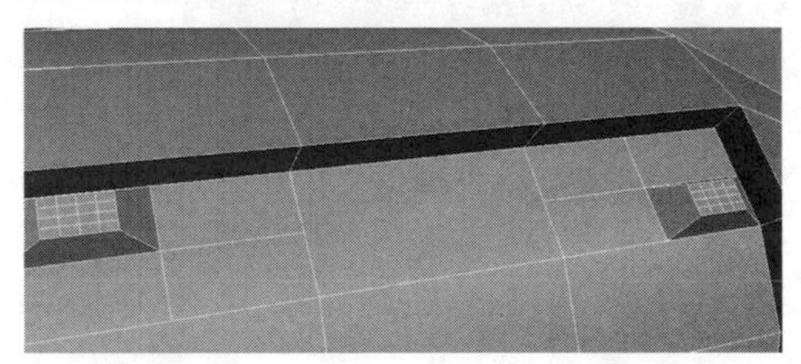

Figure 2-38

FYI: There's an easier way to do this this. Greeble is an excellent plug-in (max.klanky.com) that automatically creates geometry like on a Star Destroyer or Death Star. Best of all, it's free! Since I'm teaching you to model without plug-ins, we won't be using Greeble, but since it's free I encourage you to download it.

13. Select the polygons you just made through tessellation.

Figure 2-39

14. Zoom in tight on one, so you can better see what you're doing, and click **Bevel Settings**:

Type	Height	Outline	Apply/OK
By Polygon	0	–0.03	Apply
By Polygon	0.1	0	Apply
By Polygon	0	–0.04	OK

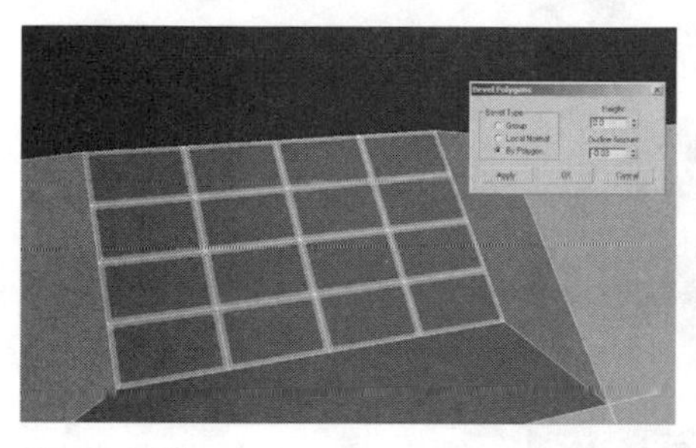

Figure 2-40

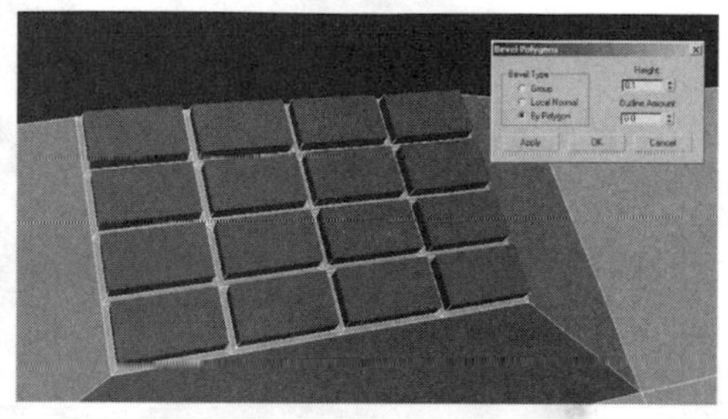

Figure 2-41

FYI: With regard to what this vent thing you're building does, Cris Robson (O'Blue) of 3d Palace, a great place for Max tutorials, said it best: "I have no idea what it does, but it looks cool." When you get a chance, check out some of the really cool (and free!) Max video tutorials available for downloading at www.3d-palace.com.

15. Scale by **50** in the local Y axis.

Figure 2-42

16. Extrude **–0.05**.

Figure 2-43

17. Under Edit Geometry, click **MSmooth**.

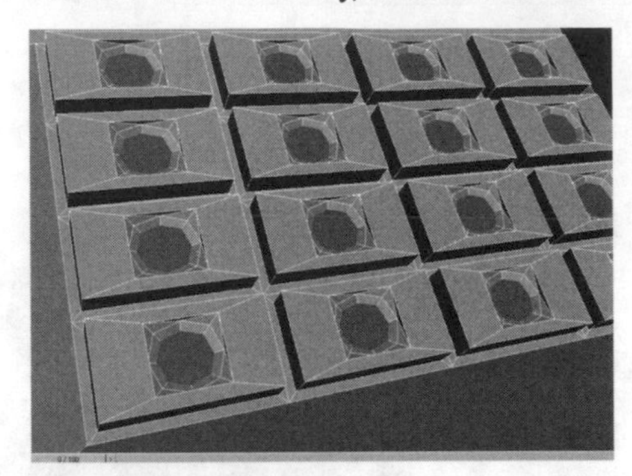

Figure 2-44

18. Click **Grow**.

Figure 2-45

19. Extrude **0.05**.

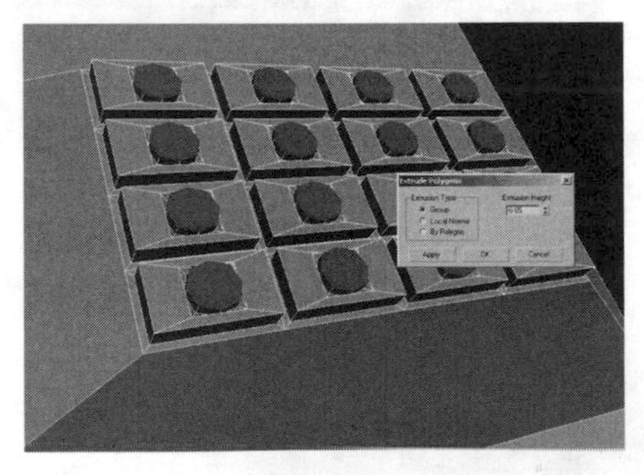

Figure 2-46

20. Click **Shrink**.

Figure 2-47

21. Click **Bevel Settings:**

Type	Height	Outline	Apply/OK
Group	–0.05	0	Apply
Group	0	–0.1	Apply
Group	0.1	0	Apply

Figure 2-48

Figure 2-49

Type	Height	Outline	Apply/OK
Group	0	–0.01	Apply
Group	0	–0.01	Apply
Group	–0.2	0	OK

Figure 2-50

22. Hit Render (**F9**).

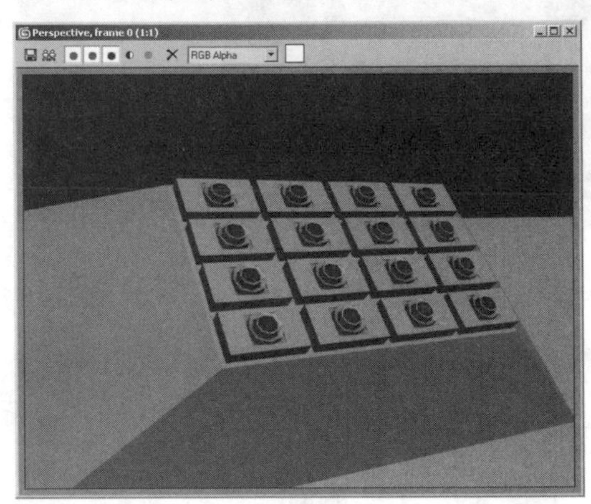

Figure 2-51

23. Switch to the Right view and zoom out so you can see both banks of jacks.
24. Under the Create panel, select the **Shapes** button.

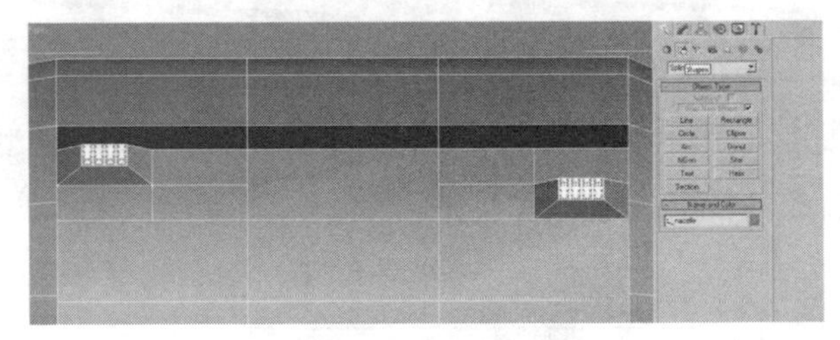

Figure 2-52

25. Click the **Line** button to create a line spline and create a spline as shown in Figure 2-53. (Each left mouse click creates a vertex, represented by the white cross. When you get to the last cross, click the right mouse button to complete the spline.) *Make sure AutoGrid is turned on!*

FYI: Don't get hung up on the exact placement of the vertices. Like polygonal modeling, you can easily move, add, and delete vertices from a spline.

Figure 2-53

26. Switch to Vertex selection mode and select the first vertex.
27. Zoom in close enough that you can see the spline and the individual jacks.
28. Use the Move tool to position the initial vertex inside the jack, as close to dead center as you can.

Figure 2-54

29. Use the Move tool to position the next vertex above the initial one, at just under a 90-degree angle.

Figure 2-55

30. With the vertex still selected, right-click and select **Smooth**.

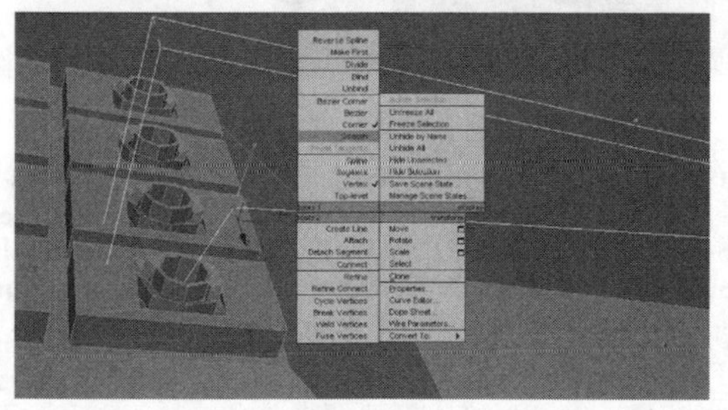

Figure 2-56

Fire Drill: As you can see from Figure 2-57, this jacks up your spline. In Figures 2-55 and 2-56, you can see the second vertex forms a corner, but this isn't conducive to smooth wires, so we had to convert it to a smooth bend, and now we have to undo the damage we did in the last step.

Figure 2-57

31. Drag the Move tool in the X axis (you may also have to move the vertex in the Y axis) until you have a smooth bend in your spline, just above the jack.

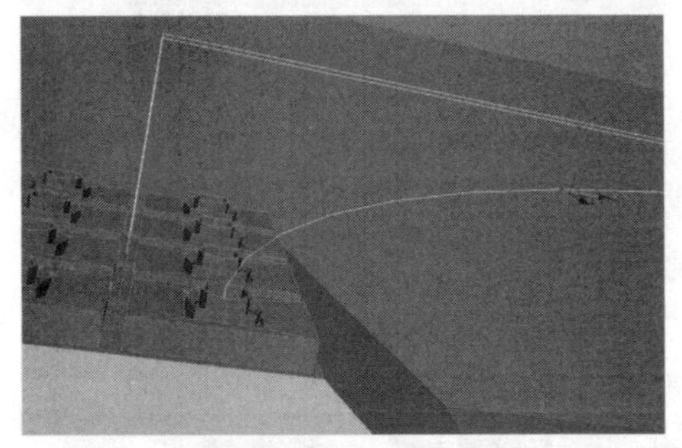

Figure 2-58

32. Convert the next two vertices to Smooth by first selecting them, right-clicking, and then selecting **Smooth**.

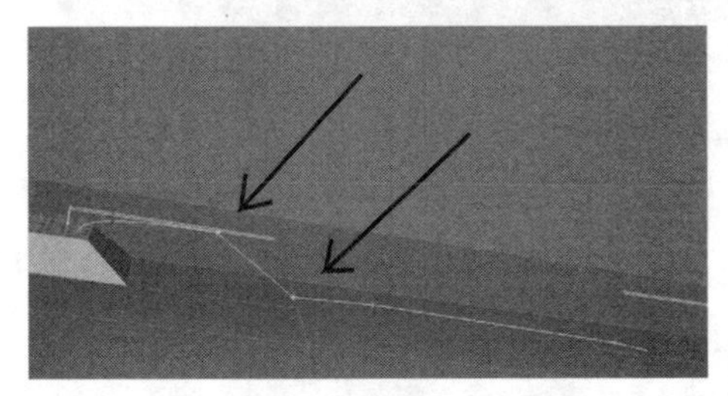

Figure 2-59

Fire Drill: Just because you smoothed vertices doesn't mean they'll be correctly aligned (Figure 2-60). You'll still need to use the Move tool to adjust the vertices (generally in the Y axis) so they don't fall beneath the surface of the nacelle, and so the spline resembles a smooth wire (Figure 2-61). If a vertex falls beneath the surface, switch to wireframe mode to find it.

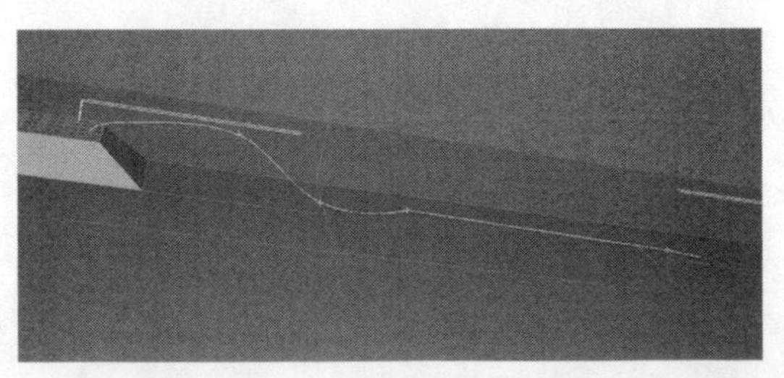

Figure 2-60

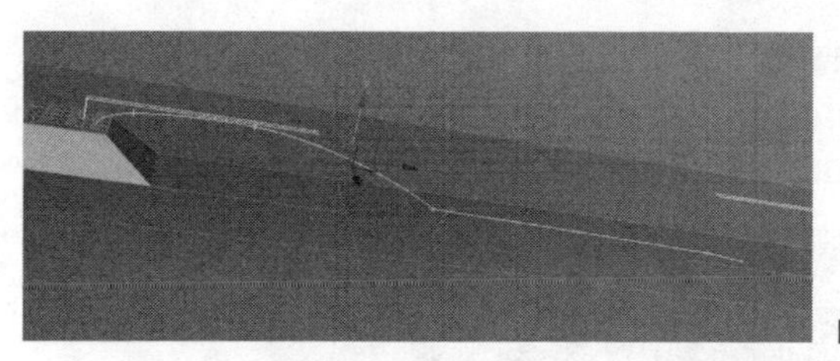

Figure 2-61

33. Continue converting vertices to Smooth and moving them until you get to the last vertex.

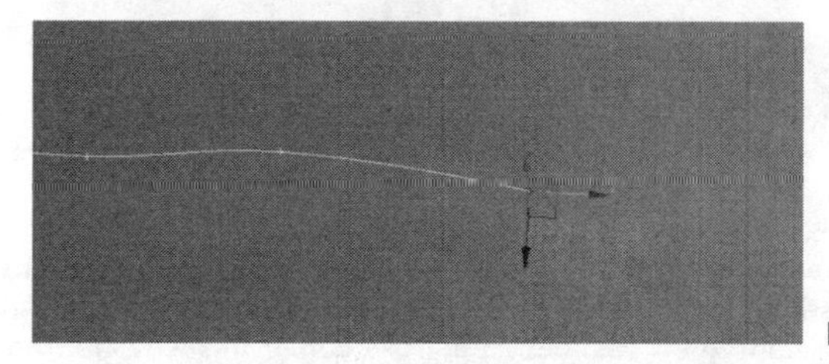

Figure 2-62

34. At the last vertex, pick a jack (it doesn't matter which one) and center the vertex inside the jack so the spline is *not* intersecting with any geometry, especially the jack's sides.

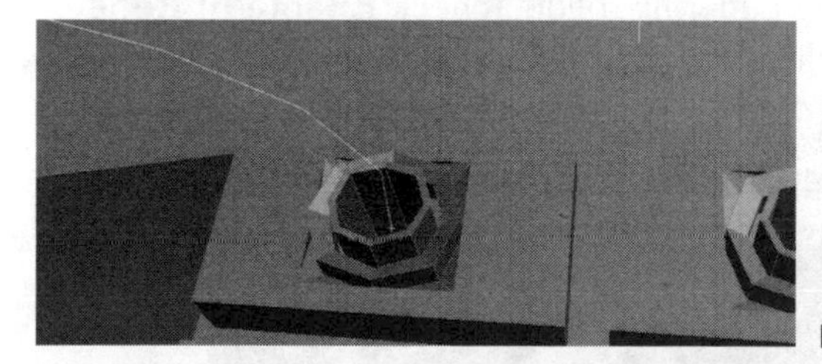

Figure 2-63

FYI: It may be necessary for you to use the Move tool to reposition some of the vertices. I had to move all of my vertices except the first one to get the positioning right. The closer you get two vertices, the sharper the corner.

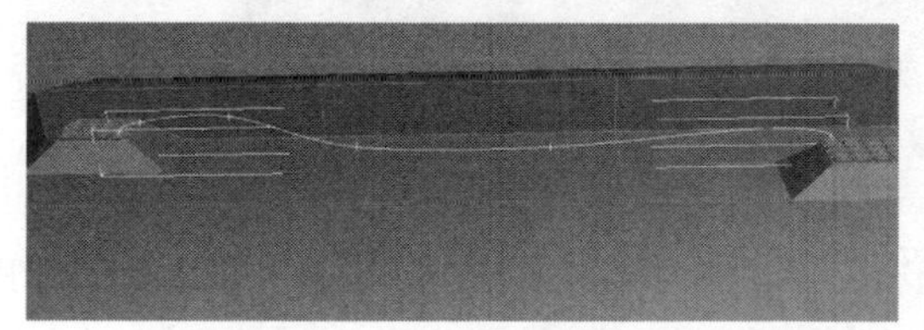

Figure 2-64

35. When you're sure the spline comes straight down into the beginning and end jacks, and none of the vertices intersect the geometry, you're ready to continue.

36. In the Command panel, find the rollout named Rendering, open it, click **Enable In Viewport**, and dial down the Radial Thickness and Sides settings until you're happy (I chose **0.09** and **18**).

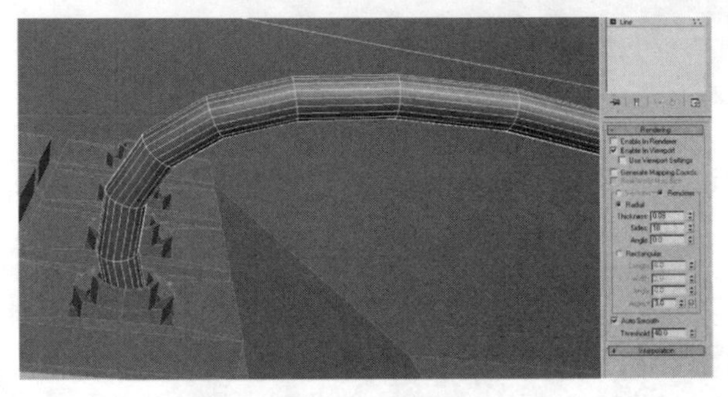

Figure 2-65

Message: A reasonable person might ask why a designer would leave the wiring exposed. If it's used for warfare, wouldn't exposed wires make it vulnerable? The answer is yes, but ... it looks cooler this way. If it really annoys you, skip this part.

37. Check again to make sure you don't have any intersections, then under the Rendering rollout, check **Enable In Renderer** (it will not render unless checked). Zoom out so you can see the entire wire, and render.

Figure 2-66

38. When you're satisfied, convert the spline to an Editable Polygon and name it **wire01**.

39. Select the nacelle, click **Attach**, and click the wire.

Urgent: Don't skip this step! When we mirror the nacelle, you want the wires to be mirrored as well. Later on, you'll want to detach them as elements so you can add a different colored material to each wire (or if you prefer, make them all black).

40. Repeat steps 26-39 to wire all the jacks, making sure you don't intersect geometry.

Message: I'll leave the wiring of the jacks to you. Wire as many or as few as you like, but more wires look more impressive. Try to insert some randomness in your wiring; wiring the same jacks together each time looks boring.

Don't Forget: You can turn off Enable In Viewport by unchecking the box. I find it easier to work with a spline; periodically Enable In Viewport to make sure the geometry isn't intersecting.

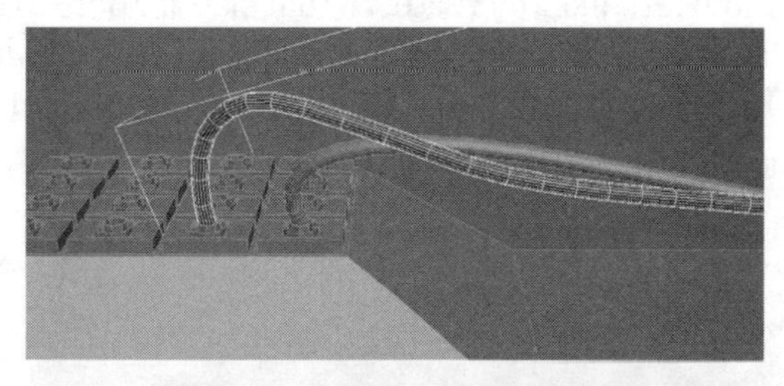

Figure 2-67

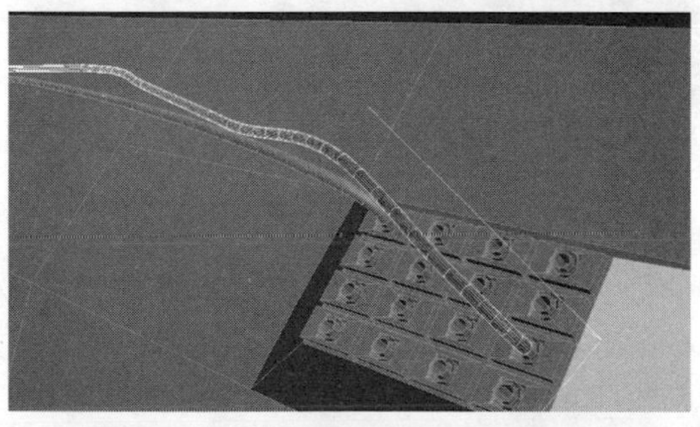

Figure 2-68

Figure 2-69

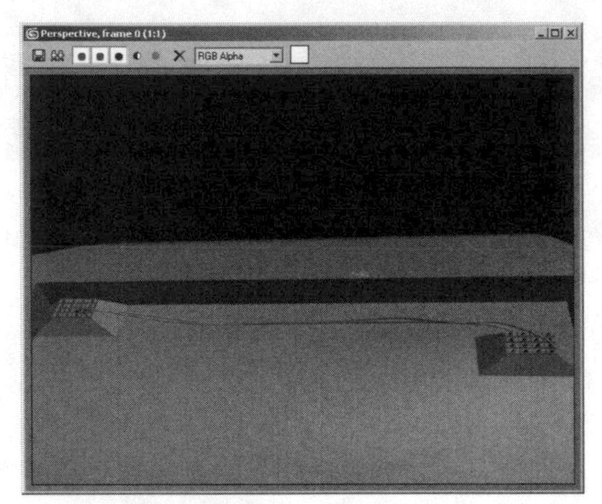

Figure 2-70

Making a "Clay" Render*

A lot of 3D modelers like to create virtual clay models to get a sense of what the model will look like using Global Illumination. Personally, I just think they look cool and that's reason enough.

1. Add a skylight to your scene: **Create panel > Lights > Standard > Skylight**.

Figure 2-71

* Thanks to Stealth Snake at http://www.oman3d.com/tutorials/3ds/clayrender_stealth/ for teaching me this.

2. Use the default settings.

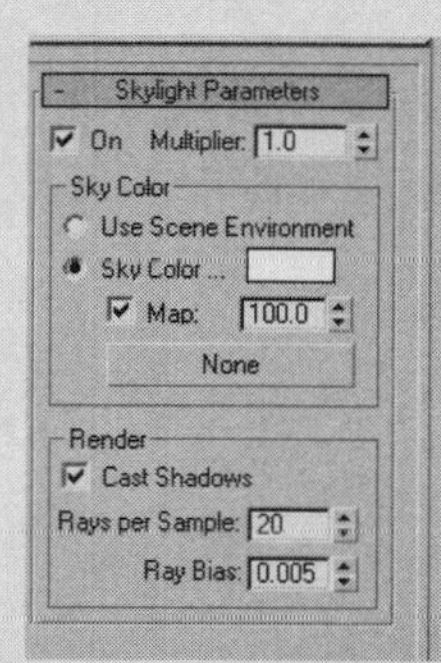

Figure 2-72

3. Position the skylight above your model.

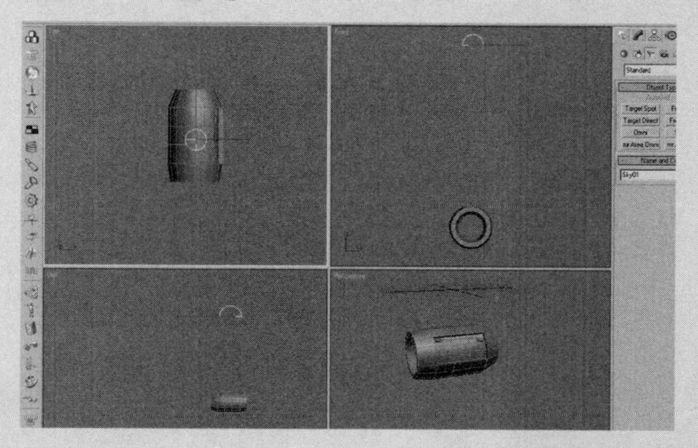

Figure 2-73

4. Press **F10** to open the Render Scene dialog, click the Advanced Lighting tab, and under Select Advanced Lighting, select **Light Tracer** from the pull-down.

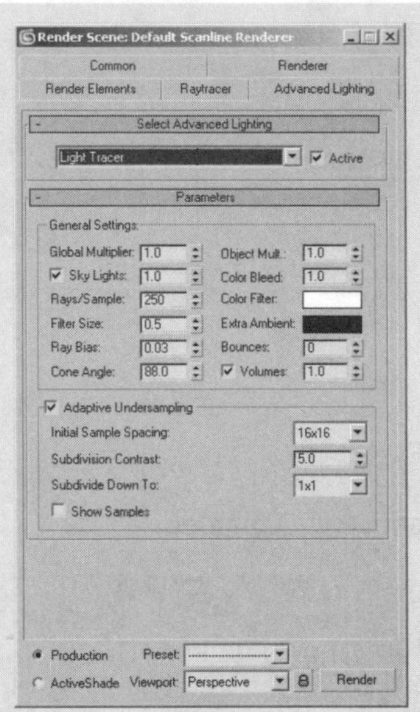

Figure 2-74

5. Close the Render Scene dialog and hit **M** to open the Material Editor.

6. Select an available slot, name the material **Clay**, change the Diffuse color to (R:**207**, G:**197**, B:**178**), and be sure the Shader is set to **Blinn**.

7. If you think you might want to do this in the future with other models, click the **Put to Library** button to save the material.

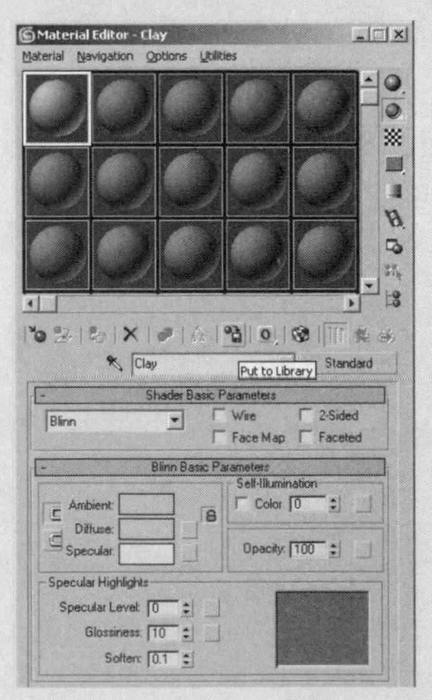

Figure 2-75

8. Apply the material to the selection and render.

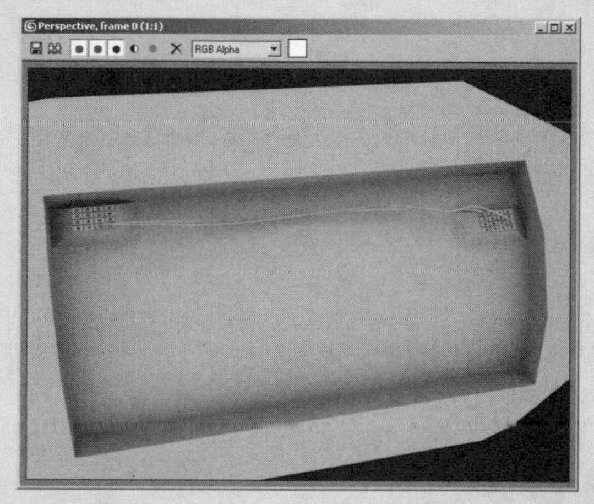

Figure 2-76

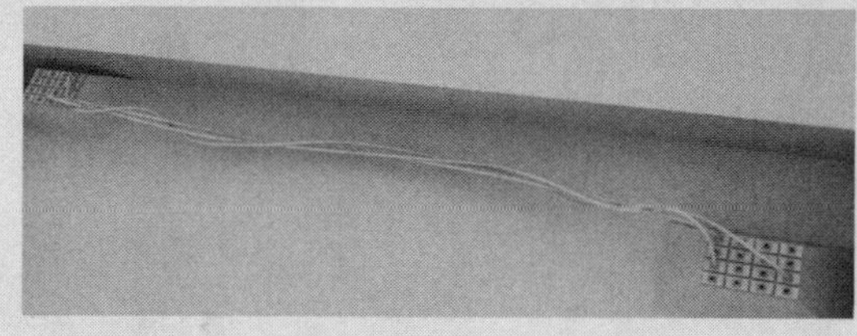

Figure 2-77

Figure 2-78

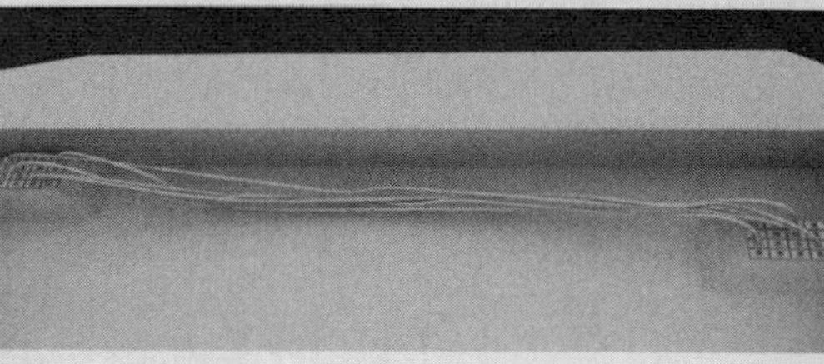

Figure 2-79

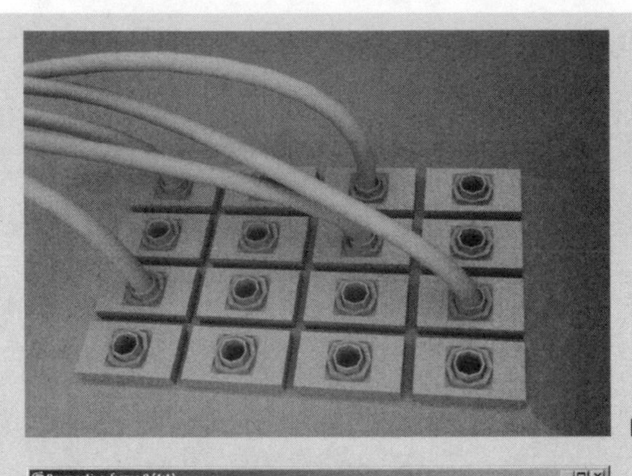

Figure 2-80

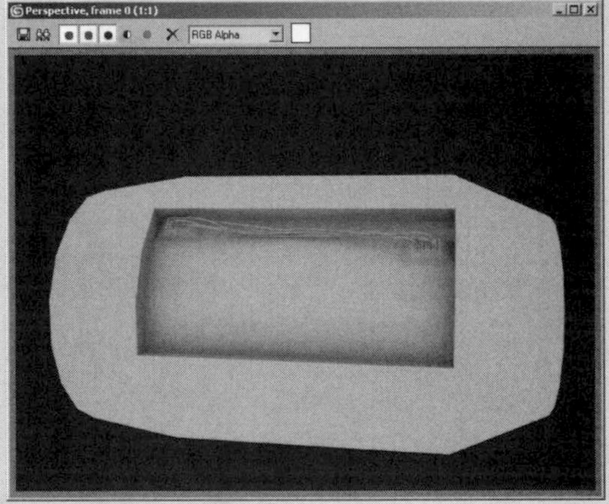

Figure 2-81

Urgent: Skylight won't work unless Light Tracer is turned on. However, Light Tracer can dramatically slow rendering! Lowering the Rays/Sample value under Global Settings will speed rendering but lower the quality. If you'd rather use Mental Ray, you don't need to add the Skylight or Light Tracer. Select Mental Ray as your renderer, apply a Mental Ray material to the object, and under Basic Shaders add an Ambient Occlusion map. Render as normal.

Day 3: Building the Engine Nacelles II

Message: I intentionally didn't wire every single jack to give the impression the unused jacks might be available for adding custom modules.

1. Select the **L_nacelle**, switch to Edge selection mode, and select the outer edges surrounding the nacelle's access port.

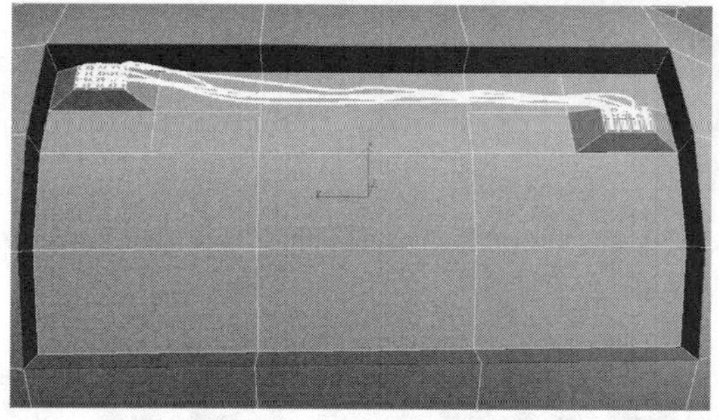

Figure 2-82

2. Under Edit Edges, select **Chamfer Settings**; chamfering subdivides edges and creates additional geometry, which makes an object look smooth.

3. Set the Chamfer Amount to **0.3** and hit **Apply**.

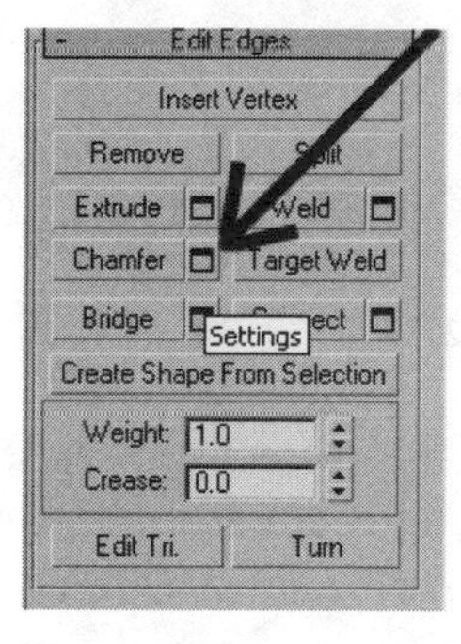

Figure 2-83

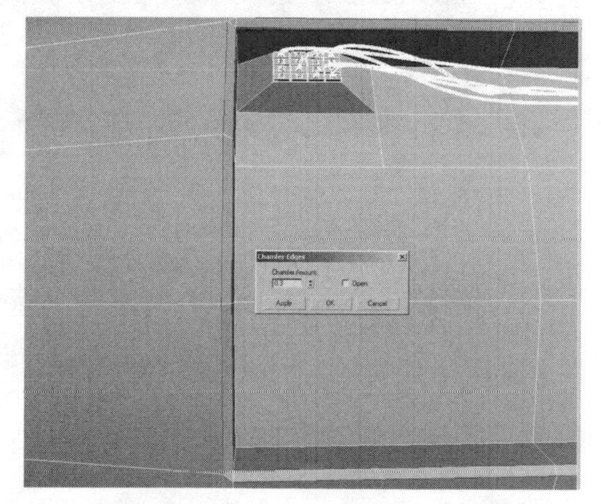

Figure 2-84

4. Set the Chamfer Amount to **0.1** and hit **OK**.

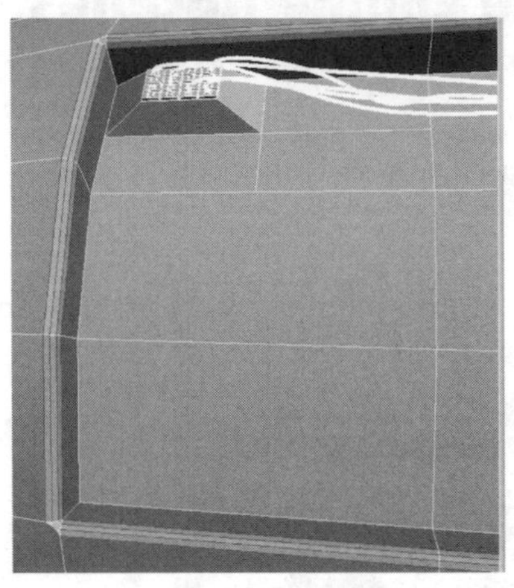

Figure 2-85

5. Do a test render and see how much the chamfering smoothed the edges.

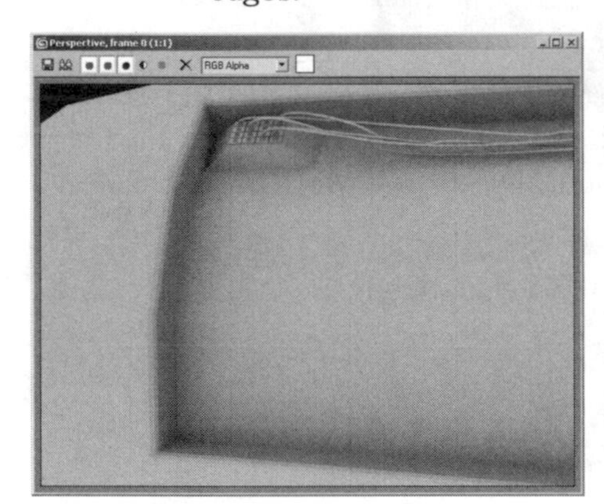

Figure 2-86

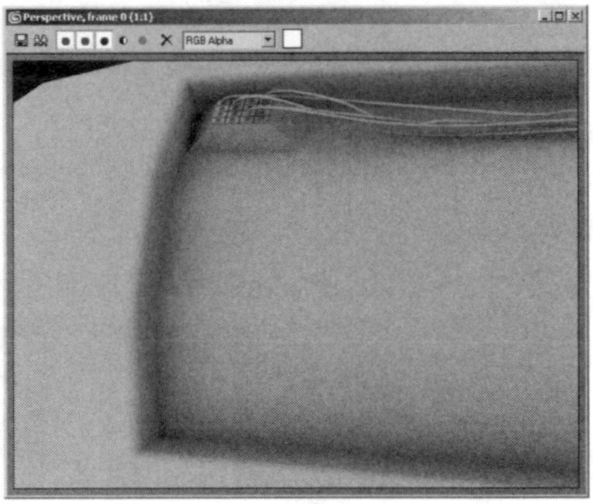

Figure 2-87

6. Switch to Perspective view, Arc Rotate to see the nacelle's intake nozzle, click one of the inner edges, and click **Loop** to select them all.

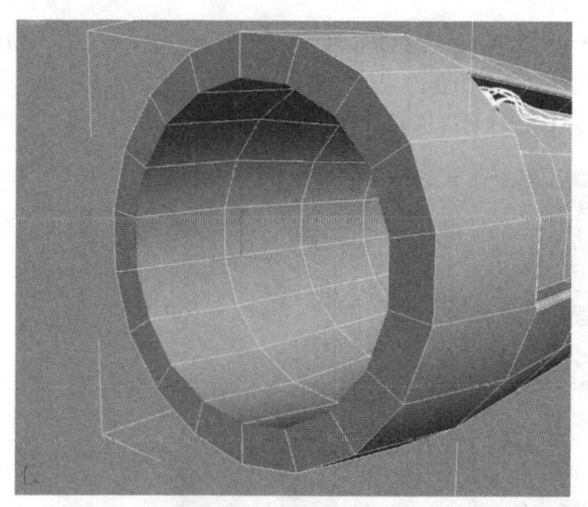

Figure 2-88

7. Chamfer the inner edge by **0.3**, hit **Apply**, and then Chamfer by **0.1**. Click **OK**.

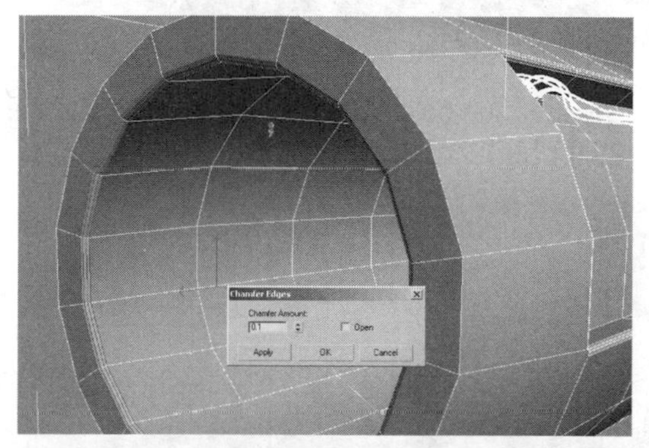

Figure 2-89

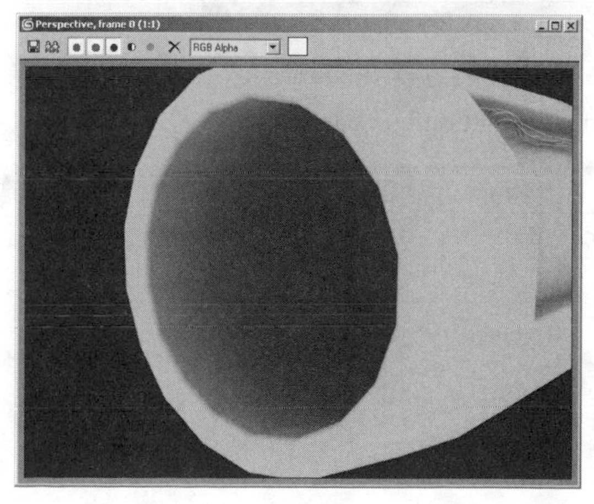

Figure 2-90

8. Repeat the same chamfering process you used for the outer rim of the front nozzle for the outer and inner edges of the rear exhaust nozzle. (I used **0.3** and **0.15** for the rear nozzle values.)

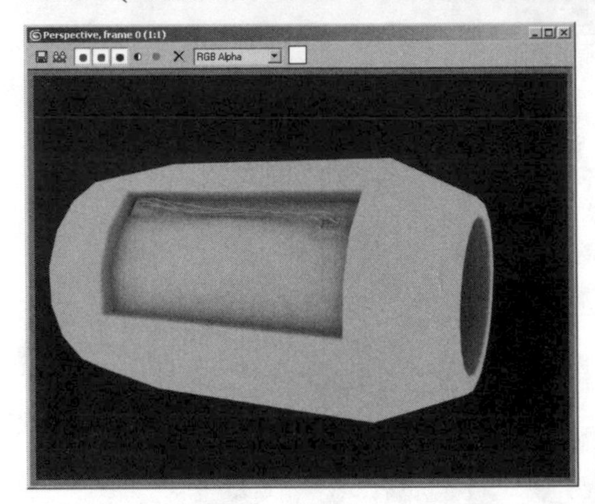

Figure 2-91

9. Zoom in on the junction boxes and polygon-select the sides shown in Figure 2-92 for both boxes.

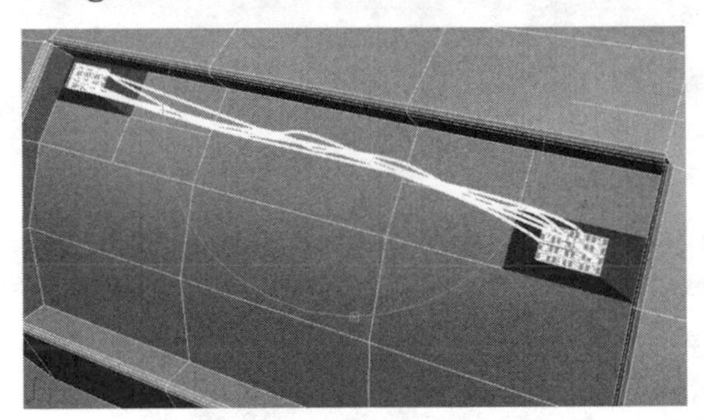

Figure 2-92

10. Bevel (to make junction box panels):

Type	Height	Outline	Apply/OK
By Polygon	0	–0.05	Apply
Group	0.05	0	OK

Figure 2-93

11. Select the two side edges of the junction boxes' bottom faces (be sure to do both sides).

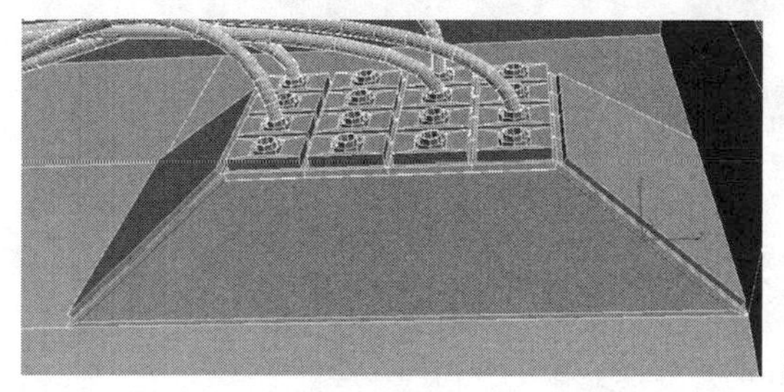

Figure 2-94

12. Click **Connect** to connect the edges.

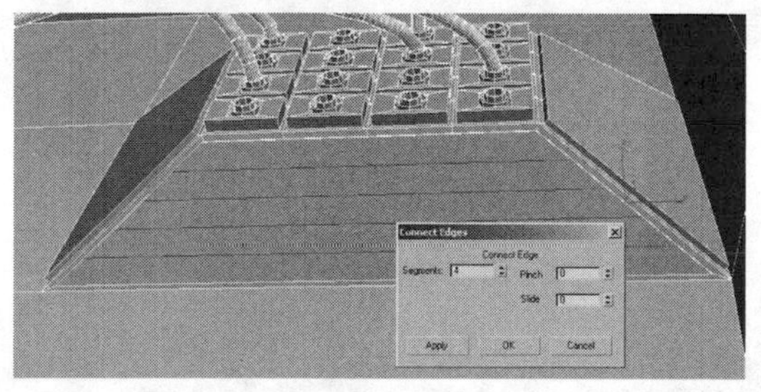

Figure 2-95

Message: If you zoom in on the top and switch to Polygon selection mode, you'll see it's really four segments interconnected by five vertices, while the bottom is one continuous edge. We need to make some cuts from the vertices connecting the top edge to the bottom edge so that both are four edges.

13. Make a vertical cut from each top vertex, between each edge, to the bottom edge.

Figure 2-96

14. Do the same for both junction boxes and select the five polys shown in Figure 2-97 for both boxes.

Figure 2-97

15. Inset the polygons by Group by **0.02**.

16. Click **Bevel Settings:**

Type	Height	Outline	Apply/OK
Group	0.03	–0.03	OK

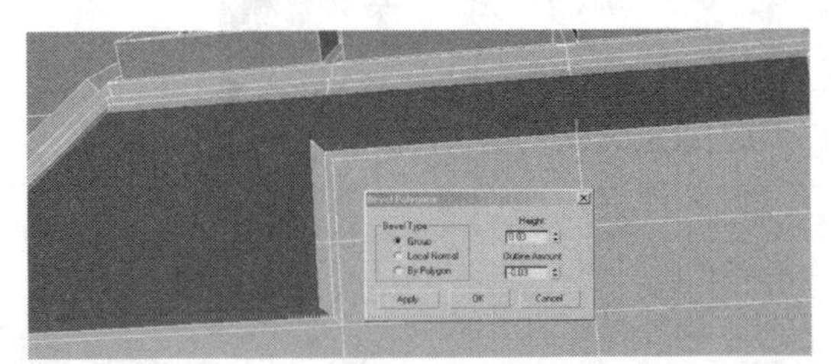

Figure 2-98

17. Select the two edges shown (for both boxes) and make a single segment Connect.

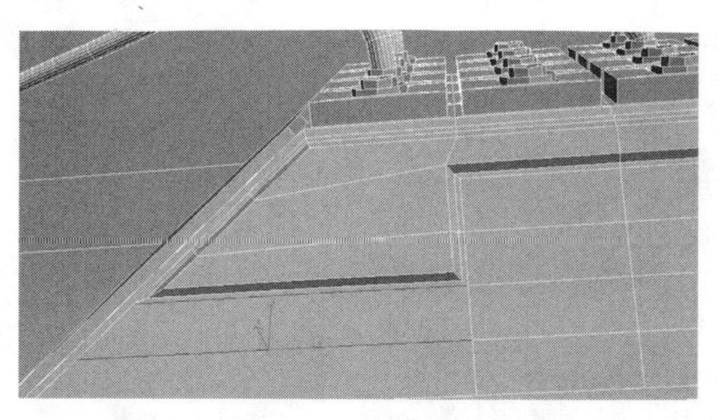

Figure 2-99

18. Select the three polygons for each box as shown in Figure 2-100.

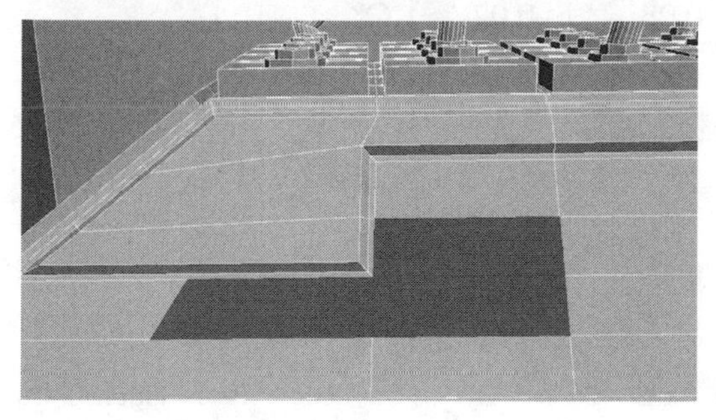

Figure 2-100

19. Group Inset them by **0.02.**
20. Click **Bevel Settings**:

Type	Height	Outline	Apply/OK
Group	0.015	–0.03	OK

21. Deselect the bottom two polygons on both boxes, leaving the top-right poly selected.

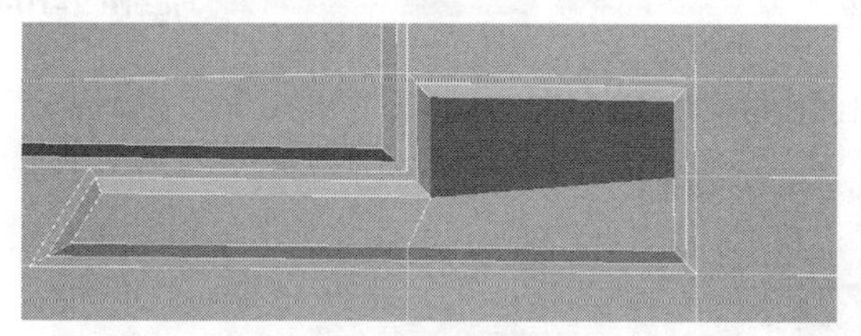

Figure 2-101

22. Hit the **Tessellate** button twice.
23. Select the polygons shown in Figure 2-102.

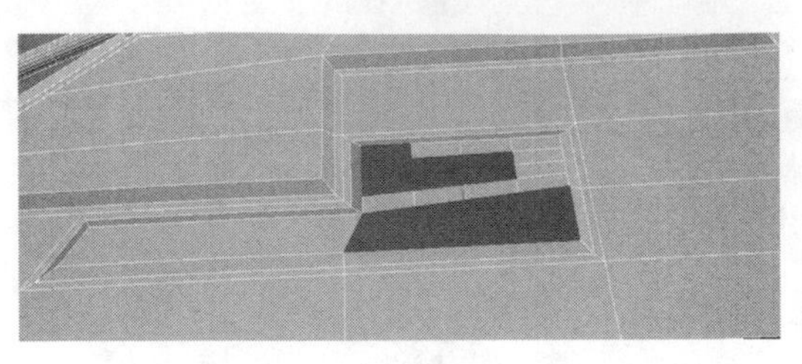

Figure 2-102

24. Click **Bevel Settings:**

Type	Height	Outline	Apply/OK
Group	0.08	–0.02	OK

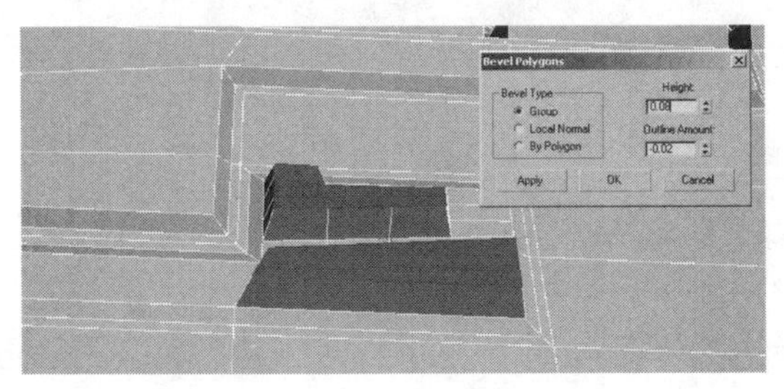

Figure 2-103

25. Select the polygons shown in Figure 2-104 (for both boxes).

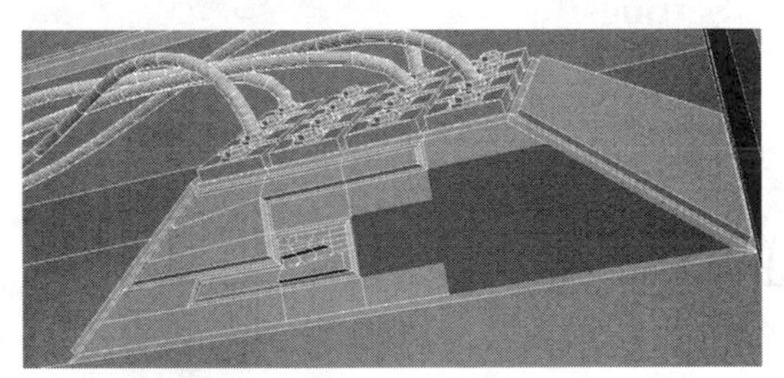

Figure 2-104

26. Group Extrude by **0.01**.
27. Group Inset by **0.03**.

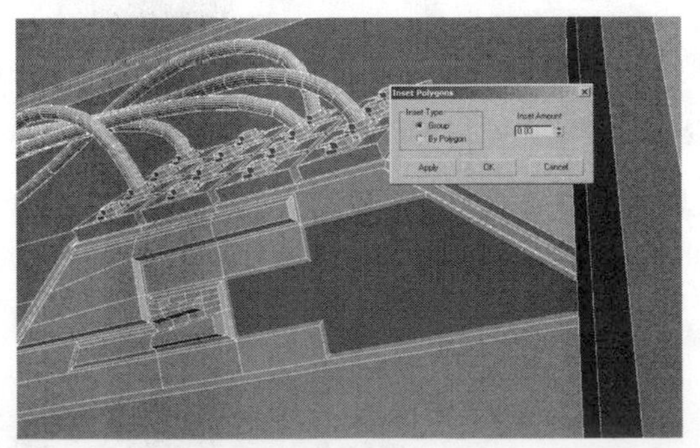

Figure 2-105

28. Delete the polygons, border-select, and then click **Cap**.

Figure 2-106

Now let's build some heat sinks ...

29. Highlight the middle three polygons.

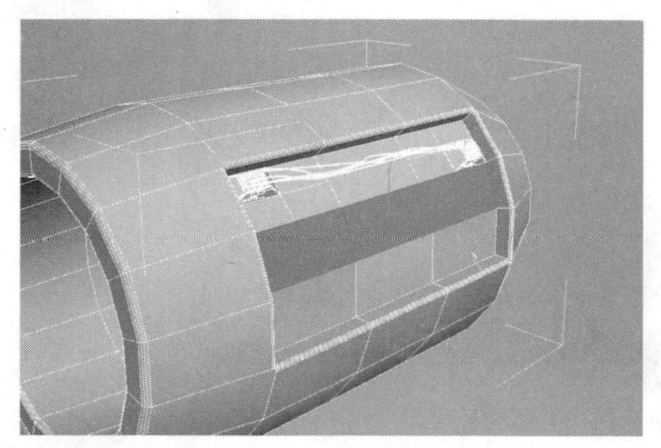

Figure 2-107

30. Click **Bevel Settings**:

Type	Height	Outline	Apply/OK
By Polygon	0.3	0	Apply
By Polygon	0	–0.3	OK

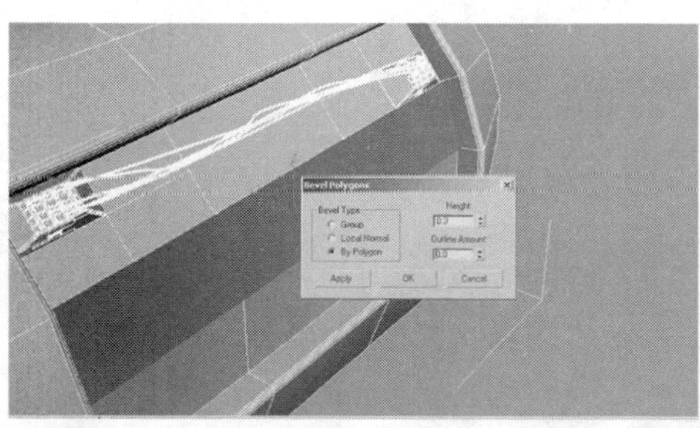

Figure 2-108

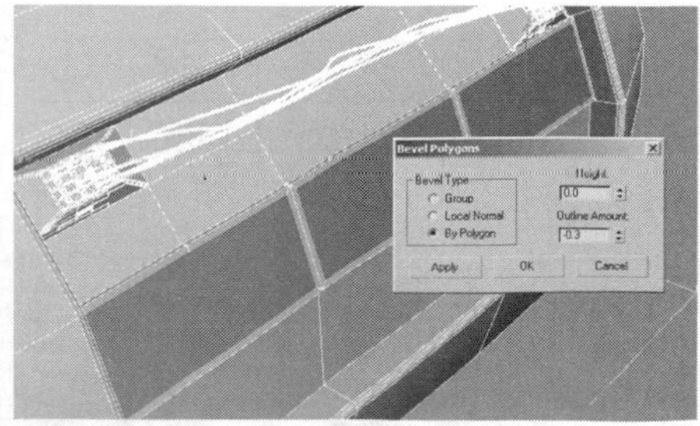

Figure 2-109

31. Edge-select the vertical edges of the inset polygons, but *not* the edges between.

Figure 2-110

32. Click **Connect Settings** and use **13** Segments.

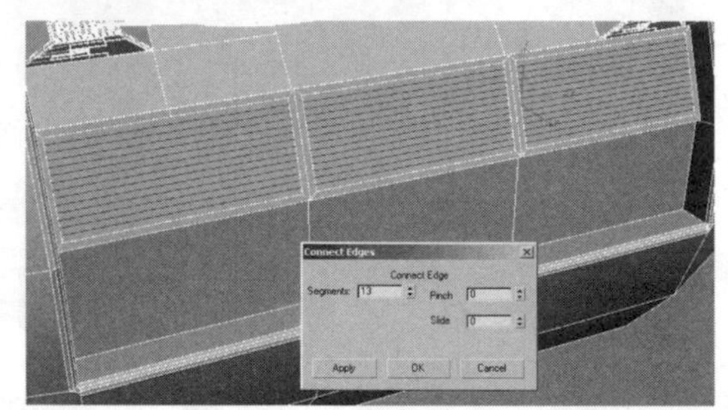

Figure 2-111

33. Select every other polygon.

Figure 2-112

34. Click **Bevel Settings**:

Type	Height	Outline	Apply/OK
By Polygon	1.38	–0.1	OK

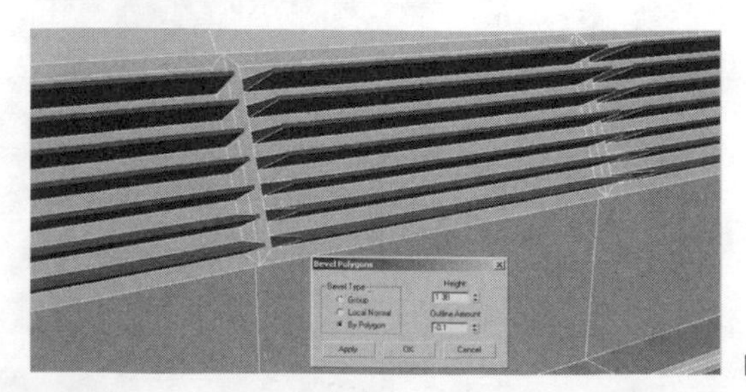

Figure 2-113

35. Select the bottom left and right polygons, and Inset them By Polygon **0.4**.

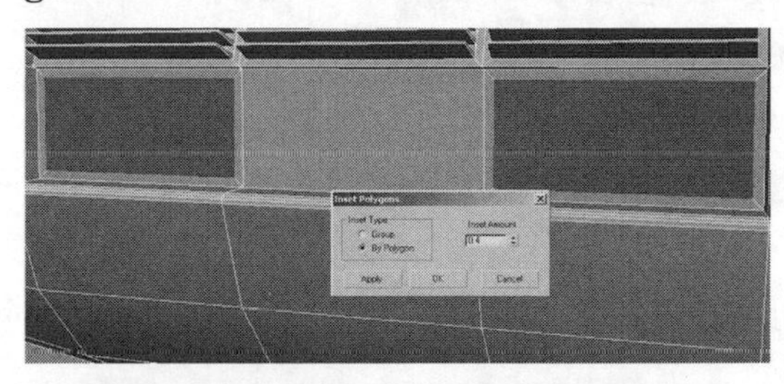

Figure 2-114

36. Scale them **30** in the Y axis.

Figure 2-115

37. Select each polygon individually. Move the right poly **3.0** in the Y axis and the left poly **–3.0** in the Y axis.

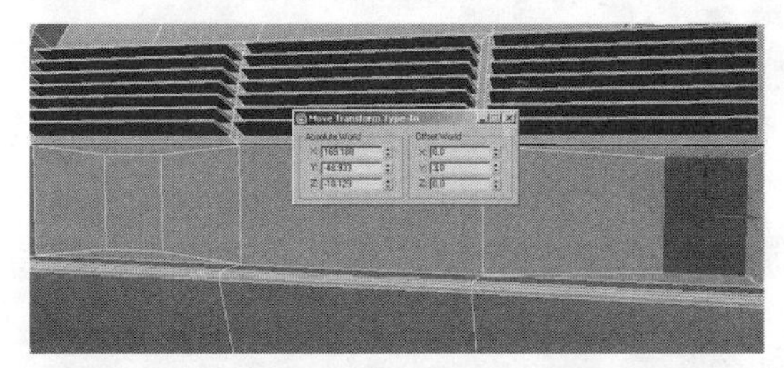

Figure 2-116

38. Select both polys and Extrude them as Local Normal by **0.01**.

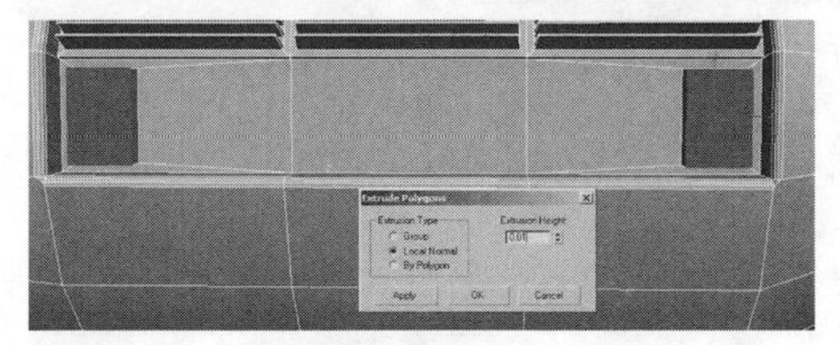

Figure 2-117

39. Click **Bevel Settings:**

Type	Height	Outline	Apply/OK
Group	0	0.2	Apply
Group	1.6	0	Apply

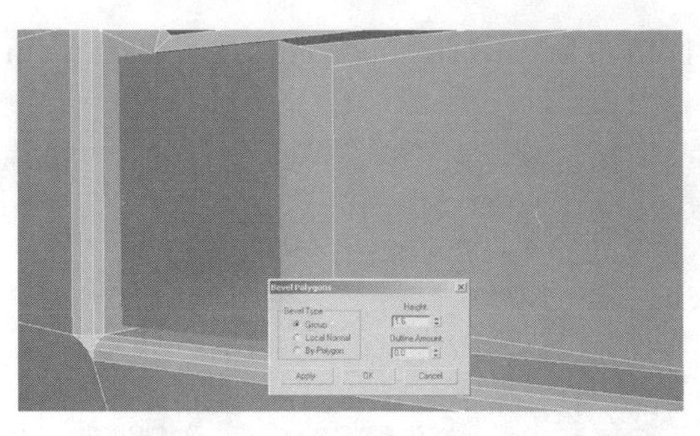

Figure 2-118

Type	Height	Outline	Apply/OK
Group	0	–0.15	Apply
Group	0.03	0	Apply
Group	0	0.15	Apply
Group	0.3	0	OK

Figure 2-119

40. Do a test render.

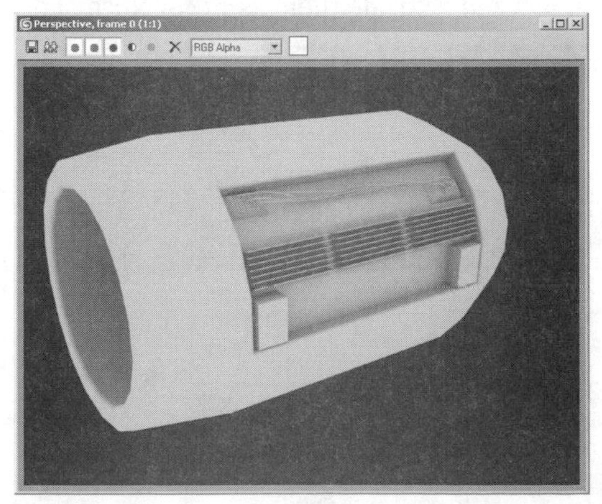

Figure 2-120

41. On the Create panel, select **Extended Primitives**, click **Chamfer Cylinder**, turn on AutoGrid, and make a Cylinder on the inside right of the left box.

Radius	Height	Fillet	Height/Fillet Segs	Sides	Cap Segs
0.5	0.3	0.08	1/4	18	2

Figure 2-121

42. Convert the chamfer cylinder to an Editable Poly and rename it **conduit01**.

43. Select one of the edges of the inner cap and click **Loop**.

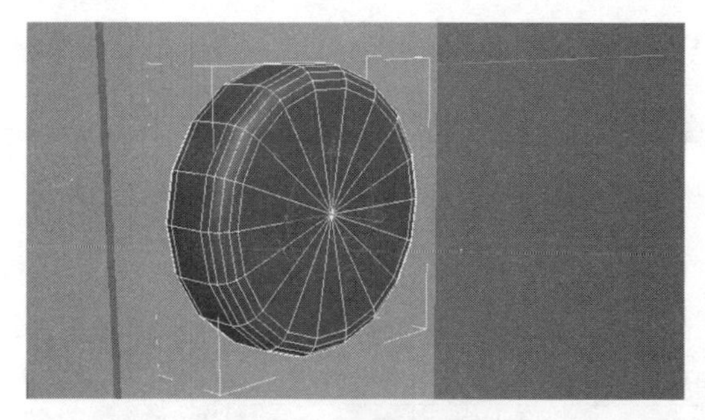

Figure 2-122

44. Uniform Scale the cap by **168**.

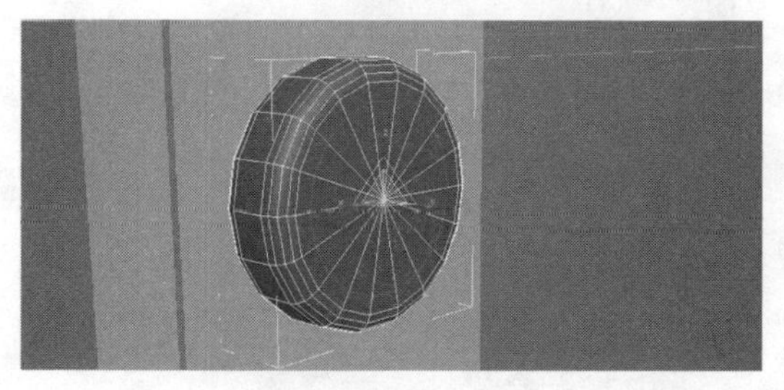

Figure 2-123

45. Highlight the interior polygons and Group Extrude them **–0.1**.

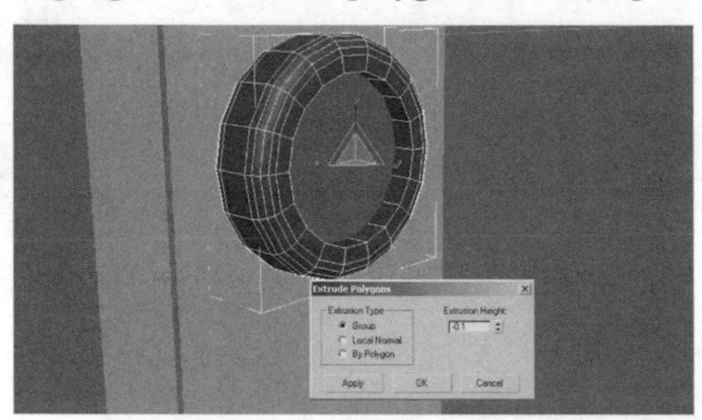

Figure 2-124

46. Inset the polygons as a Group by **0.65**.

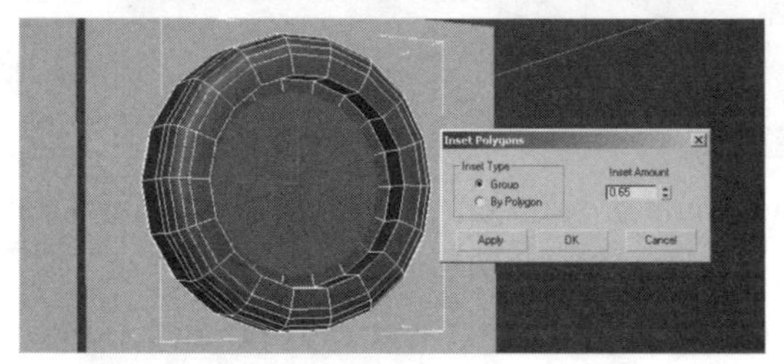

Figure 2-125

47. Click **Bevel Settings**:

Type	Height	Outline	Apply/OK
Group	1.5	0	Apply
Group	0	–0.07	Apply
Group	0.03	0	Apply
Group	0	0.07	Apply
Group	0.7	0	Apply
Group	0	–0.08	Apply
Group	9.0*	0	OK

* (or until the two ends intersect)

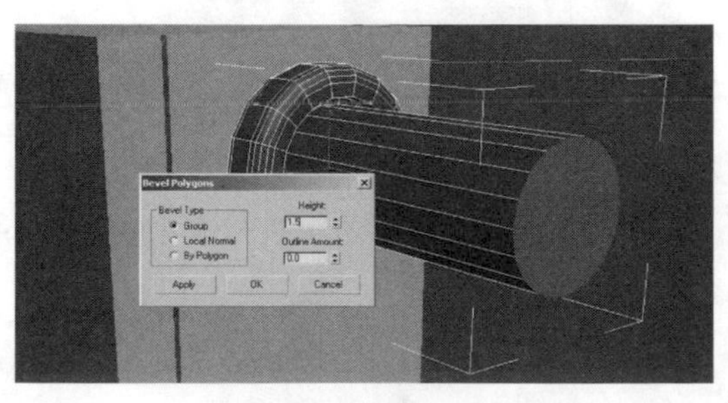

Figure 2-126

Day 3: Building the Engine Nacelles II

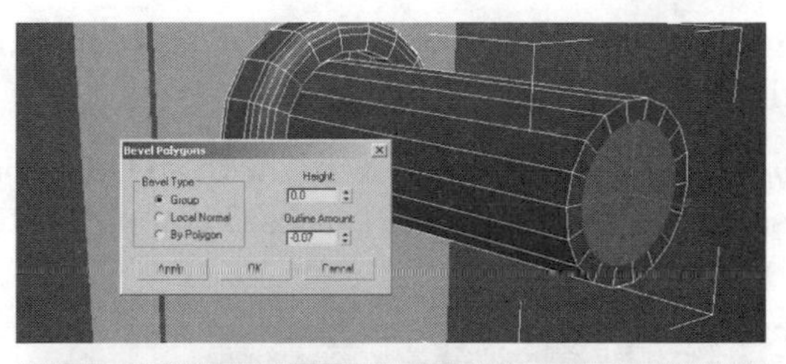

Figure 2-127

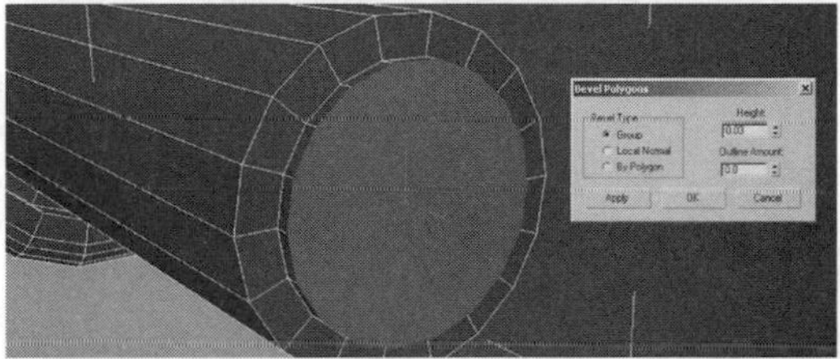

Figure 2-128

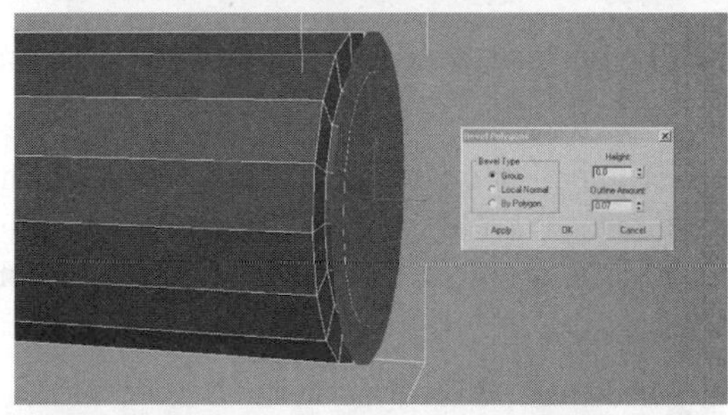

Figure 2-129

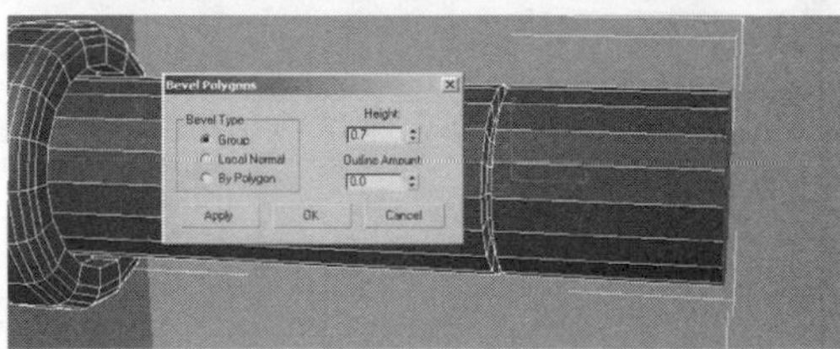

Figure 2-130

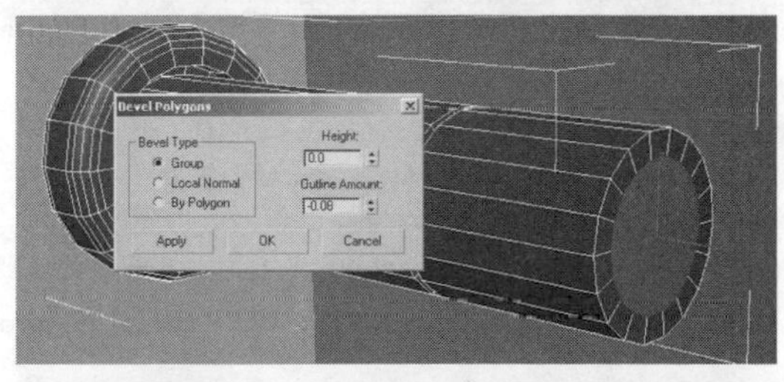

Figure 2-131

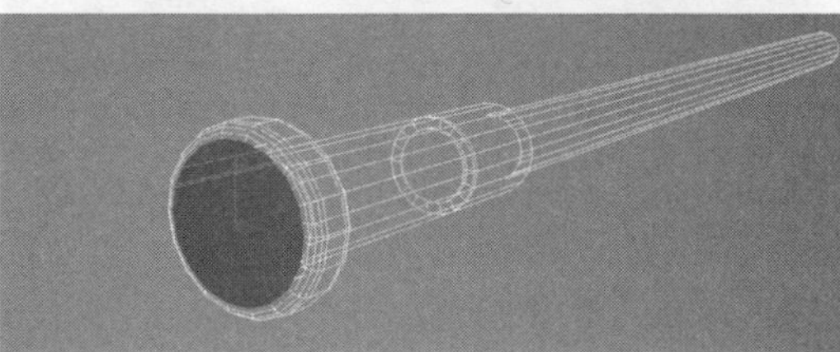

Figure 2-132

48. Delete the inward-facing polygons on both sides of the conduit, then switch to the Right view.

49. Mirror a *copy* of the conduit in the X axis with an Offset of around **11.448** (use whatever offset value causes their borders to touch in the middle).

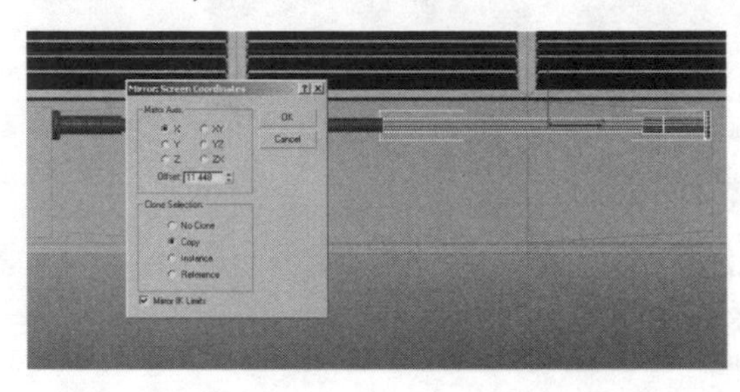

Figure 2-133

50. Select **conduit01**, click **Attach Settings**, and select **conduit02** to merge.

51. Switch to Vertex selection mode, select the 36 vertices in the center of the conduit, and click **Weld** (you make have to alter the weld settings) to complete the merge and reduce the number of middle vertices to 18.

52. Object-select **conduit01**, Shift-drag in the Y axis, and make three copies.

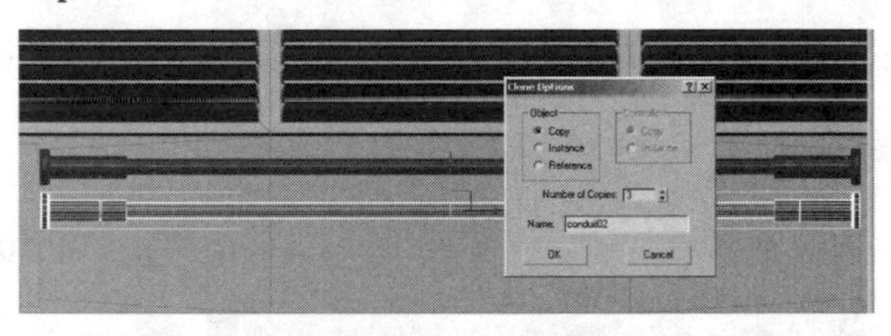

Figure 2-134

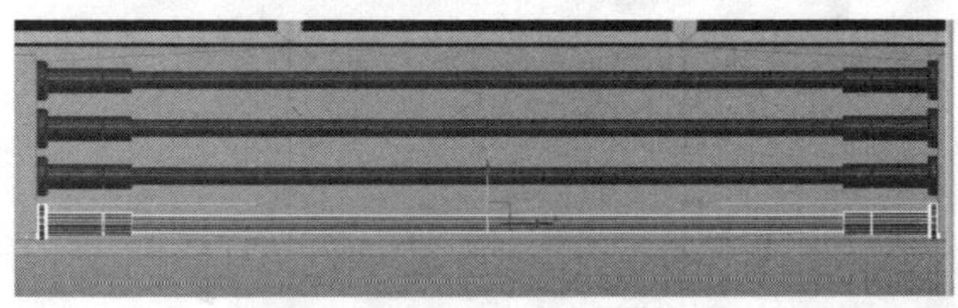

Figure 2-135

FYI: As you can tell from Figure 2-135, you may need to move some conduits to fit squarely on the boxes. Feel free to scale their diameter (in the X and Z). It's not essential they be the same *diameter* as long as their length remains constant. In fact, varying their diameter may make for a more interesting model.

Figure 2-136

53. Switch to the Perspective view, object-select **L_nacelle**, and Attach the four conduits.

54. Do a test render.

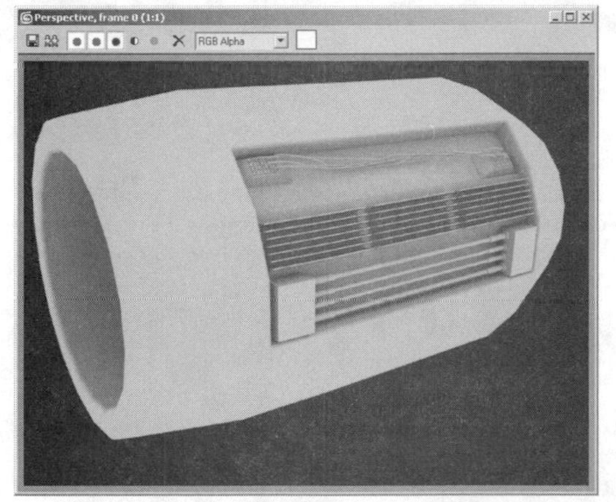

Figure 2-137

Message: That's coming along nicely. We need to do a couple more things. For starters, the boxes linking the conduits could use some spicing up. Also, the top near the wiring boxes is kinda bare. We don't want our nacelle to look "junky," but we do want it to look like a complicated bit of engineering.

55. Select the big polygon in the middle of the nacelle, beneath the wires.

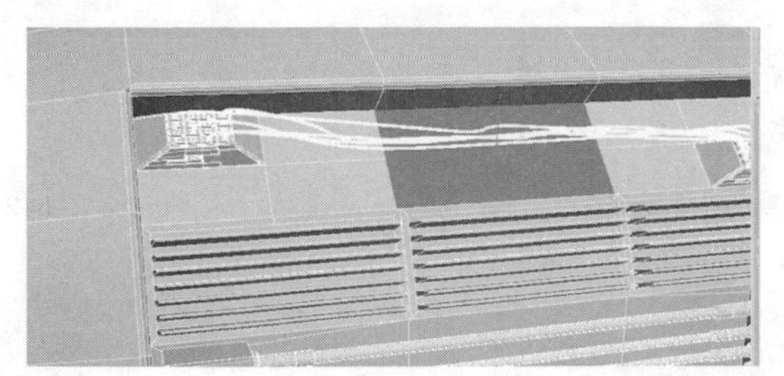
Figure 2-138

56. Click **Bevel Settings:**

Type	Height	Outline	Apply/OK
Group	–0.2	0	Apply
Group	0	–0.1	OK

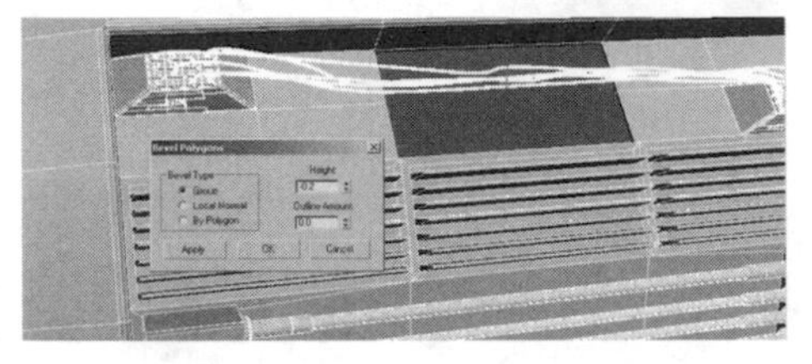

Figure 2-139

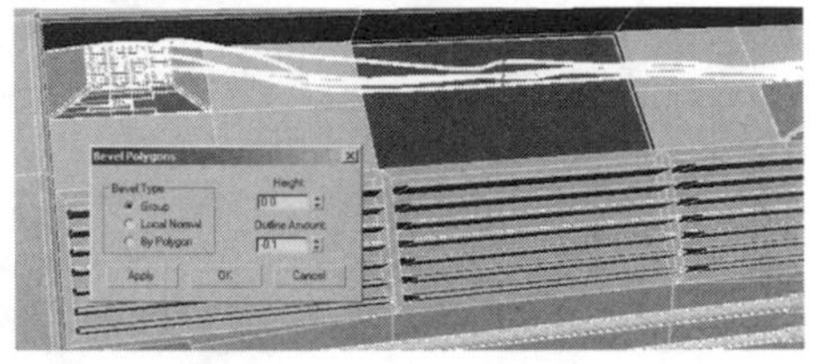

Figure 2-140

FYI: Ideally, we'd Tessellate to make a grate, but extra segments on the sides would give us trouble (see Figure 2-141). Rather than subdividing into smaller rectangles, Max merges the side verts into the center. We don't want that.

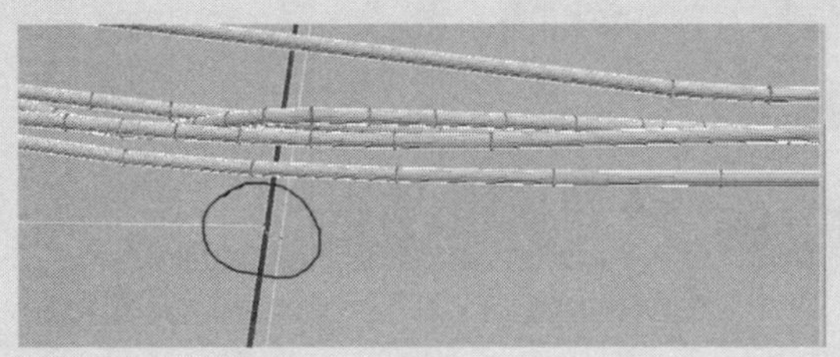

Figure 2-141

57. Use the Cut tool and cut from the segment on the left to the segment on the right, effectively cutting the larger polygon into two smaller ones.

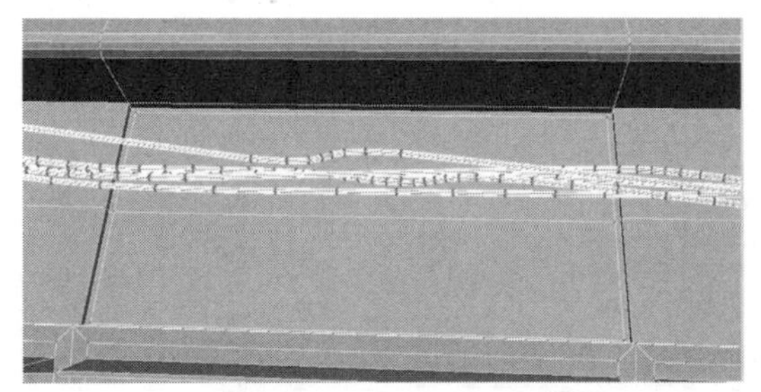

Figure 2-142

58. Select the two polygons and hit the **Tessellate** button twice.

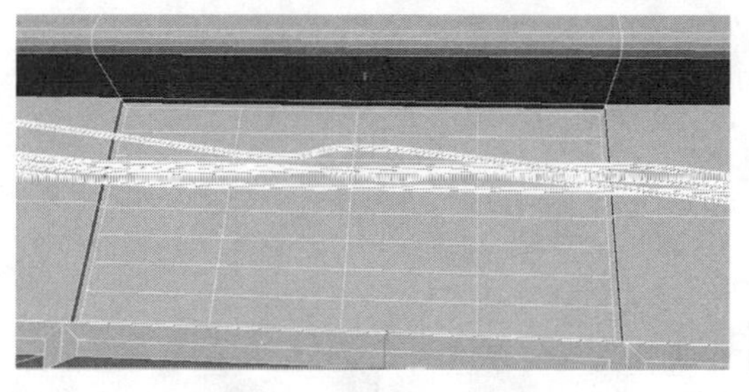

Figure 2-143

Message: Tessellate now works as it's supposed to, subdividing the two polygons into 32. But now the polys are rectangles, and we want to make a more interesting grate than that. We need square geometry to use MSmooth.

59. Select the 40 vertical edges. Use Arc Rotate to keep from selecting the wires.

Figure 2-144

60. Click **Chamfer Settings**, Chamfer by **0.62**, and click **Apply**.

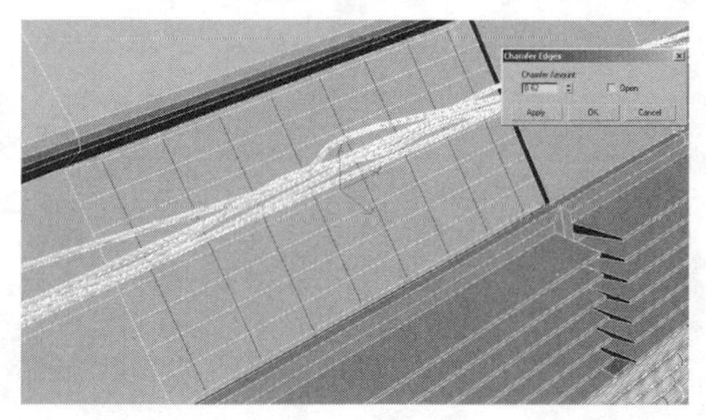

Figure 2-145

61. Change the Chamfer Amount to **0.31**, and click **OK**.

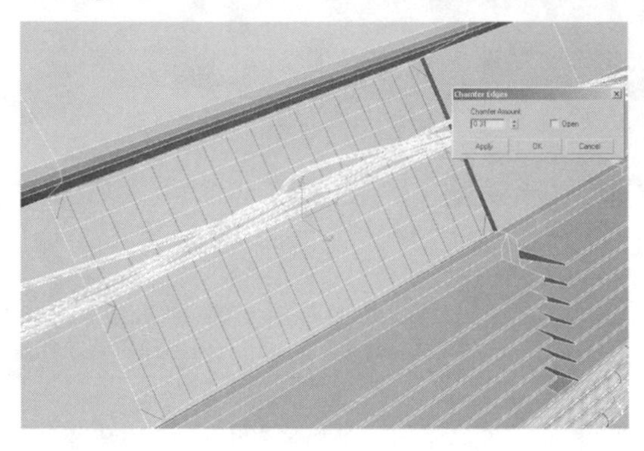

Figure 2-146

62. Select the middle polygons, being careful not to select any of the wires or any border polygons that ended up with angled segments, and then click **Bevel Settings**.

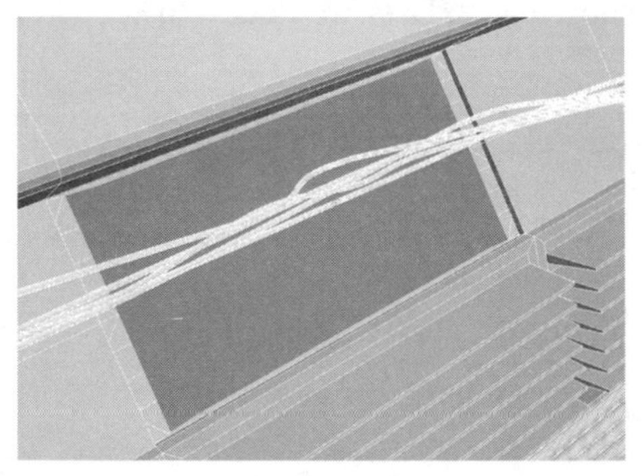

Figure 2-147

Type	Height	Outline	Apply/OK
By Polygon	0	–0.06	Apply
By Polygon	–0.1	0	OK

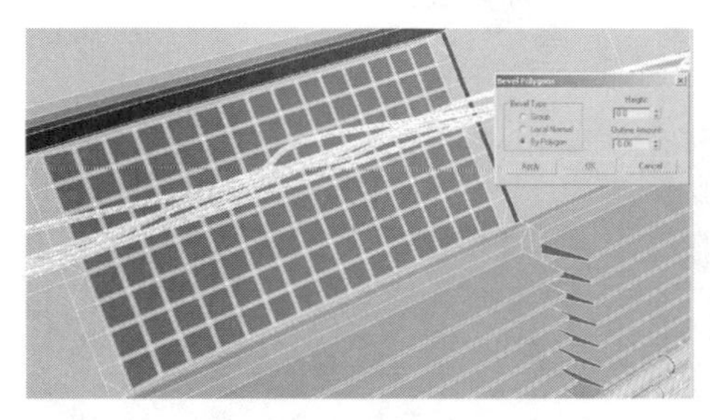

Figure 2-148

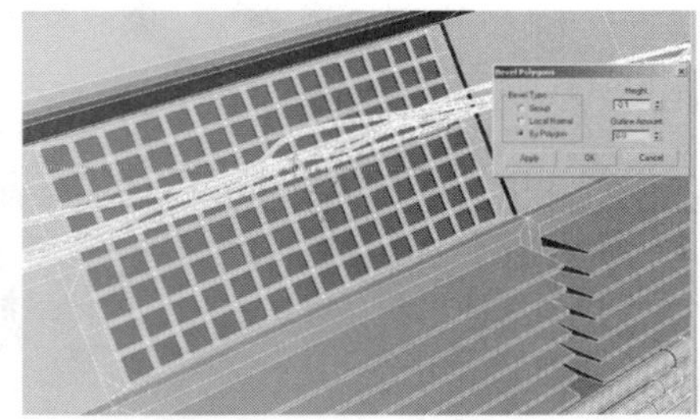

Figure 2-149

63. Click **MSmooth** (the button, not the modifier) and use **1.0** for the Smoothness.

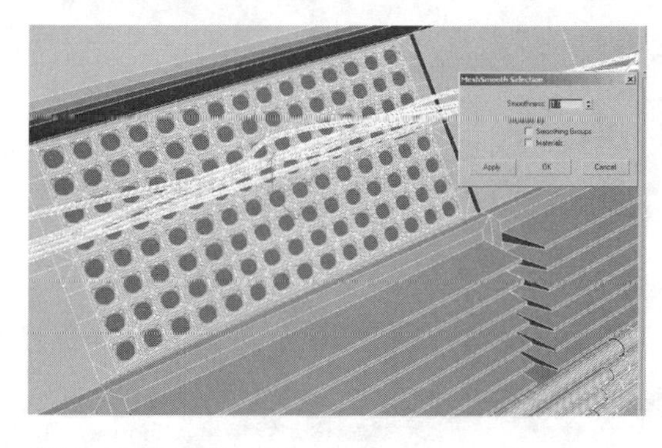

Figure 2-150

64. Click **Bevel Settings:**

Type	Height	Outline	Apply/OK
Group	0.14	–0.07	Apply
By Polygon	0	–0.01	Apply

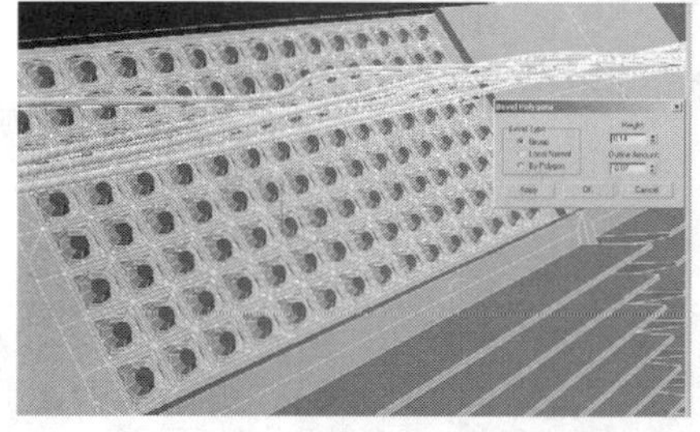

Figure 2-151

Figure 2-152

Type	Height	Outline	Apply/OK
By Polygon	–0.22	–0.01	OK

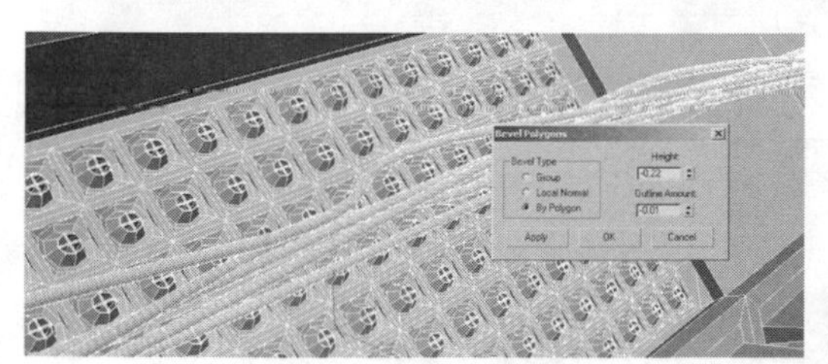

Figure 2-153

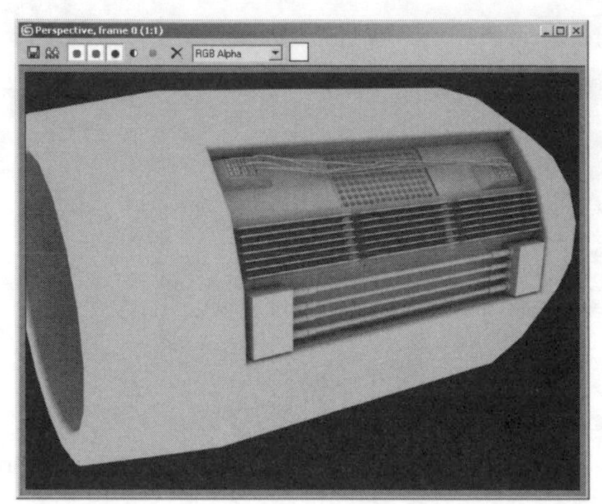

Figure 2-154

Day 4: Building the Engine Nacelles III — Pipes

1. Select the three polygons shown in Figure 2-155.

Figure 2-155

2. Click **Bevel Settings**:

Type	Height	Outline	Apply/OK
Group	0	–0.1	Apply
By Polygon	0.25	–0.1	OK

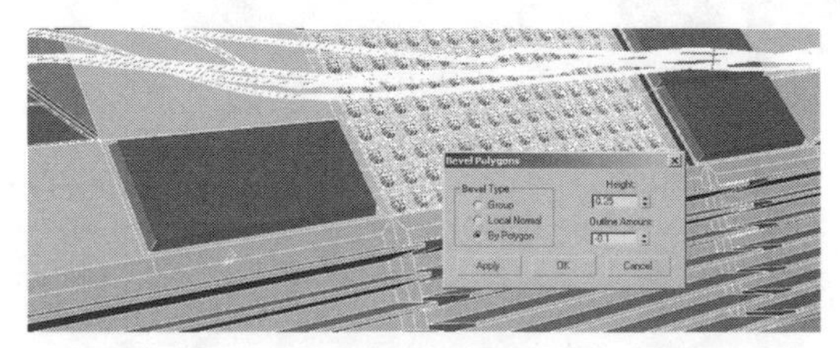

Figure 2-156

3. Hit **Tessellate** once.
4. Inset By Polygon **0.1**.

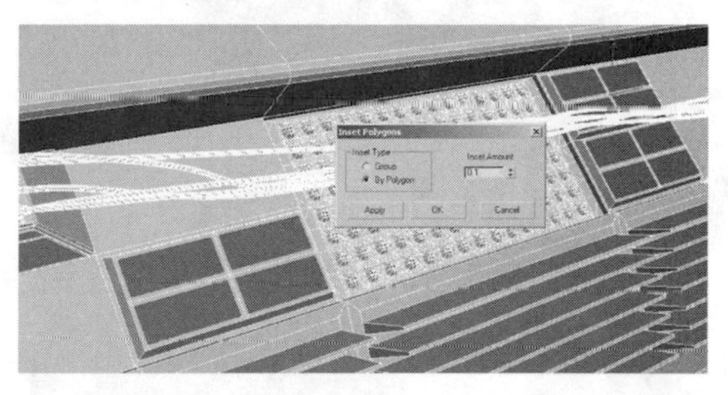

Figure 2-157

5. Scale the polygons **49** in the Y axis to square them off.

Figure 2-158

6. Extrude by Local Normal **–0.05**.

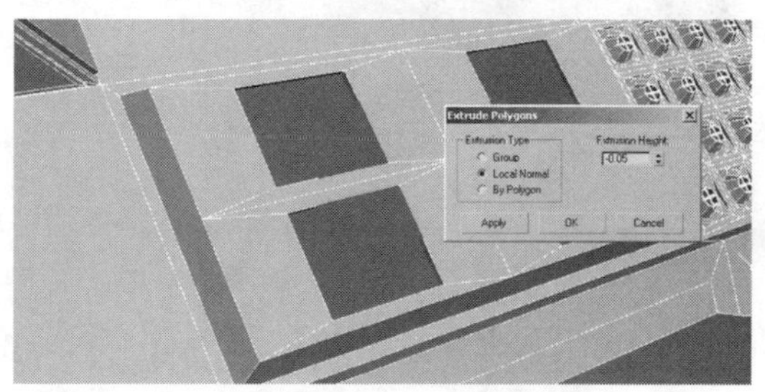

Figure 2-159

7. MSmooth with Smoothness of **1**.

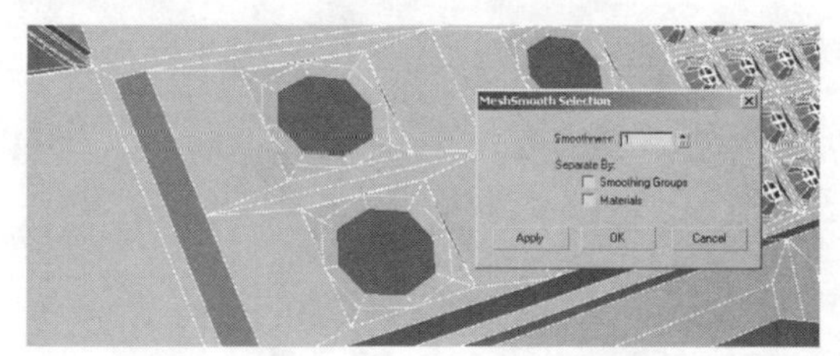

Figure 2-160

8. Click **Grow** and then Extrude by Local Normal **–0.05**.

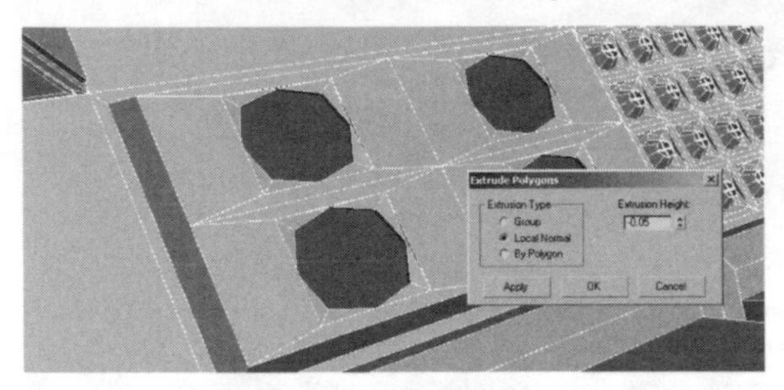

Figure 2-161

9. Group Inset by **0.03**.

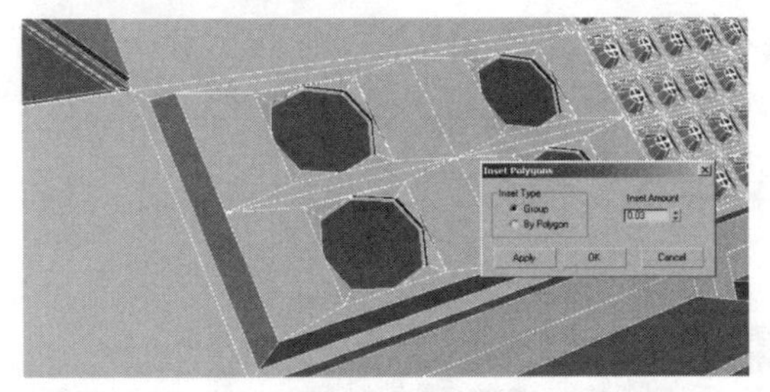

Figure 2-162

10. Group Extrude by **0.2**.

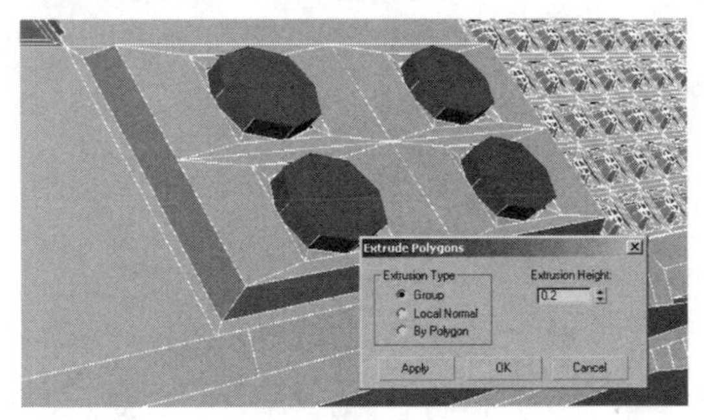

Figure 2-163

11. Click **Shrink**.

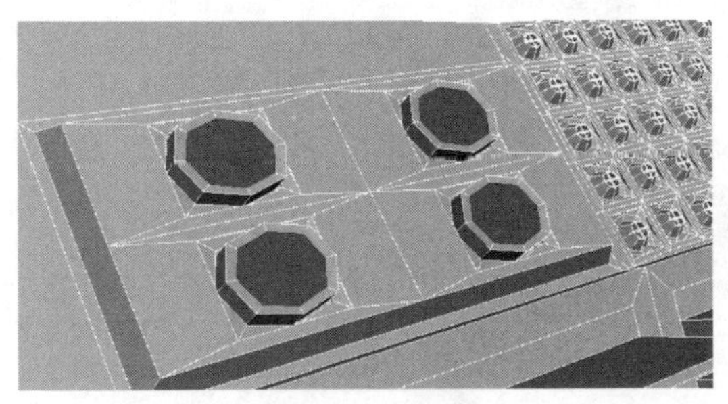

Figure 2-164

12. Group Extrude by **0.1**.

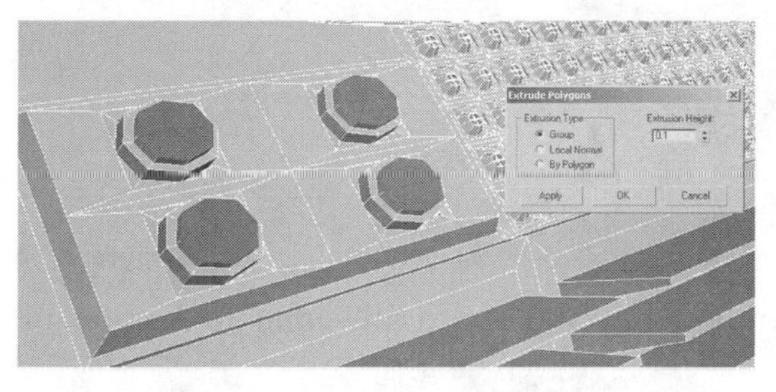

Figure 2-165

13. Delete the polygons, border-select each of them, and then Cap them; this reduces the number of polygons from four to one.

Figure 2-166

14. Select the polygon shown in Figure 2-167.

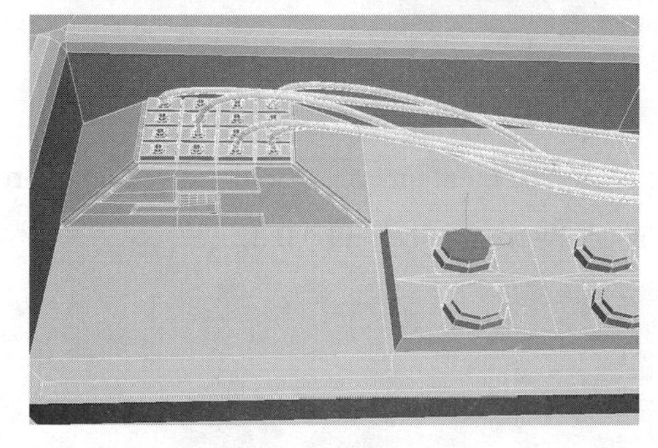

Figure 2-167

15. Switch to the Right view.
16. Shift-drag in the X axis (around **1.2**) and choose **Clone To Element**.

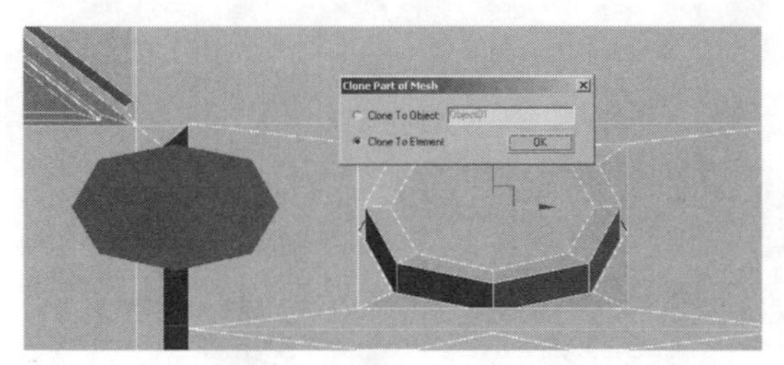

Figure 2-168

17. Turn on **Angle Snap** and rotate the clone 30 degrees in the Z axis.

Figure 2-169

18. Click **Hinge From Edge** and use the edge shown in Figure 2-170.

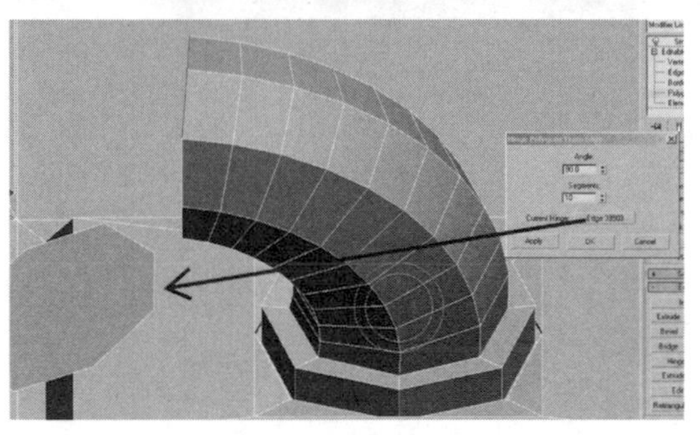

Figure 2-170

19. Delete the cloned element since we don't need it anymore.

20. Group Extrude the front polygon by **0.3**.

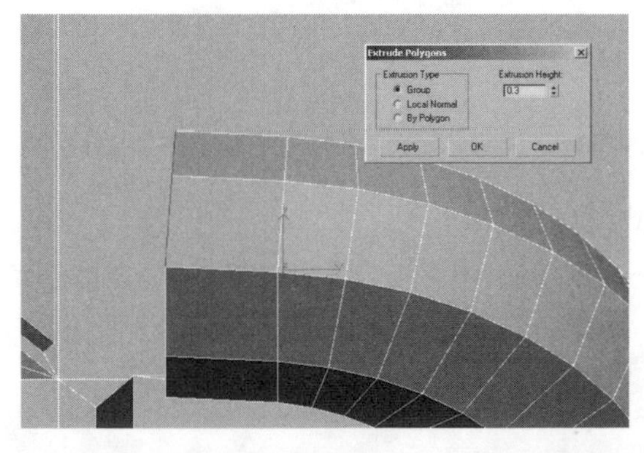

Figure 2-171

21. Shift-drag to Clone To Element in the X axis by **0.2**.
22. Switch between the Top, Right, and Perspective views, repositioning the polygon until it is at a 90-degree angle to the pipe, facing upward toward the junction box.

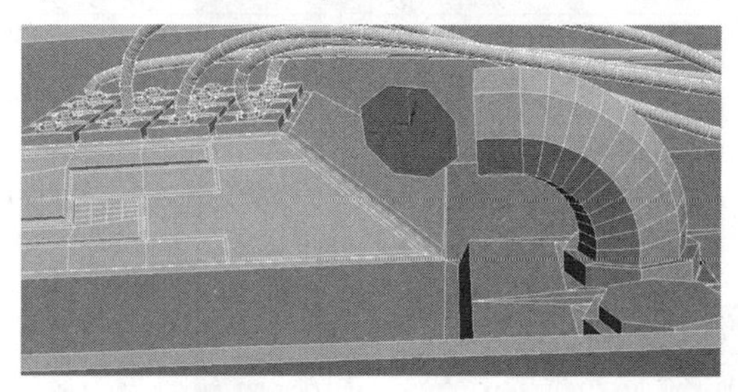

Figure 2-172

FYI: It may help you (it helps me) to border-select the clone and cap its rear, making a two-sided polygon, so when you rotate around the element it doesn't disappear.

Message: You might ask why I didn't just use a spline. Splines result in a smooth look more suited to wires. I wanted a segmented pipe. However, when your pipe starts at a strange angle and then curves, it can be challenging. You may have to play around with positioning until you get a segment you're happy with.

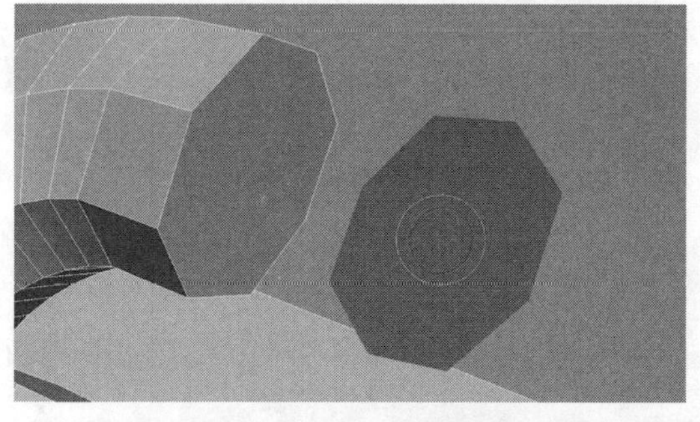

Figure 2-173

23. Move the element in the Z axis into its final position (see Figure 2-174), between the pipe and the junction box.

Figure 2-174

24. Do a Hinge From Edge of **90** degrees using the edge shown in Figure 2-174 with a Segments setting of **10.**

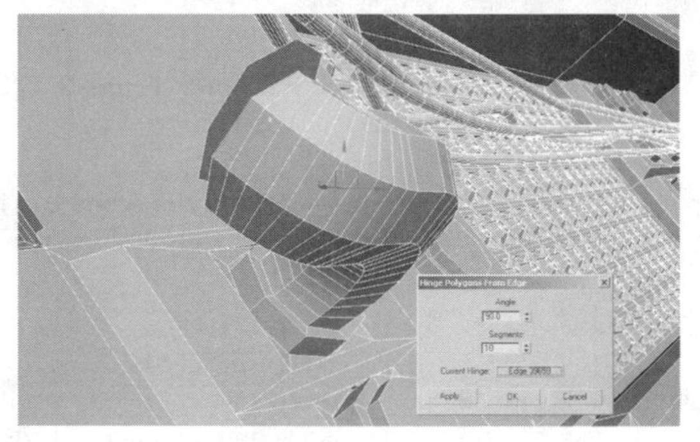
Figure 2-175

25. Delete the cloned element, as we no longer need it. Remember to delete both sides.

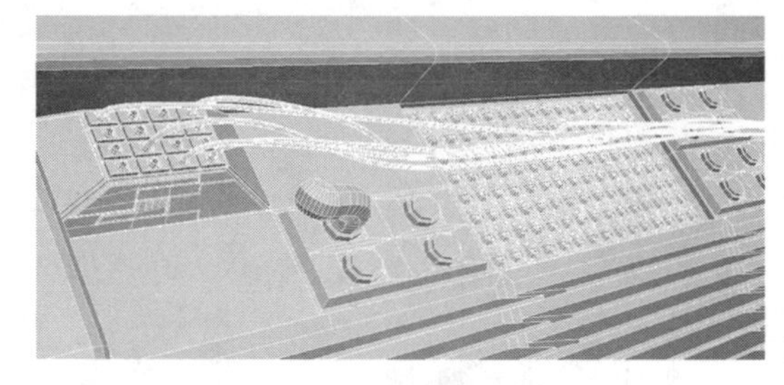
Figure 2-176

26. Click the pipe's facing polygon and Group Extrude it by **0.95**.

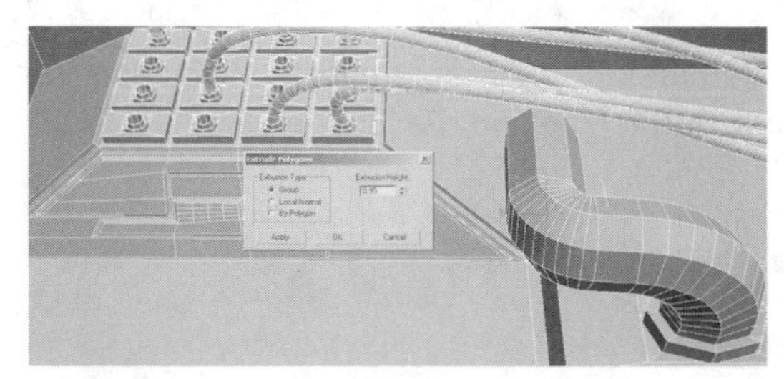
Figure 2-177

27. Shift-drag in the Z axis to Clone To Element and then flip the polygon so it's facing back toward the pipe.

Figure 2-178

28. Switch to the Top view.

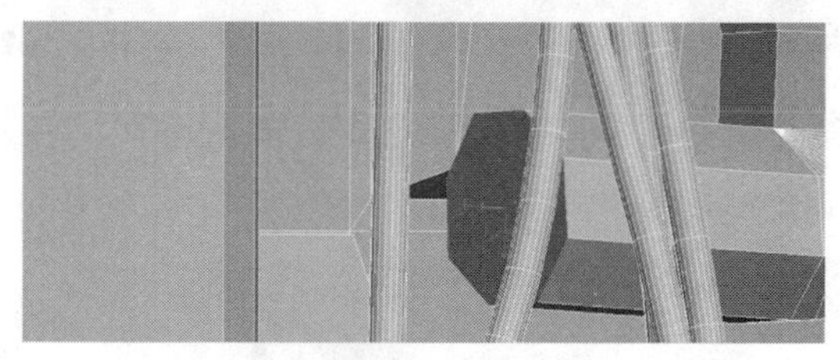

Figure 2-179

29. Rotate the polygon **5** degrees in the Y axis until it is correctly angled.

Figure 2-180

30. Hinge From Edge **90** degrees using the edge shown in Figure 2-181.

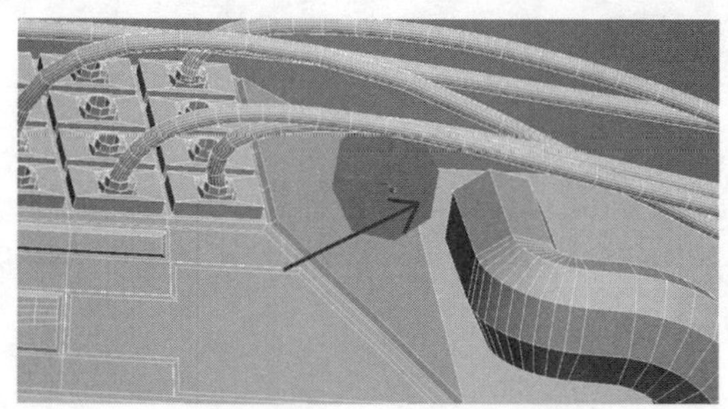

Figure 2-181

31. Extrude **0.73** (or until the polygon intersects with the surface of the junction box).

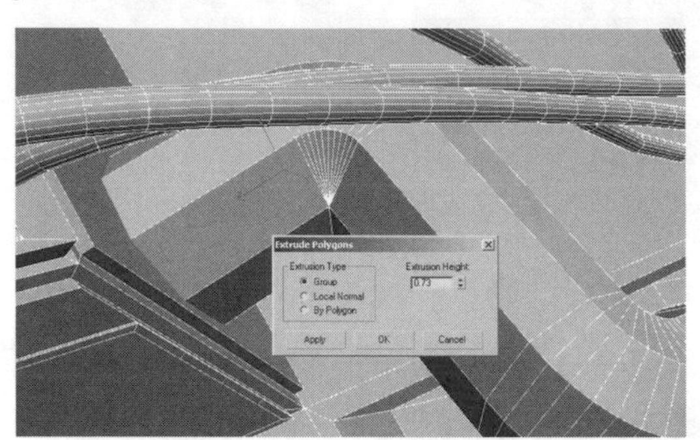

Figure 2-182

32. Zoom out in the Perspective view and do a render.

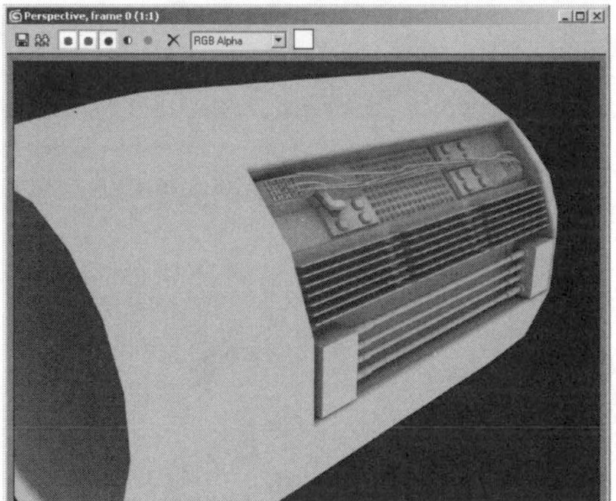

Figure 2-183

33. Select the polygon shown in Figure 2-184.

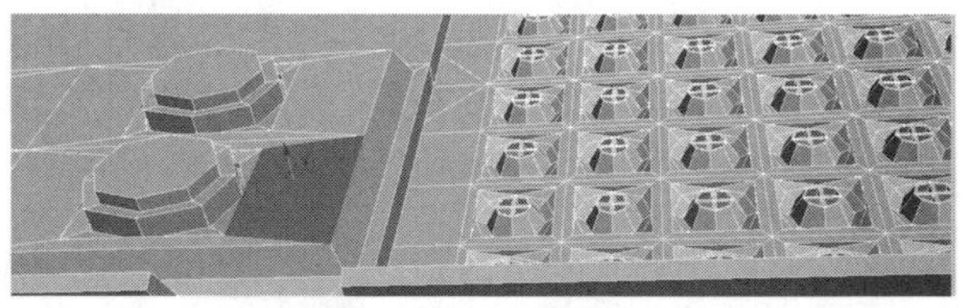

Figure 2-184

34. Shift-drag up in the Z axis to Clone To Element, and continue moving it up in the Z until it is even with the surface of the pipe fixture.

Figure 2-185

35. Select the polygon on the top of the pipe fitting and Hinge From Edge, using the left edge of the cloned element.

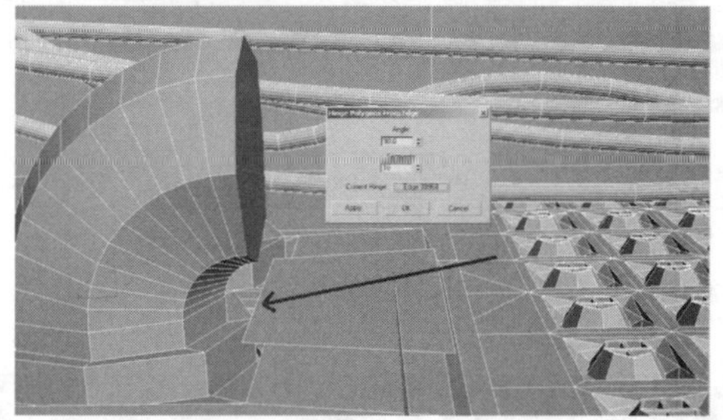

Figure 2-186

36. Select the cloned element and move it across the nacelle to the pipe fittings on the rear.

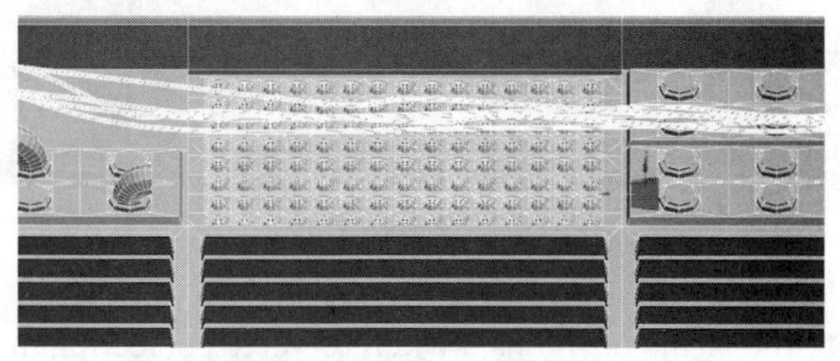

Figure 2-187

37. Select the polygon on top of the pipe fitting and Hinge From Edge **90** degrees.

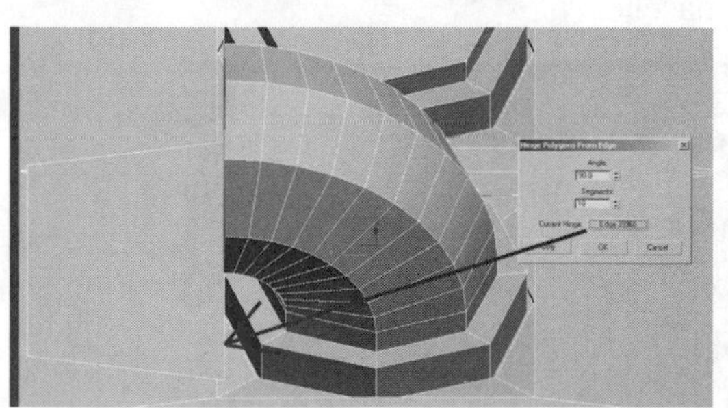

Figure 2-188

38. Delete the cloned element and select the facing surfaces on both pipes.

39. Group Extrude the polygons by **5.68.**

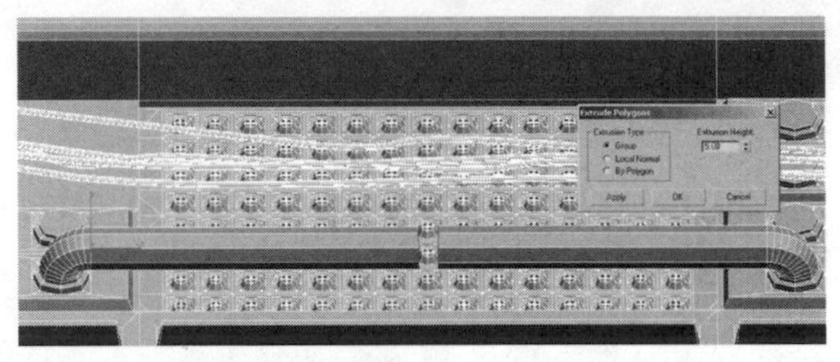

Figure 2-189

40. Click **Bevel Settings:**

Type	Height	Outline	Apply/OK
Group	0	0.3	Apply
Group	0.18	0	OK

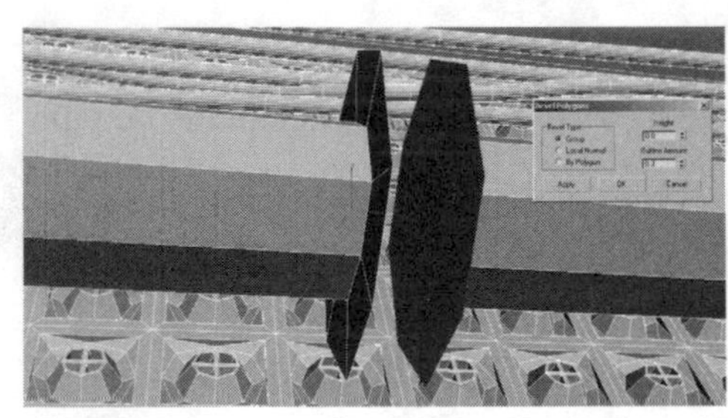

Figure 2-190

Figure 2-191

41. Delete the facing polygons, switch to Vertex selection mode, and weld the overlapping vertices.

42. Select the polygon at the left base of the lower-left pipe at the left side of the nacelle.

Figure 2-192

43. Shift-drag the polygon (Z axis) to Clone To Element, aligning with the top of the pipe fitting.

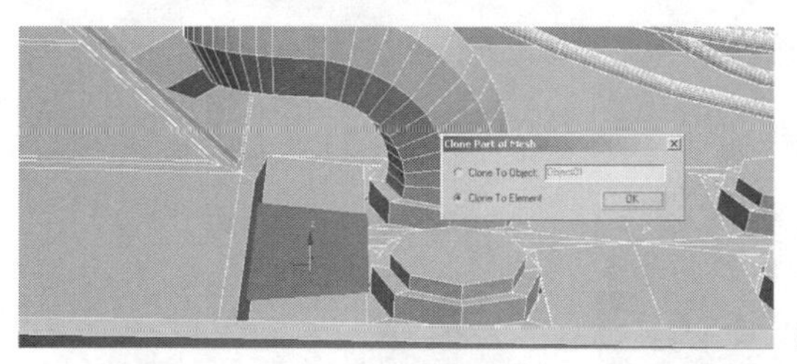

Figure 2-193

44. Hinge From Edge **90** degrees using the right edge of the cloned element as the hinge.

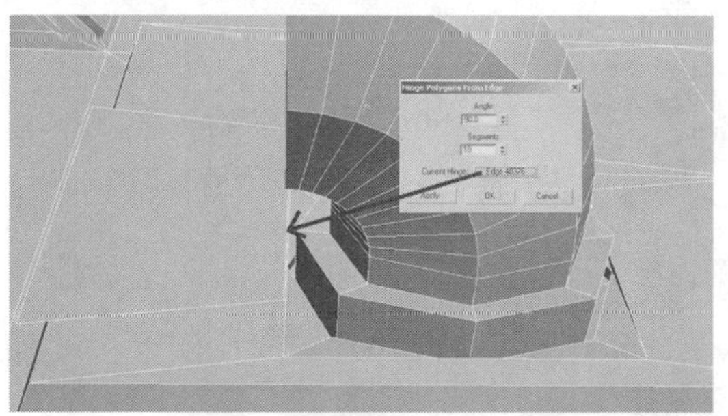

Figure 2-194

45. Move the cloned element around **1.7** in the local Y axis.

Figure 2-195

46. Select the facing polygon on the pipe and Group Extrude it by **1.55**.

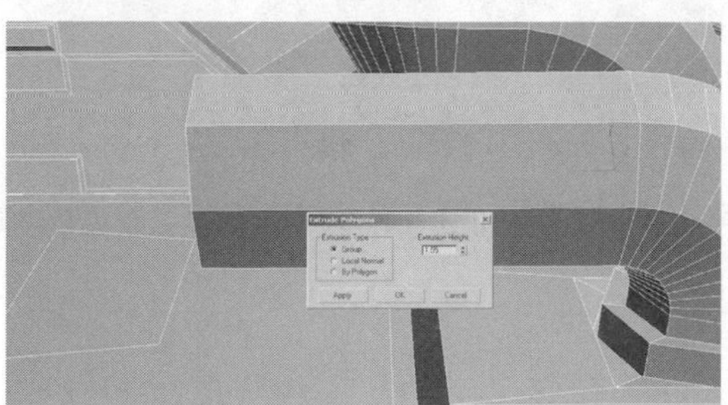

Figure 2-196

47. Switch to the Right view, select the cloned element, and rotate it **90** degrees in the X axis.

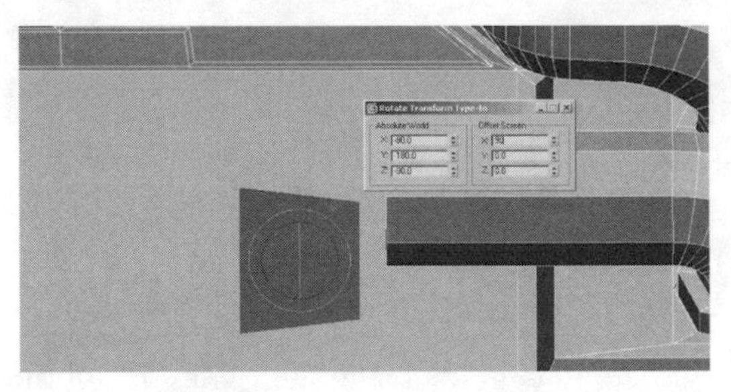

Figure 2-197

48. Move the cloned element until it's aligned with the pipe edge facing the junction box.

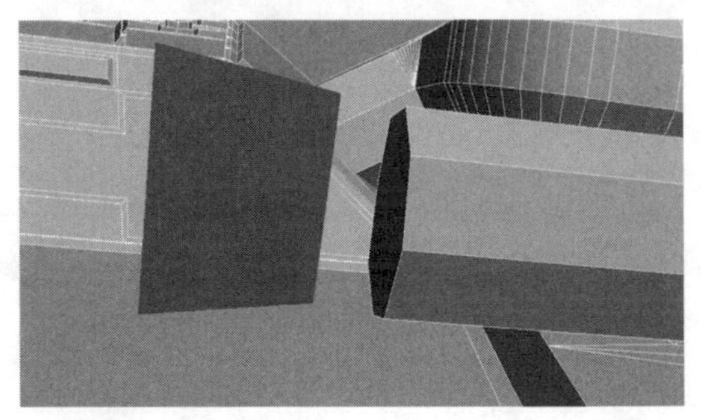

Figure 2-198

49. Select the polygon at the end of the pipe and Hinge From Edge **90** degrees.

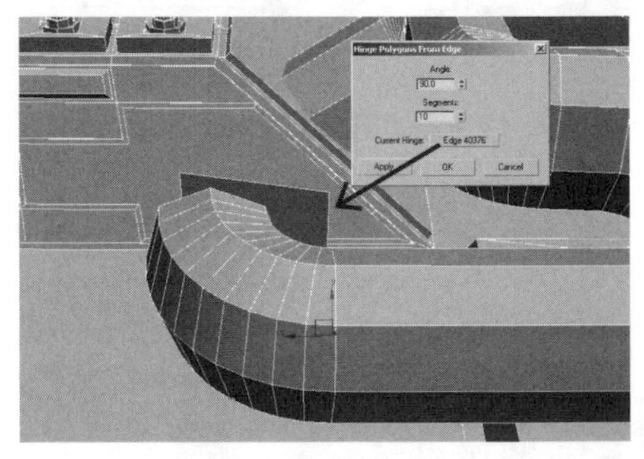

Figure 2-199

50. Delete the clone and Group Extrude the facing polygon by **0.7**.

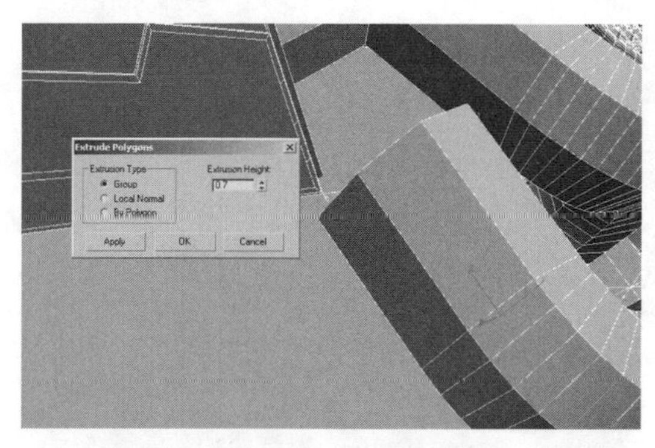

Figure 2-200

51. Extrude by **0.05** and then rotate the polygon **–5** in the Y axis.

Figure 2-201

52. Repeat step 51 ten more times.

Figure 2-202

53. Click **Bevel Settings:**

Type	Height	Outline	Apply/OK
Group	0.05	–0.03	Apply twice then OK

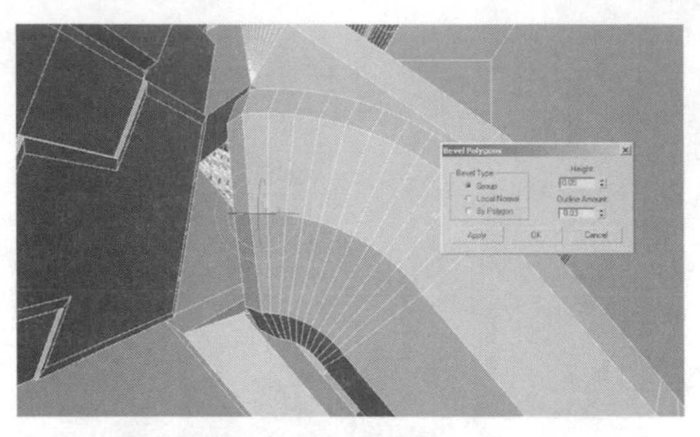

Figure 2-203

54. Group Extrude **0.4**.

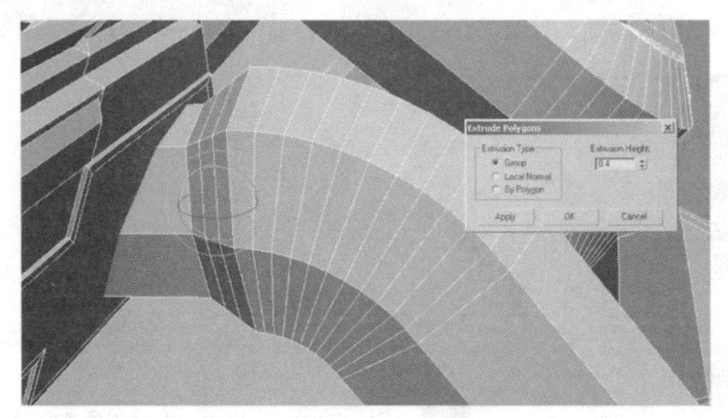

Figure 2-204

55. Select the polygons shown in Figure 2-205 and Group Extrude them by **0.8**.

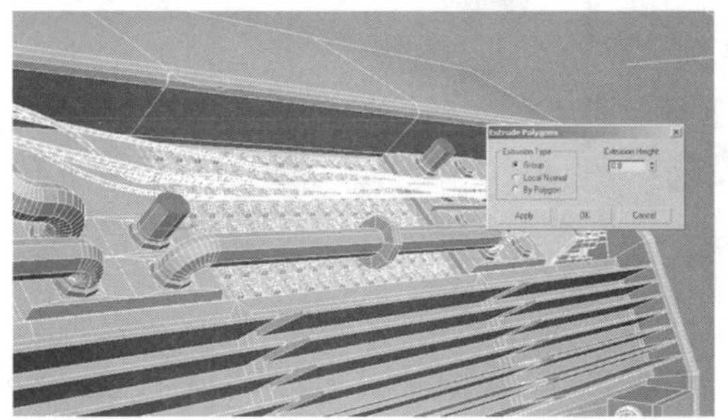

Figure 2-205

56. Select the polygon at the base to the right of the leftmost pipe.
57. Shift-drag in the Z axis to Clone To Element.

Figure 2-206

58. Align the clone with the top of the pipe and Hinge From Edge **90** degrees.

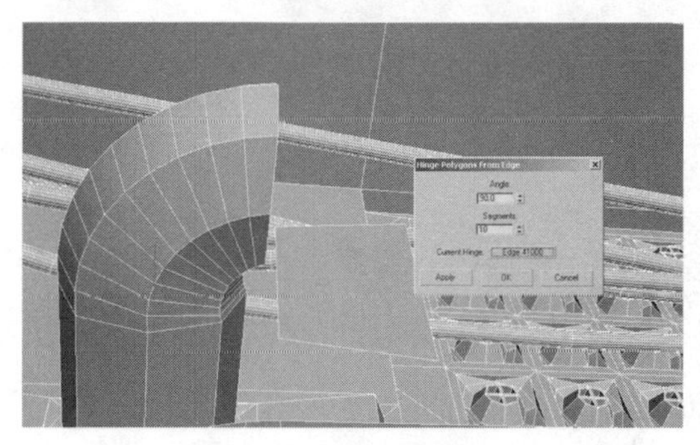

Figure 2-207

59. Delete the cloned element, Group Extrude the polygon by **4.0**, and then switch to the Right view.

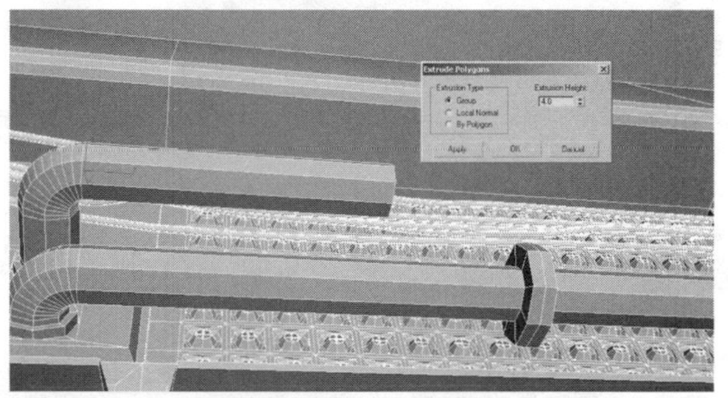

Figure 2-208

60. Extrude by **0.1** and then rotate **–10** in the X axis.

Figure 2-209

61. Repeat step 60 four times.

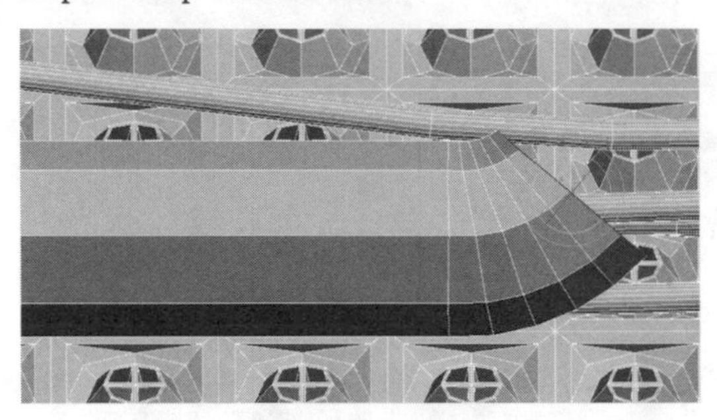

Figure 2-210

62. Extrude by **0.1** and then rotate **10** in the Y axis.

Figure 2-211

63. Repeat step 62 three times.

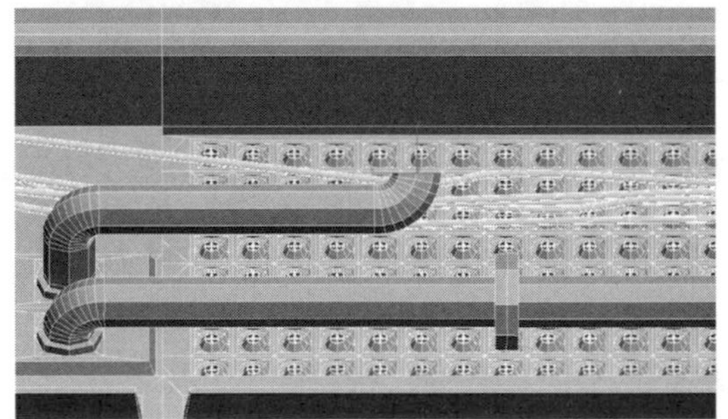

Figure 2-212

64. Select the polygon at the base of the pipe fitting on the right side.

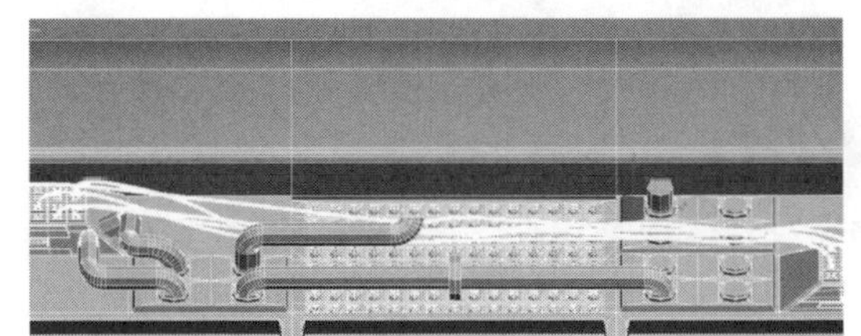

Figure 2-213

65. Clone To Element in the local Z axis and move it so it is even with the top of the pipe fitting.

Figure 2-214

66. Select the polygon atop the pipe fitting and Hinge From Edge **90** degrees.

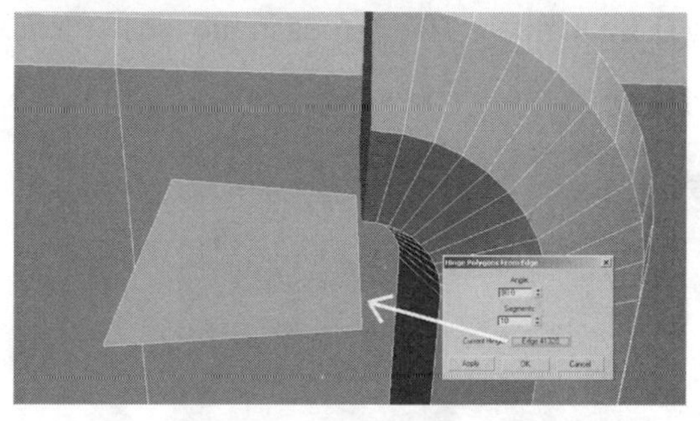

Figure 2-215

67. Extrude the polygon by **6.98** and then delete the cloned element.

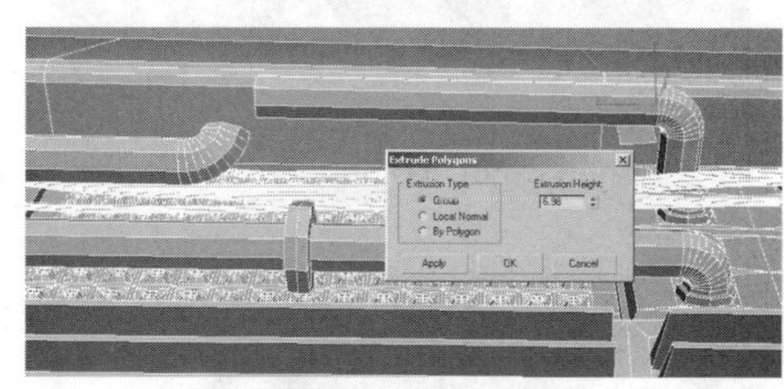

Figure 2-216

68. Switch to the Right view, select the facing polygon of the pipe fitting, and zoom in (**z**).

69. Extrude by **0.1** and rotate **10** degrees in the local Y axis.

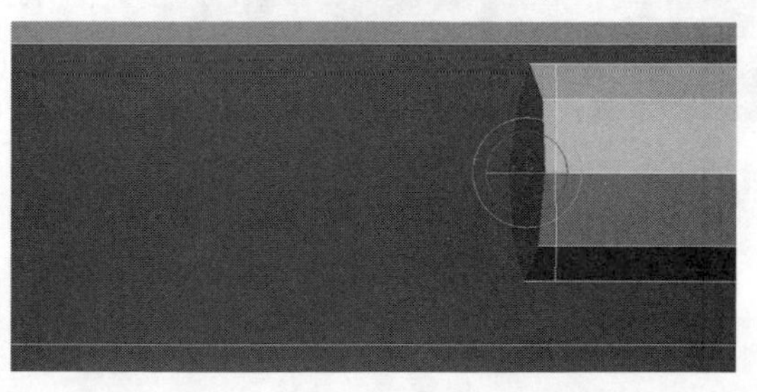

Figure 2-217

70. Repeat step 69 three more times.

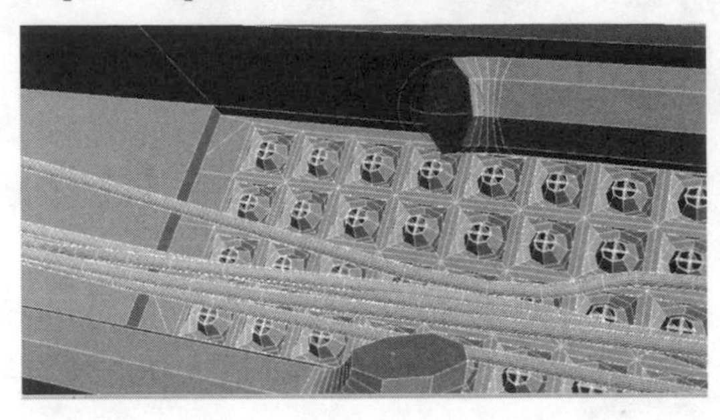

Figure 2-218

71. Extrude by **0.1** and rotate **10** degrees in the local X axis.
72. Repeat step 71 four more times.

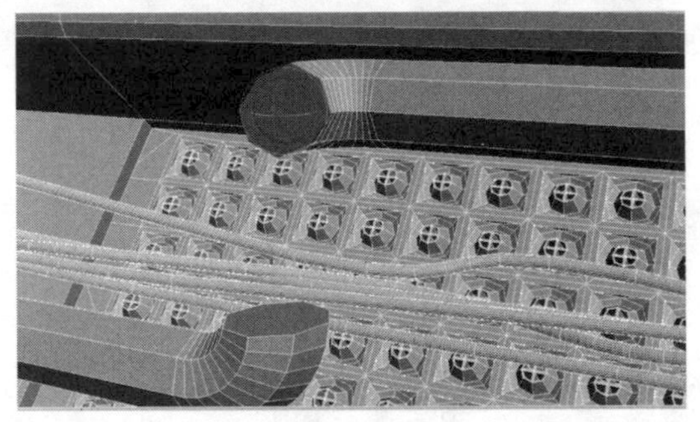

Figure 2-219

73. Extrude by **0.1** and then rotate **10** degrees in the X axis and **–10** degrees in the Y axis.

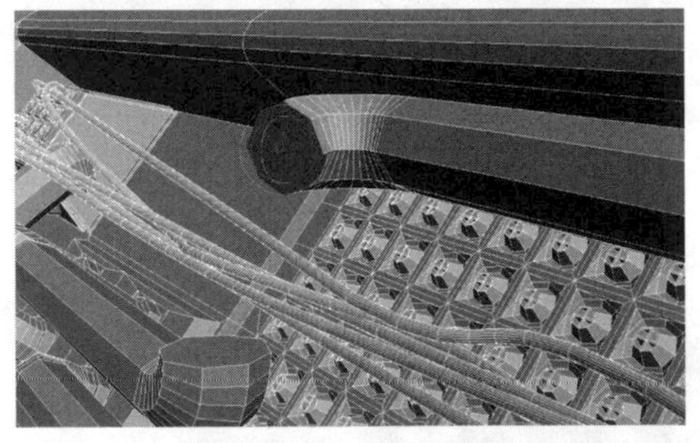

Figure 2-220

74. Extrude by **0.1**.

75. Select the facing polygon on the left lower pipe.

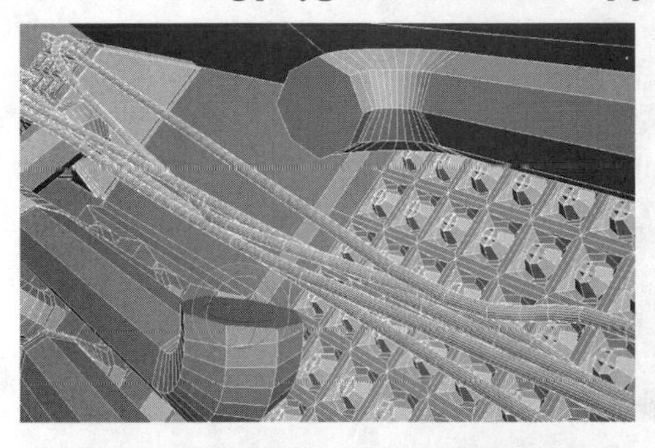

Figure 2-221

76. Extrude by **0.1** and then rotate **10** degrees in the local X axis.

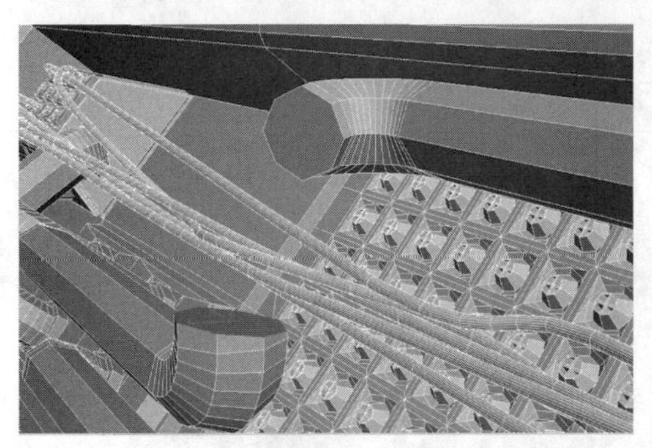

Figure 2-222

77. Repeat step 76.

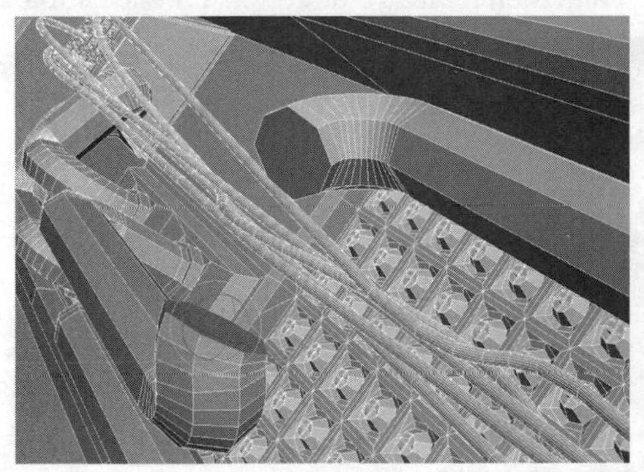

Figure 2-223

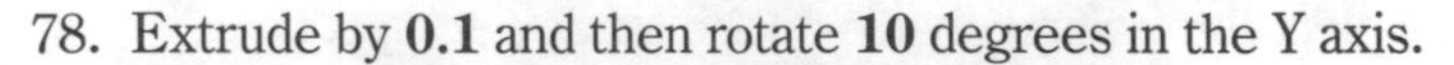

78. Extrude by **0.1** and then rotate **10** degrees in the Y axis.

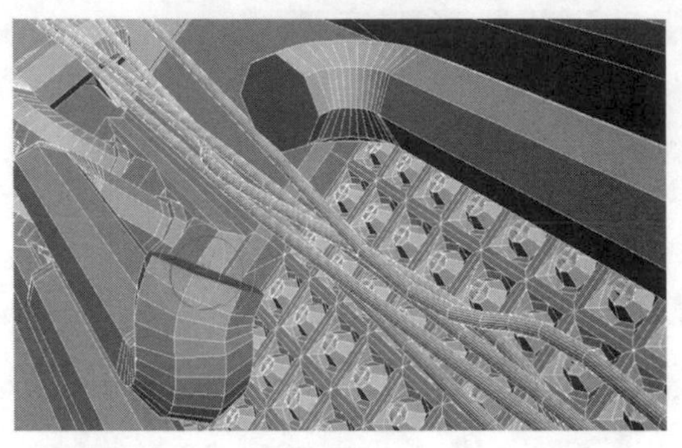

Figure 2-224

79. Repeat step 78 three times.
80. Extrude by **0.1** three times.

Figure 2-225

81. Extrude **0.1** and then rotate **10** degrees in the local X axis.

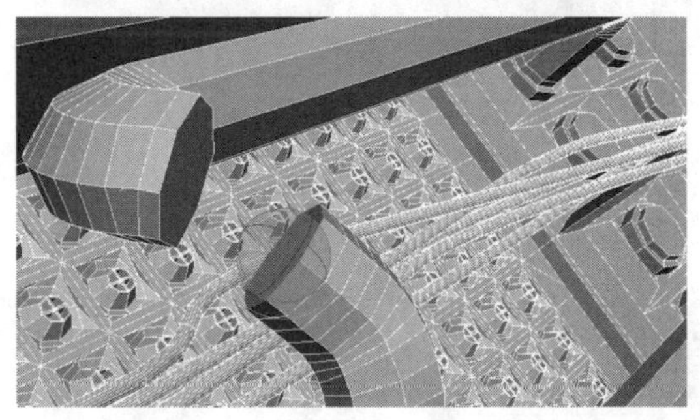

Figure 2-226

82. Select the polygon on the other pipe, Extrude it **0.1**, and rotate it **–10** degrees in the Y axis.

Figure 2-227

83. Extrude it by **0.1**, then rotate it **–10** degrees in the Y axis and **5** in the Z axis.

Figure 2-228

84. Extrude it by **0.1** and the rotate it by **5** degrees in the X axis.

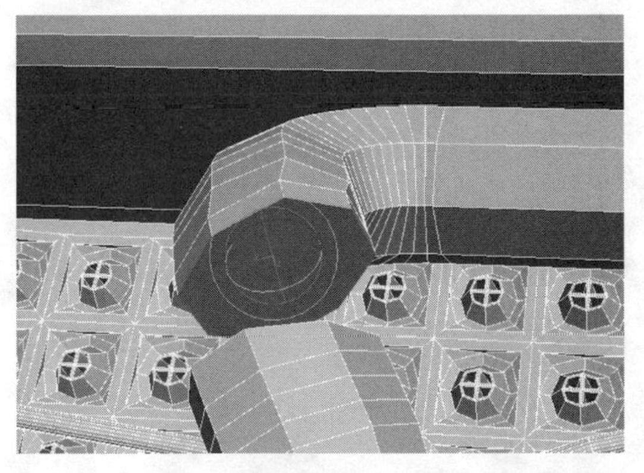

Figure 2-229

85. Select the polygons on both pipes and delete them.

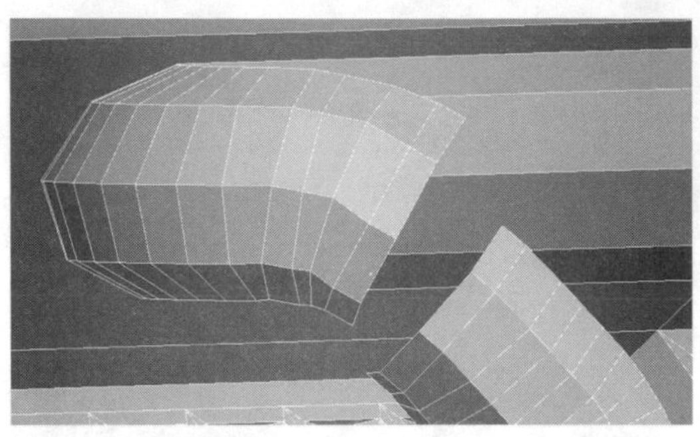

Figure 2-230

86. Click an edge on each pipe and click **Bridge**.

Figure 2-231

87. Repeat step 86 until you have bridged all the edges and have one continuous pipe.

FYI: You may want to move vertices before bridging to make your pipe smoother looking.

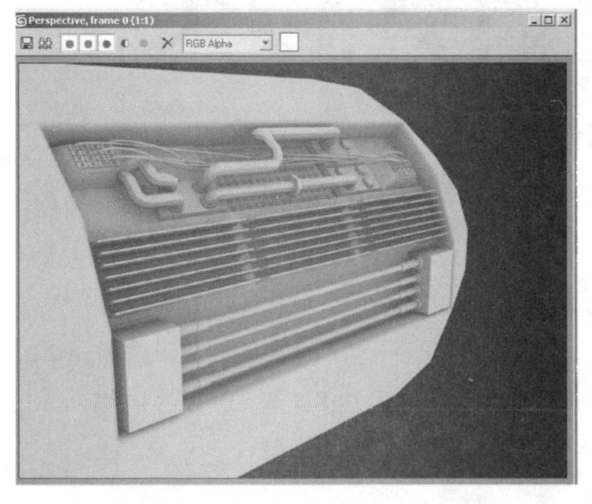

Figure 2-232

Message: I intentionally didn't straighten every vertex to make perfect contours; I wanted an irregular look. If you prefer, move the vertices until the contours are smooth.

88. Select the polygon at the base of the pipe fitting on the rightmost collection of fittings.

Figure 2-233

89. Clone To Element and move in the local Z axis to align to the top of the lower-right pipe fitting.

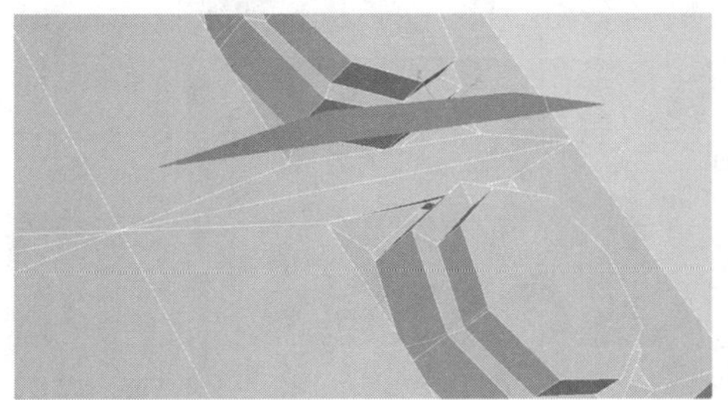

Figure 2-234

90. Click the polygon at the top of the lower-right pipe fitting and Hinge From Edge **90** degrees.

Figure 2-235

91. Move the clone **2.196** in the local X axis so it is beneath the upper-rightmost pipe fitting.

Figure 2-236

92. Select the polygon atop the upper-rightmost pipe fitting, Hinge From Edge **90** degrees, then delete the cloned element.

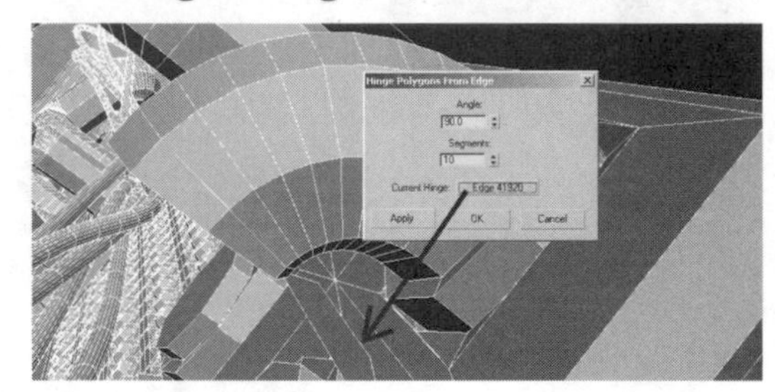

Figure 2-237

93. Select the facing polygons on both pipes and Group Extrude them until they meet (around **1.16**).

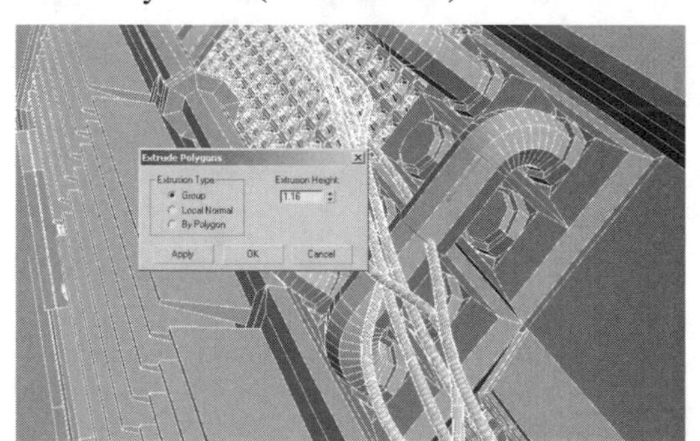

Figure 2-238

94. Delete the inward-facing polygons on both pipes.

95. To fix the problem of wires intersecting pipes, select the four polygons on the top of the pipe (two on each side of the connection).

Figure 2-239

96. Click **Grow** until the entire pipe is highlighted except for a single set of polygons at the base of each fitting.

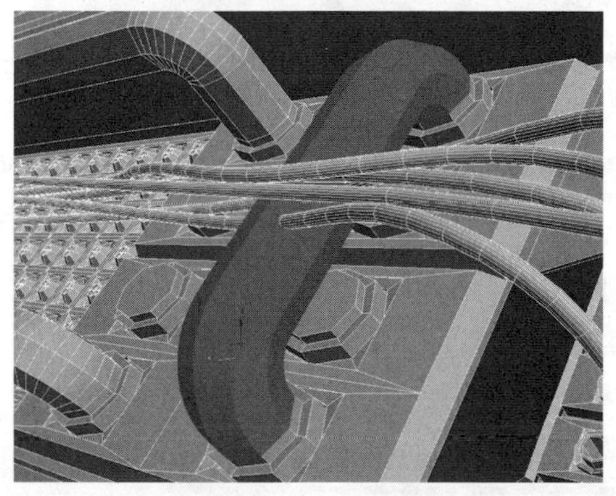
Figure 2-240

97. Right-click the **Select and Move** tool.
98. In the Transform Type-In dialog, set the Offset World X to **0.80** and the Z to **0.73**.

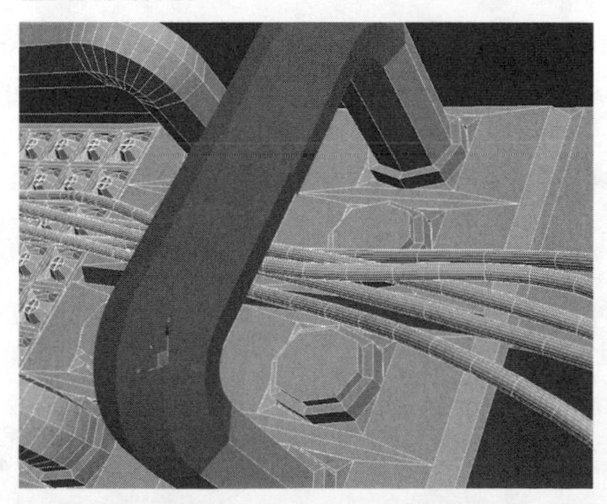
Figure 2-241

99. Switch to Vertex selection mode, highlight the vertices along the middle seam, and Weld them.

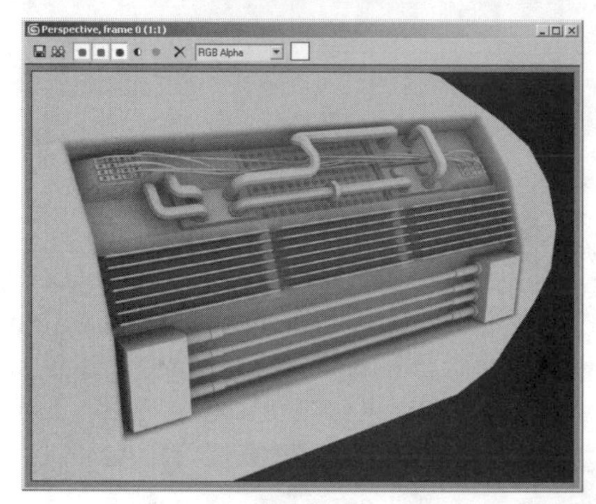

Figure 2-242

Message: At this point, I'm going to move on. Add as many pipes, wires, and hoses as you want. The more you have, the more complicated and techy your bot will look.

100. Select the polygon atop the lower-left junction box.

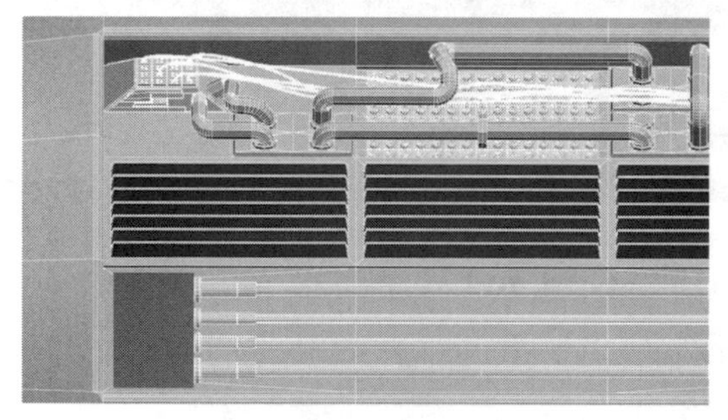

Figure 2-243

101. Zoom in on it, then go to the Create panel, select **Sphere**, turn on AutoGrid, and create a hemisphere in the upper-left corner of the junction box with a Radius of **0.2** and **32** Segments.

Figure 2-244

102. Switch to the Perspective view to make sure that the sphere is seated just below the surface of the junction box (see Figure 2-244), choose **Convert to Editable Polygon**, and then delete the sphere's polygons that are lying beneath the surface of the junction box.

103. Switch back to object mode and Shift-drag to clone the sphere (make seven copies so you have one for each junction box corner) and then position one rivet in each junction box corner with the Move tool.

Message: Because the junction boxes are seated at an angle, use the Perspective view to double-check that all the rivets are seated below the surface of the junction box.

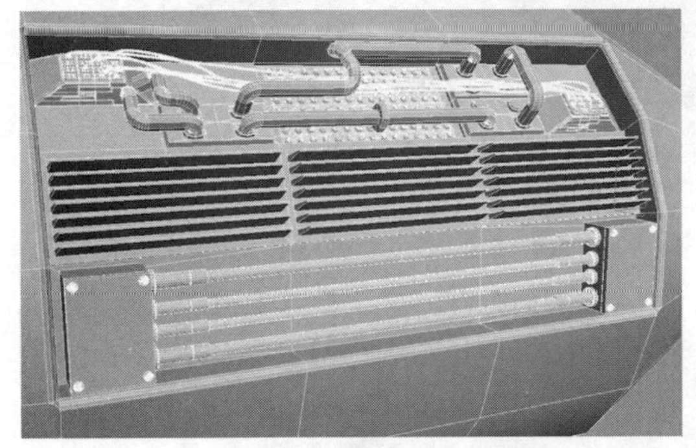

Figure 2-245

104. Object-select the **L_nacelle**, click **Attach List**, select all the spheres, and click **Attach**.

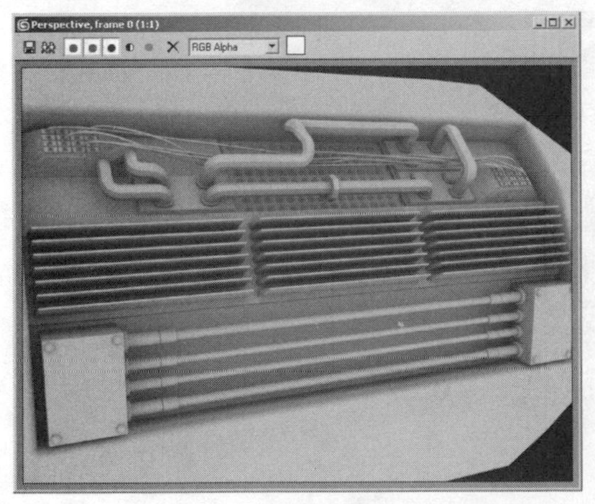

Figure 2-246

Day 5: Detailing the Nacelle

1. Select the nacelle's rear polygons, activate **Slice Plane**, and move the slice plane approximately **16** in the X axis.

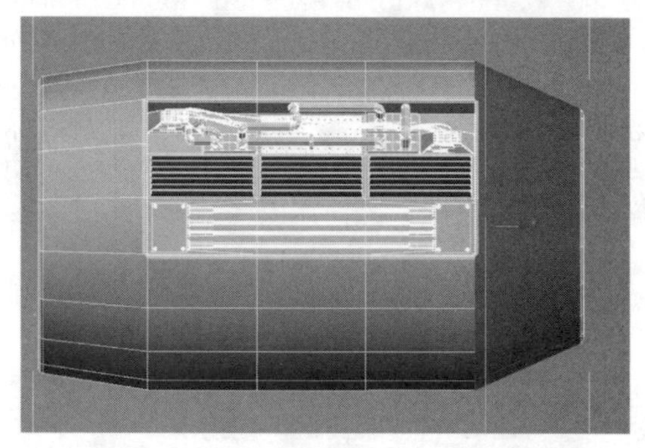

Figure 2-247

2. Click the **Slice** button and then turn off Slice Plane.
3. Select one of the segments created using Slice Plane and click **Loop**.

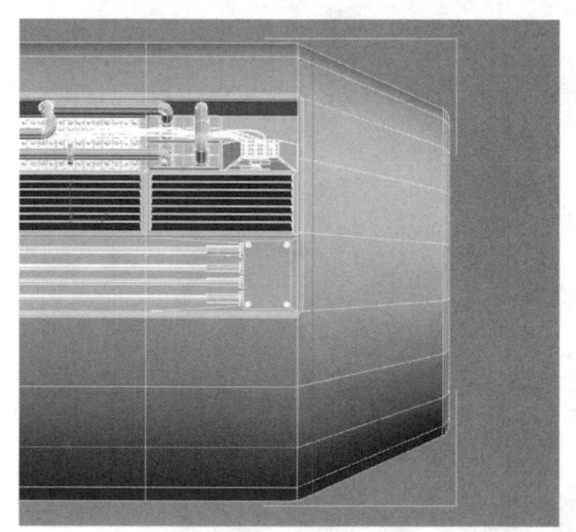

Figure 2-248

4. Chamfer the edge by **0.12**.

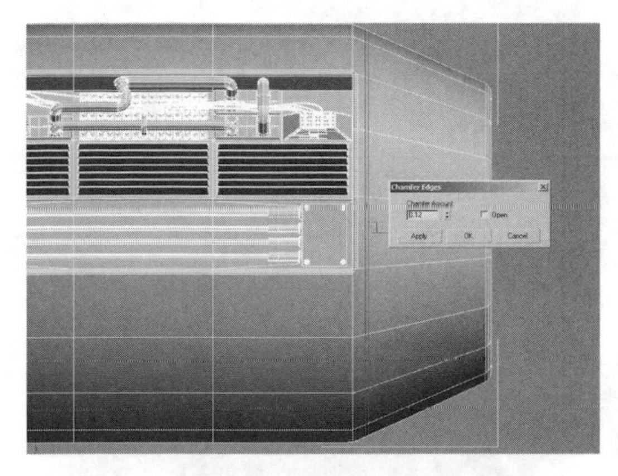

Figure 2-249

5. Highlight the new polygons you made with the chamfer.

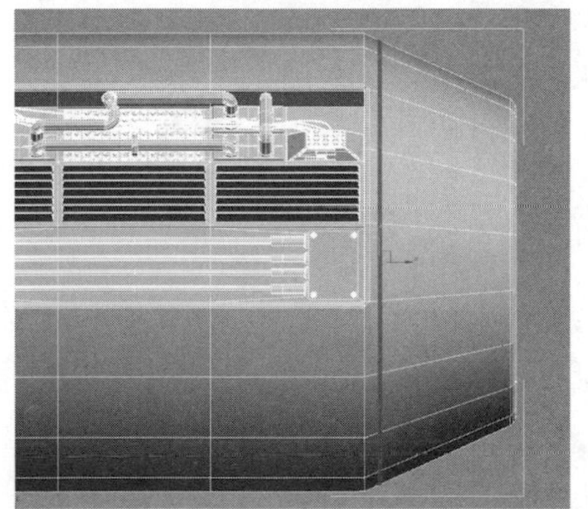

Figure 2-250

6. Extrude the Local Normals by a height of **–0.2**.

FYI: We extruded by "Local Normals" rather than by Group because you want the polys to extrude inward around the nozzle, creating a groove where the nozzle connects to the nacelle.

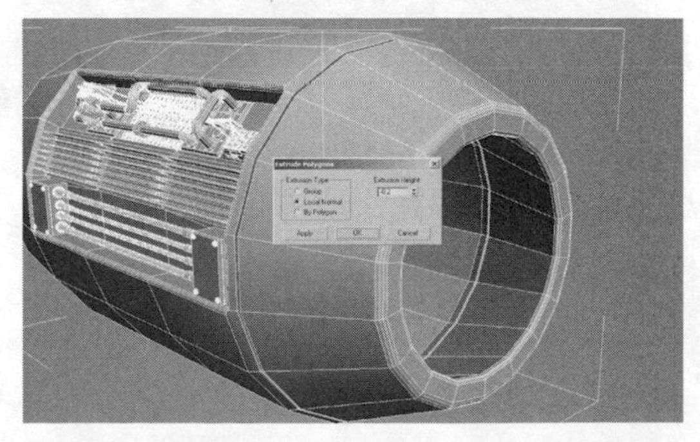

Figure 2-251

7. Select the 18 polygons shown in Figure 2-252, exercising extreme care not to select the polygons on the outer nozzle or the polygons inside the nozzle.

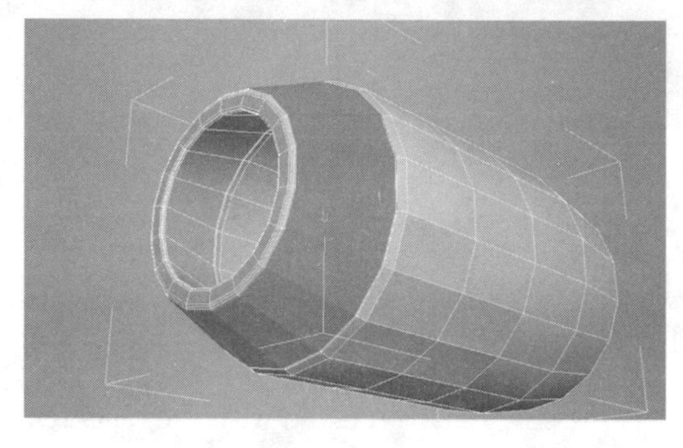

Figure 2-252

8. Click **Bevel Settings**:

Type	Height	Outline	Apply/OK
By Polygon	0	–0.25	Apply
By Polygon	–0.25	0	Apply
By Polygon	0	–0.05	Apply
By Polygon	0.3	0	Apply
By Polygon	0	–1.0	Apply
By Polygon	–0.1	0	OK

Message: These are air brakes. If I were doing this for a film, I'd detach the panels and put a hydraulic system below them.

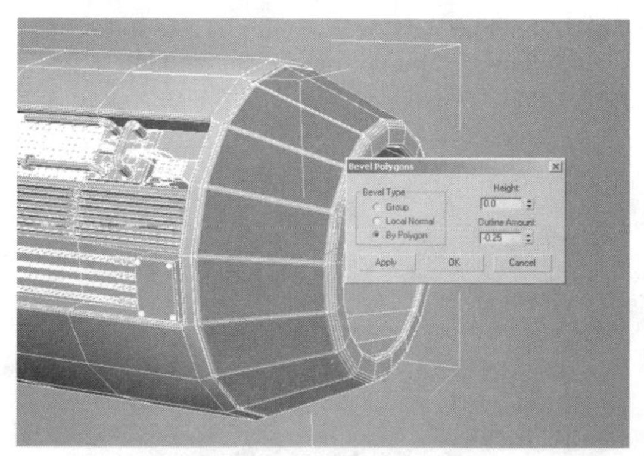

Figure 2-253

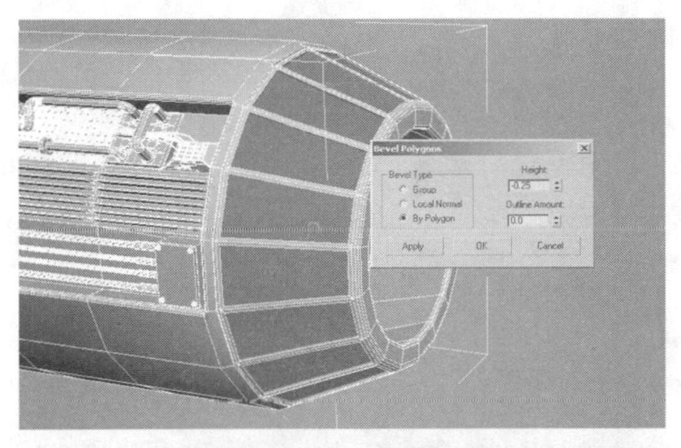

Figure 2-254

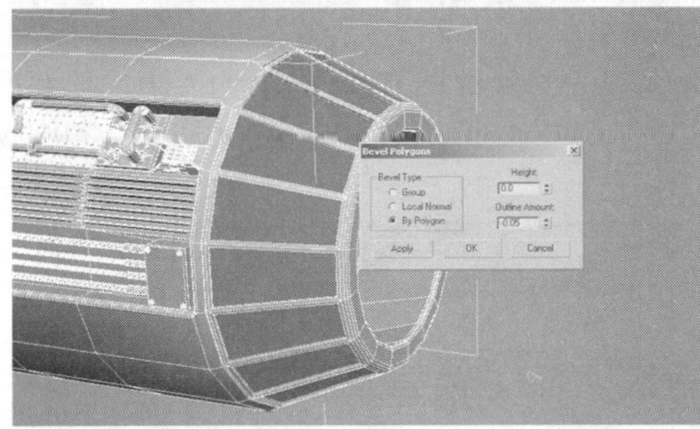

Figure 2-255

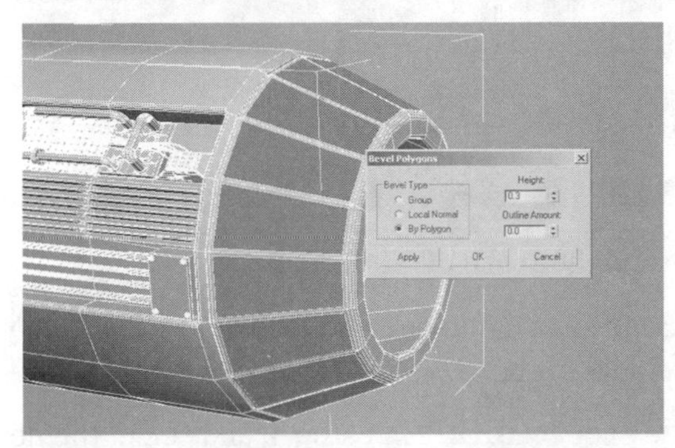

Figure 2-256

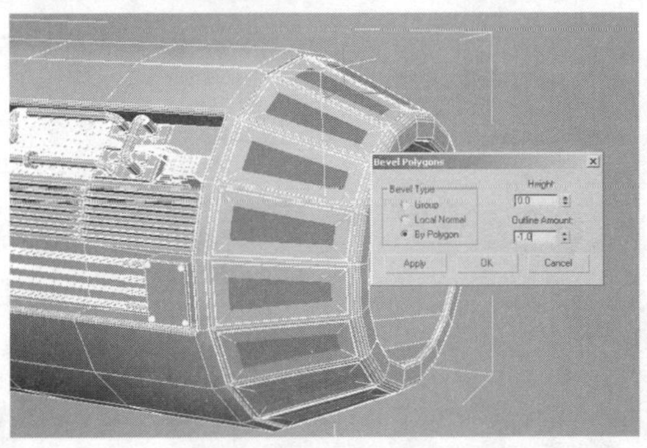

Figure 2-257

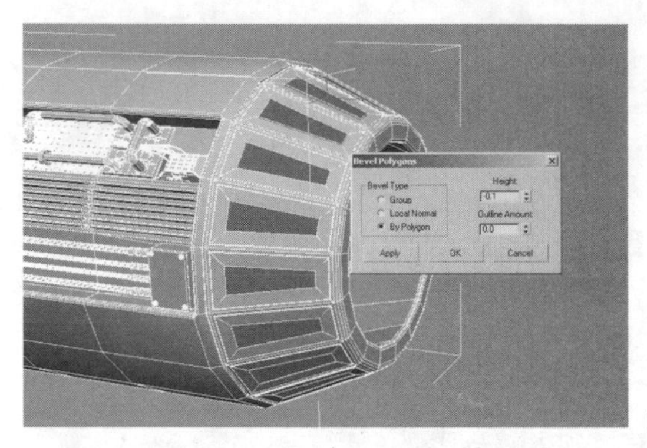

Figure 2-258

9. Switch to the Right view, select the polygons shown in Figure 2-259, click **Slice Plane**, and move the slice plane approximately **–16** in the X axis.

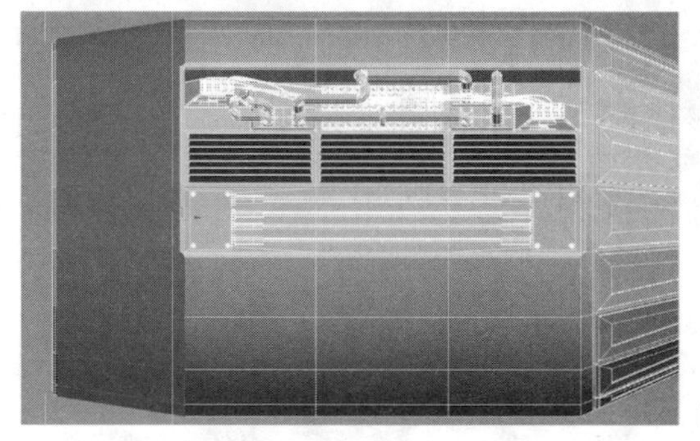

Figure 2-259

10. Click **Slice** and then turn off Slice Plane.
11. Switch to Edge selection mode and loop-select the slice you just made, as you did in step 3.
12. Chamfer the edge by **0.12**, as in step 4, and select the new polys you made, as in step 5.

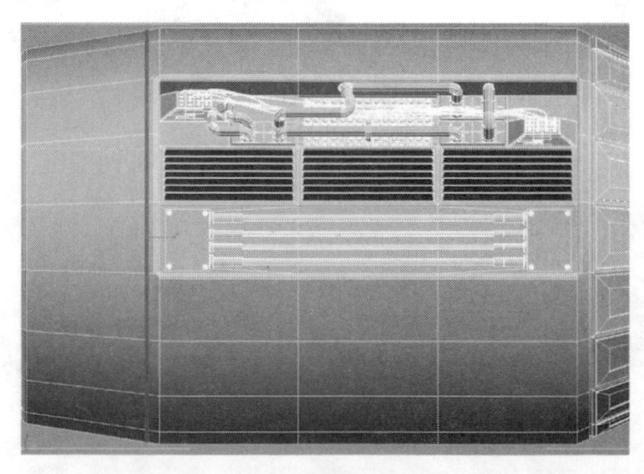

Figure 2-260

13. Extrude by Local Normals **–0.2**.

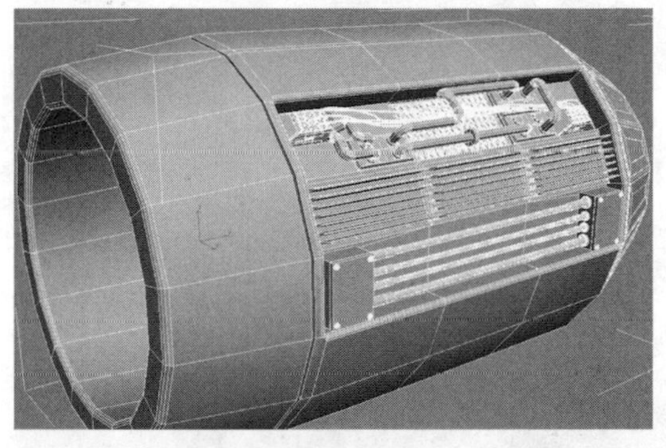

Figure 2-261

14. Highlight the polygons shown in Figure 2-262:

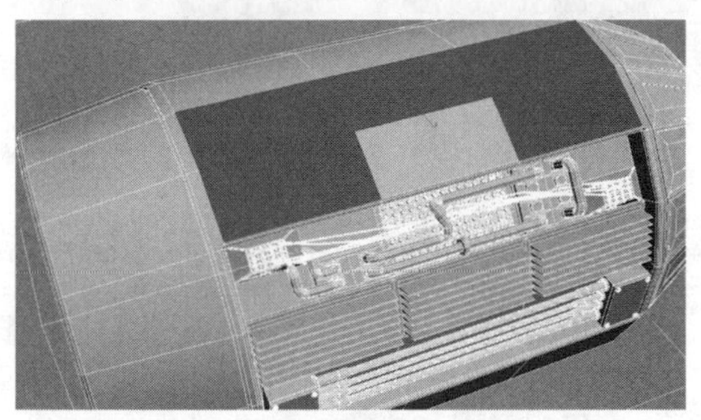

Figure 2-262

15. Click **Bevel Settings**:

Type	Height	Outline	Apply/OK
Group	–0.2	0	Apply
Group	0	–0.12	Apply
Group	0.2	0	OK

Figure 2-263

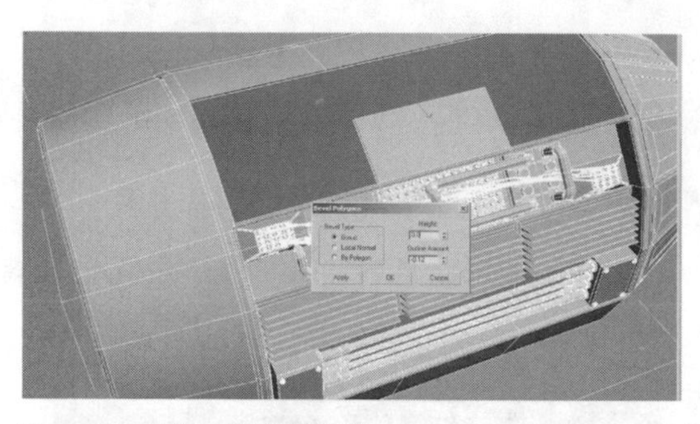

Figure 2-264

Figure 2-265

Message: A test render shows what we've been doing: creating a mechanic's access panel for working on the interior components. We're going to use the same technique to trim out the rest of the nacelle.

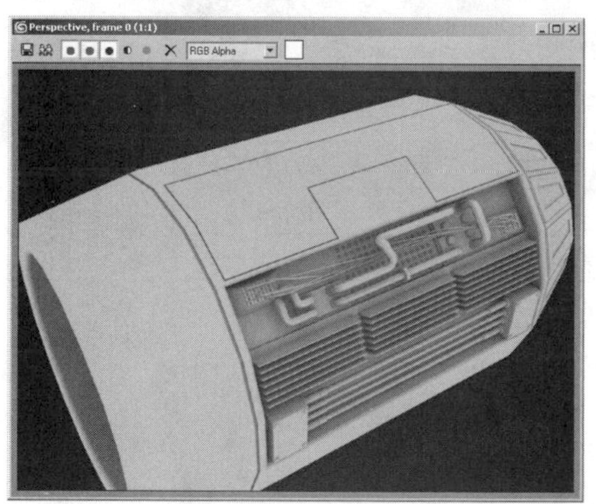

Figure 2-266

16. Highlight the polygons shown in Figure 2-267.

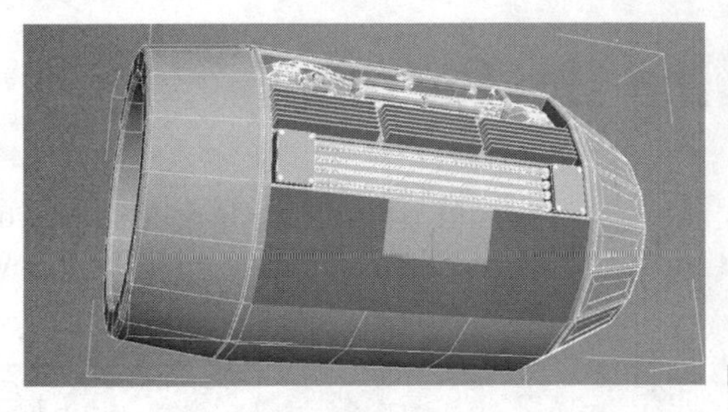

Figure 2-267

17. Repeat the Bevels from step 15.
18. Select the nine polygons on the bottom of the nacelle as shown in Figure 2-268.

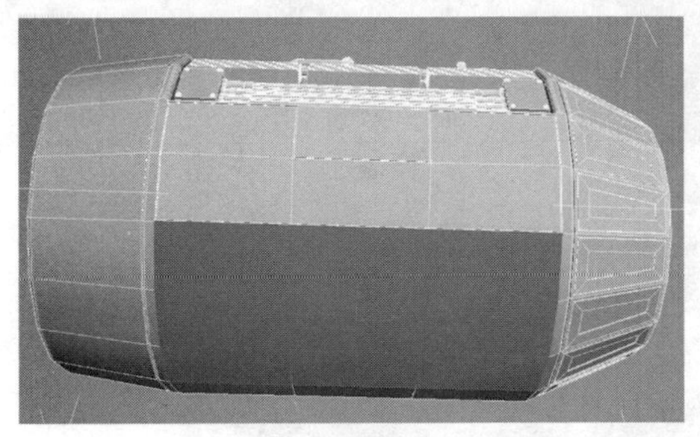

Figure 2-268

19. Repeat the Bevels from step 15 again.

Day 6: Building the Rotors

1. Switch to the Front view and, using AutoGrid, create a Cone primitive in the middle of the nacelle's air intake with the following settings:

Radius 1	Radius 2	Height	Sides	Height Segs	Cap Segs
3.0	0.03	3	32	4	1

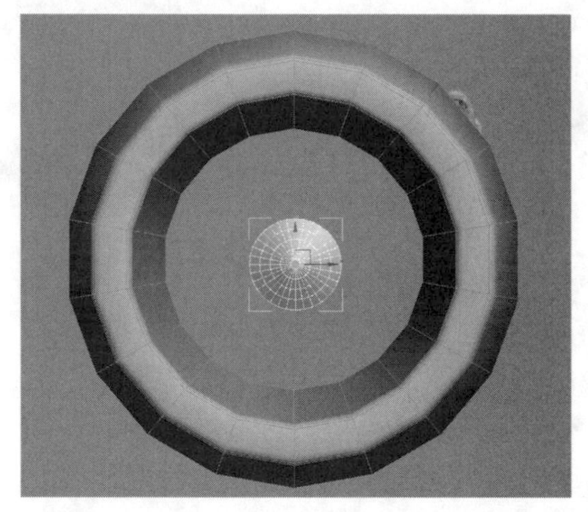

Figure 2-269

2. Switch to the Right view and move the cone into its proper position, just inside the nacelle's air intake (around **–83** in the X axis).

Figure 2-270

3. Choose **Convert to Editable Poly**, select the back-facing polygon, and click **Bevel Settings:**

Type	Height	Outline	Apply/OK
Group	0.4	0	Apply
Group	0	0.3	Apply
Group	4	0	OK

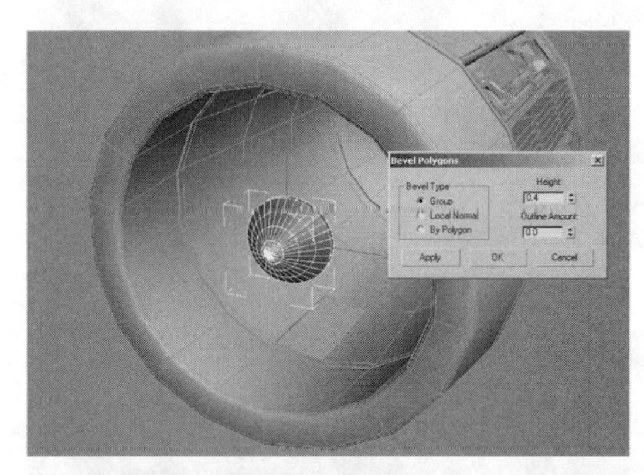

Figure 2-271

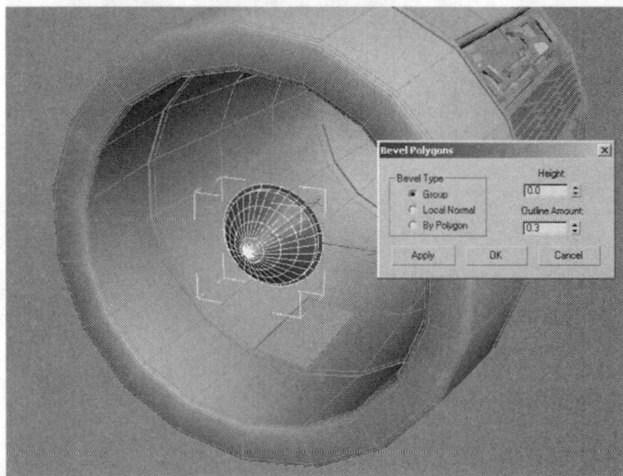

Figure 2-272

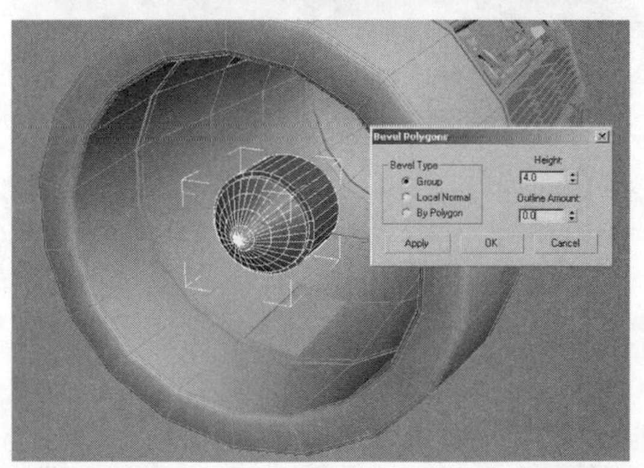

Figure 2-273

4. Select and delete the rear-facing polygons.

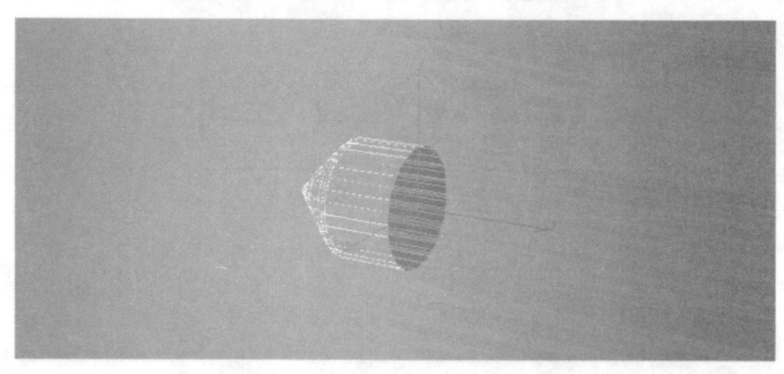

Figure 2-274

5. Select the 32 polygons at the rear of the rotor:

Figure 2-275

6. Extrude By Polygon **14**.

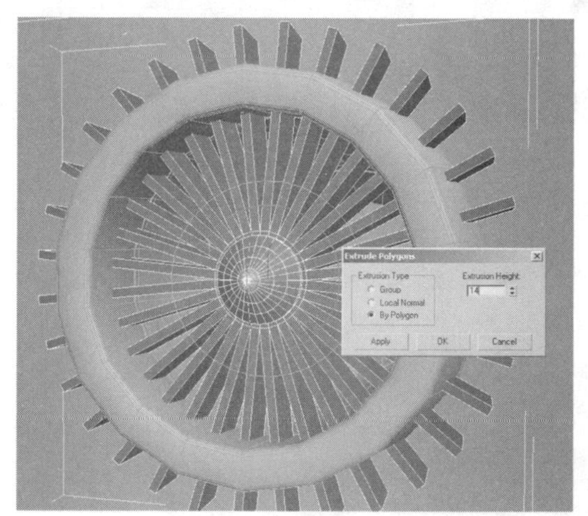

Figure 2-276

7. Switch to the Right view, turn on Vertex selection mode, marquee-select the two rear vertices of each blade (96 total), and rotate them **30** degrees in X.

Figure 2-277

8. Switch to Polygon selection mode (the tips of the blades should still be selected), go to the Front view, and scale the blades down to **30%**.

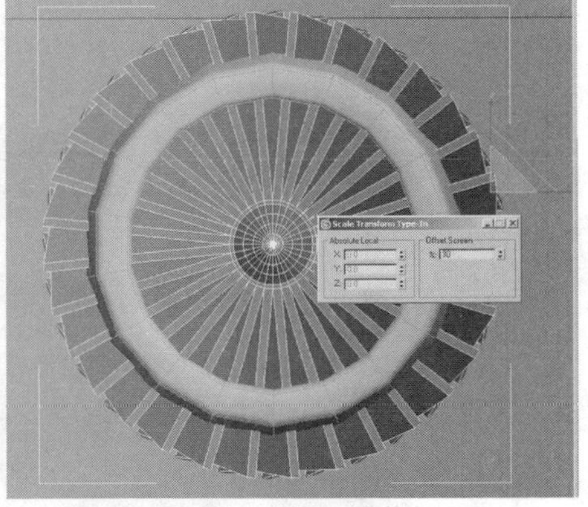

Figure 2-278

Figure 2-279

9. Switch to Object mode and the Perspective view, then scale the entire blade-rotor assembly down to **66** in the X and Z axes (or until the blades do not intersect the nacelle).

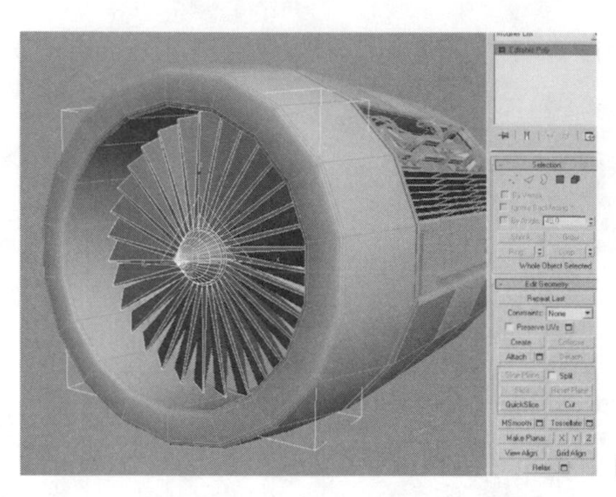

Figure 2-280

10. Apply the Clay material to the rotor assembly, rename it **rotor assembly**, and do a test render. If you prefer a rounder look, you can always use NURMS with three iterations, as shown in Figure 2-282.

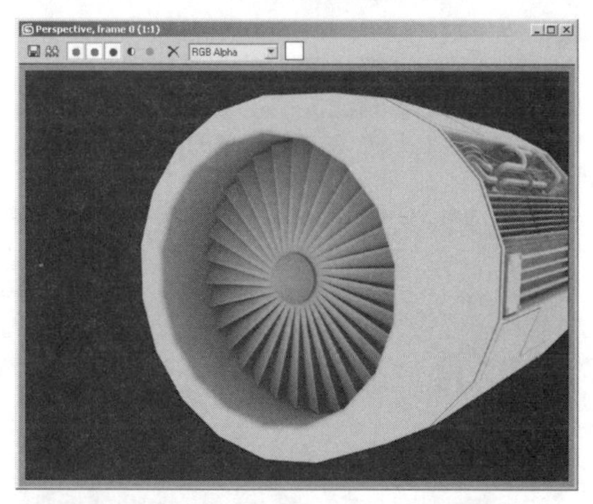

Figure 2-281

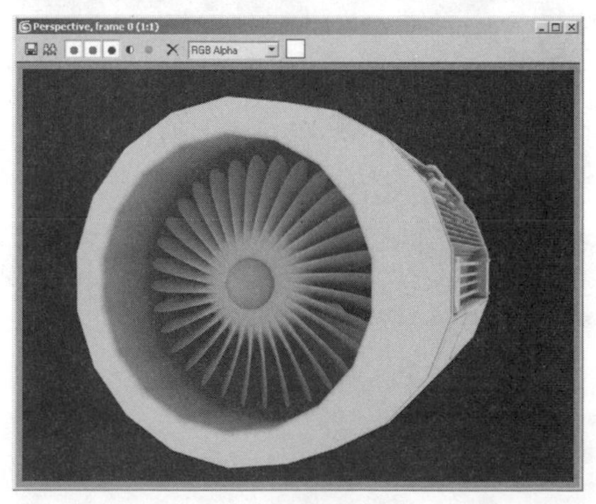

Figure 2-282

11. Switch to the Back view and, using AutoGrid, create a Cone in the rear nozzle and adjust its values to match those in the following table.

Radius 1	Radius 2	Height	Height Segs	Cap Segs	Sides
4.088	5.854	–4.136	5	1	24

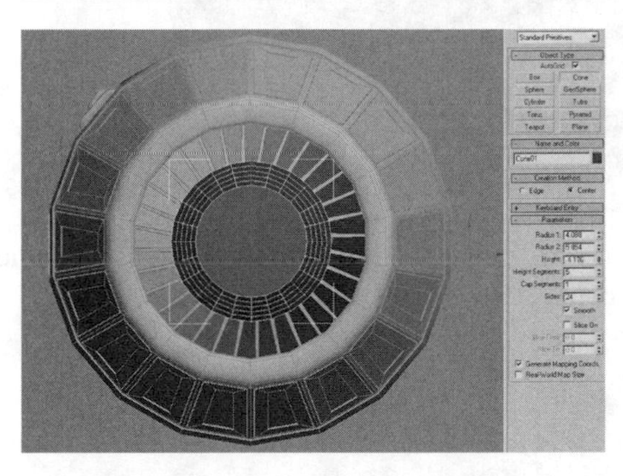

Figure 2-283

12. Convert the cone to an Editable Polygon and select the 18 segments in the center of the tip.

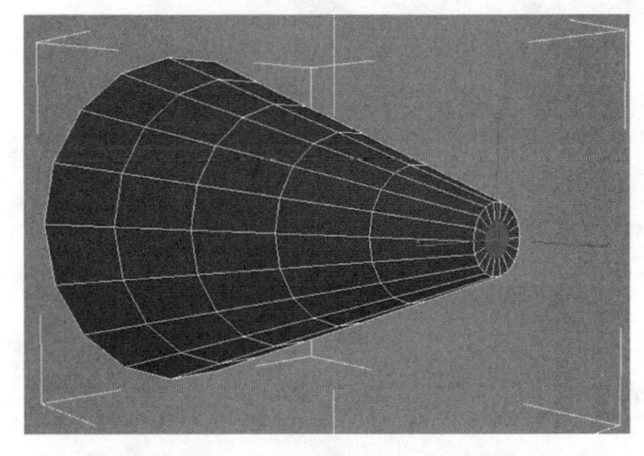

Figure 2-284

13. Group Extrude those 18 polygons **–2**.

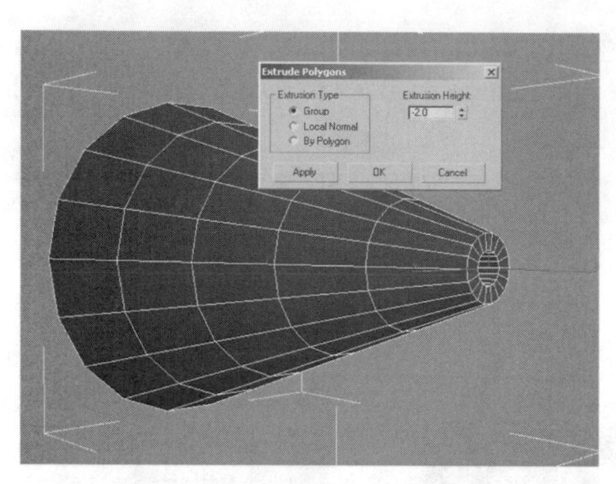

Figure 2-285

14. Select the rear 72 polygons, but not the rear-facing one nor the 18 inside the cone.

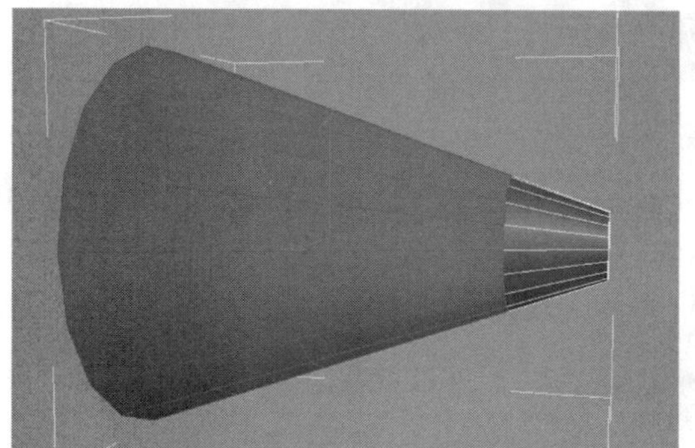

Figure 2-286

15. Click **Bevel Settings:**

Type	Height	Outline	Apply/OK
By Polygon	0	–0.1	Apply
By Polygon	–0.4	0	OK

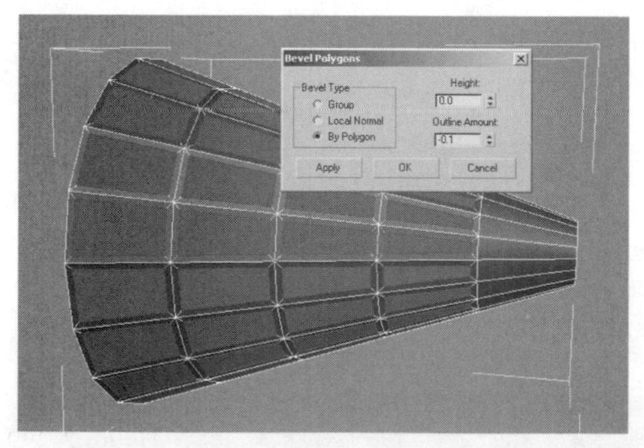

Figure 2-287

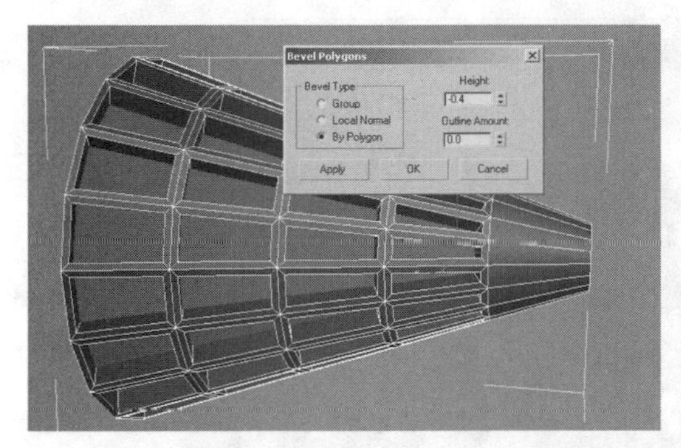

Figure 2-288

16. Select the innermost 18 rear-facing polygons and click **Bevel Settings:**

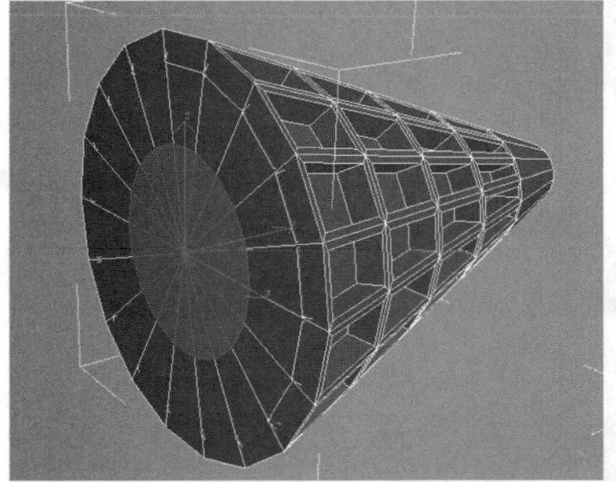

Figure 2-289

Type	Height	Outline	Apply/OK
Group	0.1	0	Apply
Group	0	3	Apply

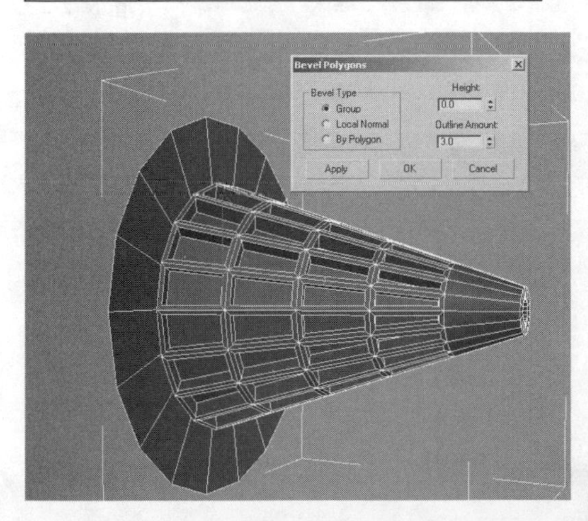

Figure 2-290

Type	Height	Outline	Apply/OK
Group	0.3	0	OK

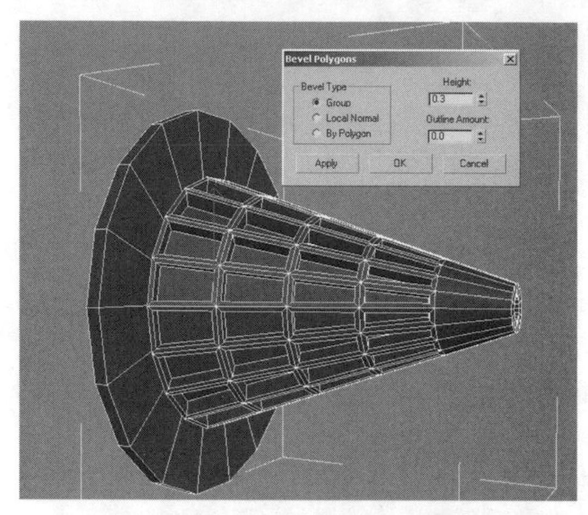

Figure 2-291

17. Move the exhaust cone into position in the nacelle exhaust nozzle.

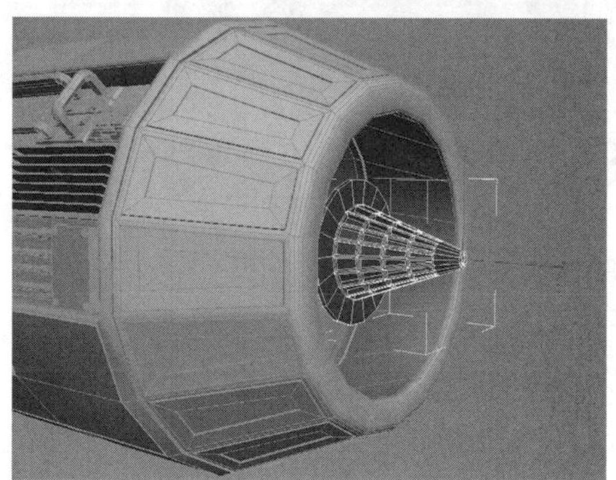

Figure 2-292

18. Switch back to Polygon selection mode and adjust the bevel settings until the cone just intersects the exhaust nozzle.

Type	Height	Outline	Apply/OK
Group	0	5.09	OK

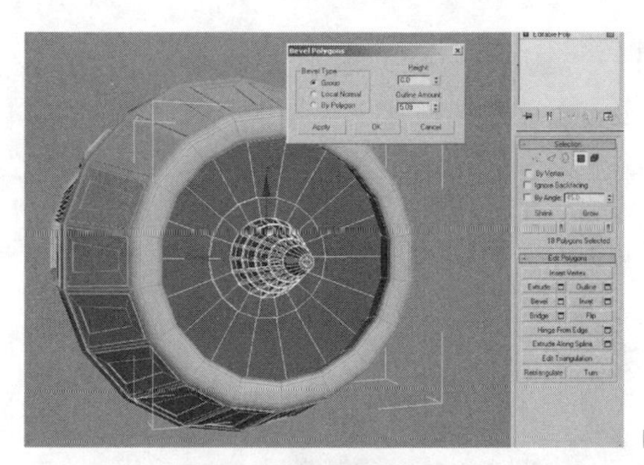

Figure 2-293

19. Select the 36 polygons behind the front cone, but be sure you leave a row of polygons unselected:

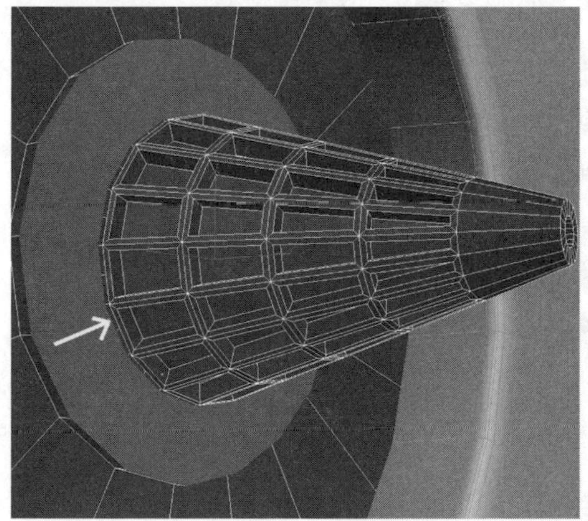

Figure 2-294

20. Click **Bevel Settings:**

Type	Height	Outline	Apply/OK
By Polygon	–0.05	–0.2	OK

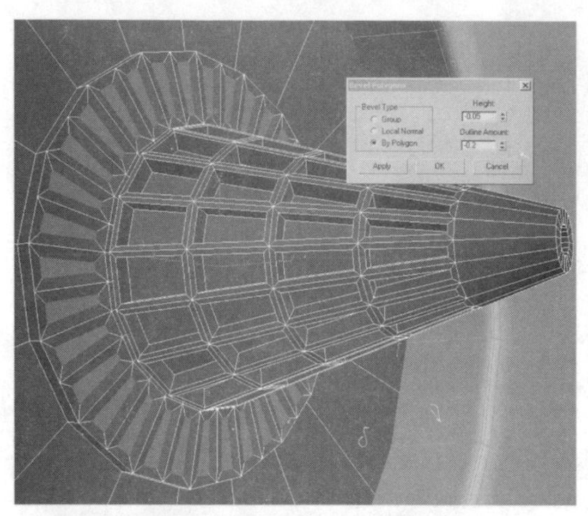

Figure 2-295

21. Extrude By Polygon **–5.0**.

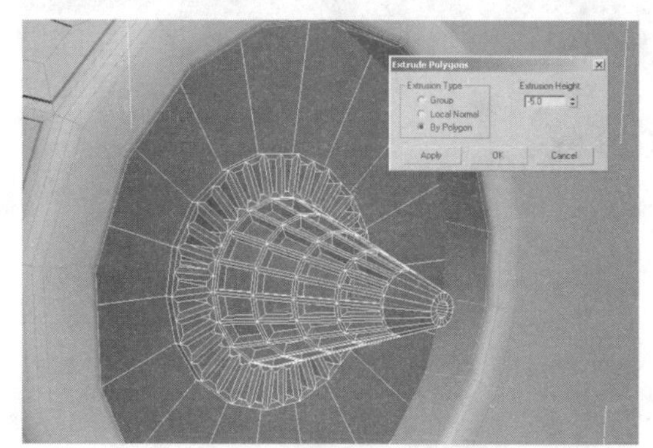

Figure 2-296

22. On the next set of polygons, select every other one:

Figure 2-297

23. Click **Bevel Settings:**

Type	Height	Outline	Apply/OK
By Polygon	0	–0.2	Apply
By Polygon	–1.0	0	OK

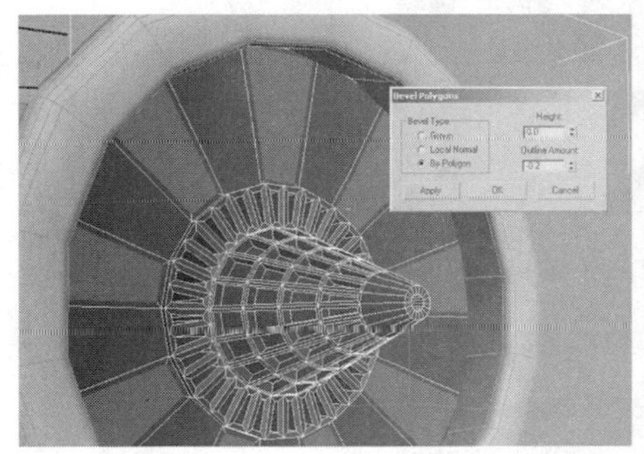

Figure 2-298

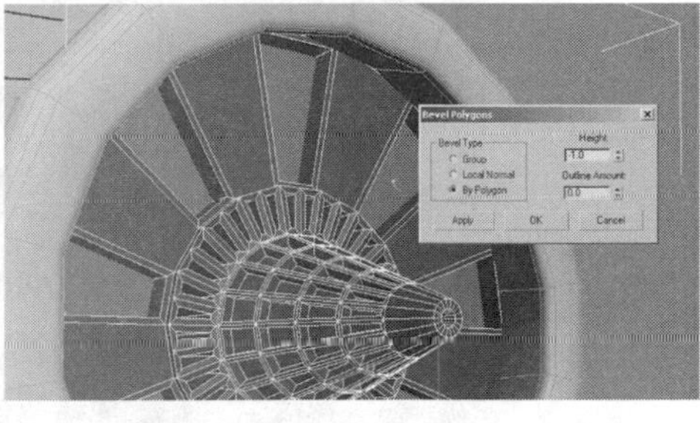

Figure 2-299

24. Select one of the polygons and zoom in until you can see the inside edge.

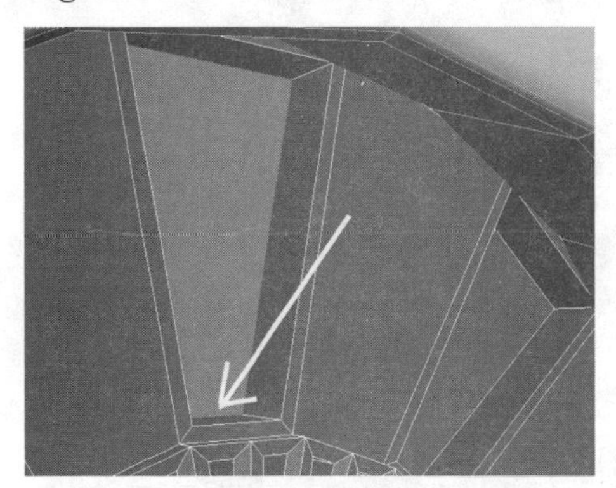

Figure 2-300

25. Hinge From Edge, **–90** degrees, with **10** Segments, using the inside edge as the hinge.

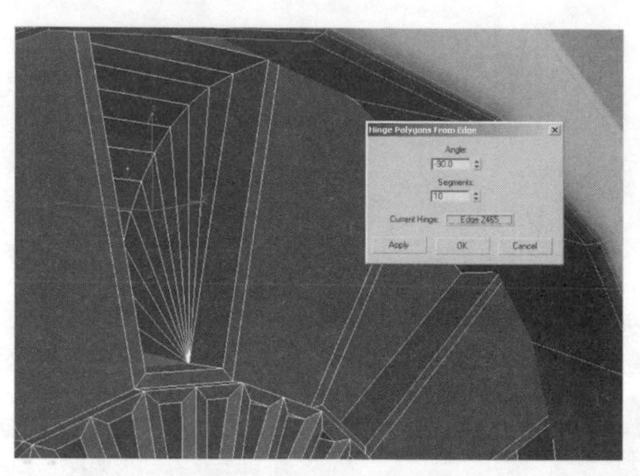

Figure 2-301

26. Repeat step 25 for the remaining eight polygons that are recessed.

Figure 2-302

27. Switch to Perspective view, add the Clay material to the object, and do a test render.

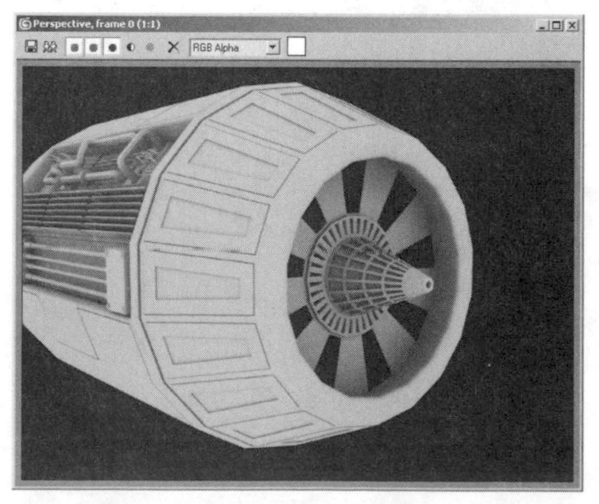

Figure 2-303

28. Click **Bevel Settings:**

Type	Height	Outline	Apply/OK
By Polygon	–1.0	0	OK

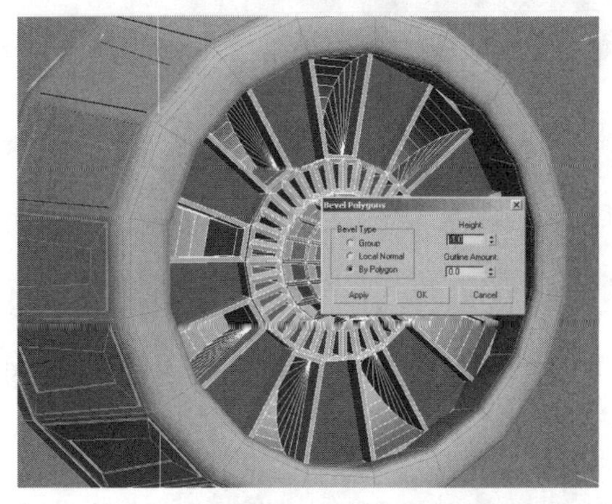

Figure 2-304

29. In one of the recesses you've made, create a Box using AutoGrid with these settings:

Length	Width	Height	Length/Width/Height Segs
0.6	1.6	0.5	1/3/1

Figure 2-305

30. Switch to Perspective view, Arc Rotate until you can see the part of the box that faces the center cone, and use AutoGrid to create a Cylinder to the left of the leftmost segment.

Radius	Height	Height Segs	Sides
0.12	2.5	10	18

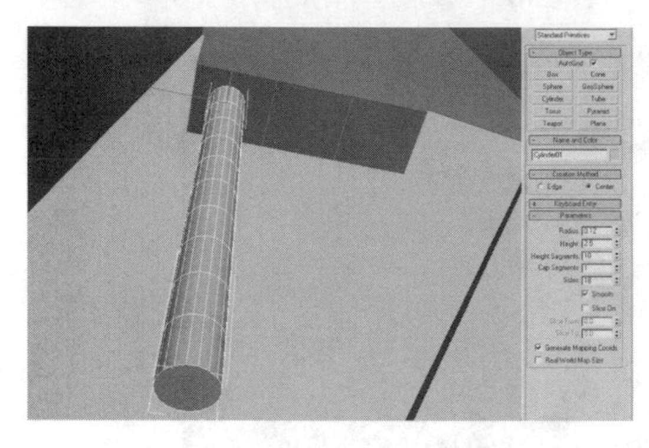

Figure 2-306

31. Add a Bend modifier to the cylinder's stack, using a Bend Angle of **57**.

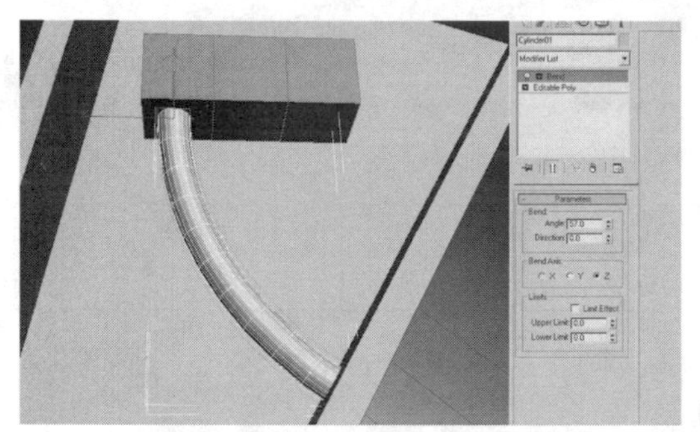

Figure 2-307

32. Add a Smooth modifier to the cylinder's stack, then right-click and choose **Convert to Editable Polygon**.

Figure 2-308

33. Delete the cylinder's end polygon, as you can't see it anyway.

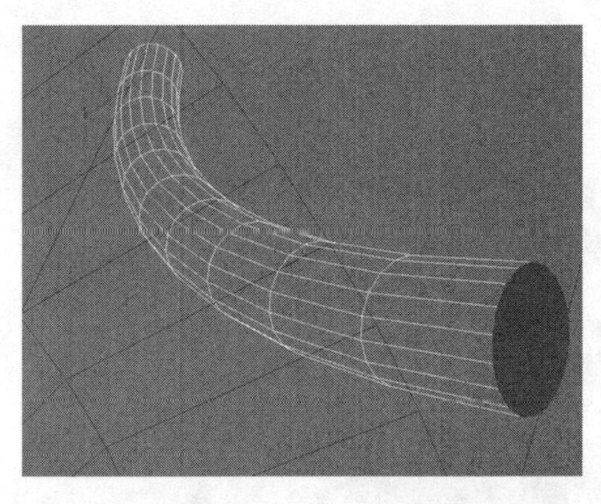

Figure 2-309

34. Using AutoGrid, create a Torus in the recessed area closest to the nozzle and then convert it to an Editable Polygon.

Radius 1	Radius 2	Segs	Sides
0.635	0.082	24	12

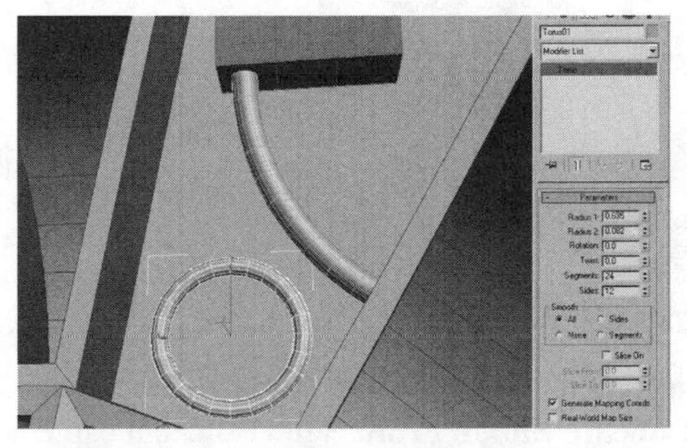

Figure 2-310

35. Using AutoGrid, create a Sphere centered inside the torus (you'll have to move it up in the Local Z axis, as you're looking for more of an egg in an egg cup than a rivet) with a Radius of **0.66** and **32** Segments. Then convert it to an Editable Polygon.

Figure 2-311

36. Highlight the top two center rings of polygons (64 total) and Group Extrude them by **0.02**.

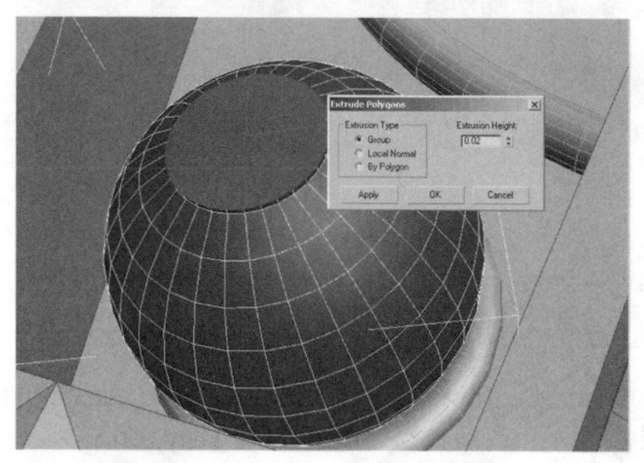

Figure 2-312

37. Click **Shrink** (to shrink the selection down to the centermost 32 polys), Group Extrude them **–0.1**, and then delete them.

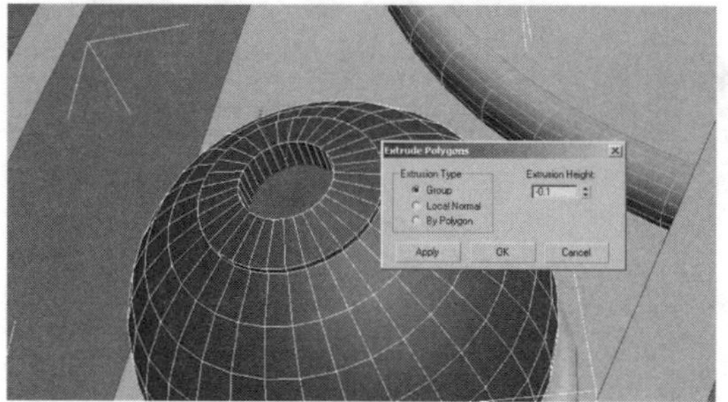

Figure 2-313

38. Border-select the border you created by deleting the center polygons, click **Create Shape From Selection**, and name it **compressor_seal**.

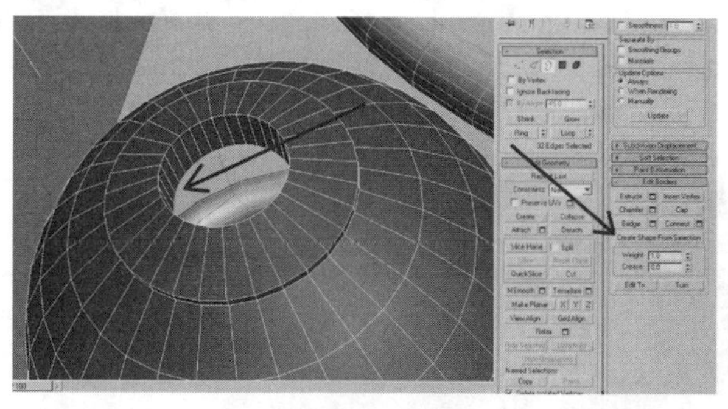

Figure 2-314

39. Open the Rendering rollout and choose the settings in the following table, then move the seal up (in the Local Z axis) to the top of the opening and convert it to an Editable Polygon.

Enable In Renderer	Enable In Viewport	Radial/Rectangular	Thickness	Sides
Checked	Checked	Radial	0.03	4

Figure 2-315

40. Using AutoGrid, create a Cylinder in the center of the seal (it's likely you'll need to switch between the Back and Perspective views to get it seated properly), and then raise it in the Local Z axis:

Radius	Height	Height/Cap Segs	Sides	Smooth
0.112	1.0	10/1	18	Checked

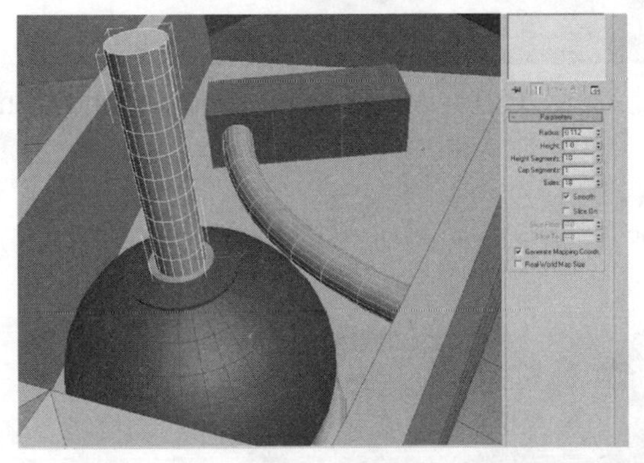

Figure 2-316

41. Convert the cylinder to an Editable Polygon and add a Bend modifier to the stack with an Angle of **90**. Use a Direction of **–65.5** to turn the bend to face the box you made in step 29.

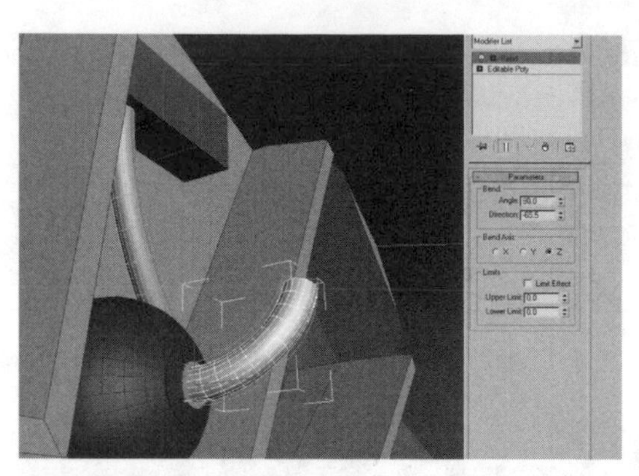

Figure 2-317

42. Click the cap polygon facing the box, Group Extrude it by **1.4**, and hit **Apply**.

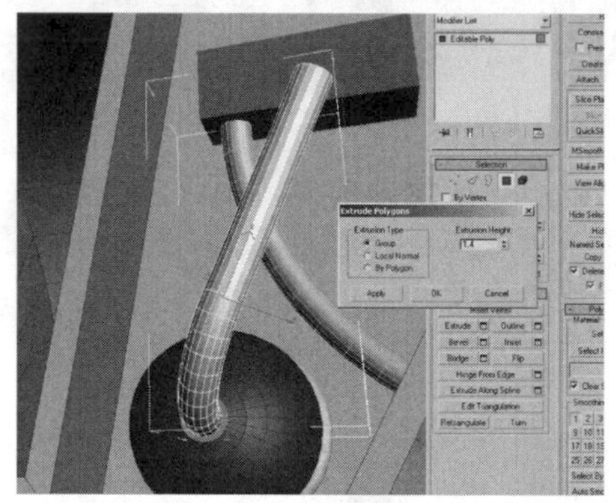

Figure 2-318

43. Reset Extrude to **0.08** and click **Apply** 14 times and then click **OK** (you should have 15 extrusions of 0.08).

FYI: When using the Bend modifier, more segments make smoother bends.

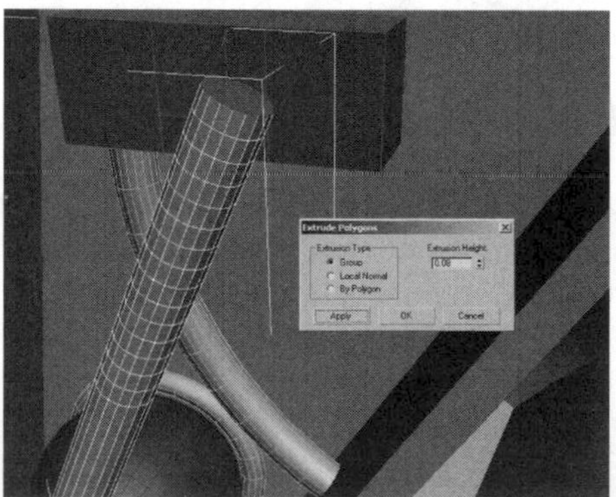

Figure 2-319

44. Click **Grow** until all the segments have been selected and then click **Detach** to detach it as an object (don't bother giving it a name as it's not going to be around long).

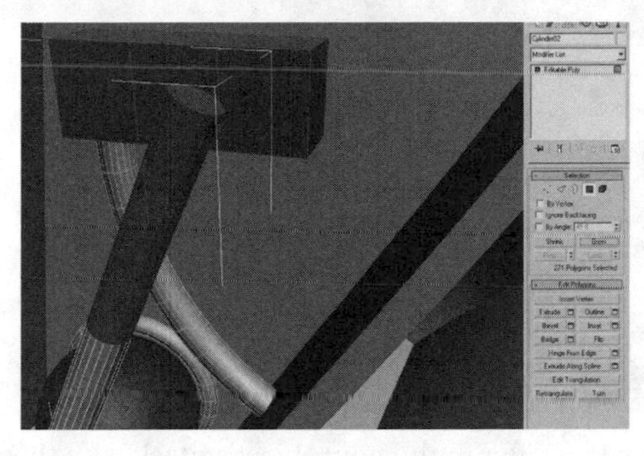

Figure 2-320

45. Hit the **H** key, select the object you just created, convert it to an Editable Polygon, click the Hierarchy tab, click **Affect Pivot Only**, and click **Center to Object**.

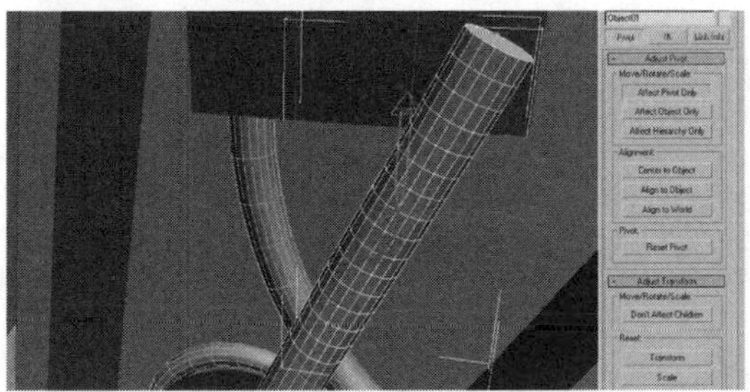

Figure 2-321

FYI: Because this new object was once part of the compressor_tube, its pivot point is the same. You have to move the new object's pivot so the Bend modifier will give you the effect you want.

46. Move the pivot until it is at the edge of the objects, where it connects to the original tube.

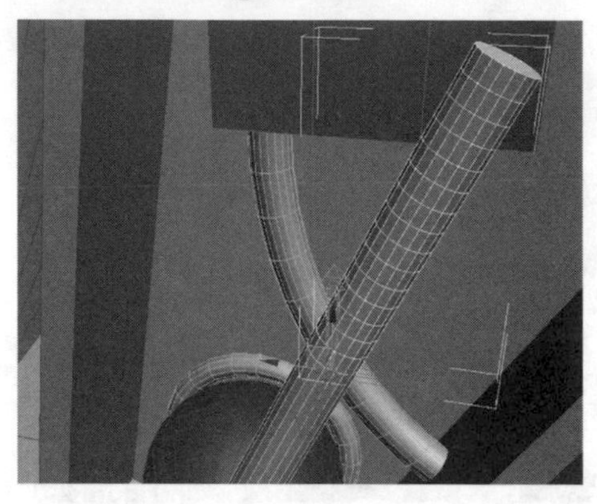

Figure 2-322

47. Apply a Bend modifier to the new object's stack with these settings:

Angle	Direction	Bend Axis	Limit Effect	Upper Limit
139	–103	Y	Checked	1.625

FYI: The Limit Effect and Upper Limit controls do what you think they do. The Bend modifier uniformly affects the object. Sometimes, as in this case, you want the pipe to either start or end straight and bend at the opposite end. Limiting the effect limits the Bend modifier's influence at the ends. If you want to make a U-shaped bend you enter values for both the Upper and Lower Limit settings.

Figure 2-323

48. Convert the new object to an Editable Polygon to collapse the stack. Select the original pipe, which exits the sphere, click **Attach List**, and attach the object to it so they once again form a single object.

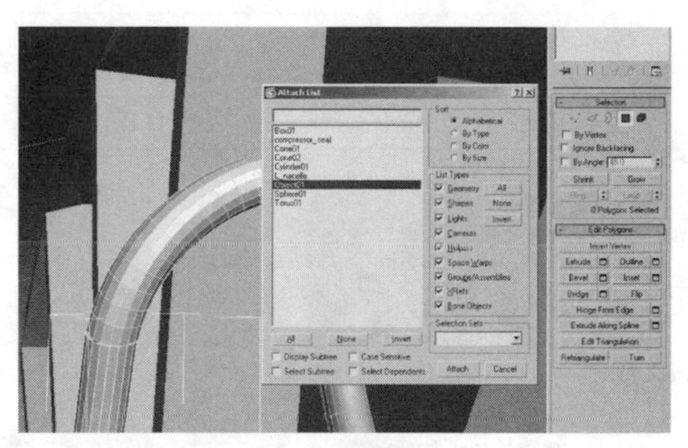

Figure 2-324

49. Switch to Vertex selection mode, select the 36 vertices that form a seam, and click **Weld Vertices**, adjusting the Weld Threshold until the number of vertices is lowered by 18 (in my case, it went from 504 to 486).

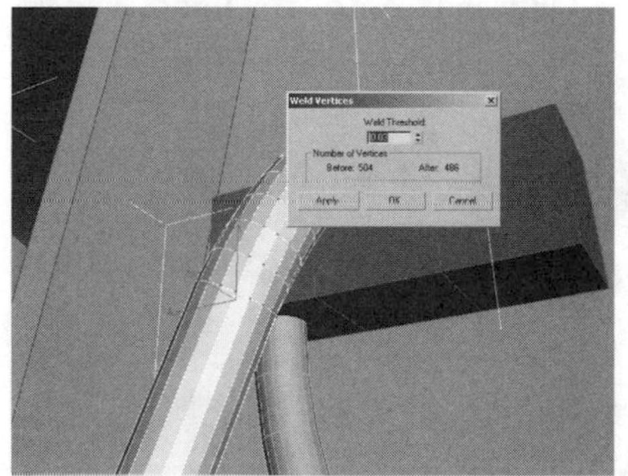

Figure 2-325

50. Select the cap polygon that faces the box, and Extrude it until it just meets the surface of the box (mine is **0.32**).

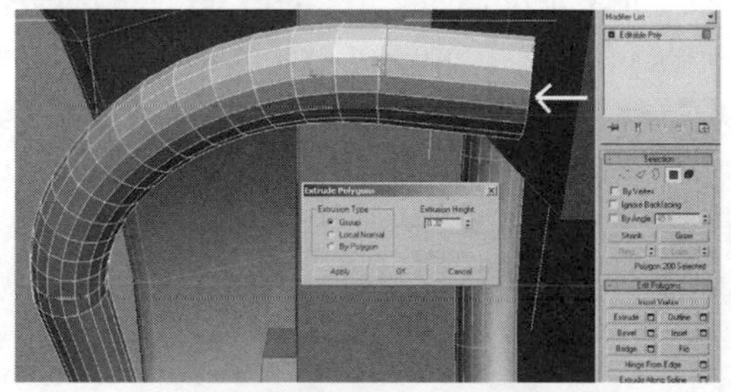

Figure 2-326

51. Delete the polygon facing the box. Border-select the border created by the deletion, click **Create Shape From Selection**, and call the new shape **compressor_seal**. Then hit **H**, select **compressor_seal** from the list, and apply these settings:

Enable In Renderer	Enable In Viewport	Radial/Rectangular	Thickness	Sides
Checked	Checked	Radial	0.06	12

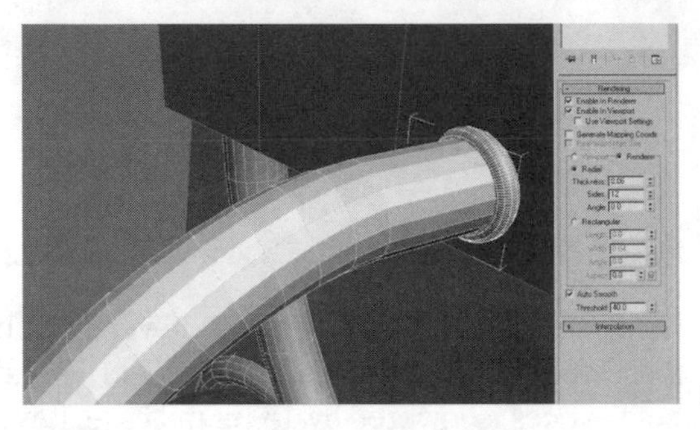

Figure 2-327

52. Convert the seal to an Editable Polygon, go to the Hierarchy tab, click **Affect Pivot Only** and **Center to Object**, and use the Move and Rotate tools to make the seal look evenly placed.

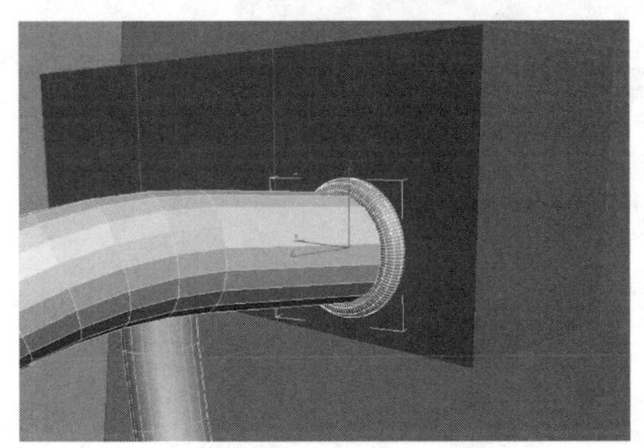

Figure 2-328

53. With the seal still selected, click **Attach List**, and click all the components making up the compressor system.

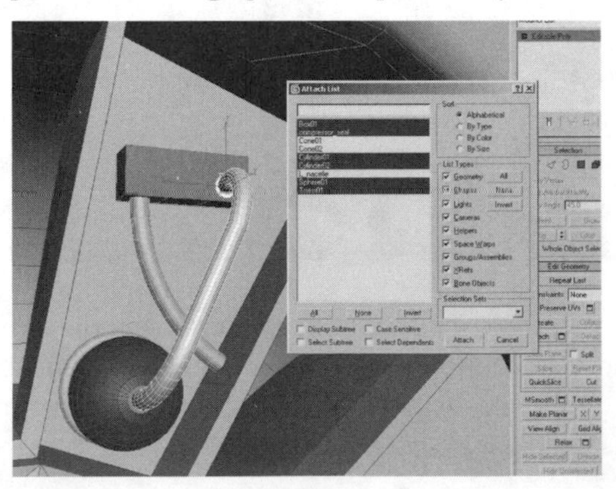

Figure 2-329

54. Name the new object **compressor.**

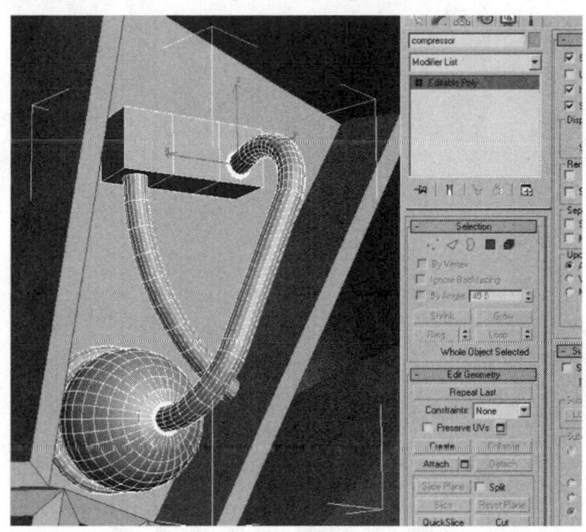

Figure 2-330

55. Switch to the Back view, zoom out so you can see the entire exhaust nozzle, click the Hierarchy tab, click **Affect Pivot Only**, and move the compressor's pivot to the center of the exhaust nozzle.

Figure 2-331

56. Shift-rotate (around **40** degrees in Z) until you have a compressor clone positioned in the next recess, select **clone**, and enter **8** for Number of Copies.

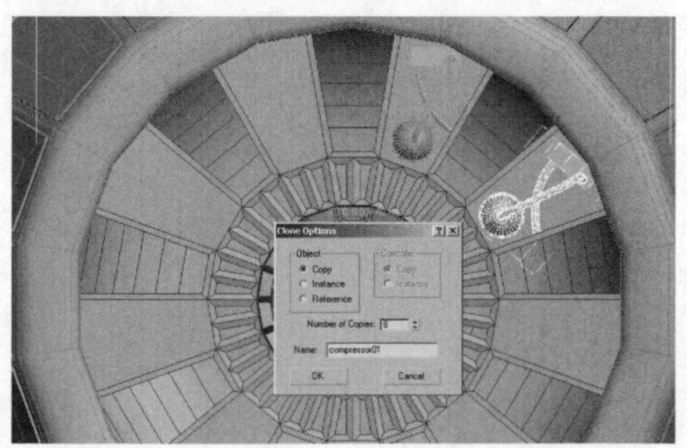

Figure 2-332

57. Object-select the exhaust cone, click **Attach List**, and select all the compressor clones. Click **OK**.

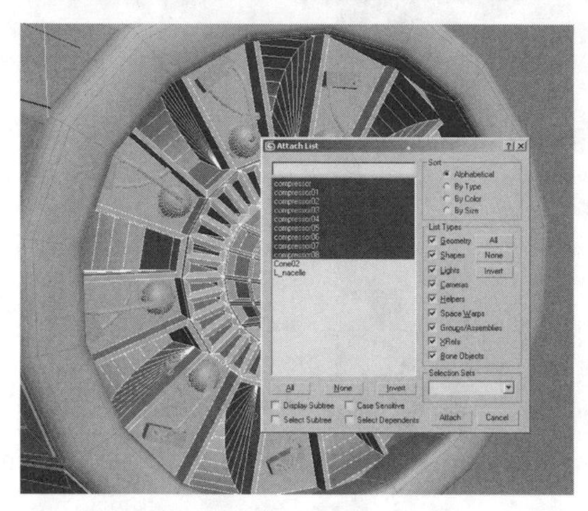

Figure 2-333

58. Switch to the Perspective view and do a test render.

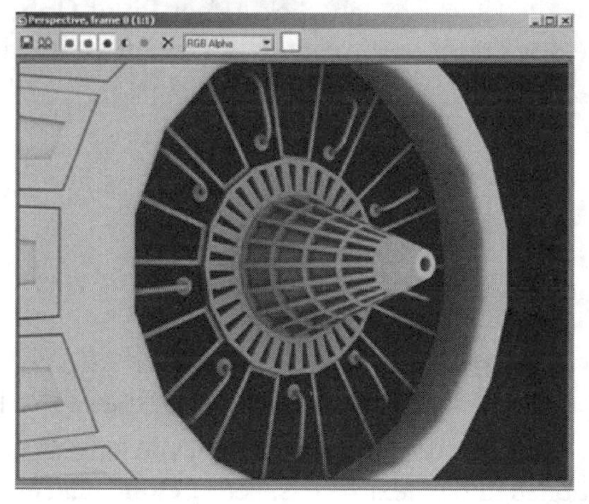

Figure 2-334

Message: Don't worry that you can't see all the compressor components; their position puts them into shadow. Once you add additional lights or animate the model, you'll see them.

59. Rename the cone **exhaust_nozzle** and Select and Link it to the L_nacelle.

Day 7: Building the Wing

1. In the Top view, create a Box adjacent to the nacelle.

Length	Width	Height	Length Segs	Width Segs	Height Segs
31	84	10	4	8	3

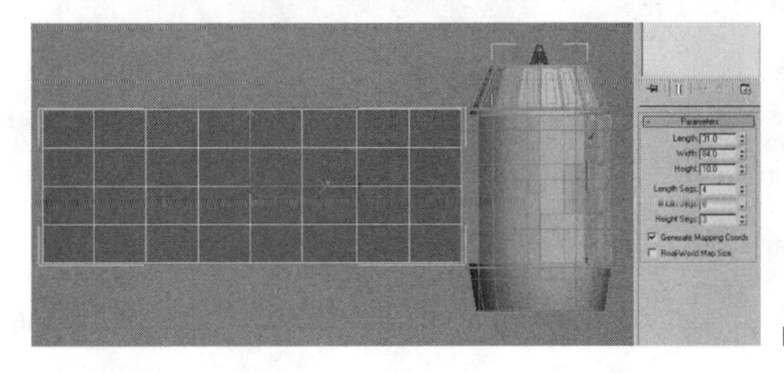

Figure 2-335

2. Convert the box to an Editable Polygon and rename it **wing**.
3. Click the Hierarchy tab, click **Affect Pivot Only**, and move the pivot in the X axis to the edge opposite the nacelle.

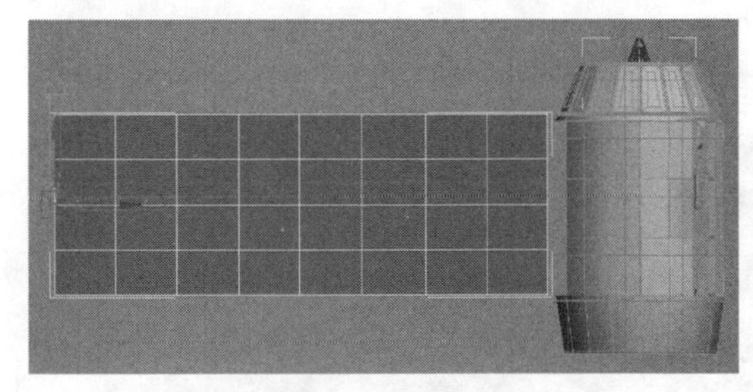

Figure 2-336

4. Add a Bend modifier to the wing's stack with these settings:

Angle	Direction	Bend Axis	Limit Effect	Upper Limit
55	0	X	Unchecked	NA

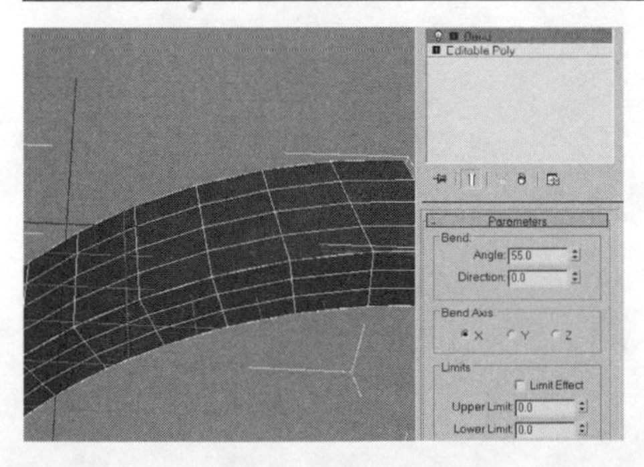

Figure 2-337

5. Hide the wing and switch to the Front view.
6. With your cursor in the center of the nacelle, using AutoGrid, create a Tube that envelopes the nacelle like a glove.

Radius 1	Radius 2	Height	Height/Cap Segs	Sides	Smooth
15.182	18	30	5/3	18	Checked

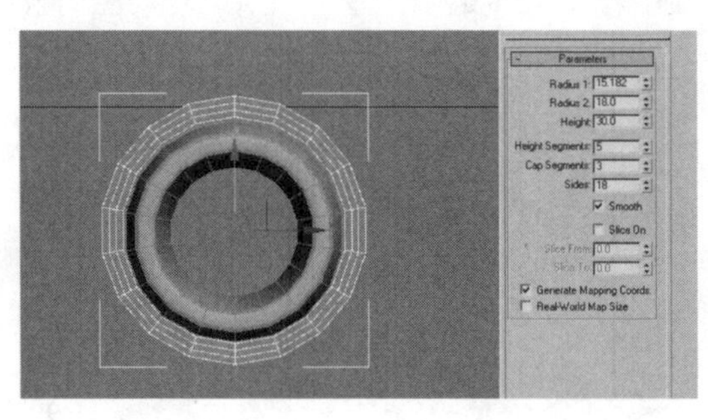

Figure 2-338

7. We don't want to cover up all that nice pipe work we worked so hard to make, so check **Slice On** under the tube's Parameters rollout, set Slice From to **–250** and Slice To to **–6.0**, and rename it **wing_ brace**.

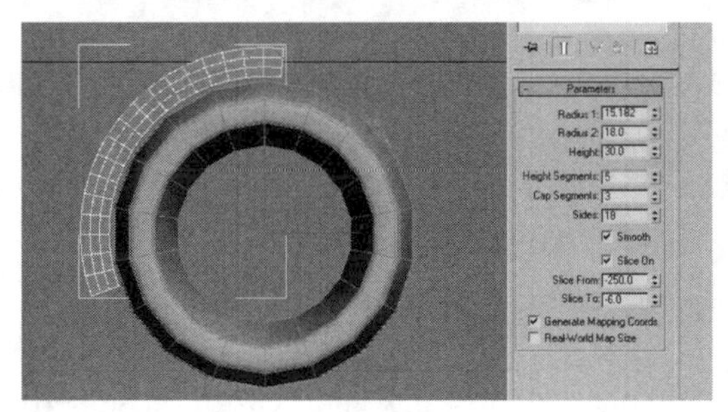

Figure 2-339

8. Switch to Perspective view and move the wing_brace into position on the nacelle.

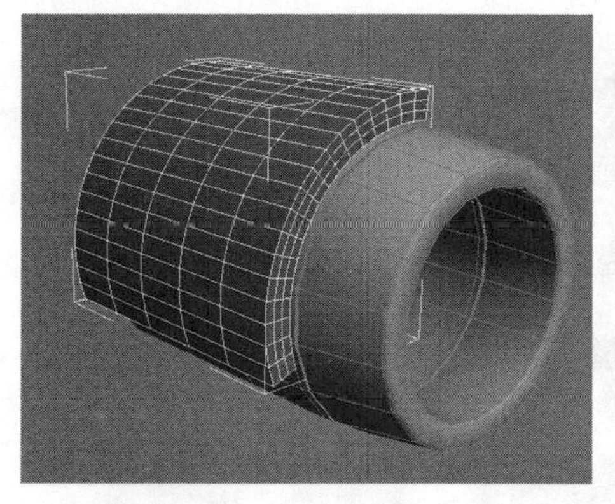

Figure 2-340

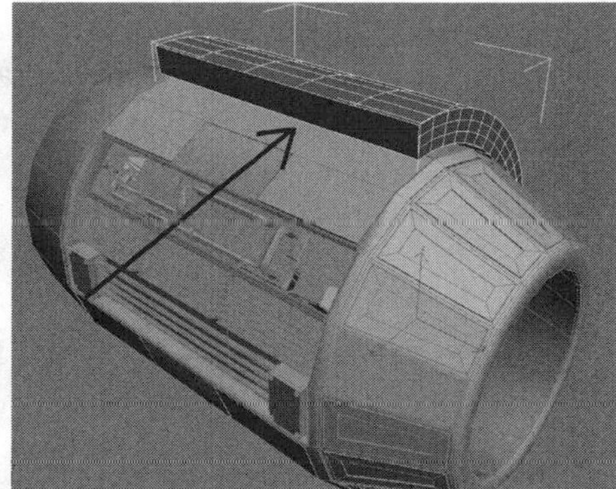

Figure 2-341

Fire Drill: One problem with Slice — at least for me — is your segments don't carry over to the sliced edge. There must be a reason it does this, but it means we're going to have to do some additional cuts and slices.

9. Convert wing_brace into an Editable Polygon and use the Cut or Slice tool — your preference — to create two horizontal and four vertical cuts so that the sliced edge is consistent with the rest of the object.

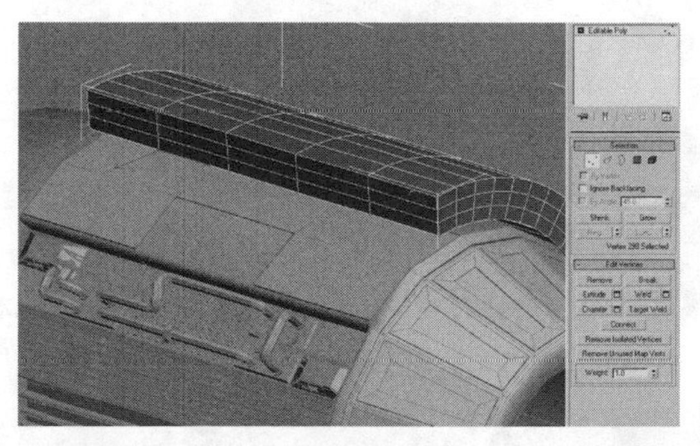

Figure 2-342

FYI: I found it to be helpful to temporarily hide the nacelle when making these cuts. Be sure you cut both the top and bottom edges!

10. Currently, our brace is covering our access port, so switch to the Front view and use the Rotate Transform Type-In dialog to rotate the wing_brace **15** in the Z axis.

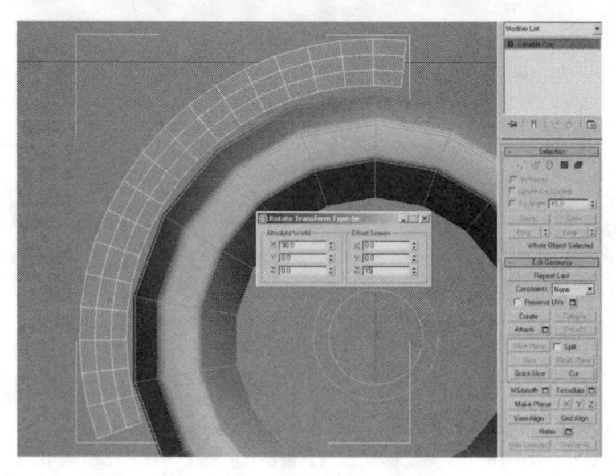

Figure 2-343

11. Switch to the Top view, use the Scale tool to scale the brace down to **96** in the Y axis, and center the brace.
12. Select the bottom two rows of polygons on the edge of the brace, on both the top and the bottom edges.

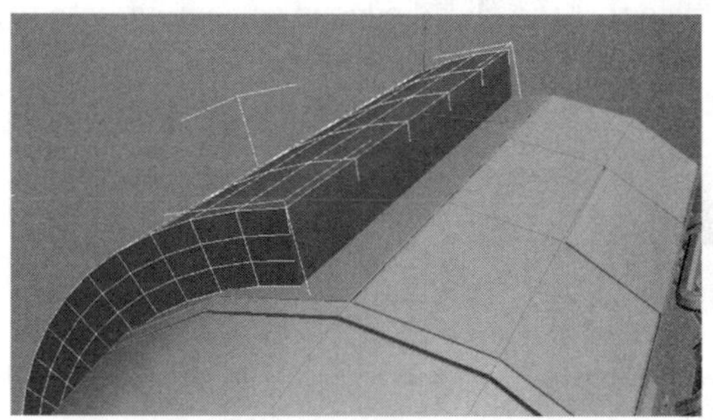

Figure 2-344

13. Group Extrude by **2.05** and click **OK**.

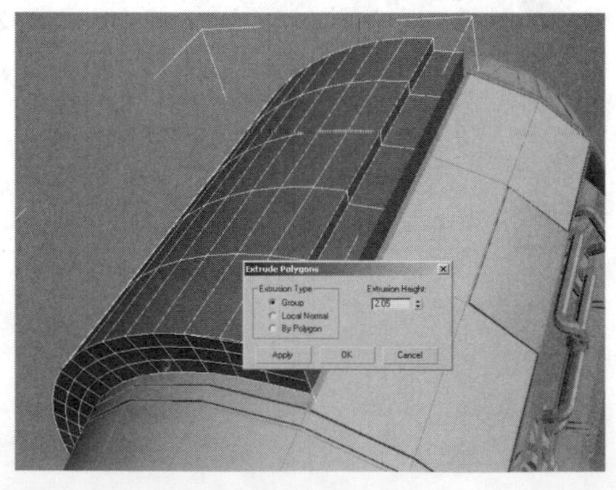

Figure 2-345

14. Select the five polygons on the top surface of your extrusion (do this on the top and bottom).

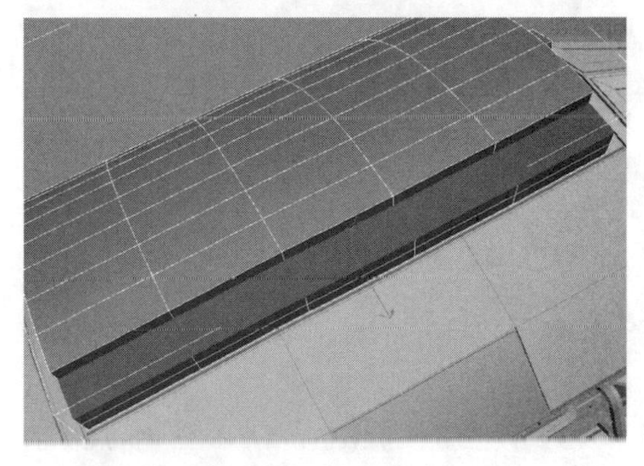

Figure 2-346

15. Click **Bevel Settings:**

Type	Height	Outline	Apply/OK
By Polygon	0	–0.3	OK

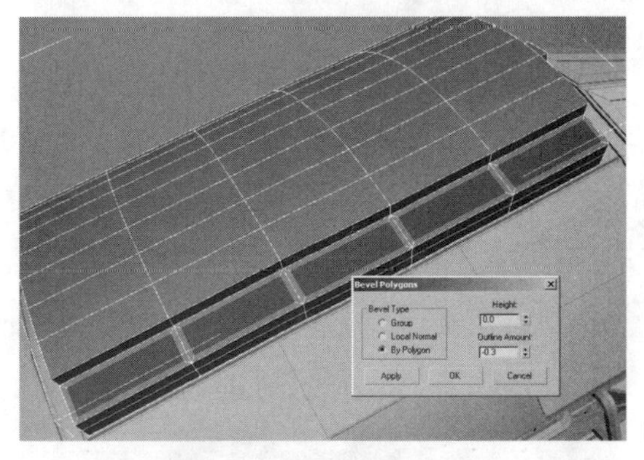

Figure 2-347

16. Scale the selection down to **30** in the Y axis to form squares.

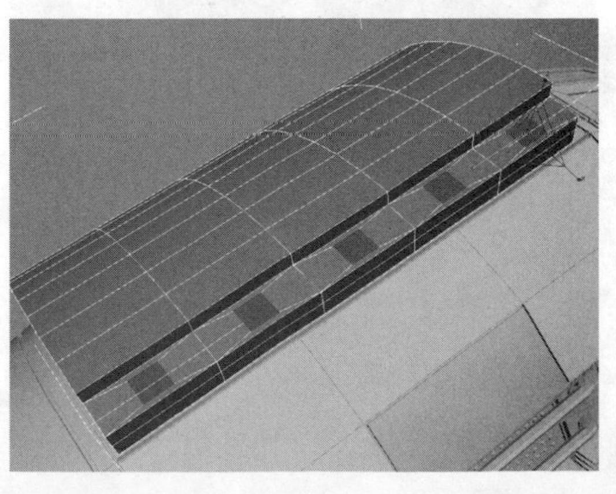

Figure 2-348

17. Group Extrude them **–0.01**.

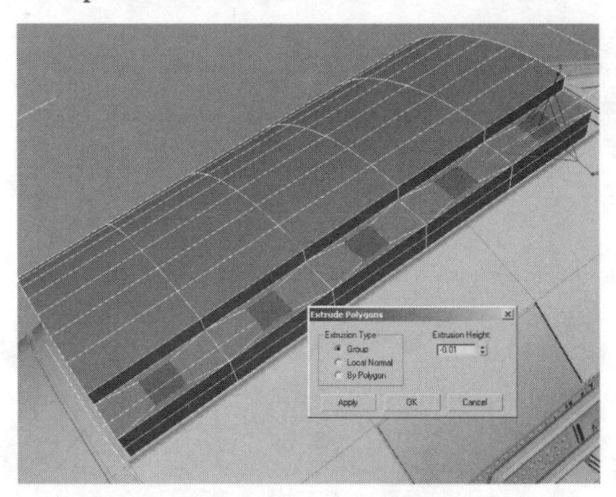

Figure 2-349

18. Under Edit Geometry, click **MSmooth**.

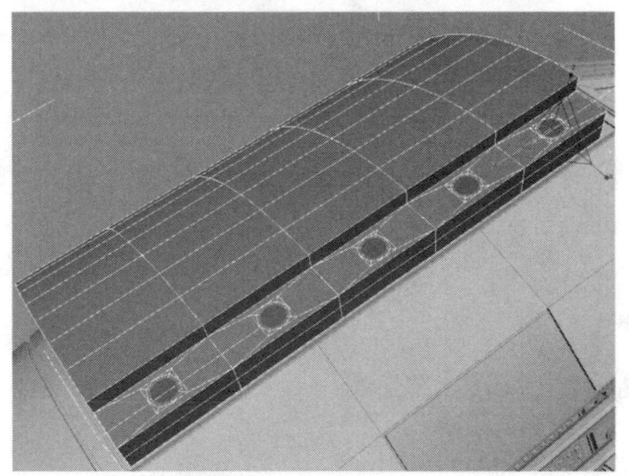

Figure 2-350

19. Click **Grow** and then do a Group Extrude of **–0.4**.

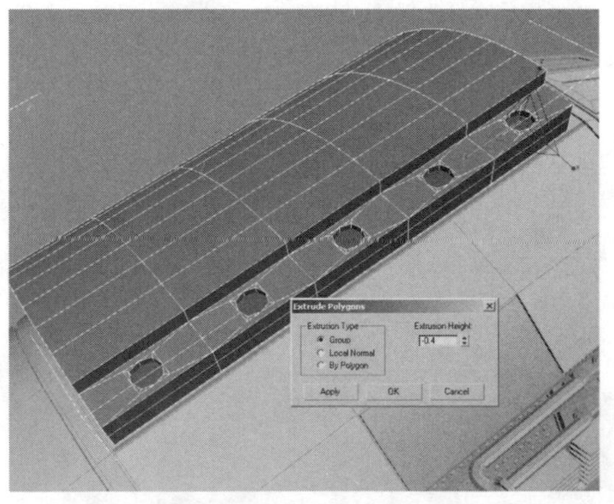

Figure 2-351

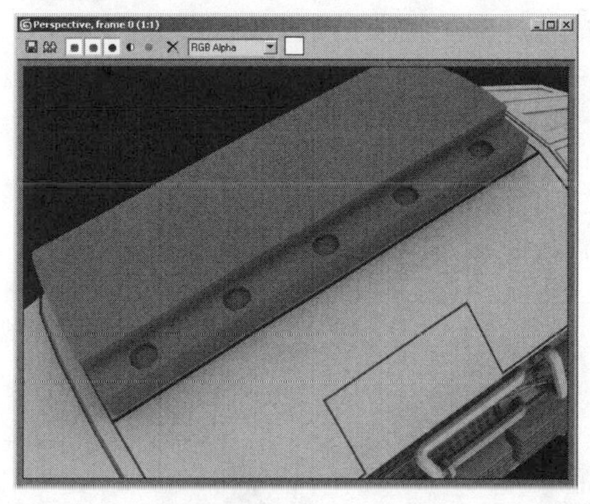

Figure 2-352

20. Click **Bevel Settings:**

Type	Height	Outline	Apply/OK
Group	0	–0.01	Apply
Group	1	–0.01	OK

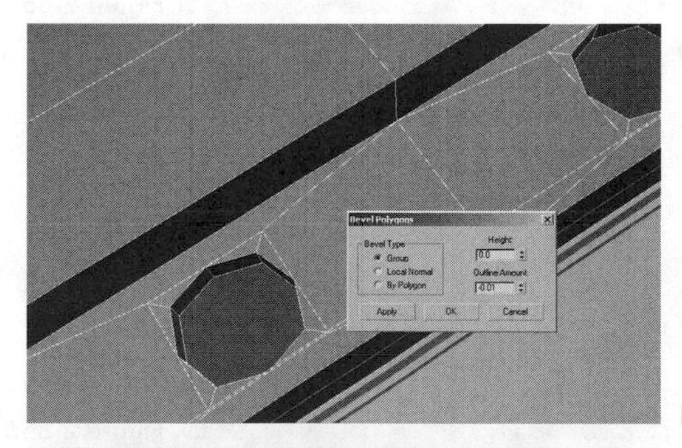

Figure 2-353

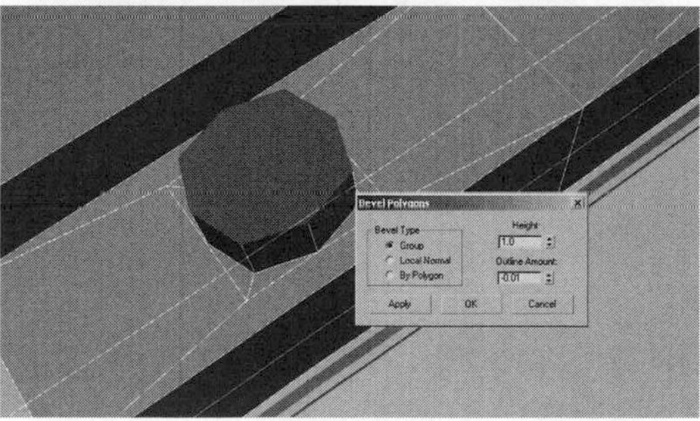

Figure 2-354

21. Click **Shrink** and then click **Bevel Settings:**

Type	Height	Outline	Apply/OK
Group	0	–0.02	Apply
Group	–0.03	0	Apply
Group	0	–0.01	Apply
Group	0.1	0	OK

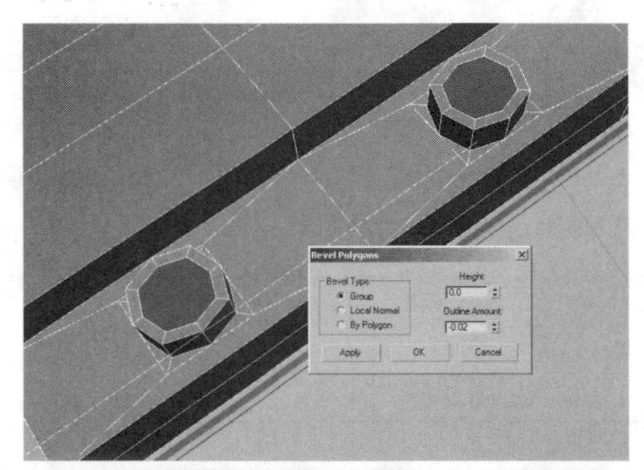

Figure 2-355

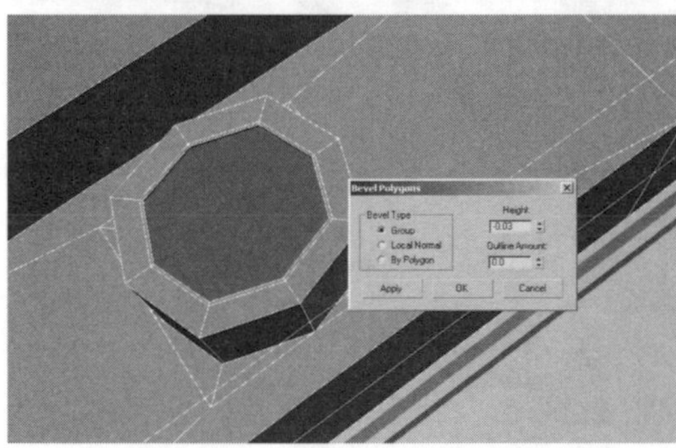

Figure 2-356

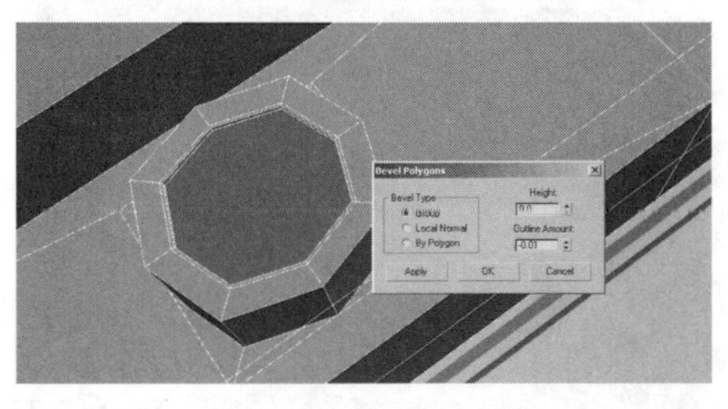

Figure 2-357

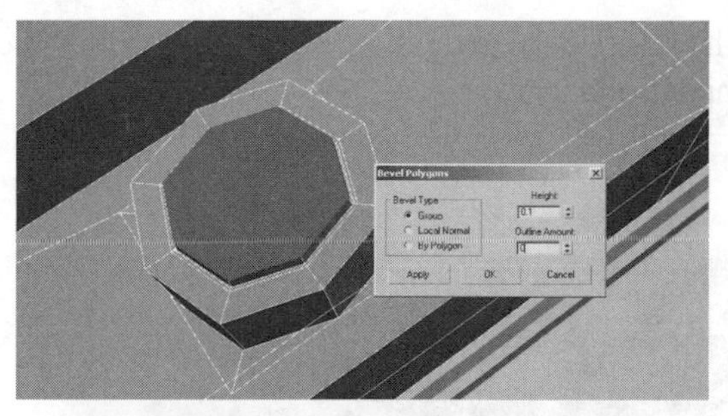

Figure 2-358

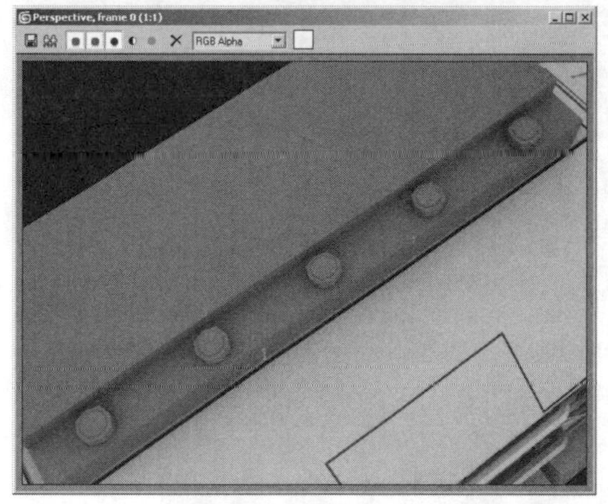

Figure 2-359

22. Select the nacelle and then Select and Link it to the wing_brace.
23. Switch to Edge selection mode and select all the sharp outer edges (there should be 122 in all); you may want to switch to wireframe to make it easier.

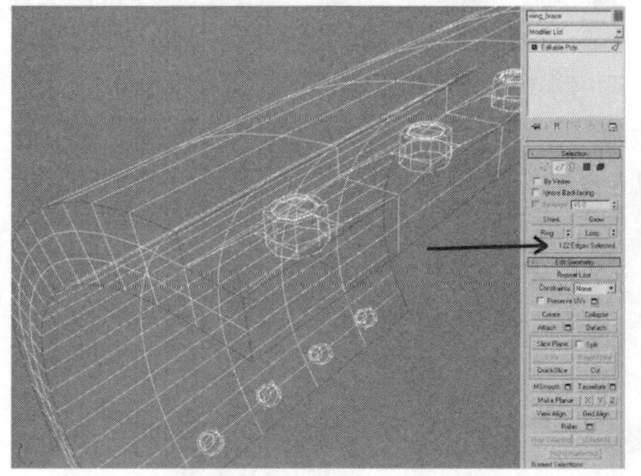

Figure 2-360

24. Chamfer the edges **0.06** and hit **Apply**, then Chamfer the edges **0.02** and hit **Apply** again.

25. Do a test render.

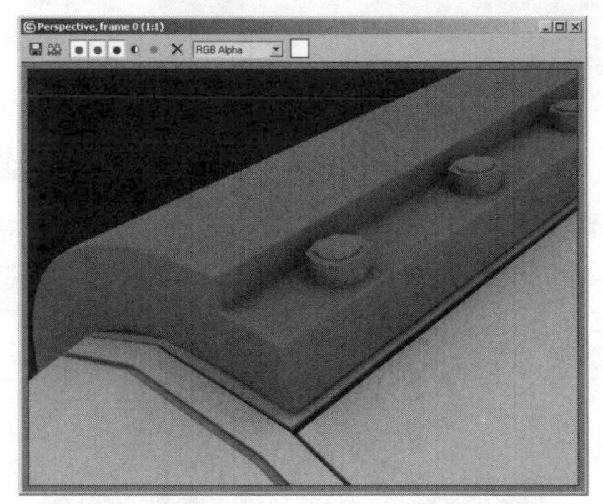

Figure 2-361

26. Unhide the wing.

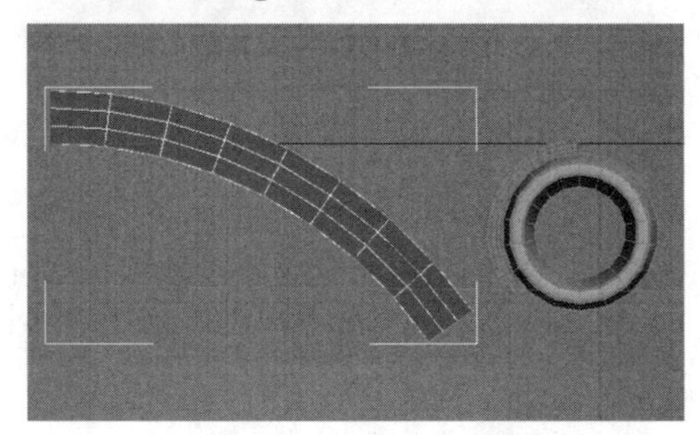

Figure 2-362

27. Move the wing **35** in the Y axis.

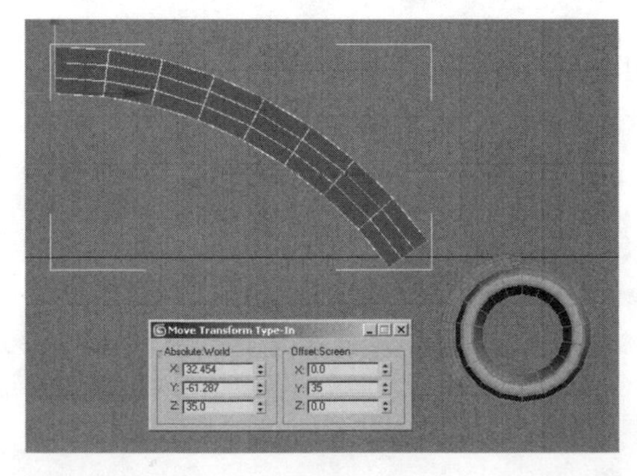

Figure 2-363

28. Move the wing **13** in the X axis.

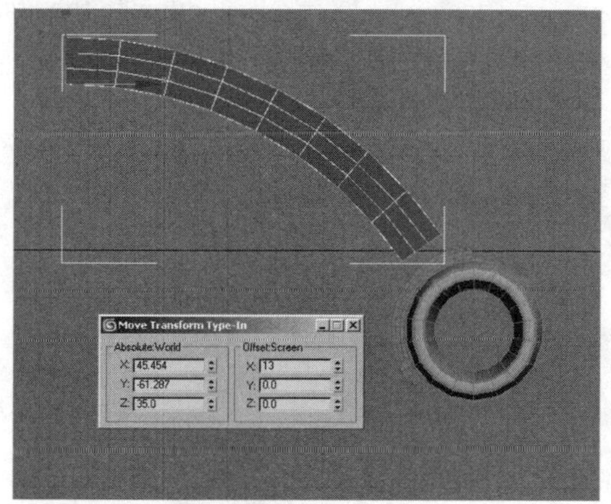

Figure 2-364

29. Move the wing in the Y axis, by eye, until it just touches the brace (**–3.709** on mine).

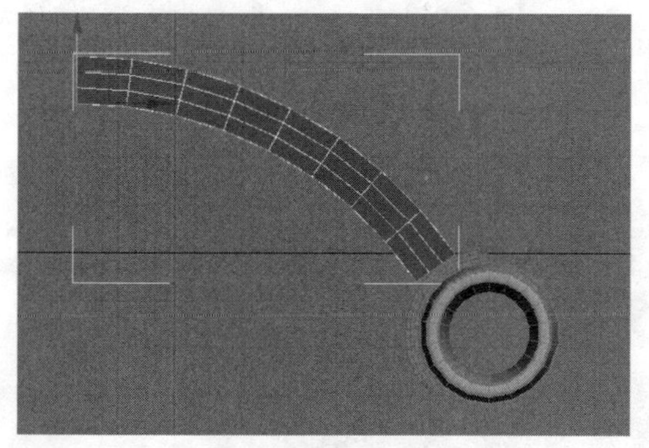

Figure 2-365

Message: Look at the wing from the Top view. It's too wide for the wing_brace. We could scale the wing, but we really want it wider at the chassis and narrower at the nacelle.

30. Right-click the wing, convert it to an Editable Polygon to collapse the stack, and then add an FFD 2x2x2 modifier to the stack.

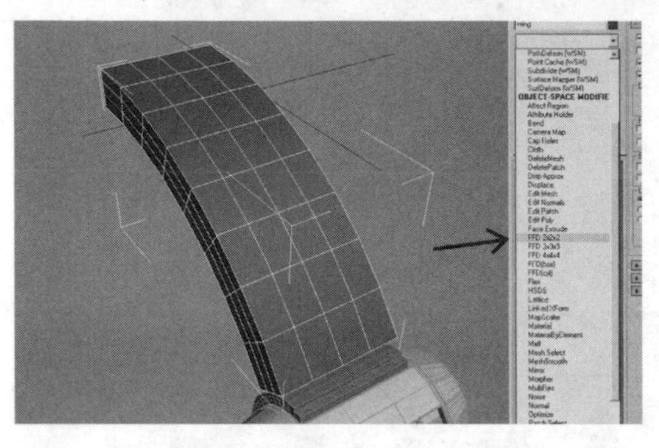

Figure 2-366

FYI: FFD stands for free form deformation. FFD modifiers are used in animation. They create a lattice around the underlying geometry, allowing you to make significant changes to the overall shape by manipulating a few control points rather than dozens of vertices. There are three flavors of FFDs: 2x2x2, 3x3x3, and 4x4x4. The values refer to the number of control points (see Figure 2-367). The higher the number of control points, the tighter the control over the underlying geometry.

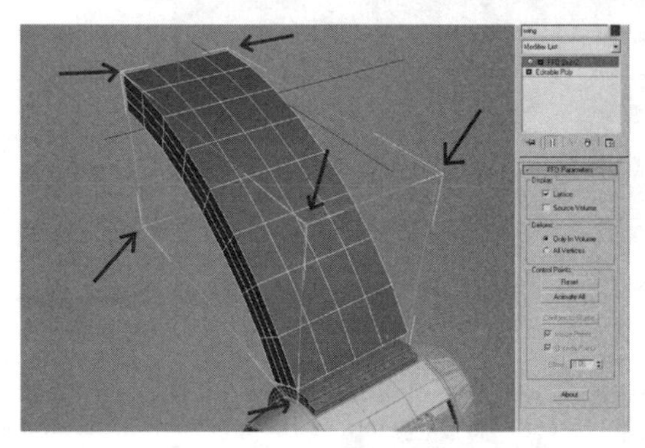

Figure 2-367

31. Click on **FFD** in the stack to open up the controls and select **Activate All** under Control Points.

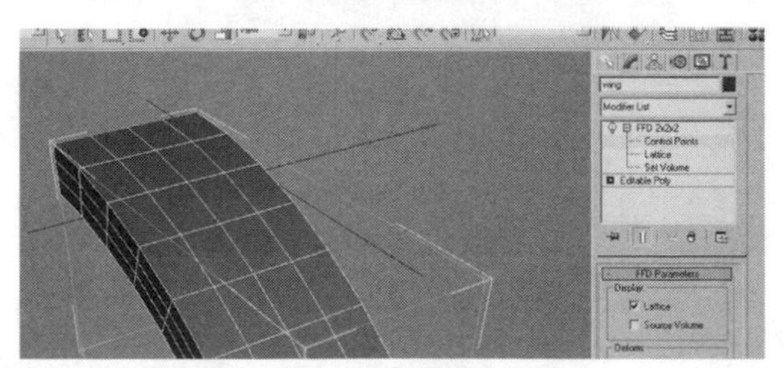

Figure 2-368

32. Select the four control points closest to the nacelle and scale them down to **45** in the X axis.

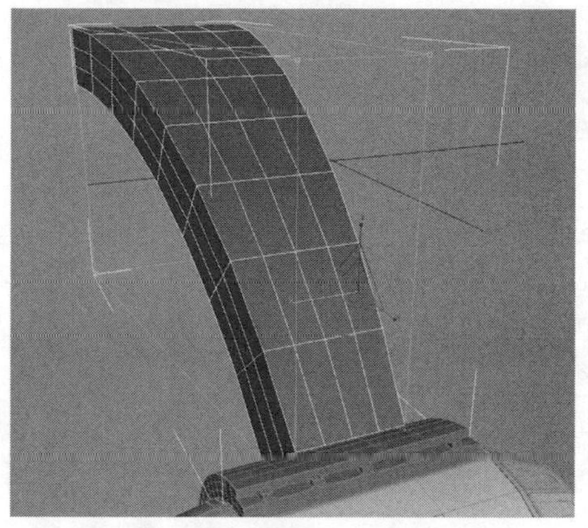

Figure 2-369

33. Arc Rotate so you can see where the wing meets the brace. Notice that the wing is not evenly spaced on the brace.

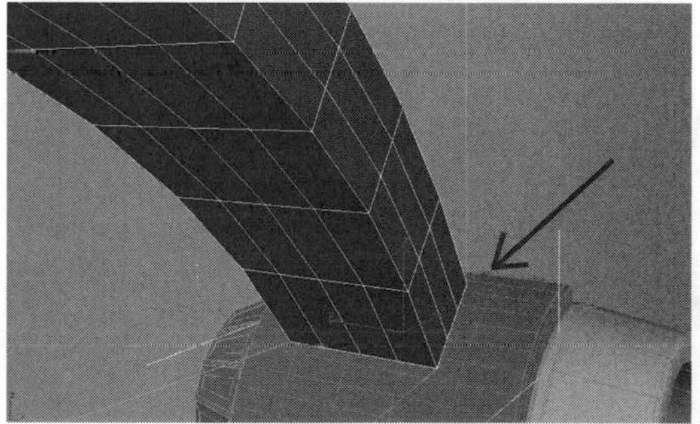

Figure 2-370

34. Right-click, choose **Convert to Editable Polygon**, and move the wing **–1.482** in the Y axis, or until it is evenly positioned on the brace.

Figure 2-371

35. Switch to wireframe mode and select the 21 polygons on the wing_brace, just below the tip of the wing.

Figure 2-372

36. Click **Bevel Settings:**

Type	Height	Outline	Apply/OK
Group	2.5	0	OK

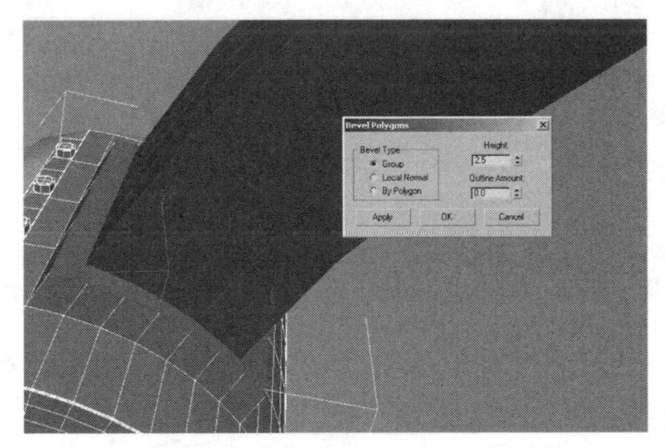
Figure 2-373

FYI: The contour of the wing makes it unevenly aligned with the contour of the brace. We need to fix that.

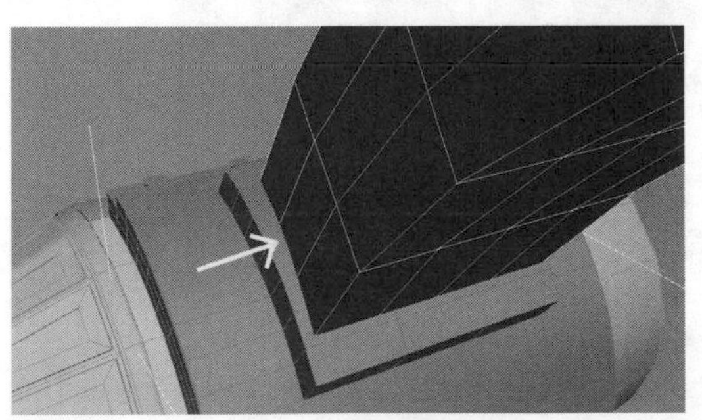
Figure 2-374

37. Switch to wireframe mode, switch to Vertex selection mode, and select the four vertices that comprise the wing tip, on the side that faces the nozzle.

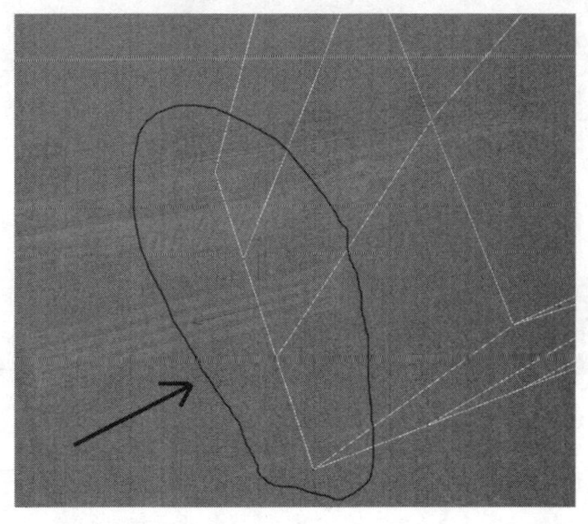

Figure 2-375

38. Switch back to shaded/edged faces mode, switch the reference coordinate system to **View**, and scale the vertices down to **0** in the Y axis to straighten them.

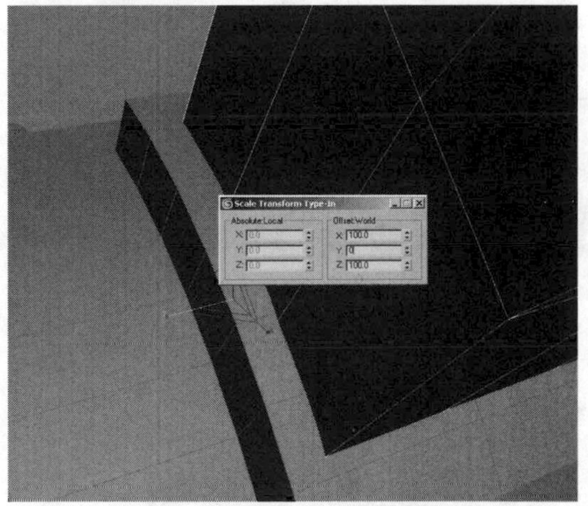

Figure 2-376

39. Now straighten the vertices on the intake side using the same technique.

40. Select the **wing_brace**, and select the 21 polygons beneath the wing tip that you selected before.

Figure 2-377

41. Click **Bevel Settings:**

Type	Height	Outline	Apply/OK
Group	0	–1.186	OK

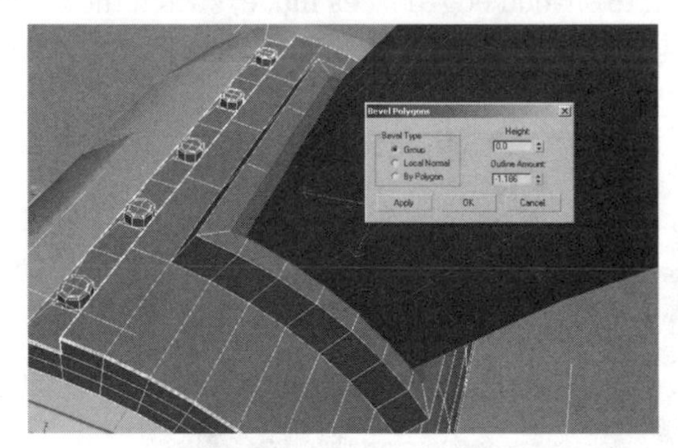

Figure 2-378

42. Scale the polygons down (**~89**) in the local Y axis until they fit tightly around the wing tip.

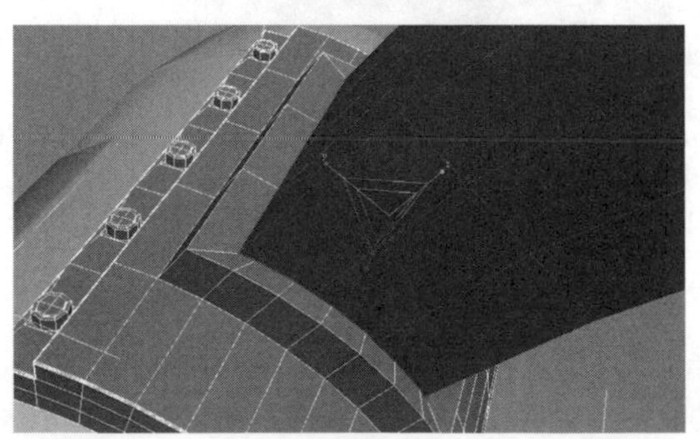

Figure 2-379

43. Group Extrude the polygons **–0.4**.

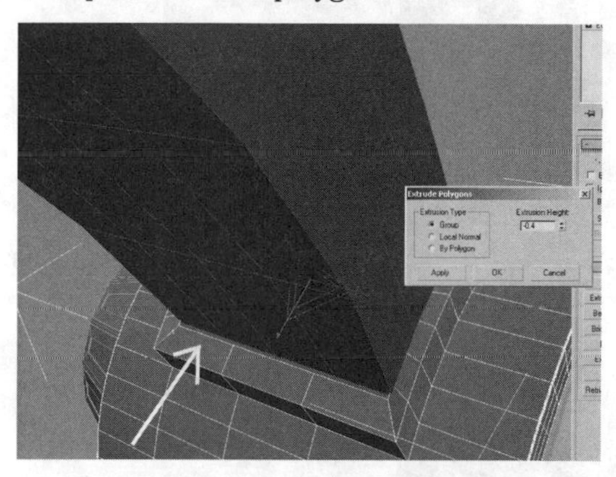

Figure 2-380

Fire Drill: If you have wide gaps between the wing tip and the wing_brace, it may be necessary to adjust the vertices of either the wing or the extrusion to make the wing fit into the wing_brace. We want a snug fit, but we also want enough of a gap so we can see it when we render. Look at the objects around you. Nearly all of them have some kind of seam.

44. Select the **wing_brace** and select the three polygons shown in Figure 2-381, on both the nozzle and the intake sides.

Figure 2-381

45. Click **Bevel Settings:**

Type	Height	Outline	Apply/OK
Group	0	–0.27	Apply
Group	–0.01	0	OK

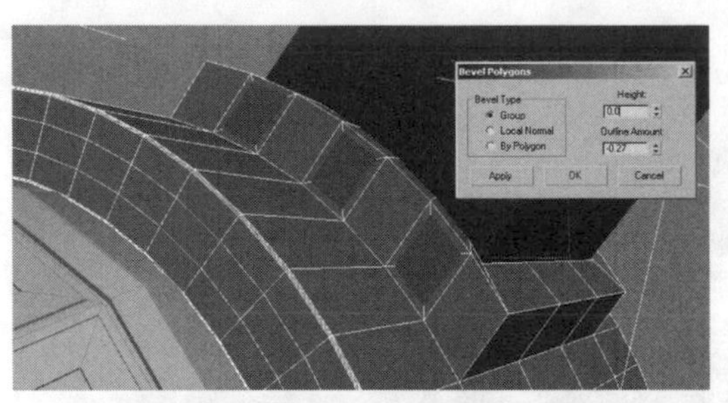

Figure 2-382

Figure 2-383

46. MSmooth the polygons.

Figure 2-384

47. Click **Grow** and then **Bevel Settings** to make the bolts:

Type	Height	Outline	Apply/OK
Group	–0.4	0	Apply
Group	0	–0.1	Apply
Group	0.75	0	OK

Figure 2-385

48. Select the middle polygon on the top and underneath sides of the wing_brace and repeat steps 45-47 to make upper and lower bolts.

Figure 2-386

Figure 2-387

49. Select the 24 sharp outer edges making up the place the wing slips into, and Chamfer by **0.06** and then **0.02**.

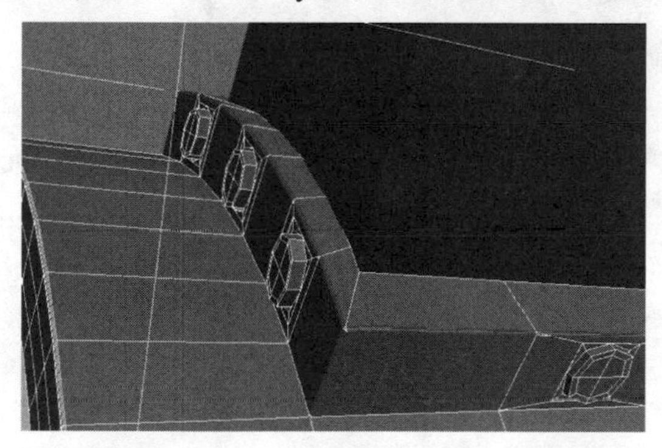
Figure 2-388

50. Select an inner edge, where the wing enters the wing_brace, click **Loop**, then Chamfer the edge by **0.06**.

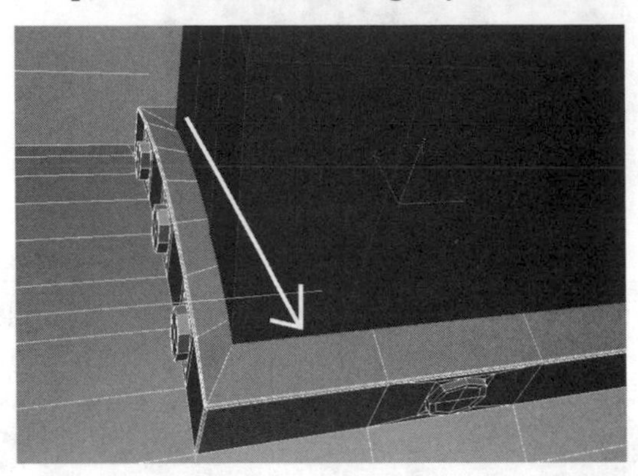

Figure 2-389

51. Unhide the rotors, zoom out so you can see the nacelle, brace, and wing, and do a test render.

Figure 2-390

52. Using the Select and Link tool, link the rotors to the nacelle, link the nacelle to the wing_brace, and link the wing_brace to the wing.

Day 8: Detailing the Wing

1. Select all the middle segments of the wing's edge, both front and back (total of 24 edges).

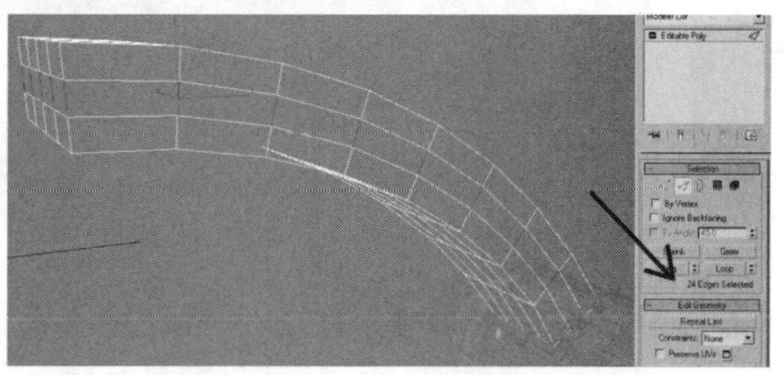

Figure 2-391

2. Click **Connect** to make a center seam.

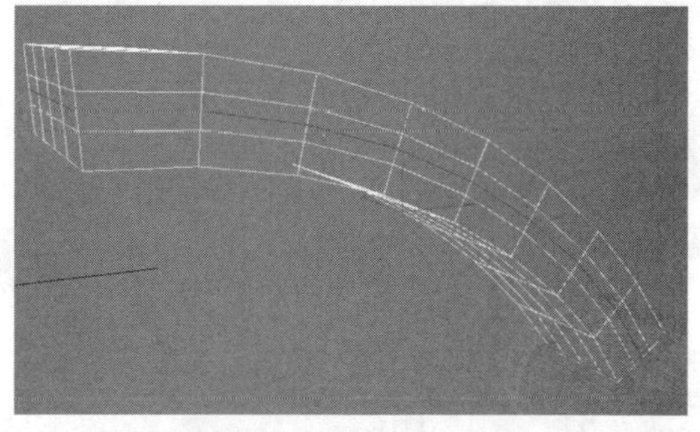

Figure 2-392

3. Select the 16 polygons on the chassis side of the wing and delete them.

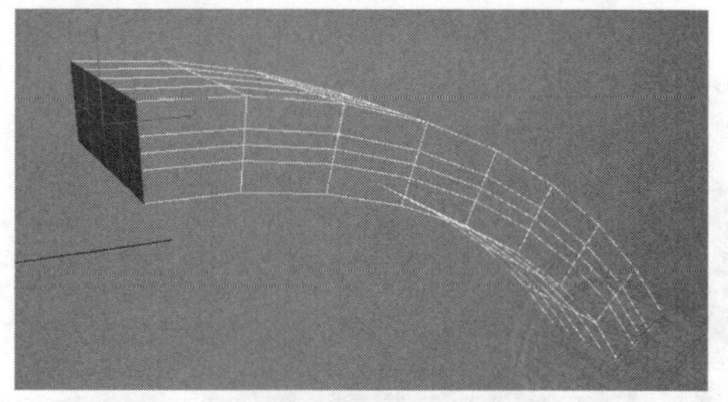

Figure 2-393

4. Target Weld the upper and lower vertices in the middle of the wing edge to the middle seam you made with the Connect tool; these target welds will result in a single seam running down the edges of the wings.

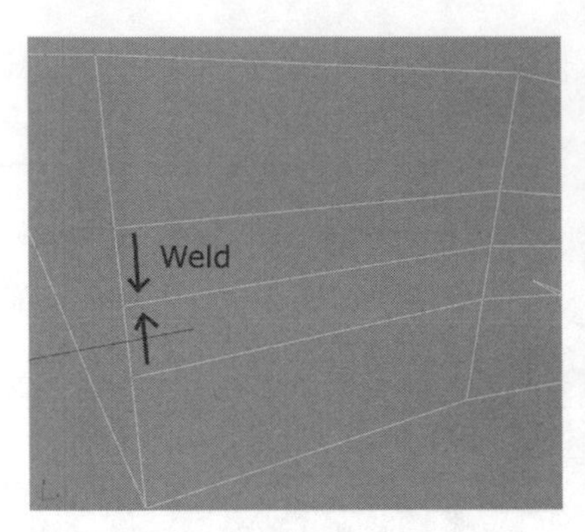

Figure 2-394

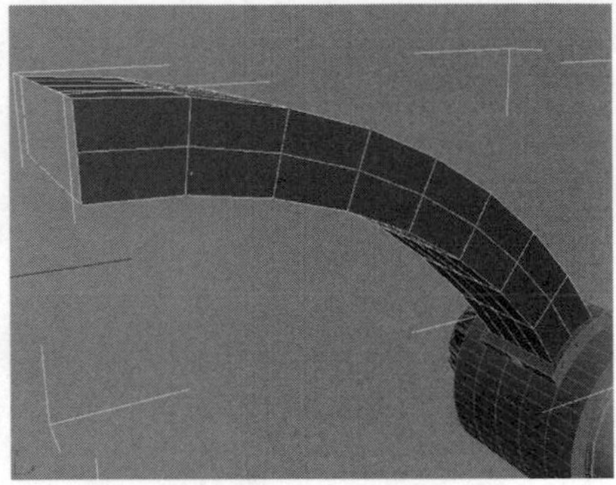

Figure 2-395

5. Select the eight top and top/side polygons that make up the rotor-side edge of the wing and click **Bevel Settings**:

Figure 2-396

Type	Height	Outline	Apply/OK
Local Normal	0	–0.01	Apply
Local Normal	1.0	0	OK

6. Bevel the six bottom polygons (Figure 2-397) using the same settings as you did in step 5.

Figure 2-397

7. Select the 14 polygons shown in Figure 2-398 (three polygons on top of the wing are not visible in the figure).

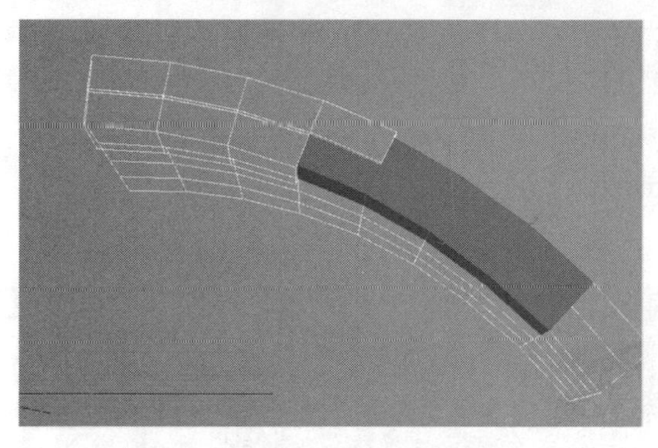
Figure 2-398

8. Bevel them using the same settings as in step 5.
9. Add the Clay material to the wing and do a test render to get a better sense of the detailing the last few steps have accomplished.

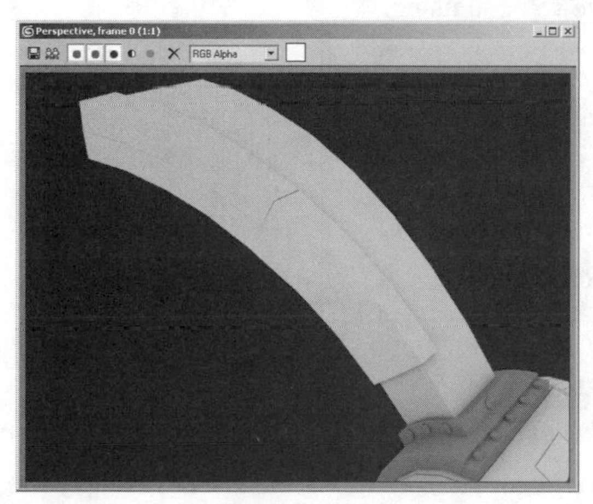

Figure 2-399

FYI: The bevel outlines make the gaps between the plates, while the bevel height forms the plates.

10. Select the polygons shown in Figure 2-400 and apply the same bevel settings we've been using.

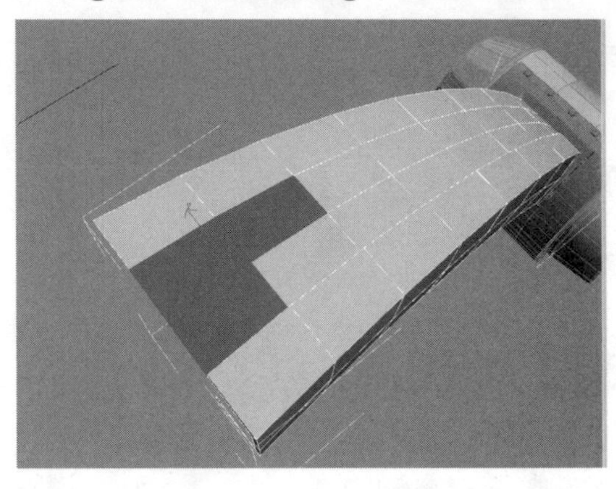

Figure 2-400

11. Select the polygons shown in Figure 2-401 and apply the same bevel settings we've been using.

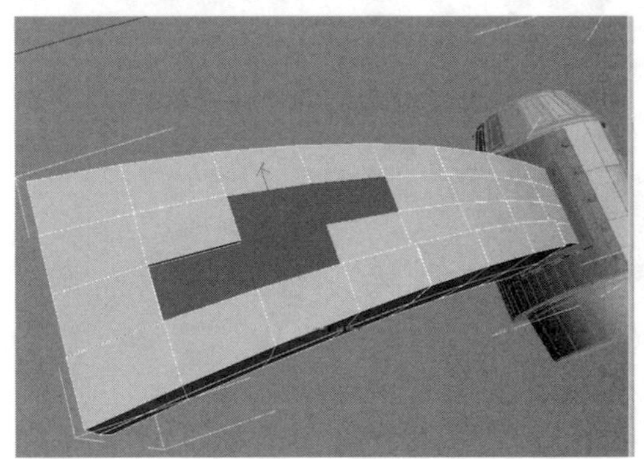

Figure 2-401

12. Select the polygons shown in Figure 2-402 and apply the same bevel settings we've been using.

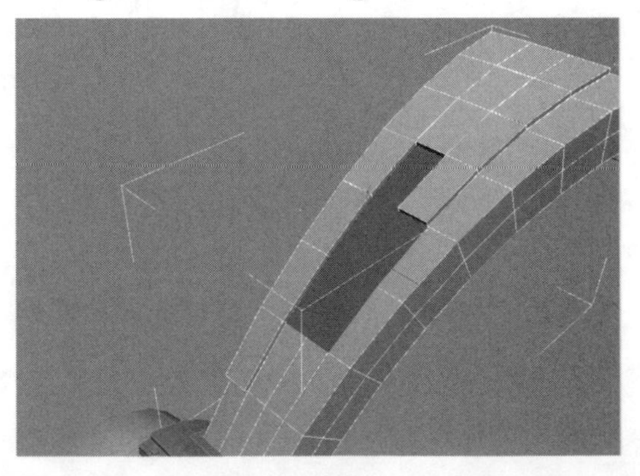

Figure 2-402

13. Select the polygons shown in Figure 2-403 and apply the same bevel settings we've been using.

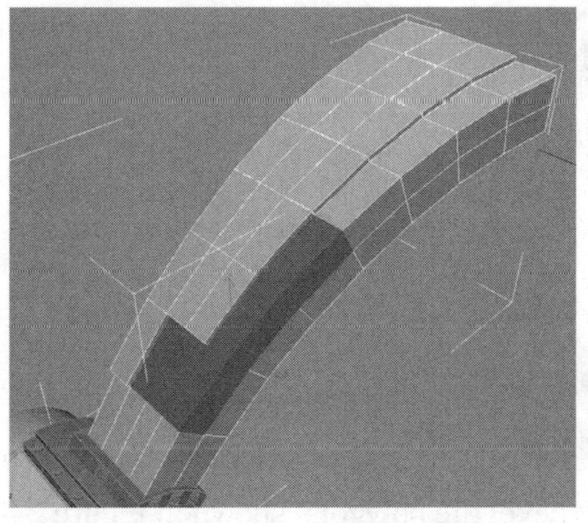

Figure 2-403

14. Select the polygons shown in Figure 2-404 and apply the same bevel settings we've been using.

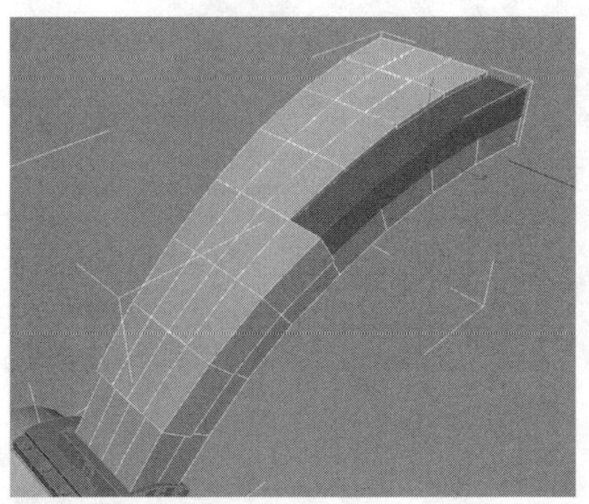

Figure 2-404

15. Select the polygons shown in Figure 2-405 and apply the same bevel settings we've been using.

Figure 2-405

16. Select the polygons shown in Figure 2-406 and apply the same bevel settings we've been using.

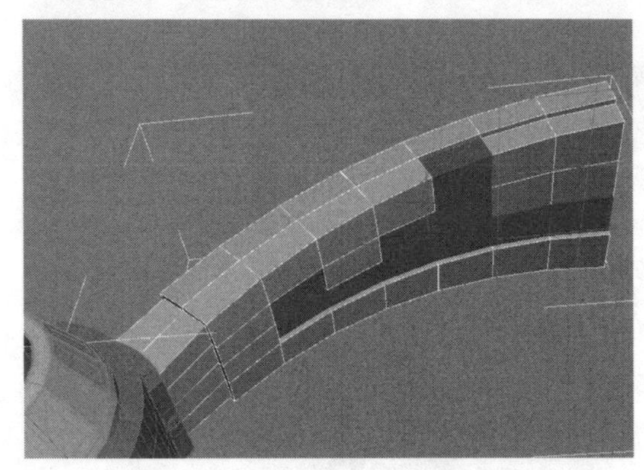

Figure 2-406

17. Select but *do not* bevel the polygons shown in Figure 2-407.

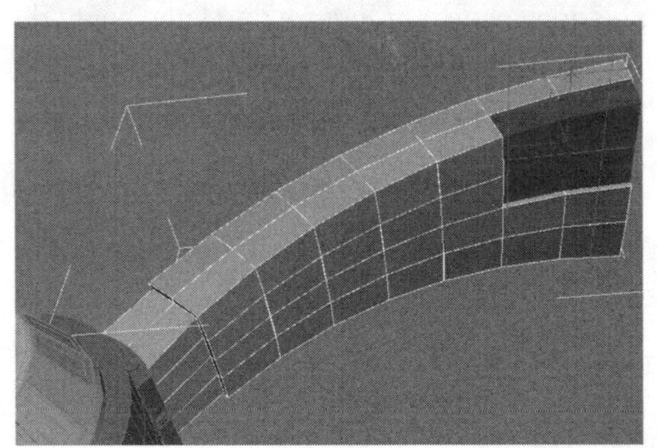

Figure 2-407

18. Do a test render.

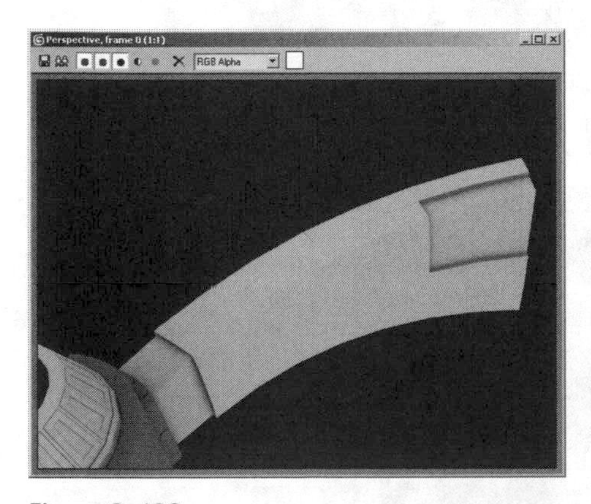

Figure 2-408

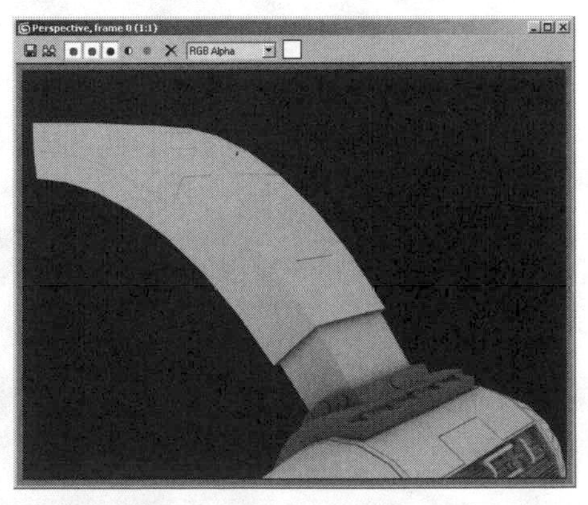

Figure 2-409

19. Select the same polygons you did in step 5 and Bevel them:

Type	Height	Outline	Apply/OK
Local Normal	0	–0.75	Apply
Local Normal	1	0	OK

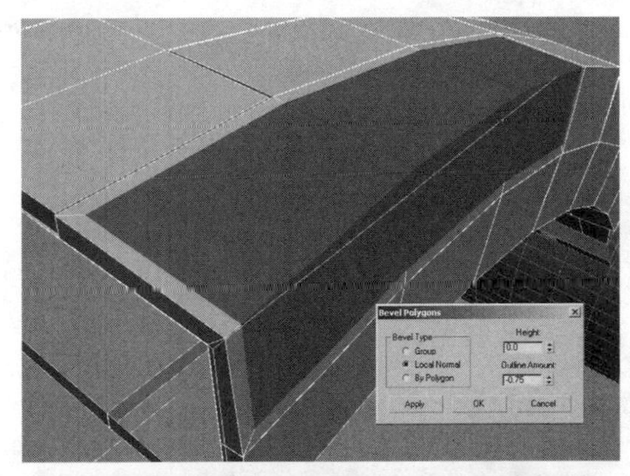

Figure 2-410

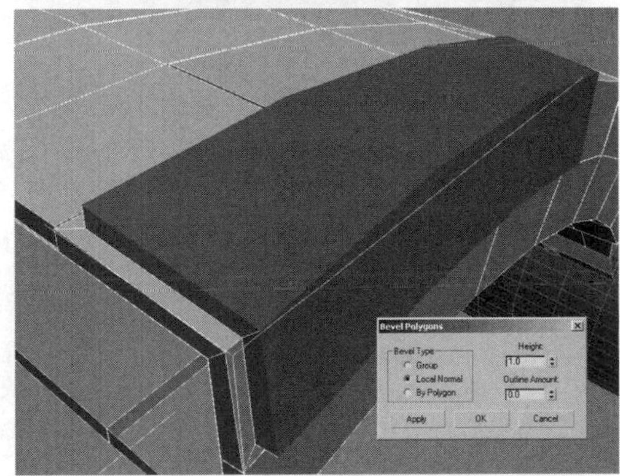

Figure 2-411

20. Hold down the **Shift** key and click the **Edge** selection mode button.

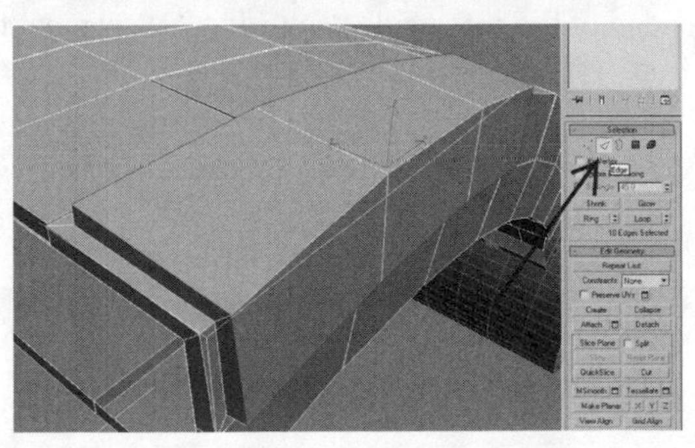

Figure 2-412

FYI: Shift+Edge selection mode switches from Polygon selection mode to Edge selection mode *and* highlights the outer edges of the selected polygons.

21. Chamfer the edges first by **0.06** and then by **0.2**.
22. Repeat steps 20-21, using the same polygon selections you used in steps 5-16 to make the armored plates.
23. Do a test render.

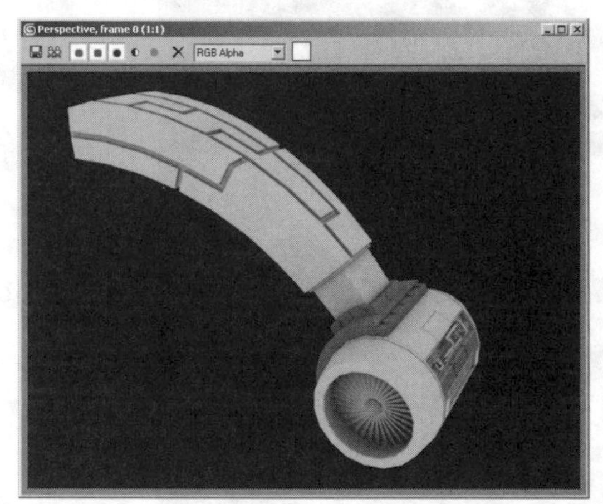

Figure 2-413

Message: You can put the rivets, which hold the armor to the wing, either on top of the plates or between them. It's just a matter of personal taste. I've also intentionally left the armor off the area closest to the wing_brace. If you want to detach it, you can set up a rigging so that this part can slide into the wing, allowing you to animate the nacelle to move closer to the wing for certain maneuvers.

24. Switch to Edge selection mode and click the innermost edge of the chamfered edge of the rotor-side armored plate, closest to the chassis connection.

Fire Drill: It should loop for you but if it doesn't, click Loop. As a last resort, because Loop is finicky, you may have to select them using Ctrl+left-click.

Figure 2-414

25. Under Edit Edges, click **Create Shape From Selection** (be sure to select Linear and *not* Smooth).
26. Hit **H** and select the shape you just made (**Shape01**).

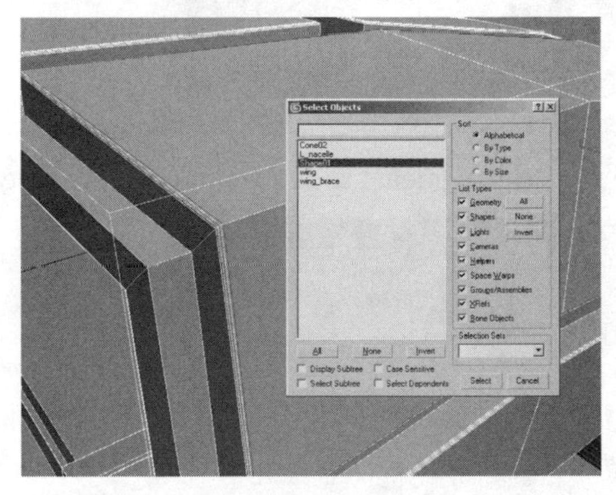

Figure 2-415

27. Select the top and side segments and move them **0.4** in the X axis. (Hit **F3** to switch between shaded and wireframe modes as needed.)

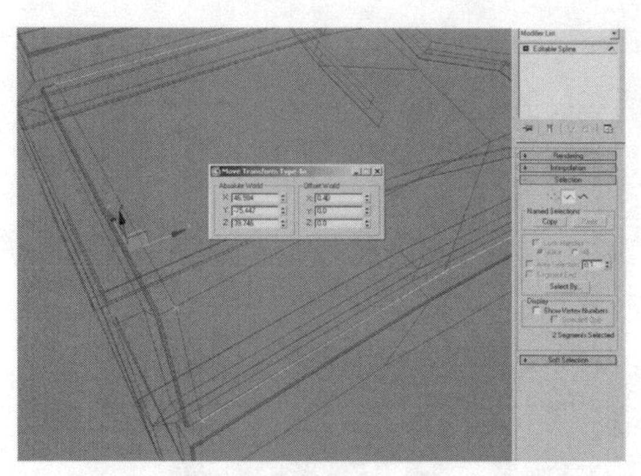

Figure 2-416

28. Select the bottom segments and move them up **0.4** in the Z axis.

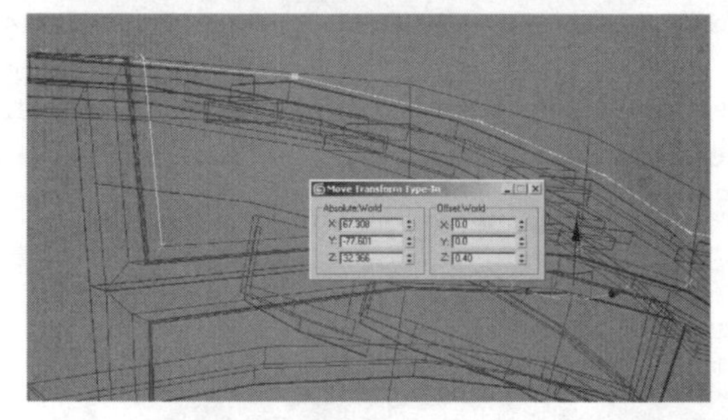

Figure 2-417

29. Select the four rear segments and move them **–0.4** in the Y axis.

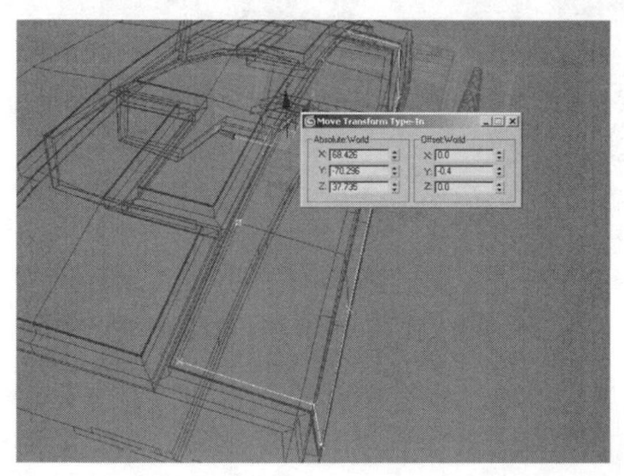

Figure 2-418

30. Select the two segments on the edge on the nacelle side and move them **–0.4** in the X axis.

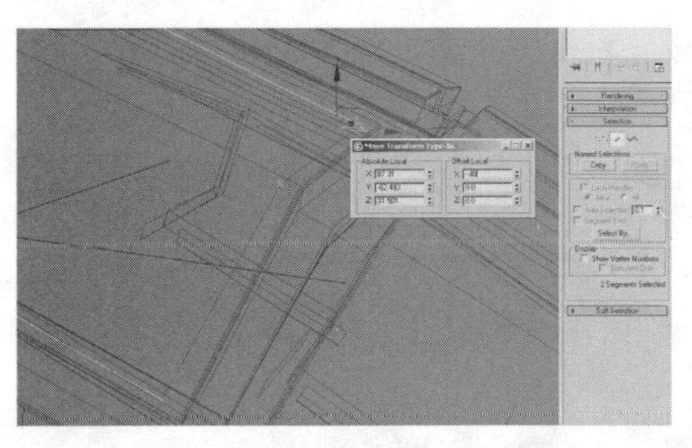

Figure 2-419

Fire Drill: If you slip back into shaded/edged faces mode, you'll see that some of the vertices have fallen below the surface of the armor plates.

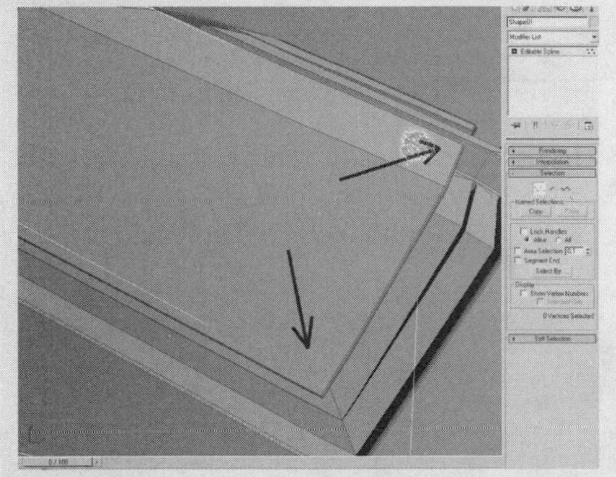

Figure 2-420

31. Use the Move tool to ensure all the vertices are just above the surface.
32. Switch to the Front viewport. Using AutoGrid, create a Sphere with a Radius of **0.25**, **18** Segments, and a Hemisphere of **0.5** at the bottom corner of the armor plate, at the location of the spline vertex.

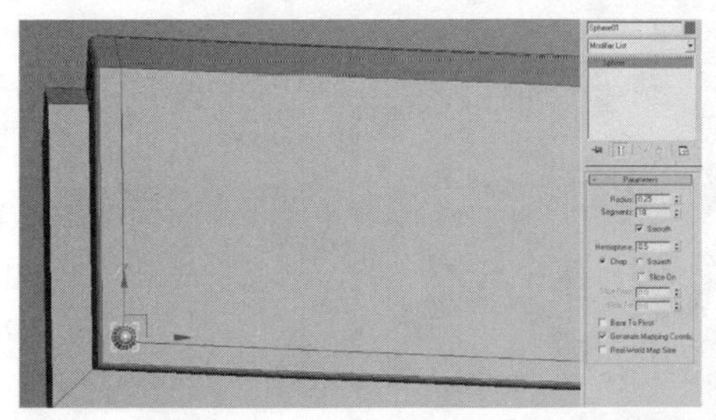

Figure 2-421

33. Convert the sphere to an Editable Polygon and delete the rear-facing polygons.
34. Object-select the sphere and select the Spacing tool (**Shift+I**) from the Tools menu.

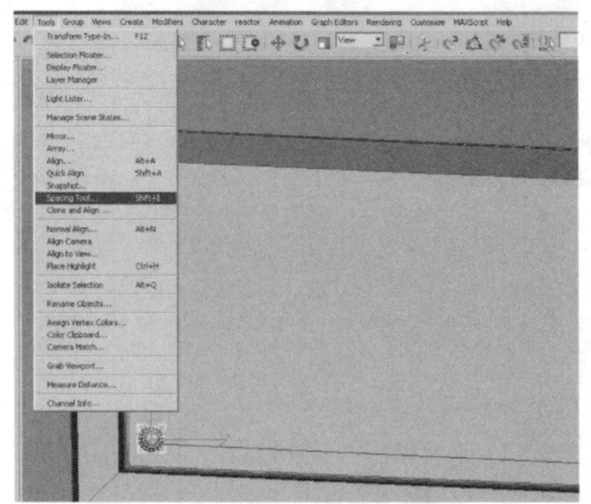

Figure 2-422

35. Click **Pick Path** and click the spline shape object you made. Type **30** into the Count field, make sure Context is set to **Centers** and Type of Object is set to **Copy**, then click **Apply** and close the window.

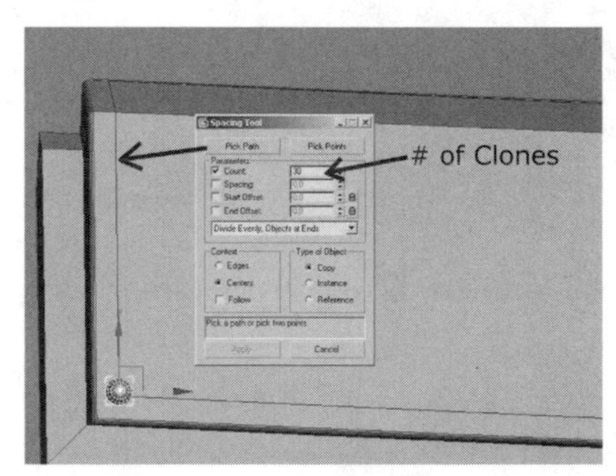

Figure 2-423

36. Delete the extra rivet and select the spline shape and delete it too.

Figure 2-424

FYI: The spline was a guide for Max to use when positioning the clones. We no longer need it.

Cloning to a path is a huge time-saver when cloning in two dimensions. However, the Spacing tool is not without problems. Specifically, when the clones follow a path over multiple axes, the clones get turned the wrong way, necessitating the use of the Rotation tool. Even so, it's quicker and more accurate than placing them by hand. Also, make sure the bottom edge of each sphere is just below the surface, so when you attach them, there won't be gaps beneath the rivets and the surface.

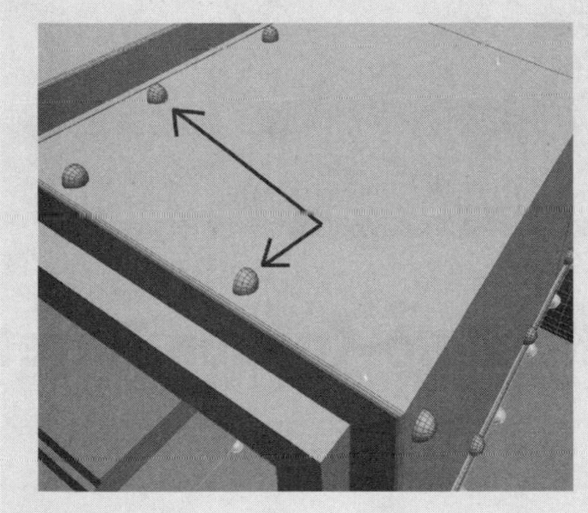

Figure 2-425

37. Select the wing, click **Attach List**, and attach all the spheres.
38. Repeat steps 25-37 for the rest of the armored plates.

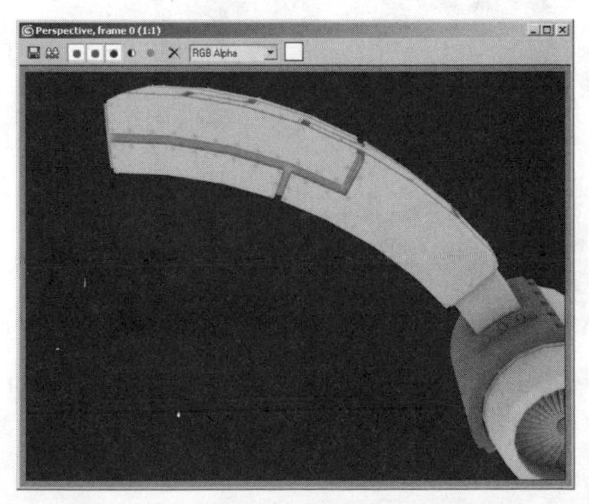

Figure 2-426

Message: Let's be real. Making all those rivets is a pain in the butt, because it's about as interesting as watching paint dry. That said, if you look at Figure 2-426, the rivets are really indispensible, because they're what sell it as being armor plating.

39. Rotate around the back and delete the extra polygons that were made from the bevels and that face where the wing connects to the chassis.

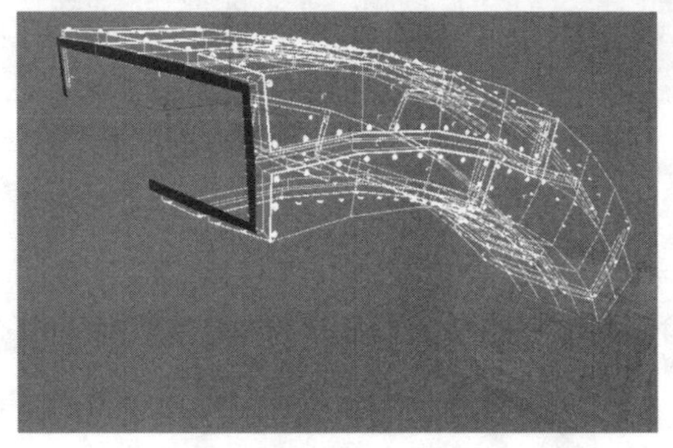

Figure 2-427

Day 9: Making the Auto-Cannon Turret Assembly

1. Switch to the Left viewport, hide everything but the bracket, and select the eight polygons shown in Figure 2-428.

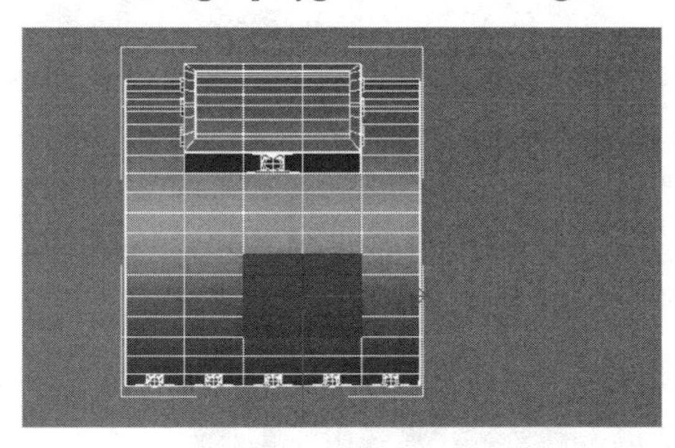

Figure 2-428

2. Detach these eight polygons as an object and then Select and Link them back to the bracket.
3. Hide the bracket so that only the eight polygons remain.

Figure 2-429

4. Select the eight polygons and Group Extrude them **1.0**.

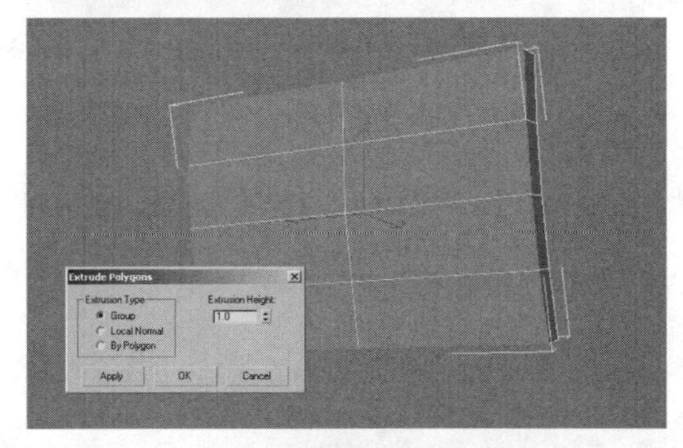

Figure 2-430

5. Select the four middle polygons.

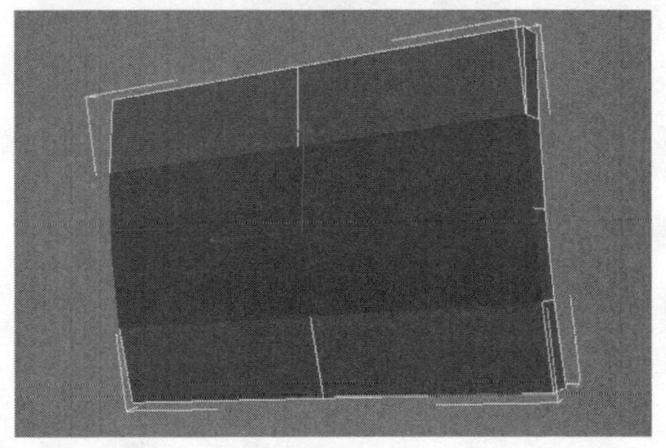

Figure 2-431

6. Click **Bevel Settings:**

Type	Height	Outline	Apply/OK
Group	0	–1	Apply
Group	0.05	0	Apply
Group	0	–0.05	Apply
Group	10	0	OK

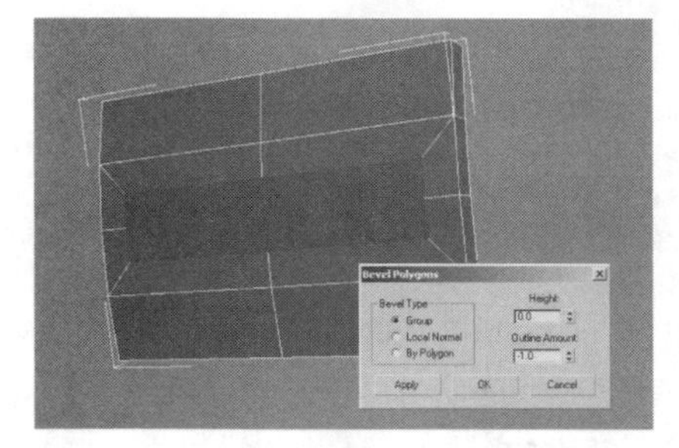

Figure 2-432

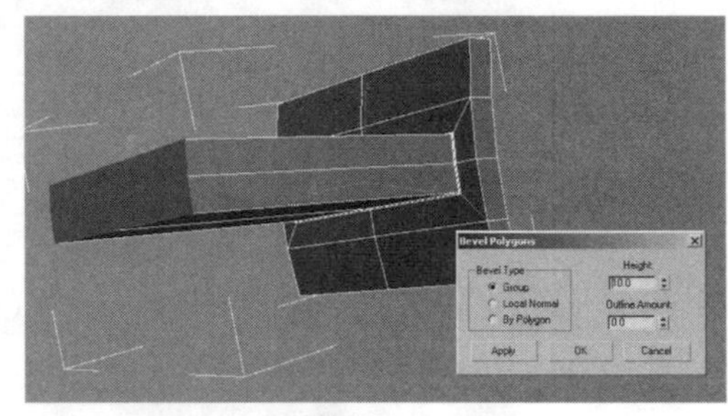

Figure 2-433

7. Unhide the nacelle and the wing_bracket so we have a frame of reference for our scale.

Figure 2-434

8. Group Extrude the end polygons by **4.0**.

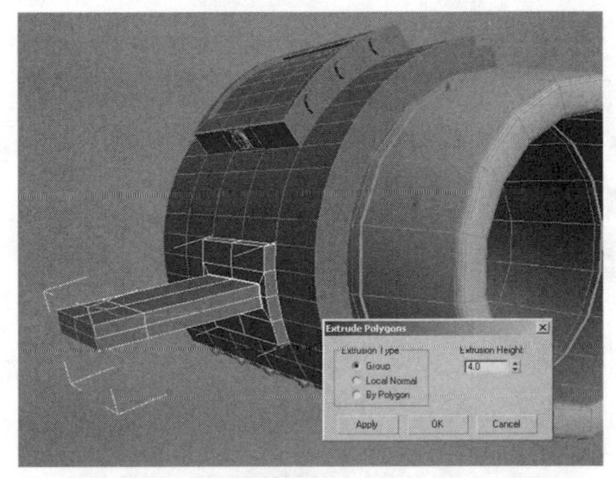

Figure 2-435

9. Delete the four end polygons.

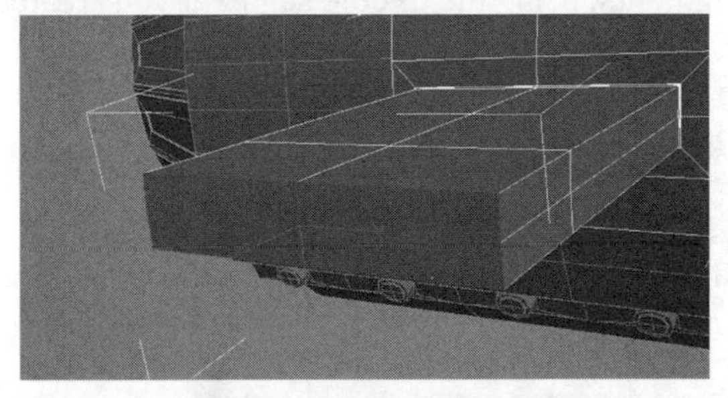

Figure 2-436

10. Select the border and then Cap it.

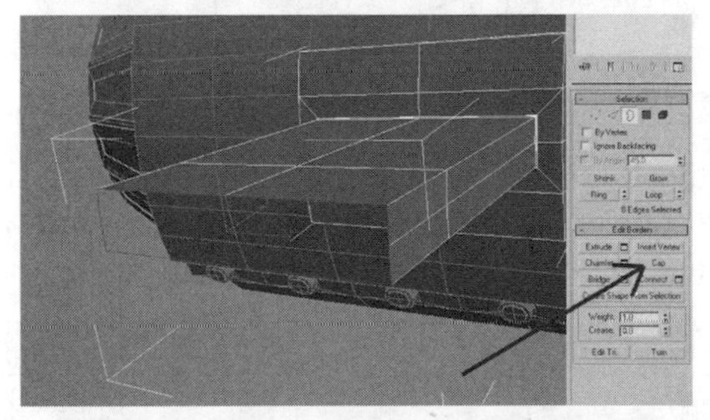

Figure 2-437

11. Using the Cut tool, split the cap into two separate polygons.

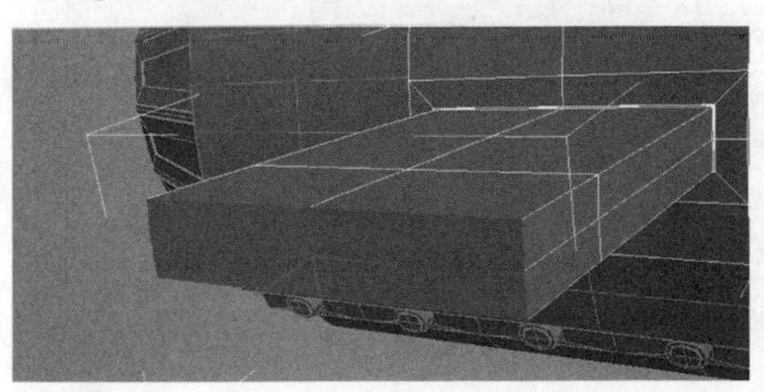

Figure 2-438

12. Select the rightmost polygon and delete it.

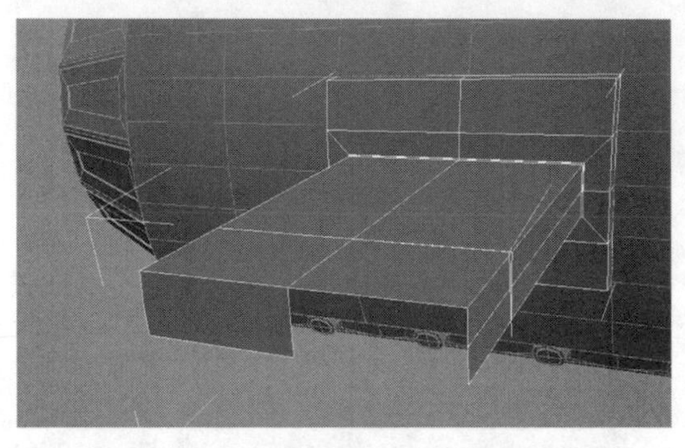

Figure 2-439

13. Select the remaining polygon and Hinge From Edge **180** degrees with **18** Segments, using the middle segment you created with the Cut tool as the hinge.

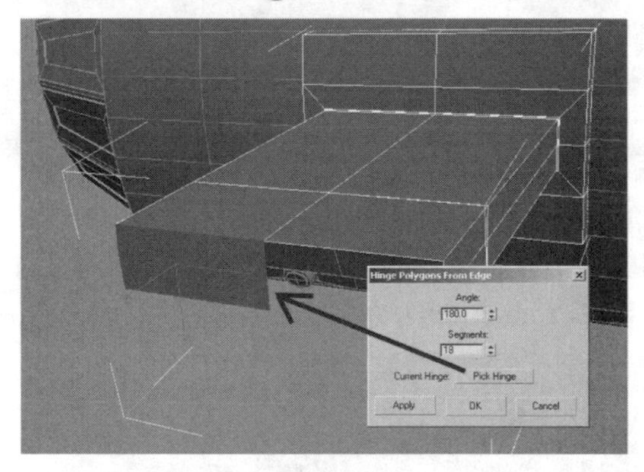

Figure 2-440

14. Switch to the Top viewport and, using AutoGrid, create a Cylinder in the middle of the rounded area you just created. Then switch to Perspective view and center the cylinder vertically.

Radius	Height	Height/Cap Segs	Sides	Smooth
3.5	4	2/1	32	Checked

Figure 2-441

15. Switch to Perspective view and move the cylinder down until it is roughly centered. Select **Compound Objects** from the Create panel and then click **Boolean.**

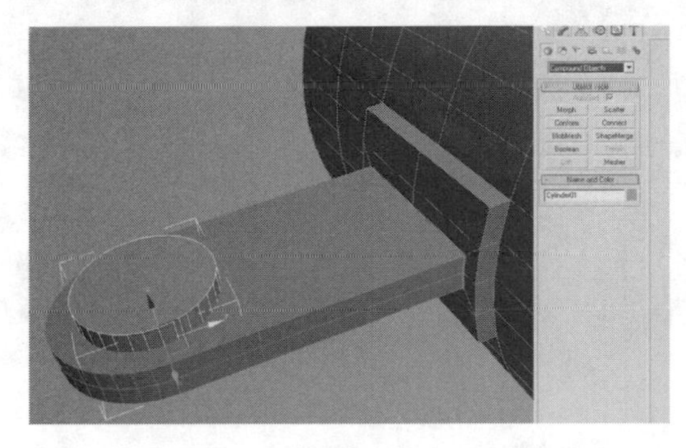

Figure 2-442

16. Click **Pick Operand B**, click the brace, and under Operation, click **Subtraction (B-A).**

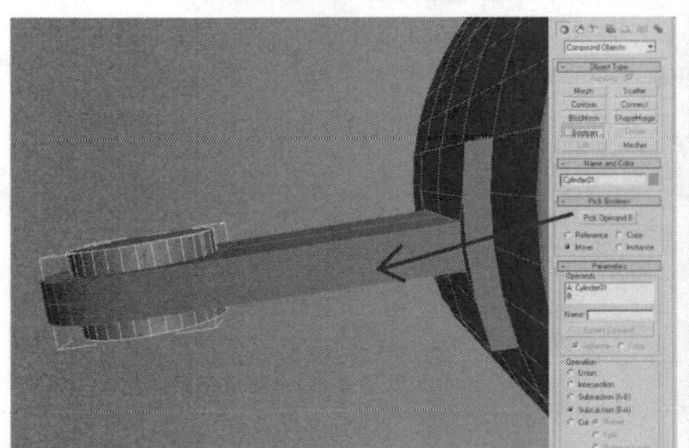

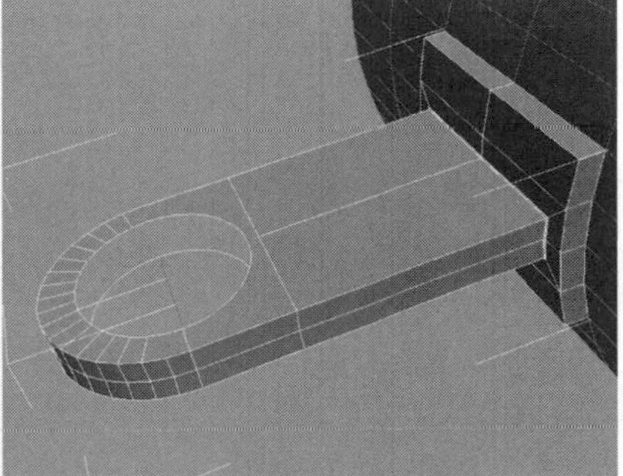

Figure 2-443

Figure 2-444

Fire Drill: The Boolean made a really nice hole. We'd be in a wee mess if we wanted to use NURMS subdivision on this (see Figure 2-445). But we're not going to use NURMS, so we're fine. Nevertheless, in the interest of good modeling practice, we'll add some cuts to mitigate the problem.

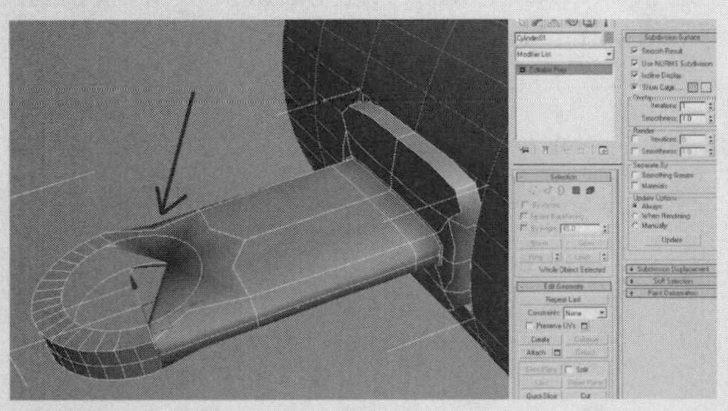

Figure 2-445

17. Make cuts where you see the dotted lines (on the top and bottom sides) in Figure 2-446.

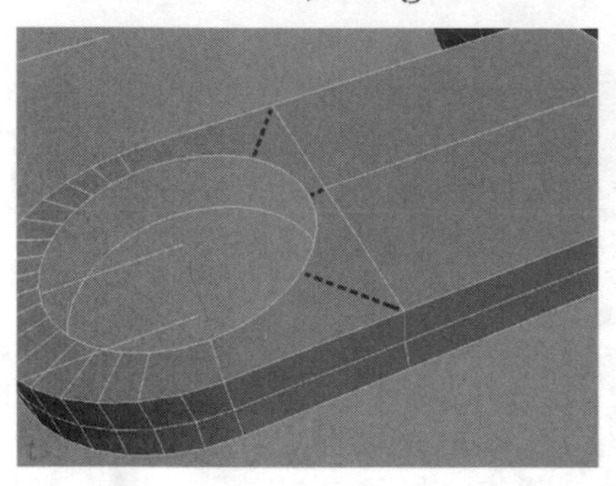
Figure 2-446

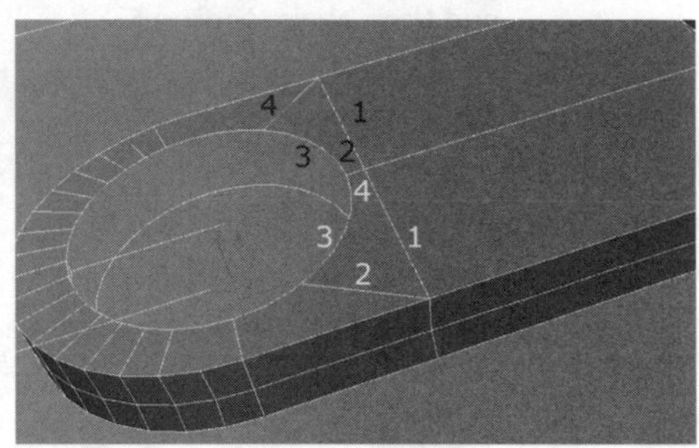

Figure 2-447

FYI: An ideal polygon has four edges. By making six judicious cuts (three on top and three below) we've turned two six-edged polygons into four four-edged polygons. Now, if you do NURMS, it's far from perfect and could benefit from some massaging, but it's light-years better than Figure 2-445.

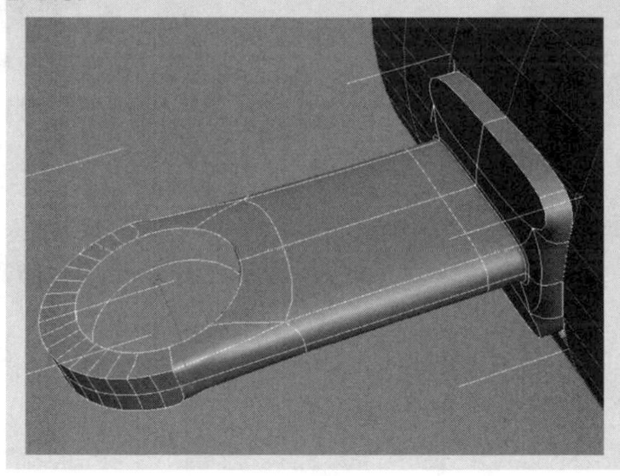
Figure 2-448

18. If you've turned on NURMS, turn it off and edge-select an edge on the inner hole and its counterpart bottom edge.

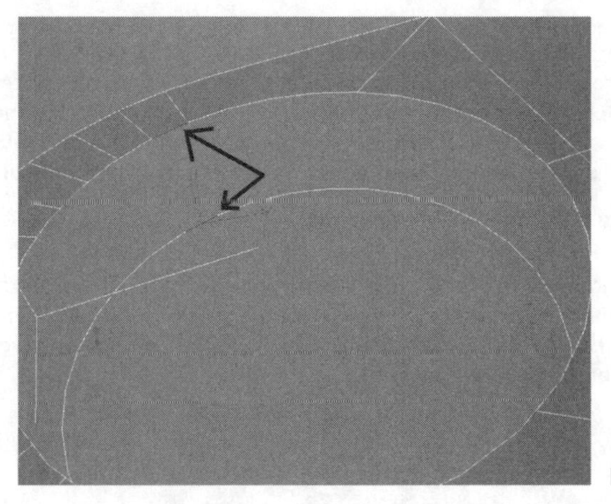

Figure 2-449

19. Click **Bridge** to connect the edges by creating a new polygon between them.

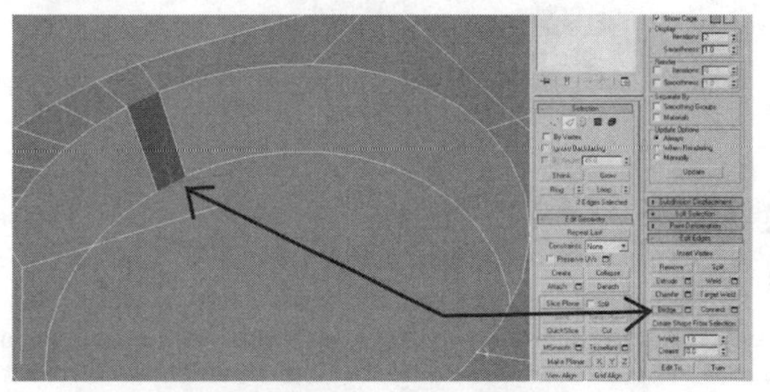

Figure 2-450

20. Bridge the remaining edges until the hole becomes a tube.

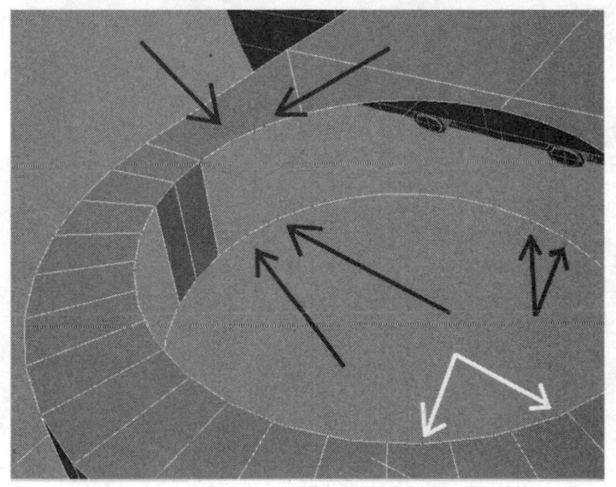

Figure 2-451

FYI: Ah, the joys of Booleans. The arrows in Figure 2-451 point to excess vertices from our cylinder having more segments than our brace. Either make matching cuts on the top and bottom so you can bridge them or remove them using the Remove tool. You can also opt to Target Weld those near other segments. Use a cut when needed to preserve the curve.

FYI: When you get to the corner, make a cut, as shown in Figure 2-452. Though the resultant polygon *looks like a triangle*, note that it has four edges (owing to the vertex indicated by the arrow). That is just what we want; don't forget to do the edges on the bottom.

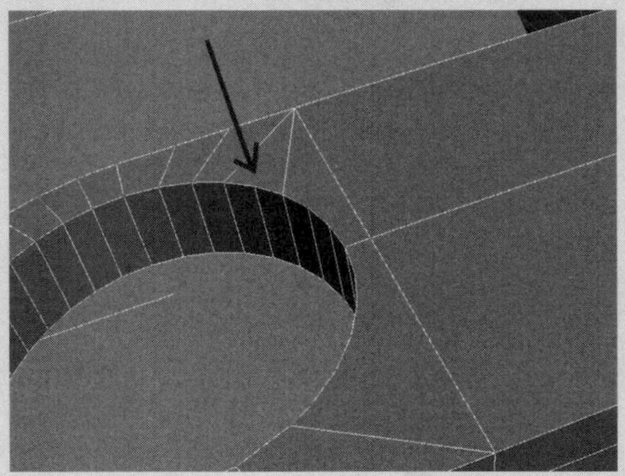

Figure 2-452

This is another pain-in-the-butt thing we have to do when using Booleans, which is why people don't like them. Mostly this occurs when punching holes in an otherwise rectangular object. Which, unfortunately, is what we most often use Booleans for.

21. Make the same kind of cut from the middle segment to the vertex shown in Figure 2-453. This will make another four-sided polygon.

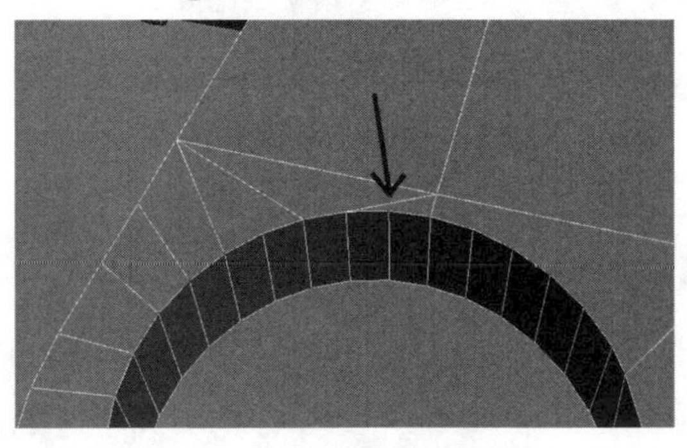

Figure 2-453

22. Repeat this on the other corner.

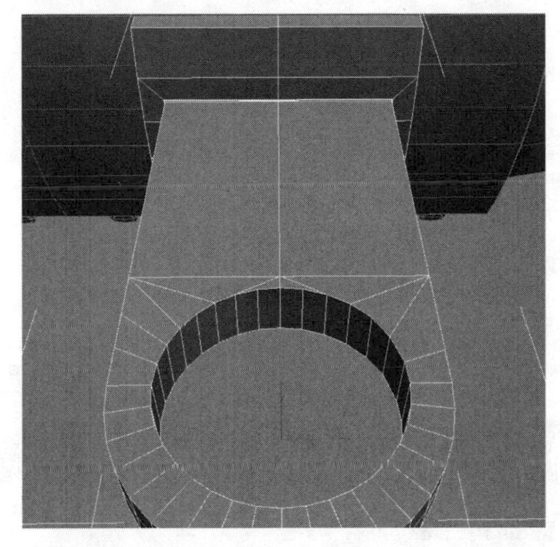

Figure 2-454

Message: Now if we use NURMS, we get a much more acceptable result (see Figure 2-455); not great, but better. Fortunately, we're not going to be using NURMS because we don't want the hardware to look overly smooth and organic. We want our hunter-killer to look cold, hard, and machined. But, as you can see, if you really must have that organic look, you can get your NURMS to look as good as you want them with some more tweaking of vertices and cutting.

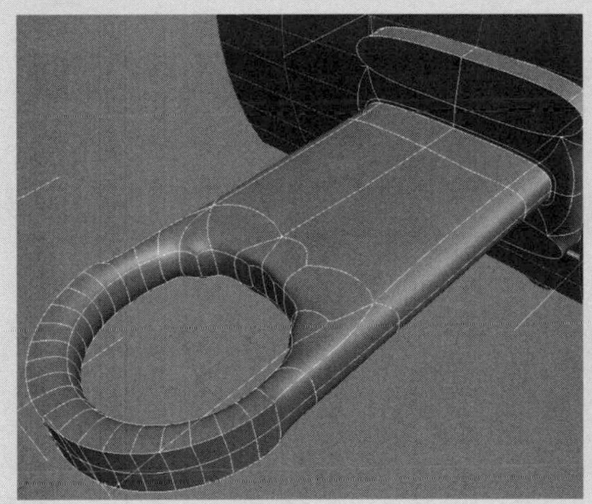

Figure 2-455

23. Edge-select the outer edges and the edges of the hole; you should have 158 edges selected.

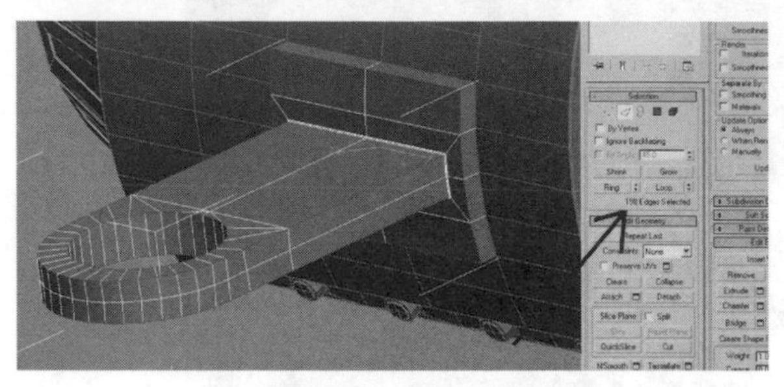

Figure 2-456

FYI: You can either select them by hand, or you can polygon-select the entire object and Shift+Ctrl on Edge select to select the edges. If you choose the latter, you'll have to deselect edges you don't need. It takes about the same amount of time either way.

24. Chamfer the edges by **0.06** and then by **0.02**.
25. Click the **wing_brace** and attach this object to it, making them a single object.
26. Do a test render.

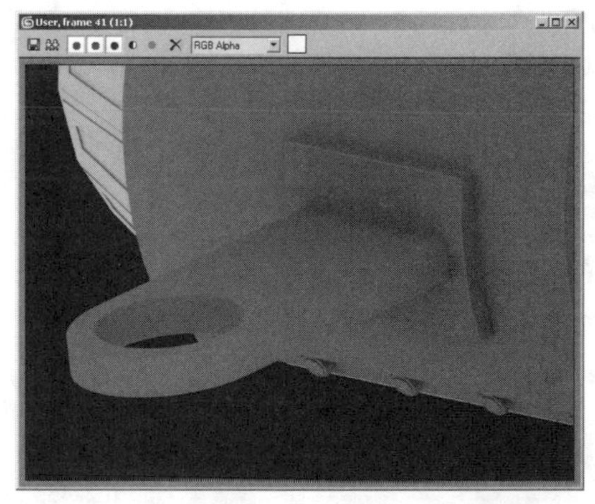

Figure 2-457

27. Zoom in on the area that attaches to the wing_brace, go to the Create panel, select **Extended Primitives**, and create a Gengon in the left corner using AutoGrid.

Sides	Radius	Fillet	Height	Side/Height/Fillet Segs	Smooth
6	0.4	0	0.3	1/1/1	Checked

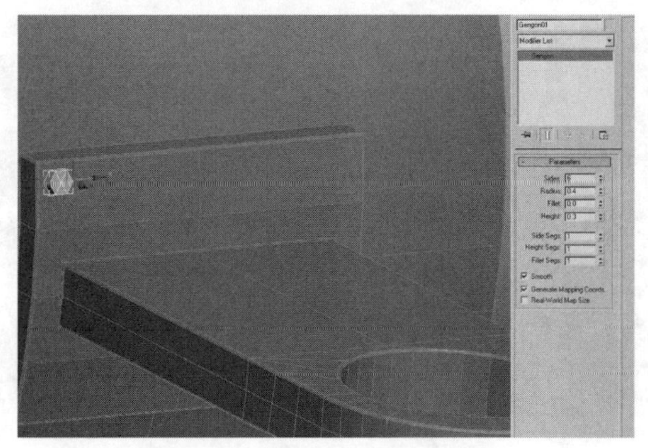

Figure 2-458

28. Make three clones, place one in each corner, and then use the Rotate tool to offset each one a little so they're not all turned in the same direction (like they were put on by hand).

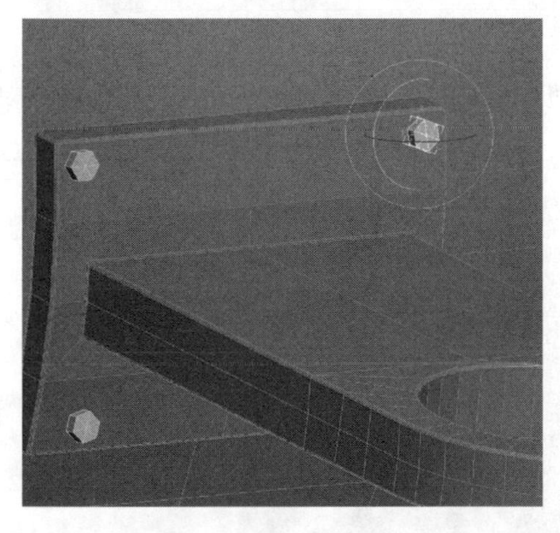

Figure 2-459

29. In the Perspective view, use the Move and Rotate tools to make sure the gengons are touching the surface of the brace (the way you did with the rivets). Hit **F9** to render.

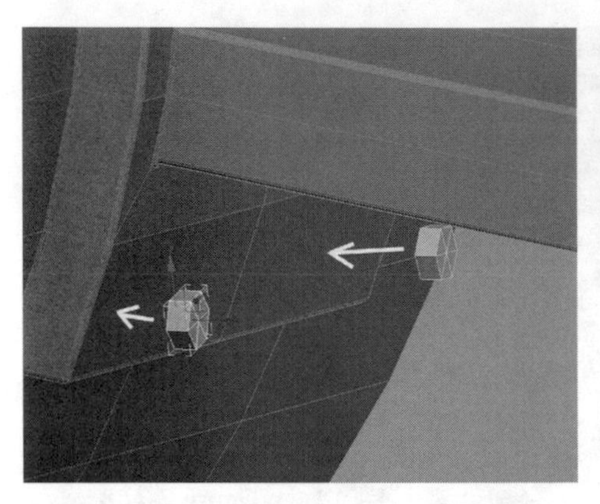

Figure 2-460

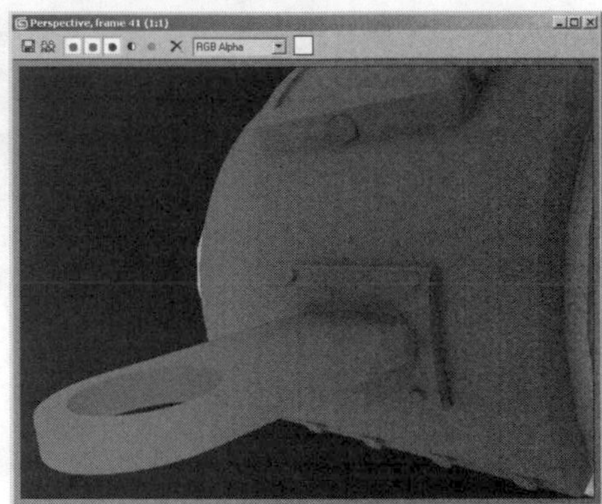

Figure 2-461

30. Switch to the Top view. Under the Create panel, pick **Extended Primitives**, and then create a Chamfer Cylinder in the center of the hole in the brace.

Radius	Height	Fillet	Height/Fillet/Cap Segs	Sides	Smooth
3.51	6	0.06	6/1/4	36	Checked

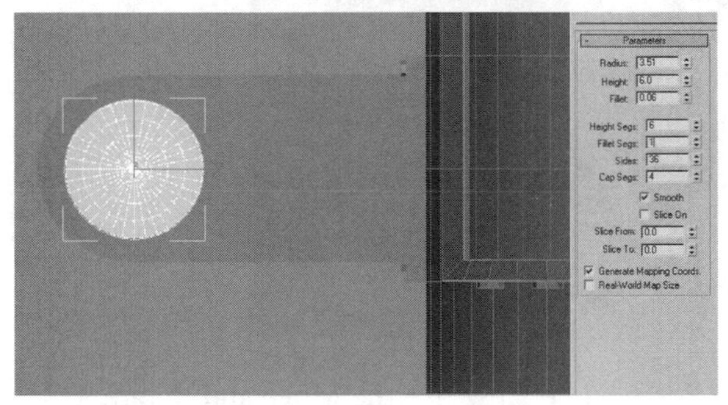

Figure 2-462

31. Switch to the Perspective view and use the Move tool to move the chamfer cylinder into place on the brace (around **–27** in the local Z axis).

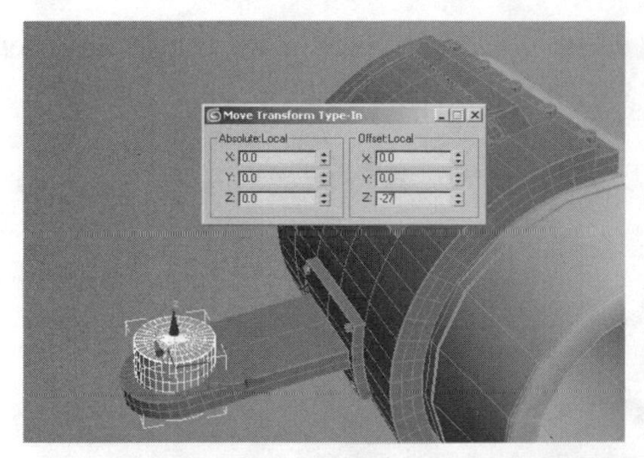

Figure 2-463

32. Use the Rotate tool to straighten the chamfer cylinder in its cradle.

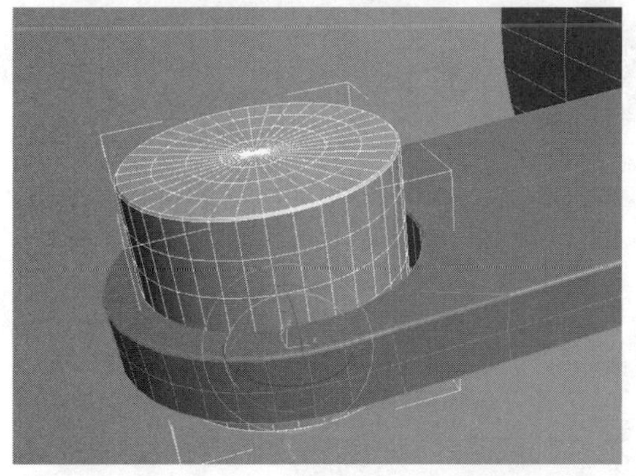
Figure 2-464

33. Center and align the chamfer cylinder.

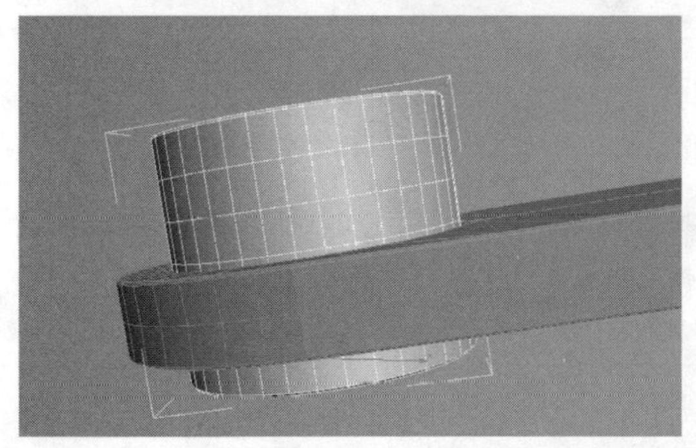
Figure 2-465

34. Rename the chamfer cylinder **cannon_turret**, convert it to an Editable Polygon, and Select and Link it to the brace.

35. Select and delete the 216 polygons in the center of the top and bottom of the cannon_turret.

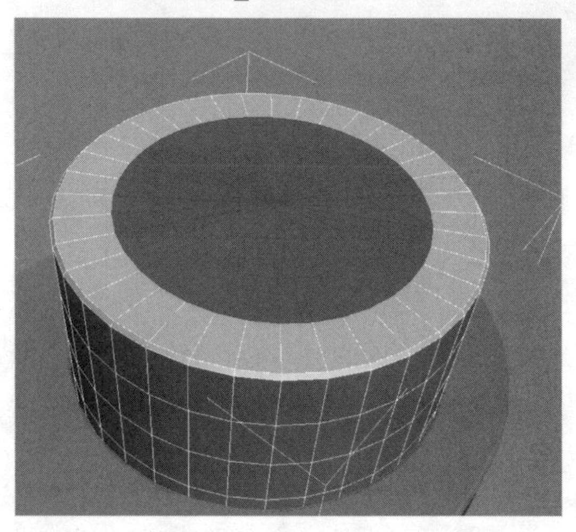

Figure 2-466

36. Border-select the top and bottom holes you made and then Cap them.

37. Select the top cap and click **Bevel Settings**:

Type	Height	Outline	Apply/OK
Group	0.4	0	Apply
Group	0	0.5	Apply
Group	0.5	0	OK

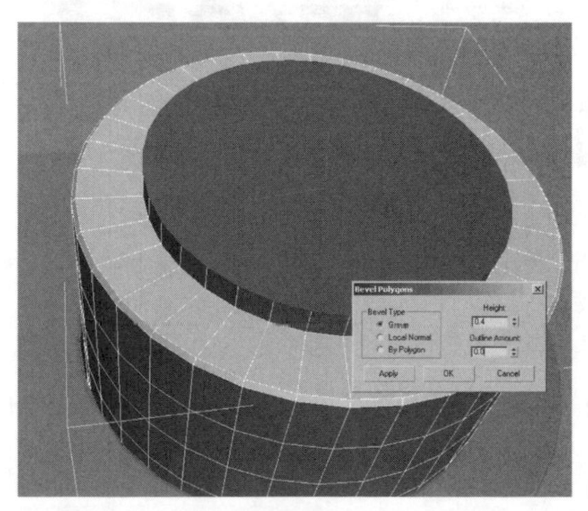

Figure 2-467

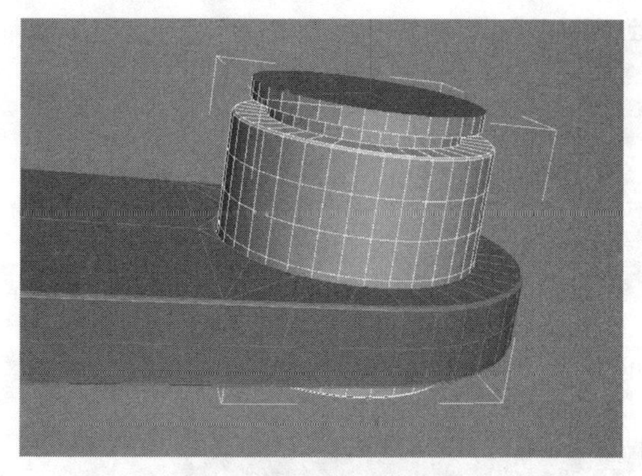

Figure 2-468

38. Click **Grow** until the top of the turret and the stem are selected.

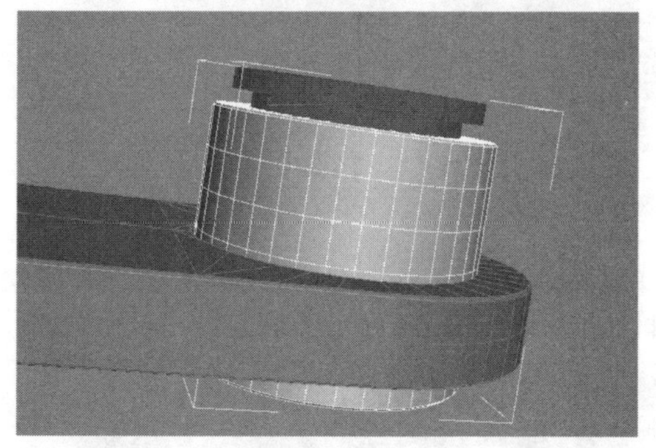

Figure 2-469

39. Click **Detach** and detach them as an object, naming the object **cannon_mount.**
40. Select and Link the cannon_turret to the wing_brace, then Select and Link the cannon_mount to the cannon_turret.

FYI: Detaching the cannon_mount from the cannon_turret allows us to rotate the mount independent of the movement of the turret. That said, it behaves as if its axle is attached to the mount, which is the reason we used Select and Link.

41. In the Top viewport, create a Box in the center of the cannon_mount using AutoGrid.

Length	Width	Height	Length/Width/Height Segs
18	3.5	0.9	5/2/1

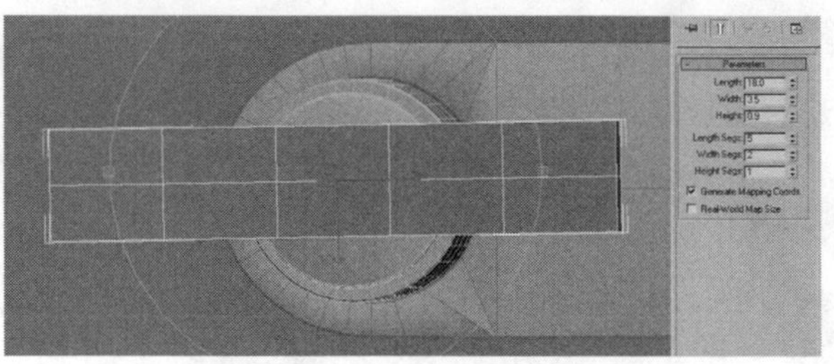

Figure 2-470

42. Convert the box to an Editable Polygon and place the box so that it is evenly positioned on the turret.

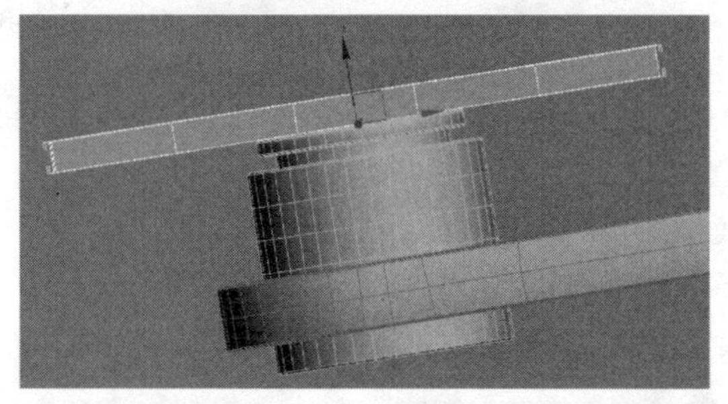

Figure 2-471

43. Select the box's rightmost edge, as shown in Figure 2-472, click **Loop**, and then move it **2.0** in the X axis.

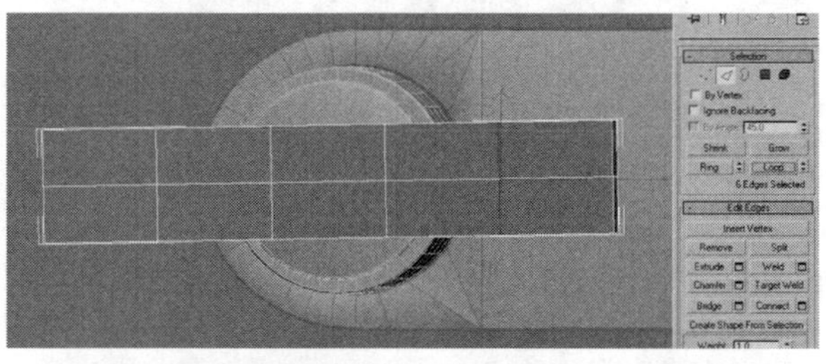

Figure 2-472

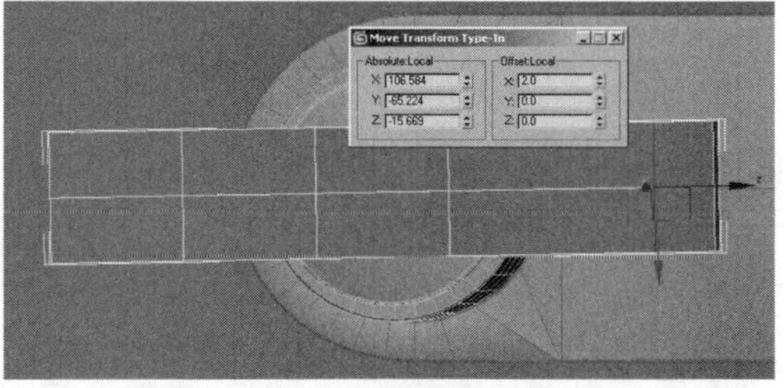

Figure 2-473

44. Repeat step 43 on the other side, but use **–2.0** for the X axis value.

45. In the Top view, select the middle two polygons and click **Bevel Settings**:

Type	Height	Outline	Apply/OK
Group	0	–0.4	OK

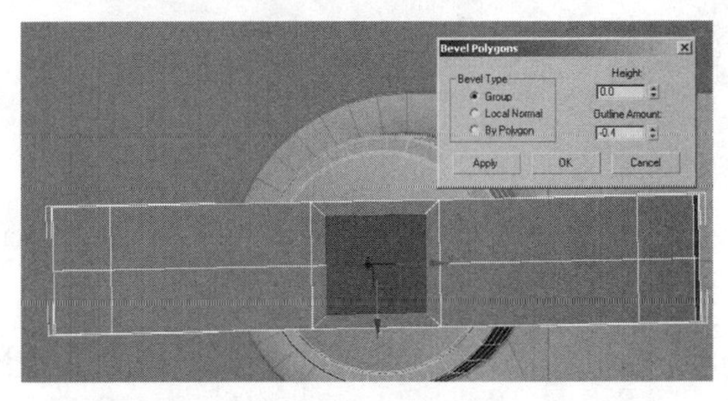

Figure 2-474

46. Scale the polygons in the Local X and Y down to **80**.

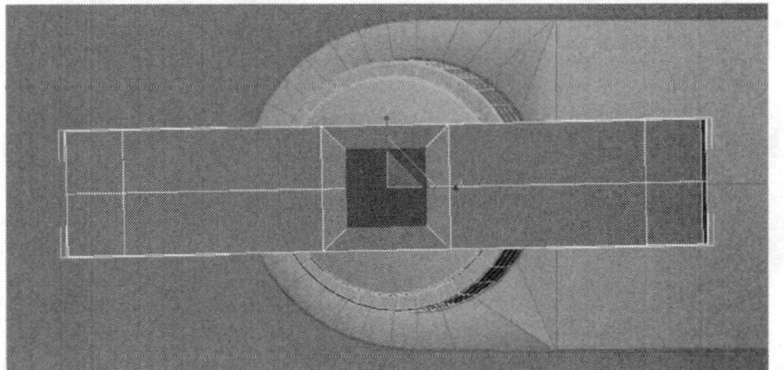

Figure 2-475

47. Extrude them by Local Normal **–0.01** and then click **MSmooth**.

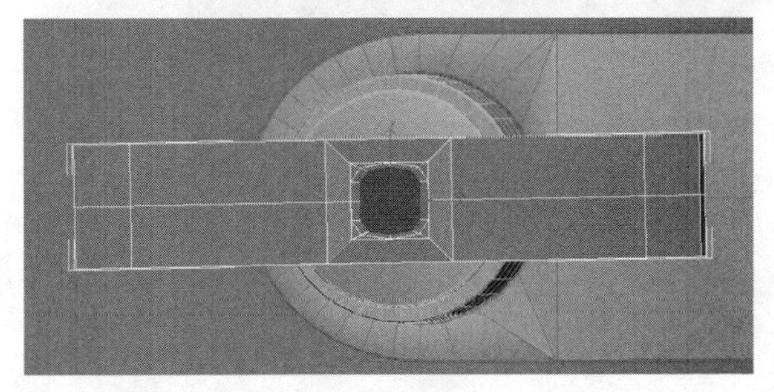

Figure 2-476

48. Extrude by Local Normal **1.2**.

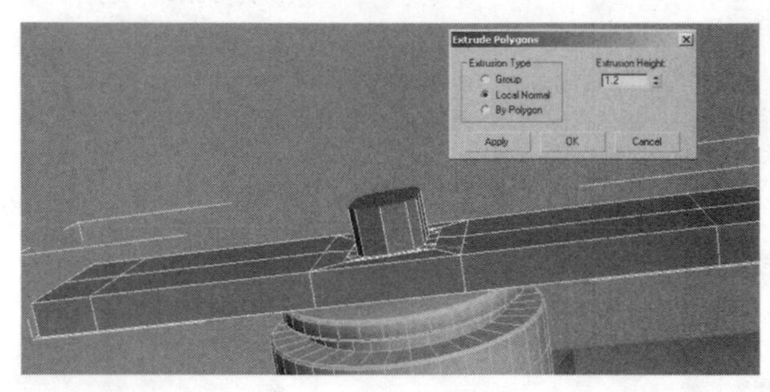

Figure 2-477

49. In the Top view, create a Gengon over the stub you just created (start with these values):

Sides	Radius	Fillet	Height	Side/Height/Fillet Segs
6	1.958	0.05	2	1/1/3

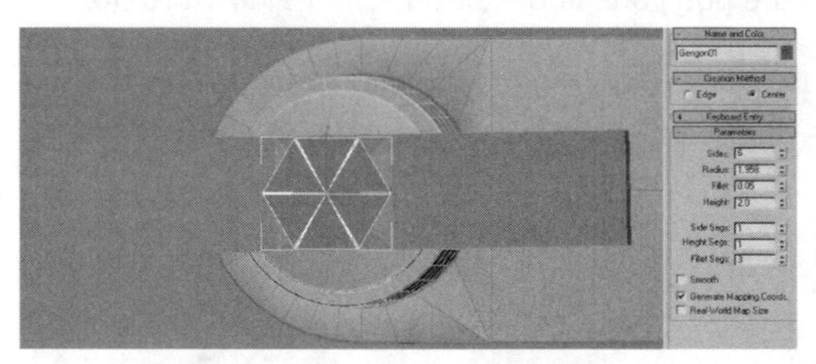

Figure 2-478

50. Switch to Perspective view and lower the gengon onto the stub and adjust it so it is properly positioned.

Figure 2-479

51. Reduce the Radius to **1.684** and the Height to **0.921**.

Figure 2-480

52. Convert it to an Editable Polygon, rename it **nut**, Select and Link the nut to the swivel, and then Select and Link the swivel to the cannon_mount.

53. Select the four polygons on the sides of the top of the swivel and scale them down to **60** in the local Y axis:

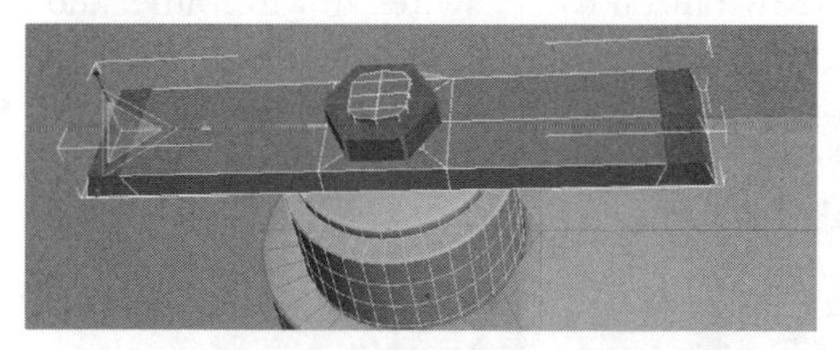

Figure 2-481

54. Group Extrude by **11**, delete the two polygons farthest from you, and then select the remaining two.

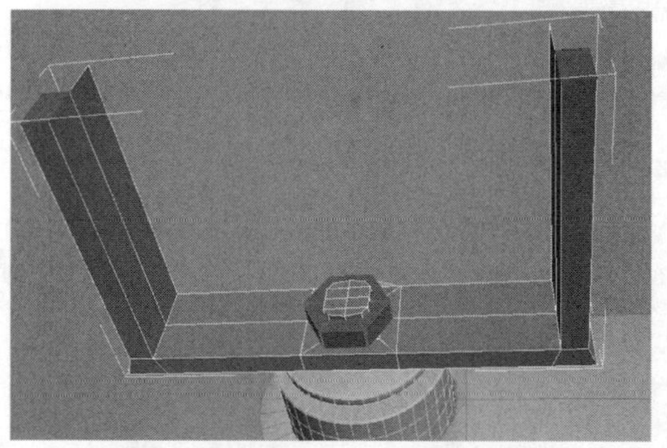

Figure 2-482

55. Hinge From Edge, **180** degrees with **18** Segments, using the far edge of the remaining polygon as the hinge. Then delete the back-facing polygons and Weld the vertices to merge.

56. Select the four center polygons on the top of the part of the swivel that pierces the bolt.

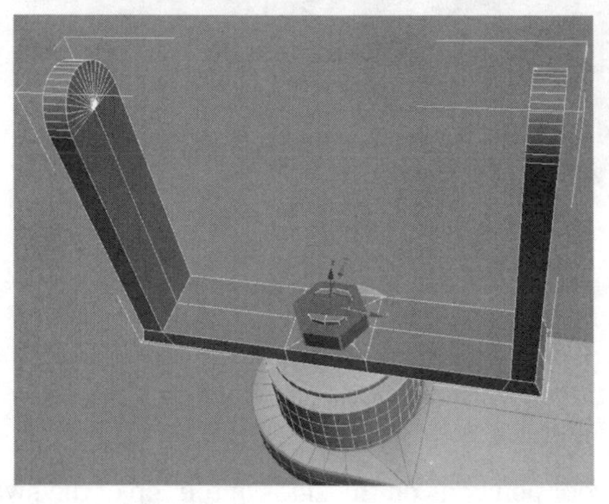

Figure 2-483

57. Click the **Grow** button twice, switch to wireframe, and deselect everything except the polygons shown in Figure 2-484.

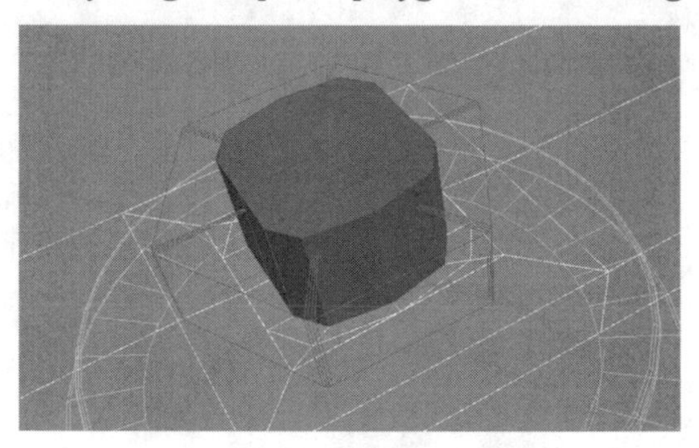

Figure 2-484

58. Click **Detach** and detach as an object.

59. Switch to Vertex selection mode and move the vertices until the object is more rounded; it doesn't have to be perfectly round.

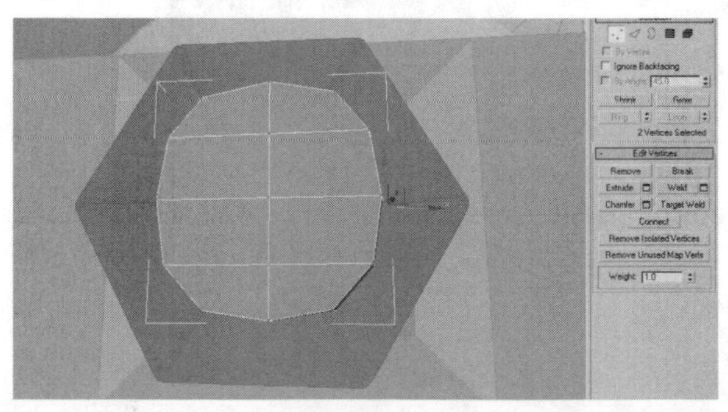

Figure 2-485

60. Add a MeshSmooth modifier to the stack and set the method to **NURMS** with **2** Iterations.

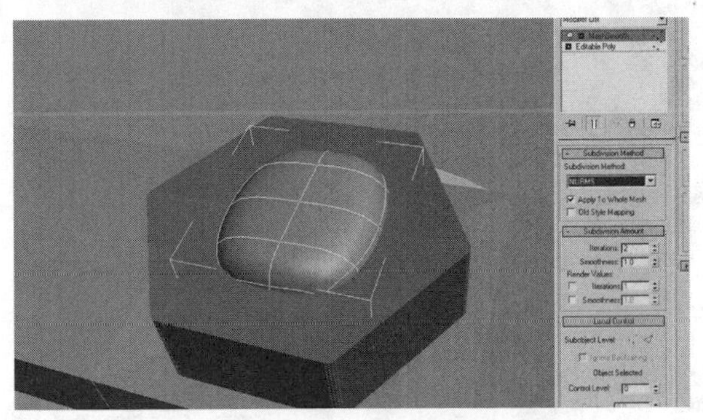

Figure 2-486

FYI: So why use a modifier instead of just clicking Use NURMS? Well you could certainly do it that way, but I want to reattach this piece to the swivel, and I want it to retain its smoothing. A MeshSmooth modifier allows me to smooth the object, then collapse the stack so the smoothing becomes a permanent part of the object.

61. Convert the object to an Editable Polygon to collapse the stack, select the swivel, click **Attach**, and reattach the object to the swivel.

62. The swivel should still be selected, so add a MeshSmooth modifier to its stack, set the Subdivision Method to **Classic** this time (to give it a boxier look), and leave the Iterations at **1** (again to give it a boxier look).

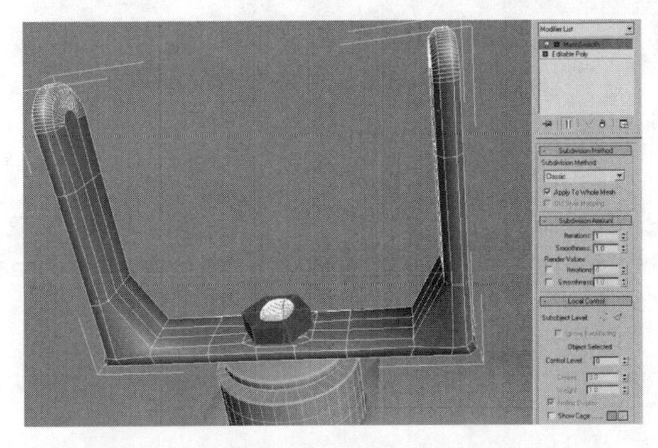

Figure 2-487

63. Convert it to an Editable Polygon to collapse the stack, then Select and Link the nut to the swivel and Select and Link the swivel to the cannon_mount. Do a quick render.

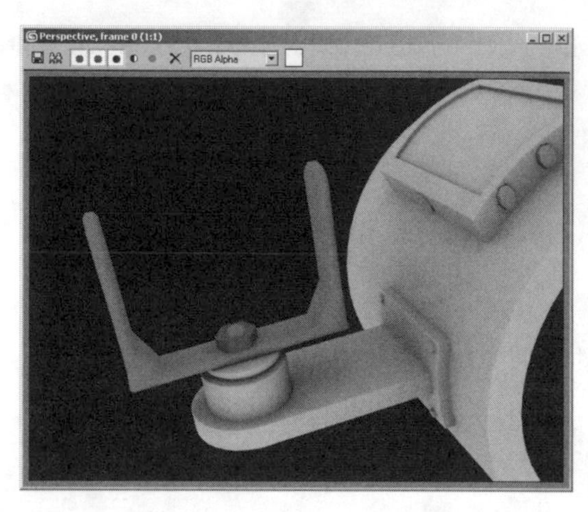

Figure 2-488

Day 10: Building the Auto-Cannon

1. Create a Box within the swivel, position it as shown, and convert it to an Editable Polygon.

Length	Width	Height	Length/Width/Height Segs
12	15	26	3/3/4

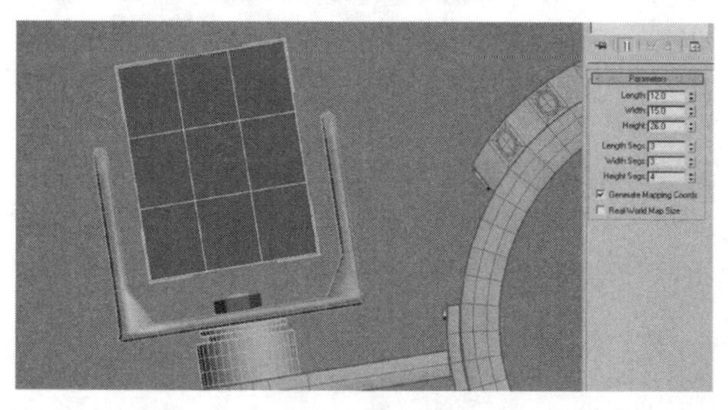

Figure 2-489

2. Select the five polygons that make up the upper-left corner and delete them.

Figure 2-490

3. Select an upper edge and a middle edge from where you deleted the polygons, and click **Bridge.**

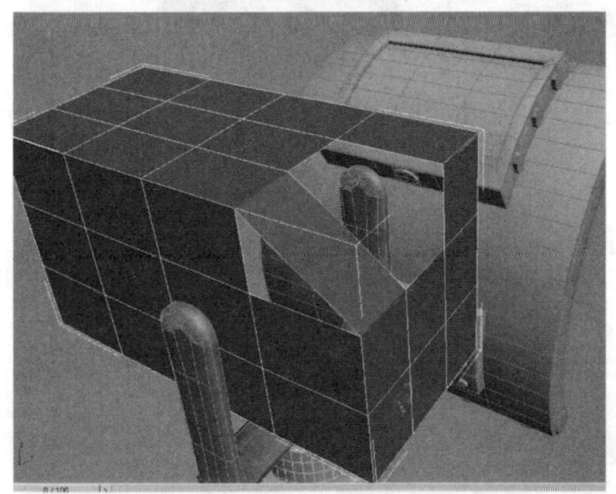

Figure 2-491

4. Bridge the next two edges.

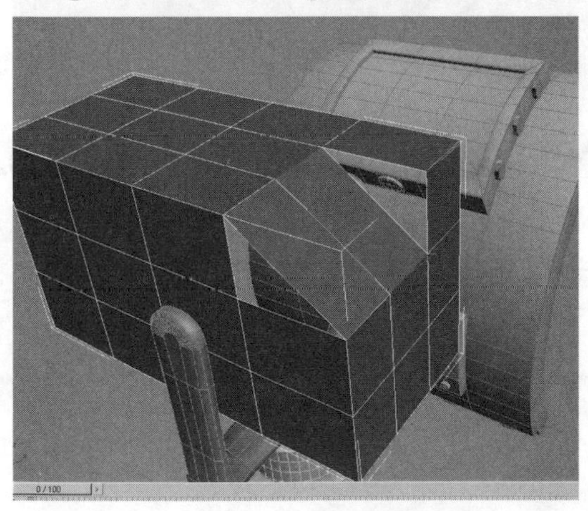

Figure 2-492

5. Cap the borders of the two triangular holes.

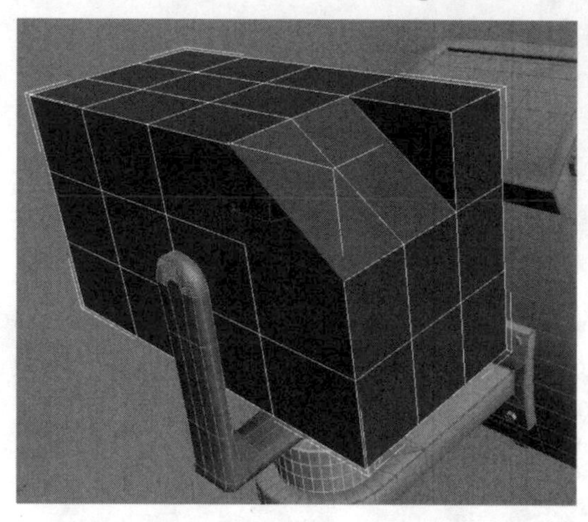

Figure 2-493

6. In the Front view, at the intersection of the horizontal and vertical edges on the lower-front left, use AutoGrid to create a Tube with these settings:

Radius 1	Radius 2	Height	Height/Cap Segs	Sides	Smooth
2.88	2.5	24	1/1	32	Checked

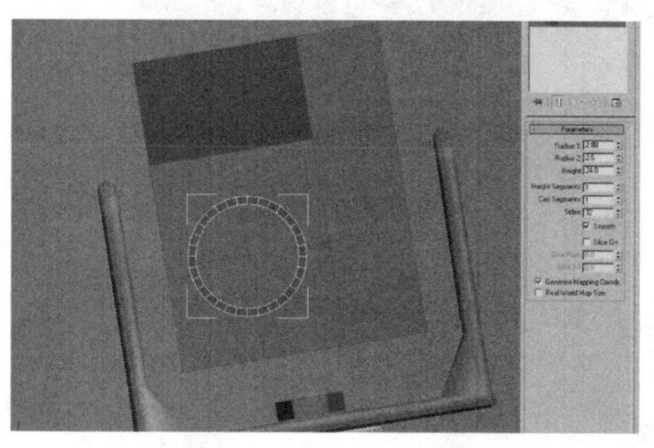

Figure 2-494

7. Convert to Editable Polygon, rename it **cannon_barrel**, select one of the edges touching the body, and then click **Loop**.

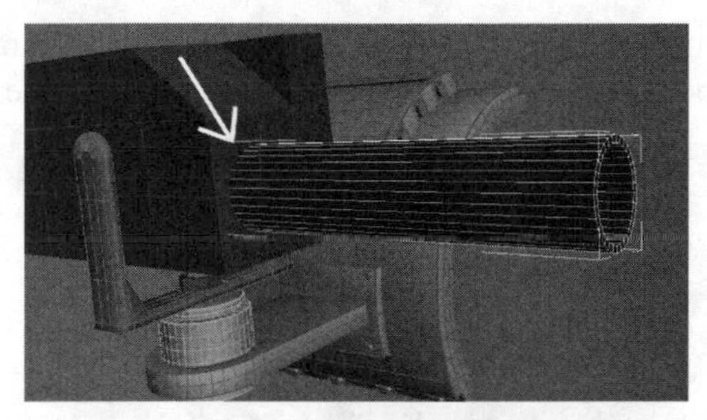

Figure 2-495

8. Click **Create Shape From Selection** and name it **gasket**.

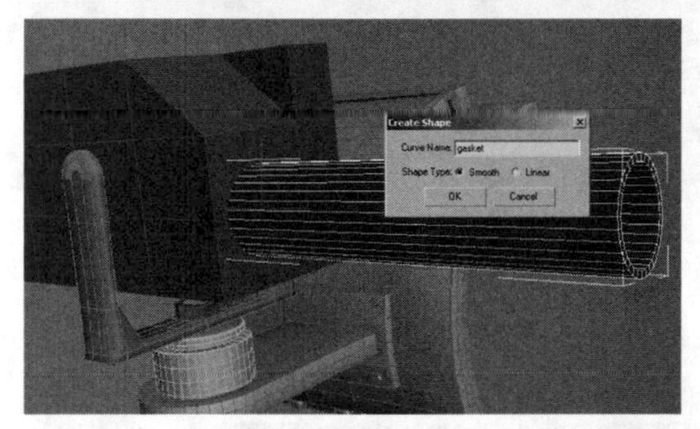

Figure 2-496

9. Hit **H**, select **gasket**, choose **Enable In Viewport** and **Enable In Renderer**, and convert it to an Editable Poly.

Figure 2-497

10. Select and Link the cannon_barrel to the gasket, then the gasket to the body, and then the body to the swivel. (To test this, rotate the swivel and the entire cannon should follow.)

11. Switch to the Front view, use AutoGrid to create a Tube over the barrel's end (think silencer), and convert it to an Editable Polygon.

Radius 1	Radius 2	Height	Height/Cap Segs	Sides	Smooth
3.84	2.853	14	5/1	32	Checked

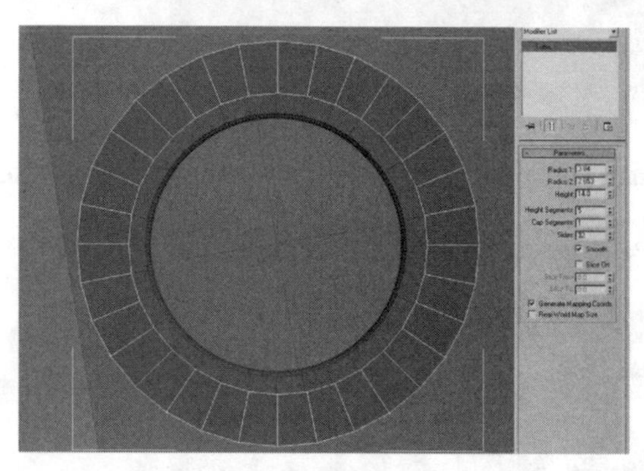

Figure 2-498

12. Rename it **flash_guard** and, in the Perspective view, position it on the end of the barrel.

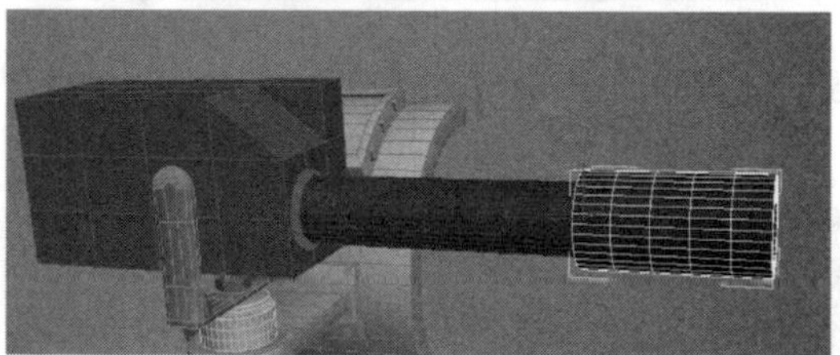

Figure 2-499

13. Switch to wireframe and select the flash_guard's middle 96 polygons, being sure not to select any of the interior polygons.

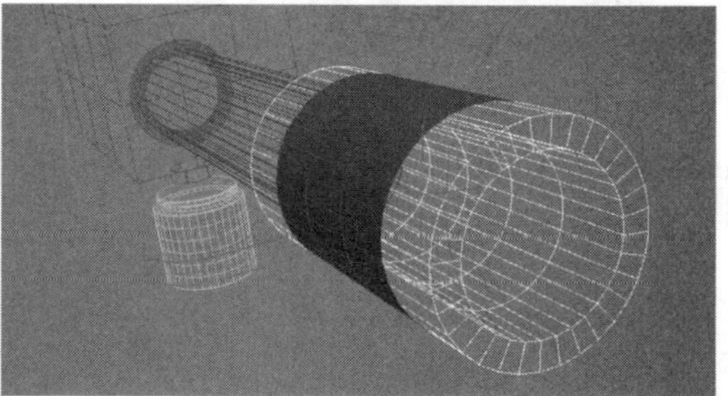

Figure 2-500

14. Extrude by Local Normal **0.6**.

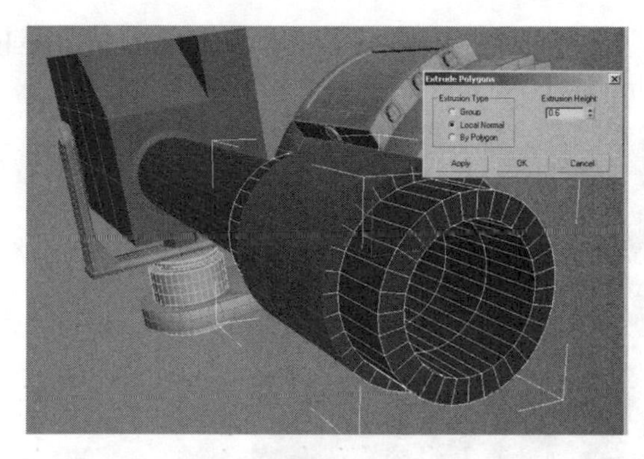

Figure 2-501

15. Click **Bevel Settings:**

Type	Height	Outline	Apply/OK
By Polygon	0	–0.1	Apply
Local Normal	–1.57	0	OK

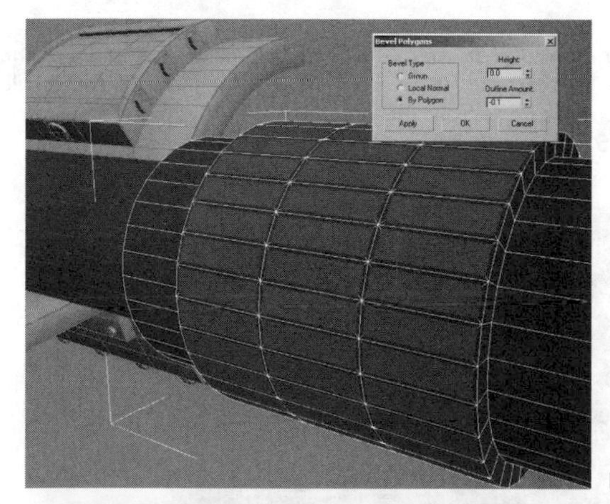

Figure 2-502

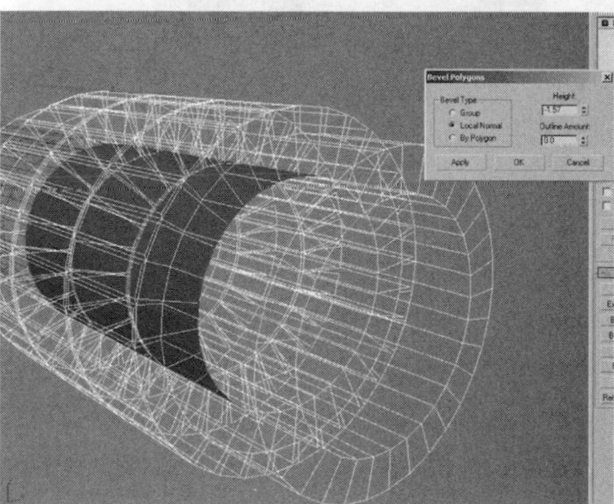

Figure 2-503

16. Delete these polygons, select the 96 polygons inside the barrel that are being intersected, and delete them too.

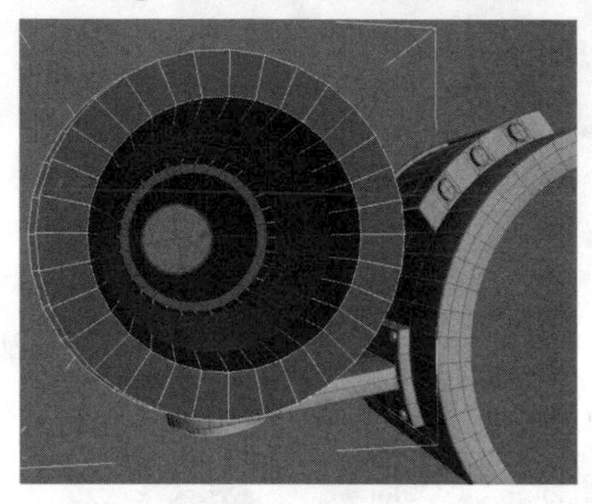

Figure 2-504

17. Marquee-select the middle vertices (1152), click **Weld Settings**, and crank up the Weld Threshold until the number of vertices drops to 960, then click **OK**.

FYI: Why these numbers? There are 192 polygons in the middle of the guard (96 on the outside and 96 on the inside), which means there will be 192 overlapping vertices from the deletion. When you weld the vertices together, 1152–192 = 960.

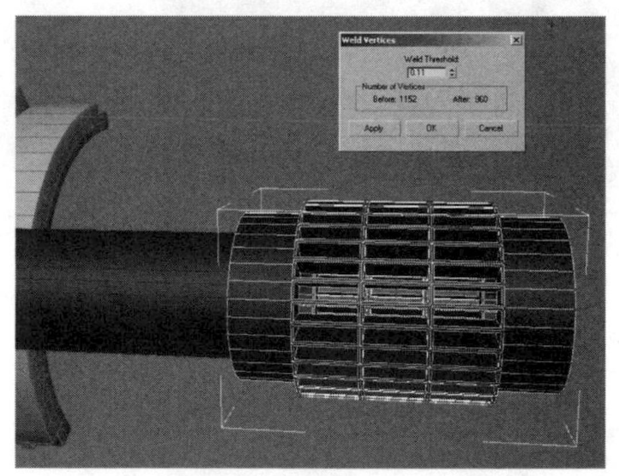

Figure 2-505

18. Select and Link the flash_guard to the barrel.

19. Where you deleted and bridged polygons on the cannon's body, you actually created two three-sided polygons. Cut the two polygons made by the Bridge to fix this problem.

Figure 2-506

Figure 2-507

20. In the Left view, object-select the cannon's body and move it in the X axis until two of the polygons are to the right of the swivel and one polygon is to the left.

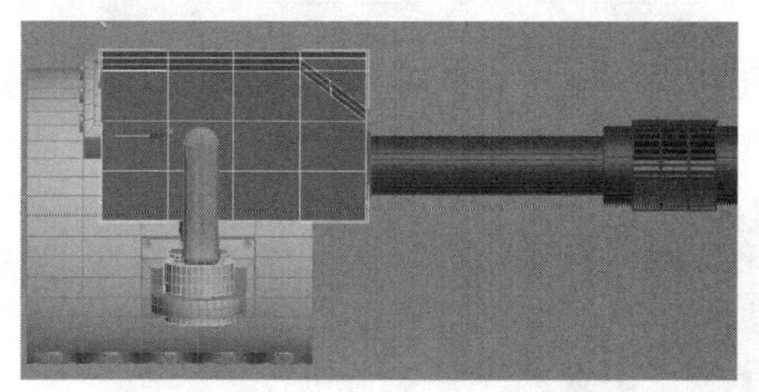

Figure 2-508

FYI: You don't have to select anything other than the body, because you've linked the barrel and flash_guard to it and they will follow (this serves as the basis for rigging and animating).

21. Select the four polygons on the bottom right and click **Tessellate**.

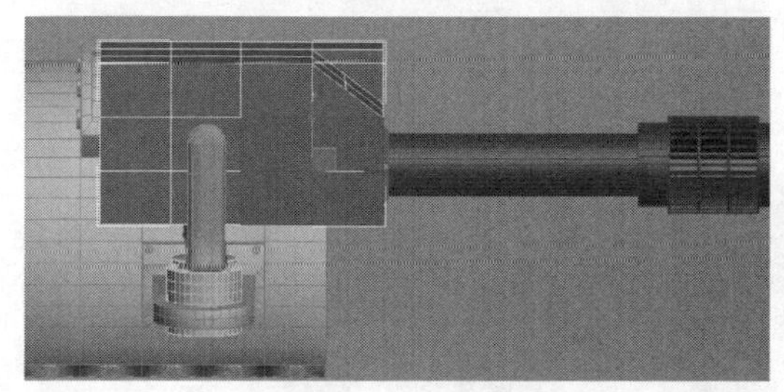

Figure 2-509

22. Select the six polygons in the middle of those you created with Tessellate.

Figure 2-510

23. Click **Bevel Settings:**

Type	Height	Outline	Apply/OK
Group	0.01	0	Apply
Group	0	1.3	Apply

Figure 2-511

Type	Height	Outline	Apply/OK
Group	1	0	Apply
Group	0	–1.35	OK

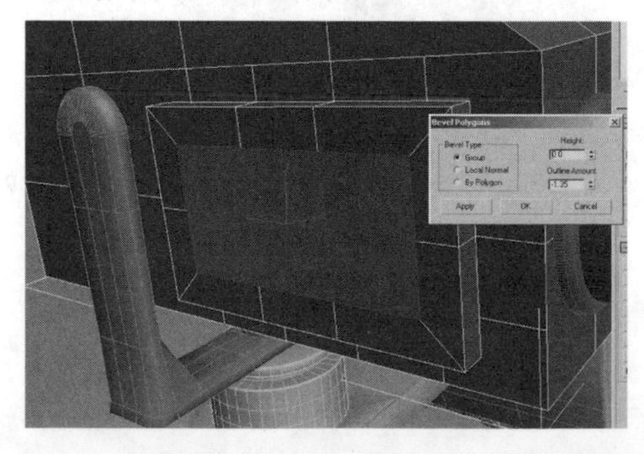

Figure 2-512

24. Extrude **–1**, hit **Apply**, and then Extrude **–10**. Click **OK**.
25. Add our Clay material to everything and do a quick render.

Figure 2-513

26. Select a segment on the inside edge of the muzzle, click **Loop**, click **Create Shape From Selection**, set the Shape Type to **Linear**, and name it **grenade**.

Figure 2-514

27. Hit **H** and select **grenade**, then move it out in front of the muzzle. Convert grenade to an Editable Polygon, border-select it, and Cap the back side.

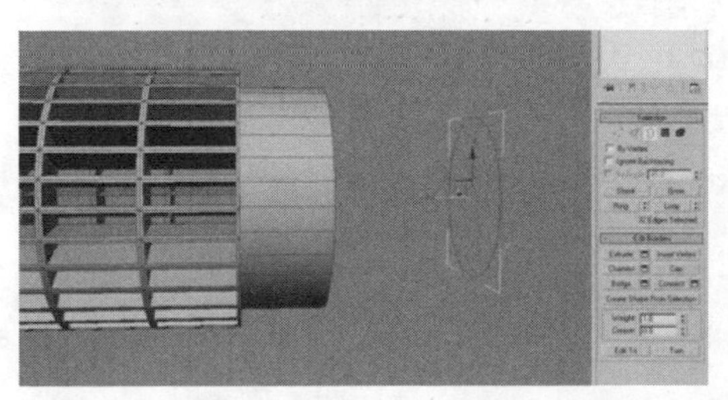

Figure 2-515

28. Polygon-select the poly facing *away* from the muzzle, Extrude it by **0.5**, and rename it **shell_casing**.

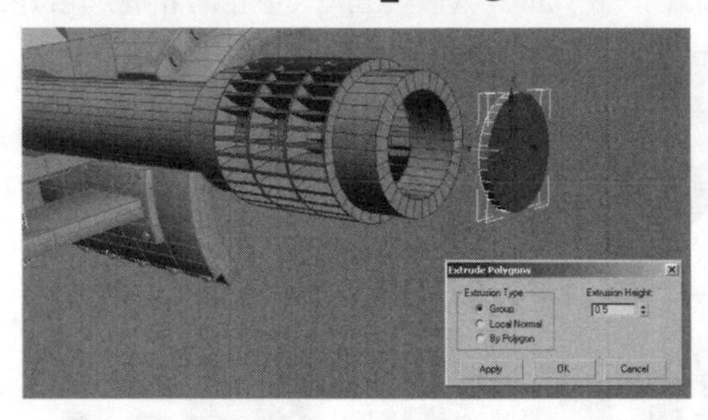

Figure 2-516

29. Click **Bevel Settings:**

Type	Height	Outline	Apply/OK
Group	0	–0.4	Apply
Group	3.5	0	Apply

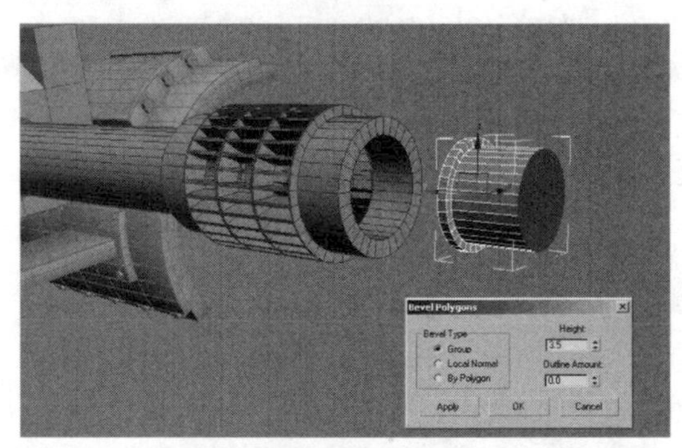

Figure 2-517

Type	Height	Outline	Apply/OK
Group	0.3	–0.2	Apply

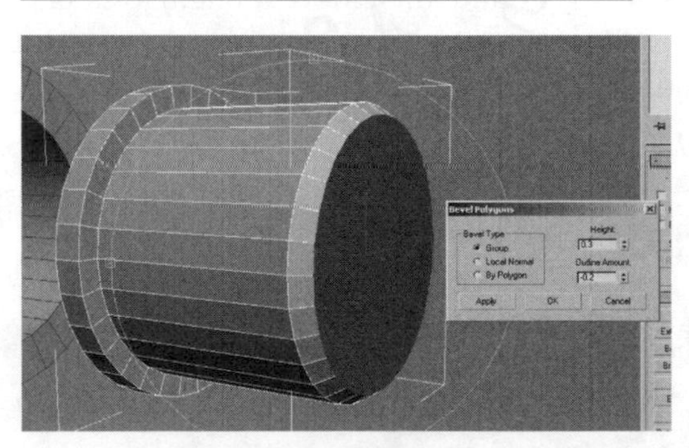

Figure 2-518

Type	Height	Outline	Apply/OK
Group	0	–0.04	Apply
Group	–0.8	0	Apply

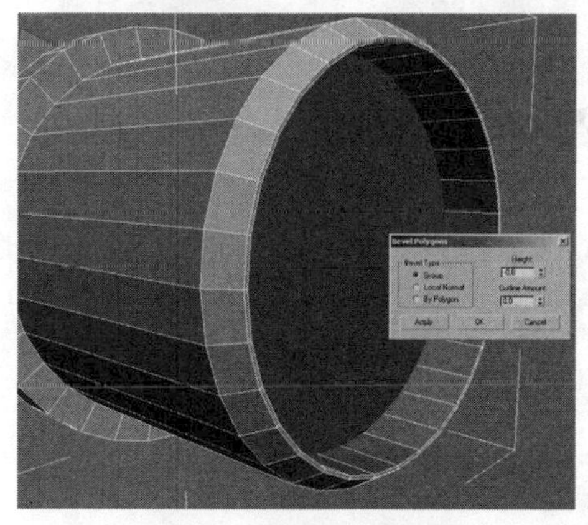

Figure 2-519

Type	Height	Outline	Apply/OK
Group	0.8	0	Apply
Group	0.3	–0.12	OK

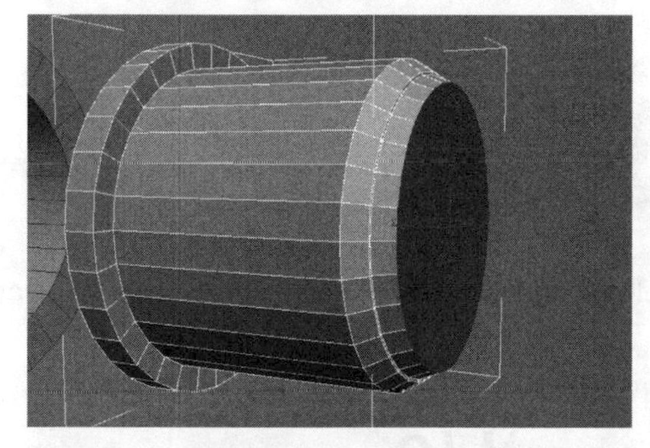

Figure 2-520

30. Delete the polygon and switch to the Front view. Create a Sphere, using AutoGrid, in the middle of the cylinder.

Radius	Segments	Hemisphere
2.076	32	0.5

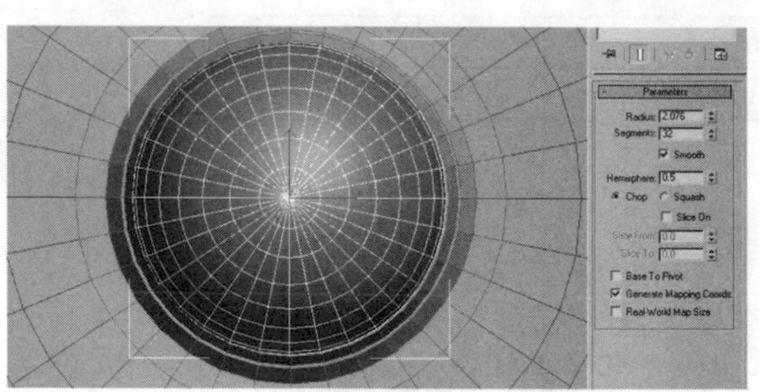

Figure 2-521

31. Convert the sphere to an Editable Polygon, delete the back-facing polygons, attach the sphere to the shell_casing, and then Weld the vertices together.

32. Scale the vertices in all three axes to **104**, or until they make a smooth contour.

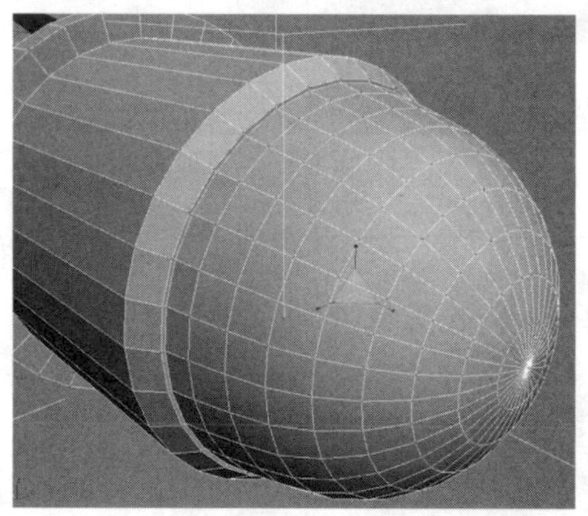

Figure 2-522

33. Border-select the bottom of the shell_casing and click **Cap**.

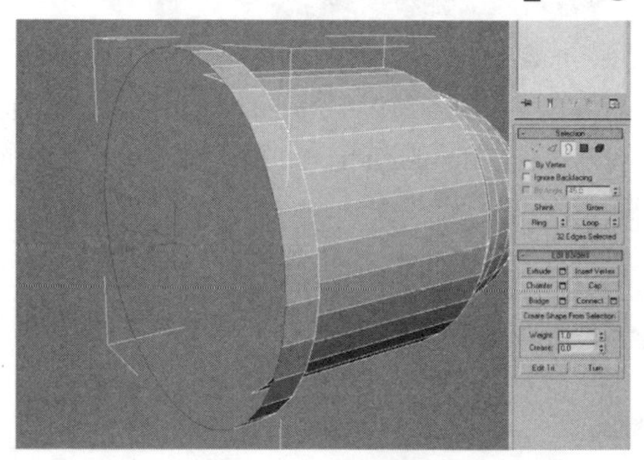

Figure 2-523

34. Click an edge on the top and bottom and click **Loop.**

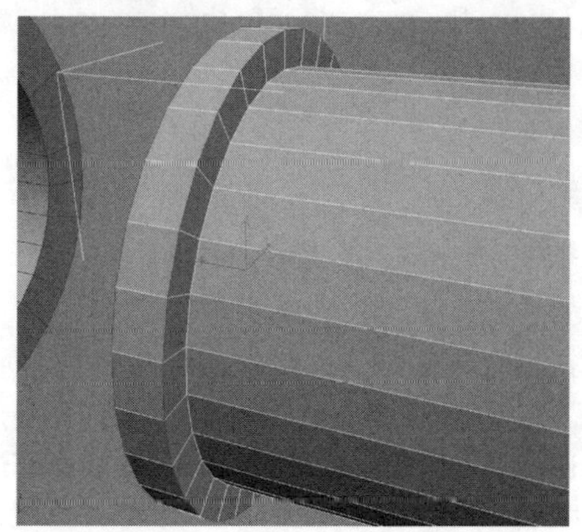

Figure 2-524

35. Chamfer **0.04**, click **Apply**, and then Chamfer again **0.015**.

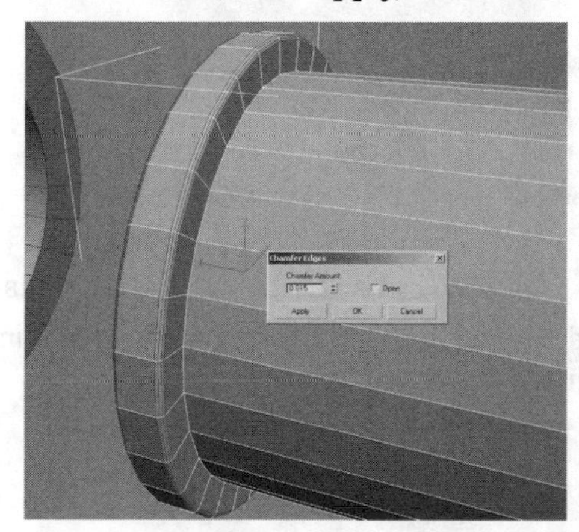

Figure 2-525

36. Add a Smooth modifier to the stack, click **Auto Smooth**, then convert it to an Editable Polygon to collapse the stack.

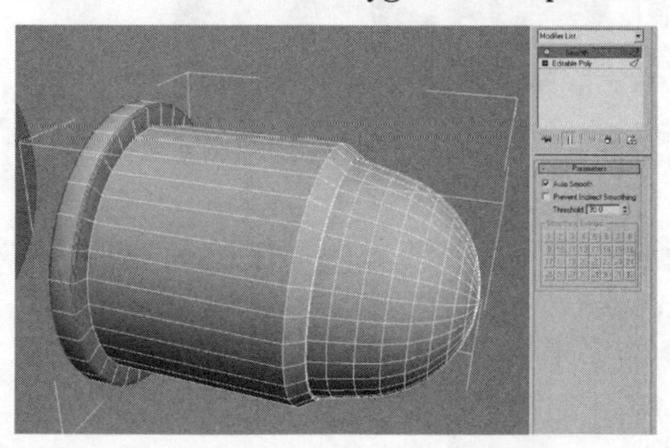

Figure 2-526

37. Object-select the grenade, click the Hierarchy tab, center the pivot to the object, and move the grenade into the ejector.

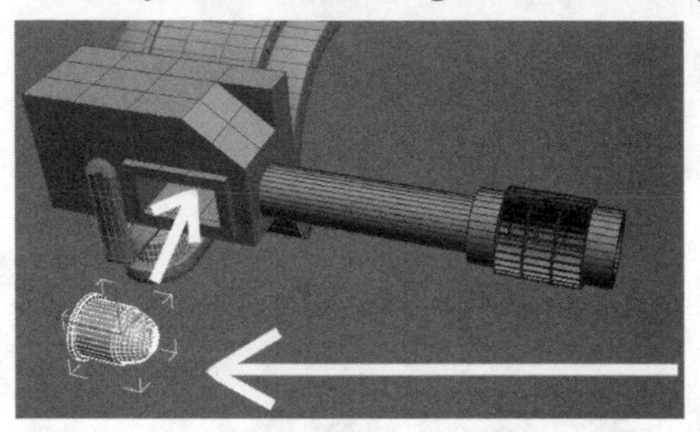

Figure 2-527

38. Scale the grenade to fit into the ejector port. (I scaled mine down to **87** in all three axes.)

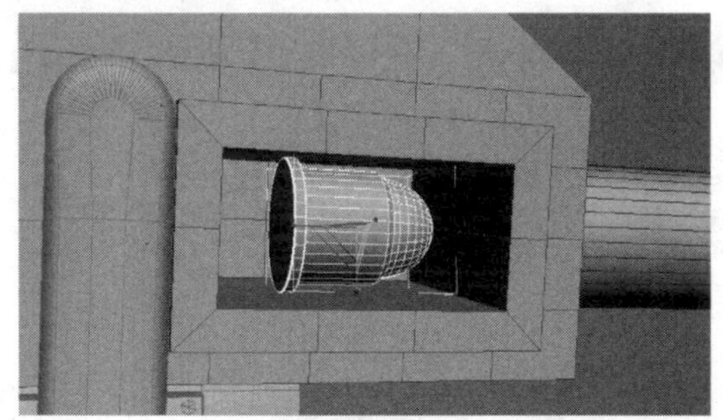

Figure 2-528

39. Scale the grenade to **165** in the Y axis and then move it in the Y axis until it is in position.

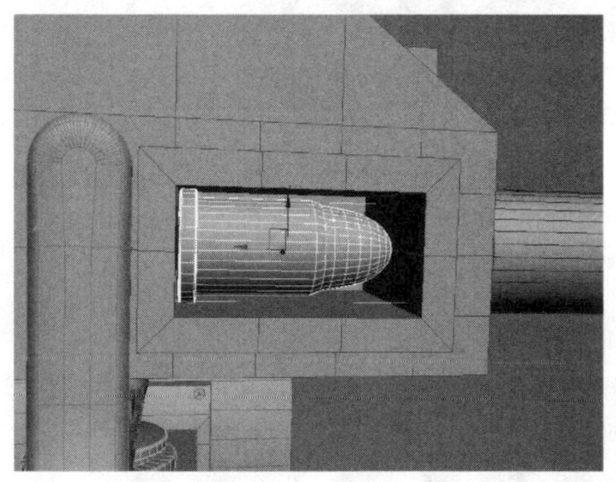

Figure 2-529

40. Do a test render.

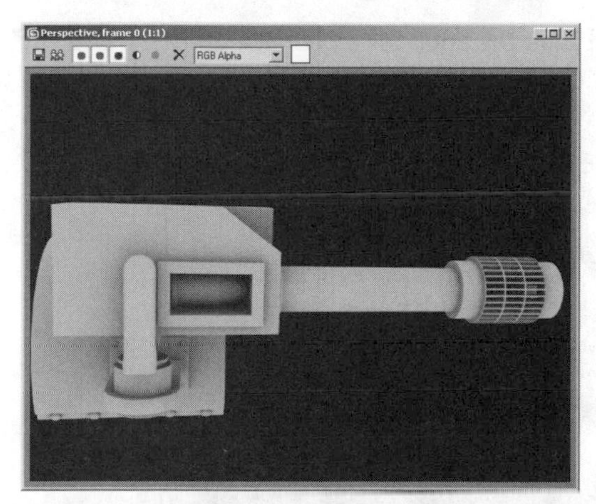

Figure 2-530

41. Select the 12 polygons in the center of the body, beneath the swivel.

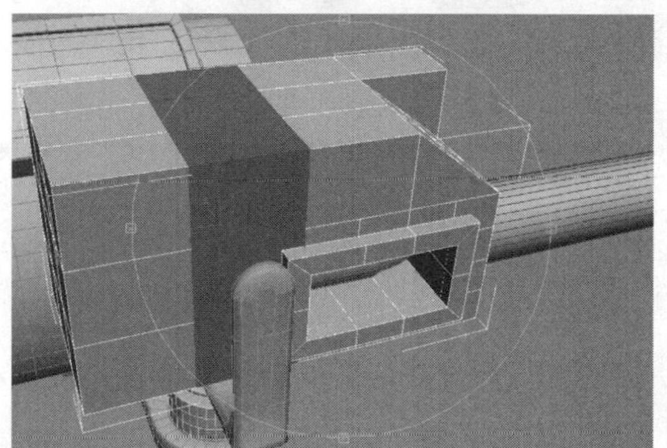

Figure 2-531

42. Activate Slice Plane and slice just behind the ejector port.

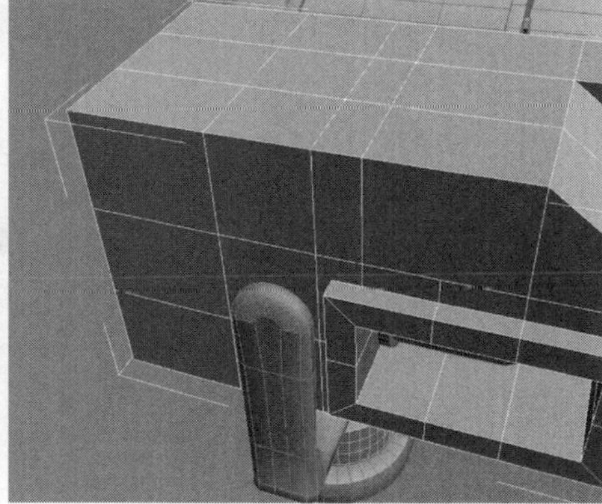

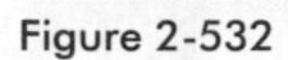

Figure 2-532

Figure 2-533

43. Select and Link the shell to the body, and then move the body forward a little bit until the slice you made is to the right of the swivel and the swivel is centered over the polygon.

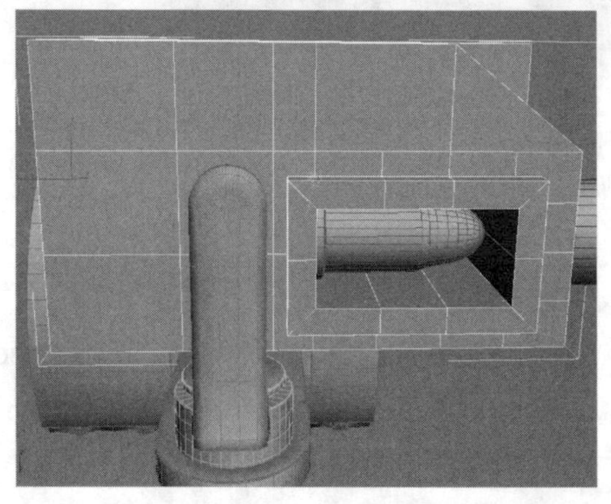

Figure 2-534

Message: Linking the shells is only necessary because we're making a static model. If we were doing an animation, I would separate the grenade from the casing and create a dual particle system (one to eject the casing and the other to propel the grenade from the barrel). I would also use a gravity space warp to hold them in place.

44. Select the polygon beneath the swivel on each side, and detach them as objects.

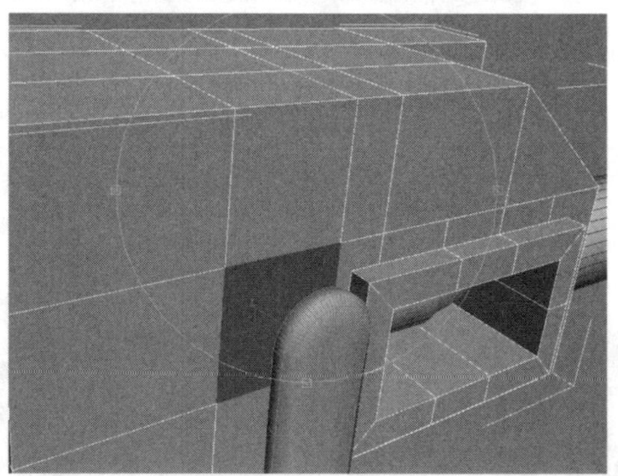

Figure 2-535

45. Hide everything except the detached polygons and then delete the polygon shown in Figure 2-536.

Figure 2-536

Don't Forget: The polygon is there; you just can't see it because you're looking at its back side and the normal is facing away from you.

46. Select the remaining polygon and Extrude it by **0.6**.

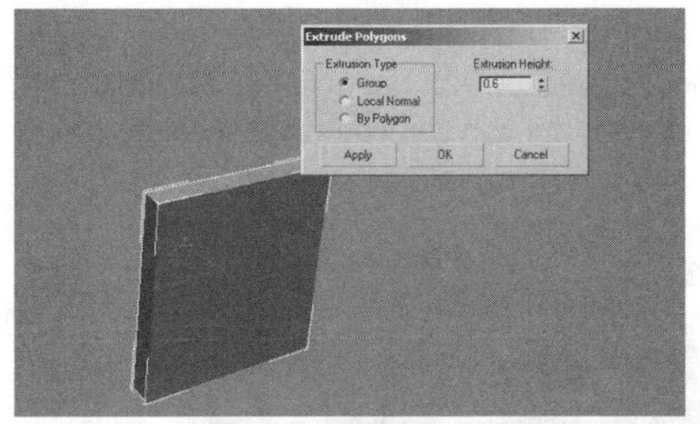

Figure 2-537

47. Arc Rotate until you are looking straight at the polygon, and use AutoGrid to create a Cylinder in the center of the polygon.

Radius	Height	Height/Cap Segs	Sides	Smooth
1.805	2.585	5/1	18	Checked

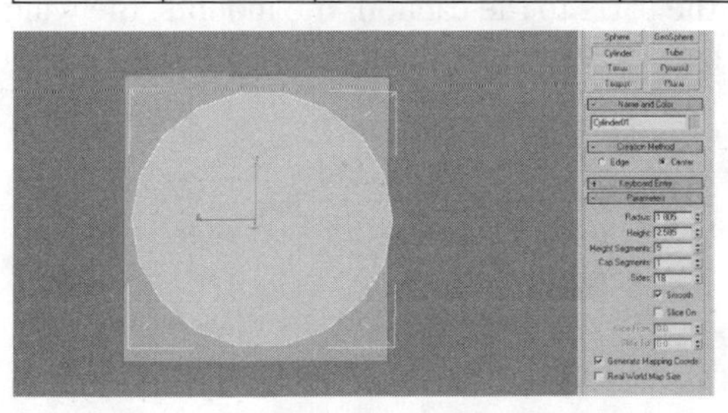

Figure 2-538

48. Unhide the swivel and Arc Rotate until you can see if the cylinder intersects with the swivel. Adjust the cylinder's parameters until it is just touching the inside surface of the swivel and then convert it to an Editable Polygon.

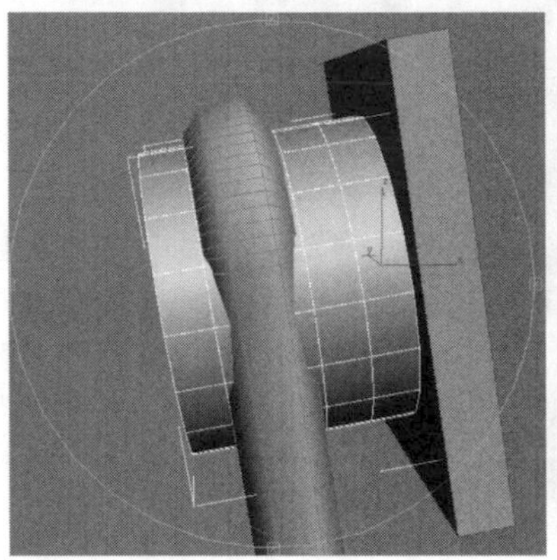

Figure 2-539

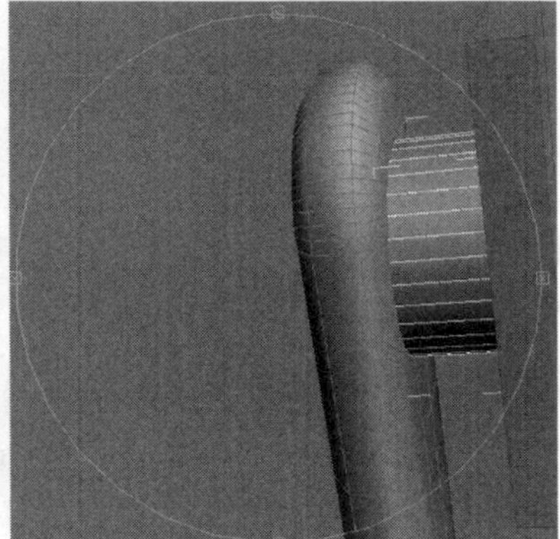

Figure 2-540

49. Create a Boolean object with the cylinder as Operand A, click **Pick Operand B**, click the polygon you extruded, and choose **Union** as the Operation.

Figure 2-541

50. Unhide all the parts to the cannon, the mounts, the wing brace, etc., then switch to the Front view and select the Boolean you made.

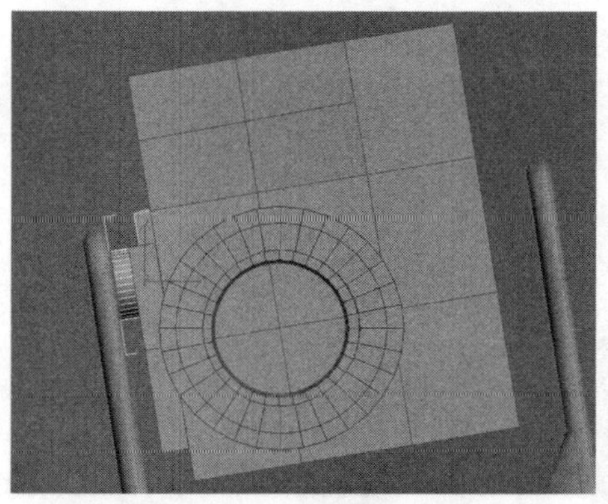

Figure 2-542

51. Switch your Reference Coordinate System to **Local**, Shift-drag the Boolean in the local Z axis to make a copy, and move it into position on the other side of the cannon.

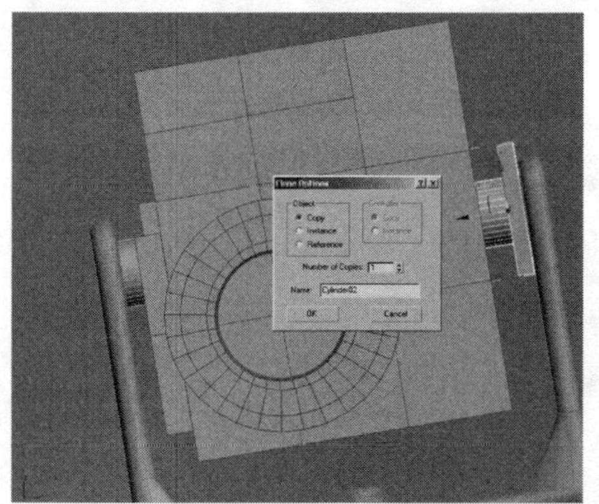

Figure 2-543

52. Rotate the copy 180 degrees, move it into position, select the cannon, click **Attach List**, and attach the Boolean and its copy (**Cylinder01** and **Cylinder02**) to the cannon.

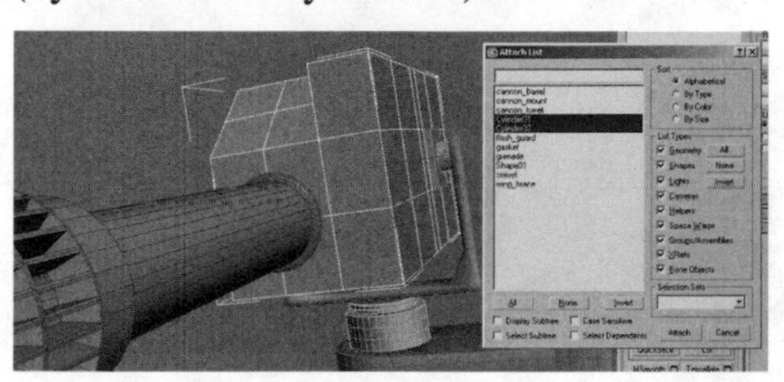

Figure 2-544

53. Select the polygon in the upper-right front corner of the cannon.

Figure 2-545

54. Click **Bevel Settings:**

Type	Height	Outline	Apply/OK
Group	0	–0.1	Apply
Group	0.2	0	OK

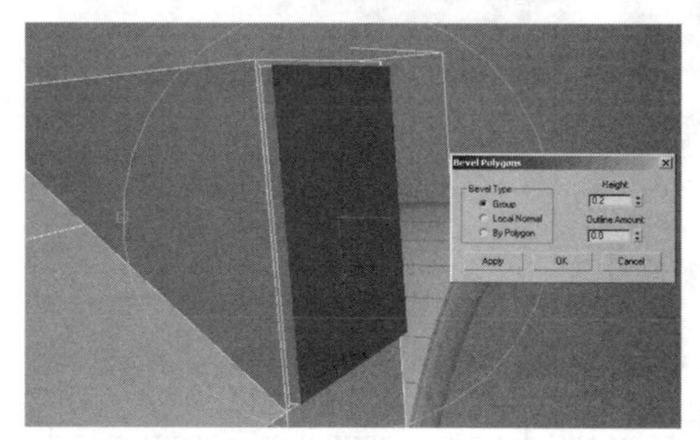

Figure 2-546

55. Select and Loop the edges as shown below, and then move them **1.2** in the X axis.

Figure 2-547

56. Select the polygons shown in Figure 2-548.

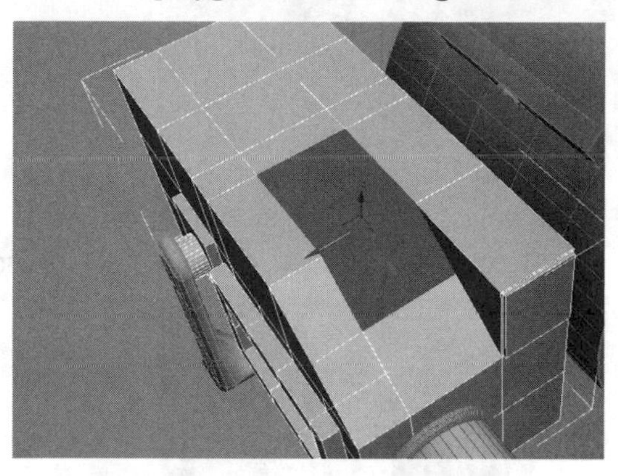

Figure 2-548

57. Click **Bevel Settings:**

Type	Height	Outline	Apply/OK
Group	0.6	0	Apply
Group	0	–0.1	Apply
Group	6	0	Apply
Group	6	0	Apply
Group	6	–0.2	Apply
Group	–6	0	Apply
Group	–6	0	Apply
Group	–6	0	OK

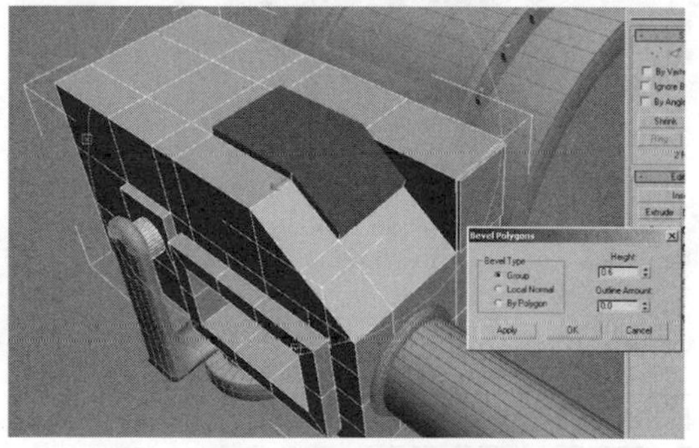

Figure 2-549

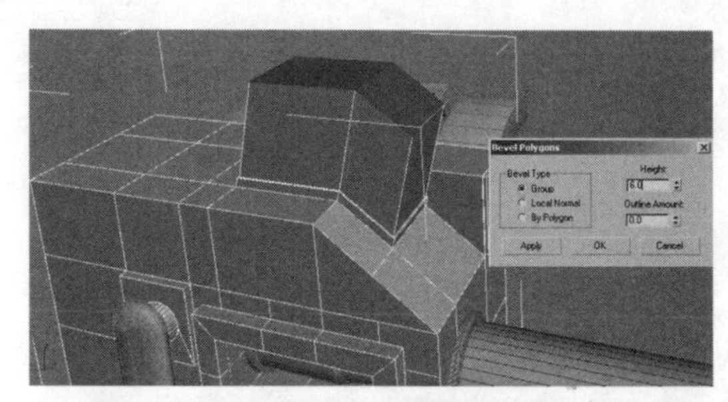

Figure 2-550

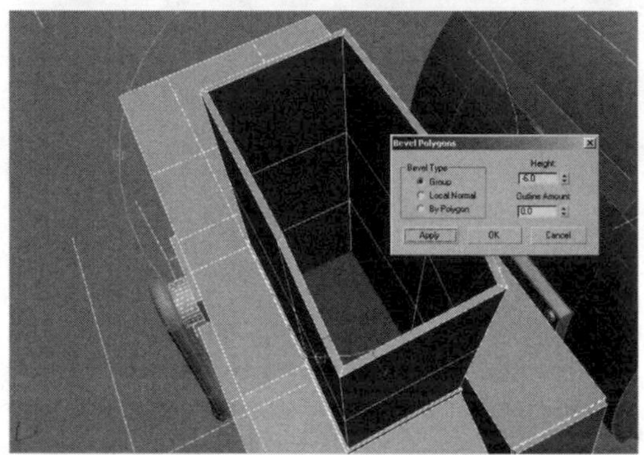

Figure 2-551

58. Select the right and left sides (inside and out) of the clip, but not the front and back.

Figure 2-552

59. Click **Bevel Settings**:

Type	Height	Outline	Apply/OK
Group	0	–0.4	OK

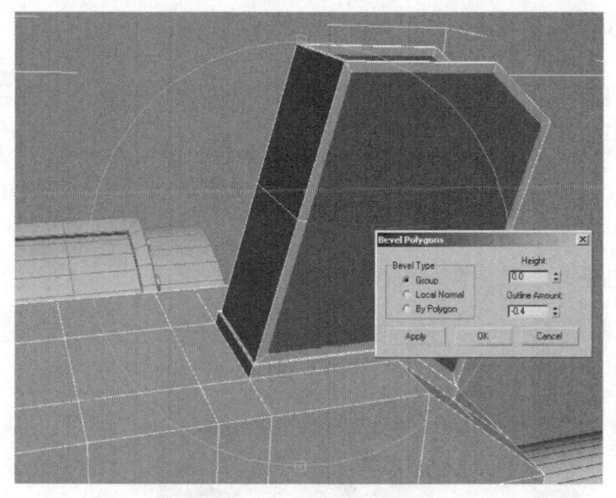

Figure 2-553

60. Select the four outside polygons, delete them, then select the matching four inside polygons and delete them.

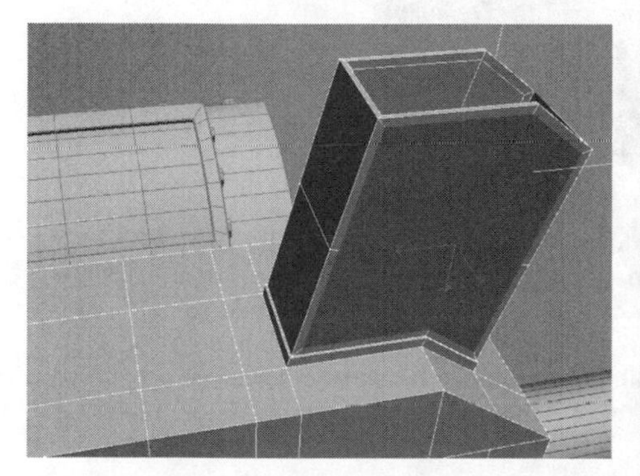

Figure 2-554

Figure 2-555

61. Use Border selection mode to select the inside and outside borders created by the deletion, and then click **Bridge**.

Figure 2-556

62. Repeat steps 60-61 for the polygons on the right side.
63. Clone the grenade and fill the clip; then Select and Link all the grenades to the cannon.
64. Unhide the wing, mounts, nacelle, rotors, etc., and do a quick render to see how everything fits together.

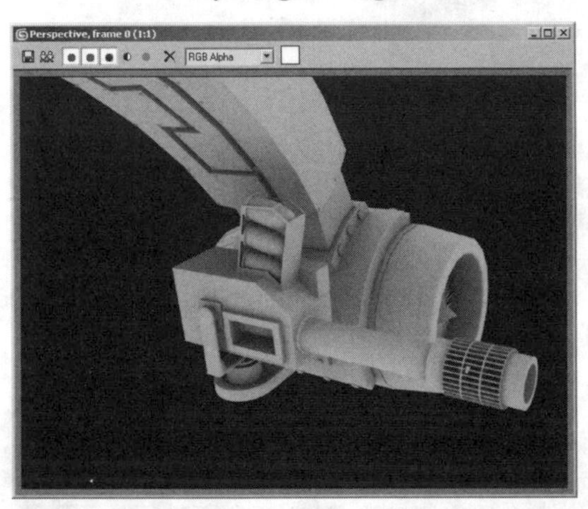

Figure 2-557

FYI: Chances are you'll have to cheat a little by scaling either the size of the clip or the size of the grenade shell. But since we're building a static model rather than an animation, no one should be able to tell. I had to scale my cannon down by about 10% to keep the clip from hitting the wing when I rotated it. If you do scale your cannon, be sure to scale all the cannon components, the turret, the brace, and the cannon mount.

Day 11: Detailing the Auto-Cannon

1. Use AutoGrid to create a Tube on the polygon in the upper-right front.

Radius 1	Radius 2	Height	Height/Cap Segs	Sides	Smooth
1.335	1.222	0.83	3/1	32	Checked

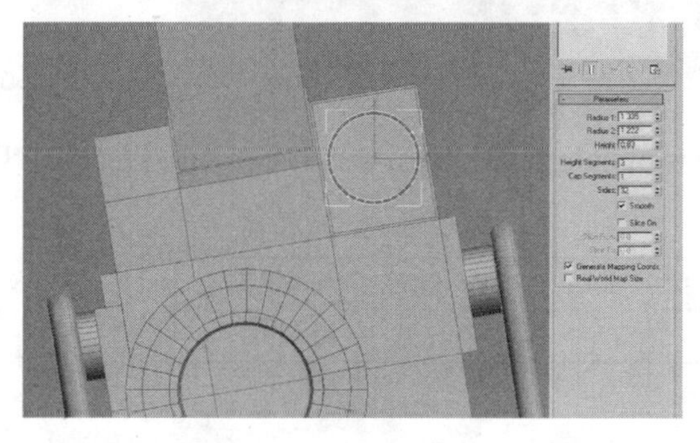

Figure 2-558

2. Use AutoGrid to create a Geosphere inside the tube.

Radius	Segs	Type
1.279	4	Icosa

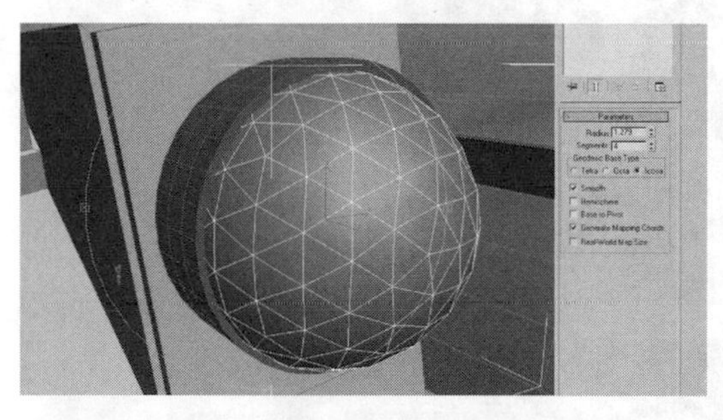

Figure 2-559

3. Convert the geosphere to an Editable Polygon, then select the half of the geosphere that will not be seen and delete it.

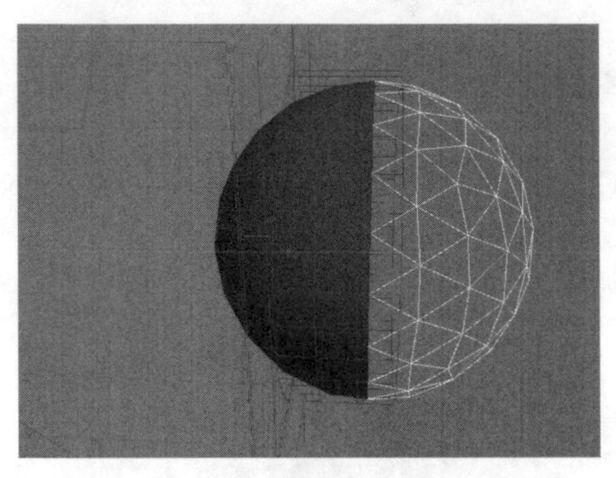

Figure 2-560

4. Select the remaining polygons, which face out, and click **Bevel Settings**:

Type	Height	Outline	Apply/OK
By Polygon	0	–0.02	Apply
By Polygon	–0.03	0	OK

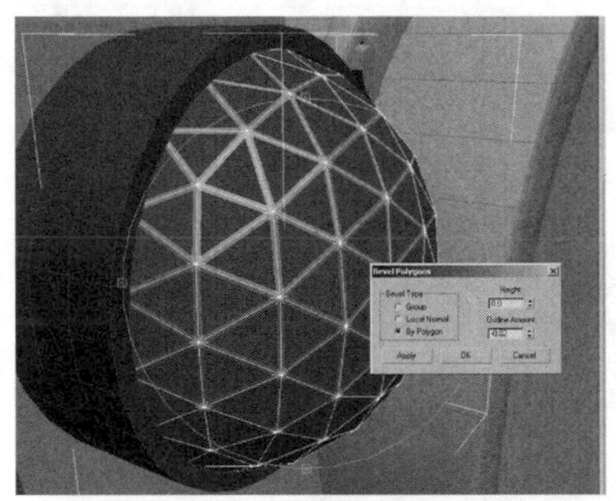

Figure 2-561

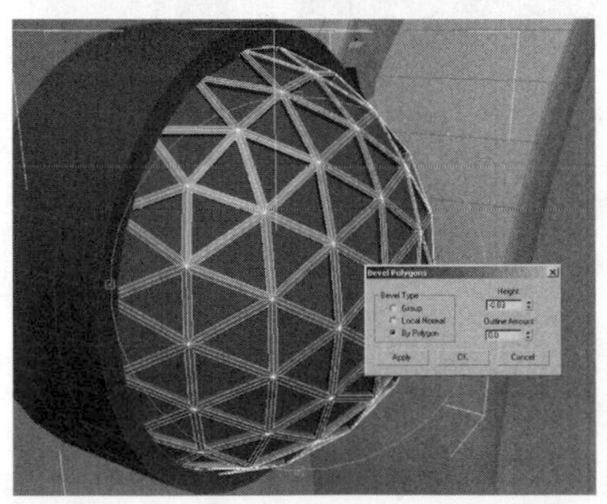

Figure 2-562

5. Select and Link the geosphere and the tube to the cannon, and then add the Clay material to both.
6. Convert the tube to an Editable Polygon and select the four polygons shown in Figure 2-563.

Figure 2-563

7. Group Extrude the four polygons **0.2**.

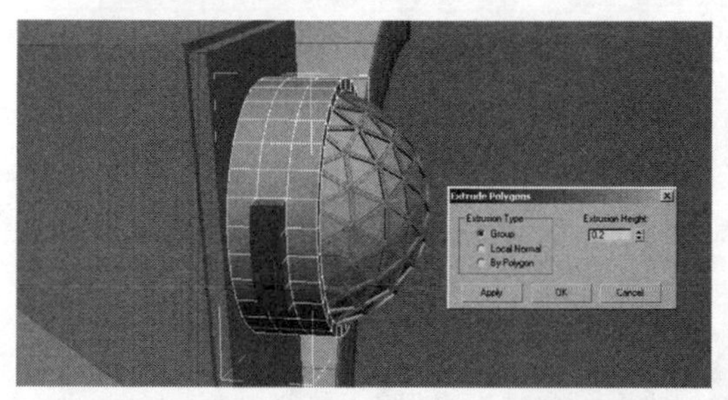

Figure 2-564

8. Scale the polygons down to **0** in the Local X axis.

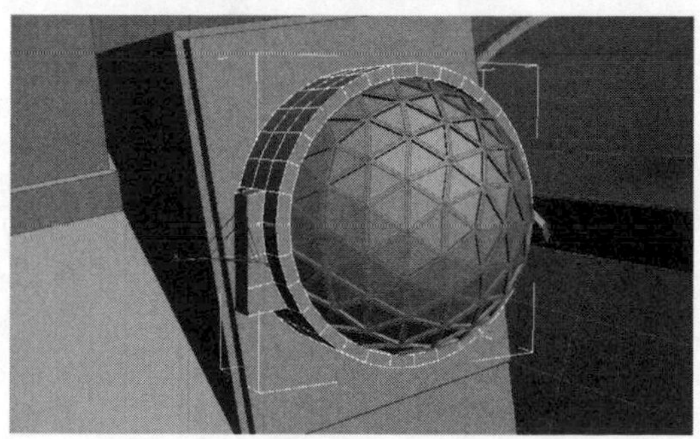

Figure 2-565

9. Rotate the polygons **–9.4** in the Y axis, or until they're straight.

Figure 2-566

10. Click **Bevel Settings:**

Type	Height	Outline	Apply/OK
Group	0	–0.04	Apply
Group	0.08	0	Apply
By Polygon	0	–0.02	OK

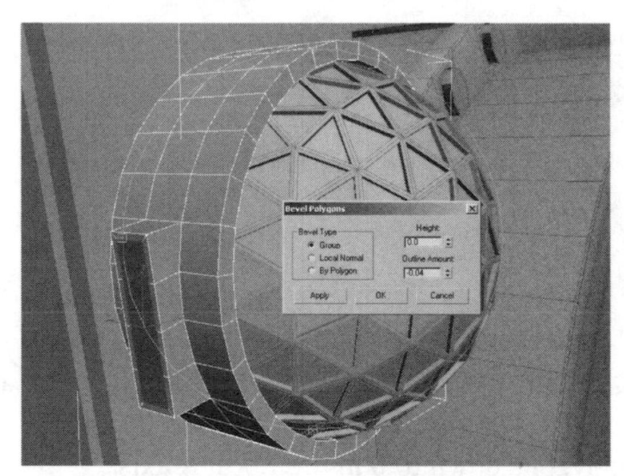

Figure 2-567

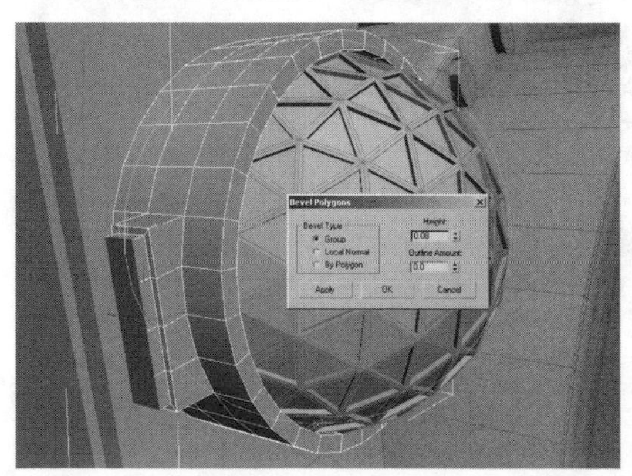

Figure 2-568

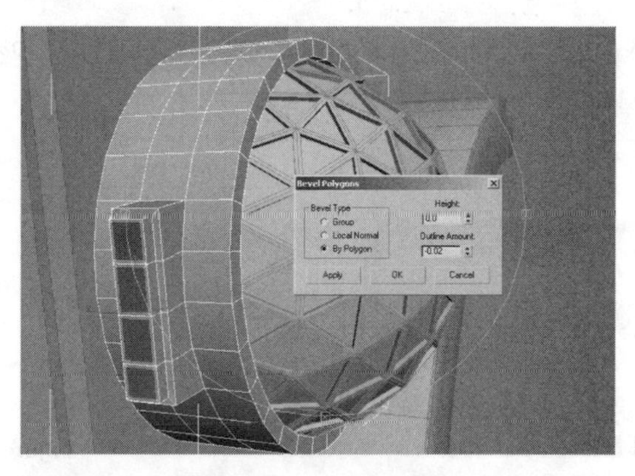

Figure 2-569

11. Select the middle two polygons and scale them down to **80** in the Z axis.

Figure 2-570

12. Select the four polygons and Extrude them **–0.01**, MSmooth them, and then delete them.

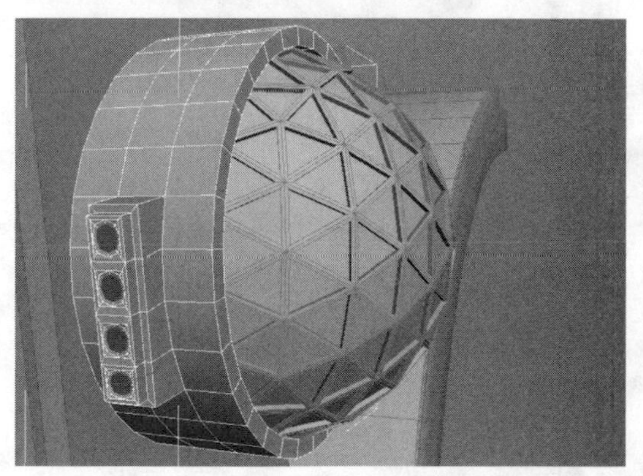

Figure 2-571

13. Use AutoGrid to create a Box on the surface above the barrel.

Length	Width	Height	Length/Width/Height Segs
1.235	2.432	0.788	3/6/1

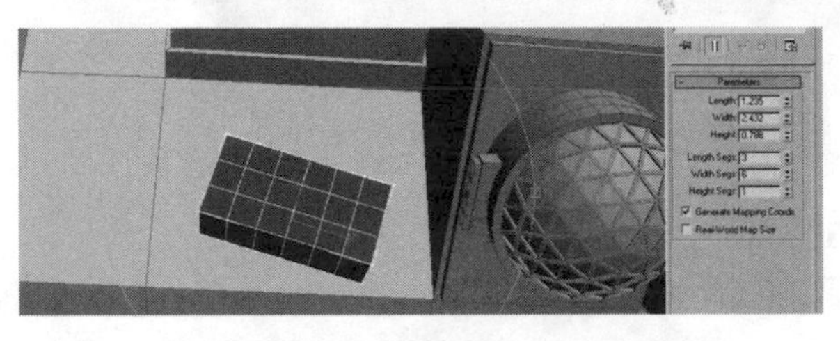

Figure 2-572

14. Select the polygons on the top of the box.

Figure 2-573

15. Click **Bevel Settings:**

Type	Height	Outline	Apply/OK
Group	0	–0.14	Apply
Group	0.55	0	OK

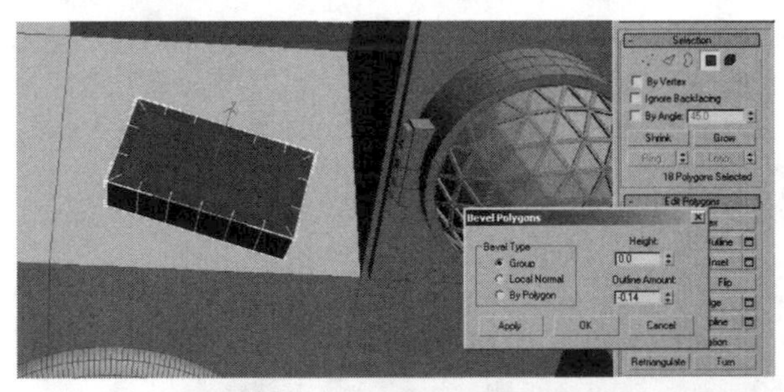

Figure 2-574

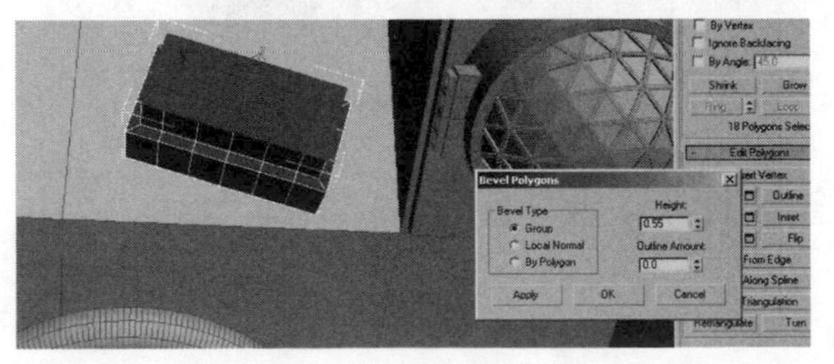

Figure 2-575

16. Click **Shrink.**

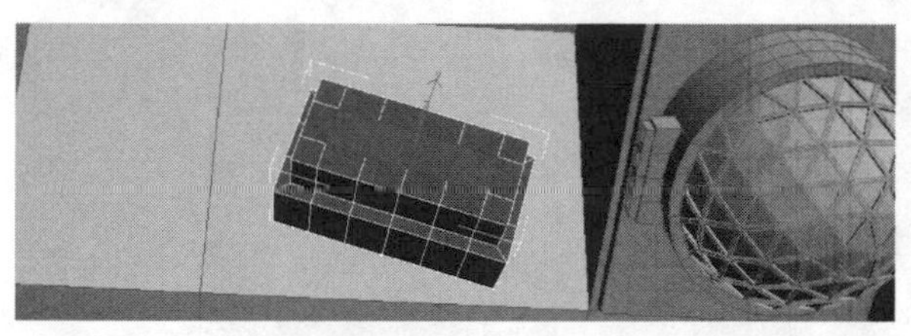

Figure 2-576

17. Extrude By Polygon **0.2.**

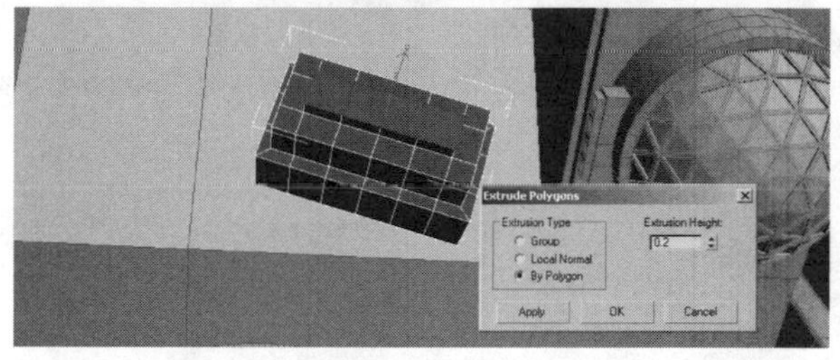

Figure 2-577

18. Click **Bevel Settings:**

Type	Height	Outline	Apply/OK
Group	0	–0.04	OK

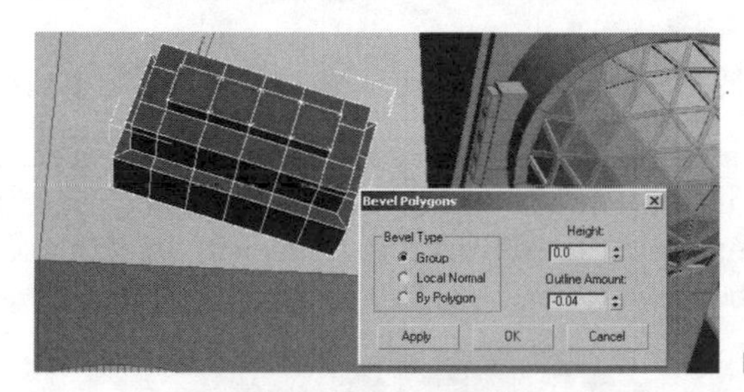

Figure 2-578

19. Extrude By Polygon **–0.01.**

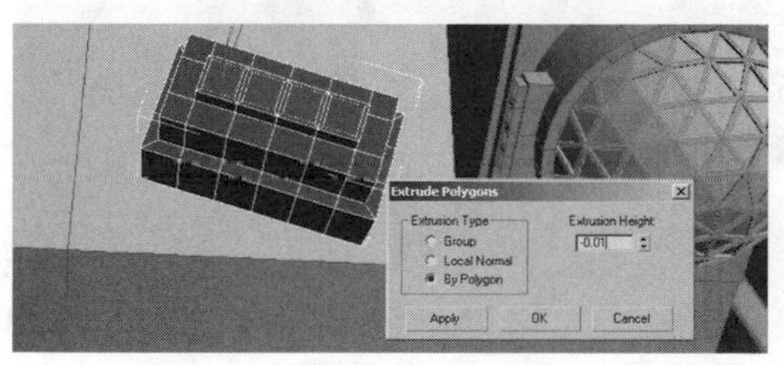

Figure 2-579

20. Click the **MSmooth** button and delete the polygons.

Figure 2-580

21. Scale the connector **50%** in all three axes.

Figure 2-581

22. Create a linear spline connecting the far right hole on the surface plug with the bottom hole on the sensor you made using the geosphere; be sure to convert the vertices to Smooth and set the spline to be viewable in the viewport and the renderer.

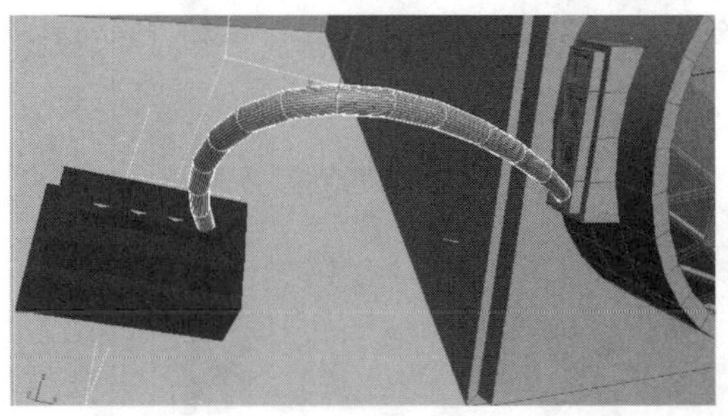

Figure 2-582

23. Move the vertices until the wire is properly aligned with both plugs.

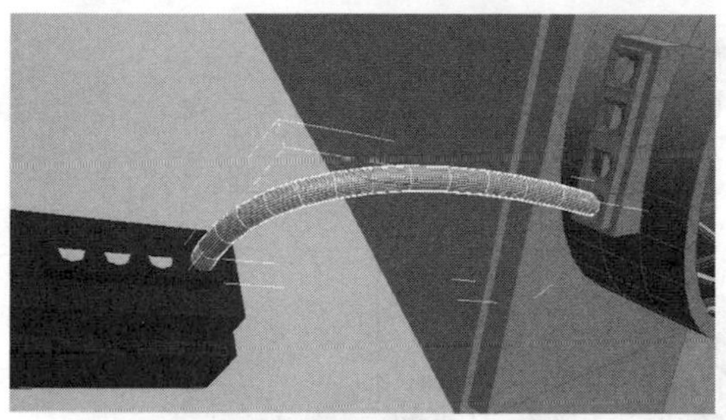

Figure 2-583

24. Clone the wire three times and move the vertices until all the wires are aligned with the plugs.

Figure 2-584

25. Select and Link all of the wires and the plug to the cannon.
26. Select the seven polygons on the left side of the cannon.

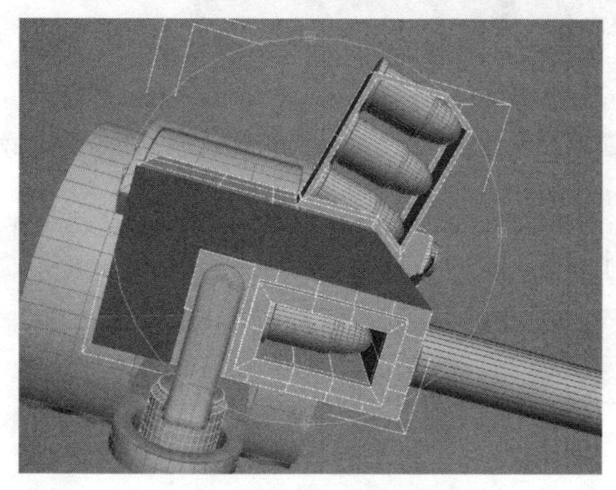

Figure 2-585

27. Click **Bevel Settings:**

Type	Height	Outline	Apply/OK
Group	0	–0.4	Apply
Group	0	–0.4	Apply
Group	–0.15	0	OK

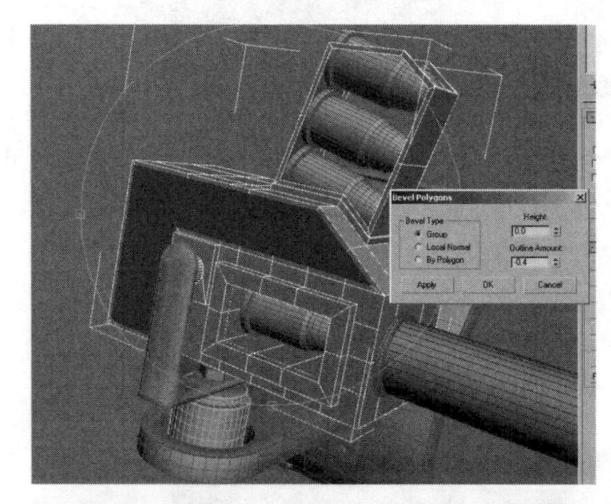

Figure 2-586

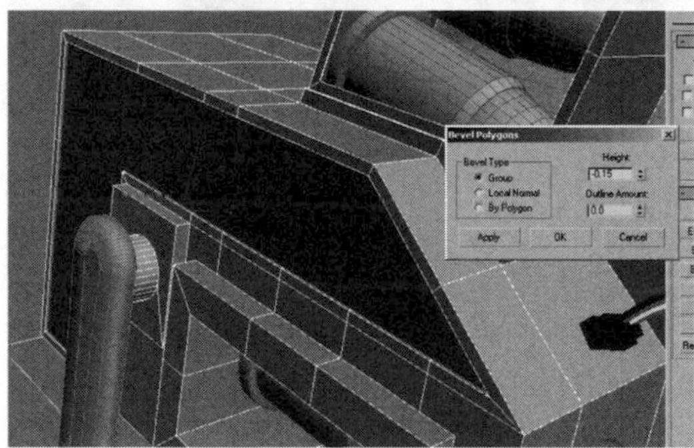

Figure 2-587

28. Using AutoGrid, create a Sphere in the upper-left corner of the bevel you just made:

Radius	Segments	Hemisphere
0.3	32	0.5

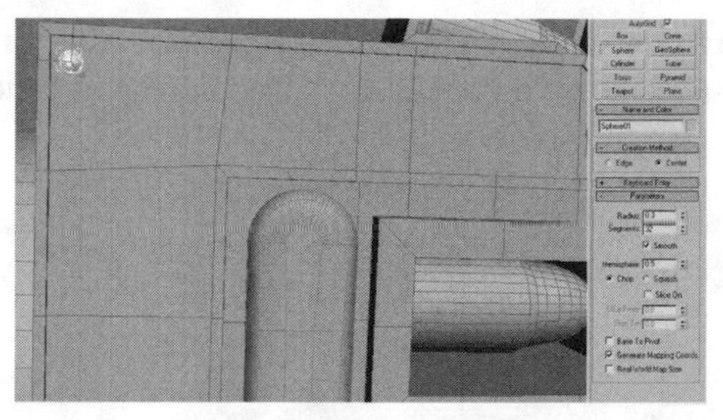

Figure 2-588

29. Convert the sphere to an Editable Polygon, delete the back-facing polys, and move the sphere so it touches the inner surface of the bevel.

Figure 2-589

30. Select the inside edges of the bevel you made on the cannon's left side.

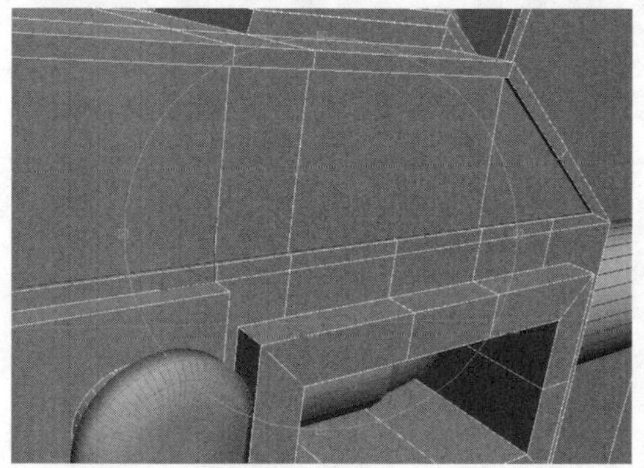

Figure 2-590

31. Click **Create Shape From Selection** and set Shape Type to **Linear**.

32. Select the shape, center its pivot, scale it until it runs through the middle of the sphere you just created, and move its vertices until it looks like this:

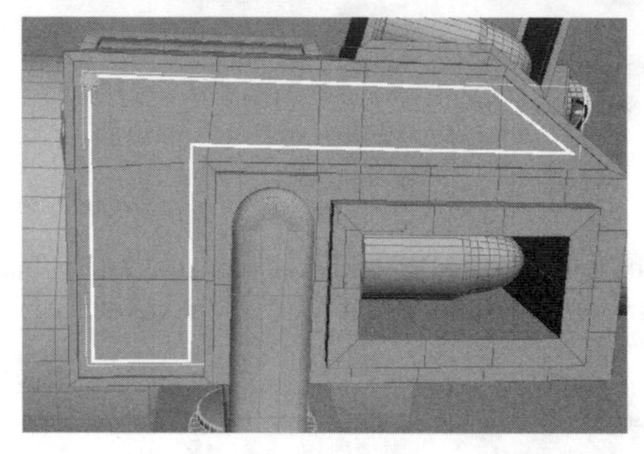

Figure 2-591

33. Select the sphere, press **Shift+I** to activate the Spacing tool, click **Pick Path**, select the spline you created in step 31, and enter **11** for Count.

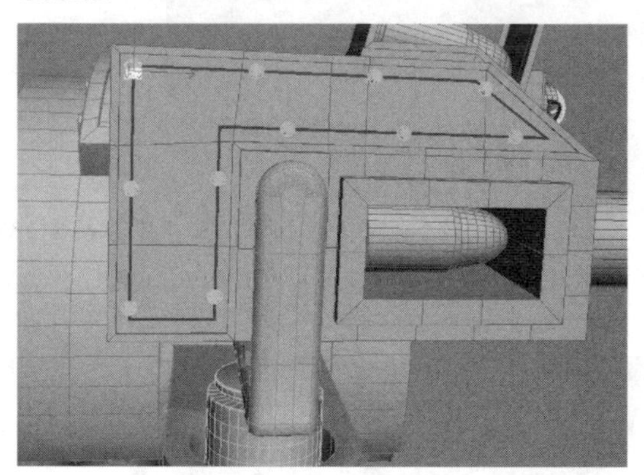

Figure 2-592

34. Move the spheres so you have one in each corner of the spline, and then delete the spline.

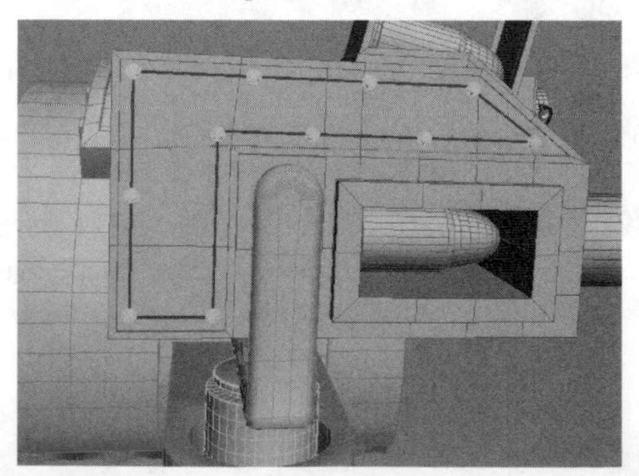

Figure 2-593

35. Make sure all the spheres connect with the cannon, select the cannon, and Attach the spheres. Do a test render.

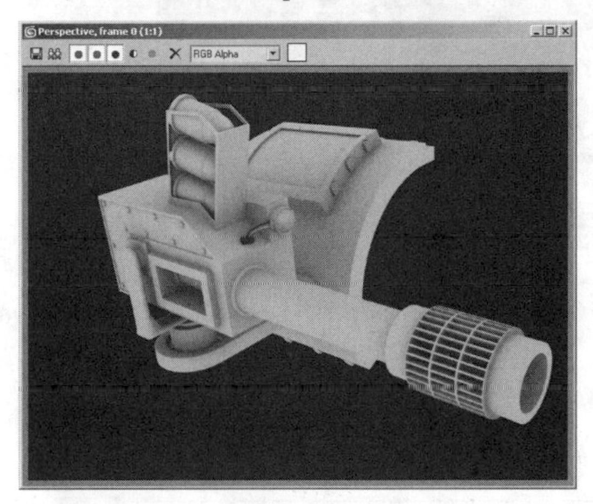

Figure 2-594

36. Select the two polygons on the front of the cannon.

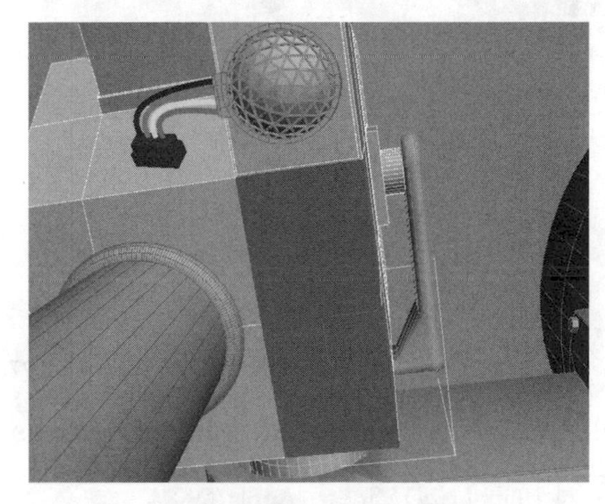

Figure 2-595

37. Click **Bevel Settings:**

Type	Height	Outline	Apply/OK
Group	0	–0.1	Apply
Group	0.2	0	OK

Figure 2-596

Type	Height	Outline	Apply/OK
By Polygon	0	–0.1	Apply
By Polygon	–0.1	0	OK

Figure 2-597

38. Hit **Tessellate** four times and then click **Bevel Settings**:

Type	Height	Outline	Apply/OK
By Polygon	0	–0.03	Apply
By Polygon	0.1	0	OK

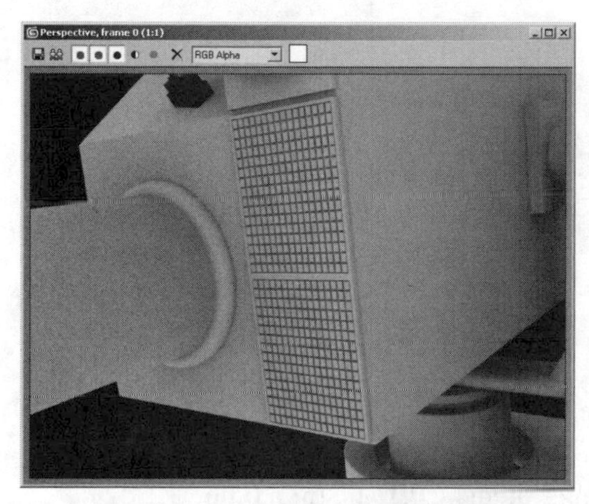

Figure 2-598

39. Select the four bottom polygons on the lower-left corner of the cannon's right side.

Figure 2-599

40. Hit **Bevel Settings:**

Type	Height	Outline	Apply/OK
Group	0	–0.5	Apply
Group	0.59	–0.5	OK

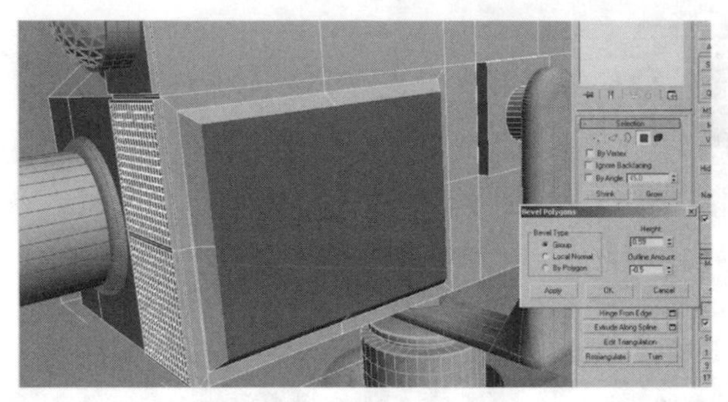

Figure 2-600

41. Control-click on the **Edge** selection mode icon, deselect the four edges in the middle so that only the outer edges are selected, and then Chamfer them by **0.1** and then **0.05**.

Figure 2-601

Figure 2-602

Urgent: When we rescaled the cannon at the end of the Day 10 section, I made a mistake. I shouldn't have scaled the turret. Now, as you can see from Figure 2-603, it doesn't fit in the brace. The hole is too big! Since we chose to Select and Link everything, if we scale the turret, then everything linked to it will scale too!

Figure 2-603

42. Click the **Schematic View** button on the main toolbar.

FYI: The schematic view provides a hierarchical display of all the linkages you've made.

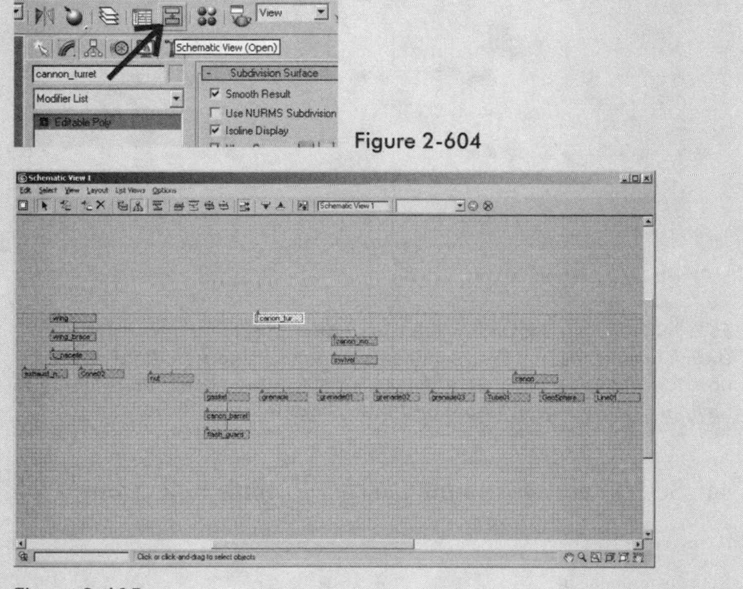

Figure 2-604

Figure 2-605

The currently selected object is displayed in white, in this case the cannon_turret. Linkages you've made are displayed by the green lines. The blue boxes are unselected items. As we can see from the schematic, the cannon_turret connects the entire cannon apparatus to the wing. What we need to do is to temporarily disconnect the cannon_turret, resize it, and then reconnect it.

43. Click **Unlink Selected** on the Schematic View toolbar to break the link with the wing.

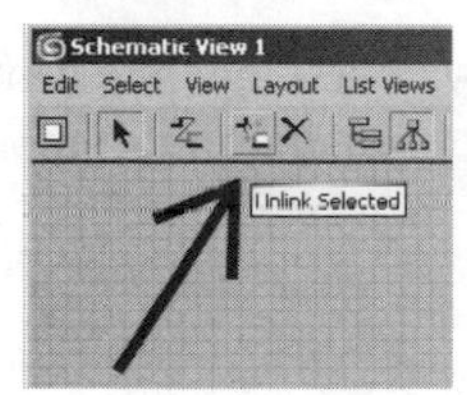

Figure 2-606

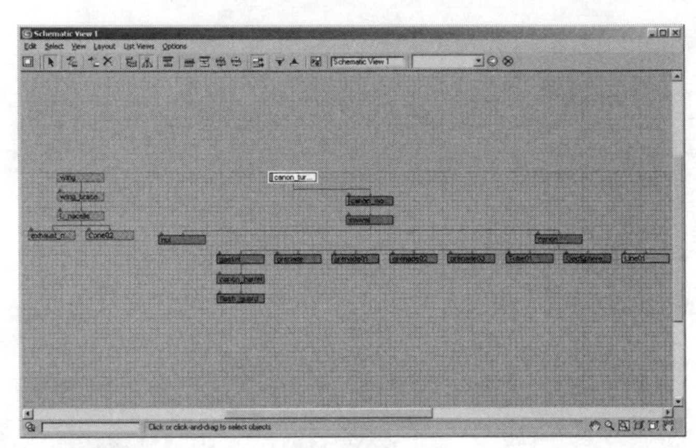

Figure 2-607

FYI: Now if we click Unlink Selection again, nothing happens. Why? Unlink breaks the link between the object and its parent. Right now cannon_turret *is* the parent. So to get cannon_turret by itself, we're going to have to select cannon_mount and then click Unlink Selection.

44. Select **cannon_mount** and click **Unlink Selection**.

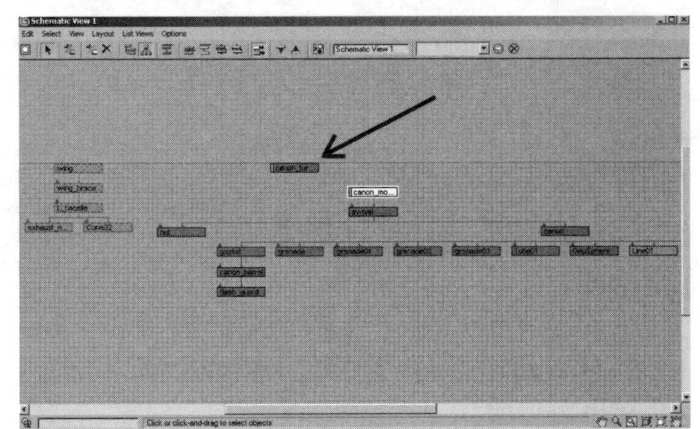

Figure 2-608

45. As you can see, cannon_turret is now by itself, while cannon_mount is now the parent to all the objects comprising the cannon. Close the schematic view.

46. Select the cannon_turret and scale it (around **125**) in the X and Y axes until it fills the hole in the wing_brace.

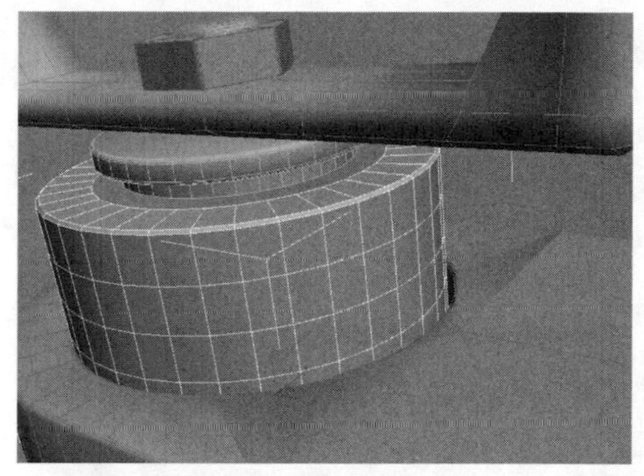

Figure 2-609

47. Border-select the hole in the middle of the cannon_turret and scale it in the X and Y axes until it closes around the cannon_mount.

Figure 2-610

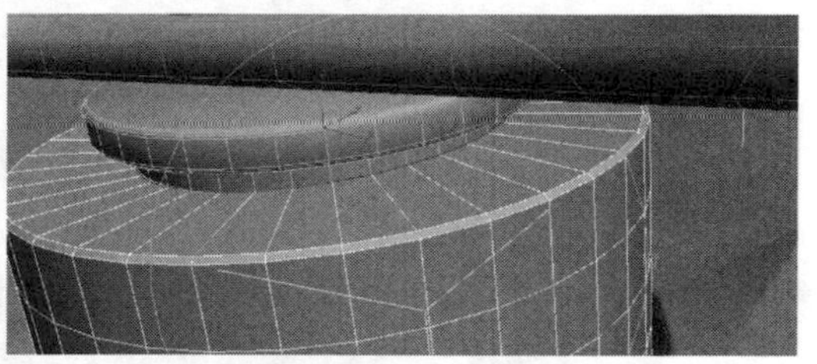

Figure 2-611

48. Click **Schematic View** to reopen the schematic view, click **cannon_mount** to select it, click the **Connect** button, and then drag a line from the cannon_mount to the cannon_turret to reparent them.

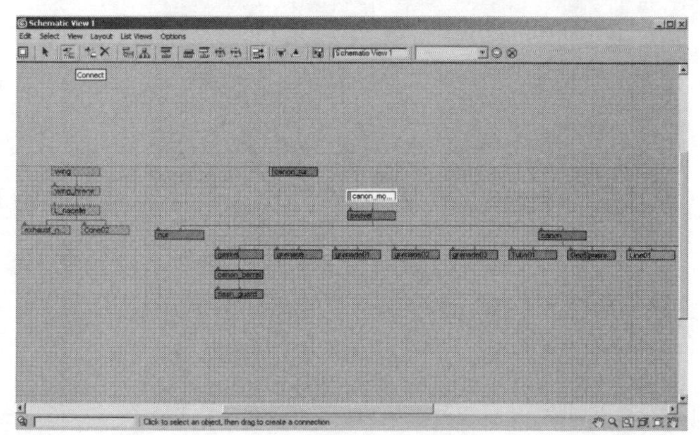

Figure 2-612

49. Click **cannon_turret** to select it, and drag a line to wing_brace to reparent it.

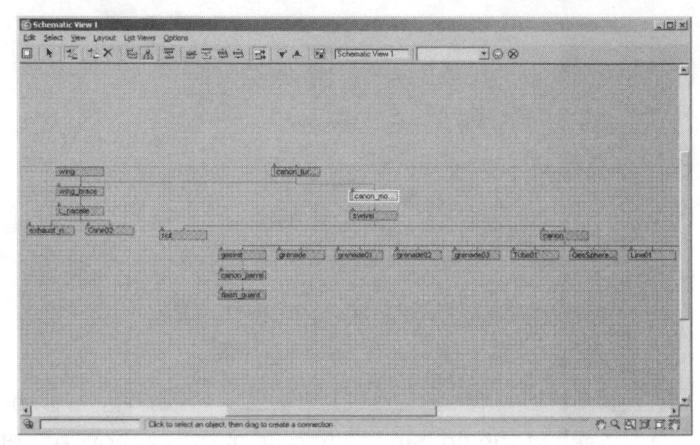

Figure 2-613

50. Close the Schematic View window.

51. Select all the sharp edges on the cannon and Chamfer them first **0.06** and then **0.02**.

52. Select the three polygons on the *outside* surface of the swivel, on both sides.

Figure 2-614

53. Group Extrude **–0.2**.

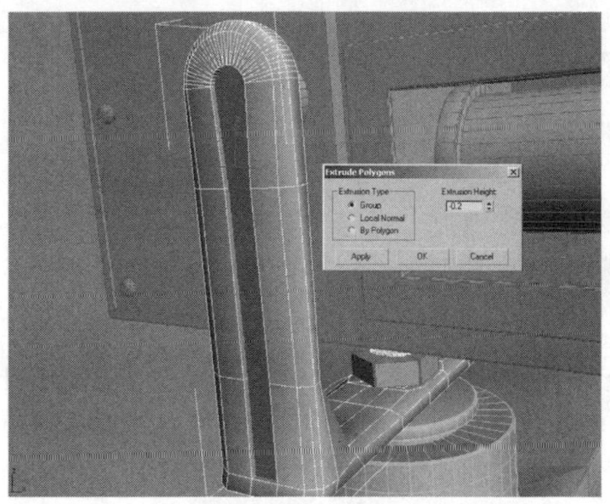

Figure 2-615

Day 12: Making the Missile Pods

1. Switch to the Front view and unhide the wing.

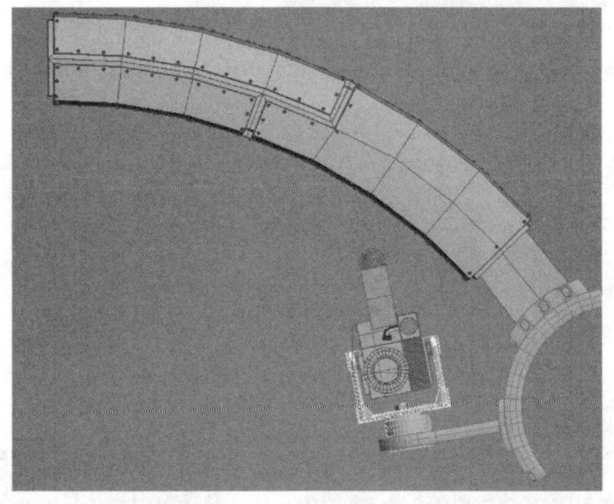

Figure 2-616

2. Using AutoGrid, create a Cylinder:

Radius	Height	Height/Cap Segs	Sides	Smooth
3	35	5/5	32	Checked

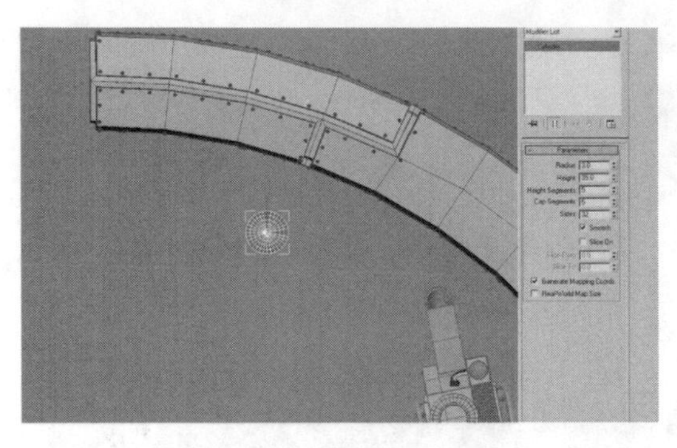
Figure 2-617

3. Switch to the Top view and center the missile beneath the wing (**–45.407** in the Y axis).

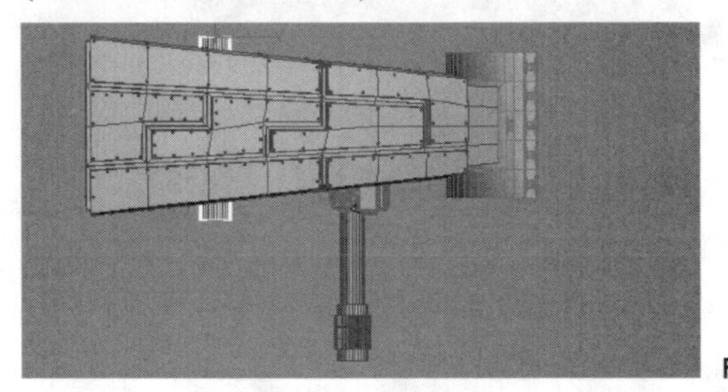
Figure 2-618

4. Hide everything except the cylinder and convert it to an Editable Polygon.

5. Select and Loop the first and third segments.

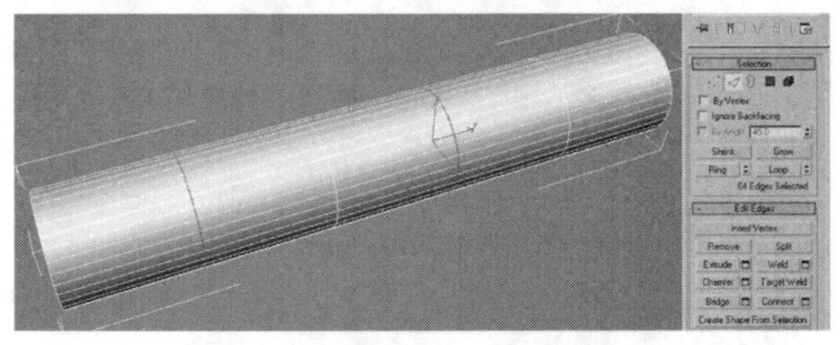
Figure 2-619

6. To make machined seams, Extrude by **–0.1** with a Base Width of **0.01**.

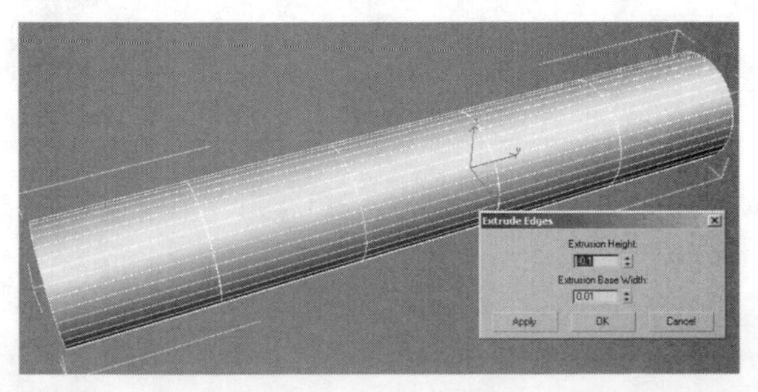

Figure 2-620

7. In the Top view, select the center two polygons at the top of the cylinder.

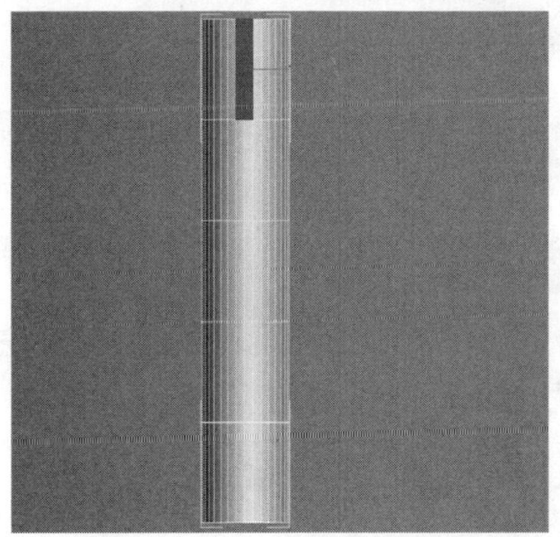

Figure 2-621

8. Switch to the Perspective view and select the center two polygons on top of the cylinder, then skip six polygons, select the next two, and so on, until you have a total of eight polygons selected (two polys at the 3, 6, and 9 o'clock positions, plus the polys selected in step 7).

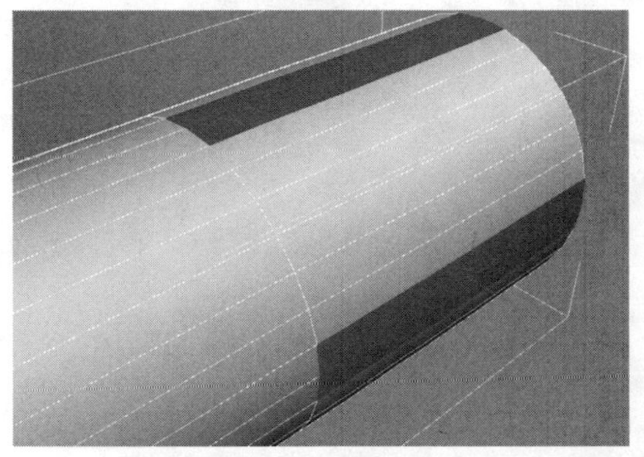

Figure 2-622

9. Group Extrude by **0.1**.

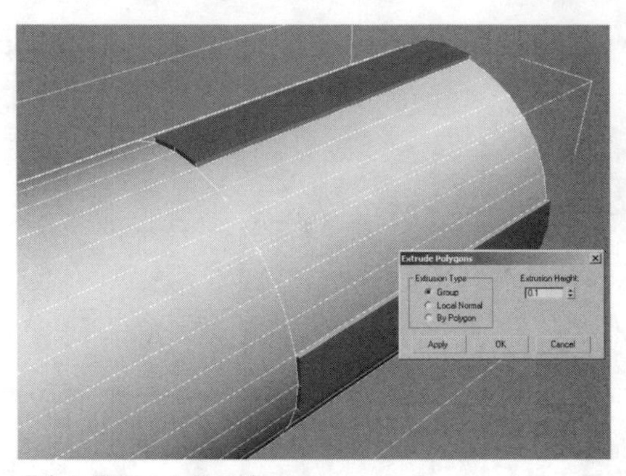

Figure 2-623

10. Click **Bevel Settings:**

Type	Height	Outline	Apply/OK
Group	0	–0.1	Apply
Group	2	–0.4	OK

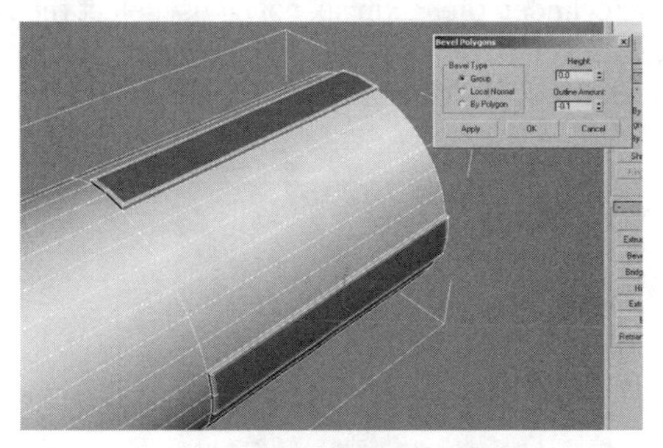

Figure 2-624

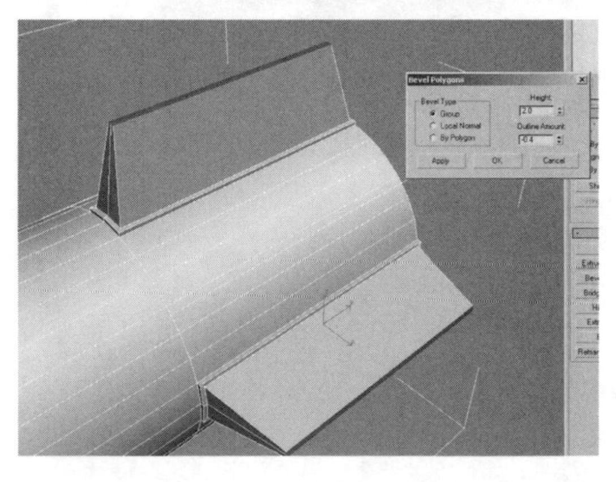

Figure 2-625

11. Select an edge one row in from the outer edge and Loop it.

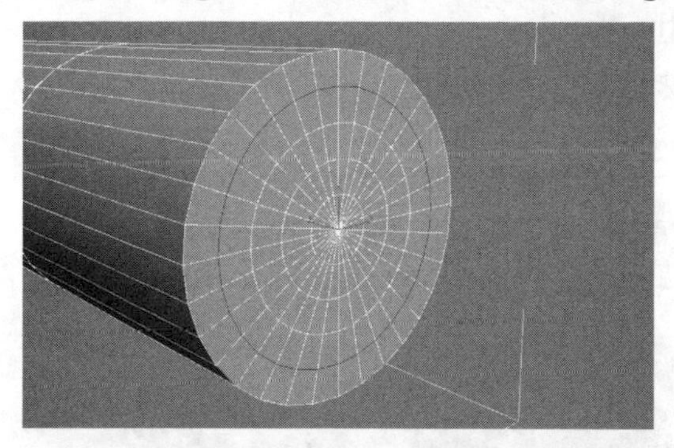
Figure 2-626

12. Scale the selected edges **120** in the X and Z axes.

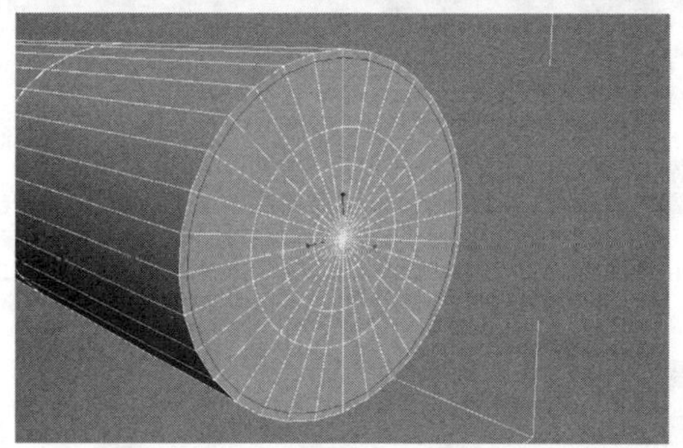
Figure 2-627

13. Select the 128 polygons in the middle of the front of the missile and extrude them by **0.01**, and then delete them.

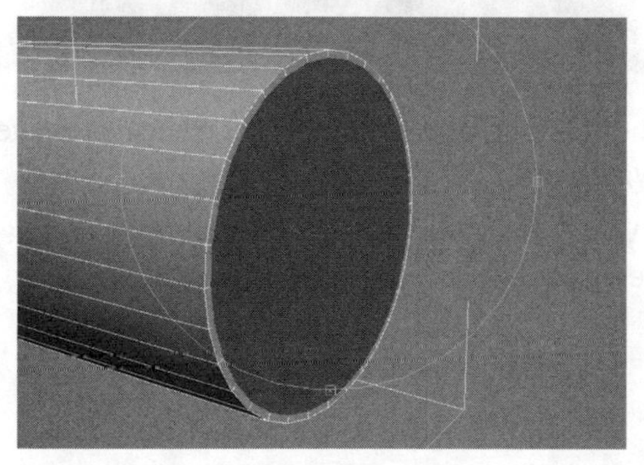
Figure 2-628

14. Switch to the Front view and use AutoGrid to create a Sphere in the center of the missile:

Radius	Segments	Hemisphere
2.871	32	0.5

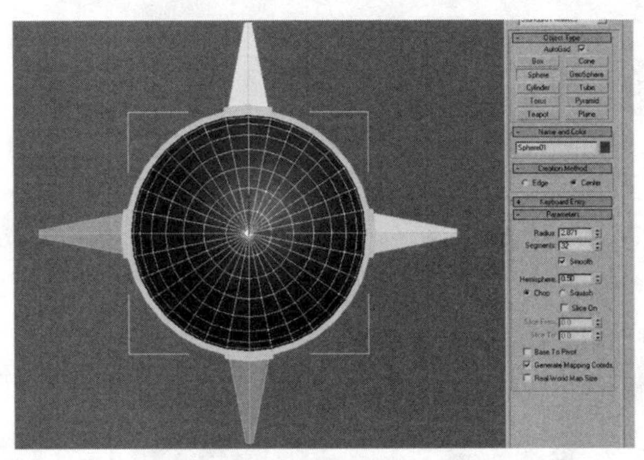

Figure 2-629

15. Move the sphere to the front of the missile (around **–80** in the X axis).

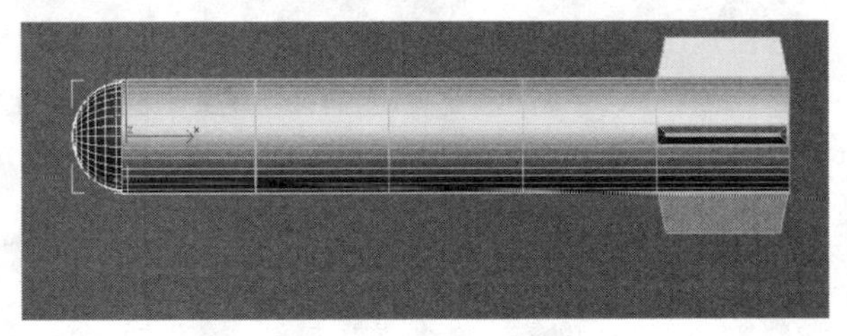

Figure 2-630

16. Convert the sphere to an Editable Polygon and delete the back-facing polygons.

17. Switch to Vertex selection mode and select the vertex at the center of the sphere (vertex 1).

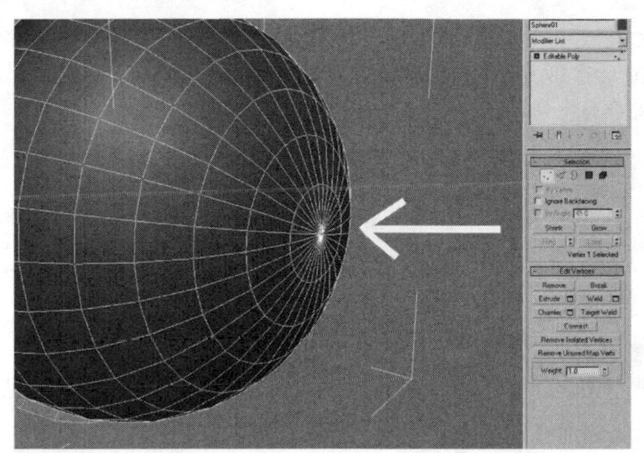

Figure 2-631

18. Turn on **Use Soft Selection**, click **Shaded Face Toggle**, and enter **4.75** for the Falloff.

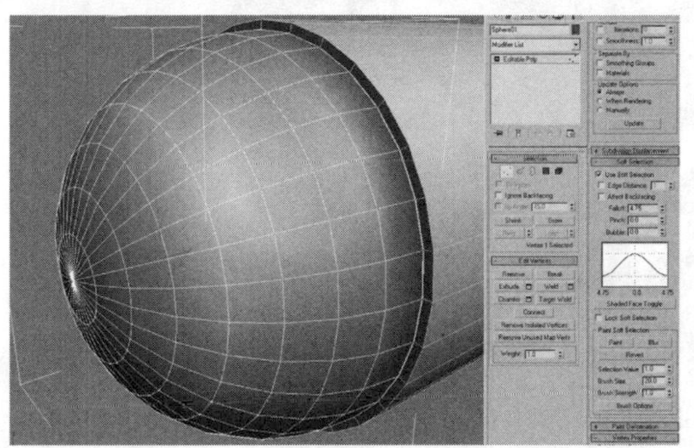

Figure 2-632

19. Move the vertex **–2.2** in the Offset World Y axis to make a cone.

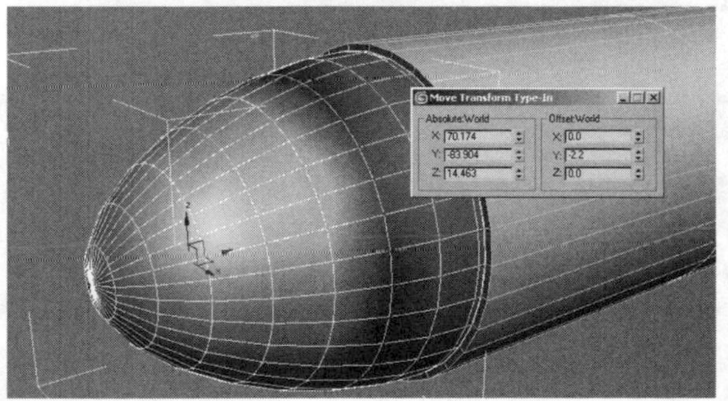

Figure 2-633

20. Uncheck Use Soft Selection, add a Smooth modifier to the stack, check **Auto Smooth**, and convert the sphere to an Editable Polygon to collapse the stack.

21. Select the cylinder, attach the sphere, select the vertices along the seam, and Weld the vertices together to merge them. (Use a threshold of **0.01**; the vertices should drop from 874 to 842.)

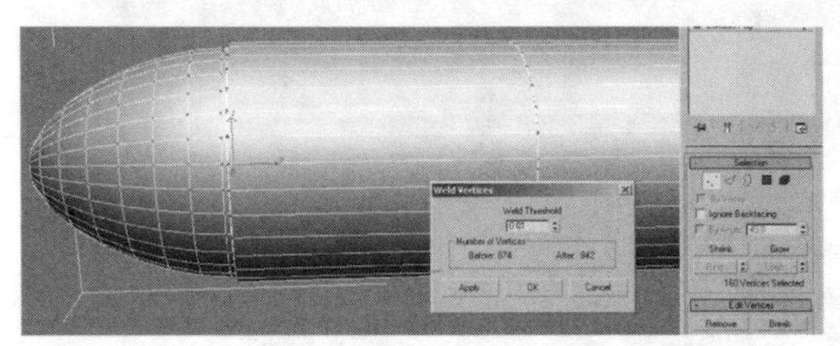

Figure 2-634

22. Switch to the Perspective view, Arc Rotate around the rear of the missile, and select the 128 polygons in the middle.

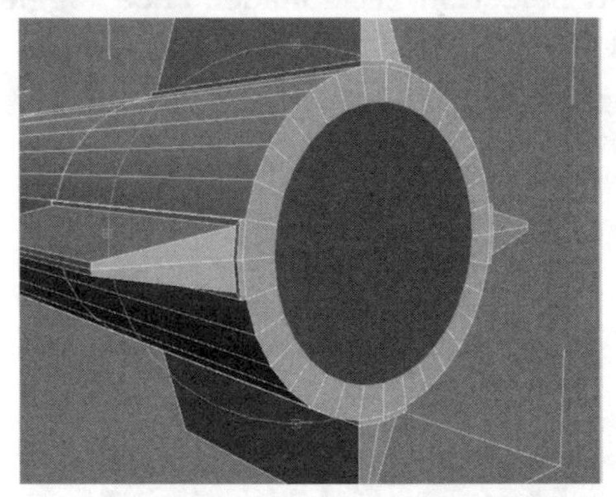

Figure 2-635

23. Group Extrude **–0.25** and then click **Shrink**.

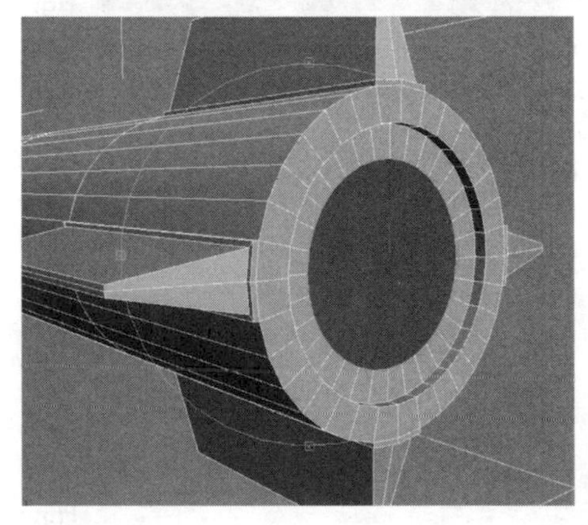

Figure 2-636

24. Move the polygons **–0.20** in the Y axis.

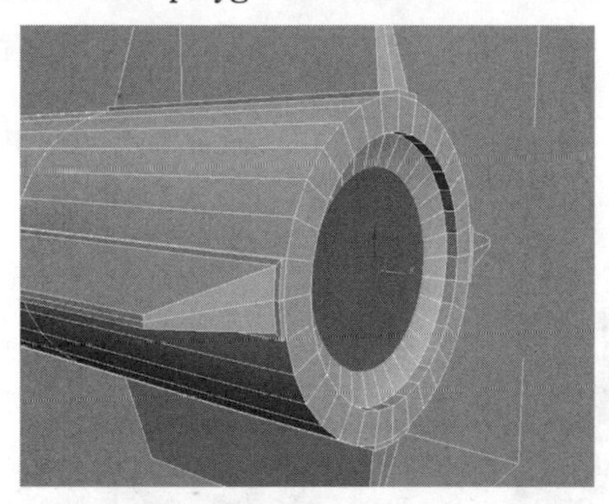

Figure 2-637

25. Click **Shrink** and move the polygons **–0.15** in the Y axis.

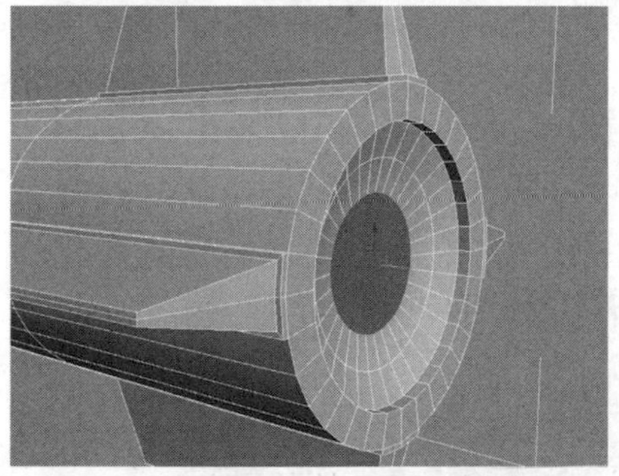

Figure 2-638

26. Click **Shrink** and move the polygons **–0.15** in the Y axis.

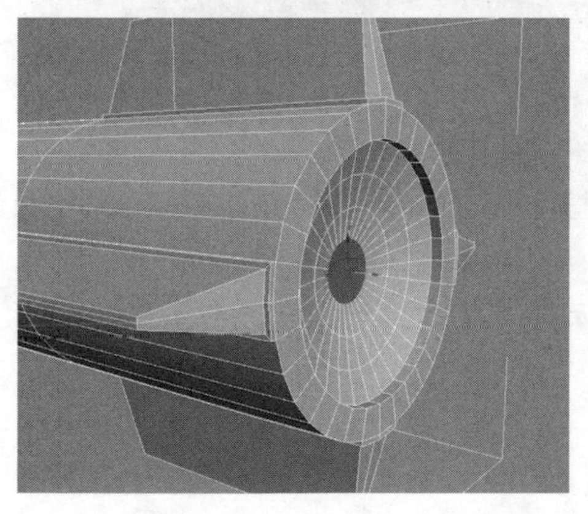

Figure 2-639

27. Click **Bevel Settings:**

Type	Height	Outline	Apply/OK
Group	–2	–0.15	OK

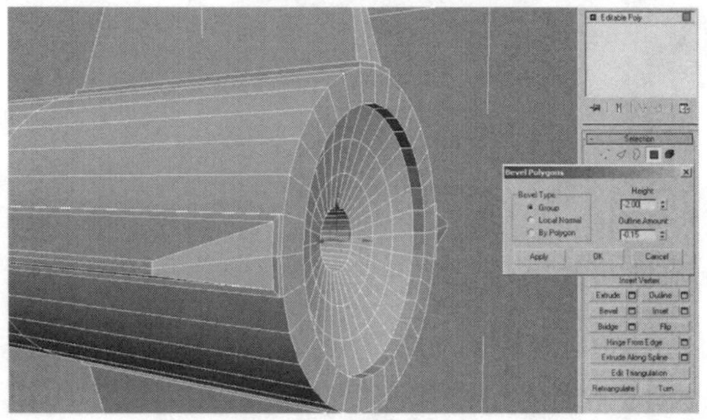

Figure 2-640

28. Add a Smooth modifier to the stack, check **Auto Smooth**, and convert to Editable Polygon. Switch to the Perspective view, Arc Rotate to get a good angle, and do a test render.

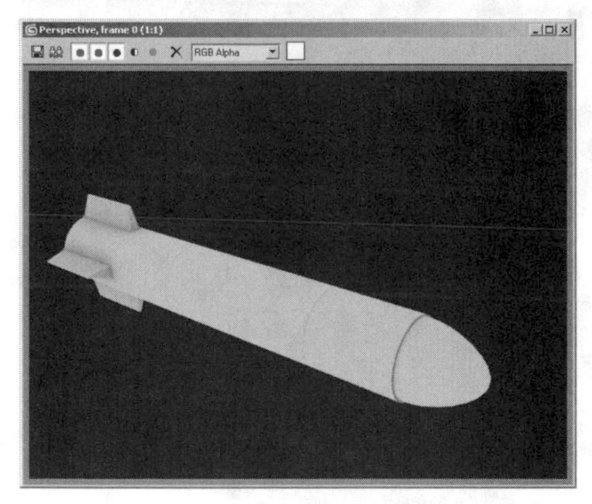

Figure 2-641

29. Switch to the Front view, and using AutoGrid, create a Tube centered around the missile:

Radius 1	Radius 2	Height	Height/Cap Segs	Sides	Smooth	Slice On/ From/To
3.029	3.349	2.5	3/1	32	Checked	Checked/ –180/0

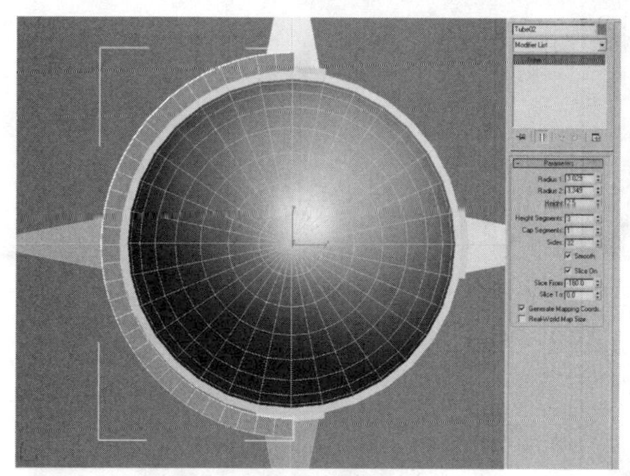

Figure 2-642

30. Switch to the Top view and move the tube into place.

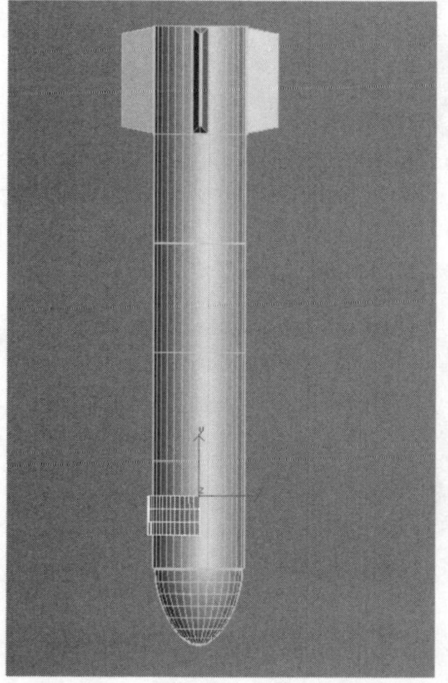

Figure 2-643

31. Convert the tube to an Editable Polygon, rename it **brace**, click a segment on the leftmost side, and click **Loop**.

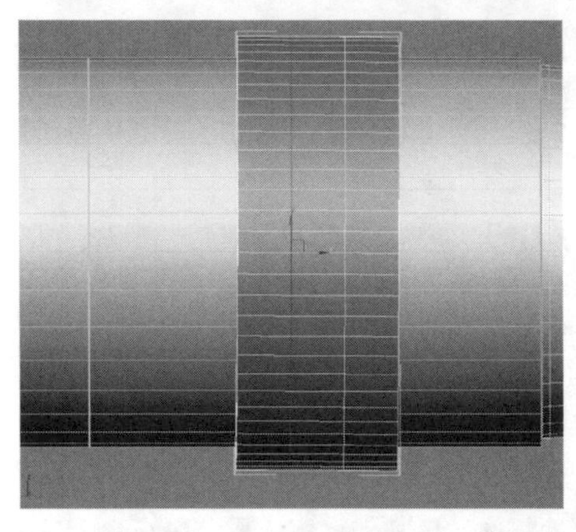

Figure 2-644

32. Move the segments **–0.30** in the X axis, then loop-select the segments to the right and move them **0.30** in the X axis.

33. Select the eight polygons shown in Figure 2-645.

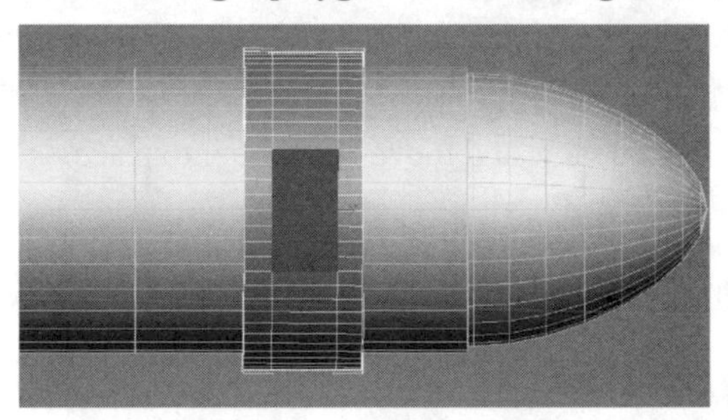

Figure 2-645

34. Extrude the polygons **0.5**.

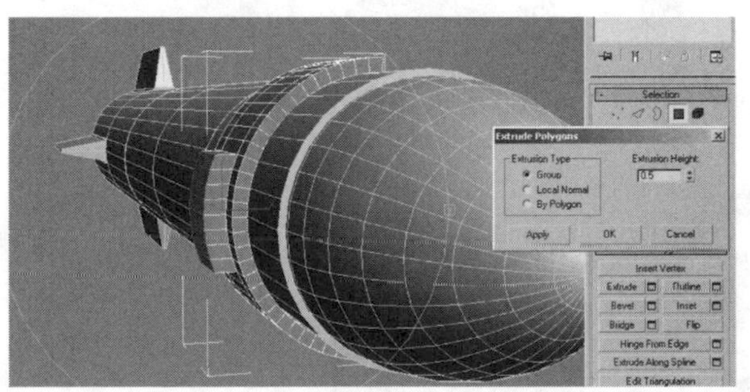

Figure 2-646

35. Scale the polygons down to **0** in the X axis.

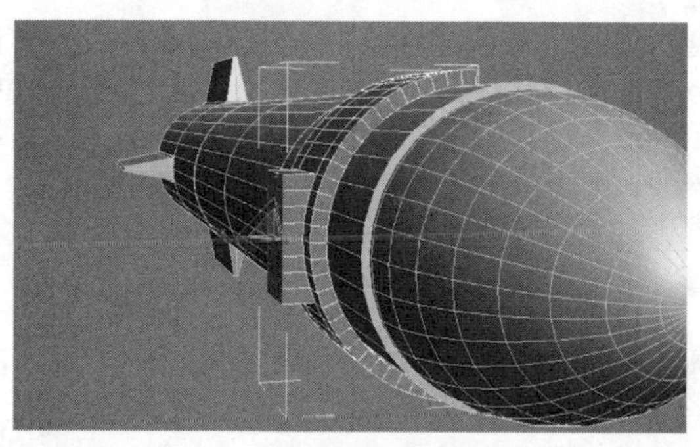

Figure 2-647

36. Group Extrude them **0.5**.

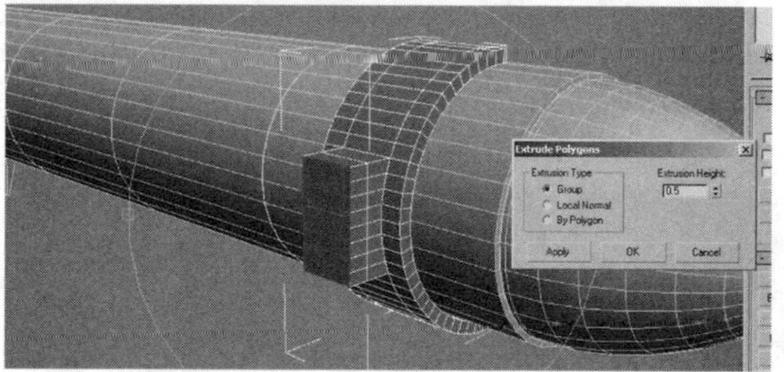

Figure 2-648

37. Arc Rotate around the back and select the eight polygons shown in Figure 2-649.

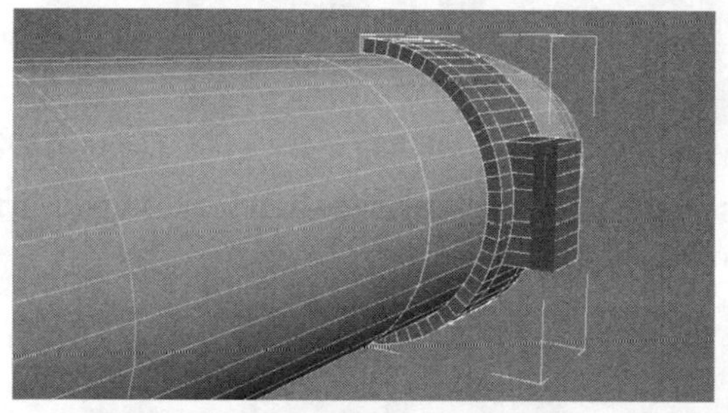

Figure 2-649

38. Zoom out, Extrude those eight polygons around **9.73** or until they reach the missile's center, and then delete them.

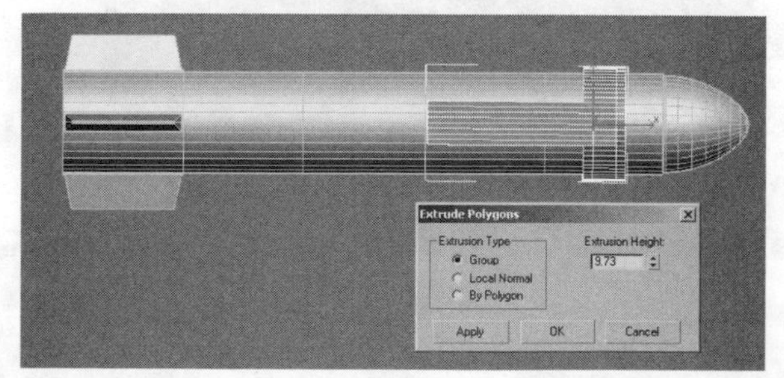

Figure 2-650

39. Object-select the brace you've been building and Mirror it, offsetting the clone (~**–18.28**) until it is just forward of the fins but still intersecting the original.

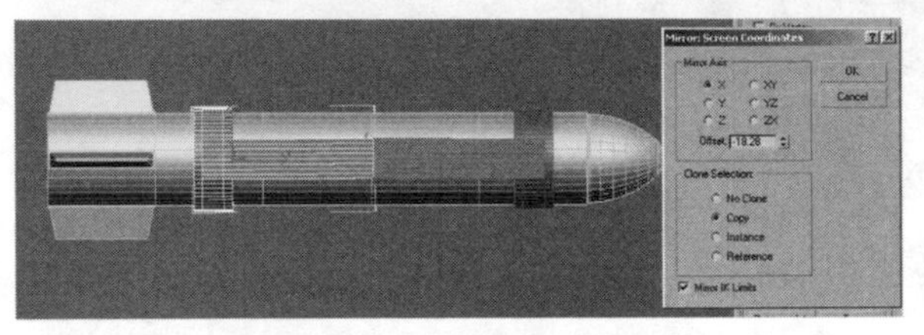

Figure 2-651

40. Select the original brace, attach the clone, select the intersecting vertices in the middle, and Weld them.

41. Select both the missile and the brace, switch to the Front view, and Shift-drag down (~**11.207**) in the Y axis to clone a missile and brace below the original.

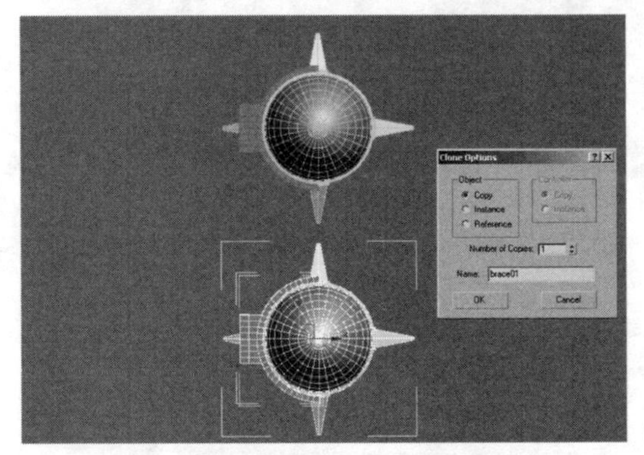

Figure 2-652

42. Marquee-select both sets of missiles and braces and Mirror them in X with an offset of **–10**.

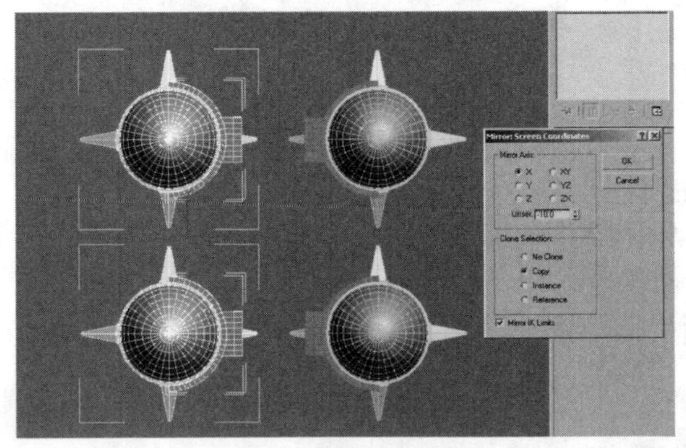

Figure 2-653

43. Attach the braces together and select the eight center, inward-facing polygons on all four braces as shown in Figure 2-654.

Figure 2-654

44. Extrude the polygons **1.812**, or until they meet in the middle.

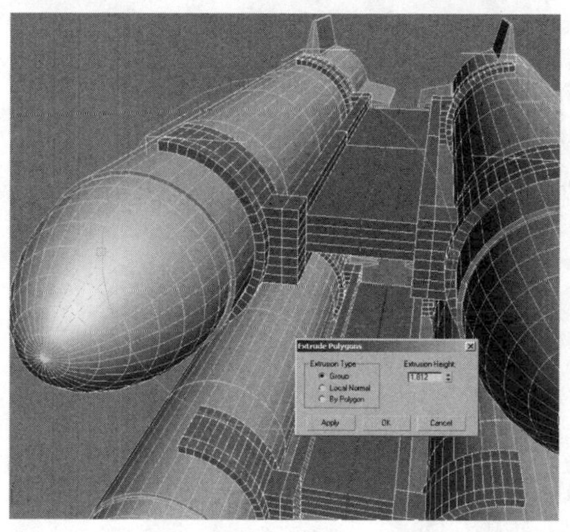

Figure 2-655

45. Delete the inward-facing polygons, switch to Vertex selection mode, select the middle vertices, and Weld the seams.

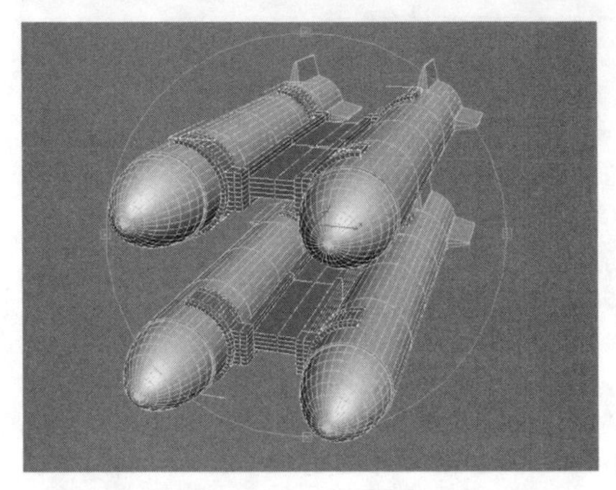

Figure 2-656

46. Select the eight inner surface polygons (top and bottom).

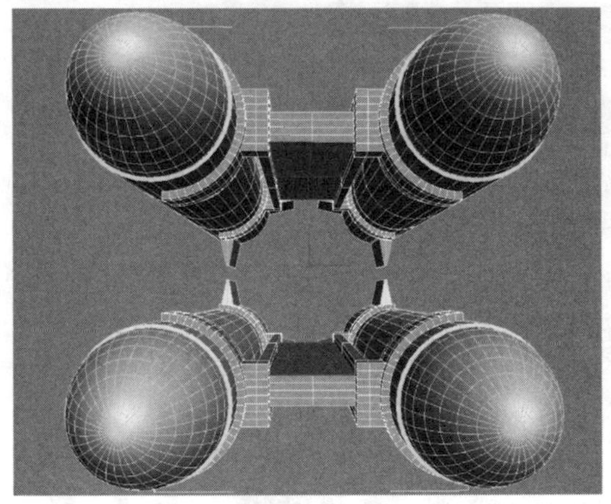

Figure 2-657

47. Click **Bevel Settings:**

Type	Height	Outline	Apply/OK
Group	0	–0.75	Apply
Group	5.0	0	OK

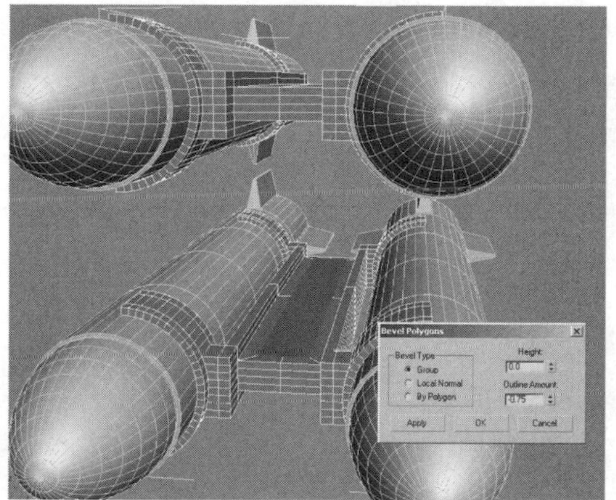

Figure 2-658

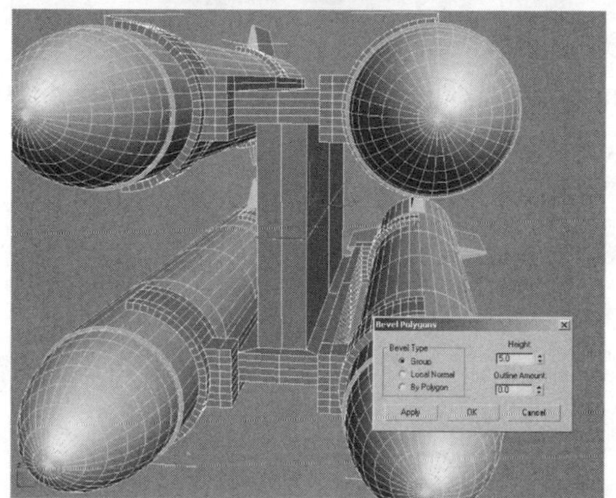

Figure 2-659

48. Delete the inward-facing polygons, switch to Vertex selection mode, select the seam vertices, and Weld. Do a test render.

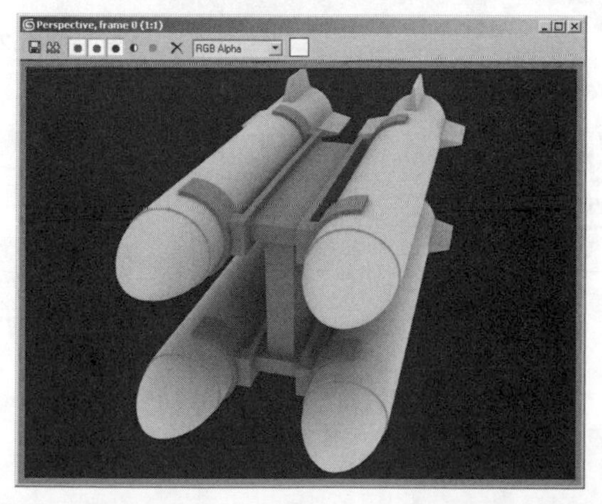

Figure 2-660

49. Select the top four polygons on the brace and Group Extrude them **3.0**.

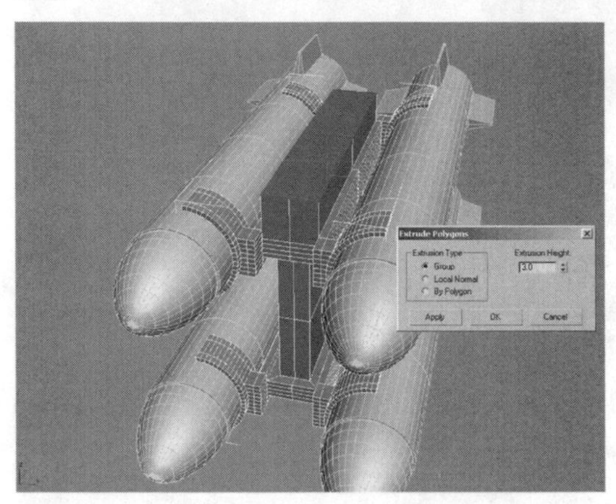

Figure 2-661

50. Unhide the wing and cannon so we can position the missiles.

Figure 2-662

51. Click **Bevel Settings:**

Type	Height	Outline	Apply/OK
Group	0	0.4	Apply
Group	0.6	0	Apply

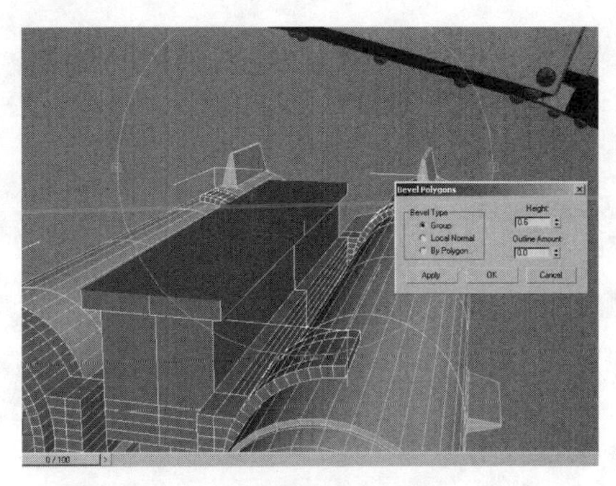

Figure 2-663

Type	Height	Outline	Apply/OK
Group	0	2	Apply
Group	2.2	0	OK

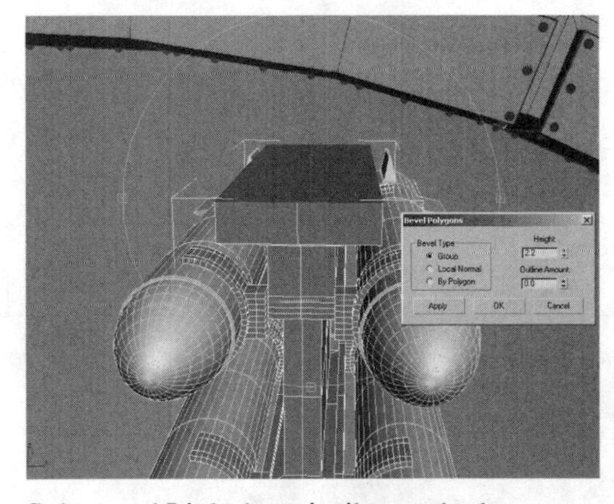

Figure 2-664

52. Select and Link the missiles to the brace.
53. Center the pivot of the brace and then move the brace and position it beneath the wing. (I rotated mine around **15.29** degrees in the Y axis.)

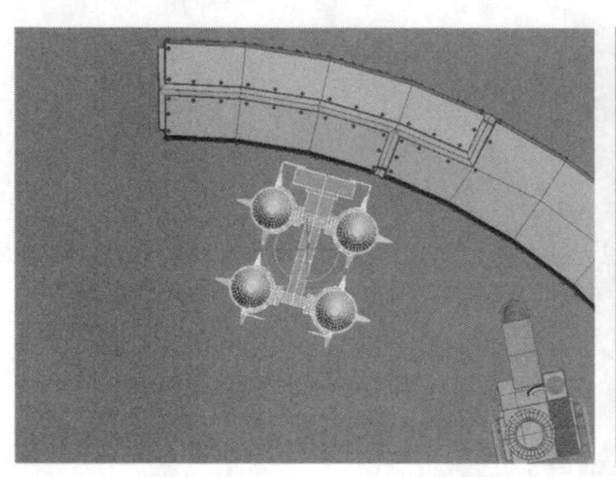
Figure 2-665

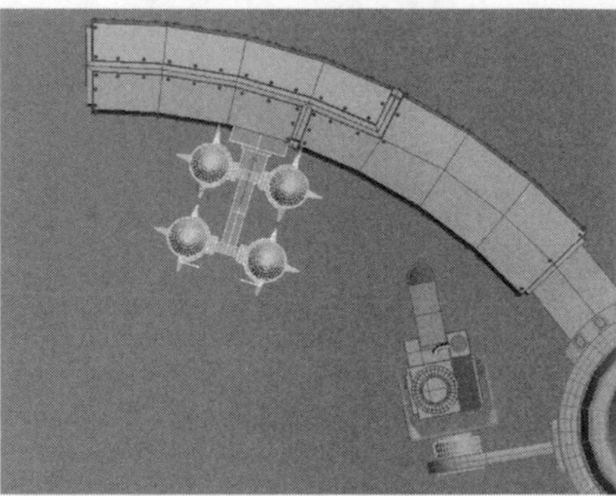
Figure 2-666

54. Add the Clay material to the brace and missiles and do a test render.

Day 13: Building the Body

1. Hide everything except the wing and switch to the Top view.
2. From the Extended Primitives, using AutoGrid, create a Chamfer Cylinder:

Radius	Height	Fillet	Height/Fillet/Cap Segs	Sides	Smooth
32.342	13.23	1.804	2/10/4	32	Checked

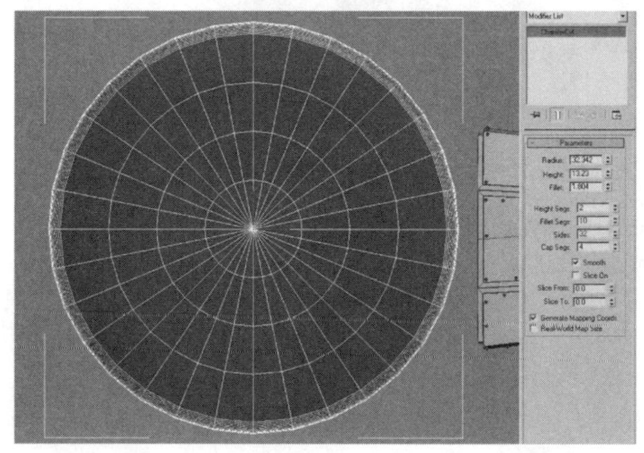
Figure 2-667

3. Switch to the Front view and move the chamfer cylinder to align it with the wing.

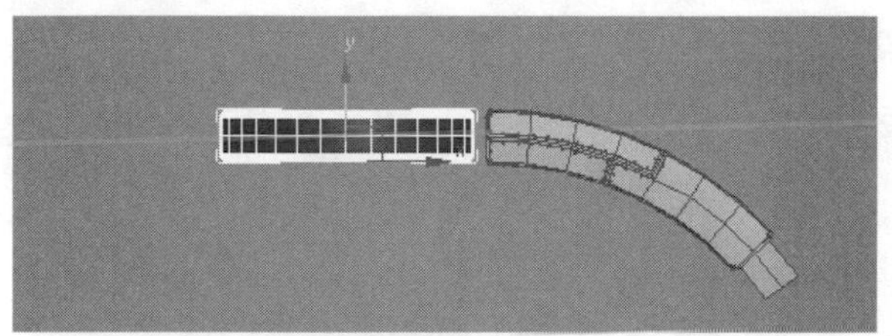

Figure 2-668

4. Increase the height of the chamfer cylinder to **26.364**, increase the height segments to **3**, and convert it to an Editable Polygon.

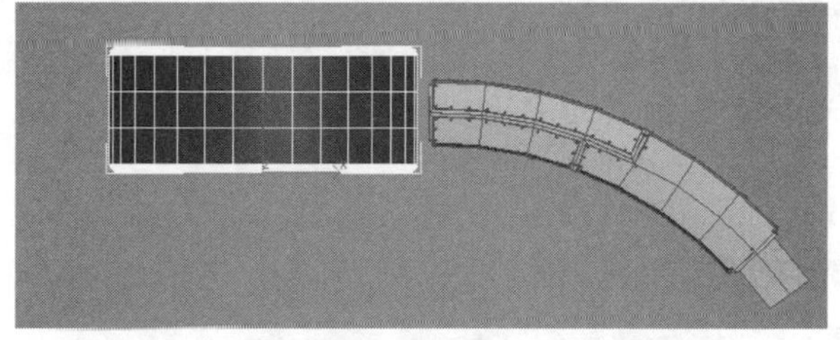

Figure 2-669

5. Select a horizontal segment, click **Loop**, and move the segments up to the lip of the wing (**3.032** in the Y axis).

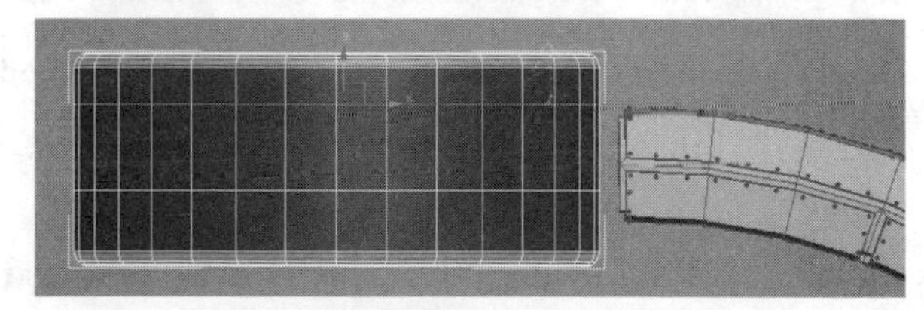

Figure 2-670

6. Select a horizontal segment, click **Loop**, and move the segments down to the lip of the wing (**–3.493** in the Y axis).

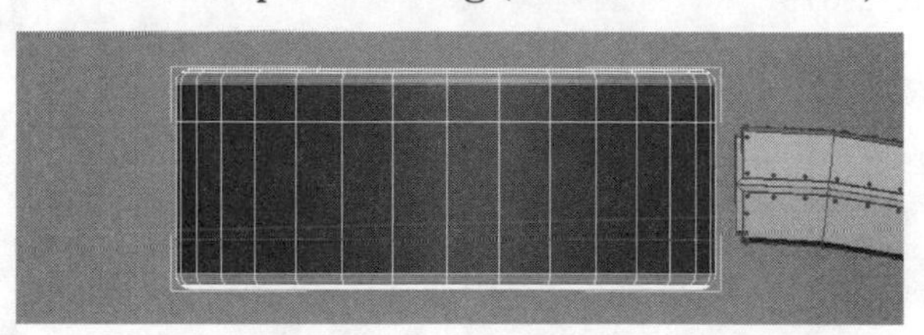

Figure 2-671

7. Switch to the Top viewport, select the cylinder half opposite the wing, and delete it.

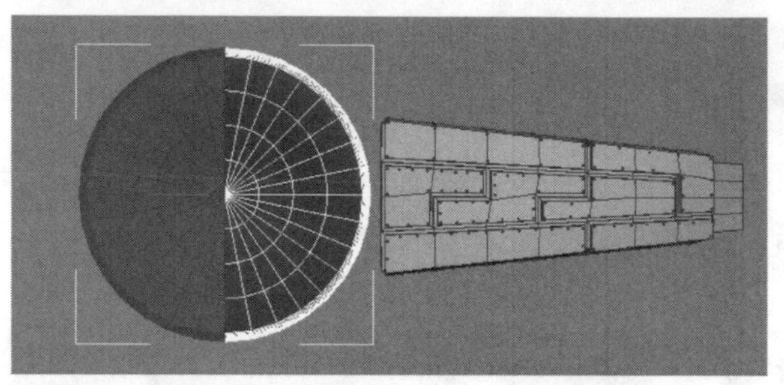

Figure 2-672

8. Add a Symmetry modifier to the stack.

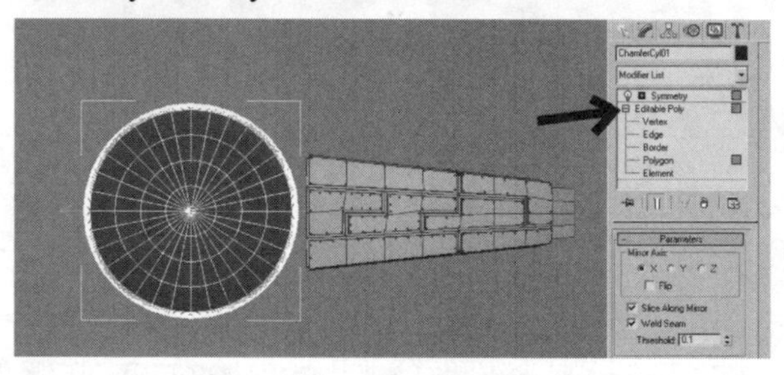

Figure 2-673

FYI: The Symmetry modifier works like mirroring, except that any modifications that are made to the mesh after the application of the modifier will be reflected in the mirrored half as well. This means that when modeling a symmetrical object like a human face, you only need to do half the work!

9. Click the plus sign to the left of Editable Poly, as indicated by the arrow in Figure 2-673, switch to Polygon selection mode, and select the six polygons on the side of the cylinder shown highlighted in Figure 2-674.

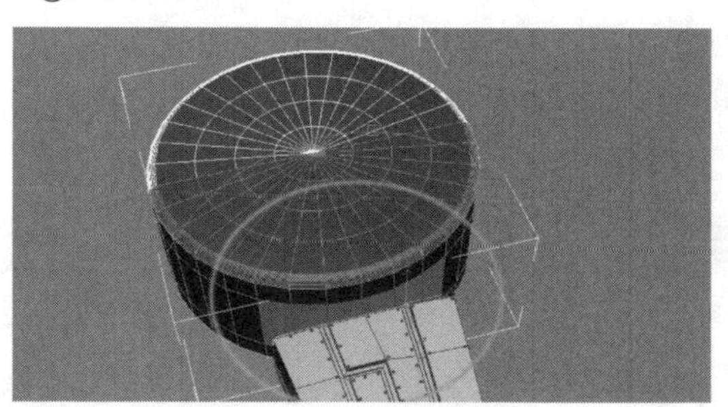

Figure 2-674

10. Group Extrude the polygons **3.36.**

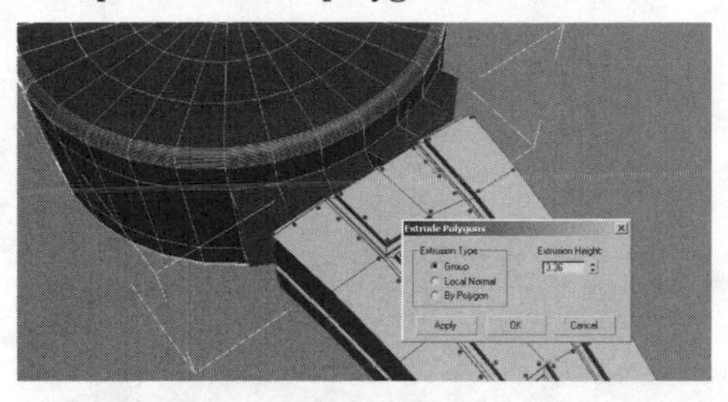

Figure 2-675

11. Hide the wing, select the middle polygons between the extrusions, and delete them.

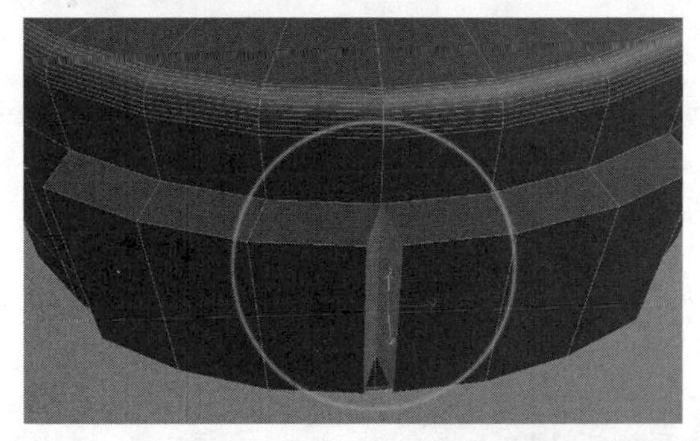

Figure 2-676

12. Select the vertices and scale them in the Y axis until the edges overlap, and then Weld the vertices.

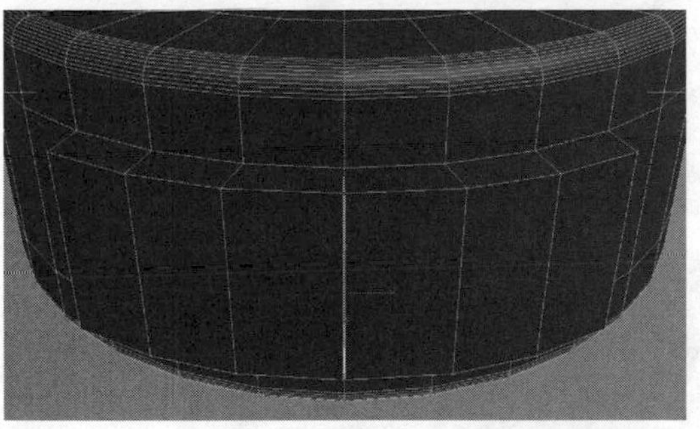

Figure 2-677

13. Unhide the wing, select the polygons, and scale them down to **0** in the X axis.

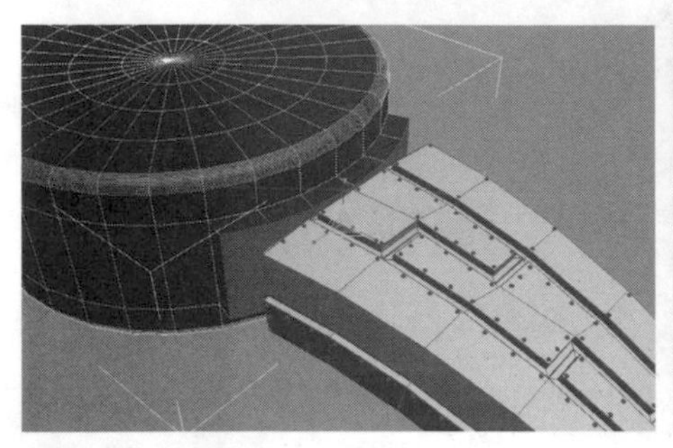
Figure 2-678

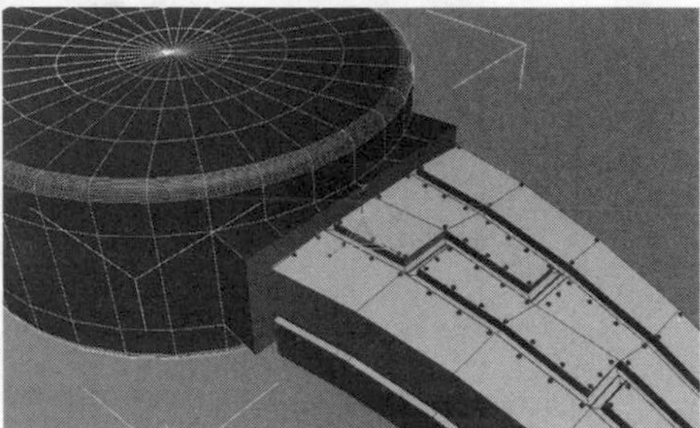
Figure 2-679

14. Zoom in tight in the Perspective viewport and click **Bevel Settings**:

Type	Height	Outline	Apply/OK
Group	0	–1.0	Apply
Group	–1.287	0	Apply

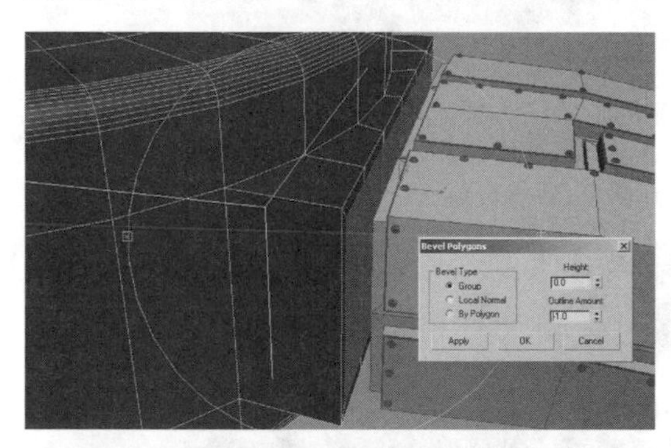

Figure 2-680

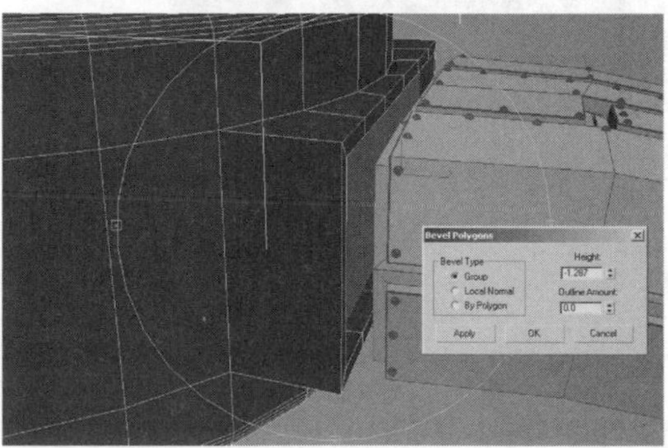

Figure 2-681

15. Delete the inside polygons.

16. Select the vertices surrounding the connection you made and move them until the connection is flush against the wing.

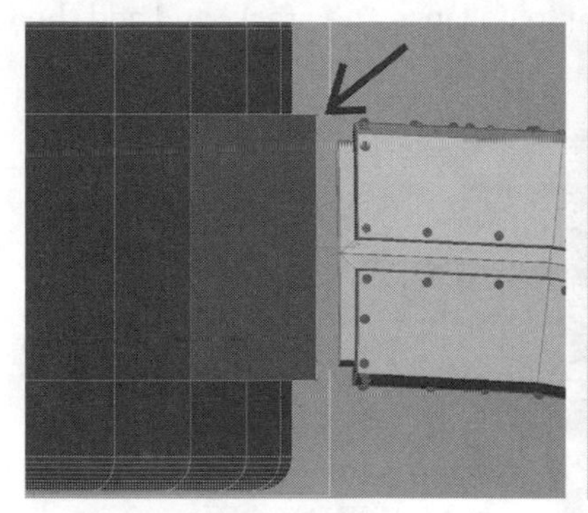

Figure 2-682

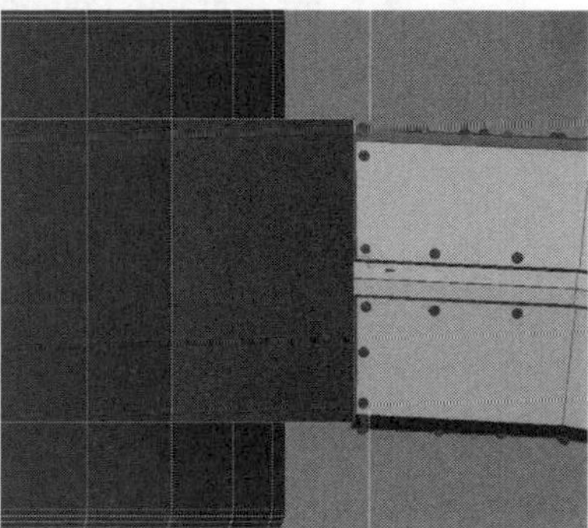

Figure 2-683

17. Move and scale the vertices until the connection is snug against the wing.

Figure 2-684

18. Select the sharp edges on the connection and Chamfer them by **0.1** and then **0.04**.

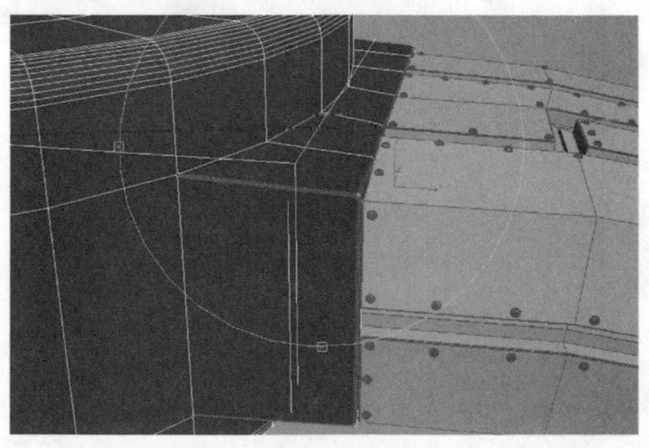

Figure 2-685

19. Add a Smooth modifier to the top of the chamfer cylinder's stack, check **Auto Smooth**, and rename the cylinder **bot_body**. Convert it to an Editable Polygon to collapse the stack, and add the Clay material to it.

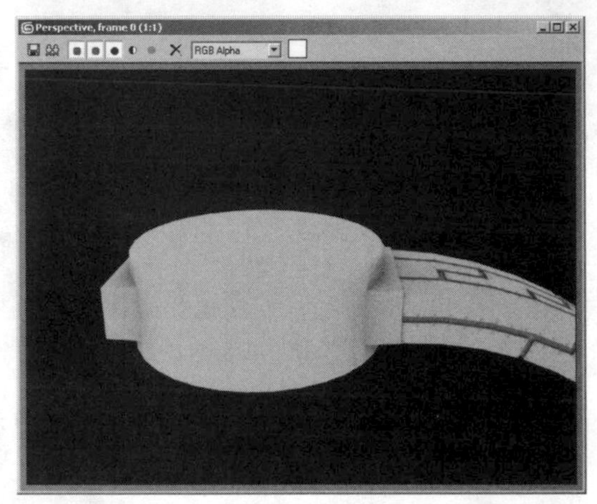

Figure 2-686

20. Select all the vertices, set the Weld setting to **0.01**, and weld all the vertices.

Fire Drill: Although collapsing the stack is supposed to weld the seams if you have it checked under the Symmetry modifier, it's been my experience that the welding is as reliable as Loop — sometimes it works and sometimes it doesn't. To be on the safe side, a weld threshold of 0.01 should only weld together vertices that are actually overlapping and should be welded.

21. Select the 96 polygons on the *top* (not the bottom) of the body.

FYI: Should there be some polygons inside of the chamfer cylinder visible through the wing connection, you'll want to delete those too. Sometimes (not often), welding symmetrical objects can leave artifacts inside an object.

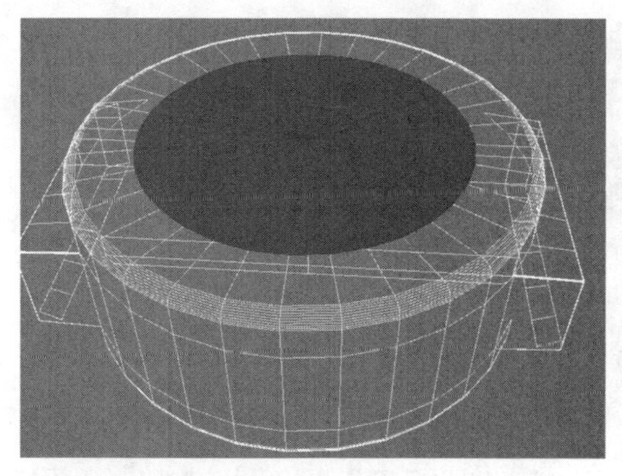

Figure 2-687

22. Click **Bevel Settings**:

Type	Height	Outline	Apply/OK
Group	–2	0	Apply
Group	0	–0.5	Apply
Group	3	0	Apply

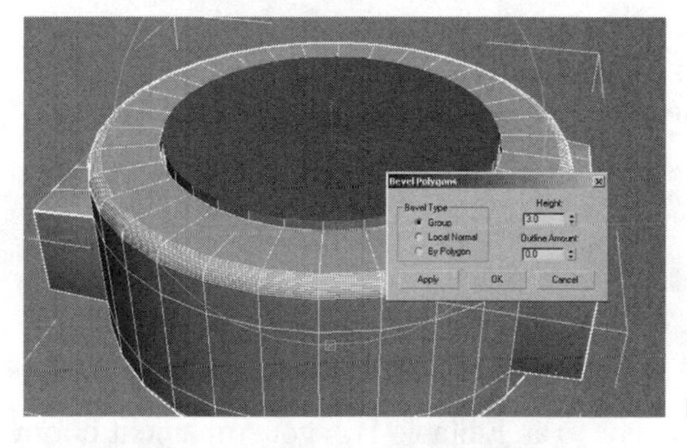

Figure 2-688

Type	Height	Outline	Apply/OK
Group	0	6	Apply
Group	8	0	OK

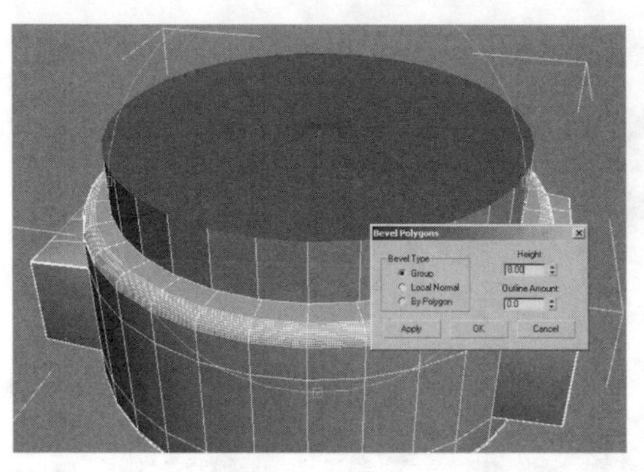

Figure 2-689

23. Switch to the Top viewport and, using AutoGrid, create a Box on the top of the body:

Length	Width	Height	Length/Width/Height Segs
10	20	2.751	1/3/1

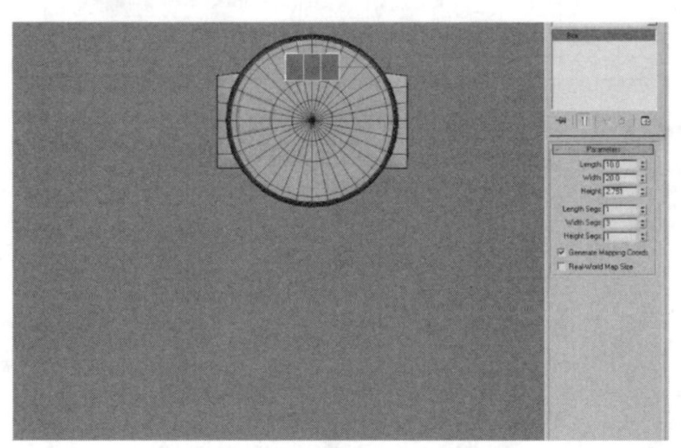

Figure 2-690

24. Convert the box to an Editable Polygon, rename it **boom_mount**, and select the right and left polygons.

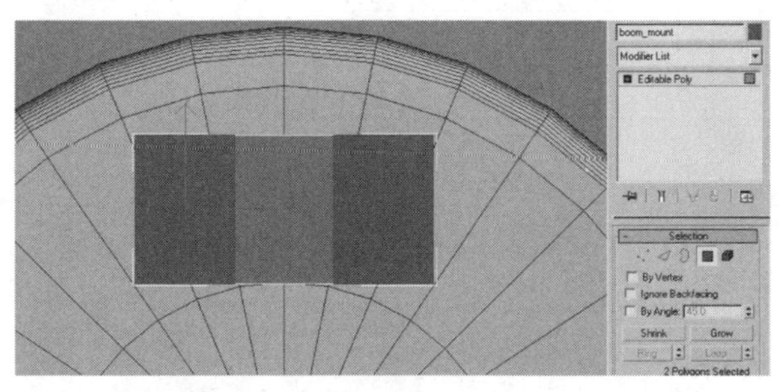

Figure 2-691

25. Click **Bevel Settings:**

Type	Height	Outline	Apply/OK
Group	0	–1.25	Apply
Group	8	0	OK

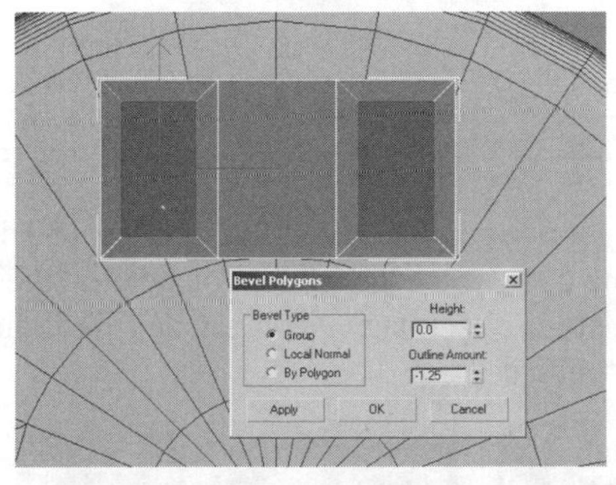

Figure 2-692

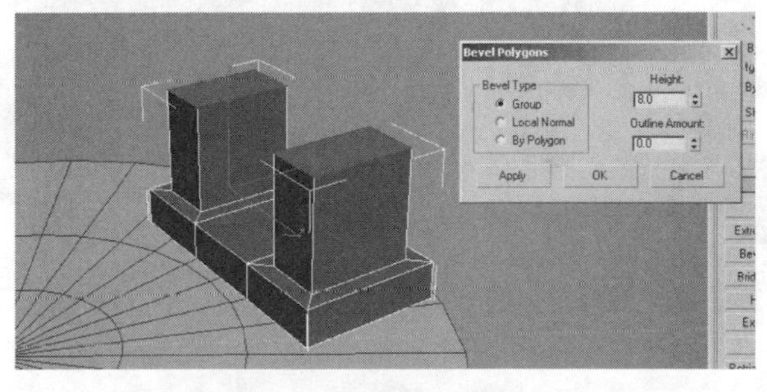

Figure 2-693

26. Select the four edges indicated in Figure 2-694 and then click **Connect.** (Connect creates a new segment that connects the two you selected, which in this case forms an H.)

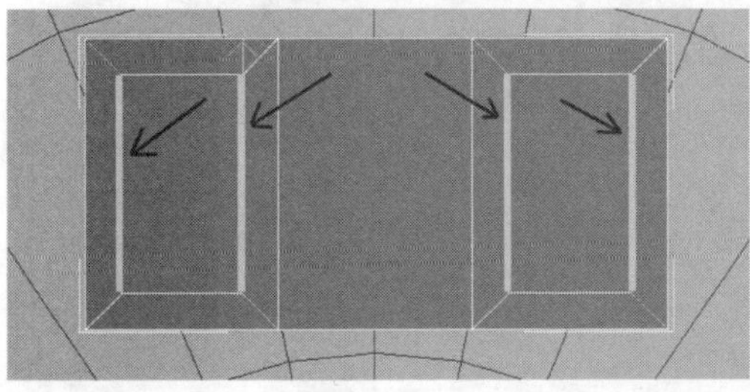

Figure 2-694

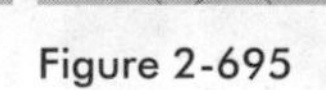

Figure 2-695

27. Select the bottom two polygons and delete them.

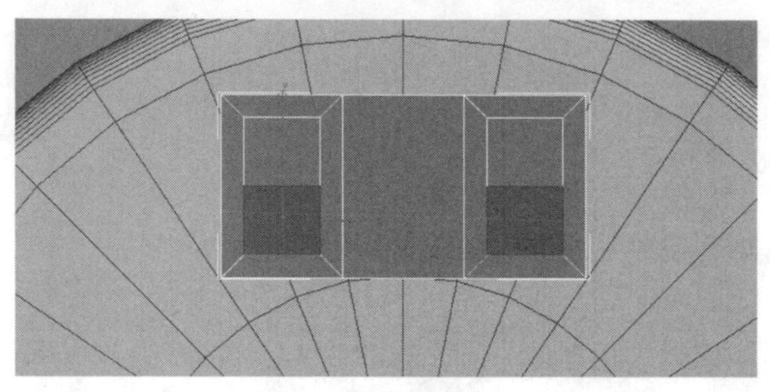

Figure 2-696

28. Select the top-right polygon and Hinge From Edge **180** degrees with **18** Segments using the edge where you deleted the polygons as the hinge. Delete the back-facing polygon and Weld the vertices. Repeat for the other side.

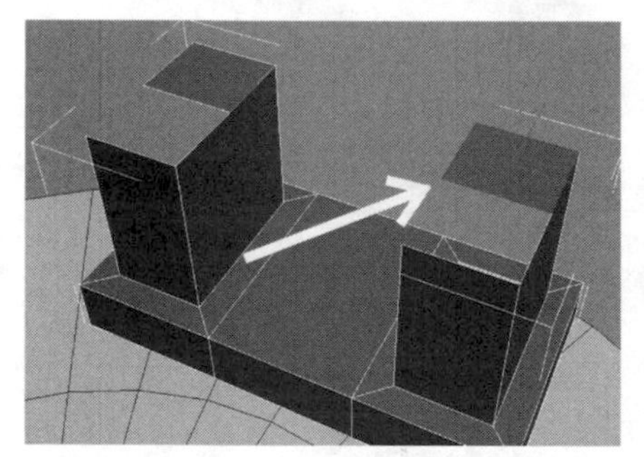

Figure 2-697

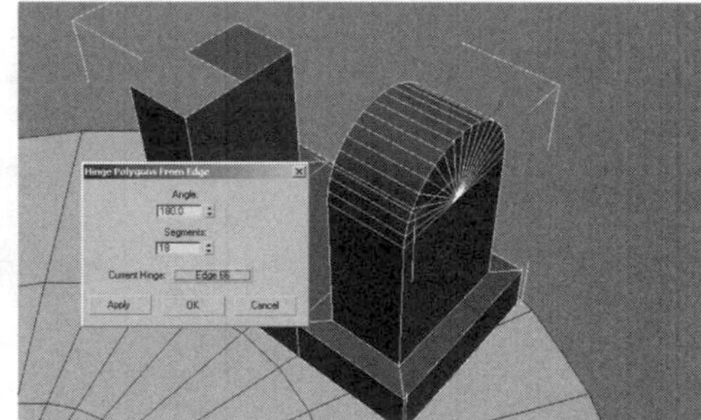

Figure 2-698

29. Switch to wireframe and select the sharp edges (84 total) and Chamfer them by **0.1** and then **0.04**.

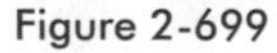

Figure 2-699

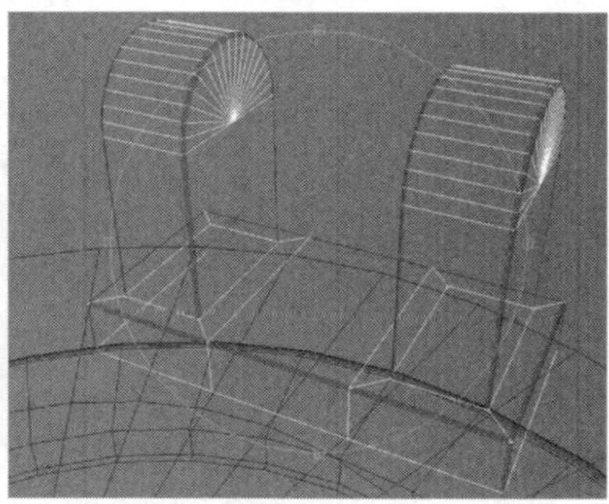

Figure 2-700

30. Add a Smooth modifier to the stack, click **Auto Smooth**, convert to an Editable Polygon, and then Select and Link to the body.

31. Switch to the Top viewport, select the **boom_mount**, and center the pivot.

32. Hold down the **Shift** key and drag down in the Y axis to make a clone and position it in the center of the turret.

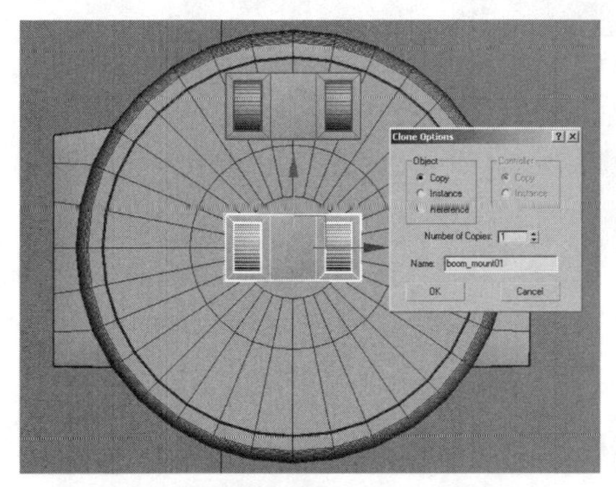

Figure 2-701

33. Select the middle 10 polygons and delete them.

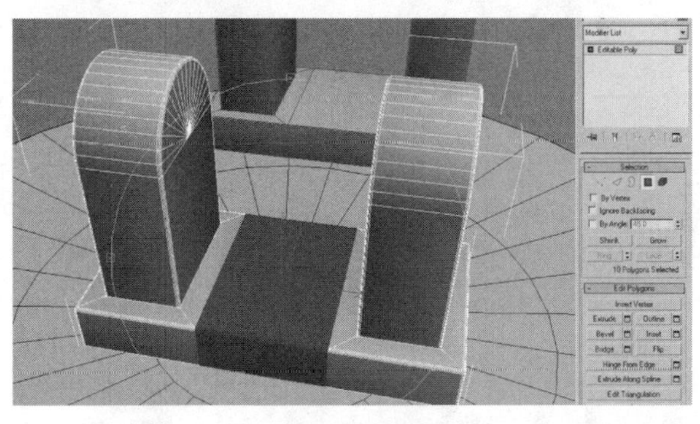

Figure 2-702

34. Select the left stanchion. Under the Edit Geometry rollout, click **Detach.**

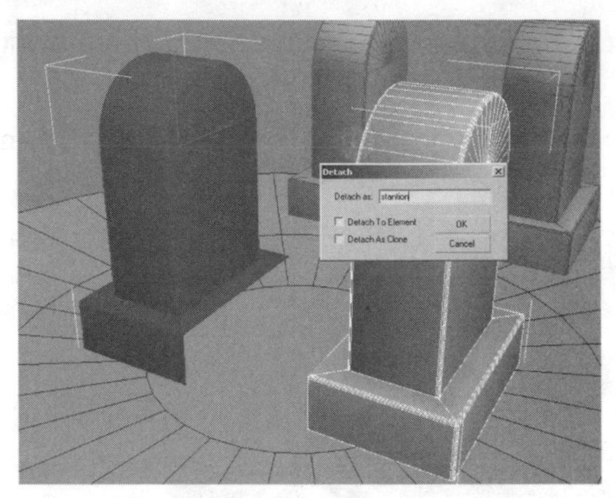

Figure 2-703

35. Select the borders on both stanchions and Cap them.

Day 14: Building the Boom Assemblies

1. Switch to the Right view and, using AutoGrid, create a Cylinder to match the curve of the frontmost stanchion.

Radius	Height	Height/Cap Segs	Sides	Smooth
3.485	–7.5	1/1	32	Checked

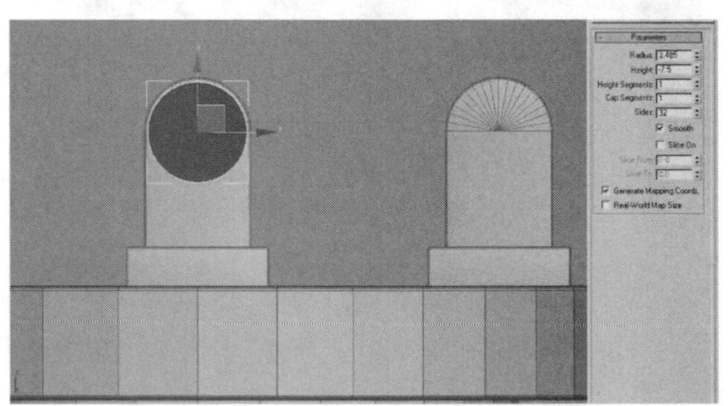

Figure 2-704

2. Switch to the Top view and center the cylinder between the vertical parts of the stanchion; adjust the position and height of the cylinder until the ends of the cylinder touch the inside edges of the stanchion, but *do not* penetrate (my final height was **–9.13**).

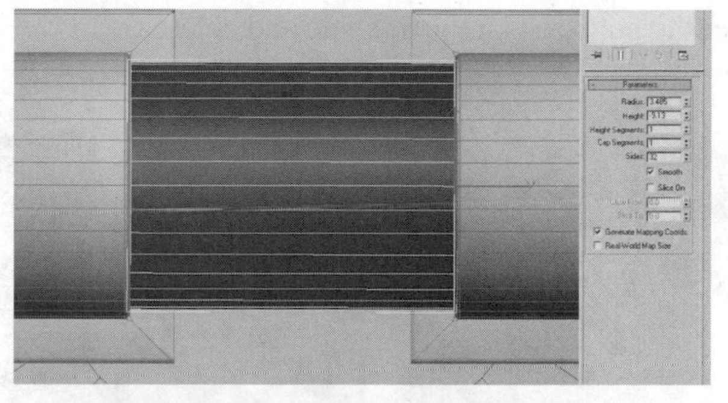

Figure 2-705

Figure 2-706

3. Convert the cylinder to an Editable Poly and center its pivot.
4. Switch back to the Top viewport, select all the edges (32 in all), and click **Connect**. A Segments setting of **1** slices the rod in half.

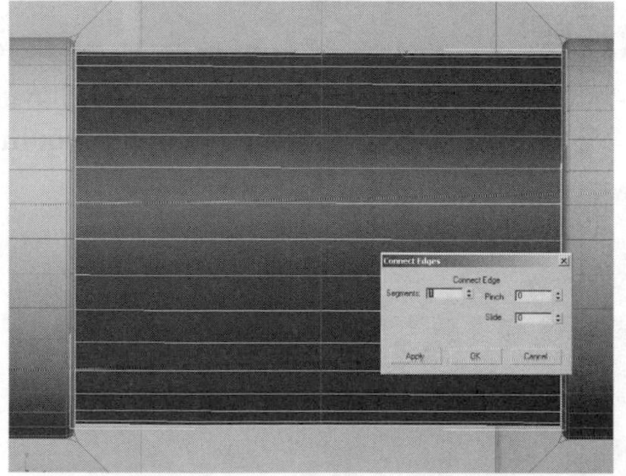

Figure 2-707

5. Select the polygons on the left side and delete them.

Figure 2-708

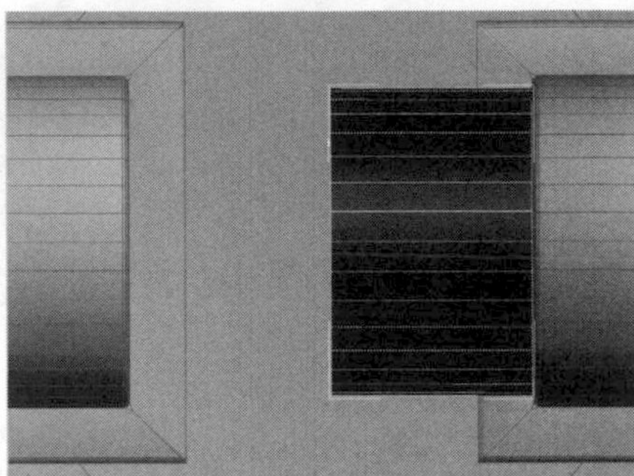

Figure 2-709

6. Select the 32 edges remaining, activate the Slice Plane, and make a slice where shown in Figure 2-710.

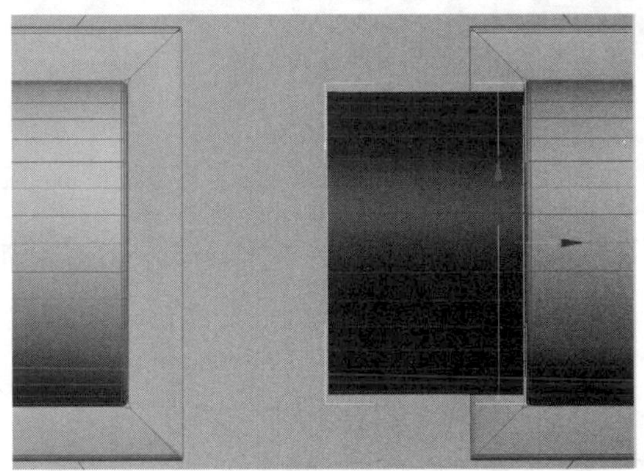

Figure 2-710

7. Object-select the cylinder, add a Symmetry modifier to its stack, switch the Mirror Axis to **Z**, and rename it **lower_boom**.

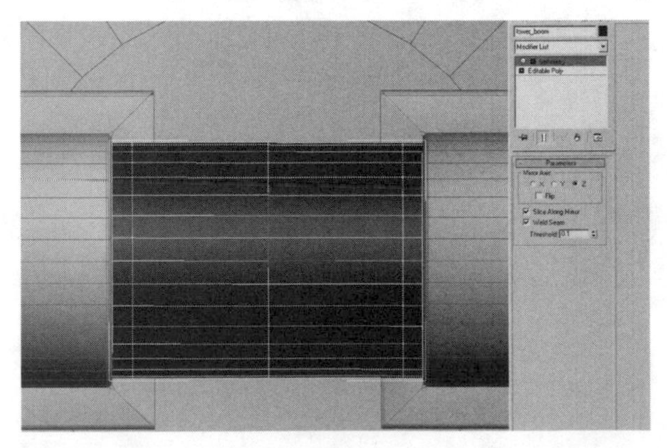

Figure 2-711

8. Select the front 26 polygons and Group Extrude them **15.0**.

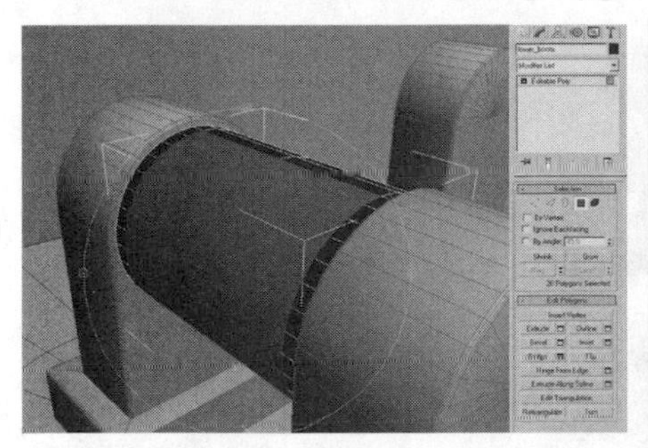

Figure 2-712

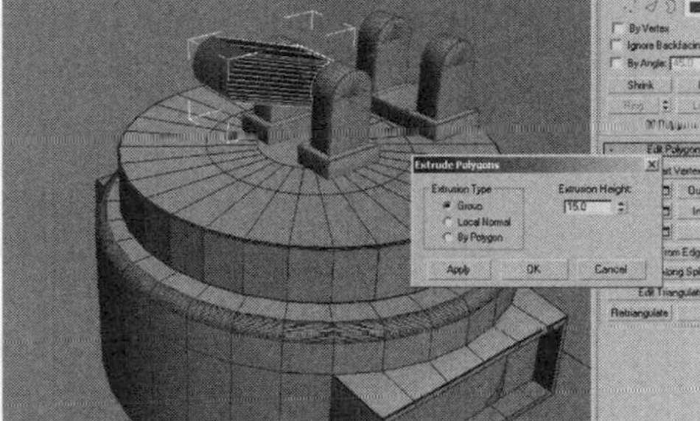

Figure 2-713

9. Switch to the Local coordinate system and scale the polygons down to **0** in the Z axis.

Figure 2-714

10. Delete the front polygons, then switch to the Right view and position the pivot as shown using the Move and Rotate tools.

Figure 2-715

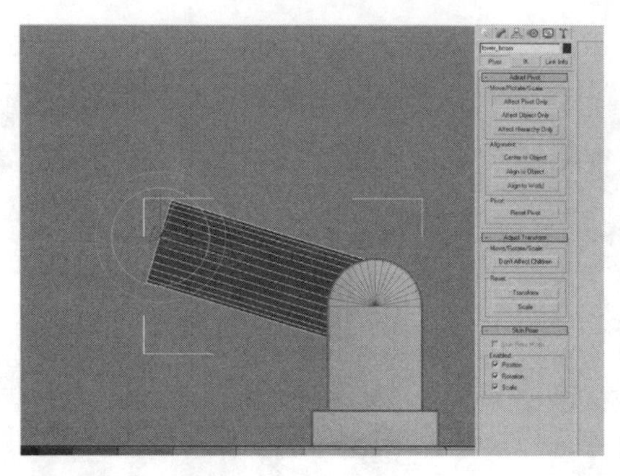

Figure 2-716

Don't Forget: You have to change the pivot; otherwise, when you mirror, Max will try to mirror from the axle part by the stanchion instead of the boom's middle. This is a mistake I *always* make and for some reason am always surprised when my mirrors don't work!

11. Mirror a copy in the X axis.

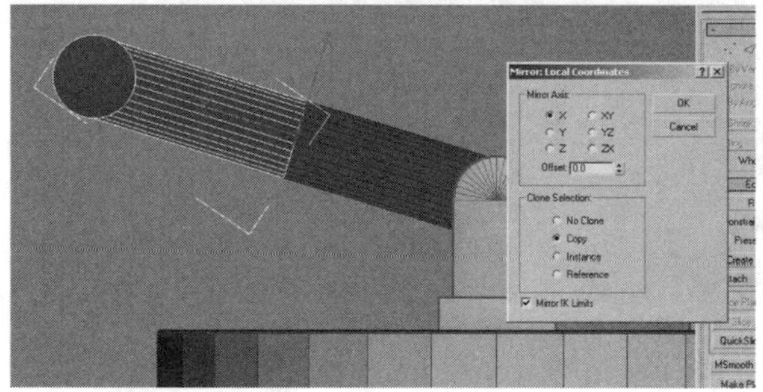

Figure 2-717

12. Attach the clone to the original, select the vertices in the middle seam, and Weld them.

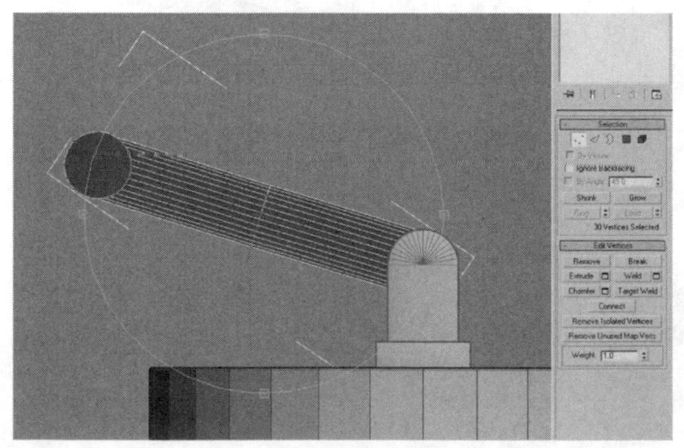

Figure 2-718

13. Select one of the seam's edges and Loop it.

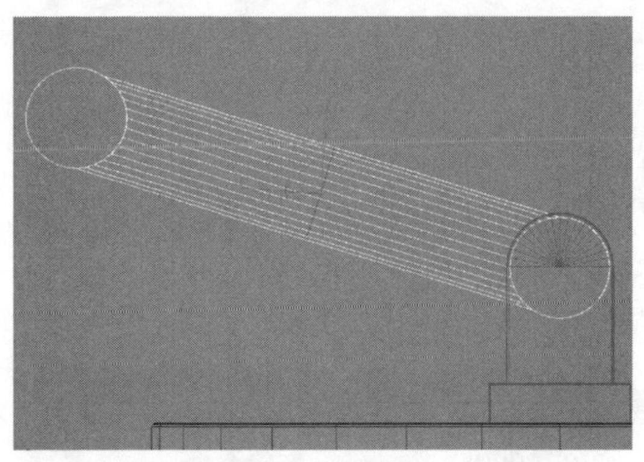

Figure 2-719

14. Chamfer the edge by **1.5**.

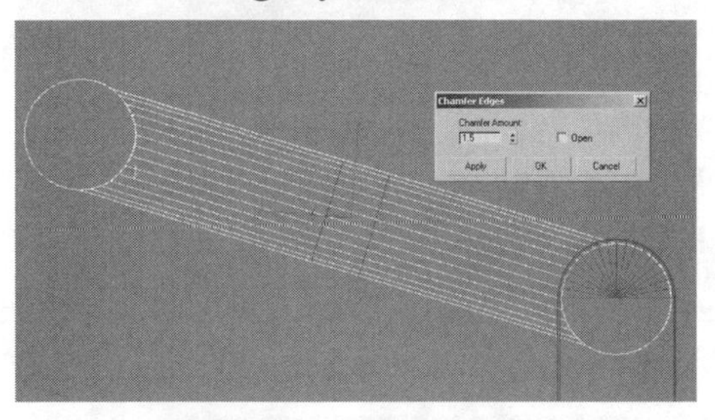

Figure 2-720

15. Rotate around until you can see the top edge, then select the middle seam between the edges you chamfered.

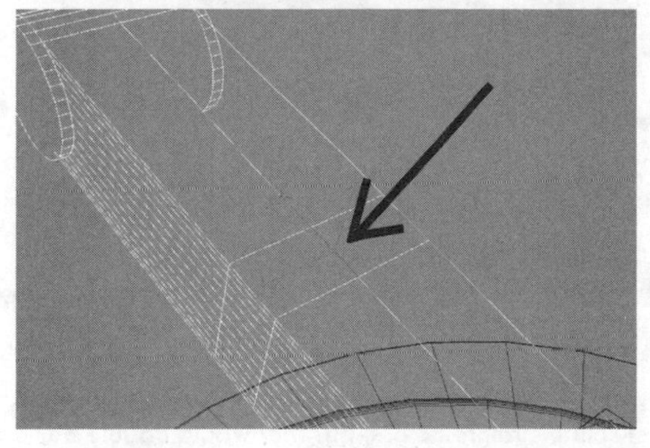

Figure 2-721

16. Chamfer the edge by **3.0**.

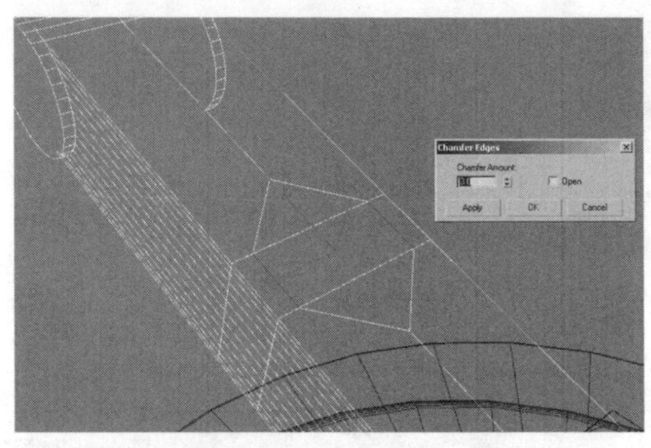

Figure 2-722

17. Select the center edges.

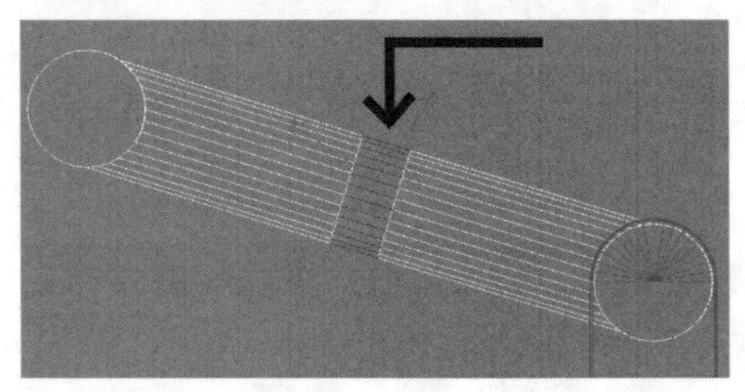

Figure 2-723

18. Click **Connect**.

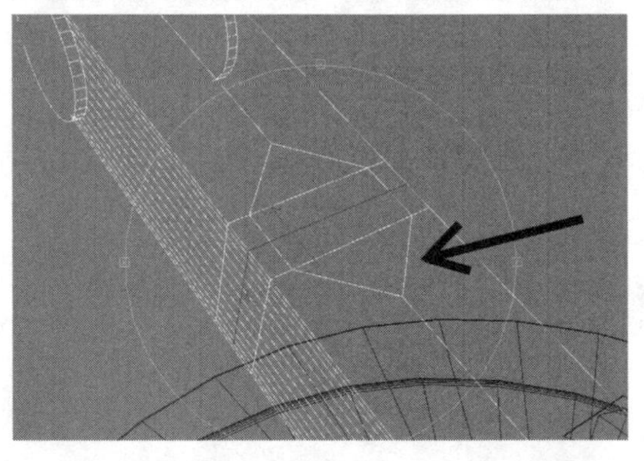

Figure 2-724

Urgent: We have a problem here. We have two triangular polygons. Now we could just split it straight across, but that would double our problem by giving us four triangles. What we need to do is connect the three middle edges. This will turn the two three-sided polygons into two four-sided polygons.

19. Select the three middle edges and click **Connect**.

Figure 2-725

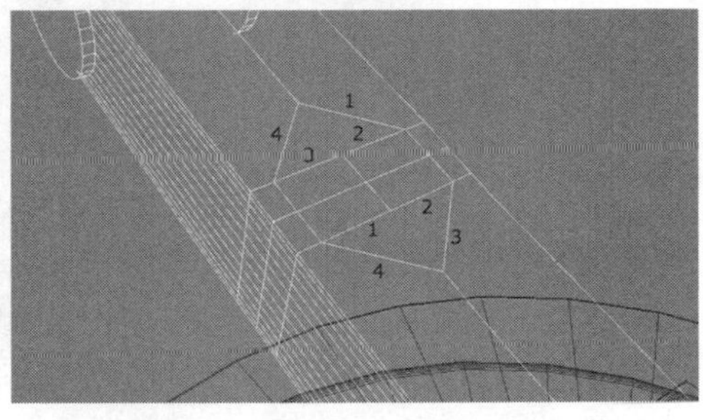

Figure 2-726

20. Select the four polygons on the edges and Extrude them by **2.5**.

Figure 2-727

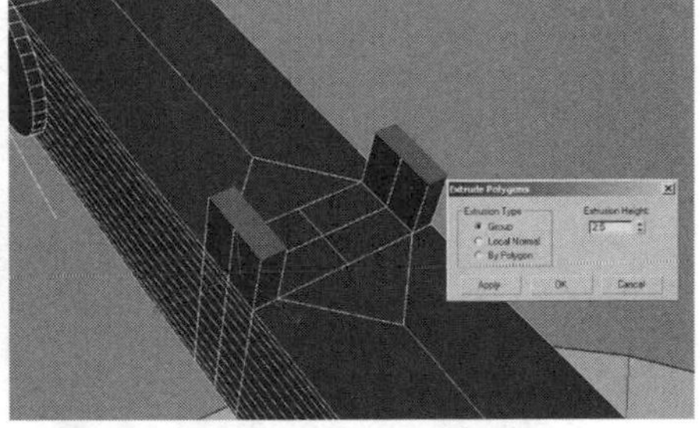

Figure 2-728

21. Select the lower two polygons, delete them, and then Hinge From Edge **180** with **10** Segments, using the edges indicated by the arrows in Figure 2-730.

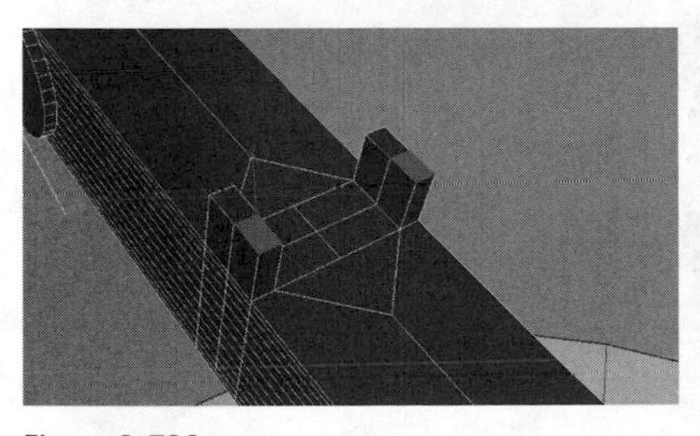

Figure 2-729

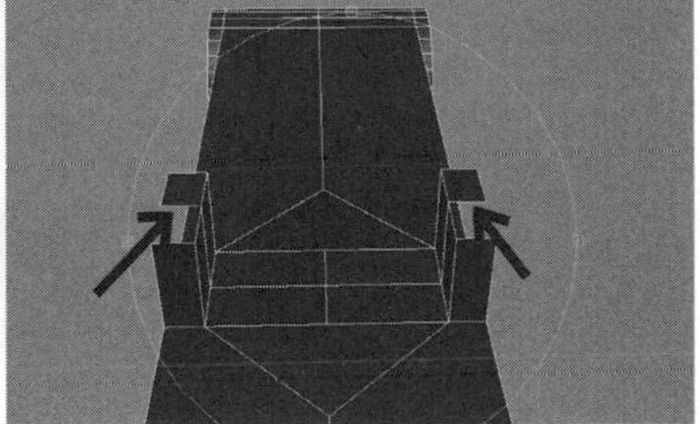

Figure 2-730

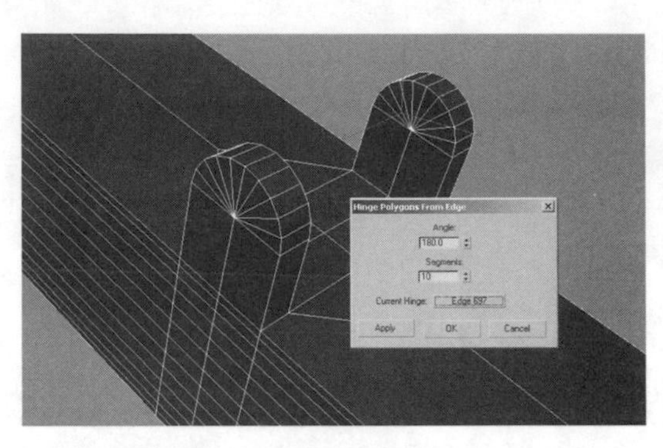

Figure 2-731

22. Select the vertices and Weld them.

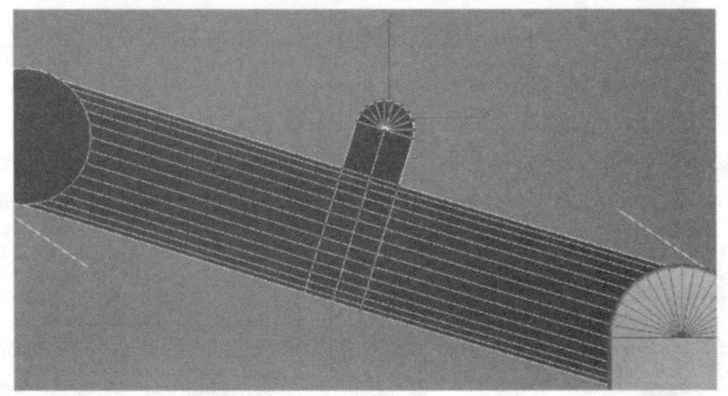

Figure 2-732

23. Object-select the boom and Mirror it in the XY axis with an Offset of **–0.45**.

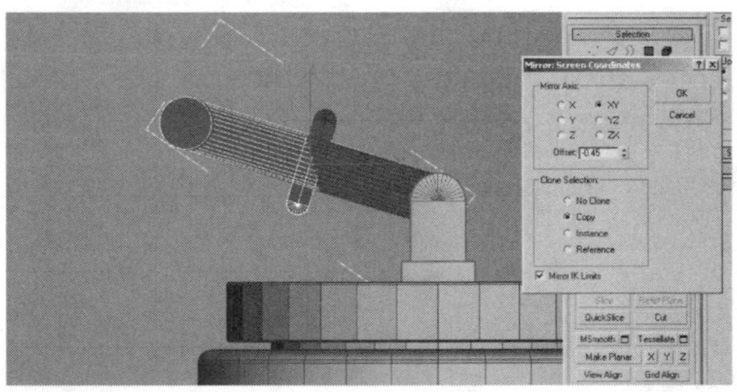

Figure 2-733

24. Move the boom in the Right, Front, and Top viewports until the two joints are superimposed.

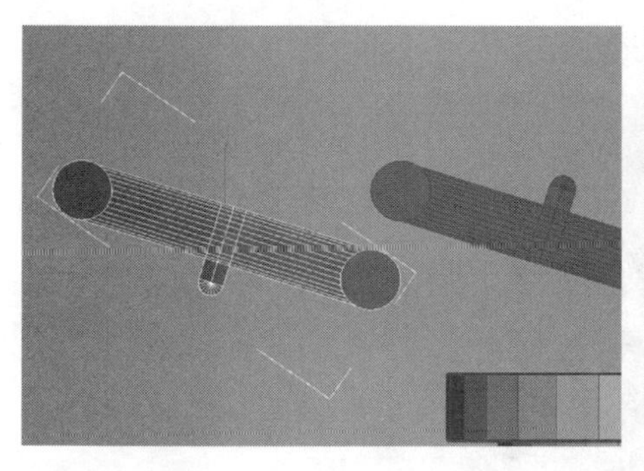

Figure 2-734

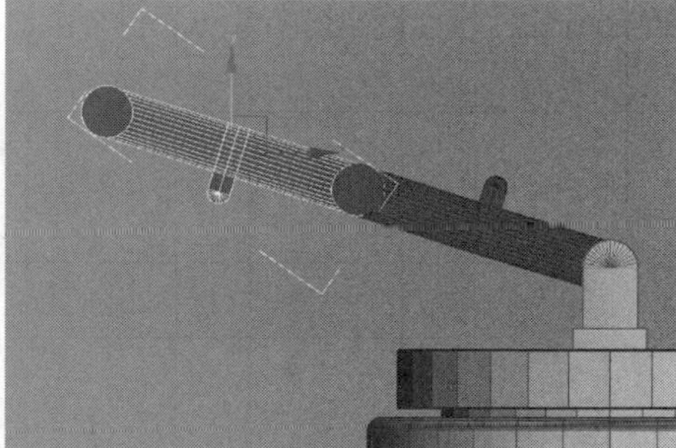

Figure 2-735

25. Rename the clone **upper_boom** and hide it.
26. Zoom in on the upper joint, select the 52 polygons shown in Figure 2-736, and then delete them.

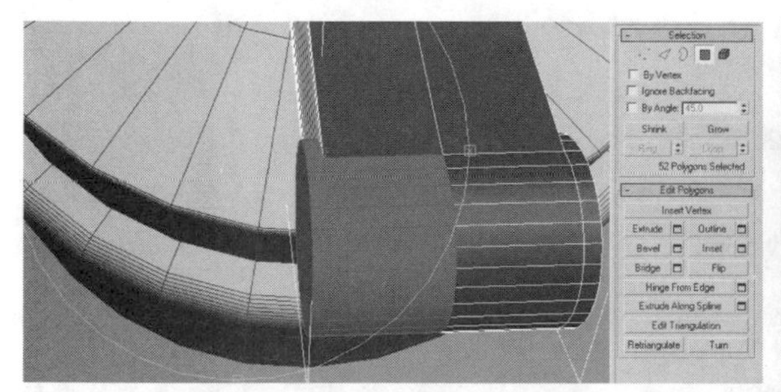

Figure 2-736

Figure 2-737

27. Switch to Polygon selection mode, click the **Create** button, and select each of the vertices clockwise until the inside of the joint has been capped.

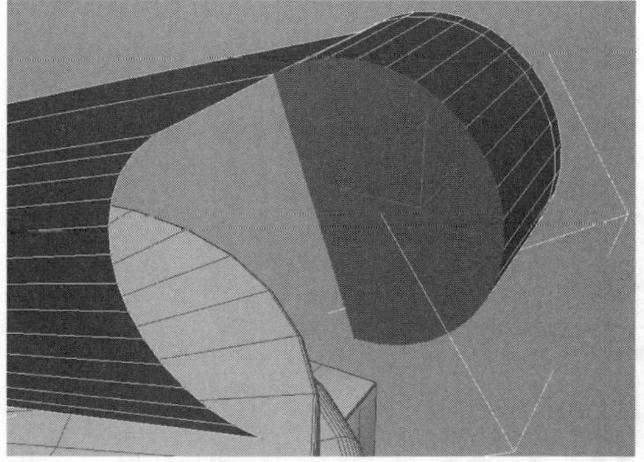

Figure 2-738

28. Bridge the upper and lower edges.

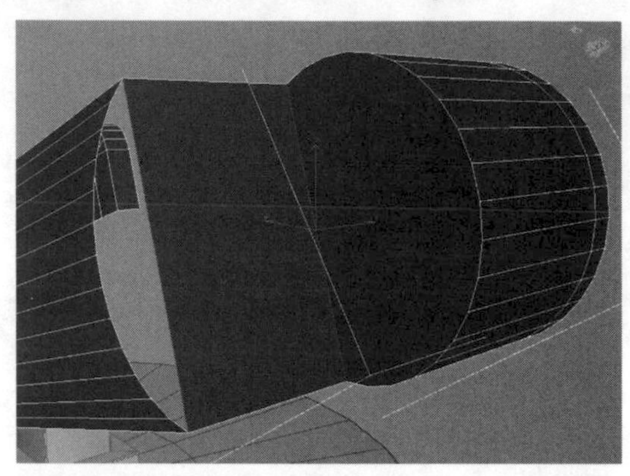

Figure 2-739

29. Select the left and right edges and then click **Connect** and enter **12** for Segments.

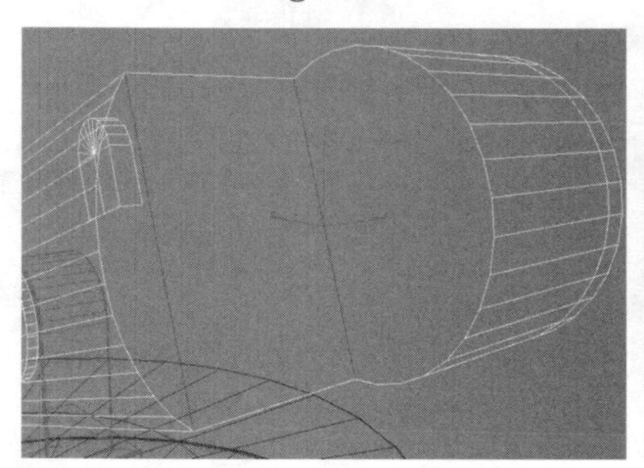

Figure 2-740

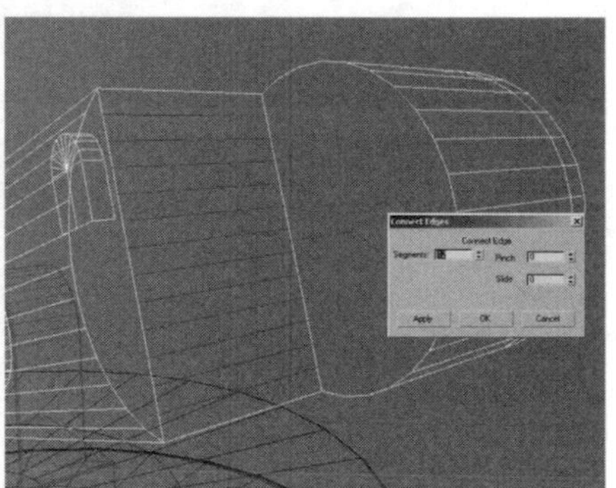

Figure 2-741

30. Select the topmost vertex on the left from the 12 segments you just created.

Figure 2-742

31. From the main menu, select **Customize**, and from the Customize menu, select **Grid and Snap Settings.**

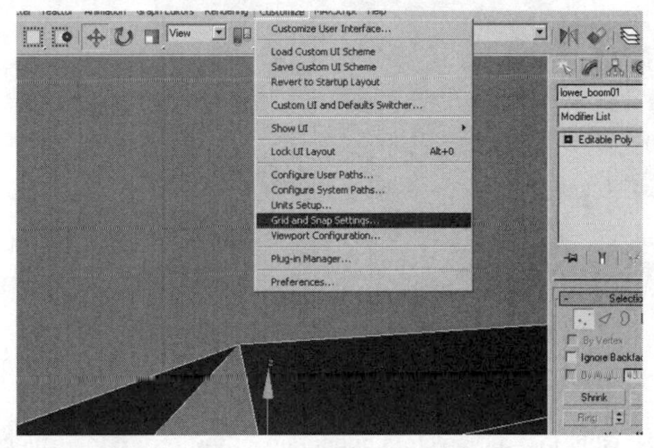

Figure 2-743

FYI: Snap allows you to very accurately align objects and subobjects. This is particularly useful when you need to superimpose objects for the purpose of welding them.

32. Make sure *only* **Vertex** is selected and close the dialog.

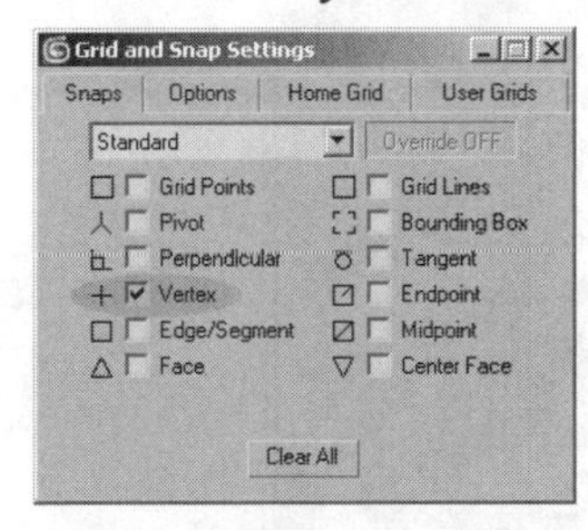

Figure 2-744

FYI: As you can see, you have a variety of snapping options available to you. You can select more than one and toggle through them using Alt+S. You might want to do that if you're a power user working on some really complex geometry. Me? I like to K.I.S.S. (Keep It Simple, Stupid). So I only turn on one snap type at a time. Personally, I find Vertex to be the most useful.

33. Select **3D Snap** from the main toolbar.

Figure 2-745

34. Select the Move tool and select the vertex you want to snap.

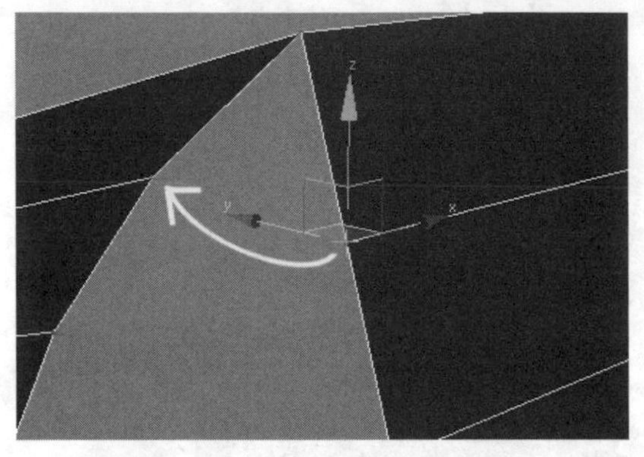

Figure 2-746

Message: Note that a cyan cross appears over the vertex, indicating that Max is ready to snap that vertex to whichever one you select.

35. Hold down the left mouse button and drag the cross until the vertex is superimposed over the one indicated by the white arrow in Figure 2-746 and release the mouse button; the vertices will snap together.

Figure 2-747

36. Select those two vertices and Weld them together.
37. Snap and Weld the remaining vertices until the gap has been closed.

Figure 2-748

FYI: What we've done here is to create a socket that the joint can turn in. Now we have to sculpt the middle verts to match the outer ones; however, since you won't really see the inner vertices, it's not essential that they be perfectly aligned.

38. Turn off Snap and use the Move tool to align the center vertices with the outer vertices; it may help to do this in the Left view in wireframe mode.

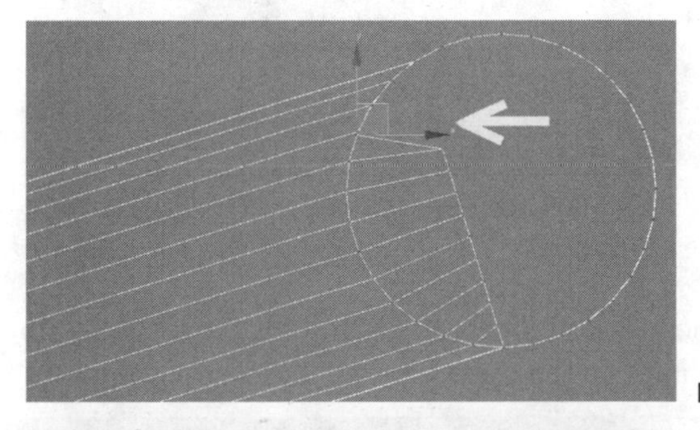

Figure 2-749

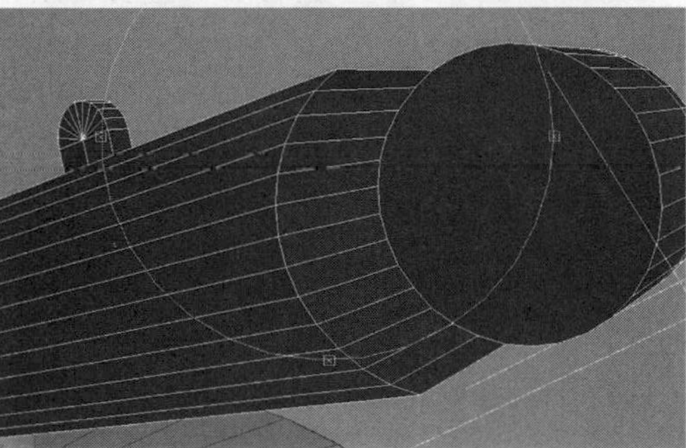

Figure 2-750

FYI: Now you can better see what we were doing in the last few steps. We now have a nicely formed socket that our upper_boom can move in.

39. Unhide the upper_boom.

Figure 2-751

Message: The booms fit together nicely. The only problem is that the right side of the upper_boom is on top of the right side of the lower_boom. Fortunately, that's easy to fix.

Figure 2-752

40. Hide the lower_boom, select all the polygons making up the duplicate right joint on the upper_boom, and delete them.

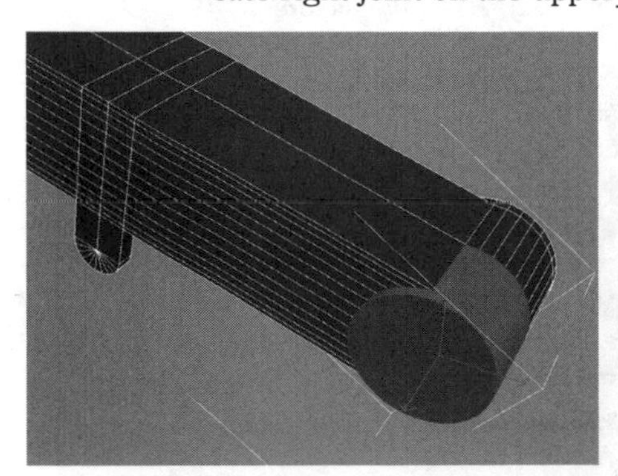

Figure 2-753

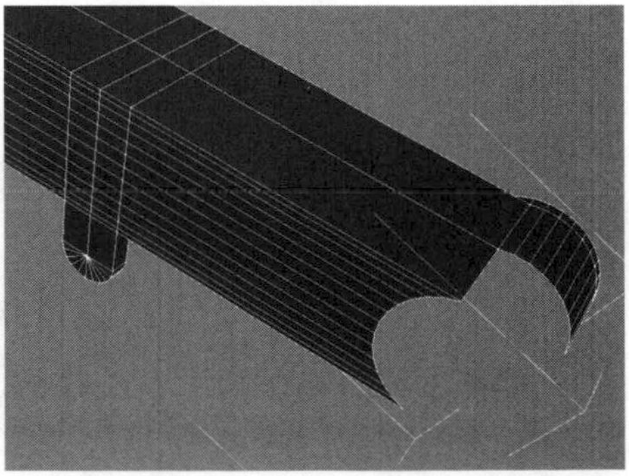

Figure 2-754

41. Repeat steps 27-38 to complete the joint.
42. Now when you unhide the lower_boom, you'll see that they fit together perfectly.

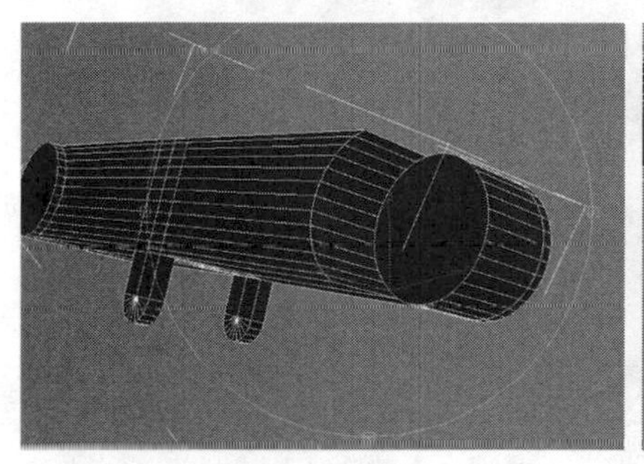
Figure 2-755

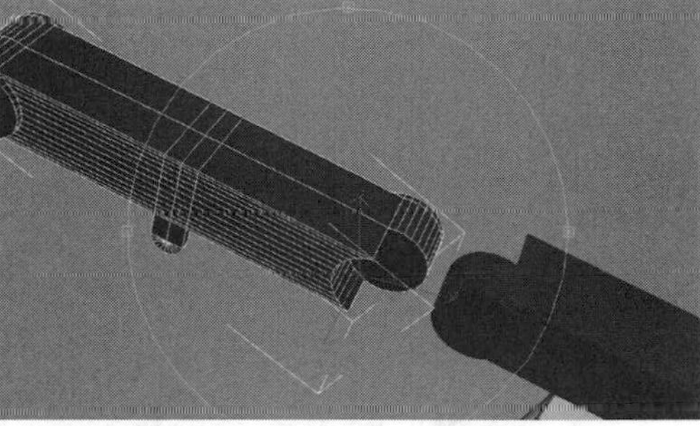
Figure 2-756

Message: Your booms should still be fitted together; I moved mine apart to show you how they fit. However, if you moved yours, move them back together now.

43. Select the polygon in the center of the lower_boom's joint.

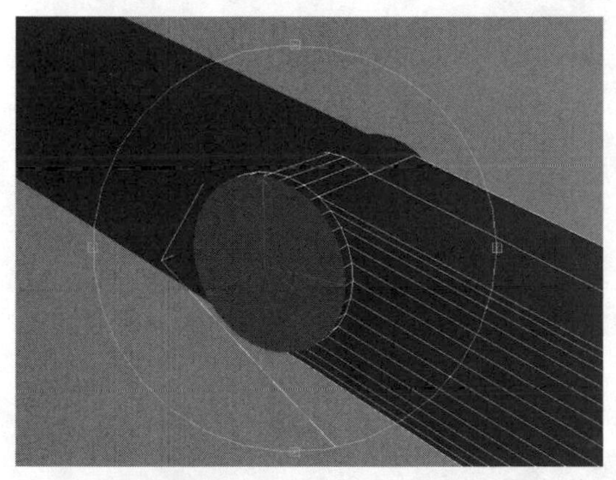
Figure 2-757

44. Click **Bevel Settings:**

Type	Height	Outline	Apply/OK
Group	0	–0.45	Apply
Group	–0.45	0	Apply

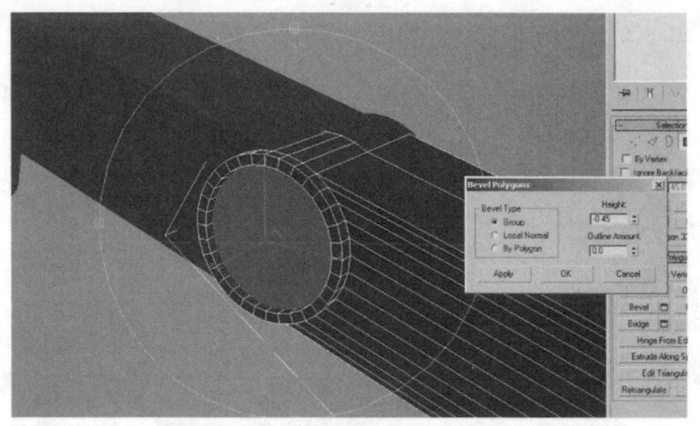

Figure 2-758

Type	Height	Outline	Apply/OK
Group	0	–0.45	Apply
Group	0.2	0	Apply

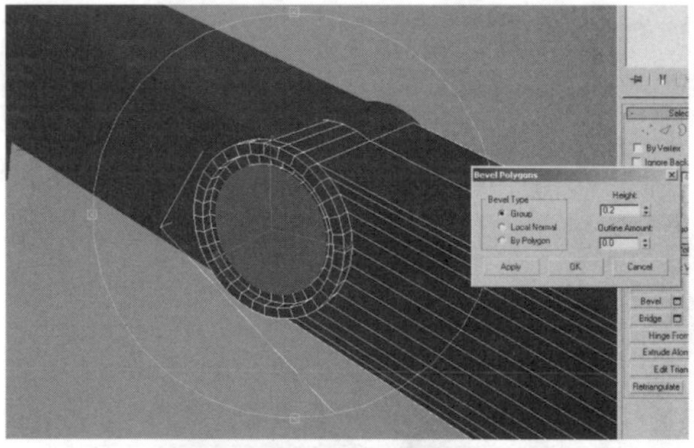

Figure 2-759

Type	Height	Outline	Apply/OK
Group	0	–0.8	Apply
Group	0.4	0	Apply

Figure 2-760

Type	Height	Outline	Apply/OK
Group	0	–0.25	Apply
Group	–0.25	0	OK

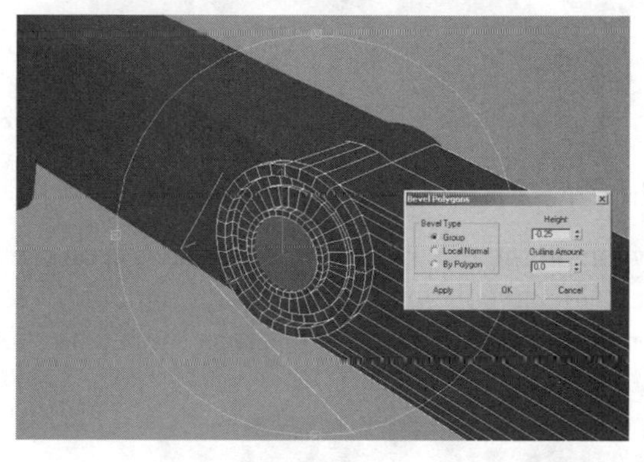

Figure 2-761

45. Apply your Clay material to the lower_boom and do a test render.

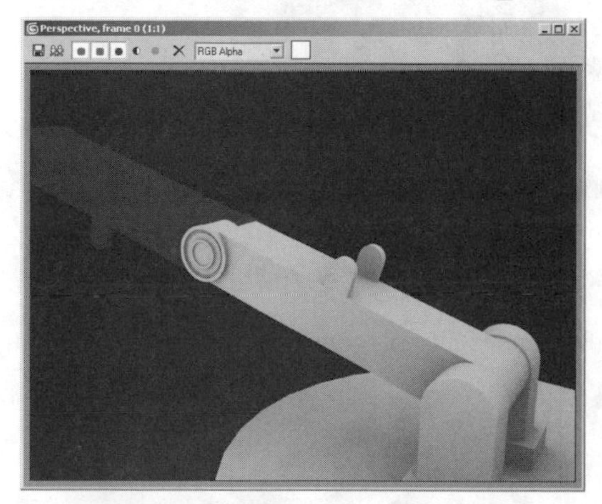

Figure 2-762

46. Using AutoGrid, create a Cylinder in the center of the joint.

Radius	Height	Height/Cap Segs	Sides	Smooth
1.3	0.25	1/1	32	Checked

Figure 2-763

47. Convert the cylinder to an Editable Polygon.
48. Pick a polygon on the top and a matching polygon on the bottom of the cylinder. Go one polygon to the left and right of these polygons and use the Cut tool to make a slice across the top as shown in Figure 2-764.

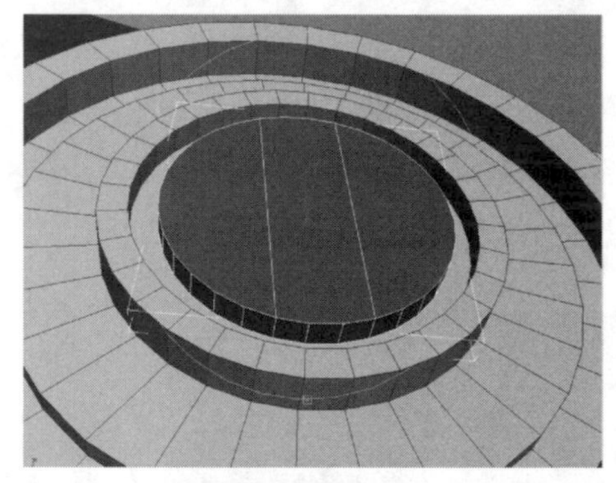
Figure 2-764

49. Select the left and right polygons created by the cuts you made.

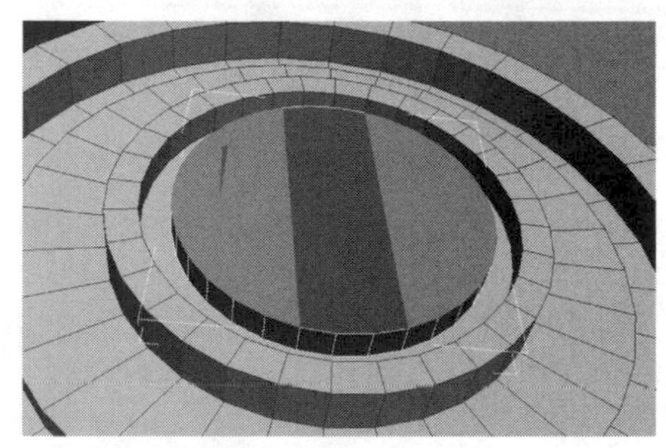
Figure 2-765

50. Click **Bevel Settings:**

Type	Height	Outline	Apply/OK
Group	0	–0.05	Apply
Group	0.3	0	OK

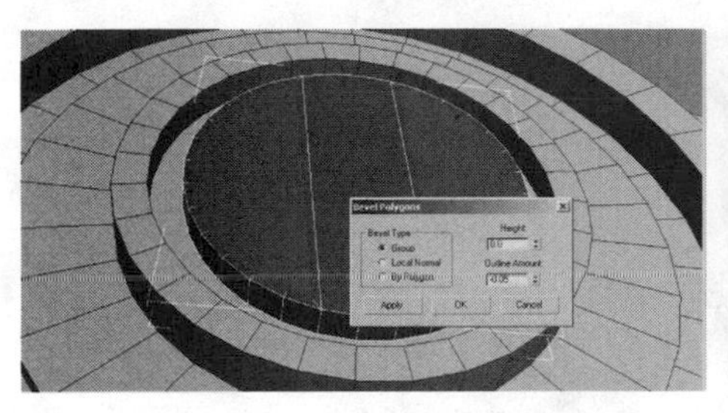

Figure 2-766

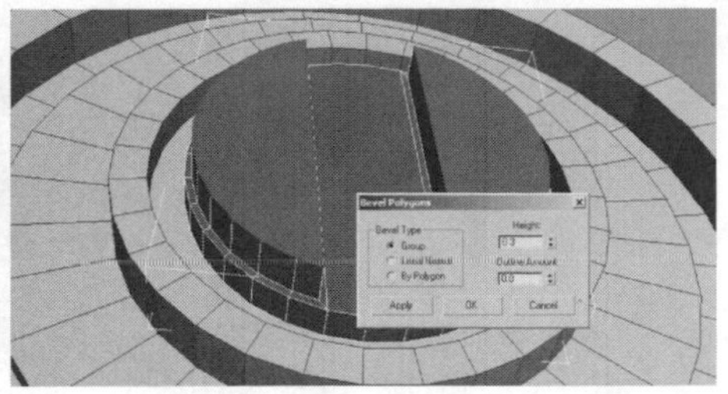

Figure 2-767

51. Rotate around the back of the screw you've just created, delete the back-facing polygon, add the Clay material to the screw, and Select and Link it to the lower_boom.

52. Do a test render.

Figure 2-768

53. Switch to the Right view and zoom in on the joint.

54. Using AutoGrid, create a Gengon on the lip next to the screw.

Sides	Radius	Fillet	Height	Side/Height/Fillet Segs	Smooth
6	0.25	0	0.15	1/1/1	Unchecked

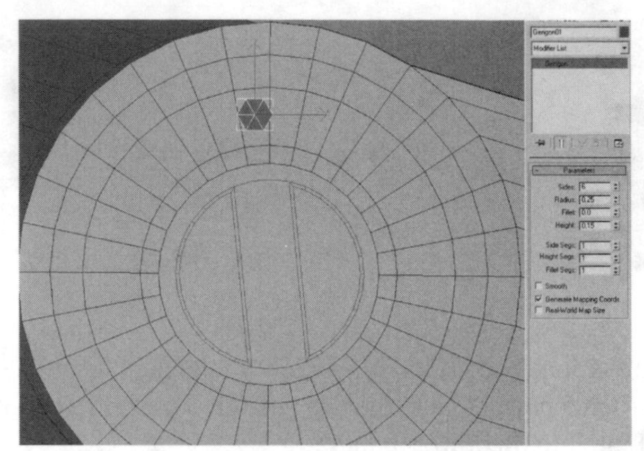

Figure 2-769

55. Convert the gengon to an Editable Polygon, delete the back-facing polygons, and move the gengon's pivot to the center of the joint.

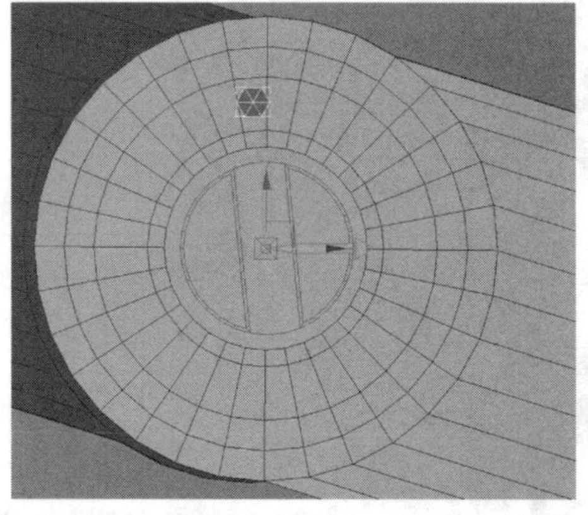
Figure 2-770

56. Add the Clay material to the gengon, turn on Angle Snap, hold down the **Shift** key, Rotate **60** degrees, and enter **5** for the Number of Copies.

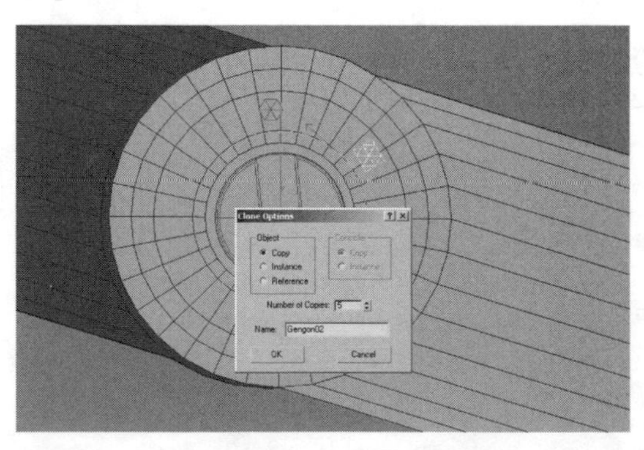

Figure 2-771

57. Select and Link the gengons to the joint and do a test render.

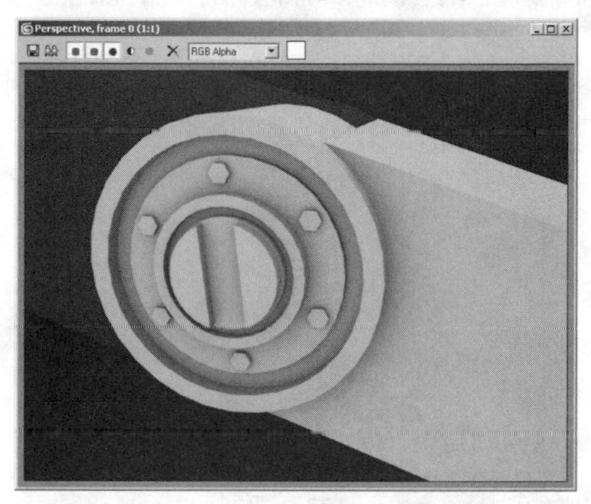

Figure 2-772

Message: Notice how simply applying gengons (nuts) and a screw can make something look mechanical.

58. Repeat steps 26-57 for the mating joint on the upper_boom.
59. Select the screw (cylinder) and nuts (gengons) and, in the Top view, move their pivots to the middle of the boom.

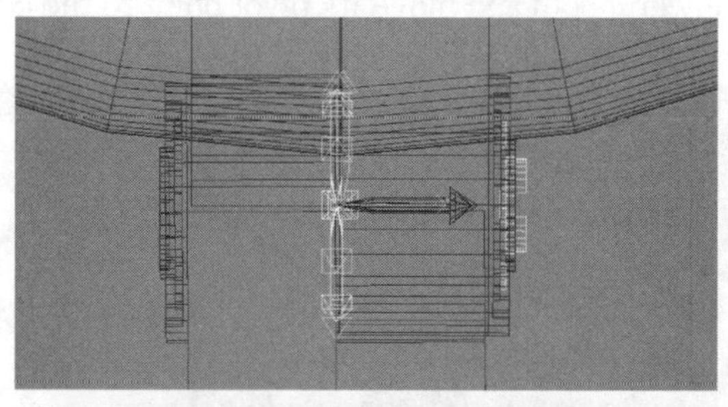

Figure 2-773

60. Click **Mirror** and copy them in the X axis.

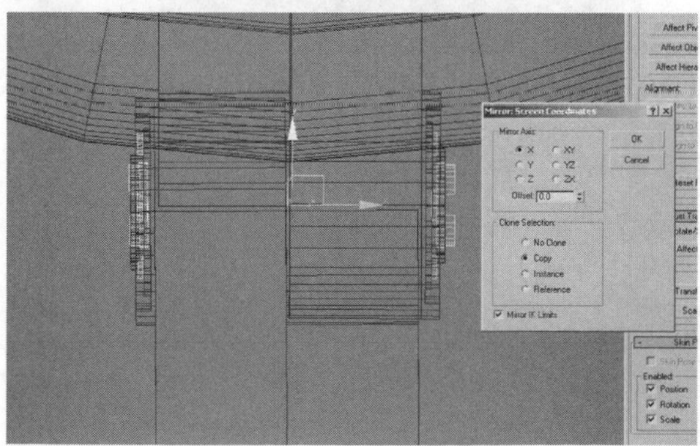

Figure 2-774

Fire Drill: Double-check the Left view to make sure the nuts and screw are properly aligned on the left side. You can think you have everything perfectly aligned and then find you don't. If they aren't aligned properly, just use the Move tool to position them before you Select and Link.

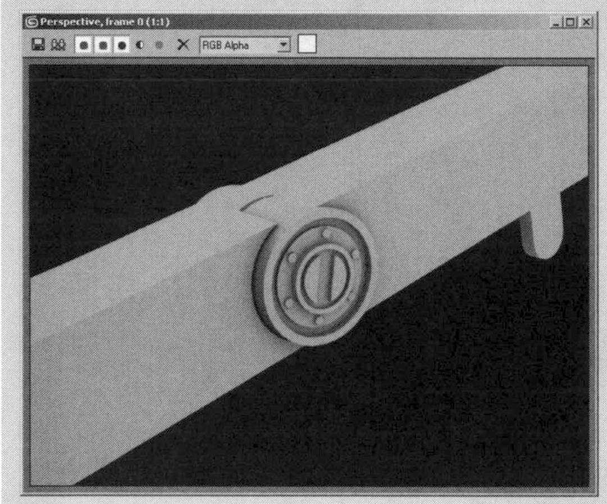

Figure 2-775

61. Select and Link the upper_boom to the lower_boom, Select and Link the lower_boom to the boom_mounts, and Select and Link the boom_mounts to the main_turret.

62. Select the lower_boom and move its pivot point to the center of the joint, beneath the mount.

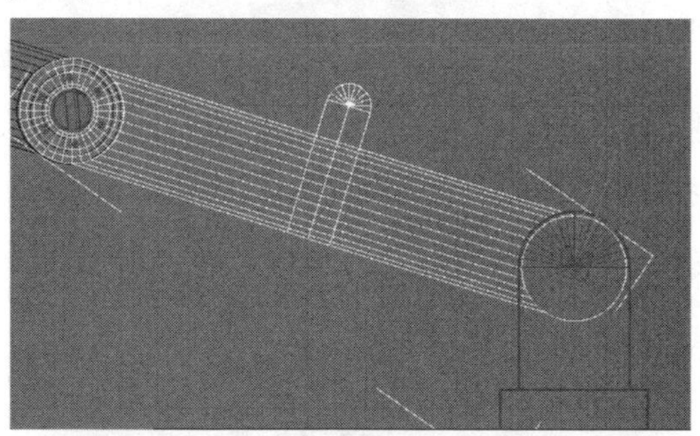

Figure 2-776

63. Select the upper_boom and move its pivot to the center of the joint.

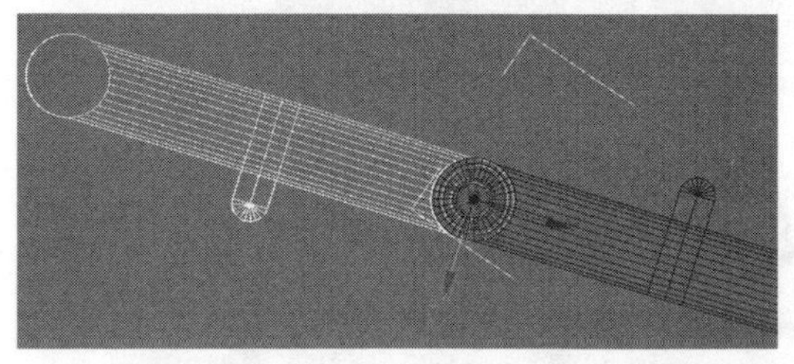

Figure 2-777

64. Polygon-select the mounts on top of the lower_boom.

Figure 2-778

65. Click **Detach As Clone.**

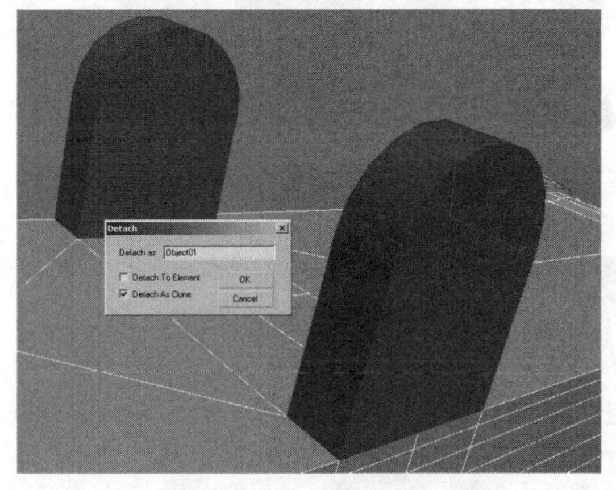

Figure 2-779

66. Click **Affect Pivot Only** and center to the object.

67. Switch to the Local coordinate system, click **Mirror**, mirror in the Y axis, choose **No Clone**, and use an offset value that gets the mount close to the bottom edge of the boom (e.g., **–10.27**).

FYI: No Clone is selected here because we merely want to flip the axis of the mounts without making a copy. We already made a copy with the Detach procedure.

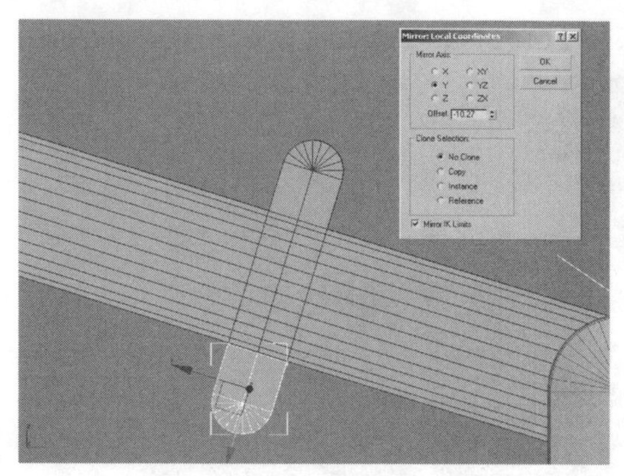

Figure 2-780

68. Edge-select the seam between the mounts, on the underside of the lower_boom.

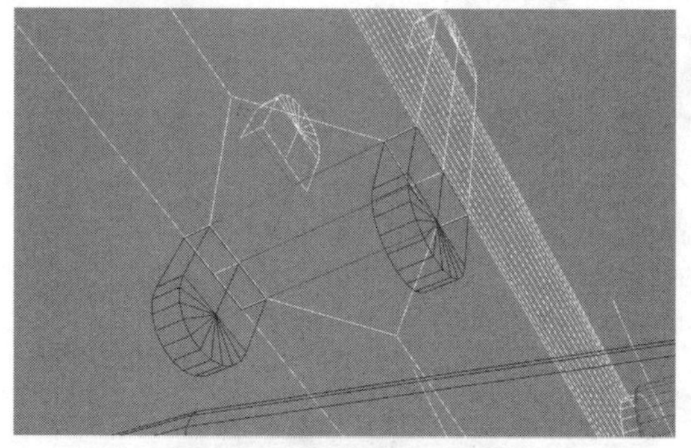

Figure 2-781

69. Chamfer the edge by **3.0**.

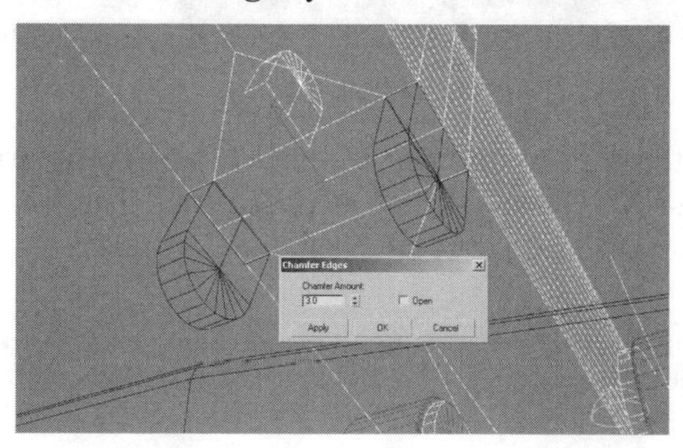

Figure 2-782

70. Select the three edges and click **Connect**, then highlight the polygons created by the chamfering and delete them.

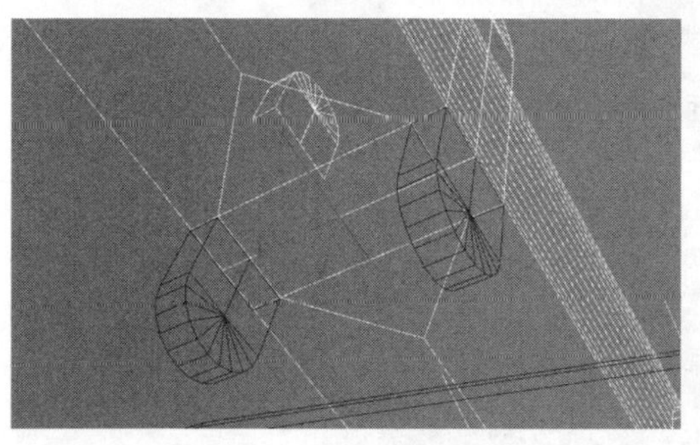

Figure 2-783

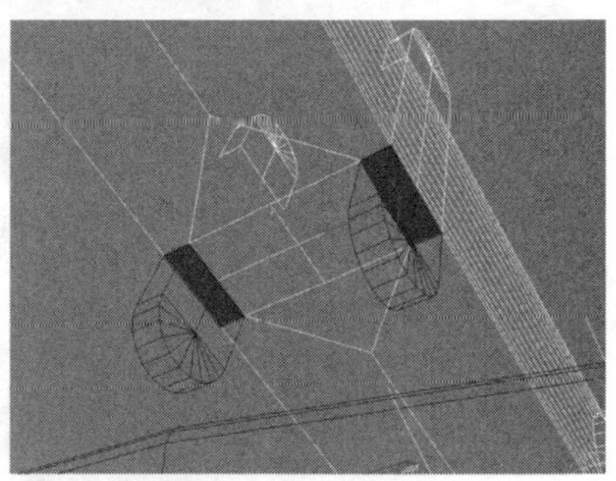

Figure 2-784

71. Attach the mounts to the lower_boom, select the vertices where the mount connects to the boom, and Weld them together.

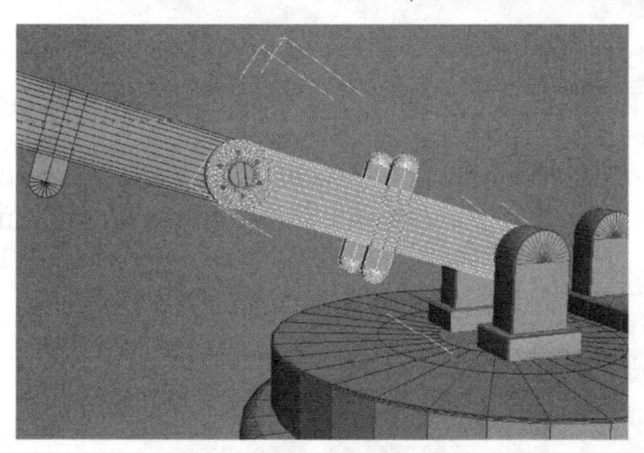

Figure 2-785

Day 15: Building the Hydraulics

1. Switch to the Bottom view and hide everything but the upper and lower booms.

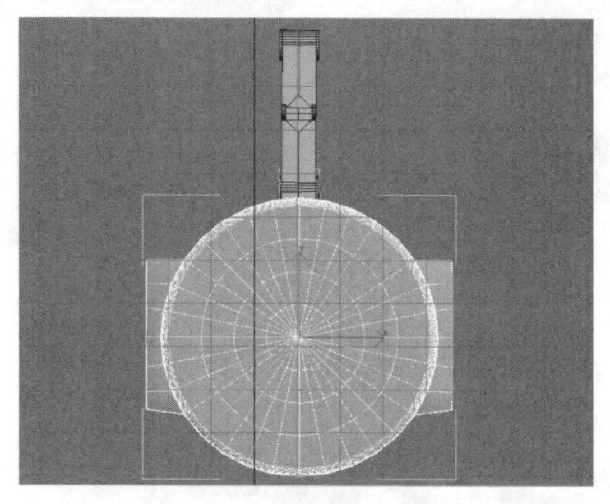

Figure 2-786

2. Using AutoGrid, create a Sphere with a Radius of **1.8** and **32** Segments between the hydraulic mounts on the lower_boom.

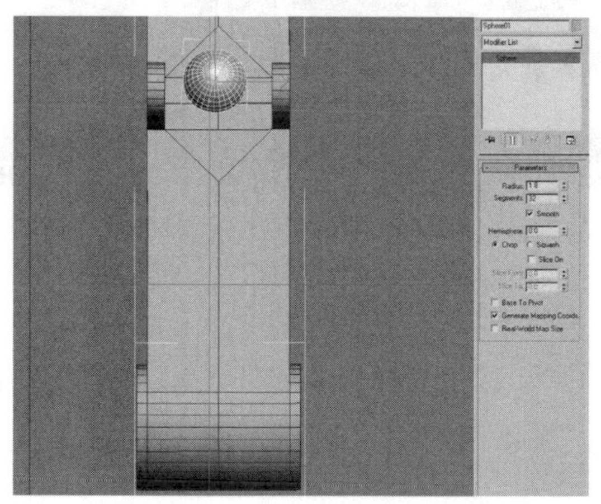

Figure 2-787

3. Move the sphere up and Rotate it **90** degrees in the Y axis, so that the poles of the sphere are facing the mounts.

Figure 2-788

4. Change the sphere's Hemisphere value to **0.5**.

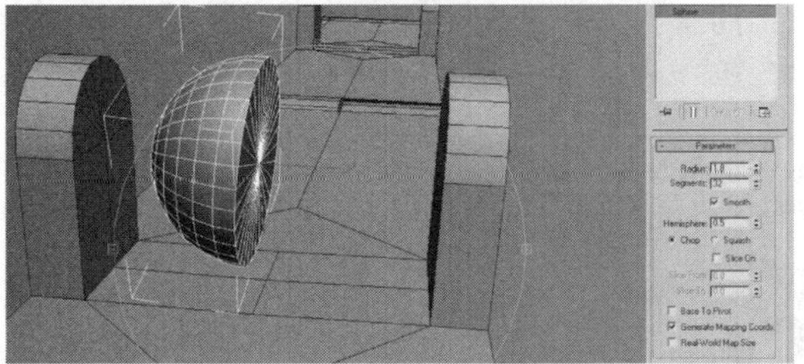

Figure 2-789

5. Convert the sphere to an Editable Polygon, delete the back-facing polys, and add a Symmetry modifier to the stack.

Figure 2-790

FYI: So why didn't I just leave it whole in the first place? Because I'll be creating axles out of the sides of the sphere. This way, I only have to do it on one side.

6. Select the first four rings of polygons (128 total).

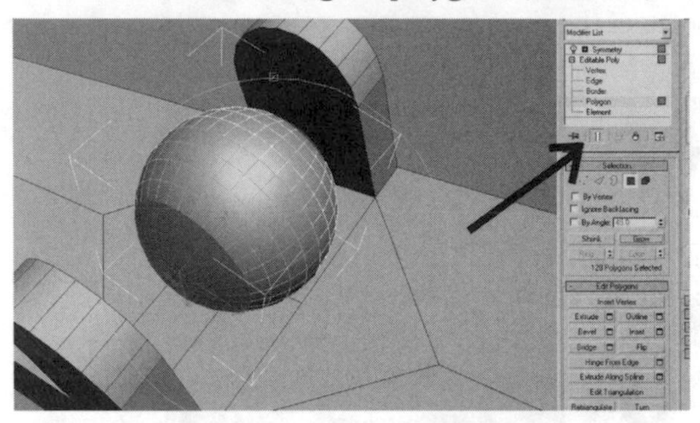

Figure 2-791

Don't Forget: To subjobject-select (polygon-select) when you've applied a modifier, you have to open up the Editable Poly rollout beneath the modifier. Also, Max does not automatically show you the results of modifiers. You have to press the little test tube icon the arrow is pointing to in Figure 2-791.

7. Delete the selected polygons and cap the border.

Figure 2-792

8. Click **Bevel Settings:**

Type	Height	Outline	Apply/OK
Group	0	–0.15	Apply
Group	–0.1	0	Apply
Group	0	–0.05	Apply
Group	1.8	0	OK

Day 15: Building the Hydraulics

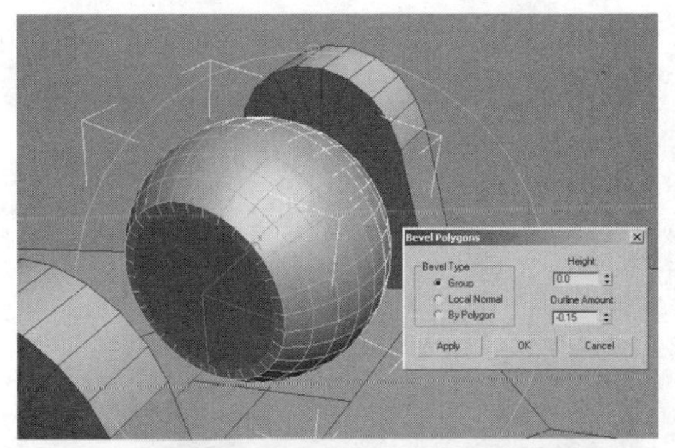

Figure 2-793

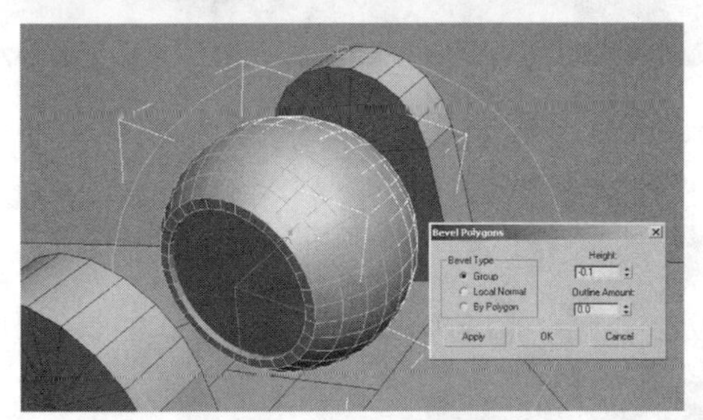

Figure 2-794

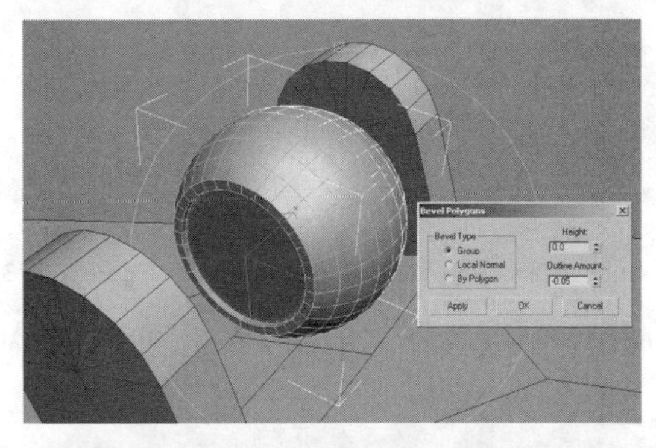

Figure 2-795

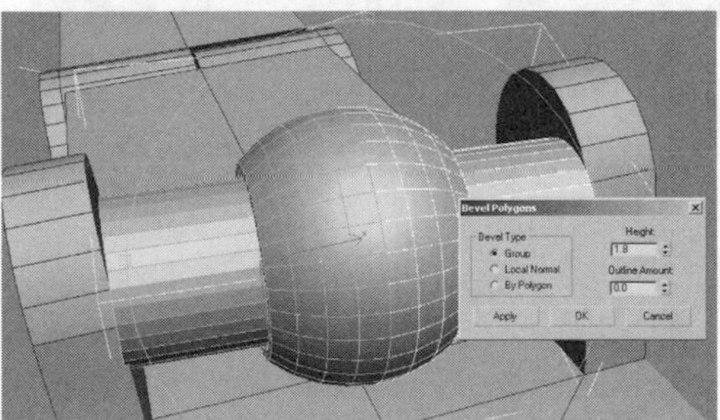

Figure 2-796

9. Use the Rotate tool to straighten the joint so that it is properly positioned between the mounts.

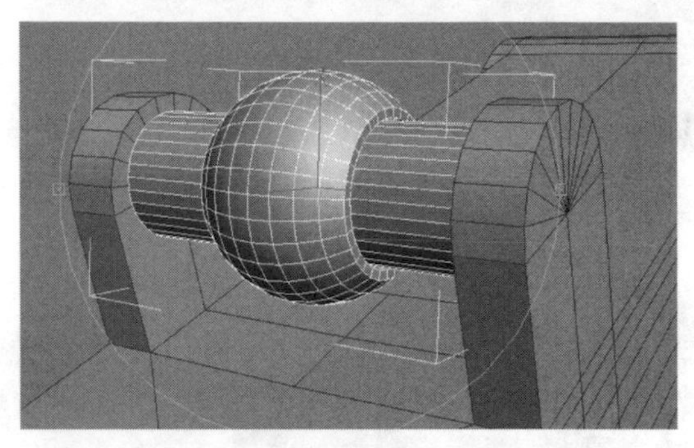

Figure 2-797

10. Do a test render.

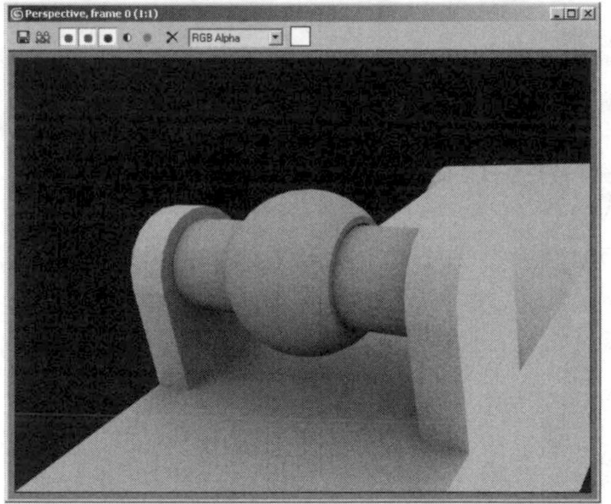

Figure 2-798

11. Add a Smooth modifier to the top of the stack and click **Auto Smooth**.

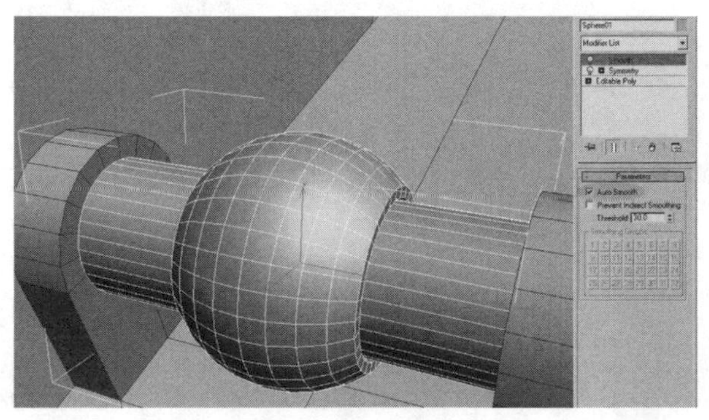

Figure 2-799

12. Switch to the wireframe mode. Select the end polygon and delete it (it'll be automatically deleted from the other side).

Figure 2-800

13. Switch to the Bottom view, hold down the **Shift** key, and move the axle to the upper mount to make a clone.

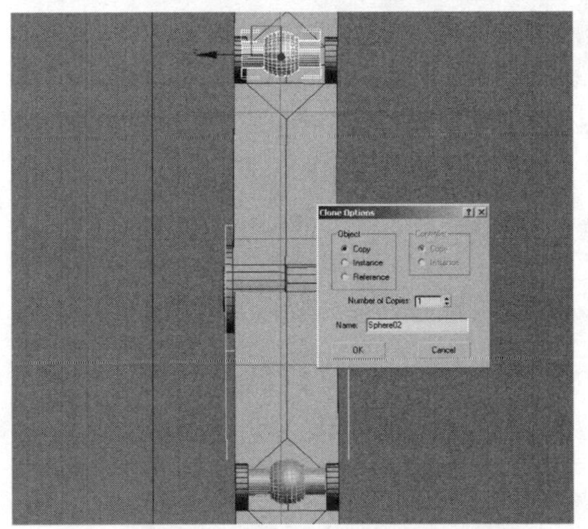

Figure 2-801

14. Arc Rotate and orient the axle between the mounts.

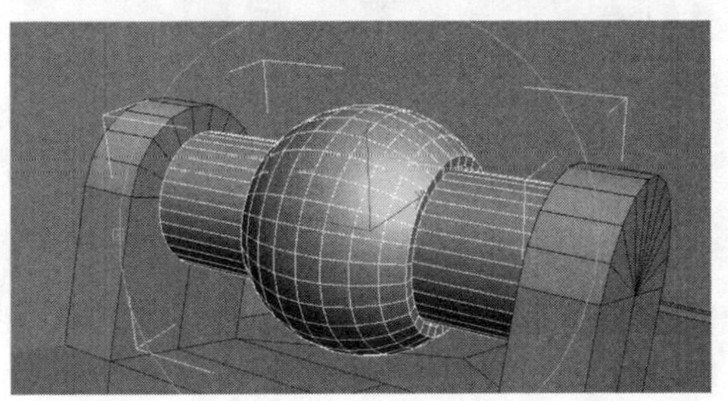

Figure 2-802

15. Select the six by six block of polygons in the center of the axle.

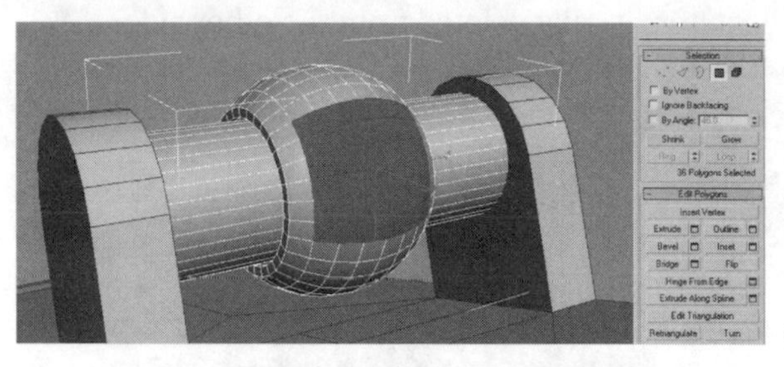

Figure 2-803

16. Group Extrude the polygons by **0.3**.

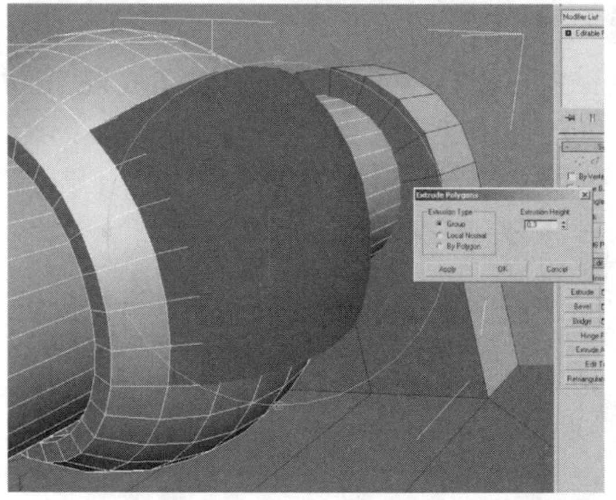

Figure 2-804

17. Scale the polygons down to **0** in the Local Z axis to flatten them.

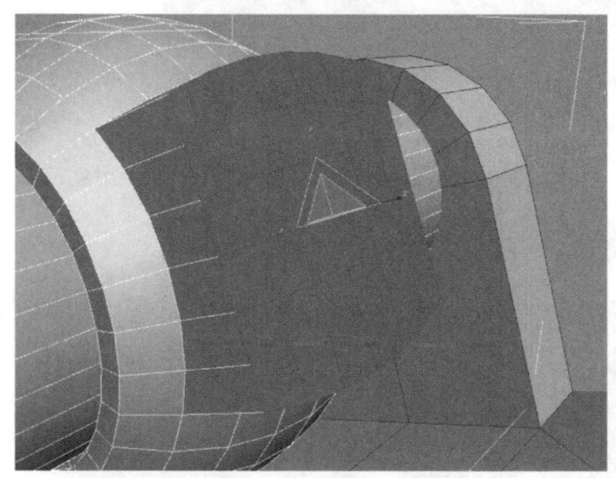

Figure 2-805

18. Select the top row of seven vertices and scale them down to **0** in the Local Y axis to flatten them. Repeat for the bottom seven. Repeat this for all the polygons (scaling in X, Y, or Z) until you get a flat surface with roughly flat tops and sides.

Message: Don't sweat trying to make them ruler straight. Just get them as close as you can without spending hours on it. After all, nothing manufactured is perfectly straight. Look at the things around you. They have bumps, and dents, and warps. The more perfect you make your geometry the *less* real it will look. For example, mine has a slight twist to it and I like that. It makes it look like the metal was poorly tempered.

Figure 2-806

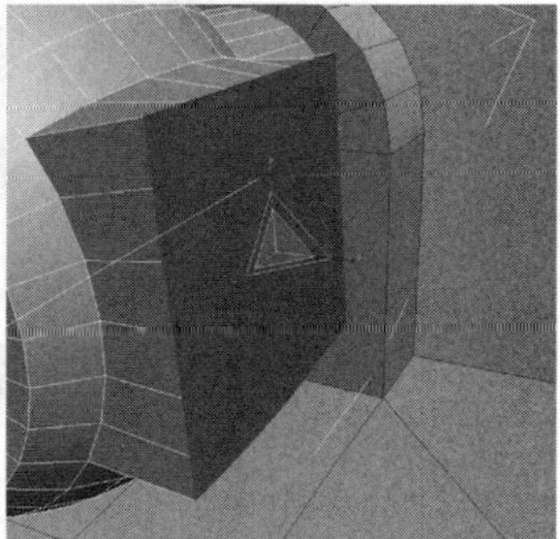

Figure 2-807

19. Select the front polygons and click **Bevel Settings**:

Type	Height	Outline	Apply/OK
Group	0	0.75	Apply
Group	0.15	0	OK

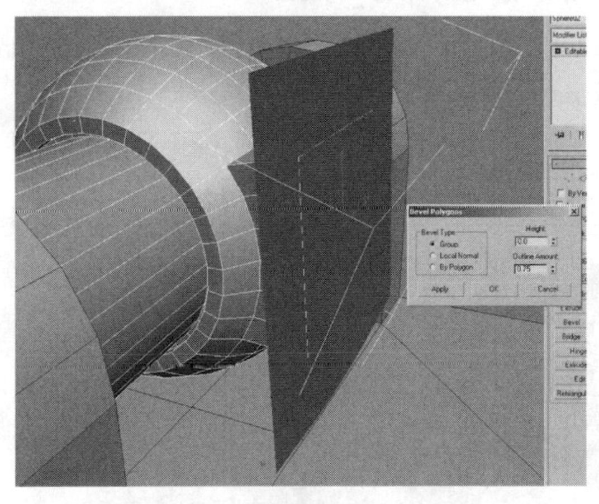

Figure 2-808

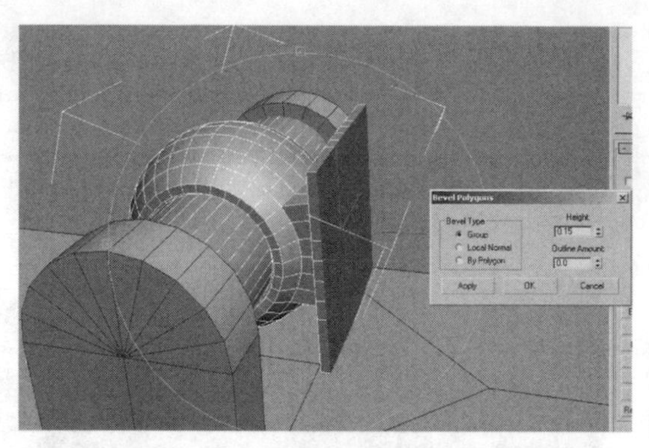

Figure 2-809

20. Delete the selected polygons and Cap the border.

Figure 2-810

21. Select and Link to the lower_boom.
22. Using AutoGrid, create a Cylinder in the center of the plate you just made.

Radius	Height	Height/Cap Segs	Sides	Smooth
1.3	12.6	1/1	32	Checked

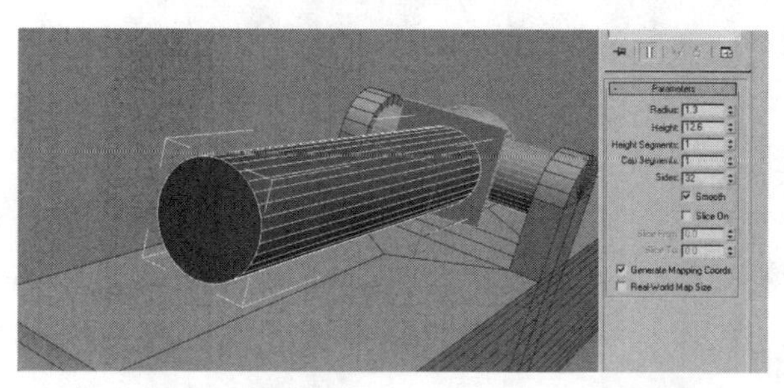

Figure 2-811

23. Convert the cylinder to an Editable Polygon, select and delete the polygon facing the plate, and Attach the cylinder to the plate.

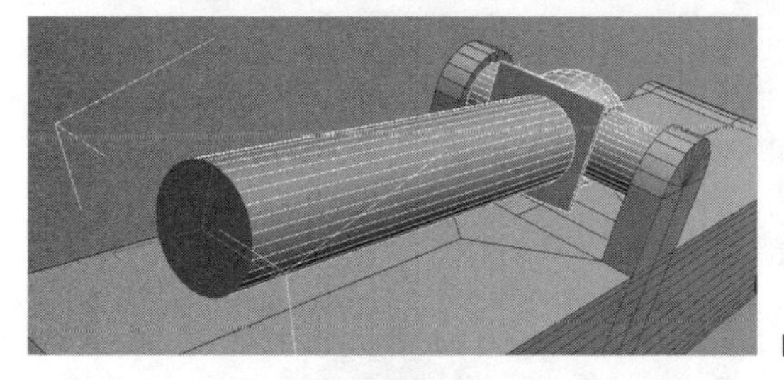

Figure 2-812

24. Select the front polygon and click **Bevel Settings**:

Type	Height	Outline	Apply/OK
Group	0	–0.3	Apply
Group	–10	0	OK

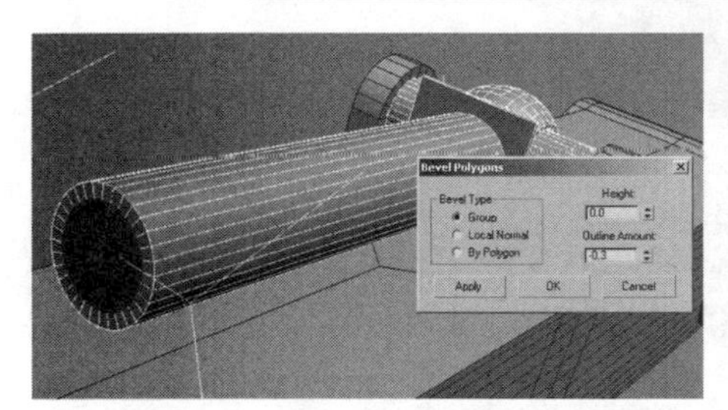

Figure 2-813

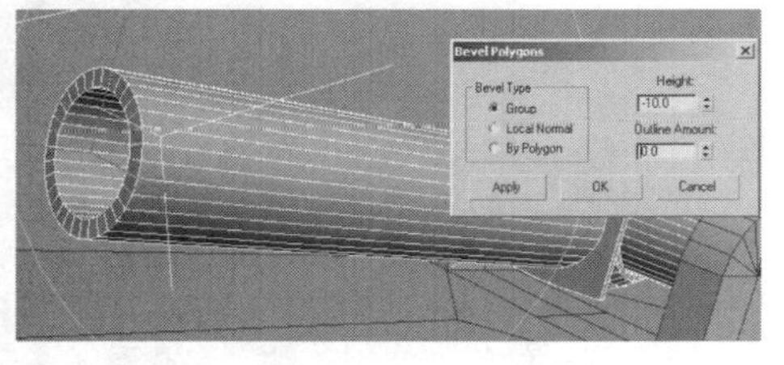

Figure 2-814

25. Although you can't see it, the polygon is still selected; click **Detach** to detach it as an object, and name the new object **piston_rod**.

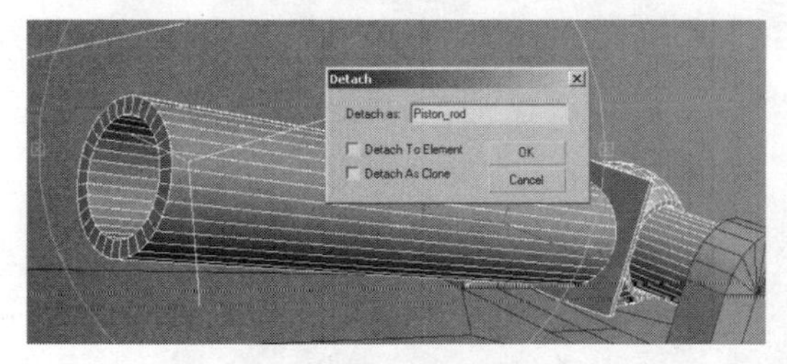

Figure 2-815

26. Switch to the Bottom view and move the piston_rod around **31** in the Y axis, until it is against the upper axle.

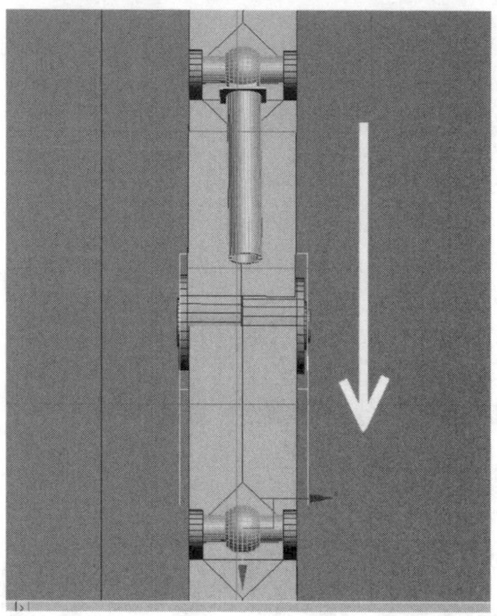

Figure 2-816

Message: The normal will be flipped away from you, making it invisible. Nice, huh? However, since your Move gizmo is attached to the object, you can use the gizmo to make your best guess. At this point, you don't need to be dead on anyway.

27. With the piston_rod polygon selected, click **Flip** to flip the normal, so that the normal is facing toward the piston; now you should see it with no problem.

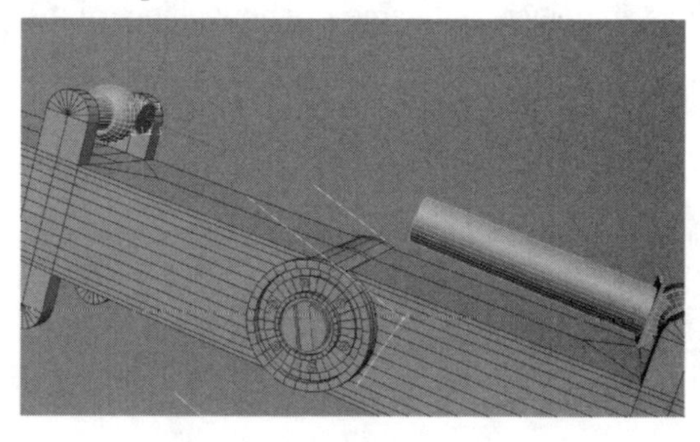

Figure 2-817

28. Extrude the piston_rod polygon until it is a little over the center of the piston (~**28**).

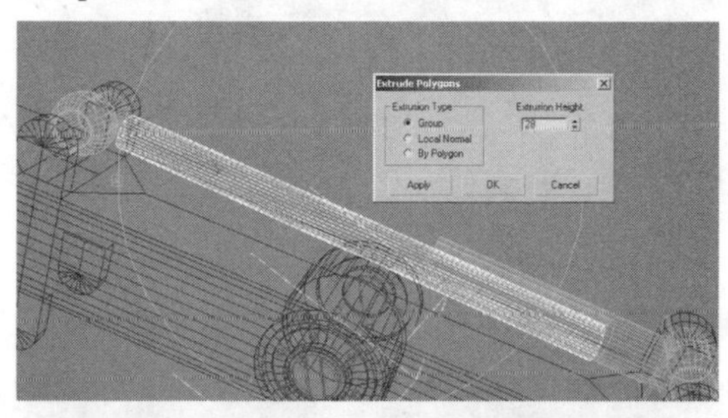

Figure 2-818

Figure 2-819

29. Click **Affect Pivot Only** and use the Rotate and Move tools to position the pivot at the end of the cylinder.

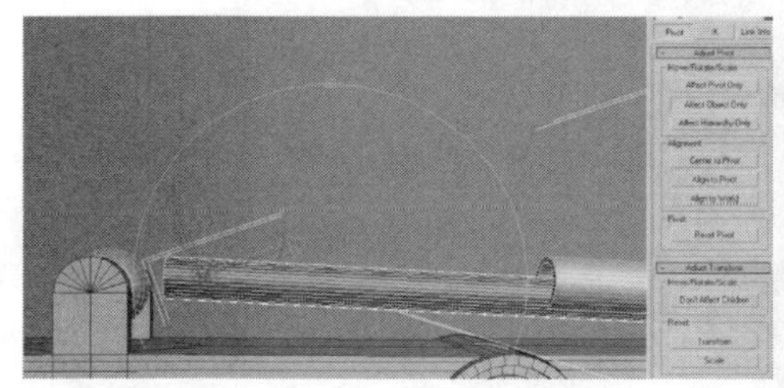

Figure 2-820

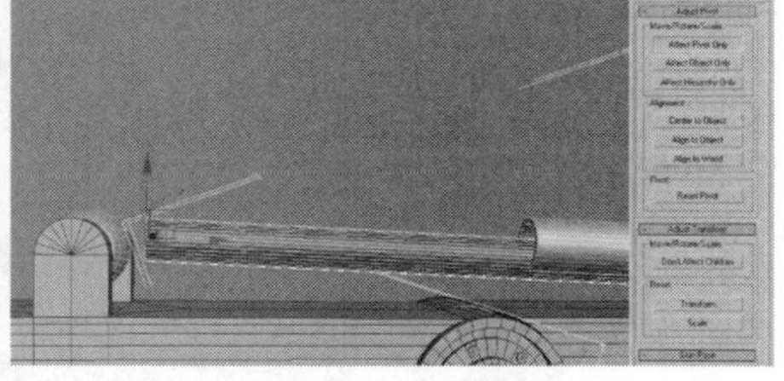

Figure 2-821

30. Rotate the cylinder so it fits into the piston.

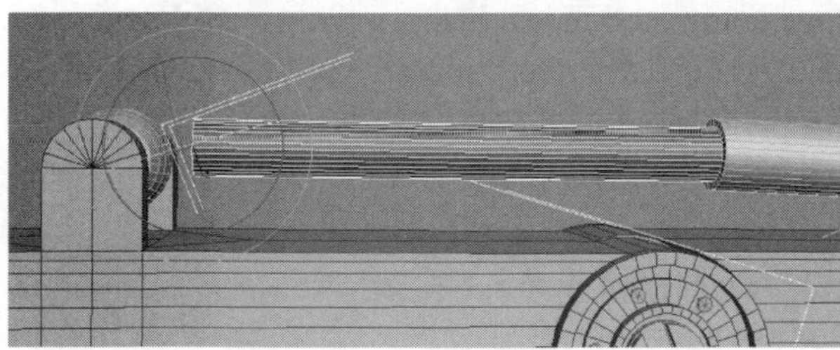

Figure 2-822

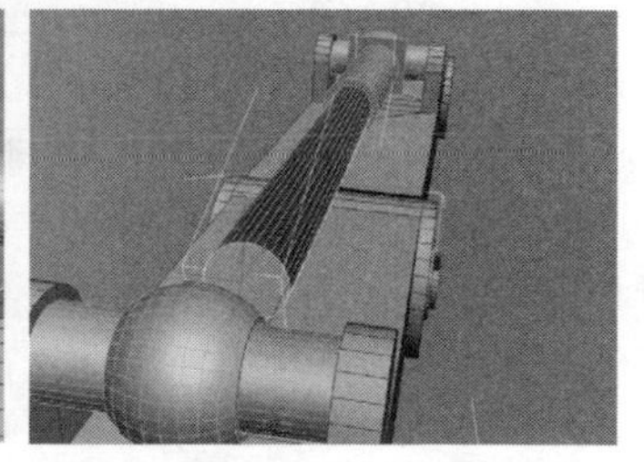

Figure 2-823

31. Align the rod so it fits into the piston.

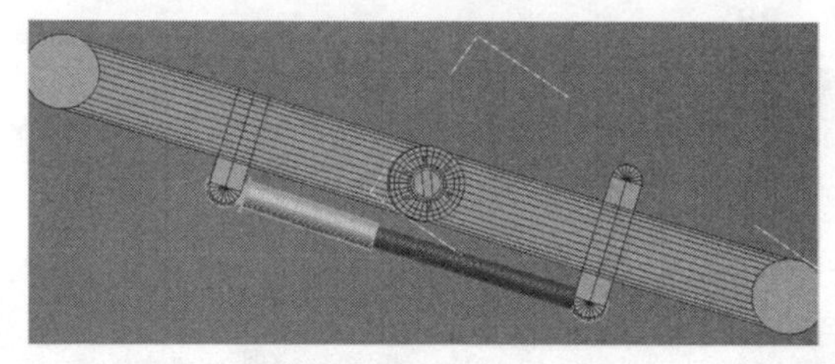

Figure 2-824

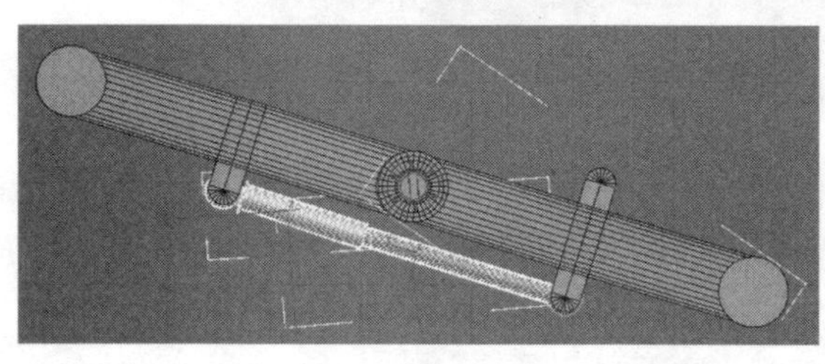

Figure 2-825

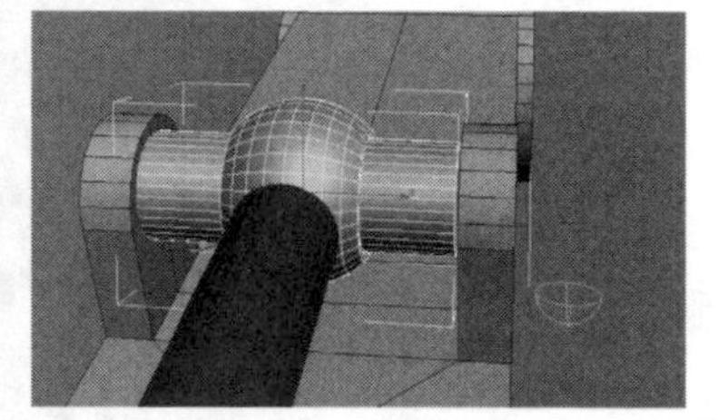

Figure 2-826

32. Under the Create panel, select **Compound Objects**, select **Boolean**, select **Union** as the Operation, click **Pick Operand B**, and click **piston_rod**.

Figure 2-827

33. Change the renamed compound object back to **piston_rod**, convert it to an Editable Polygon, add a Smooth modifier to the stack, click **Auto Smooth**, and then convert it to an Editable Polygon to collapse the stack.

34. Under the Hierarchy tab, click **Affect Pivot Only**, then make sure that the pivot is properly centered on the joint with the Y axis pointing straight at the other joint.

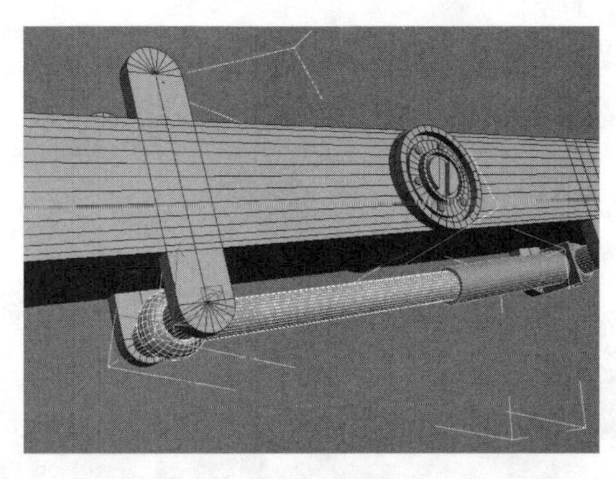
Figure 2-828

35. Repeat the previous step for the other joint, making sure its pivot is properly aligned and facing the other joint.

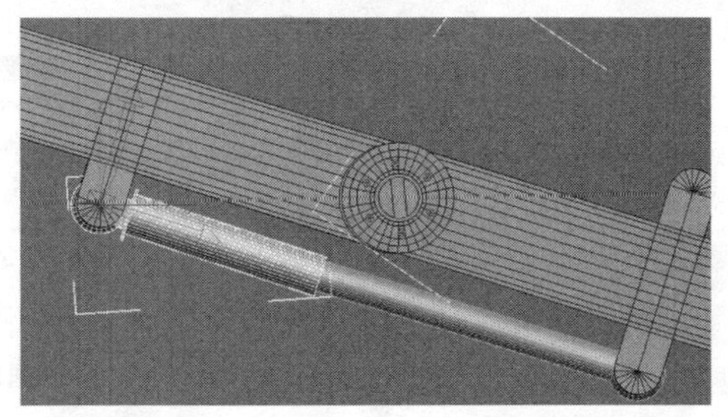
Figure 2-829

FYI: To properly link these two parts so they move together, their pivots have to be facing each other. Now comes the fun part — the linking.

36. On the Control panel, click the icon that looks like a tape measure (**Helpers**), click the **Dummy** button, and then create a dummy on the lower mount.

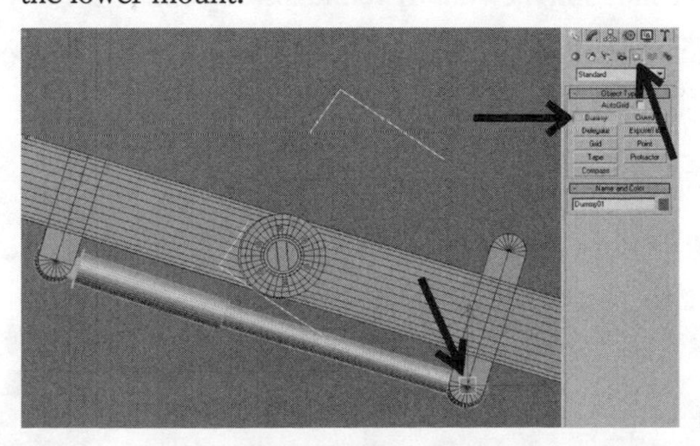
Figure 2-830

FYI: A dummy is an object that does not render. You can use a dummy for a variety of purposes, but in this instance we'll be using it to align the two parts of the hydraulic piston.

37. Position the dummy in the center of the lower joint.

Figure 2-831

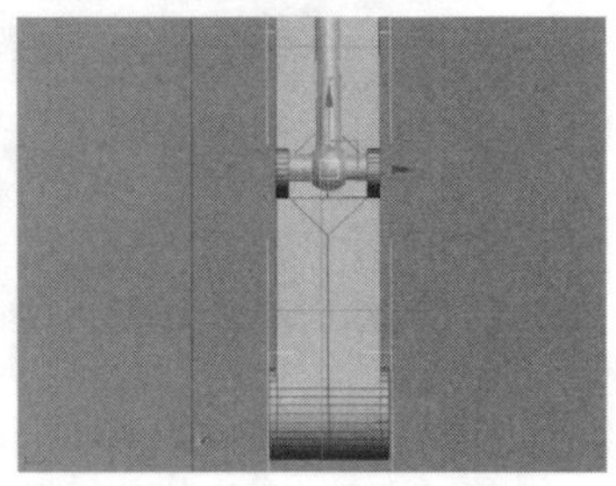

Figure 2-832

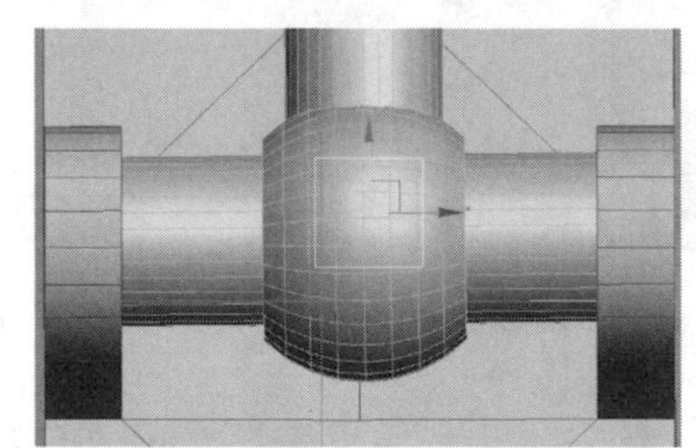

Figure 2-833

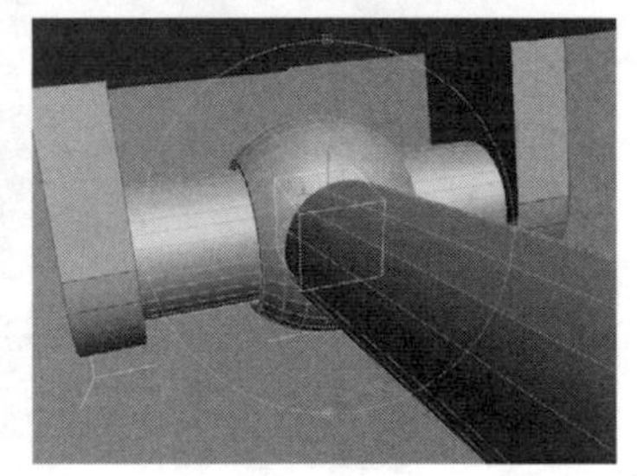

Figure 2-834

FYI: When orienting a dummy object, it is often very helpful to use the Align to Object feature (icon to the right of the Mirror Geometry button) and align the object to the target object's pivot point (which in this case is the axle).

38. Select and Link the dummy to the lower_boom.
39. Select the upper part of the piston and click on the **Motion** tab (looks like a wheel) on the Create panel.

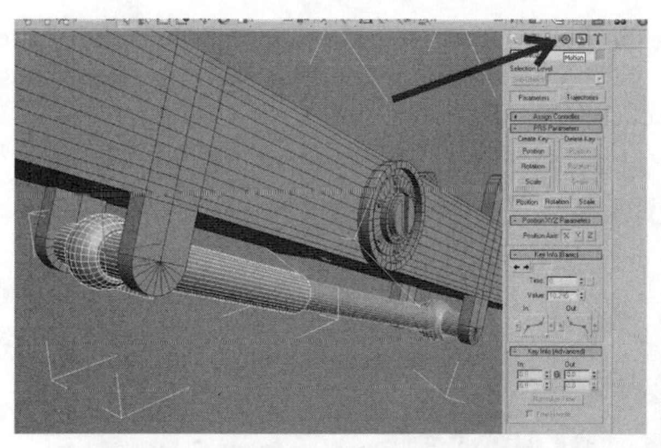

Figure 2-835

40. Click the **Assign Controller** rollout and then click **Rotation**.

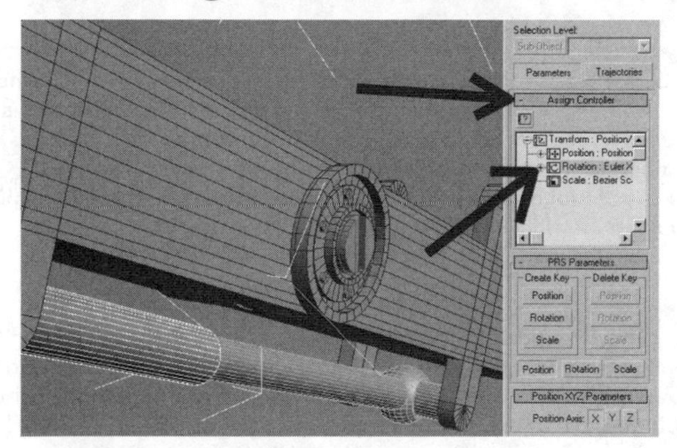

Figure 2-836

FYI: Controllers govern an object's motion, scale, or rotation. In our case, we want to control the rotation of the upper part of the piston when we rotate the upper_boom by constraining the movement of the upper part to the movement of the lower part of the piston.

41. Click the **Assign Controller** button (its icon is the ? button) to open the Assign Rotation Controller dialog, pick **LookAt Constraint**, and then click **OK.**

Figure 2-837

FYI: The LookAt constraint does what it says; it constrains the movement of an object so it is always oriented toward the target. This constraint is generally used in conjunction with eyes and a dummy object. The eyes are constrained to the dummy object, and moving the dummy object causes the eyes to follow. However, this constraint is also extremely valuable for making interlocking parts like pistons.

Don't Forget: The parts of the pistons have to be Select and Linked to their respective booms; otherwise, when you move the boom, the piston won't follow. The LookAt constraint only makes sure the two parts of the pistons look at each other.

42. Under the LookAt Constraint rollout, click **Add LookAt Target** (and nothing seems to happen). Hit the **H** key to open the Pick Object list, pick the dummy object (**Dummy01**), and then click the **Pick** button.

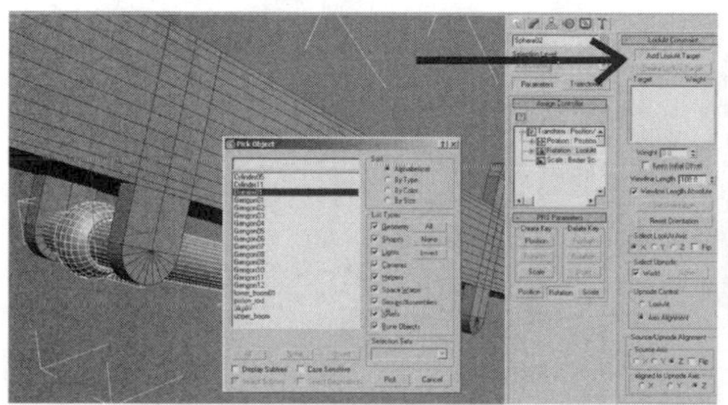

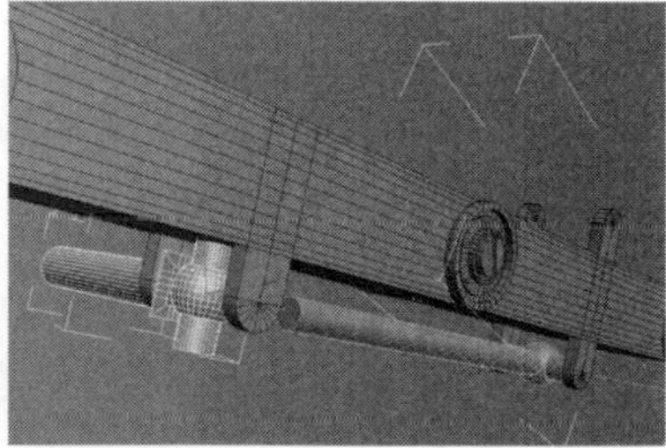

Figure 2-839

Figure 2-838

Fire Drill: Invariably, the object you're adding the constraint to will orient in the wrong direction. And this time is no exception. Fortunately, it is merely a question of realigning the axis of the object being constrained.

43. Under the LookAt Constraint rollout, you'll see a check box labeled Keep Initial Offset. Check it and the piston will return to its proper orientation.

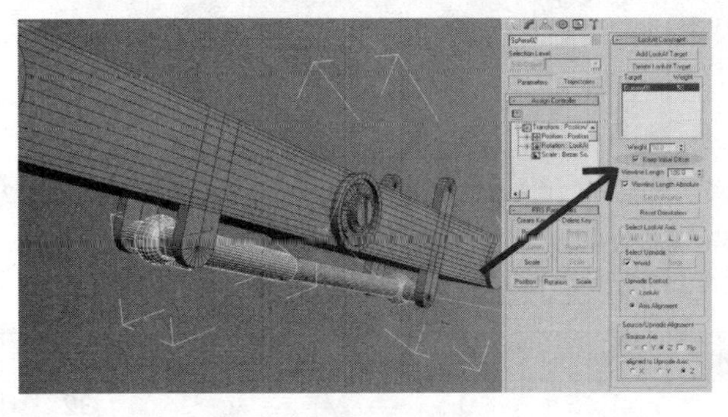

Figure 2-840

FYI: Once the LookAt constraint has been applied, a blue line will appear, indicating the sight line of the constraint. Now that we have the LookAt constraint set up for one part of the piston, we'll have to set up the constraint for the other one.

44. Click the part of the piston attached to the lower_boom, add a LookAt constraint, click the **Add LookAt Target** button, hit **H**, and select the top dummy.

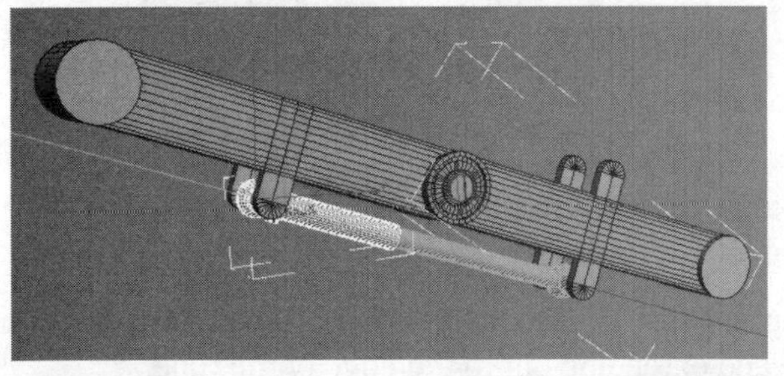

Figure 2-841

Message: Now when you rotate the upper_boom, the piston should slide in and out like a real piston. If not, first check to make sure the dummies and piston parts are attached to their respective booms. Then, check and be sure each object is aimed at the correct dummy object.

45. Hide everything except the upper part of the piston (i.e., the larger part).

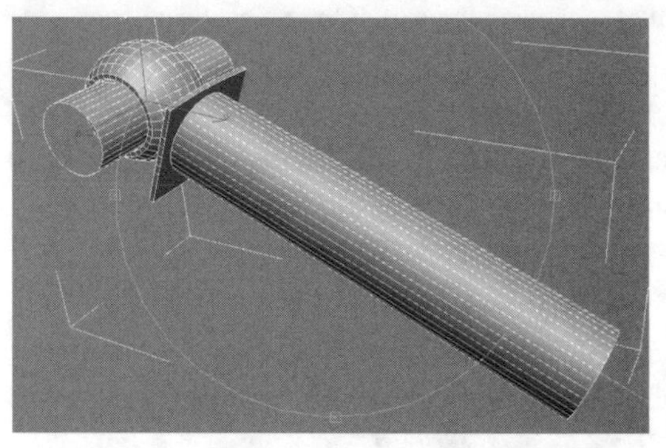

Figure 2-842

46. Arc Rotate around the end opposite the joint and create a Tube over the piston cylinder.

Radius 1	Radius 2	Height	Height/Cap Segs	Sides	Smooth
1.32	1.45	0.5	2/1	32	Checked

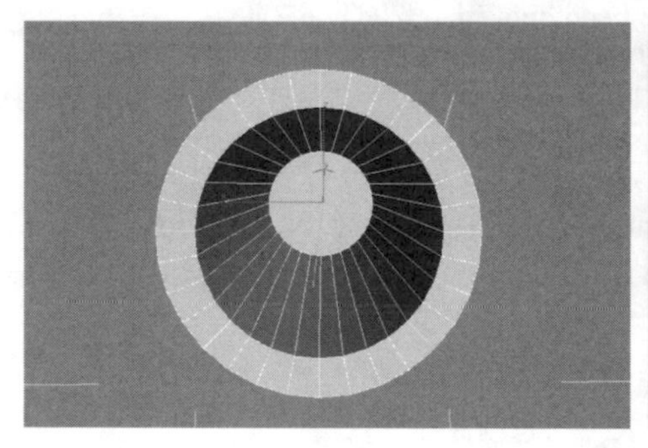

Figure 2-843

Figure 2-844

47. Move the tube to the end of the cylinder and convert the tube to an Editable Polygon.

48. Using AutoGrid, create a Cylinder in the upper-right corner of the plate and extending out to the edge of the tube.

Radius	Height	Height/Cap Segs	Sides	Smooth
0.239	12.57	1/1	32	Checked

Figure 2-845

49. Make a clone of the cylinder in the remaining three corners and then Attach them and the tube to the piston.

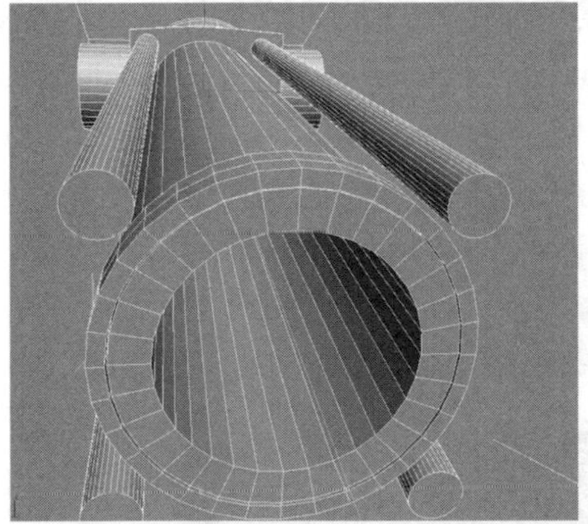

Figure 2-846

50. Using AutoGrid, create a Tube over one of the four cylinders.

Radius 1	Radius 2	Height	Height/Cap Segs	Sides	Smooth
0.23	0.33	0.36	1/1	36	Checked

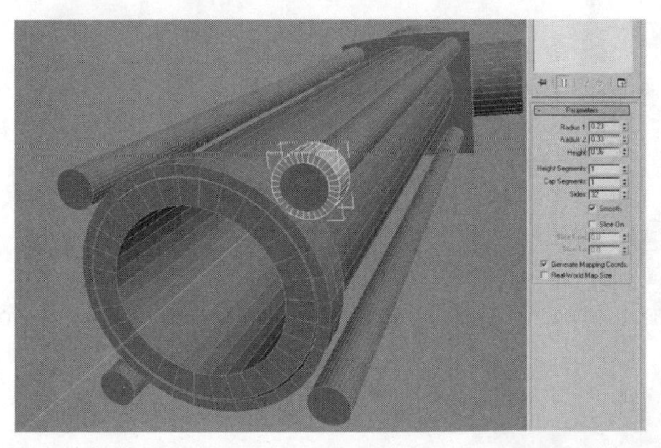

Figure 2-847

51. Clone the tube three times and place each over the top of each cylinder (you may need to scale each one a bit so that it contacts the surface of the larger tube), then Attach each tube and cylinder to the piston.

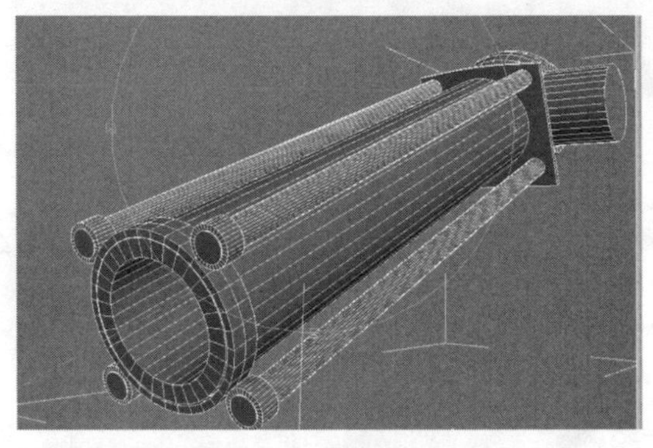

Figure 2-848

52. Unhide the piston_rod, mounts, booms, etc., and do a test render.

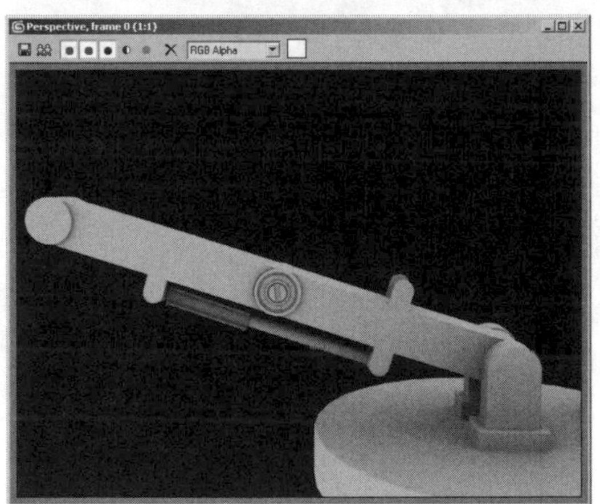

Figure 2-849

53. Select the upper part of the piston.

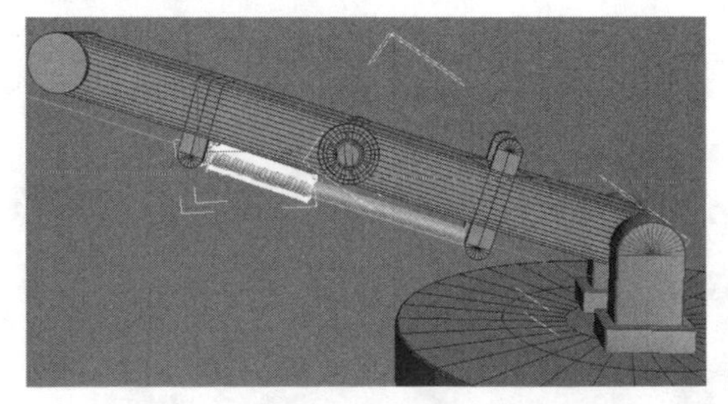

Figure 2-850

54. Clone it. Click the **Motion** tab, and under Assign Controller select **Rotation.**

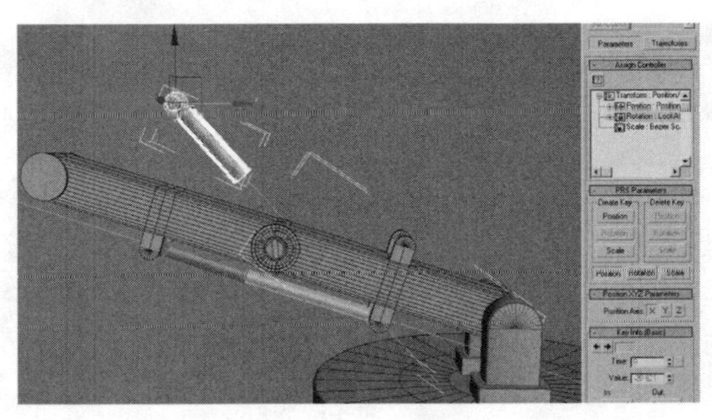

Figure 2-851

FYI: As you can see from the blue line, the clone is constrained to look at whatever the original was looking at. To properly position it, you'll have to break the clone's constraint. This step is unfortunate because it necessitates removing the LookAt constraint only to redo it. Unfortunately, Max doesn't provide a way to switch LookAt targets without removing the old one first.

55. Click **Assign Controller** and select **Euler XYZ.**

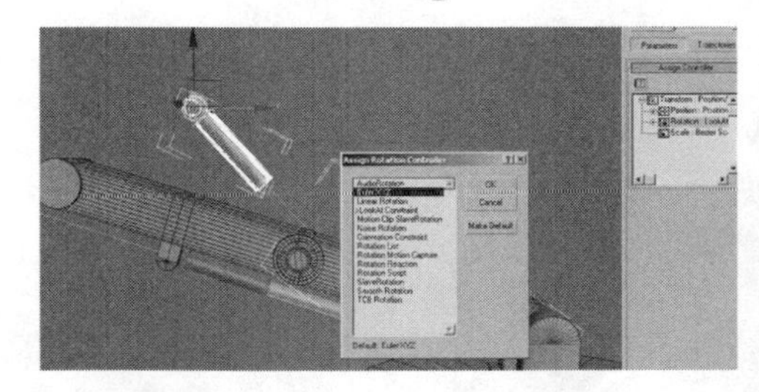

Figure 2-852

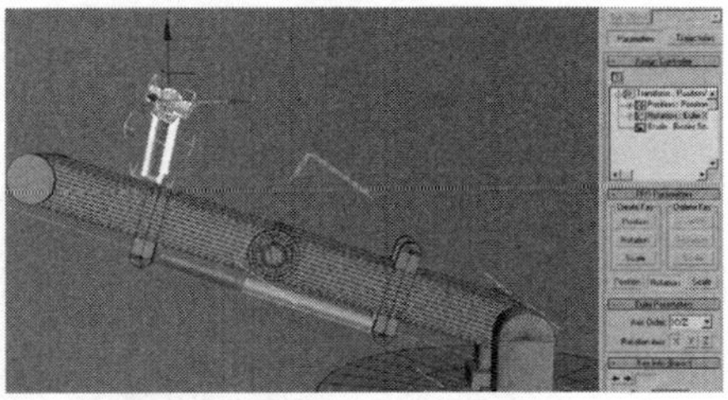

Figure 2-853

Fire Drill: As you can see, removing a constraint really jacks up your model's orientation. You'll need to reorient the clone and then readjust the pivot.

56. Use the Move and Rotate tools to adjust the piston_rod and move it into place.

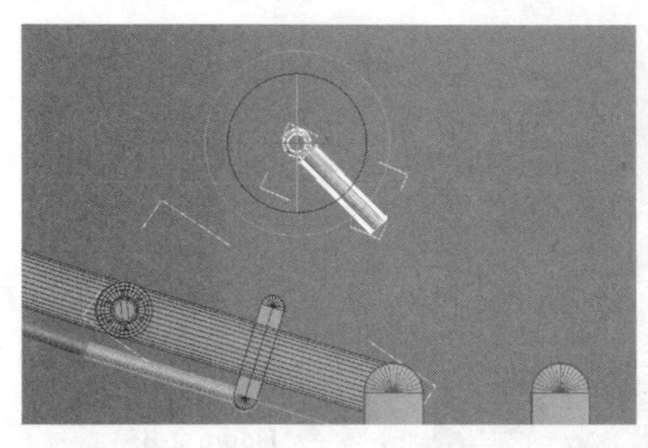

Figure 2-854

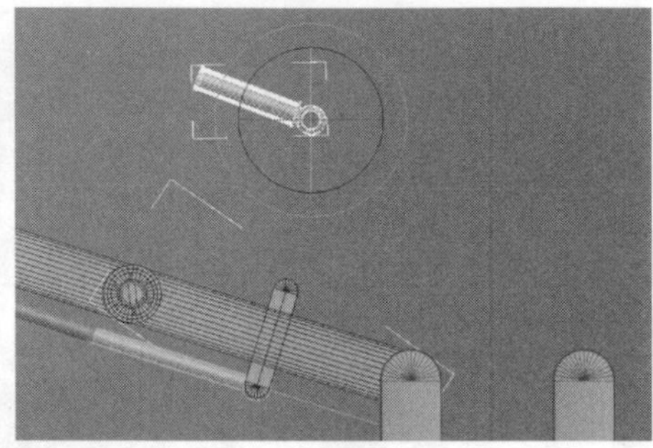

Figure 2-855

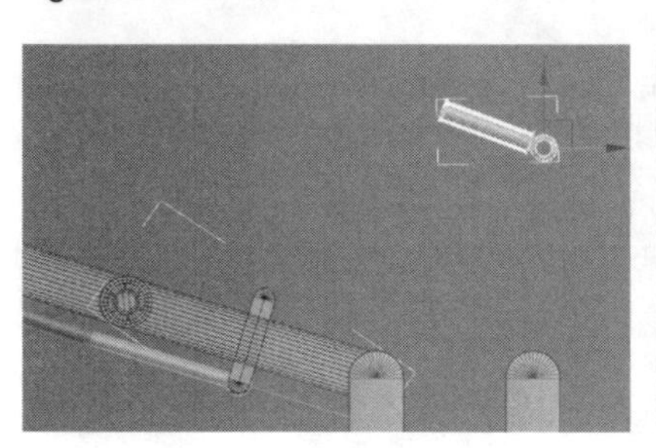

Figure 2-856

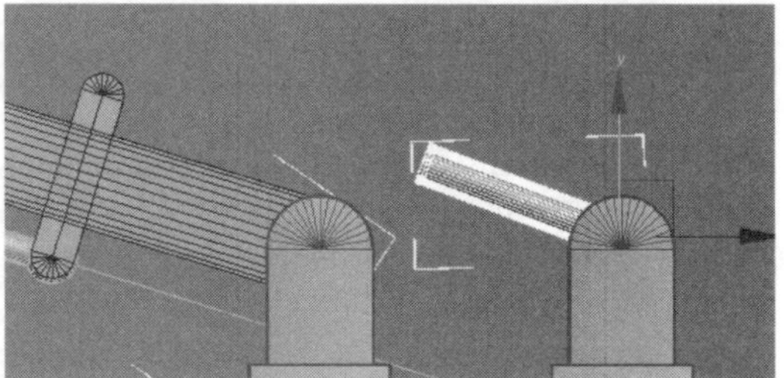

Figure 2-857

57. Scale the clone **150** percent.

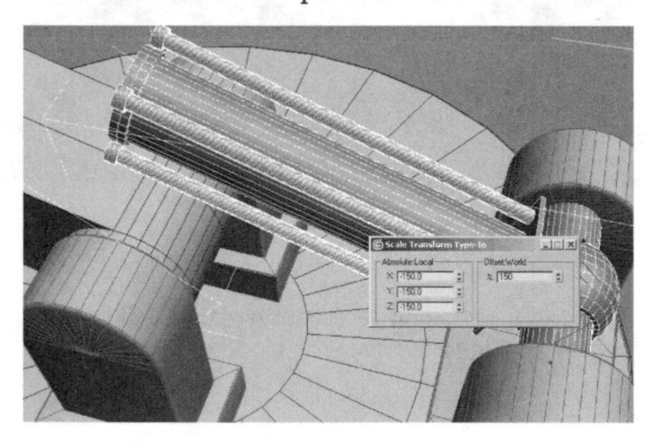

Figure 2-858

58. Clone the piston_rod.

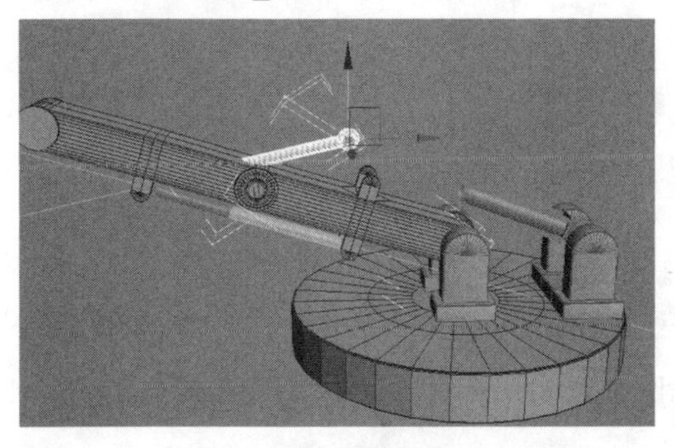

Figure 2-859

59. Open the Motion tab and replace the LookAt constraint with a **Euler XYZ**.

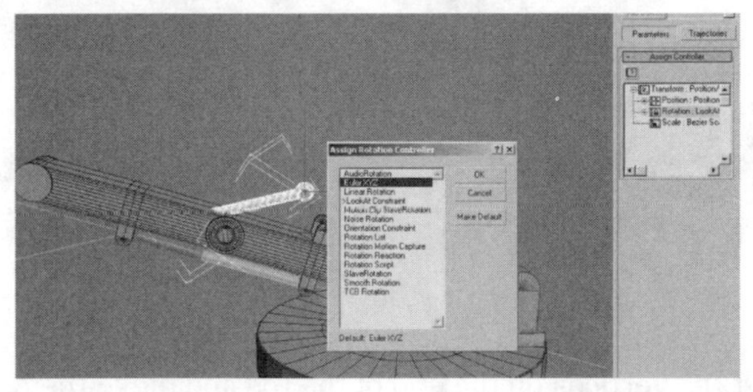

Figure 2-860

60. Use the Rotate and Move tools to orient the rod.

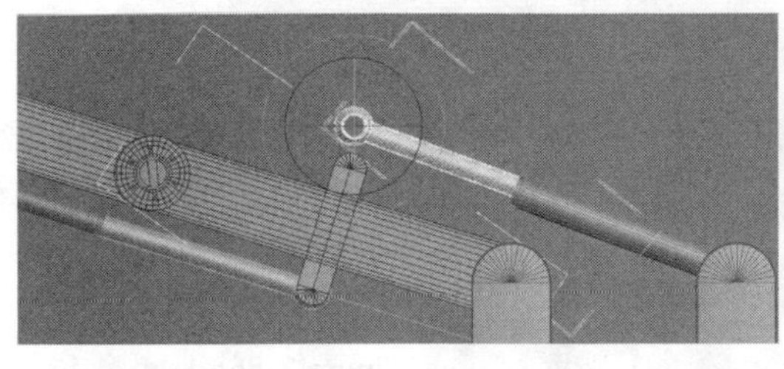

Figure 2-861

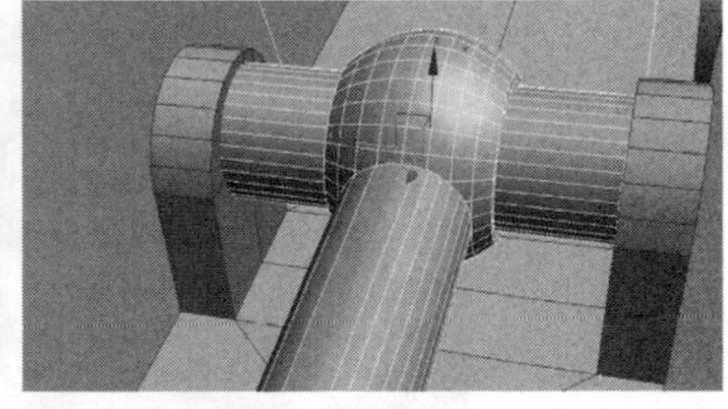

Figure 2-862

61. Scale the rod by **125** percent.

Figure 2-863

62. Select all the vertices on the sides of the axle and move them inside the mount.

Figure 2-864

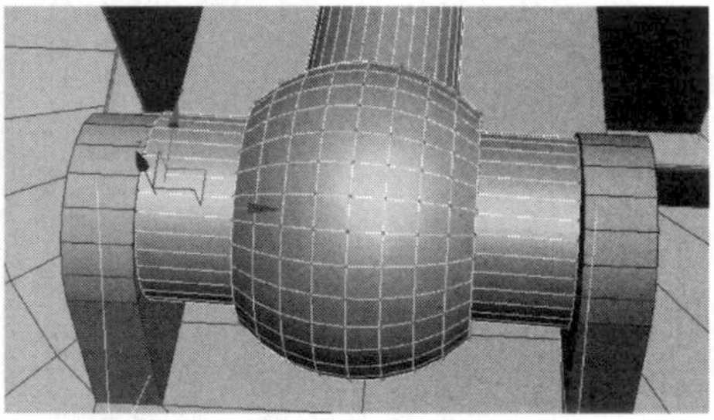

Figure 2-865

63. Select the vertices on the end of the rod and move them to reduce the length of the rod so it fits inside the piston.

Figure 2-866

64. Align the rod and the piston so they mate.

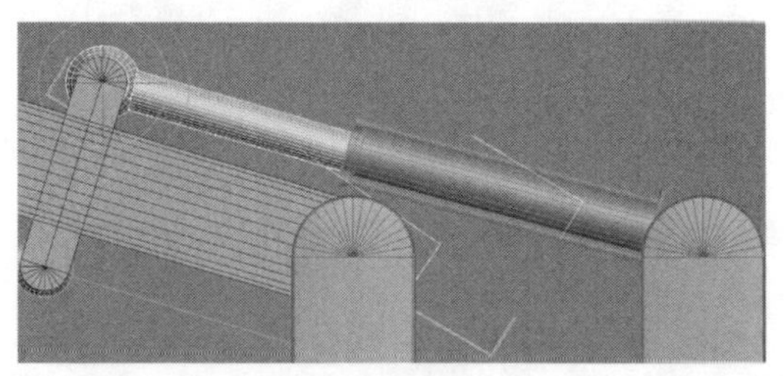

Figure 2-867

65. Switch the coordinate system to **Gimbal**, select the vertices on the end of the piston, and move them in the Y axis until they clear the other mount.

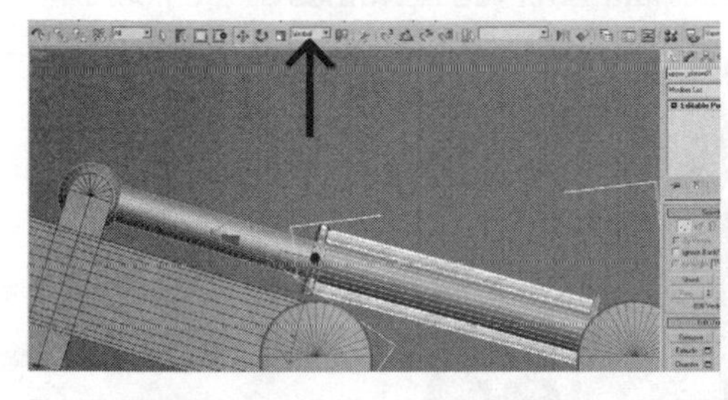

Figure 2-868

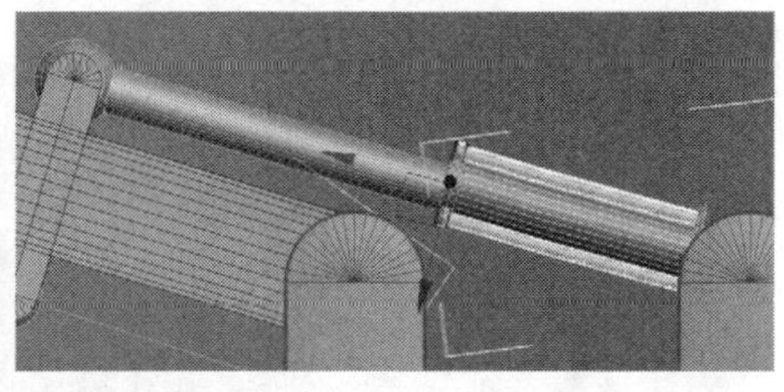

Figure 2-869

FYI: Because we are temporarily using Euler XYZ for our rotation constraint, the other coordinate systems will not work properly. Switching to Gimbal gives you a coordinate system that will allow you to smoothly move the vertices in a line.

66. Select the vertices making up the end of the piston and the supporting rods.

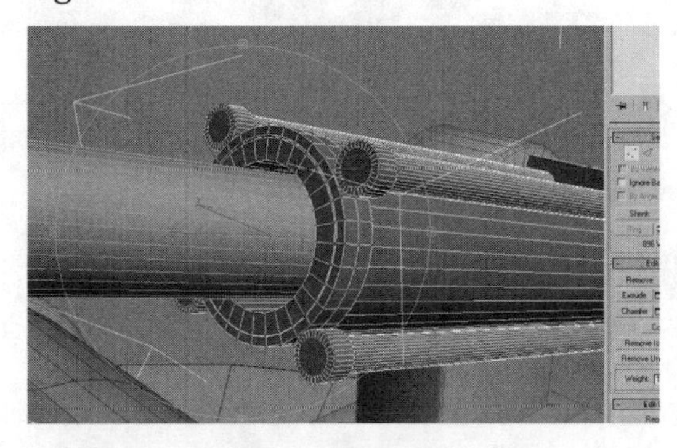

Figure 2-870

67. Scale the vertices down to **85** percent.

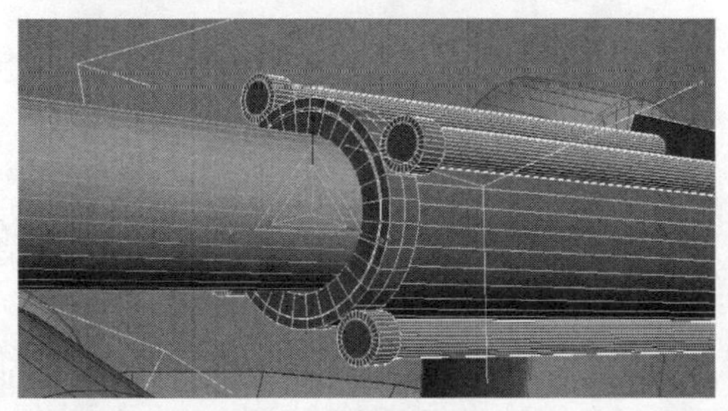

Figure 2-871

68. Select and Link the rod and the piston to the turret.
69. Create a dummy for each part of the new piston, align each to the respective piston, then Select and Link the dummies to the boom and mount.

Figure 2-872

70. Select the **piston_rod**, add a LookAt constraint, check **Keep Initial Offset**, and target the dummy (**Dummy04**) positioned at the rear of the piston cylinder.

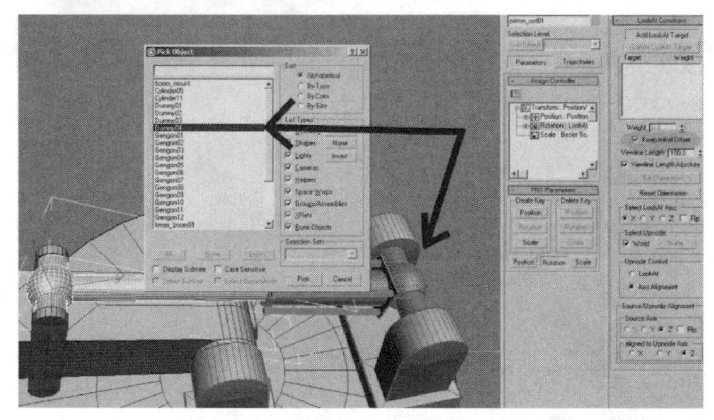

Figure 2-873

Don't Forget: You have to check Keep Initial Offset or the object will not be properly aligned.

71. Repeat the process for the piston, using Dummy03 as the LookAt target.

Message: Now if you move the booms, the pistons will work properly. However, if you hyperextend the booms, the pistons *will* come apart. Having said that, if you hyperextend the boom, you can rotate them right through the entire model. An extensive discussion of rigging and animation are beyond the scope of this book; however, the key to getting this model to behave is to add additional constraints on its movement, so that parts like the booms are prevented from moving past a certain point.

72. In the Top view, create a Box on both sides of the boom, atop the main turret.

Length	Width	Height	Length/Width/Height Segs
20	8.5	1	1/1/1

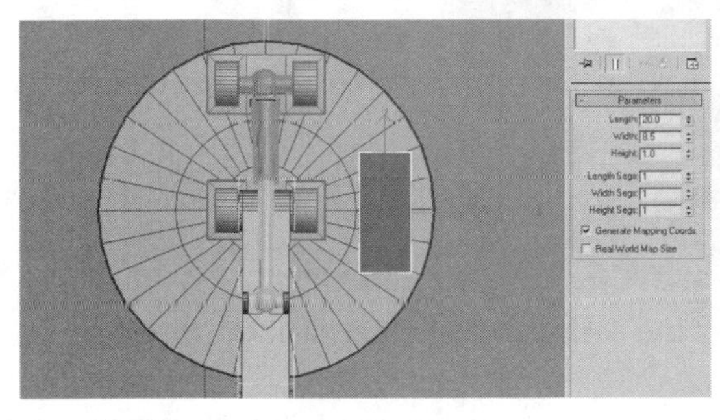

Figure 2-874

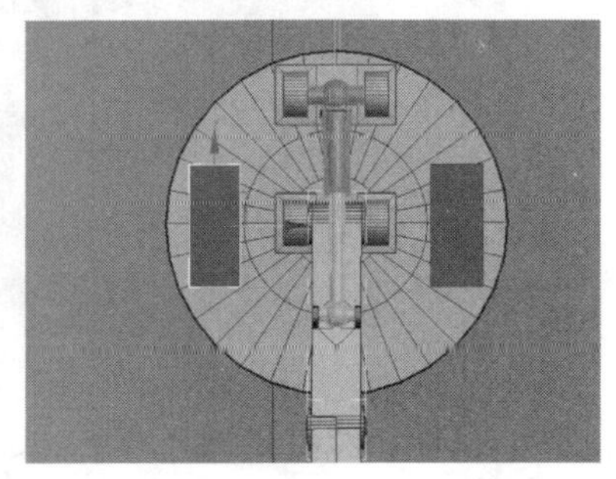

Figure 2-875

73. Convert the boxes to Editable Polygons, delete the underside faces, and Attach them to the main turret.

74. Select the top 18 polygons that make the top curve on the outside of the right stanchion.

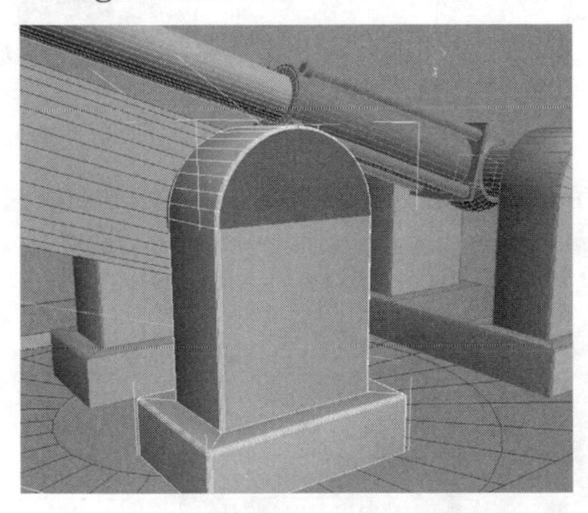

Figure 2-876

75. Extrude the polygons by **0.8**.

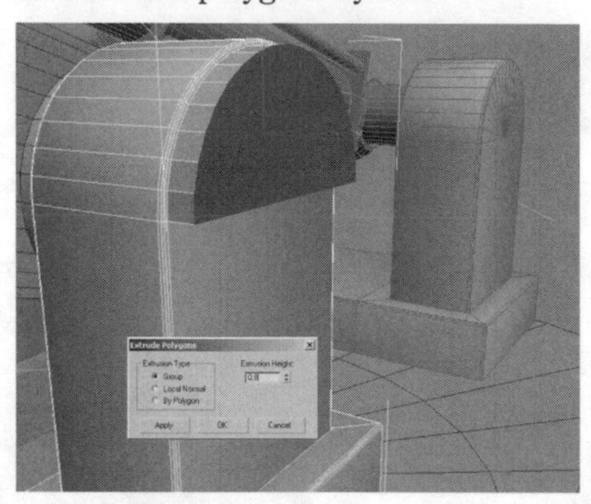

Figure 2-877

76. Select the four edges of the boxes you created, click **Connect**, and enter **2** for Segments.

Figure 2-878

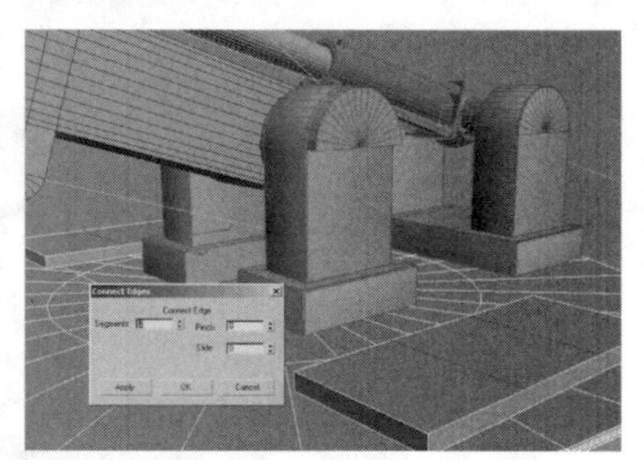

Figure 2-879

77. Select the six polygons you just made and Bevel them.

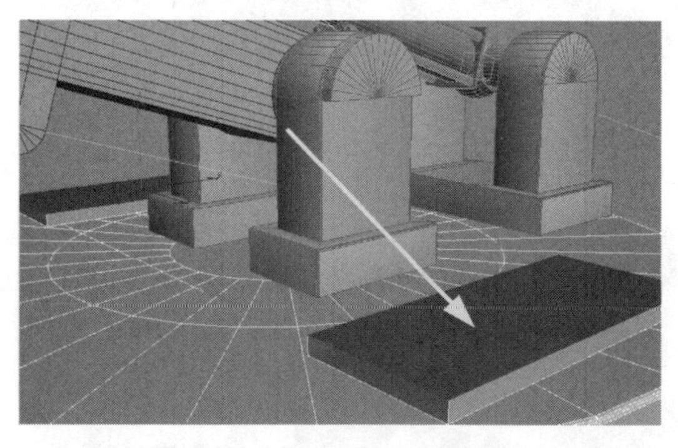

Figure 2-880

Type	Height	Outline	Apply/OK
By Polygon	0	–0.5	Apply
By Polygon	3.5	0	OK

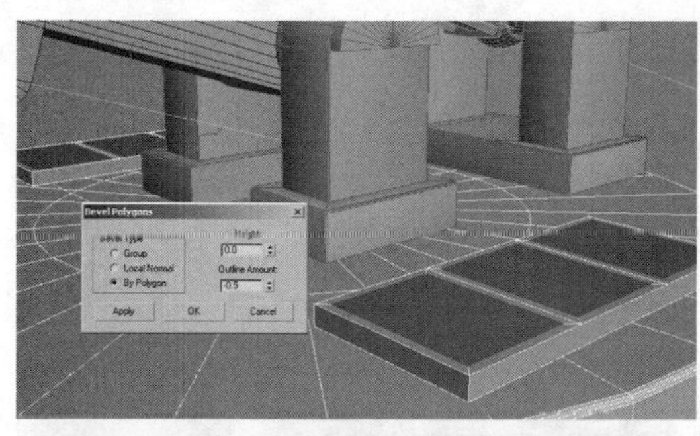

Figure 2-881

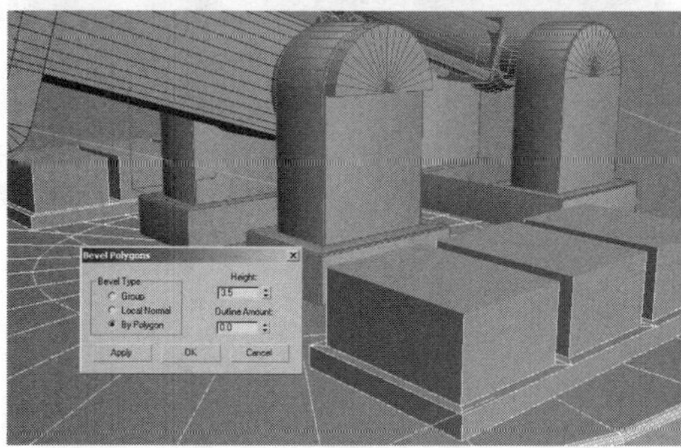

Figure 2-882

78. Create a Geosphere with a Radius of **2.45** and **4** Segments, check **Hemisphere**, convert it to an Editable Polygon, and delete the polygons beneath the hemisphere.

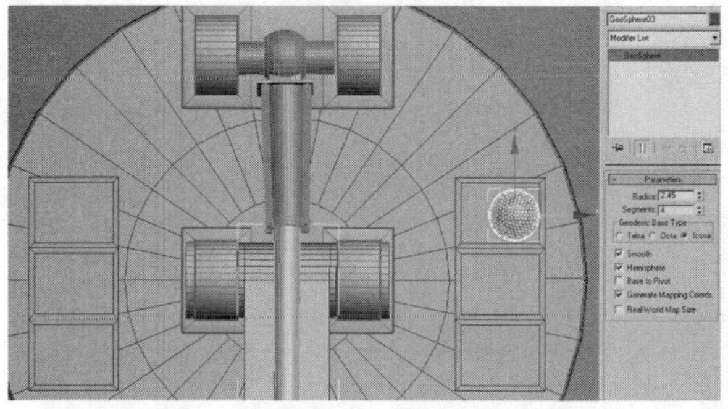

Figure 2-883

79. Select all the polygons of the hemisphere and click **Bevel Settings:**

Type	Height	Outline	Apply/OK
By Polygon	0	–0.04	Apply
By Polygon	–0.04	0	OK

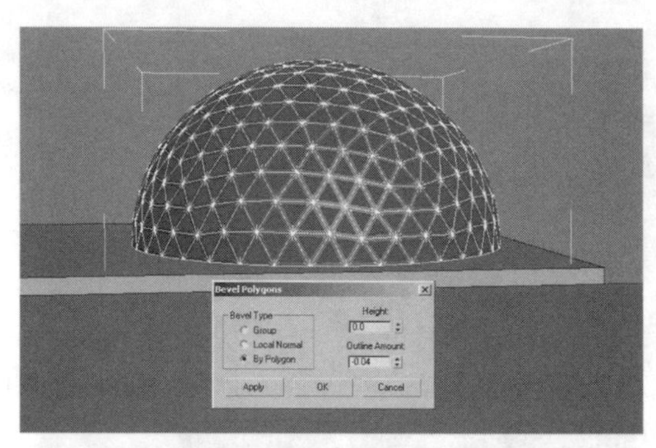

Figure 2-884

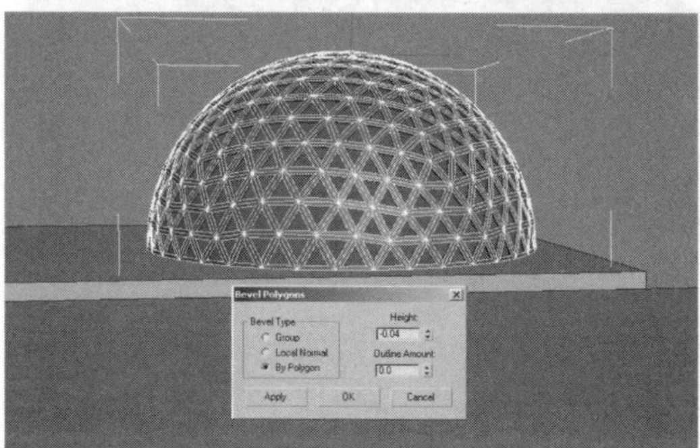

Figure 2-885

80. Border-select the bottom of the hemisphere, click **Create Shape From Selection**, and name it **seal**.

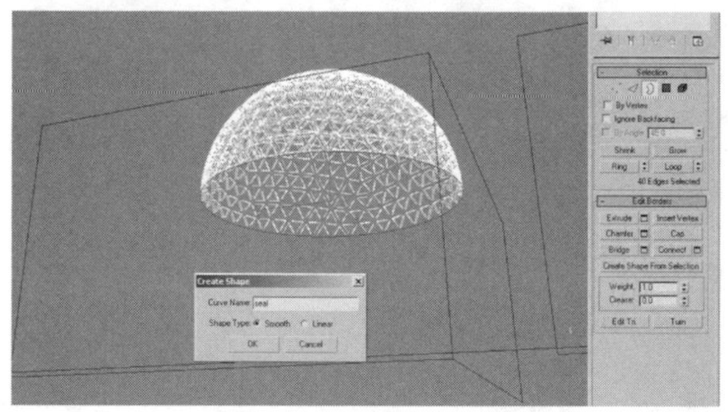

Figure 2-886

81. Select **seal** and check **Enable In Renderer** and **Enable In Viewport**; then change the Thickness to **0.3** and convert it to an Editable Polygon.

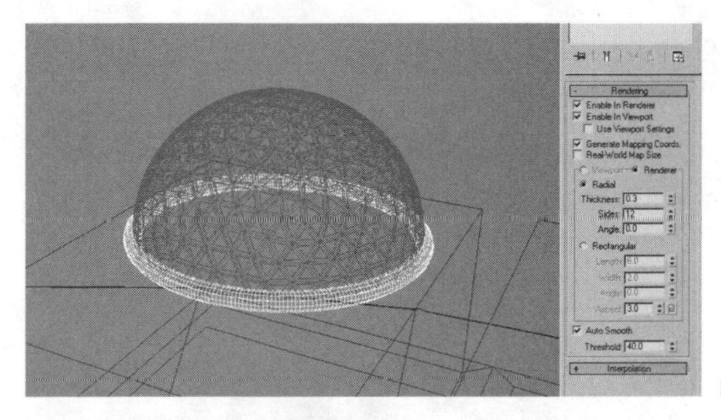

Figure 2-887

82. Attach the seal to the geosphere, switch to the Top view, and make six clones (one on top of each of the polygons you made).

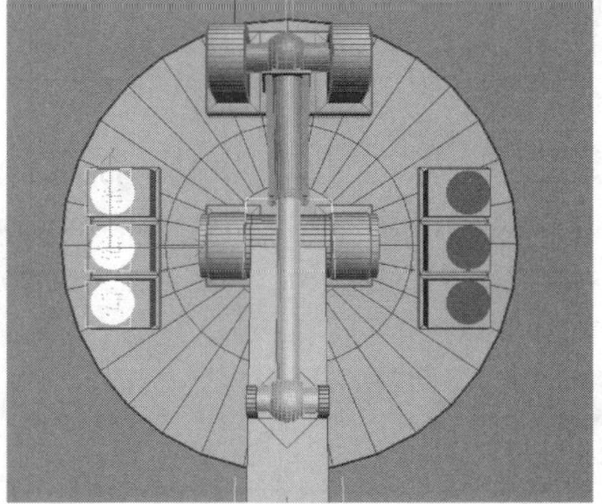

Figure 2-888

83. Attach the seal geosphere objects to the main turret and do a test render.

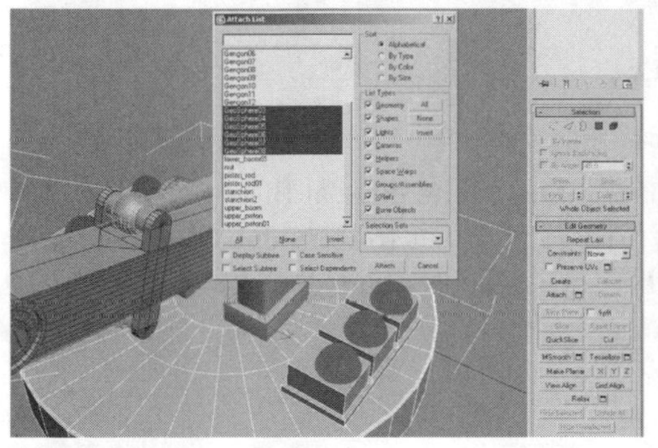

Figure 2-889

Figure 2-890

84. Switch to the Top view and create a Cylinder at the bottom-left corner of the middle box.

Radius	Height	Height/Cap Segs	Sides	Smooth
0.45	1.5	1/1	32	Checked

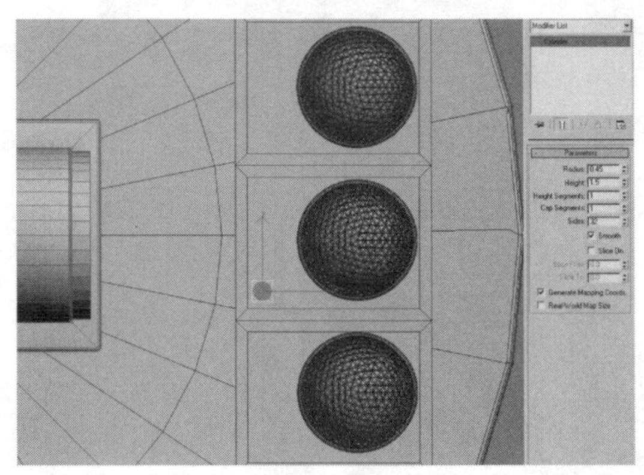

Figure 2-891

85. Convert the cylinder to an Editable Polygon, delete the downward-facing polygon, select the top polygon, enter an Extrusion Height of **0.15**, and hit **Apply** nine times.

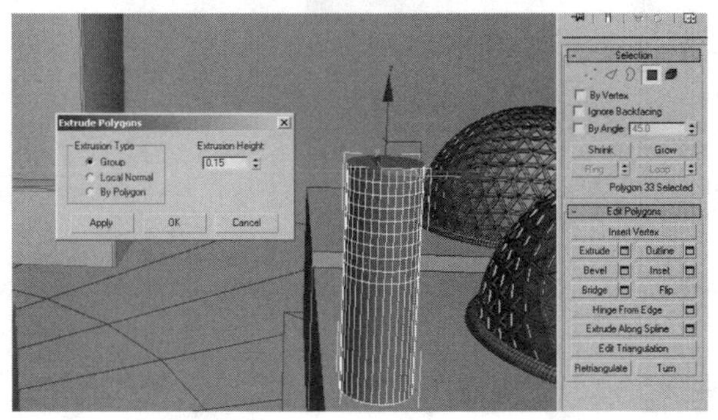

Figure 2-892

86. Move the cylinder's pivot point up to the edge at the start of the first extrusion, and apply a Bend modifier to the stack (Bend **–90** in the **Z** axis, check **Limit Effect**, and enter an Upper Limit of **1.0**).

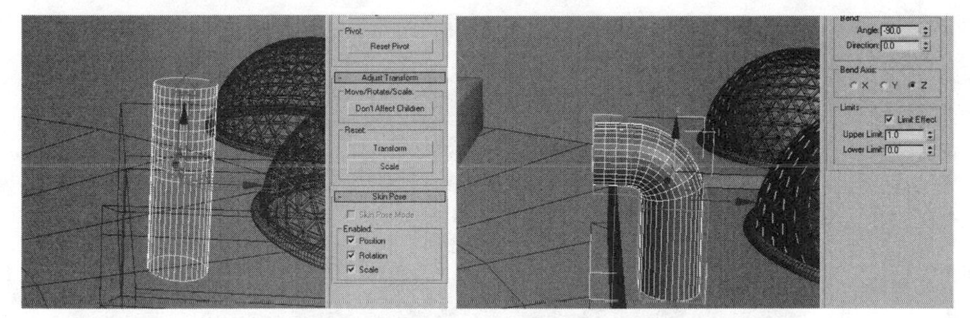

Figure 2-893

Figure 2-894

87. Convert the cylinder to an Editable Polygon to collapse the stack, then, using the Move tool, pull the polygon about halfway to the stanchion base by eye.

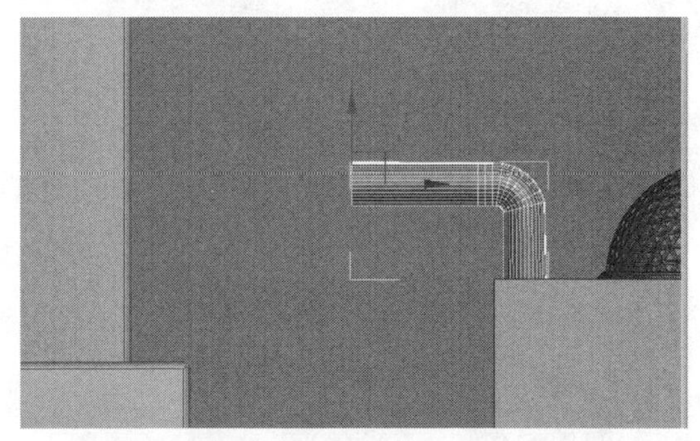

Figure 2-895

88. Click **Bevel Settings:**

Type	Height	Outline	Apply/OK
Group	0	0.1	Apply
Group	0.1	0	Apply
Group	0	–0.2	Apply
Group	2.2	0	Apply
Group	0	0.1	Apply
Group	0.1	0.0	Apply
Group	0	–0.1	Apply
Group	0.5	0	OK

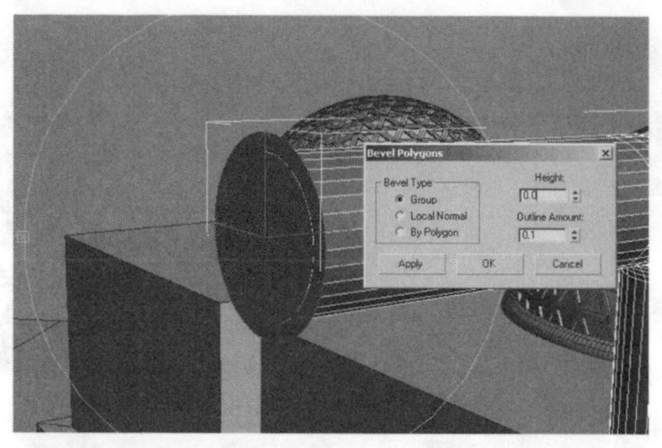

Figure 2-896

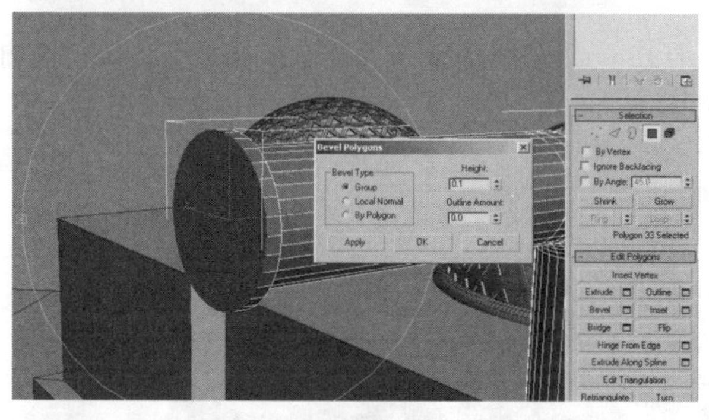

Figure 2-897

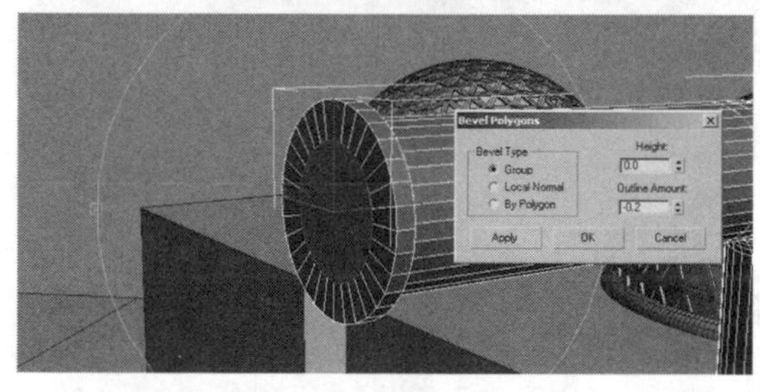

Figure 2-898

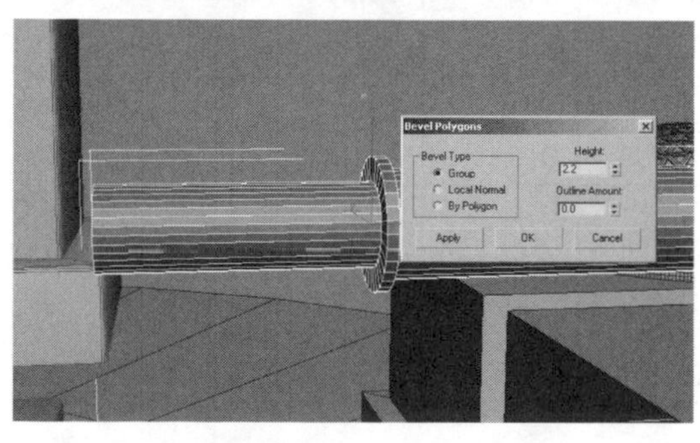

Figure 2-899

Day 15: Building the Hydraulics

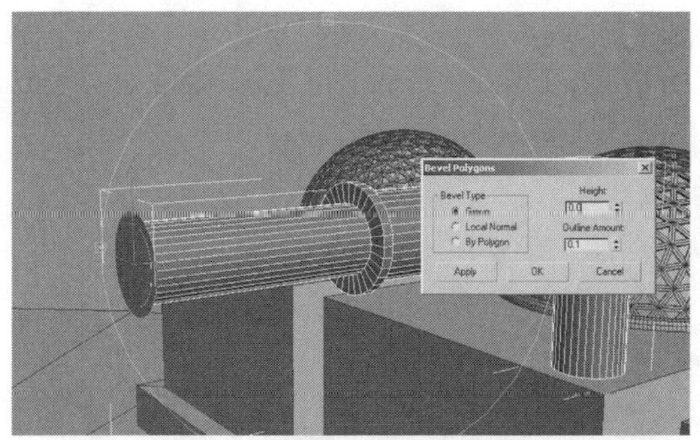

Figure 2-900

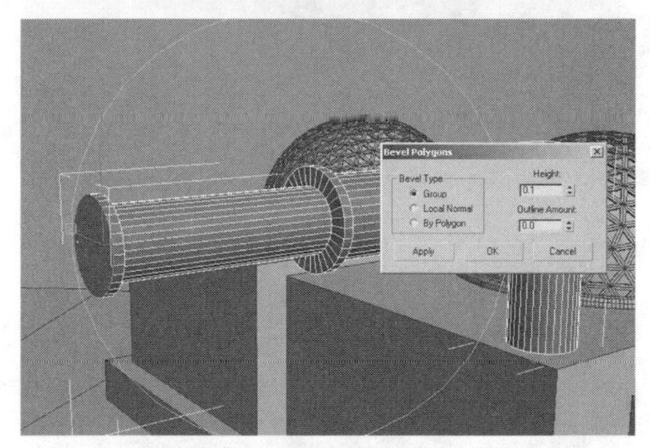

Figure 2-901

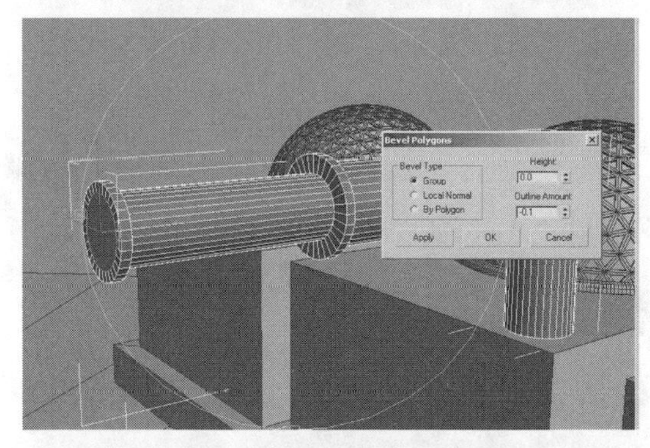

Figure 2-902

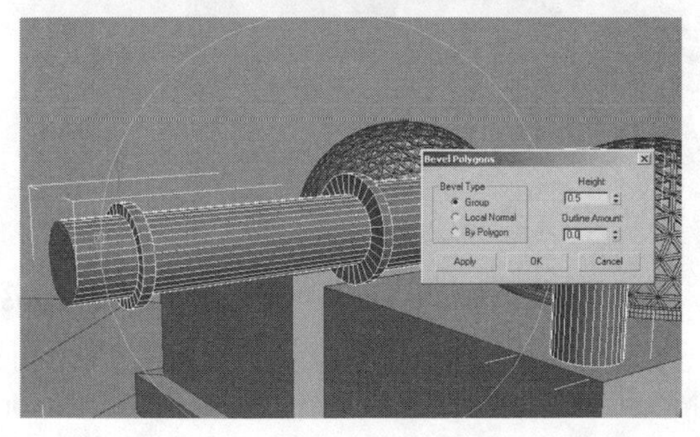

Figure 2-903

89. Switch to the Front view and use the Move tool to move the polygon until it is just below the upper part of the stanchion.

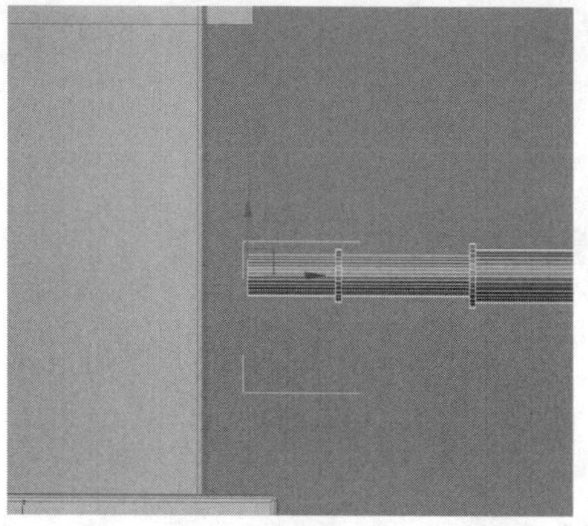

Figure 2-904

90. Extrude by **0.1** ten times.

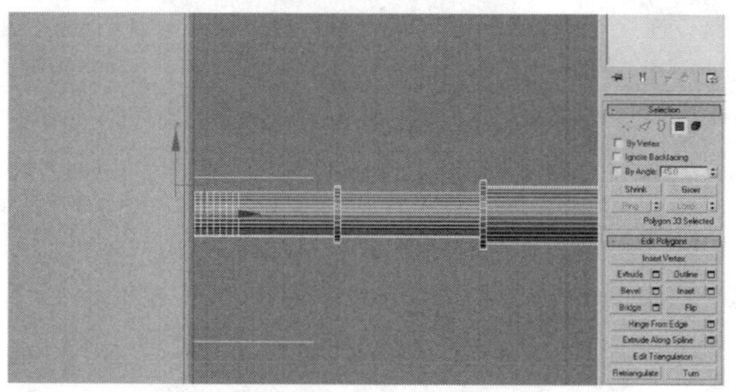

Figure 2-905

91. Move the pivot point to prepare for a bend.

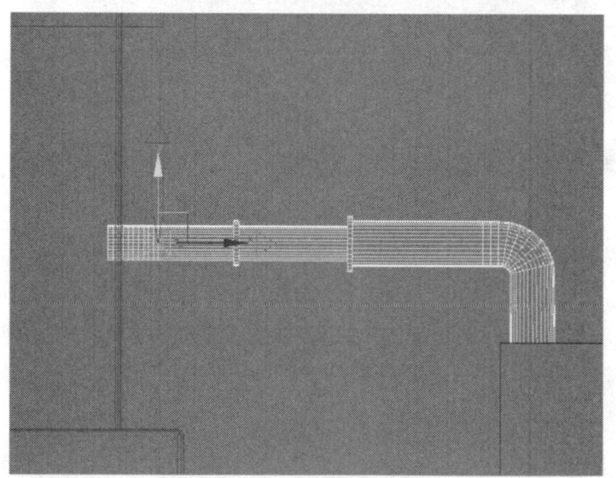

Figure 2-906

92. Add a Bend modifier to the stack with an Angle of **–90** in the X axis, and with the effect limited to a Lower Limit of **–0.56**. Convert to an Editable Polygon.

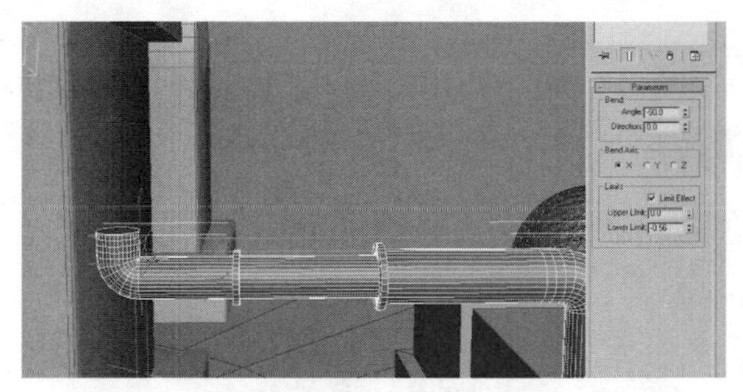

Figure 2-907

93. Polygon-select and Bevel:

Type	Height	Outline	Apply/OK
Group	0	–0.1	Apply
Group	3.5	0	OK

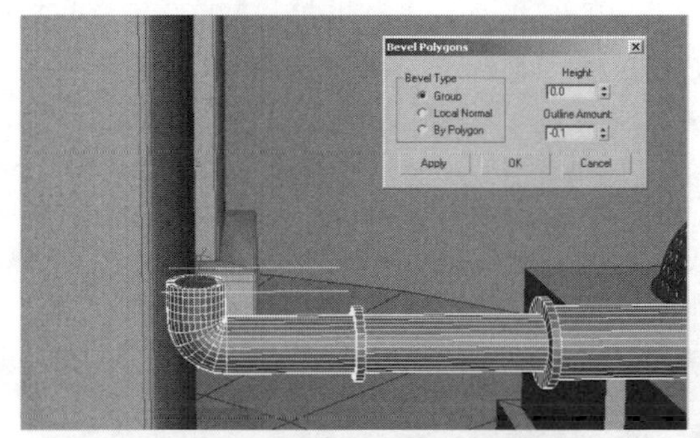

Figure 2-908

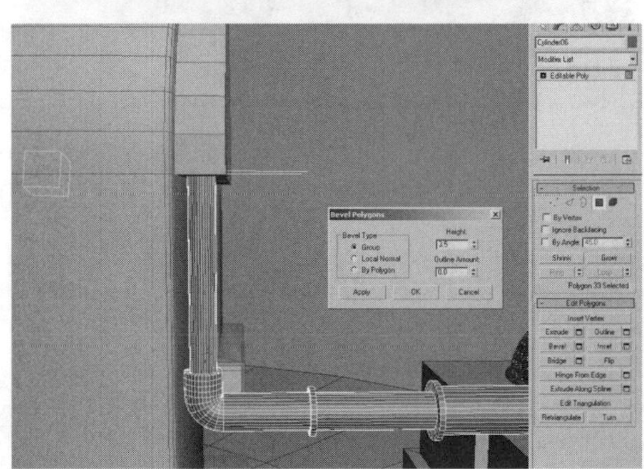

Figure 2-909

Message: I used a height of 3.5, but use whatever height you need for the tube to be flush with the bottom surface. Don't forget to delete the facing polygon!

94. Select the border between the pipe and the box, click **Create Shape From Selection**, check **Enable In Renderer** and **Enable in Viewport**, check **Generate Mapping Coordinates**, and reduce the Thickness to **0.16**.

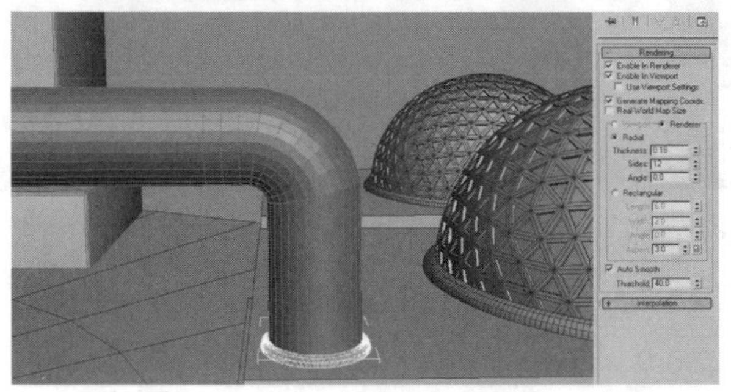

Figure 2-910

95. Select **Cylinder06**, add a Smooth modifier to its stack, turn on **Auto Smooth**, and convert it to an Editable Polygon to collapse the stack.

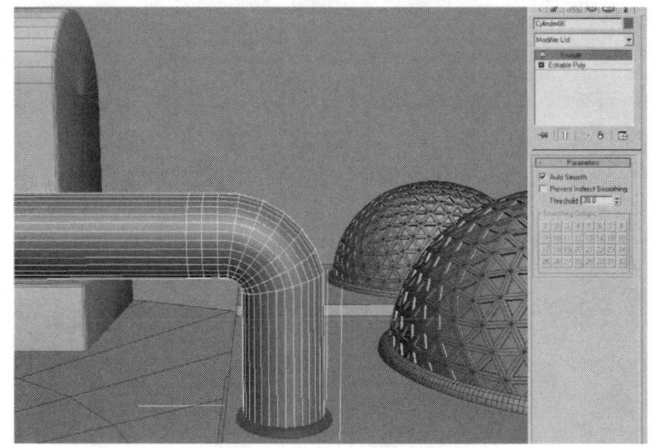

Figure 2-911

96. Convert the object to an Editable Polygon and attach it to the pipe you made.

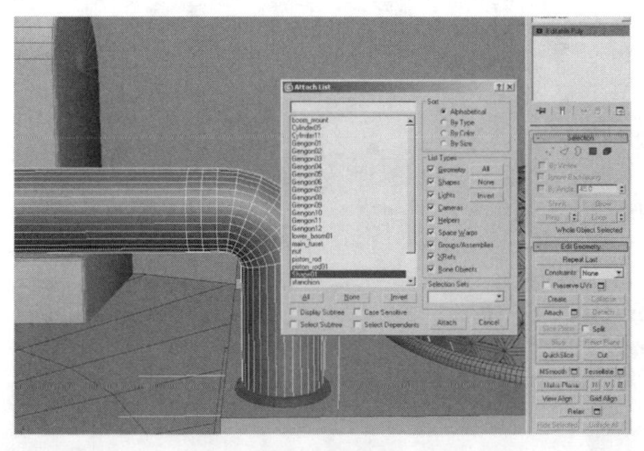

Figure 2-912

97. Switch to the Top view, select the pipe, and Shift-move it in the Y axis. Enter **3** for the Number of Copies.

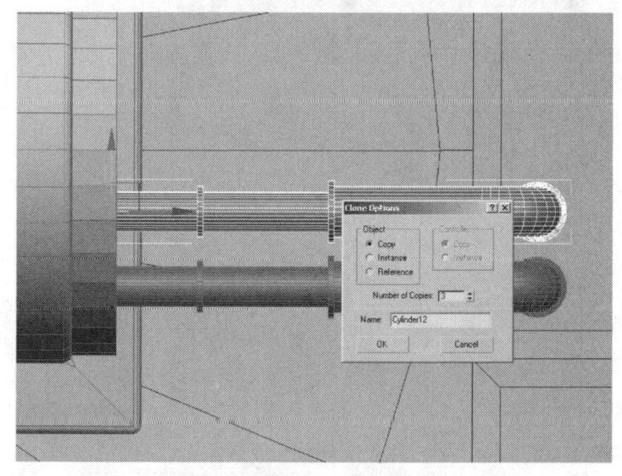

Figure 2-913

98. Do a test render.

Figure 2-914

99. Select the four pipes you just made, switch to the Top view, and Mirror copy in the X axis, with an Offset of **–19.17** (or whatever number works best to align the pipes on the left side).

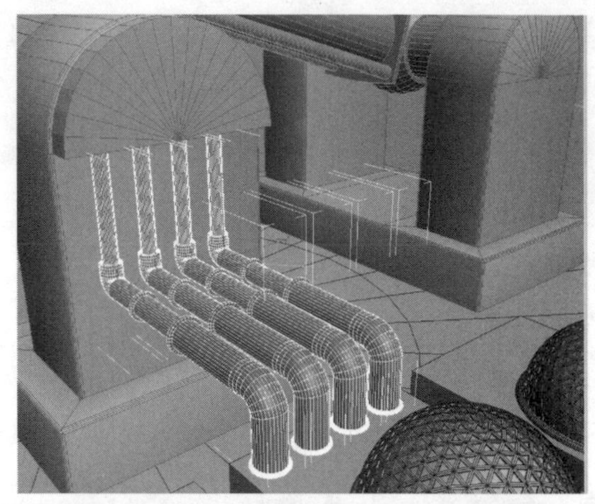

Figure 2-915

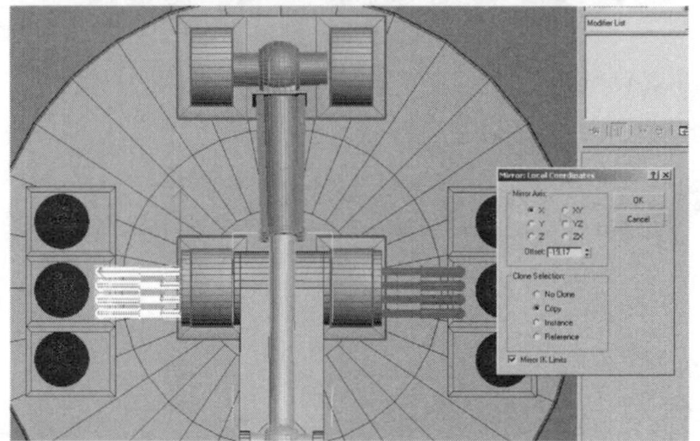

Figure 2-916

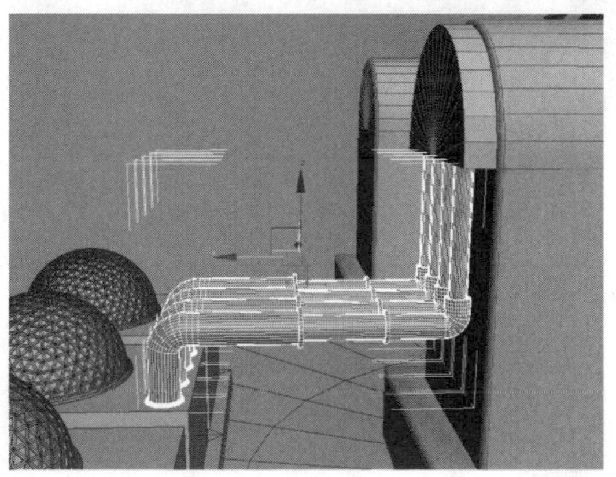

Figure 2-917

100. Select the **main_turret**, click **Attach List**, and attach the cylinders and gengons you made as part of the hydraulic system.

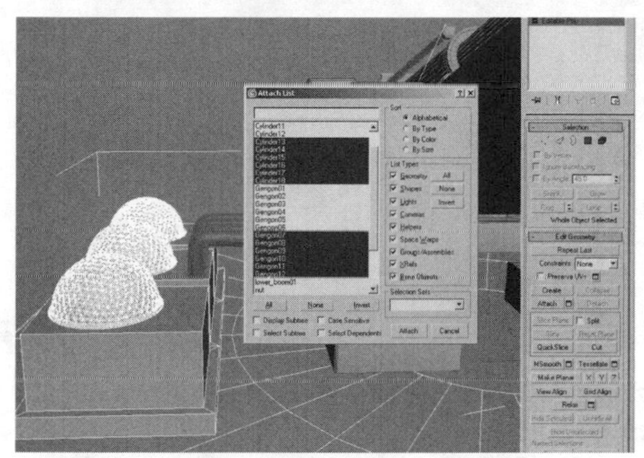

Figure 2-918

101. Do a test render.

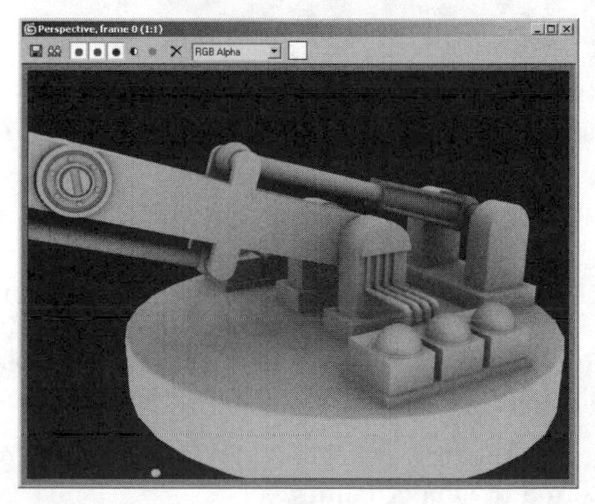

Figure 2-919

102. Switch to the Top view and create a Tube on the bottommost box.

Radius 1	Radius 2	Height	Height/Cap Segs	Sides	Smooth
0.9	0.65	0.6	1/1	32	Checked

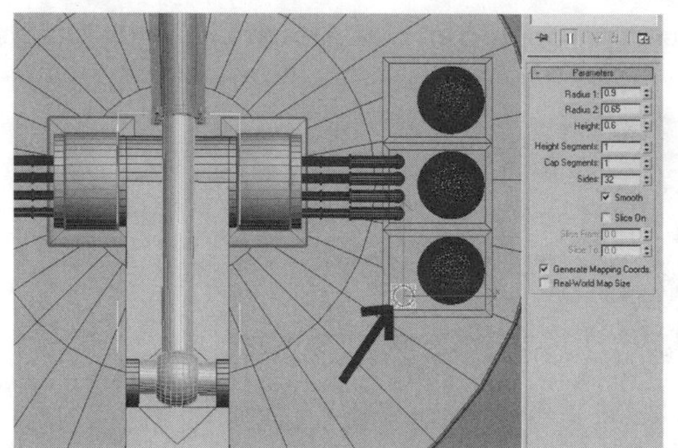

Figure 2-920

103. Make a clone of the tube and attach it to the mount for the piston on the upper_boom.

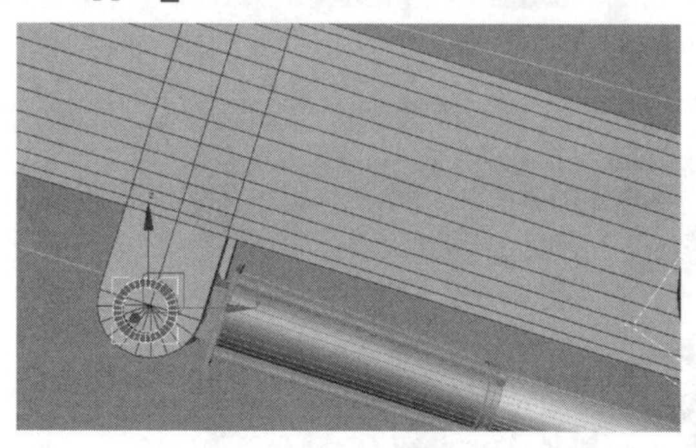

Figure 2-921

104. Switch to the Top view and, using AutoGrid, create a Hose in the center of the tube you created on the top of the box.

105. Under Hose Parameters, switch the End Point Method from Free Hose to **Bound to Object Points**.

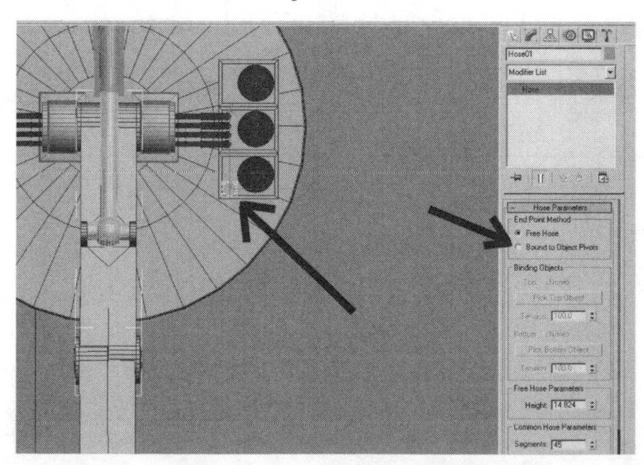

Figure 2-922

106. When you switch from Free Hose to Bound to Object Points, the Binding Objects area becomes active. Click **Pick Top Object**, hit **H** to open the object list, select **Tube04** (or whatever you called the tube you placed on the piston mount), and click **Pick.**

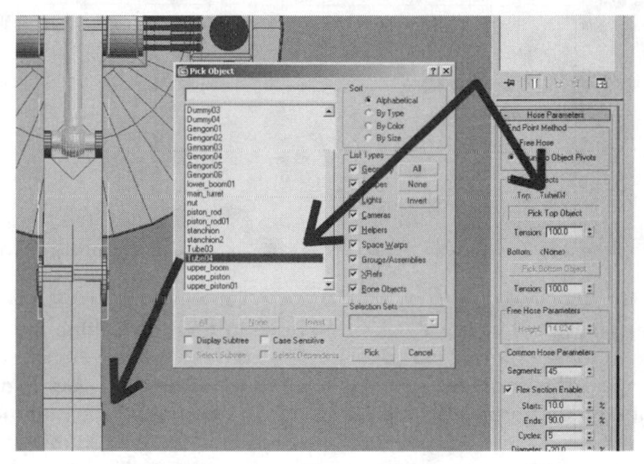

Figure 2-923

107. Click **Pick Bottom Object**, hit **H** for the object list, select **Tube03** (or whatever you called the tube you placed on the box), and click **Pick**.

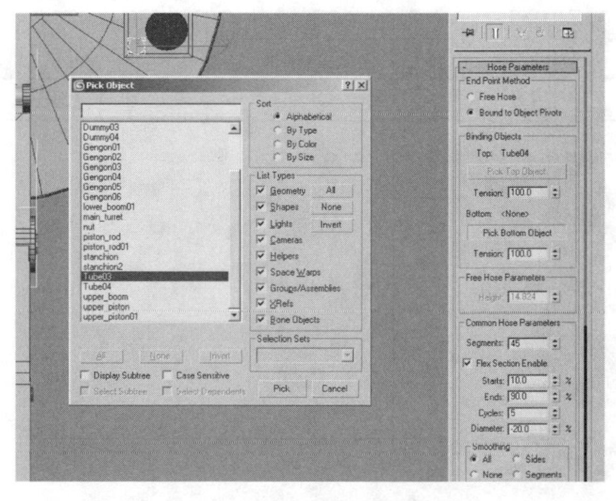

Figure 2-924

Figure 2-925

FYI: Hose is way cool because you don't have to rig it. By setting the top and bottom binding objects, you're telling Max how to make it behave like a real hose. The geometry will stay fixed to those binding objects and the geometry of the hose will stretch to match the motion of the binding objects. How cool is that? But you don't have to limit yourself to making hoses; you can use the Hose object for a rope if you're making a pirate ship.

108. Set up the hose:

Top Tension	Bottom Tension	Common Hose Segs	Hose Shape	Diameter	Sides
20	16	18	Round	1.33	18

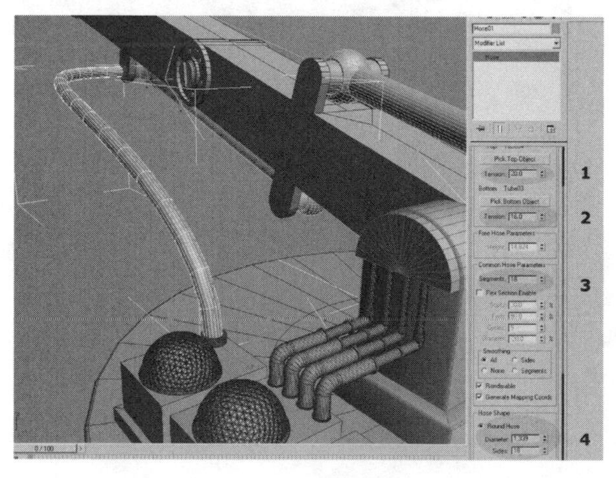

Figure 2-926

FYI: There are four required bound hose settings. The first two are tension settings. Experiment with different values; not only do they control slack, but they also control the angle at which the hose connects to the binding objects. The third value is the number of segments in the hose. Like other objects, the more segments you have, the smoother the result, but the more of a drag it will put on your machine. The Hose Shape section (three values grouped together) determines the overall shape and size of the hose. The Flex Section Enable section is used when you want to make a segmented hose. We want a smooth hose, so I left it unchecked.

109. Select and Link the tubes to mount them to the upper_boom and main_turret.
110. Make sure the hoses are connected to where they should be.
111. Repeat steps 102-110 for the left side of the model.

Fire Drill: Depending upon how asymmetric your particular model is, you may have to tweak the tension settings on the clone to get it to look right. Also check to make sure all of your objects are where they're supposed to be. If you really want to be daring, use very different settings to get an asymmetrical look.

112. Select All, add your Clay material to every object, and do a test render.

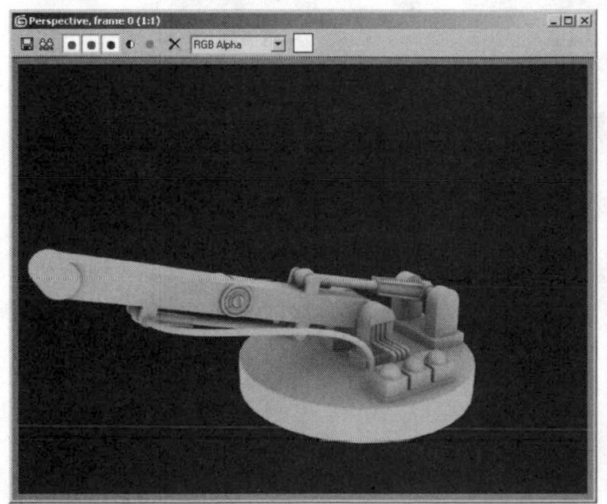

Figure 2-927

113. Repeat steps 102-110 for the rear piston as shown.

FYI: All the settings should be the same as the previous hoses. The only thing that should be different for the rear is that the top and bottom tensions should be quite different.

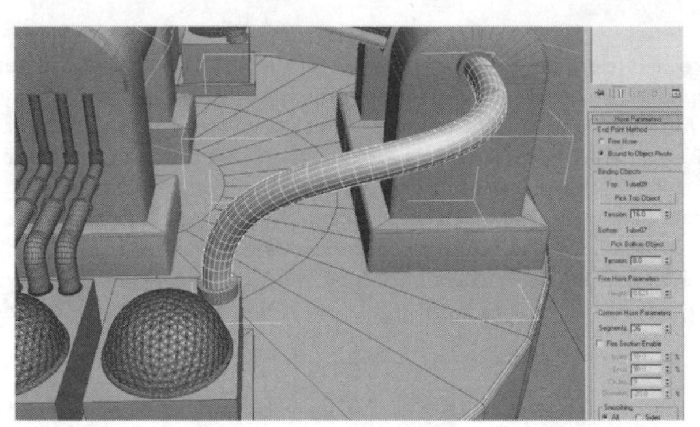

Figure 2-928

Fire Drill: Picking the proper tensions can be frustrating. Just be patient and keep tweaking the upper and lower tensions. If you're still not getting the results you think you should, check the pivot points of the binding objects. You may need to tweak those too. For example, to get my rear hose to work right, I had to rotate the binding objects' pivots.

114. Do a test render.

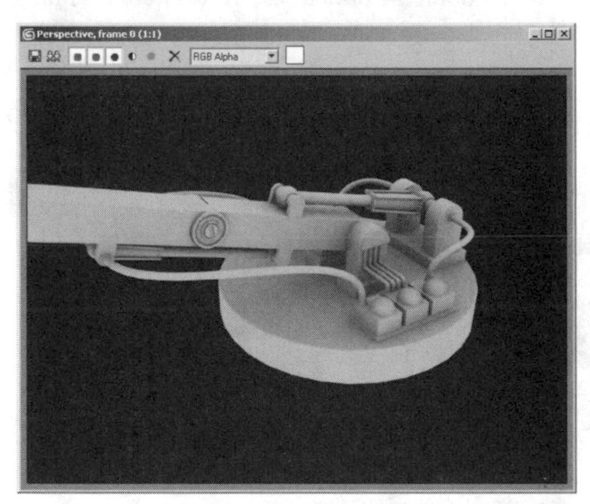

Figure 2-929

Day 16: Final Detailing

1. Switch to the Right view and polygon-select the middle polygons of the main_turret.

Figure 2-930

2. Click **Bevel Settings:**

Type	Height	Outline	Apply/OK
By Polygon	0.5	–0.5	OK

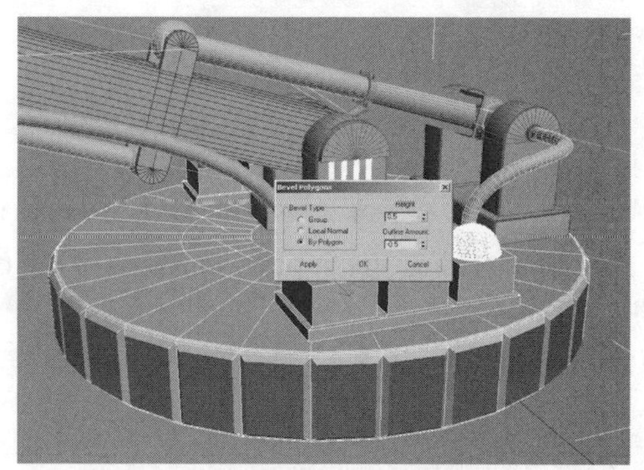

Figure 2-931

3. Select the polygons on the outer sides of the lower booms.

Figure 2-932

4. Click **Bevel Settings:**

Type	Height	Outline	Apply/OK
Local Normal	0	–0.1	Apply
Local Normal	–0.15	0	OK

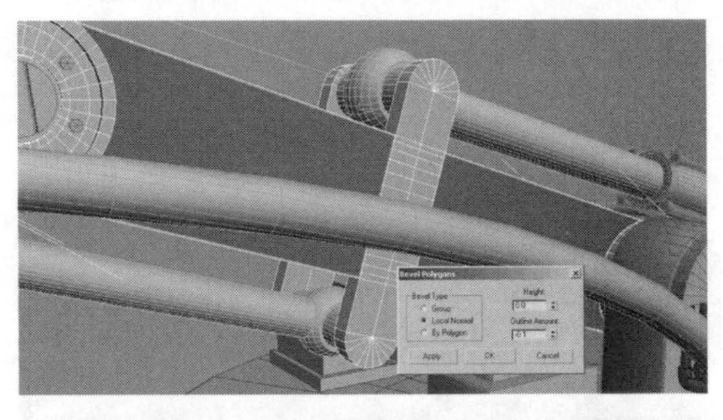

Figure 2-933

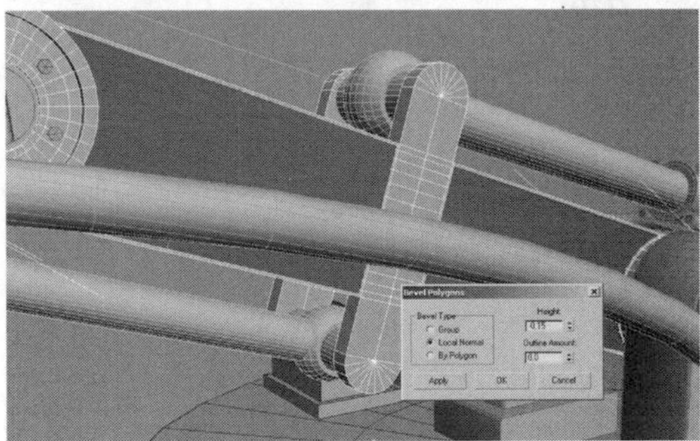

Figure 2-934

5. Select the polygons making up the outer surfaces of the mounts and Bevel them.

Figure 2-935

Type	Height	Outline	Apply/OK
Local Normal	0	–0.1	Apply
Local Normal	–0.1	0	OK

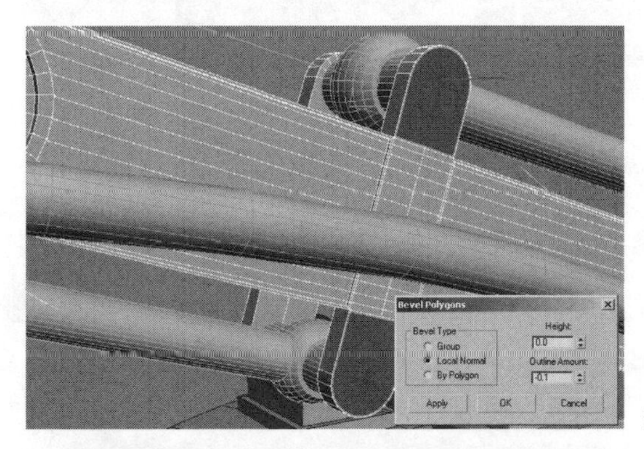

Figure 2-936

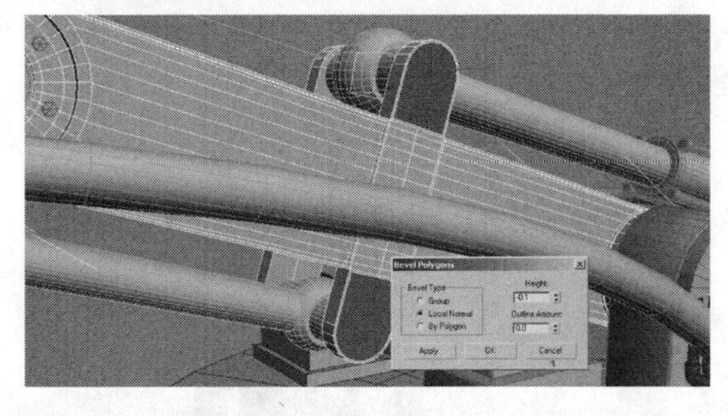

Figure 2-937

6. Create a Sphere with a Radius of **1.0**, **32** Segments, and set Hemisphere to **0.5.**

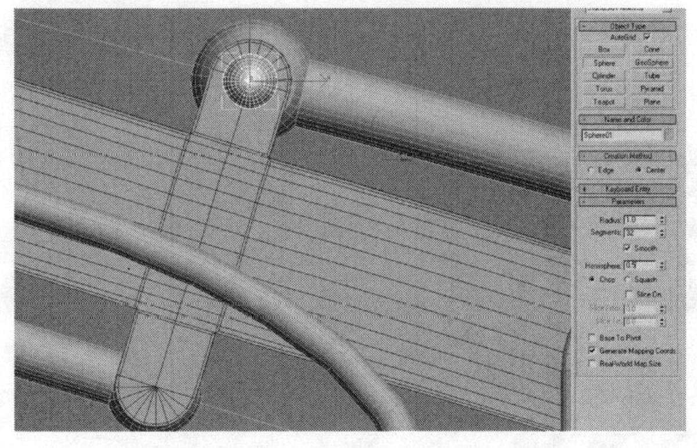

Figure 2-938

7. Convert it to an Editable Polygon, select the back-facing polygons and delete them, and make clones on both sides, for a total of four.

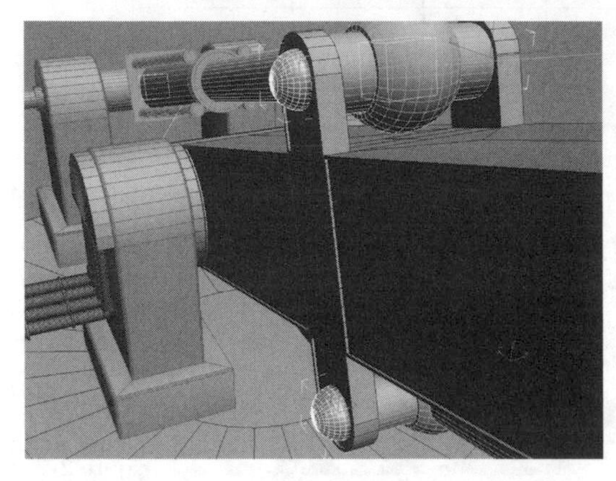

Figure 2-939

8. Attach the hemispheres to the boom.

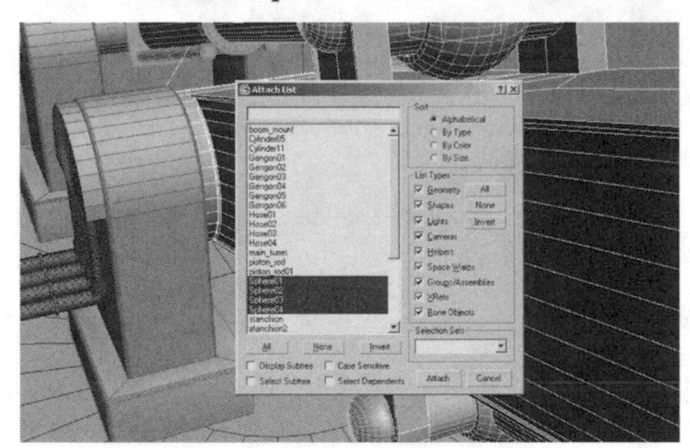

Figure 2-940

9. Select the polygons shown on both sides of the upper_boom and Bevel them:

Figure 2-941

Type	Height	Outline	Apply/OK
Local Normal	0	–0.1	Apply
Local Normal	–0.1	0	OK

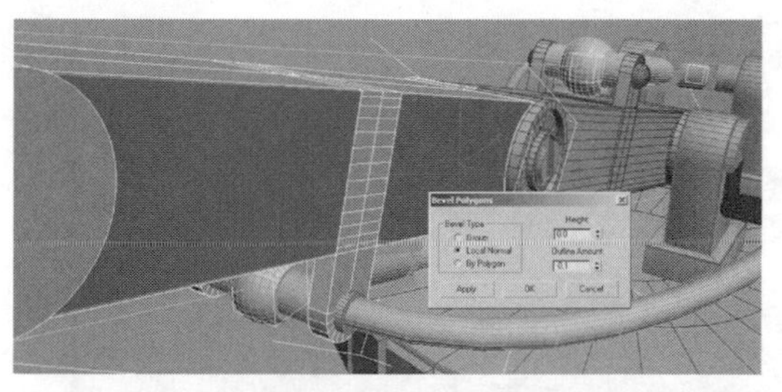
Figure 2-942

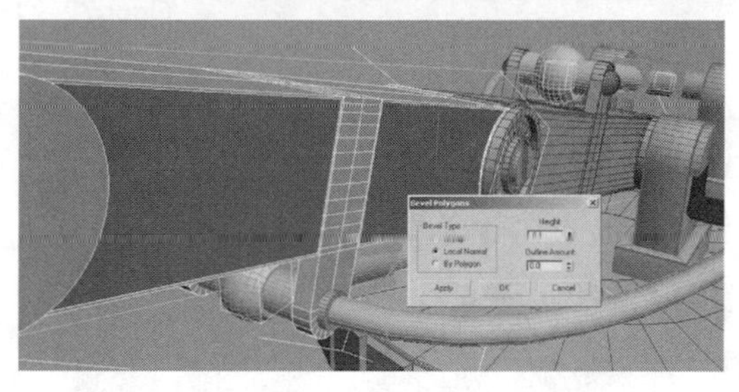
Figure 2-943

10. Select the polygons of the uppermost joint on the right side of the upper_boom.

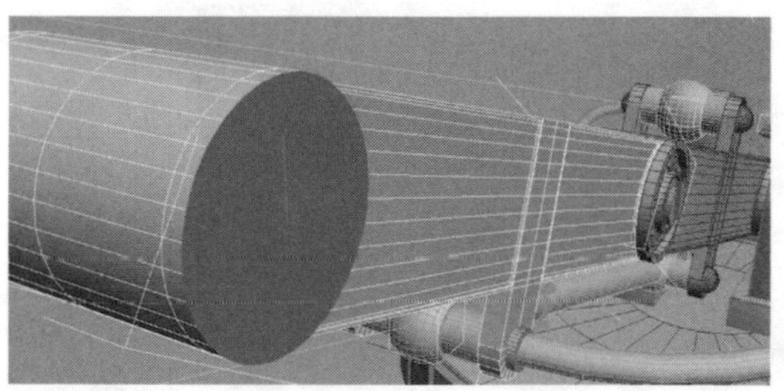
Figure 2-944

11. Click **Bevel Settings:**

Type	Height	Outline	Apply/OK
Group	0	–0.8	Apply
Group	5	0	OK

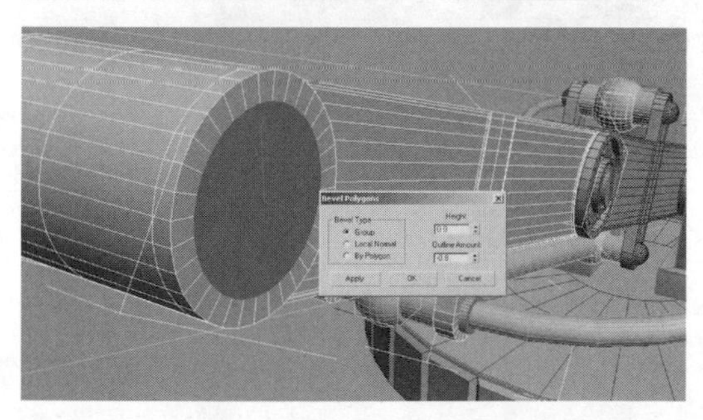
Figure 2-945

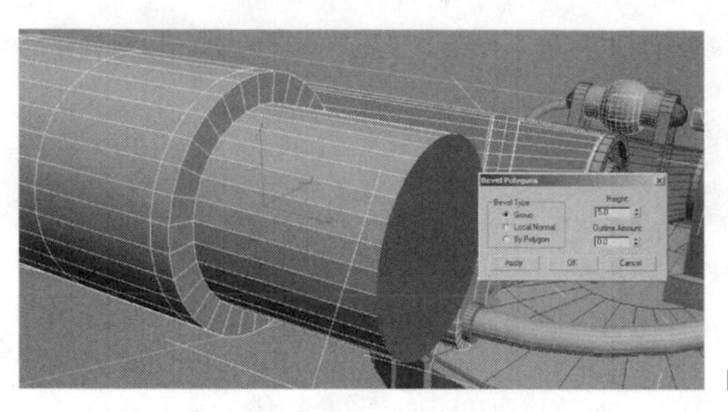

Figure 2-946

12. Group Extrude by **1.0** and hit **Apply** nine times.

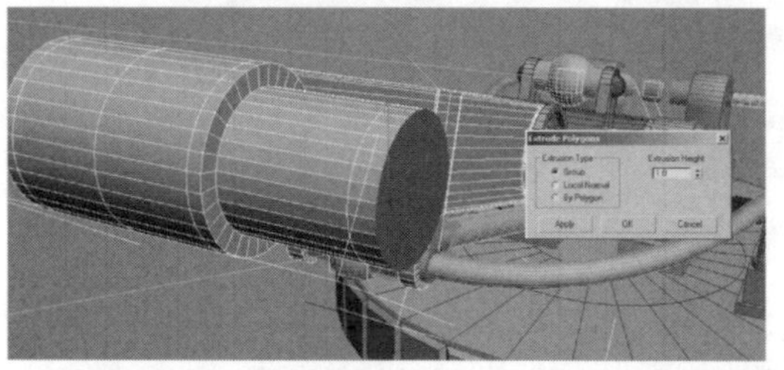

Figure 2-947

Figure 2-948

13. Click **Grow** until all the polygons are selected back to the joint (353 polys).

Figure 2-949

14. Click **Detach**, choose **Detach As Object**, and name it **eye_axle**.

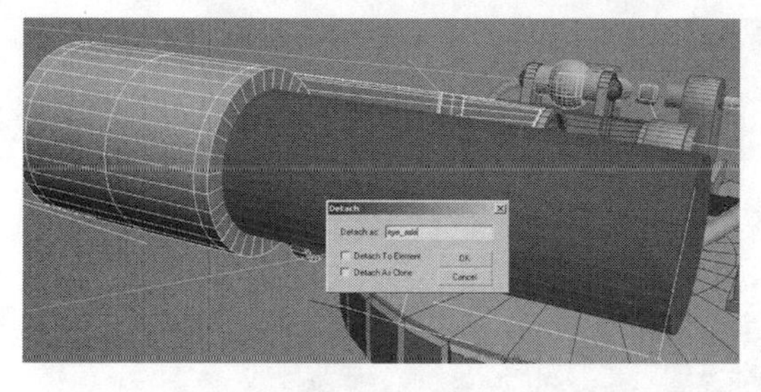

Figure 2-950

15. Move the pivot point to the fifth segment.

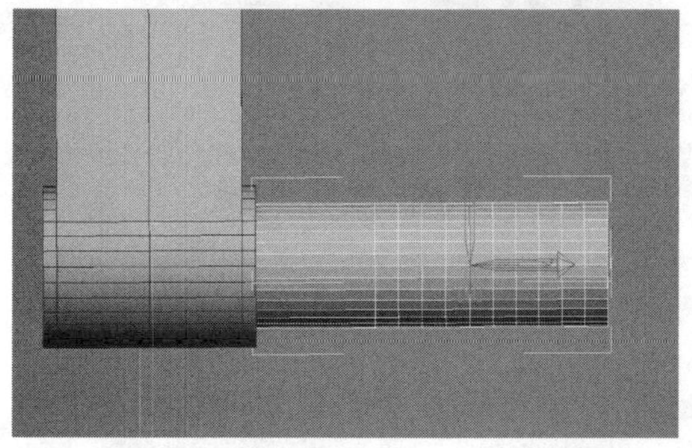

Figure 2-951

16. Add a Bend modifier to the eye_axle with an Angle of **–90**, Direction of **40**, in the Z axis, with the effect limited to an Upper Limit of **5.0**.

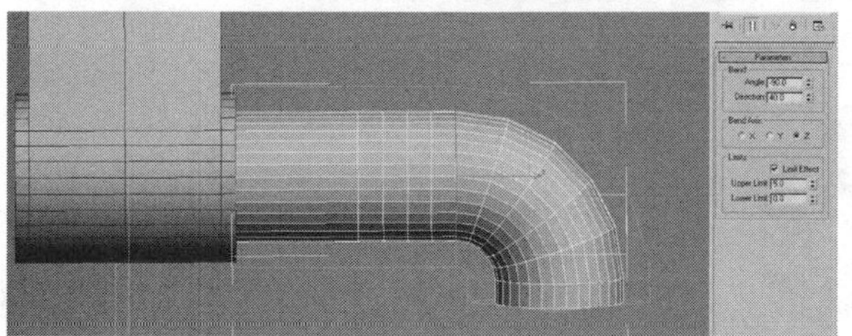

Figure 2-952

17. Convert it to an Editable Polygon and slide it inside the joint as shown in Figure 2-954.

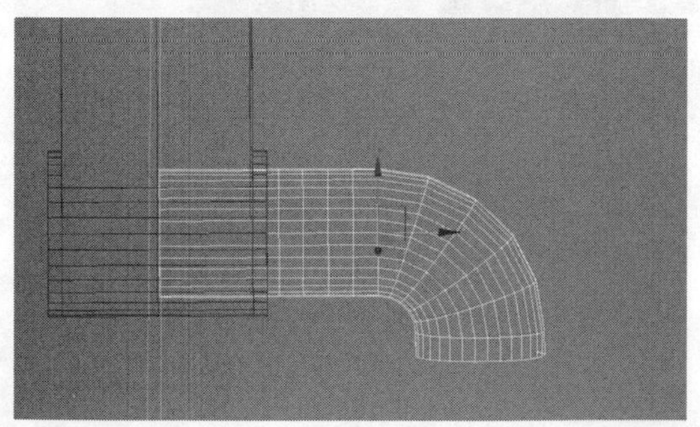

Figure 2-953

18. Unhide the eye_pod and add the Clay material to it.

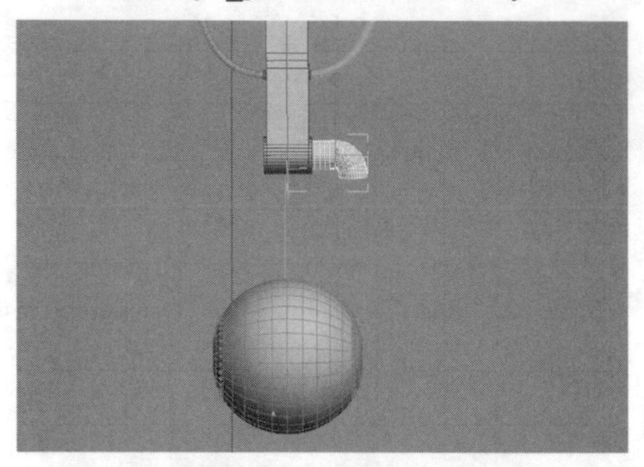

Figure 2-954

19. Select the **eye_pod** and center the pivot.

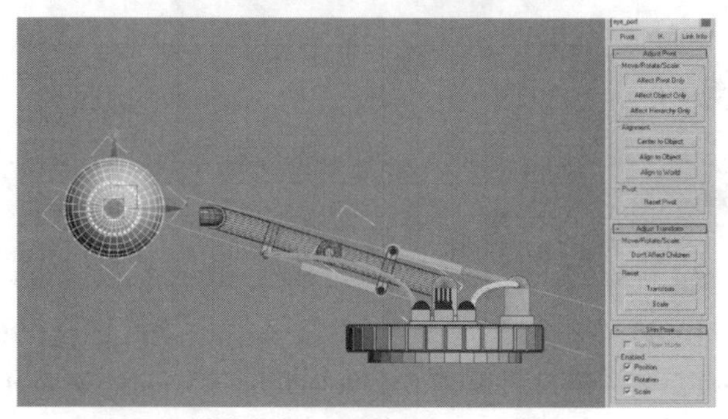

Figure 2-955

20. Scale the eye_pod down to **70** percent.

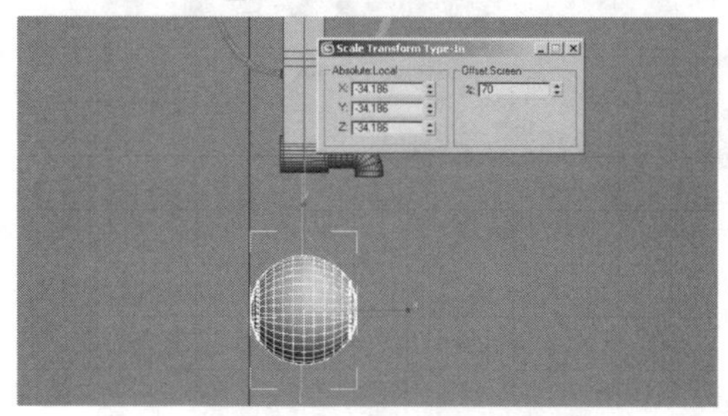

Figure 2-956

21. Select the polygon at the end of the eye_axle.

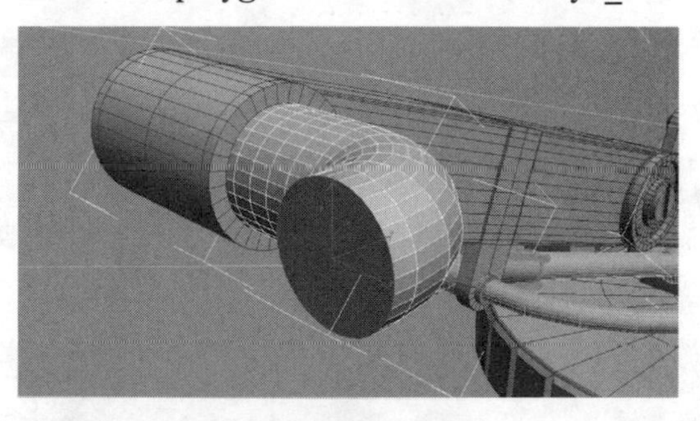

Figure 2-957

22. Extrude it by **1.0** ten times.

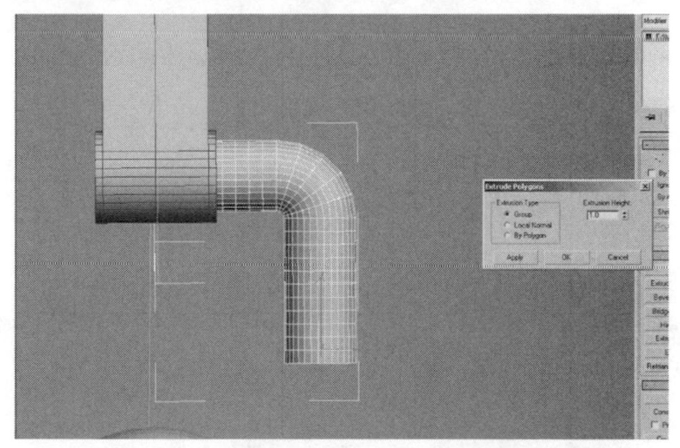

Figure 2-958

23. Rotate the front polygon by **10** degrees in the Z axis.

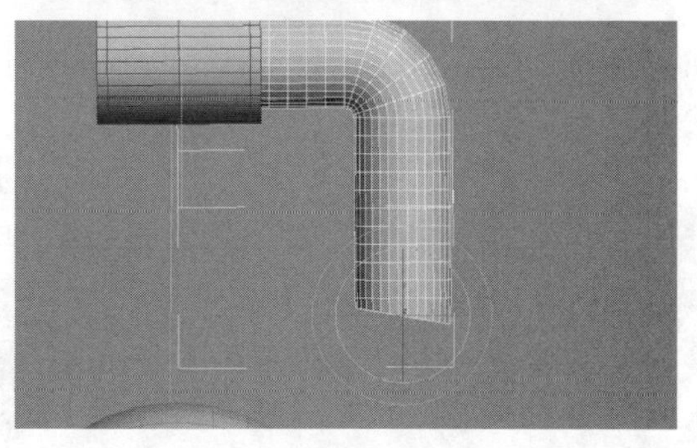

Figure 2-959

24. Extrude the polygon by **1.0** and Rotate it.

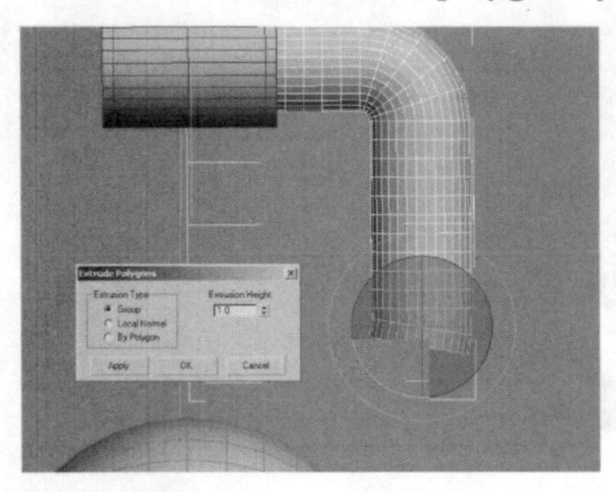

Figure 2-960

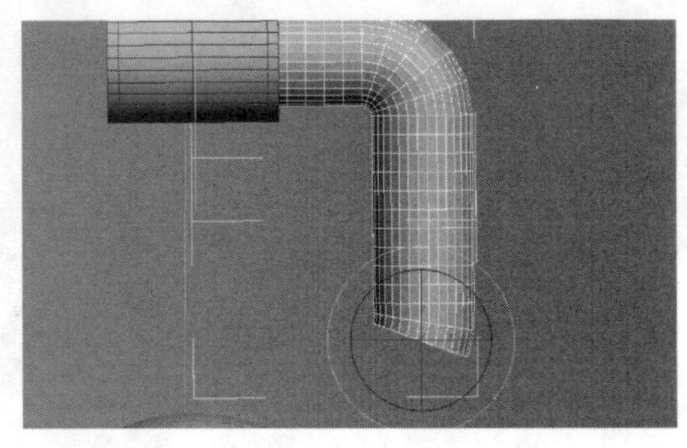

Figure 2-961

25. Repeat the last step until you achieve a 90-degree angle.

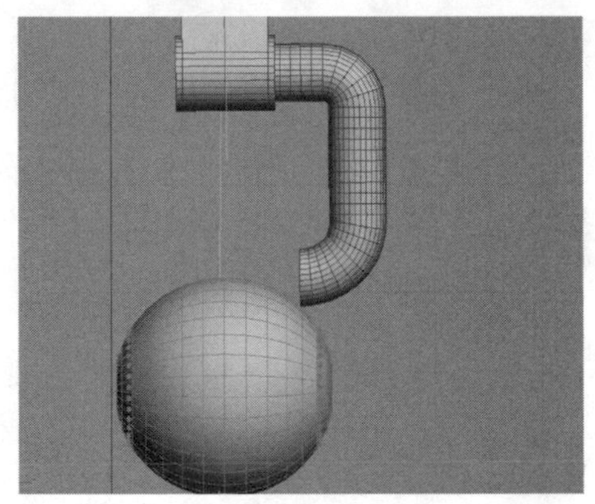

Figure 2-962

26. Position the eye_pod so that the hole in it is aligned with the end of the eye_axle.

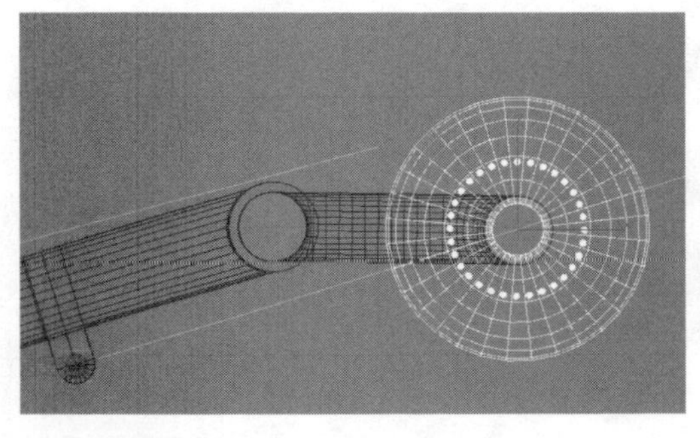

Figure 2-963

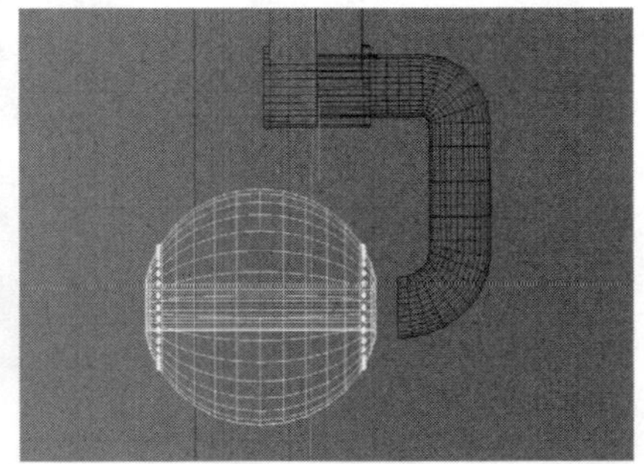

Figure 2-964

27. Select the polygon at the end of the eye_axle (facing the opening of the eye_pod), switch to the Left view, click **Bevel Settings**, and

adjust the Outline Amount until you can look through the hole in the eye_pod and see that the polygon will just fit (mine is **–0.75**). Click **OK**.

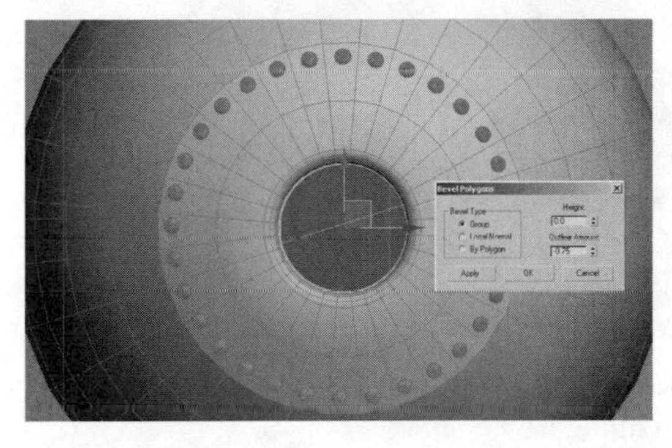

Figure 2-965

28. Switch to the Top view and Extrude the polygon until it is most of the way through the hole in the eye_pod, but not the entire way (**~17.75**).

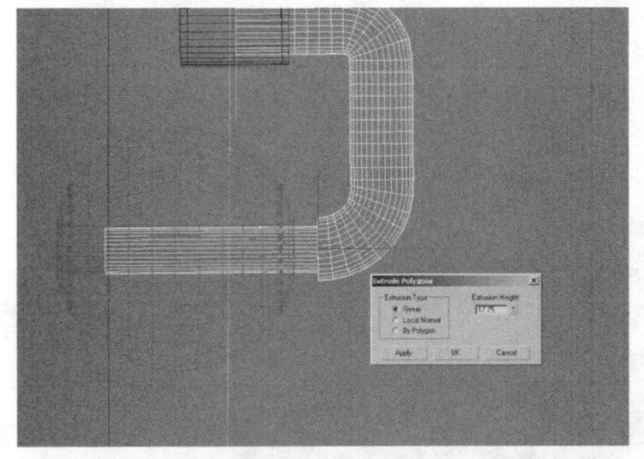

Figure 2-966

29. Move the eye_pod until it is seated against the eye_axle.

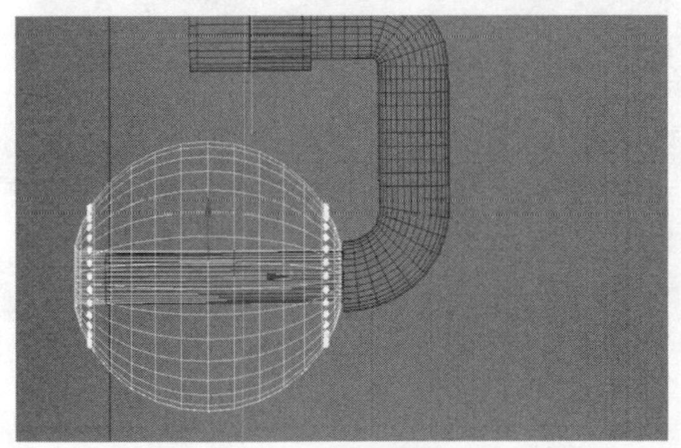

Figure 2-967

30. Select and Link the eye_pod to the eye_axle and Select and Link the eye_axle to the upper_boom.

31. Center the pivot of the eye_pod and move the eye_axle pivot to the joint that connects it to the upper_boom.

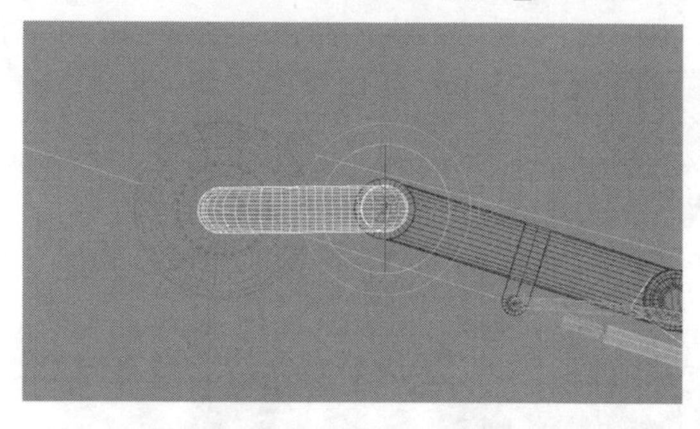

Figure 2-968

32. Unhide the eye, position it on top of the eye_pod, and scale it to the size shown in Figure 2-969.

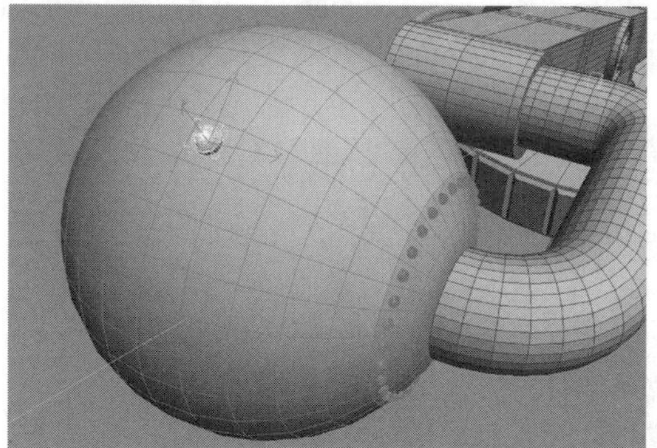

Figure 2-969

33. Select the eye.

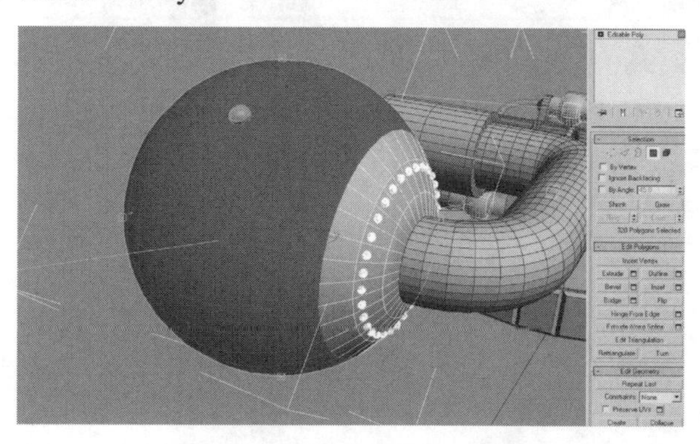

Figure 2-970

34. Object-select the eye. Under the Create panel, select **Compound Objects**, and under Object Type, press the **Scatter** button.

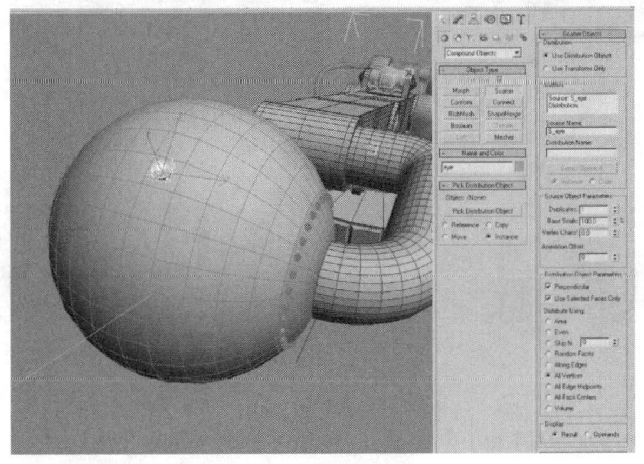

Figure 2-971

35. Make sure that **Instance** is selected, **Use Selected Faces Only** is checked, and **All Vertices** is selected.

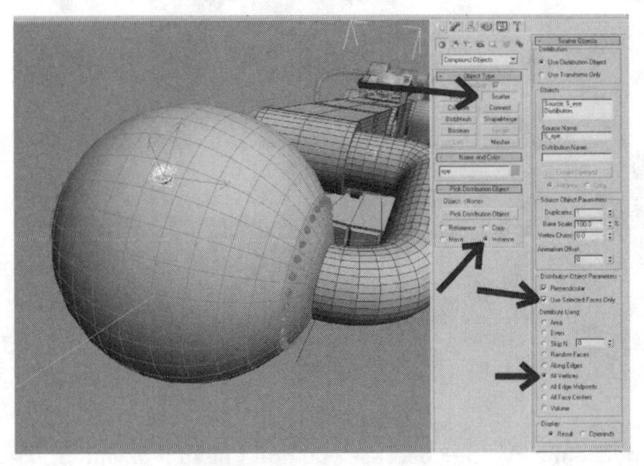

Figure 2-972

FYI: Scatter will use the faces you selected on the eye_pod and create instances at each vertex in that selection.

36. Select **Pick Distribution Object**, hit **H**, and select **eye_pod**.

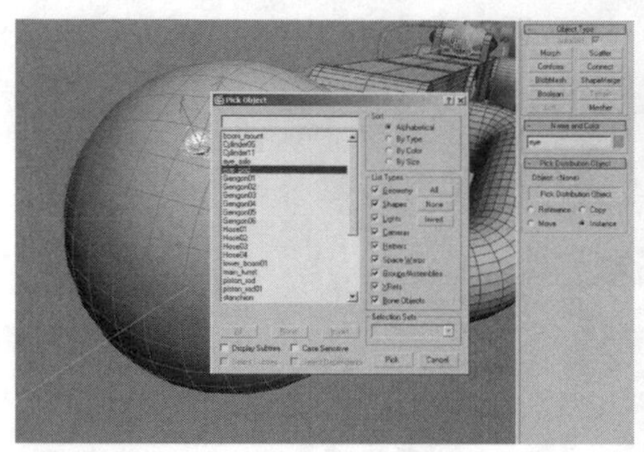

Figure 2-973

Figure 2-974

37. Convert to Editable Polygon, then select **eye_pod** and delete it.

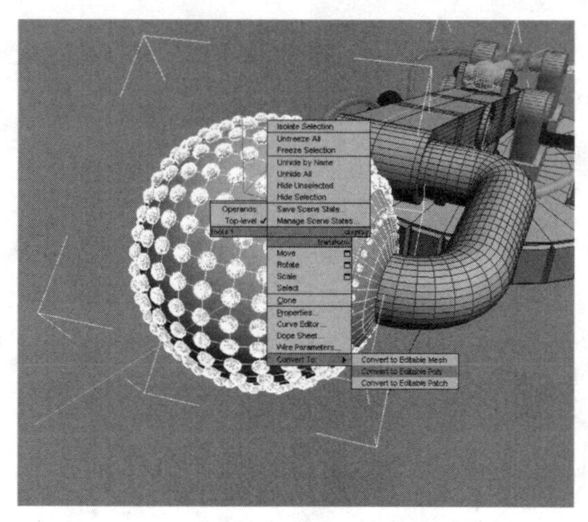

Figure 2-975

FYI: You delete the eye_pod because you don't need it anymore. It was just a matrix to create the scatter object.

38. Select and Link the eye object to the eye_axle.
39. Unhide All and add the Clay material to everything.
40. Do some renders, and ... *you're done*! Take a look:

Day 16: Final Detailing

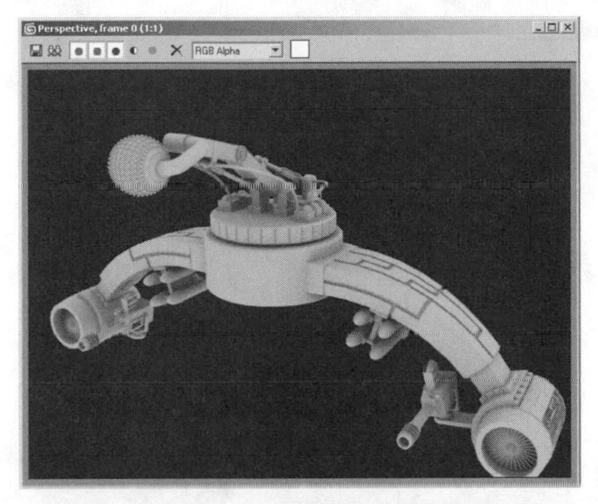

Figure 2-976

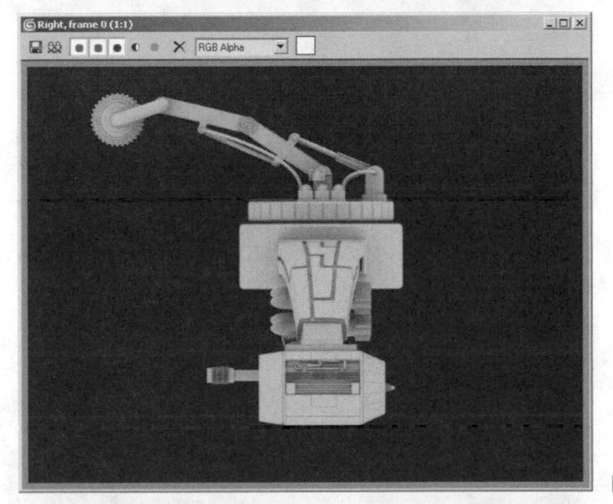

Figure 2-977

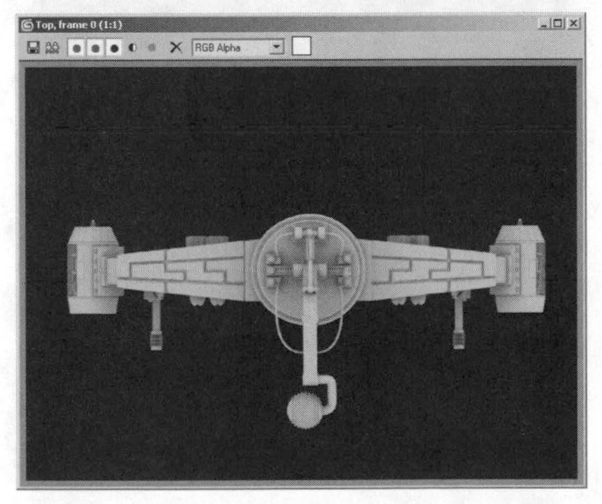

Figure 2-978

This is the battle mech we create in Chapter 3.

Chapter 3
The Battle Mech

RoboCop's ED-209. *The Matrix*'s APU. *Star Wars'* AT-ATs. They're big, they're loud, they're armed to the teeth, and they're ready to kick butt. Battle mechs are perhaps the coolest of all bots. What else is there to say?

Message: So where do you get ideas for your models? Well ... it's easy when someone gives you image planes to work from, but in models like this one, I don't use image planes. Instead, I look at a *lot* of images from the Internet. For instance, the legs and feet of the bot you'll build owe a lot to the design of a Warhammer Titan. There's also a little bit of Tiberian Sun and Battlefield 2142. I did not steal the designs, but rather used them as a starting point for the basic shape and then made it my own. For instance, I have a real affection for hoses and pipes and wires (it's all very Freudian). So while the overall shape of the leg is similar to a Titan, mine has way more hoses and pipes (that's what makes it mine). I want to point out this *isn't* cheating. Every artist I know borrows from the work of other artists they admire. To me, there's no higher compliment than for someone to build on my design. Notice I said *build* and *not* steal. Big difference.

I also use a ton of model kits. I generally get them for cheap off eBay. But here's the kicker. I generally don't build them. I use the instruction images as references and I leave the parts on the sprue (for easily handling). If I get stuck, I can break these out, look at them, look how the parts fit into the engine mounts, etc., and it can usually jump-start me when I've stalled.

Now the downside to this, as you may've noticed, is you can have some false starts and end up deleting things you've already built to make better ones. Despite the occasional redundancy or obsolescence, this is a common approach because it feels more like art, whereas working from image planes feels like drafting.

I'm starting you out with some really detailed work on the feet and legs. I've deliberately left the top of the mech somewhat bare so you can practice adding your own personal touches and make it your own. Might I suggest more pipes? ☺

Day 1: Building the Toe

1. Before starting work on the battle mech, make sure your units are set to Generic (Customize > Units Setup). Start by making a Box and converting it to an Editable Polygon:

Length	Width	Height	Length/Width/Height Segs
60	90	50	3/1/1

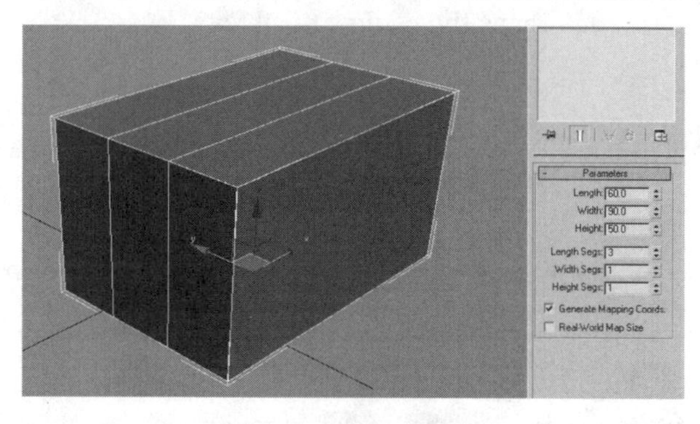

Figure 3-1

2. Select the three front edges and move them down **25** units in the Z axis to form the first segment of the toe.

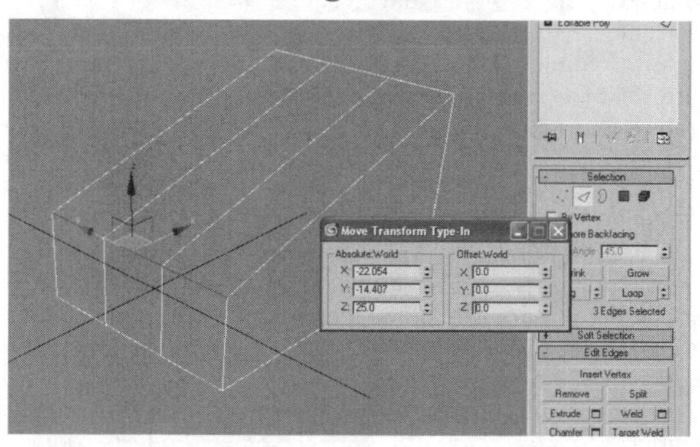

Figure 3-2

3. Select the front left and right polygons and Bevel them:

Type	Height	Outline	Apply/OK
Local Normal	22	–4	OK

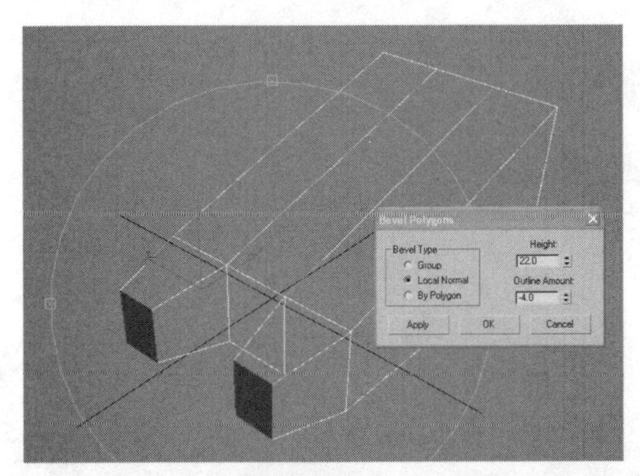

Figure 3-3

4. Select the nine polygons comprising the edge of the foot (but *not* the three in the rear).

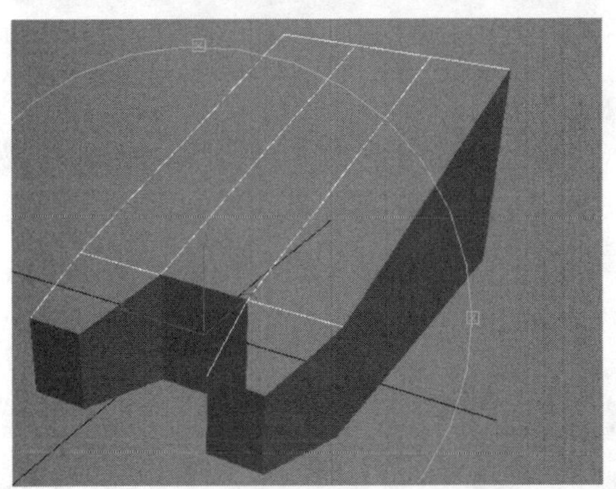

Figure 3-4

5. Click **Bevel Settings:**

Type	Height	Outline	Apply/OK
By Polygon	0	–1	Apply
By Polygon	0.4	–1	OK

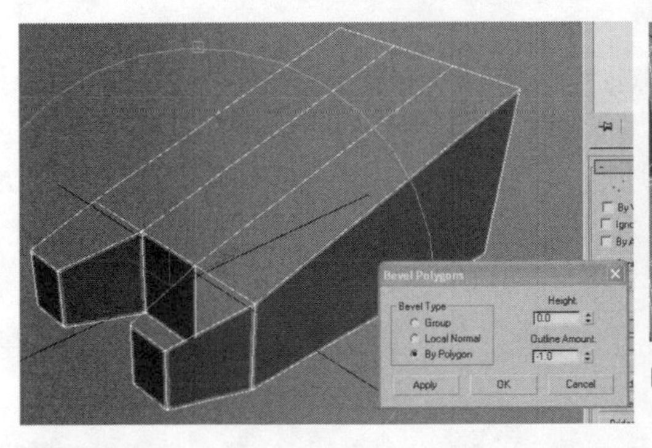

Figure 3-5

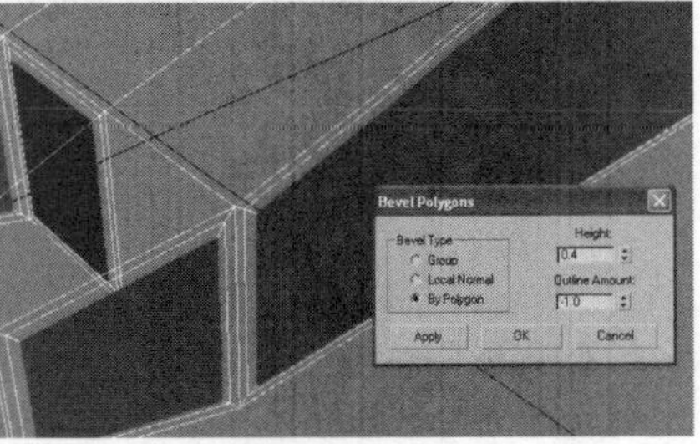

Figure 3-6

6. Select the top five polygons, click **Bevel Settings**, and then do a test render (**F9**):

Type	Height	Outline	Apply/OK
Group	0	–1	Apply
Group	0.4	–1	OK

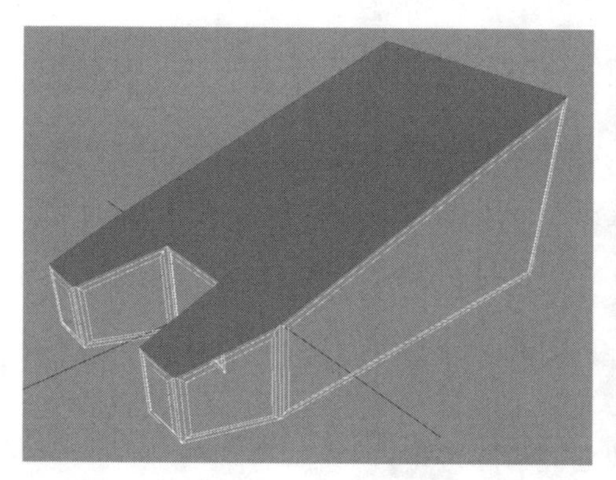

Figure 3-7

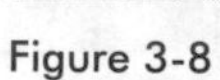

Figure 3-8

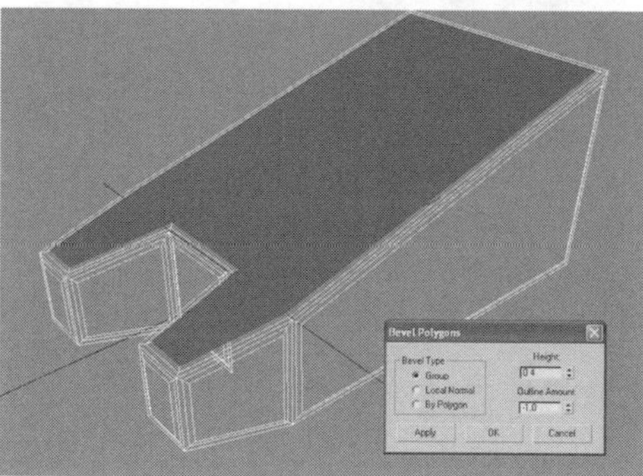

Figure 3-9

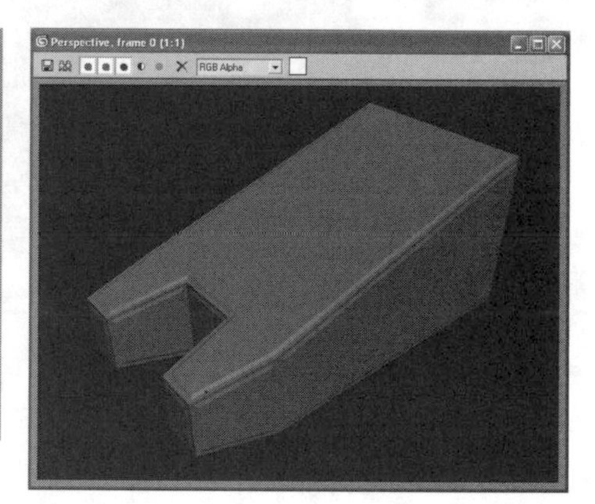

Figure 3-10

7. Select the rear three polygons, click **Bevel Settings** and use the settings in the following table, then Group Extrude the outer two by **20.**

Type	Height	Outline	Apply/OK
By Polygon	0	–1	OK

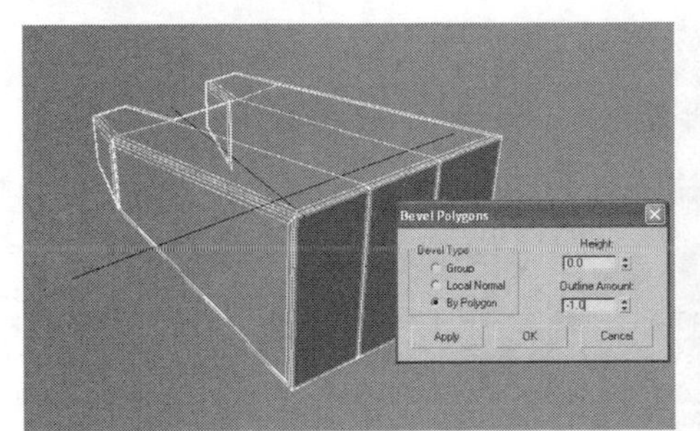

Figure 3-11

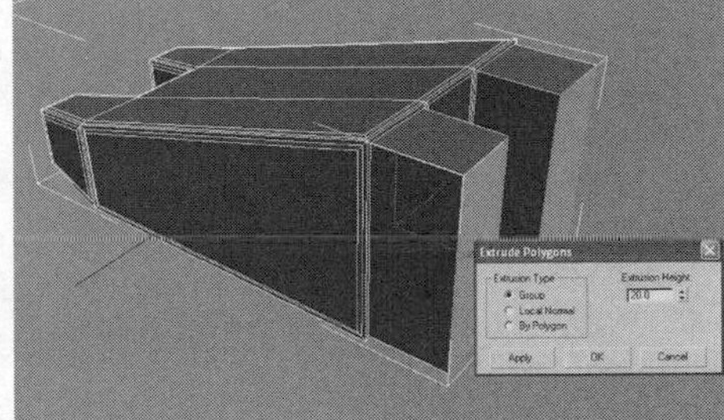

Figure 3-12

8. Select the four outer edges of the polygons you extruded in the last step and click **Connect**.

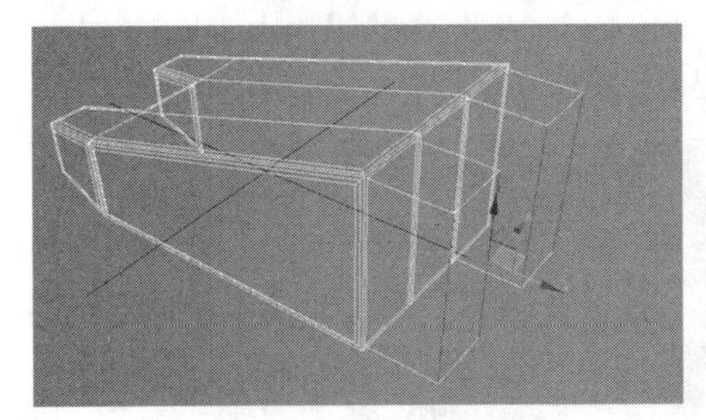

Figure 3-13

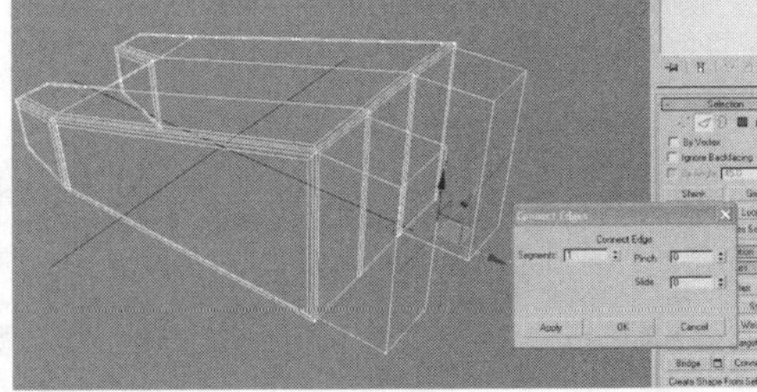

Figure 3-14

9. Select the bottom two polygons and delete them. Select the top two polygons and Hinge From Edge **180** degrees with **10** Segments, using the bottom edge of the one of the polys as the hinge. Delete the back-facing polygon and Weld the vertices.

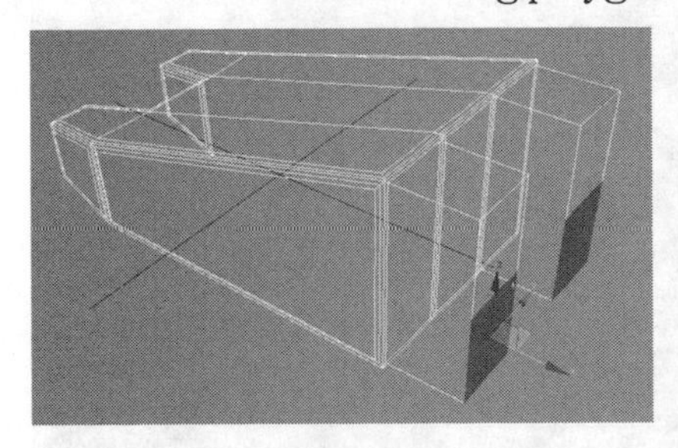

Figure 3-15

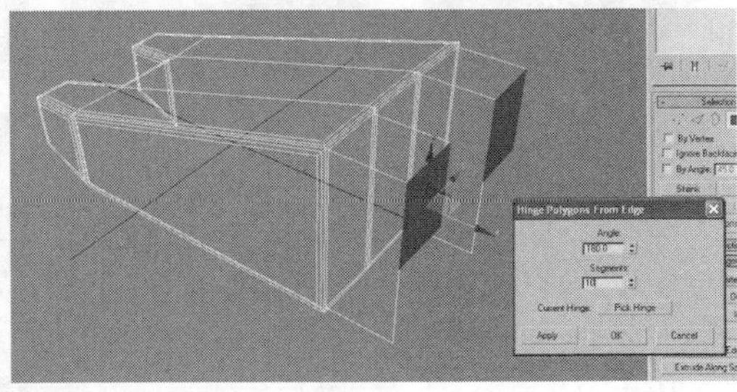

Figure 3-16

10. To make the armor plates, select the outermost polygons on the top and sides, and then click **Bevel Settings**:

Type	Height	Outline	Apply/OK
Local Normal	0.8	0	OK

Figure 3-17

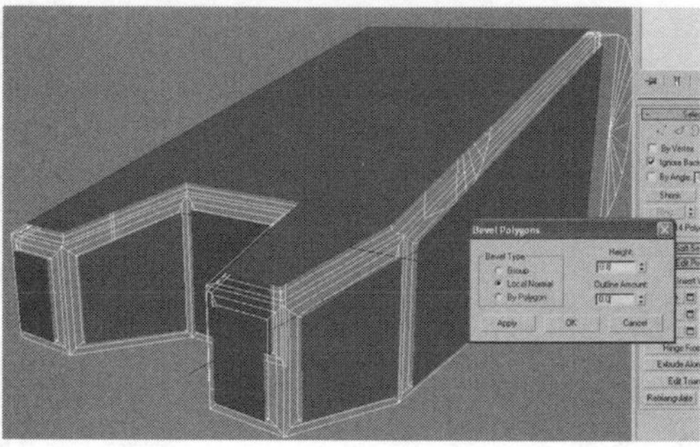

Figure 3-18

11. Select the 30 edges between the armor plates (shown with dark outlines in Figure 3-19), Chamfer Edges by **0.3**, click **Apply**, change the Chamfer Amount to **0.1**, click **OK**, and then do a test render (**F9**).

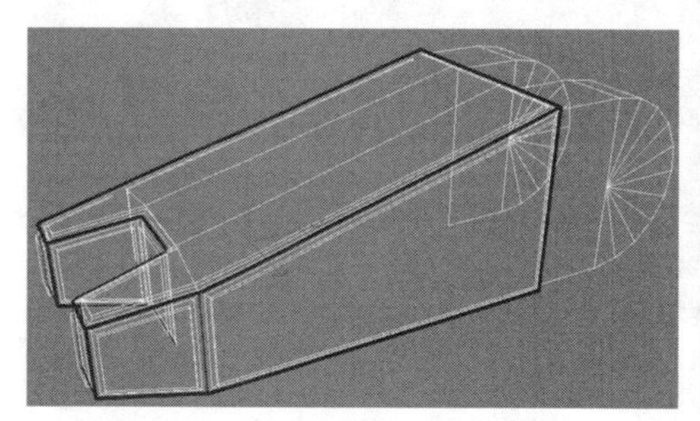

Figure 3-19

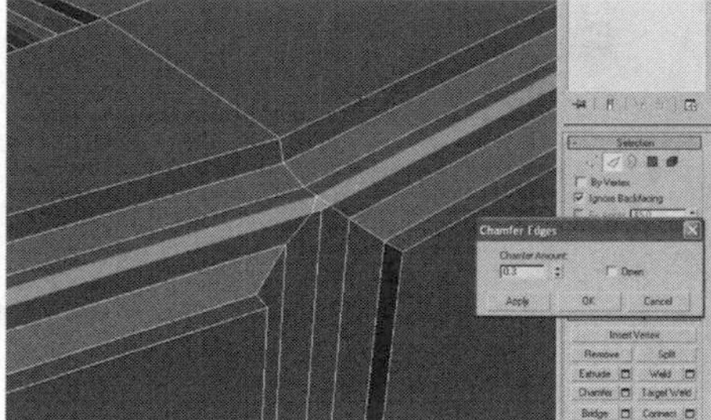

Figure 3-20

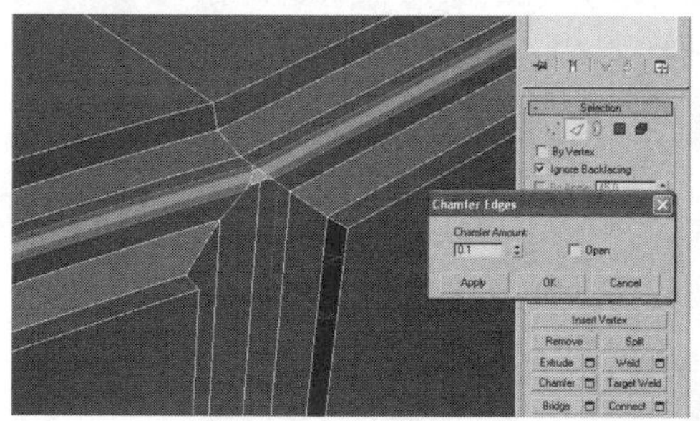

Figure 3-21

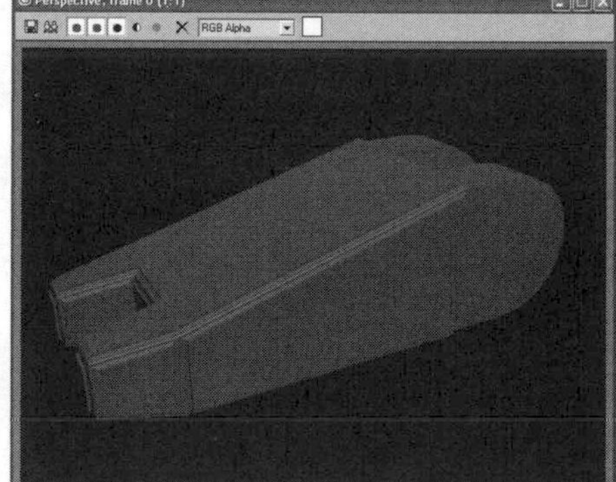

Figure 3-22

12. Select the top edges of the polygons comprising the armor plates, Chamfer Edges by **0.1**, click **Apply**, change the Chamfer Amount to **0.04**, click **OK**, and then do a test render (**F9**).

Day 1: Building the Toe

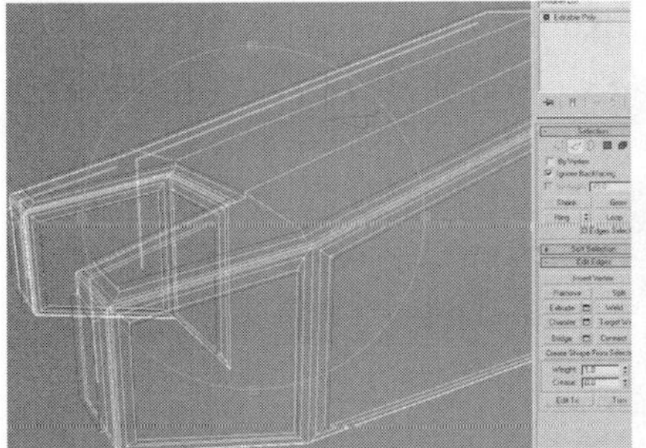

Figure 3-23

Figure 3-24

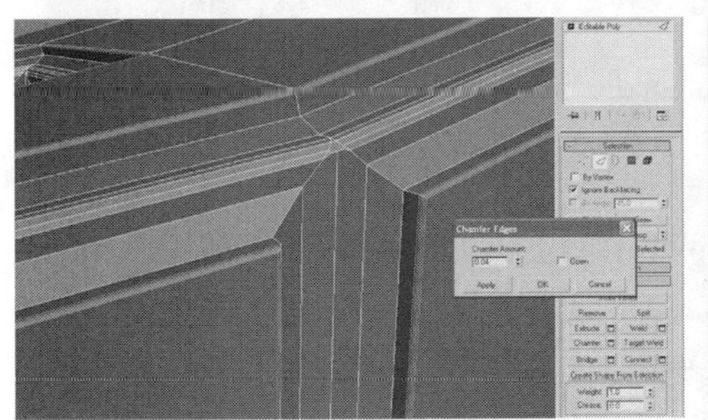

Figure 3-25

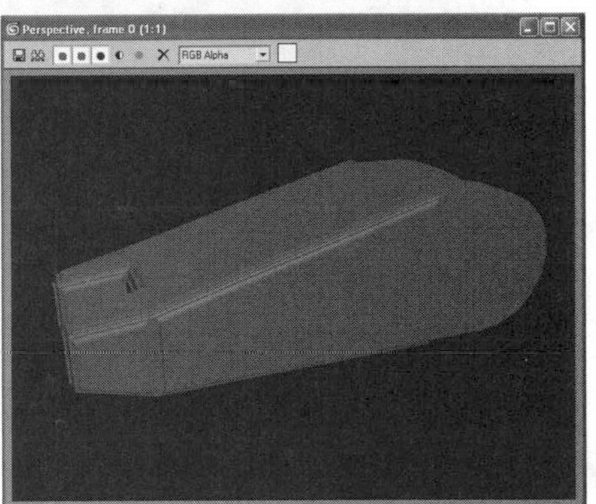

Figure 3-26

13. Create a Cylinder and center it as shown in Figure 3-27. With the cylinder still selected, click the drop-down list in the Modify panel and select **Compound Objects** from the list. Change the name of the box to **toe01**.

Radius	Height	Height/Cap Segs	Sides	Smooth
14.0	–58.6	5/1	20	Checked

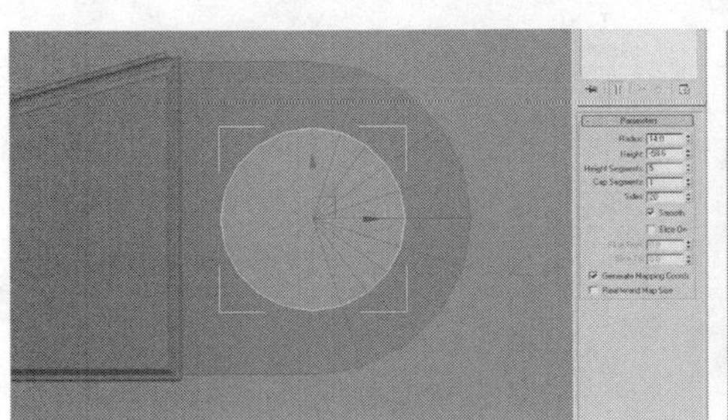

Figure 3-27

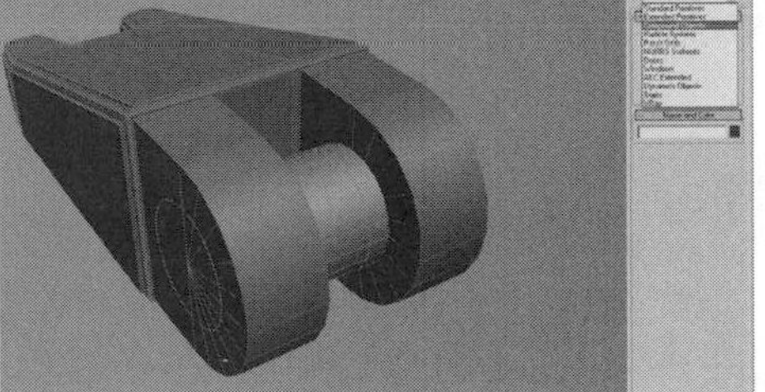

Figure 3-28

14. Under Object Type, click **Boolean**, click **Pick Operand B** (since the toe is Operand A), click the cylinder, and then under Operation click **Subtraction (A-B)**; this creates a hole for the axle.

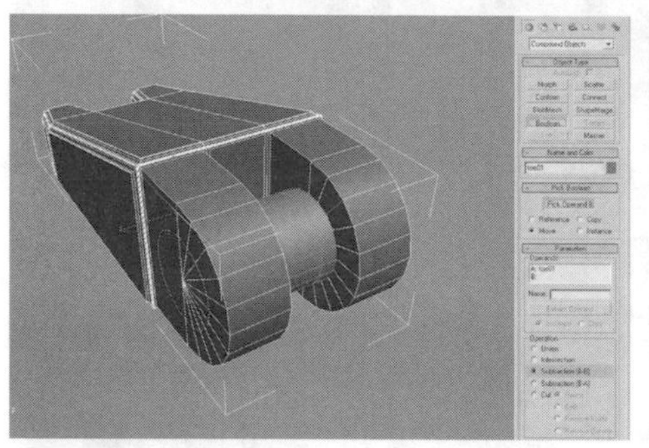

Figure 3-29

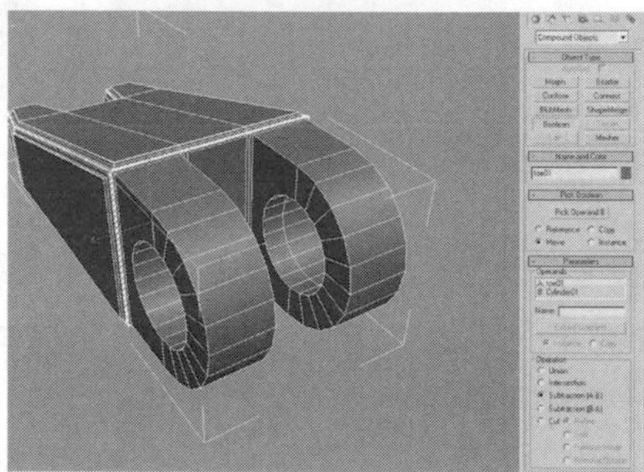

Figure 3-30

15. Convert the toe to an Editable Polygon and then select the outer edges of the hinge.

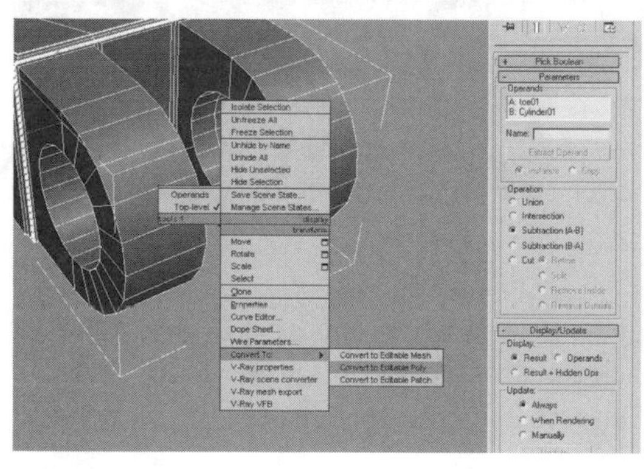

Figure 3-31

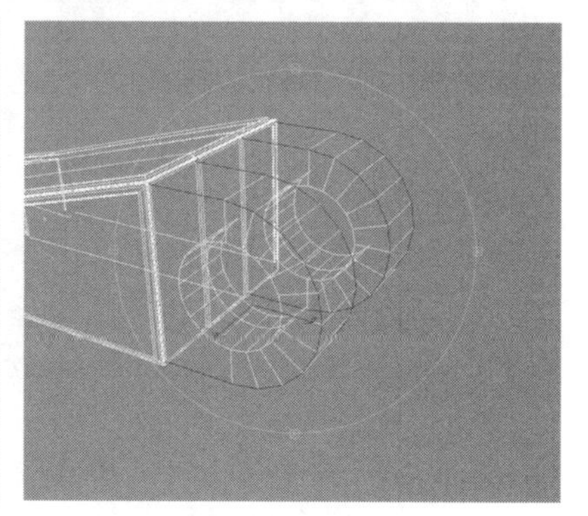

Figure 3-32

16. Chamfer the edges first by **0.4** and then by **0.15**.

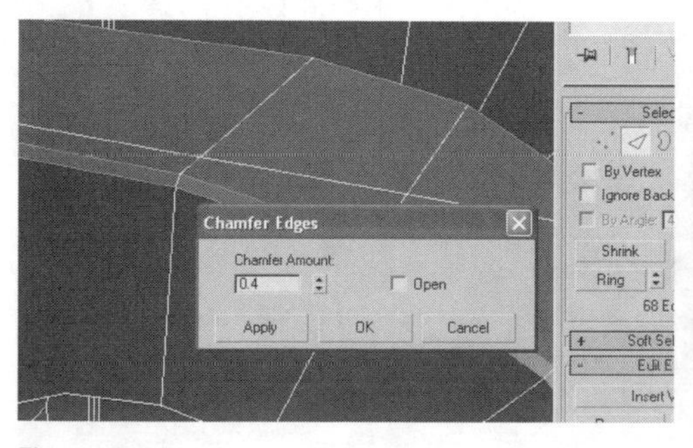

Figure 3-33

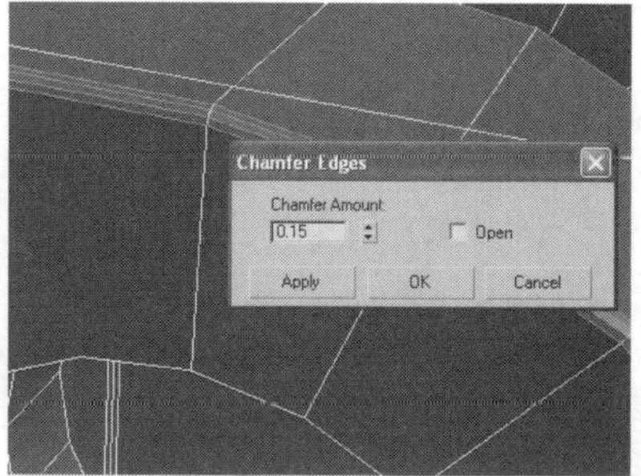

Figure 3-34

17. In the Top view, create a Box above the toe, convert it to an Editable Polygon, marquee-select across the top and bottom edges, and then click **Connect.**

Length	Width	Height	Length/Width/Height Segs
110.552	158.543	49.985	1/1/1

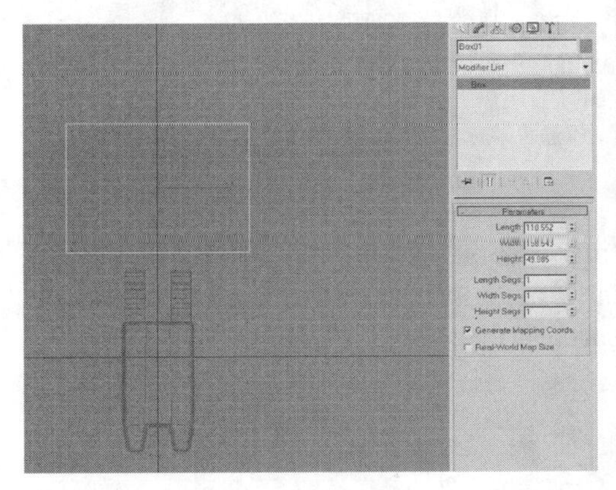

Figure 3-35

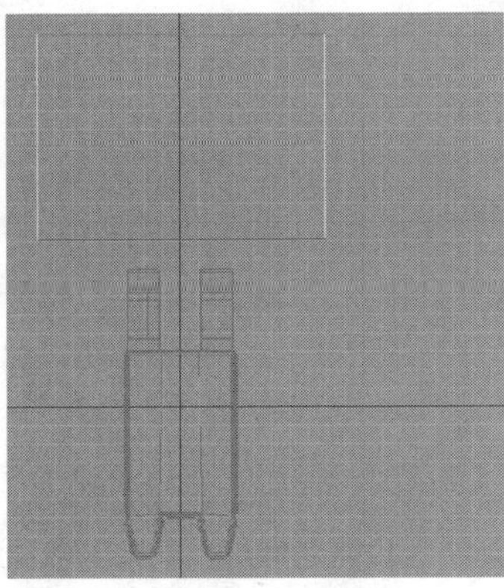

Figure 3-36

18. Select the edge you made with Connect, Chamfer it by **9.8**, then marquee-select the bottom-left and bottom-right vertices.

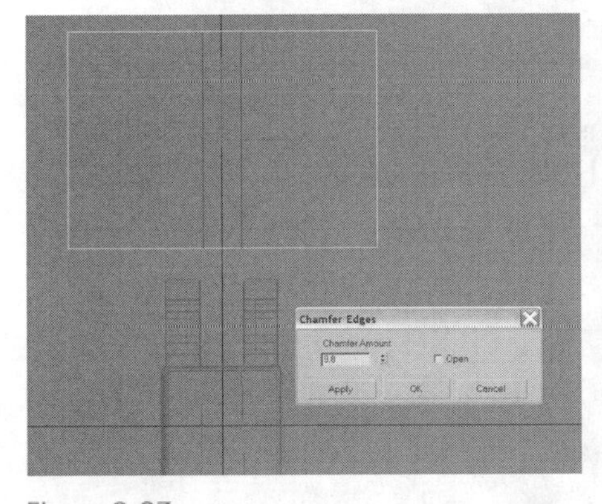

Figure 3-37

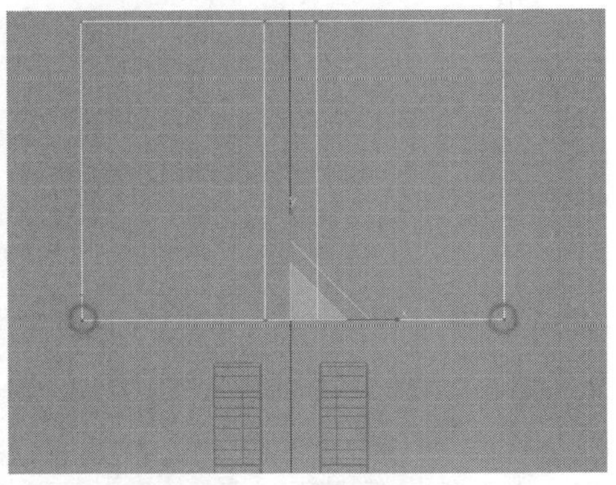

Figure 3-38

19. Scale the vertices **43** in the X axis, then select the top-left and top-right corner vertices and Scale them in the X axis until the model looks like Figure 3-40.

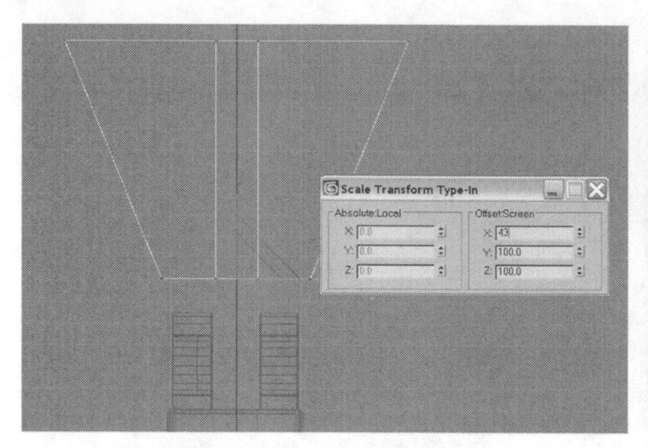

Figure 3-39

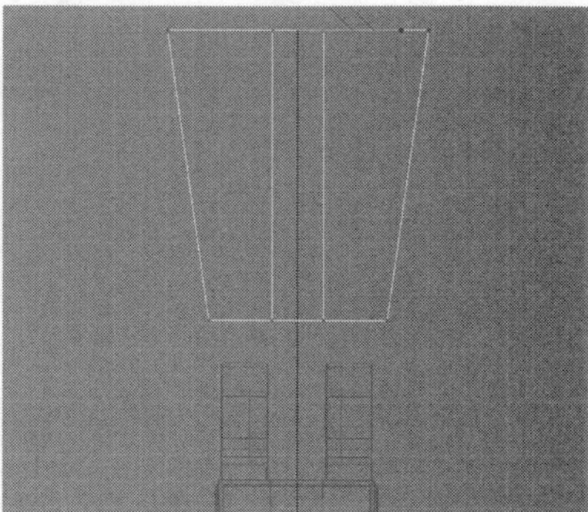
Figure 3-40

20. Switch to the Right view, marquee-select the upper-right vertices, and move them down in the Y axis until the incline of the middle toe matches the incline of the front toe.

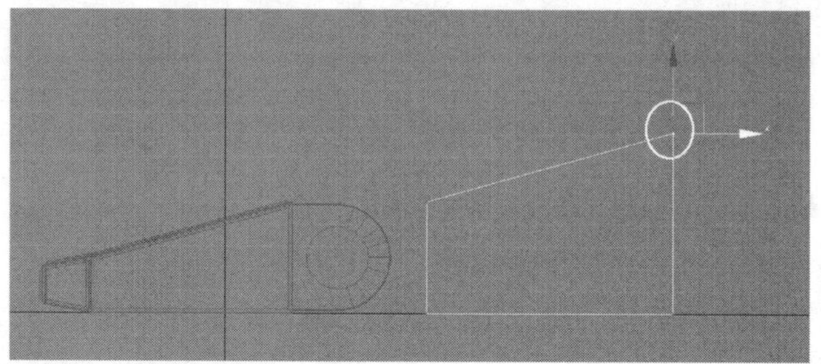
Figure 3-41

21. Select the three front polygons of the middle toe, Bevel the polygons, right-click, and choose **Hide Unselected**.

Type	Height	Outline	Apply/OK
By Polygon	0	–1	OK

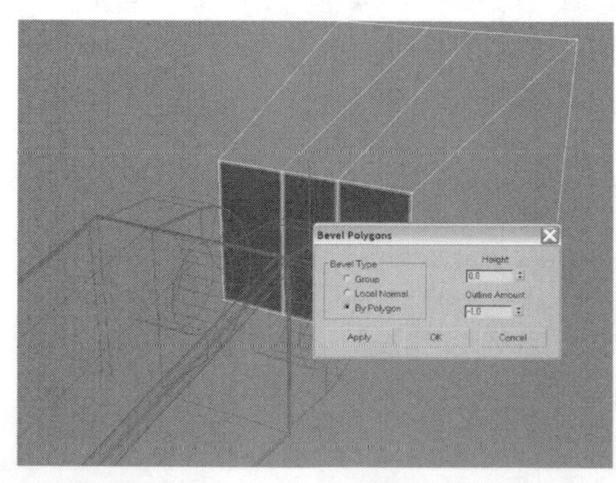

Figure 3-42

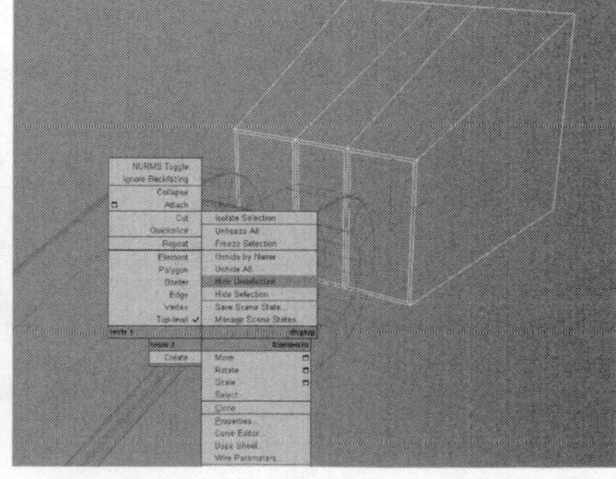
Figure 3-43

22. Select the six vertical edges of the polygons, click the **Connect** button, and then select the middle two polygons.

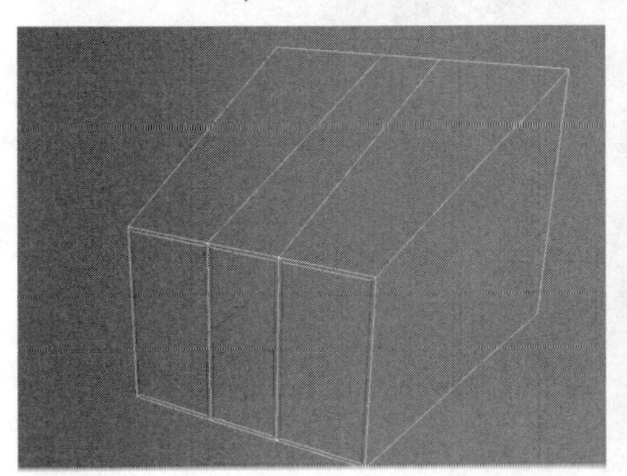
Figure 3-44

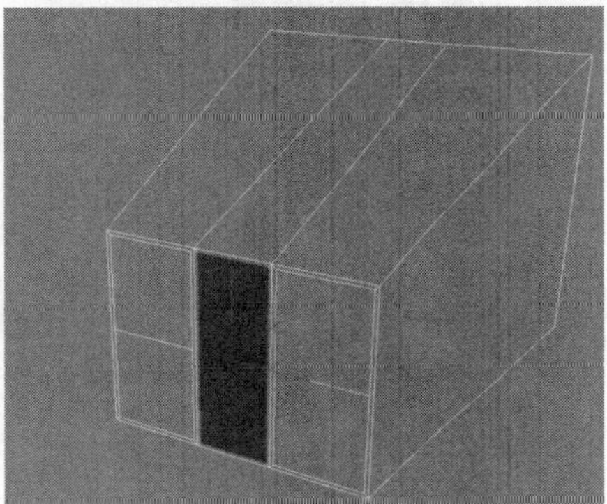
Figure 3-45

23. Switch to the Top view, Extrude the two polygons by **20**, Hinge From Edge by **180** degrees with **10** Segments using the bottom edge as the hinge, delete the back-facing polygon, and Weld the vertices.

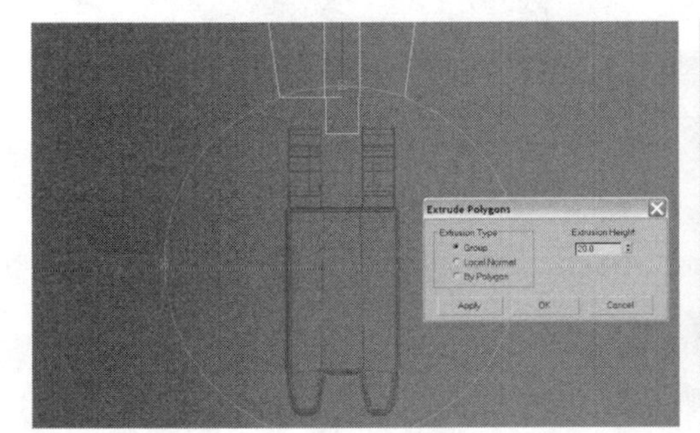

Figure 3-46

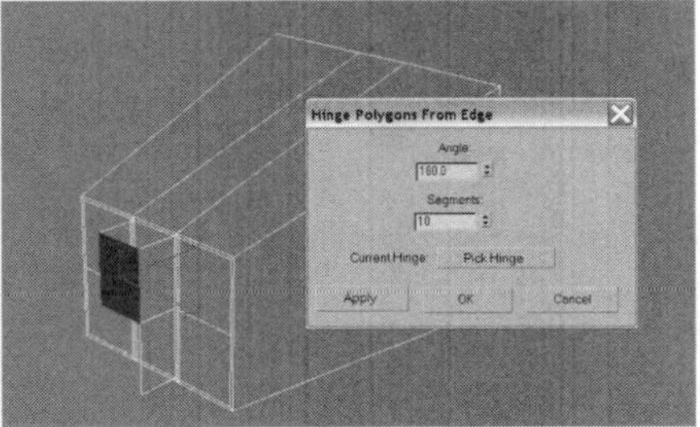

Figure 3-47

24. Create a Cylinder in the center of the joint and then convert it to an Editable Polygon.

Radius	Height	Height/Cap Segs	Sides	Smooth
14	30	1/1	20	Checked

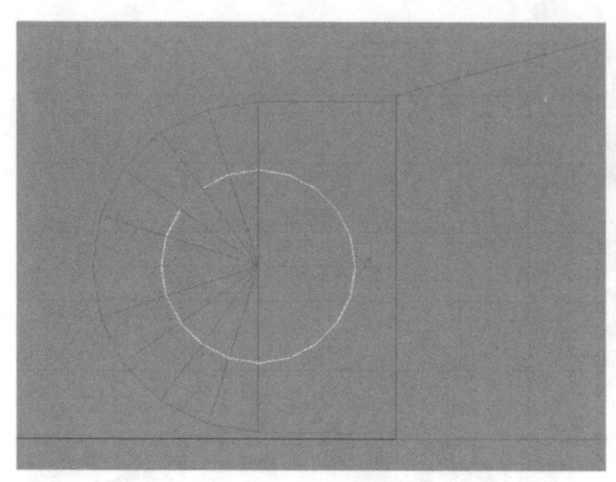

Figure 3-48

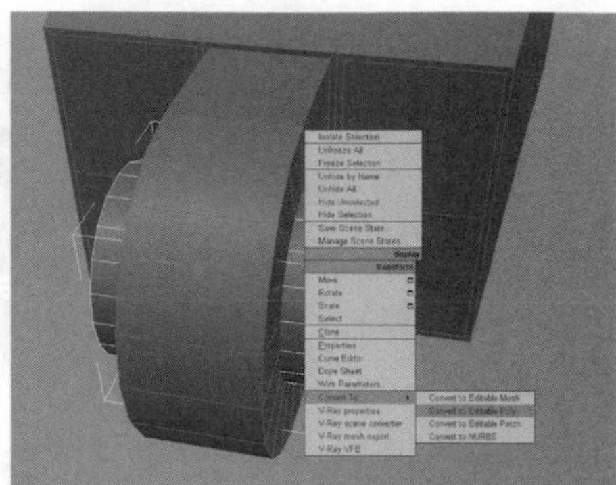

Figure 3-49

25. Create a Boolean, click **Pick Operand B**, click the cylinder (make sure **Subtraction (A-B)** is selected), convert the Boolean to an Editable Polygon, and name it **middle_toe**.

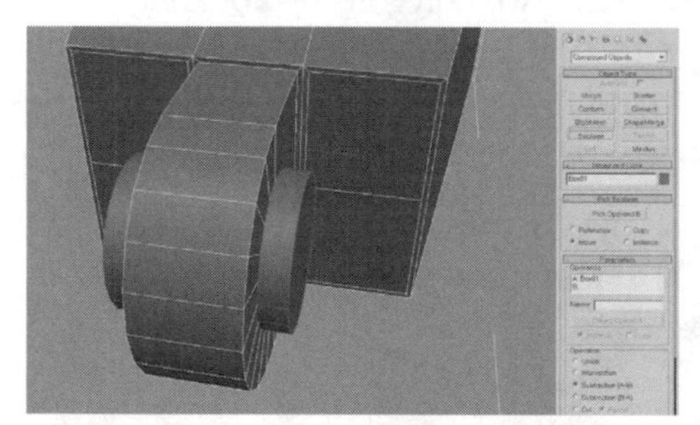

Figure 3-50

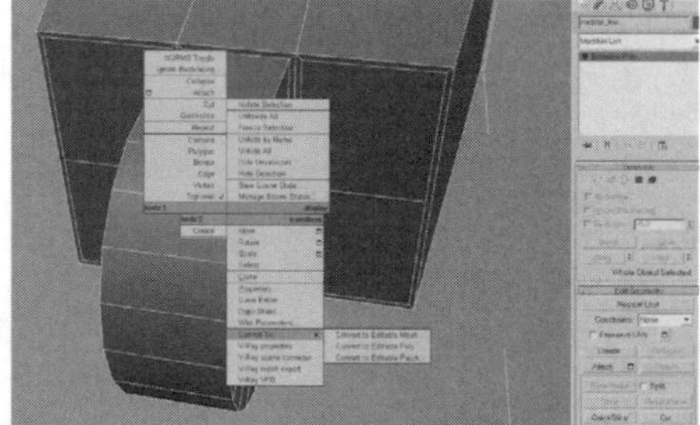

Figure 3-51

26. Select the outer and inner edges, Chamfer them by **0.4**, then Chamfer again by **0.15**.

Figure 3-52

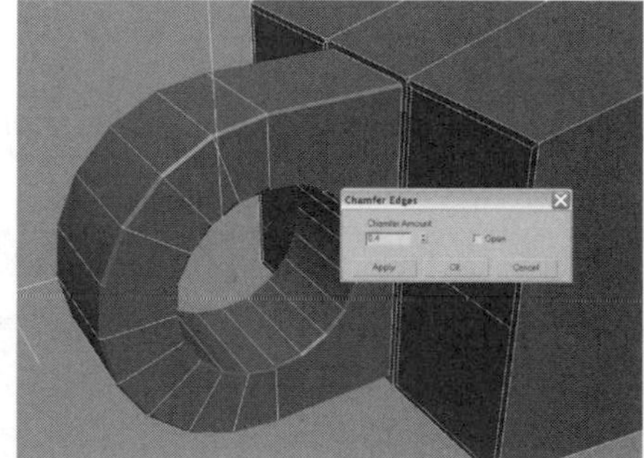

Figure 3-53

Day 1: Building the Toe

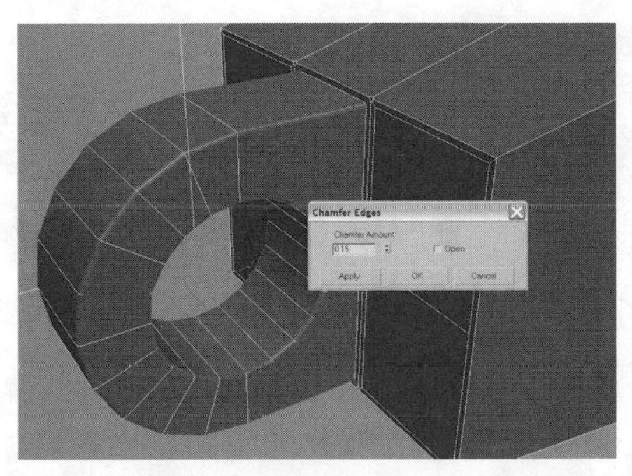

Figure 3-54

27. Align the holes in both parts of the foot (this is best done in wireframe); move vertices to better align the holes and to move the edges to give the hinges enough space to move.

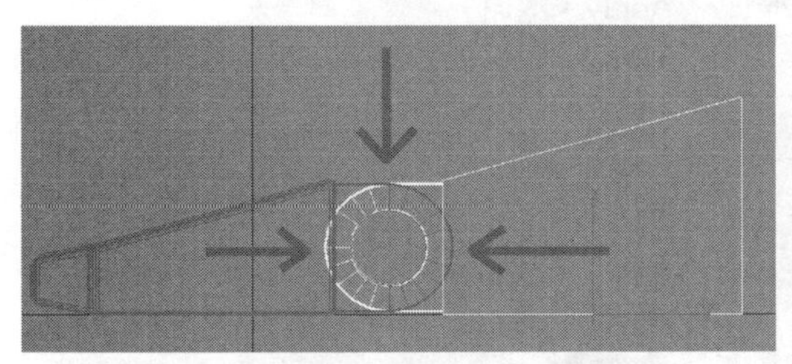

Figure 3-55

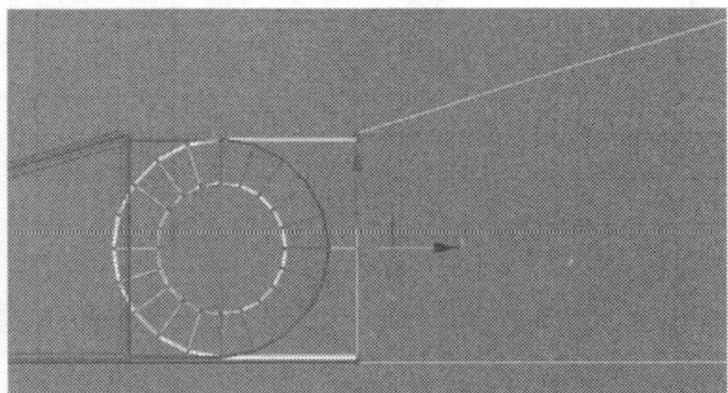

Figure 3-56

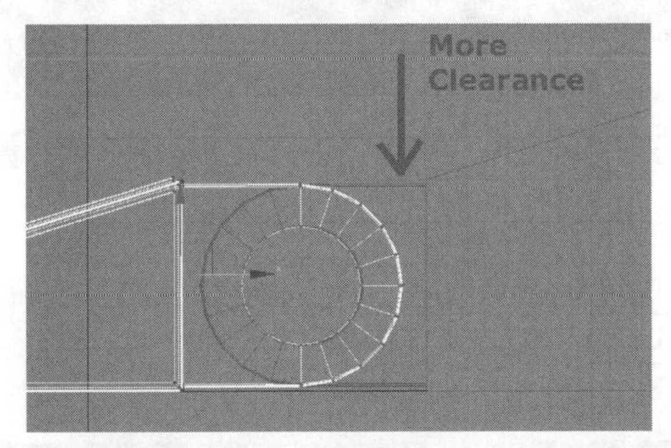

Figure 3-57

28. Using AutoGrid, create a Cylinder inside the holes in the hinges (to form an axle), and center it using the Top view.

Radius	Height	Height/Cap Segs	Sides	Smooth
13.5	16	1/1	32	Checked

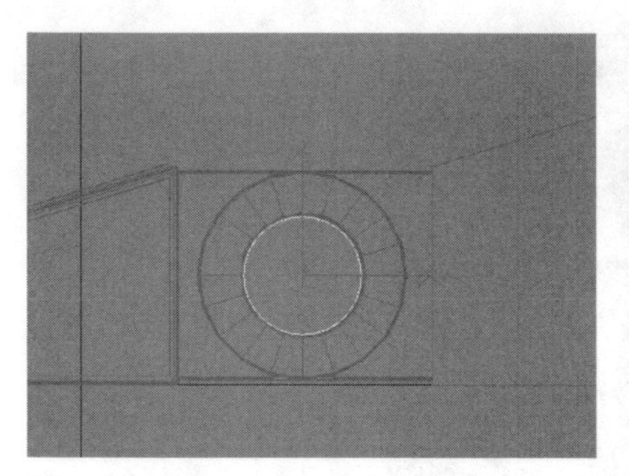

Figure 3-58

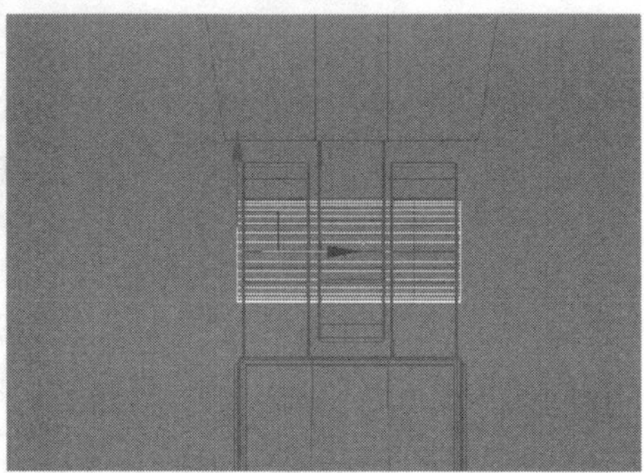

Figure 3-59

29. Convert the cylinder to an Editable Polygon, then select the two caps and Bevel:

Type	Height	Outline	Apply/OK
Group	0	3.8	Apply

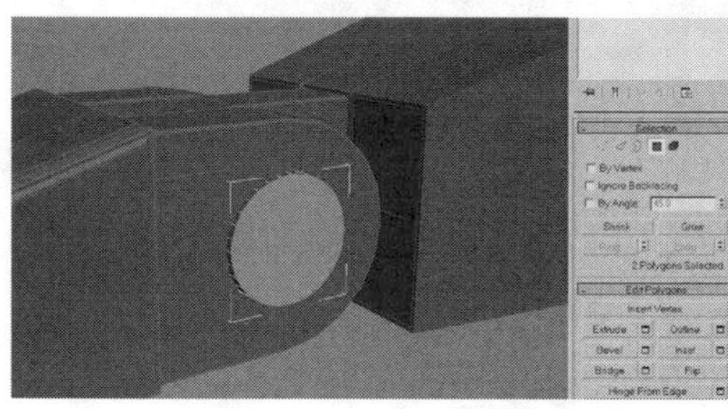

Figure 3-60

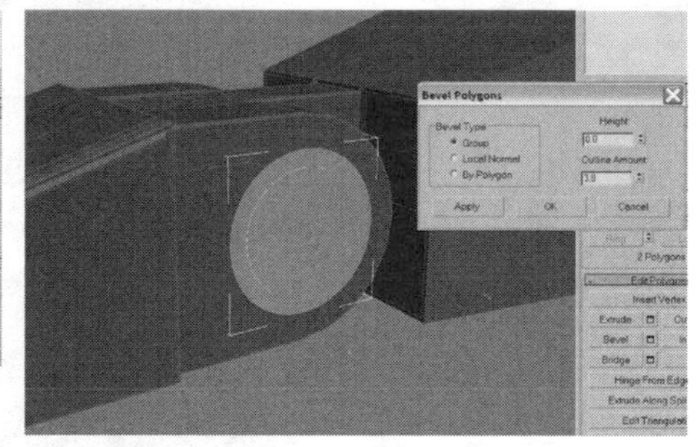

Figure 3-61

30. Continue to Bevel the caps to form axle caps:

Type	Height	Outline	Apply/OK
Group	0	–2	Apply
Group	3	0	Apply

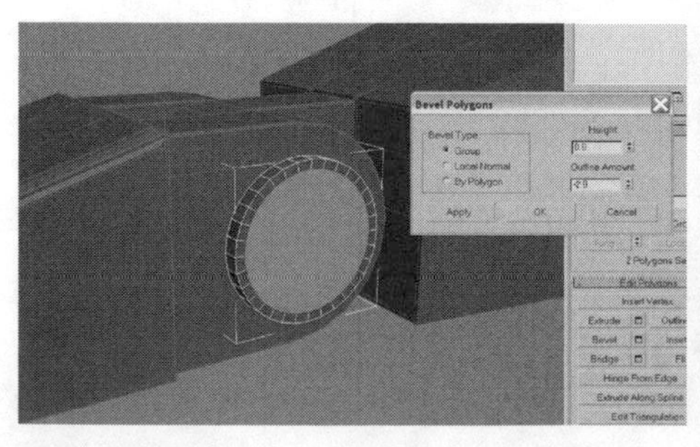

Figure 3-62

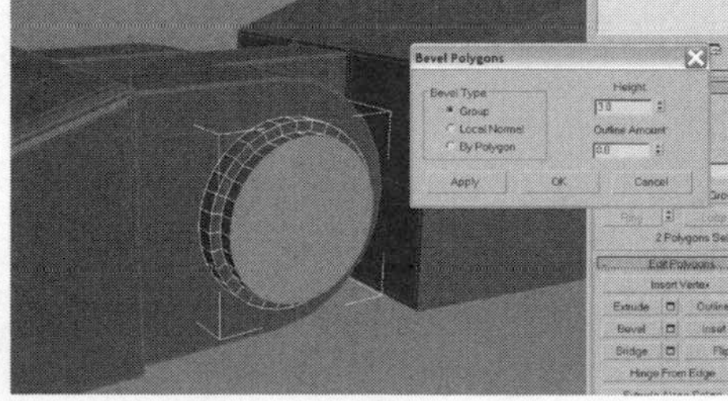

Figure 3-63

Type	Height	Outline	Apply/OK
Group	0	–4.5	Apply
Group	–1.3	0	Apply

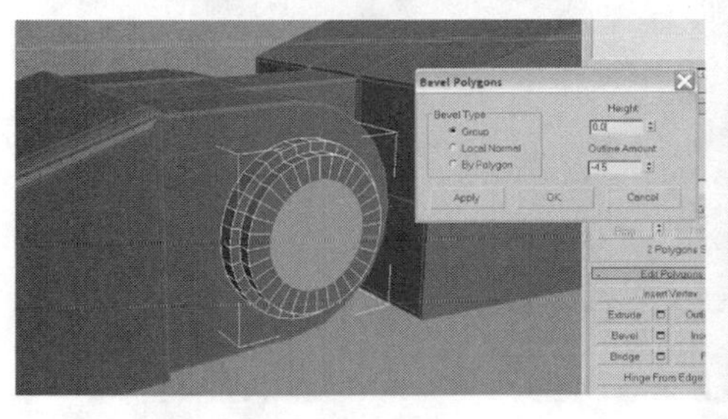

Figure 3-64

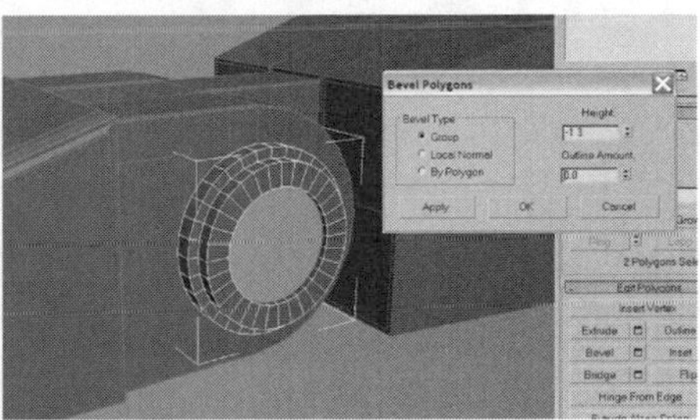

Figure 3-65

Type	Height	Outline	Apply/OK
Group	0	–0.05	OK

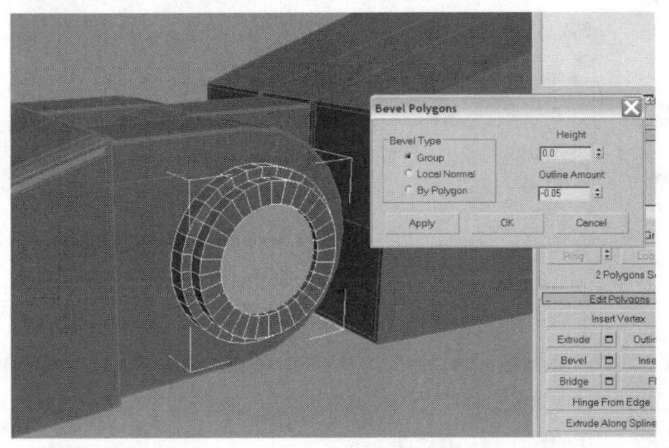

Figure 3-66

31. Click the **Snaps Toggle** button on the main toolbar, then right-click the button and make sure that Vertex is the only Snaps option selected. Use the Cut tool to slice the cap as shown in Figure 3-68; the Vertex snap will allow you to easily slice straight across the cap. Select the two outer polygons.

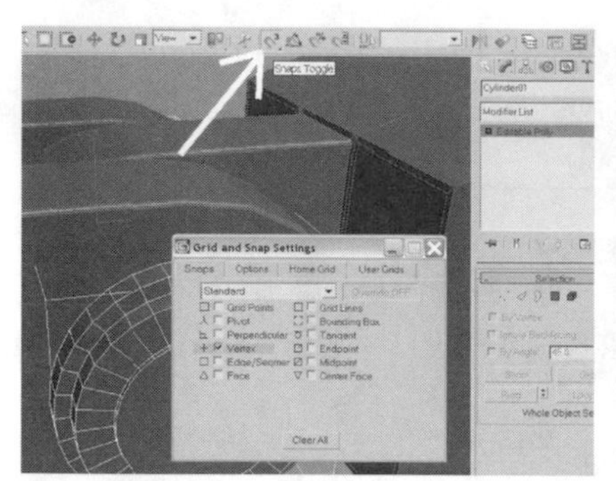

Figure 3-67

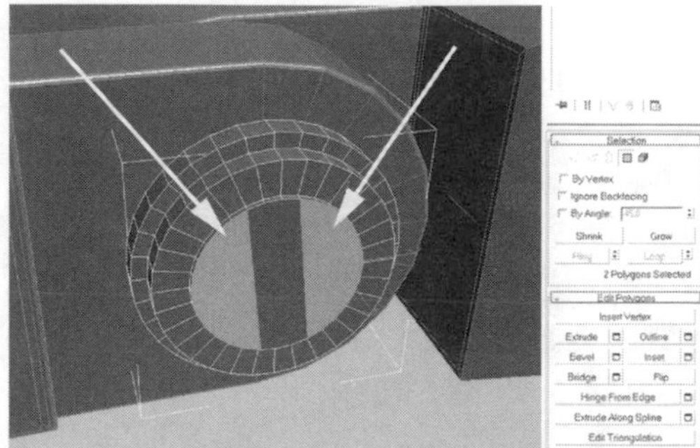

Figure 3-68

32. Extrude the polygons by **1.5** and then Select and Link the axle to the middle_toe.

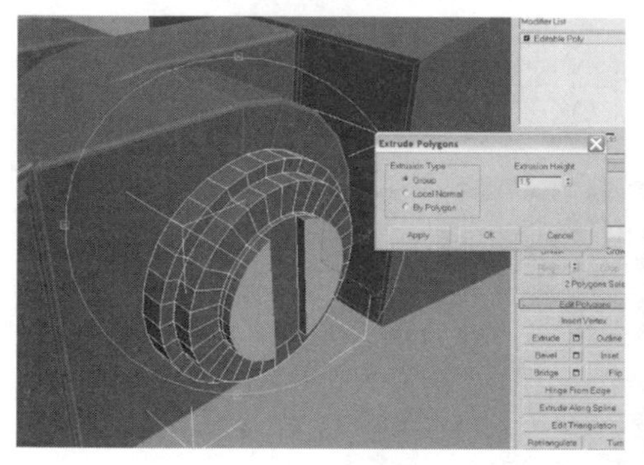

Figure 3-69

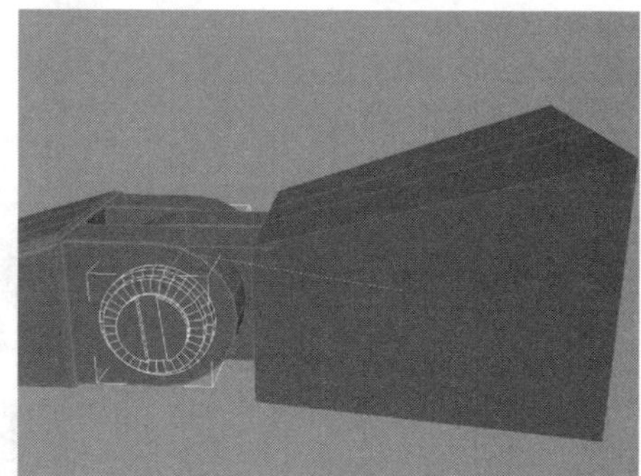

Figure 3-70

33. Select the toe, click **Affect Pivot Only**, and center the pivot over the axle. With snaps still turned on, use the Cut tool to create a side edge as shown in Figure 3-72.

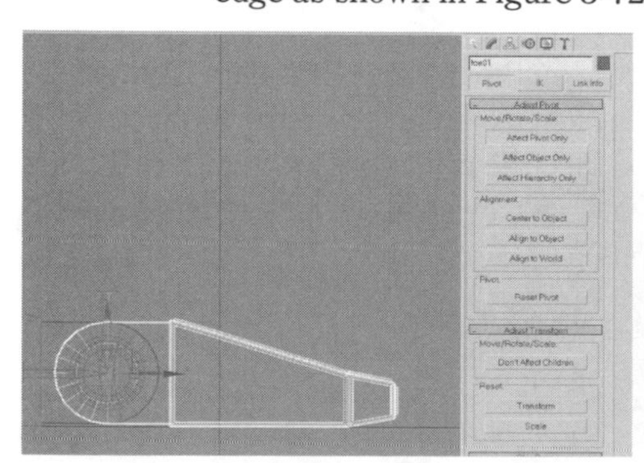

Figure 3-71

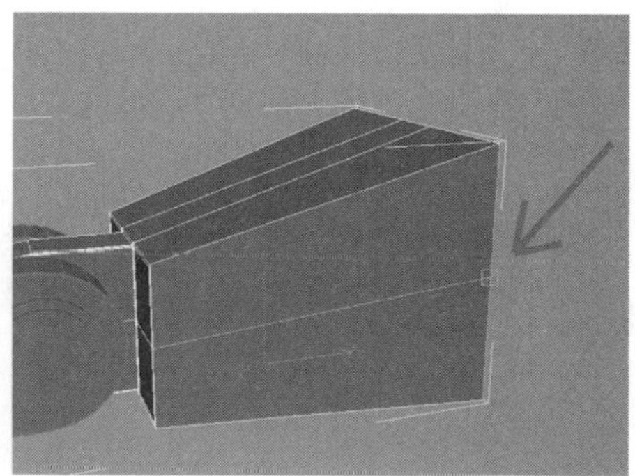

Figure 3-72

34. Rotate around the back, Slice across the back of the middle toe, and Connect the edges. Select the four vertical edges in the middle of the back of the middle_toe.

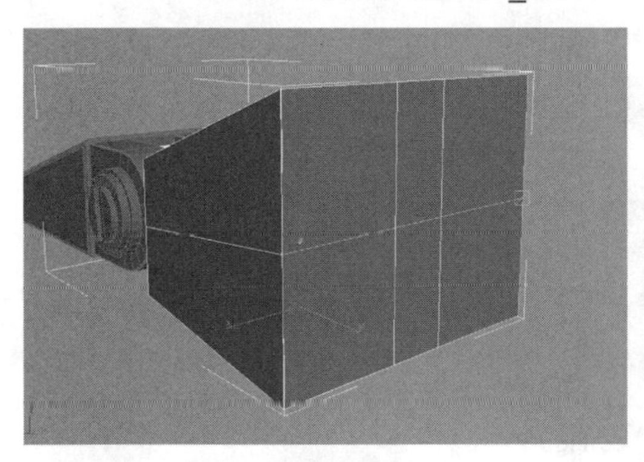

Figure 3-73

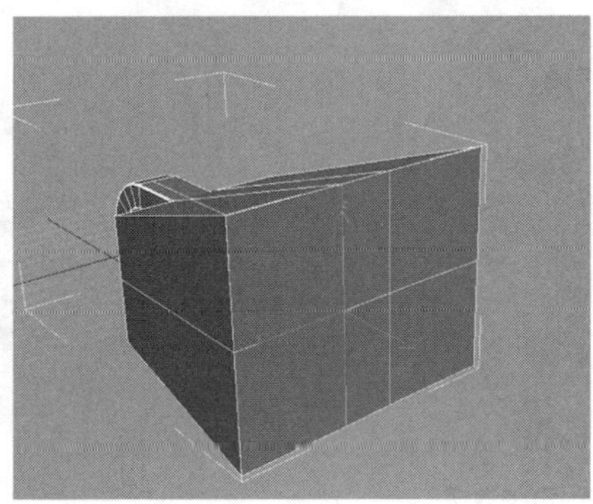

Figure 3-74

35. Chamfer the edges by **9.25** and Target Weld the center edges to form a single center seam.

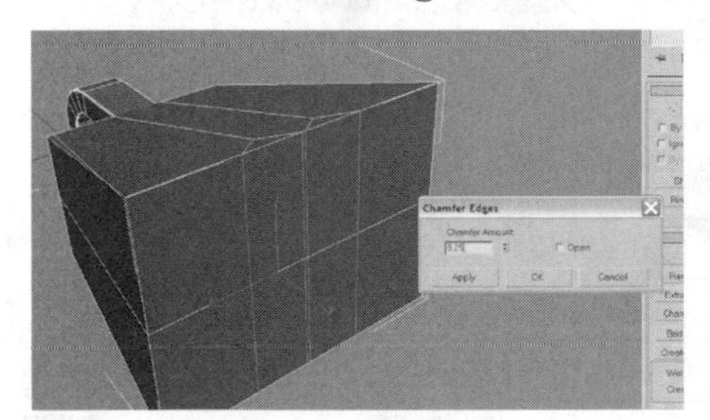

Figure 3-75

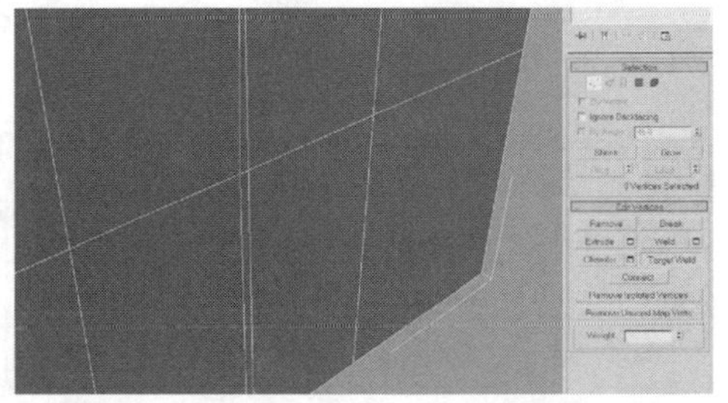

Figure 3-76

36. Select the top edges shown in Figure 3-77 and click **Remove** to remove them. Then select the vertices shown in Figure 3-78 and click **Remove.**

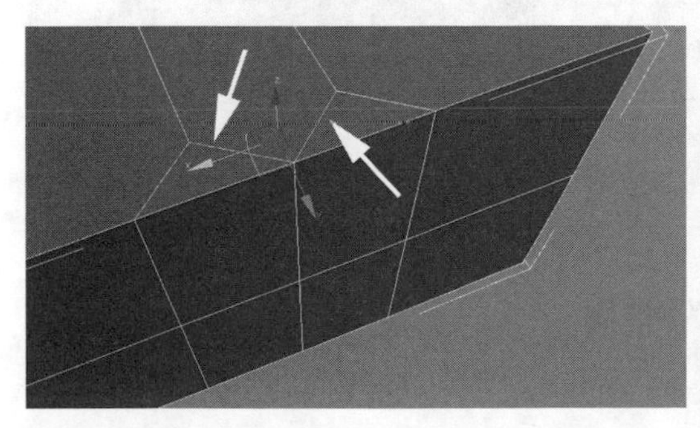

Figure 3-77

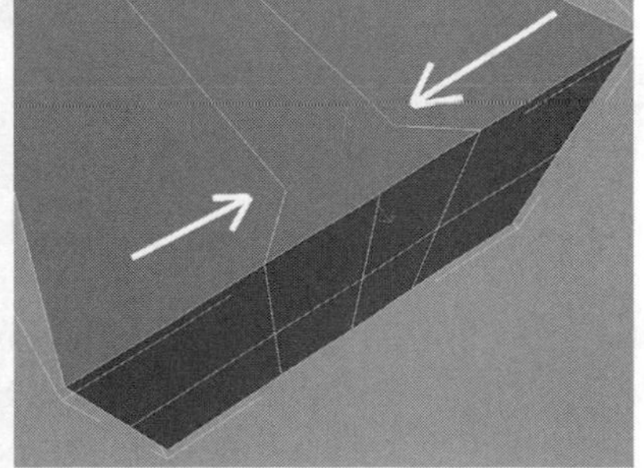

Figure 3-78

37. Select the middle seam you just made and click **Remove** to remove it. Then switch to Vertex selection mode and remove the leftover vertices.

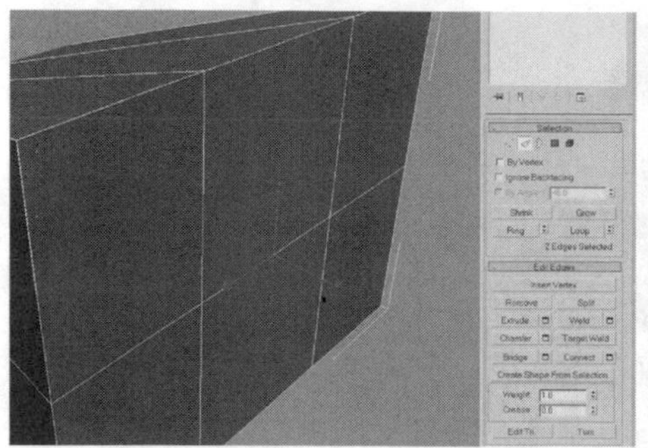

Figure 3-79

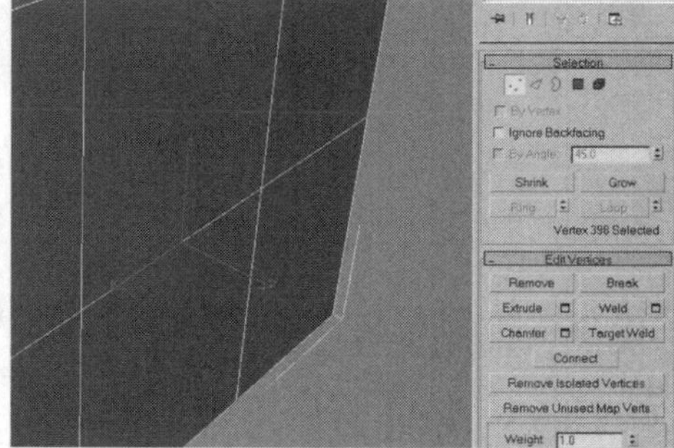

Figure 3-80

FYI: So why the heck did we go to all the trouble of making that center seam only to turn around and delete it? Because we weren't *making* the middle seam. We were spreading the two vertical seams, and welding the two middle seams together made it easier to remove.

38. Select the two middle polygons and Bevel them:

Type	Height	Outline	Apply/OK
Group	0	–2	Apply
Group	40	0	OK

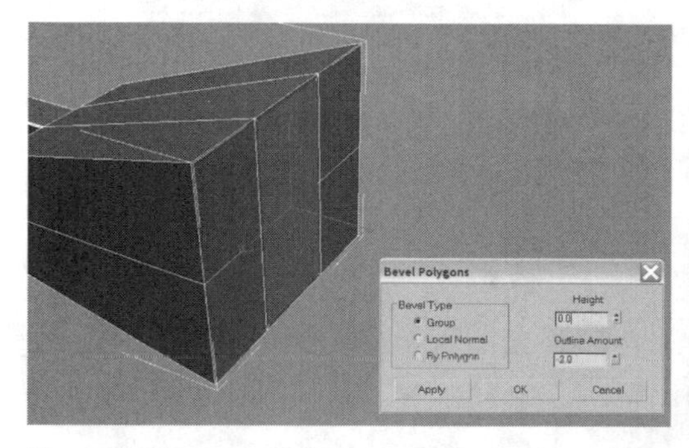

Figure 3-81

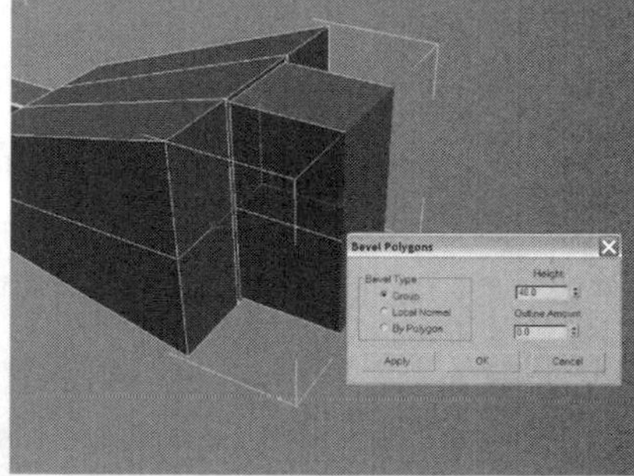

Figure 3-82

39. Delete the bottom polygon, select the top one, Hinge From Edge **180** degrees with **10** Segments, delete the back-facing polygon, vertex-select all the new vertices, and Weld.

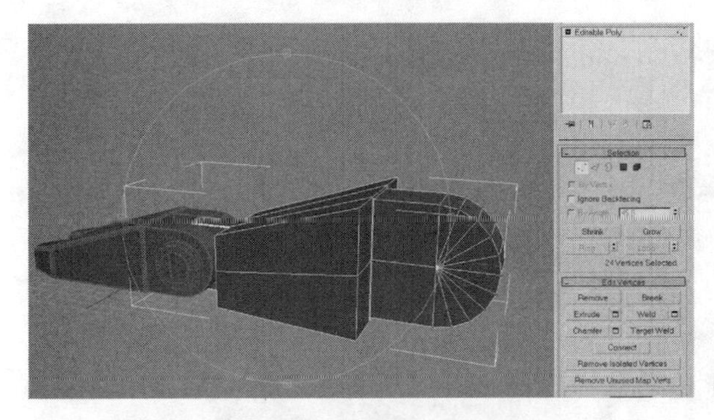

Figure 3-83

40. Switch to the Front view and create a Box behind the middle_toe.

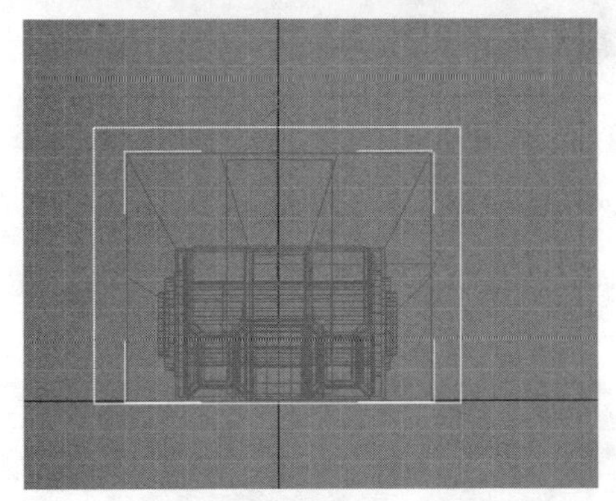

Figure 3-84

41. Switch to the Perspective view, position the box as shown in Figure 3-85 and change the box's parameters, then convert it to an Editable Polygon.

Length	Width	Height	Length/Width/Height Segs
91	120	200	2/3/1

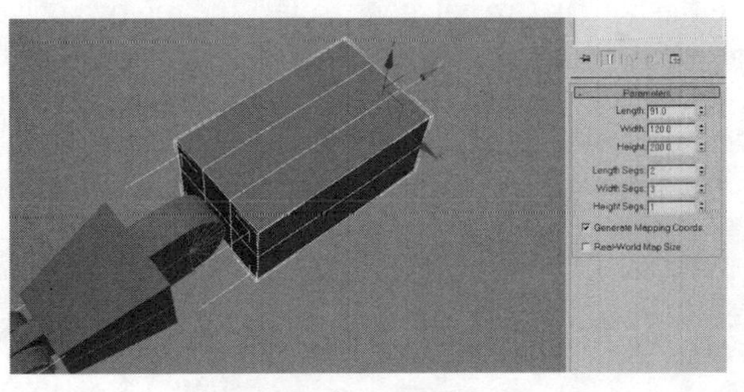

Figure 3-85

42. Select the rear polygons and Non-uniform Scale them down to **50** in the X axis.

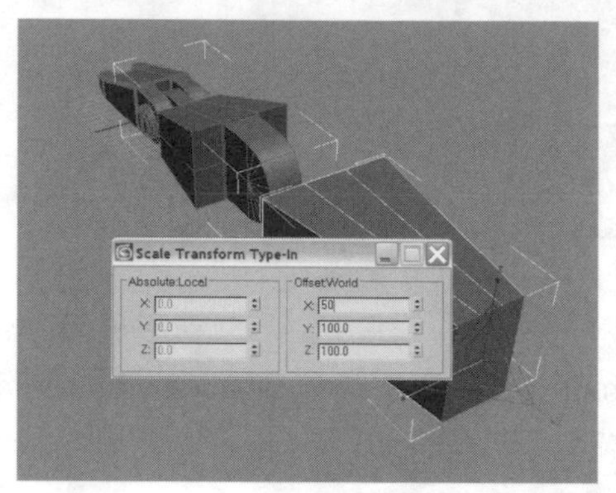

Figure 3-86

43. Select the two outer polygons and Bevel them:

Type	Height	Outline	Apply/OK
Group	0	–2.0	Apply
Group	40	0	OK

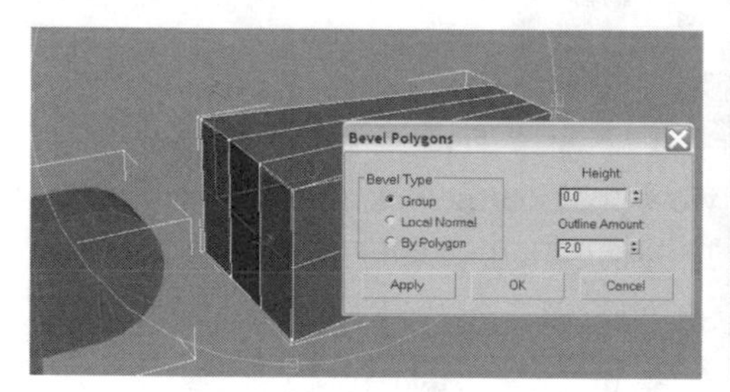

Figure 3-87

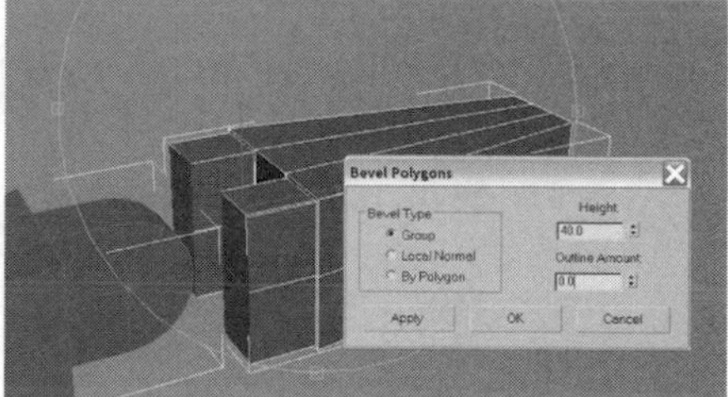

Figure 3-88

44. Delete the bottom two polygons, select the top two polygons, and Hinge From Edge **180** degrees with **10** Segments. Delete the back-facing polygons, select the vertices, and then select and Weld the vertices. Switch to the Left view, switch to wireframe, and align the hinges.

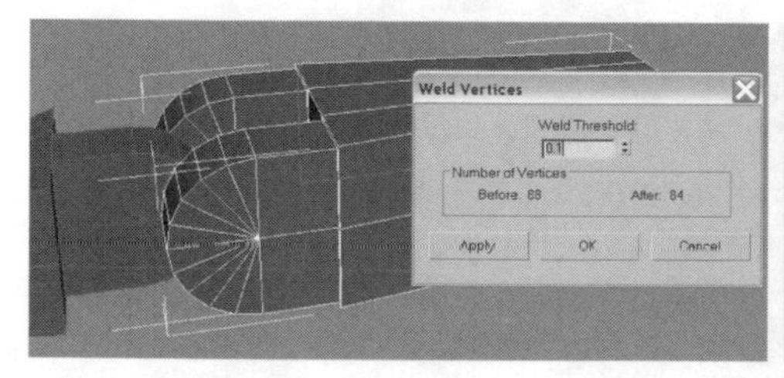

Figure 3-89

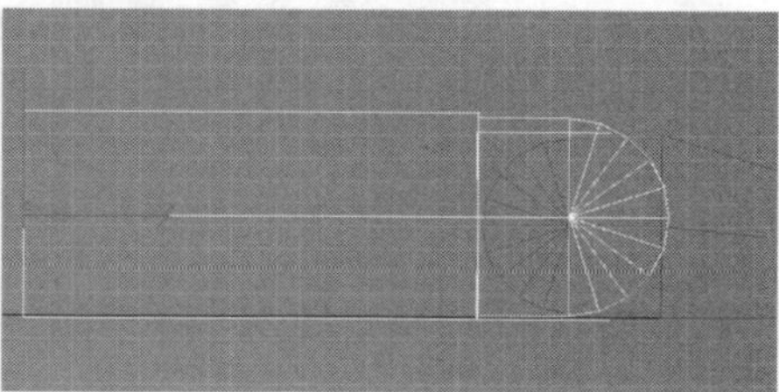

Figure 3-90

45. Marquee-select the vertices shown in Figure 3-91 and move the vertices in the X axis to increase the hinge clearance. Zoom in and notice that the center axes are not aligned.

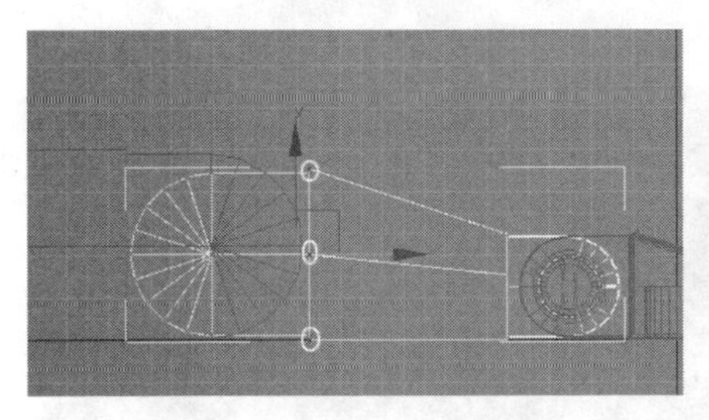

Figure 3-91

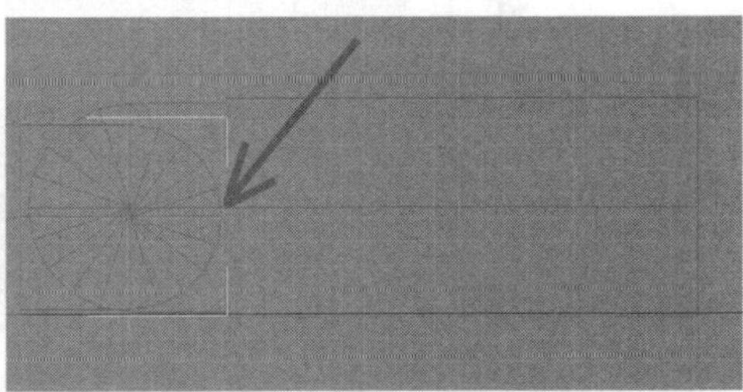

Figure 3-92

46. Marquee-select the vertices of the middle_toe hinge and Uniform Scale the vertices down to **88**. Switch to the Right view, marquee-select the upper-right corner vertices of the foot, and move them up **60** in the Y axis.

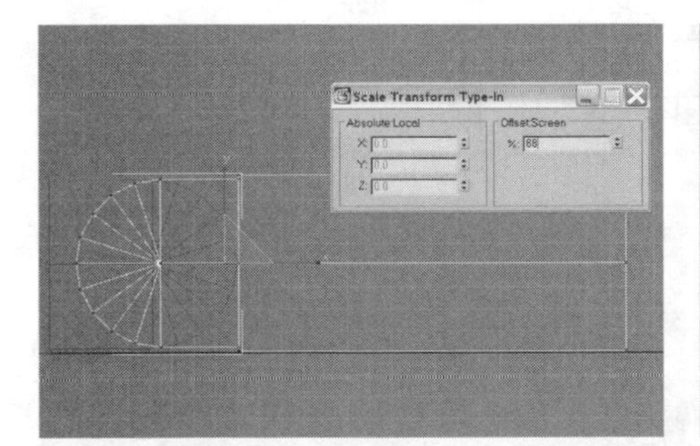

Figure 3-93

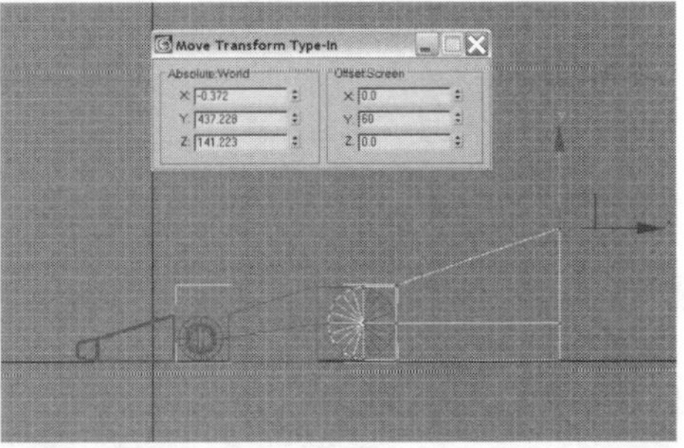

Figure 3-94

47. Marquee-select the edges on the surface of the middle toe, click **Connect Settings**, set the Segments to **2**, and then click **OK**.

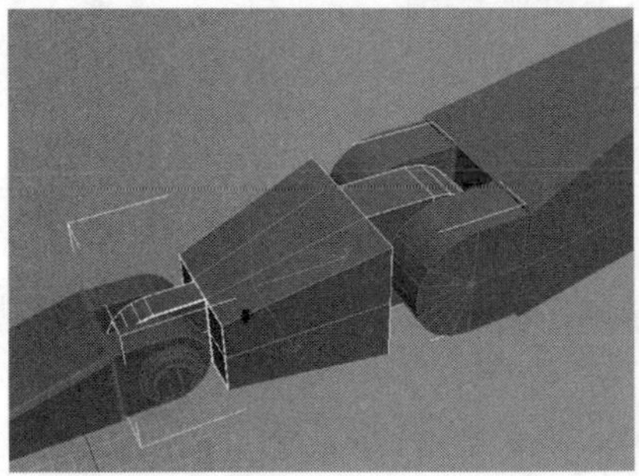

Figure 3-95

Figure 3-96

48. Switch to the Top view and Non-uniform Scale down to **0** in the Y axis to make the edges parallel. Then select the two middle vertical edges and Non-uniform Scale them down to **0** in the X axis to make them parallel.

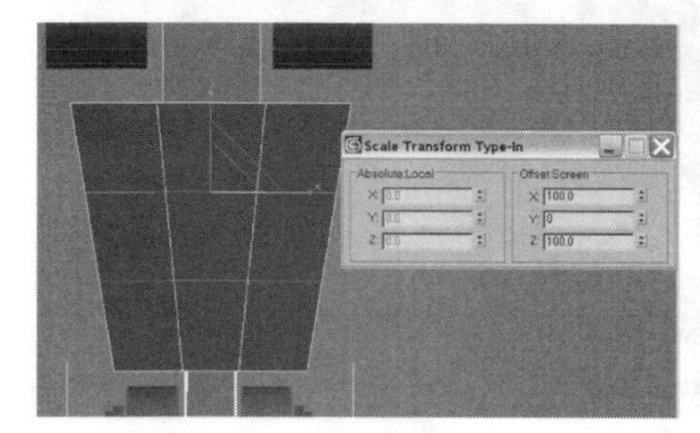

Figure 3-97

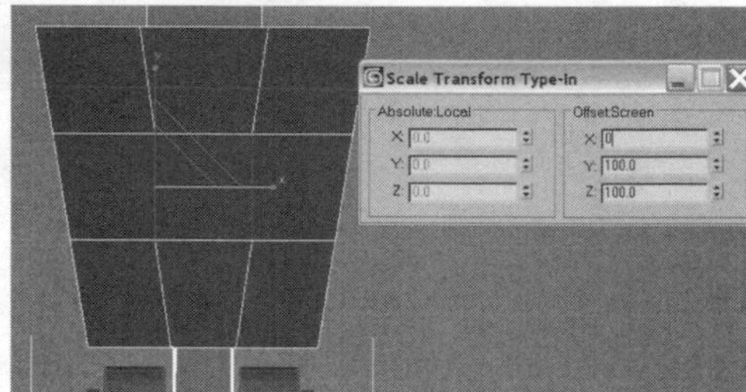

Figure 3-98

49. Select the center top polygon and then click **Bevel Settings**:

Type	Height	Outline	Apply/OK
Group	0	–2.5	Apply
Group	2.5	0	Apply

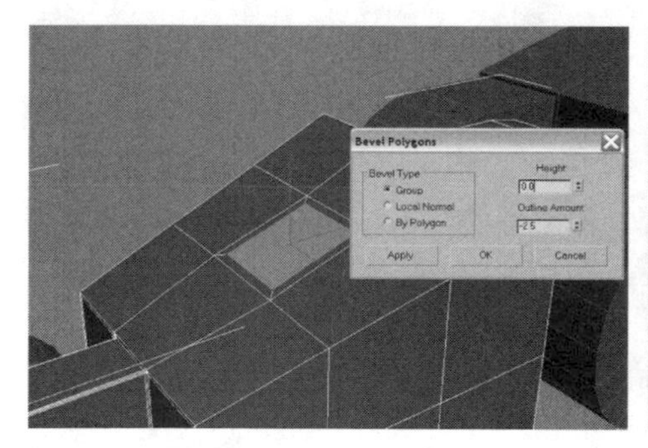

Figure 3-99

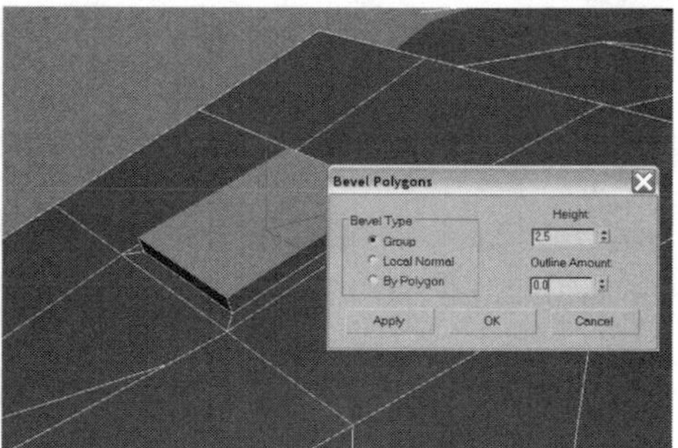

Figure 3-100

Type	Height	Outline	Apply/OK
Group	0	–5	Apply
Group	15	0	OK

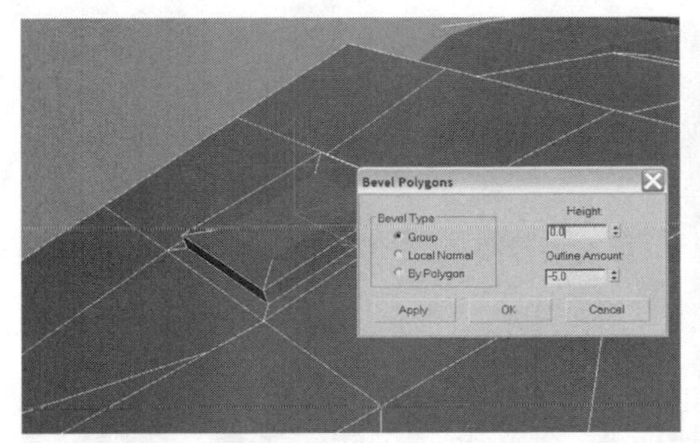

Figure 3-101

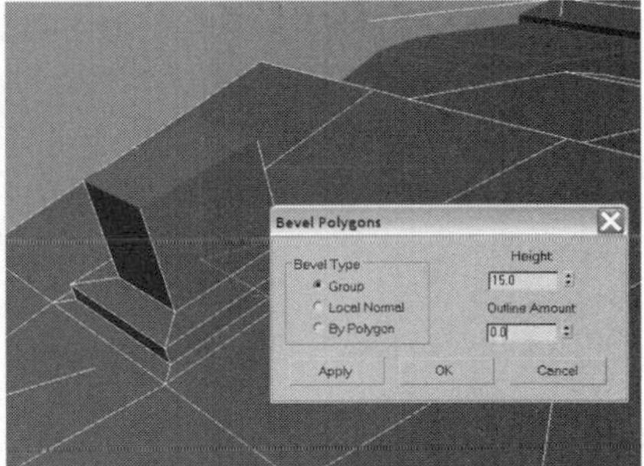

Figure 3-102

50. Select the upper side edges shown in Figure 3-103, click **Connect**, and then select the resulting bottom polygon and delete it.

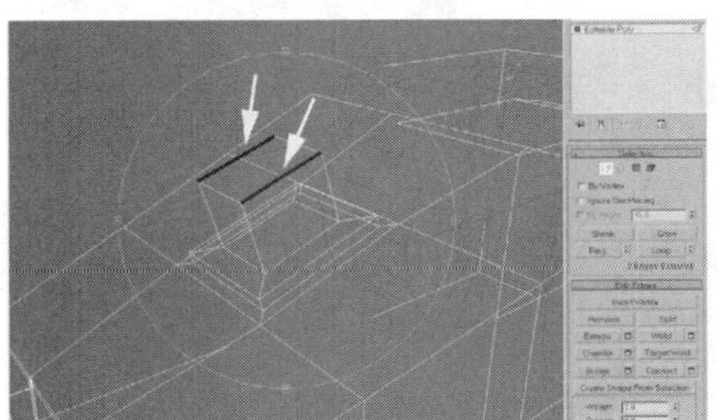

Figure 3-103

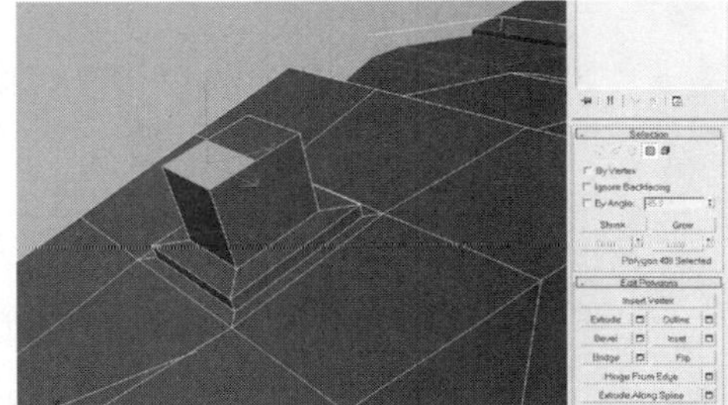

Figure 3-104

51. Select the remaining polygon, click **Hinge From Edge** with an angle of **180** degrees and **10** Segments. Delete the back-facing polygon, select the vertices, and Weld them. Switch to the Top view and element-select the toe.

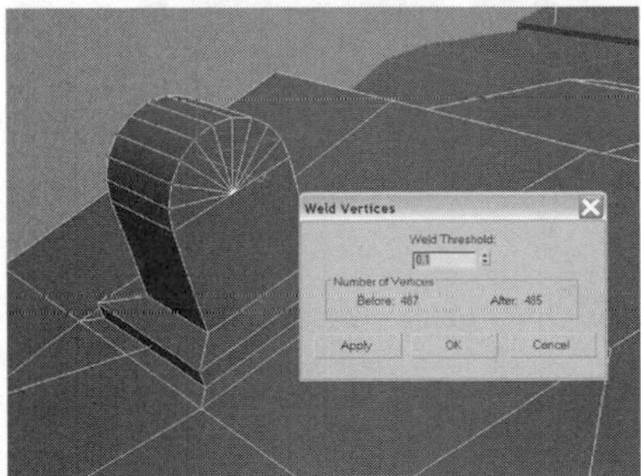

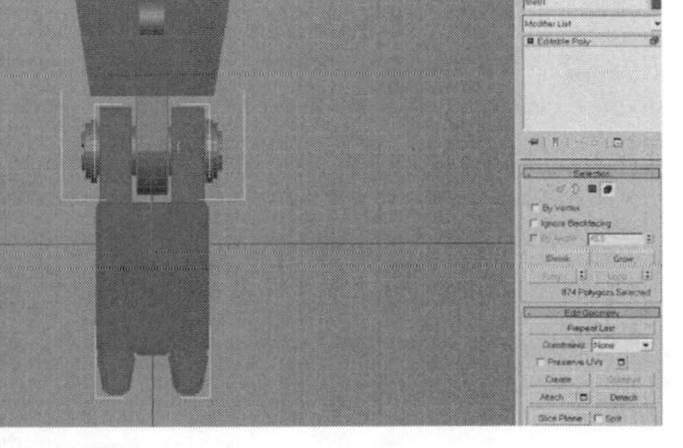

Figure 3-105

Figure 3-106

52. Click **Slice Plane**, position the slice plane around the middle of the toe (you may have to rotate it), and click the **Slice** button. Select the upper two edges as shown in Figure 3-108 and scale them in the X axis to make them parallel.

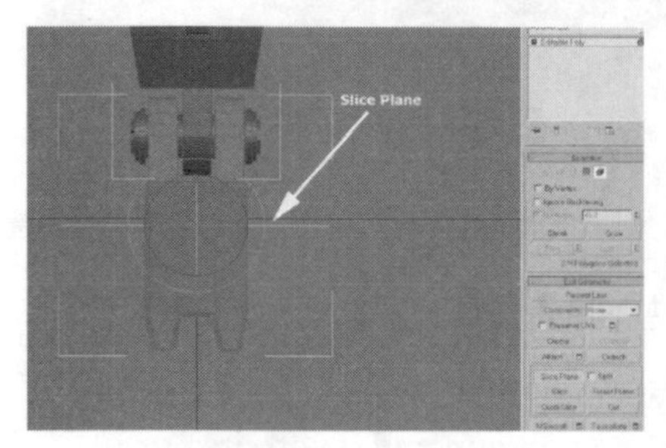

Figure 3-107

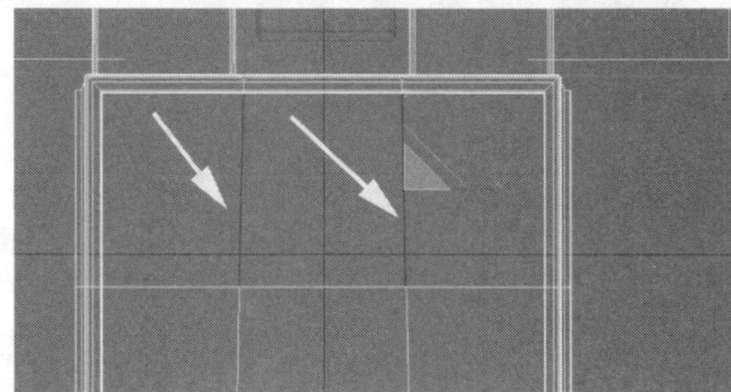

Figure 3-108

53. Select the middle polygon at the top of the toe near the hinge, and click **Bevel Settings:**

Type	Height	Outline	Apply/OK
Group	0	–0.8	Apply
Group	1.5	0	Apply

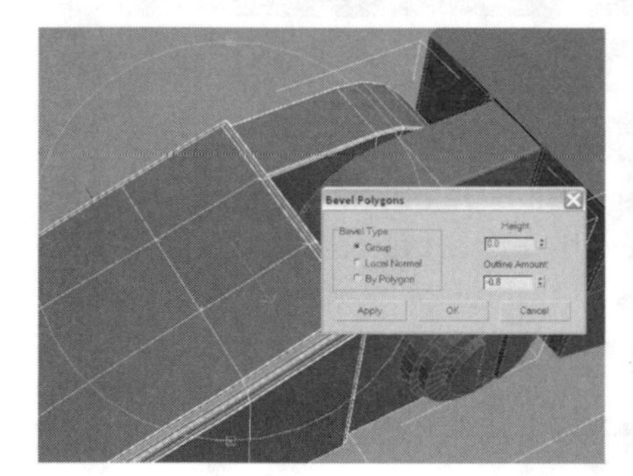

Figure 3-109

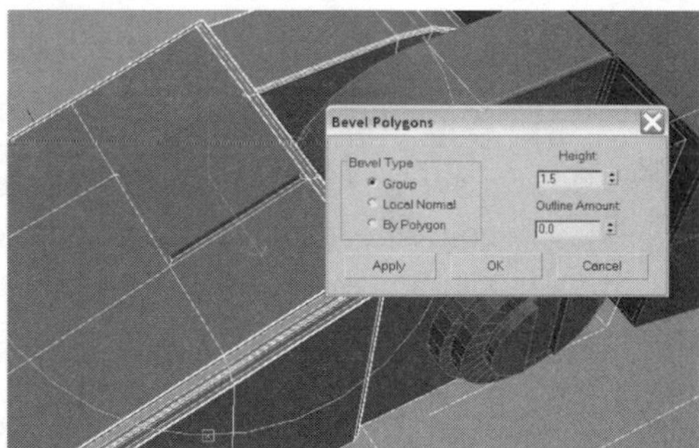

Figure 3-110

Type	Height	Outline	Apply/OK
Group	0	–3	Apply
Group	8	0	OK

Day 1: Building the Toe

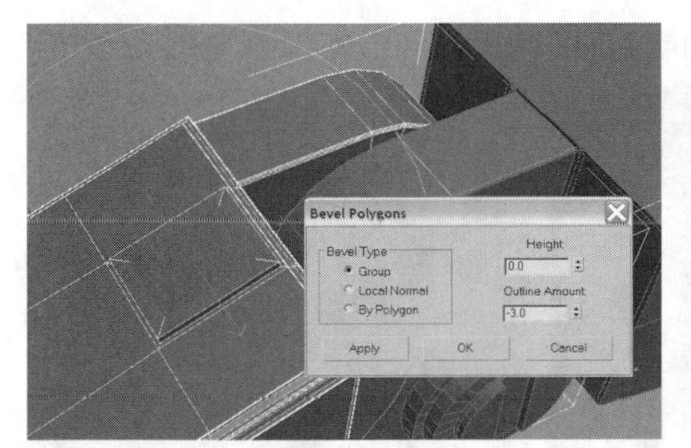

Figure 3-111

Figure 3-112

54. Select the side edges of the top polygon, click **Connect**, then select the resulting bottom polygon.

Figure 3-113

Figure 3-114

55. Hinge From Edge **180** degrees with **10** Segments, delete the back-facing polygon, vertex-select the resulting vertices, and Weld them. Edge-select the top edges of the base and the curved part of the mount. (The Loop tool can be handy, but be sure to Alt-click to unselect the four diagonal edges connecting the mount to the four corners of the base.)

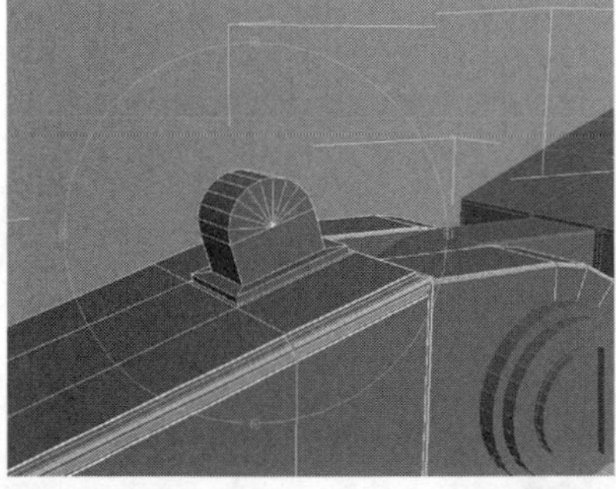

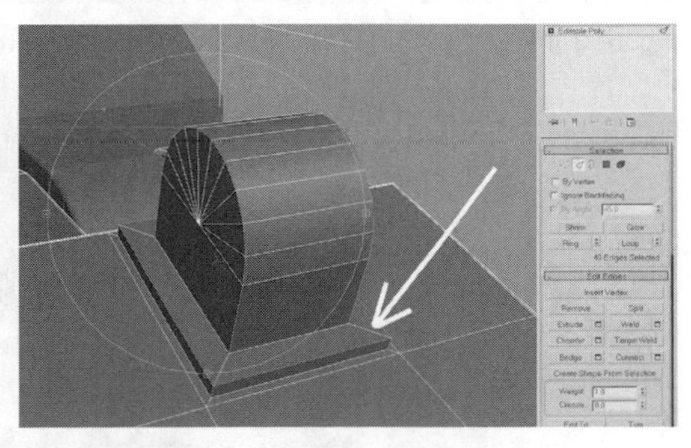

Figure 3-115

Figure 3-116

56. Chamfer the edges first by **0.3** and then by **0.13**. Click **OK**.

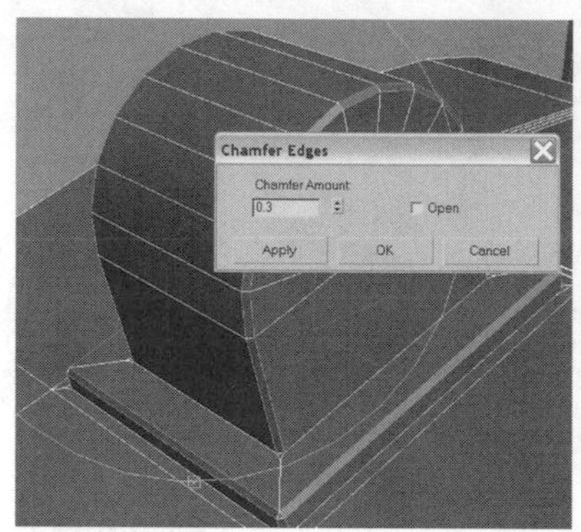

Figure 3-117

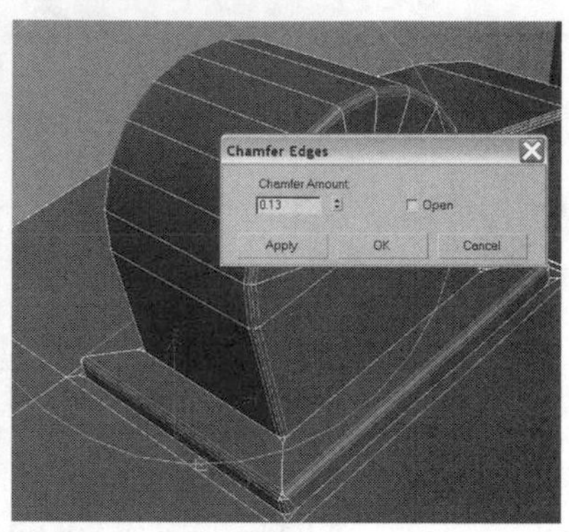

Figure 3-118

57. Select five of the side polygons on the middle_toe on *both* sides and click **Bevel Settings**:

Type	Height	Outline	Apply/OK
Local Normal	0	–0.8	Apply
Local Normal	1.9	0	OK

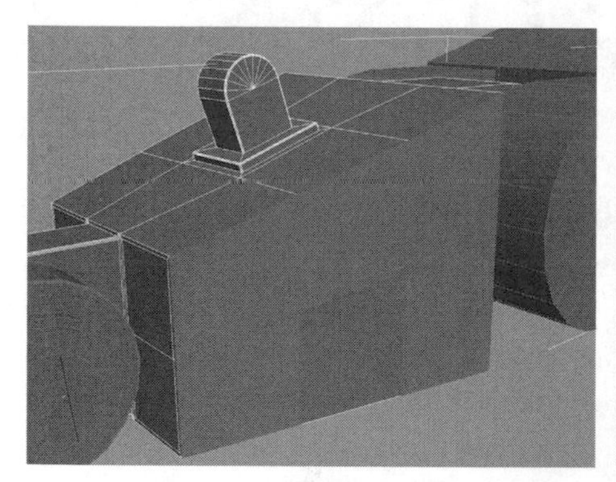

Figure 3-119

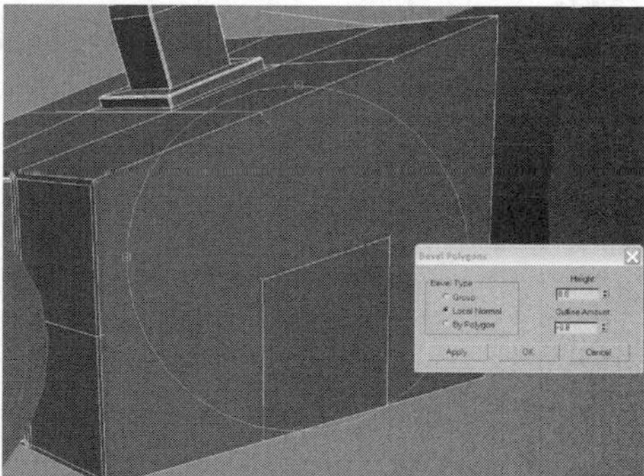

Figure 3-120

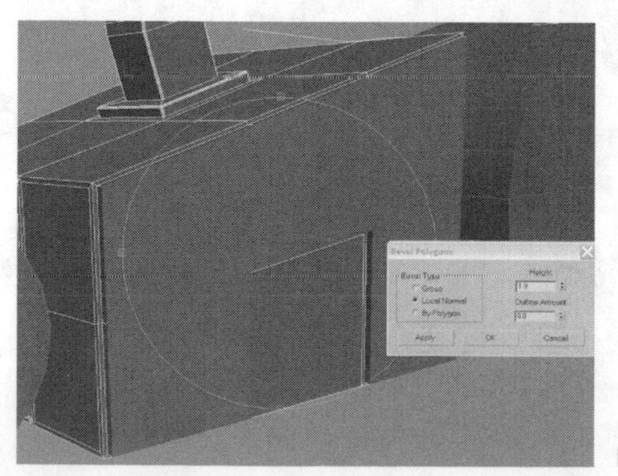

Figure 3-121

58. Select the middle and two rear polygons on both sides and then click **Bevel Settings:**

Type	Height	Outline	Apply/OK
Local Normal	0	–0.7	Apply
Local Normal	3	0	OK

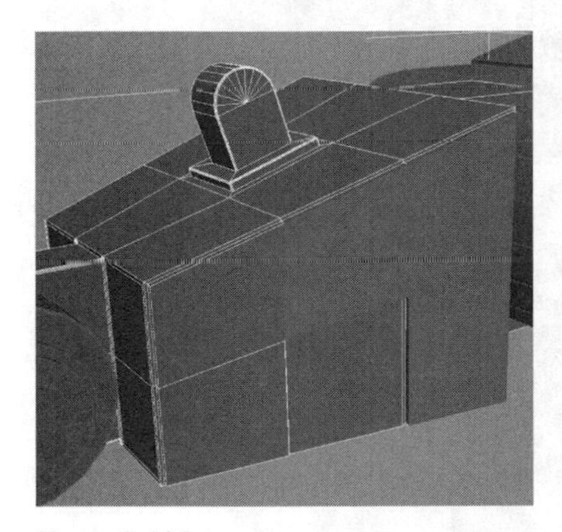

Figure 3-122

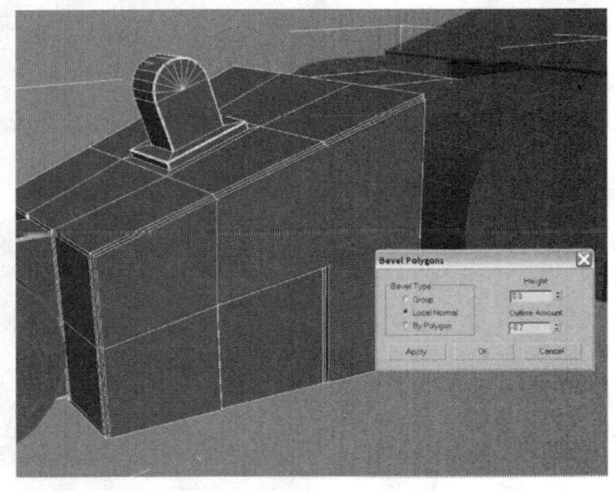

Figure 3-123

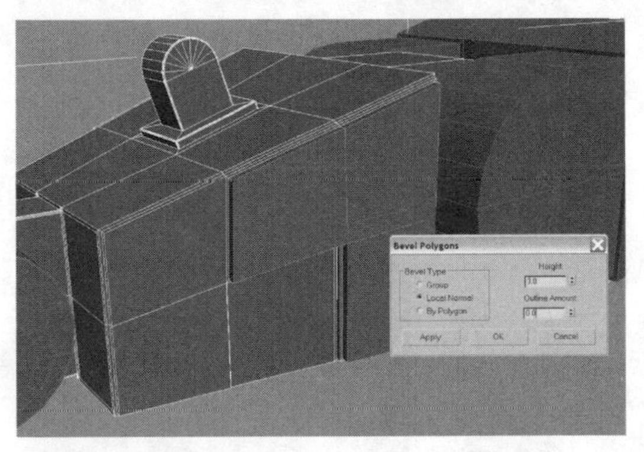

Figure 3-124

59. Select the front two polygons on both sides and click **Bevel Settings:**

Type	Height	Outline	Apply/OK
Local Normal	0	–1.5	Apply
Local Normal	3	0	OK

Figure 3-125

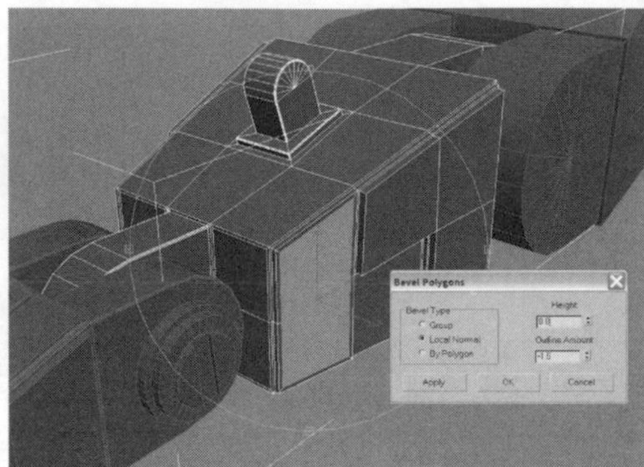

Figure 3-126

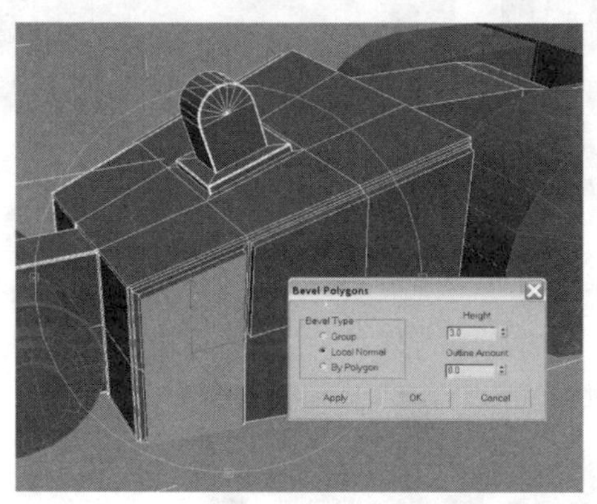

Figure 3-127

60. Select the edges of the armor panels you created using the bevels (on both sides). Chamfer the edges by **0.4**, click **Apply**, change the Chamfer Amount to **0.16**, and then click **OK.**

Figure 3-128

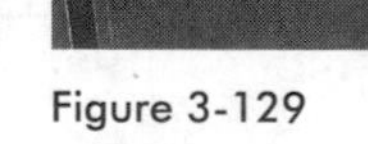

Figure 3-129

Figure 3-130

61. Hit **F9** to do a test render and check out the armor plates.

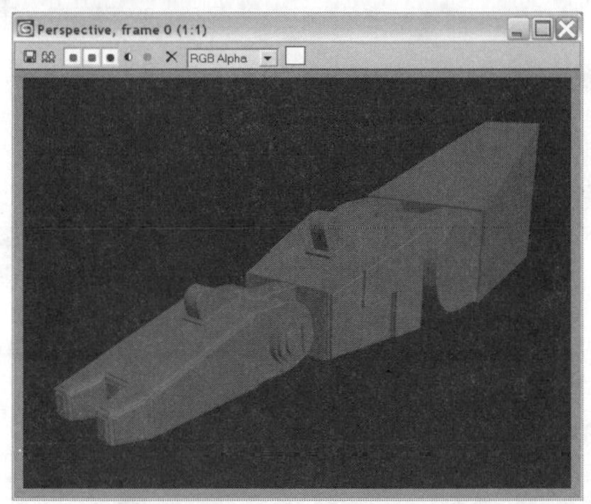

Figure 3-131

Day 2: Building the Toe Hydraulics

1. Switch to the Right viewport and create a Cylinder, then center it on the mount on the middle toe. Shift-move the cylinder to create a clone and center it on the toe mount you just made.

Radius	Height	Height/Cap Segs	Sides	Smooth
5	30	1/1	24	Checked

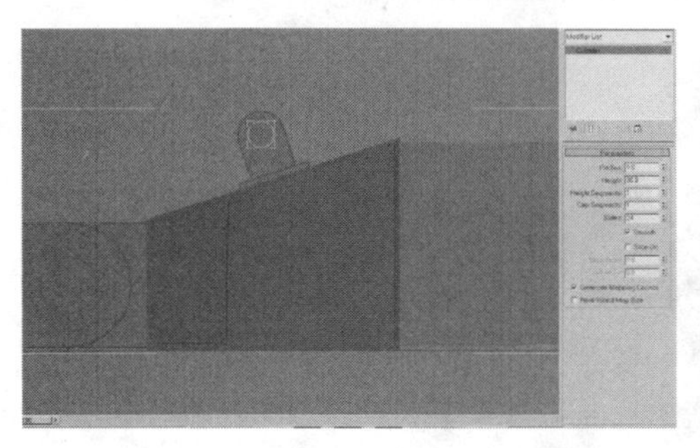

Figure 3-132

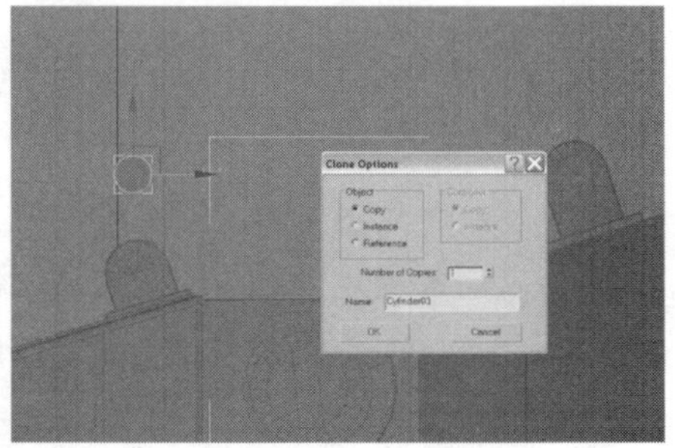

Figure 3-133

2. In the Perspective viewport, make sure both cylinders are aligned, and then link them to their respective mounts.

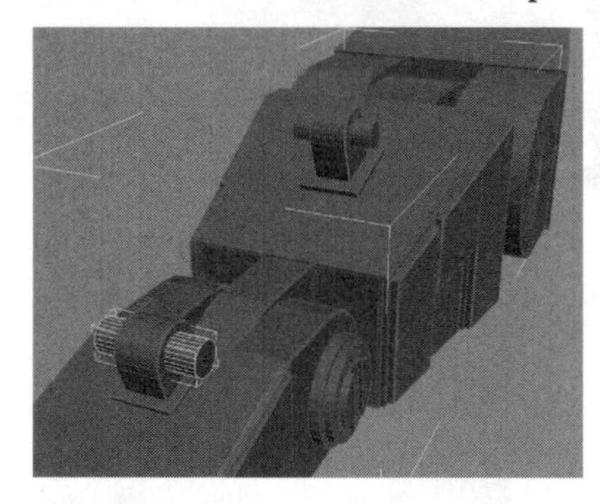

Figure 3-134

Figure 3-135

3. Create a Tube over the end of one of the cylinders, convert it to an Editable Polygon, select one of the center edges, click **Loop**, and then Chamfer the edges by **2.0**.

Radius 1	Radius 2	Height	Height/Cap Segs	Sides	Smooth
5	6	6	2/1	24	Checked

Day 2: Building the Toe Hydraulics

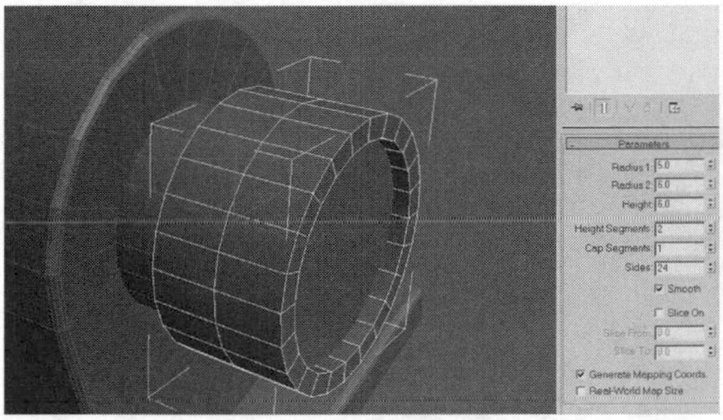

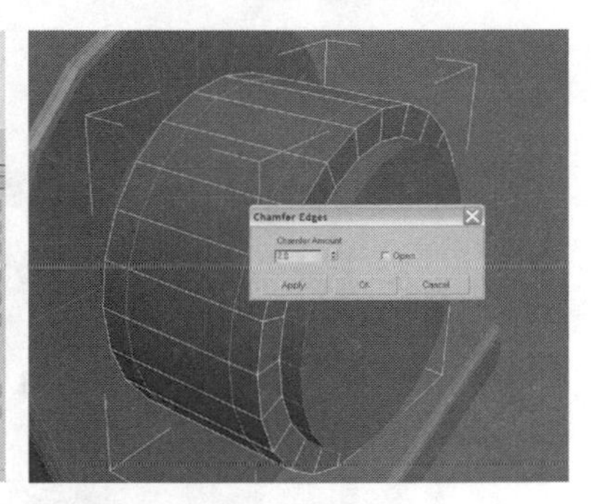

Figure 3-136

Figure 3-137

4. Select six polygons along the center of the tube and Extrude them by **7.5**.

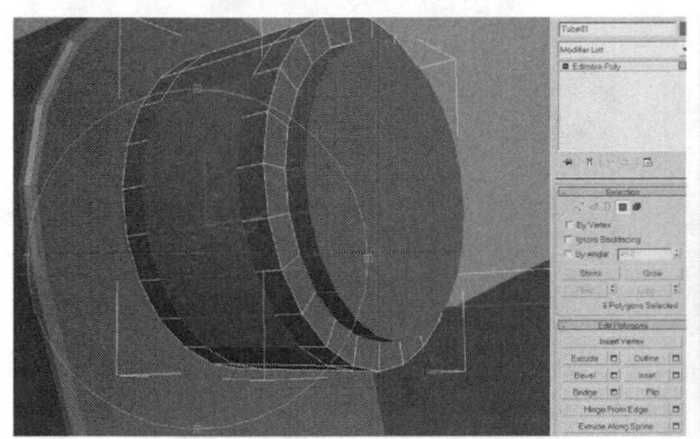

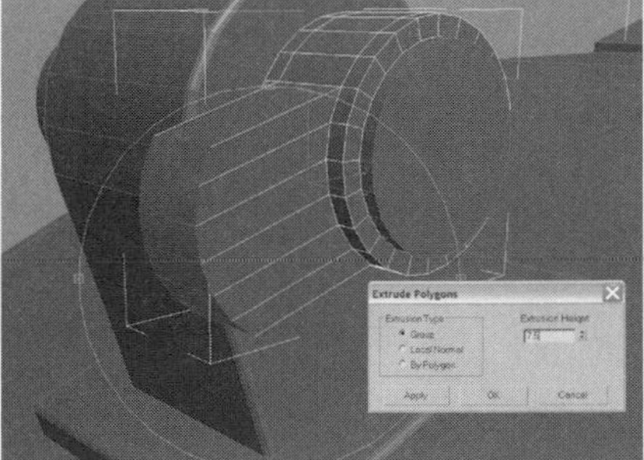

Figure 3-138

Figure 3-139

5. Switch the Coordinate System to **Local**, Non-uniform Scale the polygons down to **0** in the Z axis, and then delete them. Use Loop to select the outer edges on both the front and back of the tube, Chamfer them by **0.3** and then by **0.11**, then click **OK**.

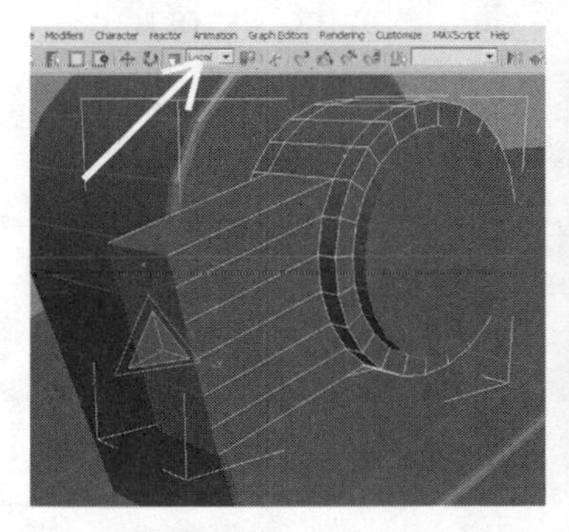

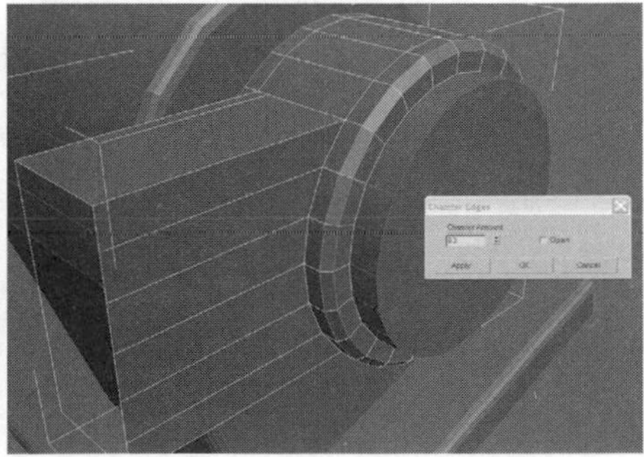

Figure 3-140

Figure 3-141

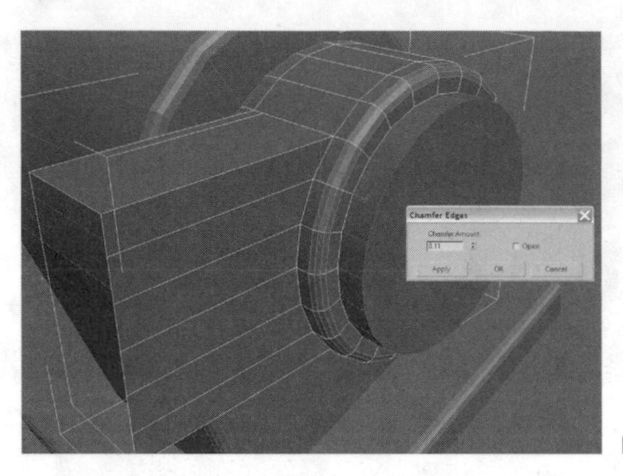

Figure 3-142

6. Select the four edges on the extruded part and Chamfer them by **0.3** and then by **0.1**.

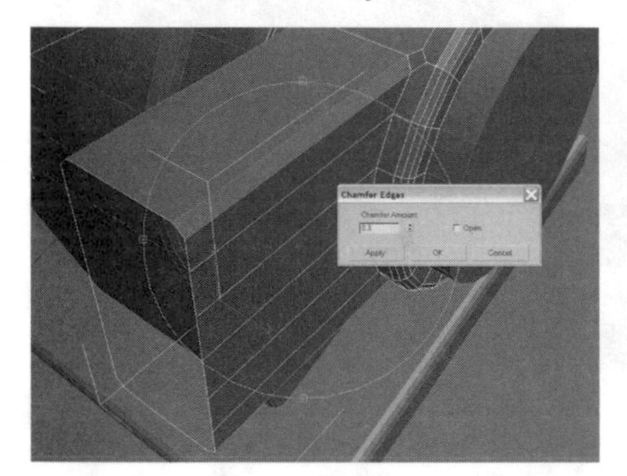

Figure 3-143

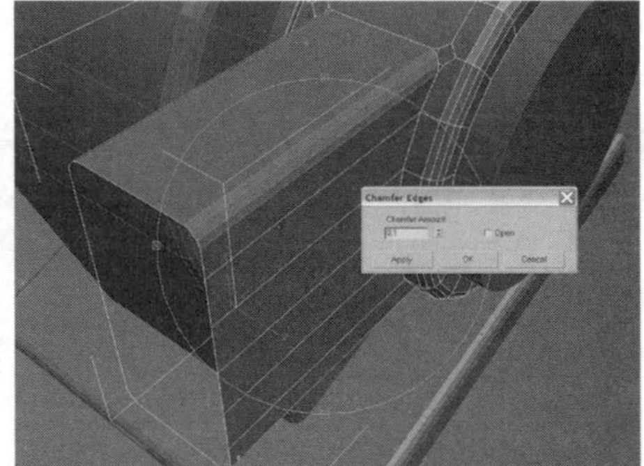

Figure 3-144

7. Object-select the extruded tube, hold down the **Shift** key and drag in the Z axis to create a clone, and position it on the opposite end of the cylinder. Create another Cylinder on the end of the extrusion.

Radius	Height	Height/Cap Segs	Sides	Smooth
5.311	6.188	1/1	24	Checked

Day 2: Building the Toe Hydraulics

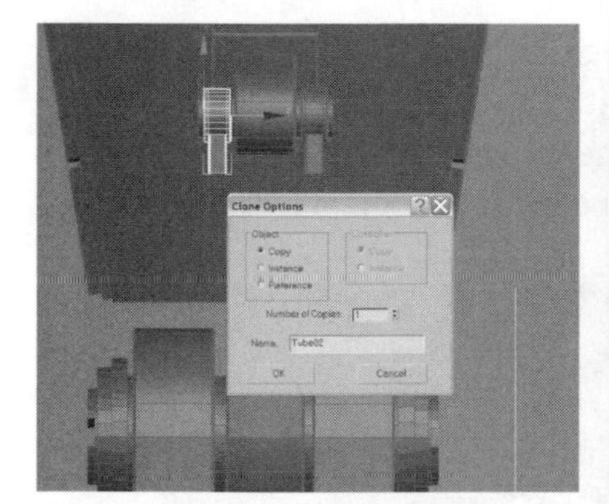

Figure 3-145

Figure 3-146

8. Increase the Radius to **8** and the Height to **60**, convert the cylinder to an Editable Polygon, select the cap, and then Bevel it:

Type	Height	Outline	Apply/OK
Group	0	–3	Apply
Group	–45	0	OK

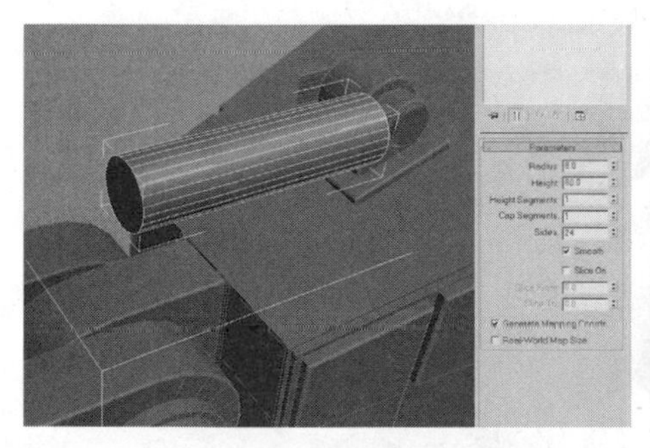

Figure 3-147

Figure 3-148

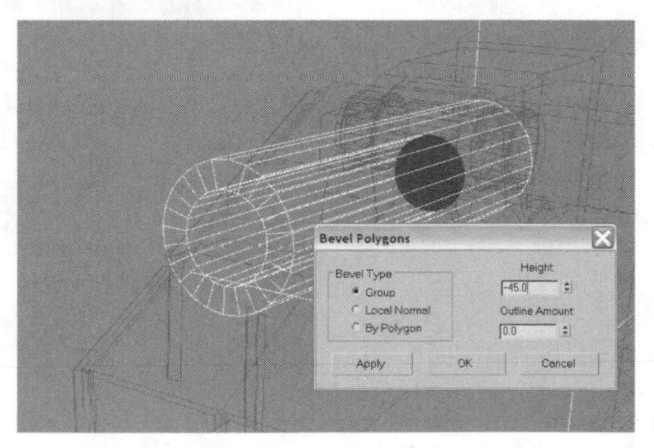

Figure 3-149

9. Object-select the new cylinder and Shift-drag it in the X axis to create a clone on the opposite side. With the clone still selected, click the **Attach** button and then click the extruded tube. Click the original cylinder, click **Attach**, and then click the original extruded tube.

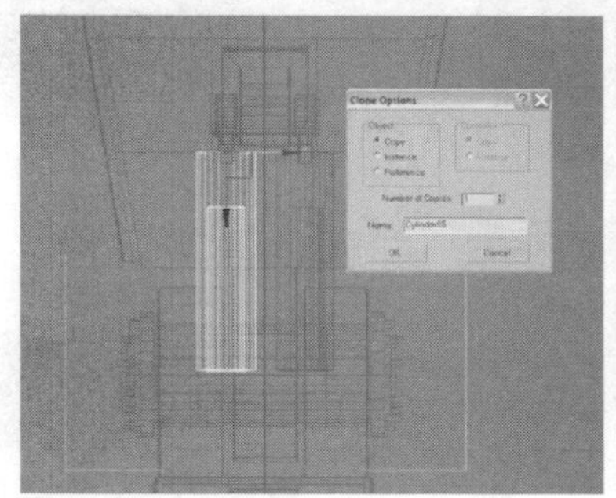

Figure 3-150

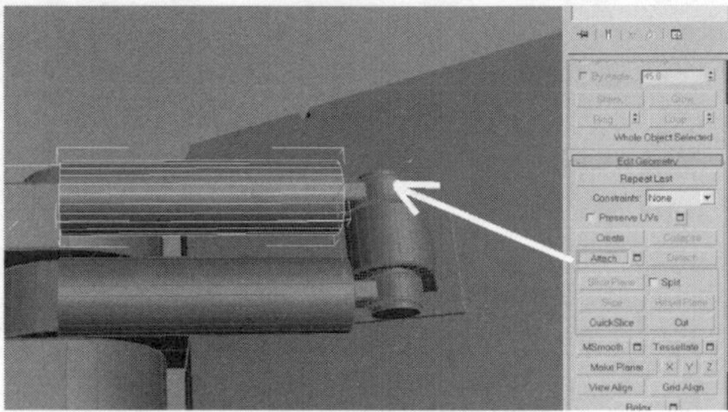

Figure 3-151

10. Select the polygon at the rear of the tube, click **Detach**, and name the new object **shaft.** Do the same for the other side and call it **shaft2**. Hit **H** and select **shaft** and **shaft2.**

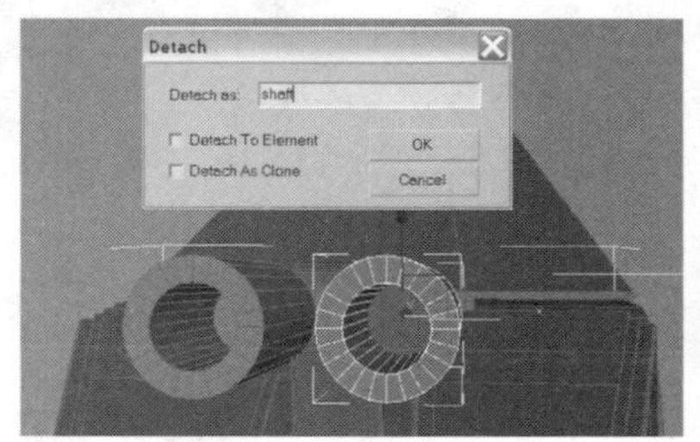

Figure 3-152

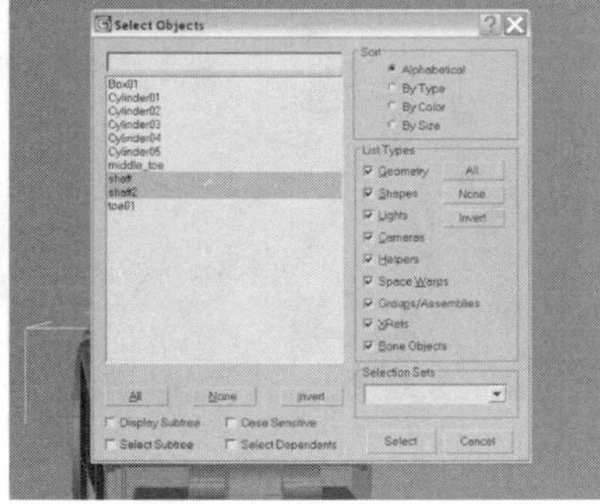

Figure 3-153

11. Move shaft and shaft2 in the Z axis until they are above the mount on the toe, and then move them down in the Y axis to align them behind the toe mount.

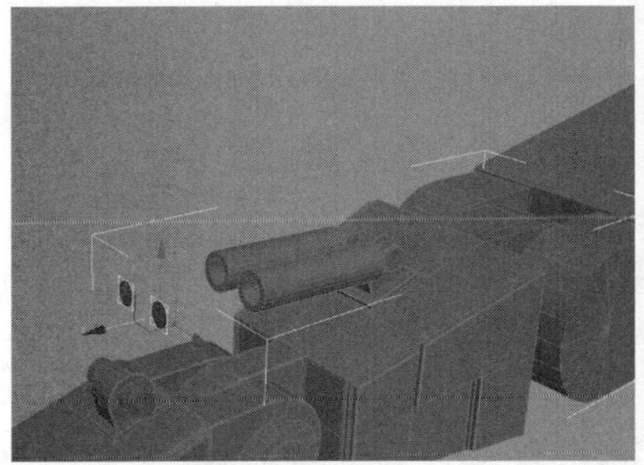
Figure 3-154

Figure 3-155

12. Select one of the pistons, click **Attach**, click the other piston, and name the new object **toePiston**. With toePiston still selected, click the Hierarchy tab, click **Affect Pivot Only**, and move the pivot until it is centered over the cylinder that goes through the mount.

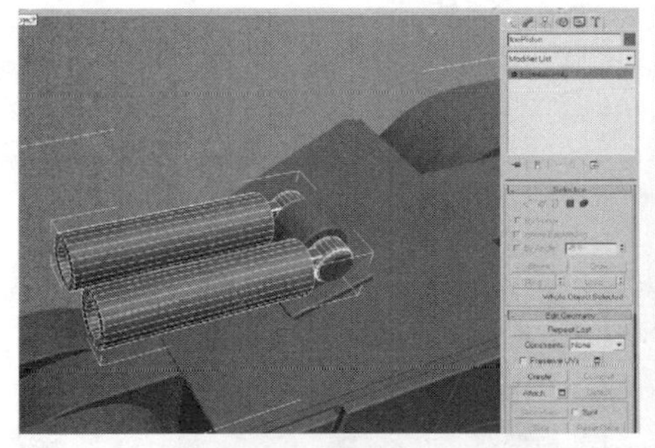
Figure 3-156

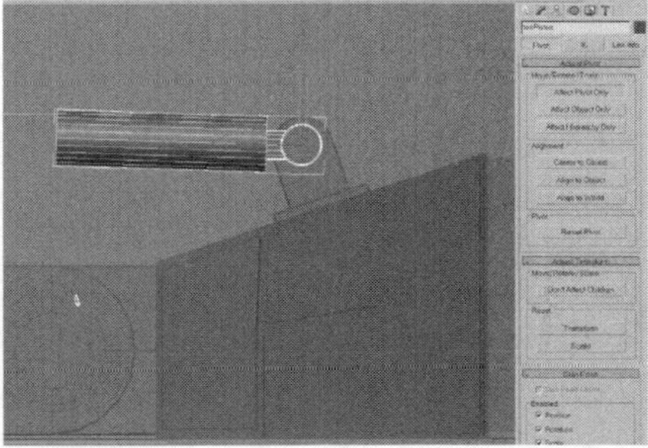
Figure 3-157

Figure 3-158

13. Create a Tube and slip it over the cylinder on the toe, convert it to an Editable Polygon, loop-select the middle edges, and Chamfer them by **2.0**.

Radius 1	Radius 2	Height	Height/Cap Segs	Sides	Smooth
5.096	6	6	2/1	24	Checked

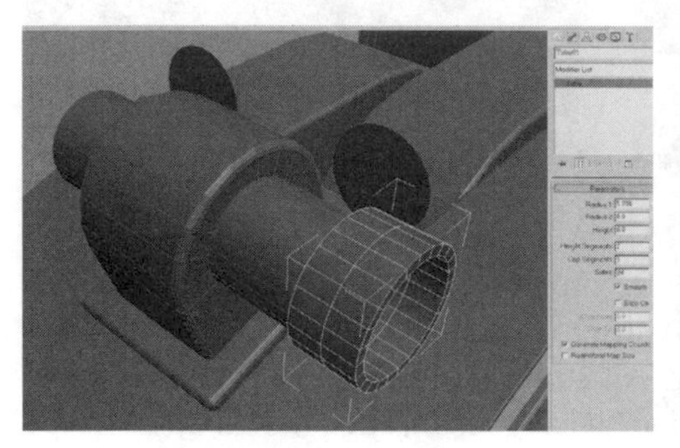

Figure 3-159

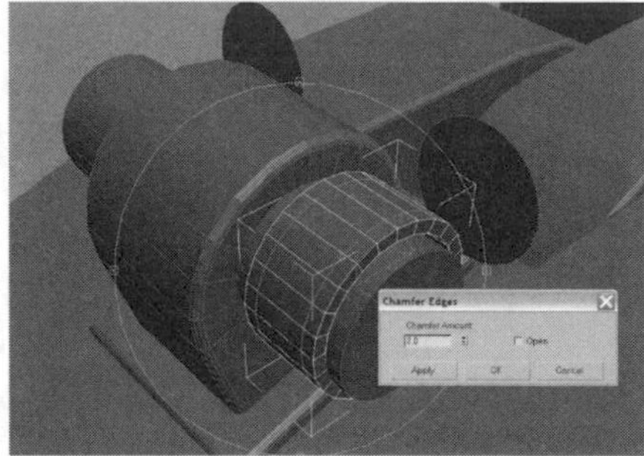

Figure 3-160

14. Select four center polygons and Extrude them by **6.0**.

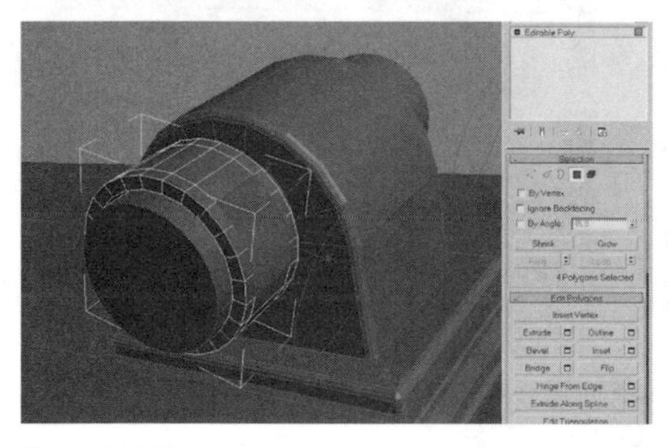

Figure 3-161

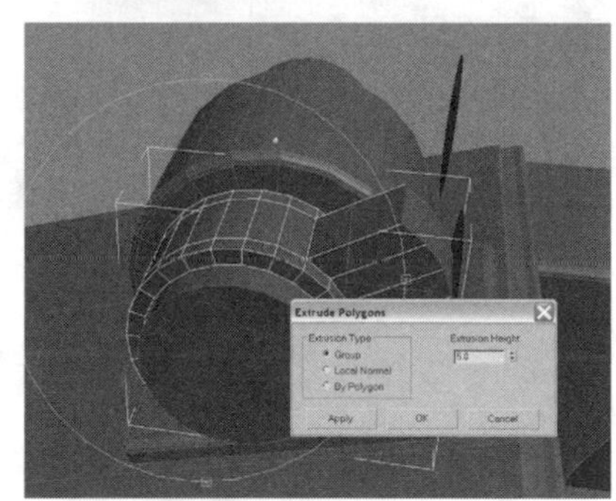

Figure 3-162

15. Switch to the Local coordinate system, Non-uniform Scale the polygons in the Z axis, and then delete them. Select one of the shafts, click **Attach**, and attach the other shaft to make them a single unit.

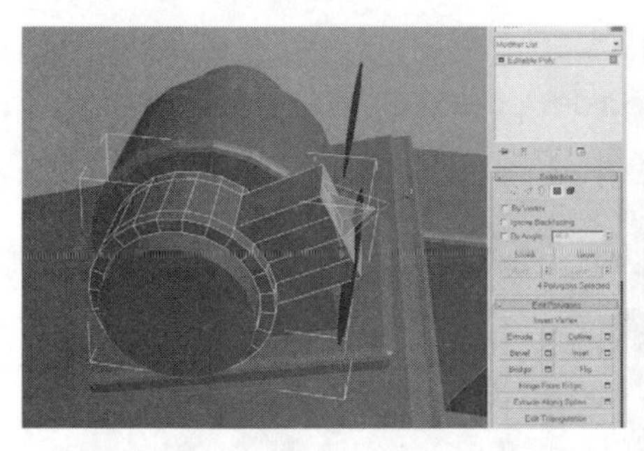

Figure 3-163

Figure 3-164

16. Click the Hierarchy tab, click **Affect Pivot Only**, click **Center to Object**, and then unclick Affect Pivot Only. Select the Rotation tool and rotate the new object **–20** in the Z axis to roughly align it with the extruded part of the tube.

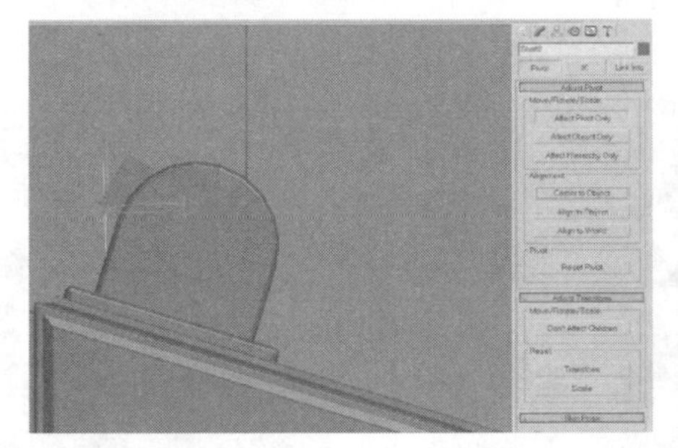

Figure 3-165

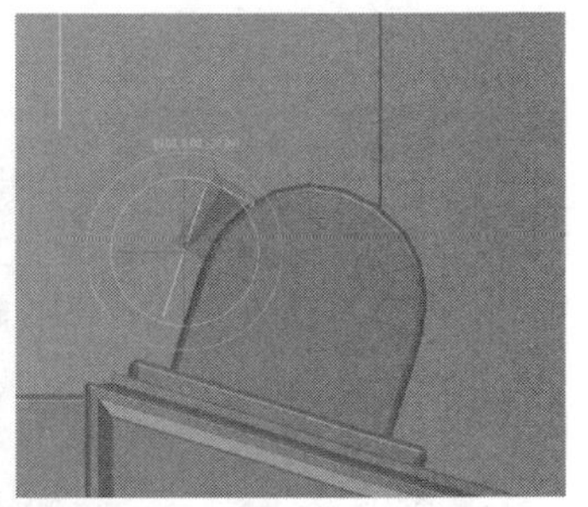

Figure 3-166

17. Select and rotate the tube so it is facing the pistons on the middle_toe. Use the Move and Rotate tools to center and align the attached shafts over the edge of the extruded part of the tube.

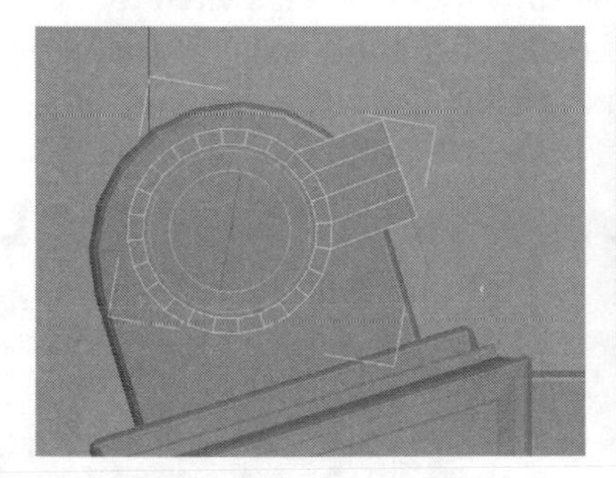

Figure 3-167

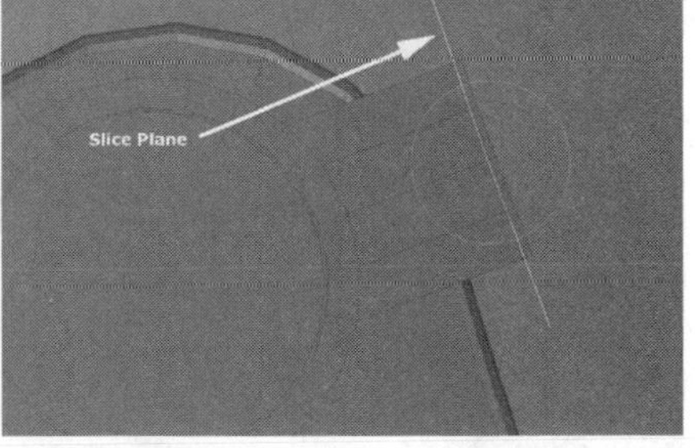

Figure 3-168

18. Object-select the extruded tube and Shift-drag in the X axis to make a clone on the other side of the axle. Click the **Attach** button and attach the other extruded tube and the two shafts to the clone.

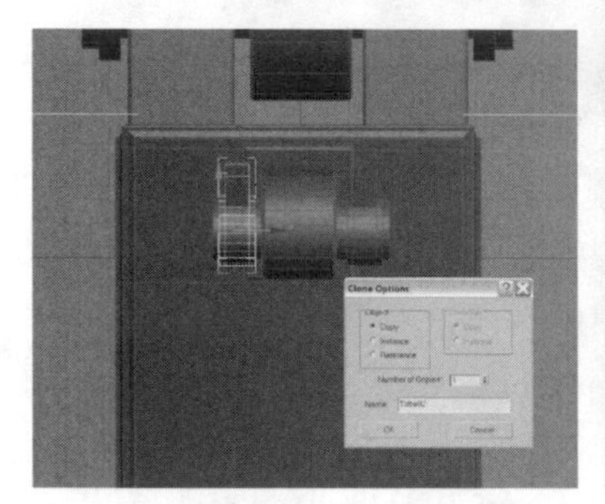

Figure 3-169

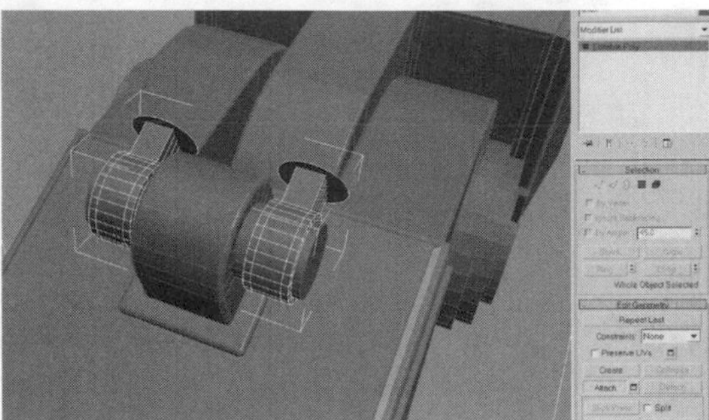

Figure 3-170

19. Border-select the two shafts and Extrude them **–82**.

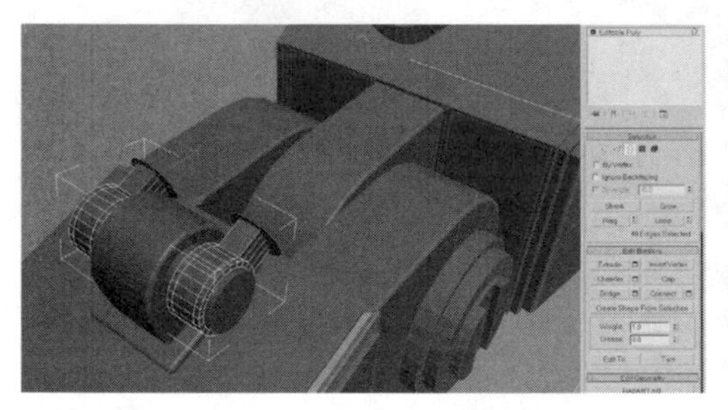

Figure 3-171

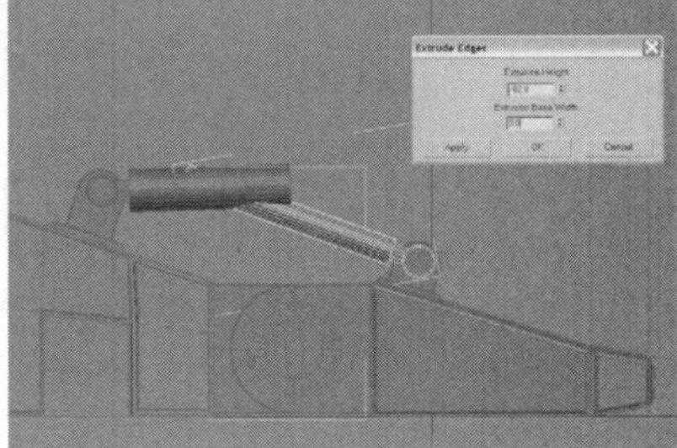

Figure 3-172

20. Click the **Hierarchy** tab, select **Affect Pivot Only**, and make sure the pivot is centered on the toe mount. Then switch to the Left view and use the Rotate tool to make sure the X axis (red arrow) is aligned with the center of the extruded shaft. Turn off **Affect Pivot Only**.

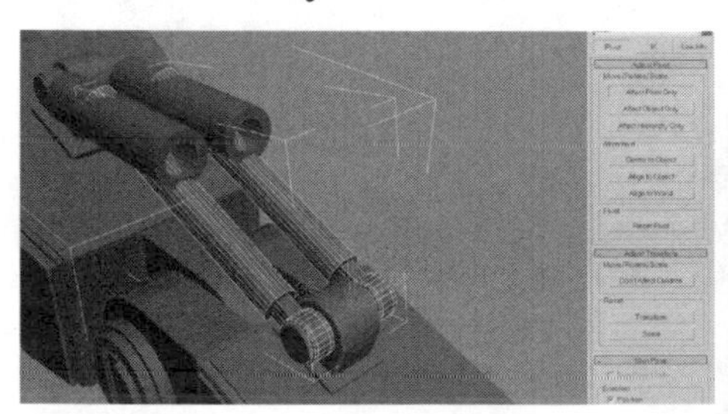

Figure 3-173

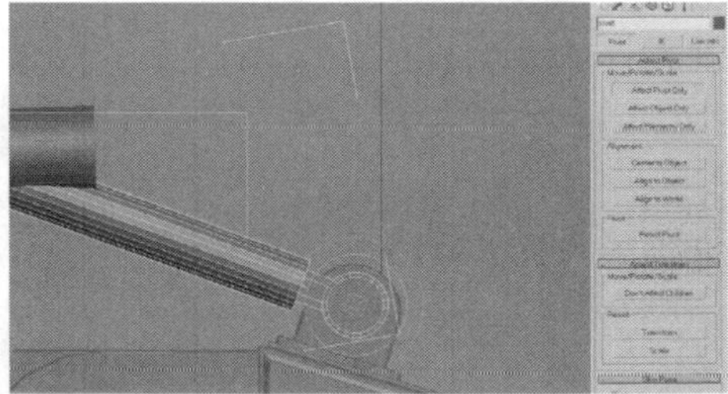

Figure 3-174

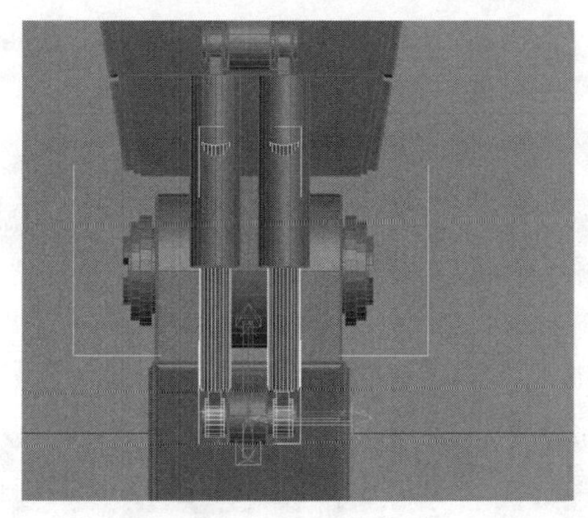

Figure 3-175

21. Click the pistons on the middle_toe, click the **Hierarchy** tab, select **Affect Pivot Only**, and make note of the orientation of the pivot. Then switch to the shaft pivot on the toe and make sure it matches the direction of the middle_toe piston.

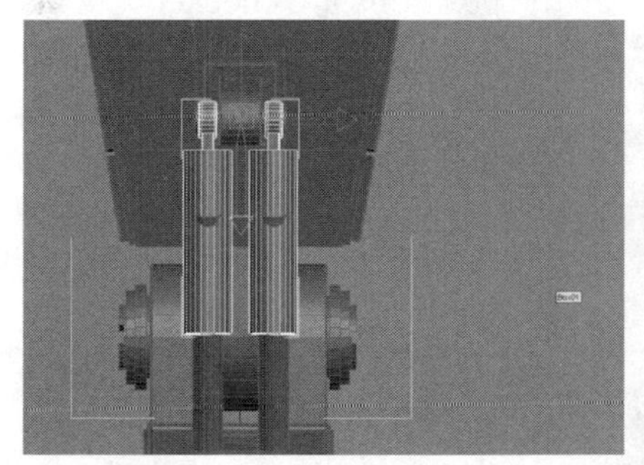

Figure 3-176

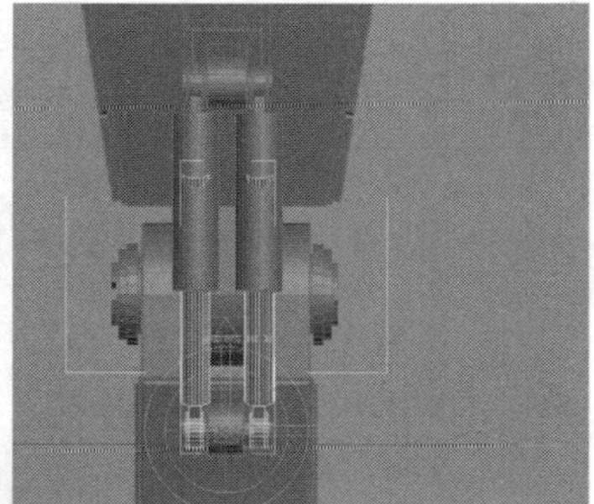

Figure 3-177

FYI: So why all the fuss about matching pivots? The pistons and shafts have to be in sync so they move together. Aligning the pivots facilitates that synchronization.

22. Create a Dummy in the center of the toe mount and adjust its pivot so it aligns with the piston's.

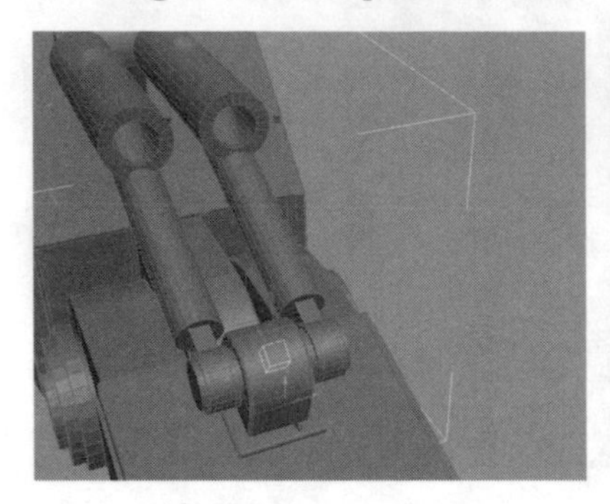

Figure 3-178

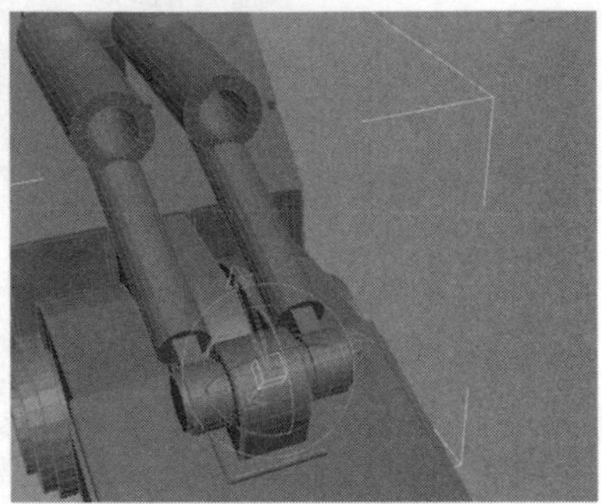

Figure 3-179

23. With the dummy still selected, click the **Align** button and then pick the cylinder that's the axle through the toe mount. Under Align Position, make sure all the positions are checked and make sure **Center** is selected for Current Object and Target Object.

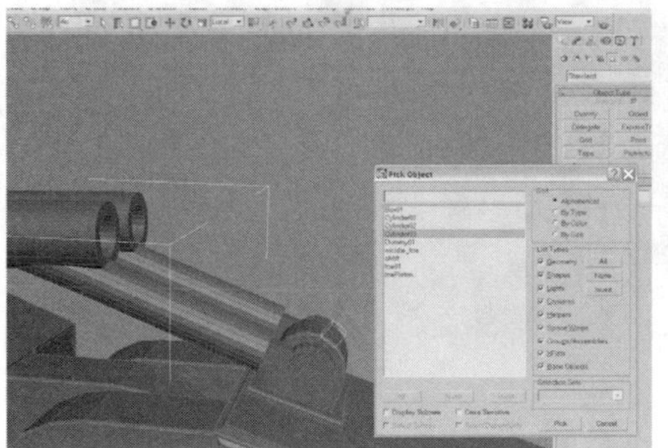

Figure 3-180

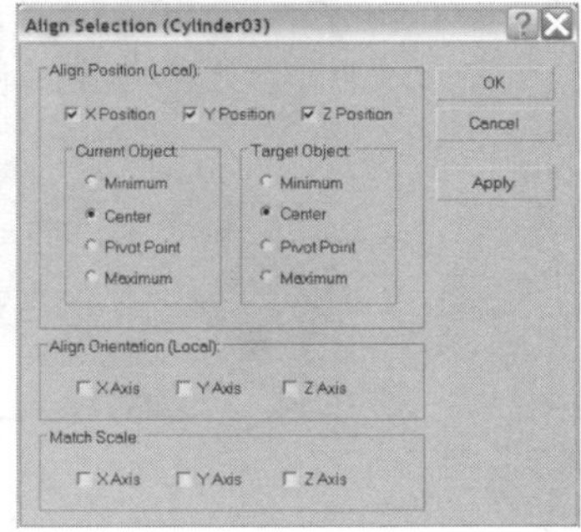

Figure 3-181

24. Rename the dummy **toe_dummy**, and then Select and Link it to the toe. Select the pistons, click the **Motion** tab, and select **Rotation: Euler XYZ** under Assign Controller.

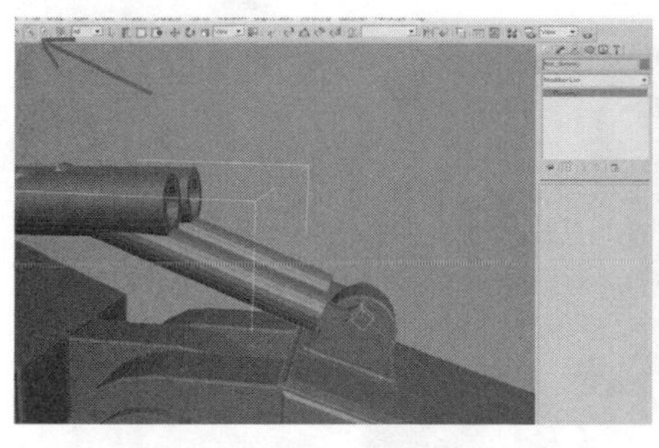

Figure 3-182

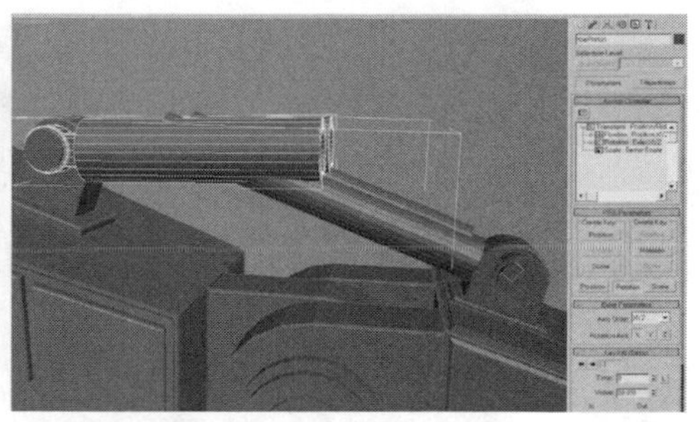

Figure 3-183

25. Click the **Assign Controller** button, pick **LookAt Constraint**, and click **OK.** Click **Add LookAt Target**, select **toe_dummy**, and click **Pick**.

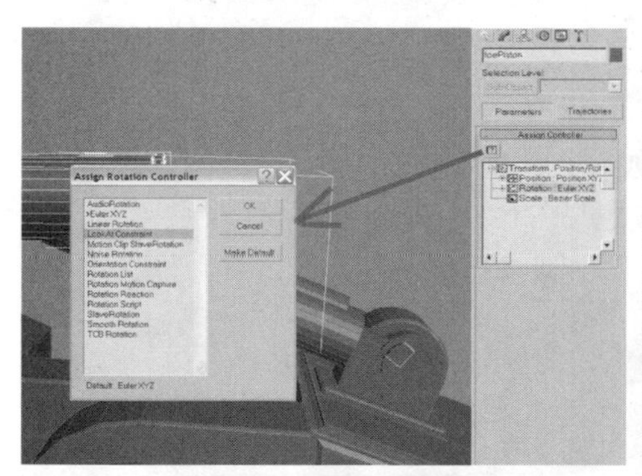

Figure 3-184

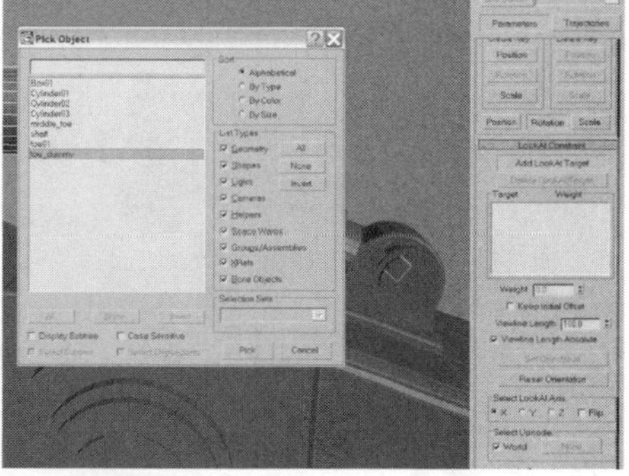

Figure 3-185

26. Set the Select LookAt Axis to **Z** and create a Dummy on the middle_toe mount named **mid_toe-Dummy**.

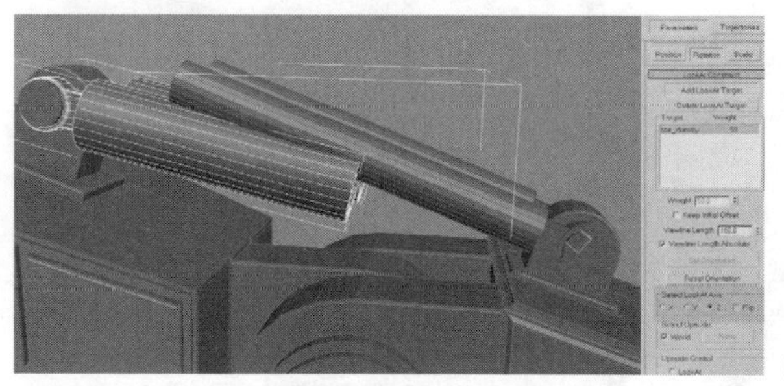

Figure 3-186

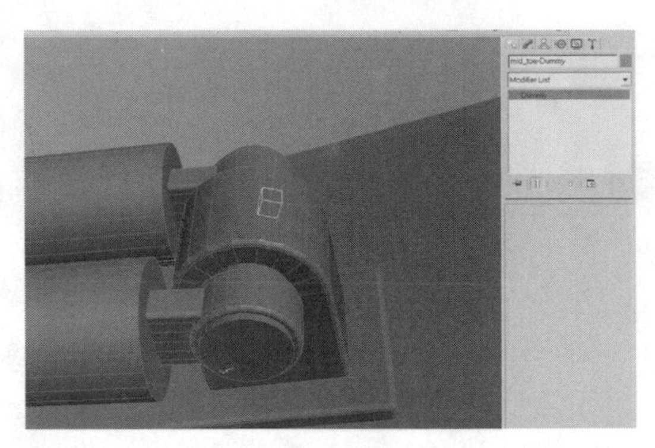

Figure 3-187

27. Make sure the pivots for the mid_toe-Dummy are oriented the same way as the pivots for the piston. Click the **Align** button on the Main toolbar, pick the cylinder corresponding to the axle of the middle_toe mount, and make sure **Center** is selected for both Current Object and Target Object.

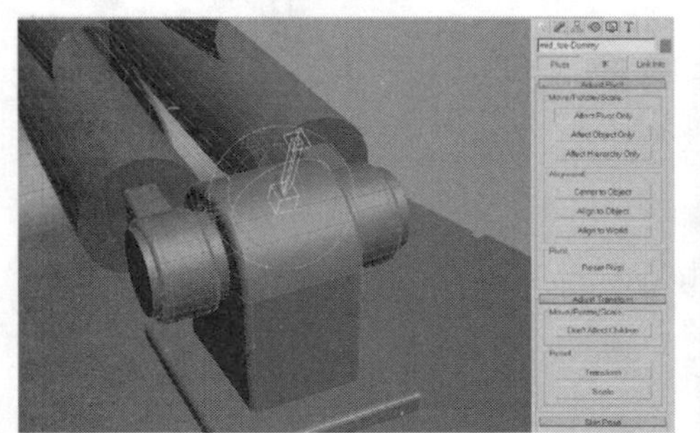

Figure 3-188

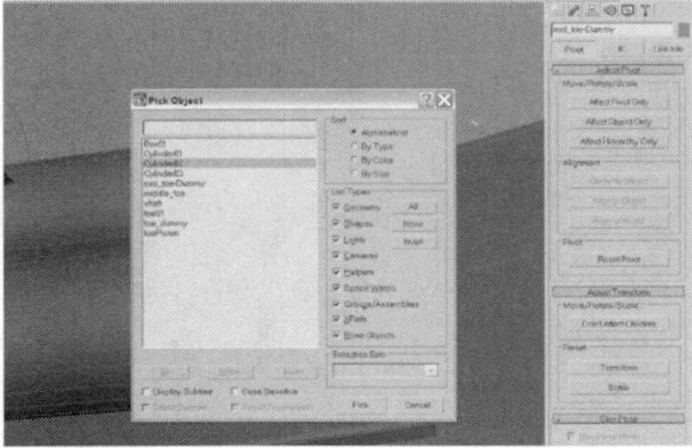

Figure 3-189

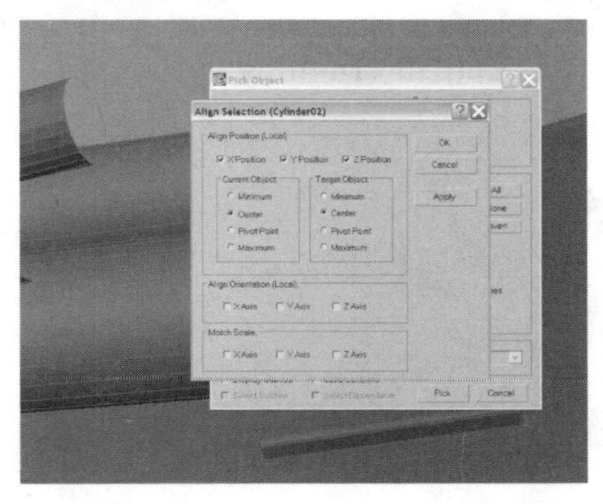

Figure 3-190

28. Select the toe shafts, click the **Motion** tab, and assign a LookAt controller to constrain their rotation.

Day 2: Building the Toe Hydraulics

Figure 3-191

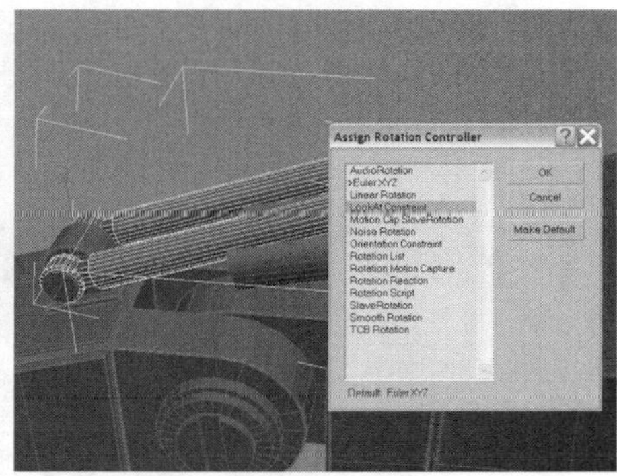

Figure 3-192

29. Click **LookAt Target**, select **mid_toe-Dummy**, and make sure the Source Axis and Aligned to Upnode Axis are both set to **Y**. If the angle of the shafts is too extreme, you may have to rotate the shaft's pivot so the shafts insert into the pistons.

Figure 3-193

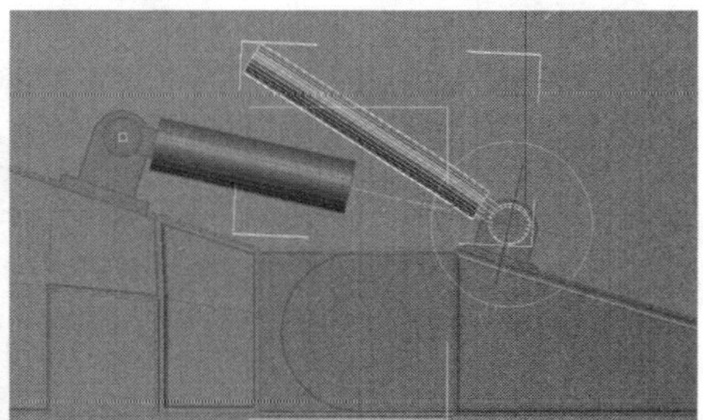

Figure 3-194

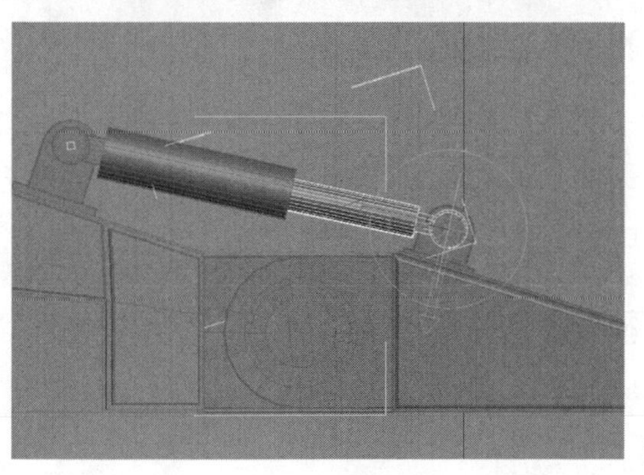

Figure 3-195

30. Make sure all the dummies have been linked to their respective toes. Rotate the toe upward and the shafts should slide in and out of the pistons. After you're done testing, press **Ctrl+Z** to undo the move and return the toe to its original position.

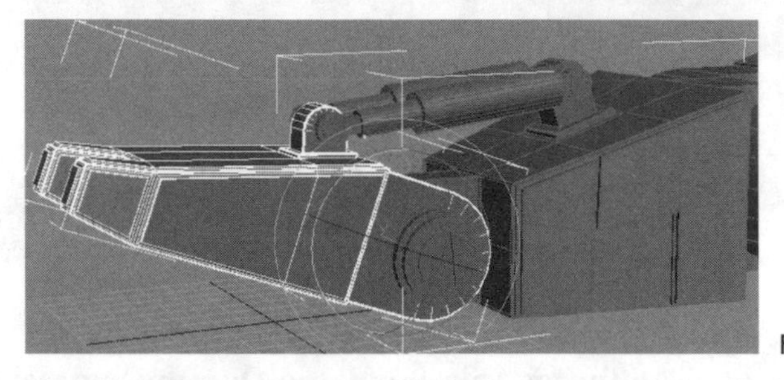

Figure 3-196

31. Use AutoGrid to create a Cylinder, center the cylinder in the hinge, and convert it to an Editable Polygon.

Radius	Height	Height/Cap Segs	Sides	Smooth
24	121	1/1	24	Checked

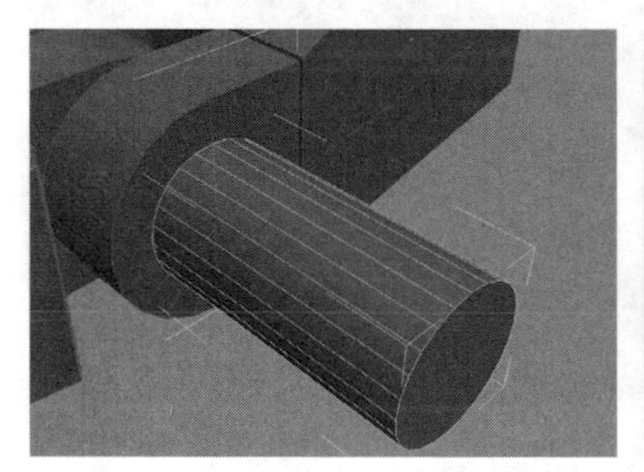

Figure 3-197

Figure 3-198

32. Select the cylinder caps and click **Bevel Settings**:

Type	Height	Outline	Apply/OK
Group	0	5	Apply
Group	5	0	Apply
Group	0	–4	Apply

Day 2: Building the Toe Hydraulics

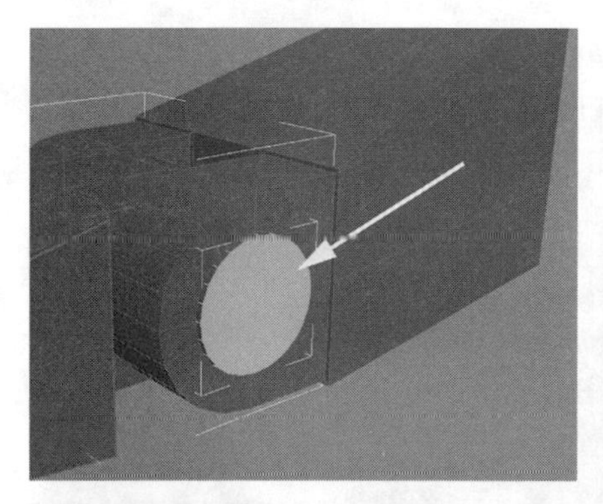

Figure 3-199

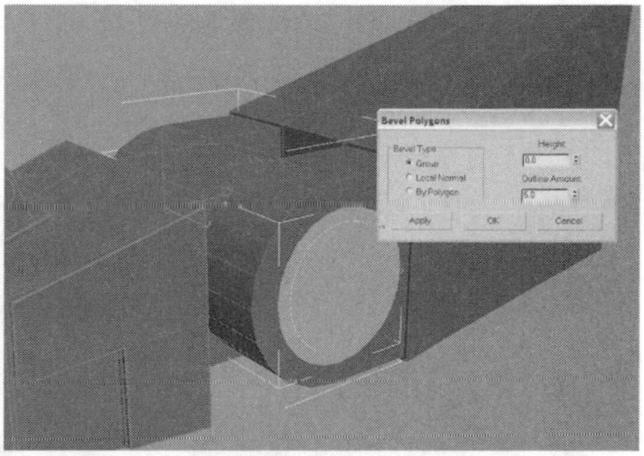

Figure 3-200

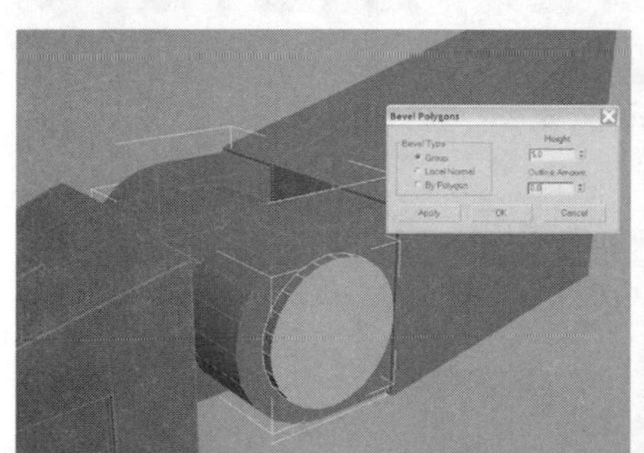

Figure 3-201

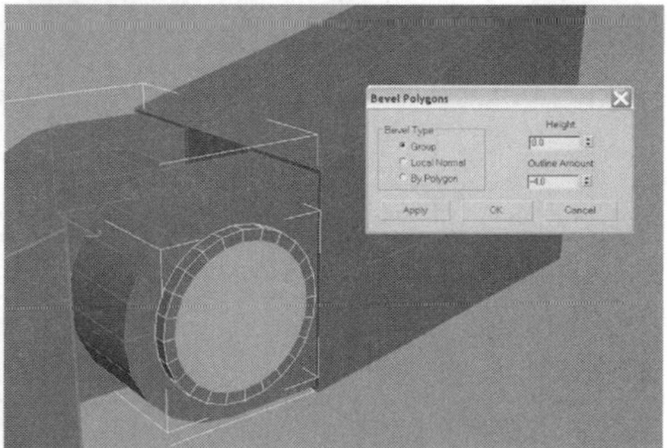

Figure 3-202

Type	Height	Outline	Apply/OK
Group	3.8	0	Apply
Group	0	–4	Apply

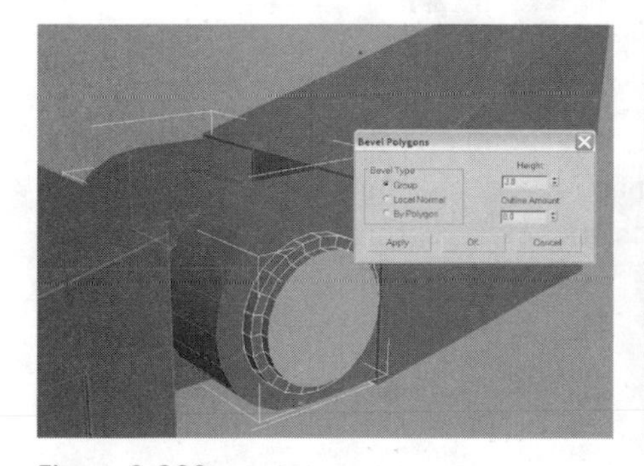

Figure 3-203

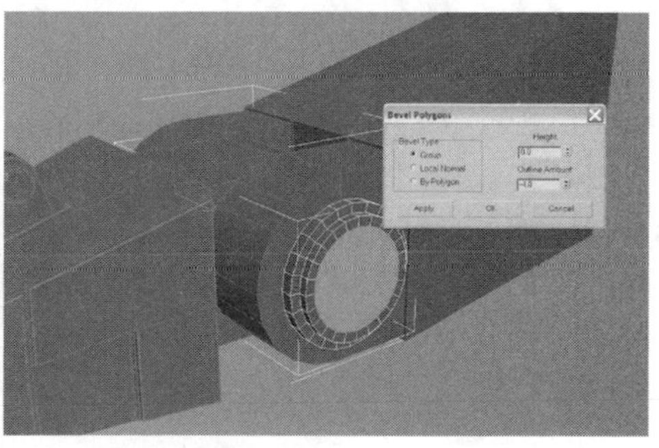

Figure 3-204

Type	Height	Outline	Apply/OK
Group	–1.75	0	Apply
Group	0	–2	Apply

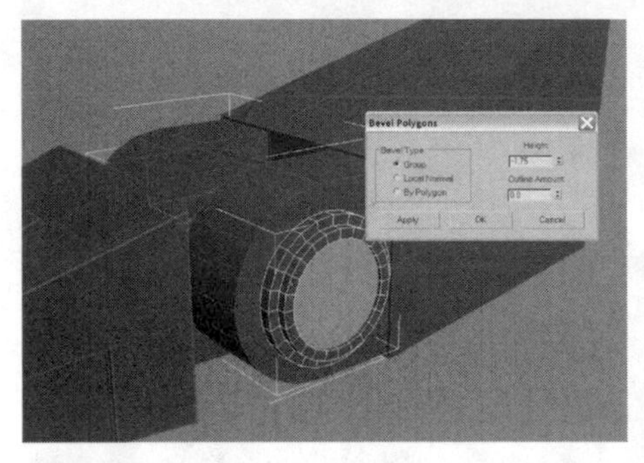

Figure 3-205

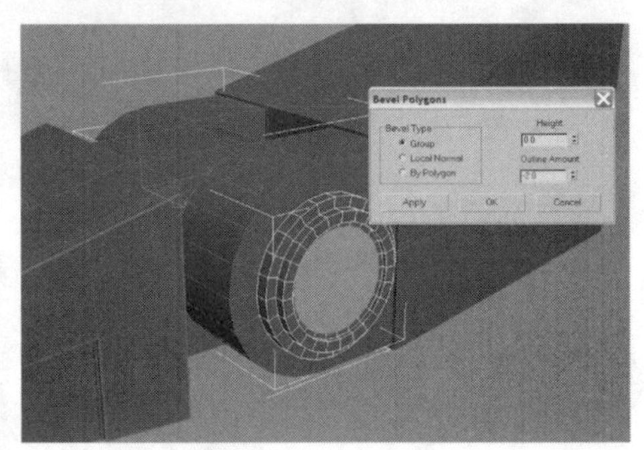

Figure 3-206

Type	Height	Outline	Apply/OK
Group	3.2	0	OK

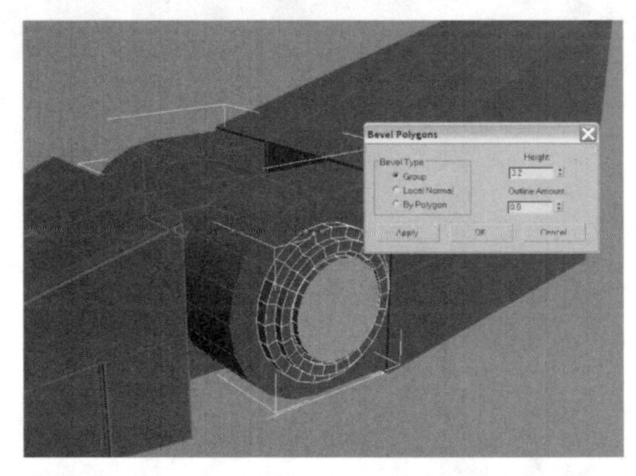

Figure 3-207

33. Click the **Snaps Toggle** button on the main toolbar, right-click and make sure that only Vertex snap is selected, and then Cut as shown. Select the two lateral polygons and Extrude them by **4.0** to make a screwhead.

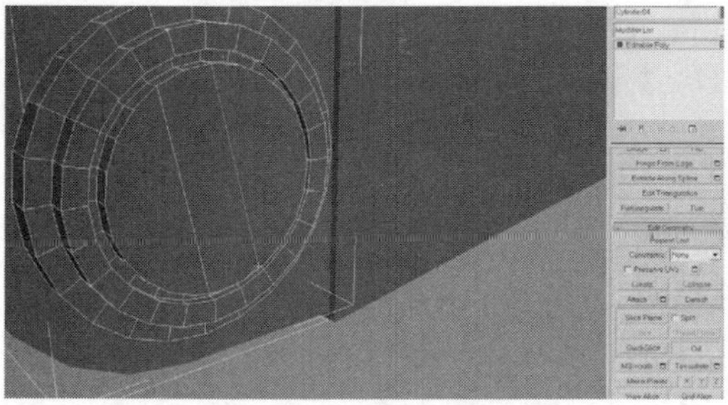

Figure 3-208

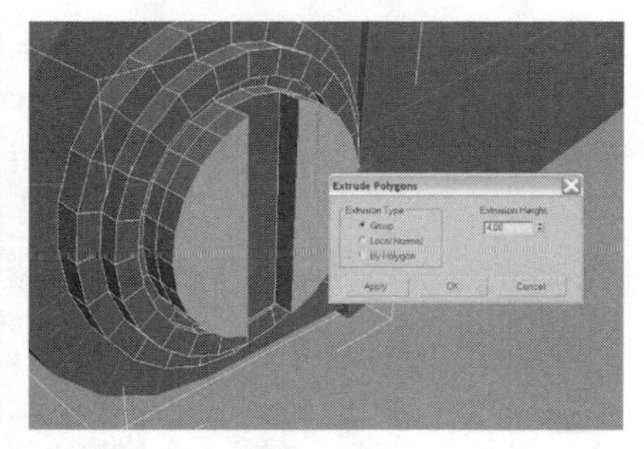

Figure 3-209

34. On the middle_toe, select the polygons that comprise the mount, click **Detach**, name it **mount**, and then Select and Link it to the middle_toc.

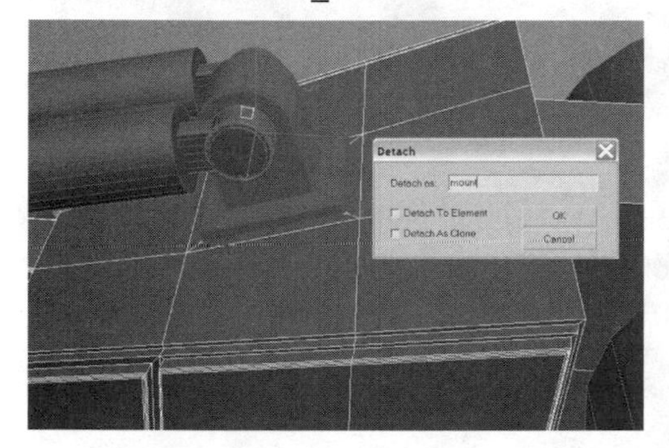

Figure 3-210

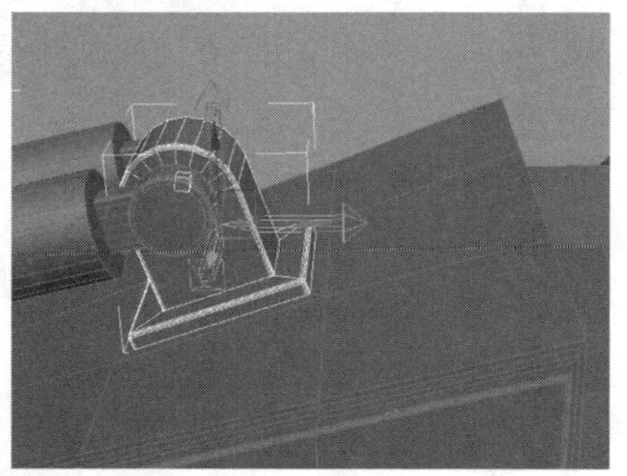

Figure 3-211

35. Shift-drag to create a clone of the mount, position the clone to the rear of the middle_toe, and Select and Link the mounts to the middle_toe. Switch to the Right view, select the **middle_toe**, click the **Hierarchy** tab, click **Affect Pivot Only**, and center the pivot over the axle that links it to the foot.

Figure 3-212

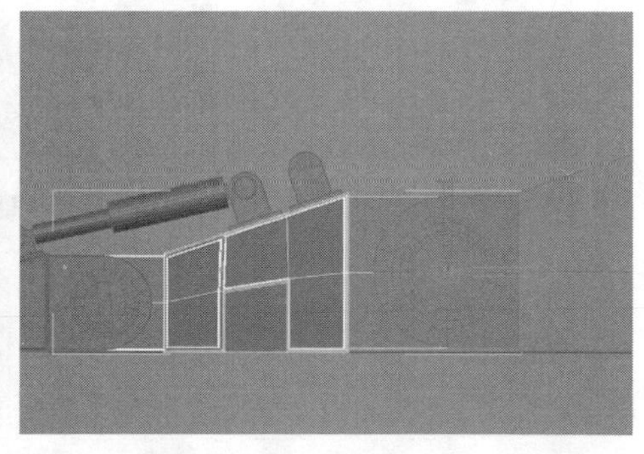

Figure 3-213

36. Turn on Slice Plane, position it near the front of the foot near the hinge, and click the **Slice** button. Move the Slice Plane in the X axis and position it as shown, and then click **Slice**. Turn off the Slice Plane.

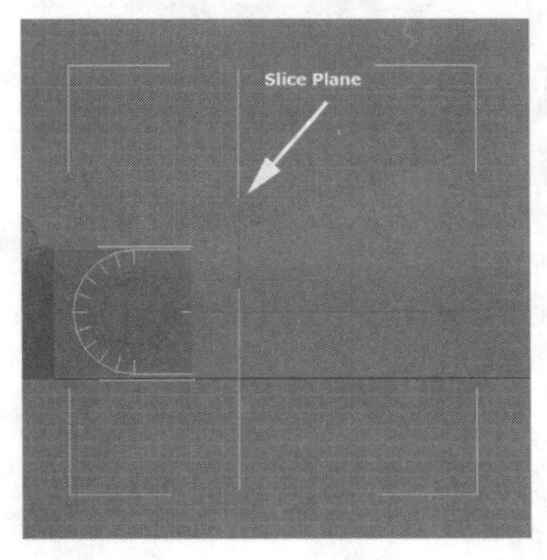

Figure 3-214

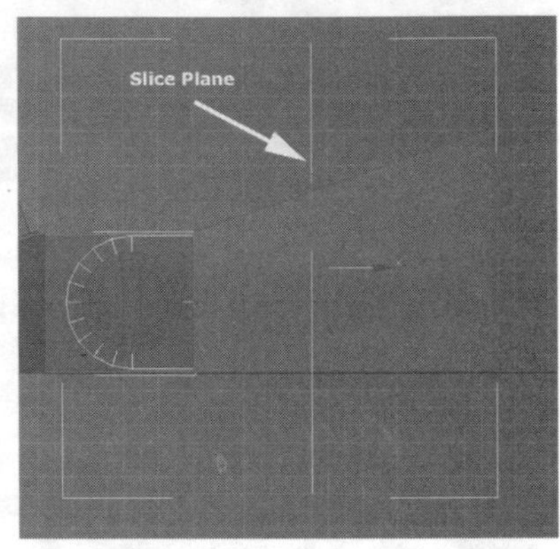

Figure 3-215

37. Select the side edges of the polygon that you created using the Slice Plane, and then Non-uniform Scale them to **0** in the Y axis (to make them parallel). Click the resulting polygon and Bevel it:

Type	Height	Outline	Apply/OK
Group	4	0	Apply

Figure 3-216

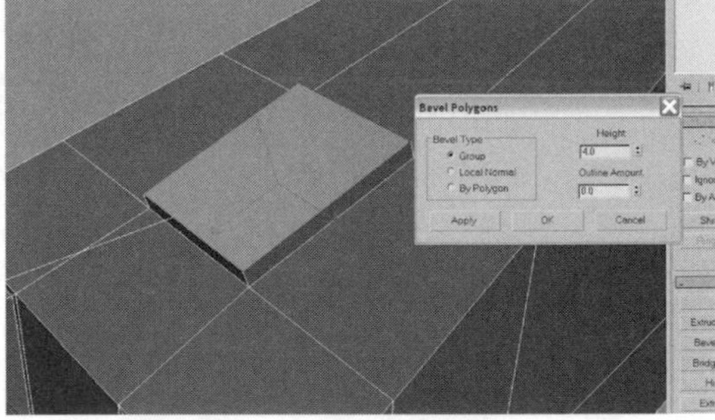

Figure 3-217

Type	Height	Outline	Apply/OK
Group	0	–8	Apply
Group	25	0	OK

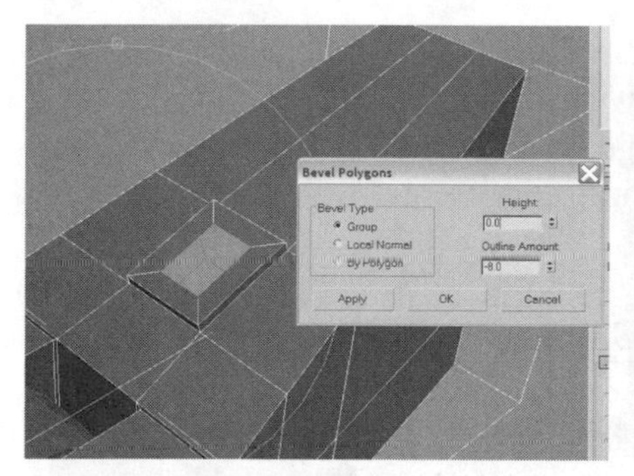

Figure 3-218

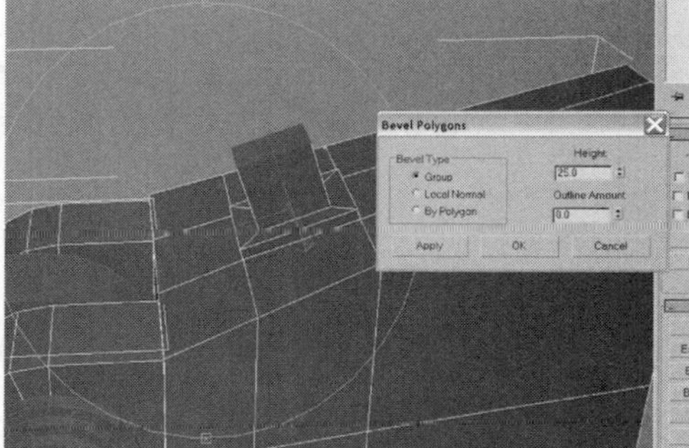

Figure 3-219

38. Select the two side top edges (the long edges) and click **Connect**. Select the bottom polygon from the two polygons created by the connection and delete it. Select the top, Hinge From Edge **180** degrees with **10** Segments, delete the back-facing polygon, and then Weld the resulting vertices.

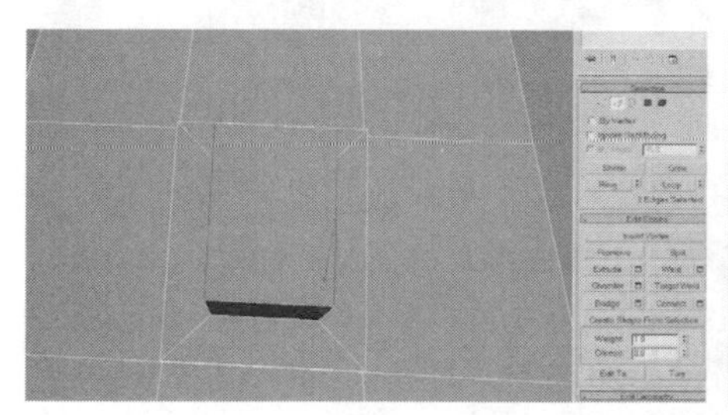

Figure 3-220

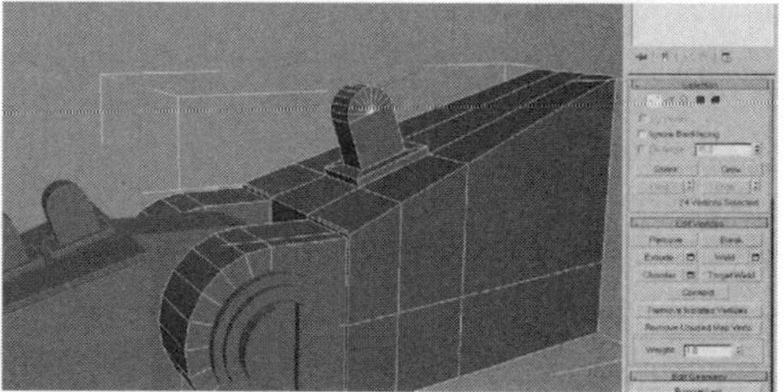

Figure 3-221

39. Select the edges of the mount, being careful to deselect the edges connecting the upper mount to the base. Chamfer the edges by **1.0** and then by **0.403**.

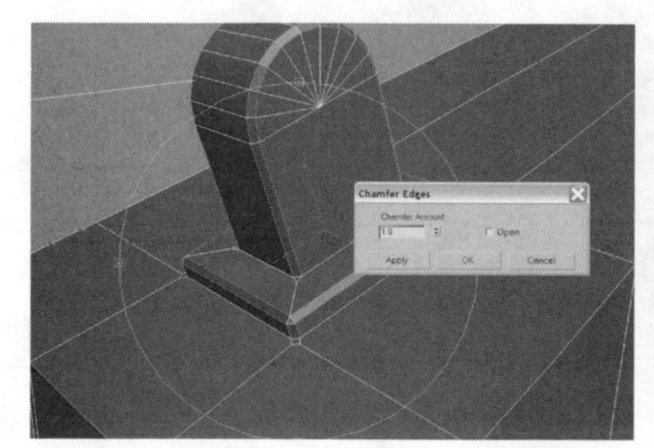

Figure 3-222

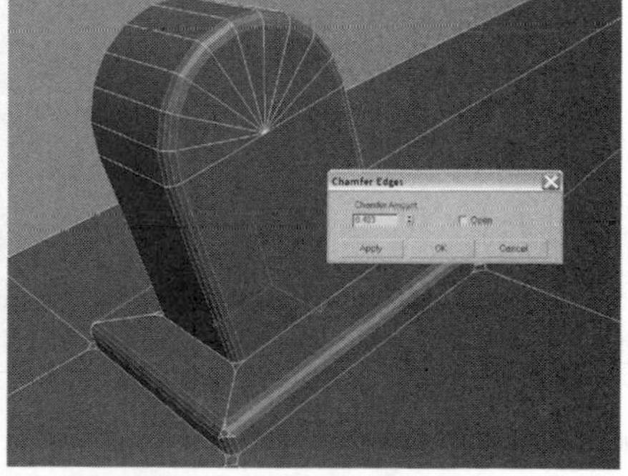

Figure 3-223

40. Create a Box and position it just to the front of the mount's center, as shown in Figure 3-224. Convert it to an Editable Polygon, select the bottom poly, delete it, Hinge From Edge **180** degrees with **10** Segments, delete the back-facing polygon, and Weld the vertices.

Length	Width	Height	Length/Width/Height Segs
16	7	10	2/1/1

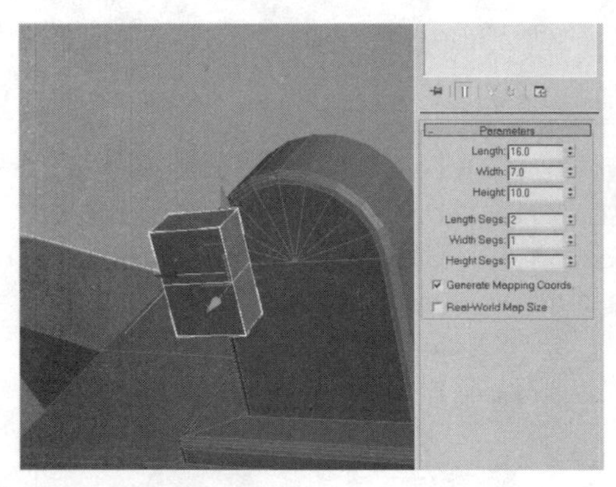

Figure 3-224

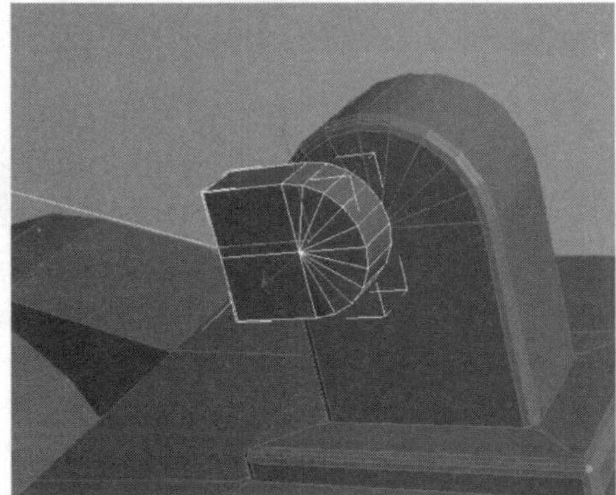

Figure 3-225

41. Switch to wireframe mode (**F3**) and align the vertical midline of the hinged box you just made with the center vertical edge of the mount. Select the vertices on the left end of the box and move them past the front edge of the mount, as shown.

Figure 3-226

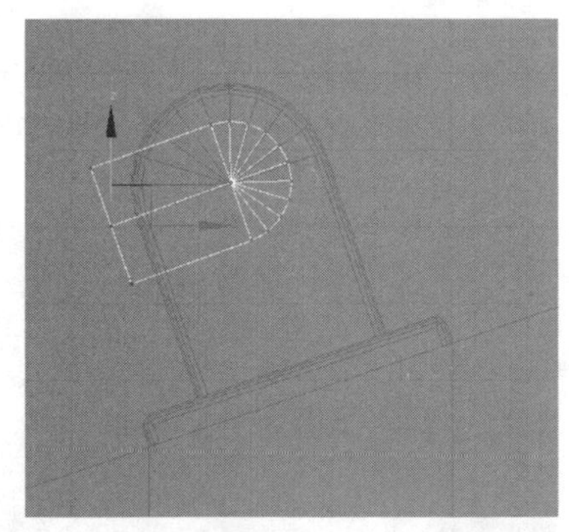

Figure 3-227

42. Switch to the Top view and clone the box, moving it to the other side of the mount. Attach the clone and the original to form a single object.

Day 2: Building the Toe Hydraulics

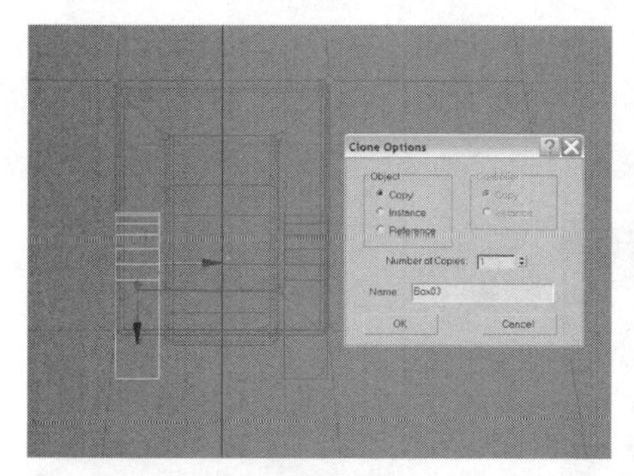

Figure 3-228

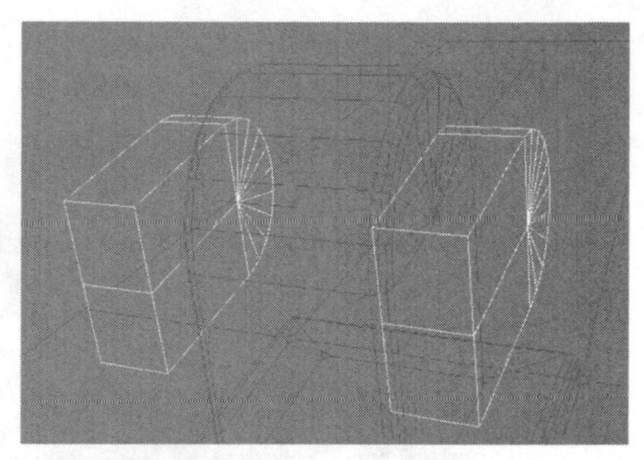

Figure 3-229

43. Select the front polygons and delete them. Select the two inside edges.

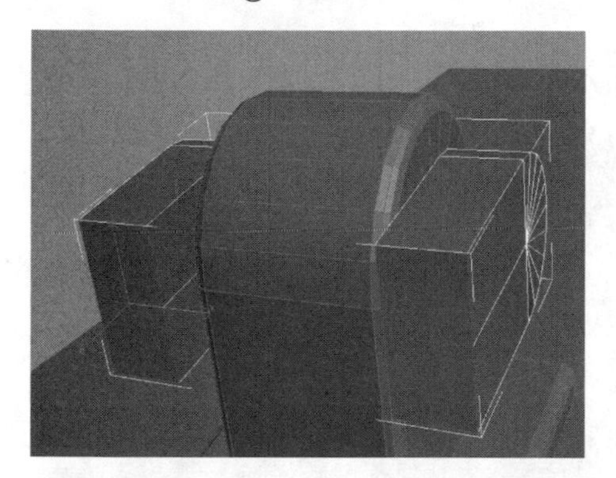

Figure 3-230

Figure 3-231

44. Click **Bridge** to connect the inside edges, then border-select it and click **Cap**.

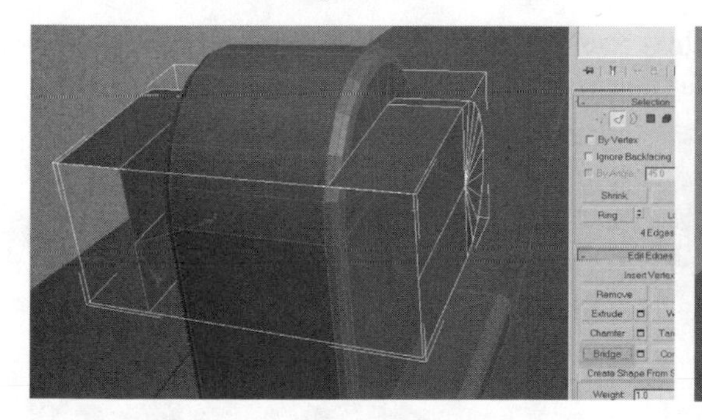

Figure 3-232

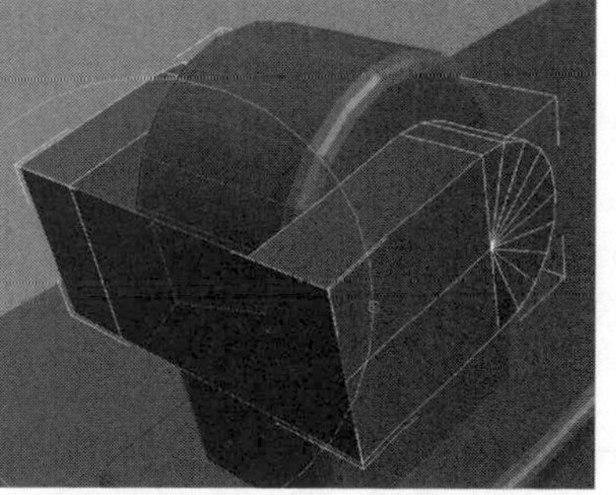

Figure 3-233

45. Extrude the cap by **2.8**, create a clone of the object, and move the clone toward the rear mount on the middle_toe.

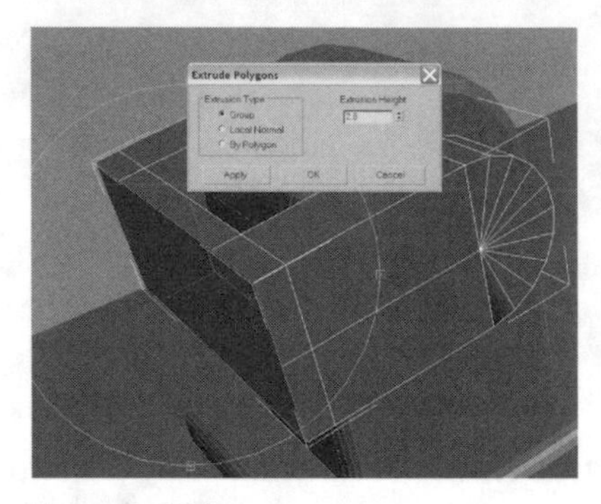

Figure 3-234

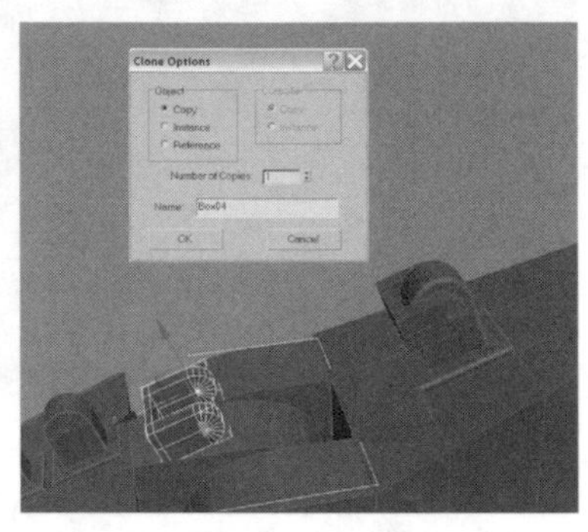

Figure 3-235

46. Rotate the clone and position it so it can turn on the middle_toe mount, as shown in Figure 3-237.

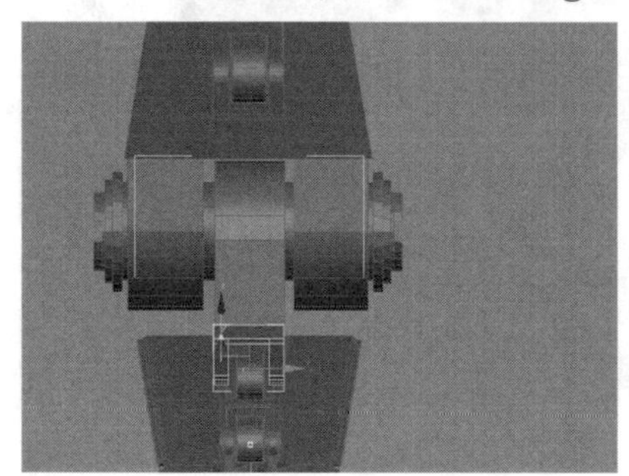

Figure 3-236

Figure 3-237

47. Click **Affect Pivot Only** and center the pivot at the center of the mount. Uniform Scale the clone down to **78** in all three axes.

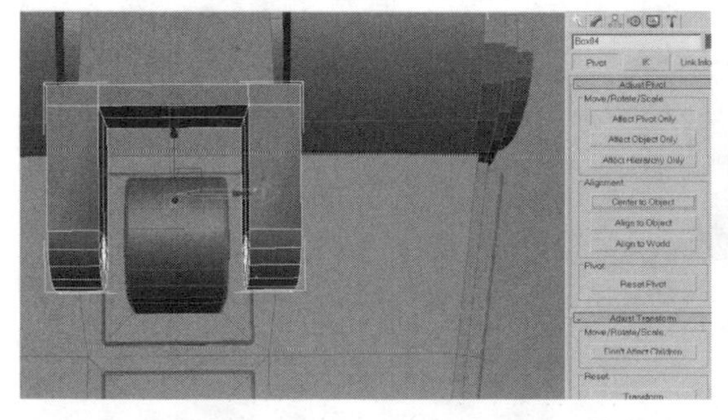

Figure 3-238

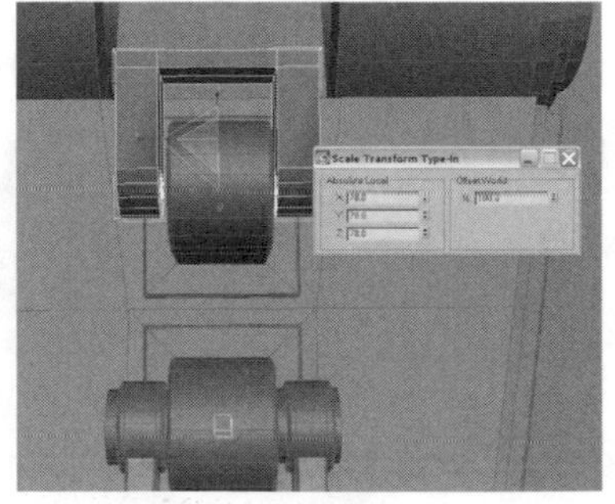

Figure 3-239

48. Select the outer vertices and scale them down to **75** in the X axis. Position the clone so it's aligned, facing the original.

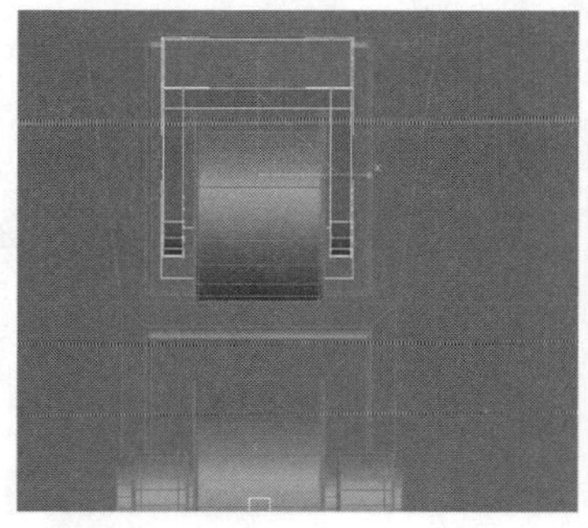

Figure 3-240

Figure 3-241

49. Create a Cylinder on the end of the hinge on the foot as shown. Increase the Height of the cylinder to **76** (to create a piston).

Radius	Height	Height/Cap Segs	Sides	Smooth
19.5	10.375	1/1	24	Checked

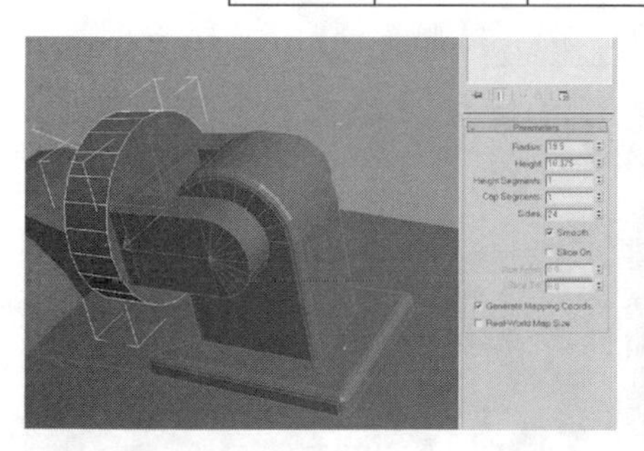

Figure 3-242

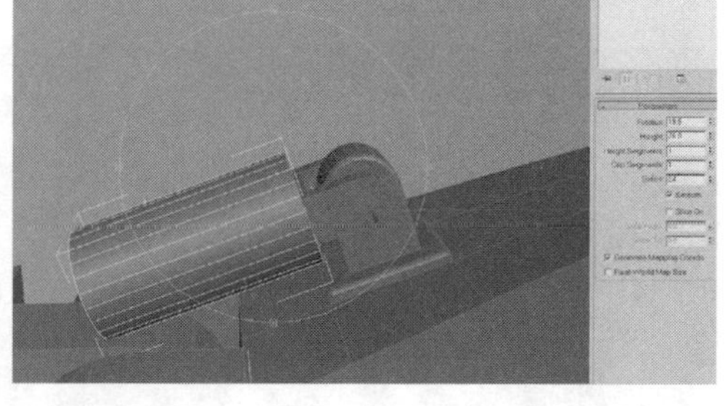

Figure 3-243

50. Attach the hinge to the cylinder and center the pivot of the new combined object over the mount (so the piston can rotate over the mount). Turn off **Affect Pivot Only**.

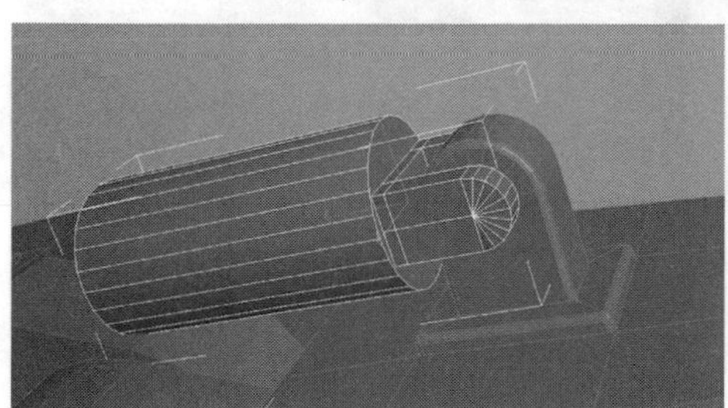

Figure 3-244

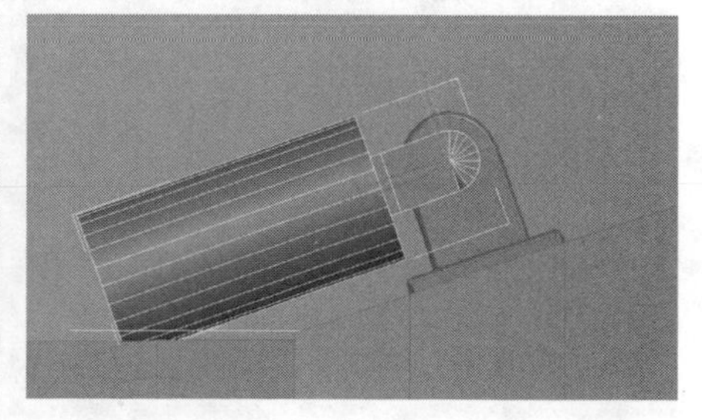

Figure 3-245

51. Rotate the piston up, so it is no longer lying in the middle_toe hinge. Rename it **big_piston**.

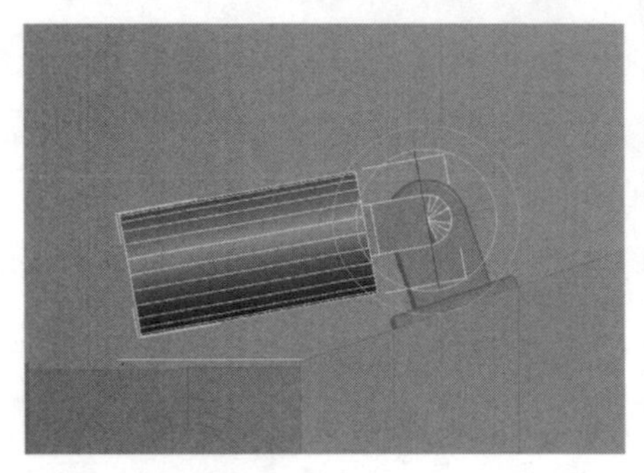

Figure 3-246

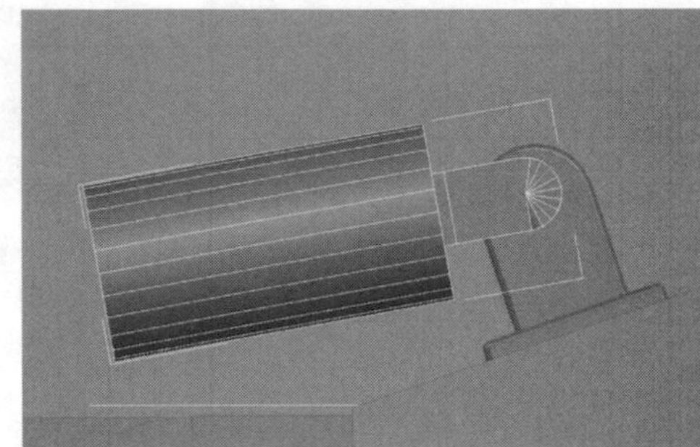

Figure 3-247

52. Select the front cap of the piston and Bevel it. Then detach the internal polygon and name it **big_shaft**.

Type	Height	Outline	Apply/OK
Group	0	–6.0	Apply
Group	–57	0	OK

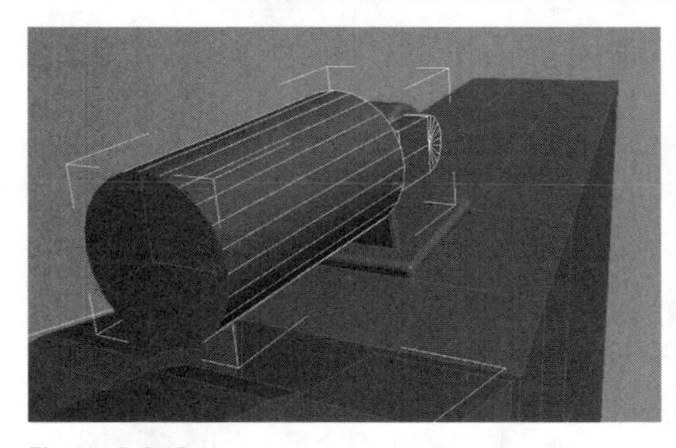

Figure 3-248

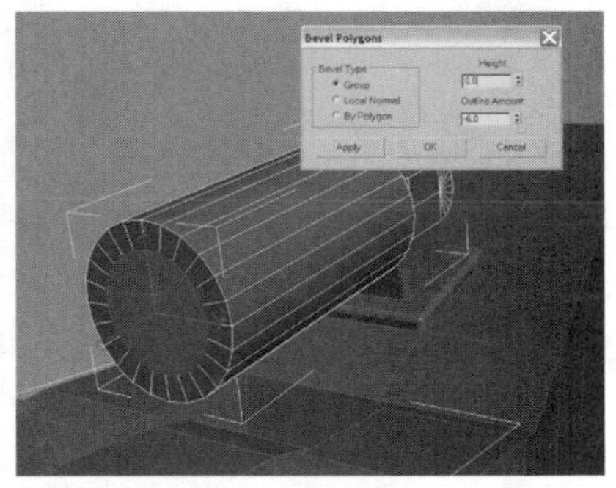

Figure 3-249

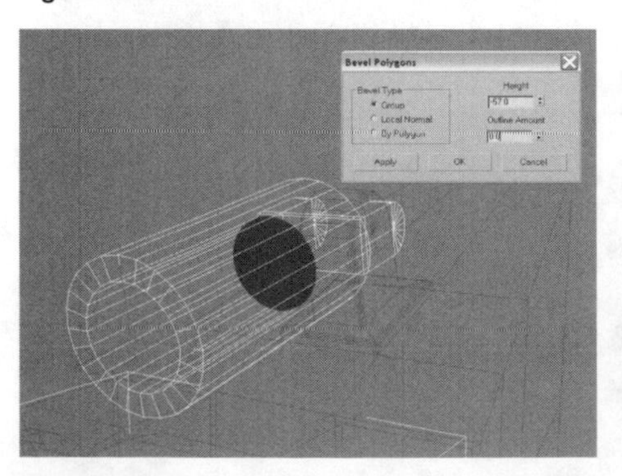

Figure 3-250

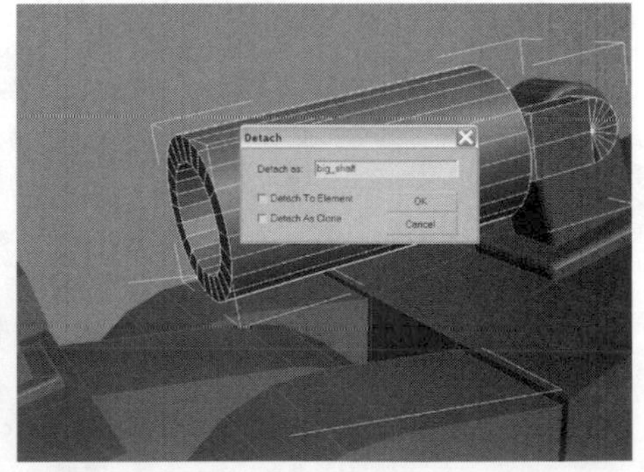

Figure 3-251

53. Move big_shaft in the Z axis and position it against the rear mount hinge on the middle_toe. Center its pivot, switch to the Left view, and then use the Rotate and Move tools to center the big_shaft against the mount hinge, as shown.

Figure 3-252

Figure 3-253

54. Attach big_shaft to the rear mount hinge on the middle_toe. Border-select big_shaft and Cap it.

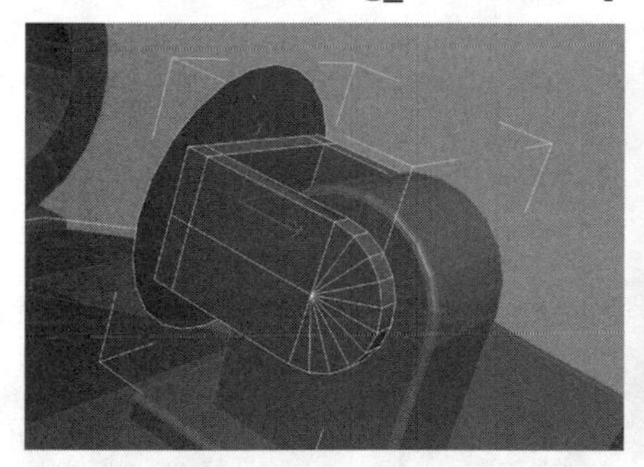

Figure 3-254

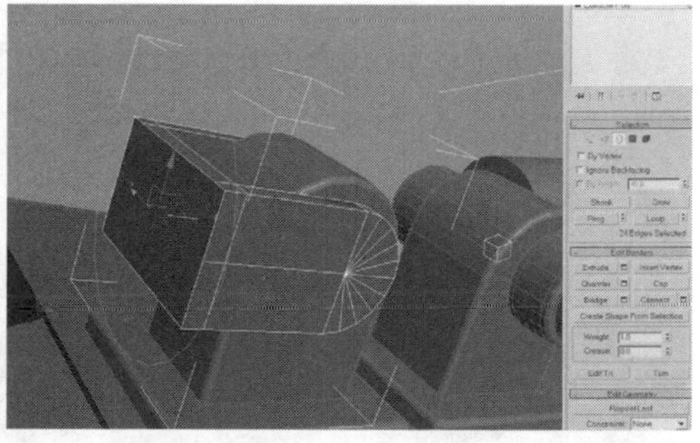

Figure 3-255

55. Poly-select the cap and Extrude it **90**. Choose **Affect Pivot Only** and position the pivot in the center of the hinge.

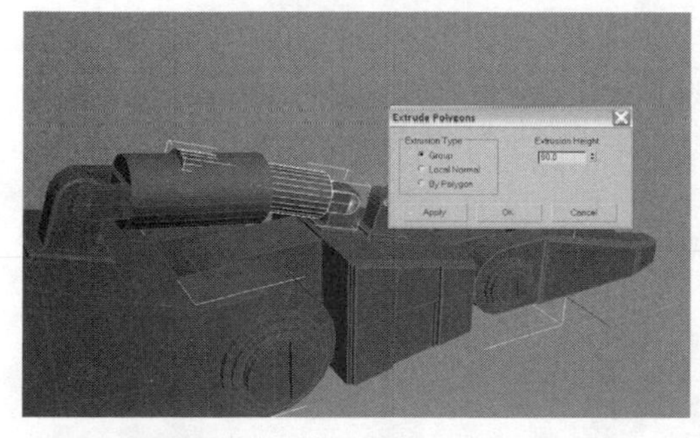

Figure 3-256

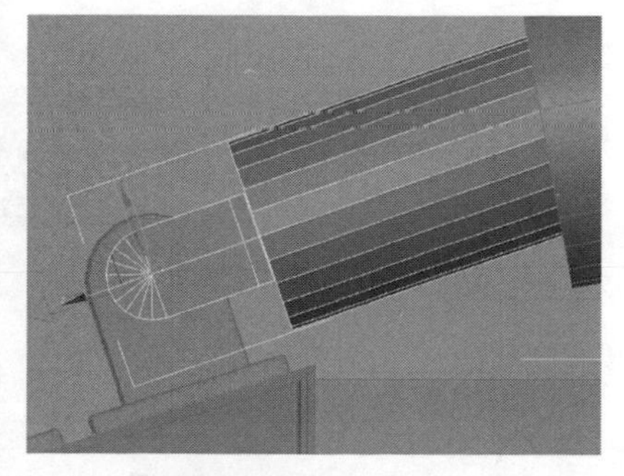

Figure 3-257

56. Poly-select the mount on the foot, detach it, and name it **big_mount**. Select and Link big_mount to the foot. Create a Dummy and center it in the big_mount.

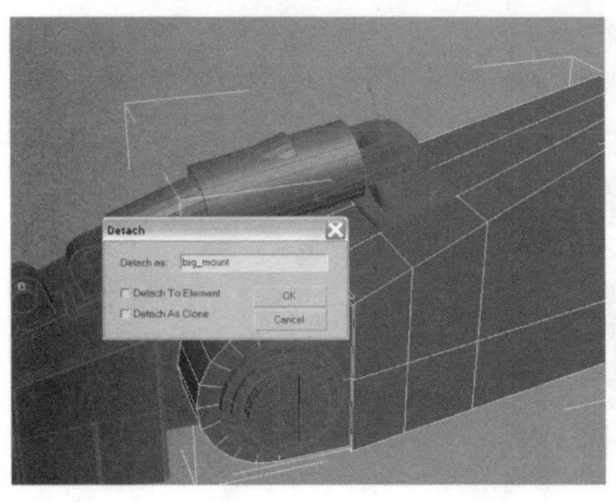

Figure 3-258

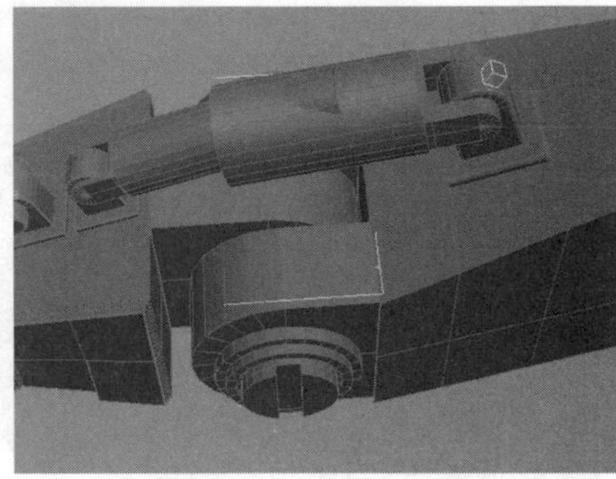

Figure 3-259

57. Click the **Align** button and align the center of the dummy with the center of big_mount, then name it **big_dummy**. Create a Dummy in the center of the mount on the rear of the middle_toe (the mount that big_shaft fits against), and call it **middle_toe_dummy**.

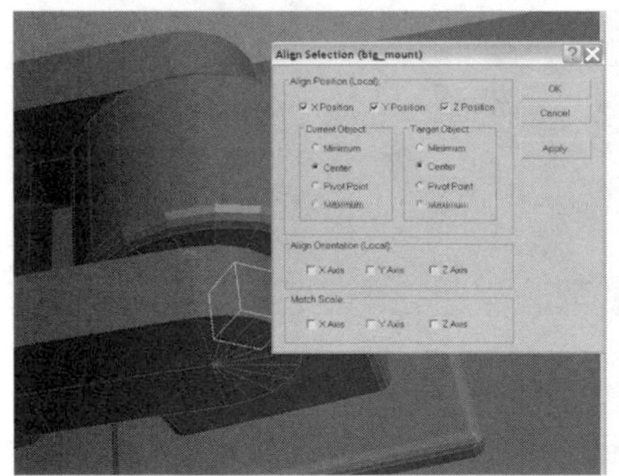

Figure 3-260

Figure 3-261

FYI: The reason we detached big_mount, only to link it back onto the foot, is so it would be a separate object and as such we could align the dummy to its center. Had we left big_mount a part of the foot, its center would've been in the middle of the foot and would not have worked for aligning the dummy.

58. Align the dummy to the mount. Select the vertices forming the top of the big_mount.

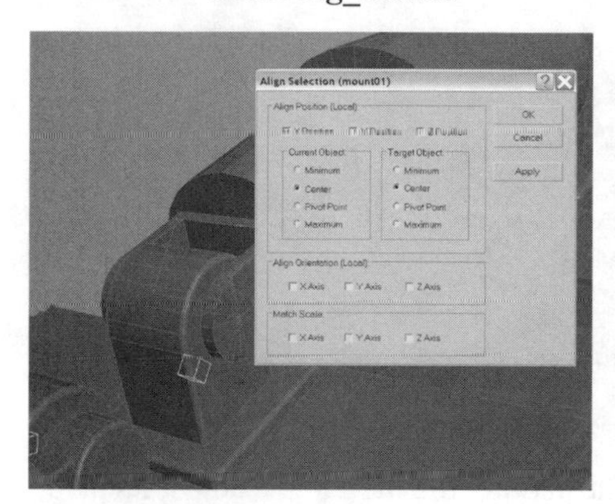

Figure 3-262

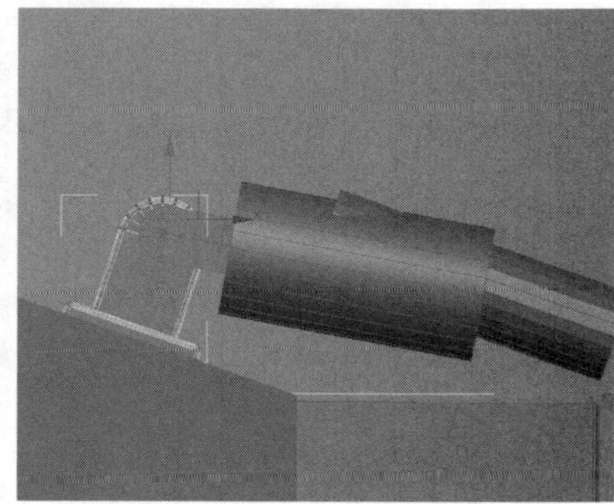

Figure 3-263

Urgent: We're going to have a problem with the big_mount. Because it is too close to the foot, it will severely limit the movement of the piston. We'll have to raise the big_mount vertically to provide more clearance.

59. Switch to the Left view and move the vertices **4.713** in the X axis and **20.831** in the Y axis. Select and move the piston into place.

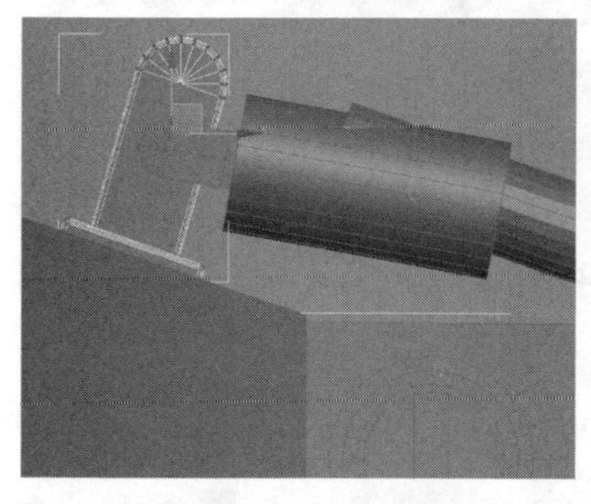

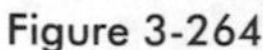

Figure 3-264

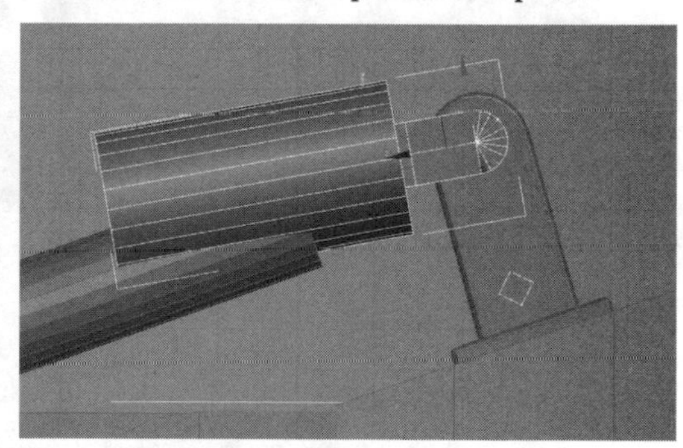

Figure 3-265

60. Move both dummies so they're positioned at the center of the mounts.

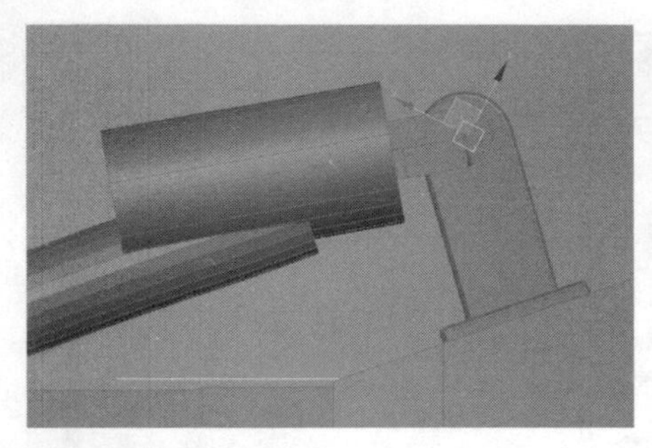

Figure 3-266

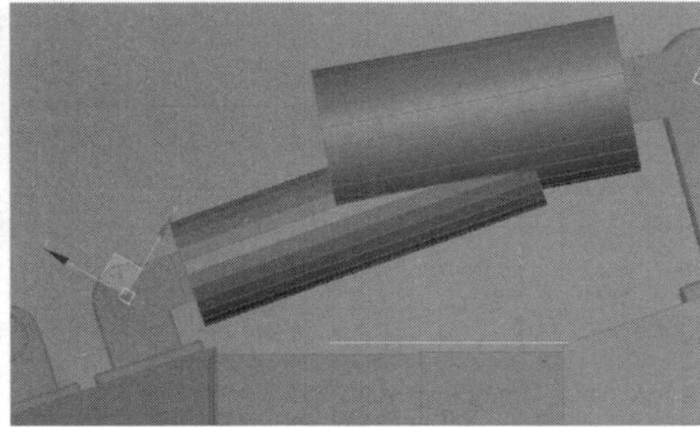

Figure 3-267

61. Select the dummy on the rear middle_toe mount and adjust its pivot so the Y axis points toward the big_piston and the arrow follows the midline of the big_shaft. Adjust the pivot of the dummy on the big_mount so that its Y axis faces front and the arrow is oriented down the midline of the piston.

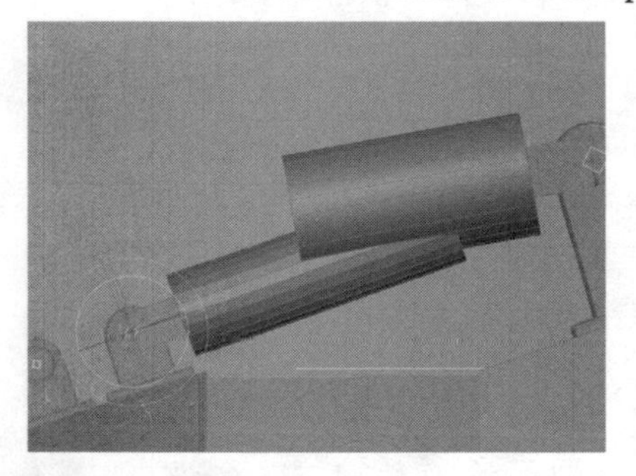

Figure 3-268

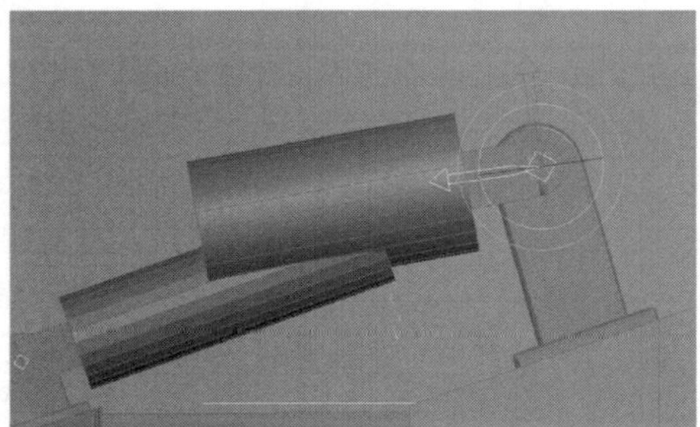

Figure 3-269

62. Select and Link each controller to the mount it is sitting on. Select the piston and assign a LookAt Rotation controller to it.

Figure 3-270

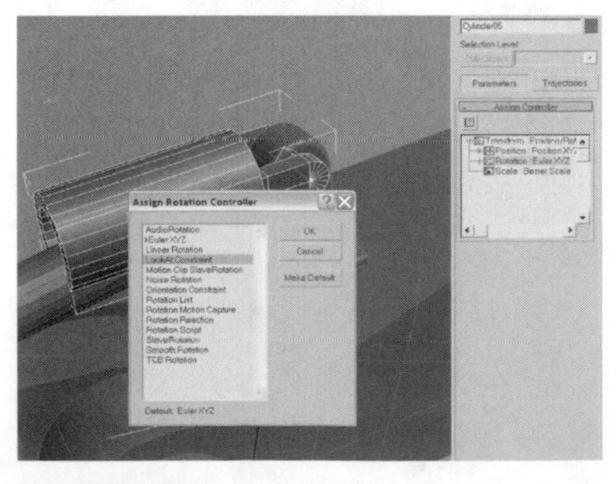

Figure 3-271

63. Click **Add LookAt Target** and pick **mid_toe-Dummy**. Set the LookAt Axis to **Z**, Upnode Control to **Axis Alignment**, and Source/Upnode Axis to **Y**; this is why you aligned their pivot axes earlier.

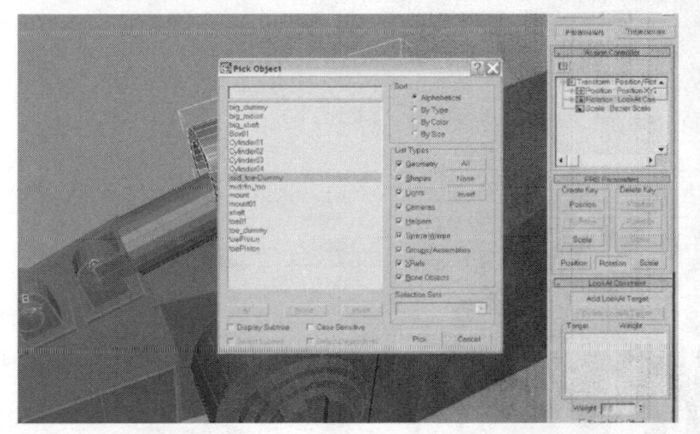

Figure 3-272

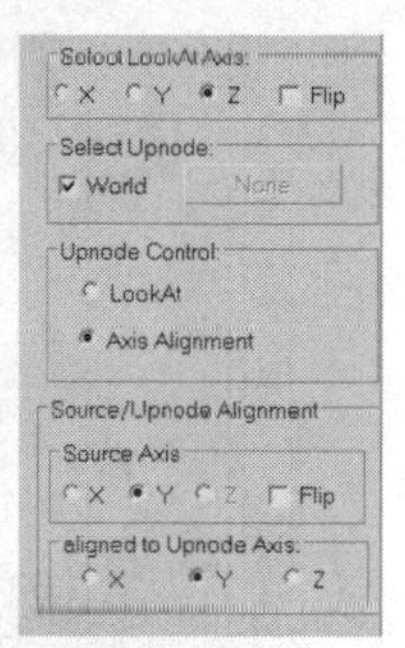

Figure 3-273

64. Assign a LookAt Rotation Controller to the **big_shaft**, click **Add LookAt Target**, and select **big_dummy**. Set the LookAt Axis to **Z**, and set the Source and Upnode axes to **Y**.

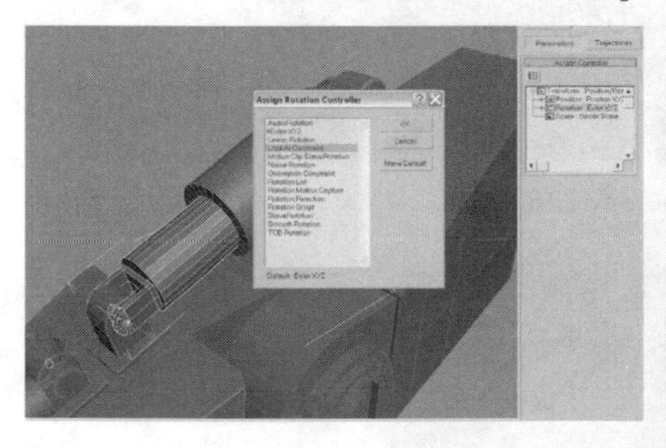

Figure 3-274

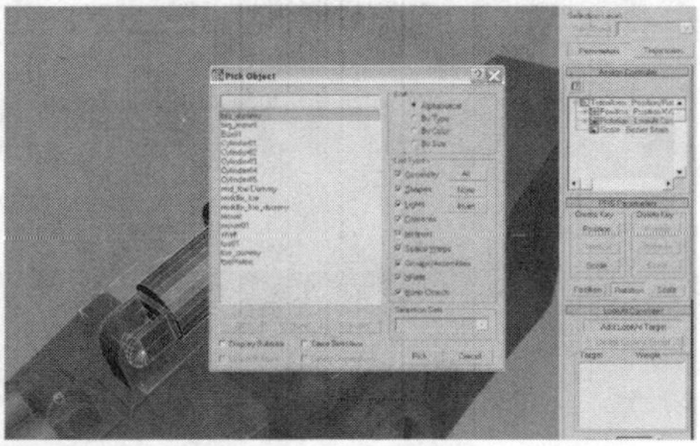

Figure 3-275

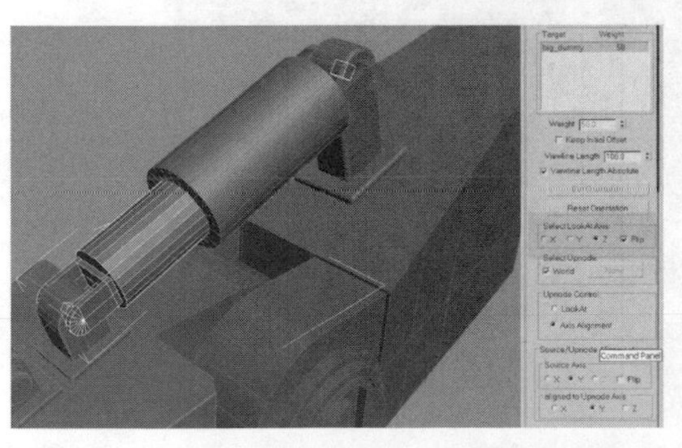

Figure 3-276

Day 3: Completing the Toe Armor and Hydraulics

1. Select the seven polygons on the top of the middle_toe that form a U shape and Bevel them:

Type	Height	Outline	Apply/OK
Group	0	–1.5	Apply
Group	2.08	0	OK

Figure 3-277

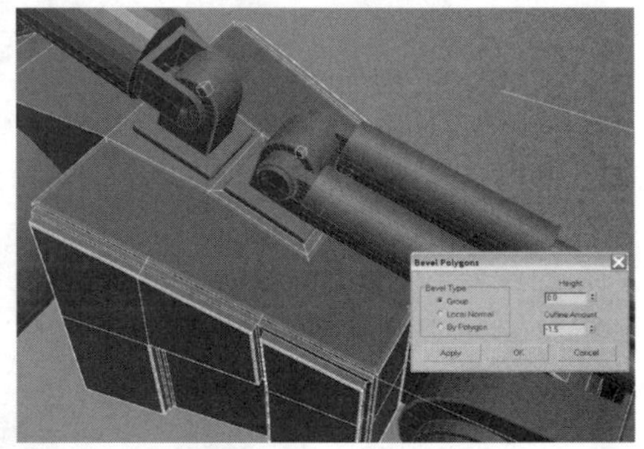

Figure 3-278

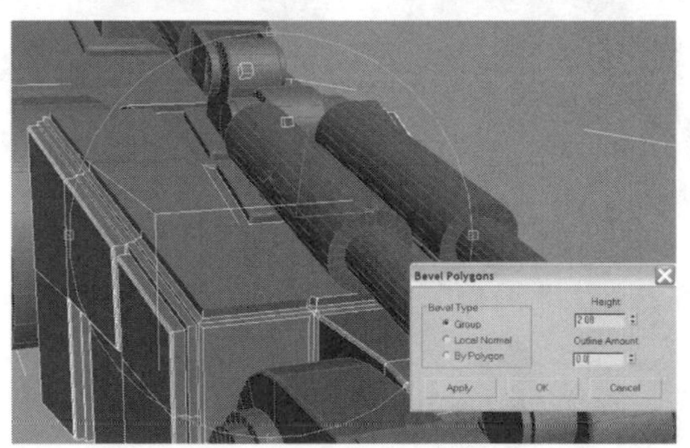

Figure 3-279

Urgent: We have some weirdness going on with our geometry because of the chamfers we did in an earlier step. We'll use Target Weld to fix it before we move on.

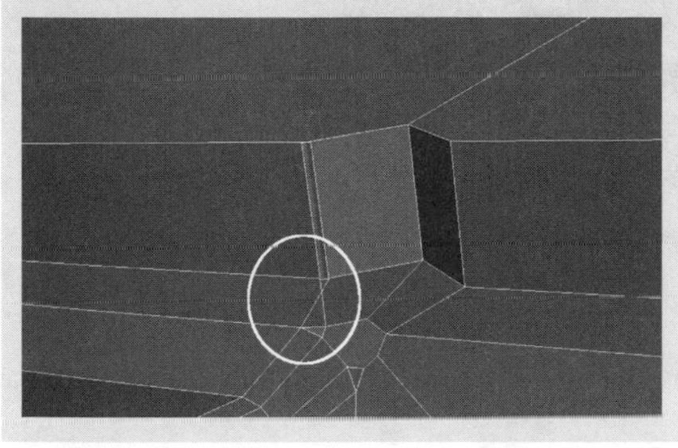

Figure 3-280

2. Each of the circles below contain two vertices. For the circles with the arrows facing left, activate **Target Weld**, click the right vertex, and snap it to the left one (vertices will automatically be welded). For the bottom circle, select the lower vertex and Target Weld it to the top vertex.

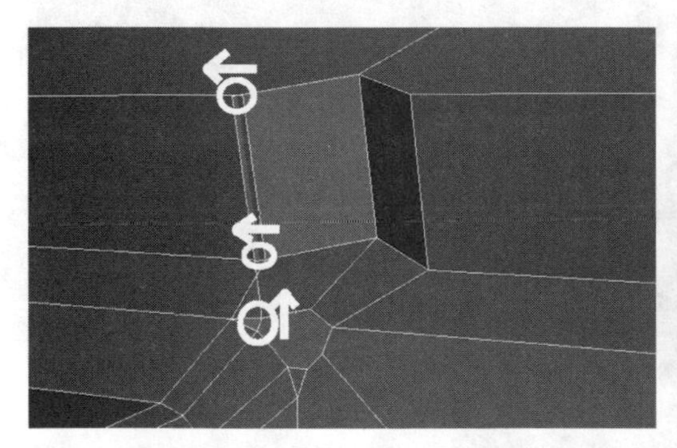

Figure 3-281

Figure 3-282

3. Select the edge indicated in Figure 3-283 and click **Remove.** Switch to Vertex selection mode and Target Weld the three vertices shown circled, going from the upper-right vertex to the lower left. Then use the same techniques to clean up the rest of the messed-up polygons on the armor. Remember: The idea is to have mostly four-sided polygons and as few three- or five-sided polys as possible.

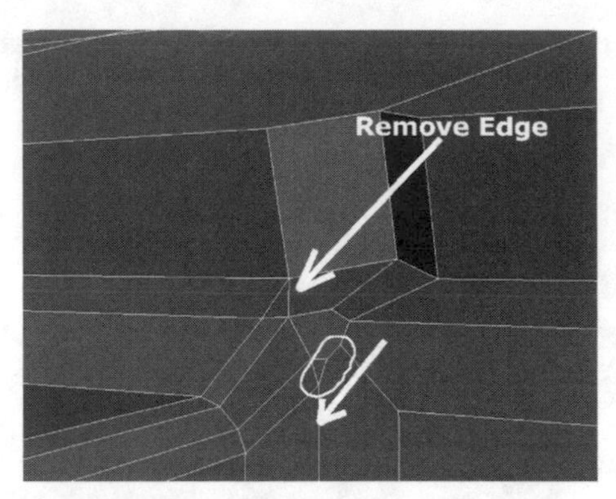

Figure 3-283

4. Select the upper edges of the armor. Chamfer them by **0.4** and then by **0.15**.

Figure 3-284

Figure 3-285

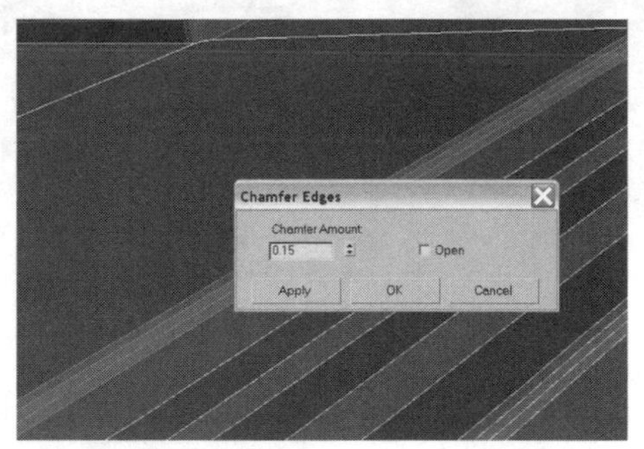

Figure 3-286

5. Select the edges of the middle_toe hinge. Chamfer them by **1** and then by **0.42**.

Day 3: Completing the Toe Armor and Hydraulics

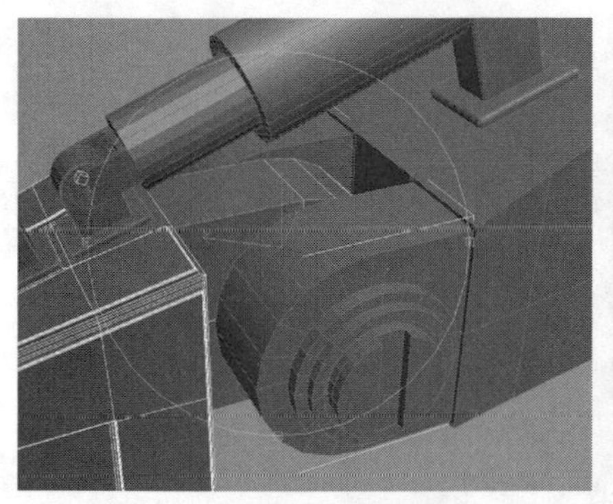

Figure 3-287

Figure 3-288

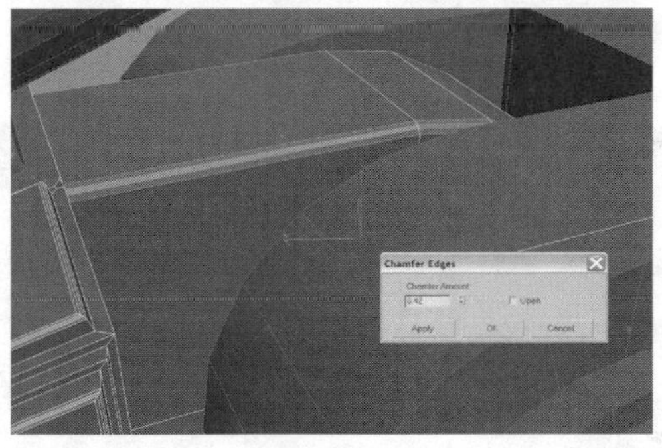

Figure 3-289

6. Select the edges of the foot hinge. Chamfer them by **1** and then by **0.42**.

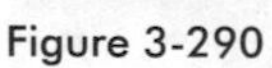

Figure 3-290

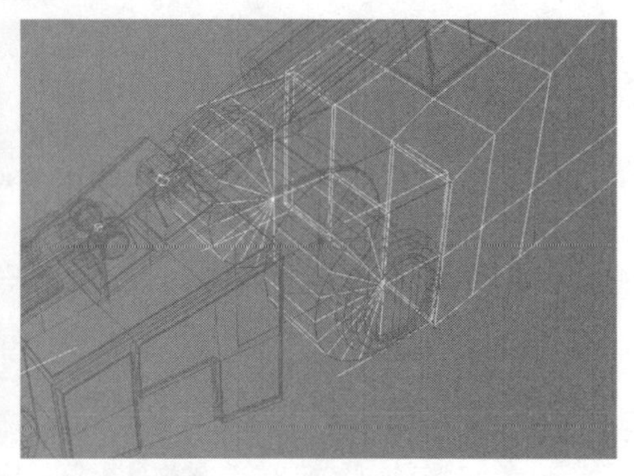

Figure 3-291

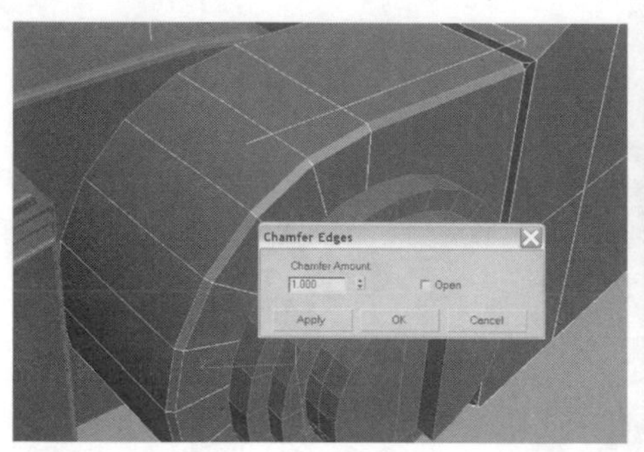

Figure 3-292

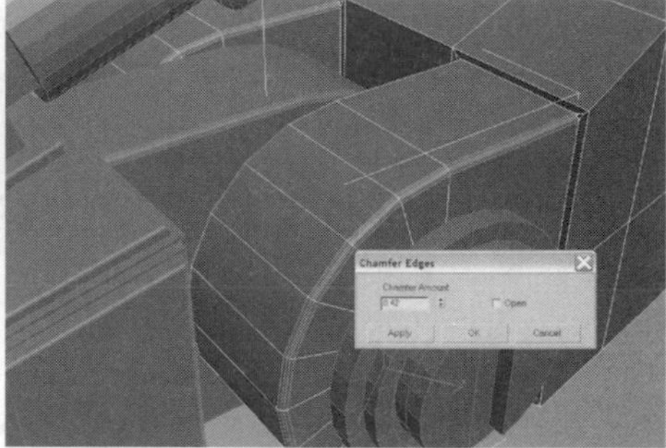

Figure 3-293

7. Select the toe, add a Smooth modifier to the stack, click **Auto Smooth**, and convert the toe to an Editable Polygon to collapse the stack.

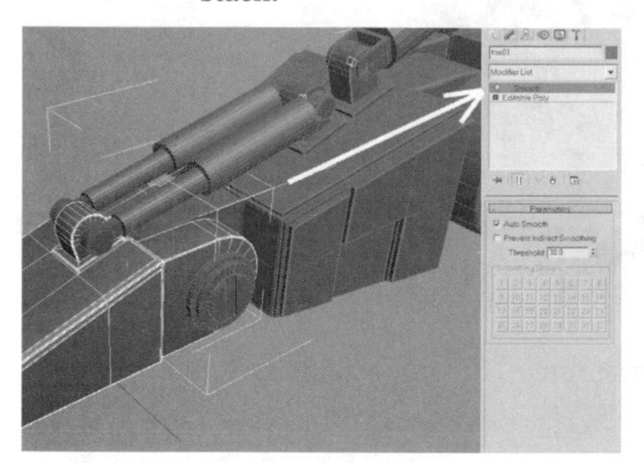

Figure 3-294

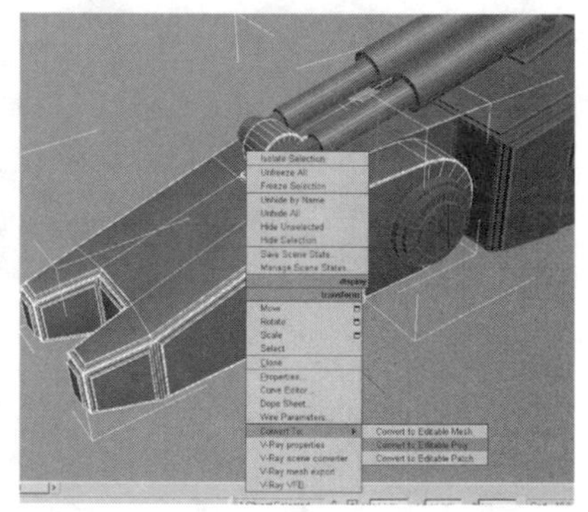

Figure 3-295

8. Add Smooth modifiers to the stacks of both the toe shafts and the axle that connects the toe and the middle_toe. Convert them to Editable Polygons to collapse the stack.

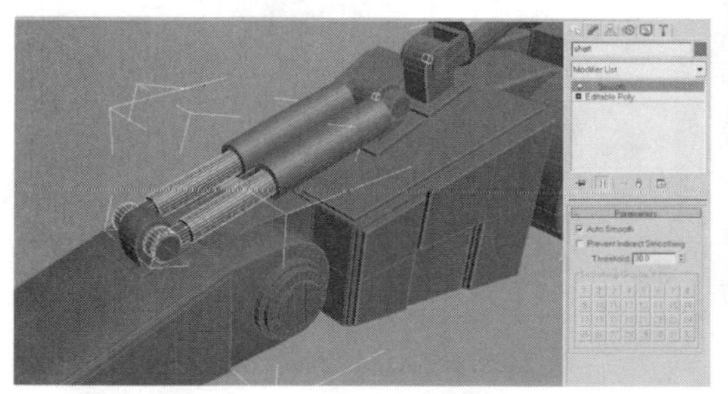

Figure 3-296

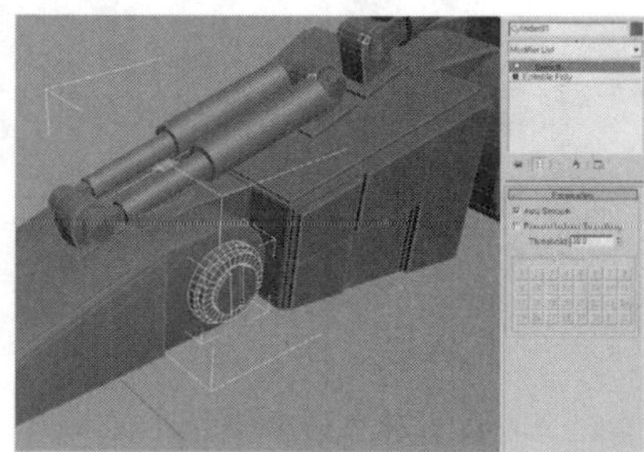

Figure 3-297

9. Hit **F9** to do a test render.

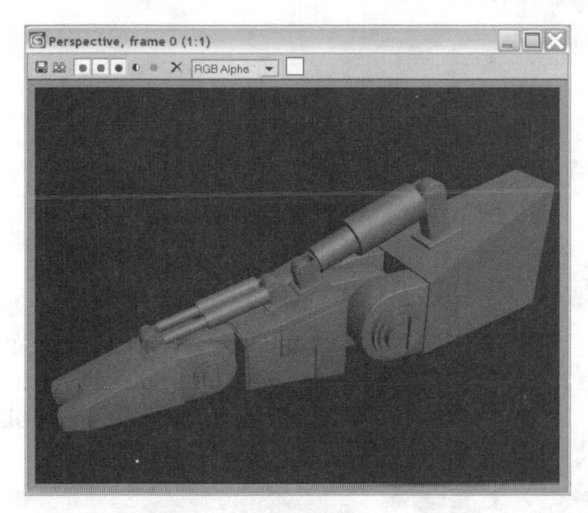

Figure 3-298

FYI: We're going to use a simple script created in MAXScript, a programming language embedded in Max. But don't let that scare you. We won't be writing any scripts in this chapter; instead, we'll be running an existing script. MAXScript allows you to add functionality that either doesn't exist in Max or augments Max by automating tedious operations. The script we'll be using gives us the ability to "paint" rivets on the armor.

FYI: Copy the object_painter.ms script from the book's DVD into the scripts folder in the 3ds Max directory on your hard disk. Generally, the directory is something like: C:\Program Files\Autodesk\3dsMax8\Scripts.

10. Create a sphere with a Radius of **1.5** and **16** Segments, and set Hemisphere to **0.5**. Name it **rivet.** Under the MAXScript menu, select **Run Script**, select **object_painter.ms**, and click **Open.**

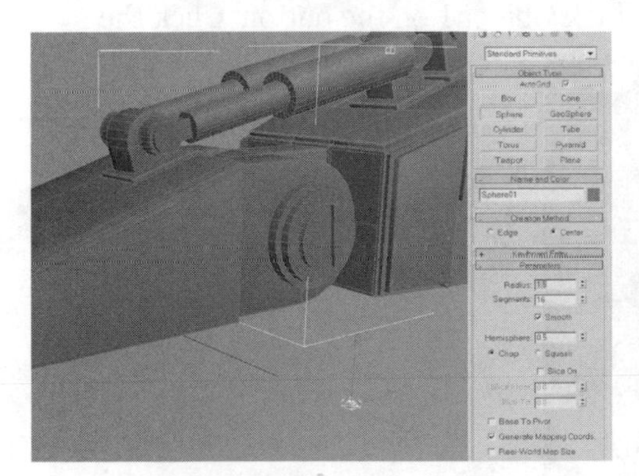

Figure 3-299

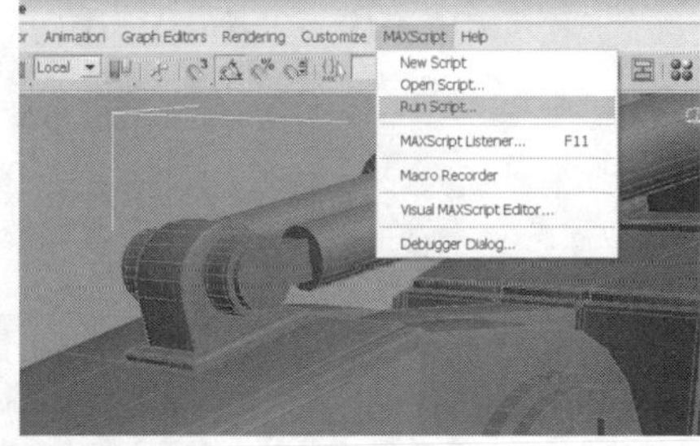

Figure 3-300

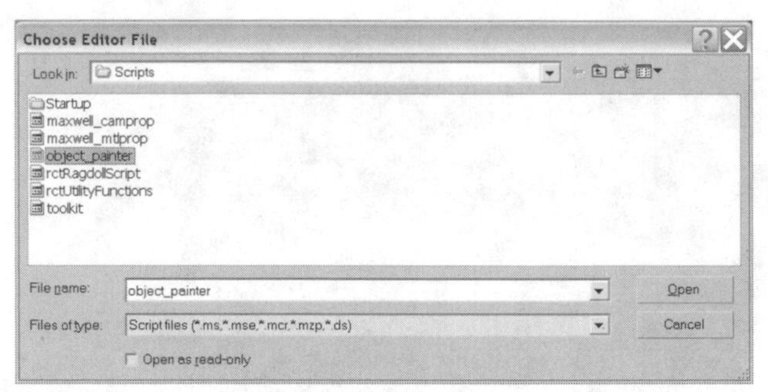

Figure 3-301

11. Make sure the toe is selected, and then click **Set Destination Object** to set the toe as the destination to have objects placed on. Click **Pick Object 1.**

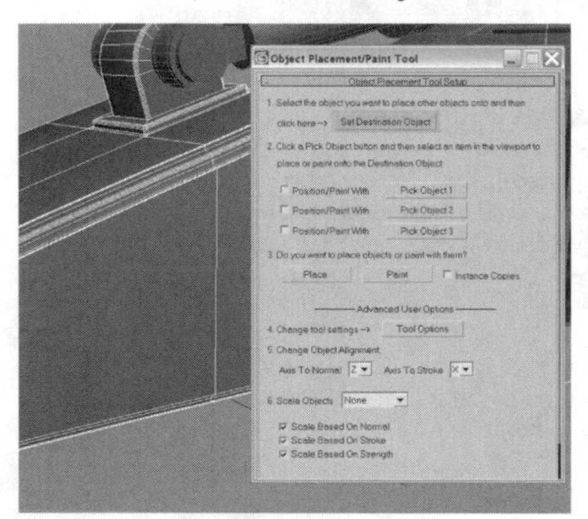

Figure 3-302

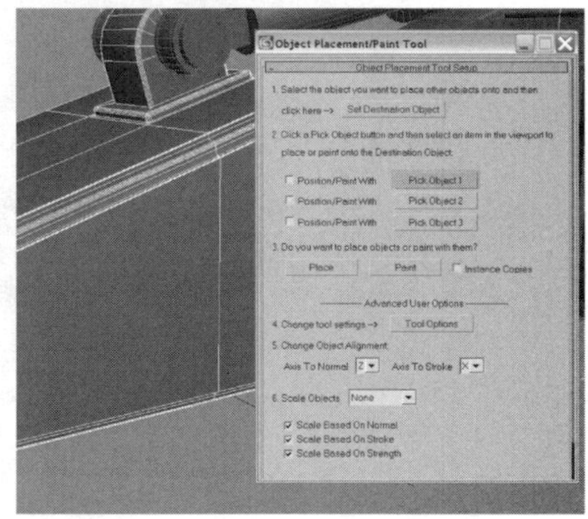

Figure 3-303

12. Hit the **H** key to open the Pick Object dialog and select **rivet**. Notice that rivet replaced Pick Object 1 on the button. Click the **Position/Paint With** check box and then click the **Place** button.

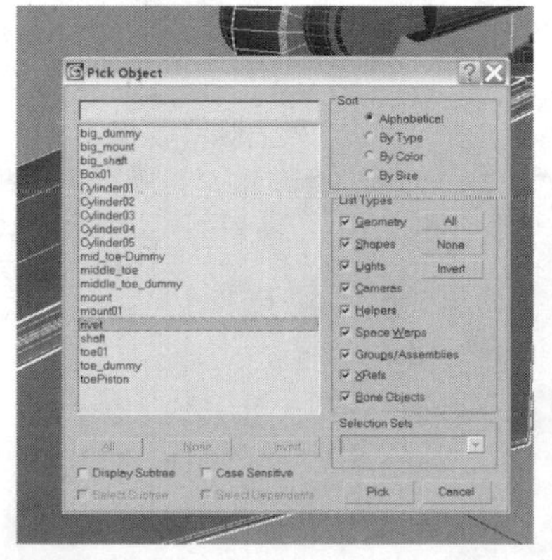

Figure 3-304

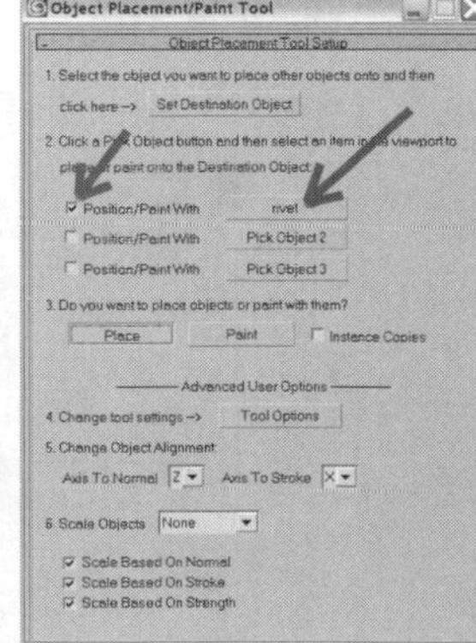

Figure 3-305

FYI: Having to check the check box may seem like an unnecessary step; however, the check boxes allow you to load the tool with multiple objects and turn them on and off.

13. A blue cross-hair cursor will appear. Place the cursor where you want to place an object, in this case a rivet, and left-click your mouse to apply the object to the destination object. Do this in each place you want a rivet on the toe.

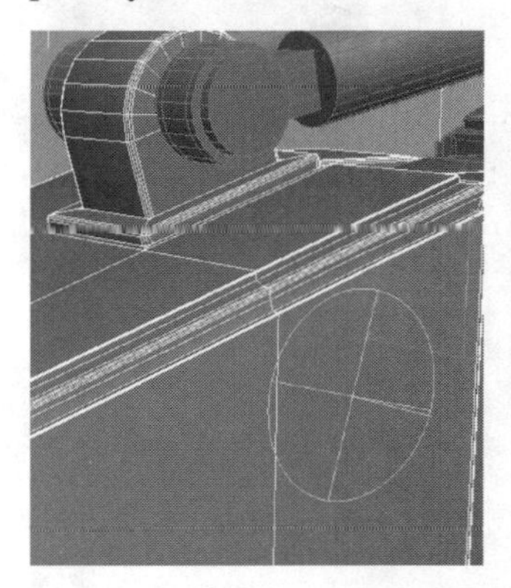

Figure 3-306

Figure 3-307

14. With the toe still selected, click **Attach List** and select all the rivets *except* the original one and then click **Attach**. Repeat using the placing tool until you've put rivets on all the armor plates on the entire foot. Attach them, as you did with the first set, and do a test render to see how the rivets have made the armor look more "real."

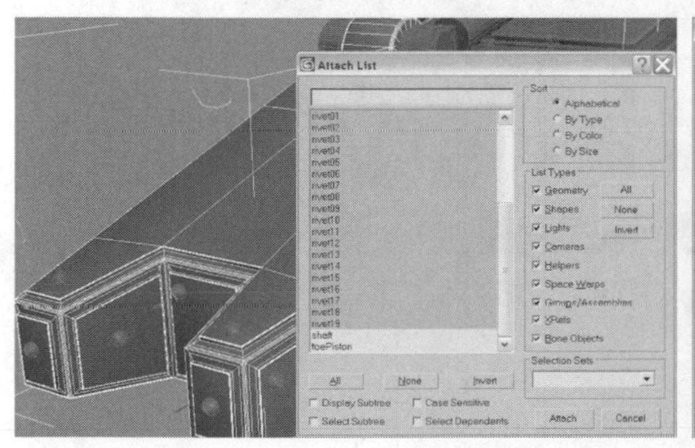

Figure 3-308

Figure 3-309

15. In the indentation of the middle_toe, where there is no armor, create a Tube and then clone it and place it on the indentation on the other side. Then create a clone of the clone you just made and place it on the piston that connects to the toe.

Radius 1	Radius 2	Height	Height/Cap Segs	Sides	Smooth
3	4	4	1/1	24	Checked

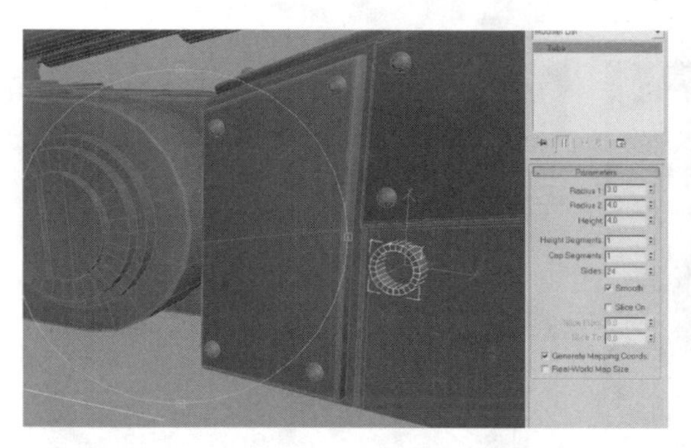

Figure 3-310

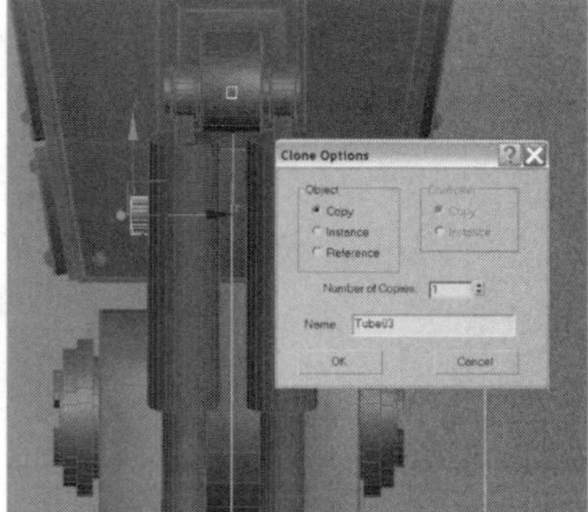

Figure 3-311

16. Create another tube clone, place it on the other piston, and Select and Link the two tubes to the pistons. Name the piston tubes **lower_hydraulic_nozzle_l** and **lower_hydraulic_nozzle_r**.

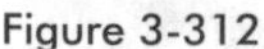
Figure 3-312

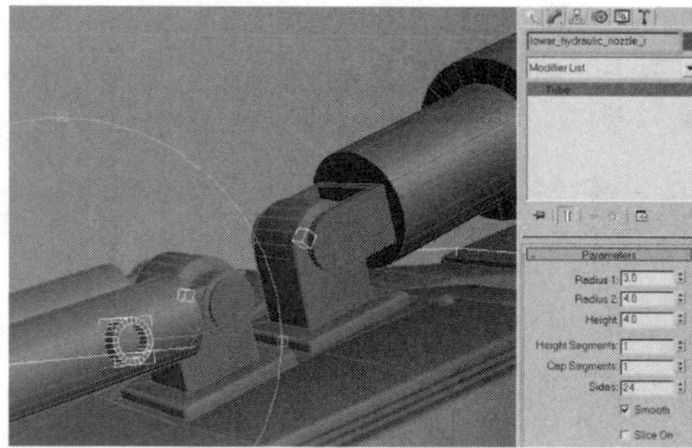

Figure 3-313

17. Name the mid_toe tubes **mid_base_hydraulic_r** and **mid_base_hydraulic_l**. Select and Link them to the middle_toe.

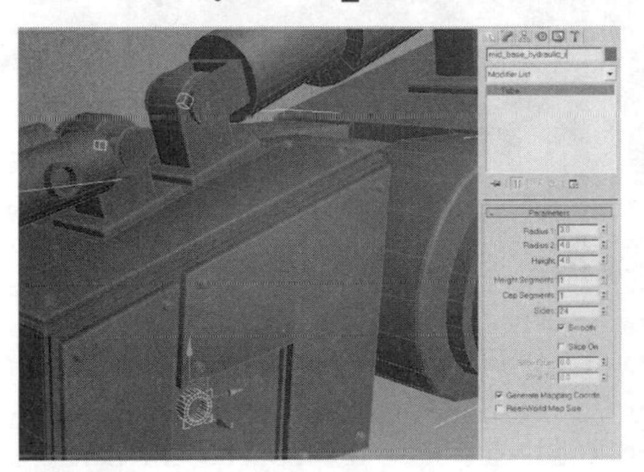

Figure 3-314

Figure 3-315

18. From the Extended Primitives drop-down select **Hose**, and create a hose next to the middle_toe. Don't worry about the dimensions. Click **Bound to Object Pivots**, click **Pick Top Object**, and click **lower_hydraulic_nozzle_r**.

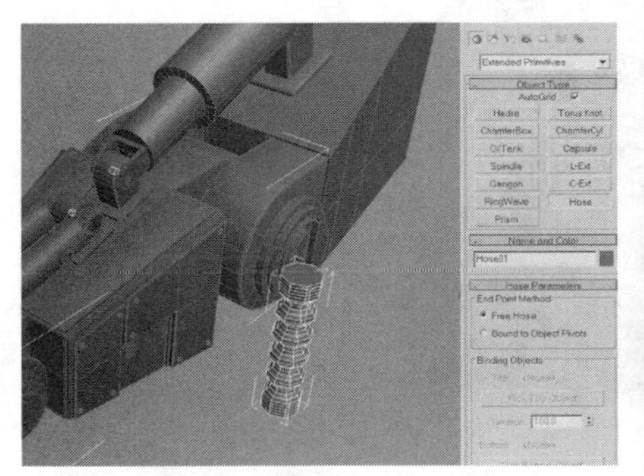

Figure 3-316

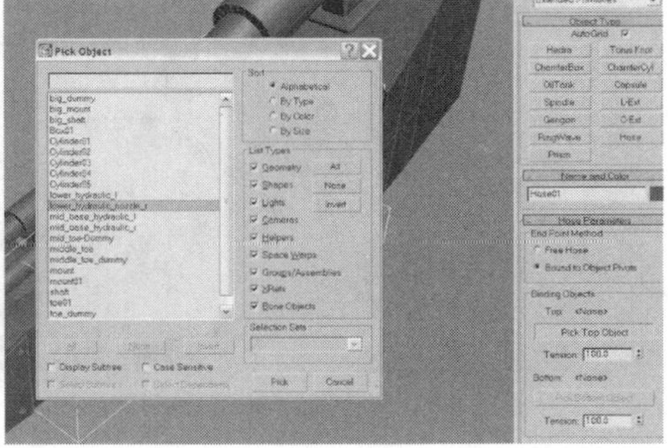

Figure 3-317

19. Click **Pick Bottom Object**, hit **H** to open the selection list, click **mid_base_hydraulic_r**, and click the **Pick** button. (Note: Picking a binding object using the selection list instead of clicking it like you did in step 18 is extremely useful when the item to be picked is small or clearances are tight.) Set the Top Object Tension to **39** and set the Bottom Object Tension to **50**, deselect Flex Section Enable (to make a smooth hose), click **Round Hose**, set the Diameter to **5.682**, and set the Sides to **16**.

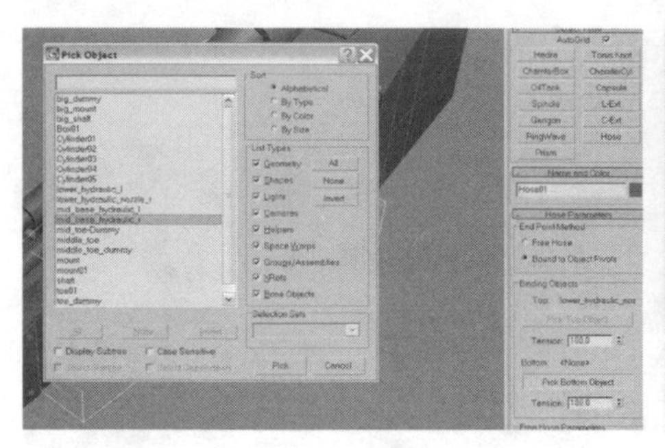

Figure 3-318

Figure 3-319

20. Do a test render. See how the presence of the rivets increases the realism of the armor? How the hoses make the model seem more complex?

Figure 3-320

21. From the Extended Primitives drop-down select **Capsule** and set Radius to **2.5**, Height to **18**, Sides to **16**, and Height Segs to **1**. Shift-drag in the Y axis and create two clones. Move them into position in the recessed part of the middle_toe.

Day 3: Completing the Toe Armor and Hydraulics

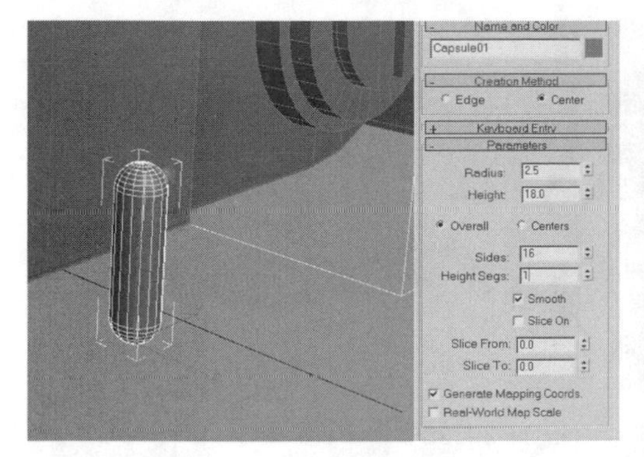

Figure 3-321

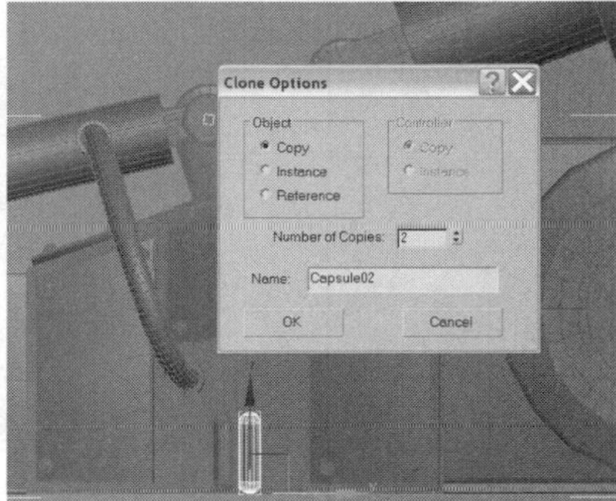

Figure 3-322

22. Convert the capsule to an Editable Polygon and attach the clones to the original.

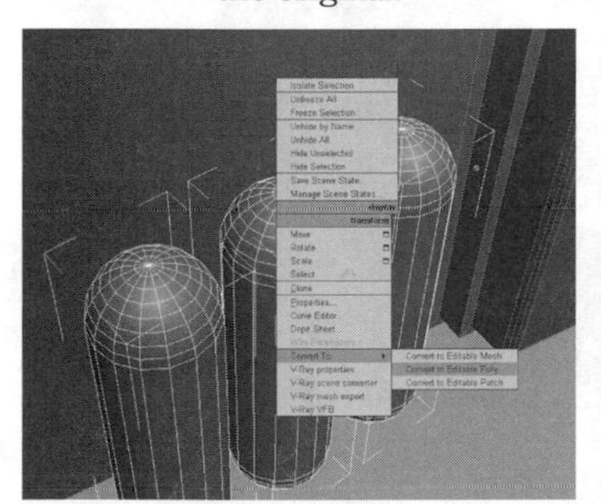

Figure 3-323

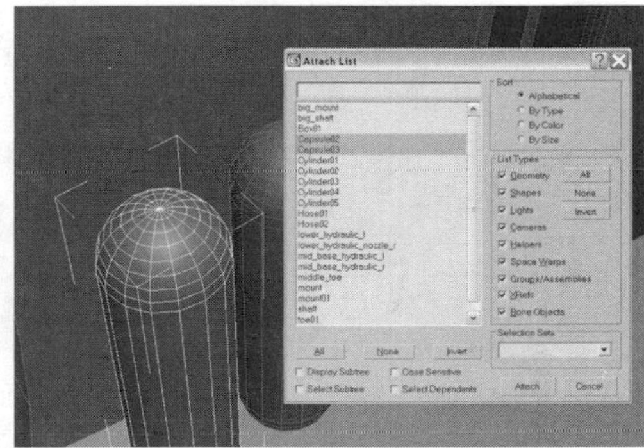

Figure 3-324

23. Select the polygons on top of both the side capsules and Extrude them by **2.0**.

Figure 3-325

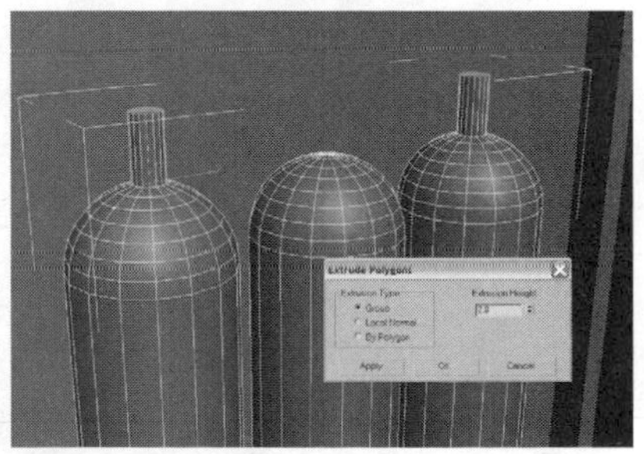

Figure 3-326

24. Extrude them by **0.1** 10 times. Polygon-select the top-left poly and click **Grow** until you've reached the top of the capsule, then click **Detach** and name it **pipe**.

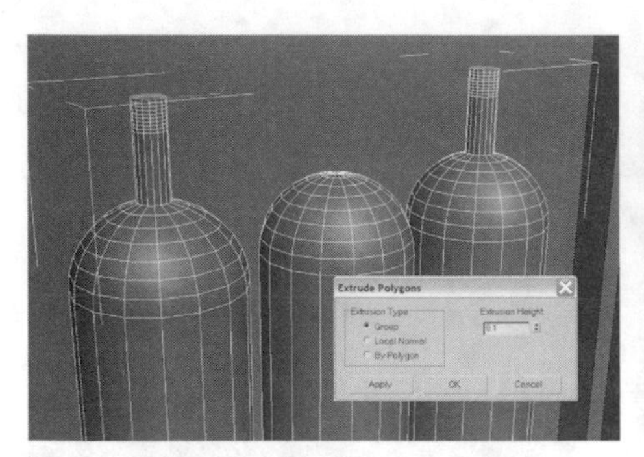

Figure 3-327

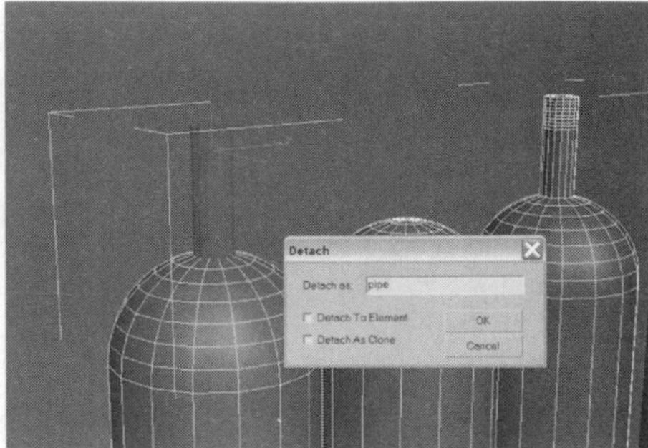

Figure 3-328

25. With the pipe still selected, move the pivot point to the start of the first of the 10 extrusions. Add a Bend modifier to the stack and set the Bend Angle to **90**, the Direction to **–90**, and the Axis to **Z**.

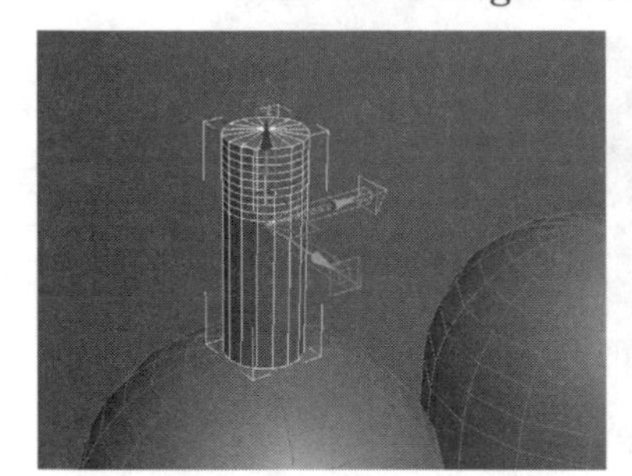

Figure 3-329

Figure 3-330

26. Add a Smooth modifier to the top of the stack (to smooth out the facets) and click **Auto Smooth**. Convert the pipe to an Editable Polygon to collapse the stack.

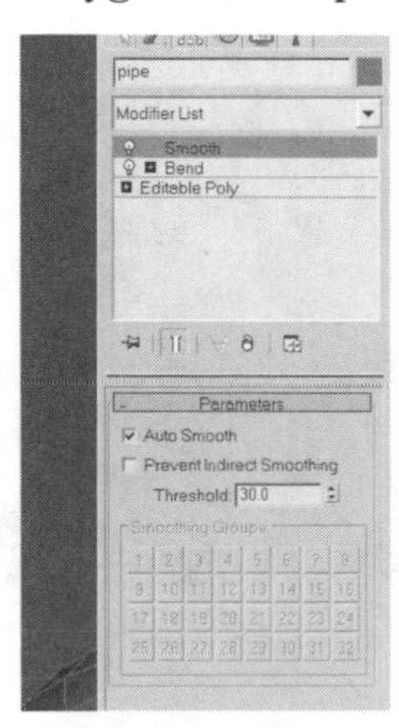

Figure 3-331

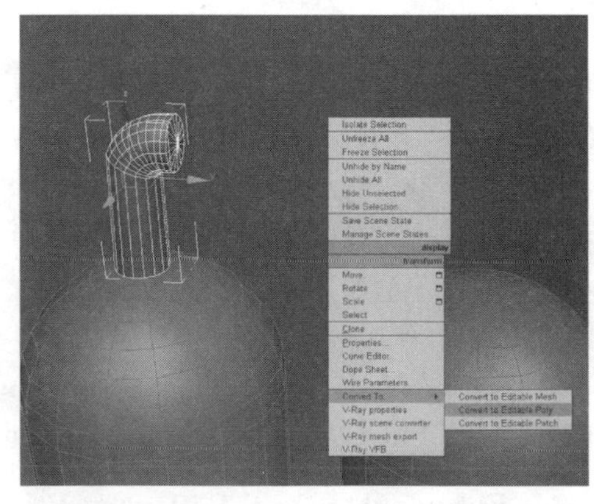

Figure 3-332

27. Select the far right tube and set its pivot to the same place. Add a Bend modifier to its stack, set the Angle to **90**, the Direction to **90**, and the Axis to **Z**.

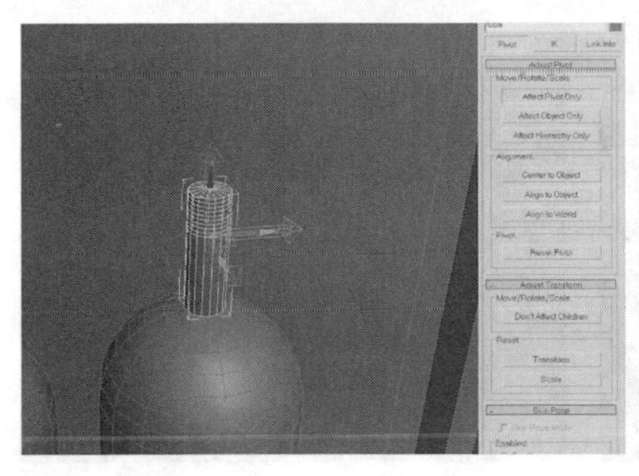

Figure 3-333

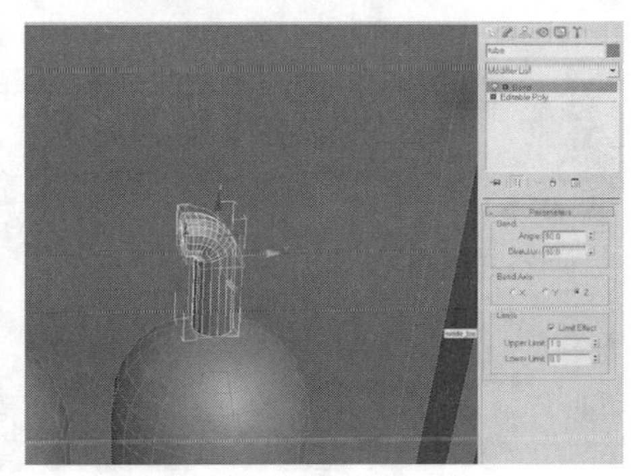

Figure 3-334

28. Add a Smooth modifier to the stack, click **Auto Smooth**, and convert it to an Editable Polygon to collapse the stack. Select the facing polygons on both the right and left pipes and delete them.

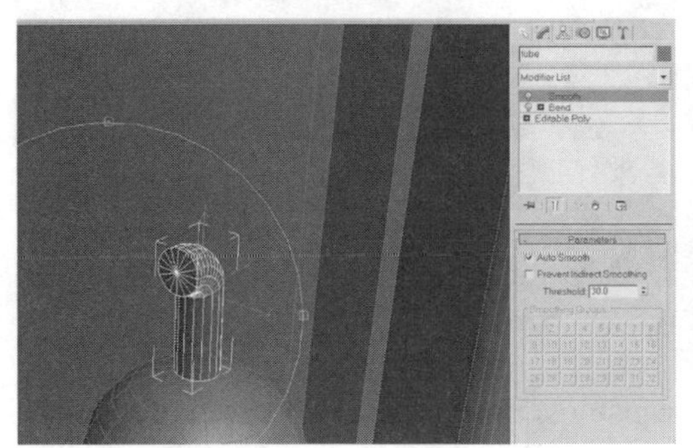

Figure 3-335

Figure 3-336

29. Border-select the right pipe and drag it in the Y axis until it is centered over the middle capsule. Then select the border of the left capsule and drag it over to meet the right pipe (until the borders overlap).

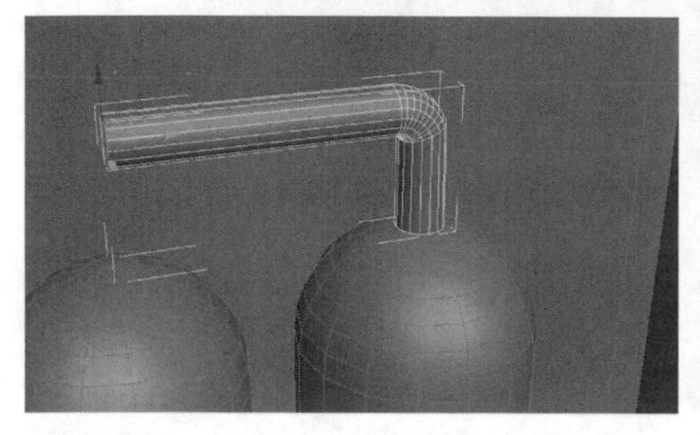

Figure 3-337

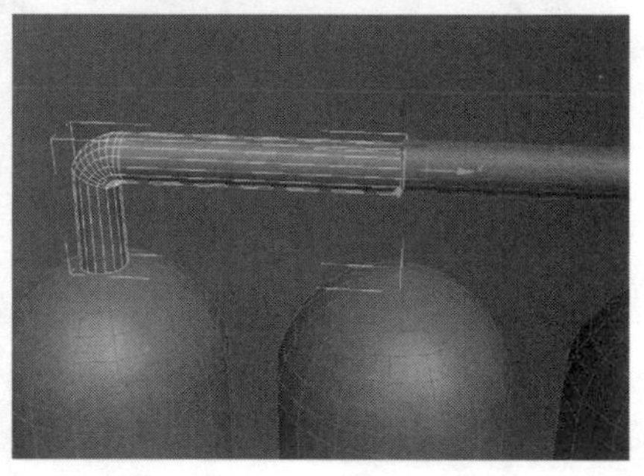

Figure 3-338

30. Attach the two pipes, select the middle vertices, and Weld.

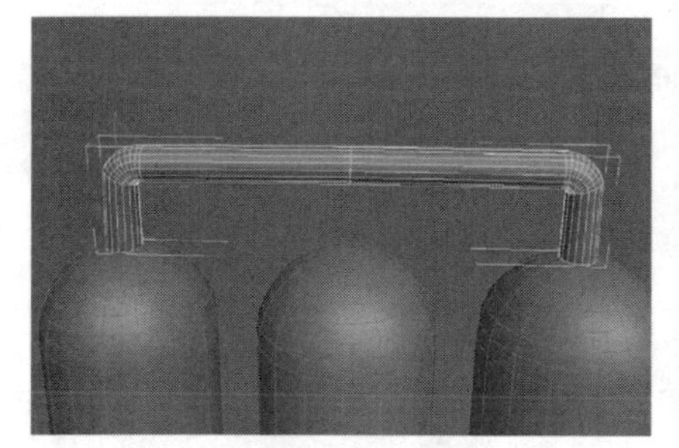

Figure 3-339

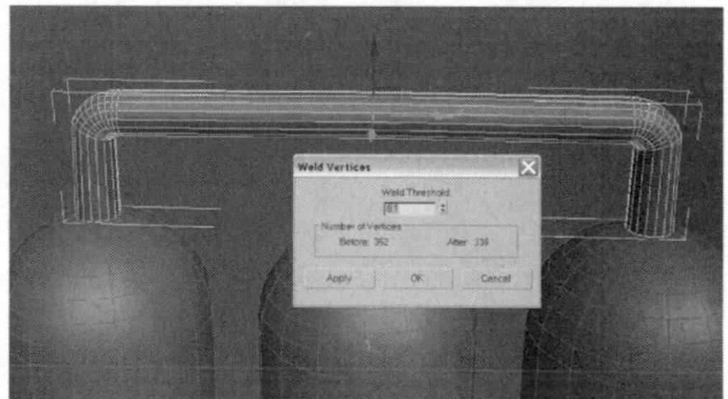

Figure 3-340

31. Reattach the pipes to the capsules. Select the top center polygons of the middle capsule.

Figure 3-341

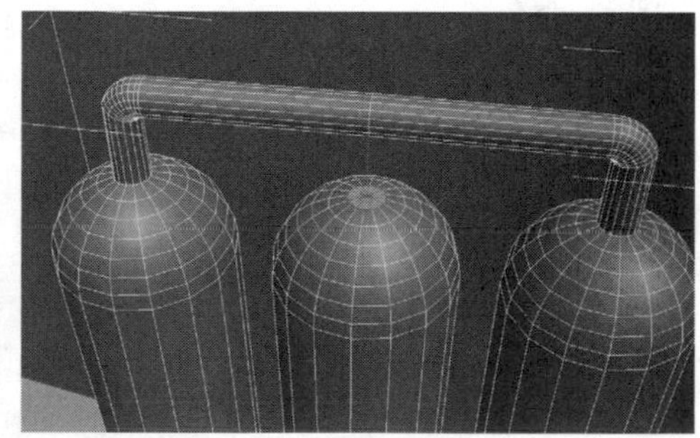

Figure 3-342

32. Extrude the polygons by **5** and then Extrude them by **0.1** 10 times.

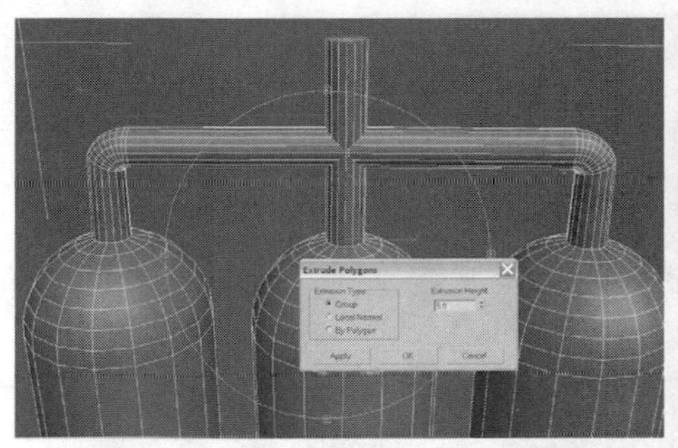

Figure 3-343

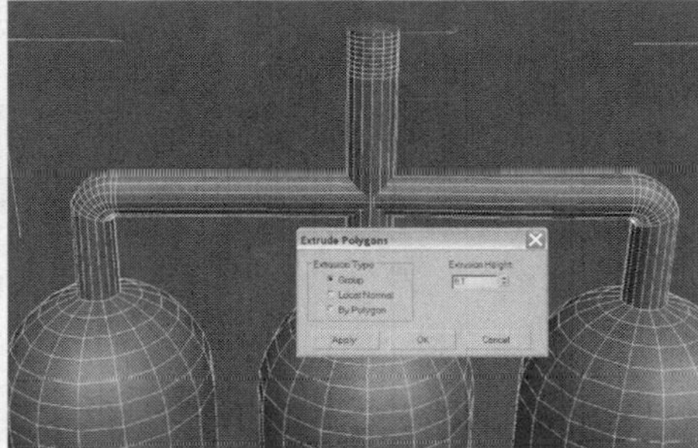

Figure 3-344

33. Polygon-select the middle pipe and detach it. Move the pivot to the first of the 10 extrusions and apply a Bend modifier to the stack with an Angle of **90**, a Direction of **90**, and the Axis set to **Z**.

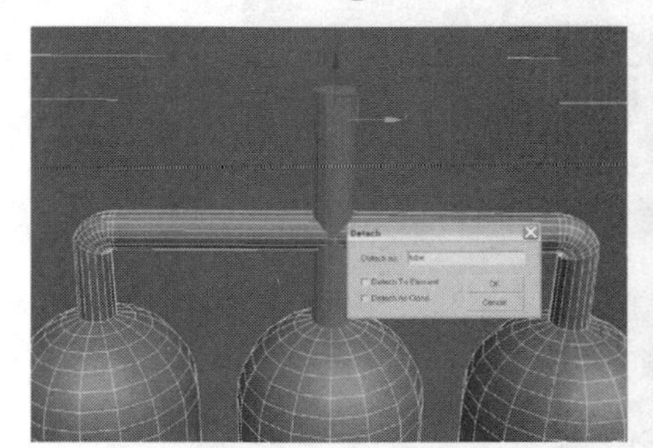

Figure 3-345

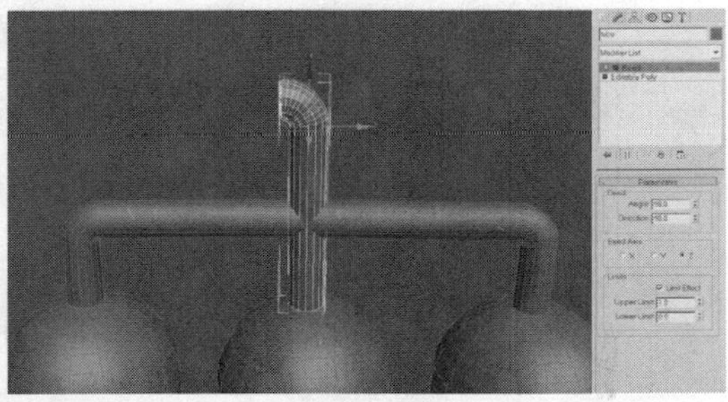

Figure 3-346

34. Add a Smooth modifier to the stack, click **Auto Smooth**, and convert to an Editable Polygon, Attach the pipe to the middle capsule and move the capsules until the pipe is directly across from the hydraulic nozzle.

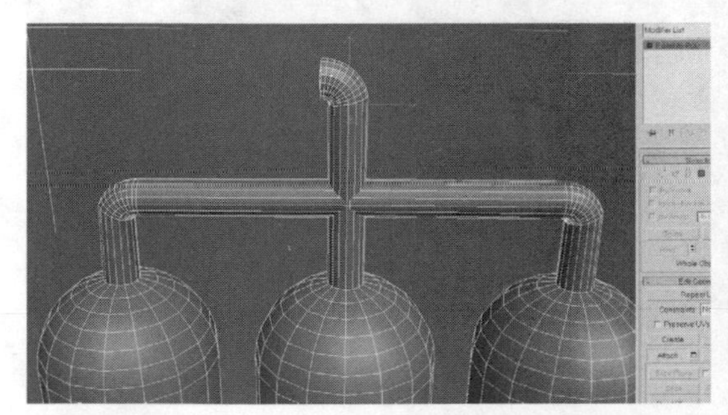

Figure 3-347

Figure 3-348

35. Select the outer facing polygons and Extrude them by **8**.

Figure 3-349

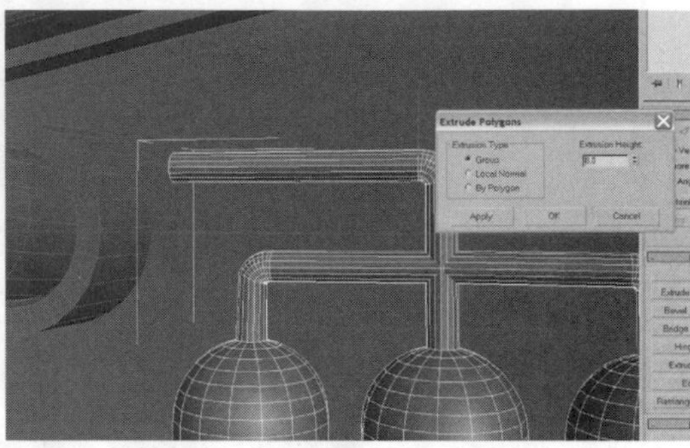

Figure 3-350

36. Switch to the Bottom view and move the capsules against the back wall of the middle_toe. Select the facing polygons and delete them.

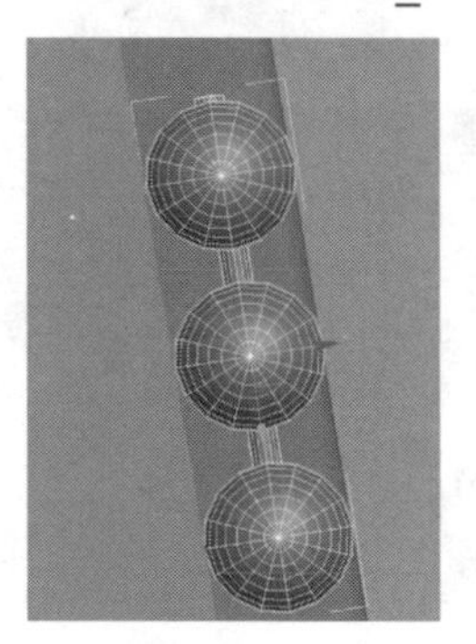

Figure 3-351

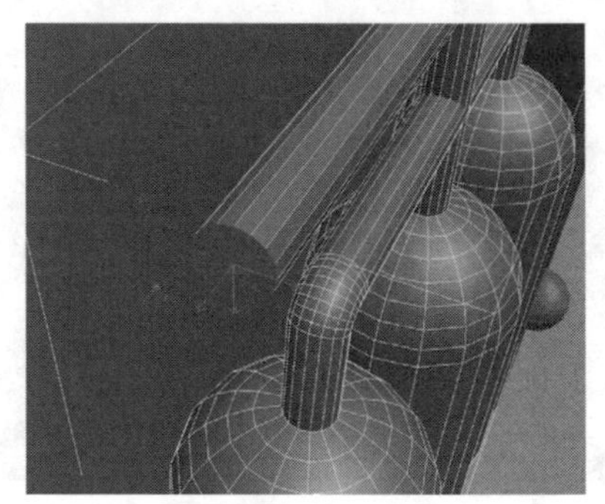

Figure 3-352

37. Select the border and move it against the hydraulic nozzle. Select the polygons on the top of the nozzle and move them in the Z axis until they've passed the pipe from the capsules.

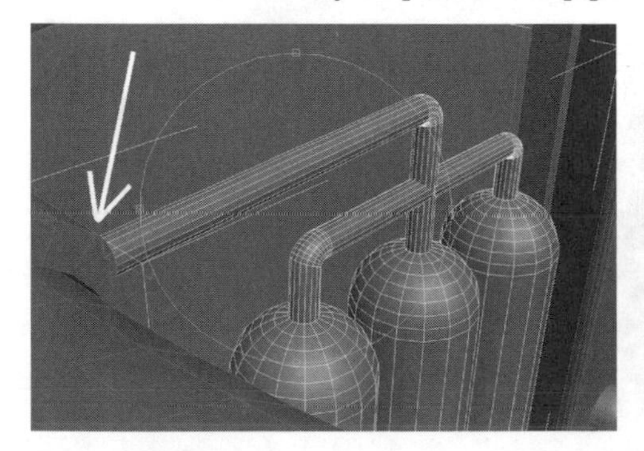

Figure 3-353

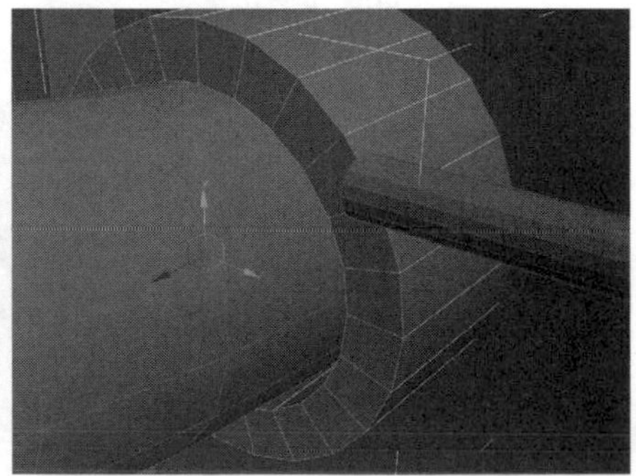

Figure 3-354

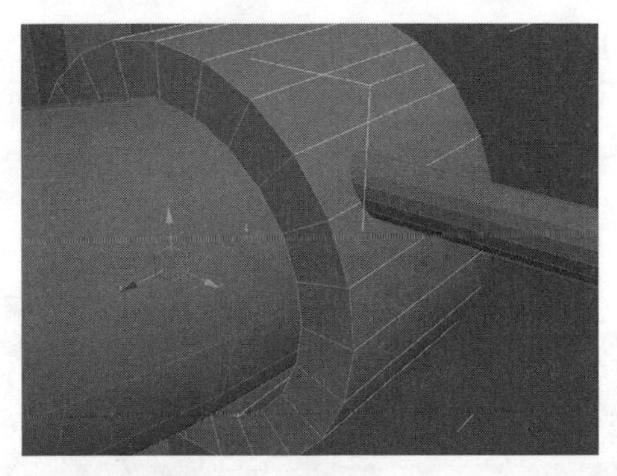

Figure 3-355

38. Add a Smooth modifier to the stack, convert to Editable Polygon, and Select and Link the capsules to the middle_toe.

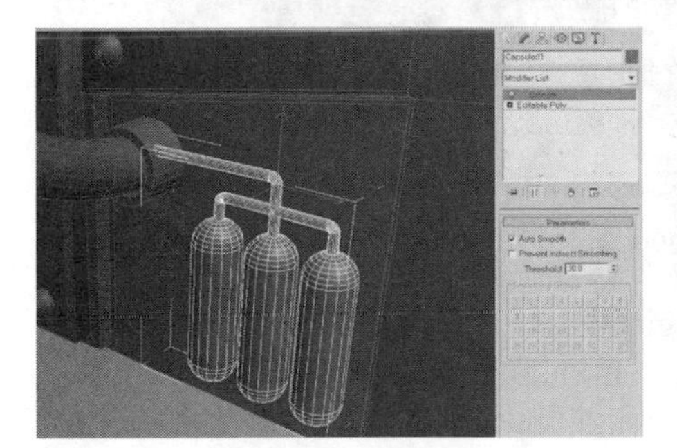

Figure 3-356

Figure 3-357

39. Hit **F9** to do a test render.

Figure 3-358

40. Clone the capsules to the other side of the middle_toe. Create a Tube on the foot, next to the base of the mount, and name it **foot_hydraulic_1**.

Radius 1	Radius 2	Height	Height/Cap Segs	Sides	Smooth
7	5	7	1/1	24	Checked

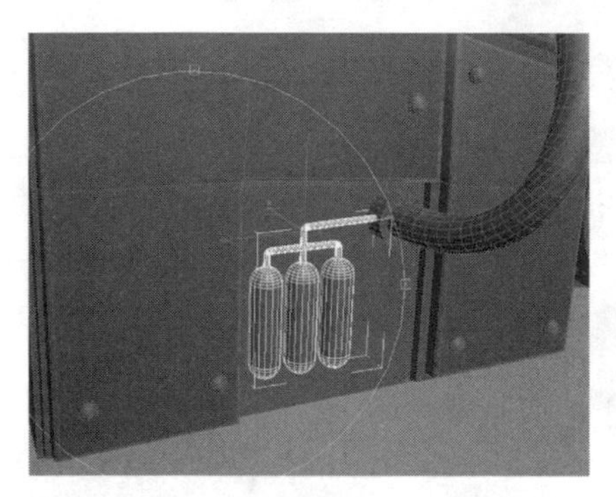

Figure 3-359

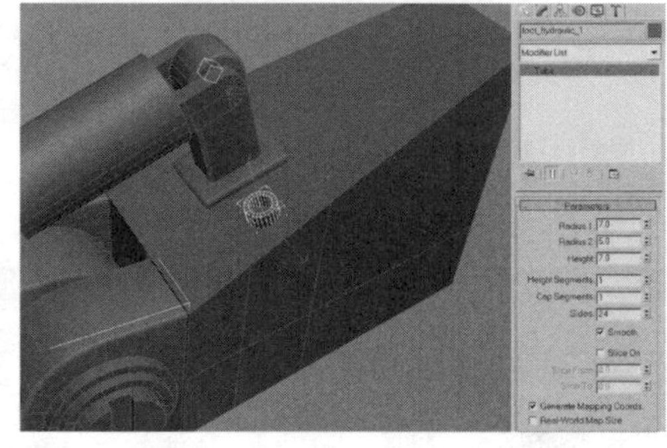

Figure 3-360

41. Clone the tube by Shift-dragging in the Z axis and move it into place, a little over halfway toward the front of the piston. Name the tube **big_piston_hydraulic**. Select and Link the big_piston_hydraulic to the piston.

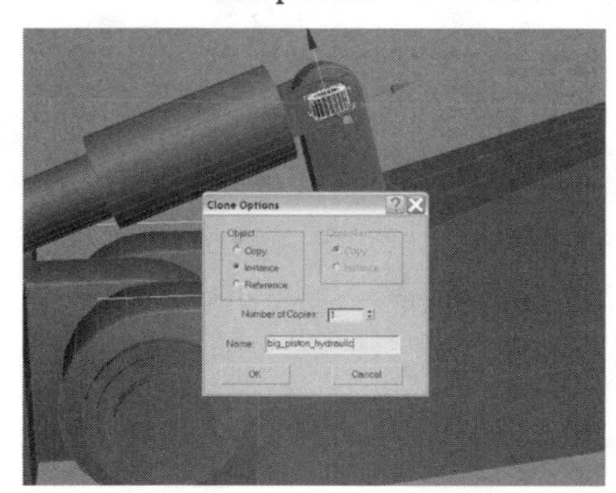

Figure 3-361

Figure 3-362

42. Create a Hose, set the Top Object to **big_piston_hydraulic**, and set the Bottom Object to **foot_hydraulic_1**.

Top Tension	Bottom Tension	Segments	Hose Shape	Diameter	Sides
100	100	45	Round	9	16

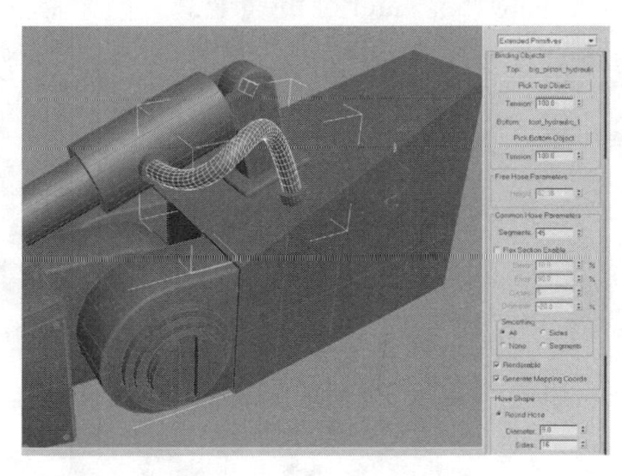

Figure 3-363

43. Hit **F9** to do a test render.

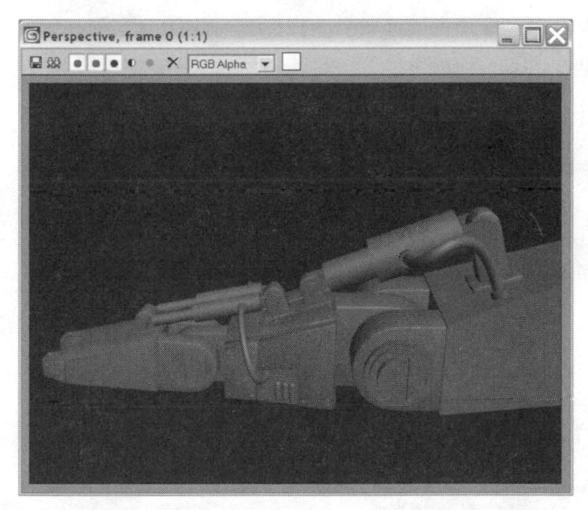

Figure 3-364

Day 4: Completing the Foot

1. Select all the objects and Group them, naming the group **Toe**. Switch to the Top view and position the Toe on the first major guideline (10 units) below the center of the grid.

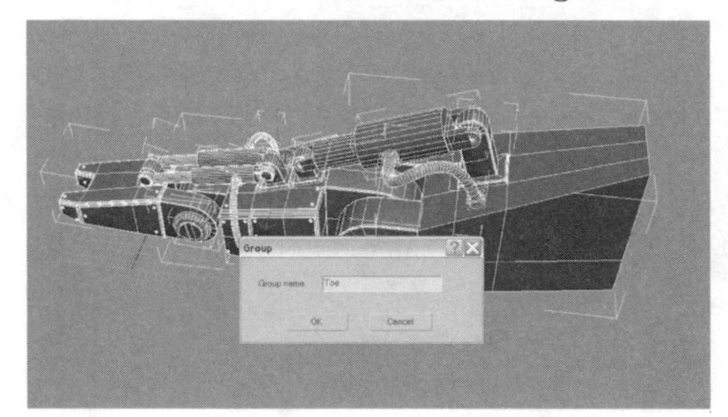

Figure 3-365

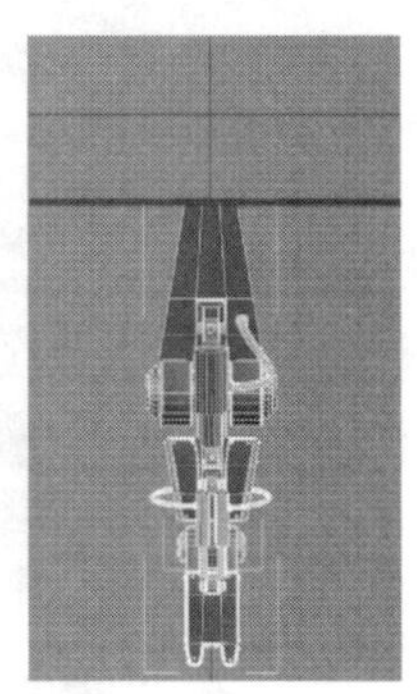

Figure 3-366

2. Move the pivot point to the center of the grid. Hold down the **Shift** key, Rotate the toe **45** degrees, and set Number of Copies to **2**.

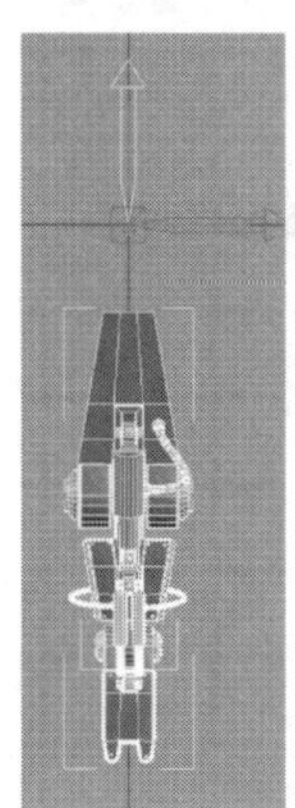

Figure 3-367

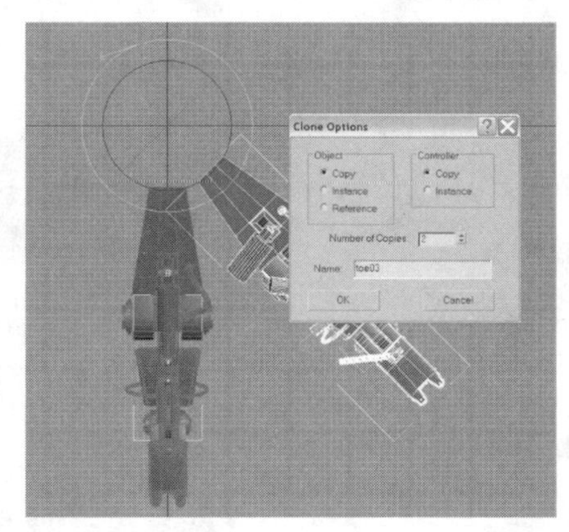

Figure 3-368

3. Cloning the toe jacks up the hoses of the clones and will need to be fixed. Ungroup each of the toes.

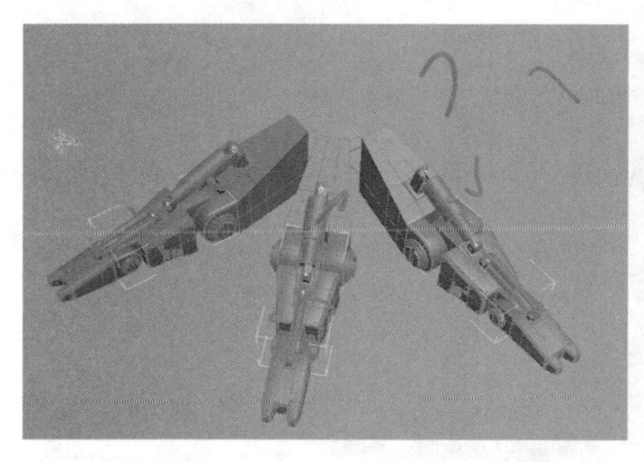

Figure 3-369

Figure 3-370

4. Compare the pivots of mid_toe-Dummy and the shafts; note how the cloning has thrown them out of alignment. Select the pivot for the shafts and rotate it until the shafts are correctly aligned. Repeat this for the other toes.

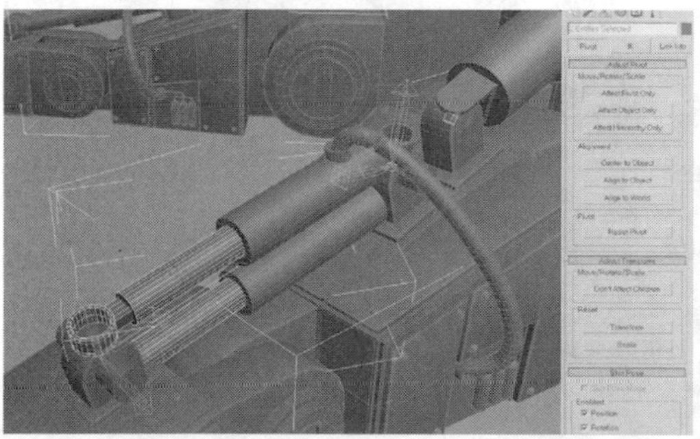

Figure 3-371

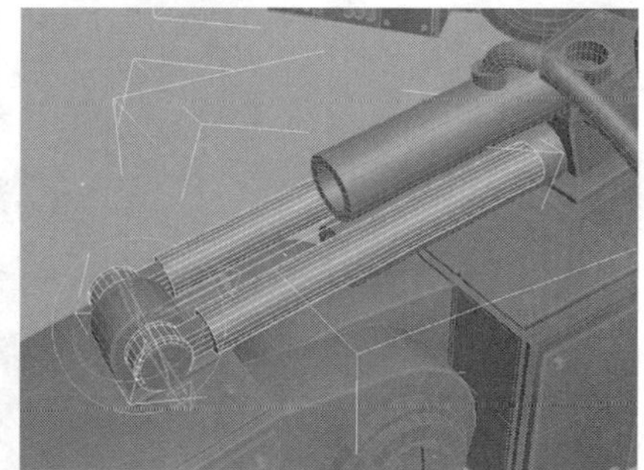

Figure 3-372

5. Select the pivot for the mid_toe pistons and rotate it to align them with the shafts. This should fix the problem with the hoses, but you may also have to tweak the pivots of the objects the hoses attach to in order to realign them.

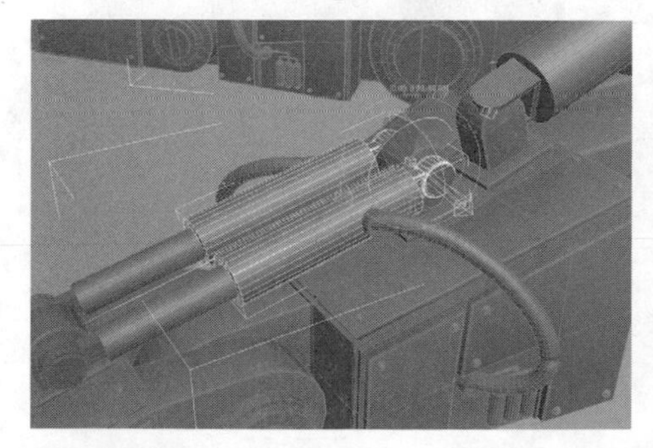

Figure 3-373

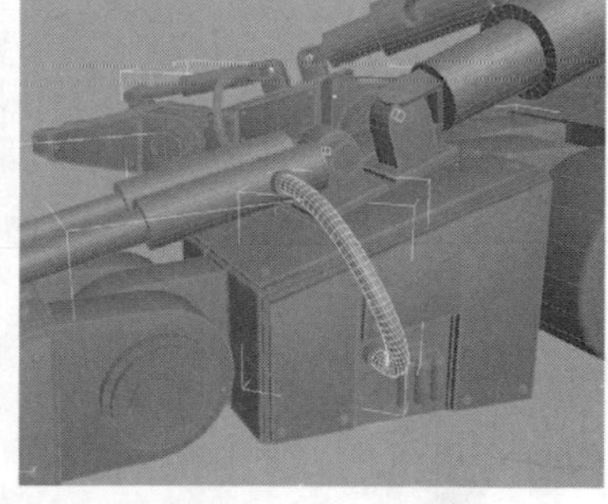

Figure 3-374

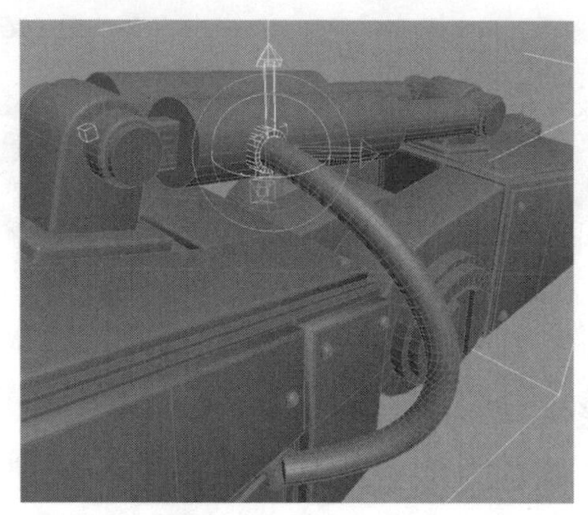

Figure 3-375

6. Select all the objects making a toe, hold down the **Shift** key, and Rotate as shown to make a rear toe. Hit **F9** to do a test render.

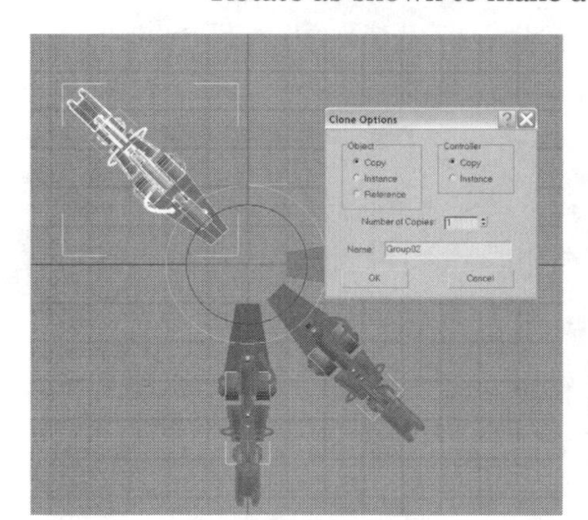

Figure 3-376

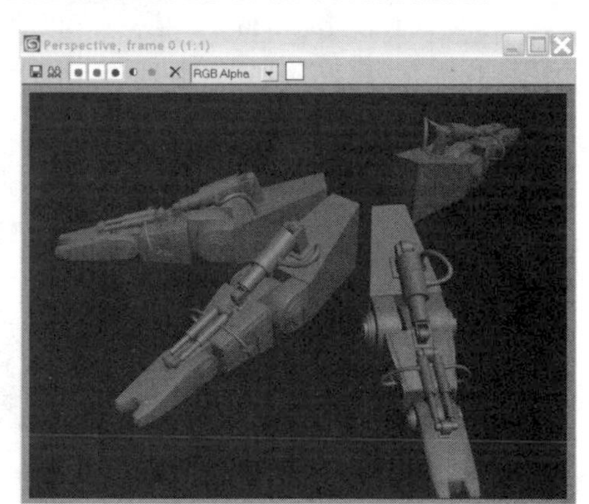

Figure 3-377

7. Select box02 and Attach box01, box03, and box04 to it. Select the inside polygons and delete them.

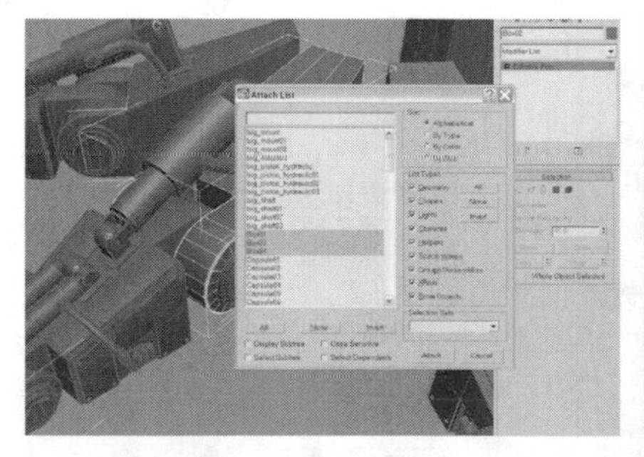

Figure 3-378

Figure 3-379

8. Select the top edges of two of the toes and click **Bridge** to connect them.

Figure 3-380

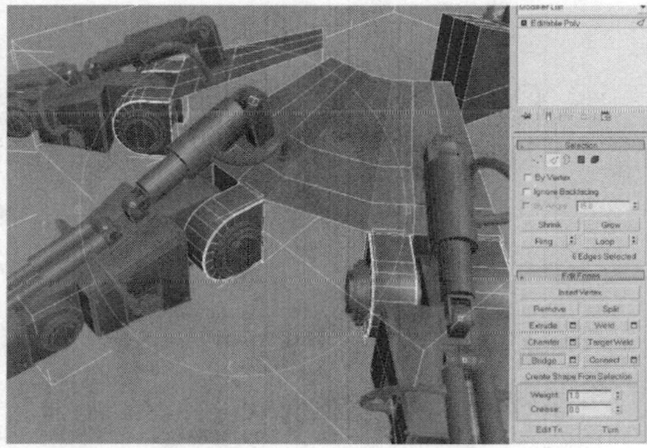

Figure 3-381

9. Bridge the top edges of the middle toe and the remaining toe and then Bridge the front edges.

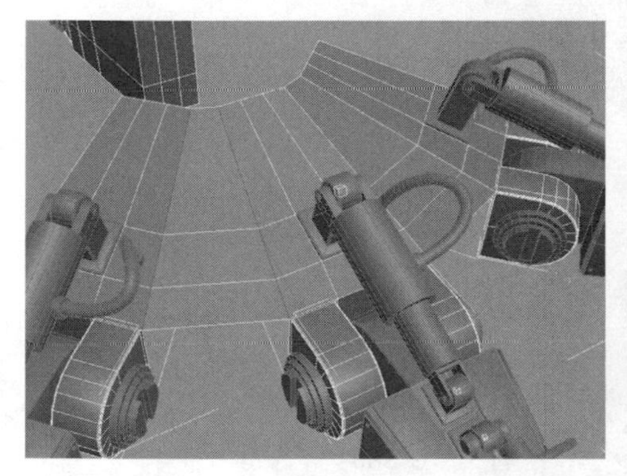

Figure 3-382

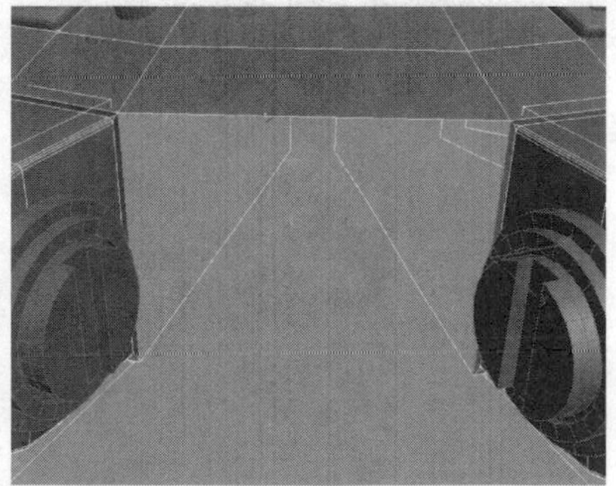

Figure 3-383

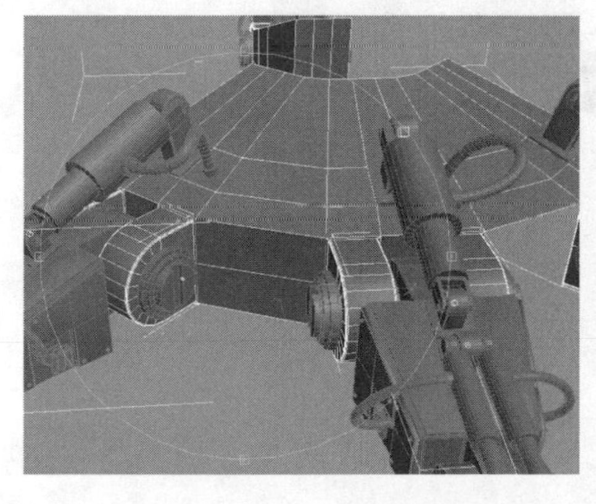

Figure 3-384

10. Switch to the Bottom view and Bridge the edges to make a foot. Rename it **foot**.

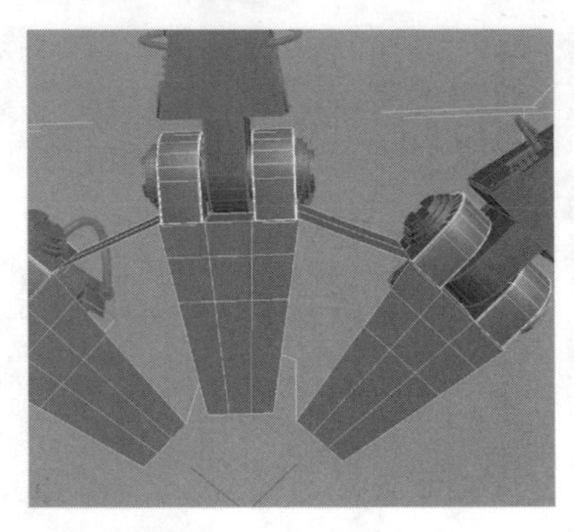

Figure 3-385

Figure 3-386

11. Attach the rear toe to the foot and then add a Smooth modifier to the stack. Adjust the rear-facing polygons to give the ankle a more rounded look.

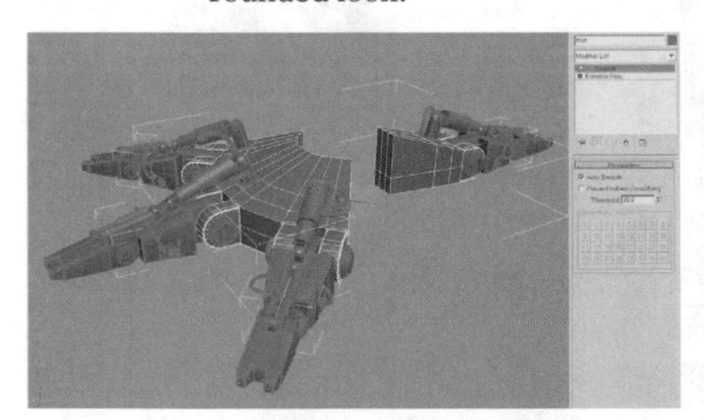

Figure 3-387

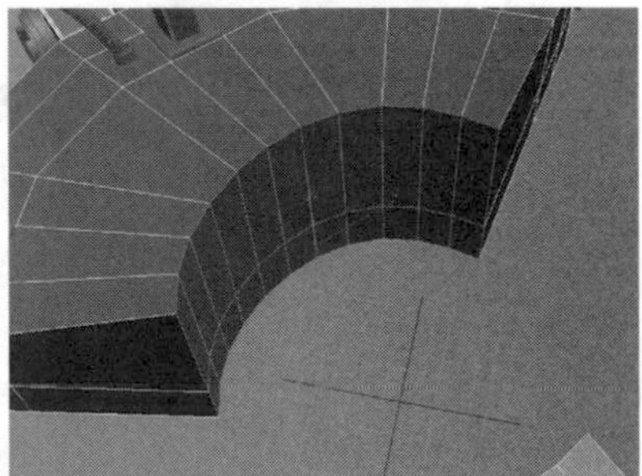

Figure 3-388

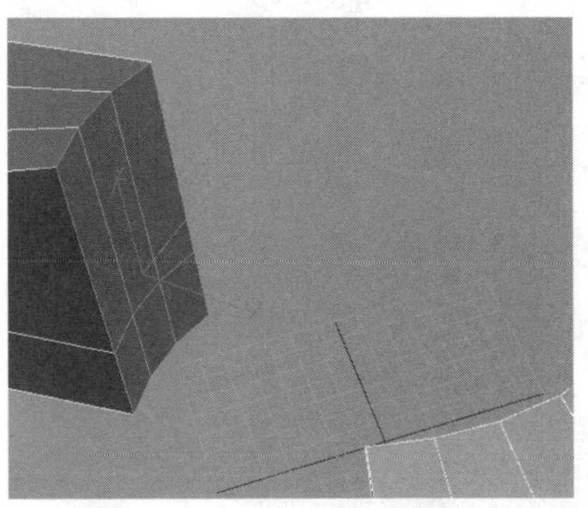

Figure 3-389

12. Create a Tube where the ankle should be and then convert it to an Editable Polygon:

Radius 1	Radius 2	Height	Height/Cap Segs	Sides	Smooth
92.343	105.658	139.791	2/1	36	Checked

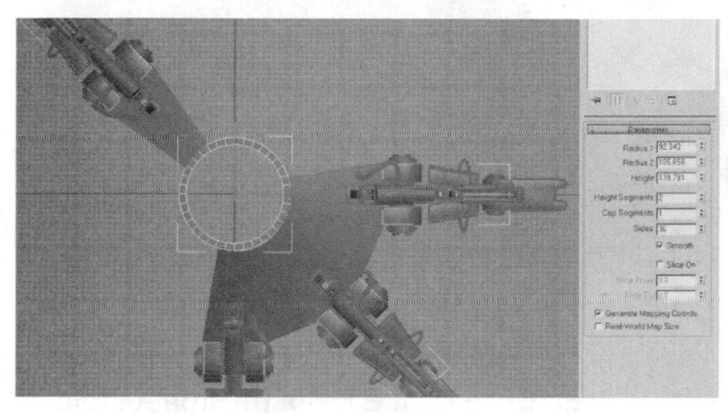

Figure 3-390

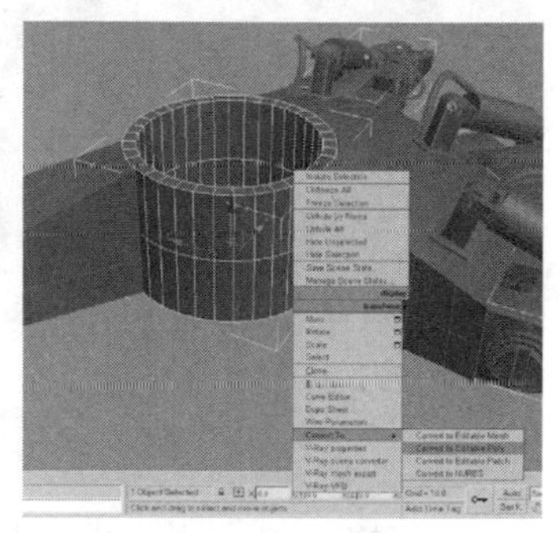

Figure 3-391

13. Loop-select the middle edges of the tube and pull them down to meet the midline of the foot. Object-select the foot, right-click, and select **Hide Selection.**

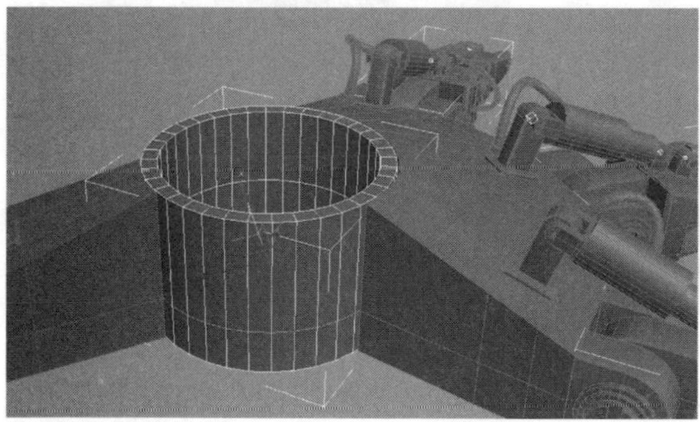

Figure 3-392

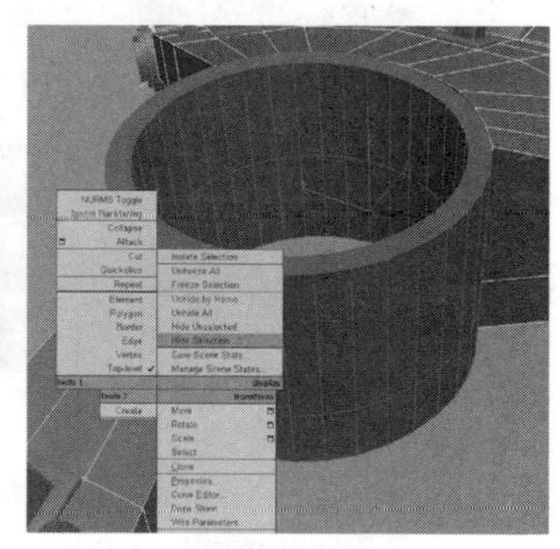

Figure 3-393

14. Select the six polygons that lie beneath the back toe and delete them. Unhide the foot.

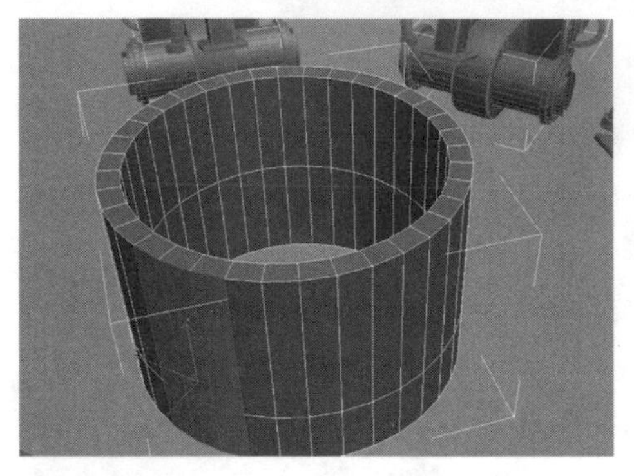

Figure 3-394

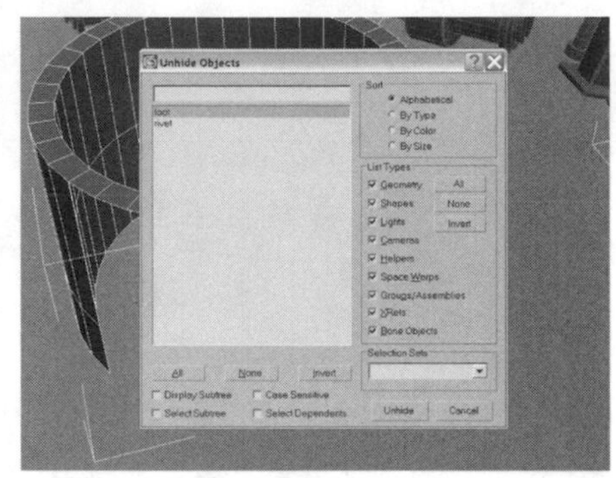

Figure 3-395

15. Select the two polygons beneath the right edge of the front of the foot and the two polygons beneath the left edge of the front of the foot (so you have a visual reference when you hide the foot again). Delete them and hide the foot.

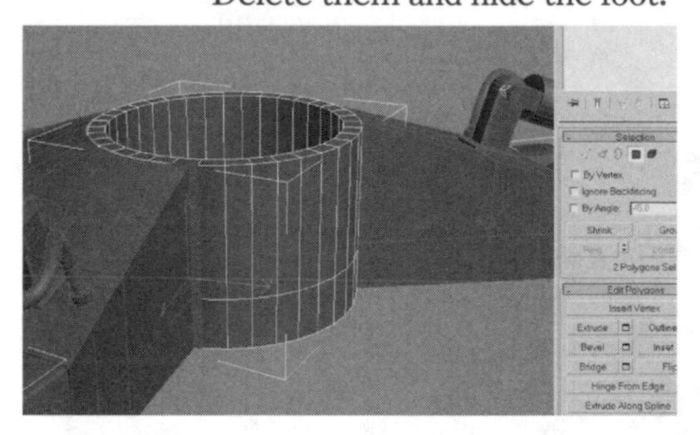

Figure 3-396

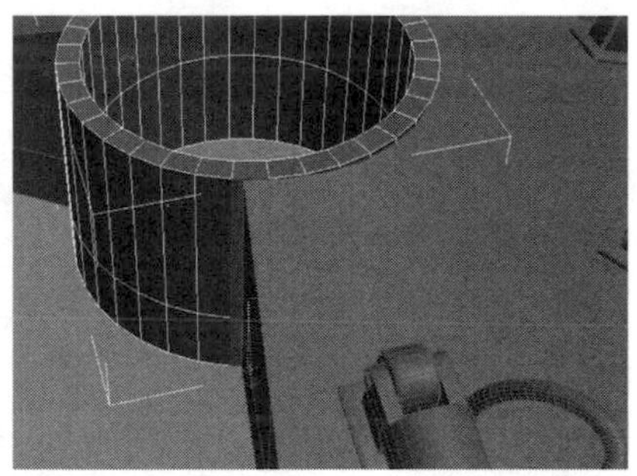

Figure 3-397

16. Select and delete the remaining polygons lying behind the foot. Unhide the foot.

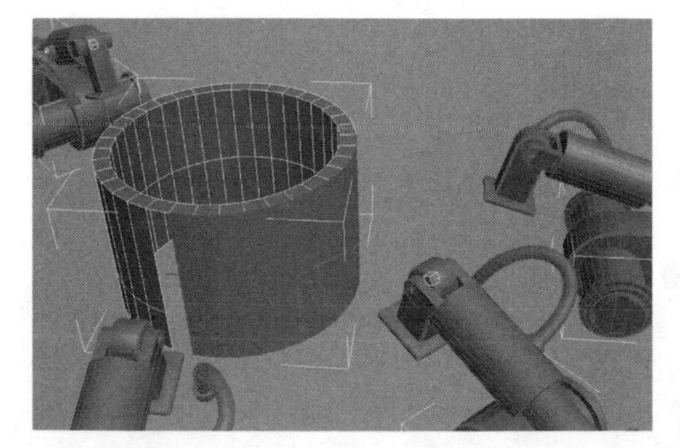

Figure 3-398

Figure 3-399

17. Select the **foot**, click **Attach List**, and attach the tube to the foot. Select the edges shown in Figure 3-401, on the foot between the toes (top, front, and bottom).

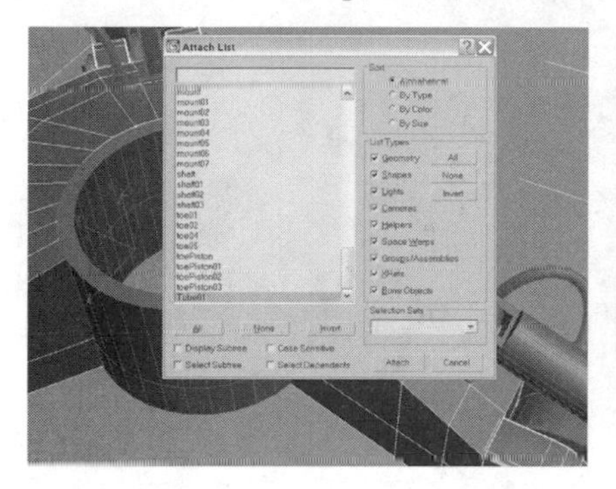

Figure 3-400

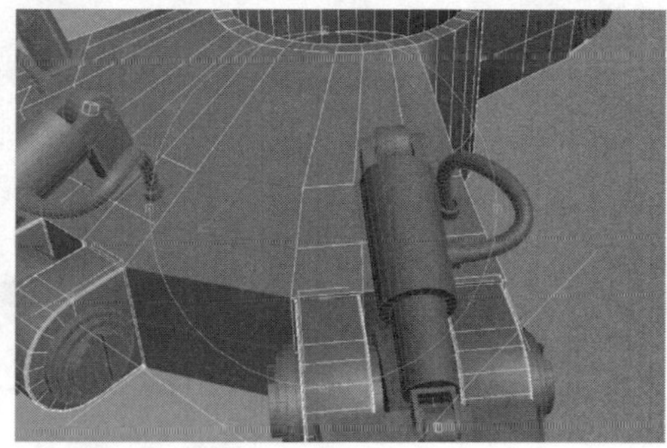

Figure 3-401

Fire Drill: Look at Figure 3-401. Compare the foot to the tube. Note how there is an extra edge on the top of the tube that does not continue through the foot between the toes. Note how the top edges of the toes align perfectly with the top edges of the tube. We'll need to fix that so our geometry is well assembled.

18. Click **Connect** to connect the edges between the toes. Repeat on the other side.

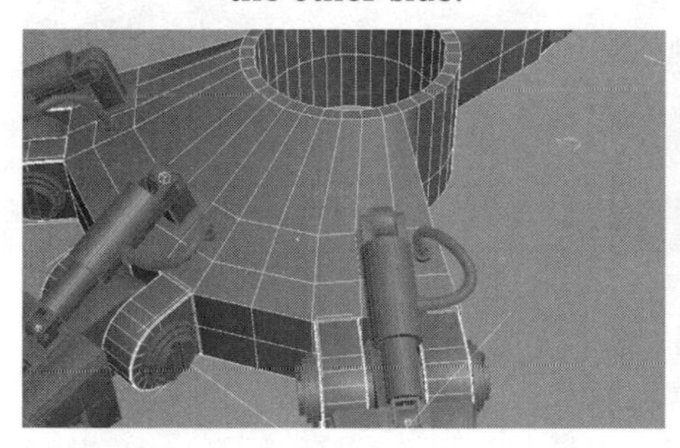

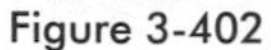
Figure 3-402

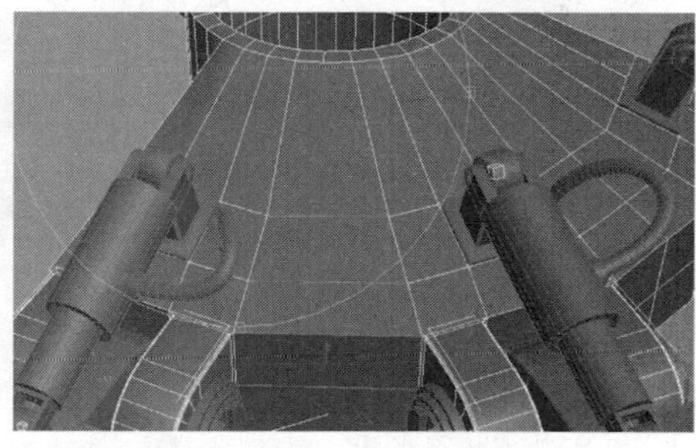

Figure 3-403

19. Switch to the Top view and create a Sphere with a Radius of **93.787** and **36** Segments in the center of the tube.

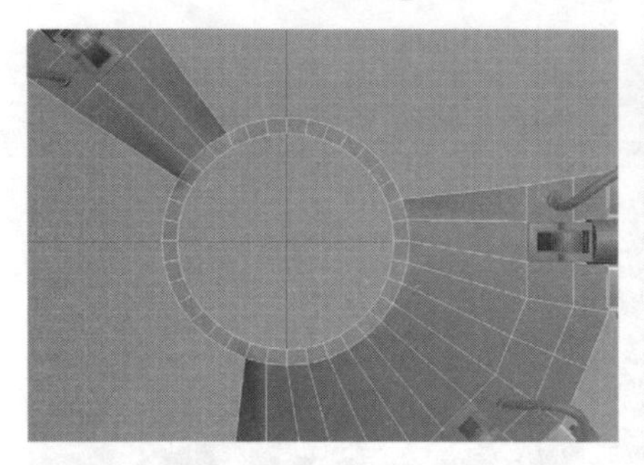

Figure 3-404

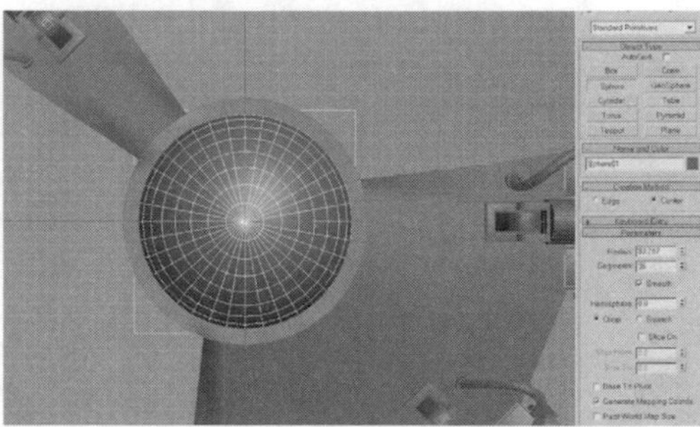

Figure 3-405

FYI: What I'm about to show you is a sneaky way of getting around those pesky Booleans. If you compare the segments of the sphere to the edges on the top of the tube, you'll see they line up exactly. If we convert the sphere to a hemisphere and Target Weld these edges together, we'll create a perfectly formed cup without all the messed-up geometry we'd get from using a Boolean.

20. Change the Hemisphere setting to **0.5** and then rotate the hemisphere **–180** degrees in the X axis so it's upside down in the tube.

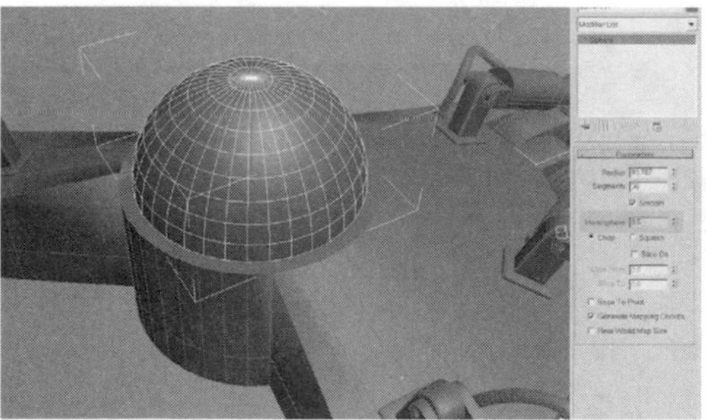

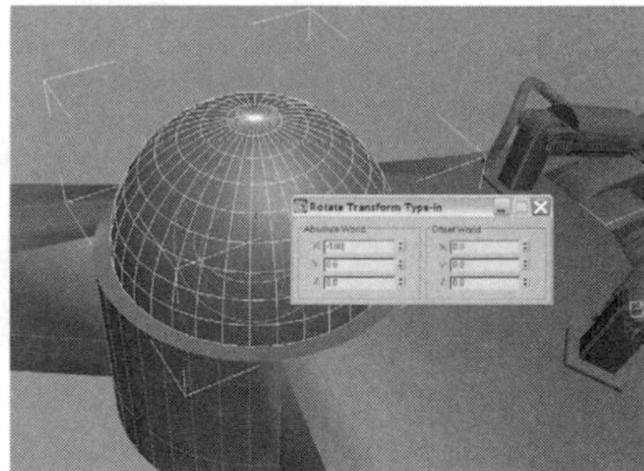

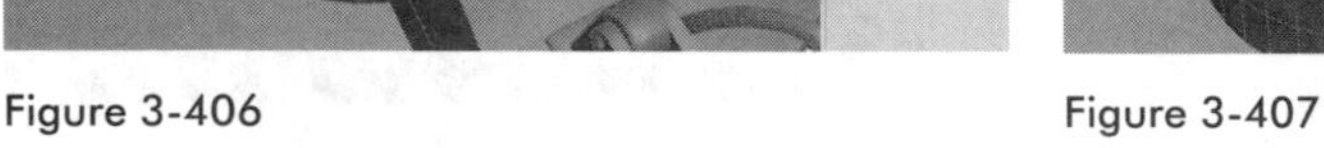

Figure 3-406

Figure 3-407

21. Convert the hemisphere to an Editable Polygon, then delete the top 36 polygons.

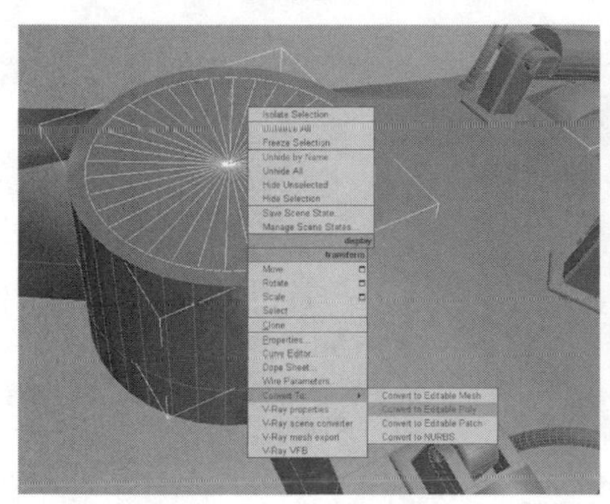

Figure 3-408

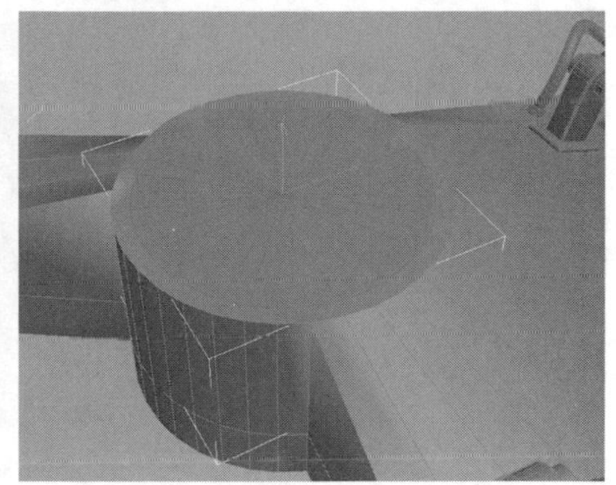

Figure 3-409

22. Hide the foot and select the polygons on the bottom of the hemisphere. Right-click and select **Flip Normals** (to turn them inside out).

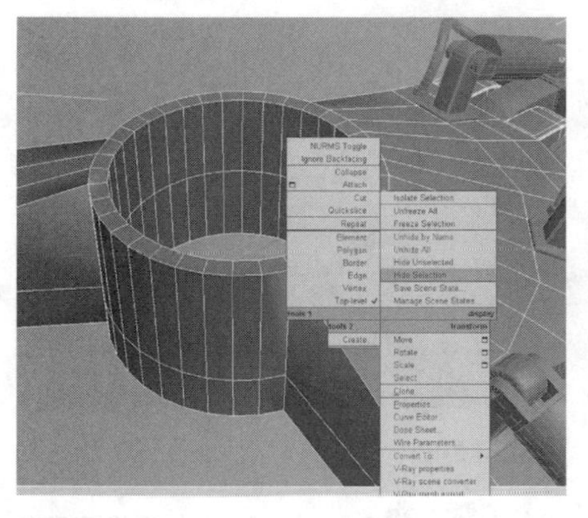

Figure 3-410

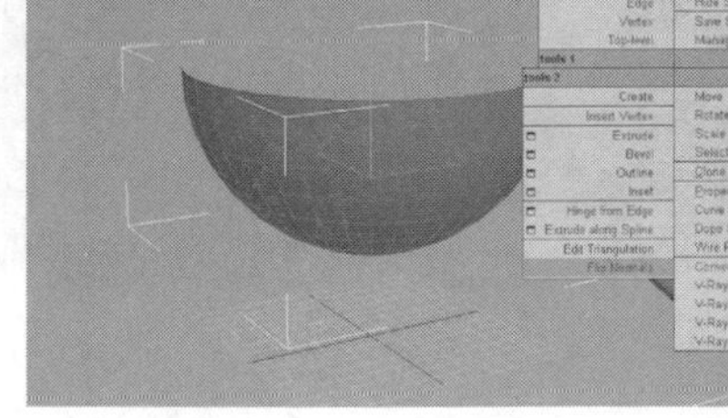

Figure 3-411

23. Hide the hemisphere, unhide the foot, and select and delete the inside top set of 36 polygons.

Figure 3-412

Figure 3-413

24. Unhide the hemisphere and Attach it to the foot, then Weld the vertices of the hemisphere to the vertices on the top of what once was the tube. Do a test render (**F9**).

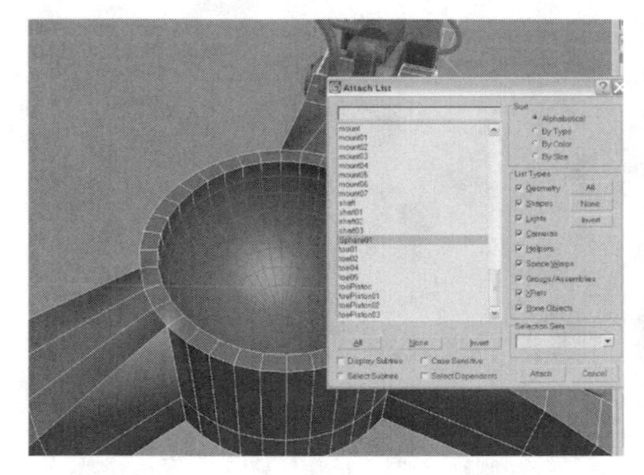

Figure 3-414

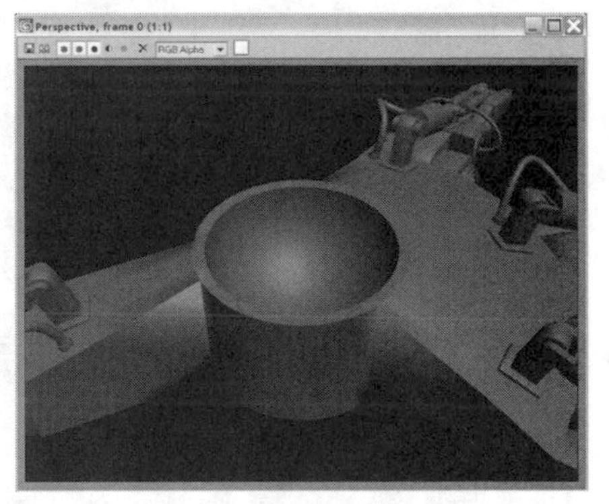

Figure 3-415

25. Create a Sphere with a Radius of **98** and **32** Segments in the cup and then convert it to an Editable Polygon. Using AutoGrid, create a Tube on top of the sphere and convert it to an Editable Polygon.

Radius 1	Radius 2	Height	Height/Cap Segs	Sides	Smooth
82	69	28	2/1	36	Checked

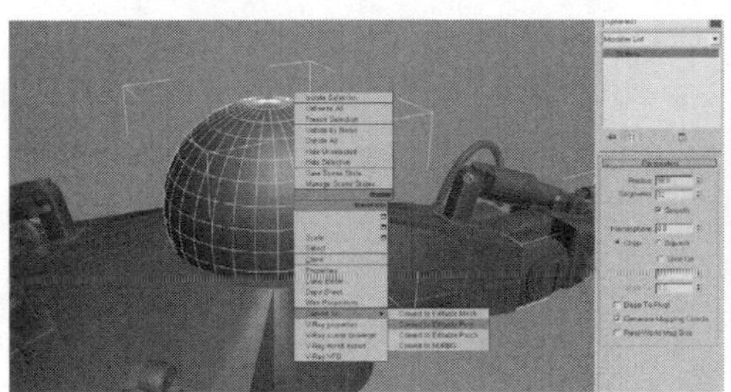

Figure 3-416

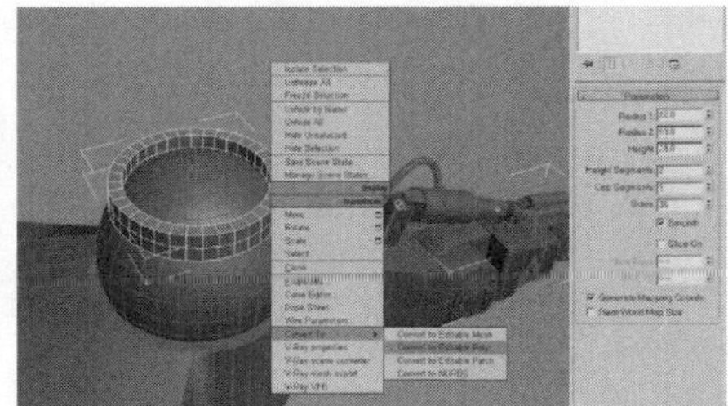

Figure 3-417

26. Select the top polygons, Bevel them, and then Extrude them by **45**.

Type	Height	Outline	Apply/OK
Group	0	–2	OK

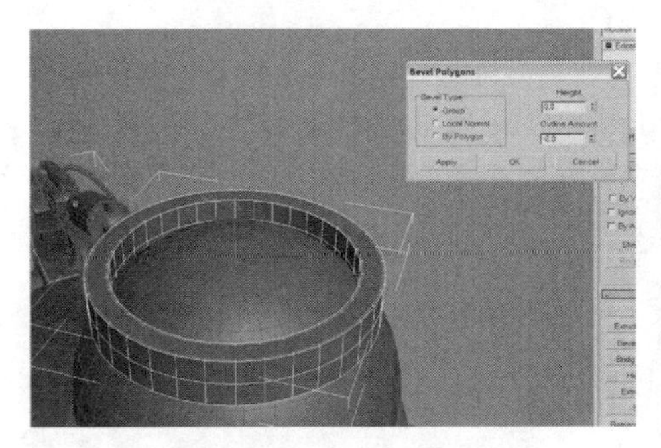

Figure 3-418

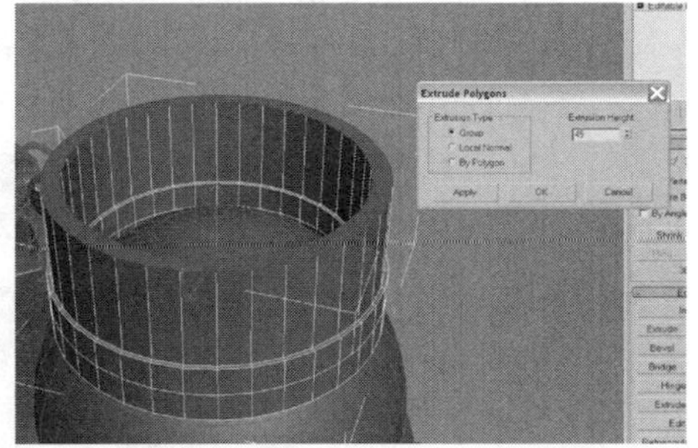

Figure 3-419

27. Uniform Scale the top polygons down to **80**. Select every ninth polygon on the bottom row of the tube and Detach them with the name **upper_mount**.

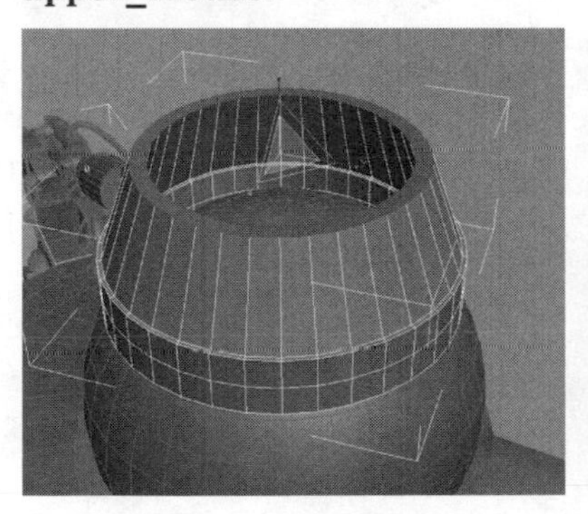

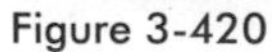

Figure 3-420

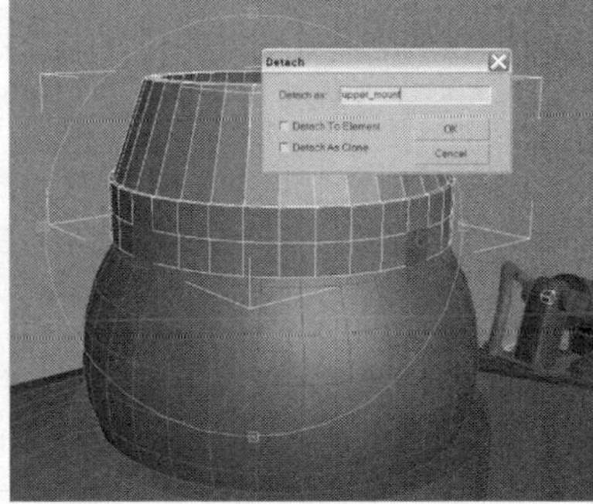

Figure 3-421

28. Clone the polygons, then move them down until they're resting on the polygons on the sphere, as shown in Figure 3-423.

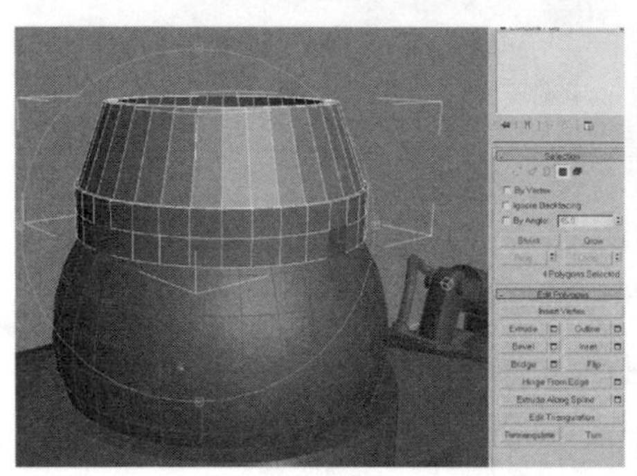

Figure 3-422

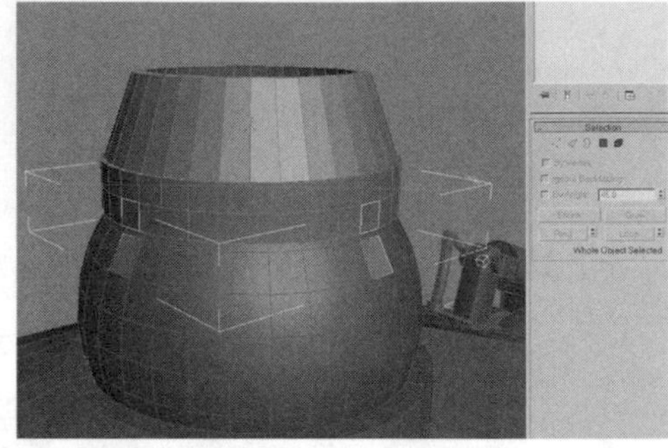

Figure 3-423

29. Select the edges on the top and bottom detached polygons and Bridge them to make a continuous piece. Do this for all the detached polygons. Select the outer edges of the bridged piece.

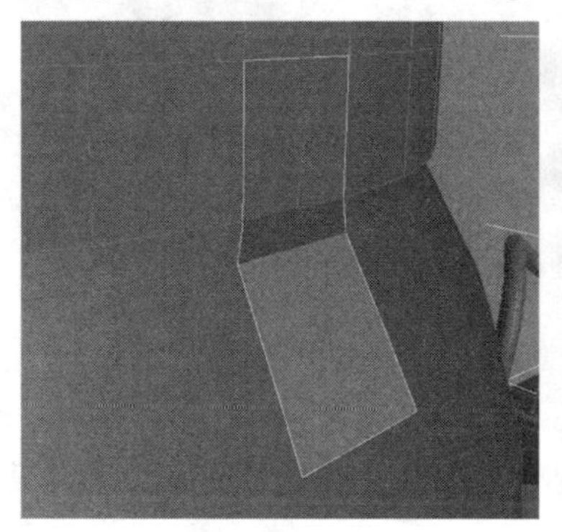

Figure 3-424

Figure 3-425

30. Click **Bridge** to connect the two side edges. Move the new edge in the X axis so that it's between the tube and the sphere, as shown in Figure 3-427.

Figure 3-426

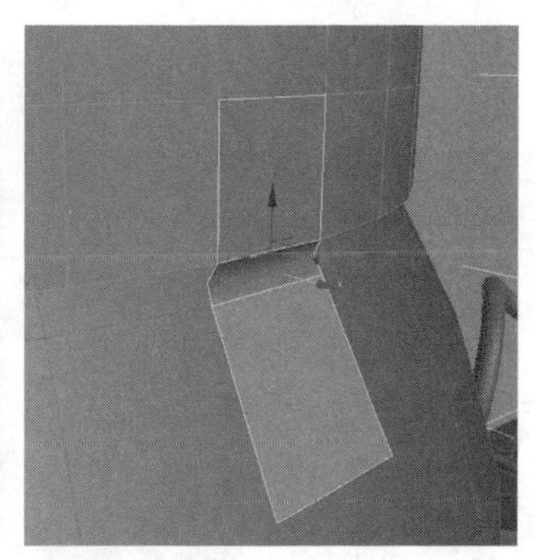

Figure 3-427

31. Chamfer the edges by **0.7**, hit **Apply**, Chamfer them again by **0.35**, then click **OK.**

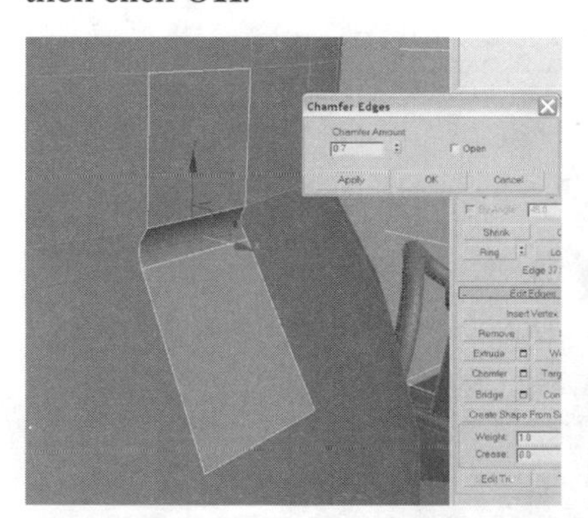

Figure 3-428

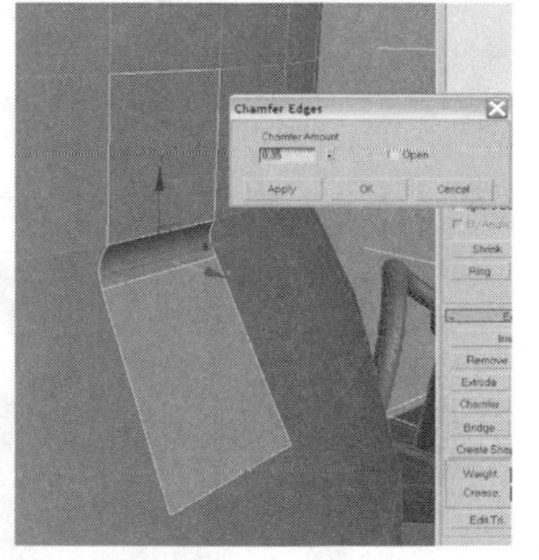

Figure 3-429

32. Select the mounts you made and Extrude by **1.5**.

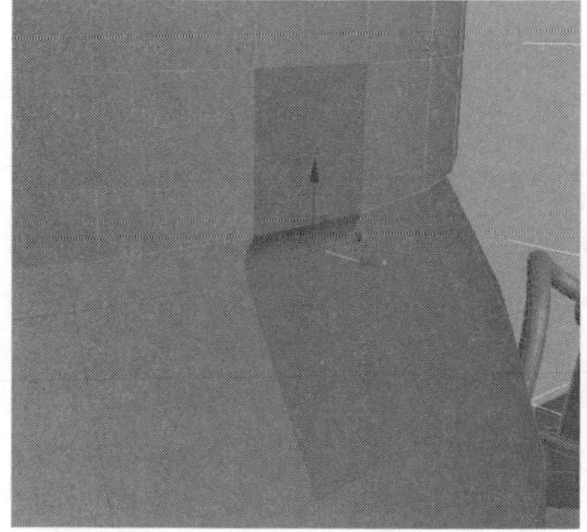

Figure 3-430

Figure 3-431

33. Select the outer edges of the mounts and Chamfer them by **0.15**. Chamfer again by **0.05**.

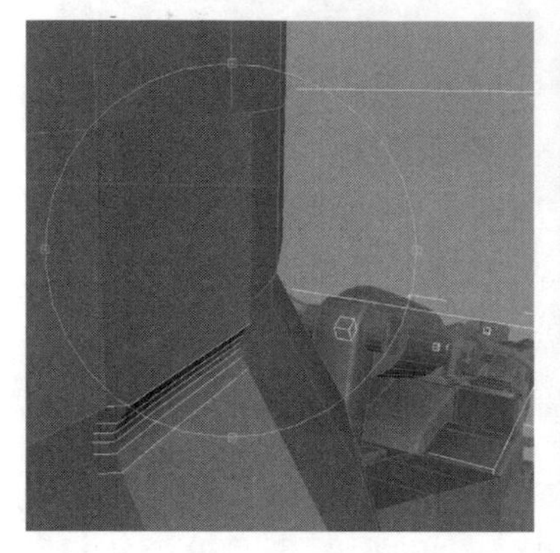

Figure 3-432

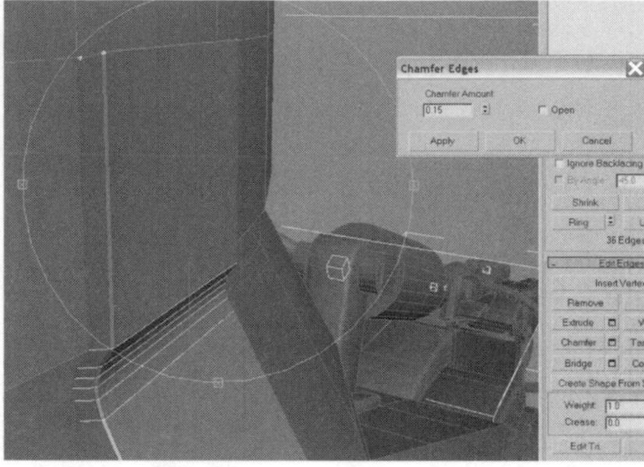

Figure 3-433

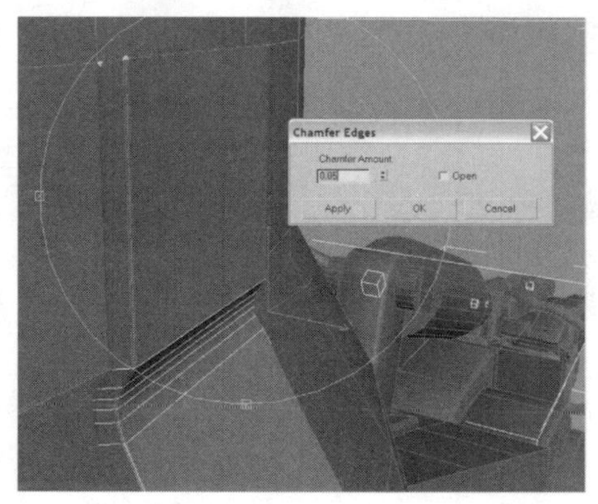

Figure 3-434

34. Add a Smooth modifier to the stack and click **Auto Smooth.** Select the tube and add a Smooth modifier to its stack too.

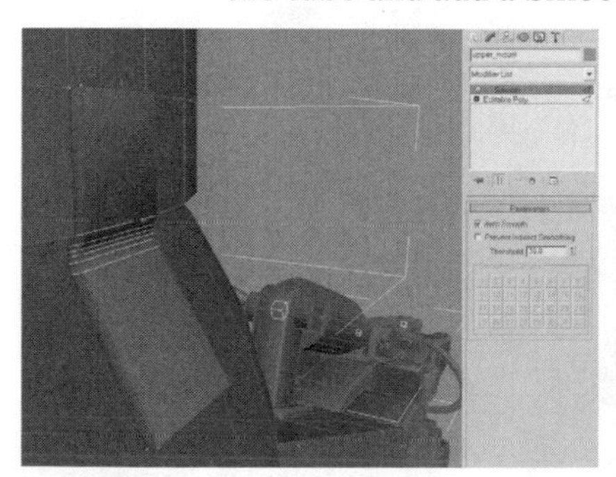

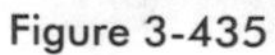

Figure 3-435

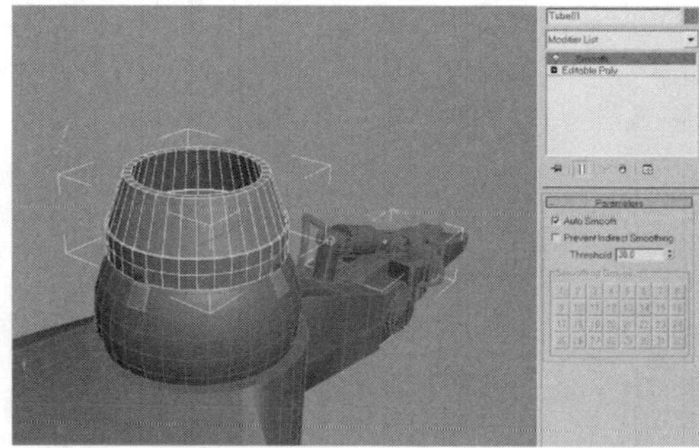

Figure 3-436

35. Create a Gengon and then clone it.

Sides	Radius	Fillet	Height	Side/Height/Fillet Segs
6	3	0	1.7	1/1/1

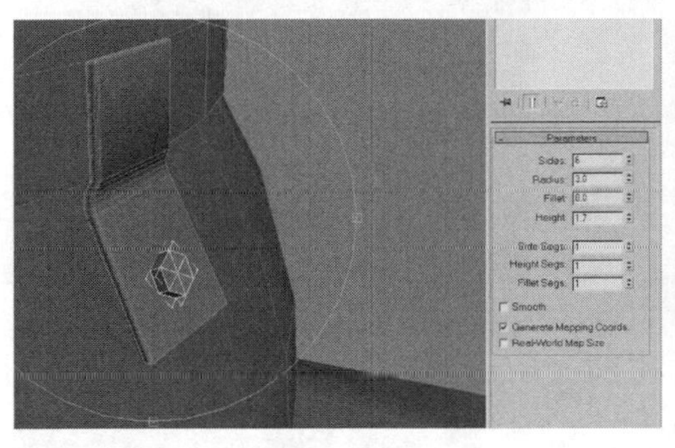

Figure 3-437

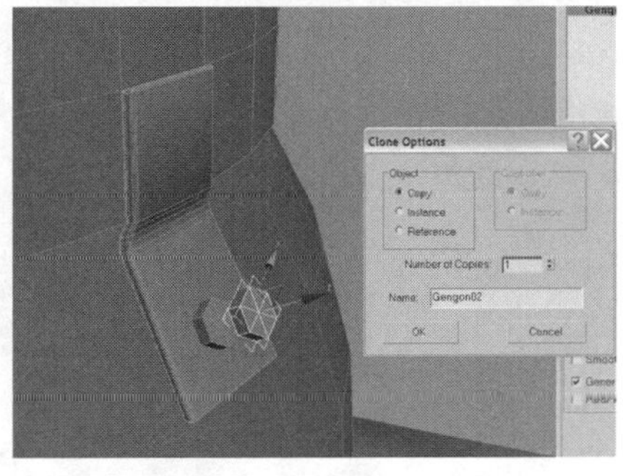

Figure 3-438

36. Create another Gengon. Select the mount and run the Object Placement script, using the mount as a destination and the gengon as the object to be placed. Click **Place**, and then place the gengon on the mounts.

Sides	Radius	Fillet	Height	Side/Height/Fillet Segs
6	3	0	1.7	1/1/1

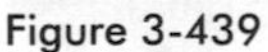
Figure 3-439

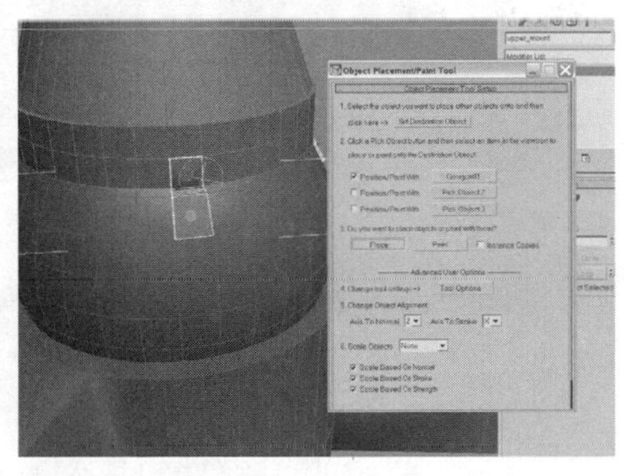

Figure 3-440

37. Select the mounts, click **Attach List**, select the gengons, and attach them to the mount. Select and Link the ankle ball to the tube.

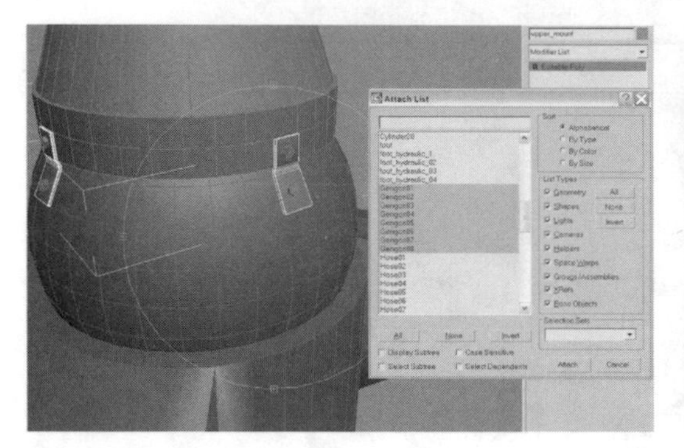
Figure 3-441

Figure 3-442

38. Create a Cylinder in the center of the tube, convert it to an Editable Polygon, select the edges on the top and bottom of the cylinder, and click **Loop**.

Radius	Height	Height/Cap Segs	Sides	Smooth
56.289	250	4/1	36	Checked

Figure 3-443

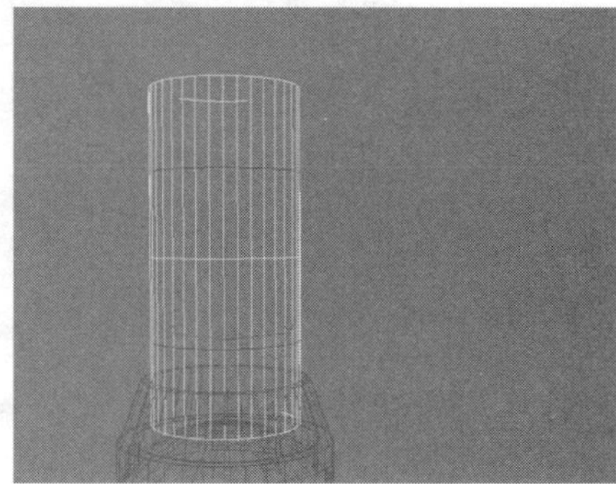
Figure 3-444

39. Extrude the edges **–1.5** with a Base Width of **1.75** to cut machine lines into the cylinder. Add a Smooth modifier to the stack and check **Auto Smooth**.

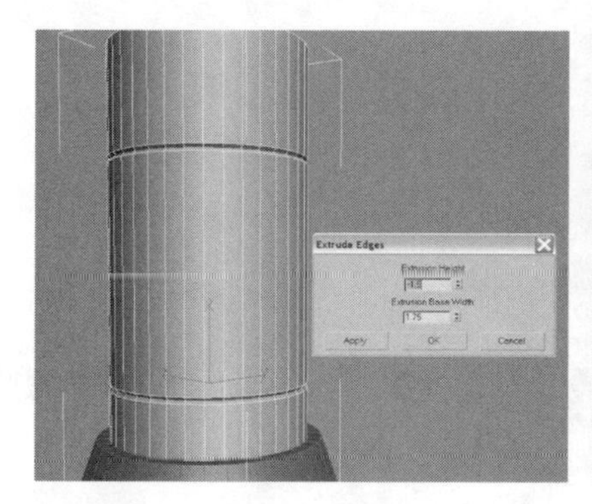

Figure 3-445

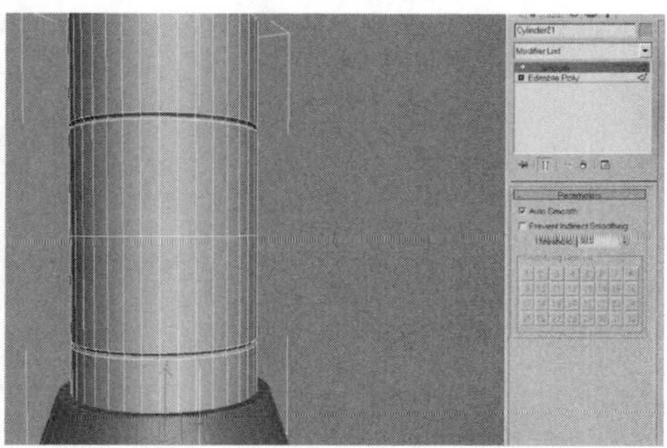

Figure 3-446

Day 5: Assembling the Foot Controllers

1. Create a Tube on the top of the cylinder, then convert it to an Editable Polygon. Select two top and two bottom polygons. Skip five polygons and repeat until you have four sets of polygons selected.

Radius 1	Radius 2	Height	Height/Cap Segs	Sides	Smooth
57	91	52	2/1	36	Checked

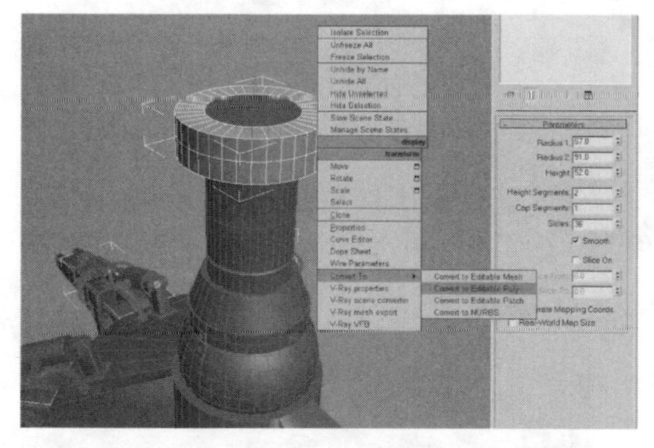

Figure 3-447

Figure 3-448

2. Bevel the selected polygons.

Type	Height	Outline	Apply/OK
Group	0	–5	Apply
Group	20	0	OK

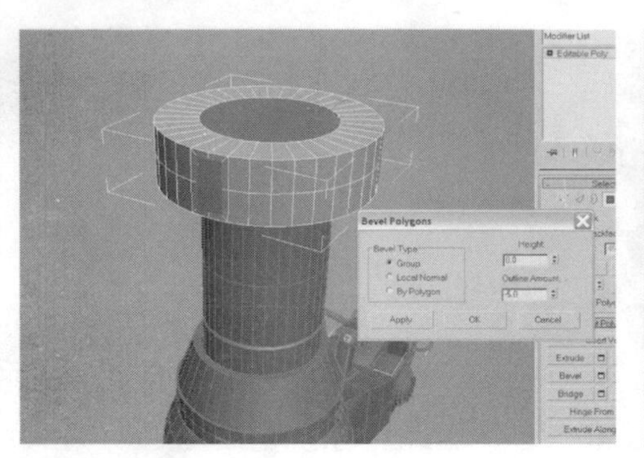

Figure 3-449

Figure 3-450

3. Scale the polygons to flatten them, delete the bottom polygon, and Hinge From Edge **180** degrees with **10** Segments, using the middle edge as the hinge.

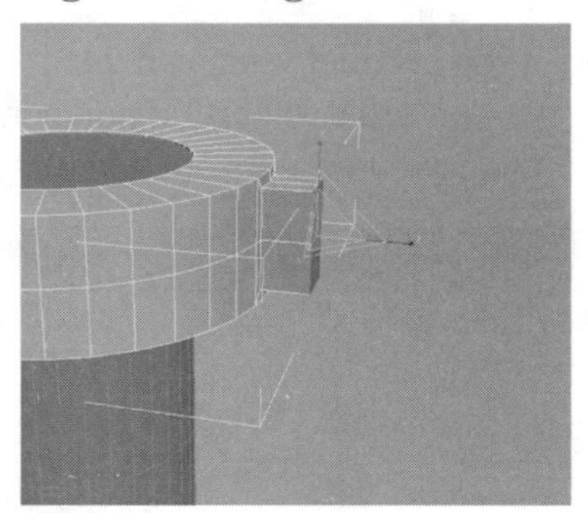

Figure 3-451

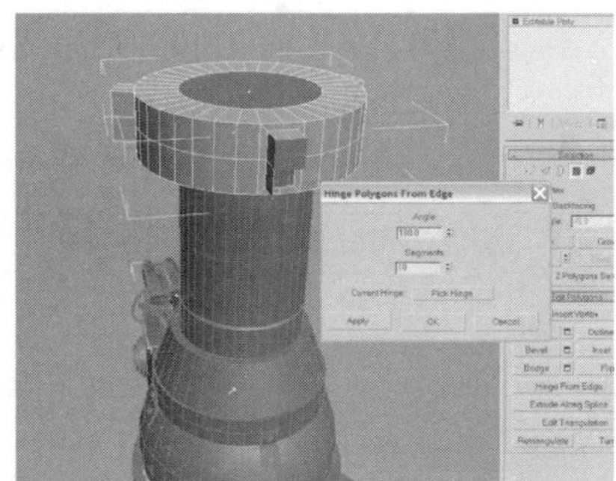

Figure 3-452

4. Create a Sphere with a Radius of **18** and **32** Segments and use **0.5** for the Hemisphere setting. Convert the sphere to an Editable Polygon, clone it, and place a clone on both sides of the braces you made with the Hinge From Edge.

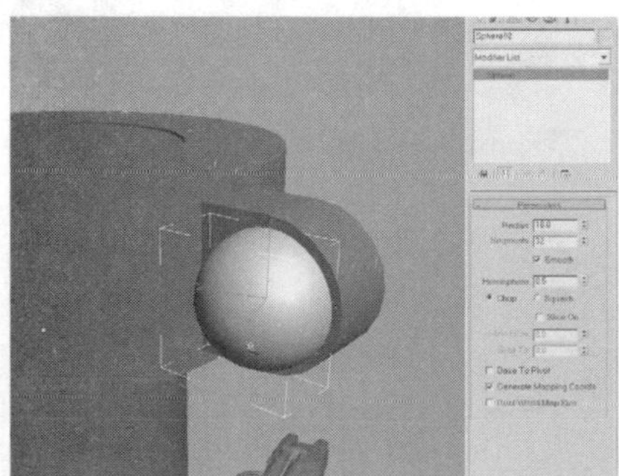

Figure 3-453

Figure 3-454

5. Select one of the spheres and Attach it to the one on the other side. Click **Affect Pivot Only** and **Center to Object**.

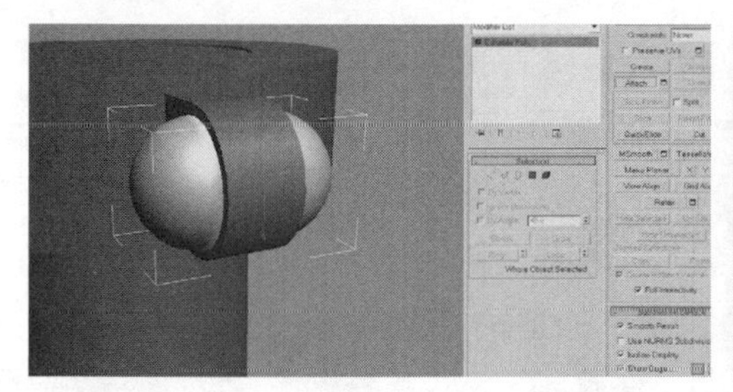

Figure 3-455

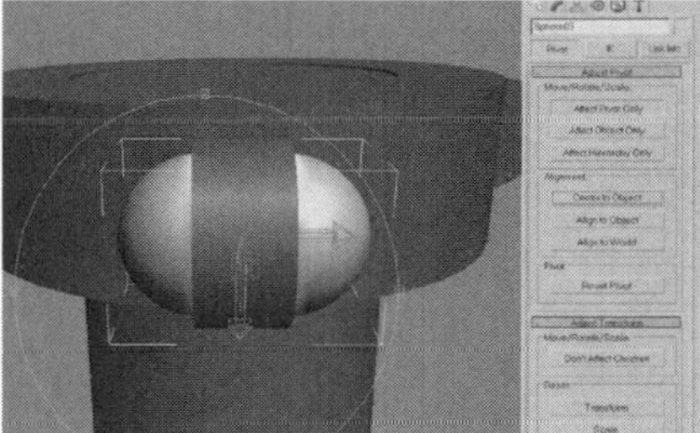

Figure 3-456

6. Clone the hemispheric joints you made and place one on each of the mounts. From the Primitives drop-down choose **Dynamics Objects**, then click the **Spring** button.

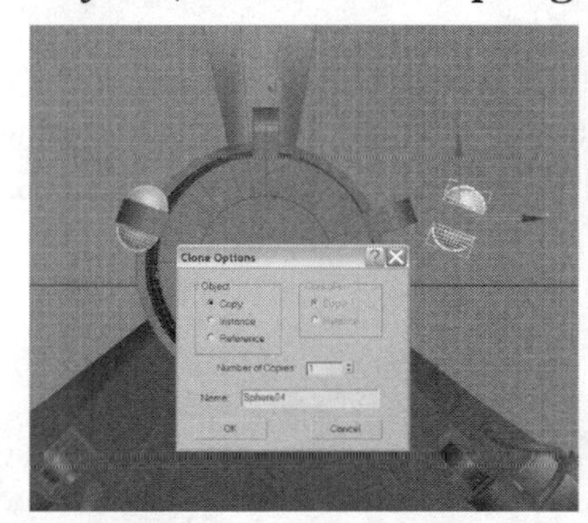

Figure 3-457

Figure 3-458

7. Create a Dummy in the ankle joint and in the middle of the tube at the top. Name them **upper_spring_mount** and **bottom_spring_mount**. Link them to their respective objects.

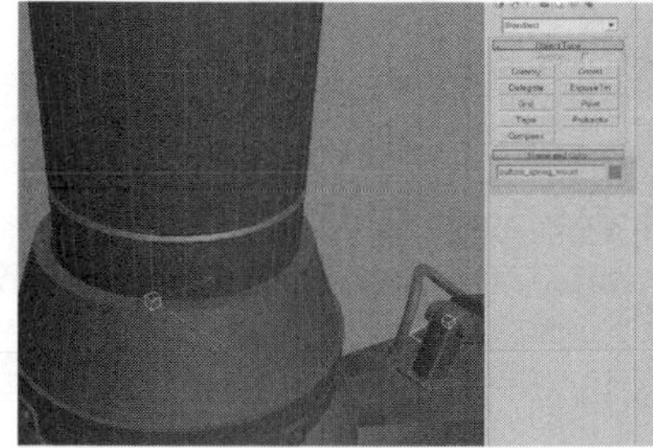

Figure 3-459

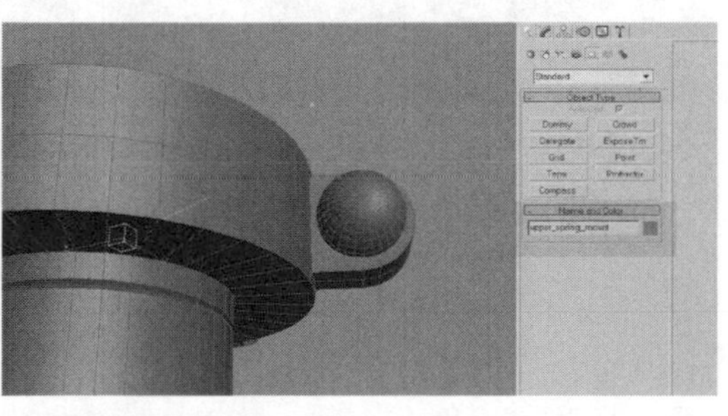

Figure 3-460

8. Click the spring, set the End Point Method to **Bound to Object Pivots**, and use the dummies you just made as the Top and Bottom binding objects, respectively.

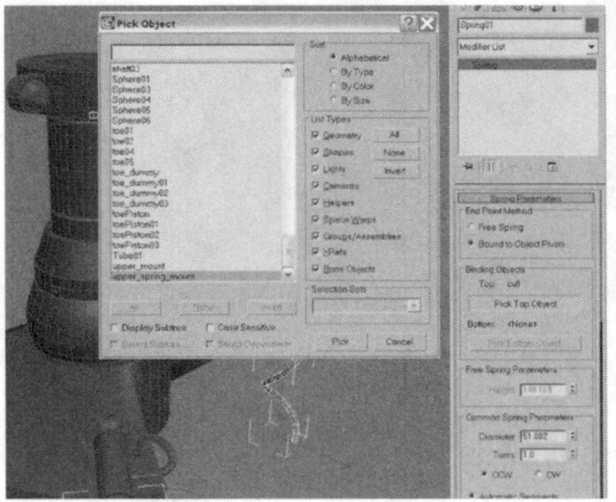

Figure 3-461

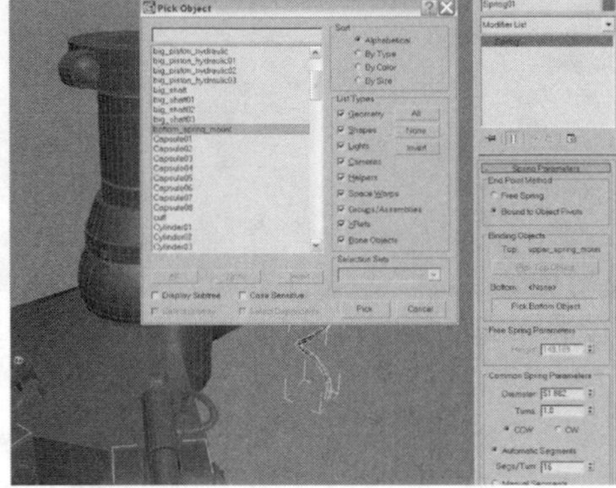

Figure 3-462

9. Set the spring's Diameter setting to **122.682** (to set the circumference of the hole inside the spring) and Turns to **6**. Scroll down and set the spring to **Round Wire** with a Diameter of **13.982** (which sets the diameter of the wire) and leave Sides set to the default of **12**.

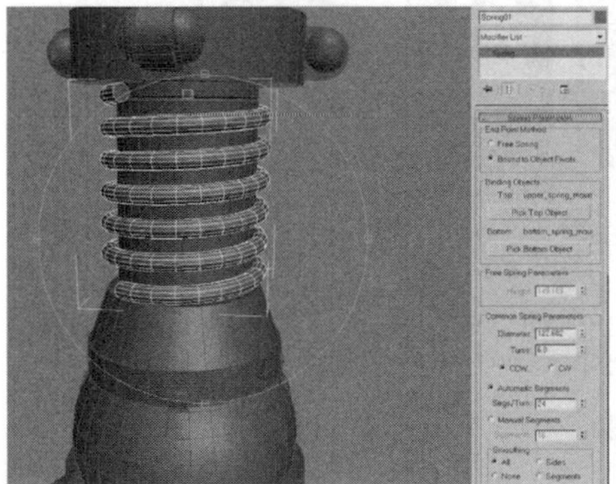

Figure 3-463

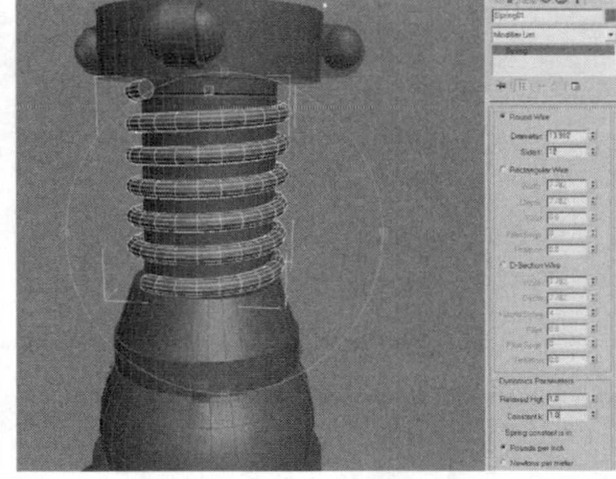

Figure 3-464

10. Clone the middle_toe mount and move it just behind the original. In the Name field, type **foot_control_mount01**. Select and Link the clone to the foot.

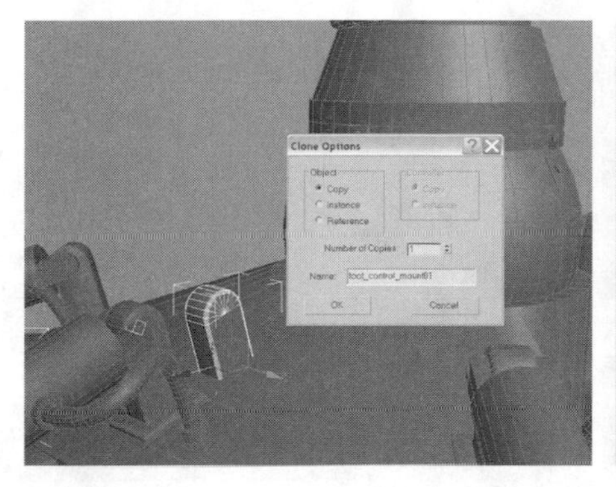

Figure 3-465

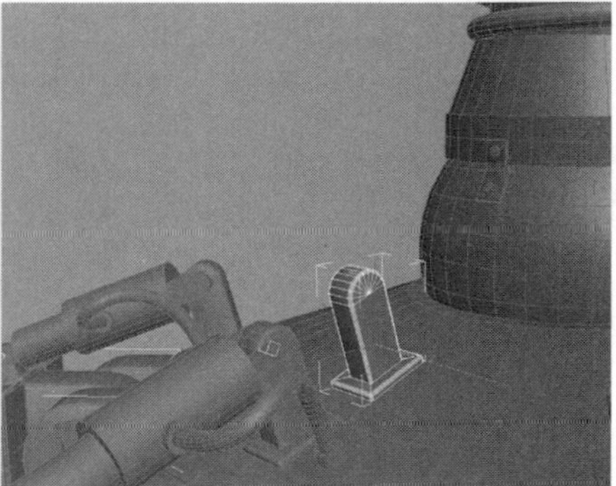

Figure 3-466

11. Orbit around and make sure the mount is properly aligned as shown in Figure 3-467. Select the top polygons on the top four rows of the hemispheres on the front of the leg.

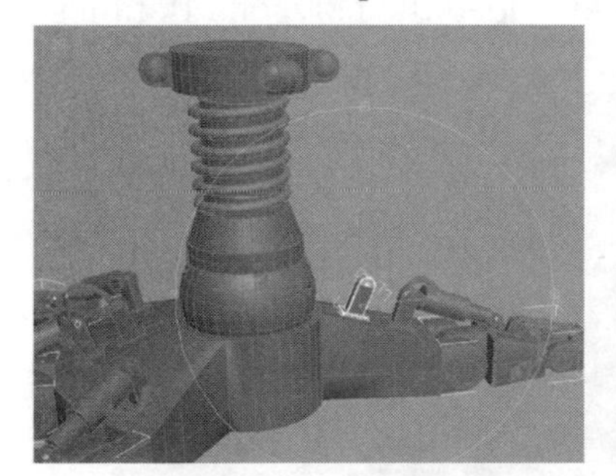

Figure 3-467

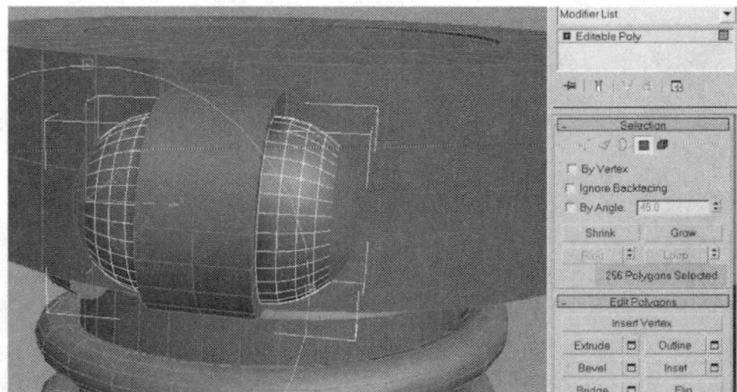

Figure 3-468

12. Delete the polygons and select the borders. Cap the borders and then Extrude them **5.0**.

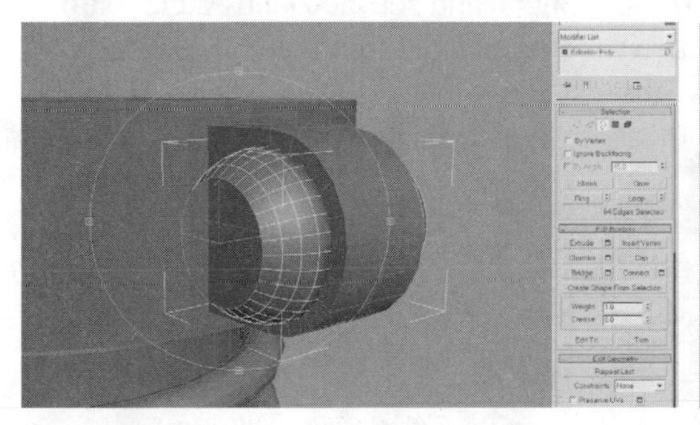

Figure 3-469

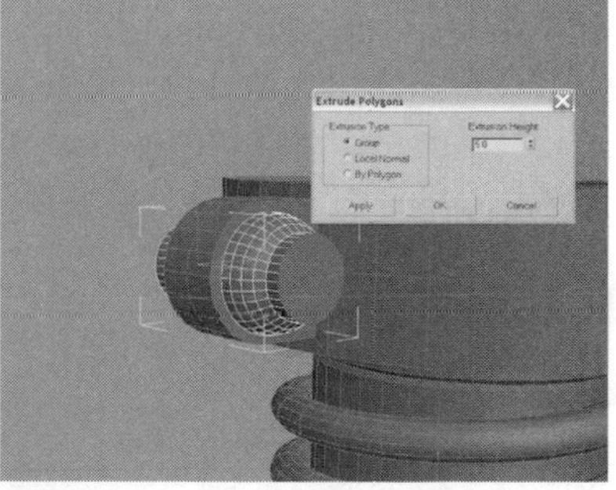

Figure 3-470

13. Extrude the polygons by **2.0** 10 times. Click **Grow** until all the polygons are selected back to the hemispheres.

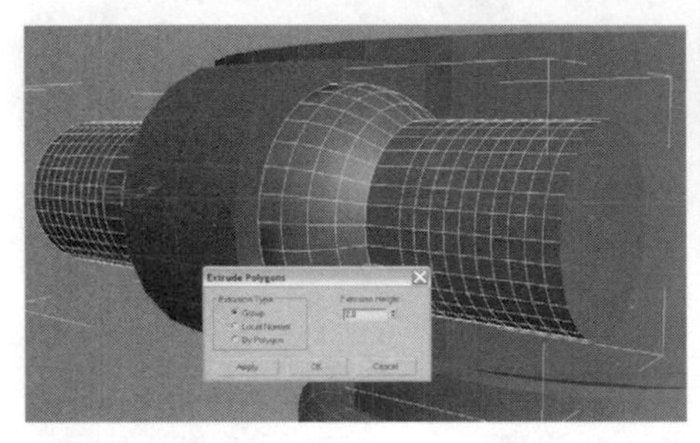

Figure 3-471

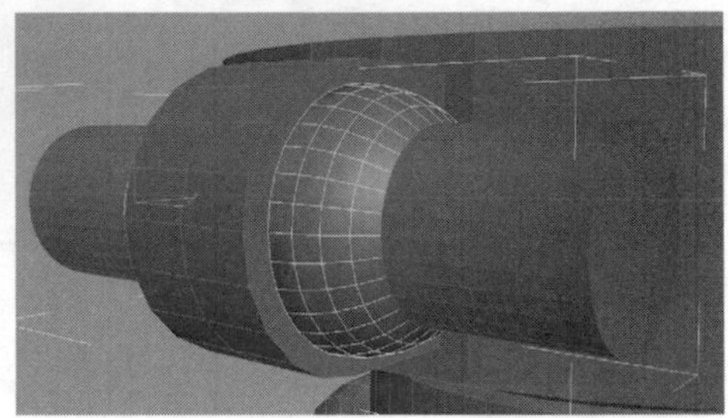
Figure 3-472

14. Click **Detach** and name them **control**. Detach the controls from each other, click **Affect Pivot Only** and move the pivot point of each control to the edge where you extruded the polygons 10 times.

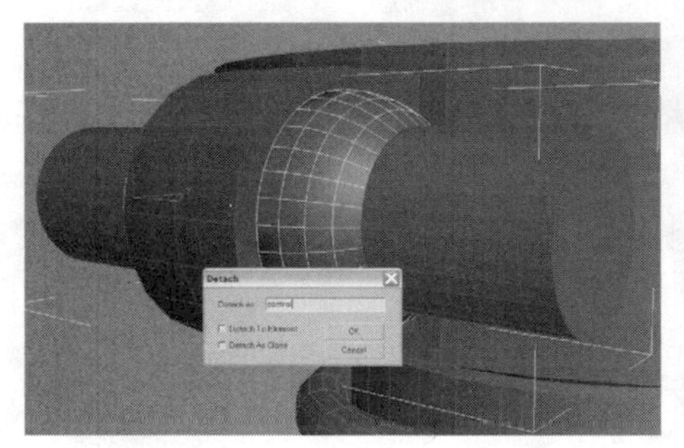

Figure 3-473

Figure 3-474

15. Add a Bend modifier to each control and set the Bend Angle to **90** degrees and the Direction to **–90**. Add a Smooth modifier to the stack and check **Auto Smooth**.

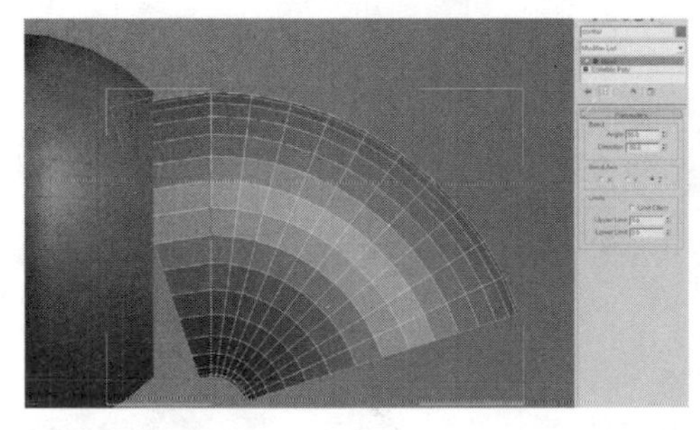
Figure 3-475

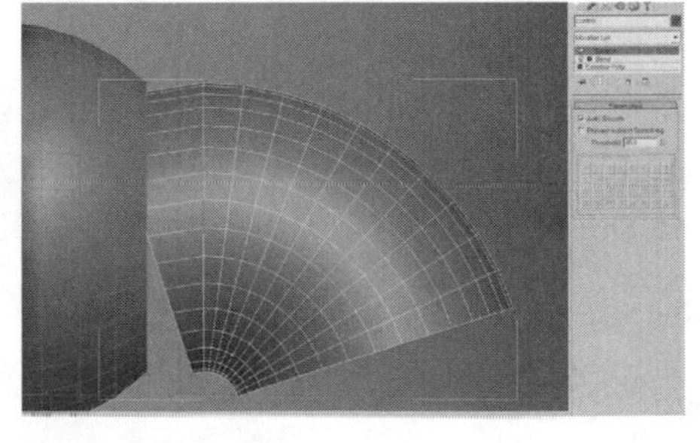
Figure 3-476

16. Rotate the controls to align them with the hemispheres you separated them from. Use the Move tool to make sure that the edges of the controls align with the edges of the original hemispheres.

Figure 3-477

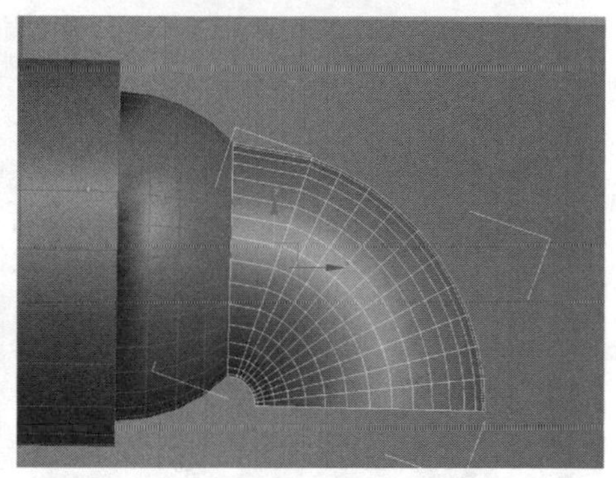

Figure 3-478

17. Reattach the controls so they form a single unit. Delete the top four rows of polygons from the hemispheres above the rear toe. Switch to the Top view, hold down the **Shift** key, and drag in the Y axis to clone the control to the back toe. Attach the controls to the front and rear hemispheres, respectively.

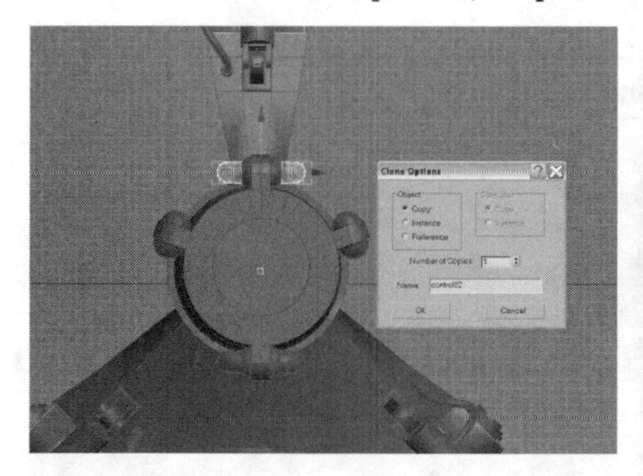

Figure 3-479

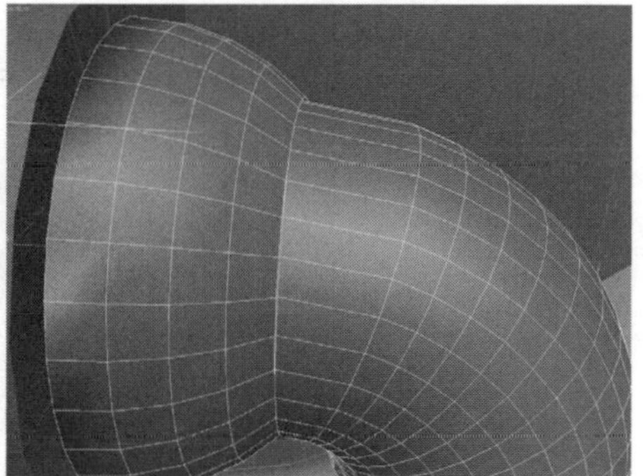

Figure 3-480

18. Select the bottom-facing polygon on the part you bent, and Extrude it by **12.0**. Bevel the polygons:

Type	Height	Outline	Apply/OK
Group	150	0	Apply
Group	0	–7	Apply
Group	–102	0	Apply

Figure 3-481

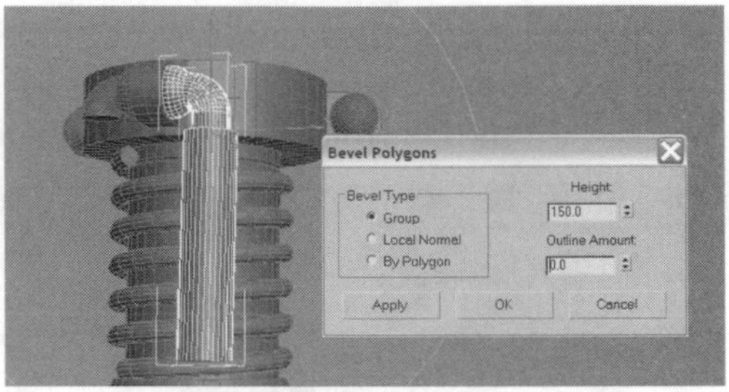

Figure 3-482

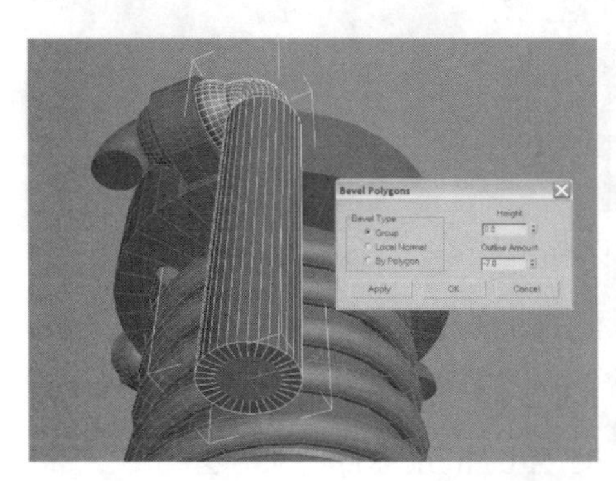

Figure 3-483

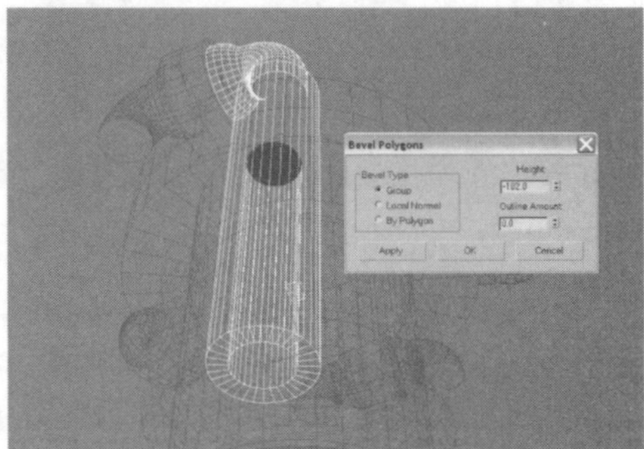

Figure 3-484

19. Mirror copy the control piston you made in the previous step. Attach the two controls together and then Shift-move it to the back to make a clone.

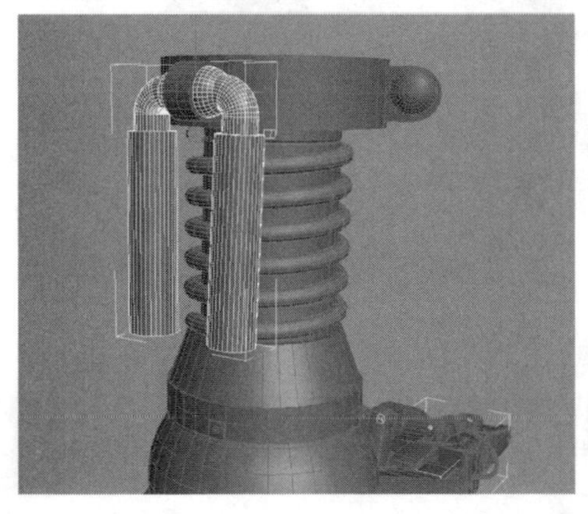

Figure 3-485

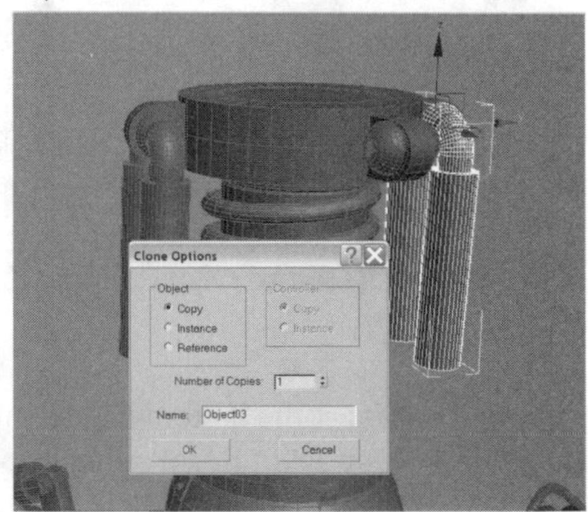

Figure 3-486

20. Select and Link the controls to the tube. Switch to Polygon selection mode, make sure the polygons inside the pistons are still selected, and Detach them.

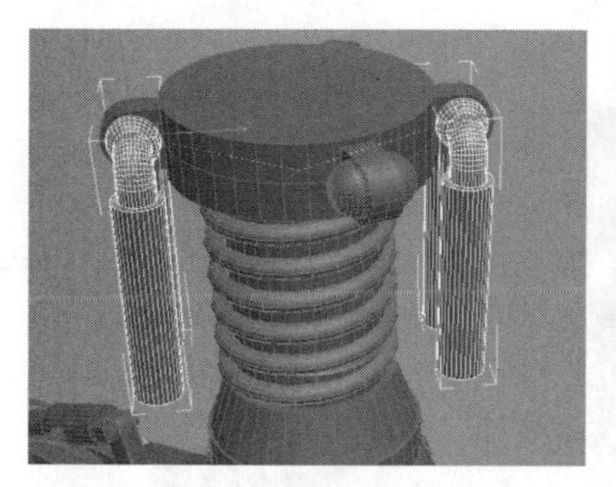

Figure 3-487

Figure 3-488

21. Position the disks adjacent to the foot mount. Border-select the disks and Extrude the edges **–230** with a Base Width of **0.**

Figure 3-489

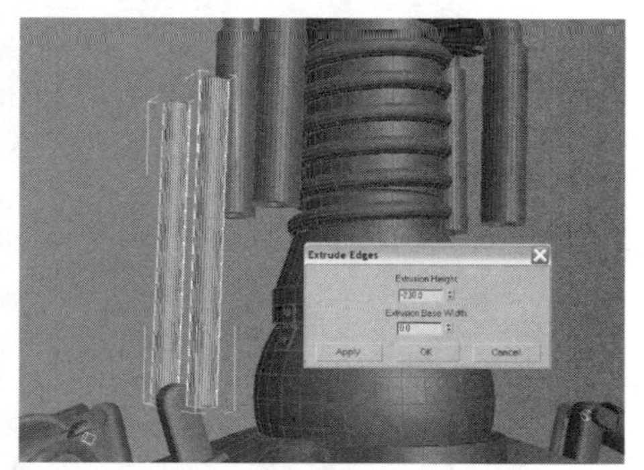

Figure 3-490

22. Right-click and select **Hide Selection**. Create a Cylinder using AutoGrid in the center of the mount.

Radius	Height	Height/Cap Segs	Sides	Smooth
9	40	1/1	18	Checked

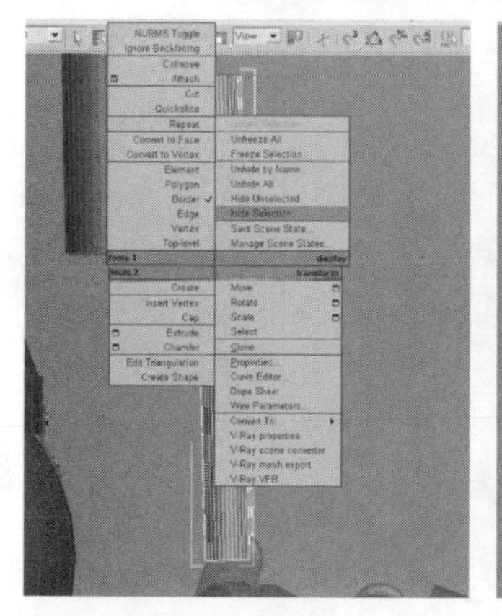

Figure 3-491

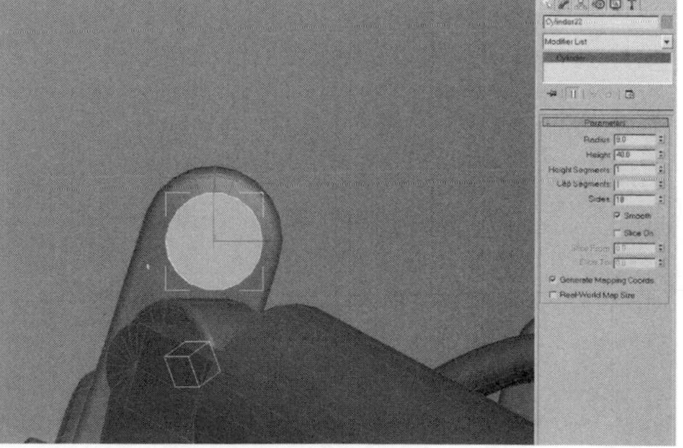

Figure 3-492

23. Center the cylinder in the mount.

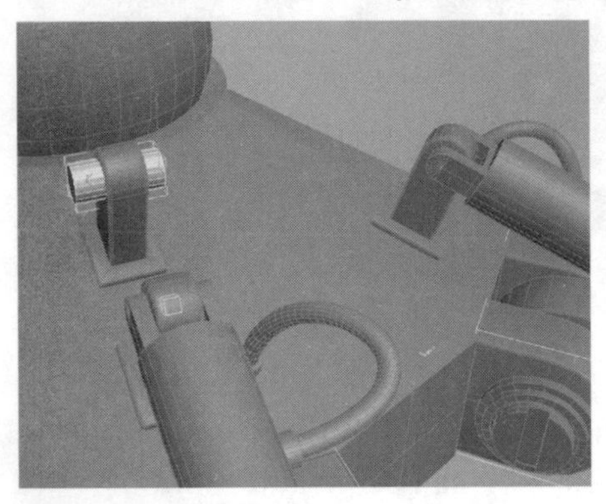

Figure 3-493

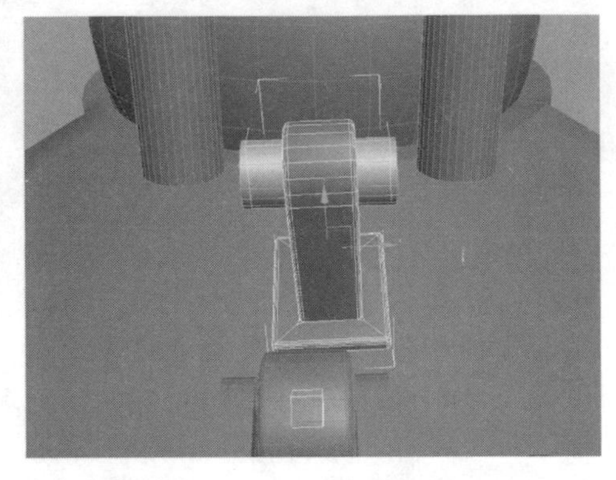

Figure 3-494

24. Change the number of Sides on the cylinder to **24** and then create a Sphere, with a Radius of **16** and **32** Segments, on the bottom of the shaft.

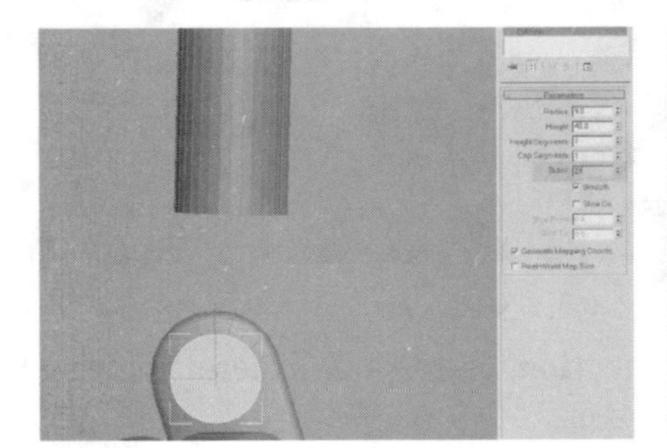

Figure 3-495

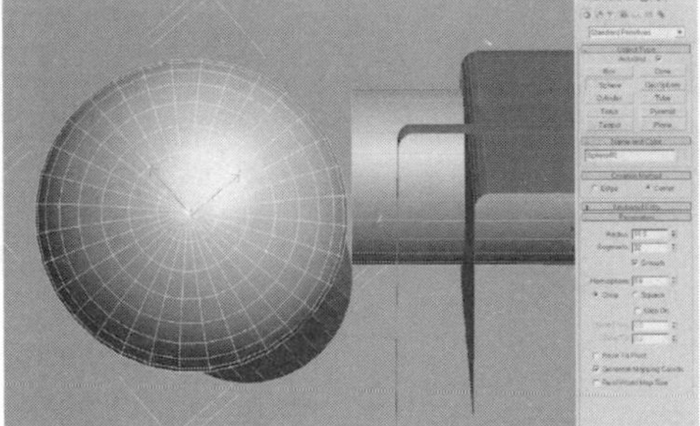

Figure 3-496

25. Center the sphere on the bottom of the shaft and convert it to an Editable Polygon. Select the four rows of polygons on the top of the sphere and delete them.

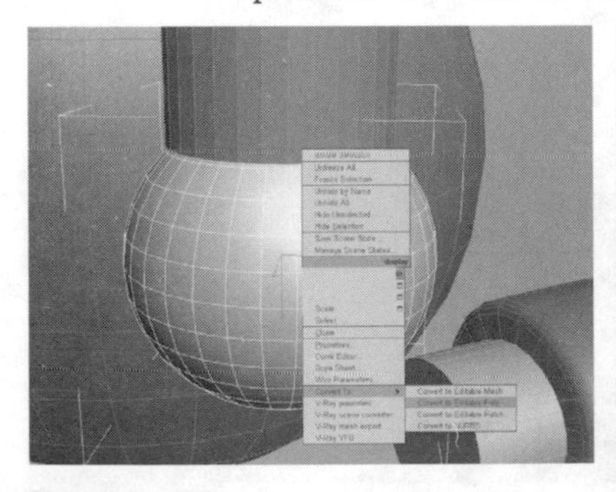

Figure 3-497

Figure 3-498

26. Select and delete the polygons on the bottom of the shafts, then clone the sphere and move it to the bottom of the other shaft.

Figure 3-499

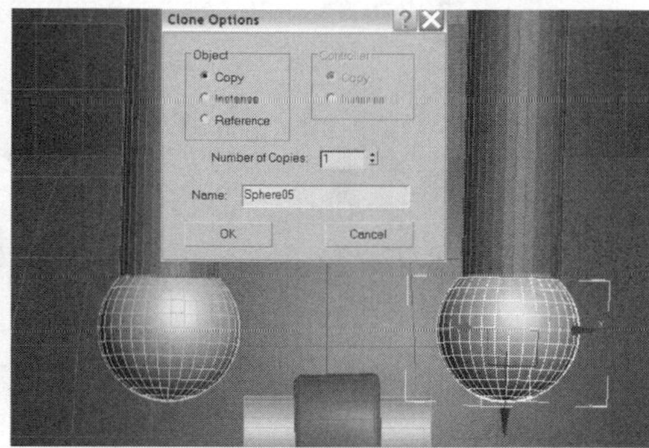

Figure 3-500

27. Attach the spheres to the bottoms of the shafts and align the pivots at the center of the spheres.

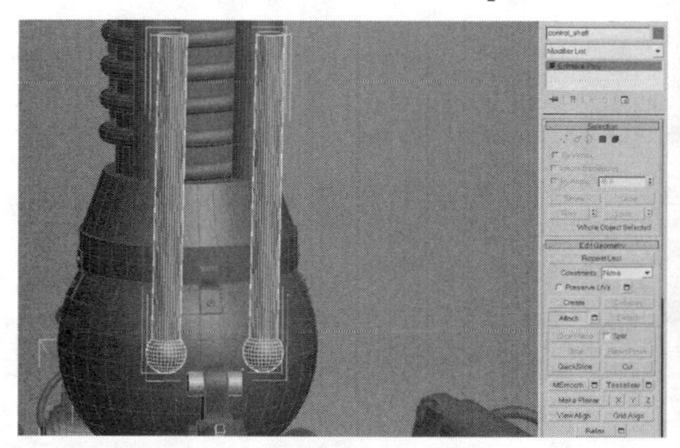

Figure 3-501

Figure 3-502

28. Increase the Height to **104** and center the cylinders between the shafts and the mount. Convert the cylinders to Editable Polygons.

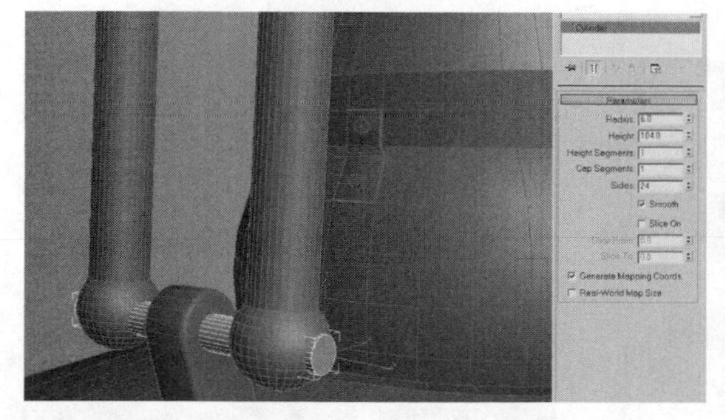

Figure 3-503

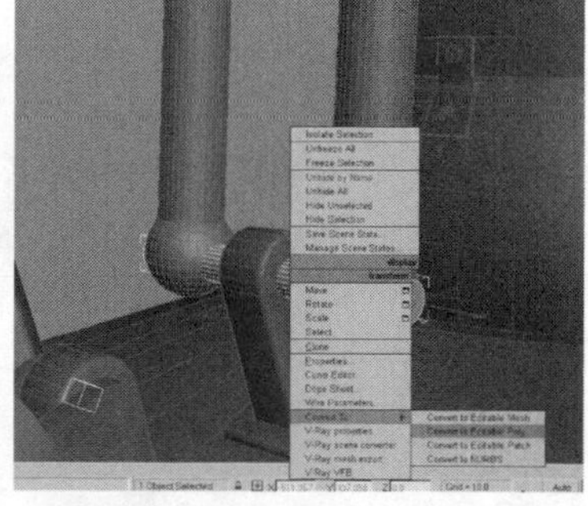

Figure 3-504

29. Attach the cylinder to the two vertical shafts. Create a Dummy, name it **upper_front_foot_control**, and center it on the top mount, then Select and Link the dummy to the mount.

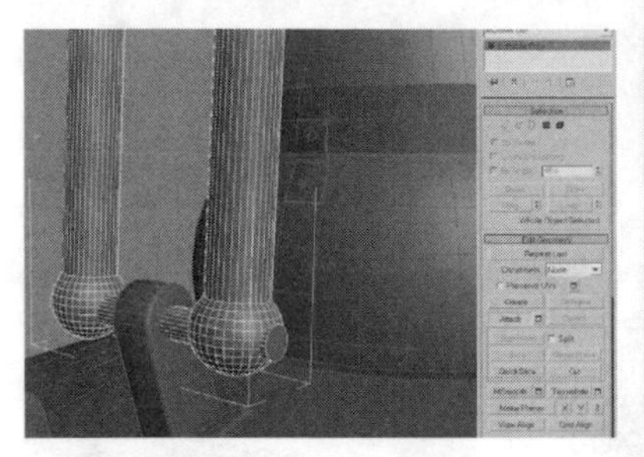

Figure 3-505

Figure 3-506

30. Detach the front mount and rename it **cuff_front_mount** (this is so we'll be able to properly align the dummy to the mount). Hit the **H** key and select **upper_front_foot_control**.

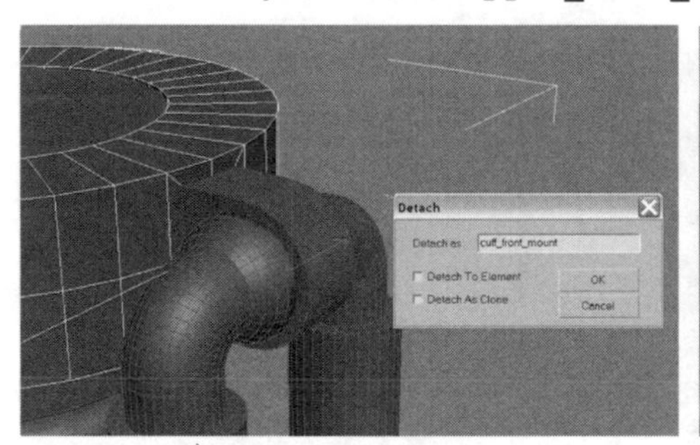

Figure 3-507

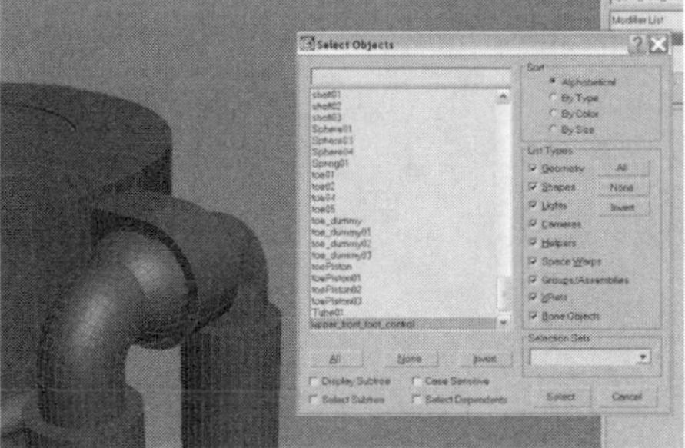

Figure 3-508

31. Click the **Align Selection** button, click the **cuff_front_mount**, and make sure **Center** is checked for both Current Object and Target Object. Select the shafts and assign a LookAt controller set to **Rotation.**

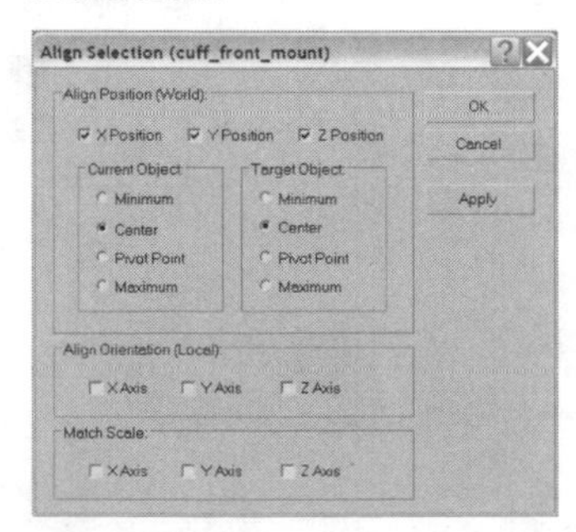

Figure 3-509

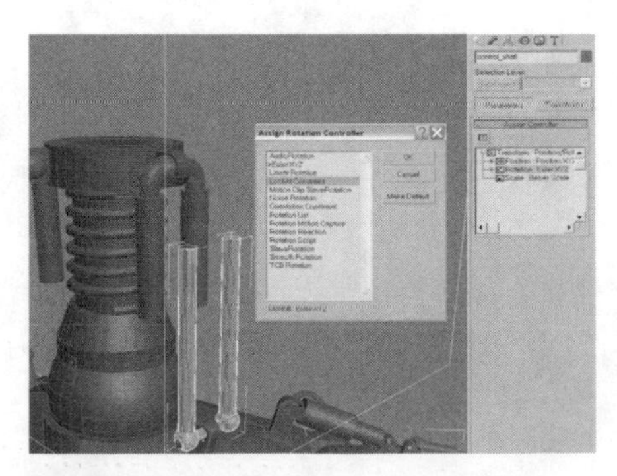

Figure 3-510

32. Click **Add LookAt Target**. Select the **upper_front_foot_control**, go to the Hierarchy tab, click **Affect Pivot Only**, and Rotate the object's pivot **–180** in the X axis.

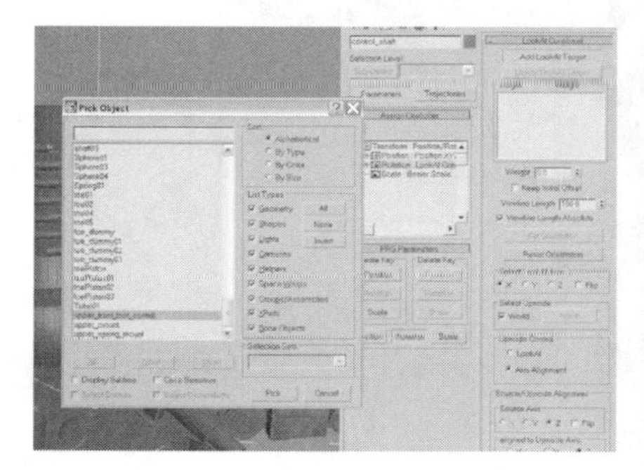

Figure 3-511

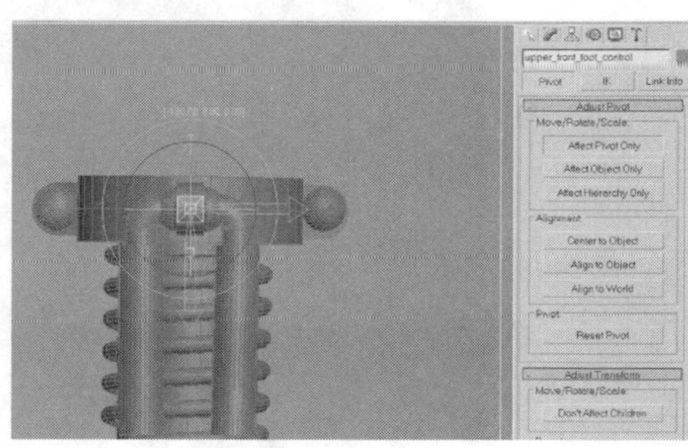

Figure 3-512

33. Set the LookAt Axis to **Y**, click **Flip**, set the Upnode Control to **LookAt**, and set the Source Axis to **X.** Select and Link the shafts to the foot.

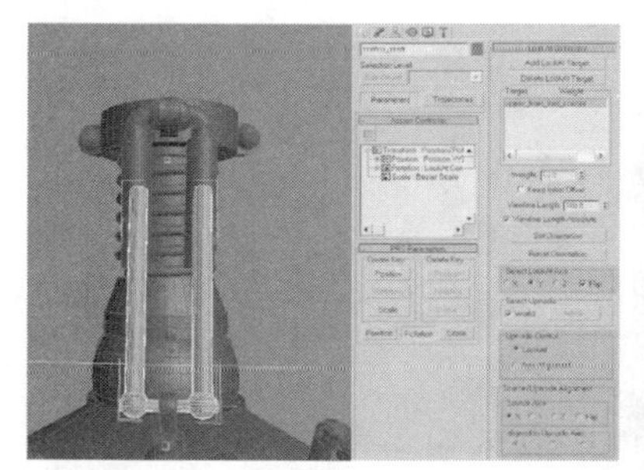

Figure 3-513

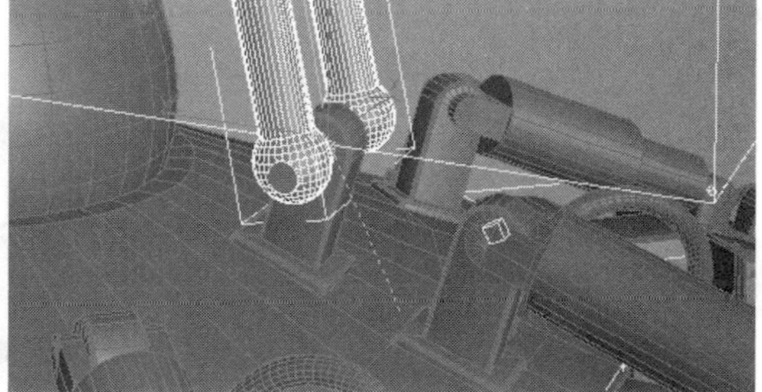

Figure 3-514

34. Create a Dummy in the center of the front foot mount. Align the dummy to the center of big_mount04.

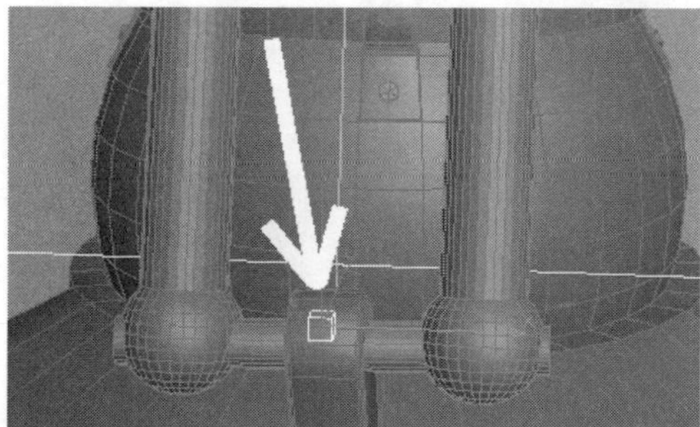

Figure 3-515

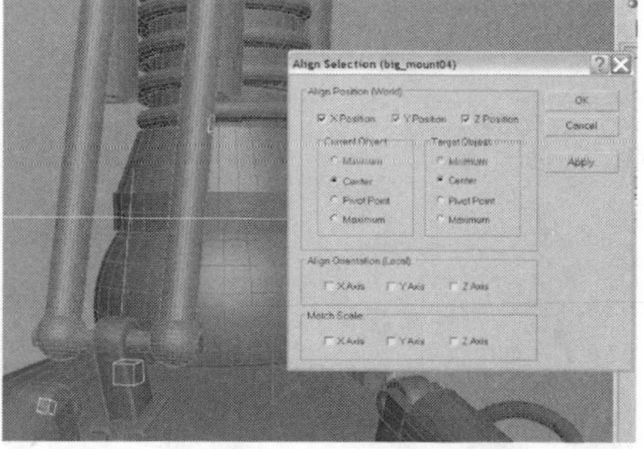

Figure 3-516

35. Select and Link the dummy to the foot and name it **front_foot_control**.

Figure 3-517

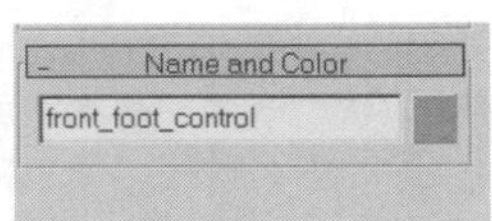

Figure 3-518

36. Select the top front pistons and assign a LookAt controller to its Rotation. Click **Add LookAt Target** and pick the **front_foot_control** dummy object.

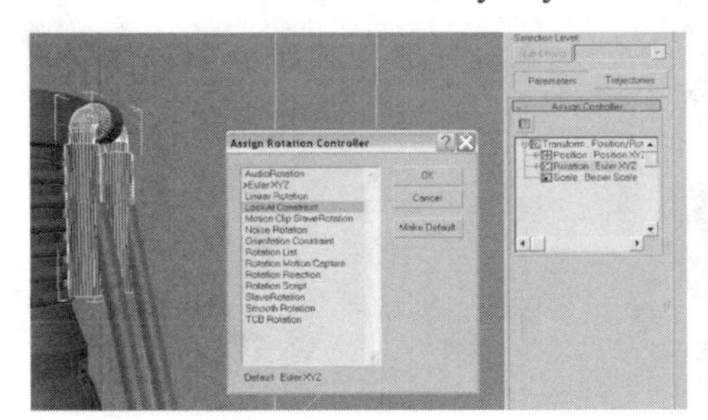

Figure 3-519

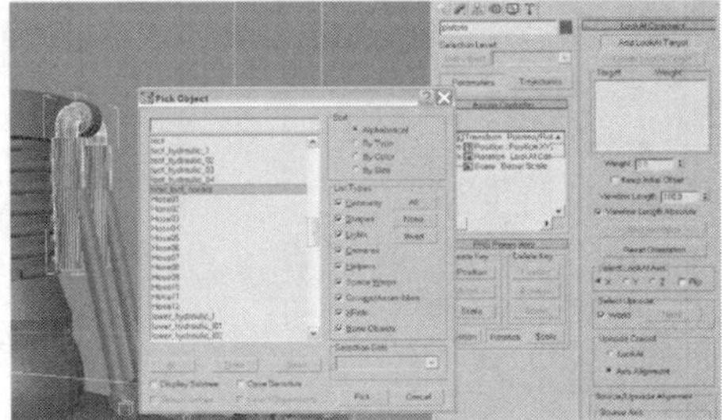

Figure 3-520

37. Select **Affect Pivot Only** and rotate until the pistons align with the shafts.

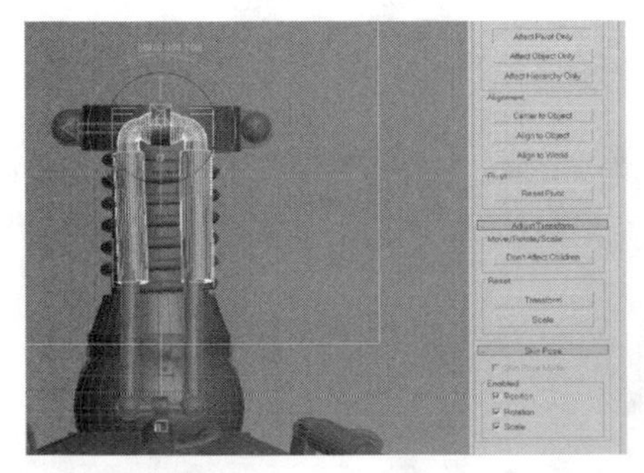

Figure 3-521

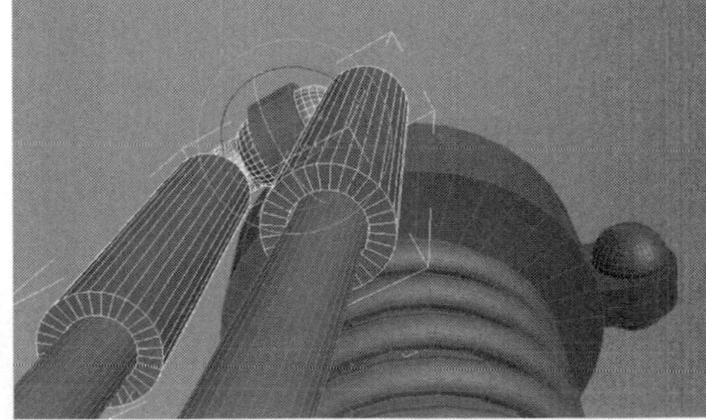

Figure 3-522

38. Switch to Vertex selection mode, select the vertices on the bottom of the pistons, and move them to tweak their alignment with the control shafts. Clone the front control shaft and move it to the rear.

Figure 3-523

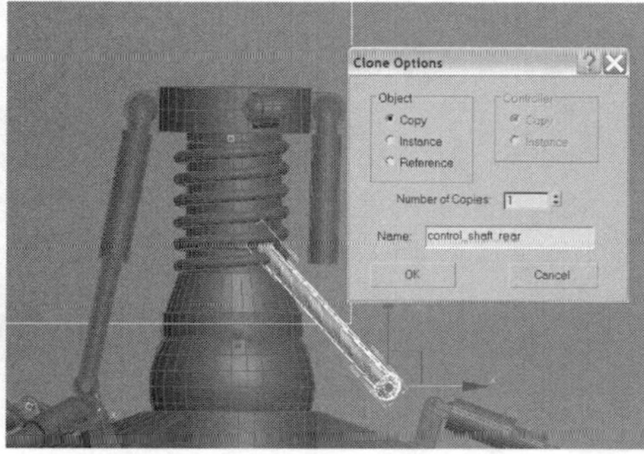

Figure 3-524

39. Clone the front foot mount and move it to the rear. Select and Link the cloned mount to the rear of the foot.

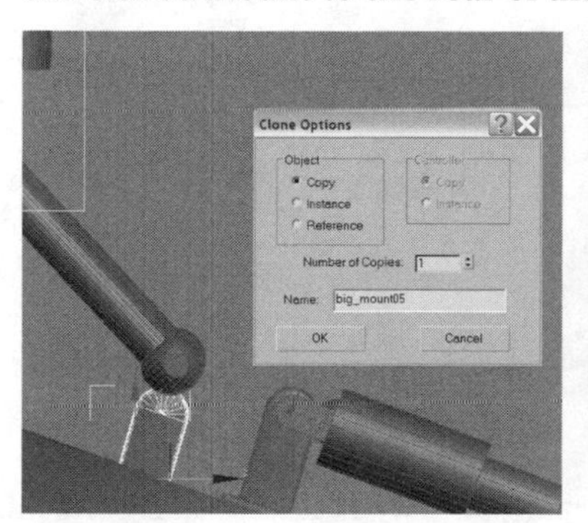

Figure 3-525

Figure 3-526

40. Create a Dummy in the center of the top rear mount and name it **upper_foot_control_rear**. Detach the rear mount, just as you did with the front, Select and Link it to the tube, and align the centers of the dummy you just made and the upper_rear_foot_mount.

Figure 3-527

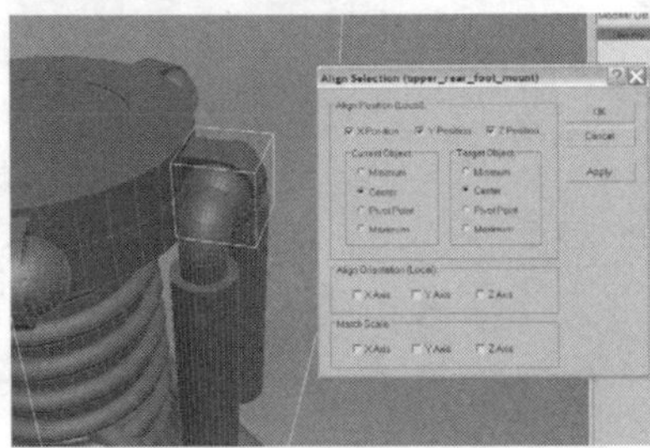

Figure 3-528

41. Assign a LookAt controller to the Rotation of the rear control shafts. Click **Add LookAt Target** and choose the **upper_foot_control_rear** dummy.

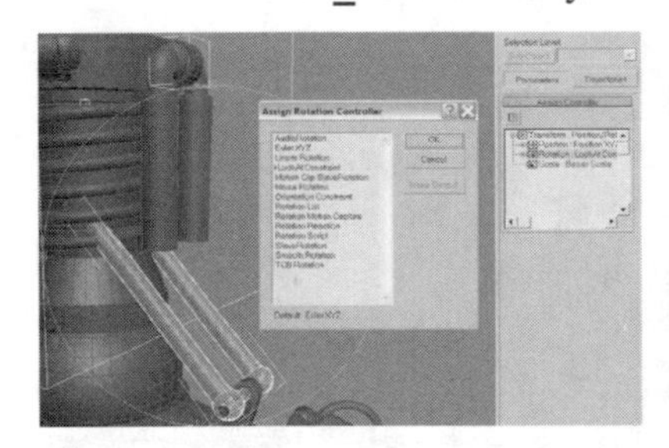

Figure 3-529

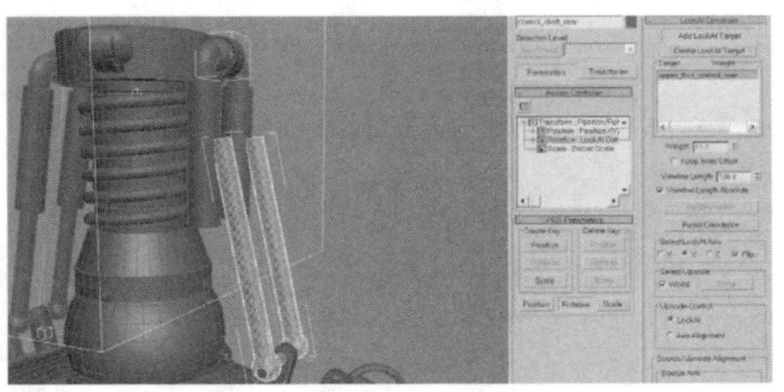

Figure 3-530

42. Create a Dummy and name it **lower_rear_foot_control**. Align it to the center of the big_mount05 that you moved to the rear.

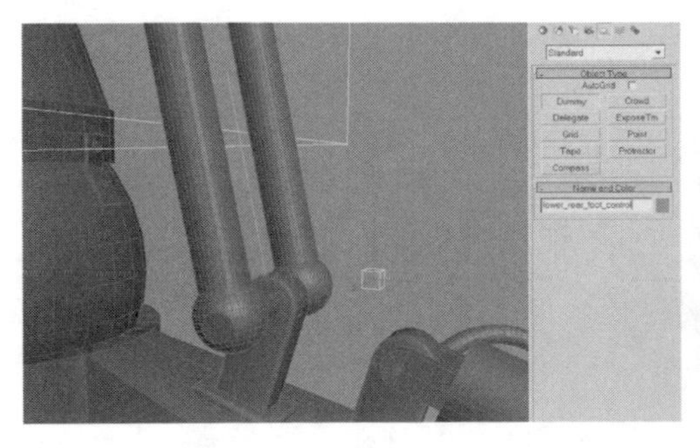

Figure 3-531

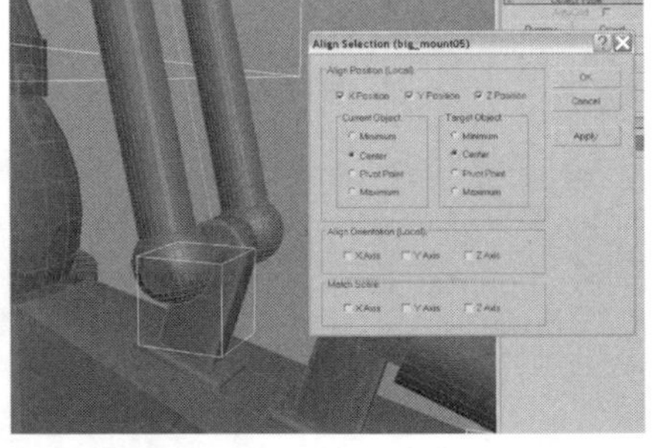

Figure 3-532

43. Assign a LookAt controller to the Rotation of the top rear pistons. Assign the LookAt Target to **lower_rear_foot_control**.

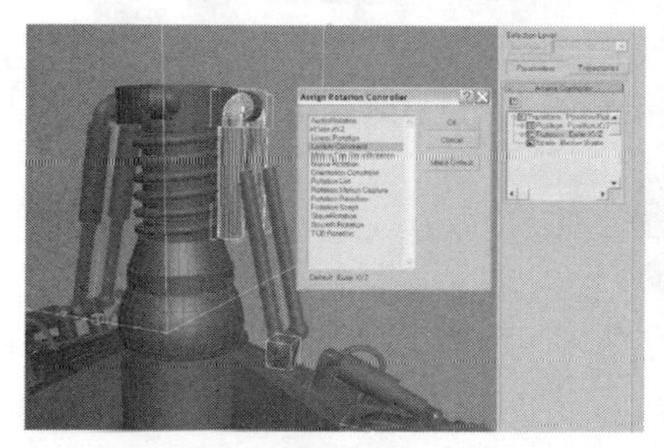

Figure 3-533

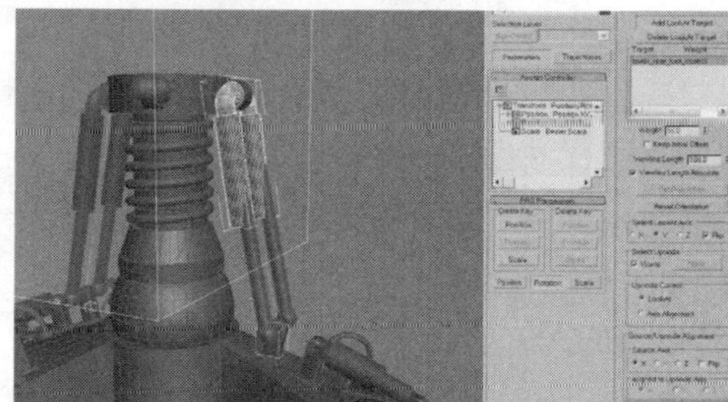

Figure 3-534

44. Select the rear piston assembly, click the **Hierarchy** tab, click **Affect Pivot Only**, and rotate the pivot until the pistons and the rear control shafts align.

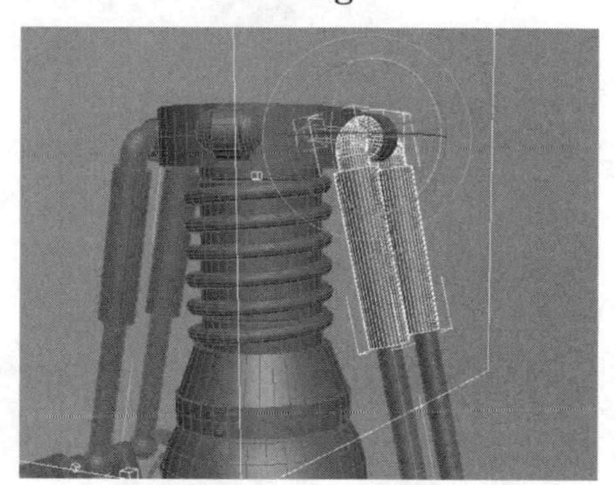

Figure 3-535

Day 6: Assembling the Middle Leg

1. Select the polygon on top of the cylinder and Bevel it:

Type	Height	Outline	Apply/OK
Group	3	0	Apply
Group	0	13	Apply
Group	55	0	OK

Figure 3-536

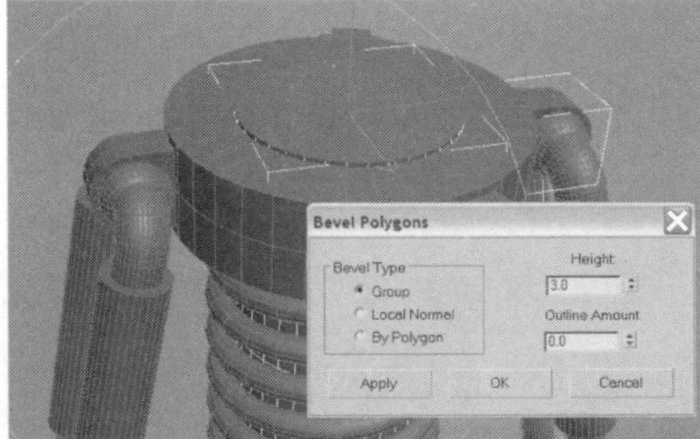

Figure 3-537

Figure 3-538

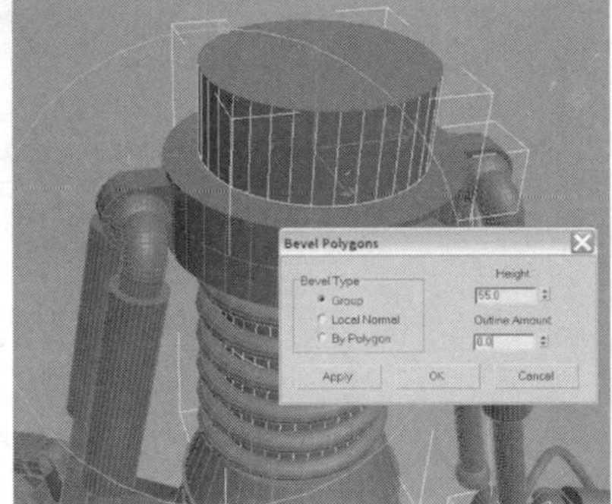

Figure 3-539

2. Create a Box on top of the cylinder and then convert it to an Editable Polygon.

Length	Width	Height	Length/Width/Height Segs
195.636	196.502	206.674	1/1/1

Day 6: Assembling the Middle Leg

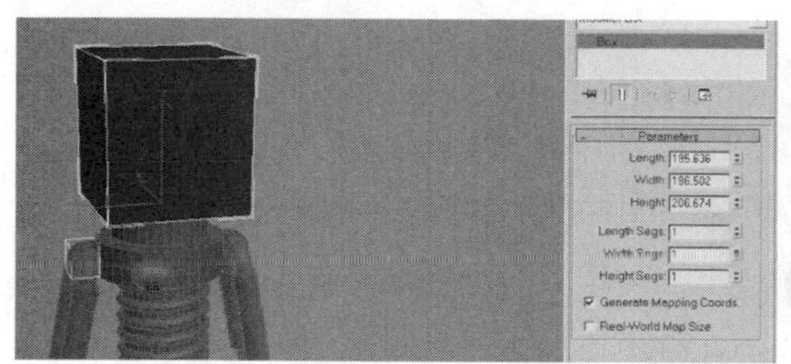

Figure 3-540

Figure 3-541

3. Create a Cylinder and position it over the corner of the box as shown. Convert it to an Editable Polygon, select the box, go to the Create panel and select **Compound Objects**, and then click the **Boolean** button.

Radius	Height	Height/Cap Segs	Sides	Smooth
105	216	1/1	36	Checked

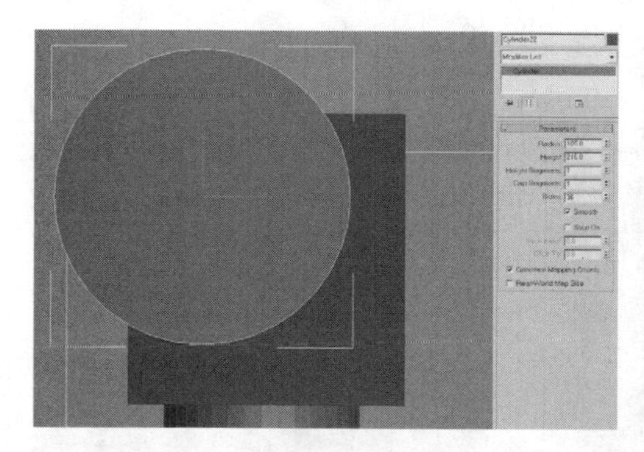

Figure 3-542

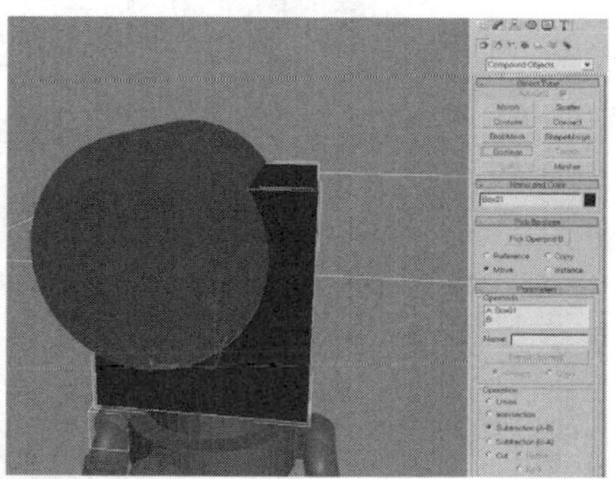

Figure 3-543

4. Click **Pick Operand B** and click **Cylinder22** to subtract it from the box.

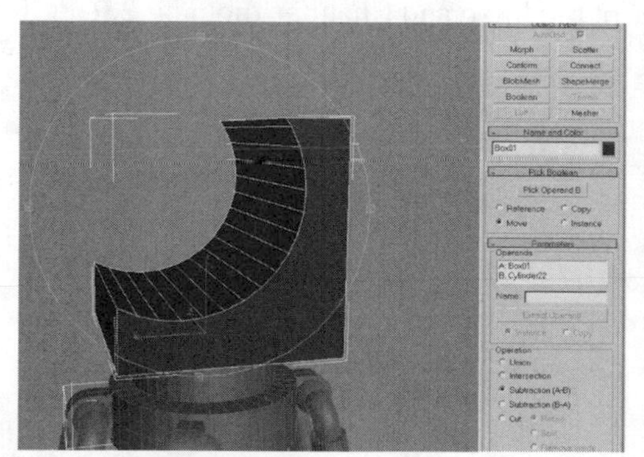

Figure 3-544

Figure 3-545

5. Select and Link the knee to the collar at the ankle (you could connect it to the cylinder, but it's kinda hard to get to with the spring in the way). Move its pivot to the middle of the knee.

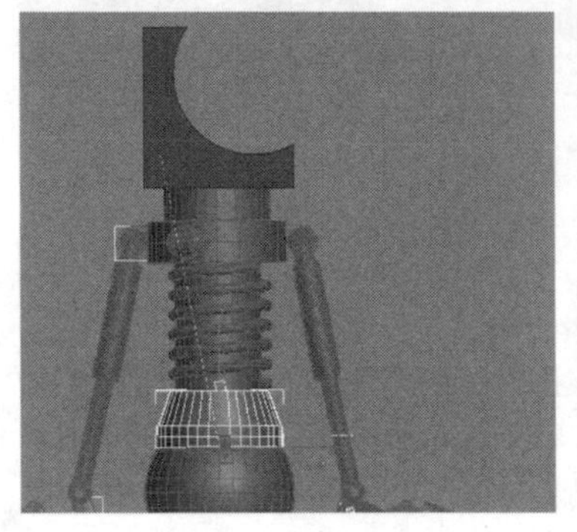

Figure 3-546

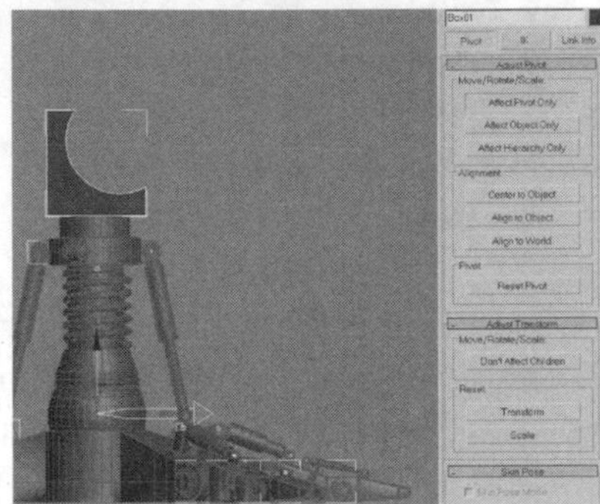

Figure 3-547

6. Use Rotate to angle the leg slightly back and then convert the knee from a Boolean to an Editable Polygon.

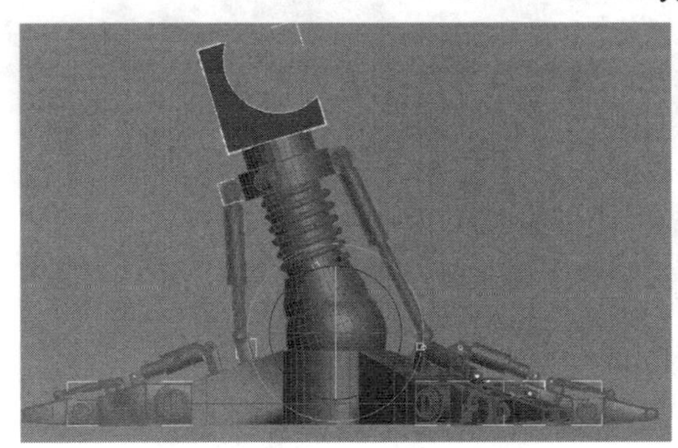

Figure 3-548

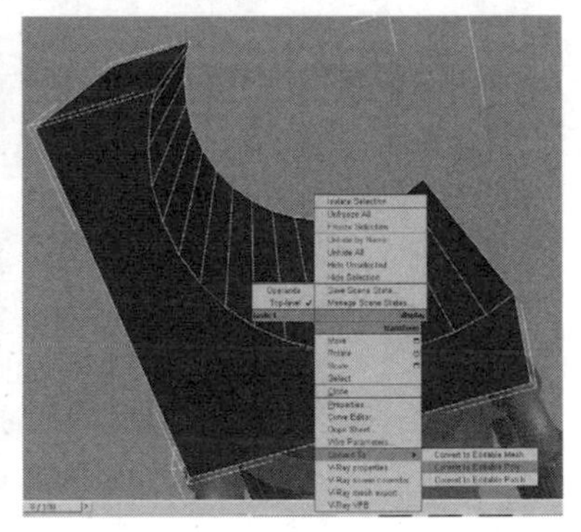

Figure 3-549

7. Select the outer edges of the knee and Chamfer them by **2.0** and then by **0.812**.

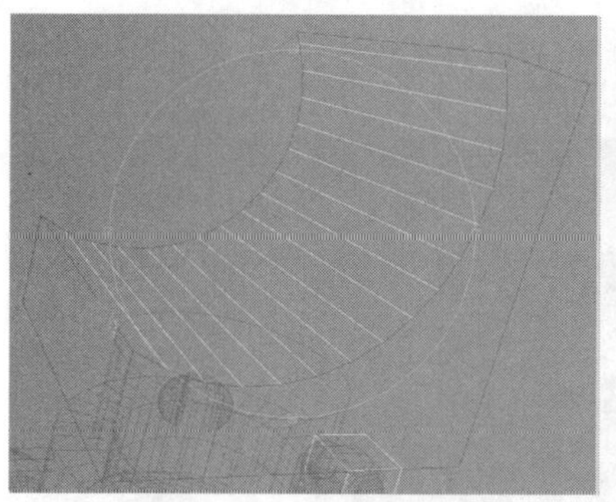

Figure 3-550

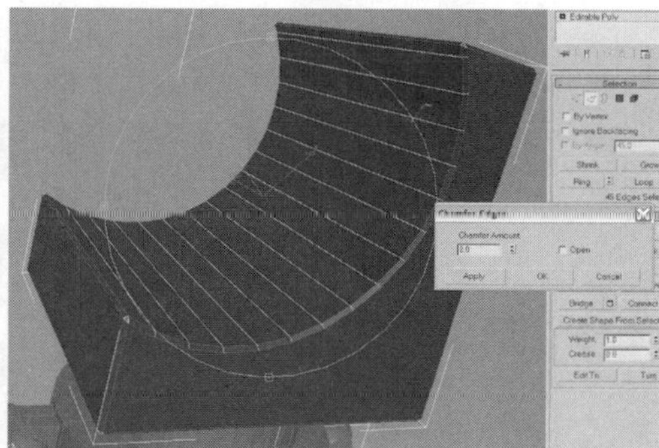

Figure 3-551

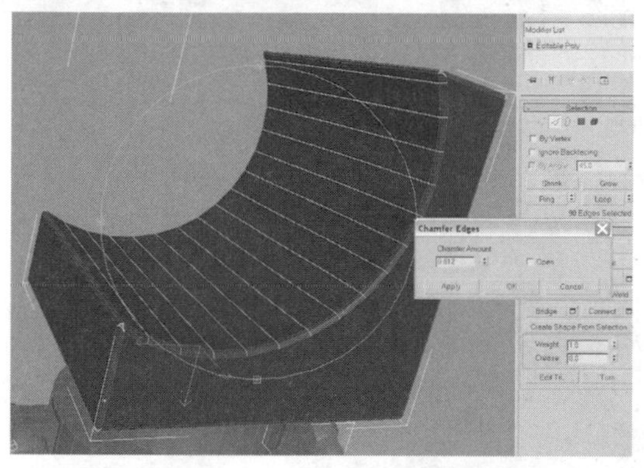

Figure 3-552

8. Add a Smooth modifier to the stack and create a Box in the lower-left corner of the rear.

Length	Width	Height	Length/Width/Height Segs
76	98	5	4/3/1

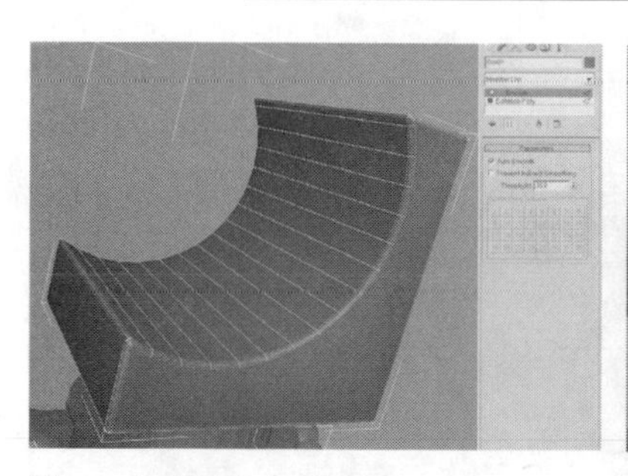

Figure 3-553

Figure 3-554

9. Convert the box to an Editable Polygon, select the top edges, and Chamfer them by **0.4** and then **0.14**.

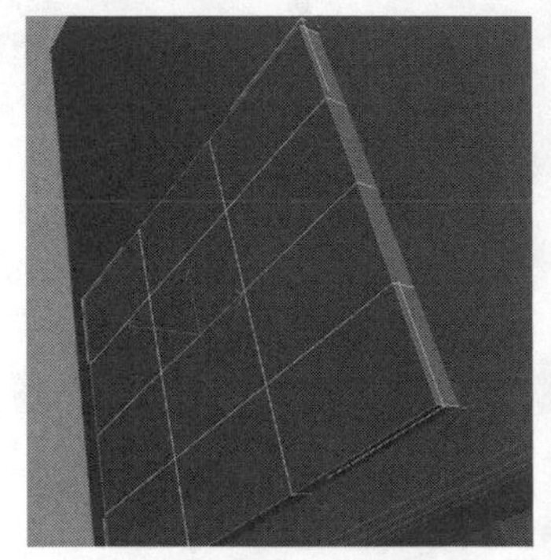

Figure 3-555

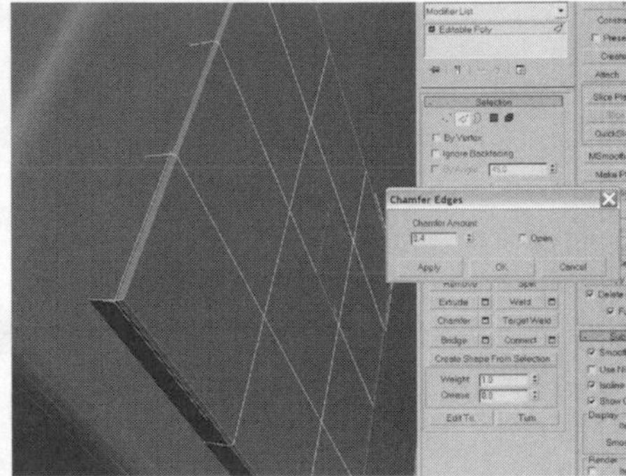

Figure 3-556

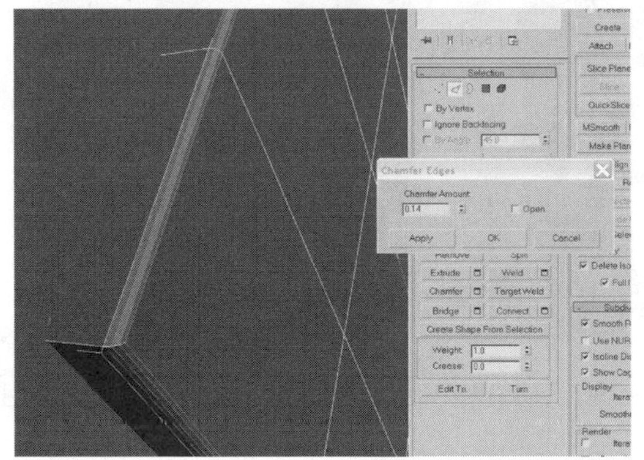

Figure 3-557

10. Select the two polygons as shown in Figure 3-558 and Bevel them:

Type	Height	Outline	Apply/OK
Group	0	–2	Apply
Group	15.01	0	OK

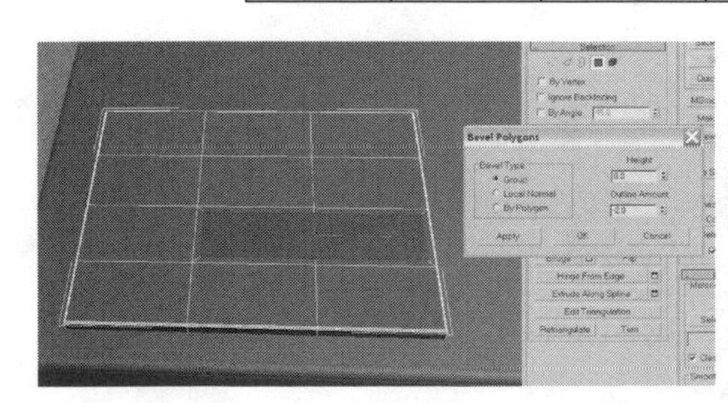

Figure 3-558

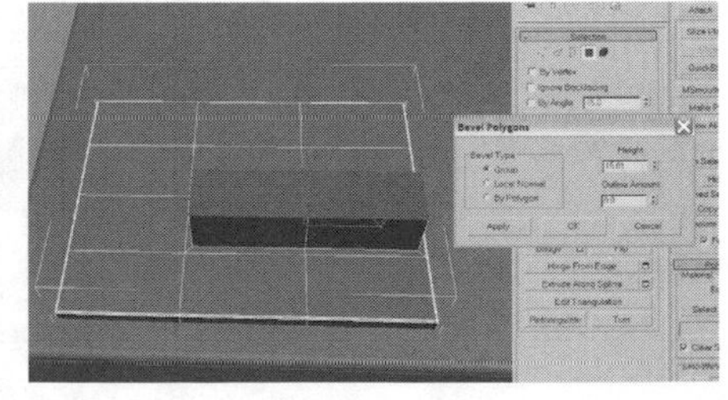

Figure 3-559

11. Select the lower middle polygon as shown and Bevel it:

Type	Height	Outline	Apply/OK
Group	0	–2	Apply
Group	4	0	OK

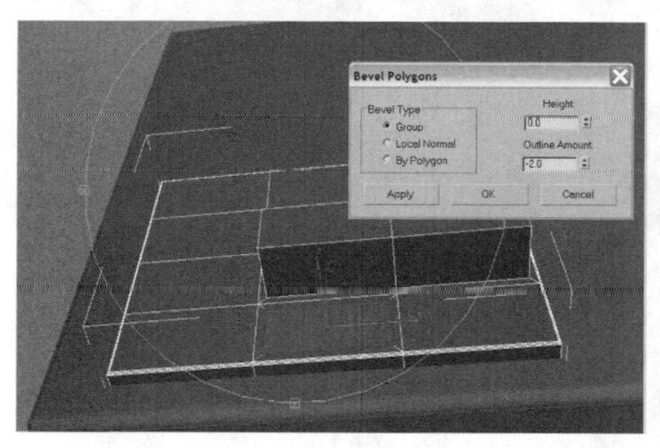

Figure 3-560

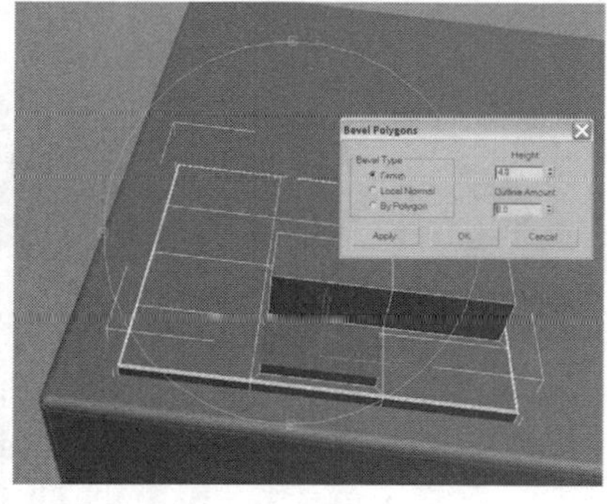

Figure 3-561

12. Create a Cylinder on the polygon you extruded in the previous step, and then convert the cylinder to an Editable Polygon.

Radius	Height	Height/Cap Segs	Sides	Smooth
3	2.5	1/1	36	Checked

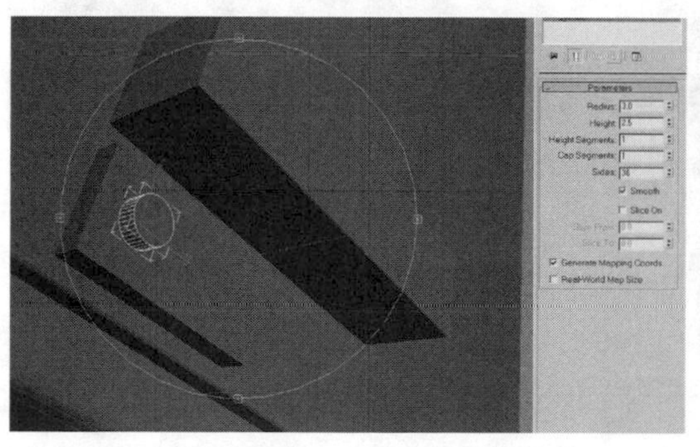

Figure 3-562

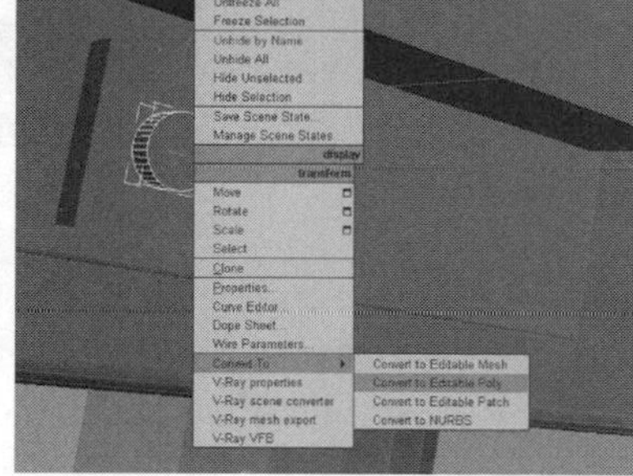

Figure 3-563

13. Select the cylinder cap and Extrude it **1.0** 10 times. Move the pivot point to the edge just before the extrusions.

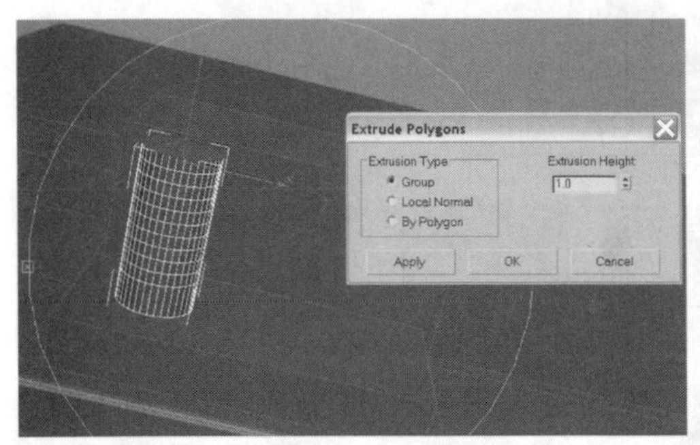

Figure 3-564

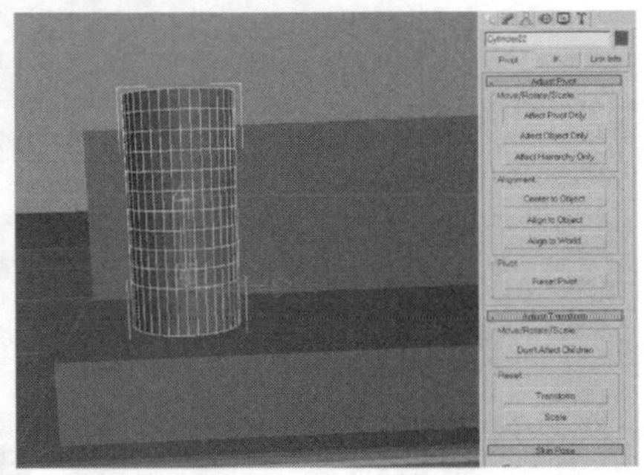

Figure 3-565

14. Add a Bend modifier with an Angle of **90** and a Direction of **–90** to the stack. Click the **Limit Effect** check box and set the Upper Limit to **9.8**. Right-click and convert the pipe to an Editable Polygon.

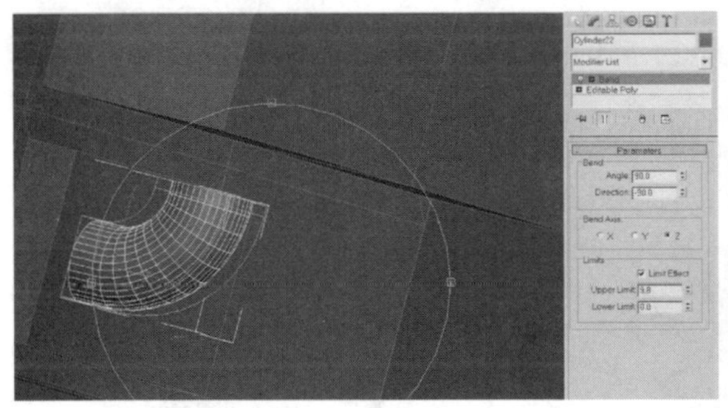

Figure 3-566

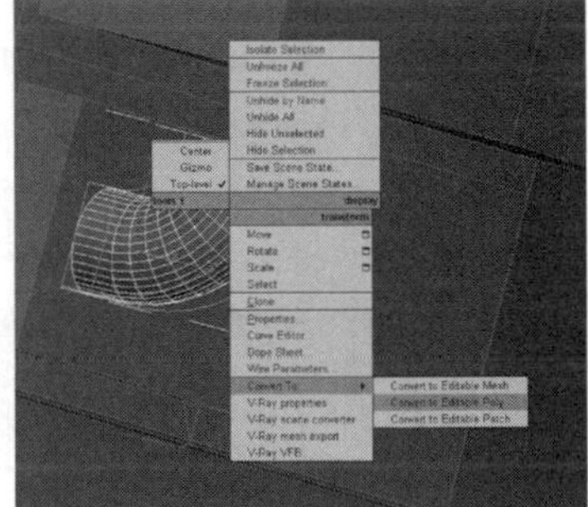

Figure 3-567

15. Use the Move tool to position the edge of the pipe just below the surface of the box. Select the cylinder cap and use the Move tool to stretch it up under the upper edge of the upper box.

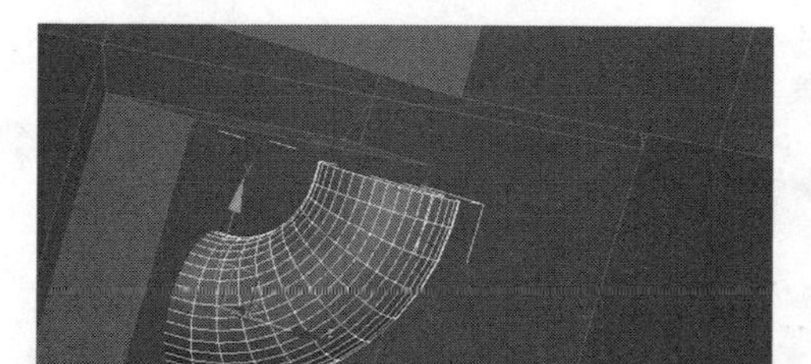

Figure 3-568

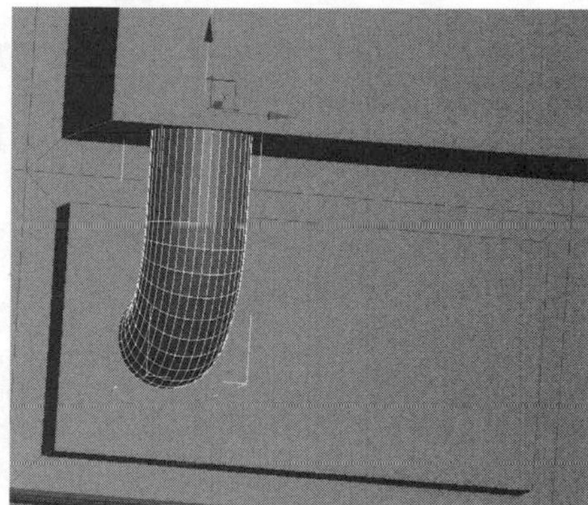

Figure 3-569

16. Make two clones of the pipe, position them as shown, and Select and Link them to the box above.

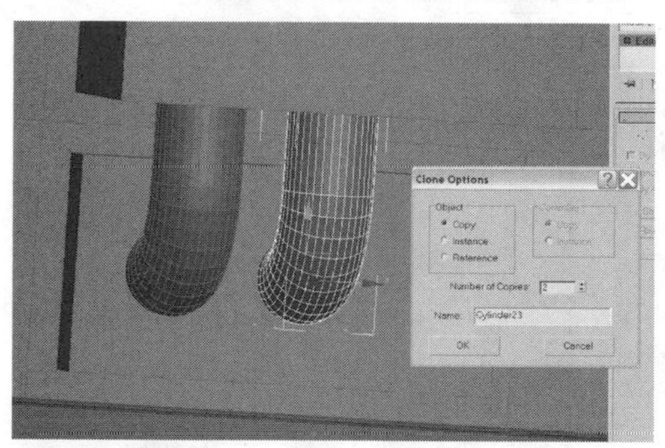

Figure 3-570

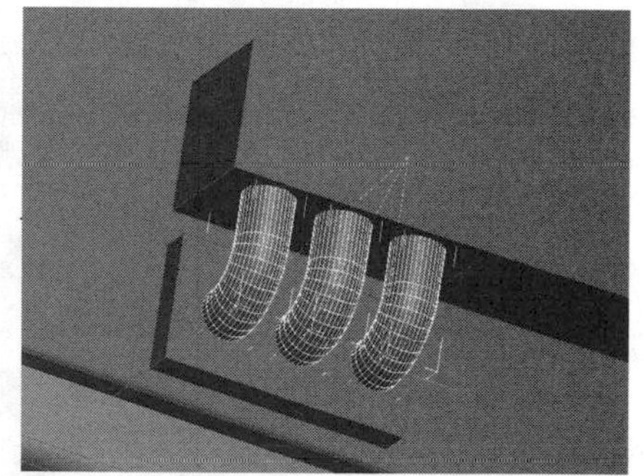

Figure 3-571

17. Create a Box at the upper-right corner of the other box and convert it to an Editable Polygon.

Length	Width	Height	Length/Width/Height Segs
30	60	15	1/1/1

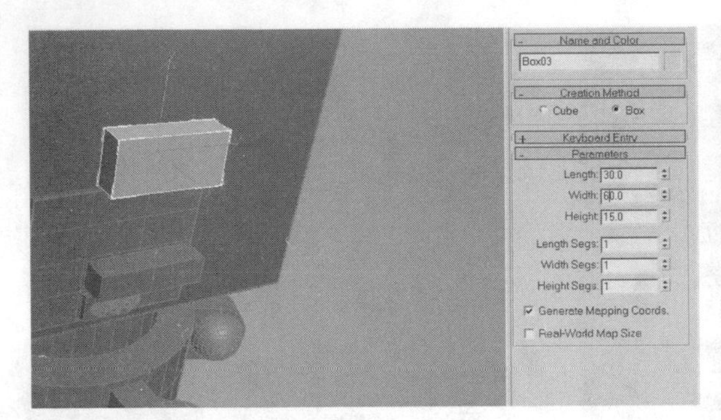

Figure 3-572

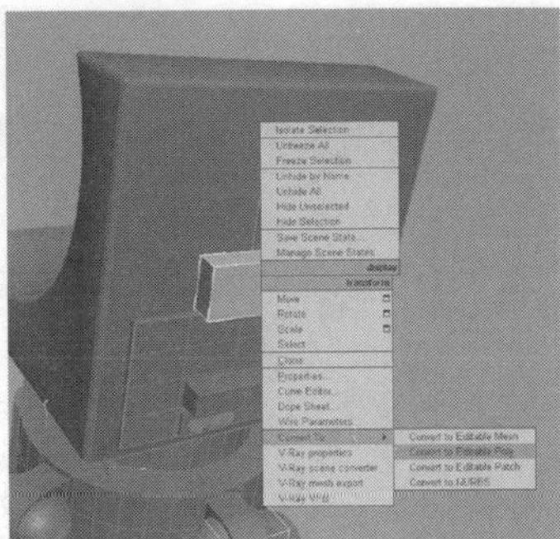

Figure 3-573

18. Select the top of the box you just made and Bevel it.

Type	Height	Outline	Apply/OK
Group	0	–1.6	Apply
Group	1.5	0	Apply

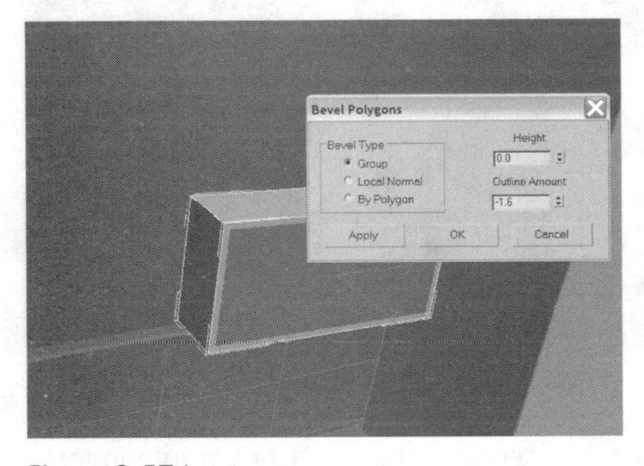

Figure 3-574

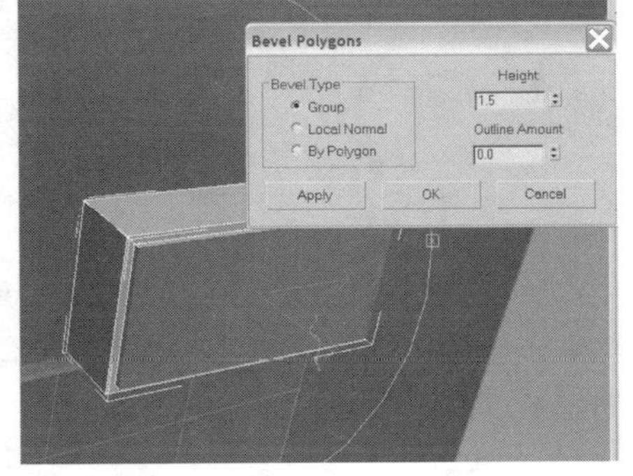

Figure 3-575

Type	Height	Outline	Apply/OK
Group	0	–1.75	Apply
Group	–1.6	0	OK

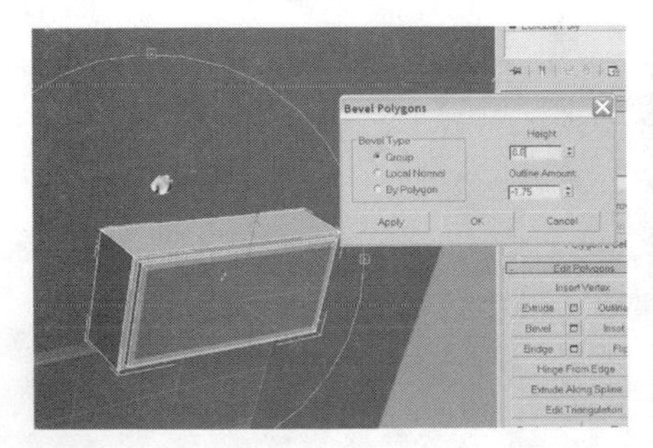

Figure 3-576

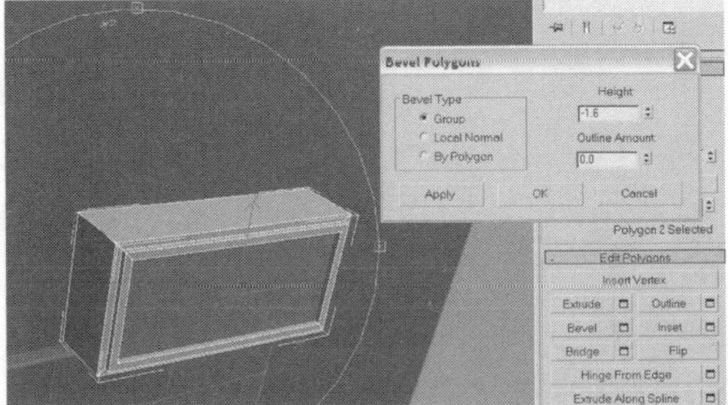

Figure 3-577

19. Click **Tessellate** and hit **Apply** five times, then hit **OK**. Click **Bevel Settings**:

Type	Height	Outline	Apply/OK
By Polygon	0	–0.5	Apply
By Polygon	–2.6	0	OK

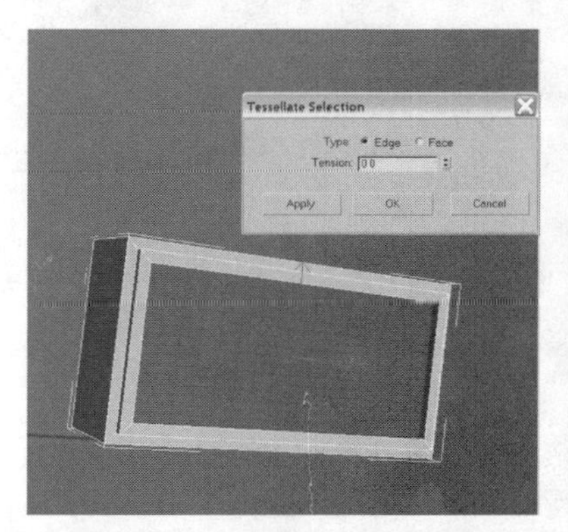

Figure 3-578

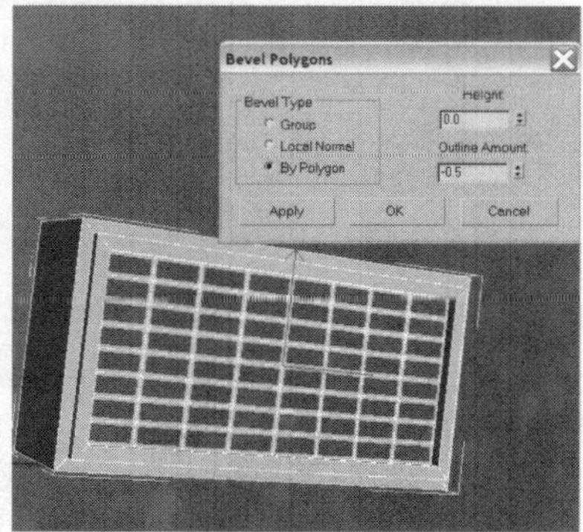

Figure 3-579

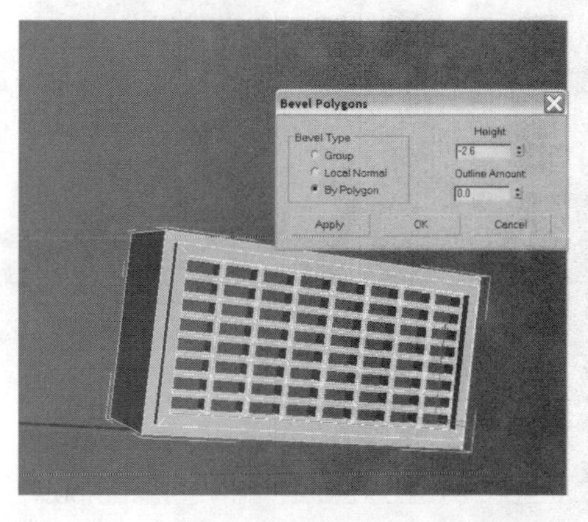

Figure 3-580

20. Create a Cylinder and clone it three times.

Radius	Height	Height/Cap Segs	Sides	Smooth
2.6	61	1/1	24	Checked

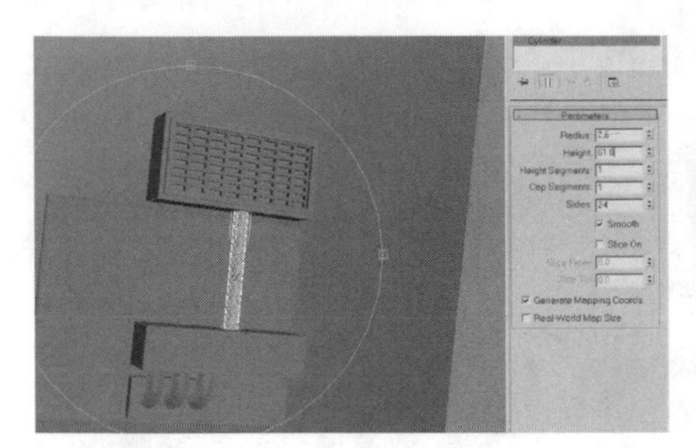

Figure 3-581

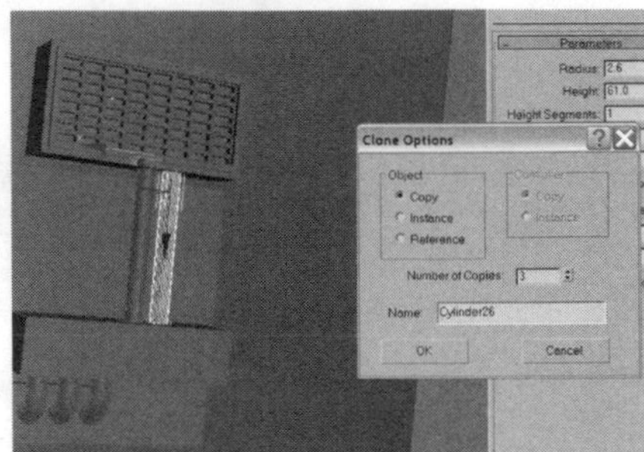

Figure 3-582

FYI: You can put the pipes wherever you like. There is nothing special about where I placed them, other than I thought it was more visually interesting to place them opposite the bent pipes.

21. Select all the pipes and Select and Link them to the knee. Create a GeoSphere with a Radius of **5**, **2** Segments, and a Type of **Icosa.**

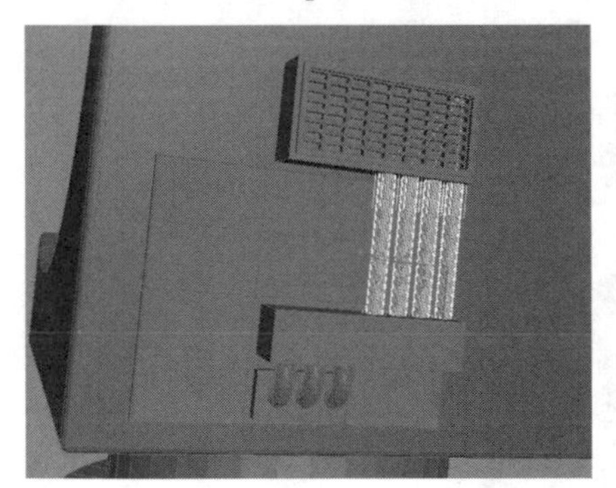

Figure 3-583

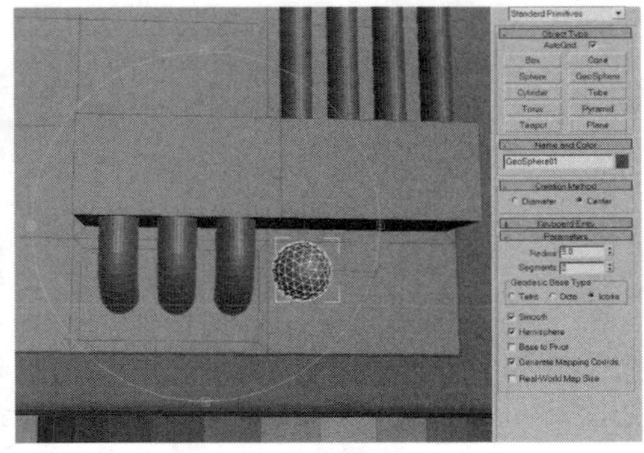

Figure 3-584

22. Convert the geosphere to an Editable Polygon and polygon-select the entire object. Click **Bevel Settings**:

Type	Height	Outline	Apply/OK
By Polygon	0	–0.2	Apply
By Polygon	–0.32	0	OK

Day 6: Assembling the Middle Leg

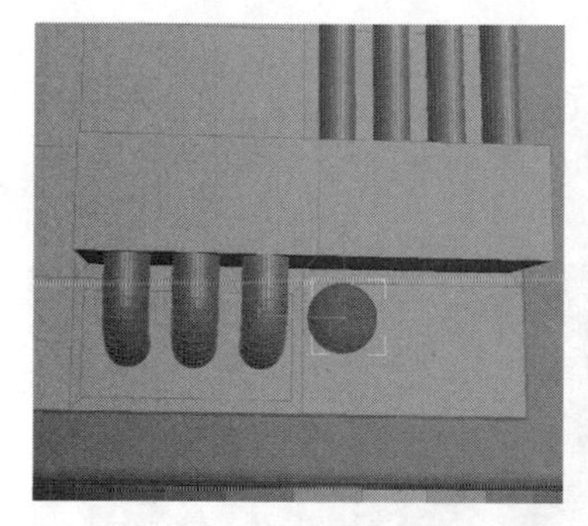

Figure 3-585

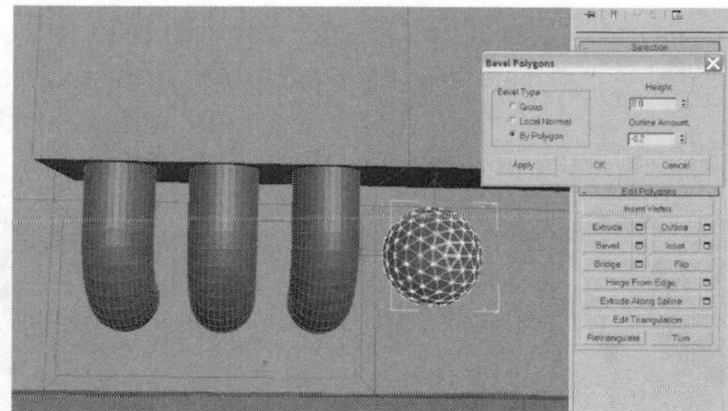

Figure 3-586

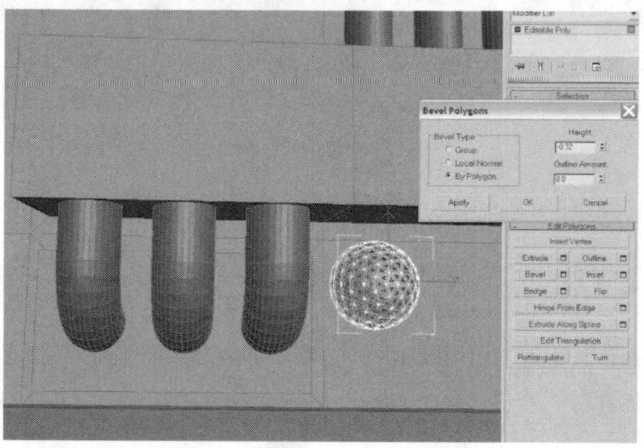

Figure 3-587

23. Create a Tube to the left of the boxes above the curved pipes. (*Note: The location of this object is important.*) Name the tube **lower_knee_hydraulic01**.

Radius 1	Radius 2	Height	Height/Cap Segs	Sides	Smooth
5.75	7.45	3.5	1/1	18	Checked

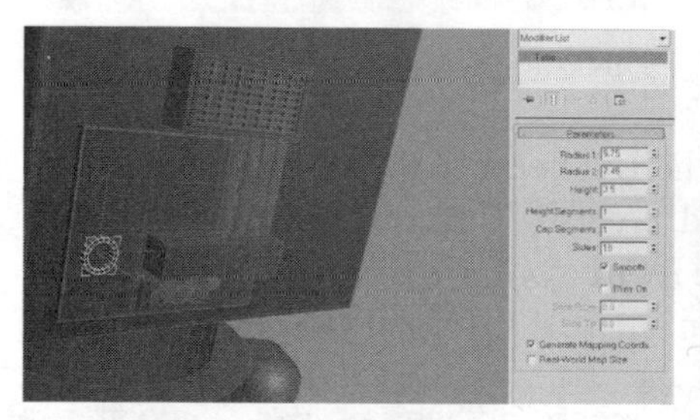

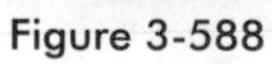

Figure 3-588

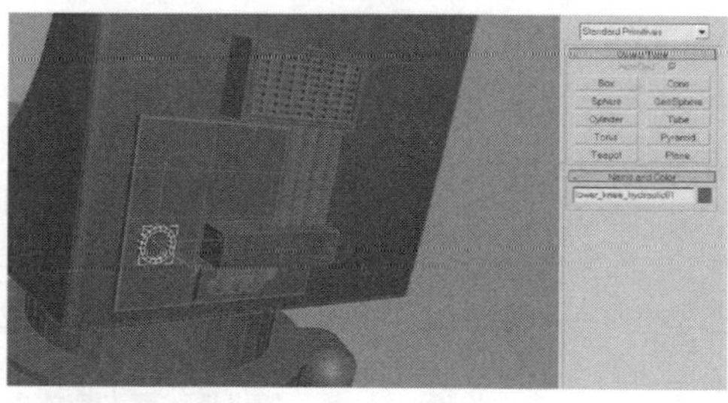

Figure 3-589

24. Create a Dummy and center it in the tube you just created, and name it **calf_hydraulic_link_front.** Clone the dummy and move it down to the hemispheric mount on the left side, and name it **lower_knee_hydraulic02.**

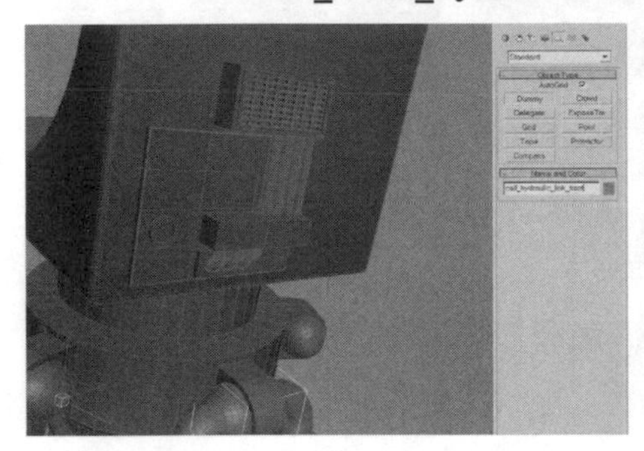

Figure 3-590

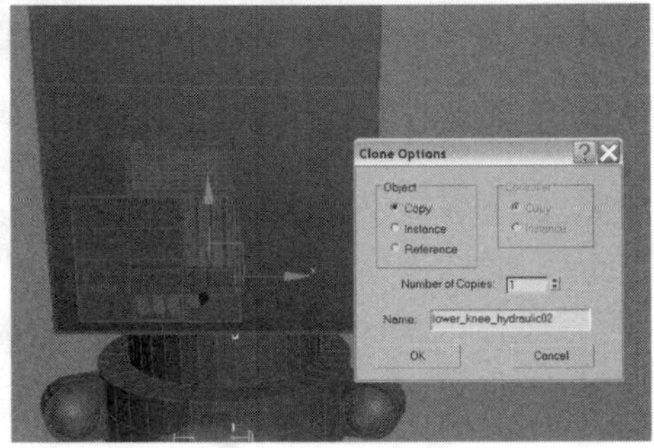

Figure 3-591

25. Create a Hose, switch the End Point Method to **Bound to Object Pivots**, and set the Top Binding Object to **lower_knee_hydraulic**, and the Bottom Binding Object to to **calf_hydraulic_link_front.**

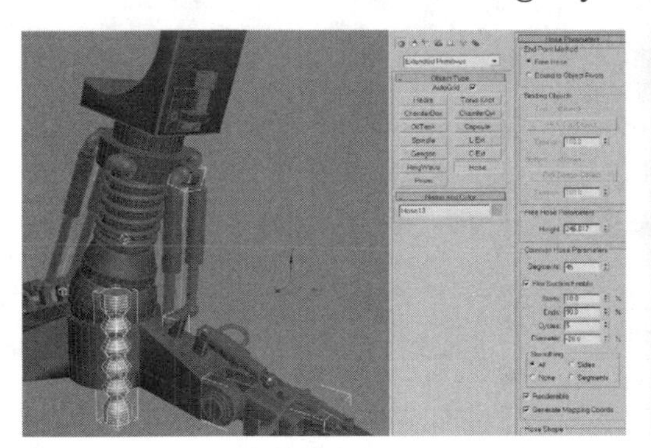

Figure 3-592

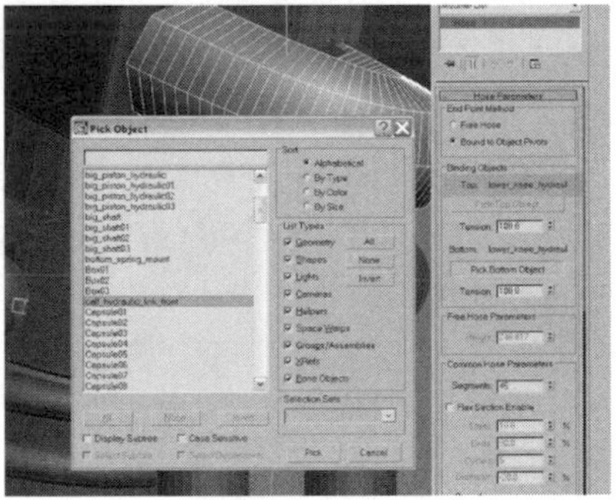

Figure 3-593

26. Set the hose type to **Round**, the Diameter to **9.242** and the number of Sides to **18.** Using AutoGrid, create a Tube on the left front control piston, and name the tube **front_foot_piston-nozzle.** Select and Link the tube to the piston.

Radius 1	Radius 2	Height	Height/Cap Segs	Sides	Smooth
5.75	7.45	3.5	1/1	18	Checked

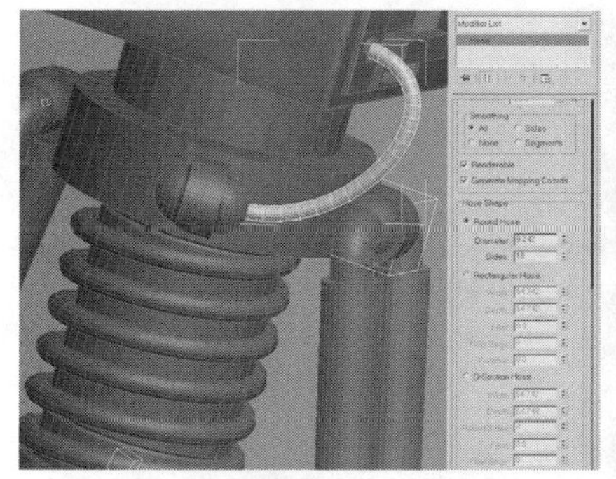

Figure 3-594

Figure 3-595

27. Create a Dummy on the front side of the hemisphere you connected the hose to in the last step, and name the dummy **front_hose_conduit**. Create another Hose.

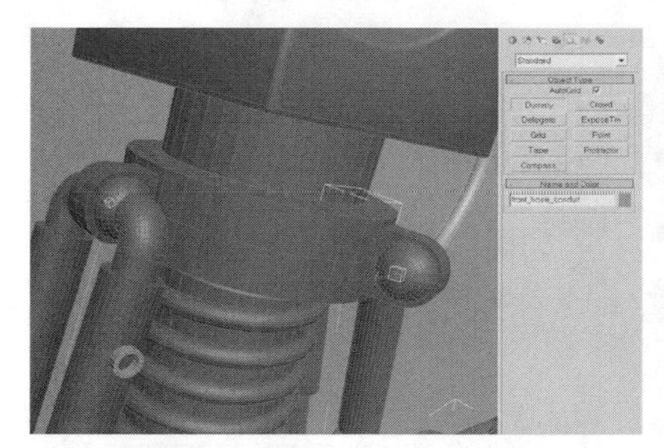

Figure 3-596

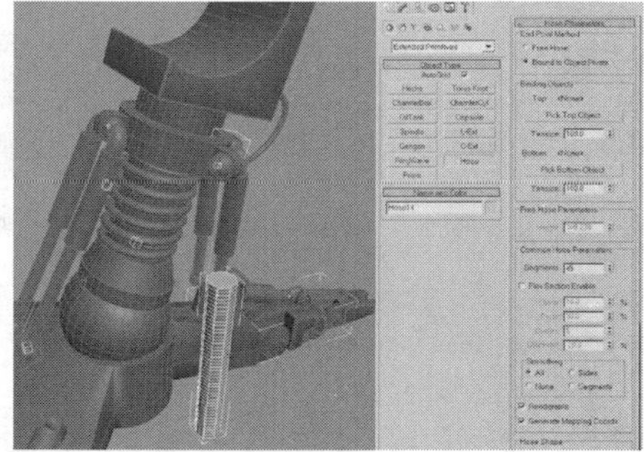

Figure 3-597

28. Set the Top Binding Object to **front_hose_conduit** and the Bottom Binding Object to **front_foot_piston-nozzle.** Set the hose to be **Round** and set both the Diameter and Sides to **12**.

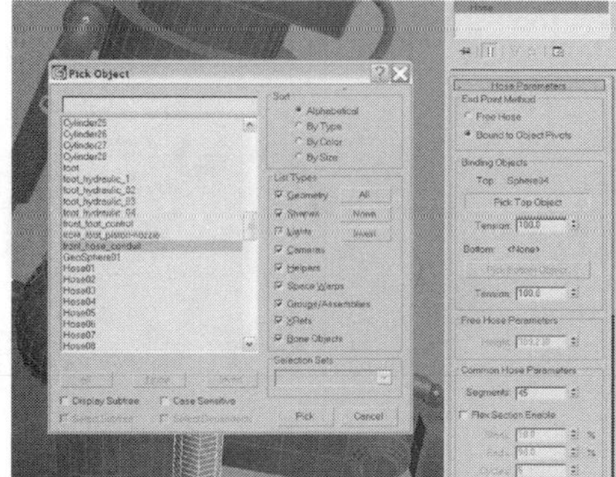

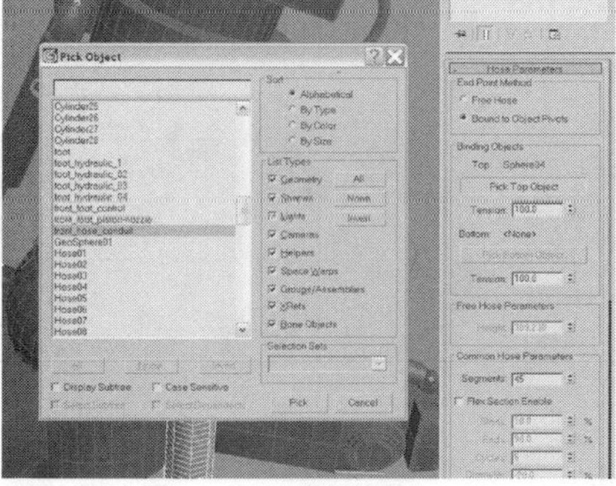

Figure 3-598

Figure 3-599

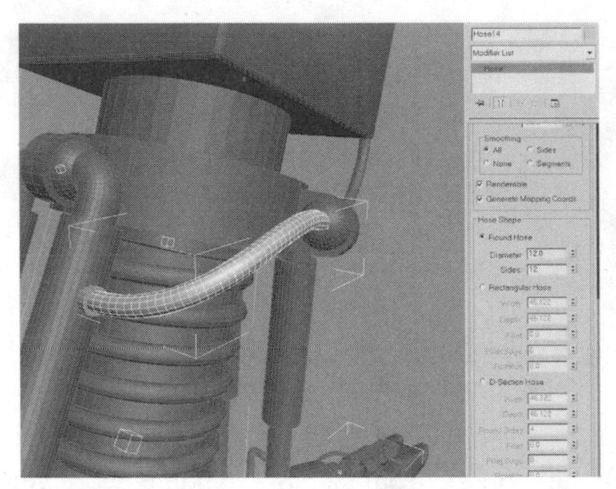

Figure 3-600

29. Create a Dummy on the right rear hemisphere, name it **rear_foot_hydraulic**, and create another Hose.

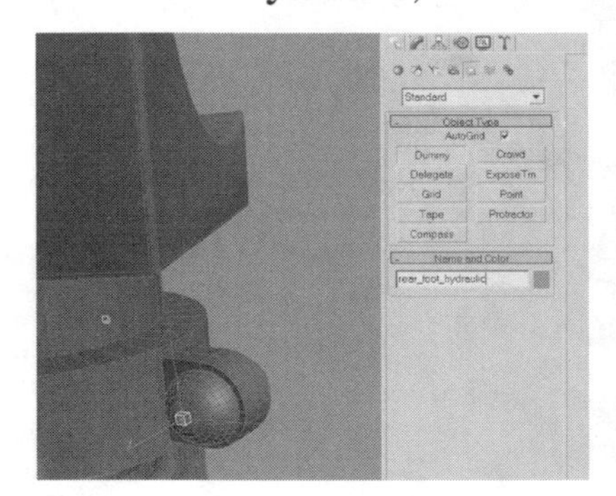

Figure 3-601

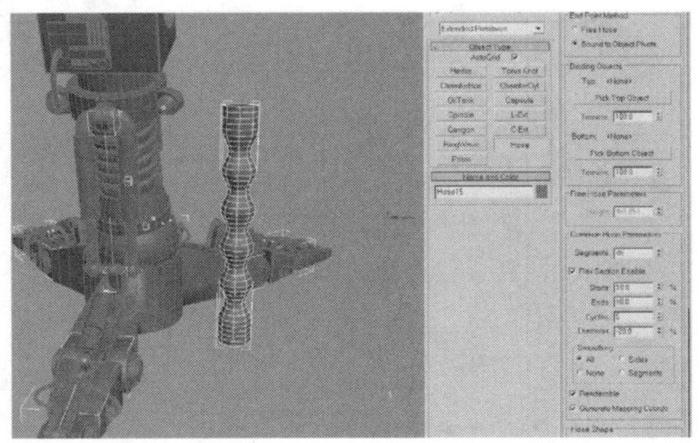

Figure 3-602

30. Set the hose's Top Binding Object to the clone of the tube you made on the lower-right corner (**lower_knee_hydraulic02**). Set the Bottom Binding Object to the **rear_foot_hydraulic**, make the hose **Round**, and set the Diameter to **11** and Sides to **12.** Create another Tube on the right rear control piston and name it **rear_foot_hydraulic_nozzle.**

Radius 1	Radius 2	Height	Height/Cap Segs	Sides	Smooth
9.4	7.4	10	1/1	18	Checked

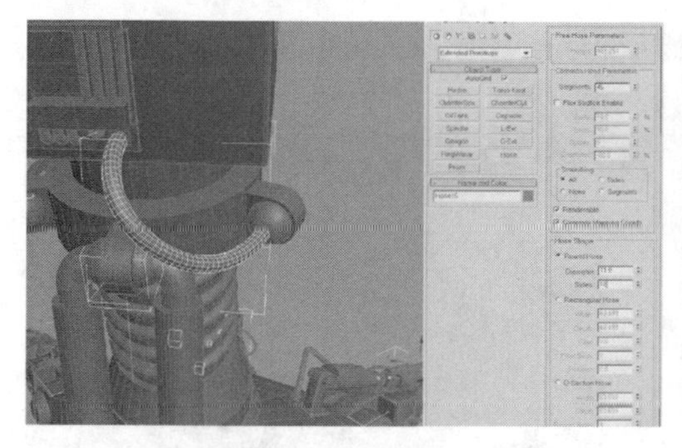

Figure 3-603

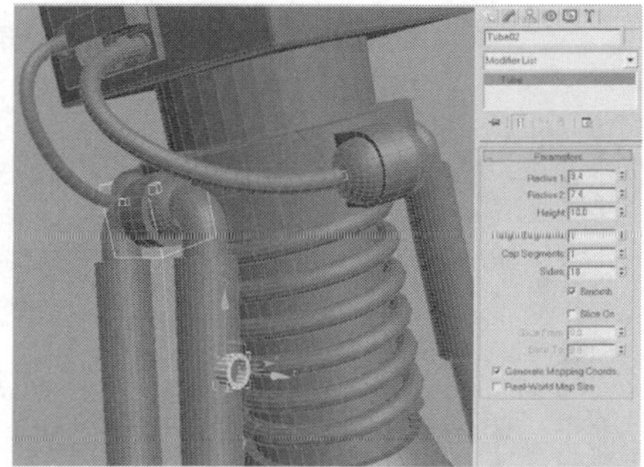

Figure 3-604

31. Create a Hose on the other side, using the same settings as in the previous step. Set its Top Binding Object to the **rear_foot_hydraulic_nozzle**. Set the Bottom Binding Object to the tube you made on the rear control piston in the previous step. Create a Cylinder in the kneecap you made using the Boolean object.

Radius	Height	Height/Cap Segs	Sides	Smooth
104.189	194.922	2/1	36	Checked

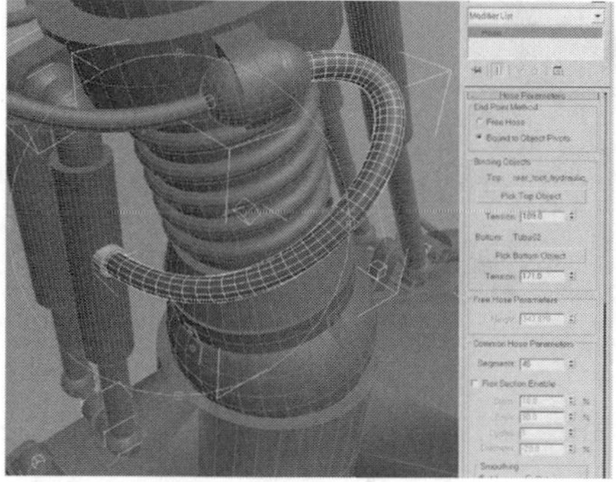

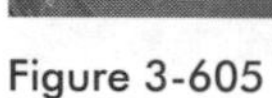

Figure 3-605

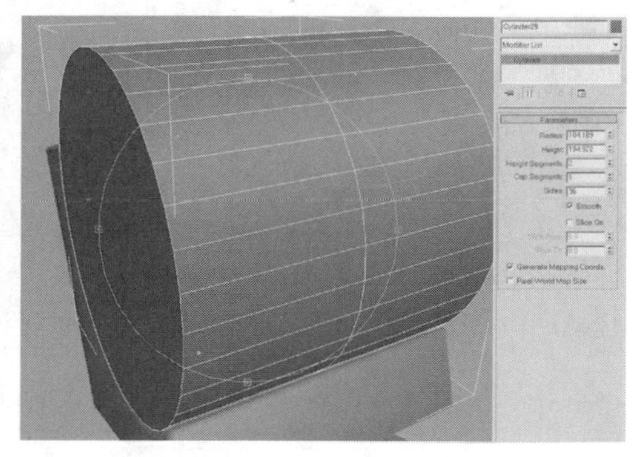

Figure 3-606

32. Convert the cylinder to an Editable Polygon and loop-select the middle edges. Chamfer the edges by **50**.

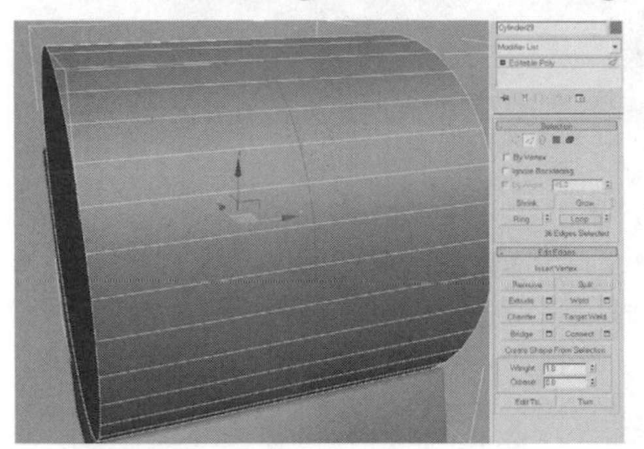

Figure 3-607

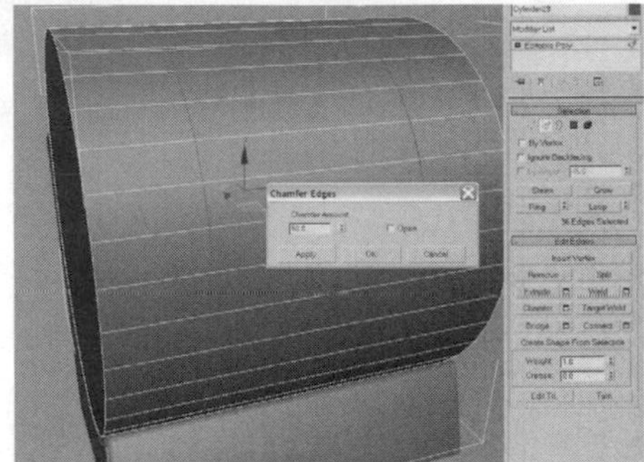

Figure 3-608

33. Select the middle polygons and Detach them as **lower_knee_hinge_middle**.

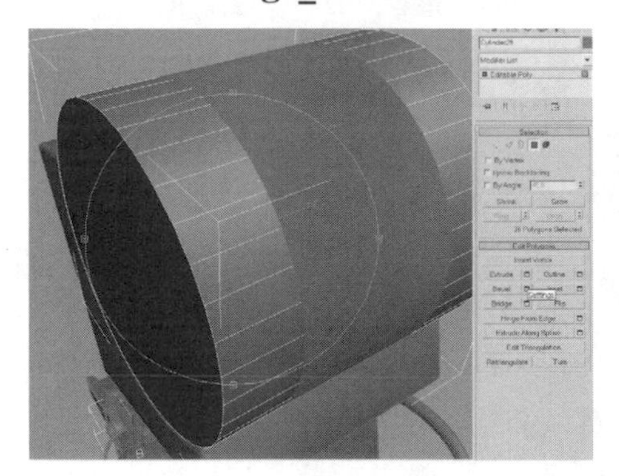

Figure 3-609

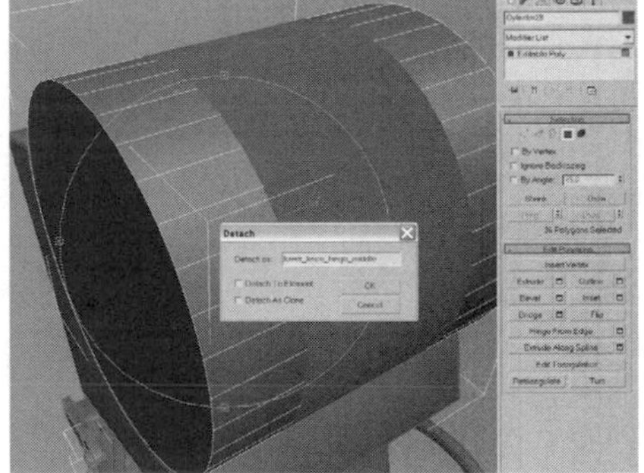

Figure 3-610

34. Select the cylinder's cap polygons and Bevel them:

Type	Height	Outline	Apply/OK
Group	0	10	Apply

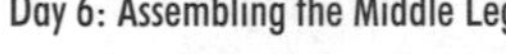

Day 6: Assembling the Middle Leg

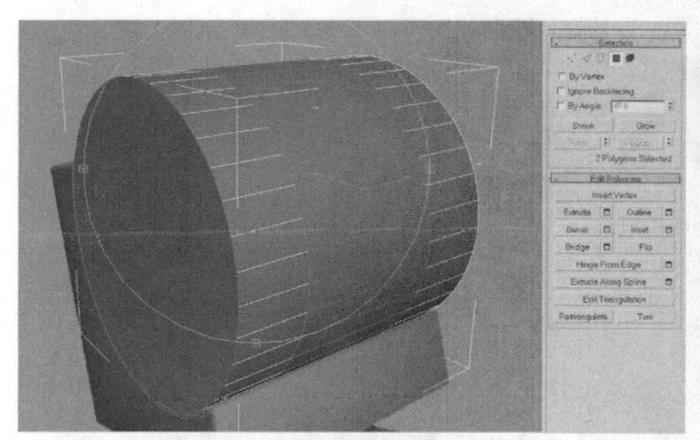

Figure 3-611

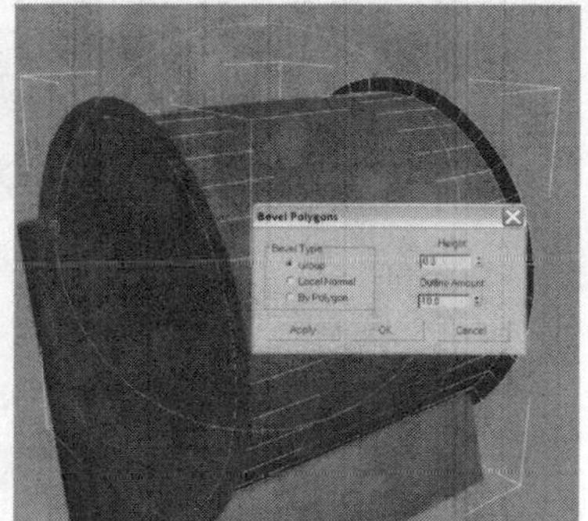

Figure 3-612

Type	Height	Outline	Apply/OK
Group	25.0	0	Apply
Group	0	–22	Apply

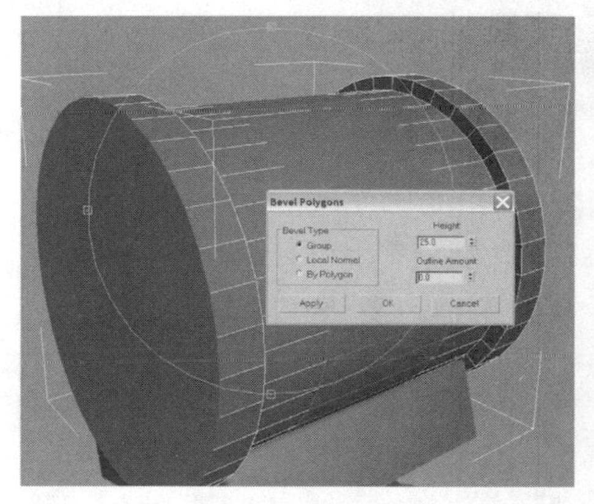

Figure 3-613

Figure 3-614

Type	Height	Outline	Apply/OK
Group	20	0	Apply
Group	0	–30	Apply

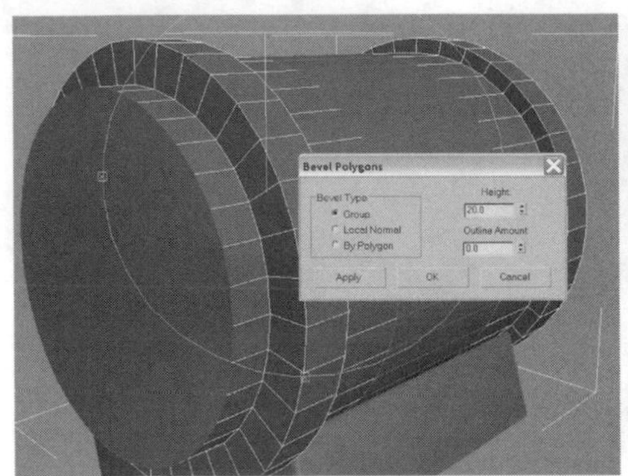

Figure 3-615

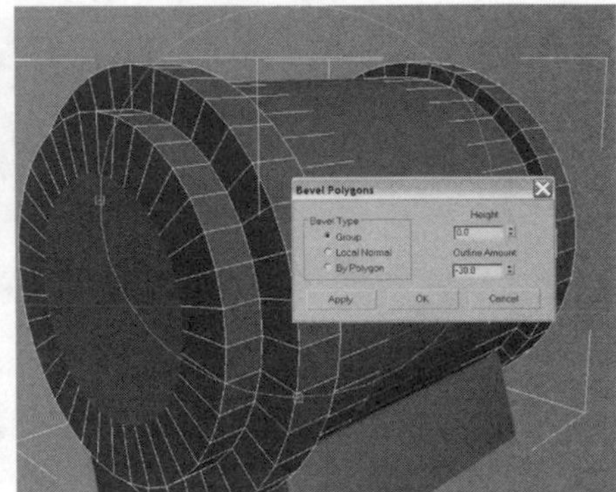

Figure 3-616

Type	Height	Outline	Apply/OK
Group	–6	0	Apply
Group	0	–25	Apply

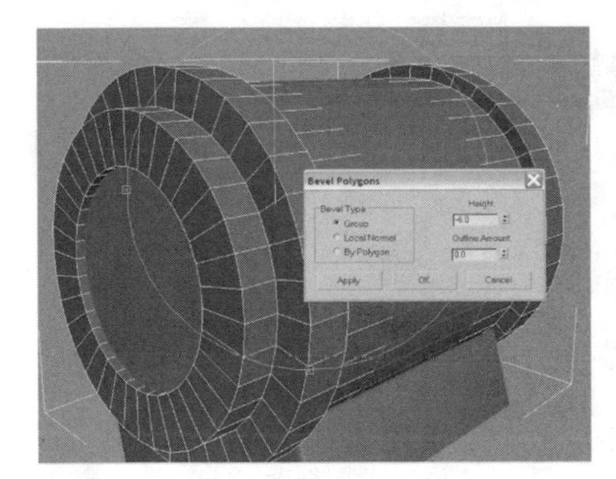

Figure 3-617

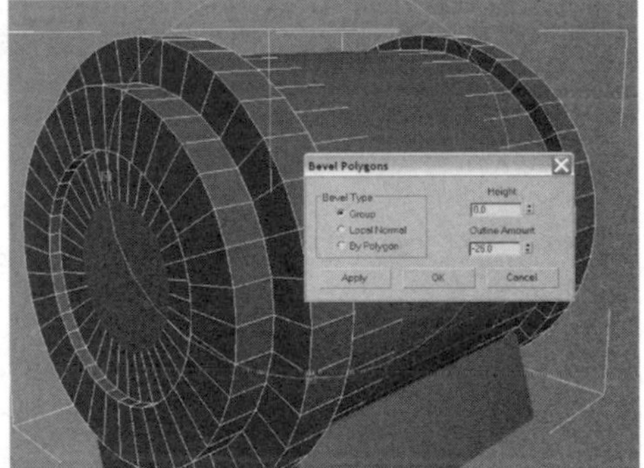

Figure 3-618

Type	Height	Outline	Apply/OK
Group	–5	0	Apply
Group	0	–1	Apply

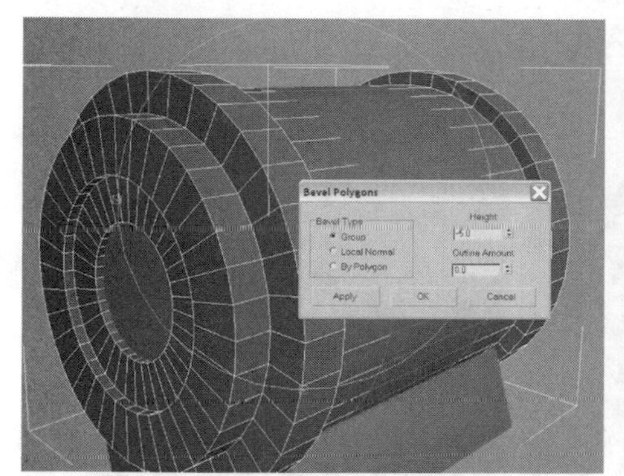

Figure 3-619

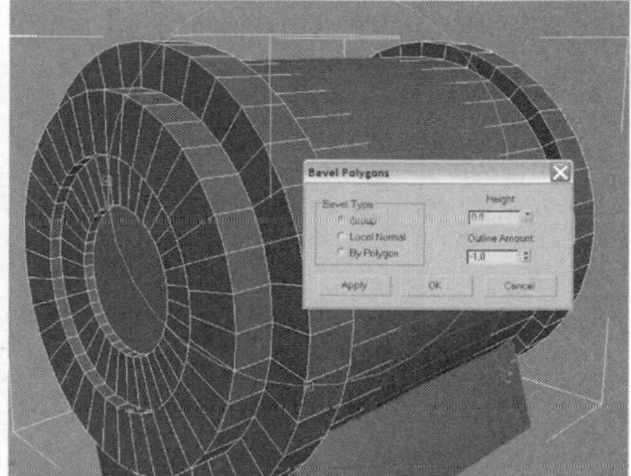

Figure 3-620

Type	Height	Outline	Apply/OK
Group	9	0	OK

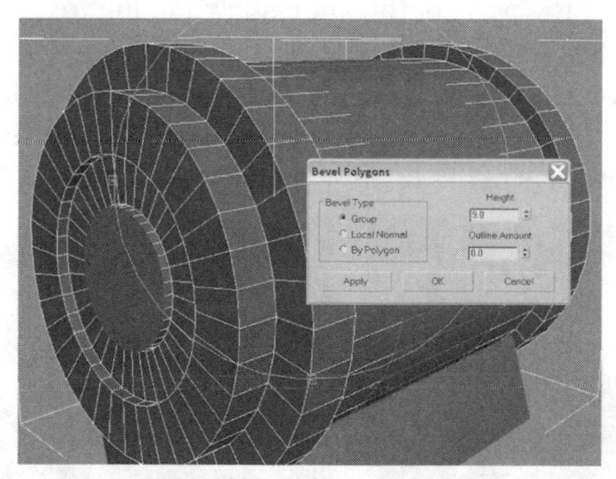

Figure 3-621

35. Using the Cut tool, make four slices in the top of the extrusion to form a cross. Be sure to do this on both the right and left sides of the knee.

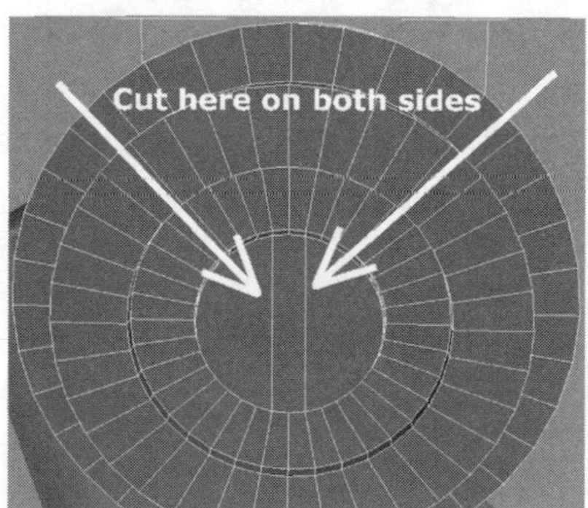

Figure 3-622

Figure 3-623

36. Select the outer four corners formed by the cuts, on both sides, and Extrude them by **10**.

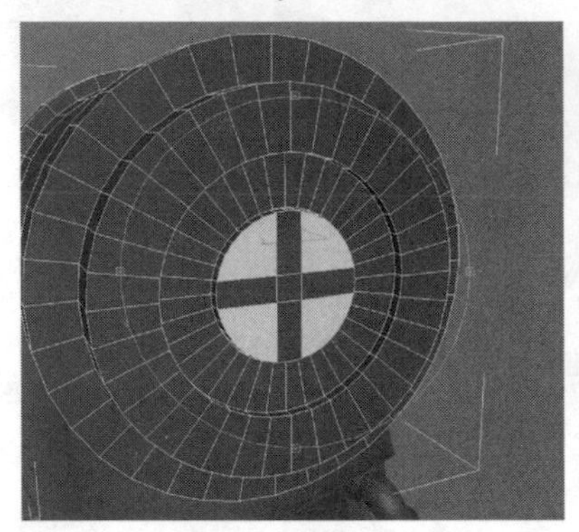

Figure 3-624

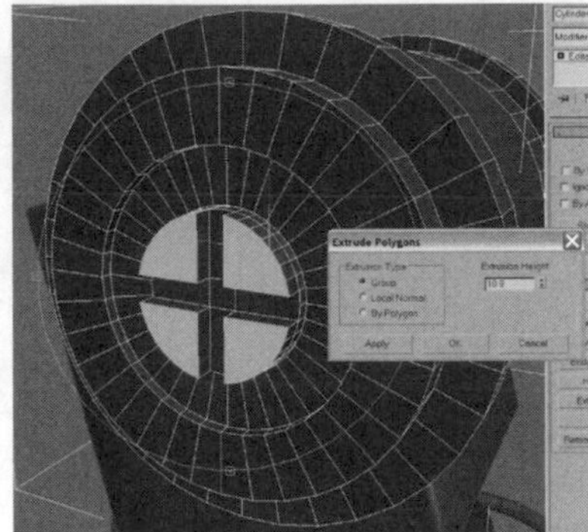

Figure 3-625

37. Element-select the parts of the knee shown in Figure 3-626 and Non-uniform Scale them **88** in the X axis so that they better fit in the indentation of the knee. Then border-select the borders of the middle part of the knee and stretch them until they close the gap with the outer parts of the knee.

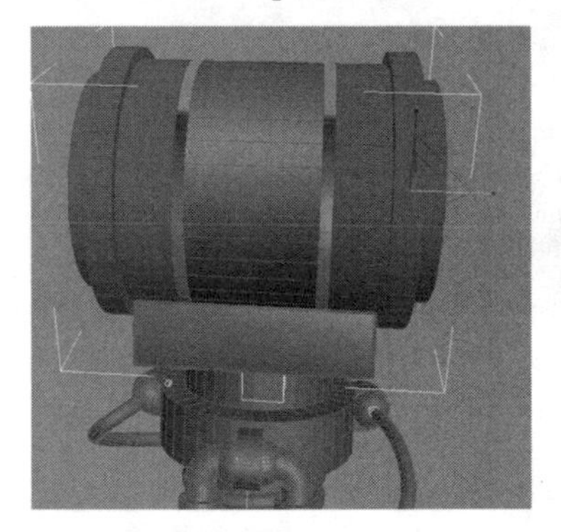

Figure 3-626

Figure 3-627

38. Loop-select the outer edges of the knee joint and Chamfer them by **1.0** and then by **0.403**.

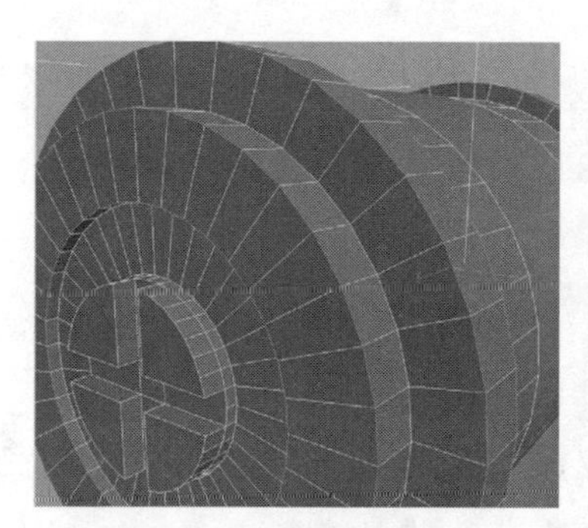

Figure 3-628

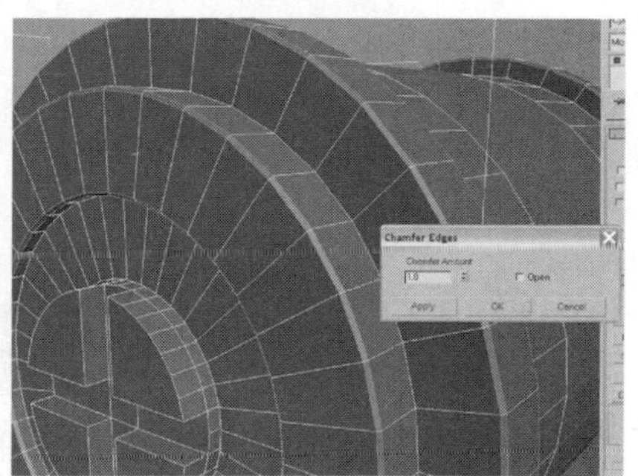

Figure 3-629

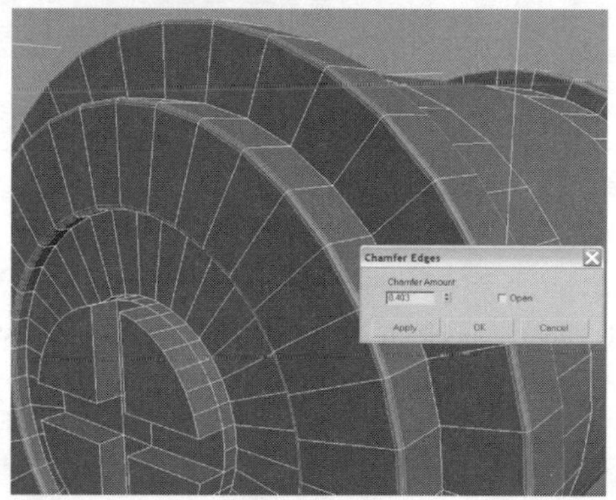

Figure 3-630

39. Add a Smooth modifier to the stack and then convert to Editable Polygon to collapse the stack. Select the six middle polygons of the middle object and Extrude them by **13**.

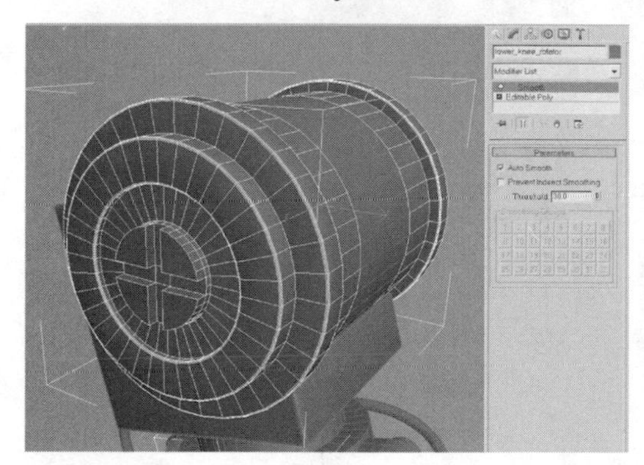

Figure 3-631

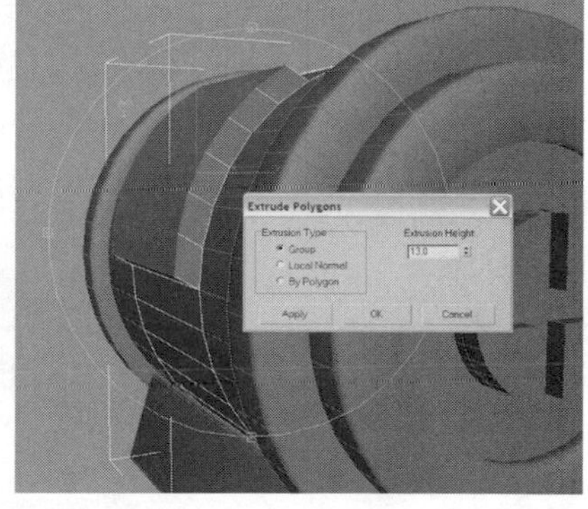

Figure 3-632

40. Extrude the polygons again by **13** to make a top stack. Select the polygons on both sides of the stack you extruded and extrude them by **72**, so they just cover the outer rim of the knee.

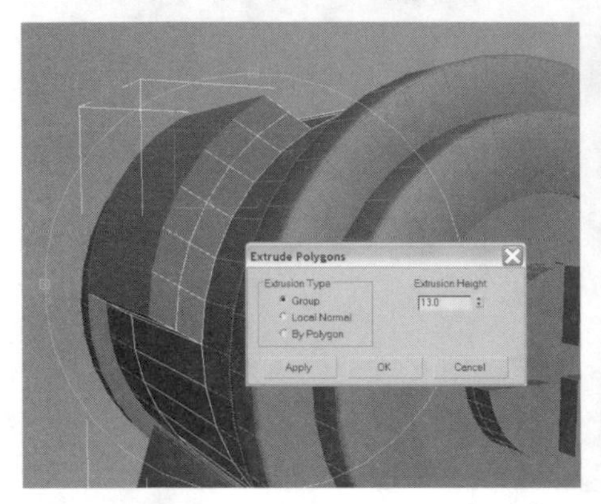

Figure 3-633

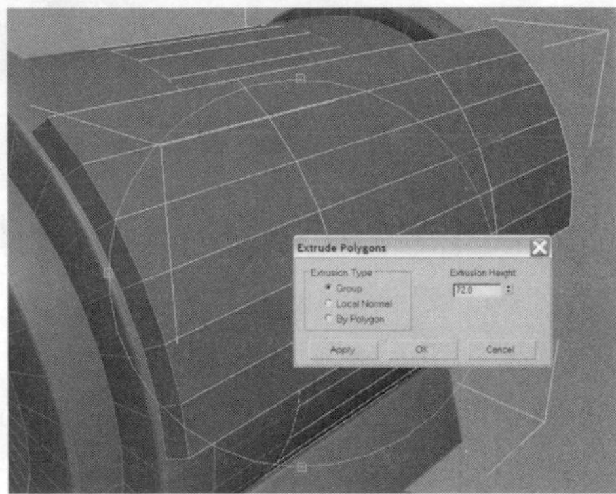

Figure 3-634

41. Select the top polygons and Non-uniform Scale them down to **0** in the Z axis to flatten them. Then Extrude the polygons by **100**.

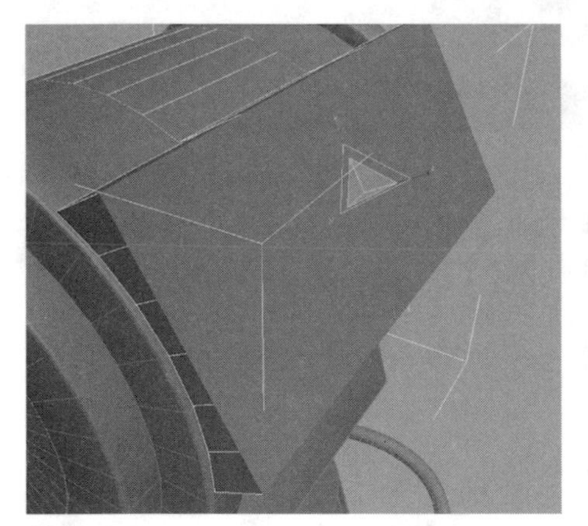

Figure 3-635

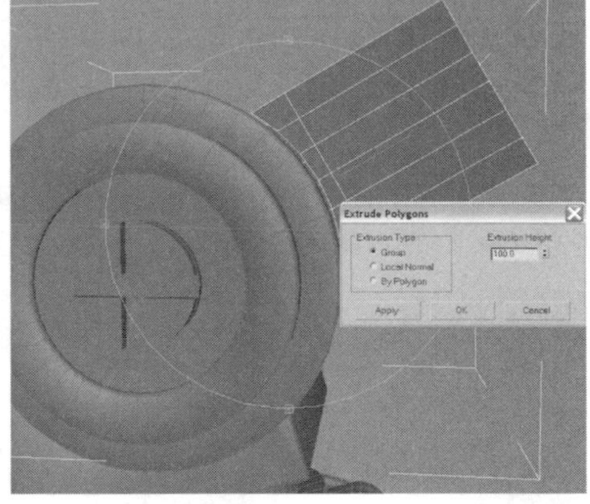

Figure 3-636

42. Select the front bottom two rows of polygons and Extrude them by **100**.

Figure 3-637

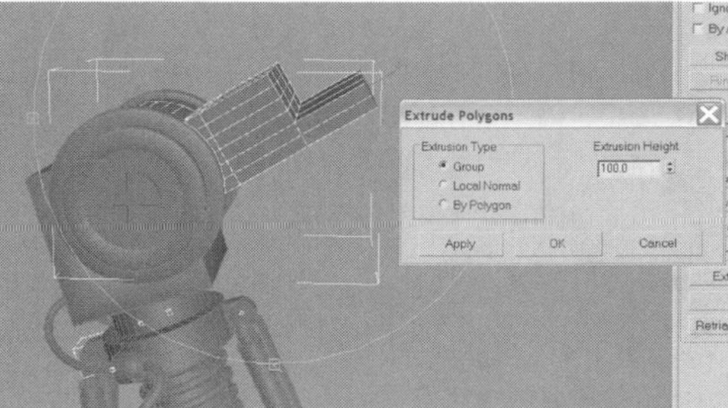

Figure 3-638

43. Select the bottom three rows of polygons and Extrude by **Local Normal 120**.

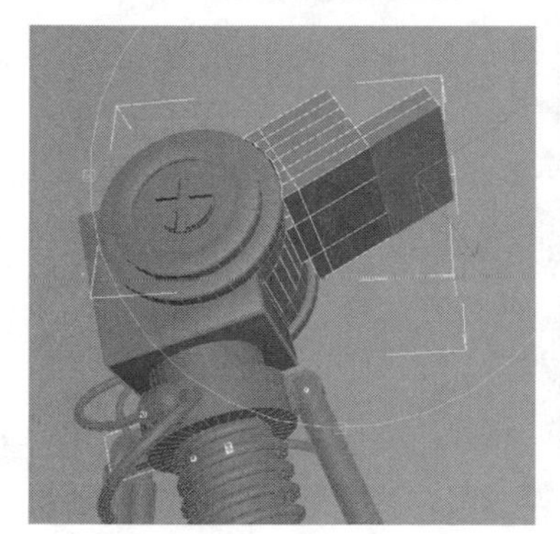

Figure 3-639

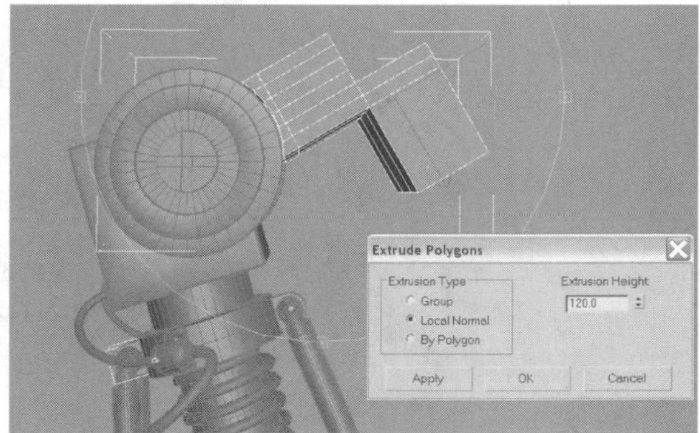

Figure 3-640

44. Select the polygon on the bottom of the kneecap and Bevel it:

Type	Height	Outline	Apply/OK
Group	0	–6	Apply
Group	28	0	OK

Figure 3-641

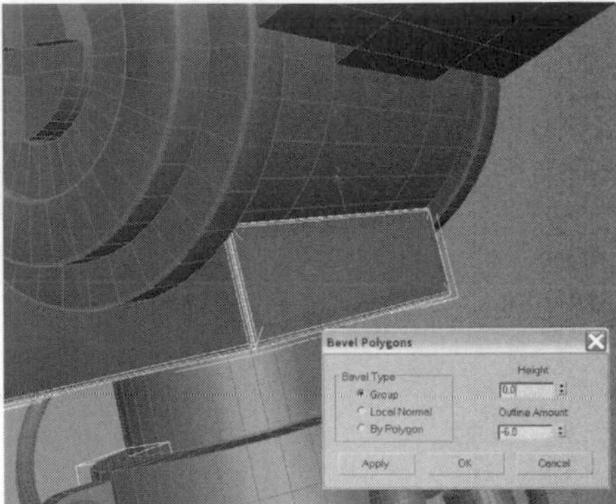

Figure 3-642

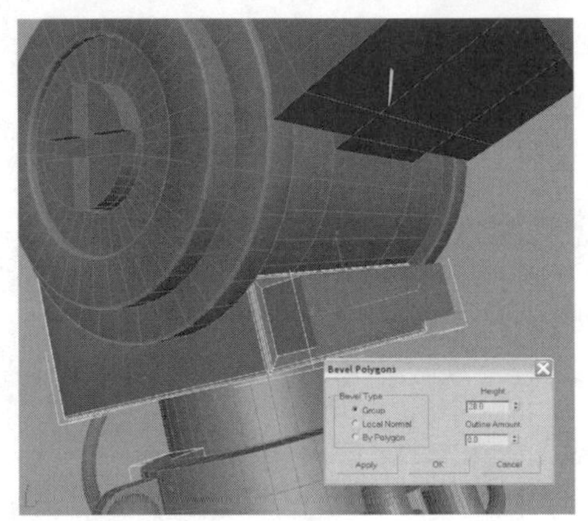

Figure 3-643

45. Select the edges of the extruded polygon, then Chamfer the edges by **0.5** and then by **0.2**.

Figure 3-644

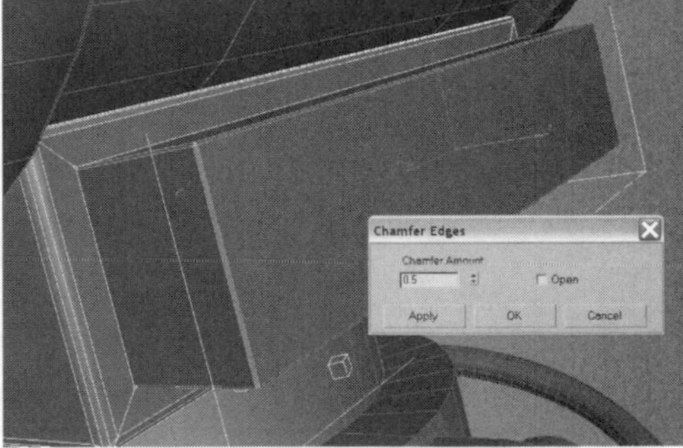

Figure 3-645

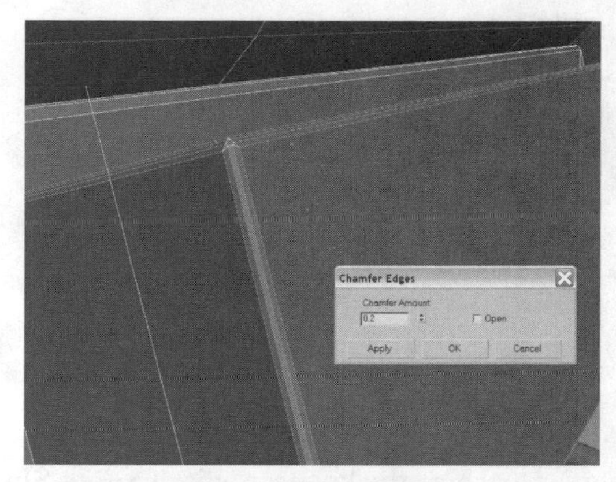

Figure 3-646

46. Select the polygons on the inside polygons and the bottom (so they form a 90-degree angle) and then Bevel them:

Type	Height	Outline	Apply/OK
Group	0	–10	Apply
Local Normal	10	0	OK

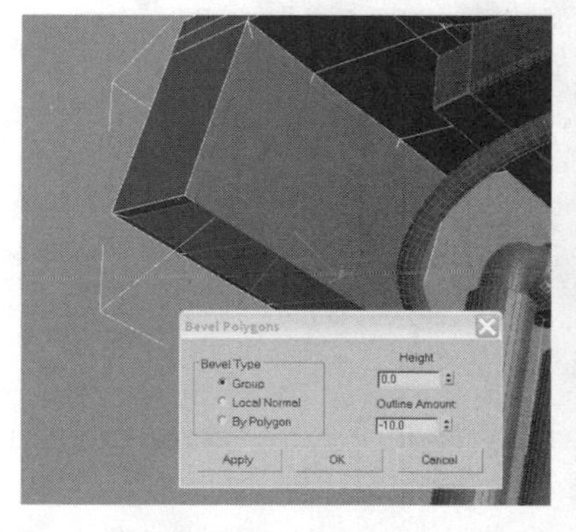

Figure 3-647

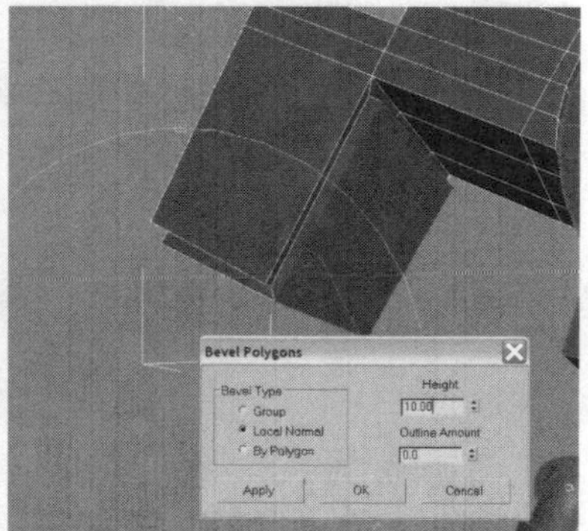

Figure 3-648

47. Create a Cylinder on the inside of the joint facing back toward the axle. Delete the polygon cap that touches the joint.

Radius	Height	Height/Cap Segs	Sides	Smooth
25	88	1/1	18	Checked

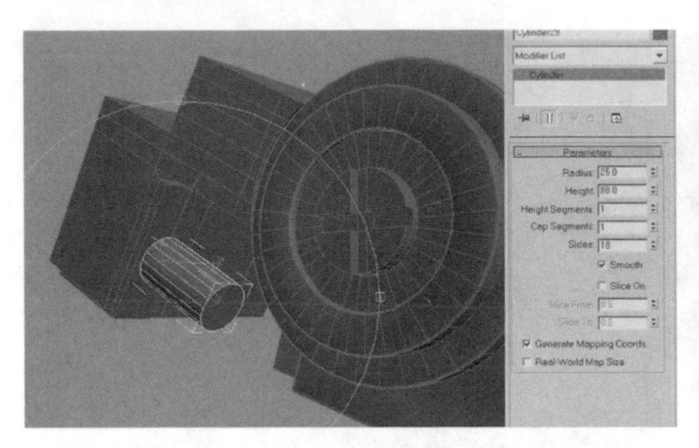

Figure 3-649

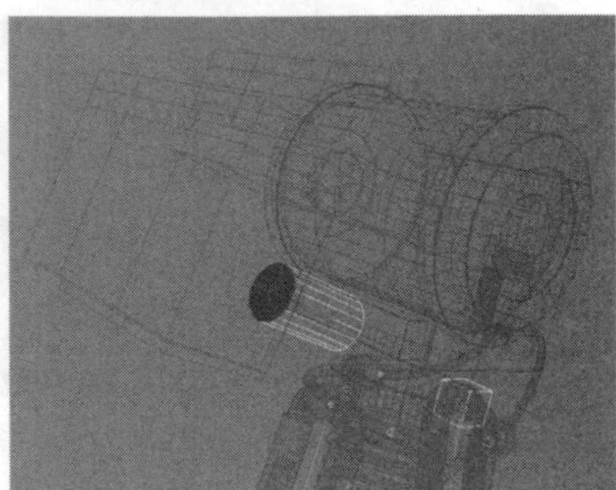

Figure 3-650

48. Select the border touching the kneecap, click **Create Shape From Selection**, and name it **knee_piston_seal**. Hit **H** and select **knee_piston_seal** from the list.

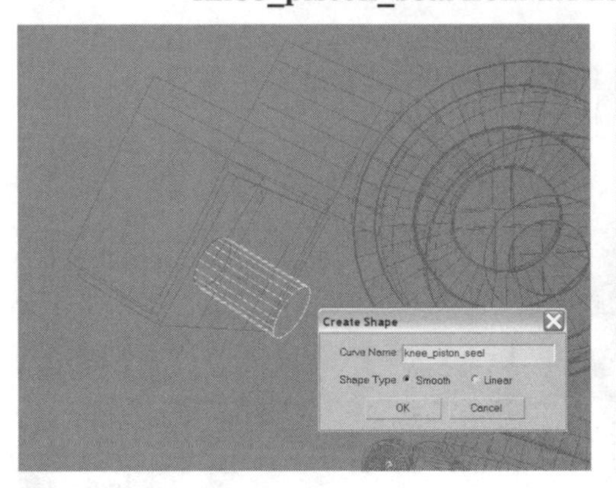

Figure 3-651

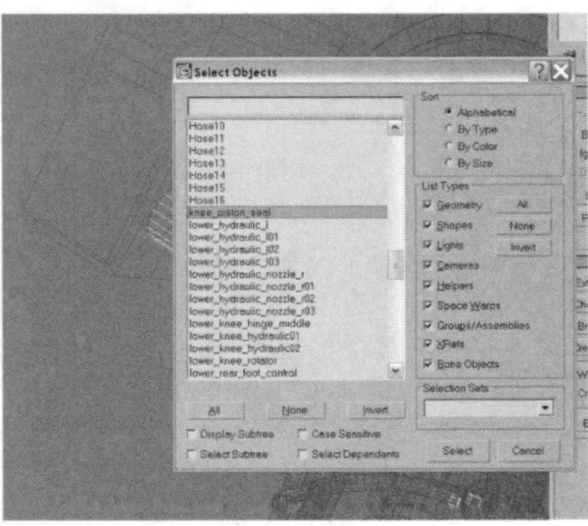

Figure 3-652

49. Select the seal and turn on rendering. Select the cap of the cylinder and Bevel it:

Type	Height	Outline	Apply/OK
Group	0	–12	Apply
Group	–80	0	OK

Day 6: Assembling the Middle Leg

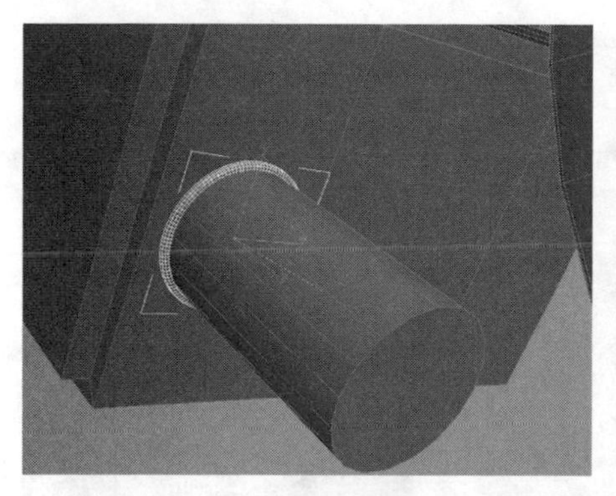

Figure 3-653

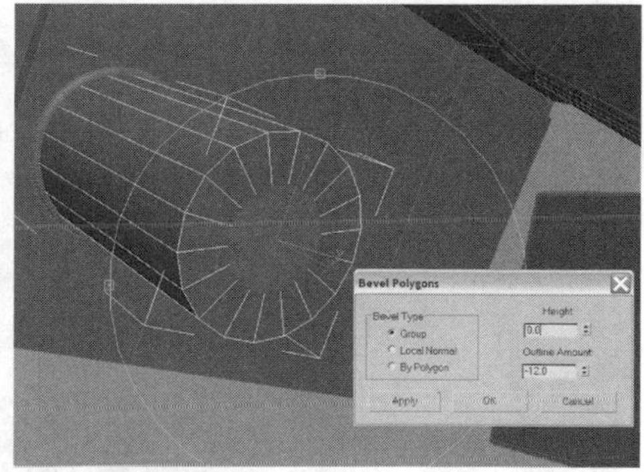

Figure 3-654

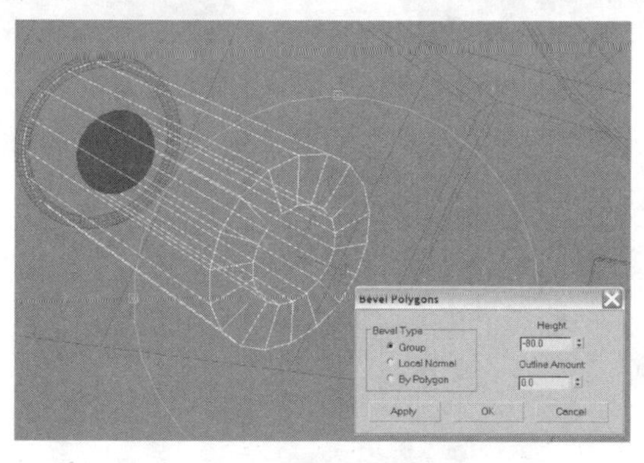

Figure 3-655

50. Select the outer edge and Chamfer it by **1.4** and then by **0.542**.

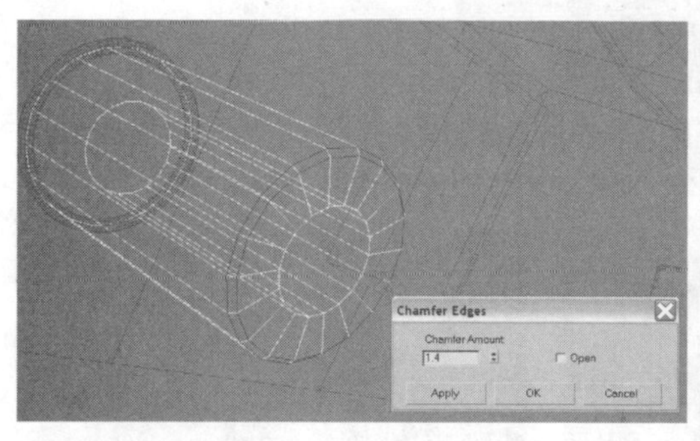

Figure 3-656

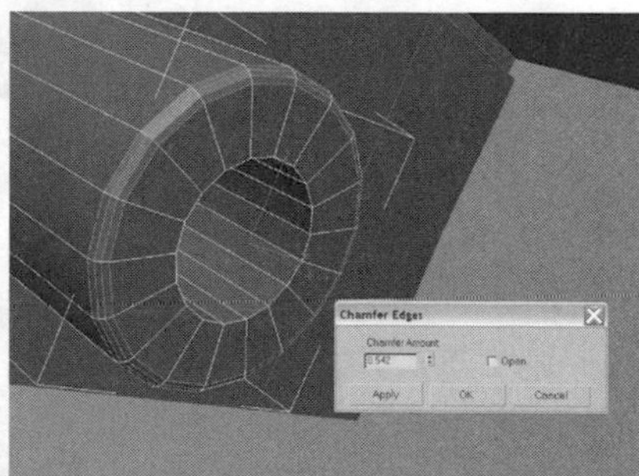

Figure 3-657

51. Add a Smooth modifier to the stack and then convert it to an Editable Polygon. Create two clones. Attach the clones to the original.

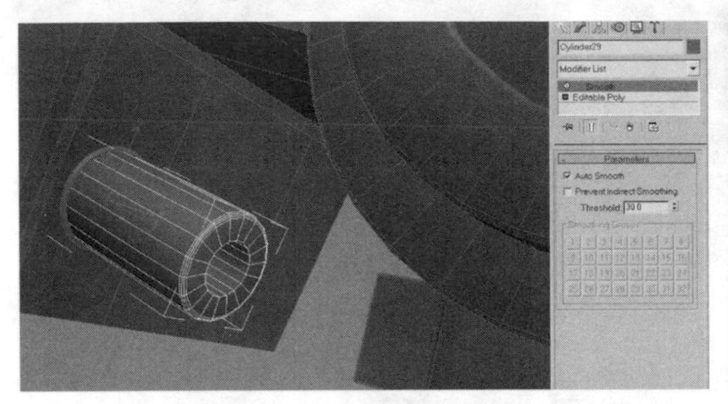

Figure 3-658

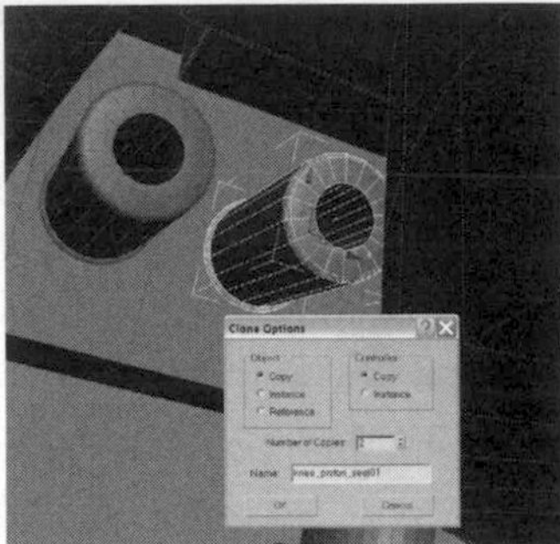

Figure 3-659

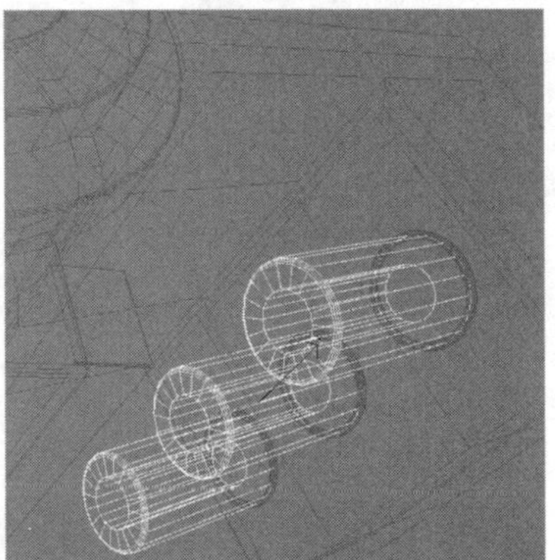

Figure 3-660

52. Select the three internal polygons and Detach them as **knee_piston_shafts**. Hit the **H** key and select **knee_piston_shafts**.

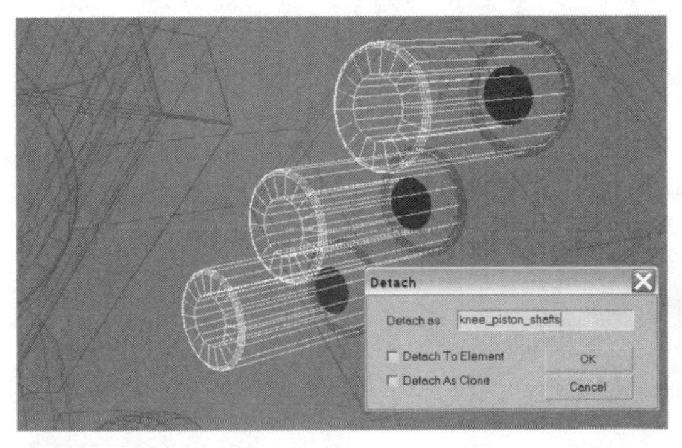

Figure 3-661

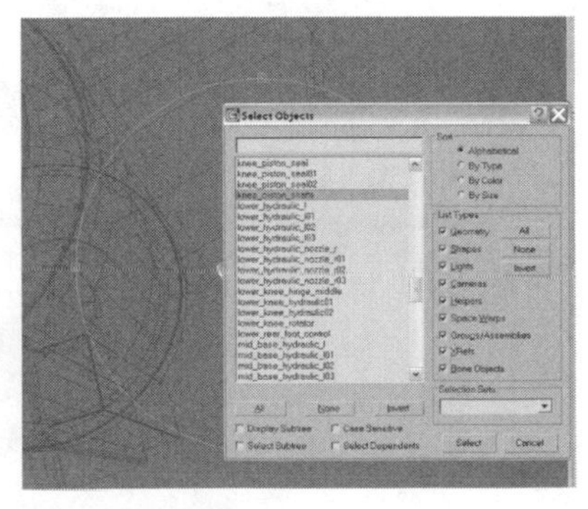

Figure 3-662

53. Pull them out of the pistons by moving them in the Z axis.

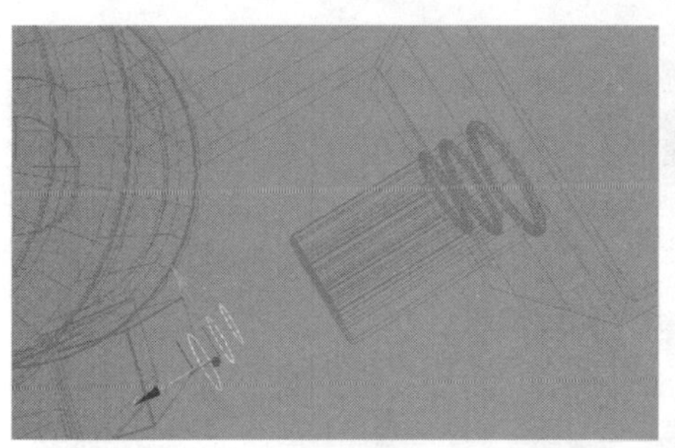

Figure 3-663

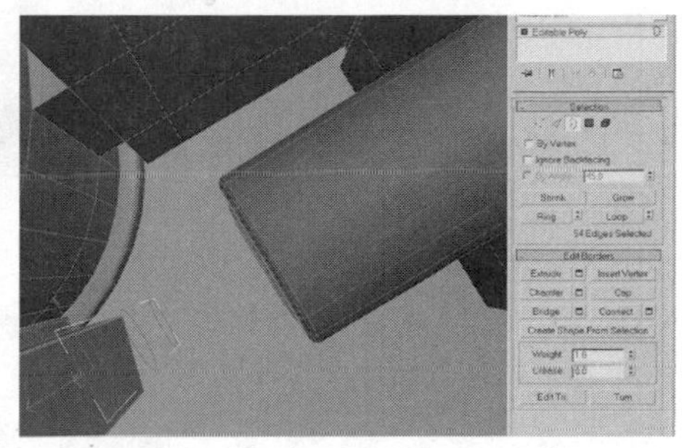

Figure 3-664

54. Use the Move tool to move them into place, border-select them, and then Extrude the edges by **–180** to create the shafts that will enter the pistons. Select the shafts and pistons, right-click, and select **Hide Unselected**.

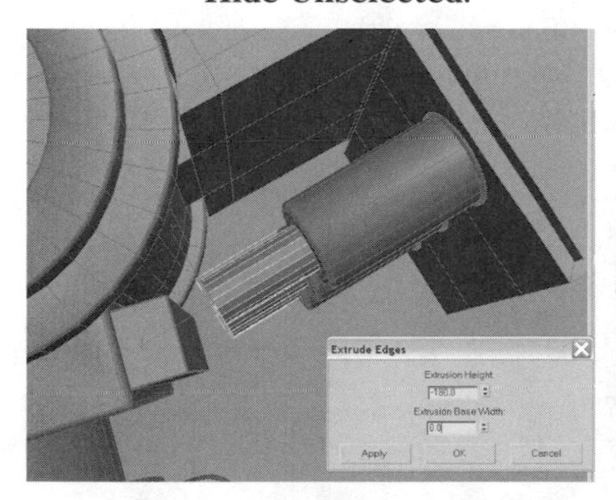

Figure 3-665

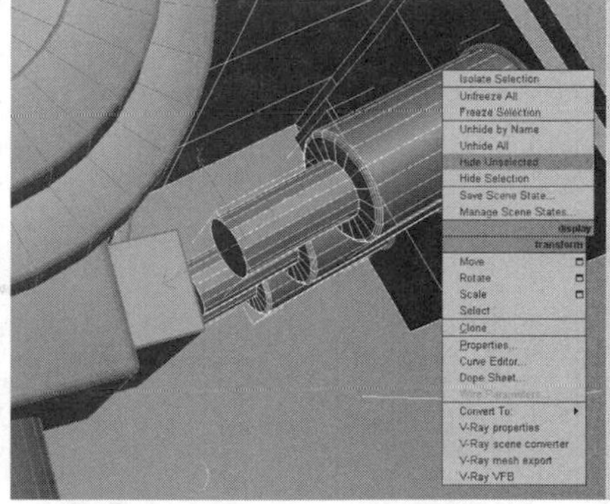

Figure 3-666

55. Use the Cut tool to cut the ends of the shafts as shown in Figure 3-667. Edge-select the cuts you just made, and use the Connect tool to connect them as shown in Figure 3-668.

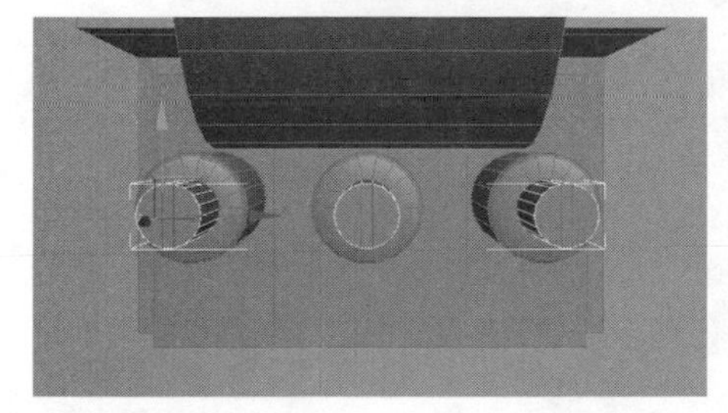

Figure 3-667

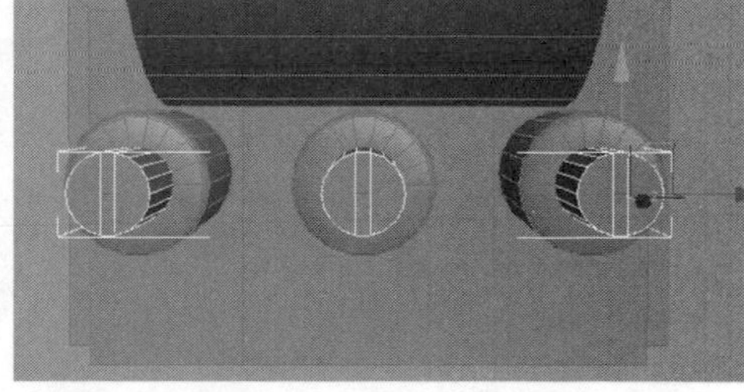

Figure 3-668

56. Select the polygons you made from the cuts and Extrude them by **15**.

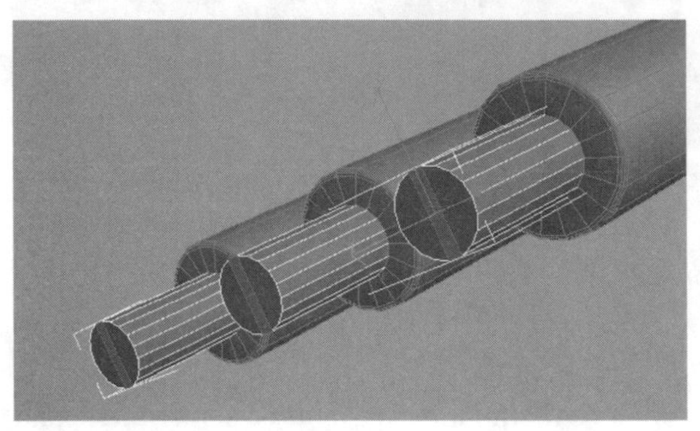

Figure 3-669

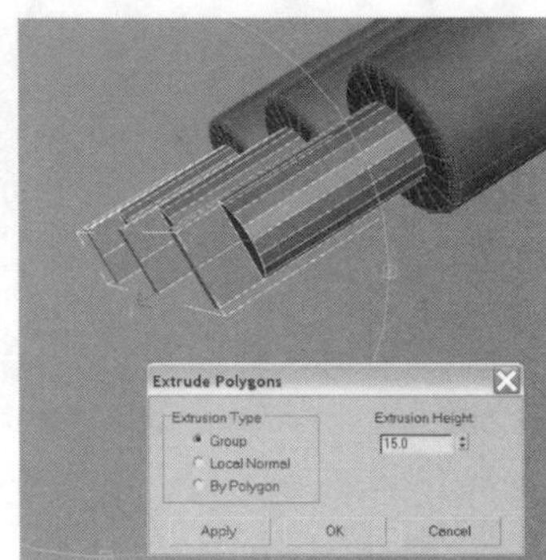

Figure 3-670

57. Select the bottom polygons and delete them. Select the top polygons and Hinge From Edge **180** degrees with **10** Segments, using the middle edge as the hinge. Delete the back-facing polygon. Select the vertices and Weld them before adding a Smooth modifier to the stack and then converting to an Editable Polygon object to collapse the stack.

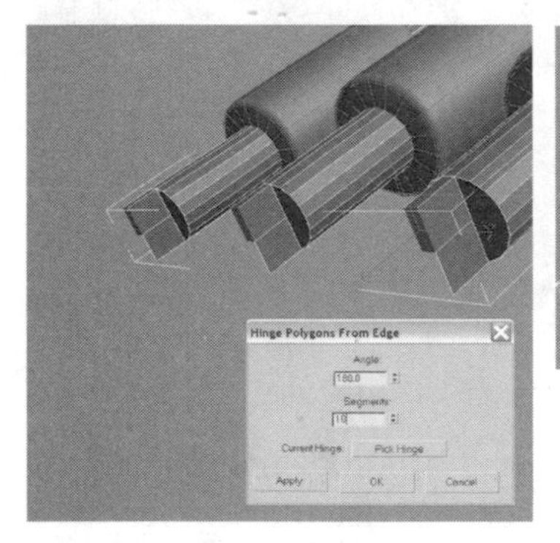

Figure 3-671

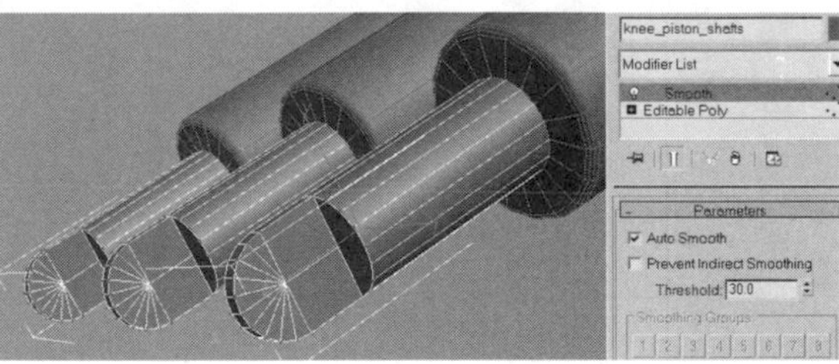

Figure 3-672

58. Clone the shafts and Rotate them **180** degrees in the X axis.

Day 6: Assembling the Middle Leg

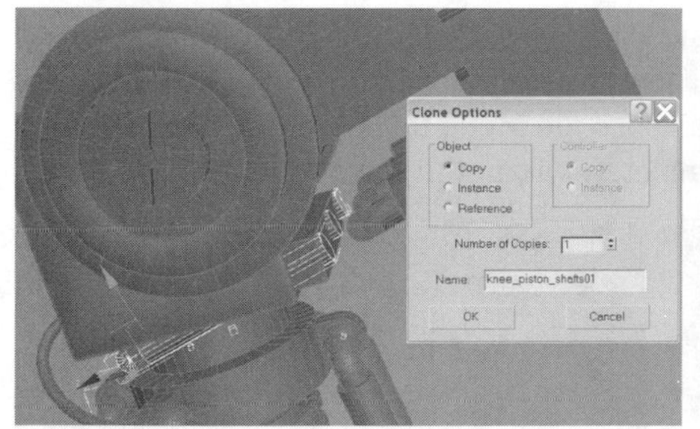

Figure 3-673

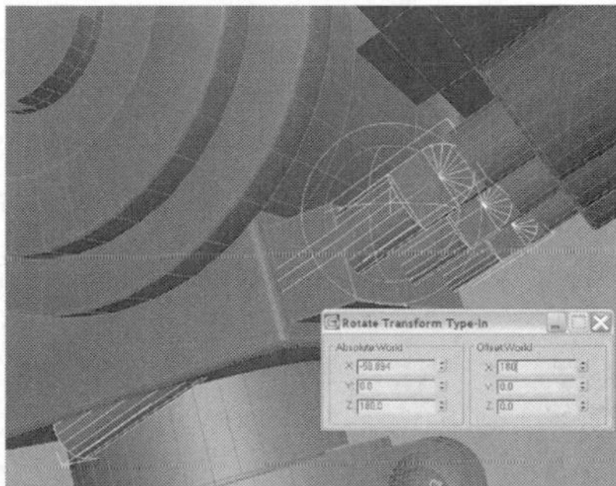

Figure 3-674

59. Make sure the rounded parts of the shafts overlap exactly and then delete the rounded parts of the clones to make a notch. Select the original, right-click, and choose **Hide Selection**.

Figure 3-675

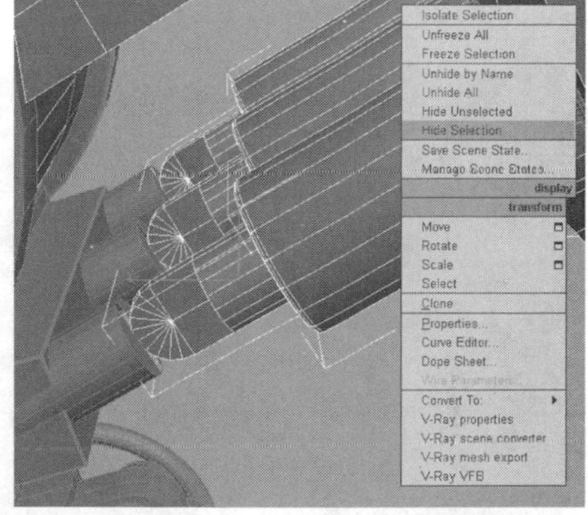

Figure 3-676

60. Border-select the open parts of the shafts and Cap them. Unhide the pistons and then select them and the shafts.

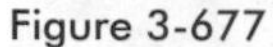

Figure 3-677

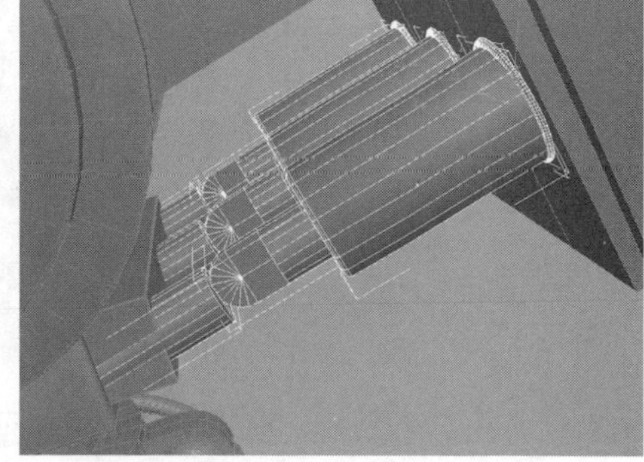

Figure 3-678

61. Scale the pistons and the shafts until they comfortably fit beneath the knee (don't worry about the length of the shafts). Border-select the ends of the shafts and use the Move tool to reduce their length until their ends are completely within the joint.

Figure 3-679

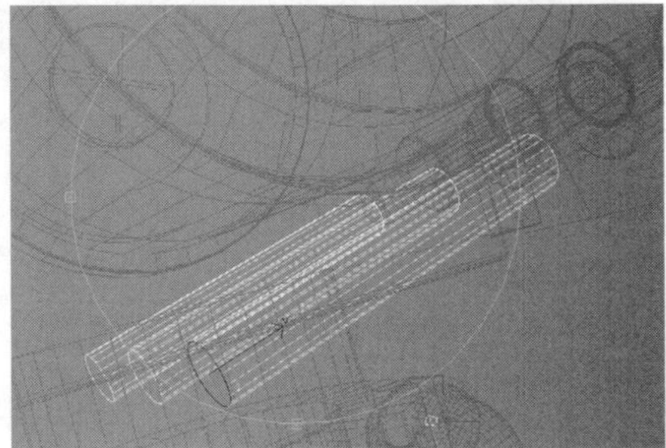

Figure 3-680

Figure 3-681

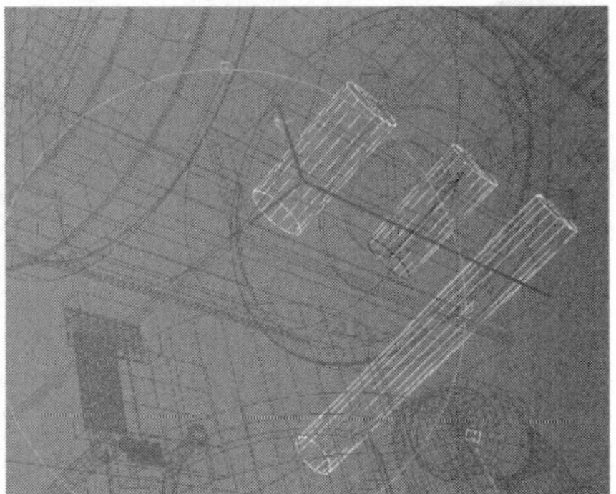

Figure 3-682

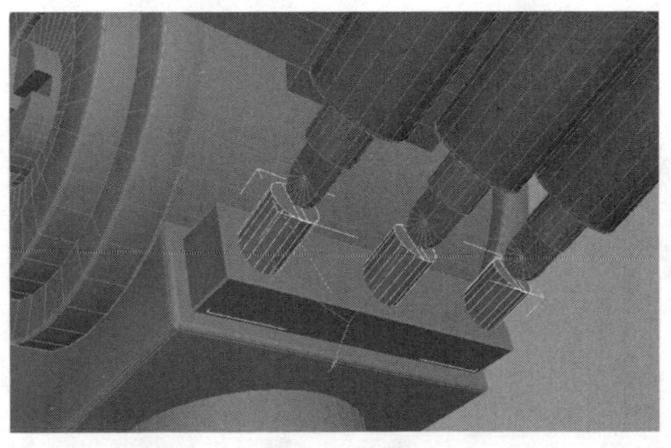

Figure 3-683

62. Select the polygons on the caps of the cloned shafts and Extrude them by **18**.

Figure 3-684

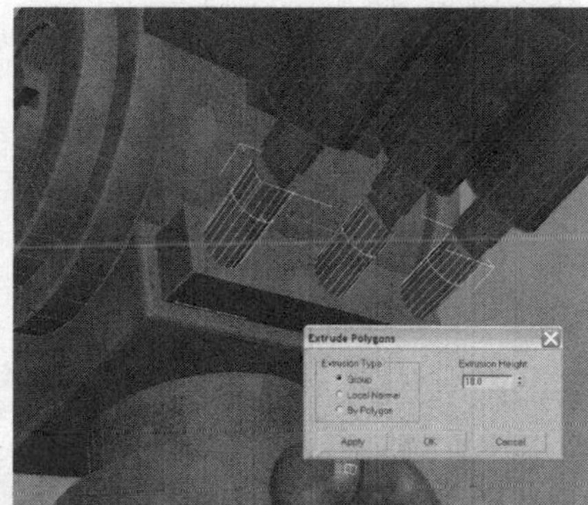

Figure 3-685

63. Add a Smooth modifier to the stack of shafts and then convert to an Editable Polygon to collapse the stack. Choose **Affect Pivot Only** and position it on the center of the middle shaft.

Figure 3-686

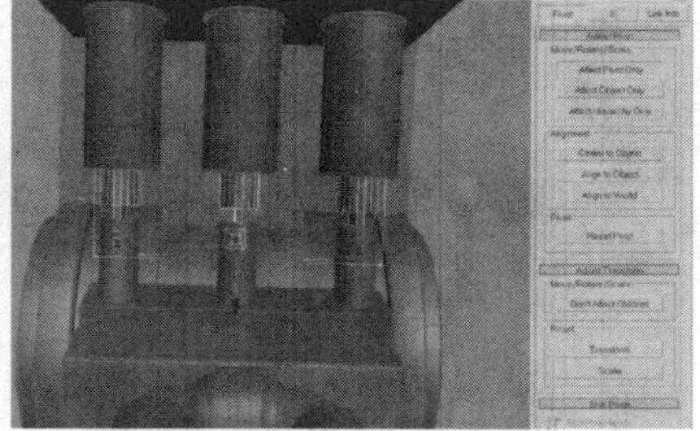

Figure 3-687

64. Create a Dummy, position it roughly in the center of the three pistons, and name it **lower_knee_piston_dummy**. Use Align Selection to center the dummy on the center of the pistons.

Figure 3-688

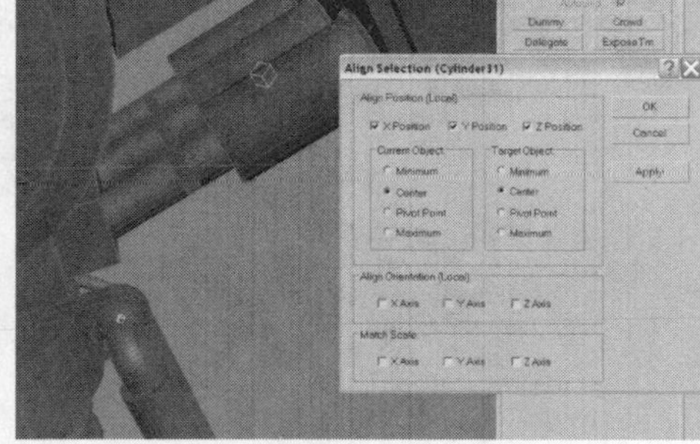

Figure 3-689

65. Select and Link the dummy to the pistons and then add a LookAt controller to the shaft's Rotation controller.

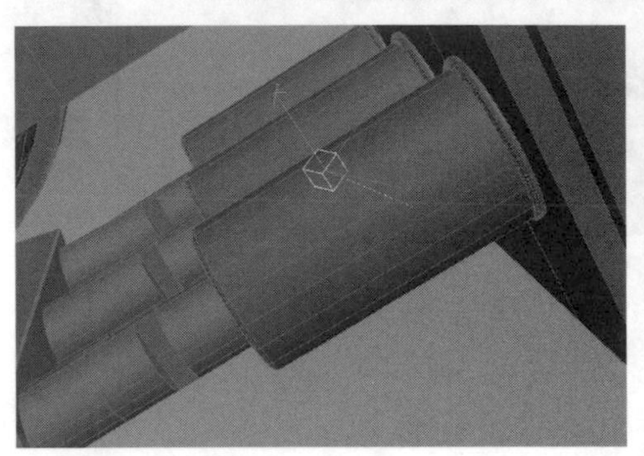

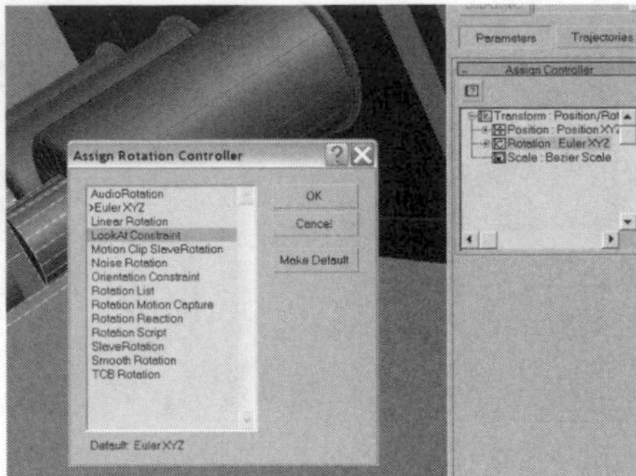

Figure 3-690

Figure 3-691

66. Assign the LookAt Target to **lower_knee_piston_dummy**. Set the LookAt Axis to **Z** and click the **Flip** check box. Set the Upnode Control to **LookAt** and the Source Axis to **Y**.

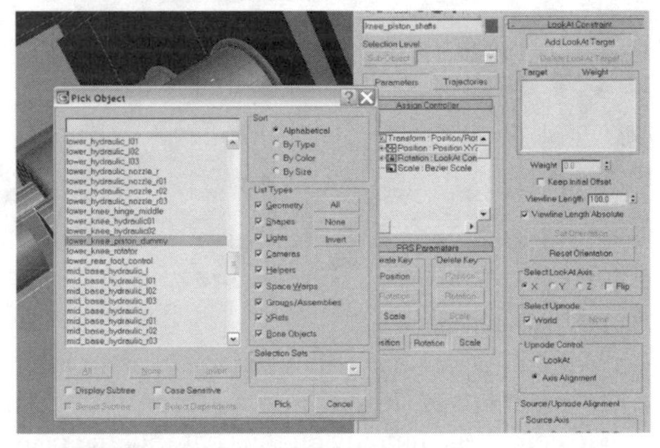

Figure 3-692

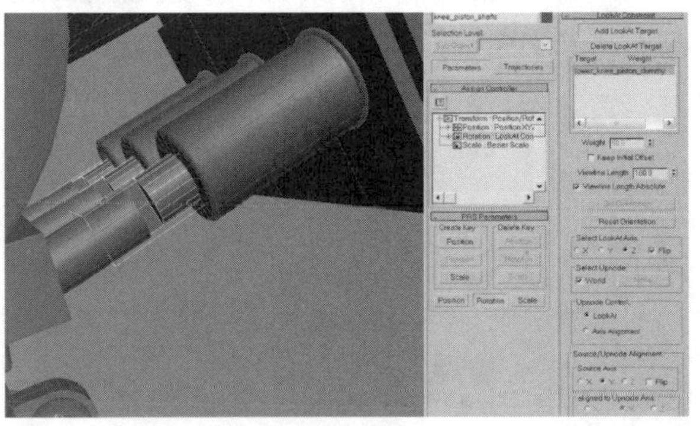

Figure 3-693

Day 7: Assembling the Upper Leg

1. Select the front three polygons shown in Figure 3-694 and Extrude them by **180** and then select the top three edges.

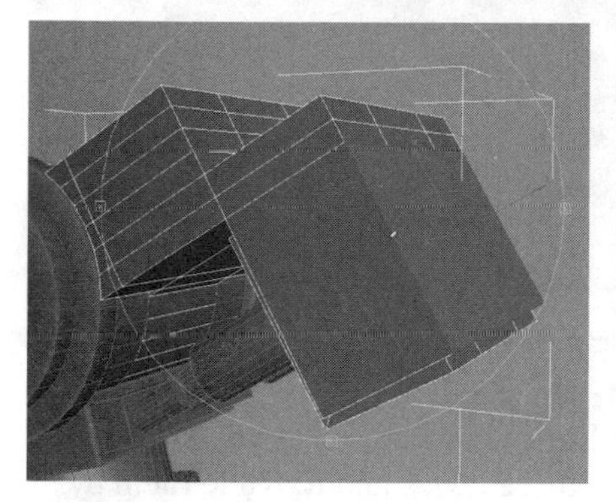

Figure 3-694

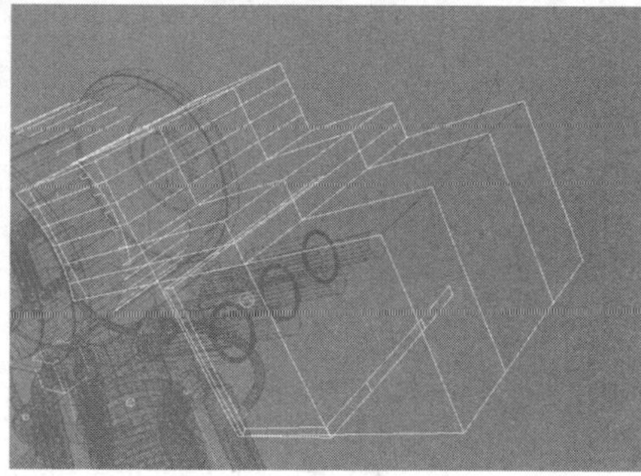

Figure 3-695

2. Chamfer the top three edges by **90** and then select the three bottom polygons.

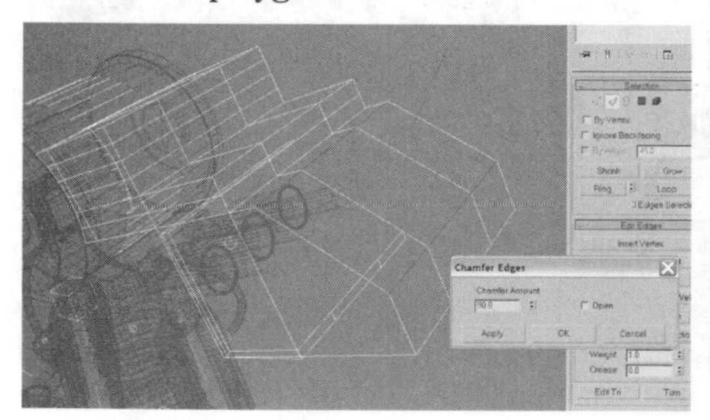

Figure 3-696

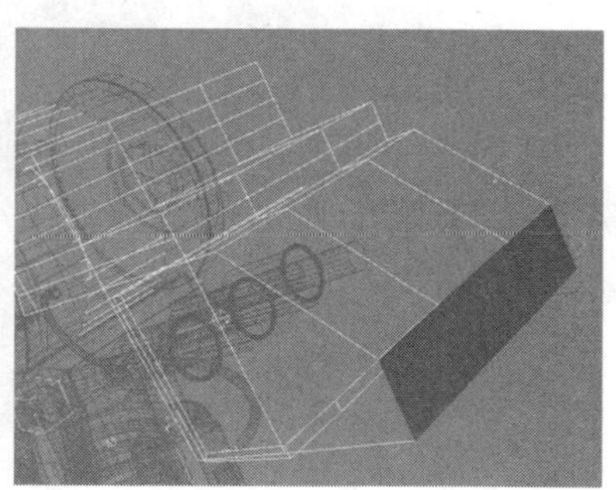

Figure 3-697

3. Extrude the three polygons by Local Normal to a Height of **48**. Select the top 10 rows of polygons.

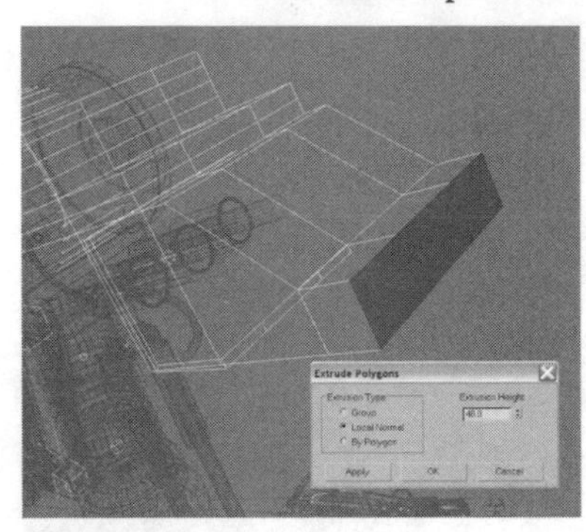

Figure 3-698

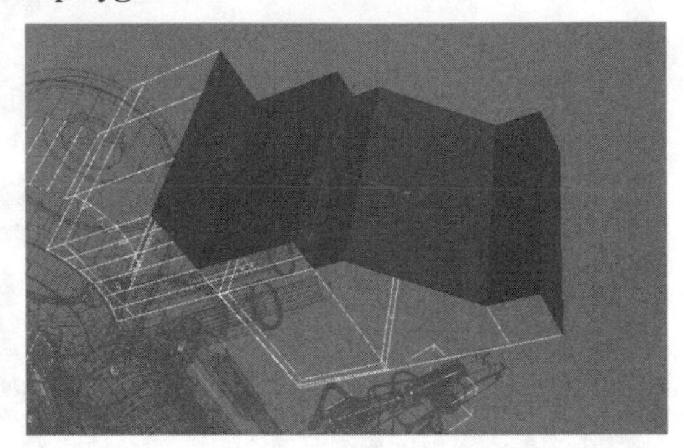

Figure 3-699

4. Click **Detach**, name it **upper_knee_cowl**, and click the Detach As Clone check box. Select the top three edges and Extrude them by **397**.

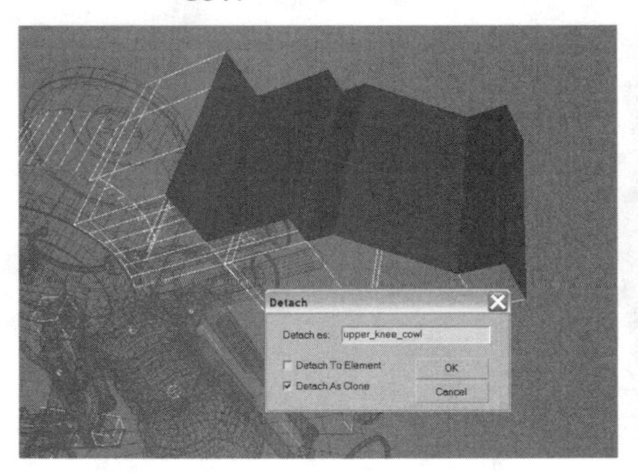

Figure 3-700

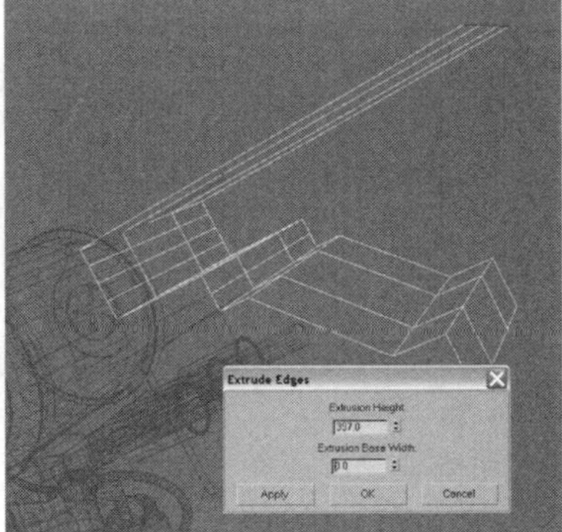

Figure 3-701

5. Hold down the **Shift** key and drag the edge downward until it is aligned with the bottom edge of the upper_knee_cowl (~221 units). Hold down the **Shift** key, select the three edges on the bottom of the upper_knee_cowl, and click the **Bridge** button (in the Edit Edges rollout).

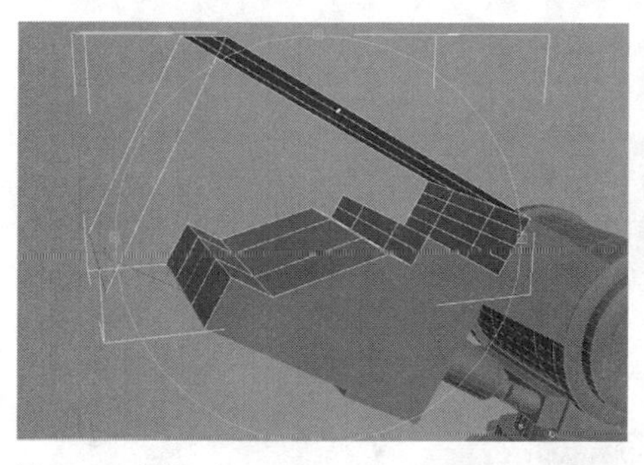

Figure 3-702

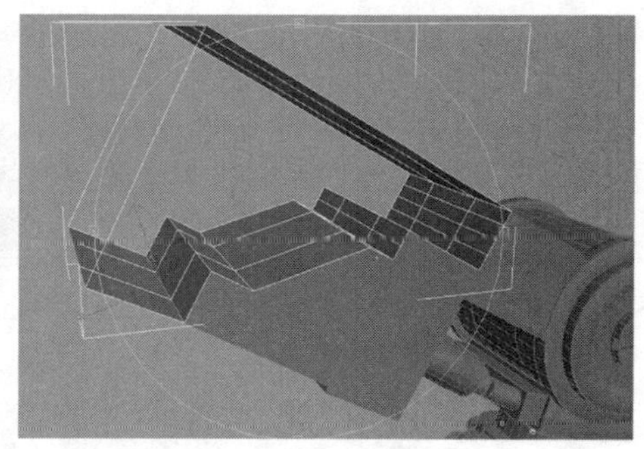

Figure 3-703

6. Switch to Polygon selection and select the polygons on the top and front inside surfaces, then click the **Grow** button (in the Selection rollout) until all the inner surface polys have been selected. Right-click and select **Flip Normals** (it's the last selection on the menu). Border-select the outer edges.

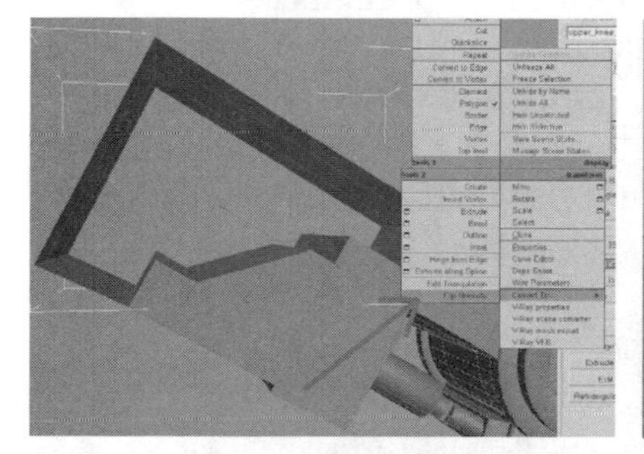

Figure 3-704

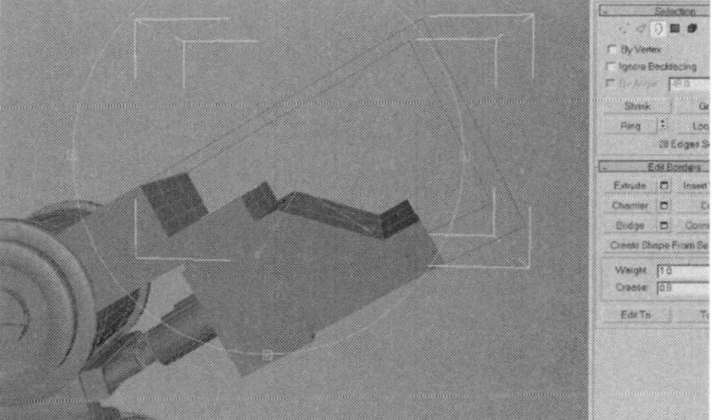

Figure 3-705

7. Border-select both sides and Cap them. Create a Cylinder and position it in the upper corner of the new joint.

Radius	Height	Height/Cap Segs	Sides	Smooth
120	300	2/1	36	Checked

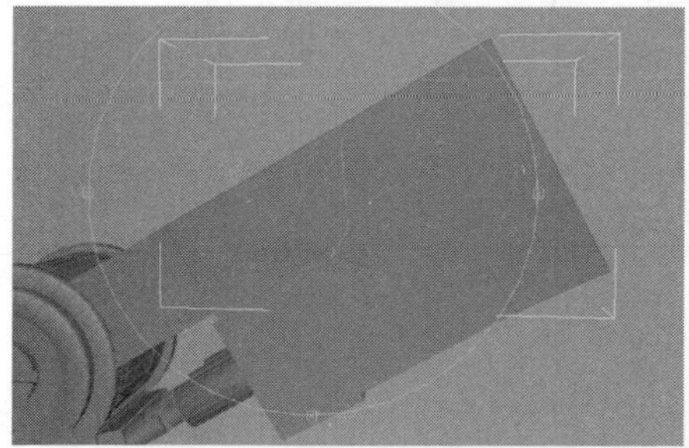

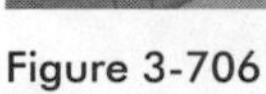

Figure 3-706

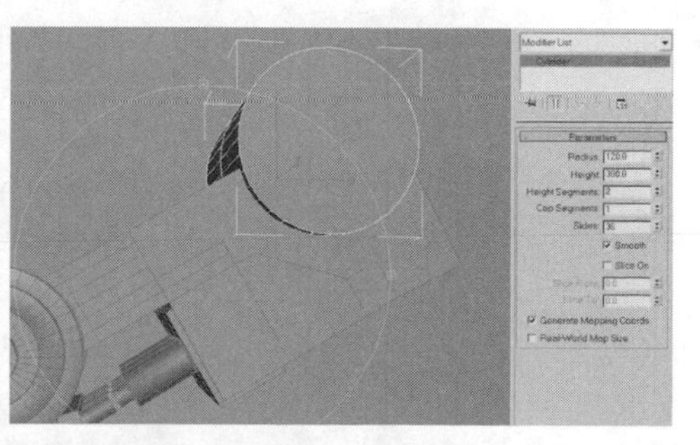

Figure 3-707

8. Select the cylinder and convert it to an Editable Polygon. Loop-select the middle edges on the cylinder.

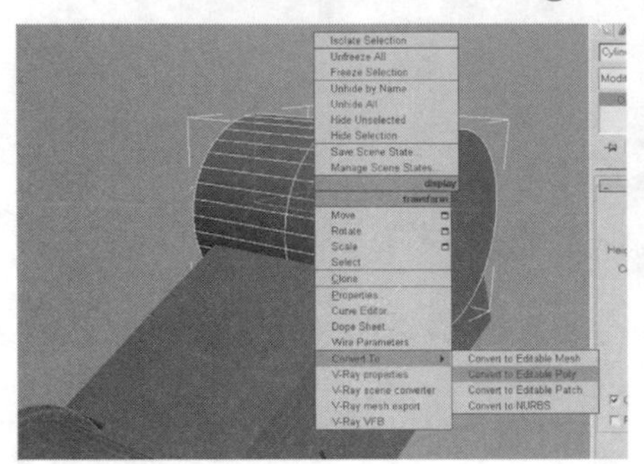

Figure 3-708

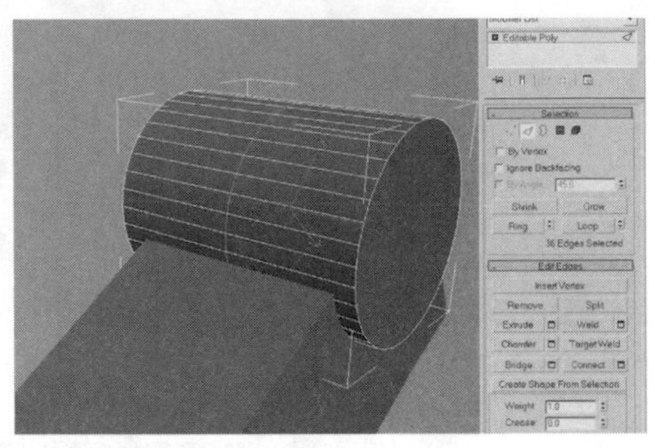

Figure 3-709

9. Chamfer the edges (around **50.3**) until they are aligned with the edges on the leg. Move the cylinder until the chamfered edges on the cylinder line up with the edges on the upper_knee_cowl. In order to make a socket for the knee, select the **upper_knee_cowl**, create a Boolean object (select **Compound Object** in the Create panel and click the **Boolean** button), click **Pick Operand B**, click the cylinder (**Cylinder29**), and choose **Subtraction (A–B)**.

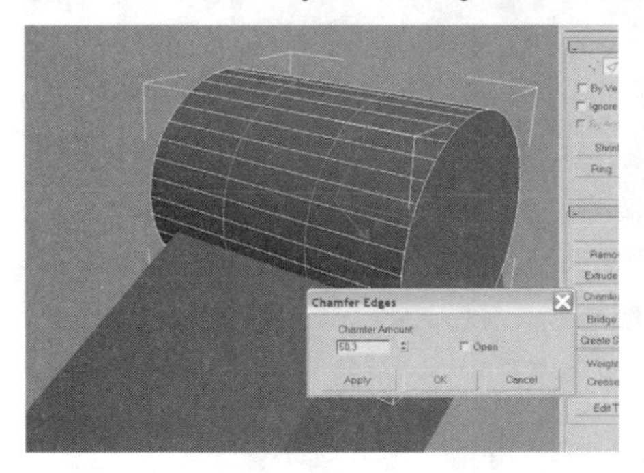

Figure 3-710

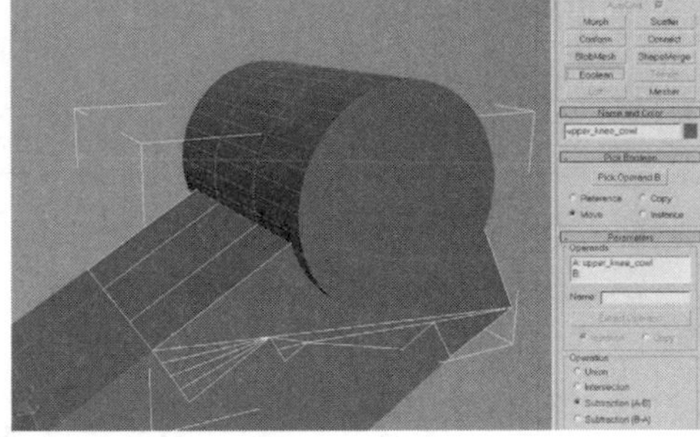

Figure 3-711

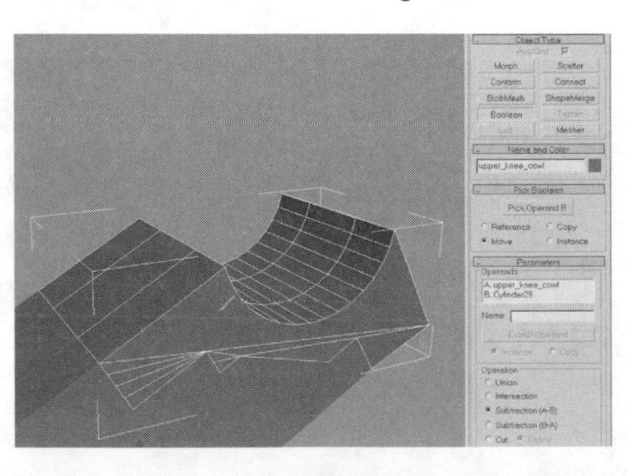

Figure 3-712

10. Select the Boolean object and convert it to an Editable Polygon. Select any extra edges made on the outer surfaces by the Boolean operation and click **Remove**. (Note: Depending on where you positioned the cylinder, you may have more or fewer edges than those shown in my figures.)

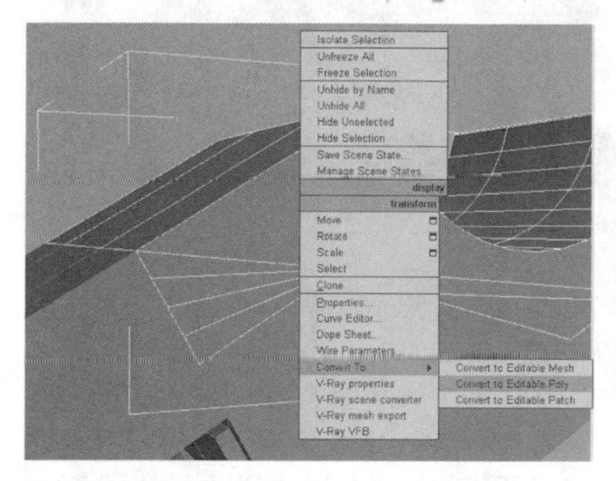

Figure 3-713

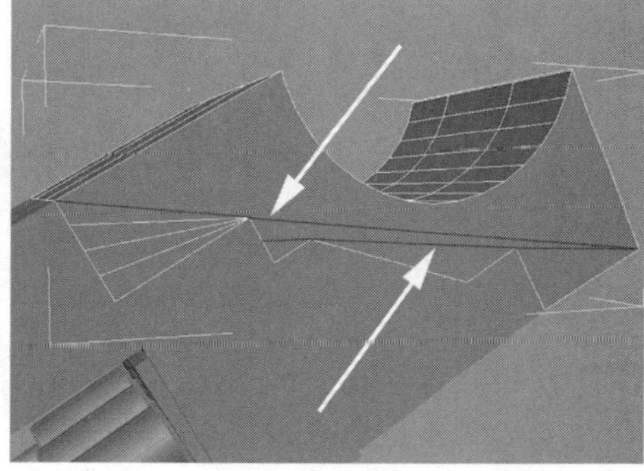

Figure 3-714

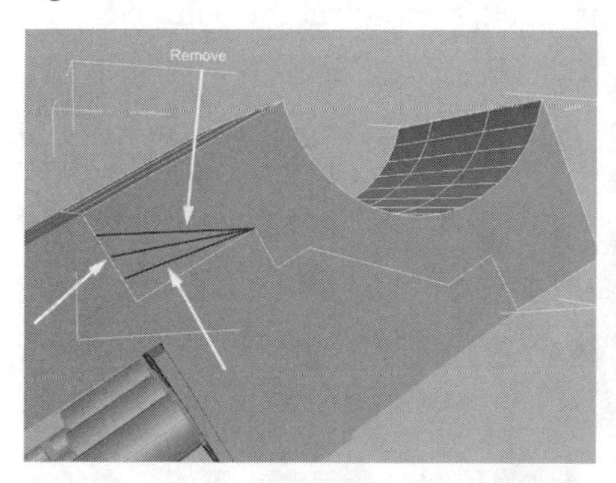

Figure 3-715

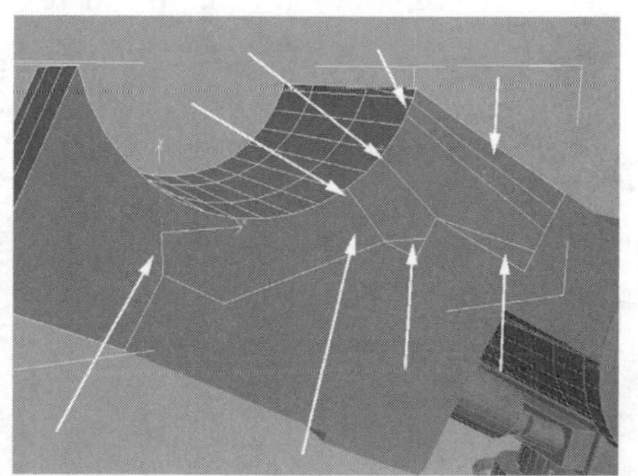

Figure 3-716

11. Select and Remove, or Target Weld, the isolated vertices indicated in the following figures, then continue to remove isolated, unnecessary edges and vertices.

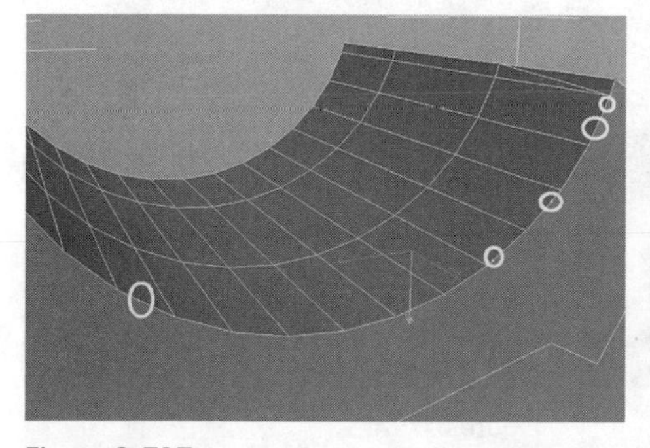

Figure 3-717

Figure 3-718

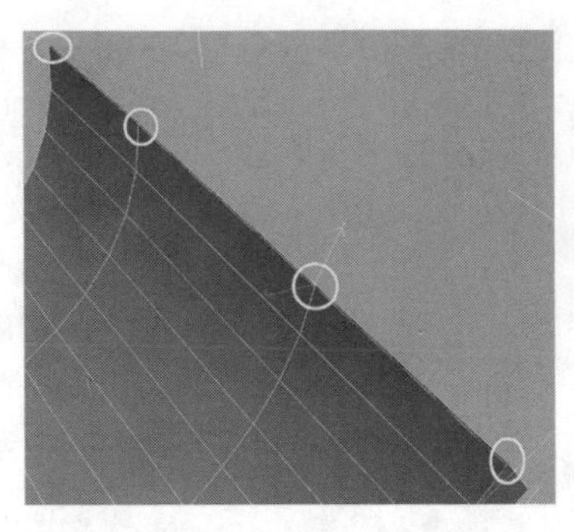

Figure 3-719

Figure 3-720

12. Select all the vertices in the upper_knee_cowl and click the **Weld Settings** button. Set the Weld Threshold fairly high (around **1.25**) and click **Weld** to weld any overlapping vertices you may've missed. Select **upper_knee_cowl** and add a Smooth modifier to the stack, making sure to check the Auto Smooth check box. Convert it to an Editable Polygon to collapse the stack, then select the outer edges.

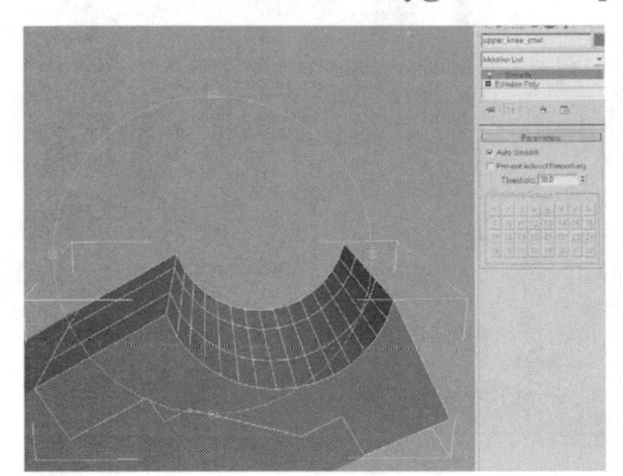

Figure 3-721

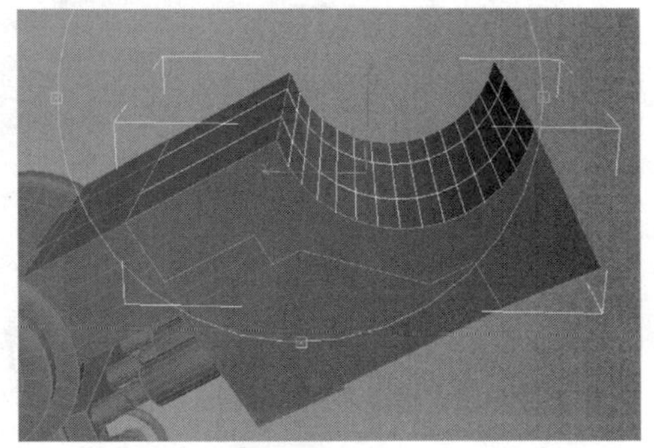

Figure 3-722

13. Chamfer the edges by **2.0** and then by **0.79**.

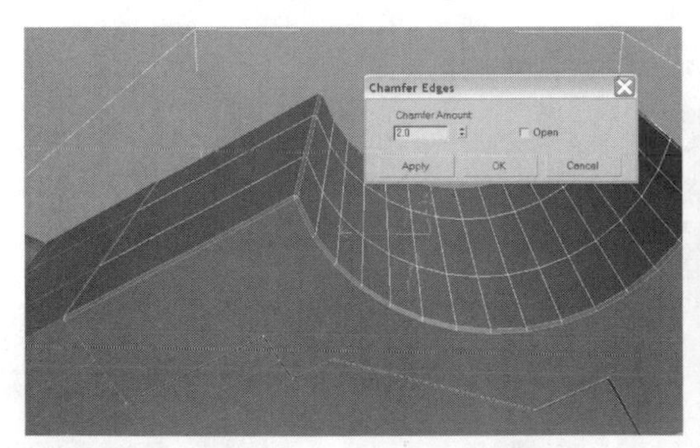

Figure 3-723

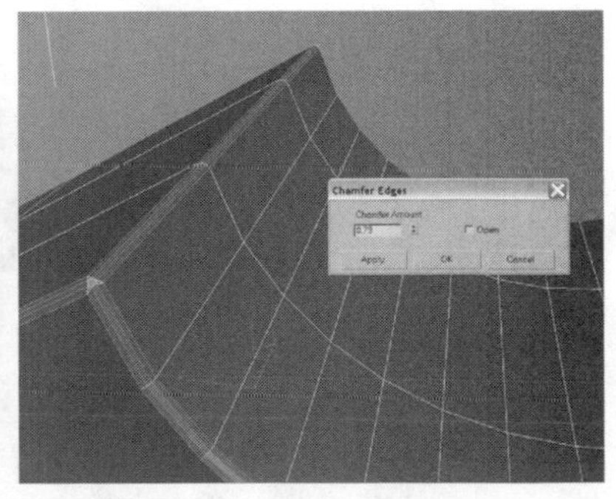

Figure 3-724

14. Select the inside surface, click **Detach**, and name the new object **knee_sleeve.**

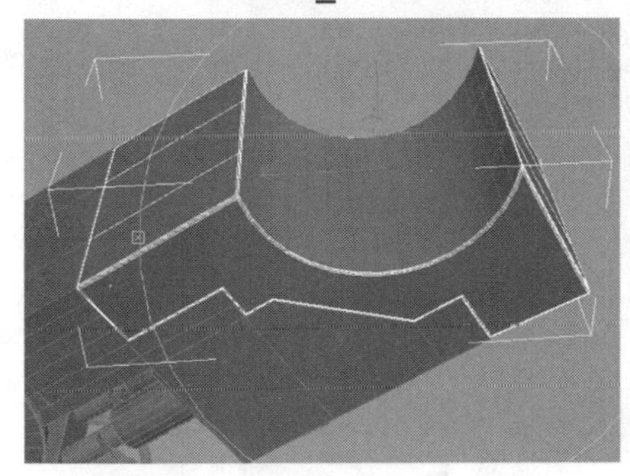
Figure 3-725

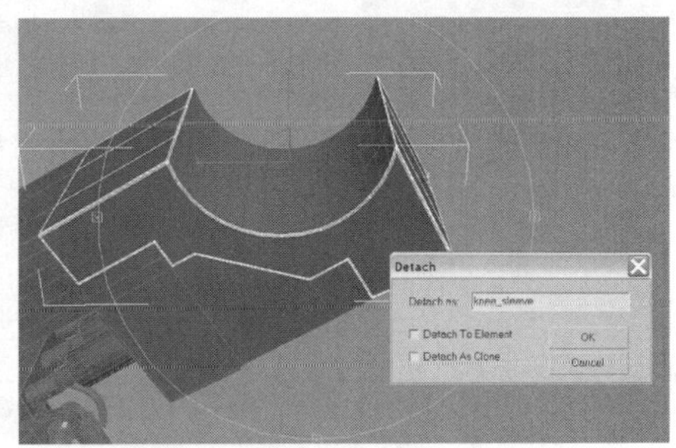

Figure 3-726

15. Do a quick render. If there is a problem with the outer surface, try selecting the cap and deleting it and then recapping it. That should work.

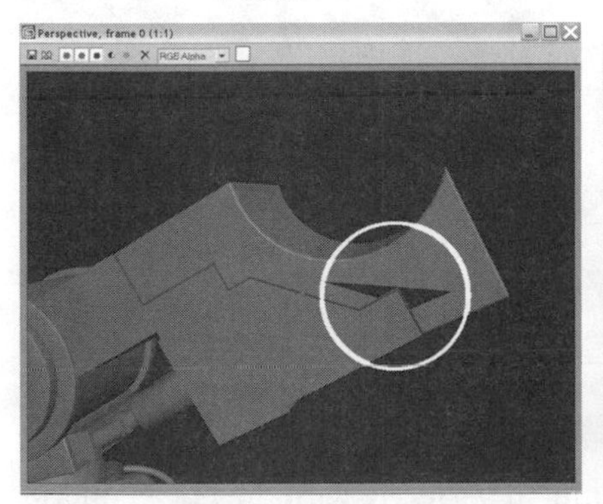

Figure 3-727

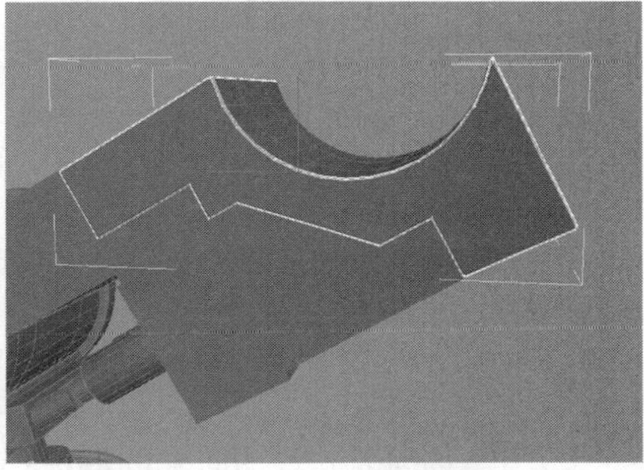
Figure 3-728

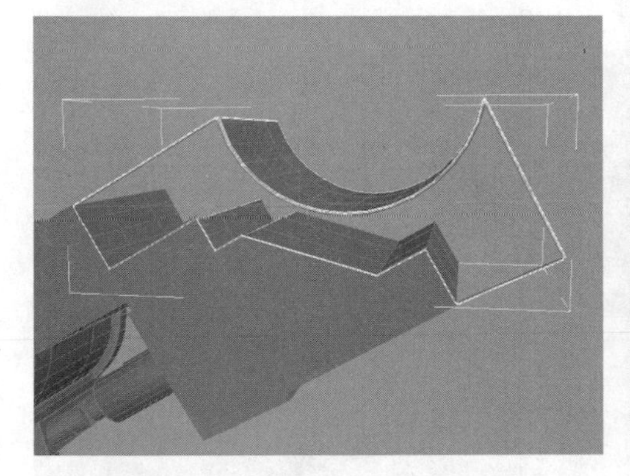
Figure 3-729

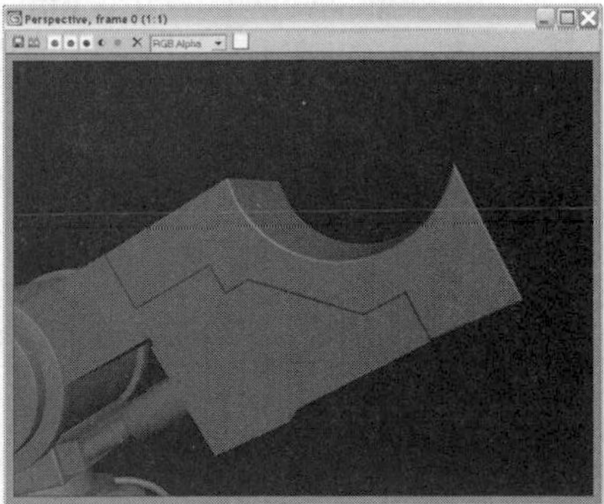

Figure 3-730

Fire Drill: So why did that happen, and why did simply deleting the cap and adding it back fix it? Don't know. Most people hate to use Booleans because they can result in unpredictable outcomes. Sometimes, as in this case, Booleans are the only way to get the shape you're looking for. In those cases, expect to suck it up and do some fixing. Incidentally, this problem with Booleans is not unique to Max. It's the same with every 3D package I've used.

16. Create a Cylinder in the joint and loop-select the middle edges of the cylinder.

Radius	Height	Height/Cap Segs	Sides	Smooth
129.411	254.426	2/1	36	Checked

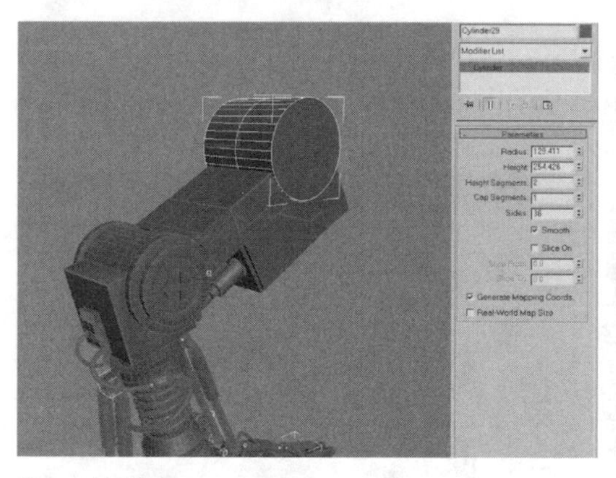

Figure 3-731

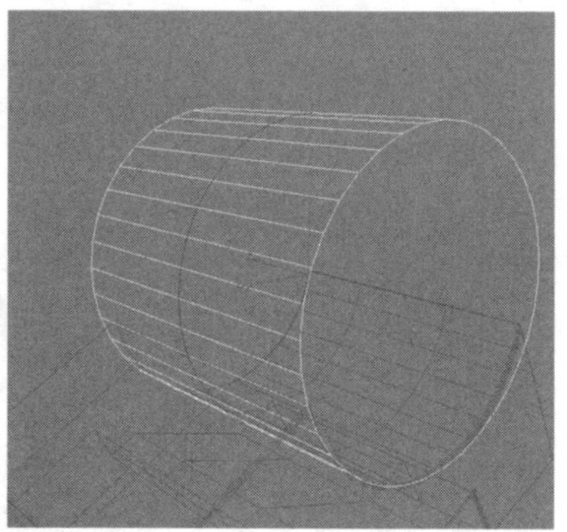

Figure 3-732

17. Chamfer the edges until they line up perfectly with the edges on the joint below (in my case it was **49.538**). Select the middle polygons and Detach them as **upper_knee**.

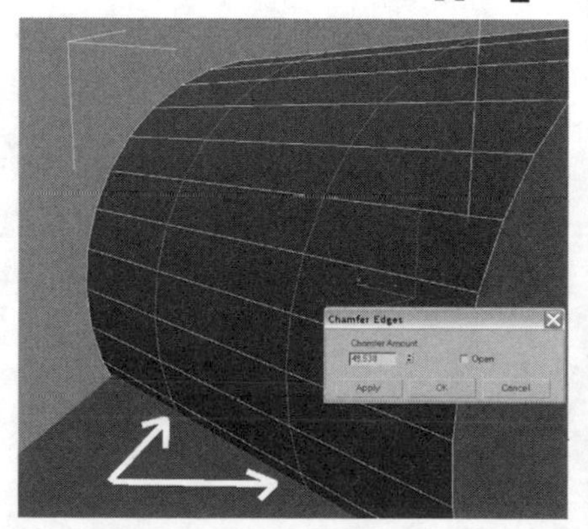

Figure 3-733

Figure 3-734

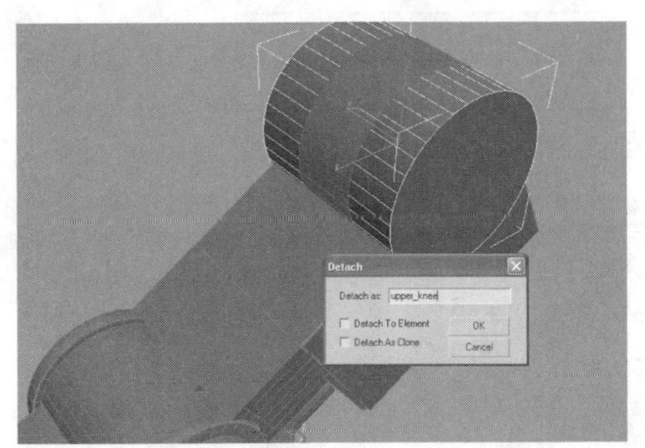

Figure 3-735

18. Select the caps on the new knee and Bevel them:

Type	Height	Outline	Apply/OK
Group	0	16	Apply
Group	25	0	Apply
Group	0	–40	Apply

Figure 3-736

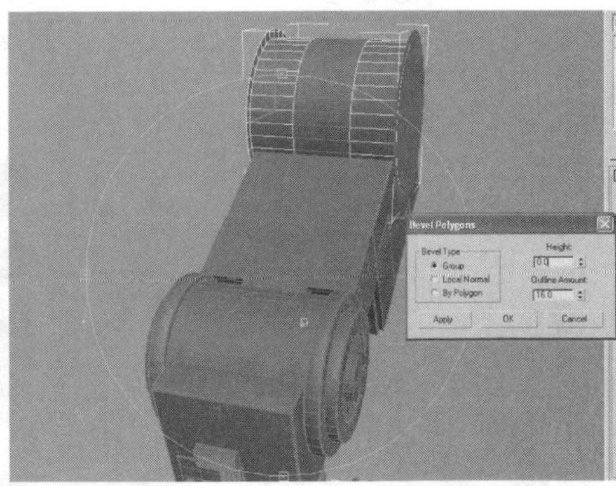

Figure 3-737

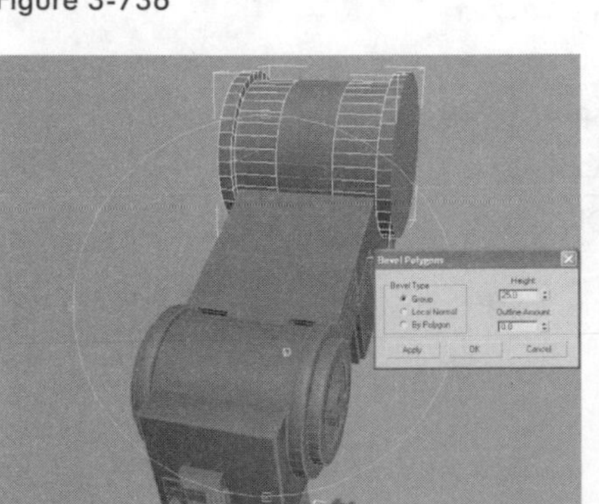

Figure 3-738

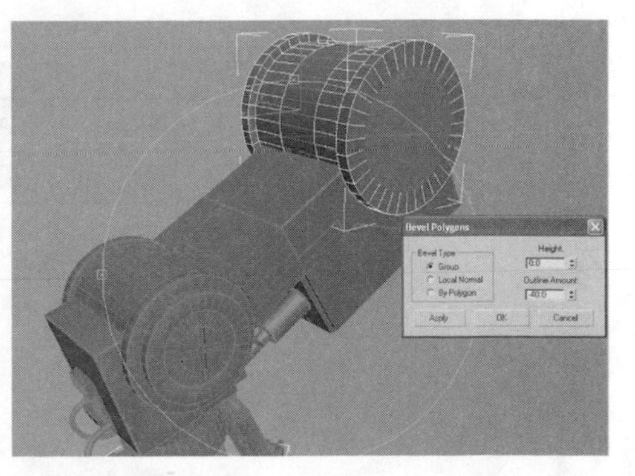

Figure 3-739

Type	Height	Outline	Apply/OK
Group	25	0	Apply
Group	0	–25	Apply

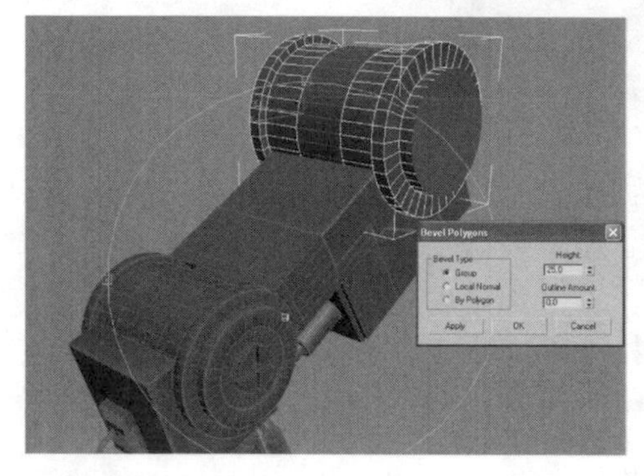

Figure 3-740

Figure 3-741

Type	Height	Outline	Apply/OK
Group	–15	0	Apply
Group	0	–25	Apply

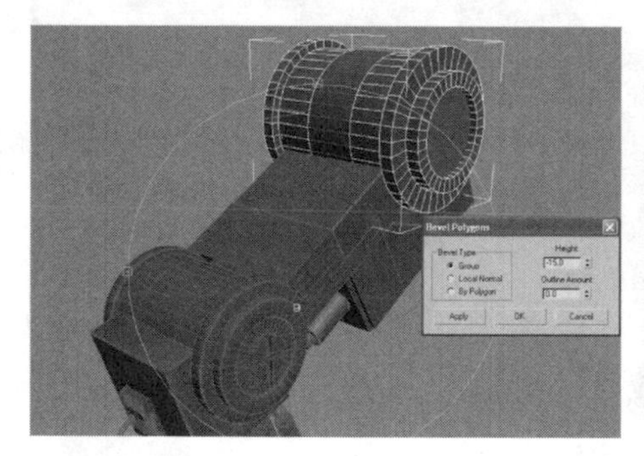

Figure 3-742

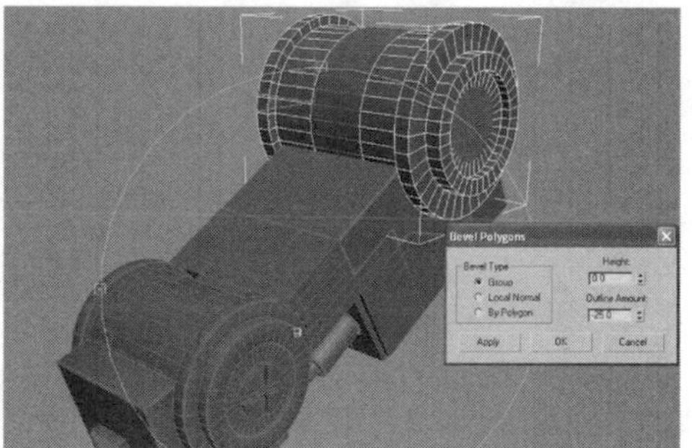

Figure 3-743

Type	Height	Outline	Apply/OK
Group	3	0	Apply
Group	0	25	OK

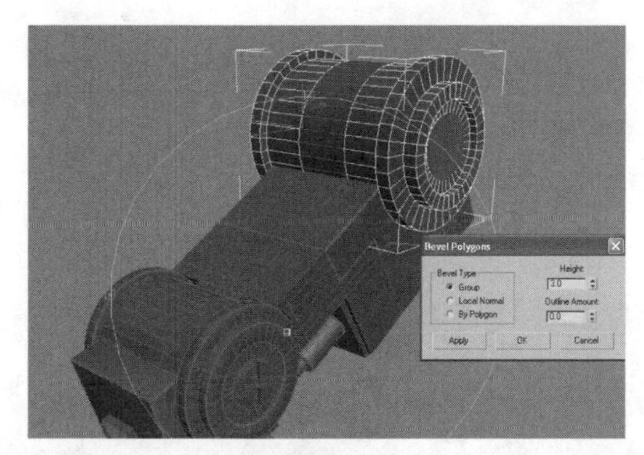

Figure 3-744

19. Cut four slices to form a cross, then select the outer four corners and Extrude them by **10**. You do this the same way you did for the lower knee, in steps 35 and 36 of the previous section (Day 6).

20. Select the outer edges of the kneecaps and Chamfer them by **3.5** and then by **1.41**.

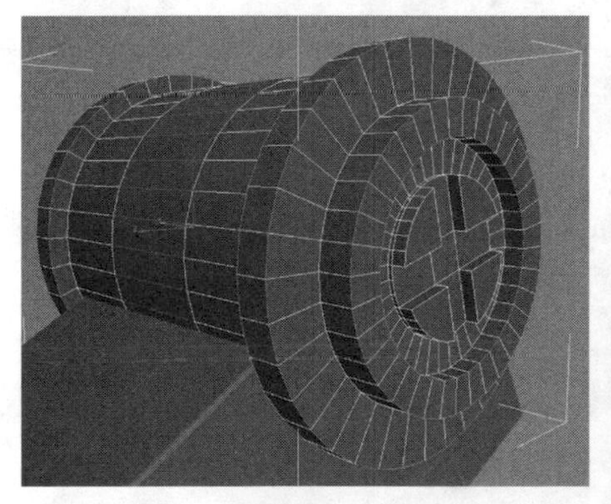

Figure 3-745

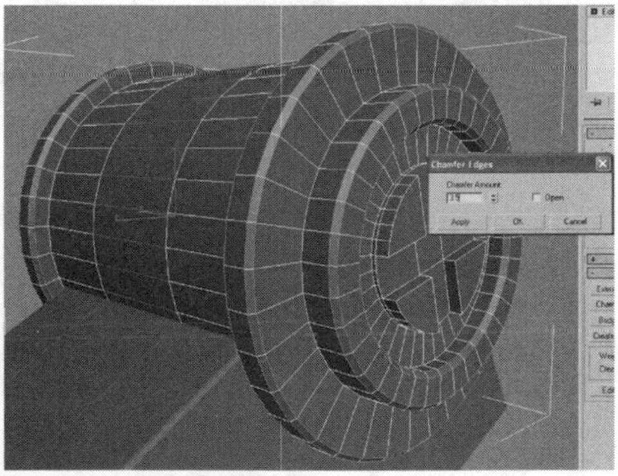

Figure 3-746

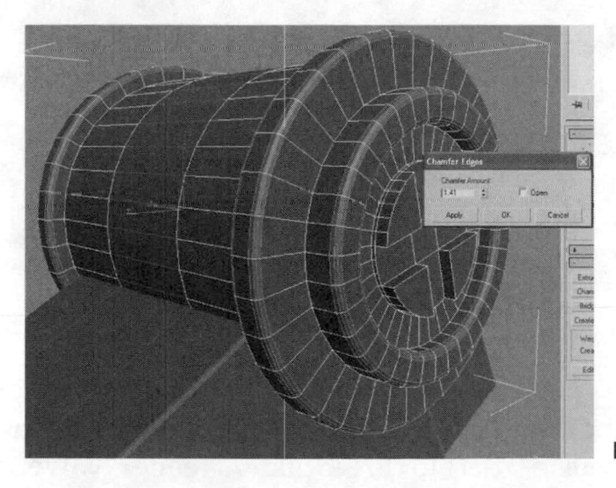

Figure 3-747

21. Add a Smooth modifier to the stack, convert it to an Editable Polygon to collapse the stack, and add a Tube named **upper_knee_hydraulic_valve**:

Radius 1	Radius 2	Height	Height/Cap Segs	Sides	Smooth
21	15	22	1/1	18	Checked

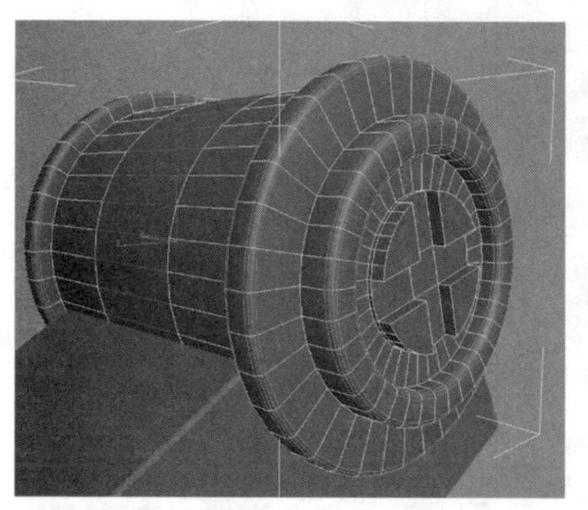

Figure 3-748

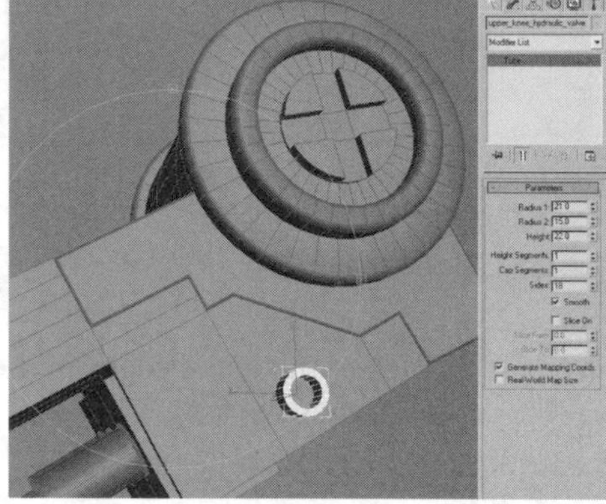

Figure 3-749

22. Create a Tube on the piston closest to the tube you just created, and name it **three_piston_feeder_valve**. Select and Link it to the piston. Create a new Hose.

Radius 1	Radius 2	Height	Height/Cap Segs	Sides	Smooth
12	15	18	1/1	18	Checked

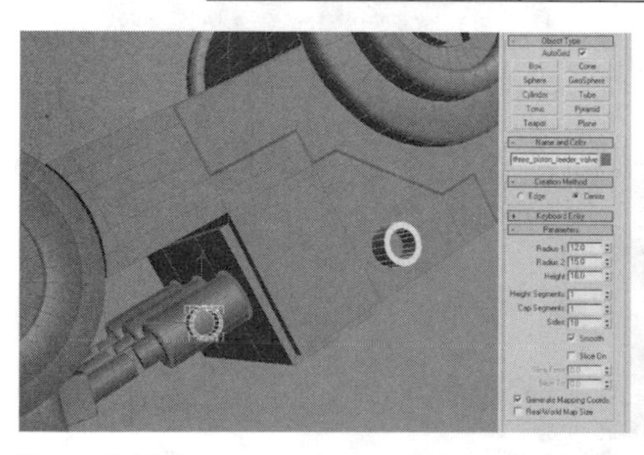

Figure 3-750

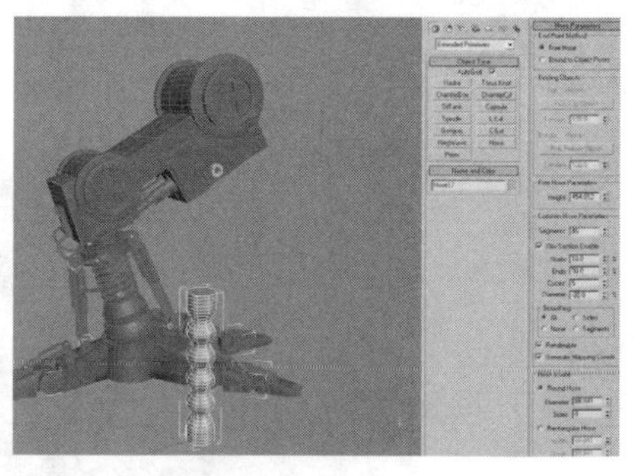

Figure 3-751

23. Change the End Point Method to **Bound to Object Pivots**, set the Top Binding Object to **upper_knee_hydraulic_valve**, and set the Bottom Binding Object to **three_piston_feeder_valve**.

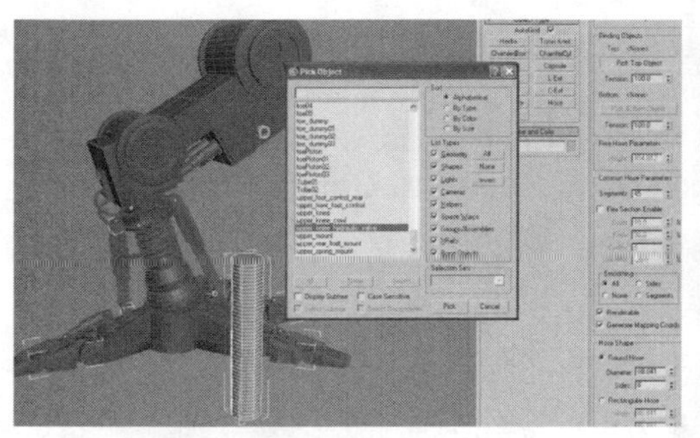

Figure 3-752

Figure 3-753

24. Set the top Tension to **191**, leave the bottom Tension at **100**, and change the hose Diameter to **22.541** with **16** Sides. Change the upper_knee_hydraulic_valve's Radius 2 to **11.858**.

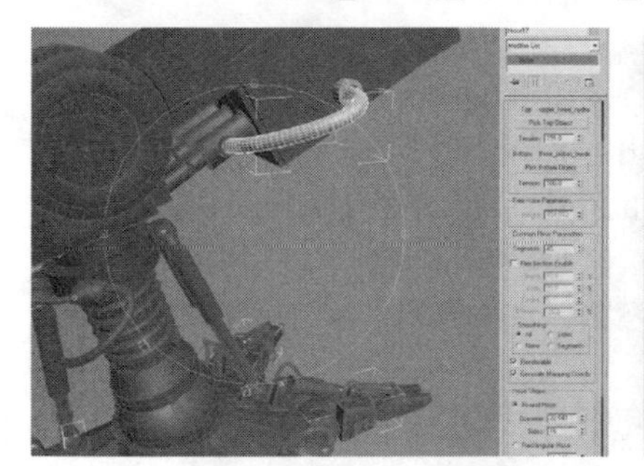

Figure 3-754

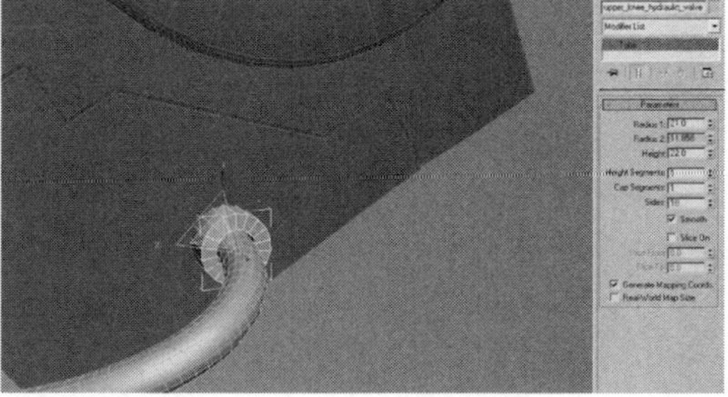

Figure 3-755

25. Make two clones of the upper_knee_hydraulic_valve, Rotate them, and move them to the far bottom surface of the knee (at right angles to the three pistons). Select three_piston_feeder_valve and make two clones.

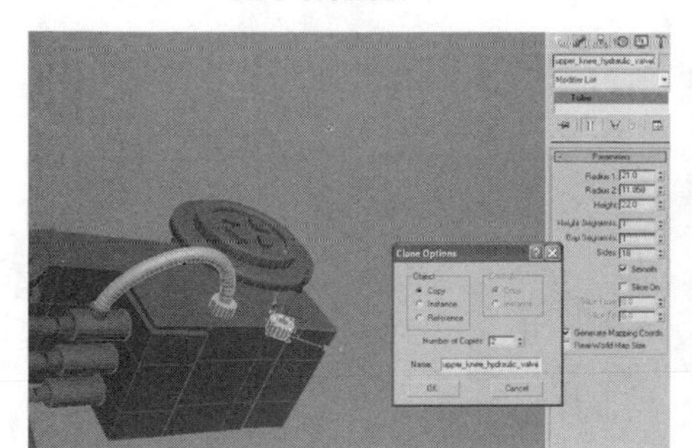

Figure 3-756

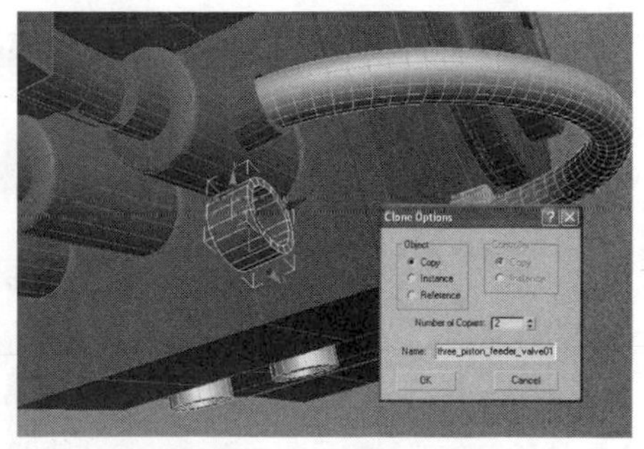

Figure 3-757

26. Move the clones you just made, Rotate them **90** degrees, and apply them to the far two pistons that do not, as yet, have valves attached to them. Select and Link them to the pistons. Create another Hose with the End Point Method set to **Bound to Object Pivots.**

Figure 3-758

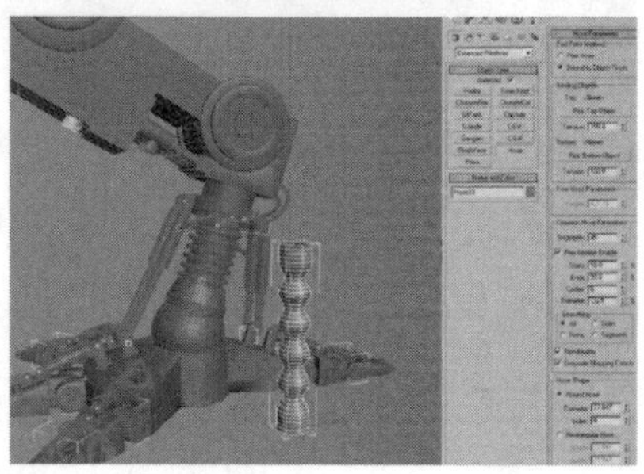

Figure 3-759

27. Set the Top Binding Object to the **upper_knee_hydraulic_valve** and set the Tension to **169.** Set the Bottom Binding Object to **three_piston_feeder_valve** and set the Tension to **138.** Set the Diameter of the hose to **18.647** and the Sides to **16.** Select the eight polygons on the center of the upper knee as shown in Figure 3-761.

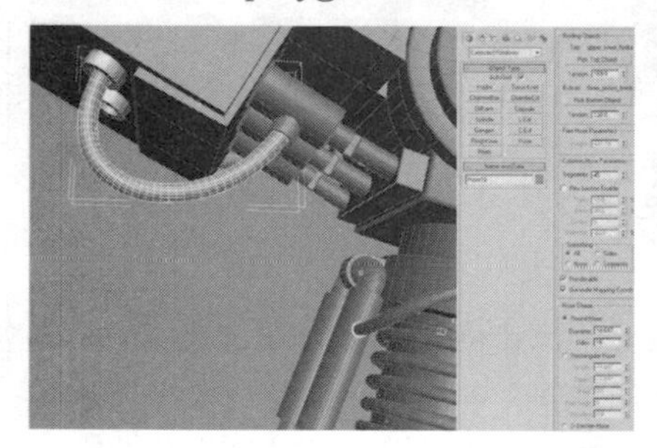

Figure 3-760

Figure 3-761

28. Extrude the polygons by **18.5**, hit **Apply**, Extrude them again by **37**, and then click **OK**.

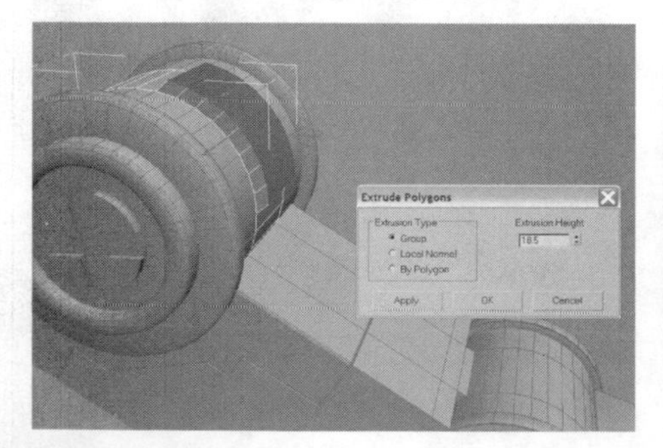

Figure 3-762

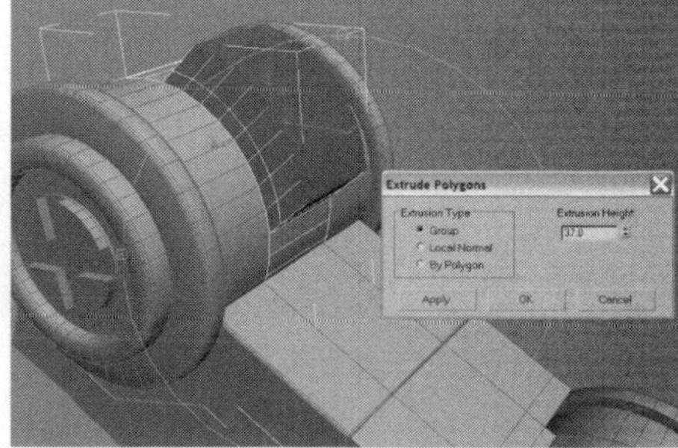

Figure 3-763

29. Select the side polygons of the top row of the extrusion and Extrude them by **92.15**.

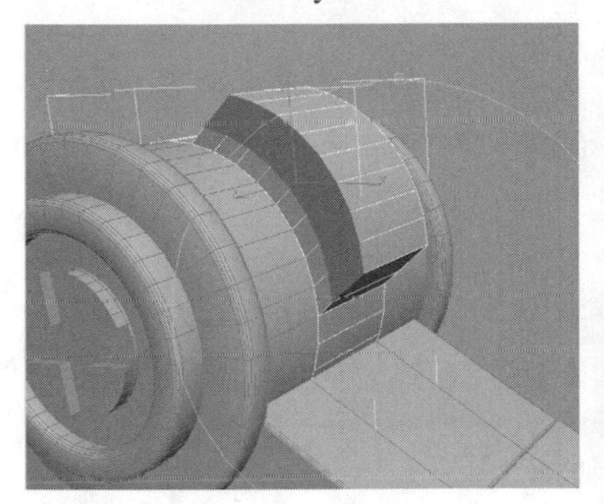
Figure 3-764

Figure 3-765

30. Select the top polygons of the extrusion, set the Coordinate System to **Local**, and then Non-uniform Scale them down to **0** in the Z axis.

Figure 3-766

Figure 3-767

31. Extrude the polygons by **180** and select only the polygons in the last three rows as shown in Figure 3-769.

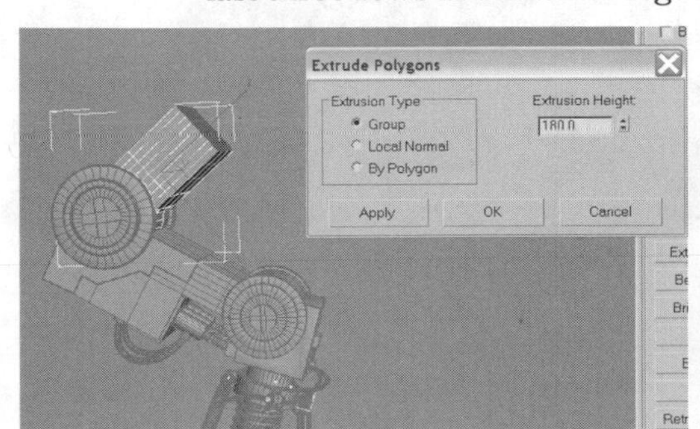

Figure 3-768

Figure 3-769

32. Extrude the polygons by **150** and then select the three polygons on the bottom of the extrusion.

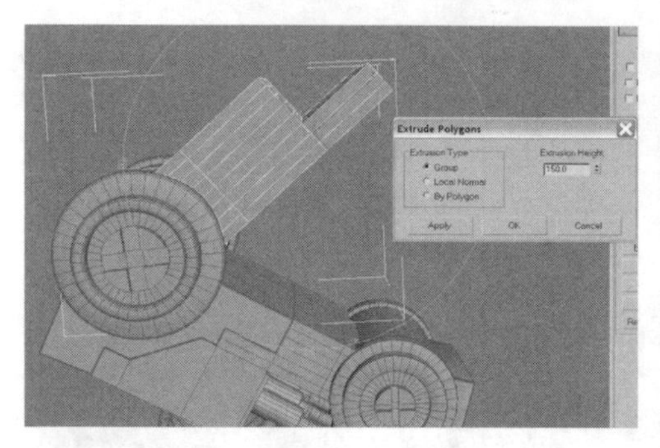

Figure 3-770

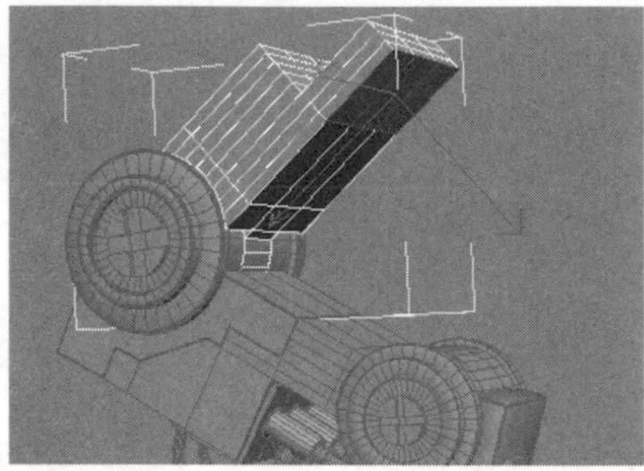

Figure 3-771

33. Extrude the polygons by **120**. Select the front three lower bottom polygons, as shown in Figure 3-773.

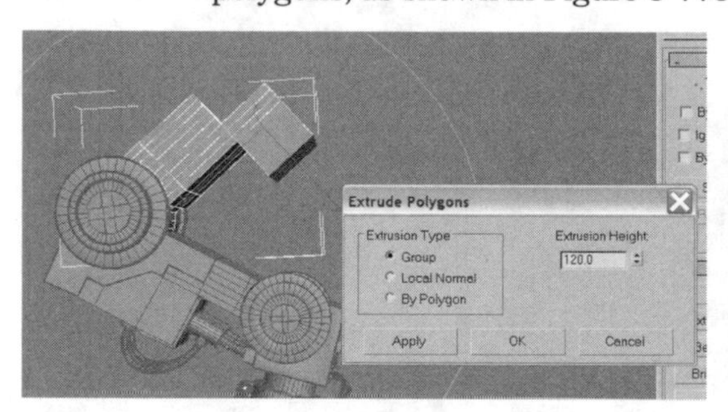

Figure 3-772

Figure 3-773

34. Extrude the polygons by **180**. Select the upper three edges of the polygons you just extruded.

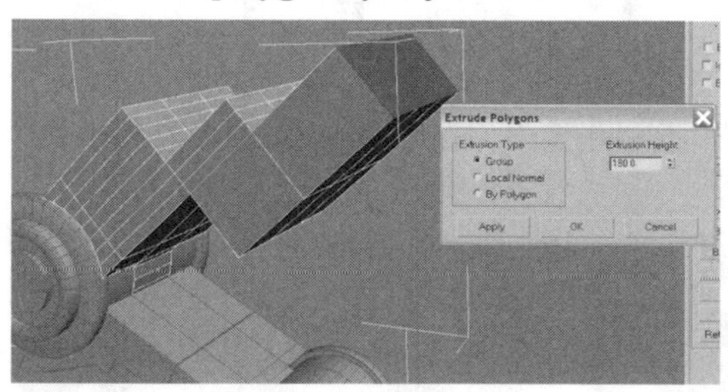

Figure 3-774

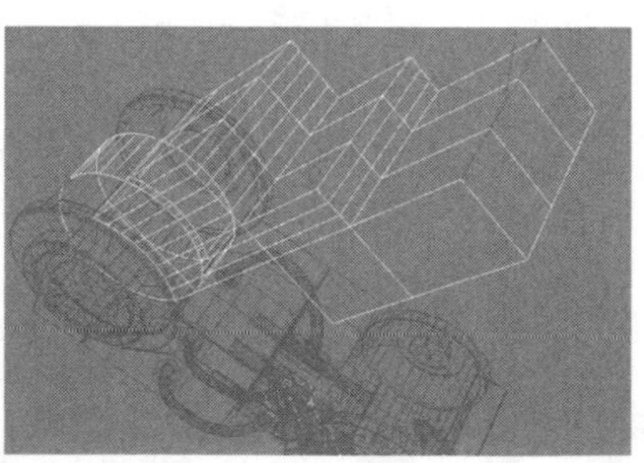

Figure 3-775

35. Chamfer the edges by **90** and then select the lower front three polygons.

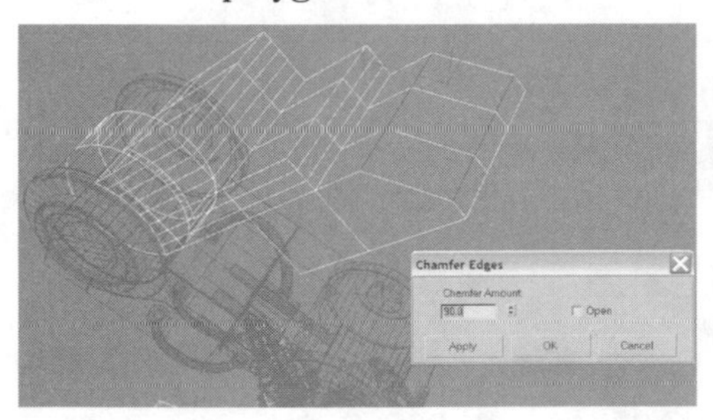

Figure 3-776

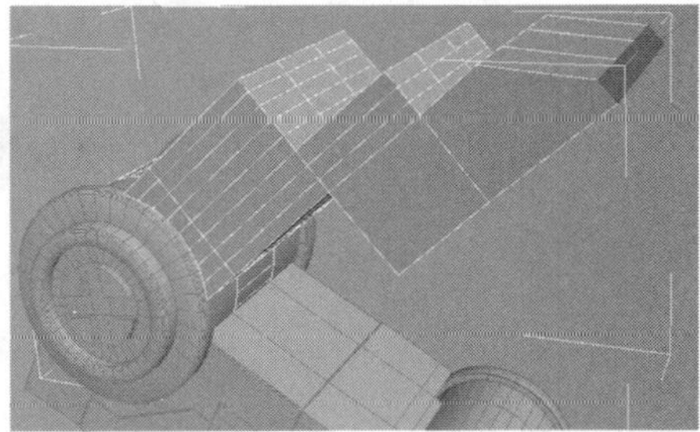

Figure 3-777

36. Extrude those three polygons by **50** and then select the top polygons the way you did before.

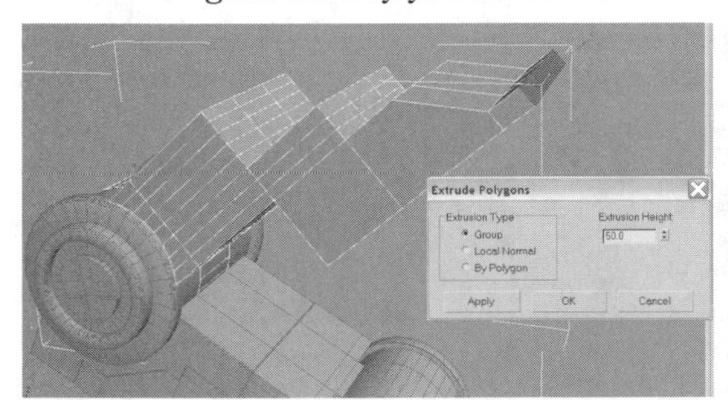

Figure 3-778

Figure 3-779

37. Detach the polygons and name it **upper_thigh**. Select the top upper three edges, as shown in Figure 3-781.

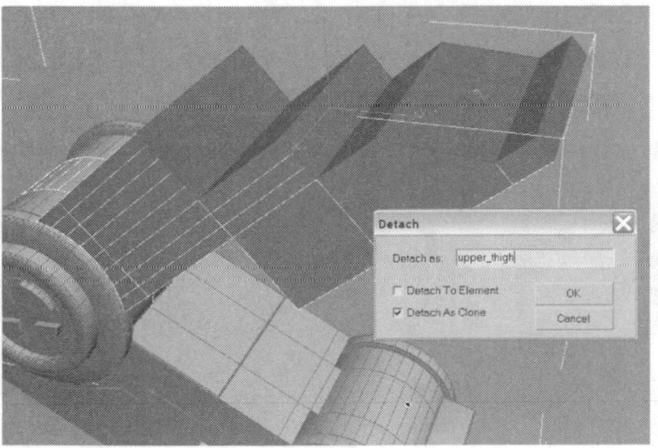

Figure 3-780

Figure 3-781

38. Extrude the edges by **550** and then drag them downward like you did before.

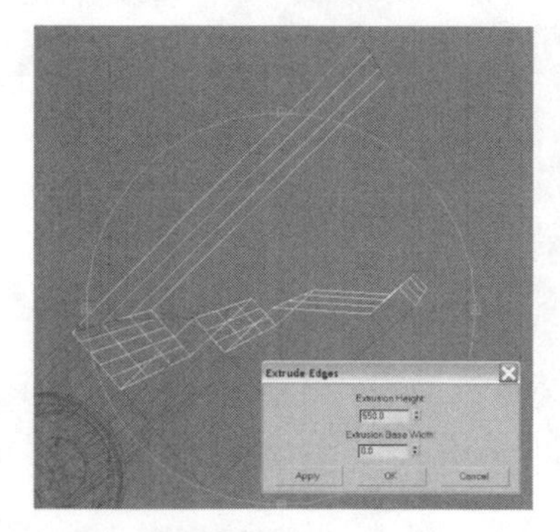

Figure 3-782

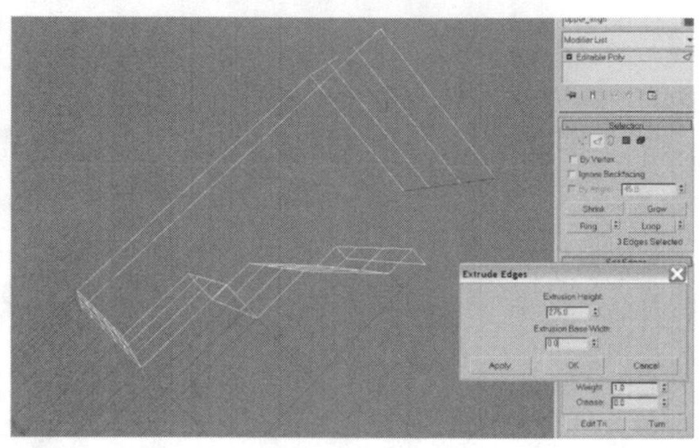

Figure 3-783

39. Select the two outer rows of edges and then click **Bridge**.

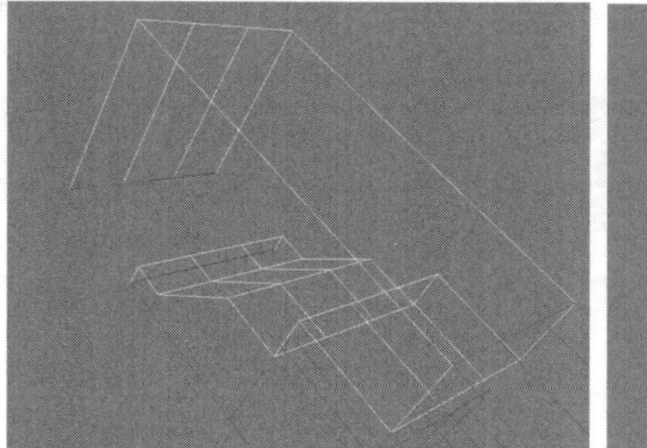

Figure 3-784

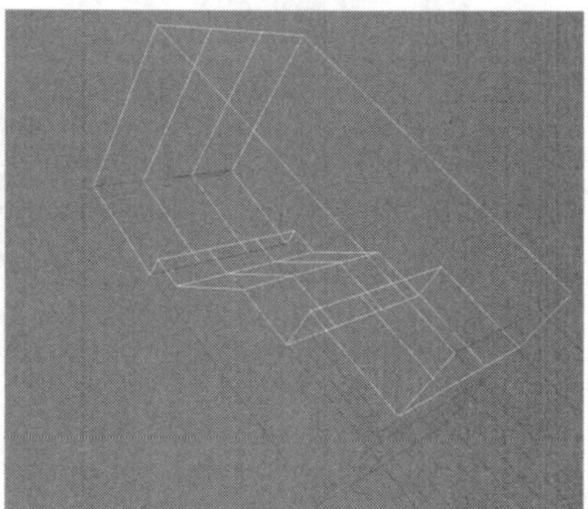

Figure 3-785

40. Select the inside polygons, like you did previously, and Flip them. Border-select the outer borders and Cap them.

Figure 3-786

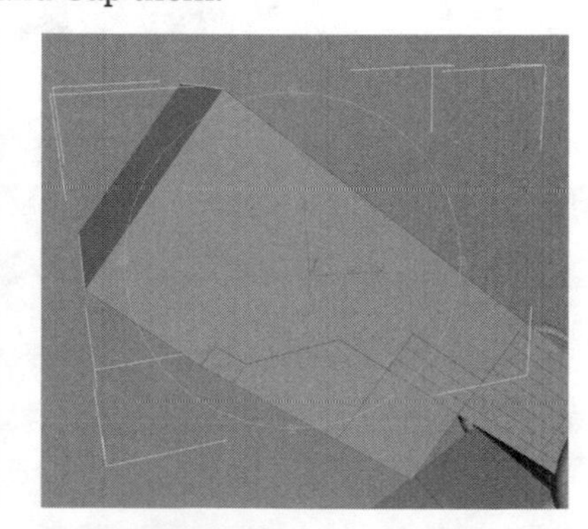

Figure 3-787

41. Create a Cylinder in the upper corner and convert it to an Editable Polygon. Use Loop to select the middle edges, as you did before, and chamfer them by about **48** (or until they're aligned with the edges on the upper_thigh). Select the **upper_thigh**, create a Boolean object, choose **Subtraction (A–B)**, click **Pick Opcrand B**, and then click the cylinder. Remove the extra edges created by the Boolean operation the way you did before. (Don't forget to remove the residual vertices.)

Radius	Height	Height/Cap Segs	Sides	Smooth
215	310	3/1	36	Checked

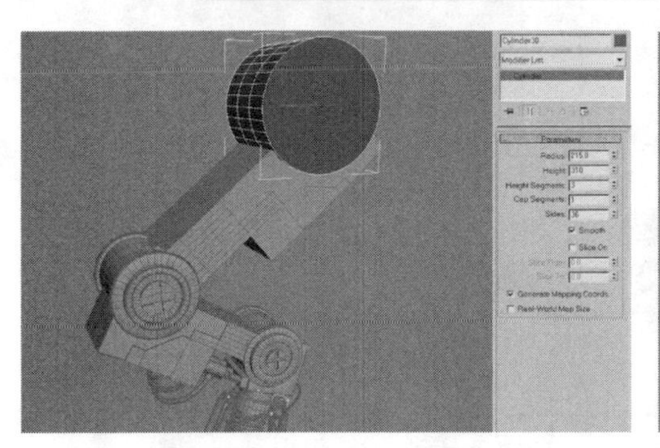

Figure 3-788

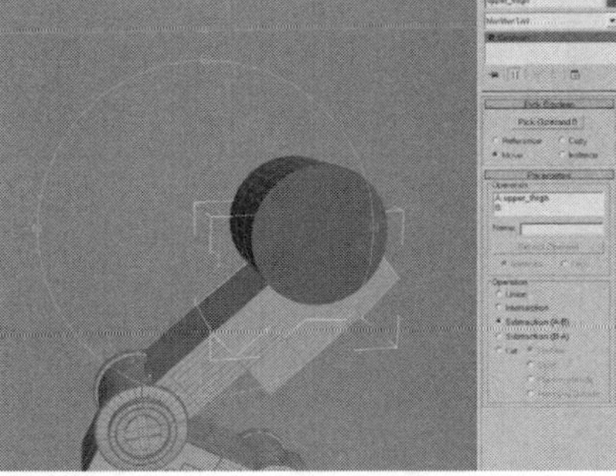

Figure 3-789

42. Select the Boolean object and convert it to an Editable Polygon. Create a Chamfer Cylinder in the socket created by the Boolean.

Radius	Height	Fillet	Height/Fillet/Cap Segs	Sides	Smooth
215	350	22.56	1/4/1	36	Checked

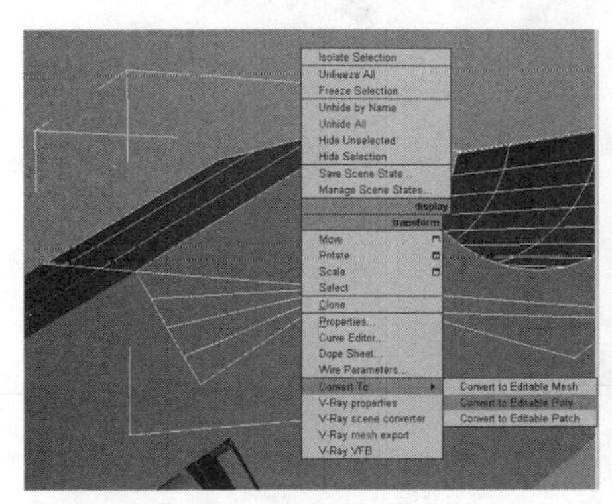

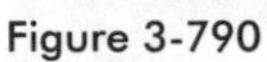

Figure 3-790

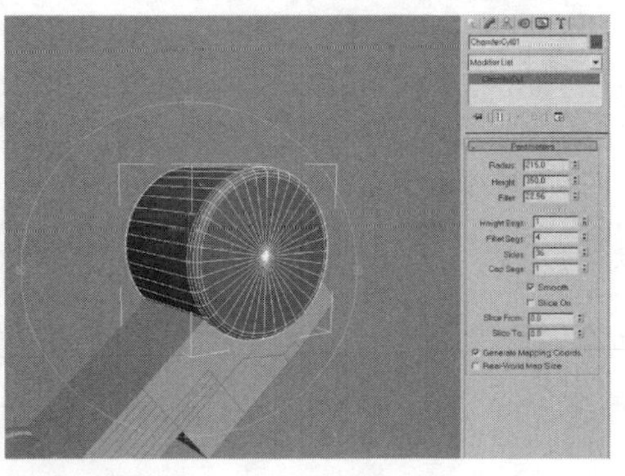

Figure 3-791

43. Convert the chamfer cylinder to an Editable Polygon and name it **Hip**. Polygon-select the outside cap only.

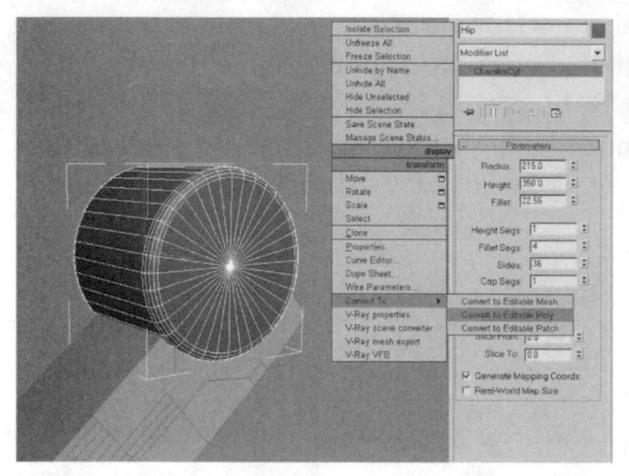

Figure 3-792

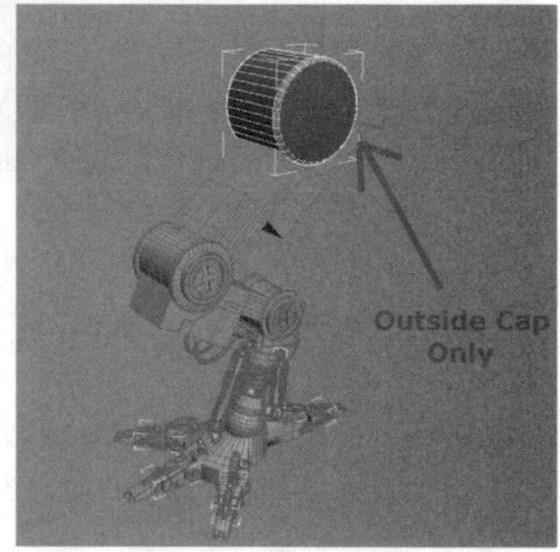

Figure 3-793

44. Bevel the cap:

Type	Height	Outline	Apply/OK
Group	50	–1	Apply
Group	0	–45	Apply

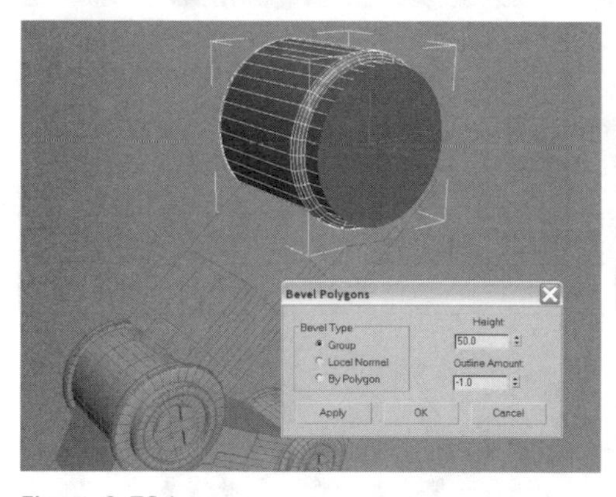

Figure 3-794

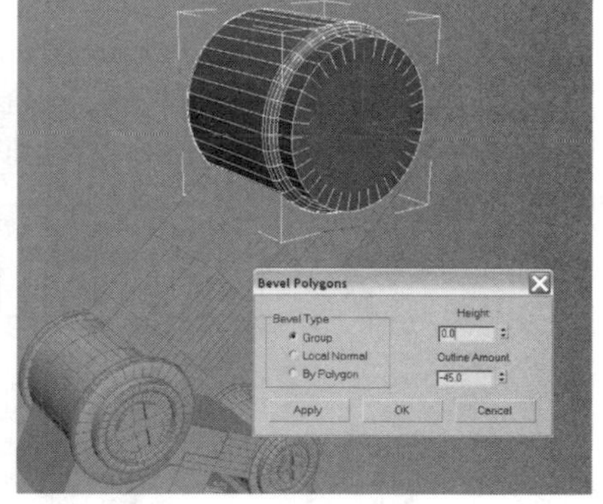

Figure 3-795

Type	Height	Outline	Apply/OK
Group	–25	0	Apply
Group	0	–7	Apply

Day 7: Assembling the Upper Leg

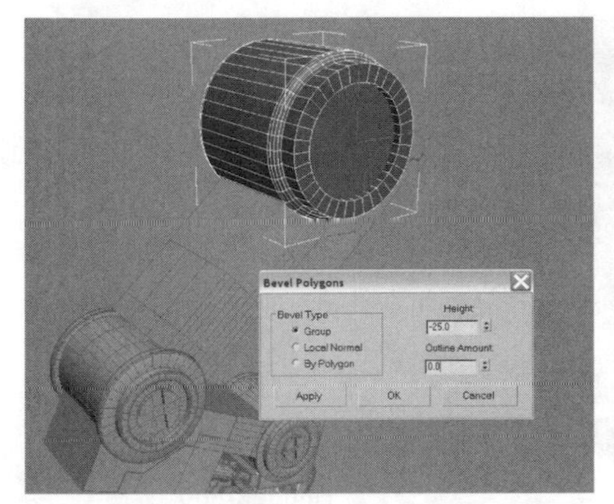

Figure 3-796

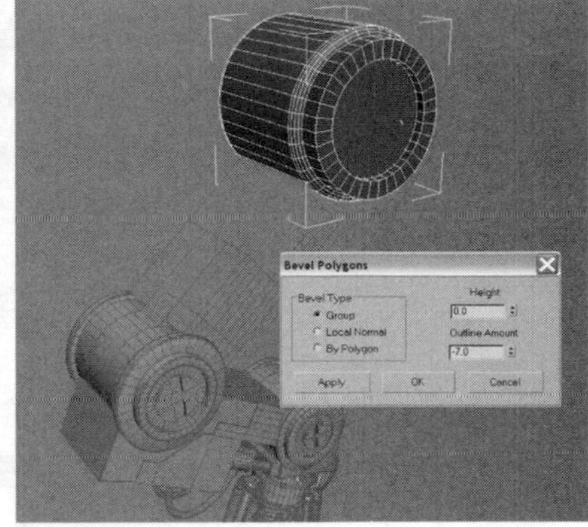

Figure 3-797

Type	Height	Outline	Apply/OK
Group	10	0	Apply
Group	0	–47	Apply

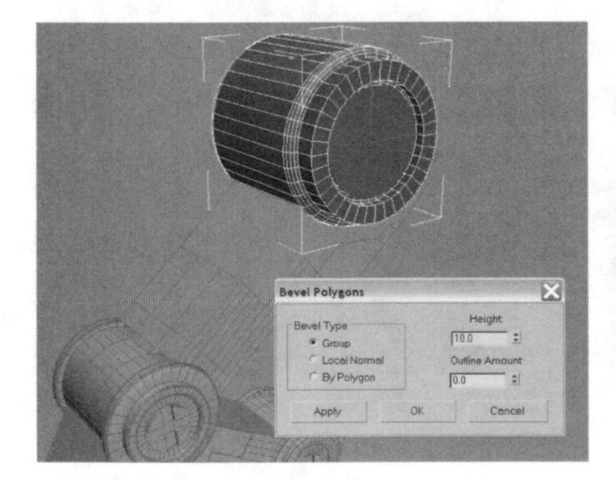

Figure 3-798

Figure 3-799

Type	Height	Outline	Apply/OK
Group	25	0	OK

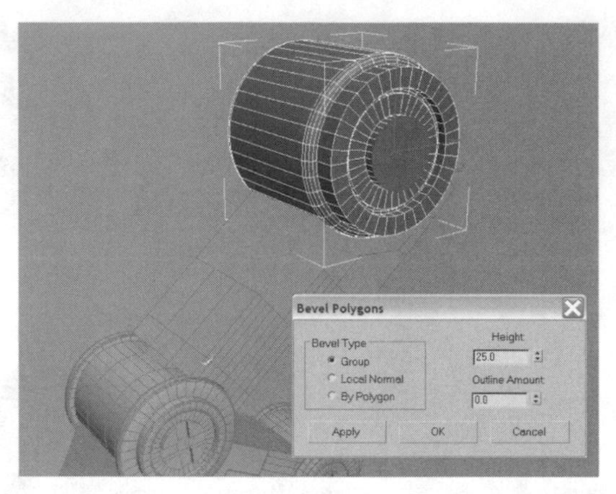

Figure 3-800

45. Delete the cap. Using AutoGrid, create a Sphere with a Radius of **88.418** and **36** Segments, and set Hemisphere to **0.5**. Align the segments, convert it to an Editable Polygon, and name the hemisphere **axle_cap**.

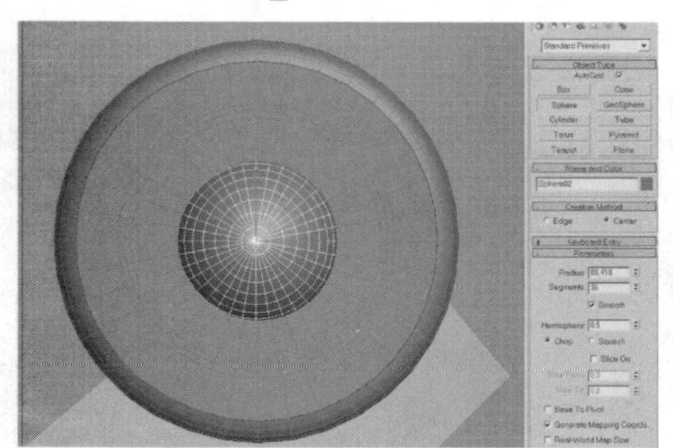

Figure 3-801

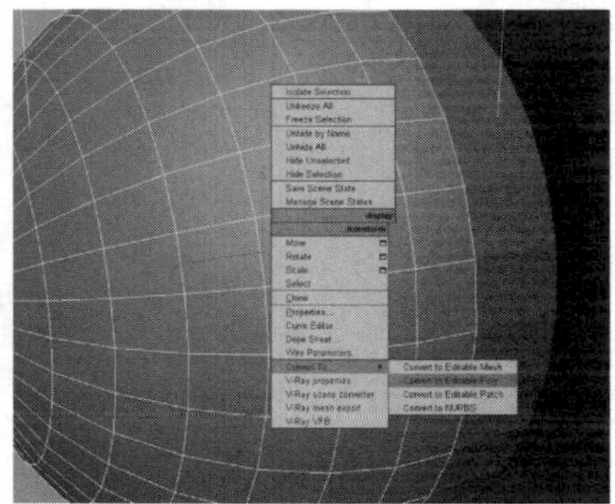

Figure 3-802

46. Select the back-facing polygons of the hemisphere and delete them. Align the segments of the hemisphere with those of the chamfer cylinder, select the chamfer cylinder, click **Attach**, and select **axle_cap**.

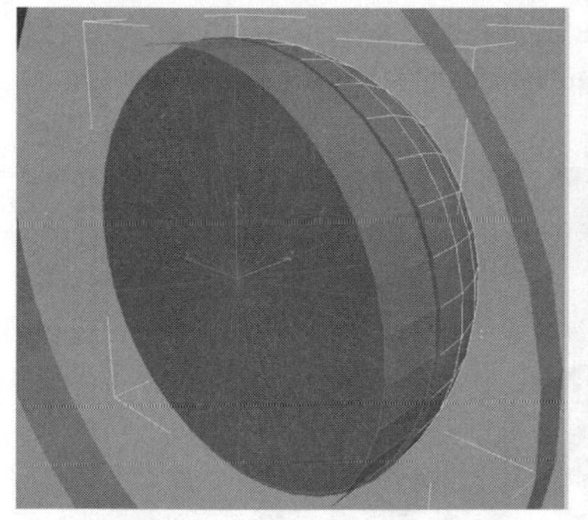

Figure 3-803

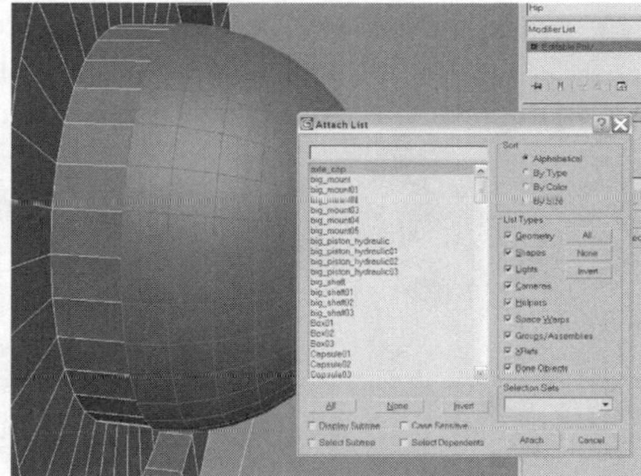

Figure 3-804

47. Create a Gengon and name it **lugnut.** Click the **Hierarchy** tab, select **Affect Pivot Only**, and move the pivot to the center of the axle_cap.

Sides	Radius	Fillet	Height	Side/Height/Fillet Segs	Smooth
6	15	0.65	8	1/1/1	Checked

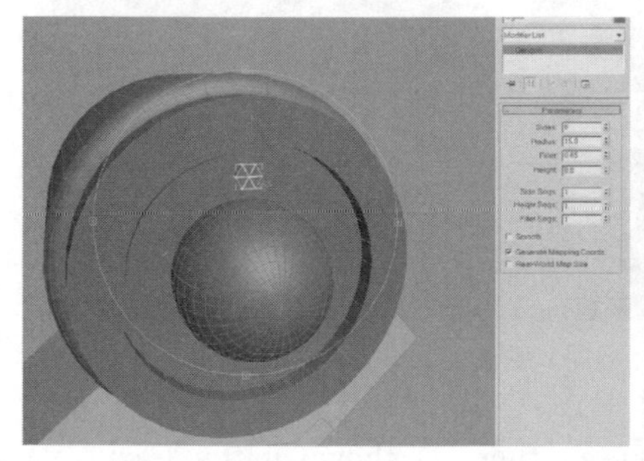

Figure 3-805

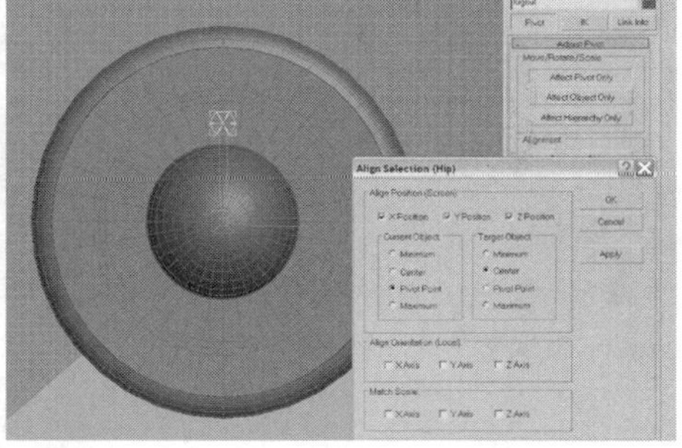

Figure 3-806

48. Hold down the **Shift** key, Rotate by **40**, and set the Number of Copies to **8**. Select the chamfer cylinder, click **Attach List**, select all lugnut clones, and click **Attach**.

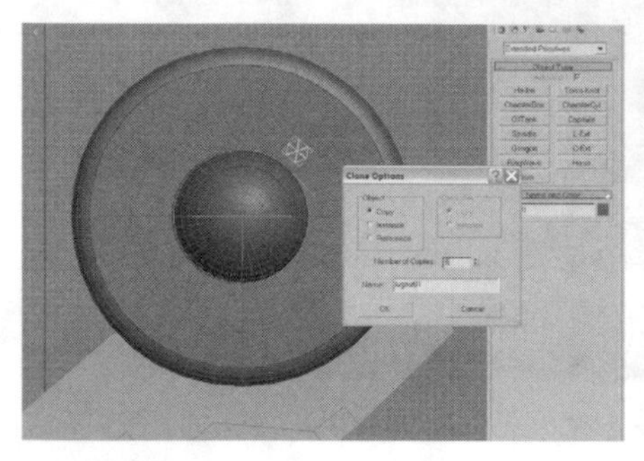

Figure 3-807

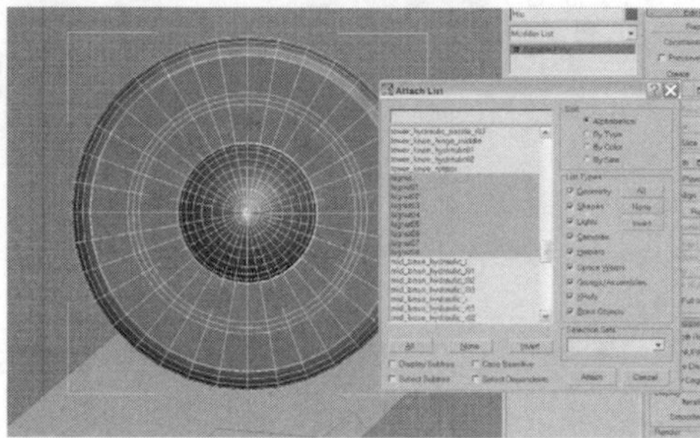

Figure 3-808

49. Select and Link the chamfer cylinder to the upper_thigh. Select the two outer polygons on the top of the middle leg.

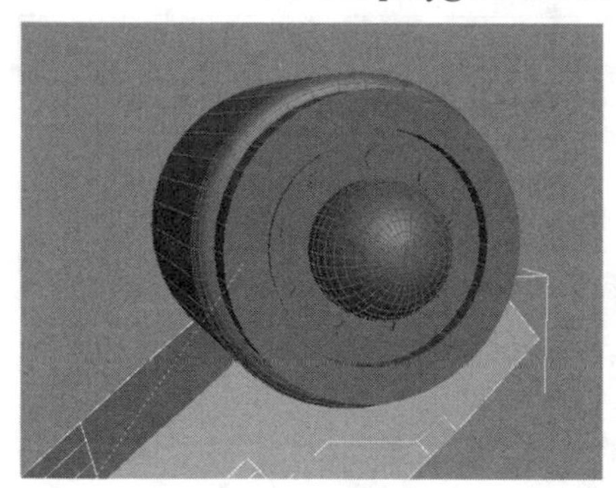

Figure 3-809

Figure 3-810

50. Bevel the polygons and then scale them, as shown, in the X axis.

Type	Height	Outline	Apply/OK
Local Normal	0	–8	OK

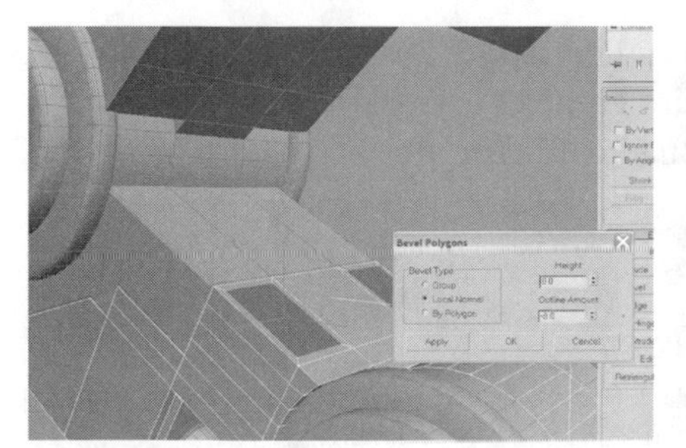

Figure 3-811

Figure 3-812

51. Extrude the polygons by Local Normal **–70**. Select the matching two polygons on the upper leg and Bevel them:

Type	Height	Outline	Apply/OK
Group	0	–25	OK

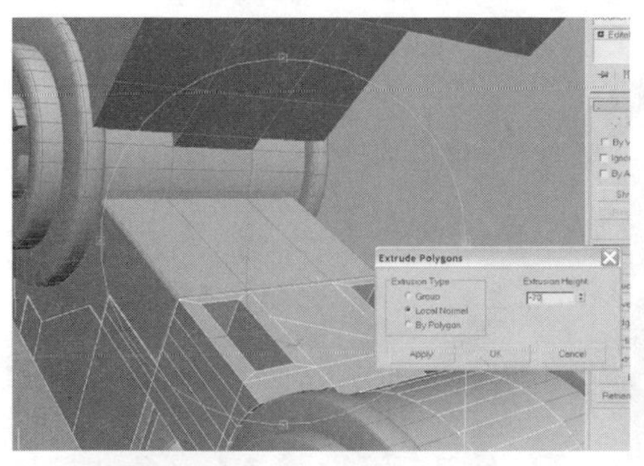

Figure 3-813

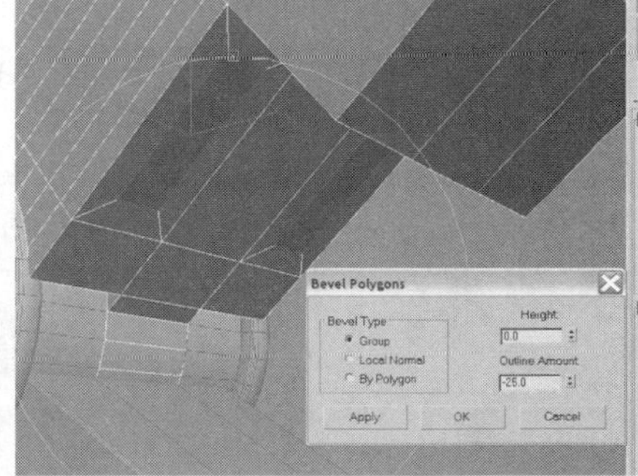

Figure 3-814

52. Scale the polygons as shown. Extrude them by **50** but hit **Apply**, *not* OK.

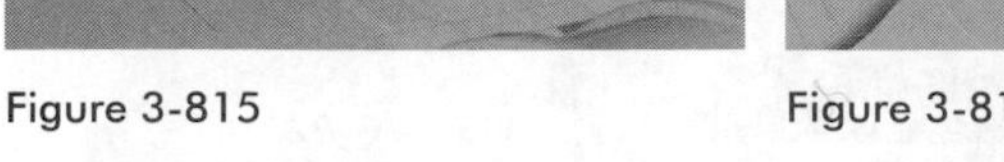

Figure 3-815

Figure 3-816

53. Extrude the polygons by **10** and hit **Apply** 20 times and then hit **OK**. Hit **Grow** until the entire group of extrusions has been selected, click **Detach**, and name it **lifter_gears**.

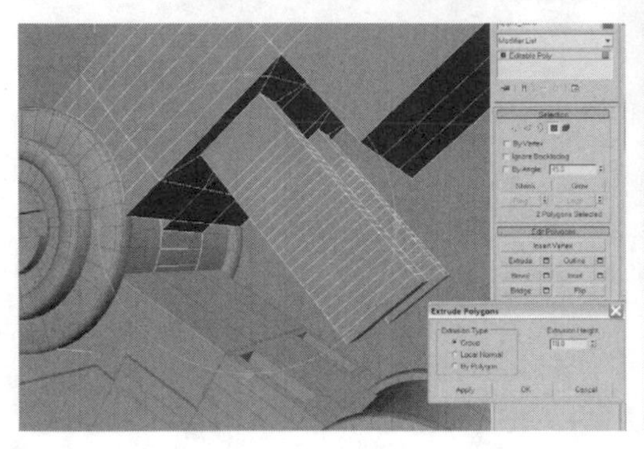

Figure 3-817

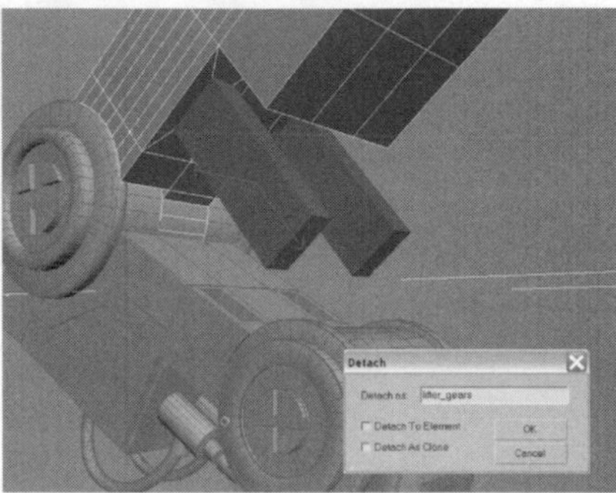

Figure 3-818

54. Select and Link the lifters to the top leg. Move the pivot point to the first segment.

Figure 3-819

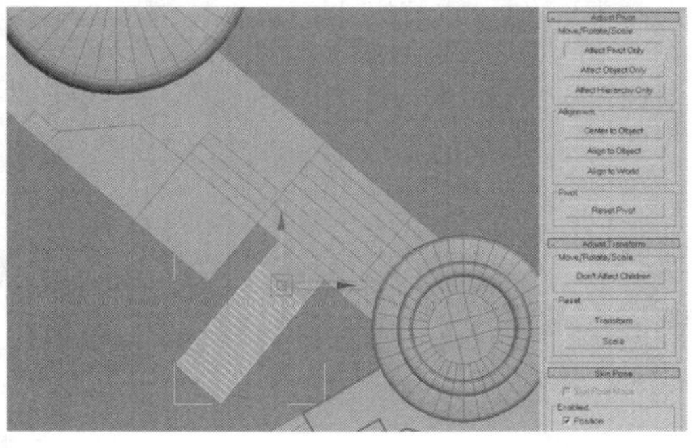

Figure 3-820

55. Add a Bend modifier to the stack with an Angle of **60** and a Bend Axis of **Y**, check **Limit Effect**, and set the Lower Limit to **–147.277**.

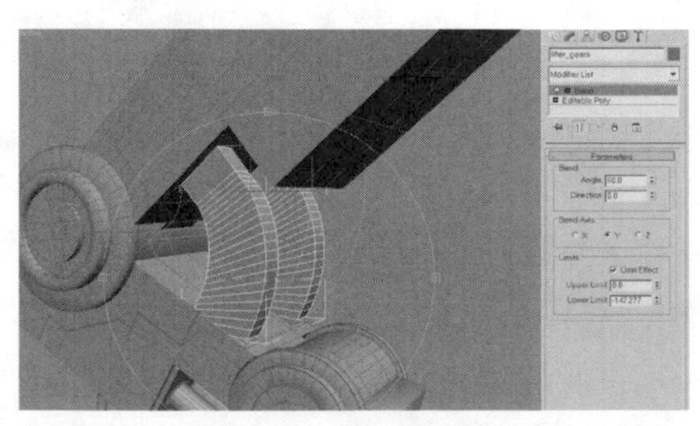

Figure 3-821

FYI: This is an iterative process. Unless you are a *lot* better than me at visualizing how long and wide these lifters have to be once the Bend modifier is attached, then you, like me, will need a couple of tries to get it right. The important thing is to *not* collapse the stack right away. Click the Editable Polygon node beneath the Bend modifier, roll it out, and tweak the subobjects, switching back and forth between the Editable Polygon level and the Bend level in the stack until you get a good fit. What follows is what I did. This not the "right" way or the "best" way. It is just one way. At this point, you should really start experimenting on your own, testing the limits of the tools. That's the only way to achieve a deep understanding of the way the tools work, both individually and together.

56. I selected the bottom 20 extrusions and used the Move tool to move them around **40** in the Z axis to stretch the lifters to compensate for the shortening that occurs from the bend.

Figure 3-822

Figure 3-823

57. Click the Bend modifier in the stack and check the alignment. It's better, but still not lining up perfectly with the holes. Non-uniform Scale the selection to **80** in the Y axis (so the ends of the lifters will be smaller and more easily fit into the holes.)

Figure 3-824

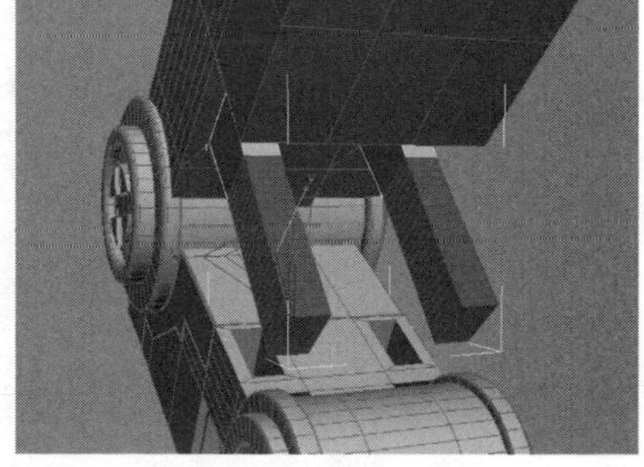

Figure 3-825

58. Under the Bend modifier, change the Lower Limit to **–168.954.** Switch to Non-uniform Scale and scale down to **80** in the Y axis again.

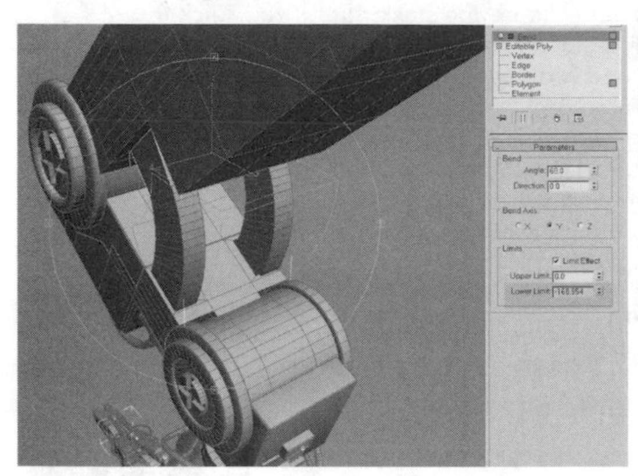

Figure 3-826

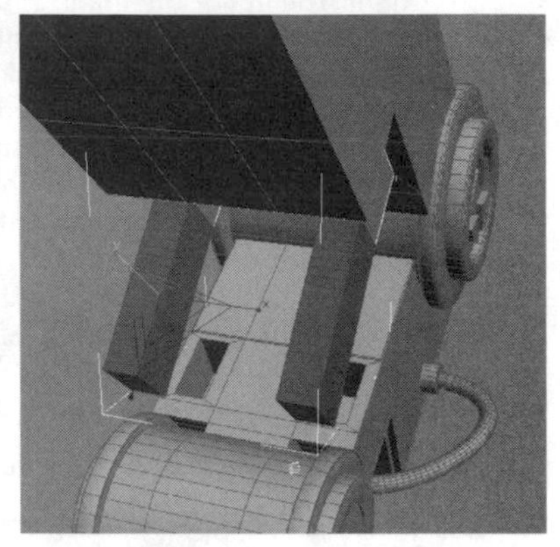

Figure 3-827

59. Switch back to the Bend modifier and check the fit. Change the Lower Limit to **–159.48**. Switch to Non-uniform Scale and scale down to **80** in the Y axis. With the Bend modifier still selected, scale the X axis to **91**.

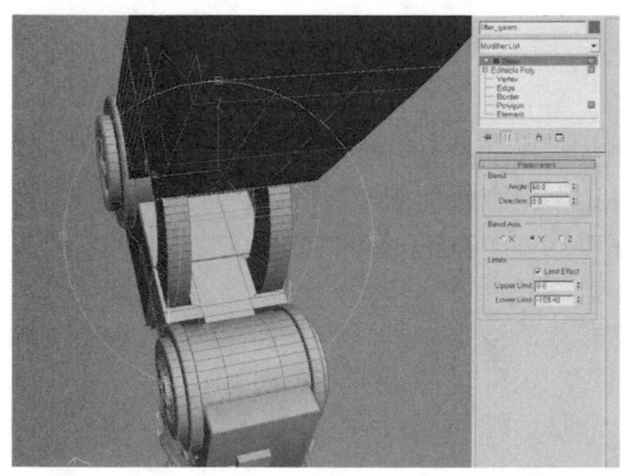

Figure 3-828

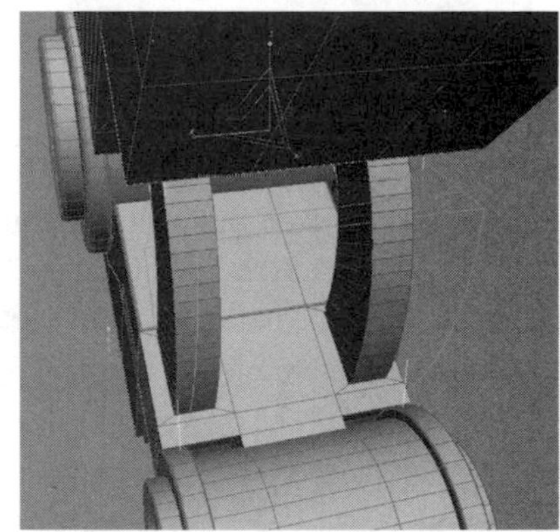

Figure 3-829

60. Convert the lifter_gears to an Editable Polygon. Attach it to the **upper_thigh**.

Day 7: Assembling the Upper Leg

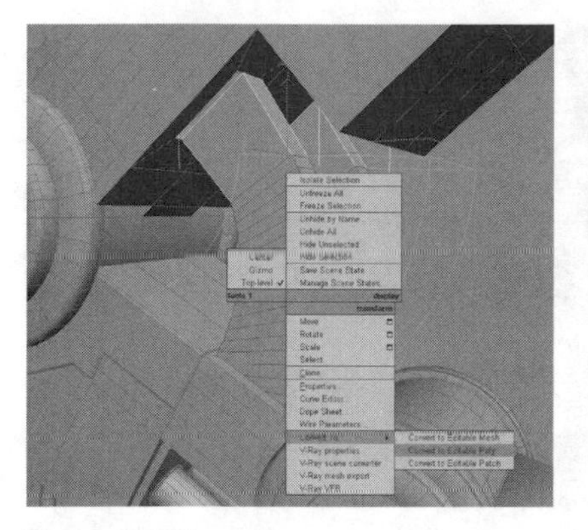

Figure 3-830

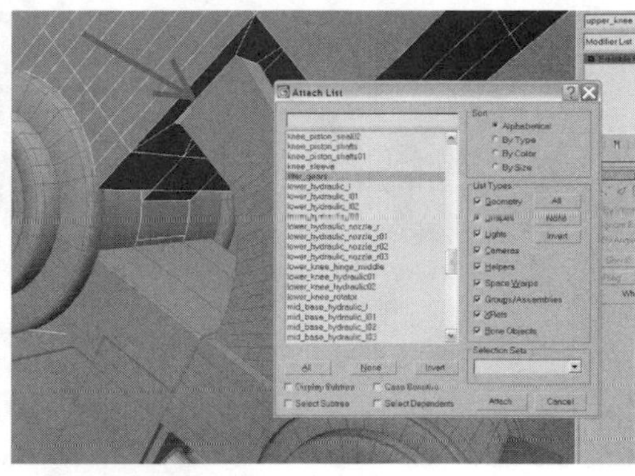

Figure 3-831

61. Select every other polygon and Bevel them:

Type	Height	Outline	Apply/OK
Group	0	–2.5	Apply
Group	–5	–2.5	OK

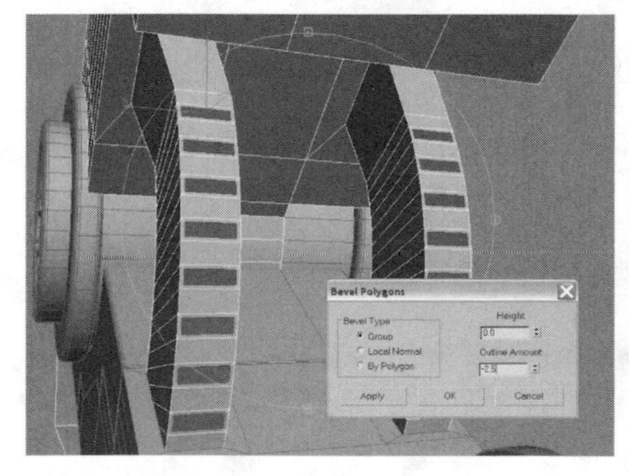

Figure 3-832

Figure 3-833

62. Select the outer and inner polygons and Bevel them:

Type	Height	Outline	Apply/OK
Group	0	–9.5	Apply
Local Normal	–2.3	–9.5	OK

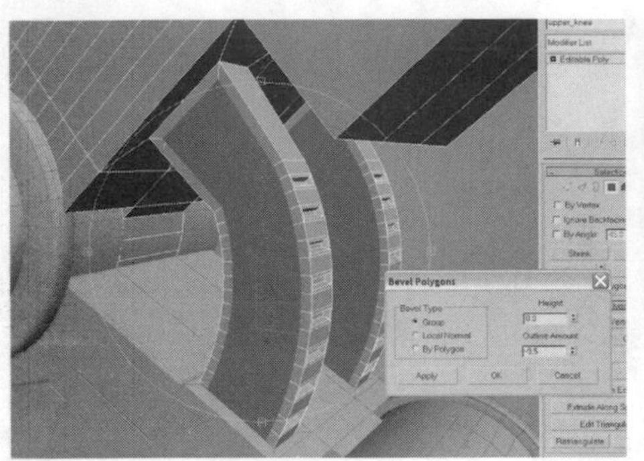

Figure 3-834

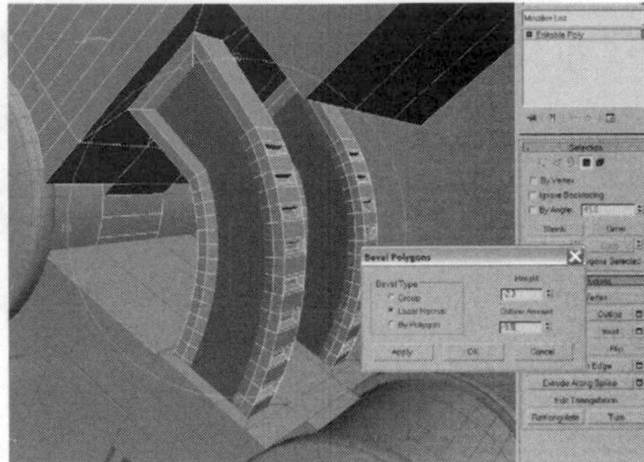

Figure 3-835

63. Extrude the polygons by **–10**. Add a Smooth modifier to the Hip and then convert it to an Editable Polygon.

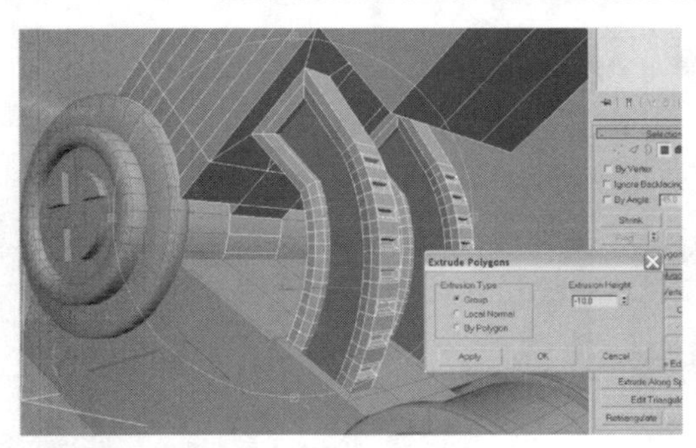

Figure 3-836

Figure 3-837

Urgent: Before continuing, it is important that you evaluate the upper_thigh. Since you created it with a Boolean, it's likely there are some problems that need fixing. Now is the time to fix them, before proceeding with the next few modeling steps.

64. Select the bottom four polygons and Bevel them:

Type	Height	Outline	Apply/OK
Local Normal	–2.5	–11	OK

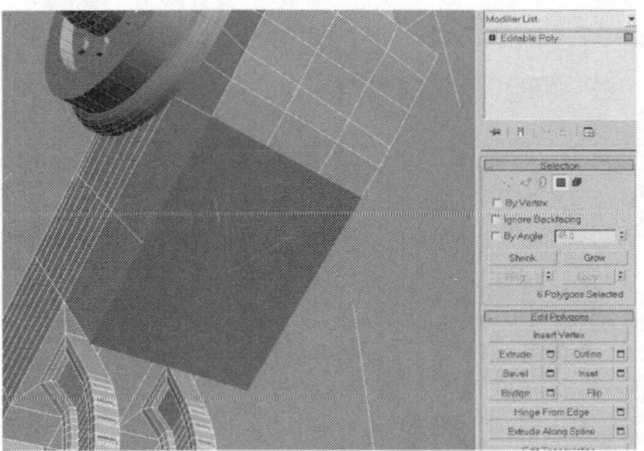

Figure 3-838

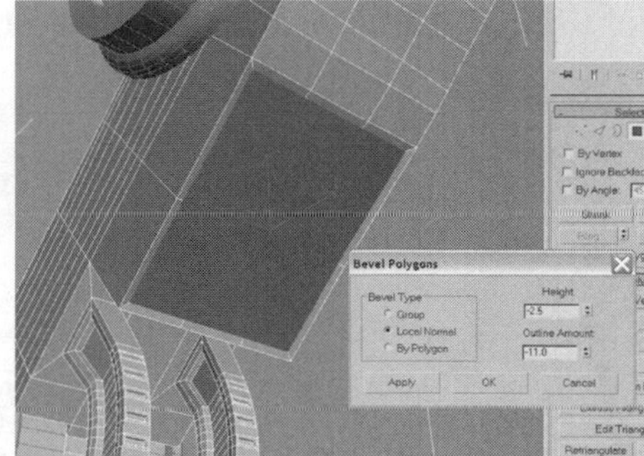

Figure 3-839

65. Extrude the polygons to a Height of **6**. Bevel them with the settings in the table below, Non-uniform Scale them to **50** in the Y axis, and Extrude them **–0.1**.

Type	Height	Outline	Apply/OK
By Polygon	0	–2.5	OK

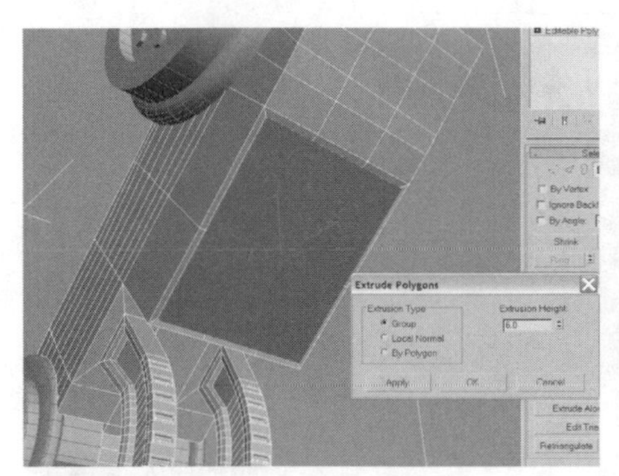

Figure 3-840

Figure 3-841

Figure 3-842

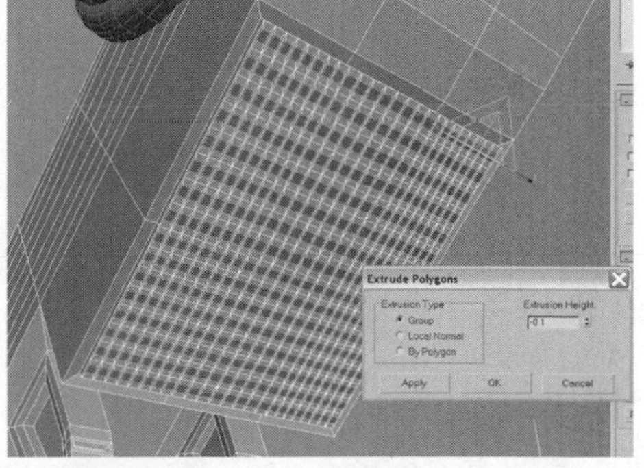

Figure 3-843

66. Click the **MSmooth** button and then Extrude by Local Normal **–25**.

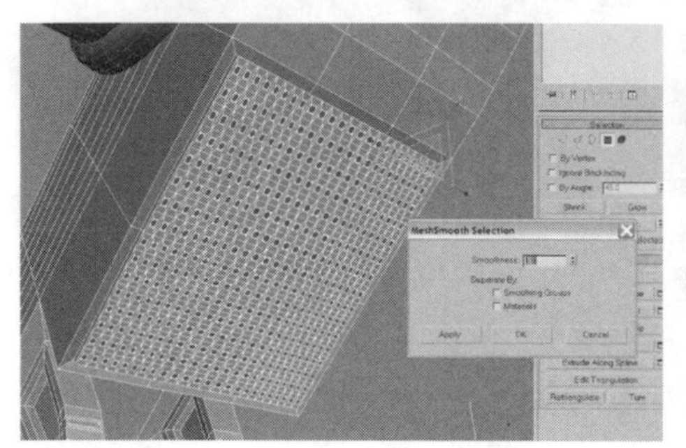

Figure 3-844

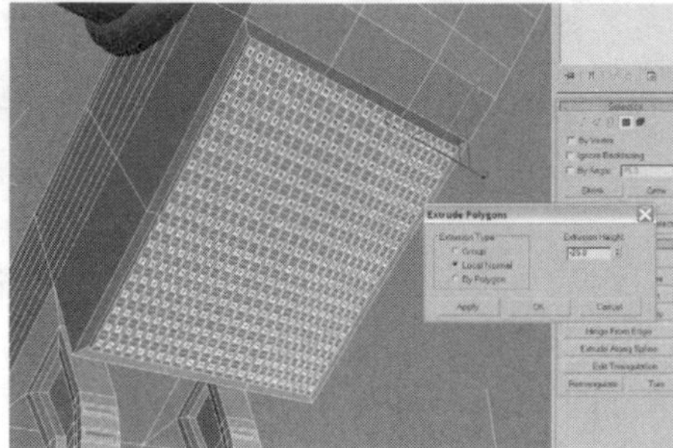

Figure 3-845

67. Select the polygons shown in Figure 3-846, Bevel them, and then select the outer edges for chamfering.

Type	Height	Outline	Apply/OK
Group	0	–8	Apply
Local Normal	20	–8	OK

Figure 3-846

Figure 3-847

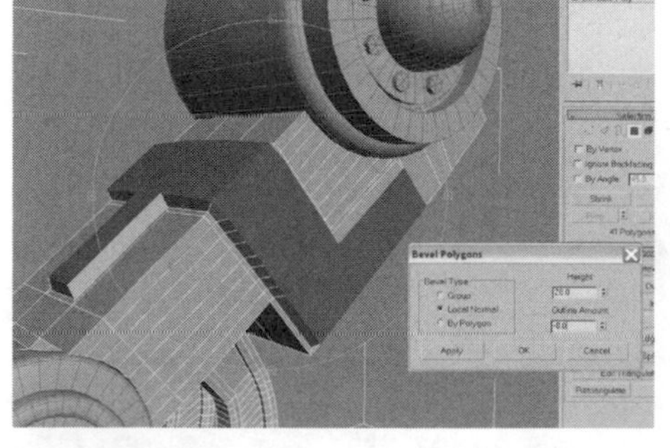

Figure 3-848

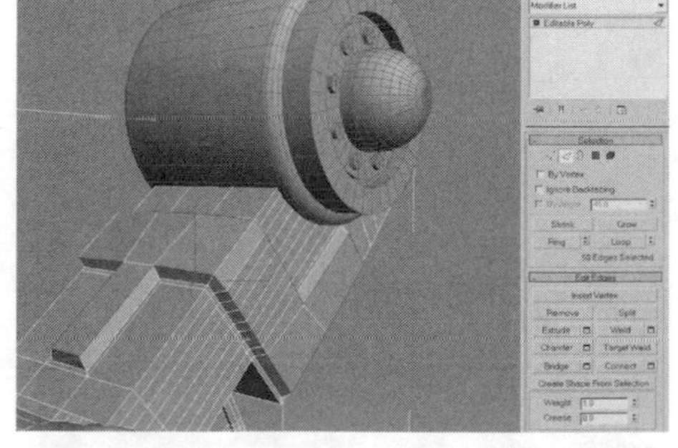

Figure 3-849

68. Chamfer the edges first by **3** and then by **1.32**.

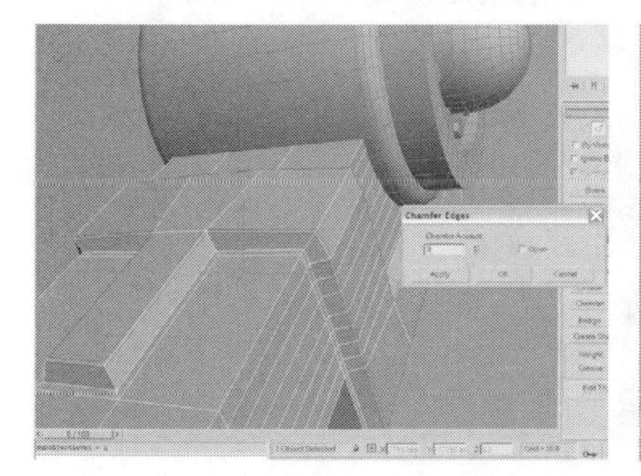

Figure 3-850

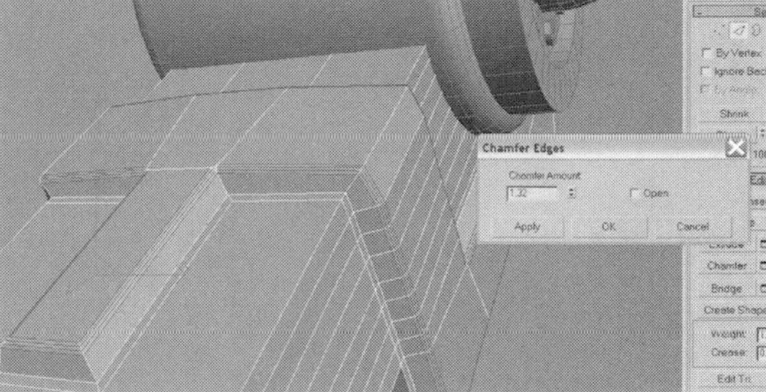

Figure 3-851

69. Create a Sphere with a Radius of **9.177**, **16** Segments, and a Hemisphere of **0.5**. Create 15 clones and position them as shown (or use your own layout), like rivets on the brace, and then Attach them to the brace.

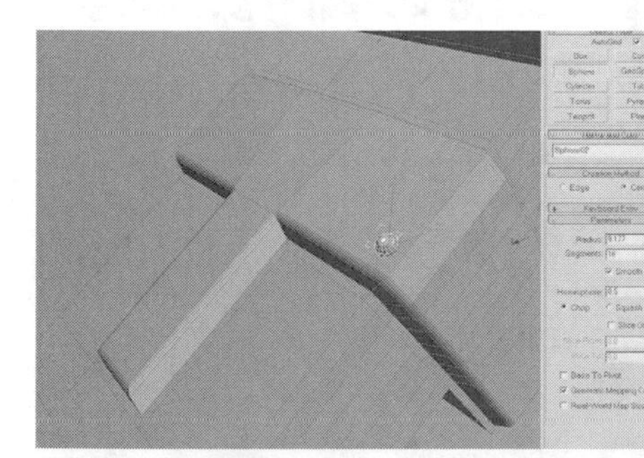

Figure 3-852

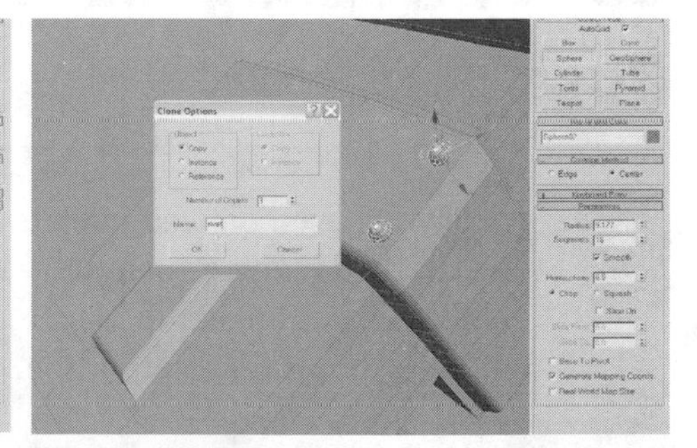

Figure 3-853

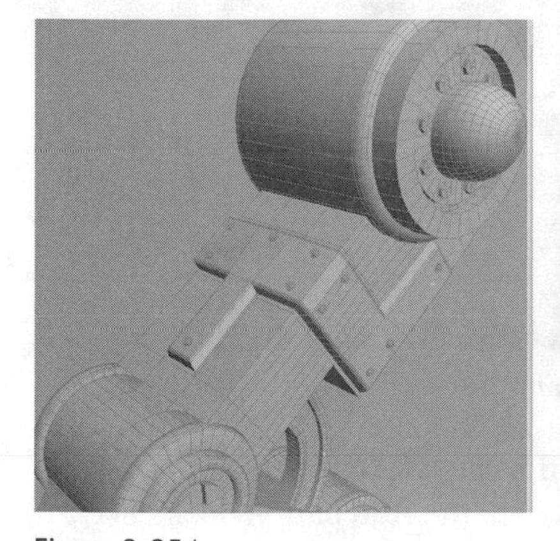

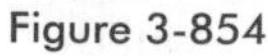

Figure 3-854

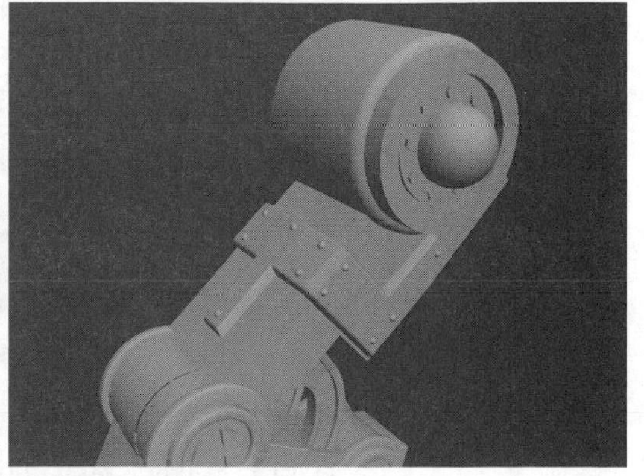

Figure 3-855

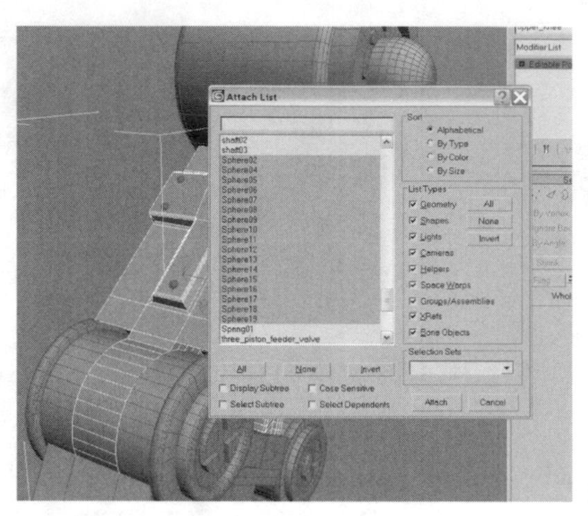
Figure 3-856

Day 8: Creating the Second Leg, Hips, and Base

1. If you haven't already, delete the rivet. We won't be needing it again. Hit the **H** key to open the selection list and click **All.** Click the **Layer** button on the Main toolbar. When the Layer Manager opens, click the **Add Layer** button.

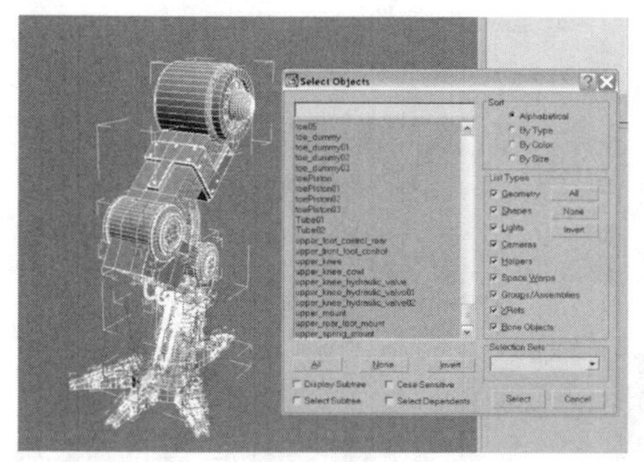
Figure 3-857

Figure 3-858

2. Double-click on the new layer and name it **left_leg.** Make sure the left_leg layer is still selected and click the **Add** button (looks like a big + sign) to add the leg components to the new layer. With all the leg components still selected, select **Group** from the Main menu and name the new group **left_leg.**

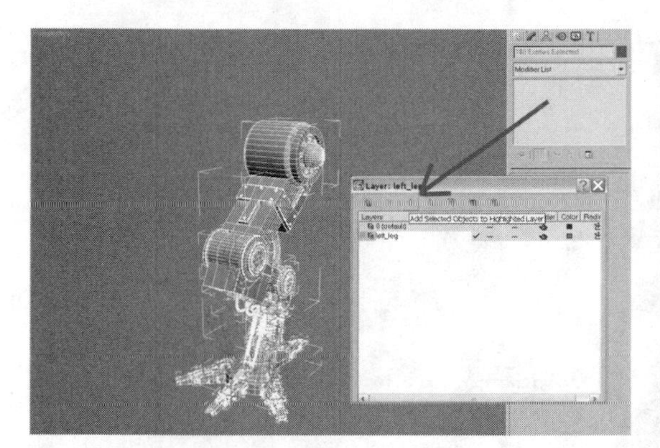

Figure 3-859

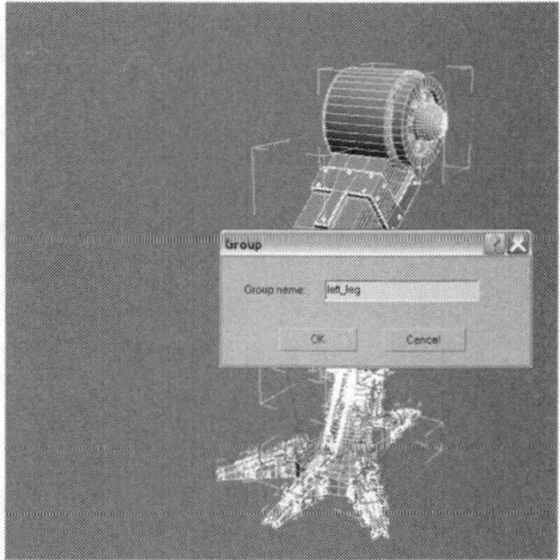

Figure 3-860

FYI: So what was the purpose of the last step? We're getting to the point where there are so many polygons we'll be starting to experience some slowdowns when we move in the viewport (maybe you've already experienced this). Putting the leg into a layer will allow us to hide it to speed up the display.

Adding all the parts of a group will make it easier to clone them to make a second leg. Grouping them will ensure that we don't miss anything.

3. Switch to the Front view and, with the leg selected, click the **Mirror** button. Set the Mirror Axis to **X**, the Offset to **–2000**, and Clone Selection to **Copy**.

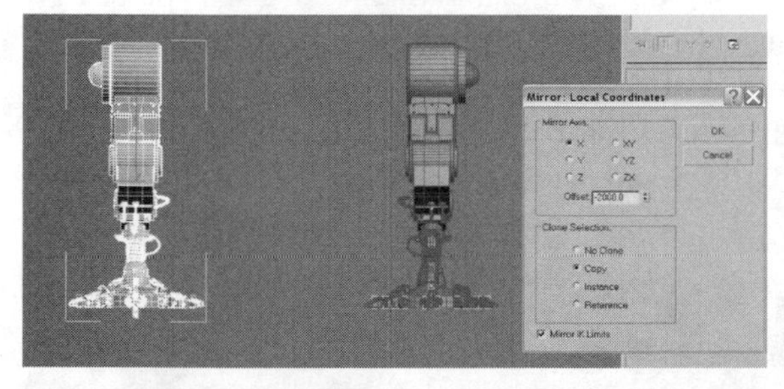

Figure 3-861

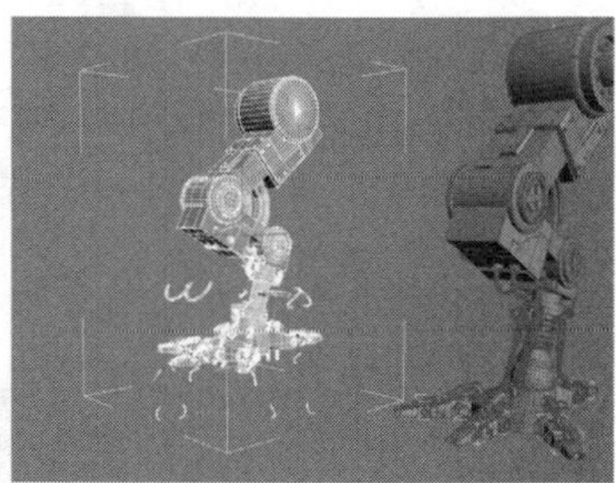

Figure 3-862

Urgent: You'll notice that when you copied the leg, your constraints and hoses they got ... um ... what's the technical term? Jacked up. Fortunately, it's not difficult to fix, but it's a major pain.

4. Ungroup the clone. Select the **mid_base_hydraulic** on the foot of the clone, as shown. Open the Hierarchy tab and go to the Adjust Transform rollout. Under Reset click the **Transform** button. Click

the **Reset Pivot** button to reset the tube's pivot point and click **Center to Object**.

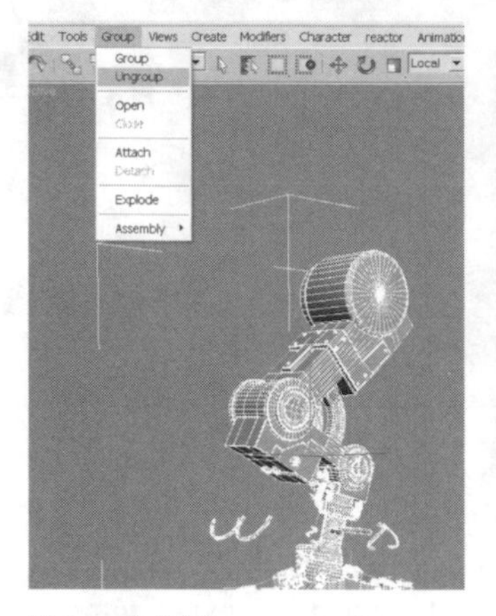

Figure 3-863

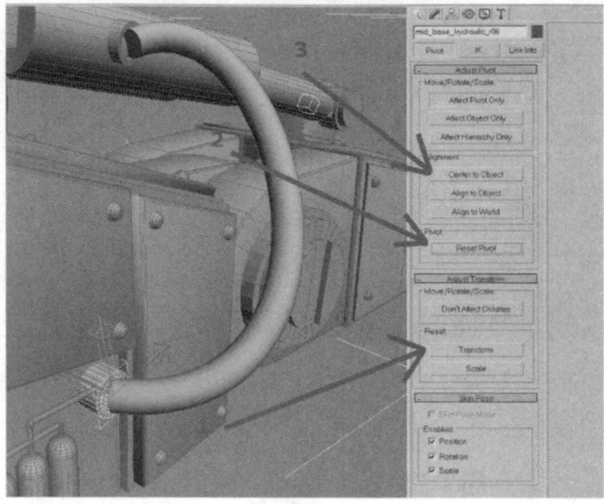

Figure 3-864

FYI: Rather than realigning the pivots, I find it easier to just delete the hose and create a new one; especially since hoses are not that difficult to make. As you know from doing the original foot, realigning the pistons and shafts can represent more of a challenge.

5. Make sure the pivots for the Top and Bottom binding objects are identically aligned, with the blue Z axis facing out and away from the foot, the red X axis facing downward, and the green Y axis pointing forward; this will make binding the new hose easier. Create a new hose. Set the Top and Bottom tensions to **45**. Choose **Bound to Object Pivots** and choose **lower_hydraulic_nozzle** for the Top Binding Object and **mid_base_hydraulic** for the Bottom Binding Object.

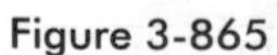
Figure 3-865

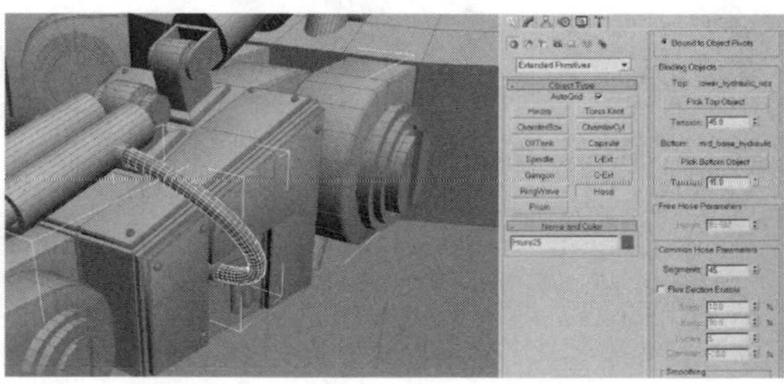

Figure 3-866

Fire Drill: Because there are so many hoses and pistons to realign, for space reasons, I'll leave you to realign them yourself. The process for hoses is identical to what you've just done. As for the pistons, the process is identical to the fixes you made at the beginning of Day 4.

6. Ungroup the original leg. Select the original Hip, click **Attach List**, select **Hip01** (the clone), and click **Attach.**

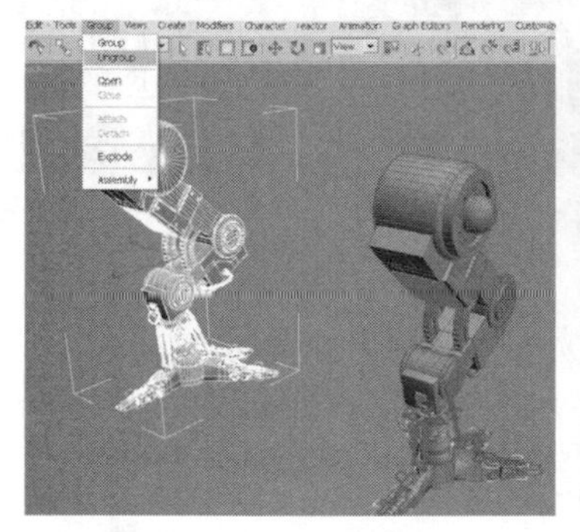

Figure 3-867

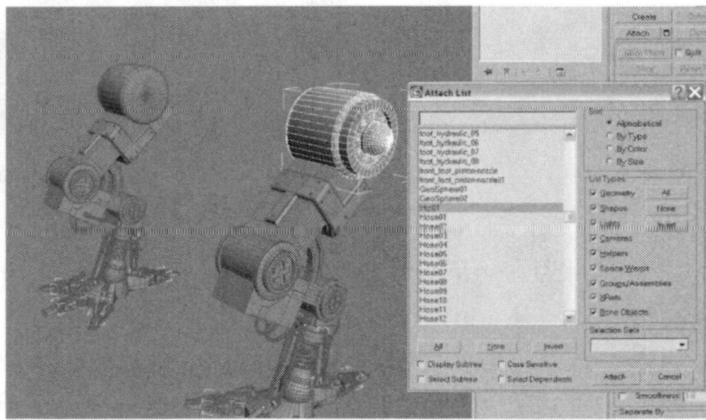

Figure 3-868

7. Select the hips and the upper legs of both legs. Right-click, choose **Hide Unselected**, and then select the inner 36 polygons on both hips.

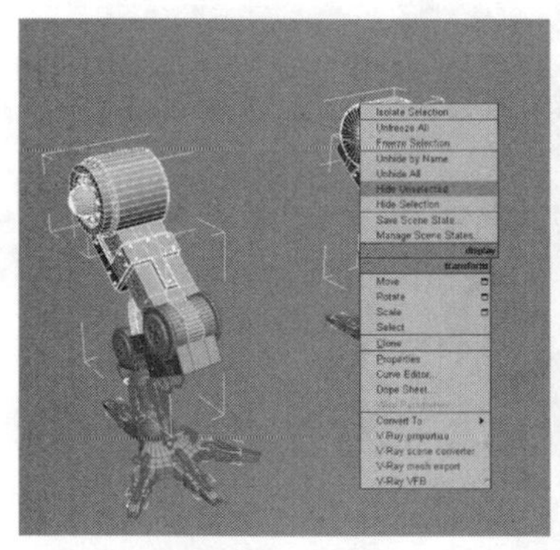

Figure 3-869

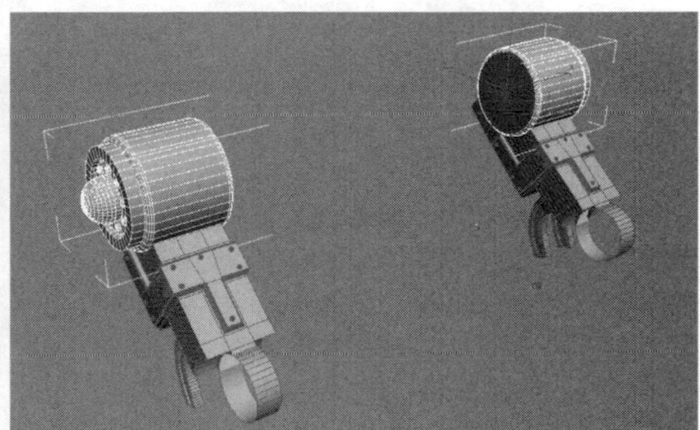

Figure 3-870

8. Bevel the polygons and then delete them.

Type	Height	Outline	Apply/OK
Group	180	–1	OK

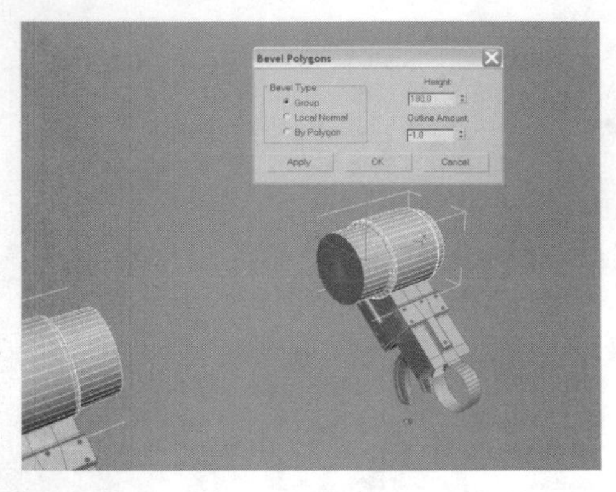

Figure 3-871

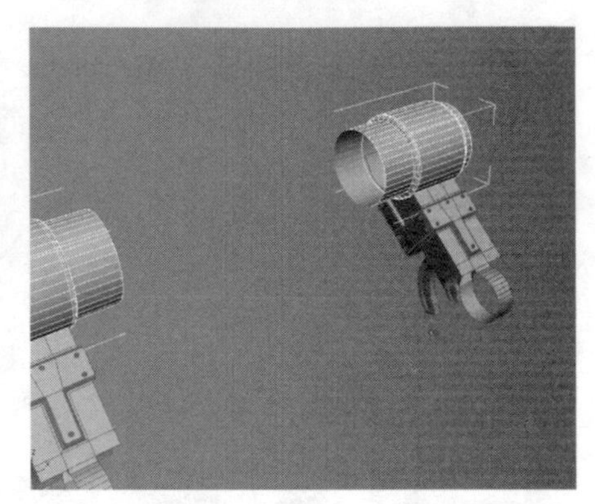

Figure 3-872

9. Switch to the Front view. Create a Sphere using AutoGrid with a Radius of around **200** and **36** Segments. Rotate it **90** degrees, so the top faces the other leg as shown. Move the sphere into the hole created by deleting the polygons and adjust its Radius (**~198**) until the segments on the sphere align with the segments on the Hip, as shown. (Note: The sphere is situated so that two rings of segments below the centerline meet the edge of the Hip. This will be important for welding).

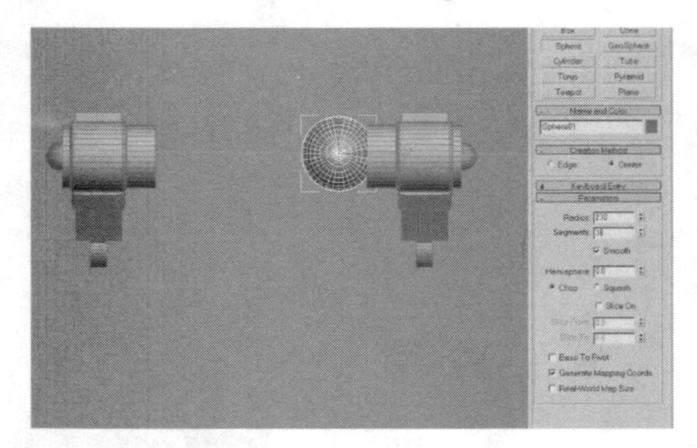

Figure 3-873

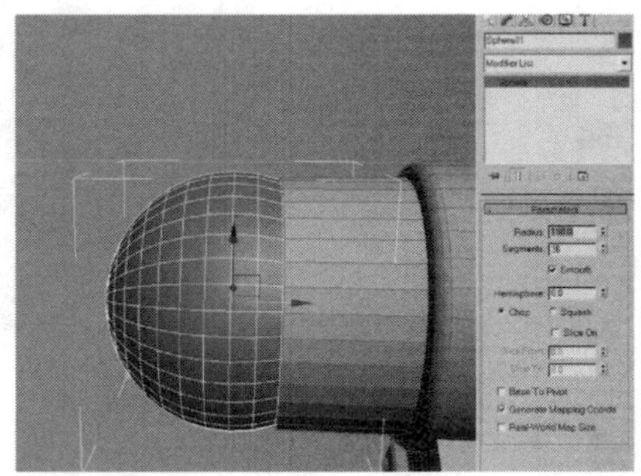

Figure 3-874

10. Switch to wireframe (**F3**) and select and delete the polygons of the sphere that lie below the surface of the Hip. Object-select the sphere, Mirror it in the X axis, and make a copy.

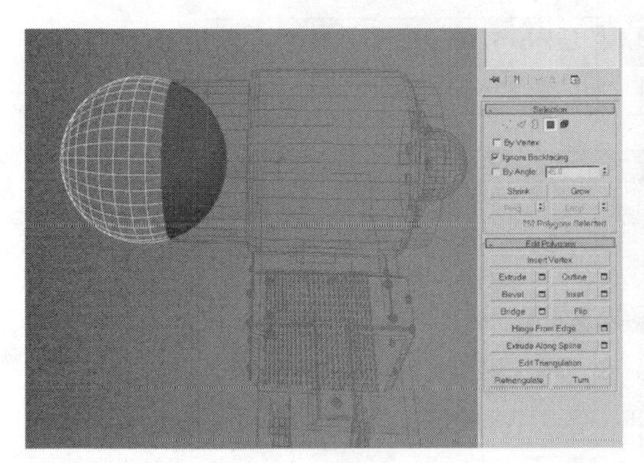

Figure 3-875

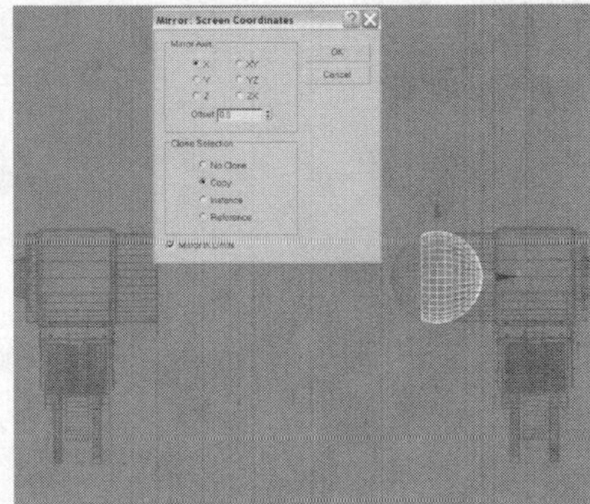

Figure 3-876

11. Move the clone to the other Hip as shown. Select the Hips and attach the spheres to create a hip joint.

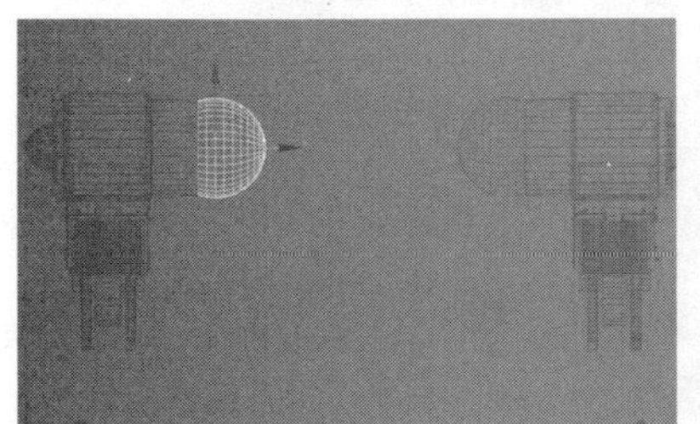

Figure 3-877

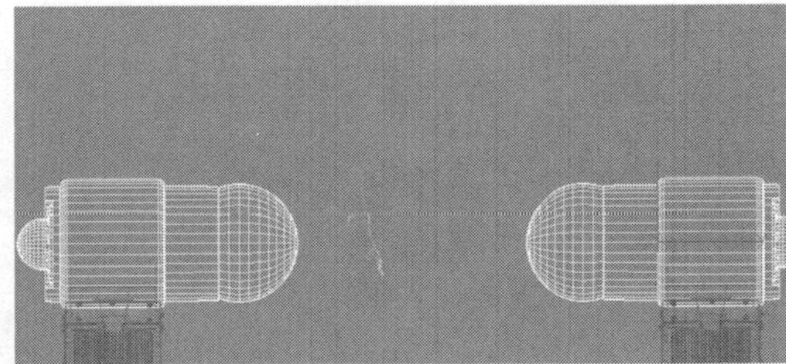

Figure 3-878

12. Vertex-select the vertices where the sphere connects with the Hip and then click **Weld.** (You'll probably need to increase the Weld Threshold; watch the Before and After values and adjust the threshold until After is 36 less than Before.)

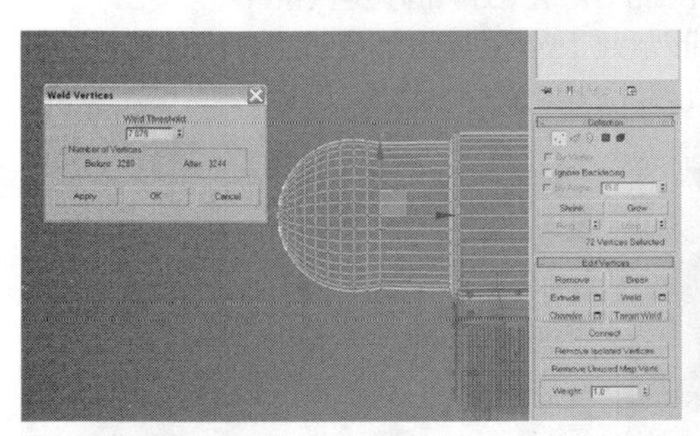

Figure 3-879

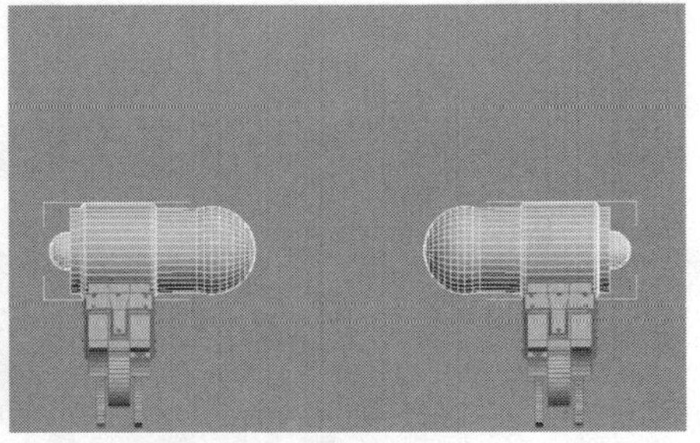

Figure 3-880

13. Create a Box between the legs and convert it to an Editable Polygon. Hide the box and then create a Sphere with a Radius of **200** and **36** Segments.

Length	Width	Height	Length/Width/Height Segs
780	1089	1434	2/2/2

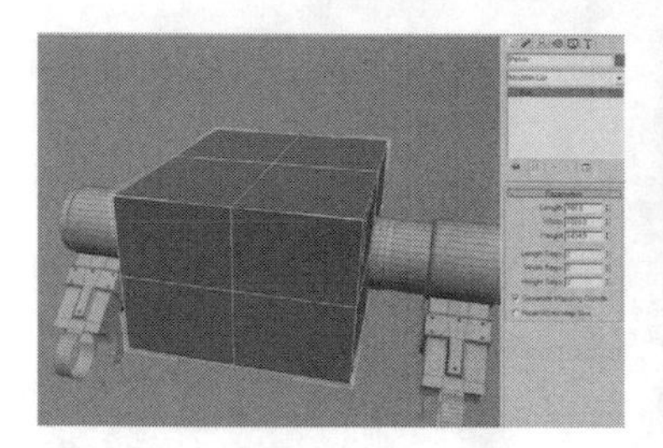

Figure 3-881

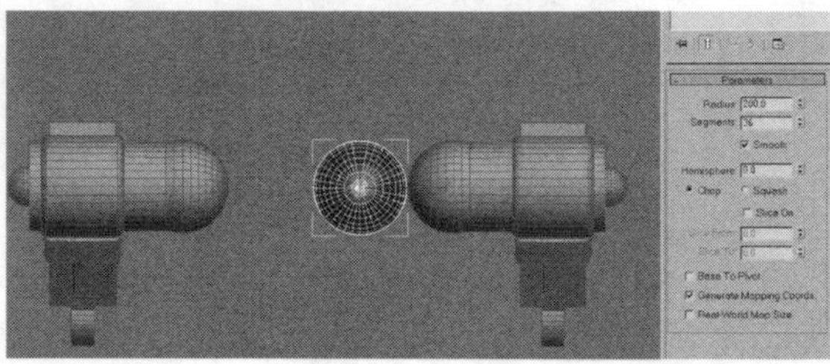

Figure 3-882

14. Rotate the sphere **90** degrees, then superimpose the sphere over the hip joint. Change the Radius to **204.304** (so that it is slightly larger than the hip joint), set Hemisphere to **0.5**, and convert it to an Editable Polygon.

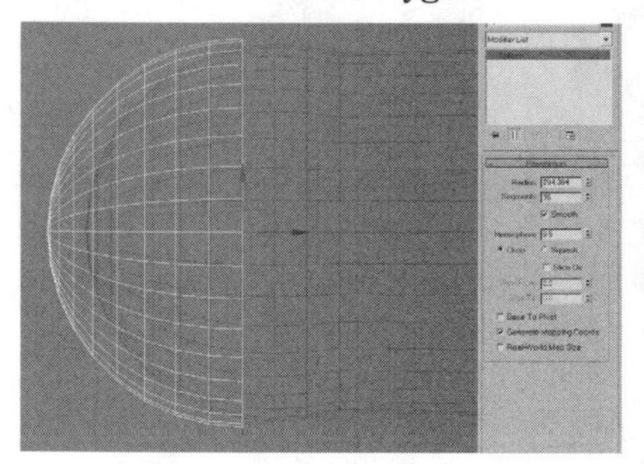

Figure 3-883

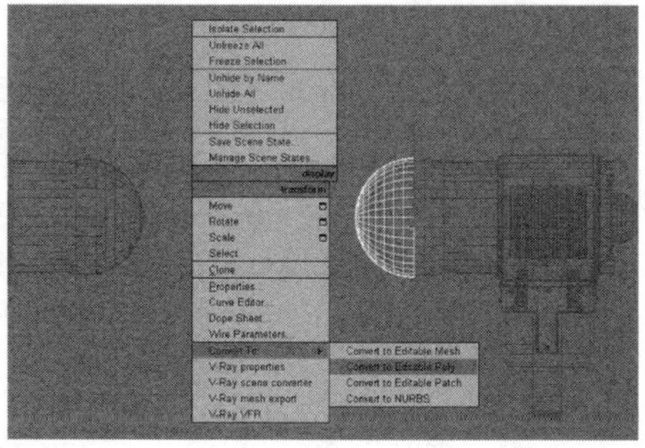

Figure 3-884

15. Mirror-copy the hemisphere in the X axis and set the Offset to **–1100**. Select both hemispheres, right-click, and click **Hide Unselected** so that only the hemispheres are visible.

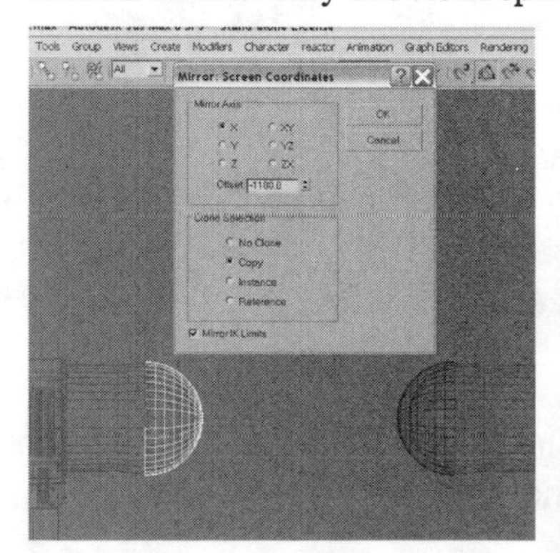

Figure 3-885

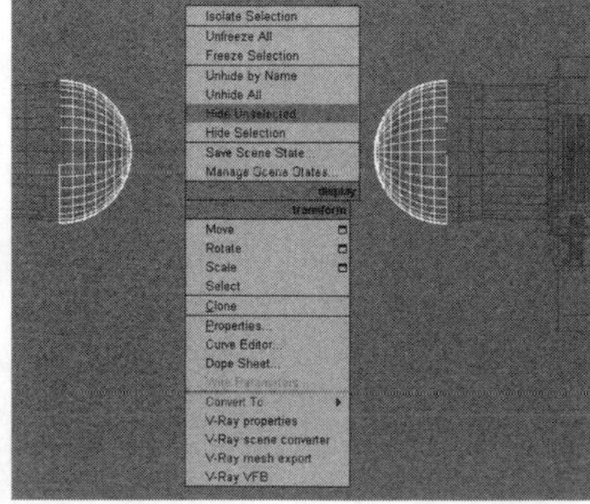

Figure 3-886

16. Switch to the Front view if necessary. Unhide the box and move the hemispheres until they are positioned as shown below, with their outer edges just above the surface of the box. Switch to the Perspective view and loop-select the vertical edges that separate the box into front and back pieces.

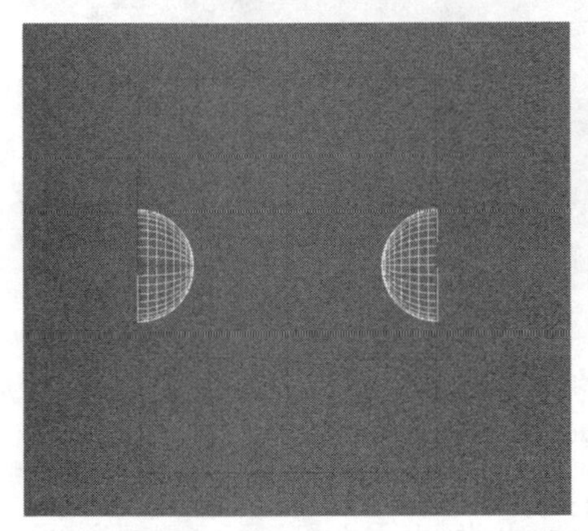

Figure 3-887

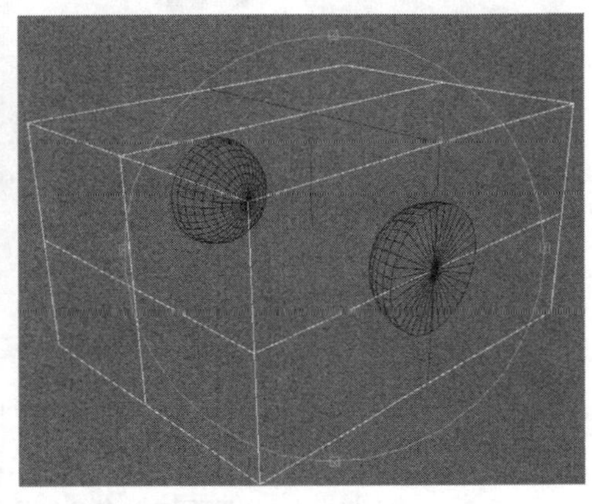

Figure 3-888

17. Chamfer the edges (**~208**) so that two edges are created (one on each side of the hemisphere). Loop-select the horizontal edges that separate the box into top and bottom sections.

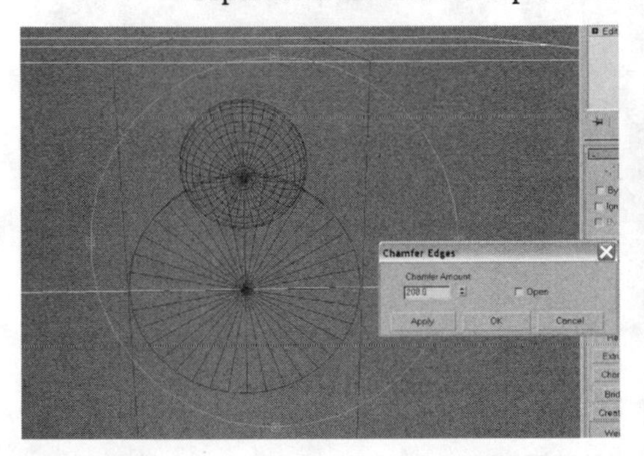

Figure 3-889

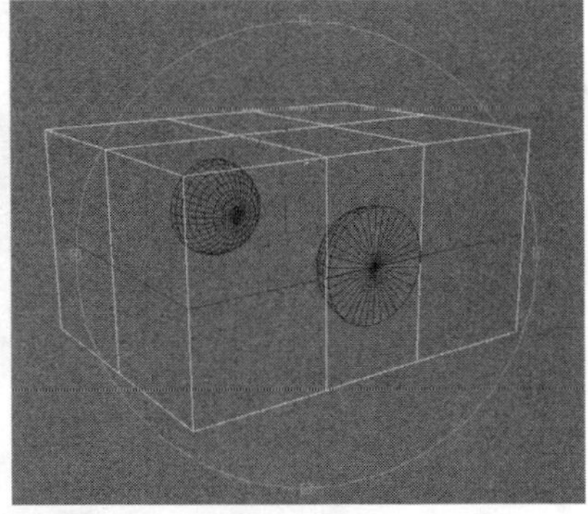

Figure 3-890

18. Chamfer the edges (**~208**) so that two edges are created (one on the top and one on the bottom of the hemisphere, forming a square with the edges you previously chamfered). Object-select the box, rename it **Pelvis**, and create a Boolean object.

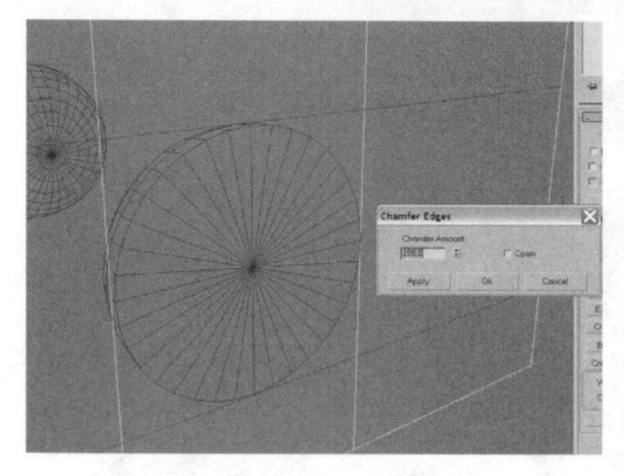

Figure 3-891

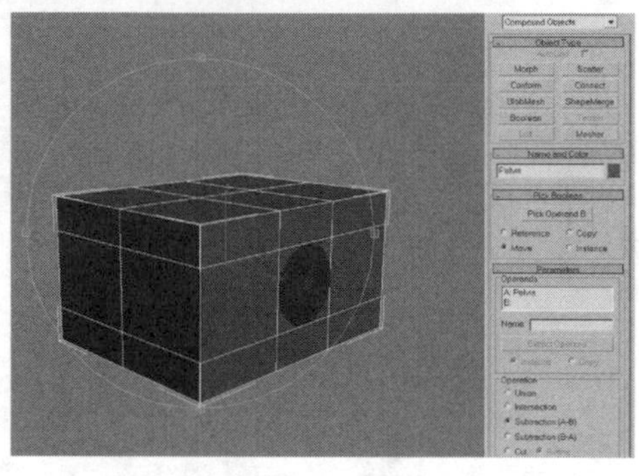

Figure 3-892

19. Click **Pick Operand B** and then select a hemisphere to create a hip socket. Convert the Boolean to an Editable Polygon. Make another Boolean and repeat the process for the hemisphere on the other side.

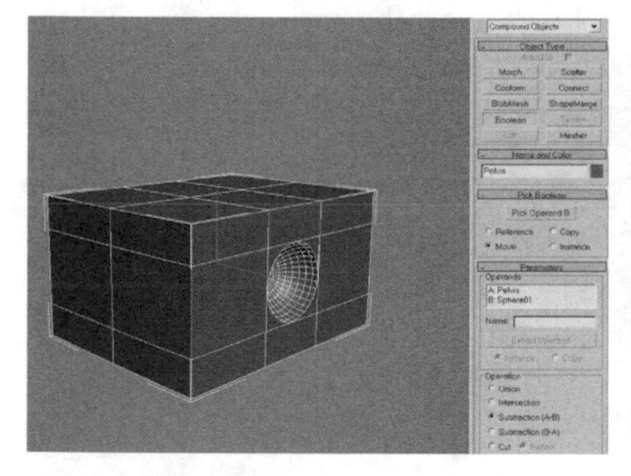

Figure 3-893

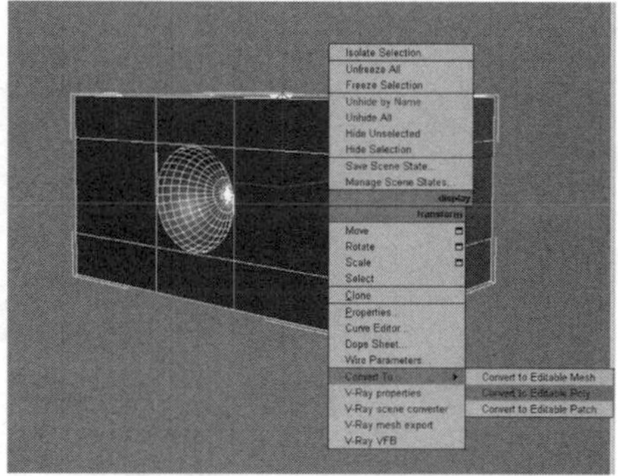

Figure 3-894

20. Unhide the Hips so you have them as a frame of reference. Select the edges on the front corners of the box and Chamfer them by **202**. Select the two front polygons and Bevel them:

Type	Height	Outline	Apply/OK
By Polygon	0	–20	Apply
By Polygon	–150	0	OK

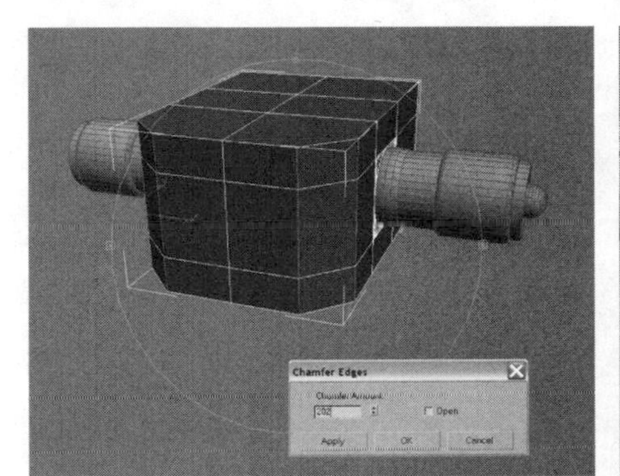

Figure 3-895

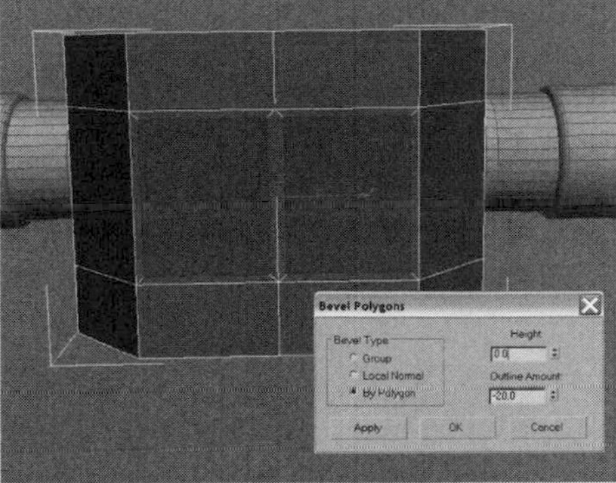

Figure 3-896

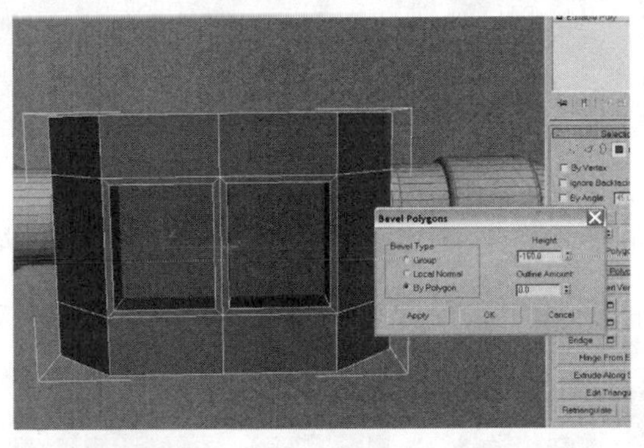

Figure 3-897

21. Detach the polygons, name them **missle_mount**, and convert them to an Editable Polygon.

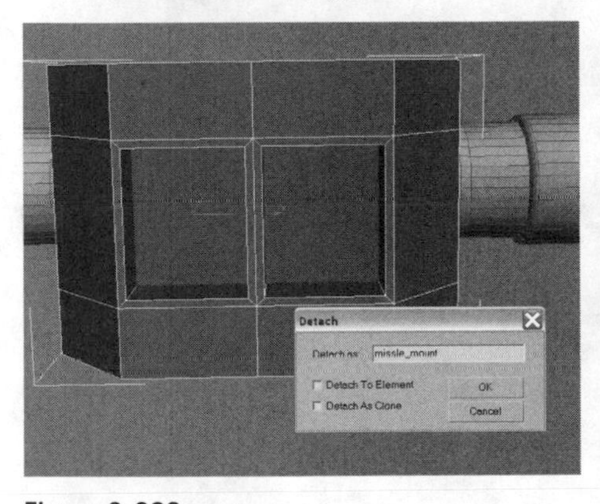

Figure 3-898

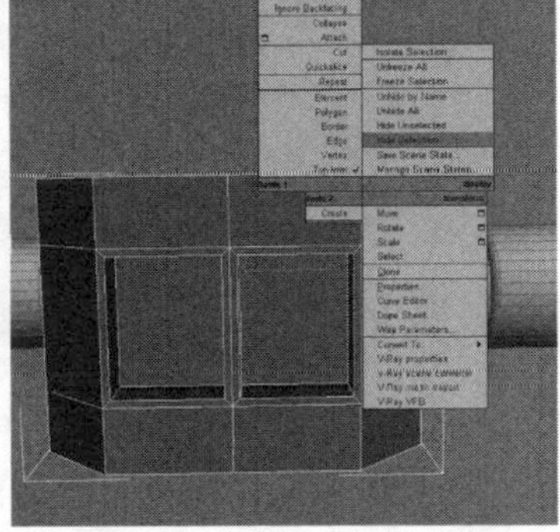

Figure 3-899

22. Create a Tube in the upper-left corner of the missle_mount and convert it to an Editable Polygon.

Radius 1	Radius 2	Height	Height/Cap Segs	Sides	Smooth
50	45	350	3/1	18	Checked

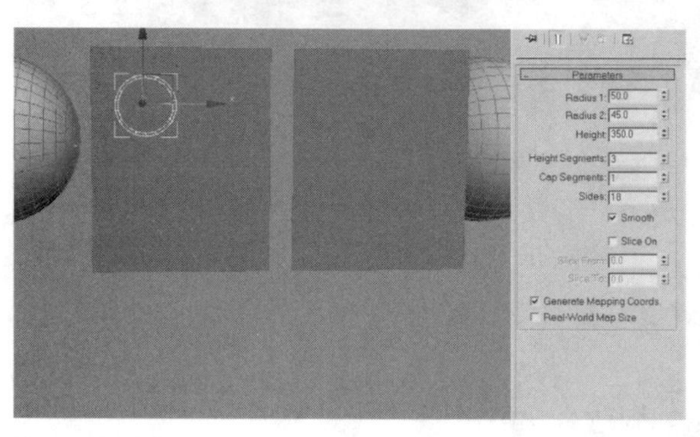

Figure 3-900

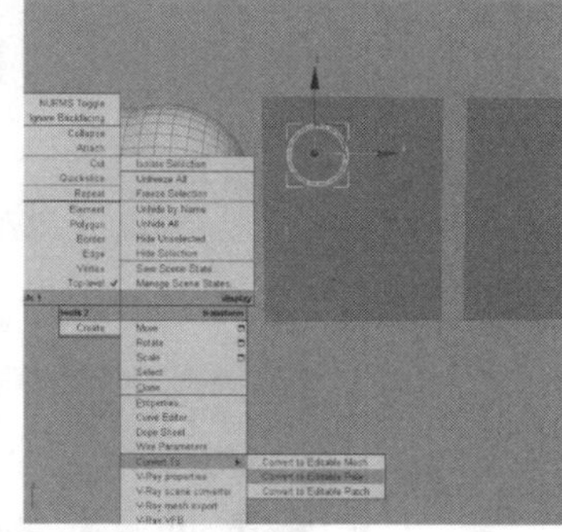

Figure 3-901

23. Use the Move tool and position the tube as shown below. Switch to the Front view and Shift-clone the tube in the X axis so that there is a clone in the right corner.

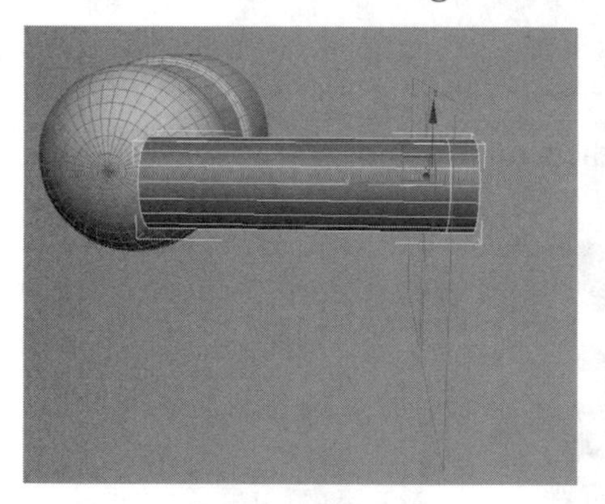

Figure 3-902

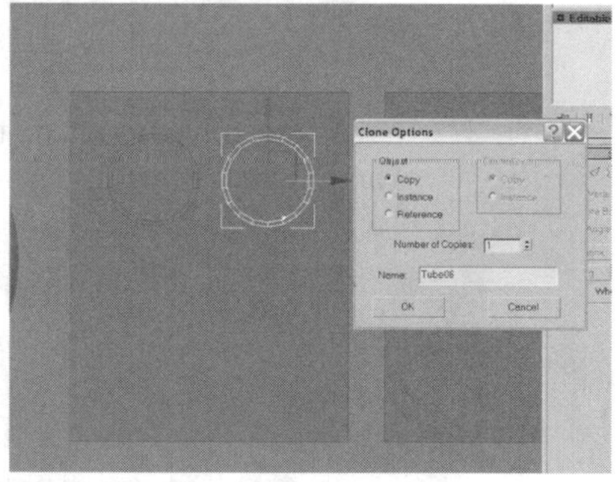

Figure 3-903

24. Select the two tubes and Shift-clone them in the Y axis to make two copies. Select the original tube and Attach the clones to it.

Figure 3-904

Figure 3-905

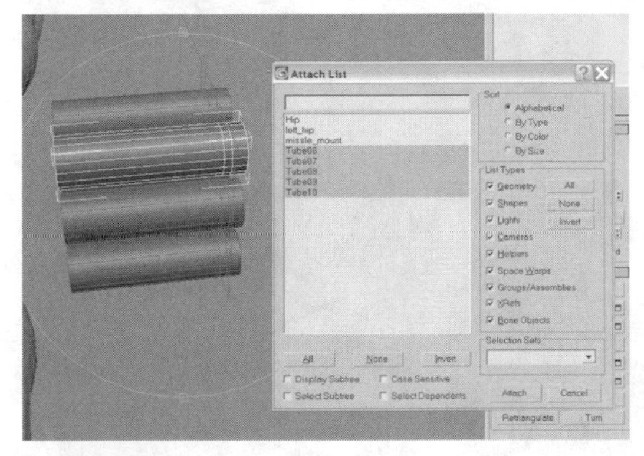

Figure 3-906

25. Select the five middle polygons on the edges of the tubes, as shown in Figure 3-907. Extrude them by **32**.

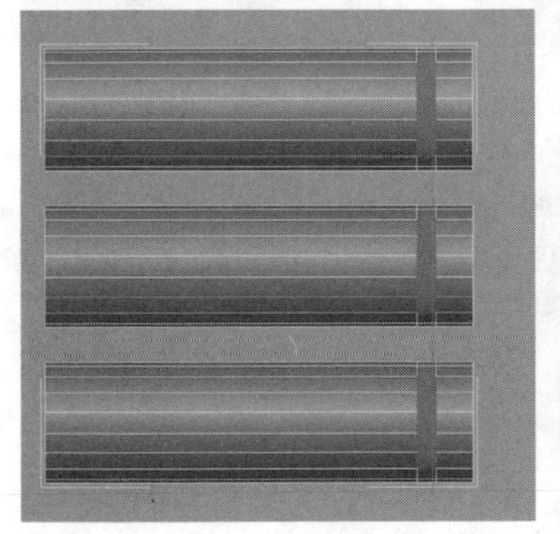

Figure 3-907

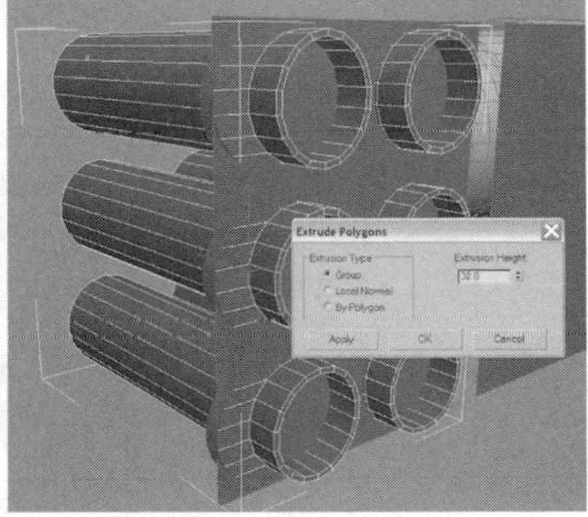

Figure 3-908

26. Scale the extrusions down to **0** in the X axis. Repeat this for the other side.

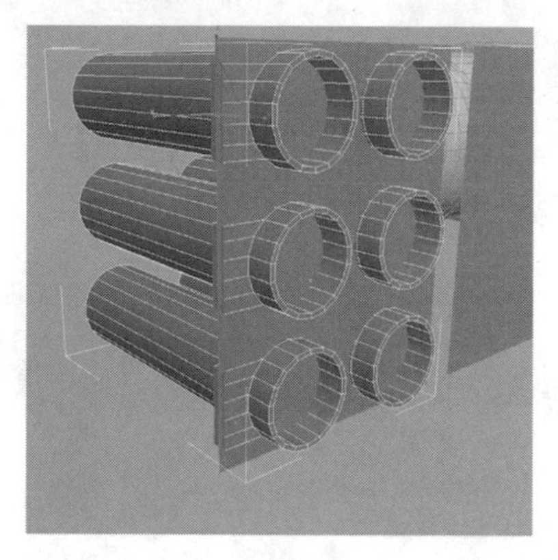

Figure 3-909

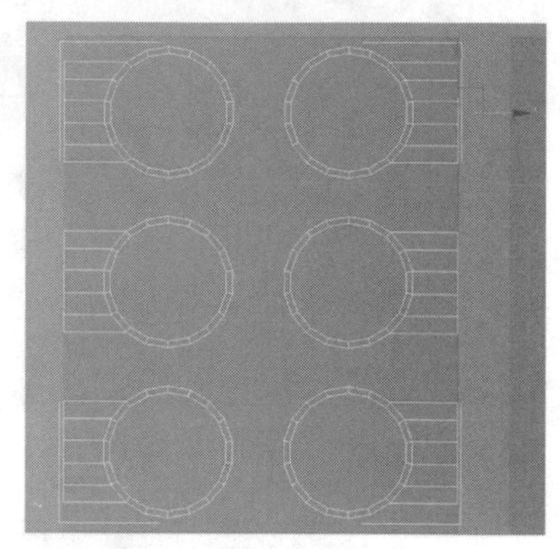

Figure 3-910

27. Select the top polygons and click the **Bridge** button to bridge them.

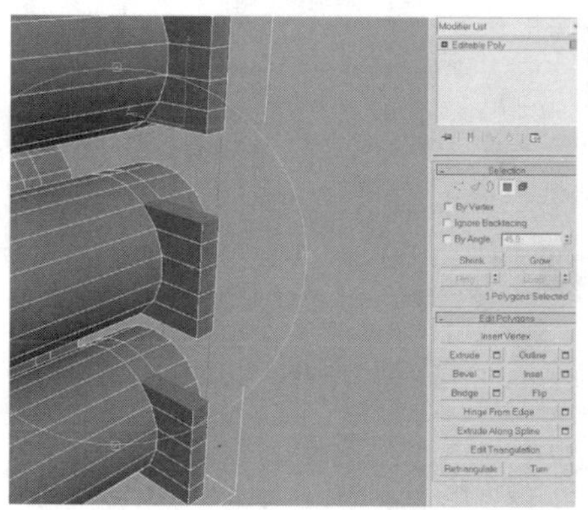

Figure 3-911

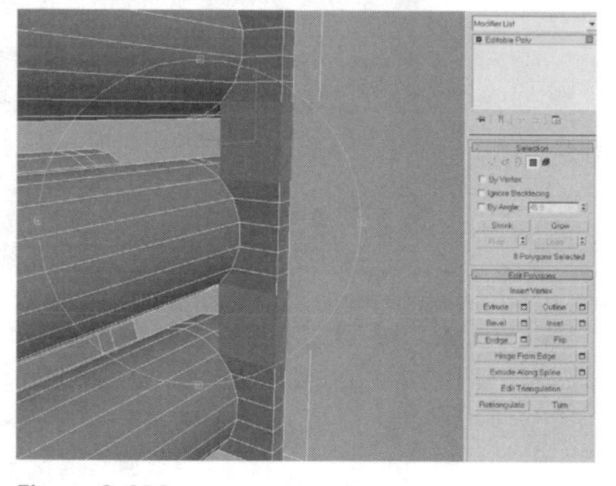

Figure 3-912

28. Bridge the polygons across the front. When you get to the last tube, the Bridge operation may try to twist on you. Should this happen, adjust the Twist value until it straightens.

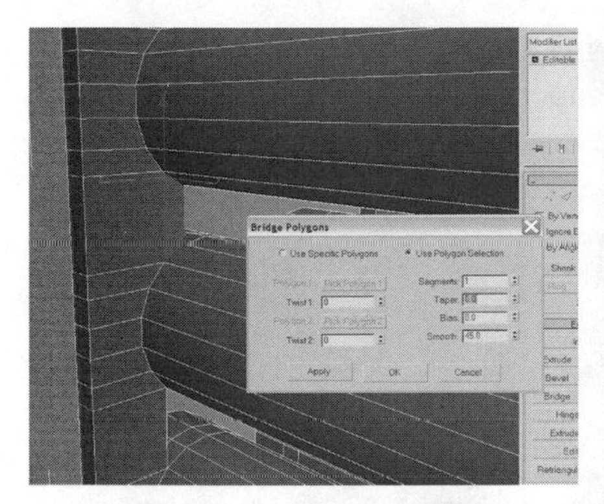

Figure 3-913

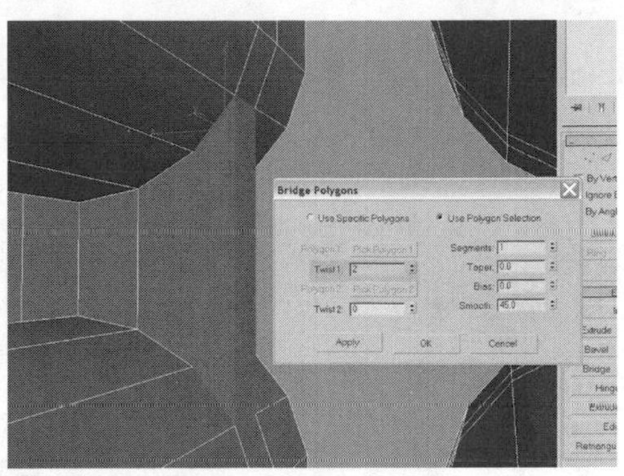

Figure 3-914

29. When you get the front completed, you'll also need to Extrude polygons (**~22.08**) on the top and bottom to match the template you made by detaching the polygons (missle_mount). Use the Non-uniform Scale tool to flatten them and use the Move tool to make them flush with the template.

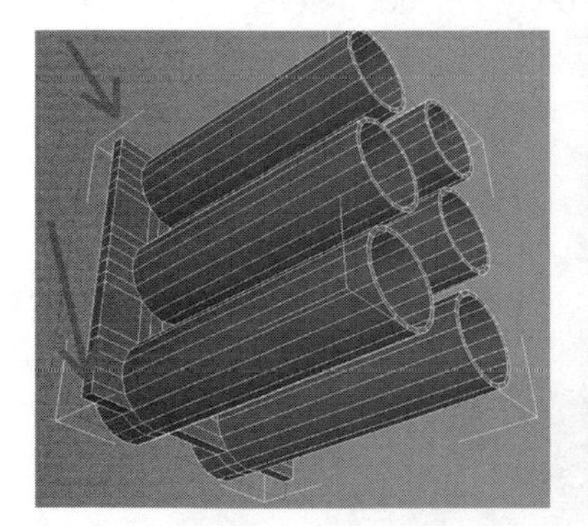

Figure 3-915

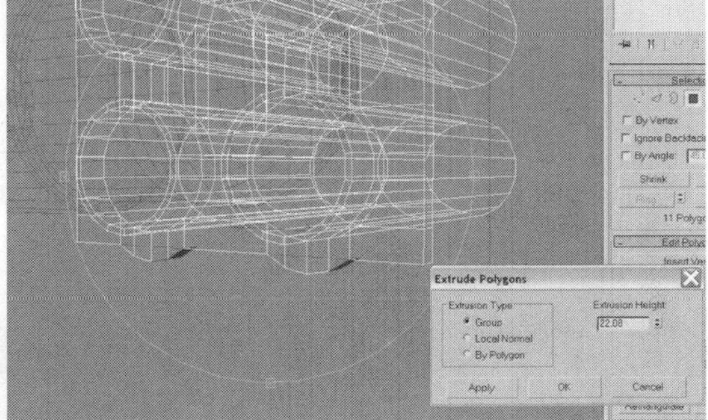

Figure 3-916

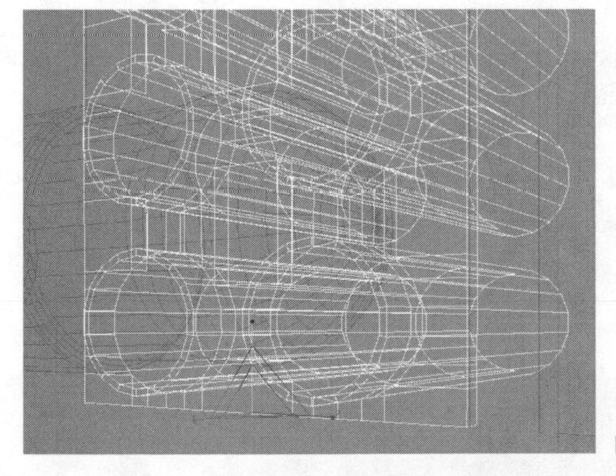

Figure 3-917

30. Clone the missile mounts you made with the extrusions and the tubes, move it to the left, and superimpose it on the missle_mount template. Hit the **H** key and select **missle_mount**. Delete it, since you don't need it anymore.

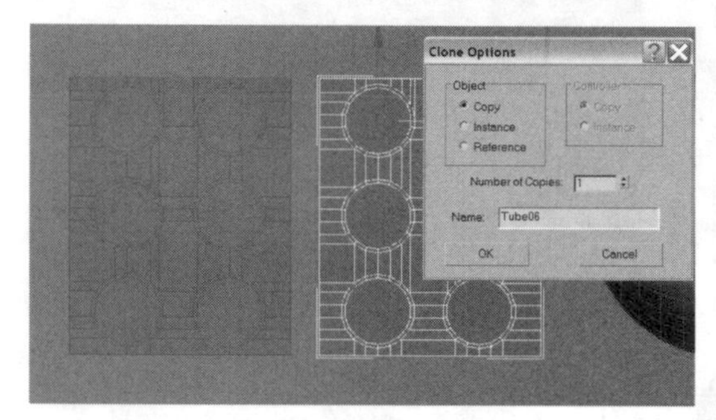

Figure 3-918

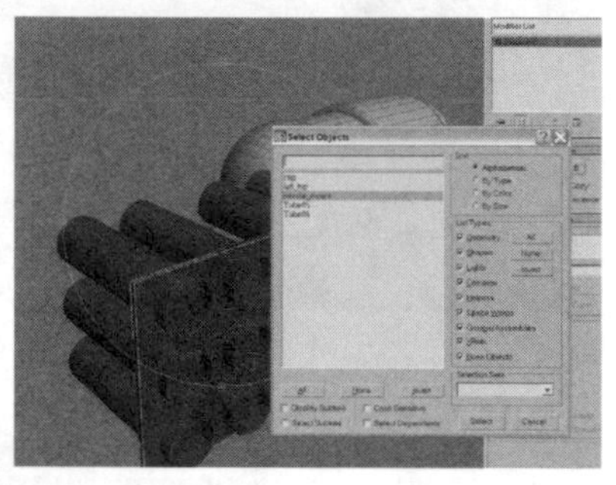

Figure 3-919

31. Select the body, click **Attach List**, and attach the two tubes (missile tubes made with extrusions) to the body. Use loop-select to select the bottom edges of the body.

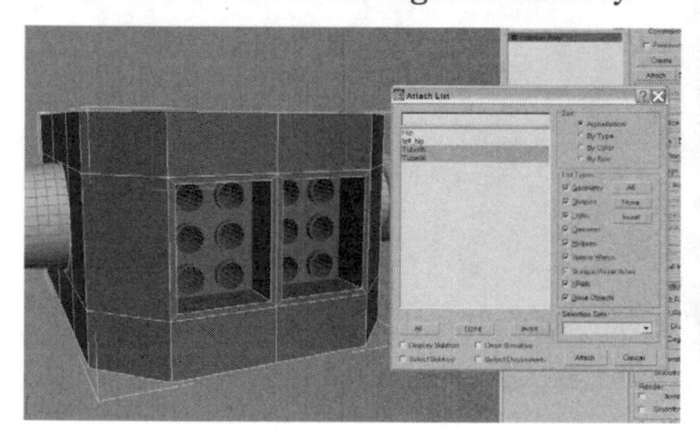

Figure 3-920

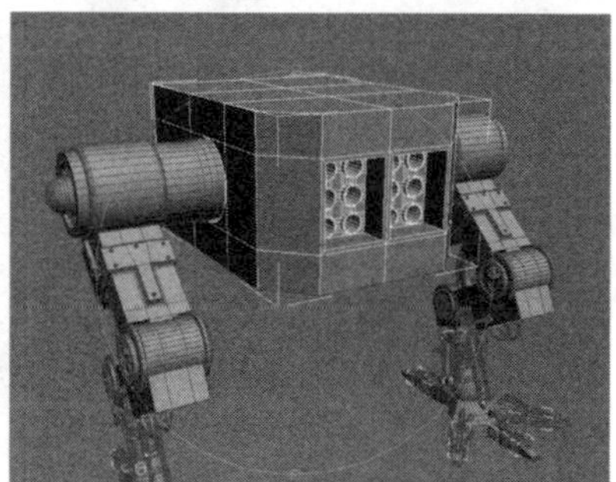

Figure 3-921

32. Right-click on the Move tool icon to open the Move Transform Type-In dialog. Set the Offset World Z axis to **121** (to raise the bottom edge, lowering the overall profile of the body). Switch to the Left viewport, click **Slice Plane**, and position the Slice Plane as shown in Figure 3-923. Click **Slice**.

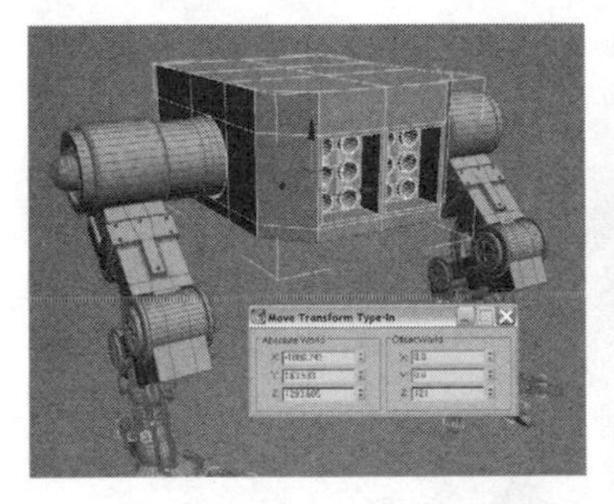

Figure 3-922

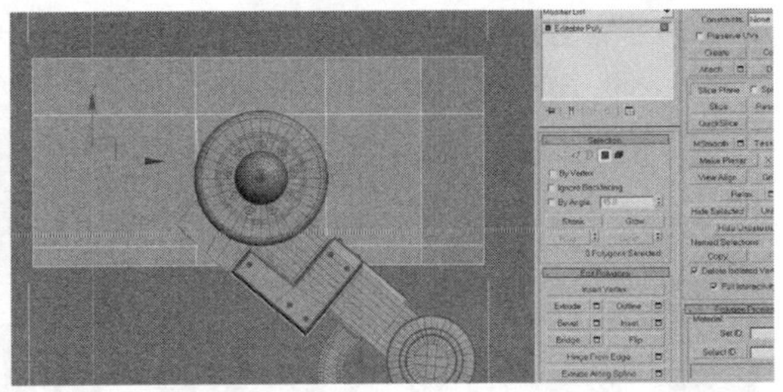

Figure 3-923

33. Target Weld the rear corners to chamfer the rear end. Activate the Slice Plane and switch to the Left viewport, then Rotate the slice plane and position it as shown in Figure 3 925, with the slice plane overlaying the bottom vertex you made with the previous slice plane. Click **Slice**.

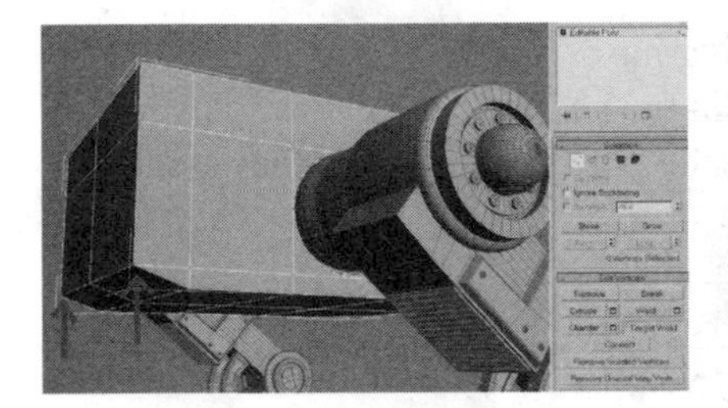

Figure 3-924

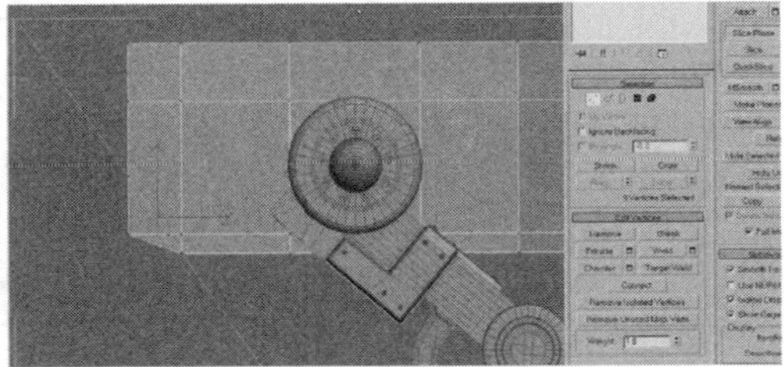

Figure 3-925

34. Select the bottom rear polygons and Target Weld the remaining segment. Select the two bottom rear segments and Bridge them.

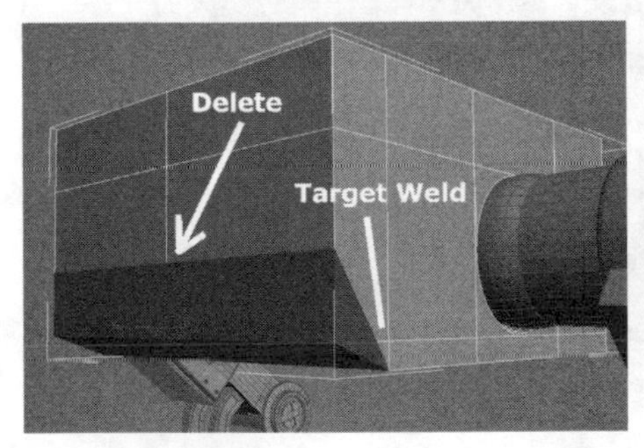

Figure 3-926

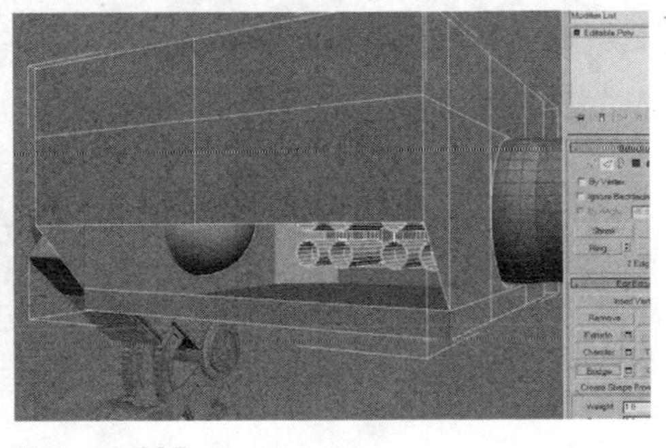

Figure 3-927

35. Border-select the remaining hole and cap it. Click **Snap Settings** and set the snaps to **Vertex.**

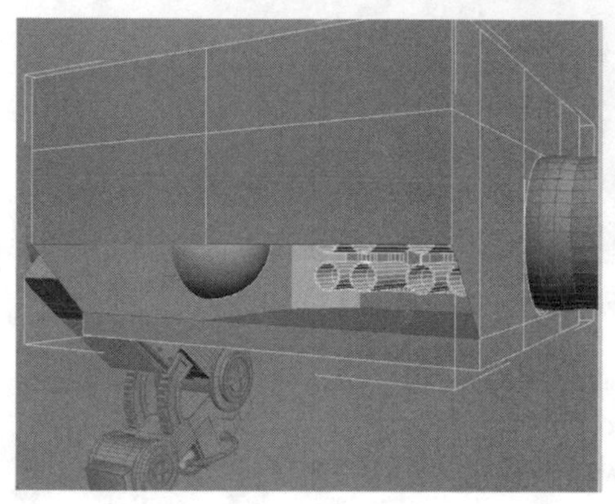

Figure 3-928

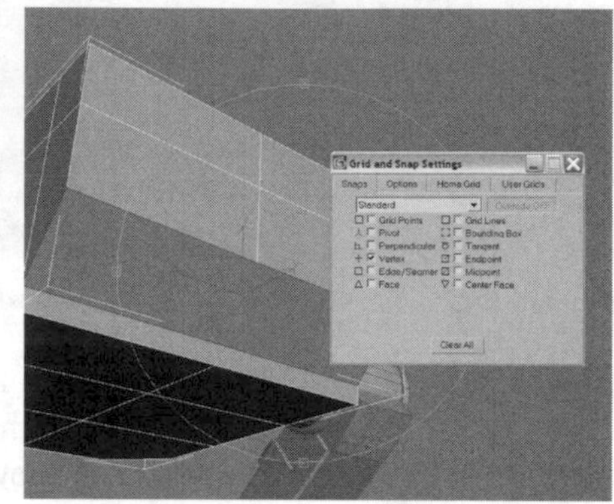

Figure 3-929

36. Use the Cut tools to cut the polygons as shown in Figure 3-930 (the Snap setting should snap the tool to the vertices, making cutting the polys easier). Select the two upper polygons from the four made from the cut and Bevel them.

Type	Height	Outline	Apply/OK
By Polygon	0	–25	Apply
By Polygon	–50	0	OK

Figure 3-930

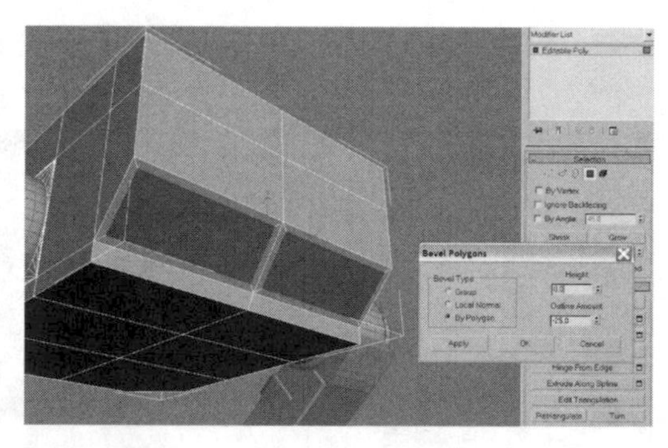

Figure 3-931

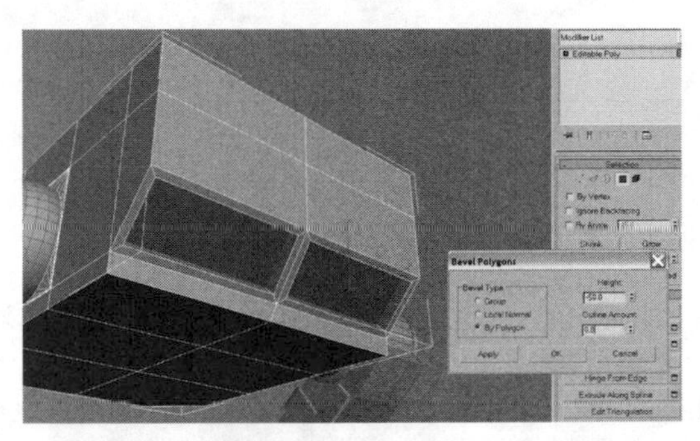

Figure 3-932

37. Select the four vertical edges, click **Connect**, and set the Segments to **5.** With the edges still selected, Extrude them by **–70** with a Base Width of **9.**

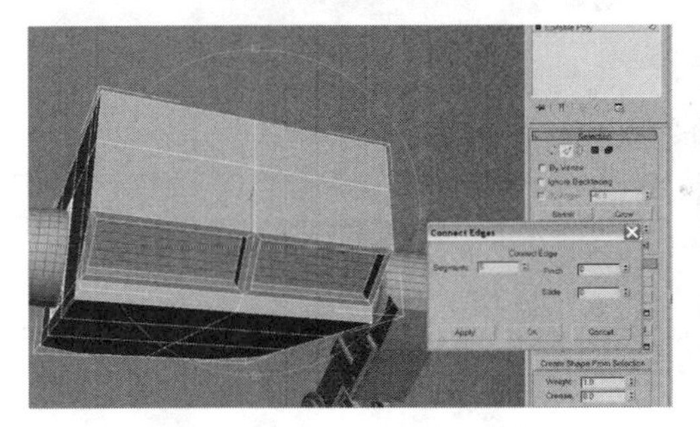

Figure 3-933

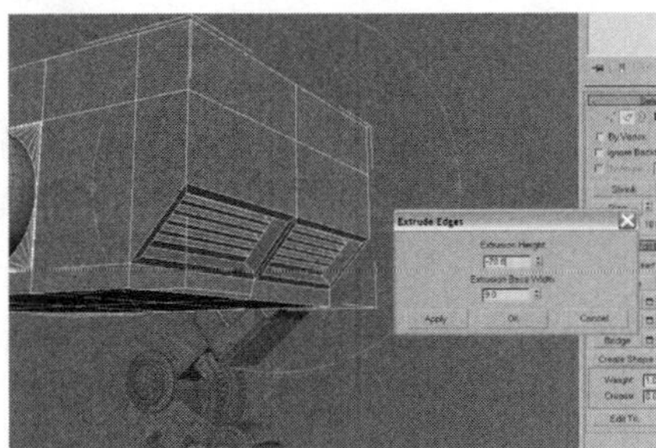

Figure 3-934

38. Select the polygons shown in Figure 3-935, on both sides, and Bevel them:

Type	Height	Outline	Apply/OK
Local Normal	0	–25	Apply
Local Normal	15	–13.5	OK

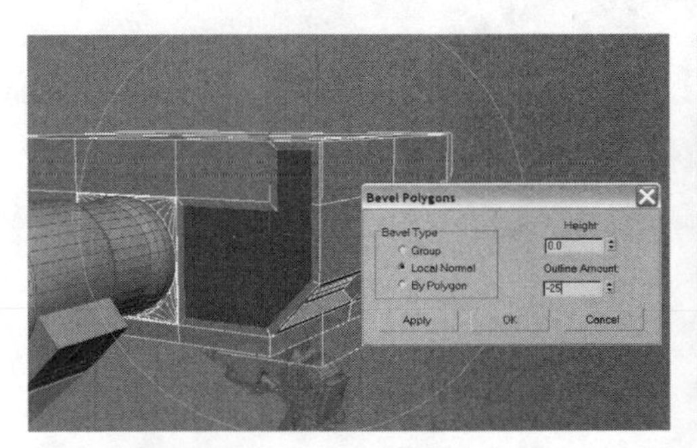

Figure 3-935

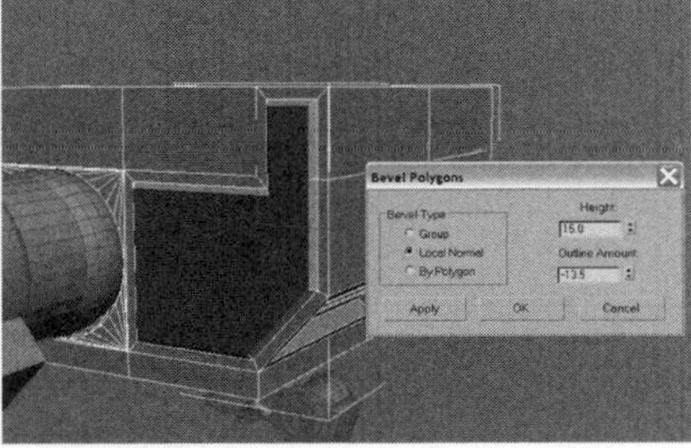

Figure 3-936

39. Select the remaining polygons, on both sides, and Bevel them:

Type	Height	Outline	Apply/OK
Local Normal	0	–25	Apply
Local Normal	15	–13.5	OK

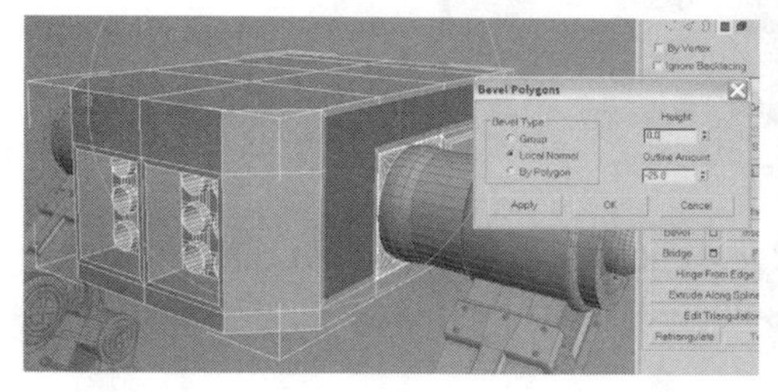

Figure 3-937

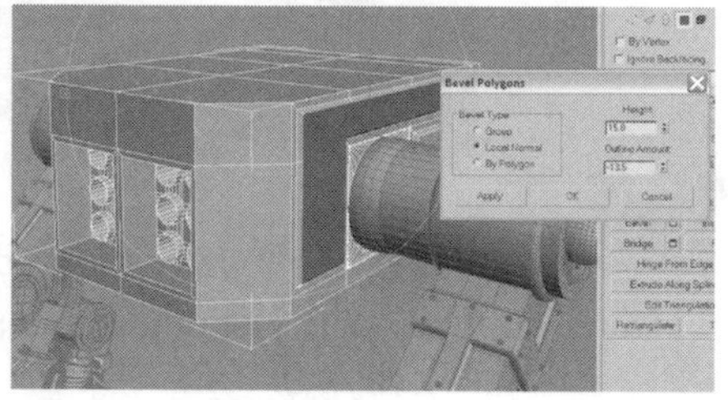

Figure 3-938

40. Select the two front panels as shown in Figure 3-939 and Bevel them:

Type	Height	Outline	Apply/OK
Local Normal	0	–30	Apply
Local Normal	–30	0	Apply
Local Normal	0	–50	Apply
Local Normal	20	0	OK

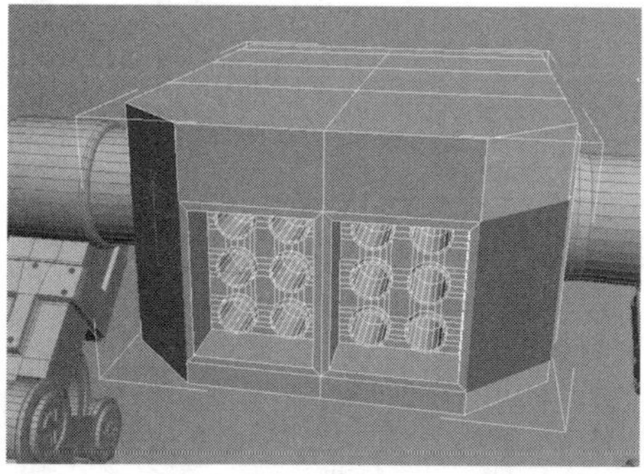

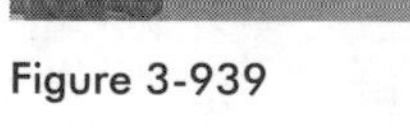
Figure 3-939

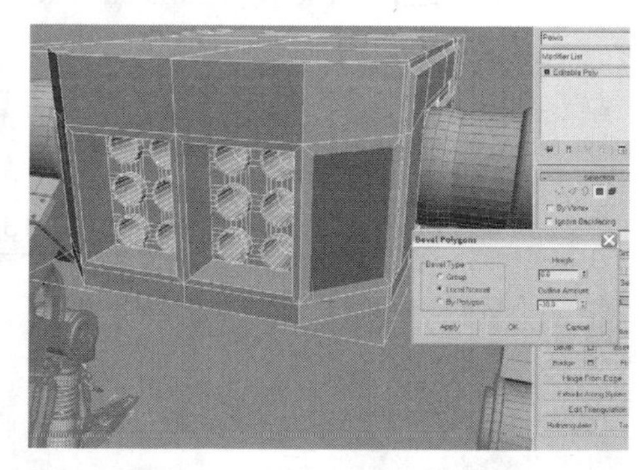

Figure 3-940

Day 8: Creating the Second Leg, Hips, and Base

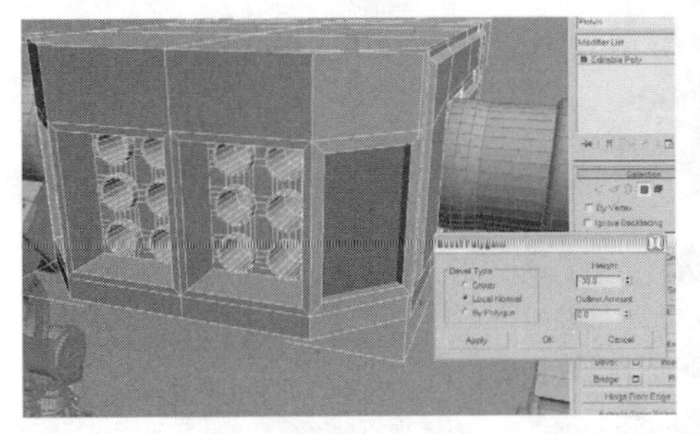

Figure 3-941

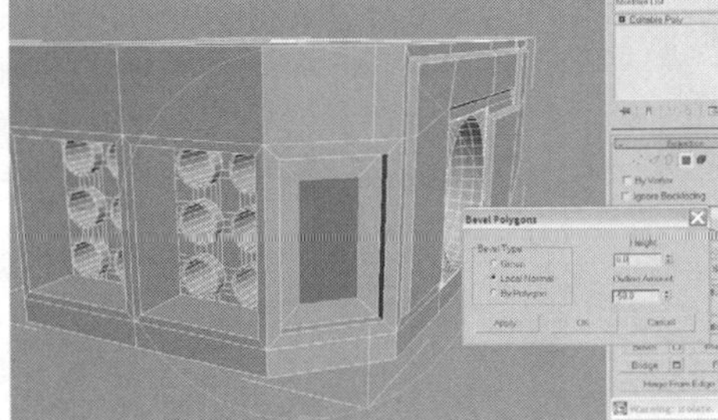

Figure 3-942

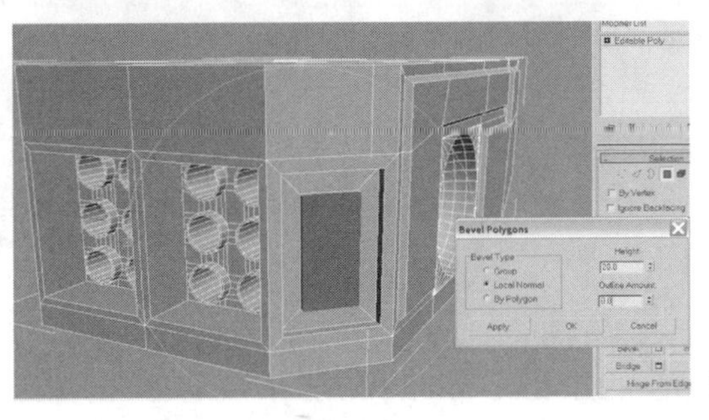

Figure 3-943

41. Create a Cylinder using AutoGrid in the upper-left corner of the indentation. Extrude it by **5** 10 times.

Radius	Height	Height/Cap Segs	Sides	Smooth
6	88	1/1	36	Checked

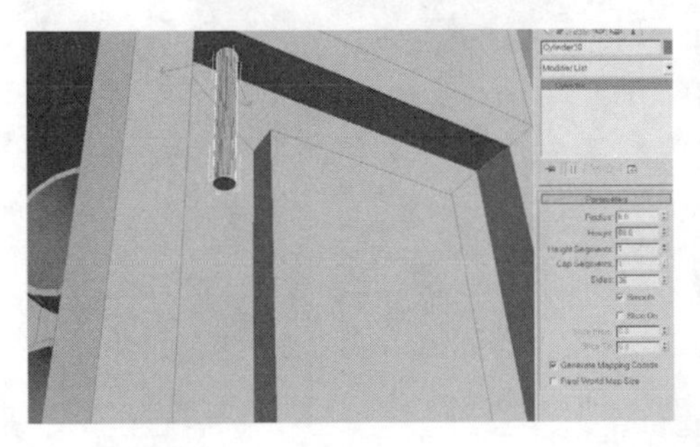

Figure 3-944

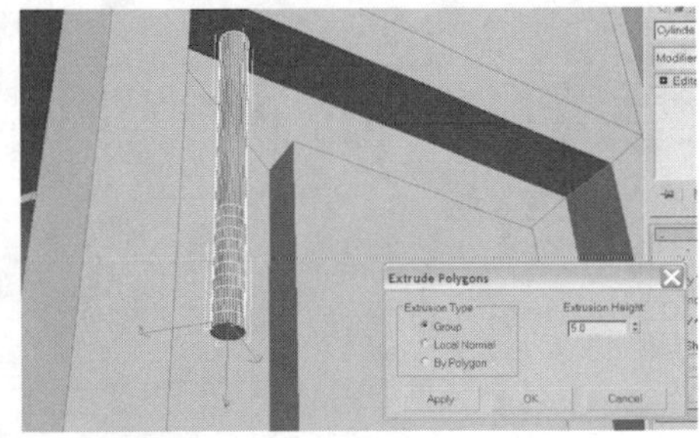

Figure 3-945

42. Clone the cylinder five times and move one of the clones to the upper-right corner. (We may not use all the clones, but keep them nearby for a while.) Move the pivot of the original to the segment at the start of the 10 extrusions.

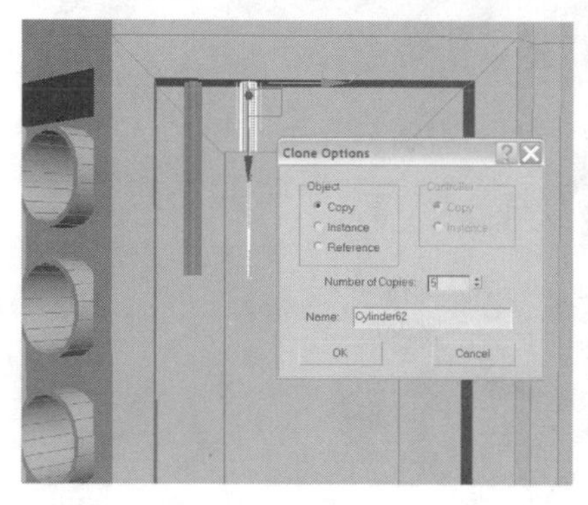

Figure 3-946

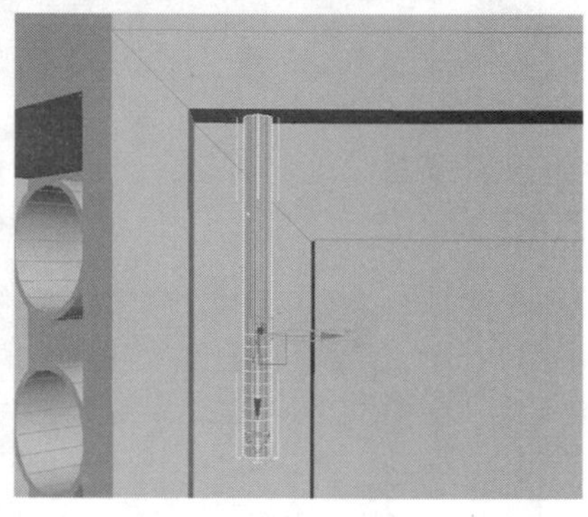

Figure 3-947

43. Select the original cylinder, add a Bend modifier to its stack with the Angle set to **90**, Direction to **222.5**, **Z** for the Bend Axis, Limit Effect checked, and Upper Limit set to **30**, and convert it to an Editable Polygon. Select the top polygon and lower it in the Z axis until it's beneath the bent cylinder.

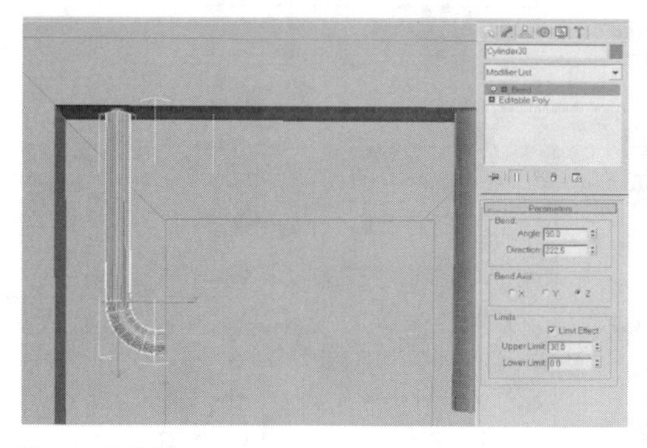

Figure 3-948

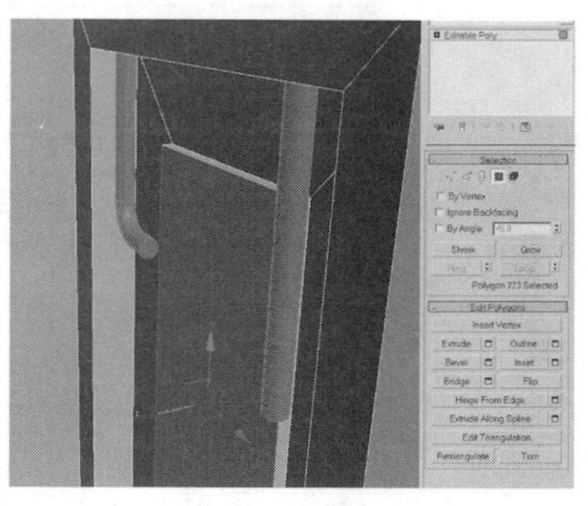

Figure 3-949

44. Select the cap of the bent cylinder and pull it in the Z axis until it's a quarter of the way across the surface of the rectangle beneath it. Add a Smooth modifier to its stack and convert it to an Editable Polygon to collapse the stack.

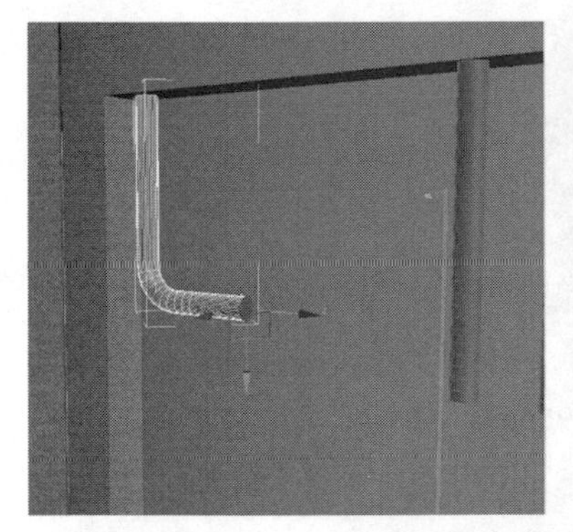

Figure 3-950

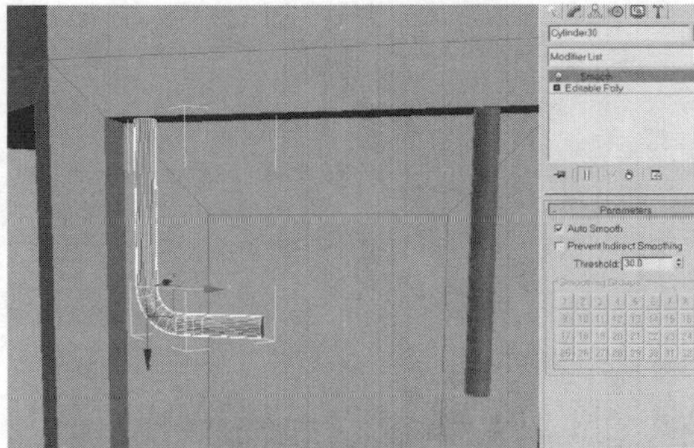

Figure 3-951

45. Select and Clone the bent cylinder two times. Move the clones until they're positioned as shown in Figure 3-953.

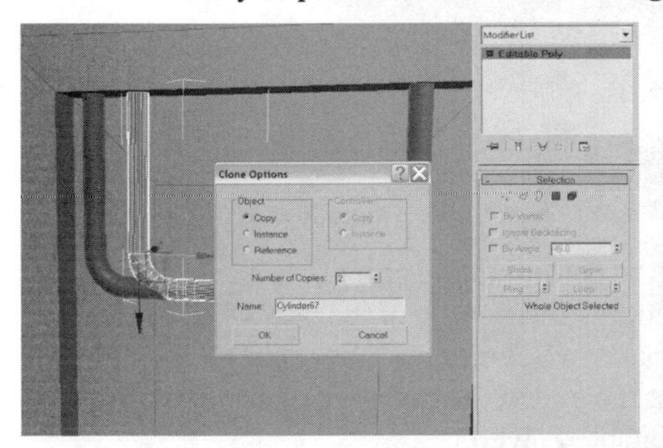

Figure 3-952

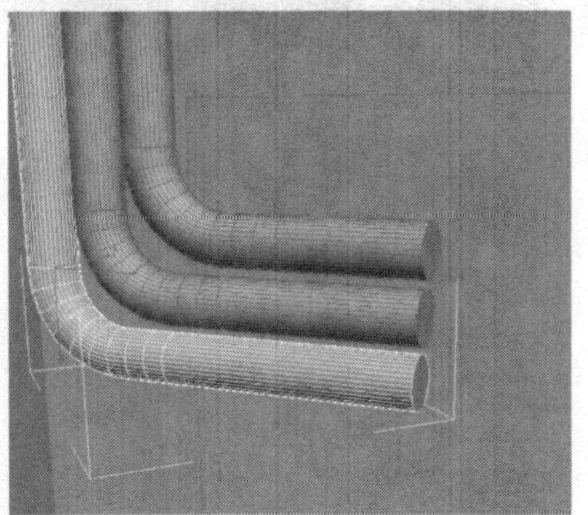

Figure 3-953

46. Create a Box at the end of the three cylinders. Convert the box to an Editable Polygon, select the two outer polygons on the bottom, and Bevel them.

Length	Width	Height	Length/Width/Height Segs
50	45	23	1/3/1

Type	Height	Outline	Apply/OK
Group	0	–3.8	Apply
Group	60	0	OK

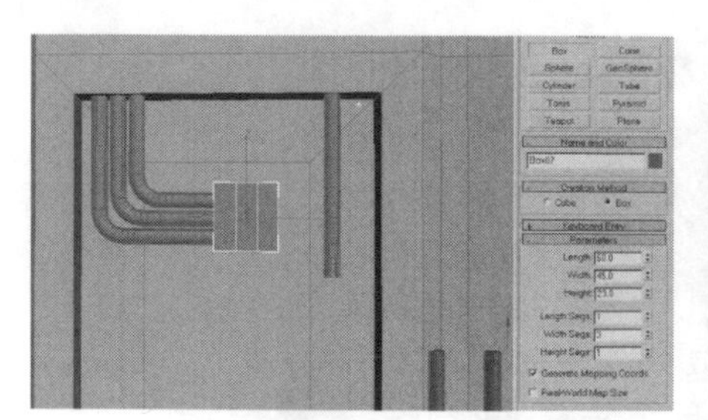

Figure 3-954

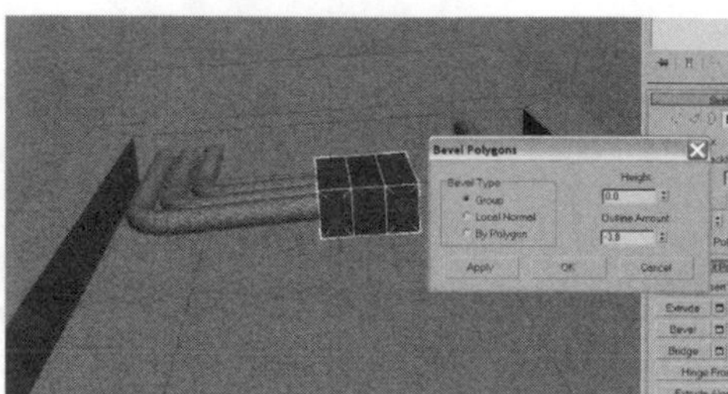

Figure 3-955

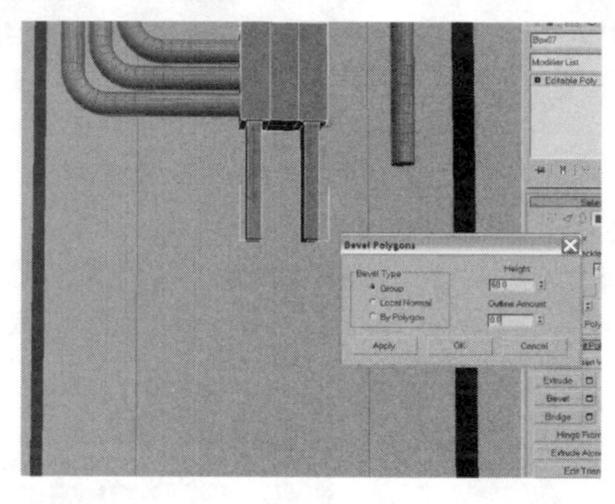

Figure 3-956

47. Select the polygon on the bottom of the straight cylinder and drag it down until it just penetrates the bottom of the box. Object-select the straight cylinder and make two clones and line them all up in the corner. Create a Box at the end of the two rectangular extrusions and convert it to an Editable Polygon.

Length	Width	Height	Length/Width/Height Segs
118	110	10	3/3/1

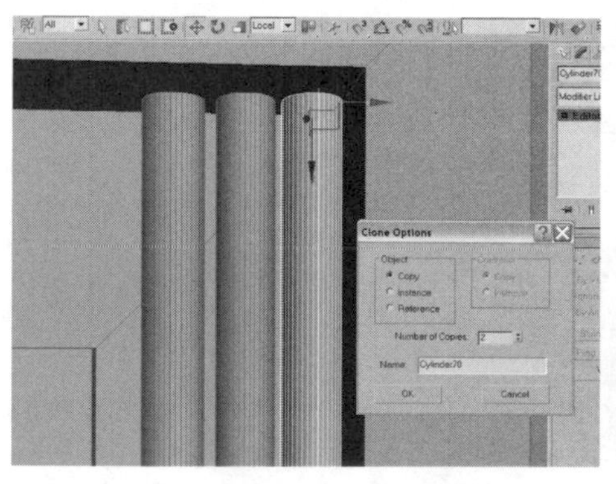

Figure 3-957

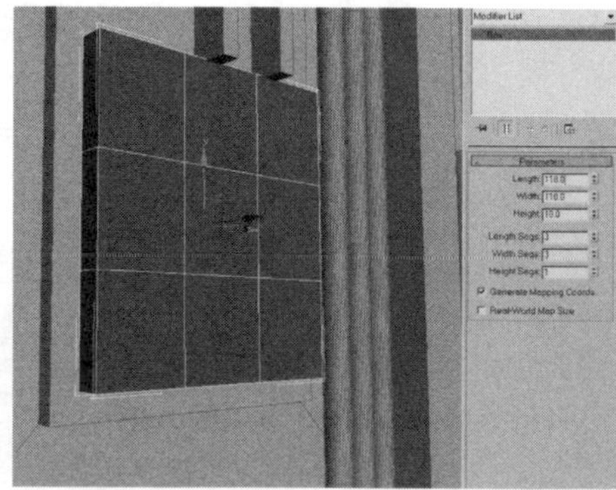

Figure 3-958

48. Select the top two polygons and Extrude them by **10**. Bevel the polygons:

Type	Height	Outline	Apply/OK
Group	0	–3	Apply
Group	–2.5	0	OK

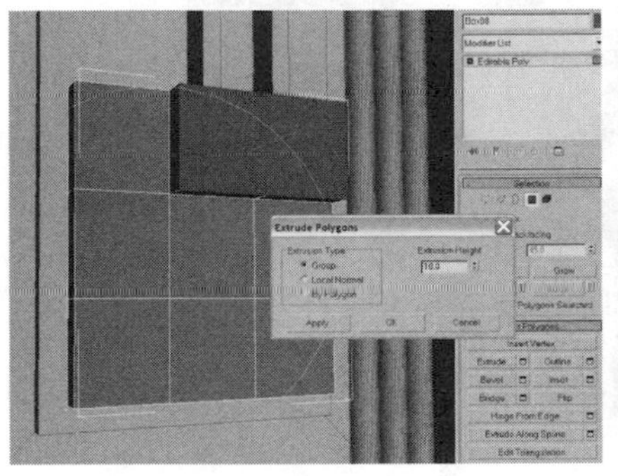

Figure 3-959

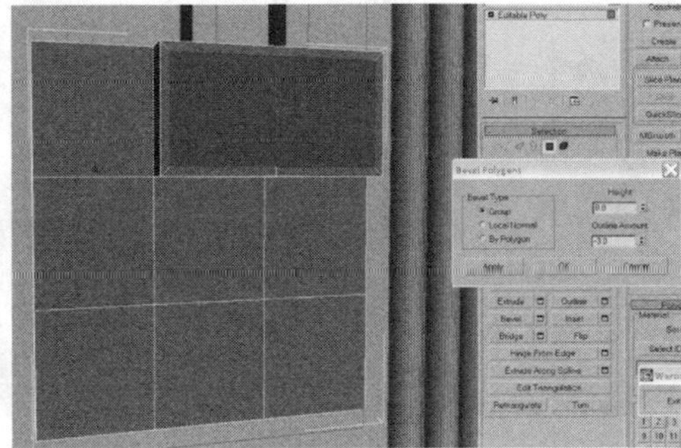

Figure 3-960

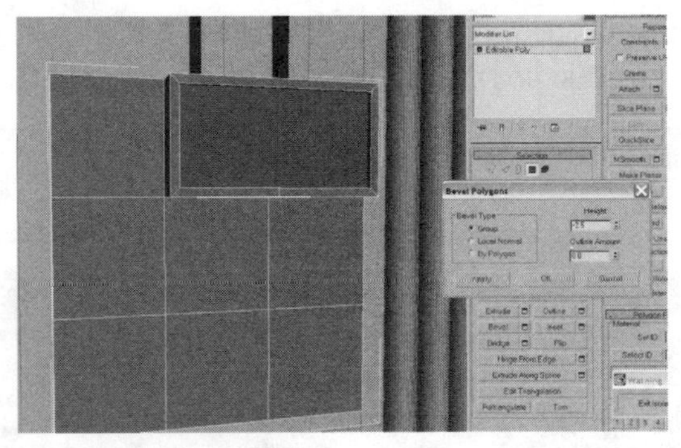

Figure 3-961

49. Select the three vertical segments and Connect the edges with **5** Segments. Extrude the edges to **6** with a Base Width of **2.25**.

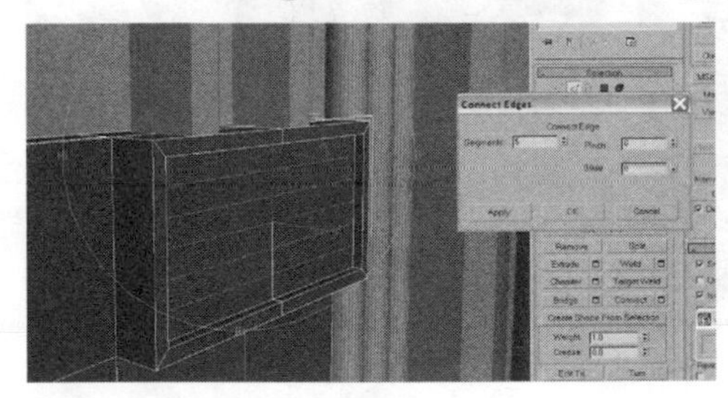

Figure 3-962

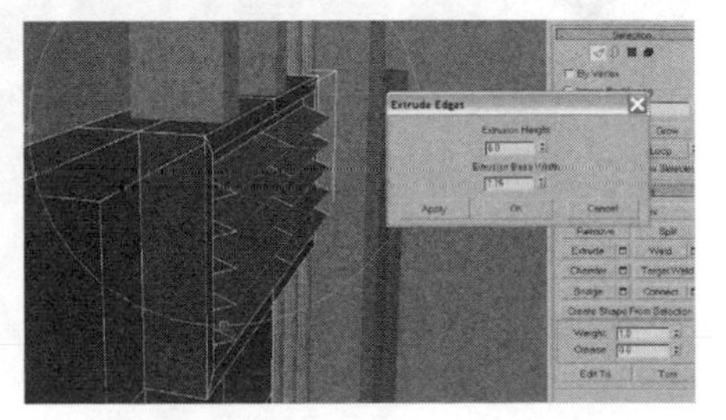

Figure 3-963

50. Push the edges down in the Y axis so they're not sticking straight out. Create a Tube beneath the vents you just made.

Radius 1	Radius 2	Height	Height/Cap Segs	Sides	Smooth
35	30	20	1/1	36	Checked

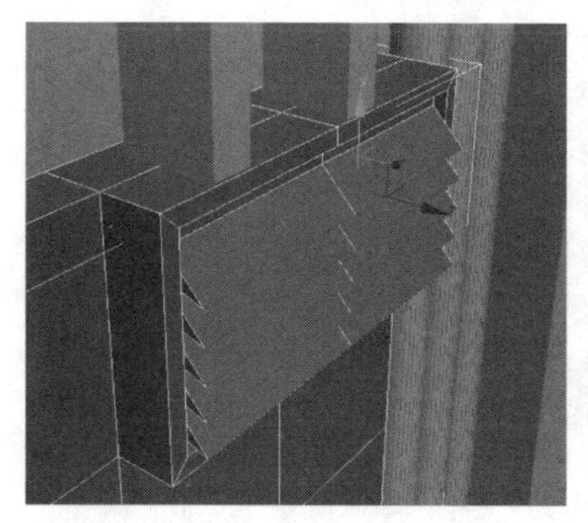

Figure 3-964

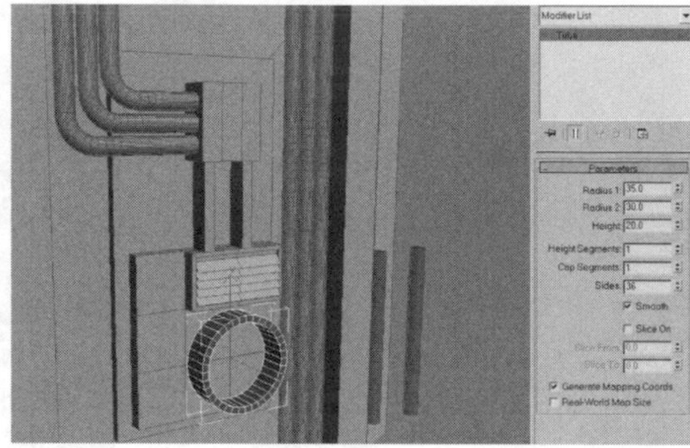

Figure 3-965

51. Create a Tube inside the tube you just made. Select every other polygon on the middle ring on the outside of the inner tube.

Radius 1	Radius 2	Height	Height/Cap Segs	Sides	Smooth
25	20	25	3/1	36	Checked

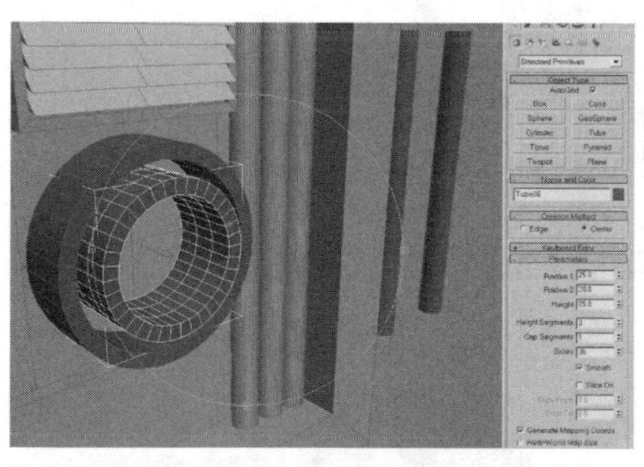

Figure 3-966

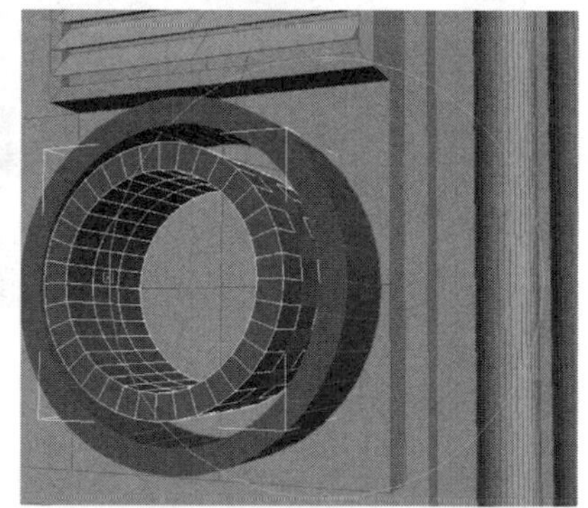

Figure 3-967

52. Extrude the polygons by **8.775**, so they form spokes. Take one of the cylinder clones you made in step 42 and Rotate it **90** degrees, then move it into the the middle tube and position it near the top. Center the cylinder's pivot point at the center of the middle tube.

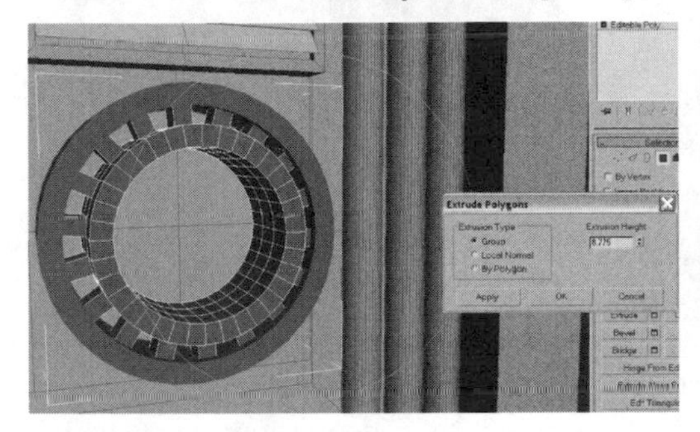

Figure 3-968

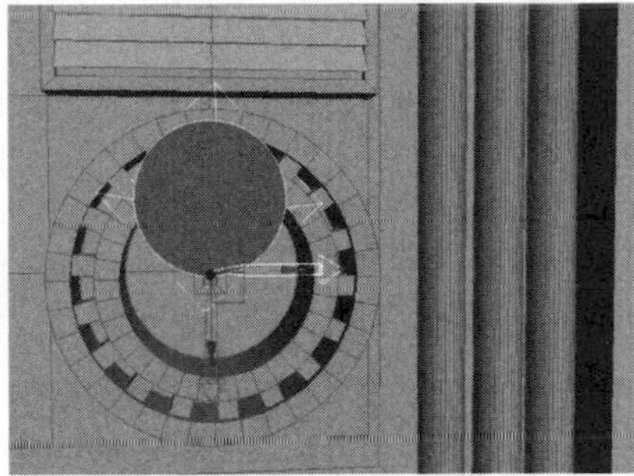

Figure 3-969

53. Uniform Scale the cylinder to **75**. Hold down the **Shift** key and Rotate **–40** degrees in the Z axis, then make eight clones. (Remember that Angle Snap will help limit the rotation to five-degree increments.)

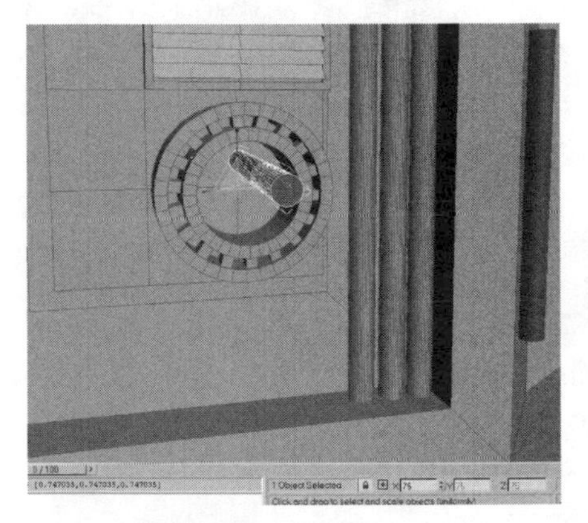

Figure 3-970

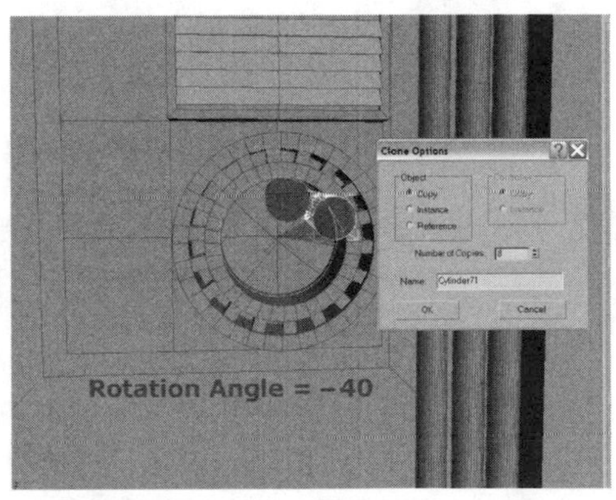

Figure 3-971

54. Using AutoGrid, create a Capsule in the upper-left missile tube on the right side of the body. Clone the capsule five times and place one in each of the tubes on the *right* side only.

Radius	Height	Sides	Height Segs	Smooth
43.857	400	10	1	Checked

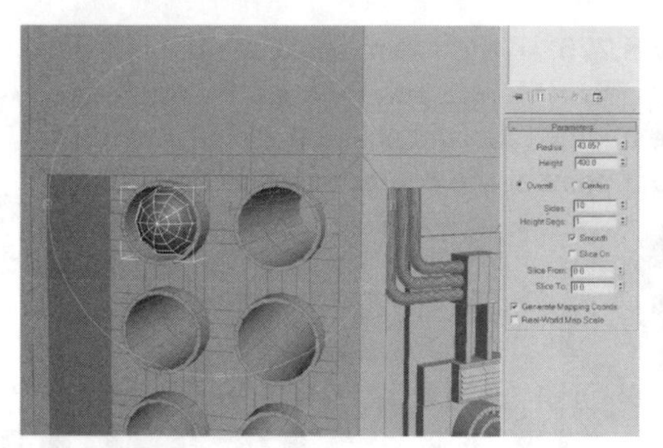

Figure 3-972

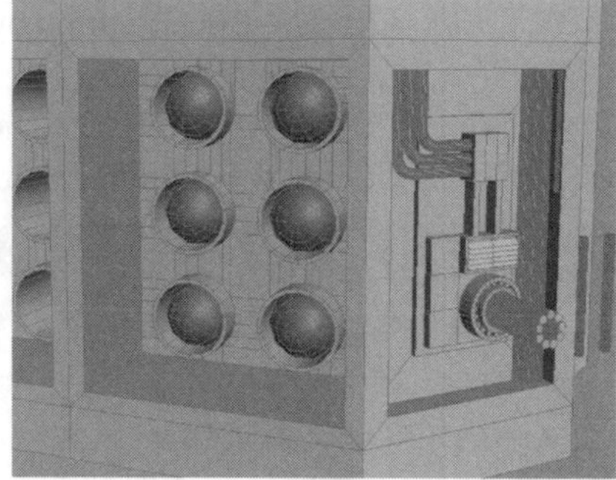

Figure 3-973

55. Select the body, click **Attach List**, and select everything on the body and Attach them. Marquee-select the side without missiles in the tubes and delete it.

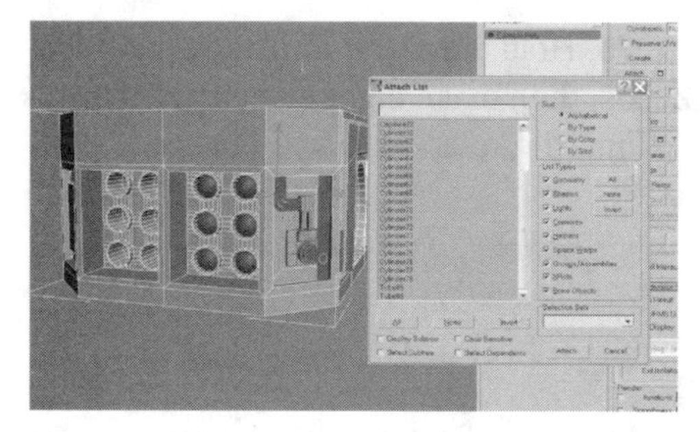

Figure 3-974

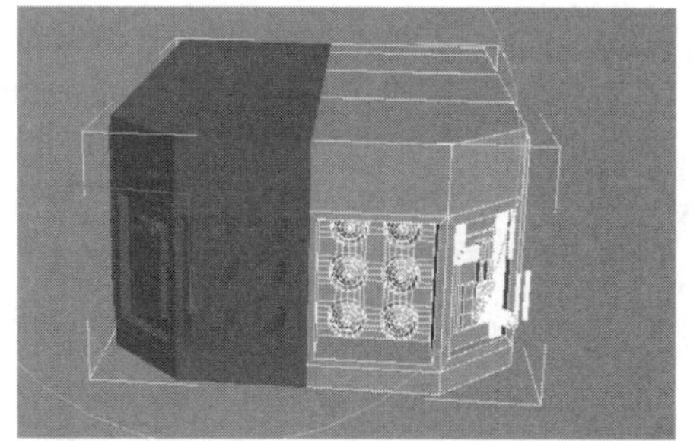

Figure 3-975

56. Select the body, add a Symmetry modifier to the stack, and click the little test tube to show it in the viewport. Open the Editable Polygon rollout in the stack, and polygon-select the front two upper polygons (you only need to select on one side because the Symmetry modifier will select the polys for you on the other). Bevel them:

Type	Height	Outline	Apply/OK
Group	0	–33.75	OK

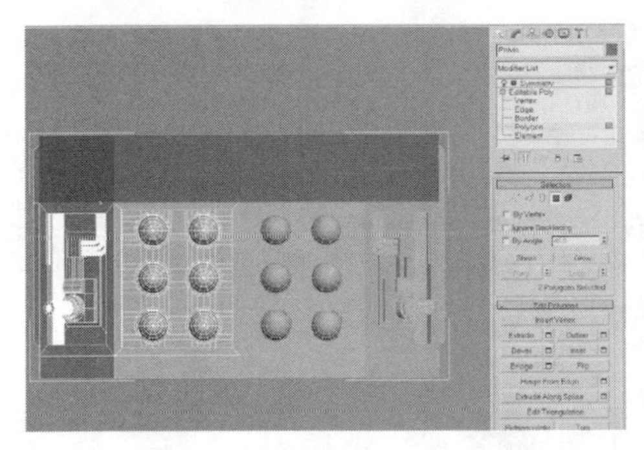

Figure 3-976

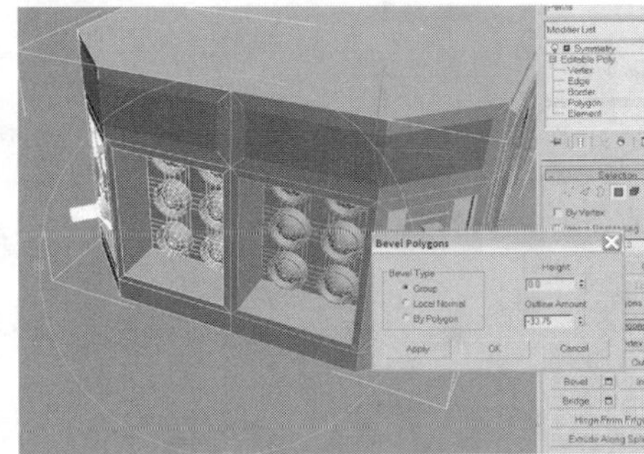

Figure 3-977

57. Create the two horizontal cuts shown in Figure 3-978. Select the edges shown in Figure 3-979, and Remove them. This will create two uninterrupted horizontal edges across the front of the body.

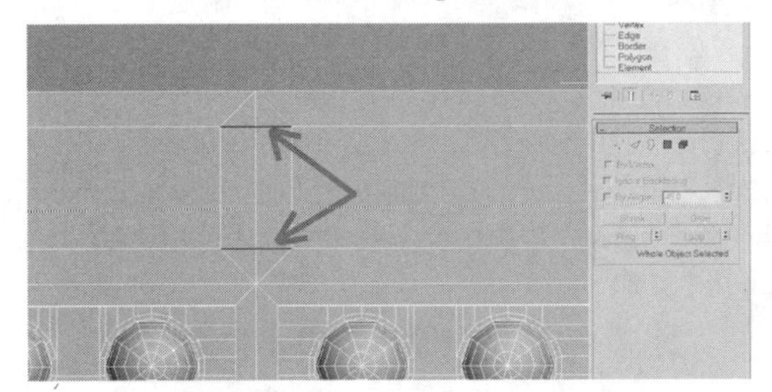

Figure 3-978

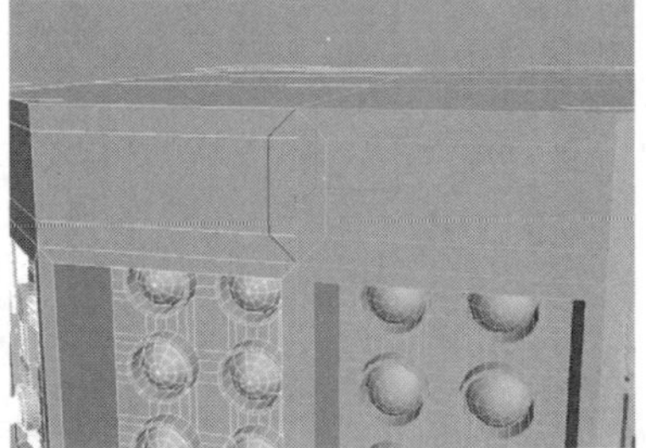

Figure 3-979

58. Select the top two polygons made from the bevel and Extrude them by **–50**. Look on the inside upper and lower ledges created by the extrusion. You'll see some edges there that we don't want. Select and Remove them.

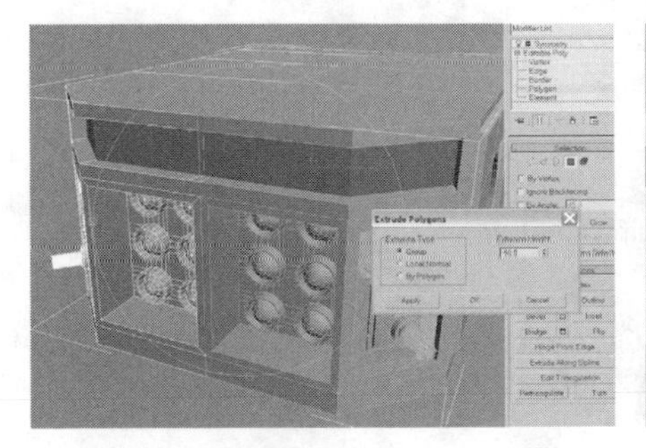

Figure 3-980

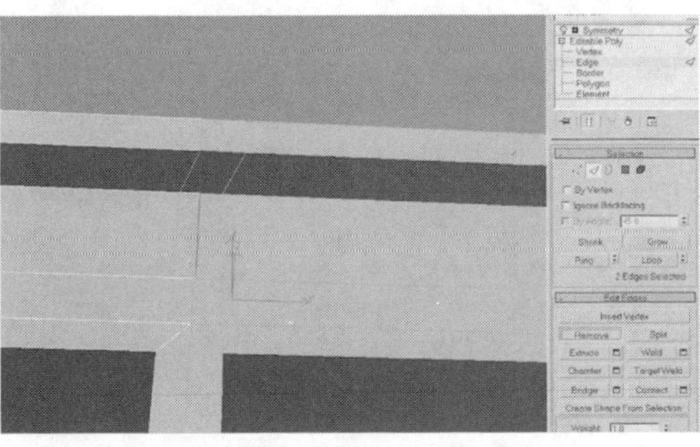

Figure 3-981

Don't Forget: Remove may've removed the edges, but it left behind some isolated vertices. Don't forget to remove those too or you may end up with nasty surprises in your geometry later!

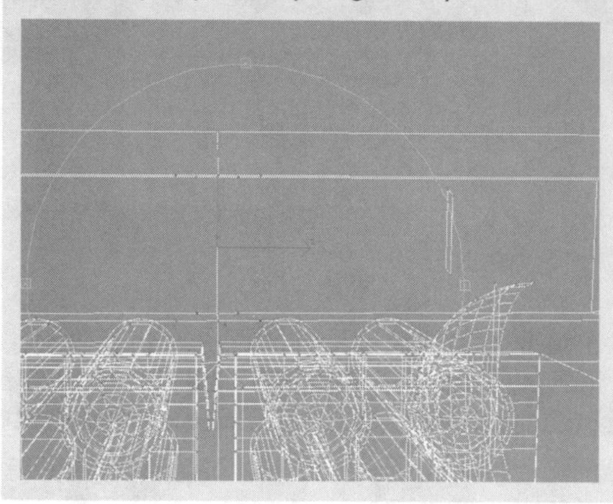

Figure 3-982

59. Be sure Weld Edges is checked under the Symmetry modifier options and then convert the Hip to an Editable Polygon to collapse the stack, merging the two halves together. Select the upper and lower edges on the inside of the recess.

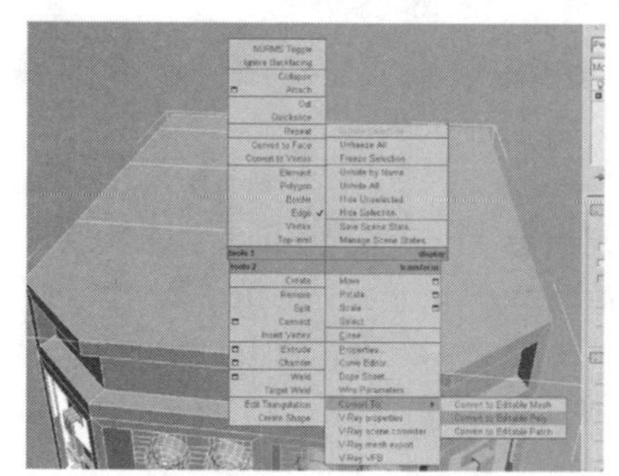

Figure 3-983

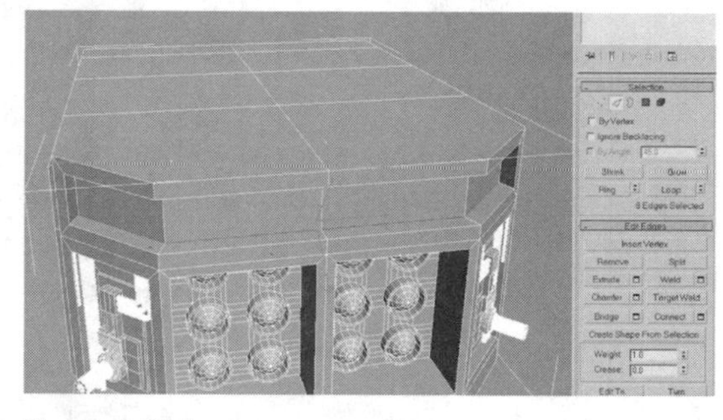

Figure 3-984

FYI: You might be wondering why we didn't keep the Symmetry modifier around for longer. But consider all the pipes and greebles we didn't have to make on the other side. And since we won't be animating the missiles, we didn't have to fully model them; just the fronts. Speaking of pipes, you should have some extras lying around. You can either delete them or hide them and use them later, as we will be making more pipes. Personally, I'd just hide them and save myself some work.

60. Connect the inner edges with **10** Segments. Extrude the edges to a Height of **42** with a Base Width of **29.788** to make vents.

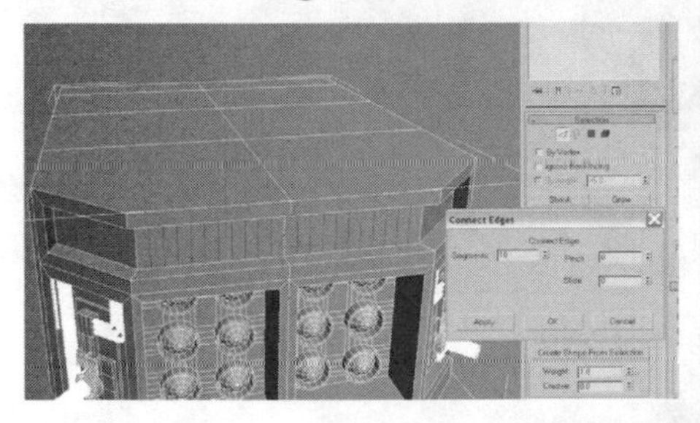

Figure 3-985

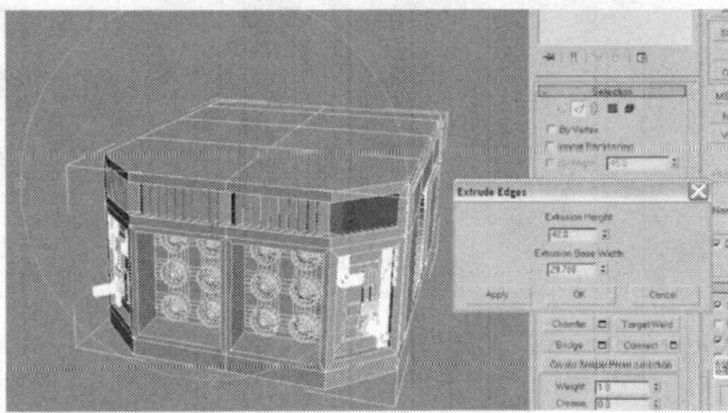

Figure 3-986

61. There are some big gaps in our vents that we could spend a lot of time correcting, or … we could add some interesting widgets. Zoom into the right corner, make a Cylinder, and Bevel it:

Radius	Height	Height/Cap Segs	Sides	Smooth
13.622	4.208	1/2	36	Checked

Type	Height	Outline	Apply/OK
Group	10	–1	Apply

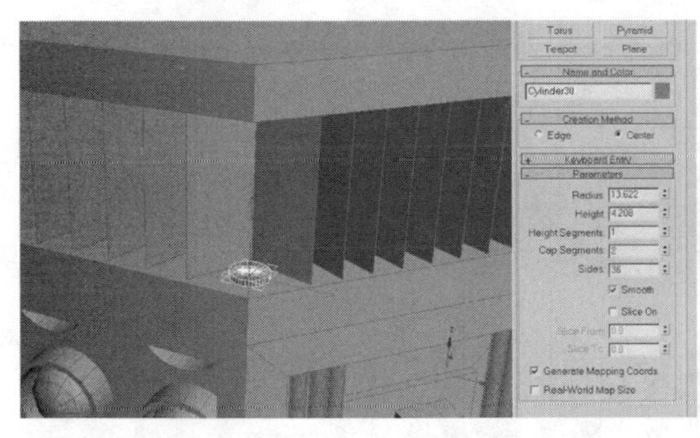

Figure 3-987

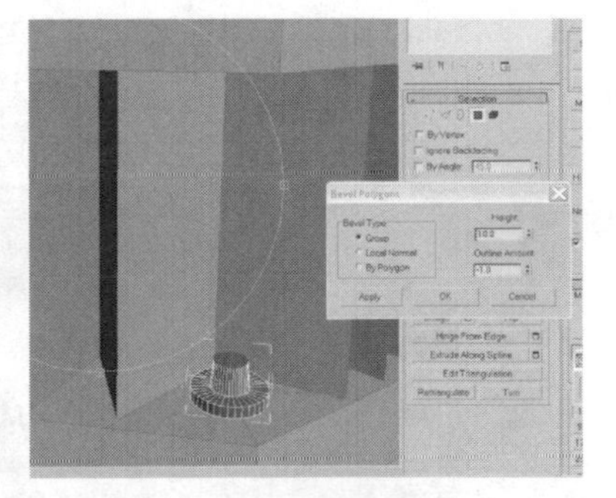

Figure 3-988

Type	Height	Outline	Apply/OK
Group	10	–1	Apply
Group	0	–1.25	Apply
Group	5	0	Apply five times then OK

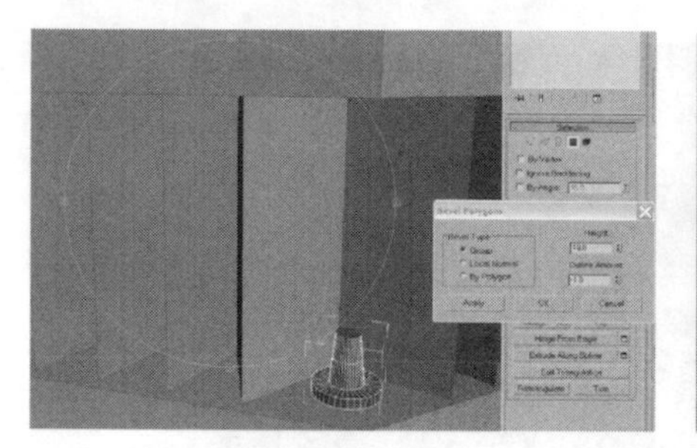

Figure 3-989

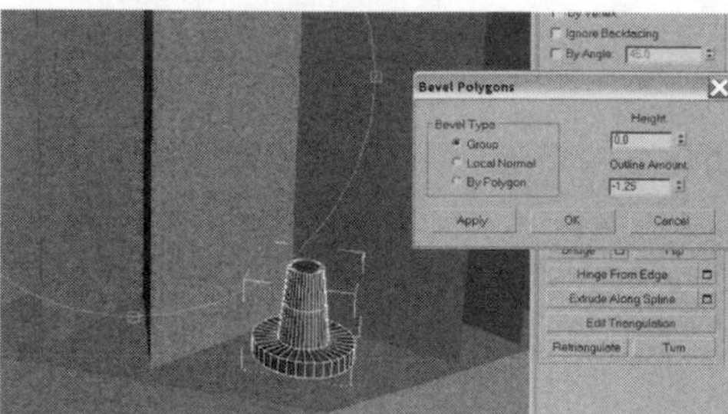

Figure 3-990

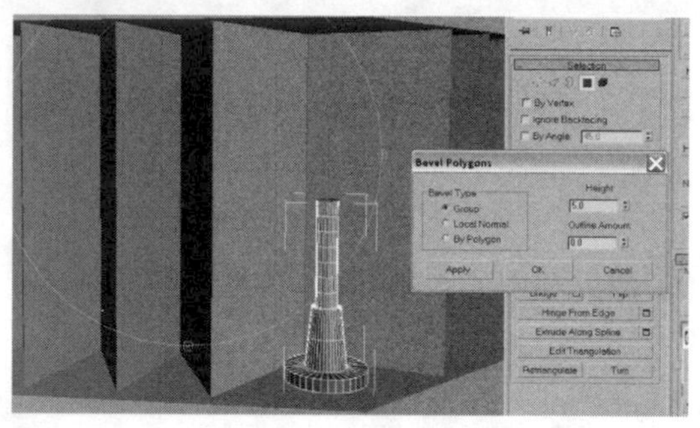

Figure 3-991

62. Select every other row of polygons on the extrusions and Bevel them By Polygon:

Type	Height	Outline	Apply/OK
By Polygon	5	0	OK

Figure 3-992

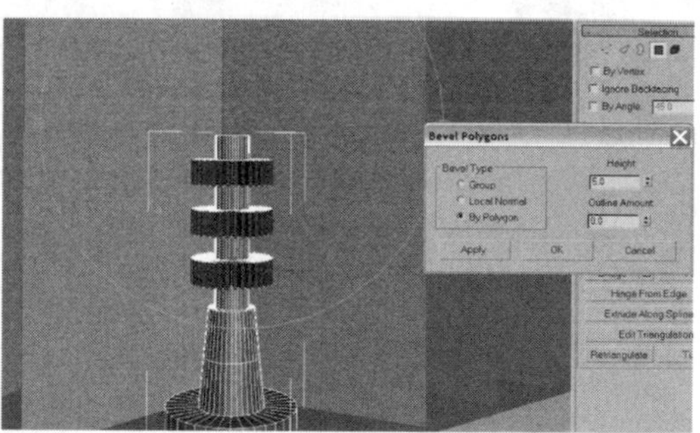

Figure 3-993

63. Select the top polygon and delete it. Object-select it and Mirror-clone it in the Z axis, with an Offset of **116**, then name it **shield_emitter**.

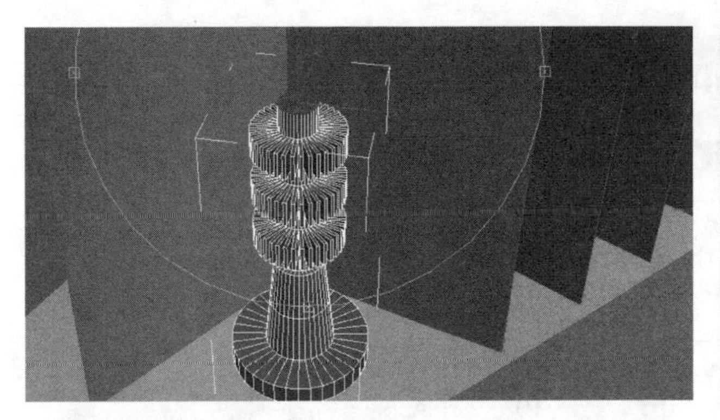

Figure 3-994

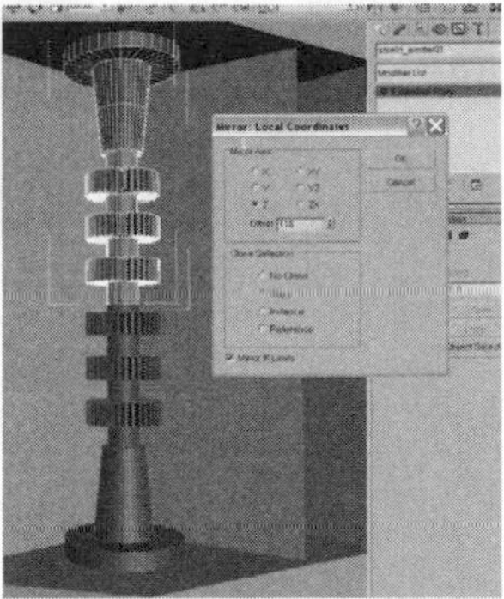

Figure 3-995

64. Attach the two parts together and Weld the center vertices.

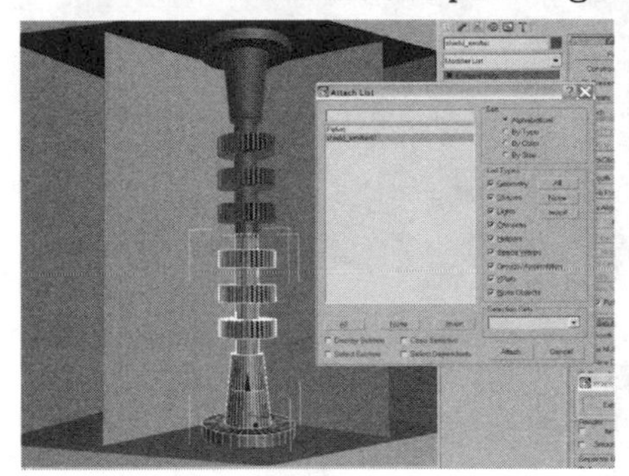

Figure 3-996

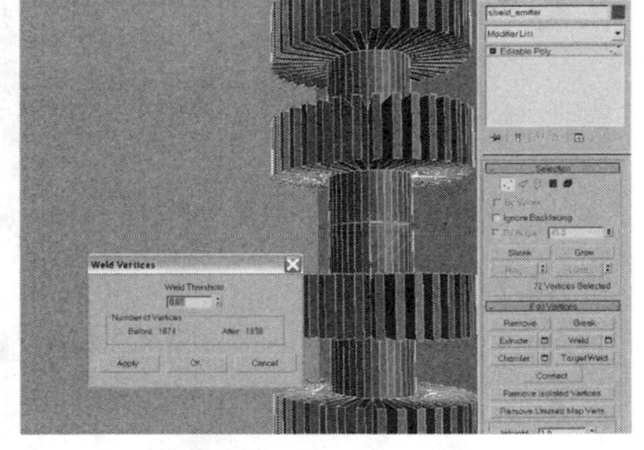

Figure 3-997

65. Shift-drag the shield_emitter in the X axis to make two clones, and place one in the center gap in the grill and one in the far left corner. Select the body, click **Attach List**, and attach the shield_emitters to the body.

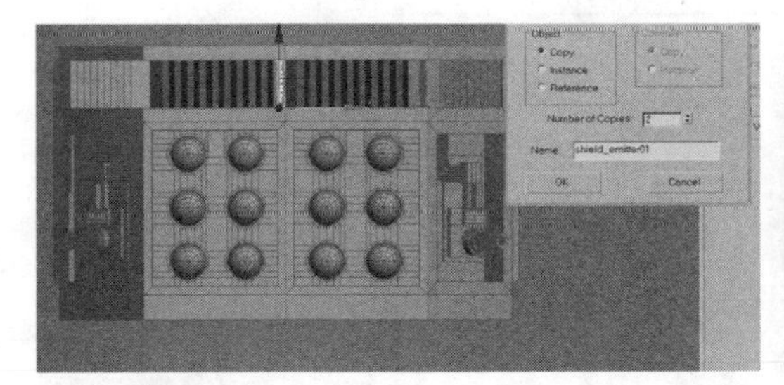

Figure 3-998

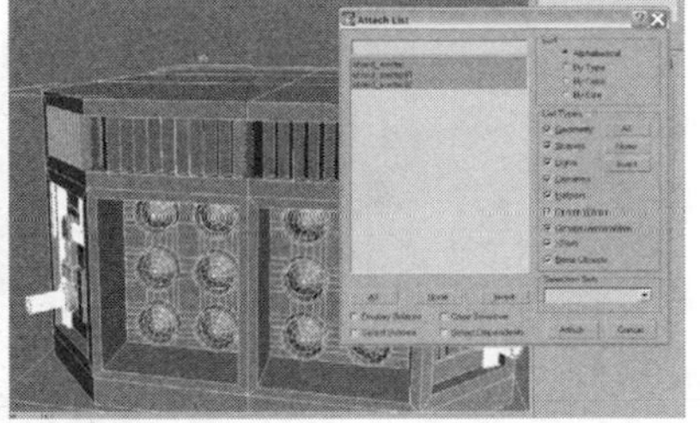

Figure 3-999

Day 9: Detailing the Rear Base and Adding the Turret and Upper Body

1. Orbit around the rear of the body, select the top two polygons, and Bevel them:

Type	Height	Outline	Apply/OK
Local Normal	0	–10	Apply
Local Normal	25	0	Apply

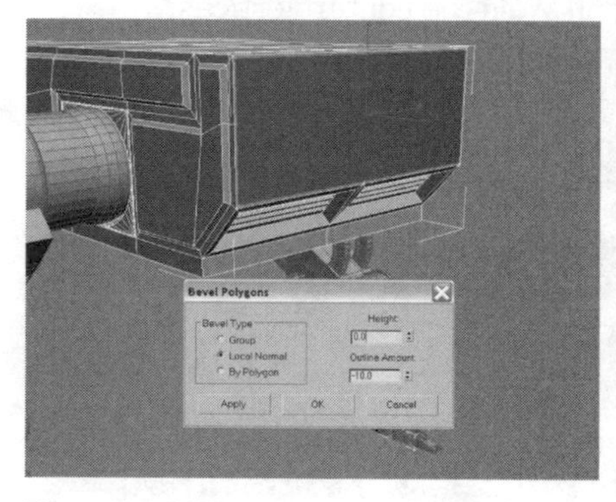

Figure 3-1000

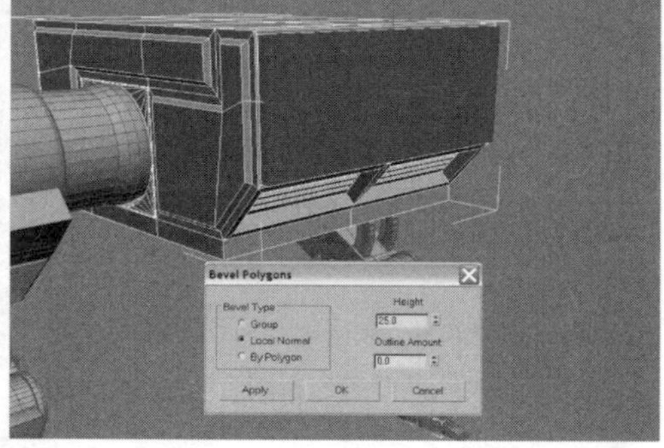

Figure 3-1001

Type	Height	Outline	Apply/OK
Local Normal	0	–25	Apply
Local Normal	–50	0	Apply
Local Normal	30	–25	OK

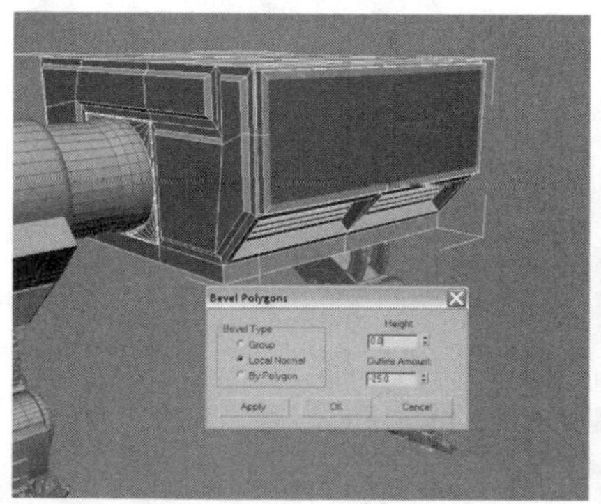

Figure 3-1002

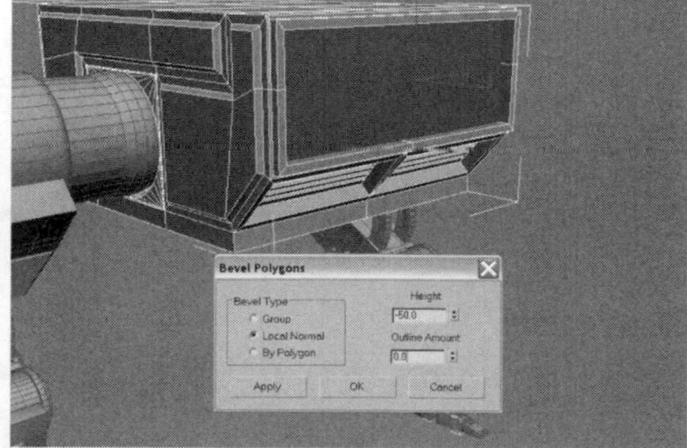

Figure 3-1003

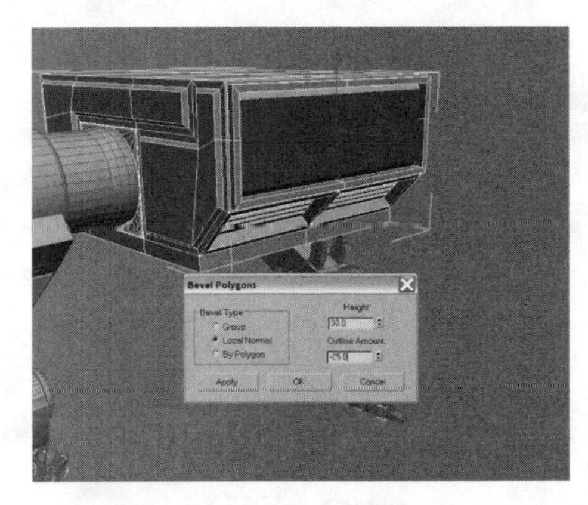

Figure 3-1004

2. Select the left two polygons and Bevel them, then create a Cylinder in the upper-left corner:

Type	Height	Outline	Apply/OK
Local Normal	30	–25	OK

Radius	Height	Height/Cap Segs	Sides	Smooth
37	16	1/1	24	Checked

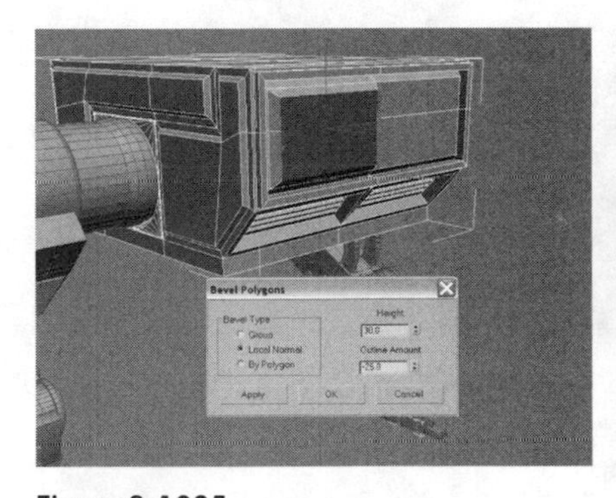

Figure 3-1005

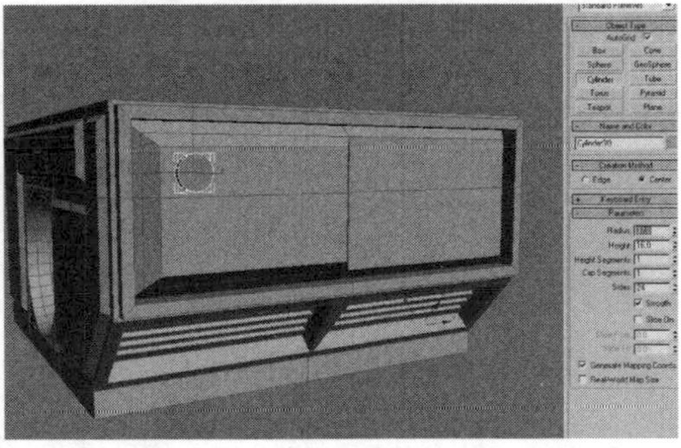

Figure 3-1006

3. Convert the cylinder to an Editable Polygon. Select the cylinder cap.

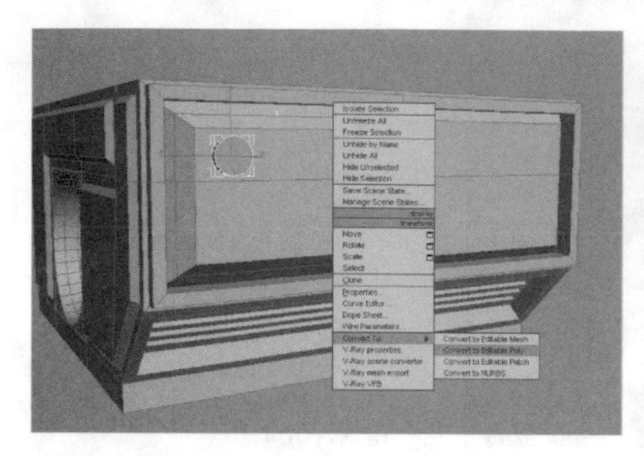

Figure 3-1007

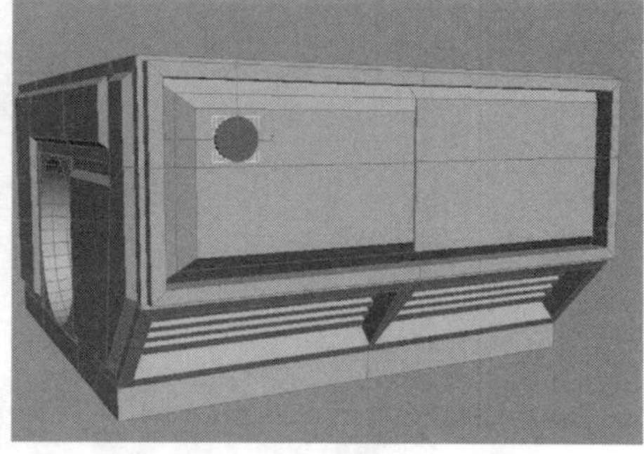

Figure 3-1008

4. Bevel the cap:

Type	Height	Outline	Apply/OK
Group	0	–8	Apply
Group	25	0	Apply

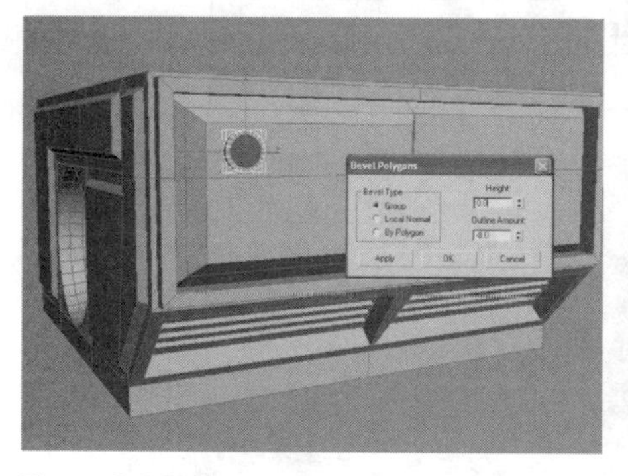

Figure 3-1009

Figure 3-1010

Type	Height	Outline	Apply/OK
Group	0	–6	Apply
Group	–26	0	OK

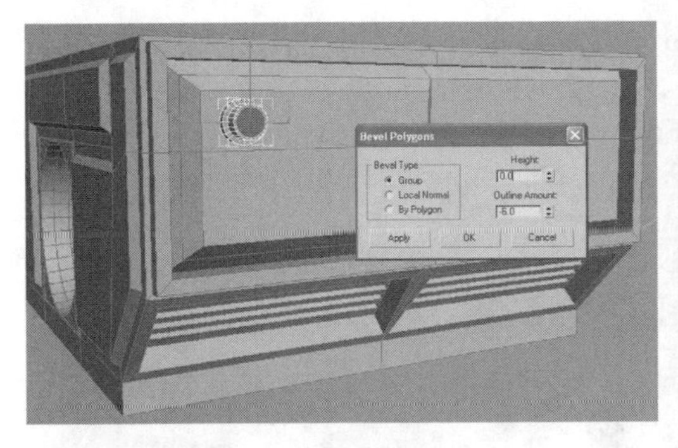

Figure 3-1011

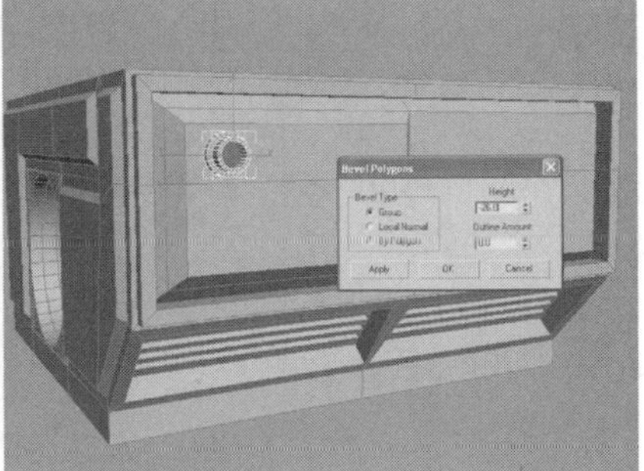

Figure 3-1012

5. Object-select the cylinder and Shift-drag it in the Z axis to make two clones, then position them as shown in Figure 3-1014.

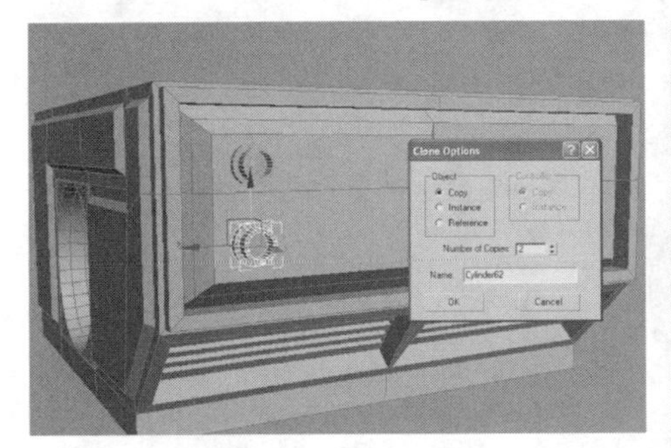

Figure 3-1013

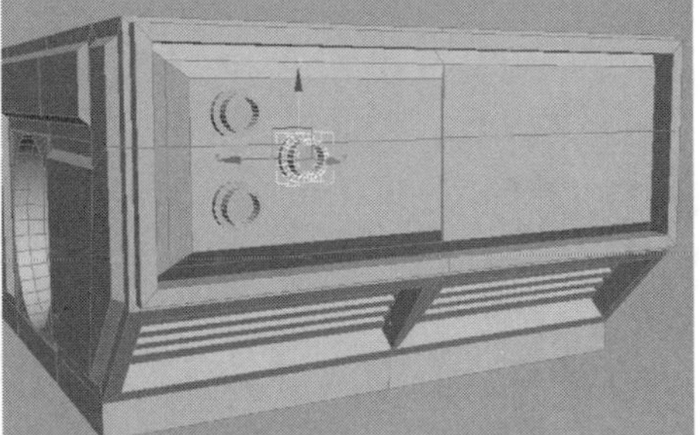

Figure 3-1014

6. Make another clone and move it to the far side of the rear, as shown. Select the body and Attach the cylinders.

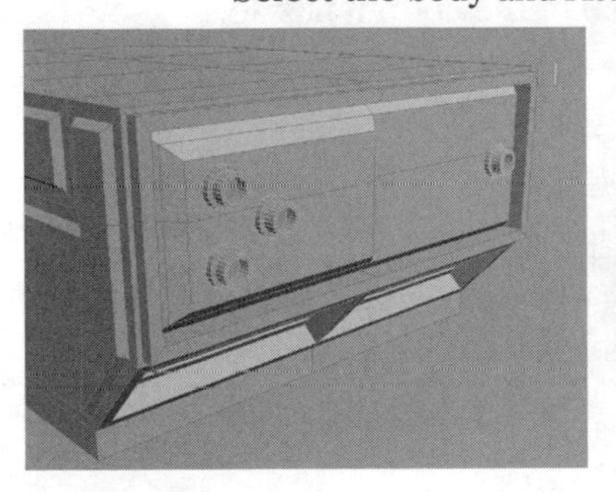

Figure 3-1015

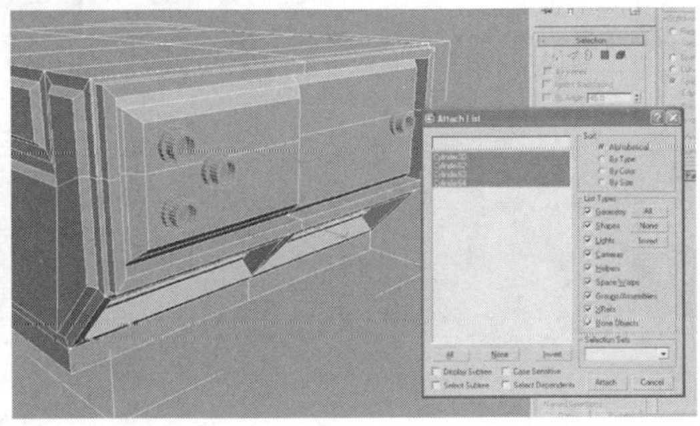

Figure 3-1016

7. Create a Line Spline from the nozzle on the right to one on the far side, as shown in Figure 3-1017. (Be sure to select each vertex, right-click, and make it Smooth so you get a curving hose.) Create a three-point Spline traveling from the topmost nozzle to the first spline.

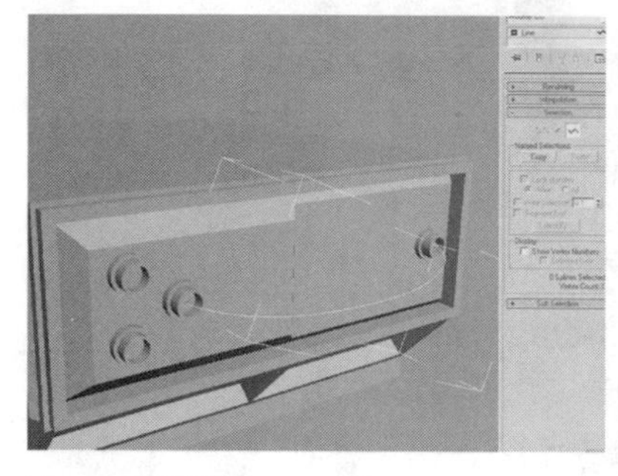

Figure 3-1017

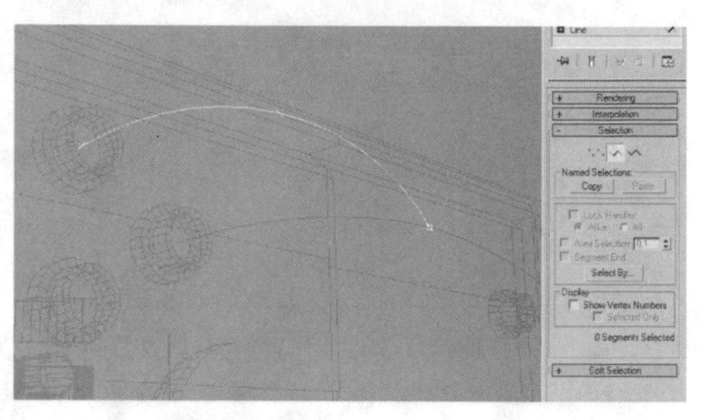

Figure 3-1018

Fire Drill: This is a workaround, because, to the best of my knowledge, there is no graceful way to make a hose that splits, like one you might find on a manifold or a distributor. If someone knows a better way to do this, *please* email me; I've been looking for a better way for a while. The way I'm going to show you *works*, but the results are not very satisfying. You could create multiple polygonal cylinders, add Bend modifiers to them, and then connect them using Bridge to merge the polygons or edges, but I can't imagine that approach's results would be sufficiently better to justify the extra work. This approach is, at least, pretty simple.

8. Create another three-point Spline from the vertex where the last spline intersected with the original to the bottom nozzle.

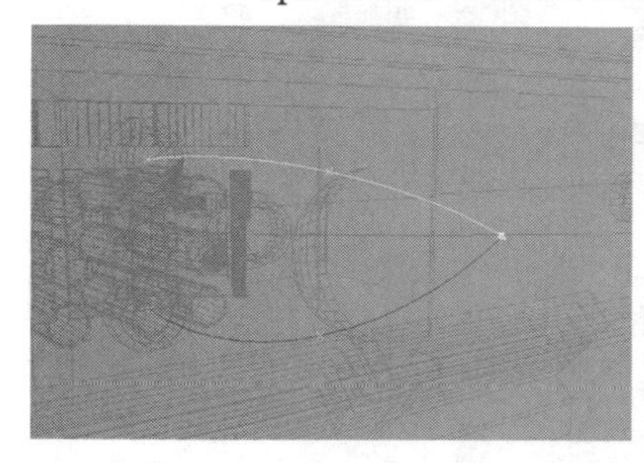

Figure 3-1019

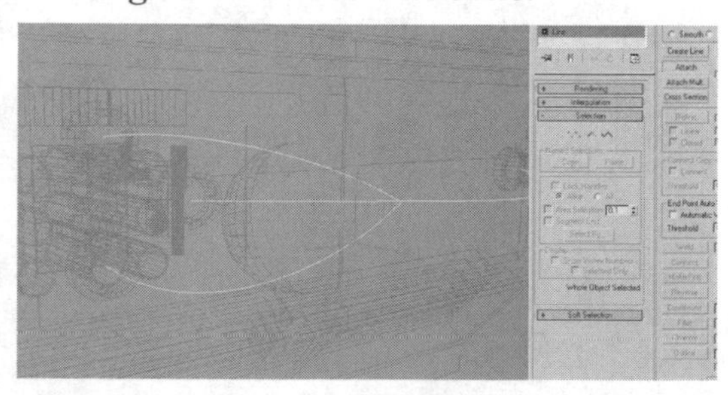

Figure 3-1020

9. Attach the ancillary splines to the original, then select the three intersecting vertices and click **Weld**. Under Rendering, select **Enable In Renderer** and **Enable In Viewport**. Click **Radial**, and set the Thickness to around **45** (mine was 45.11) and the Sides to **16**.

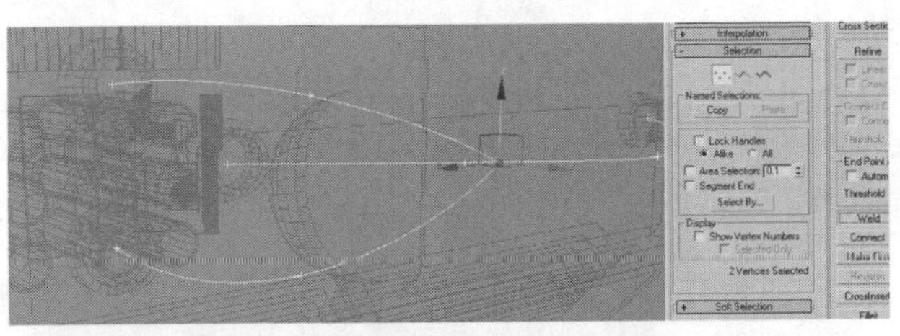

Figure 3-1021

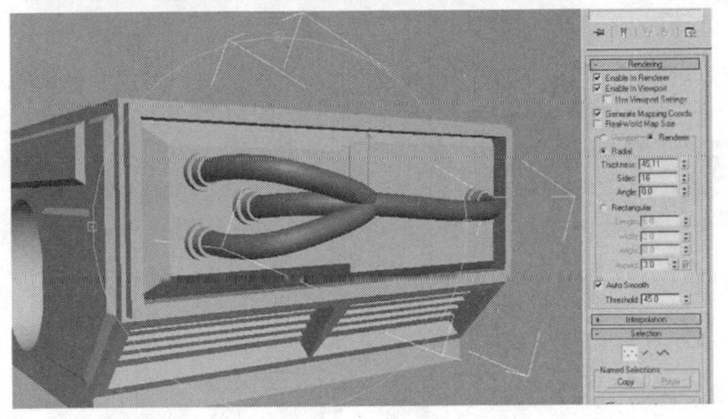

Figure 3-1022

10. Convert the line to an Editable Polygon (or Patch or NURBS).

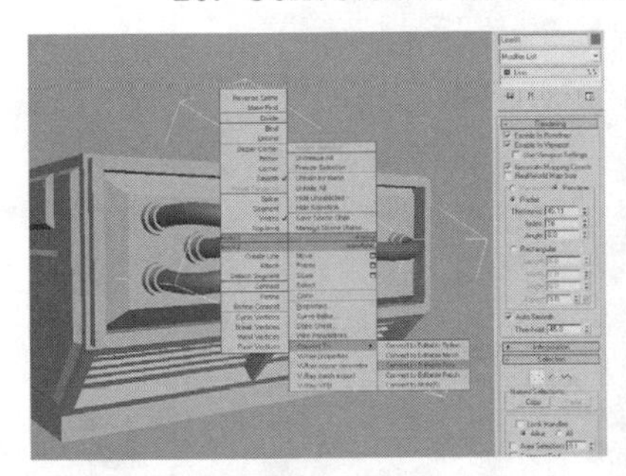

Figure 3-1023

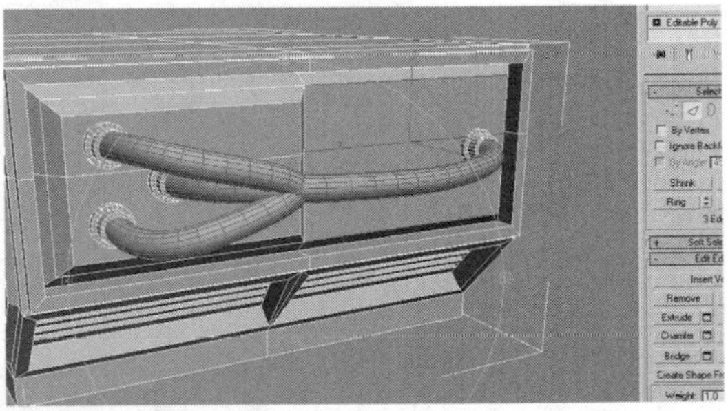

Figure 3-1024

11. In the recessed part of the rear, select the top, middle, and bottom edges and Connect them with **1** Segment. Chamfer the new edge by **80** to create two edges.

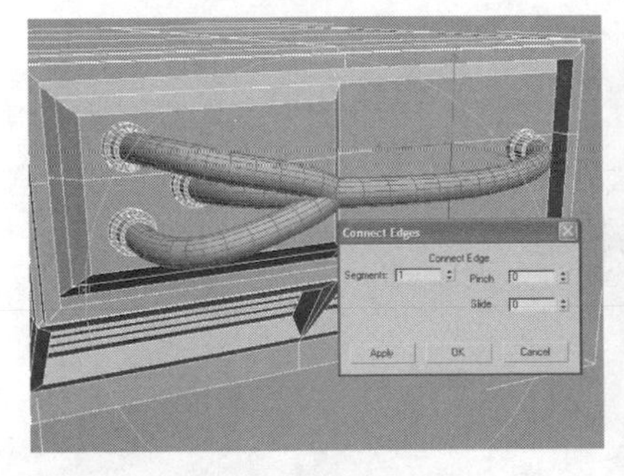

Figure 3-1025

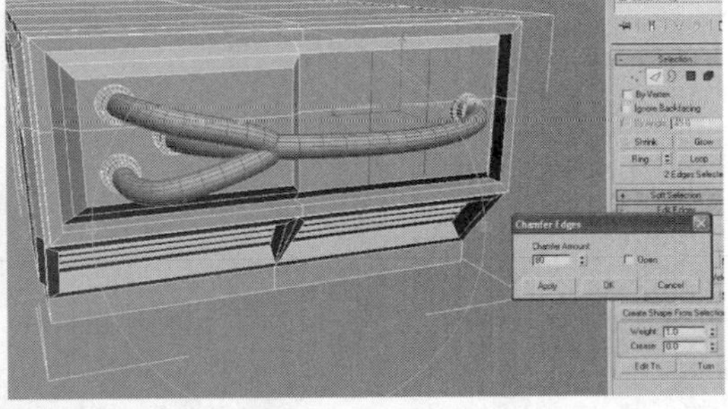

Figure 3-1026

12. Select the far left vertical edges and move them to the left in the X axis, as shown. Exact values are not important; just eyeball it. Select the polygons between the edges you made with the Chamfer.

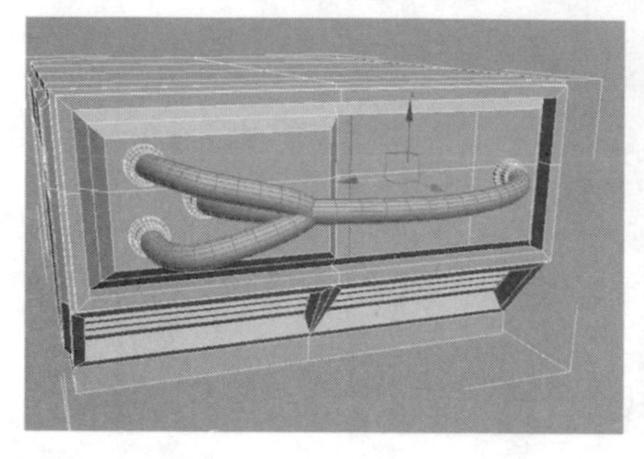

Figure 3-1027

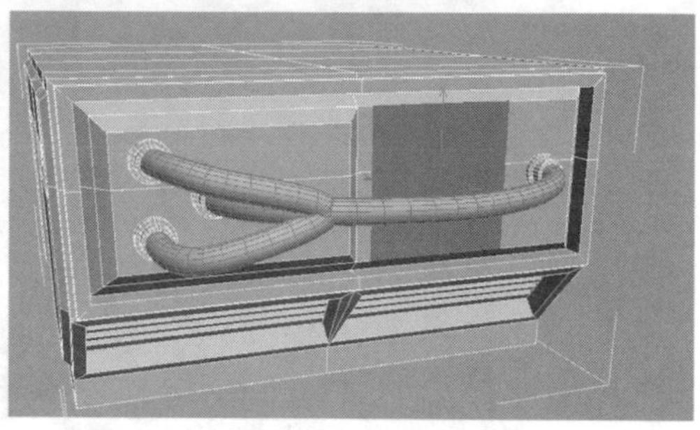

Figure 3-1028

13. Just to be different, select the outer polygons and Bevel them:

Type	Height	Outline	Apply/OK
Local Normal	0	–25	OK

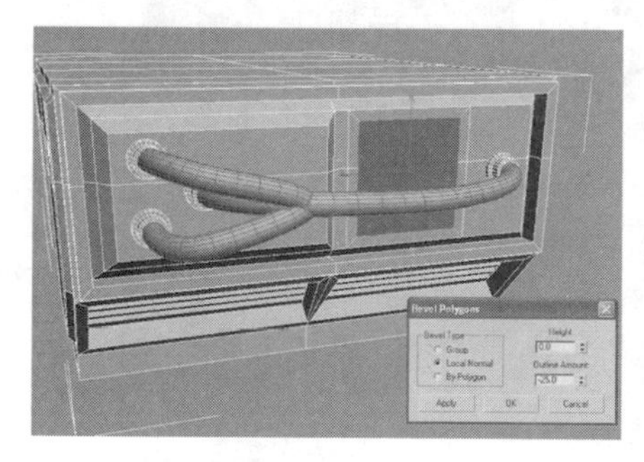

Figure 3-1029

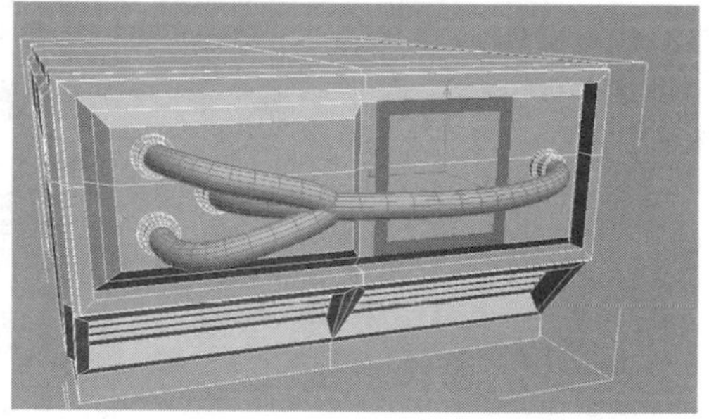

Figure 3-1030

14. Extrude the polygons by **10**. Select the top, middle, and bottom edges. (Yes, we're about to make more vents!)

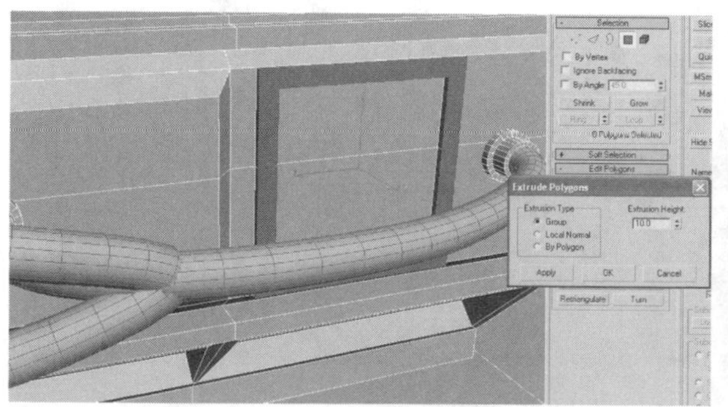

Figure 3-1031

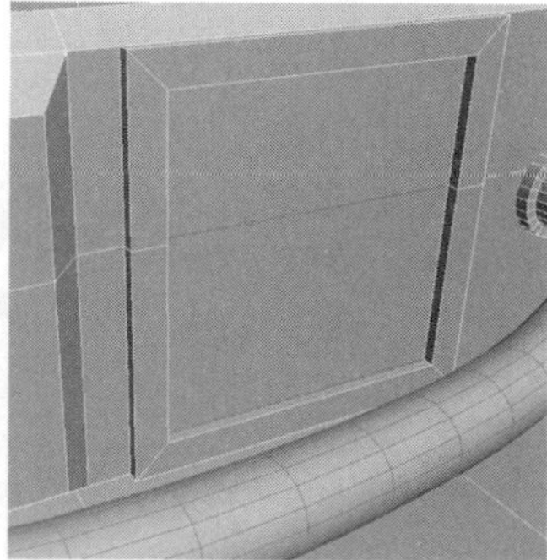

Figure 3-1032

15. Connect the edges with **6** Segments. Extrude them by **42** with a Base Width of **30**.

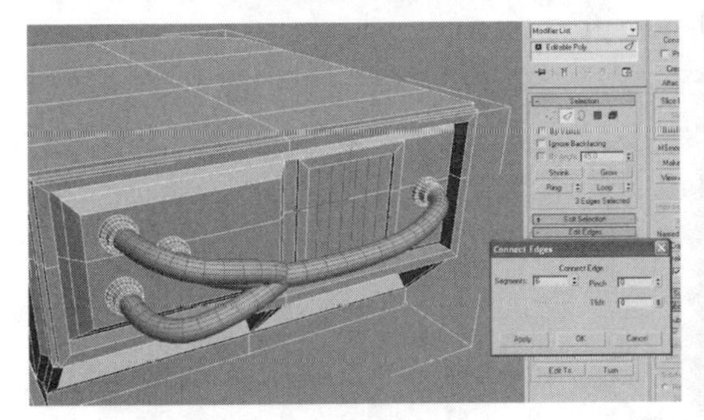

Figure 3-1033

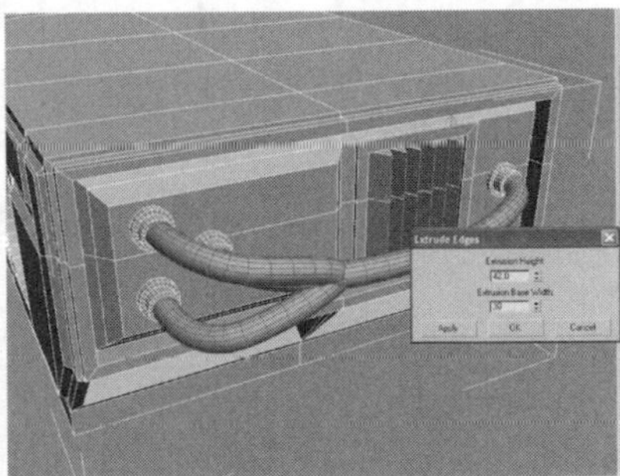

Figure 3-1034

16. Create a Torus, center it atop the base, and submerge it halfway into the base. Create a Cylinder in the center of the torus.

Radius 1	Radius 2	Rotation	Twist	Segments	Sides	Smooth
390	80	0	0	36	18	All

Radius	Height	Height/Cap Segs	Sides	Smooth
312	100	1/2	36	Checked

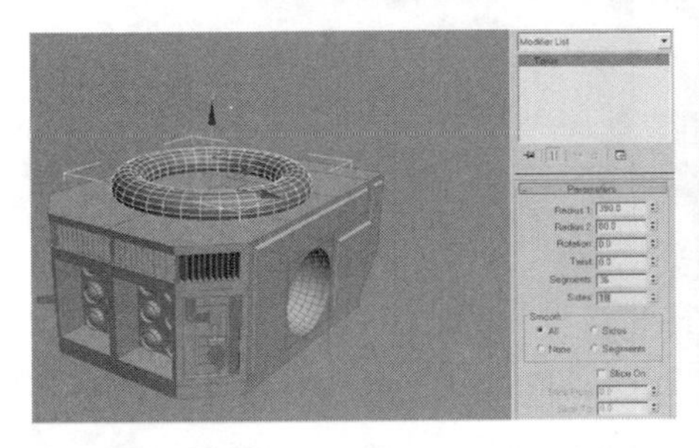

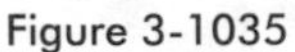

Figure 3-1035

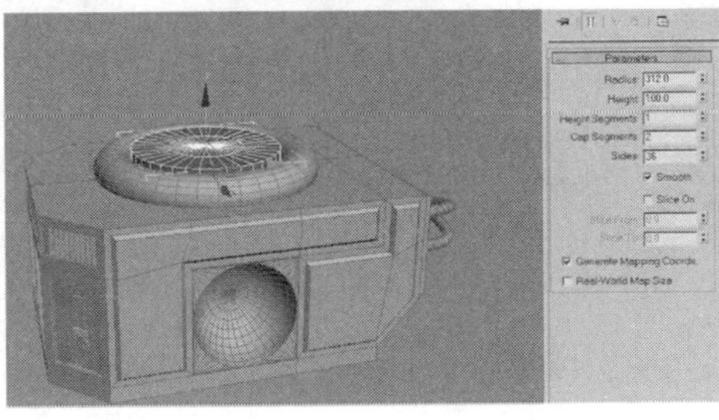

Figure 3-1036

17. Convert the cylinder to an Editable Polygon, select the inner cap segments, and Scale them up to **130**. Select the inner 36 polygons and six of the outer polygons to form a keyhole shape.

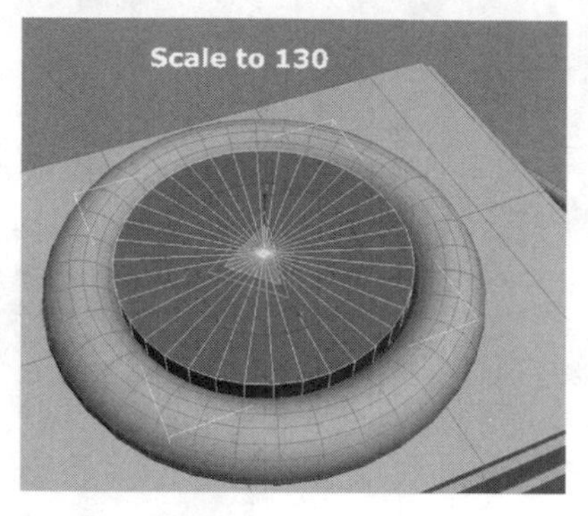

Figure 3-1037

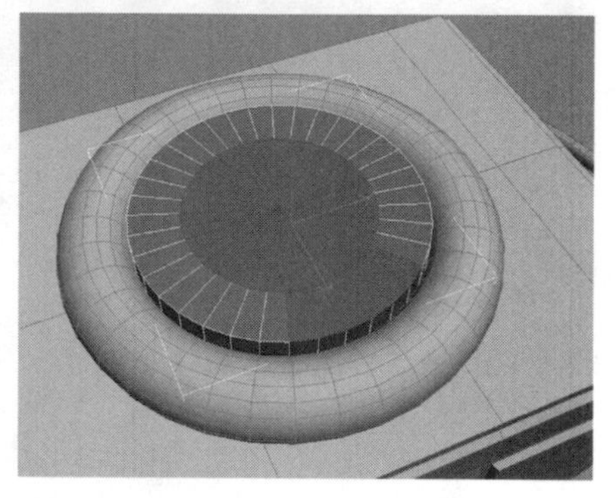

Figure 3-1038

18. Extrude the polygons by **200**. Create a Tube over the top of the extrusion:

Radius 1	Radius 2	Height	Height/Cap Segs	Sides	Smooth
316	400	380	1/1	36	Checked

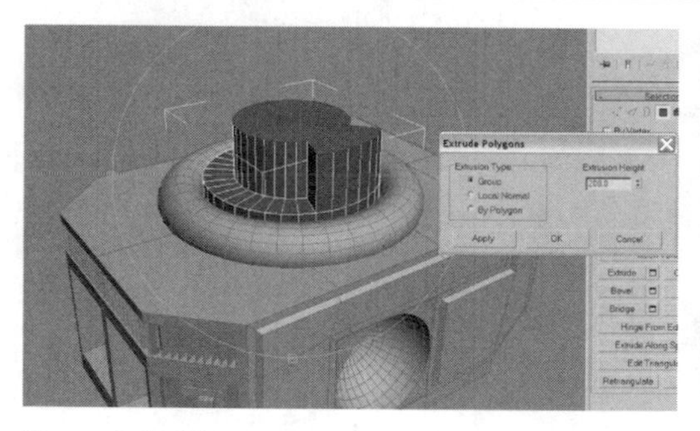

Figure 3-1039

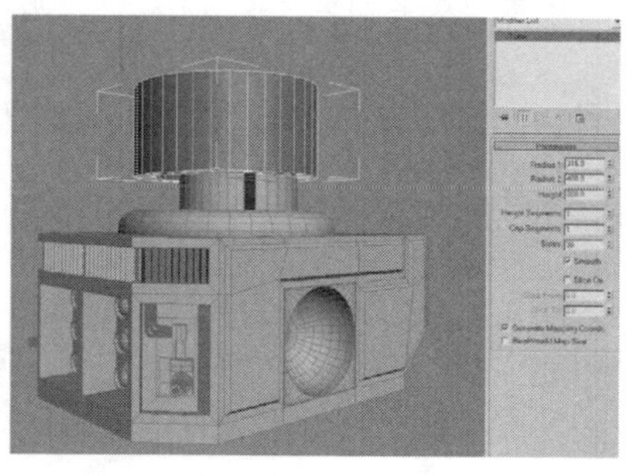

Figure 3-1040

19. Add a Smooth modifier to the stack. Create a Box centered on top of the tube:

Length	Width	Height	Length/Width/Height Segs
2100	545	650	6/4/3

Day 9: Detailing the Rear Base and Adding the Turret and Upper Body

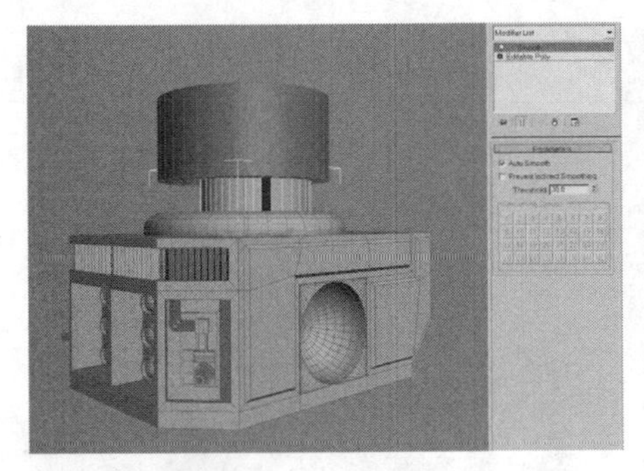

Figure 3-1041

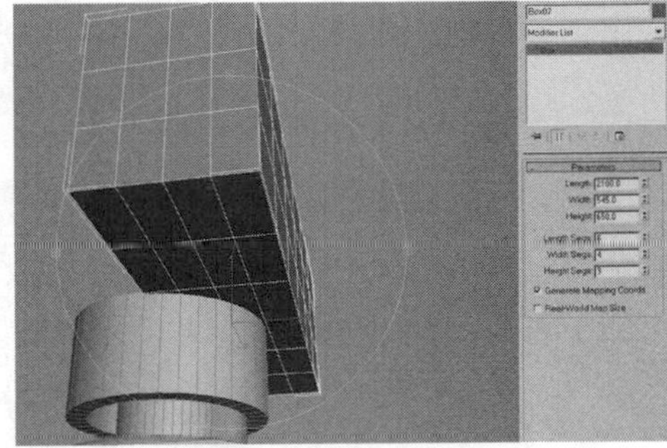

Figure 3-1042

20. Convert the box to an Editable Polygon. Select the polygons facing the center and delete them. Add a Symmetry modifier to the box's stack with the Mirror Axis set to **X**.

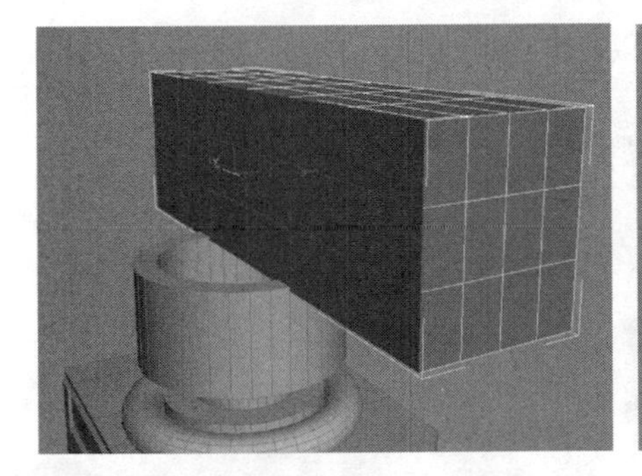

Figure 3-1043

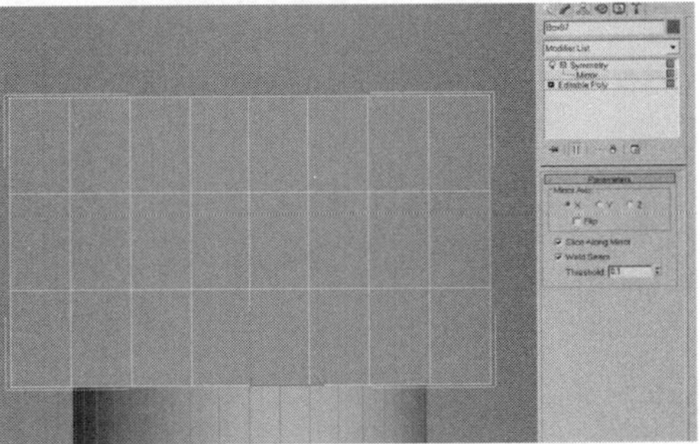

Figure 3-1044

21. Select the four bottom-facing polygons on the front of the box, and Extrude them by **300** to form a lip that extends down from the front. Select the edges forming the front corner and Chamfer them by **62**.

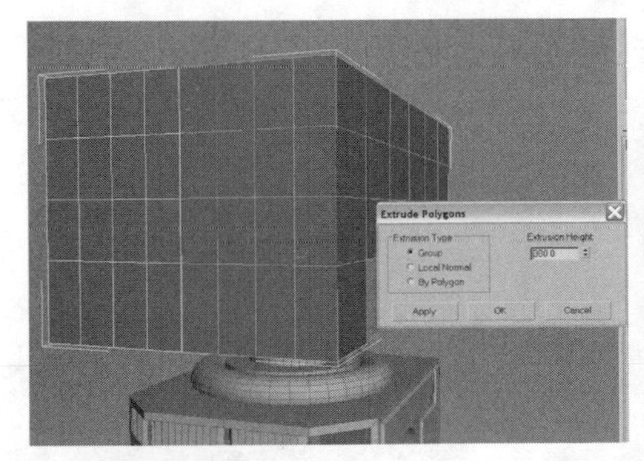

Figure 3-1045

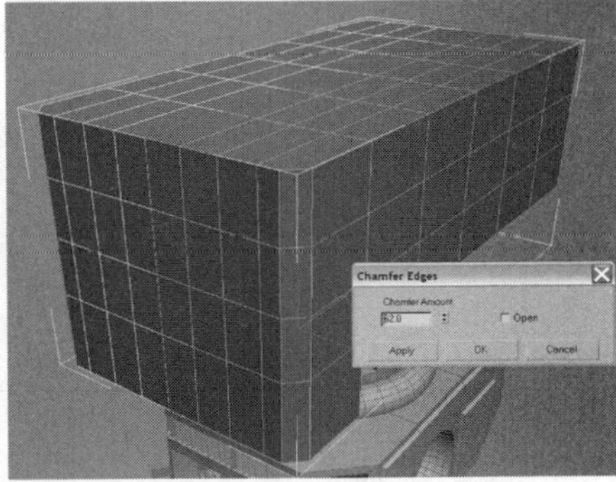

Figure 3-1046

22. Select the back four polygons on the top side and top surface of the box, and Extrude them by **475**. Select the middle four polygons on the extrusion you made.

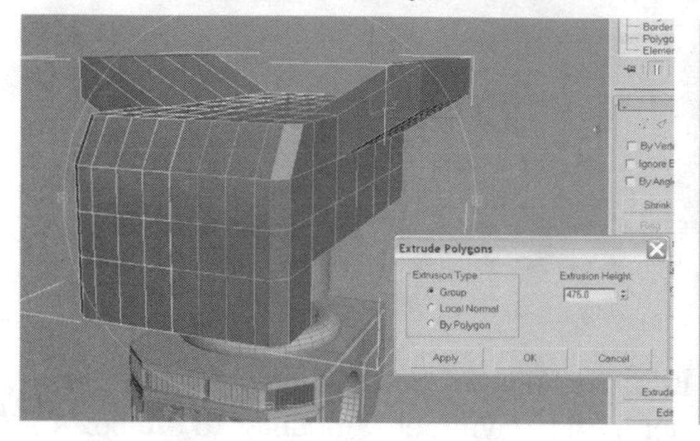

Figure 3-1047

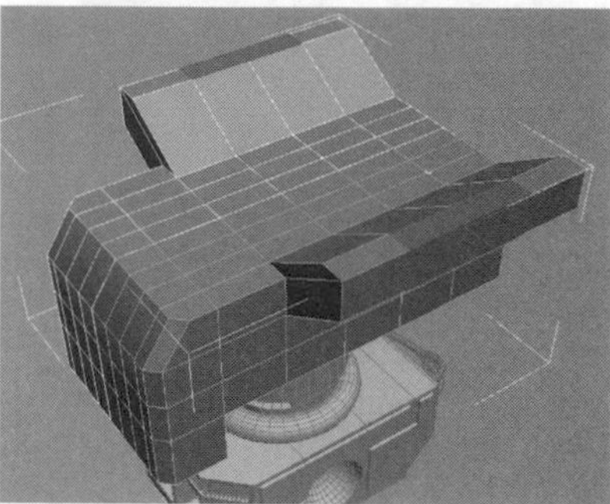

Figure 3-1048

23. Delete the selected polygons. Select the resulting four edges, as shown in Figure 3-1050.

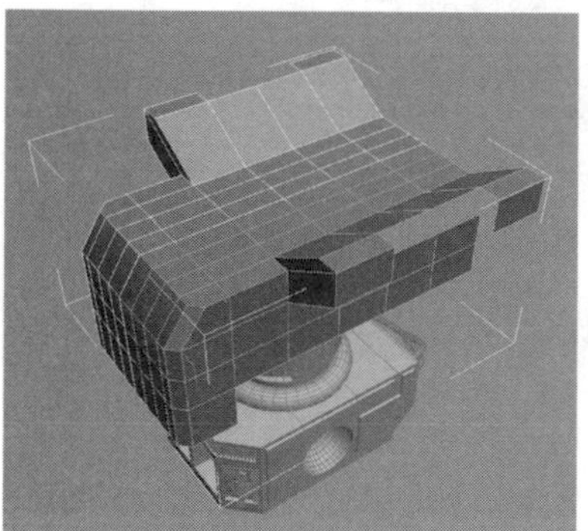

Figure 3-1049

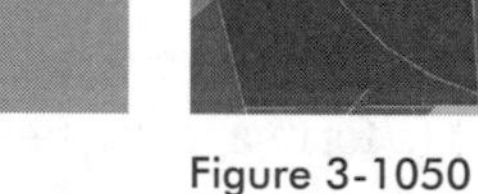

Figure 3-1050

24. Click **Bridge** to bridge the gap. Border-select the remaining empty holes and Cap them.

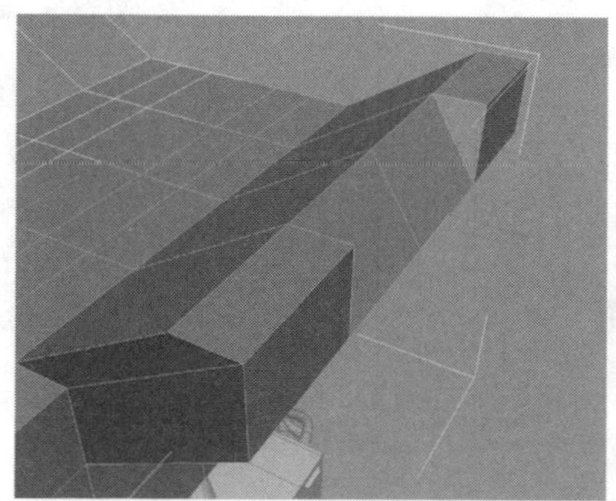

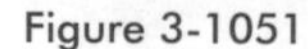

Figure 3-1051

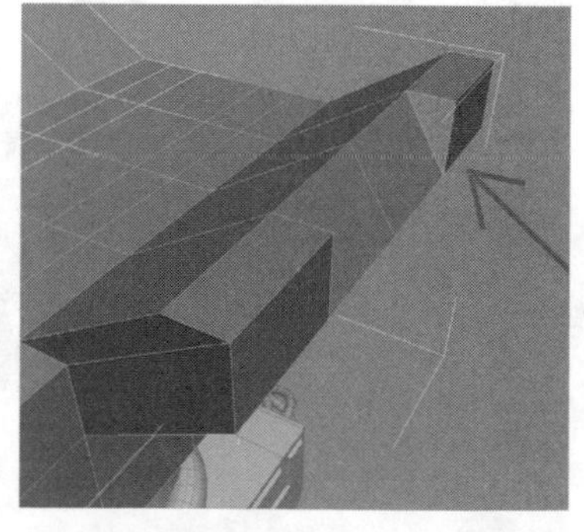

Figure 3-1052

25. Connect the three vertical edges with **1** Segment. Select the bottom front and rear polygons on the extrusion and Extrude them by **350**.

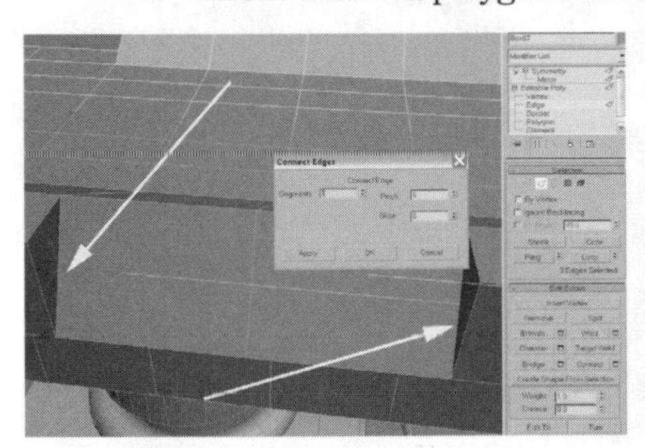

Figure 3-1053

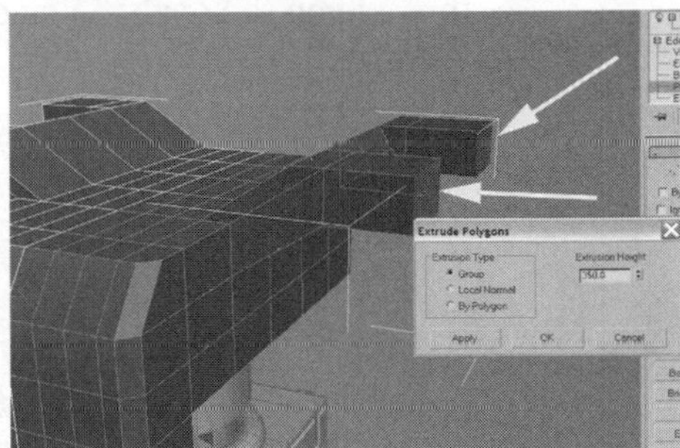

Figure 3-1054

26. Select the front polygon and Shift-drag it to clone it to element, then move it in the Y axis until the left edge of the polygon coincides with the middle segment in the recess. Hinge From Edge **180** degrees with **10** Segments, using the left edge of the cloned element. Delete the back-facing polygon and Weld the resulting vertices.

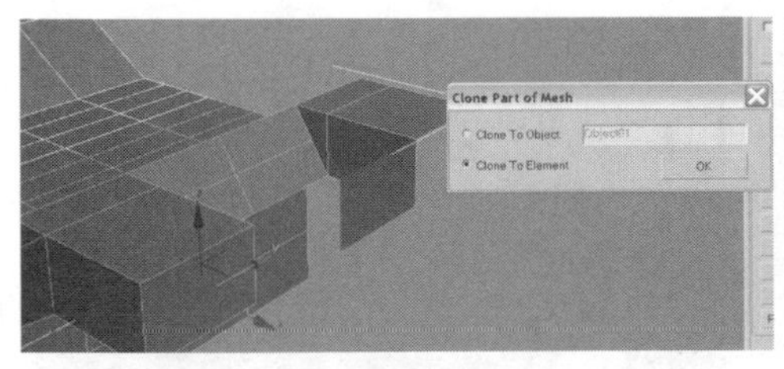

Figure 3-1055

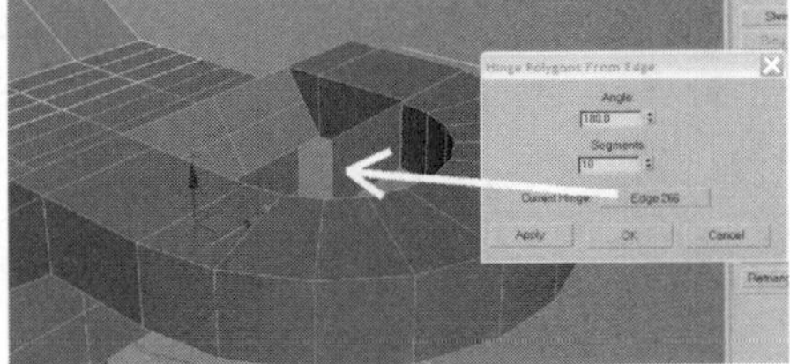

Figure 3-1056

27. Delete the cloned polygon and create a Cylinder in the hole.

Radius	Height	Height/Cap Segs	Sides	Smooth
332	300	1/1	36	Checked

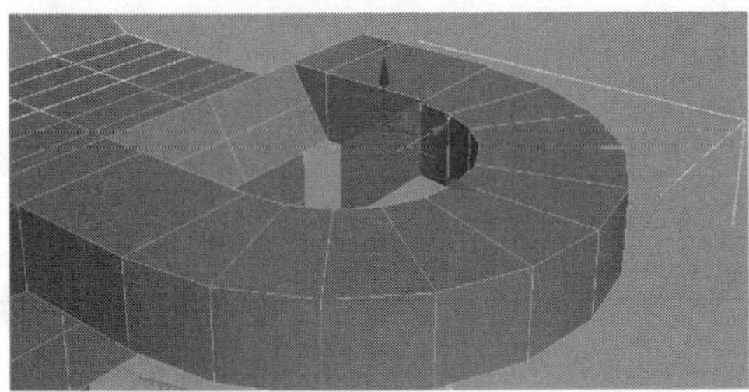

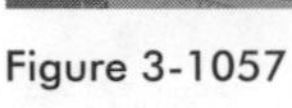

Figure 3-1057

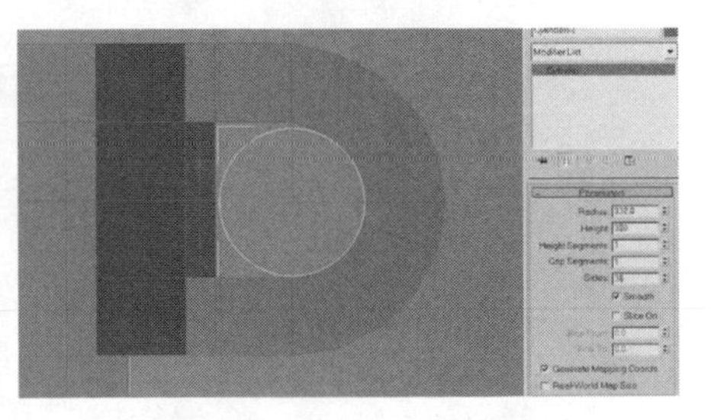

Figure 3-1058

28. Vertically center the cylinder in the hole. Reduce the cylinder's Height to **280** and Instance Mirror a clone of it on the X axis into the hole on the opposite side of the body (Offset should be around **–2575.5**).

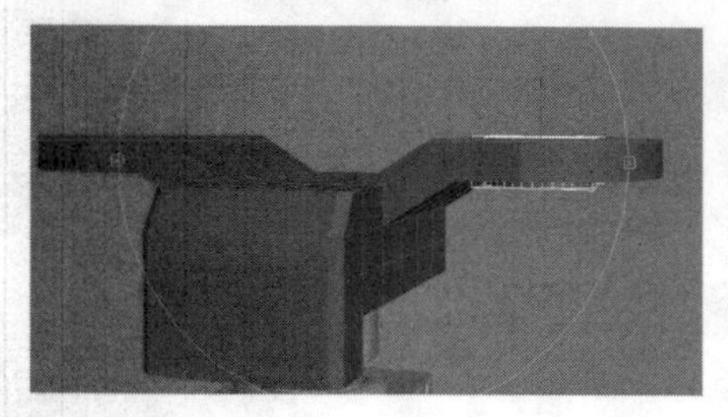

Figure 3-1059

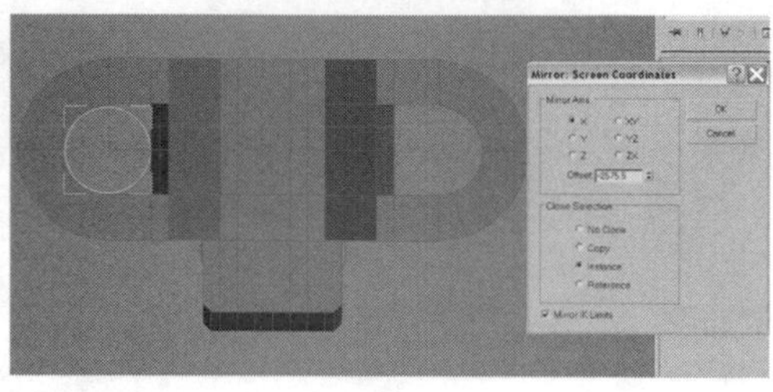

Figure 3-1060

29. Select the cylinders' caps and Bevel them (since it's an instance copy, you do not have to repeat for the opposite side):

Type	Height	Outline	Apply/OK
Group	0	90	Apply
Group	50	0	Apply

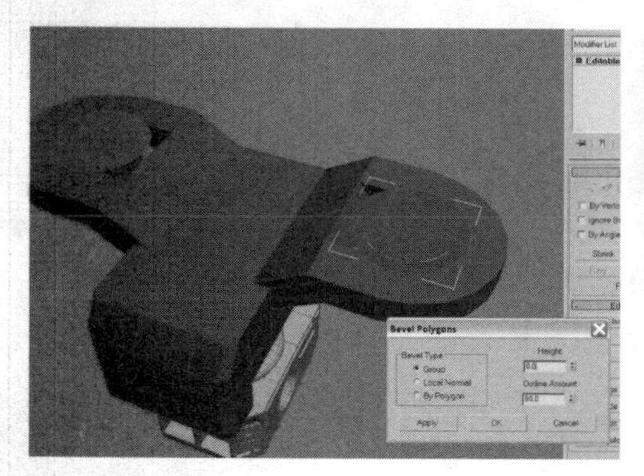

Figure 3-1061

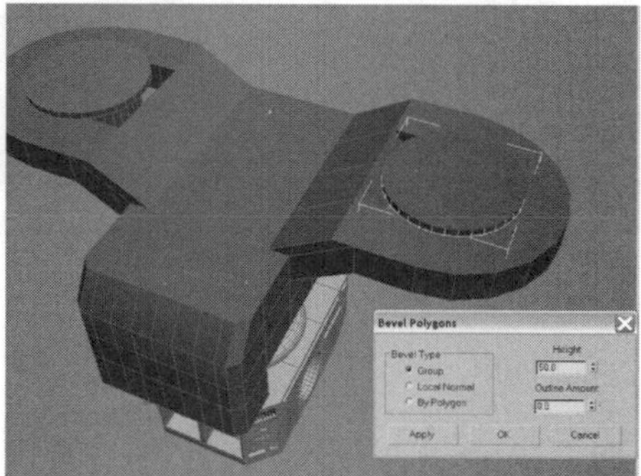

Figure 3-1062

Type	Height	Outline	Apply/OK
Group	0	–80	Apply
Group	90	0	Apply
Group	0	–60	OK

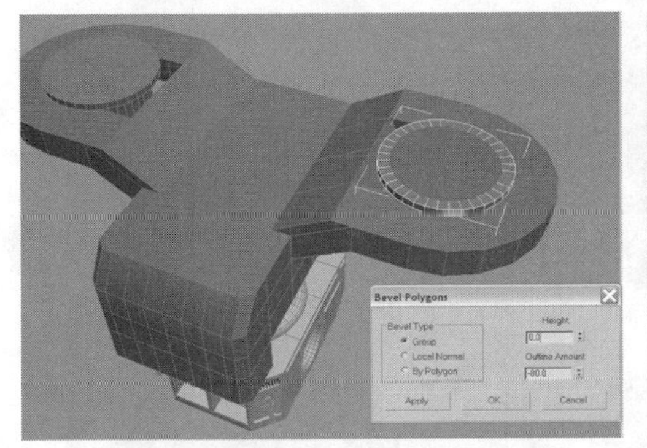

Figure 3-1063

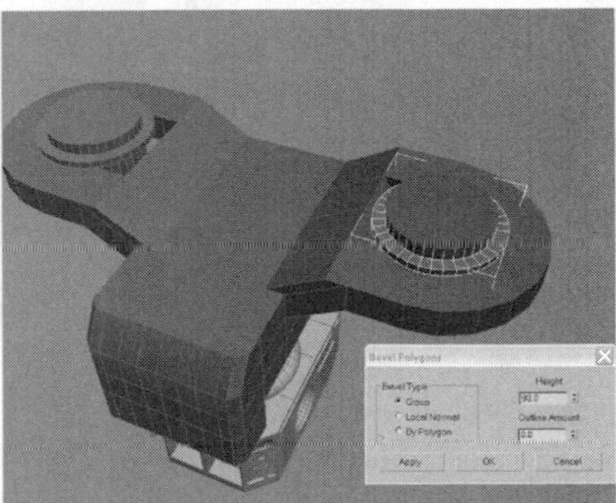

Figure 3-1064

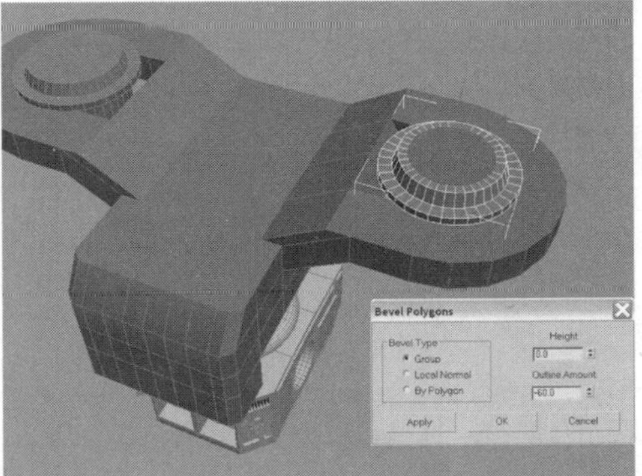

Figure 3-1065

30. Cut the cylinder cap as shown in Figure 3-1066, then select the four edges and Connect them with **1** Segment.

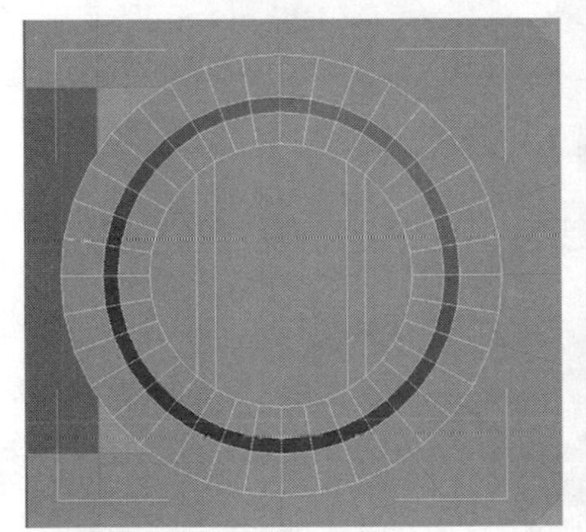

Figure 3-1066

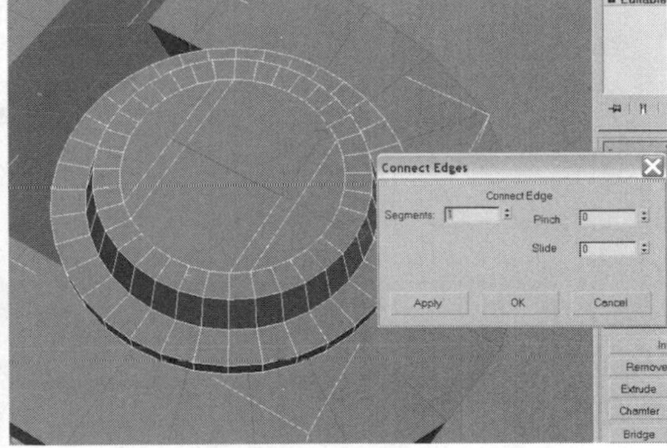

Figure 3-1067

31. Chamfer the new edge by **108** to make two edges. Select the resulting polygons and Extrude them by **20** to form an H.

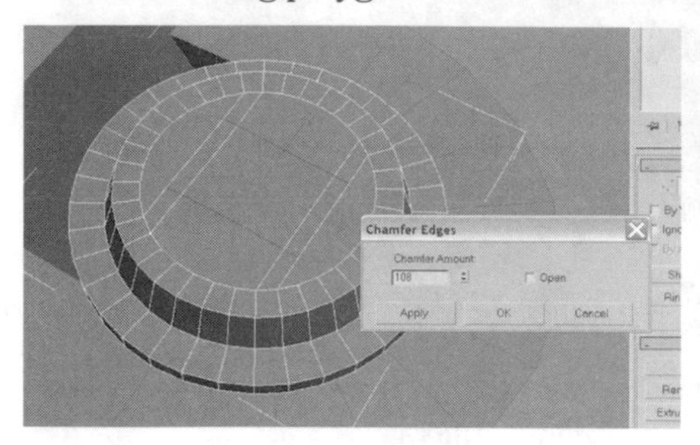

Figure 3-1068

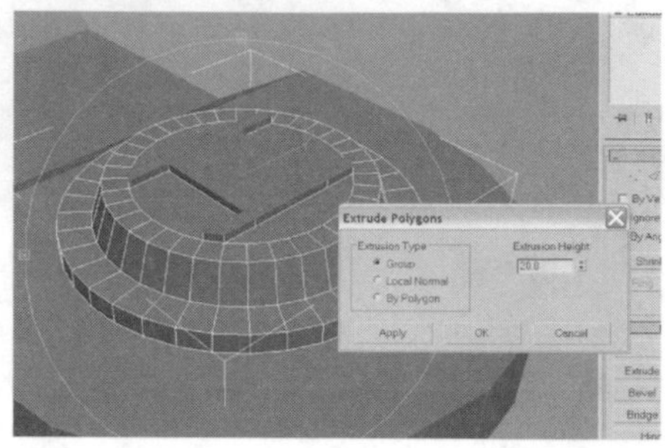

Figure 3-1069

32. Select the polygons that form the vertical parts of the H and Extrude them by **40**.

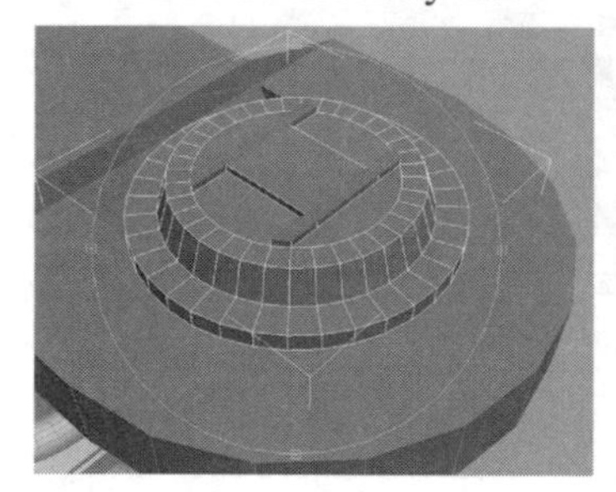

Figure 3-1070

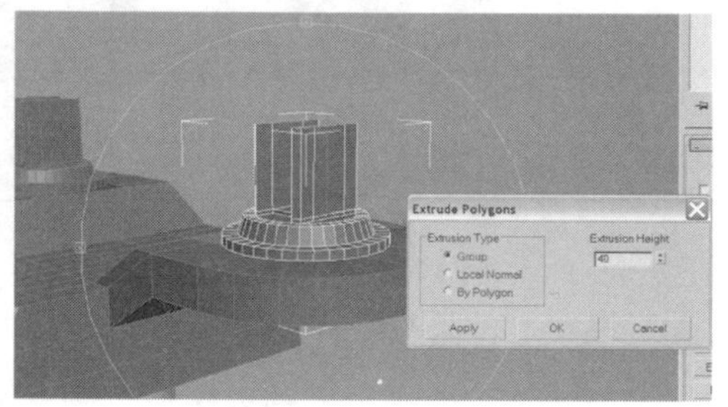

Figure 3-1071

33. Select the front eight vertices and move them by **120** in the Y axis. Create a ChamferBox between the vertical sides of the fork.

Length	Width	Height	Fillet	Length/Width/Height/ Fillet Segs	Smooth
266	240	–800	38	2/2/3/4	Checked

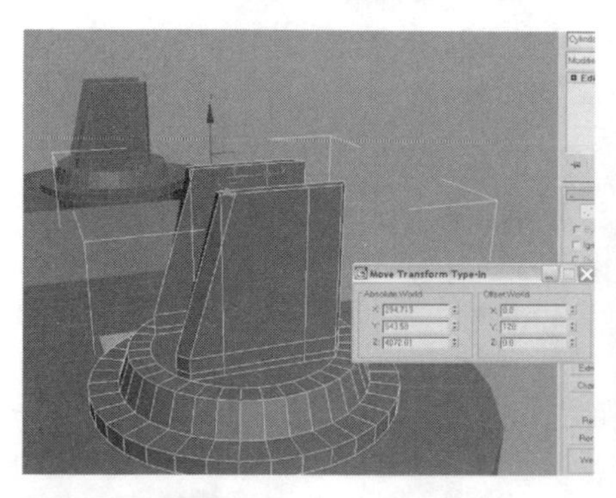

Figure 3-1072

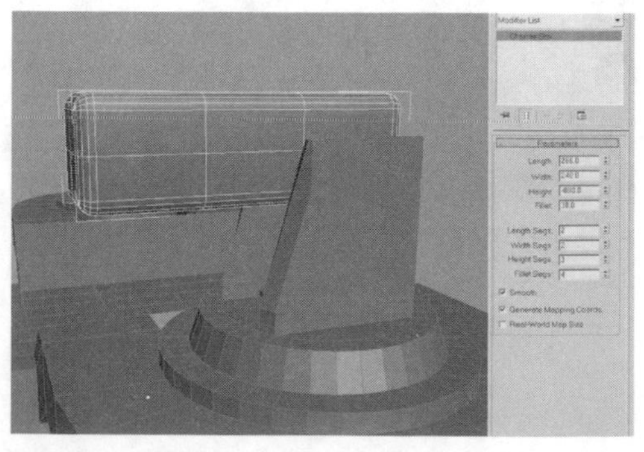

Figure 3-1073

34. Target Weld the front four vertices of each side of the fork to make it look raked.

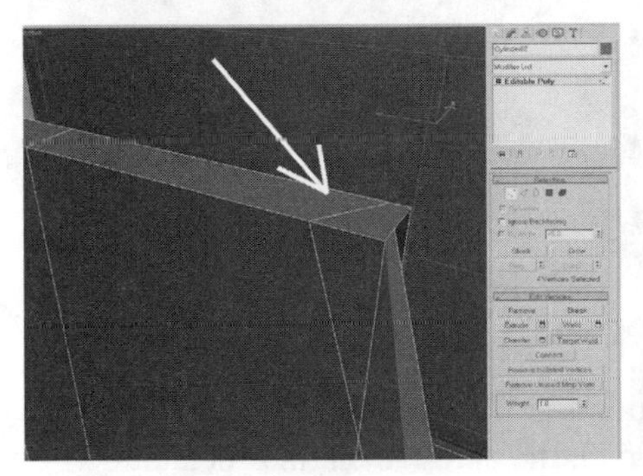

Figure 3-1074

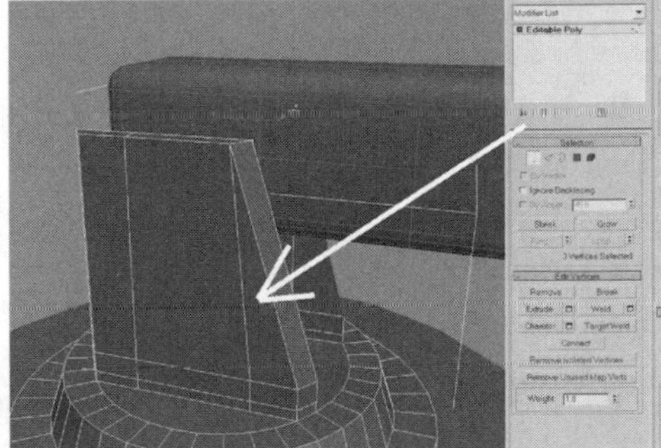

Figure 3-1075

35. Select the tops of the mounts, Extrude them by **140**, and Scale them down to **50** in the Y axis.

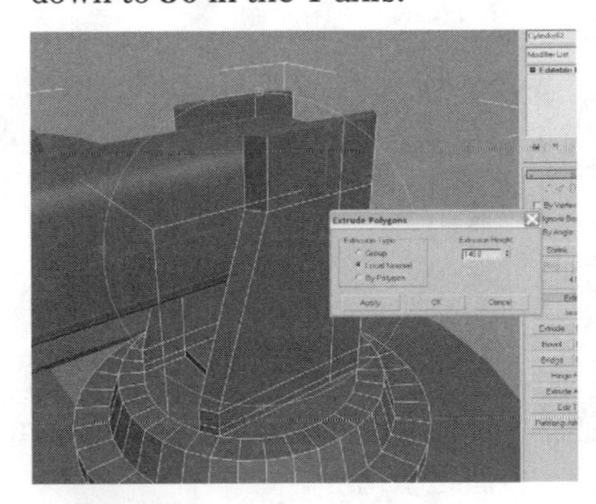

Figure 3-1076

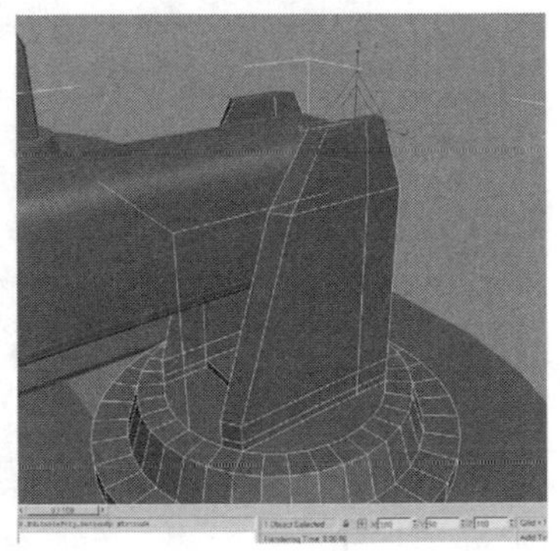

Figure 3-1077

36. Create a Chamfer Cylinder and convert it to an Editable Polygon. Select the center cap, position it as shown in Figure 3-1078, and Extrude it by **10**.

Radius	Height	Fillet	Height/Fillet/Cap Segs	Sides	Smooth
90	15	7.5	1/1/2	36	Checked

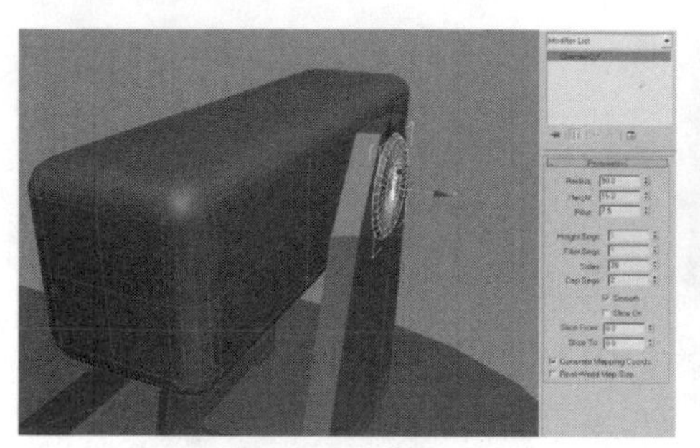

Figure 3-1078

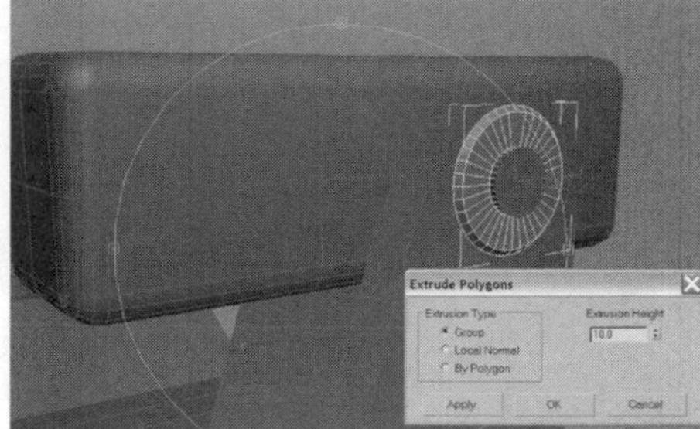

Figure 3-1079

37. Select the center of the cylinder and Bevel it. Add a TurboSmooth modifier to the stack and leave all the settings on their defaults. Hide the chamfer box to give yourself some space.

Type	Height	Outline	Apply/OK
Group	0	–12	OK

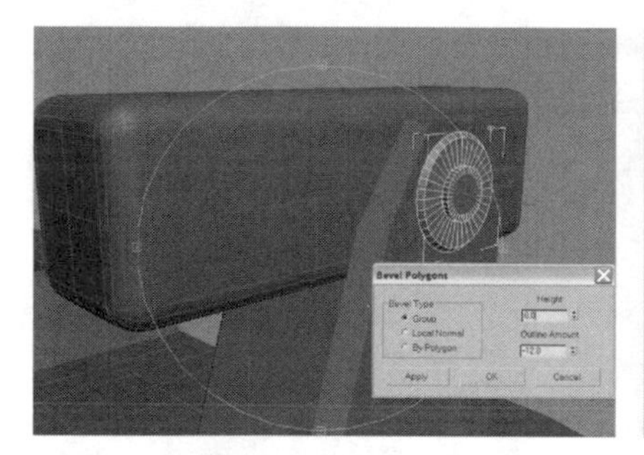

Figure 3-1080

Figure 3-1081

38. Mirror-copy the chamfer cylinder to the other side of the brace. Select the two chamfer cylinders you've already made and clone to the opposite side.

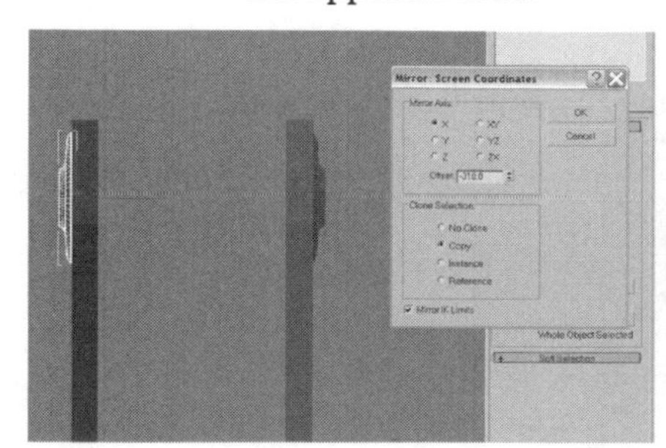

Figure 3-1082

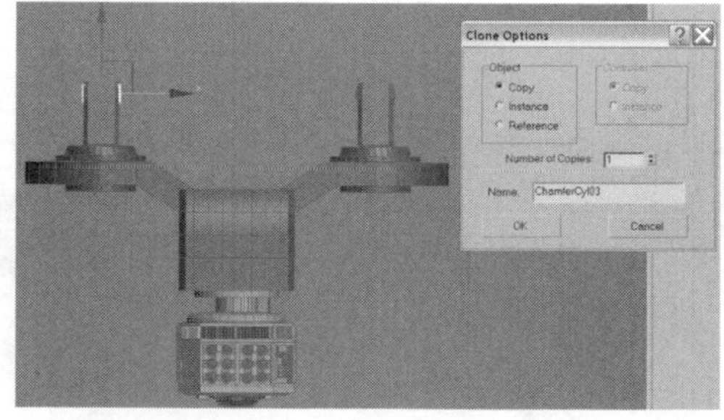

Figure 3-1083

39. Select all the top objects (e.g., body, braces, gun turrets, etc.) and Scale them down to **88** to balance the top with the size of the base.

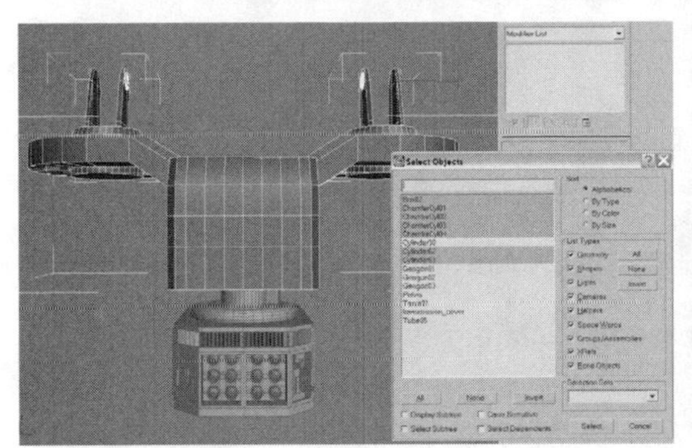

Figure 3-1084

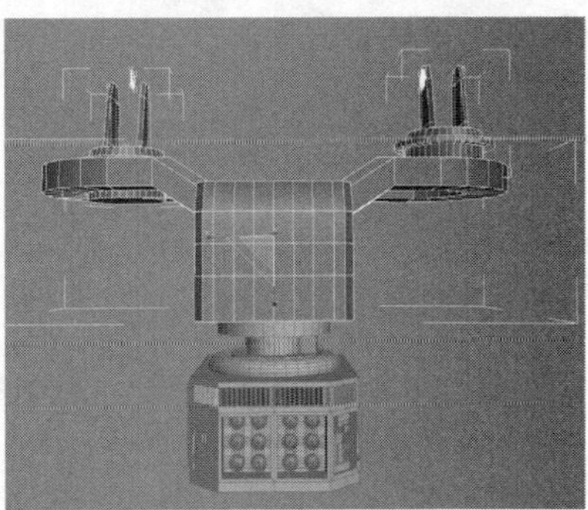

Figure 3-1085

40. Select the gun turret and Attach the chamfer cylinders to it. Unhide the chamfer box and convert it to an Editable Polygon.

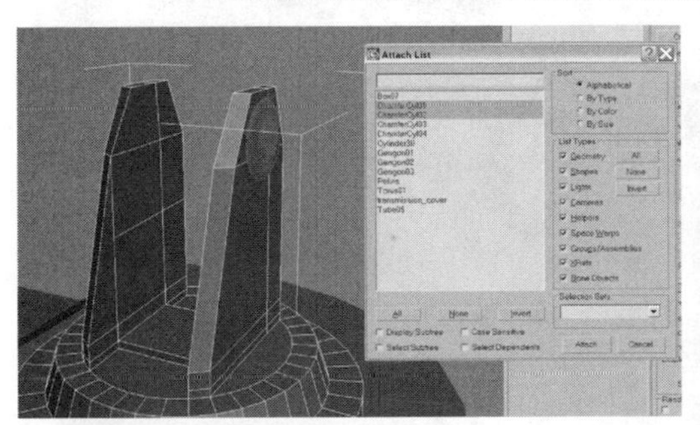

Figure 3-1086

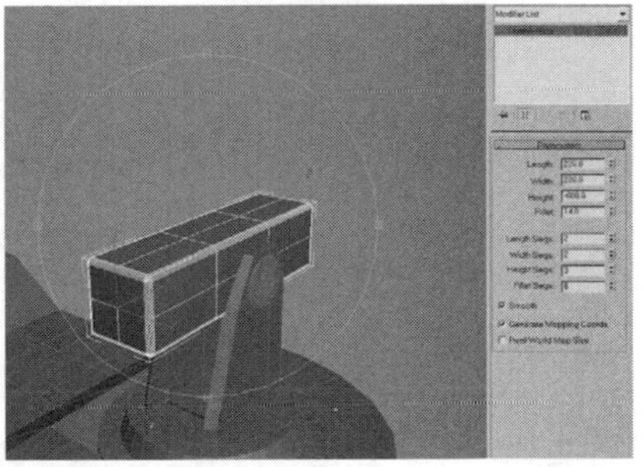

Figure 3-1087

41. Select the front four polygons and Bevel them:

Type	Height	Outline	Apply/OK
By Polygon	0	–13.99	Apply
By Polygon	–1.0	0	OK

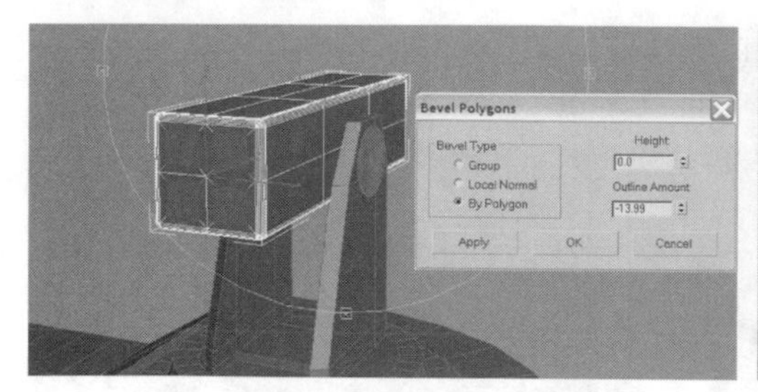

Figure 3-1088

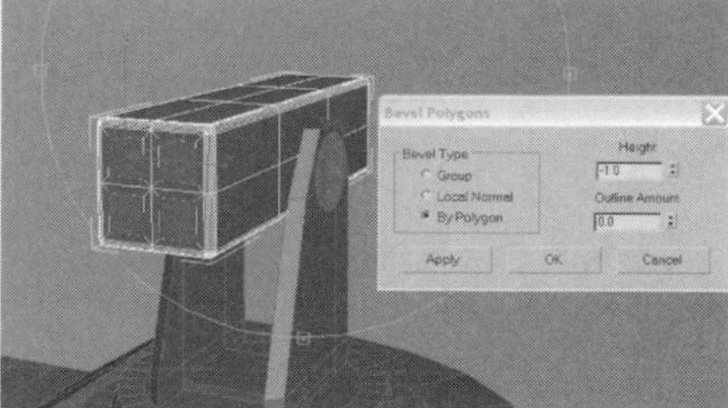

Figure 3-1089

42. Click **MSmooth** and leave the default setting of **1.0**. Extrude the polygons by **–70**.

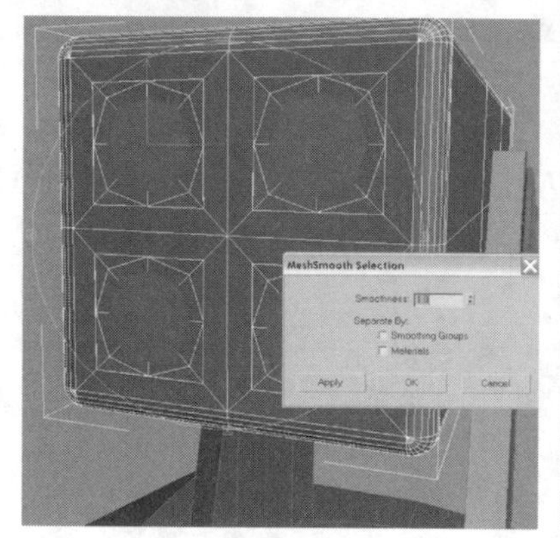

Figure 3-1090

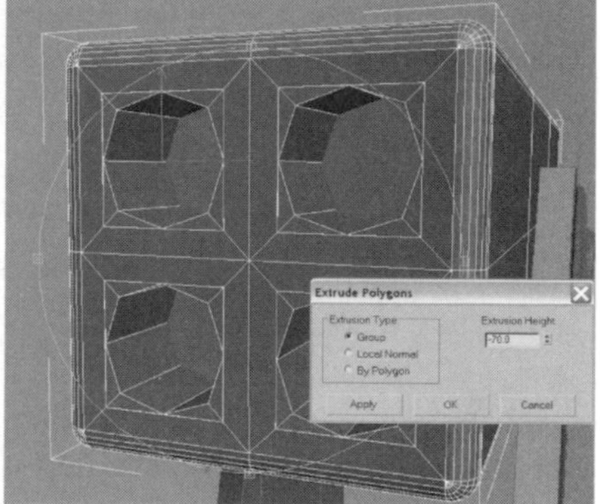

Figure 3-1091

43. Bevel the polygons:

Type	Height	Outline	Apply/OK
Group	0	–2.5	Apply
Group	300	0	OK

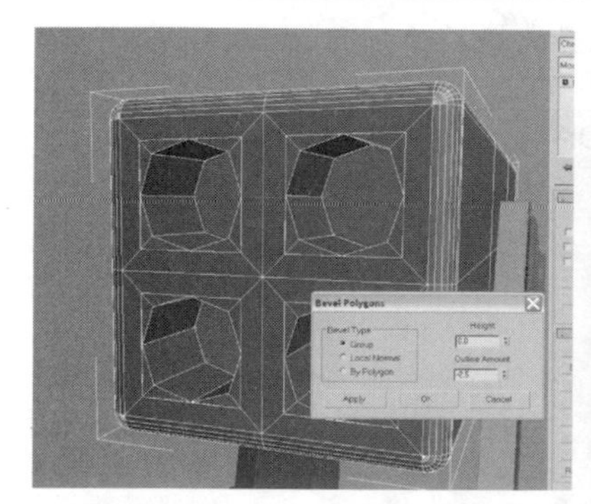

Figure 3-1092

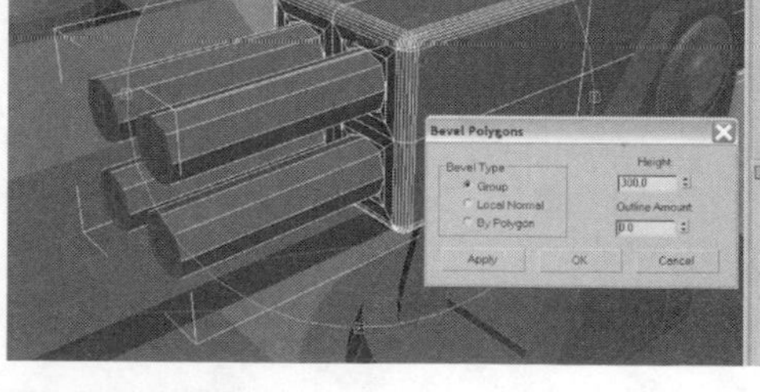

Figure 3-1093

44. Extrude the polygons by Local Normal by **400**, and then Bevel them:

Type	Height	Outline	Apply/OK
Group	12	0	Apply
By Polygon	0	–6.5	Apply
By Polygon	55	–6.5	OK

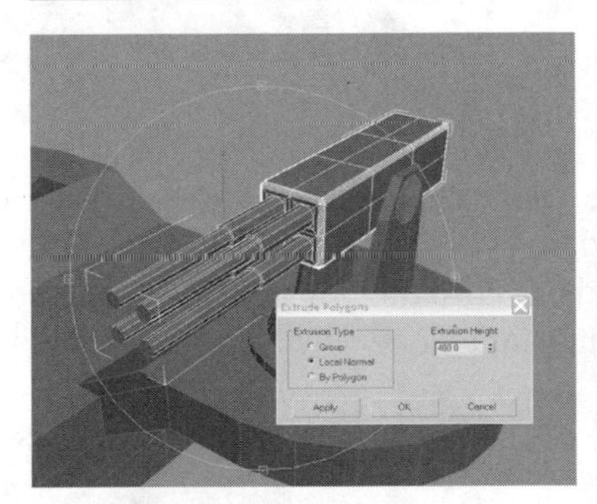

Figure 3-1094

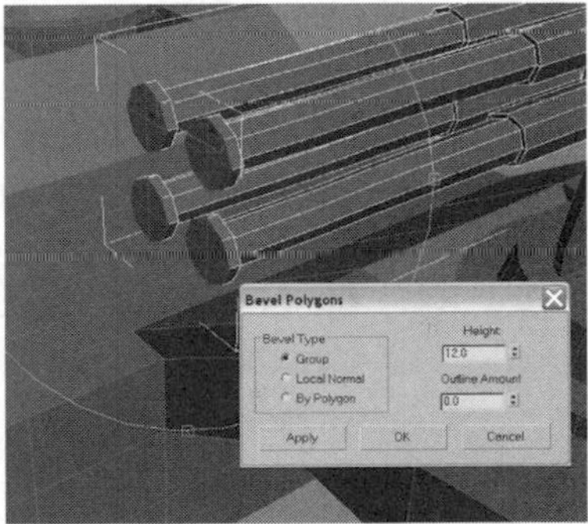

Figure 3-1095

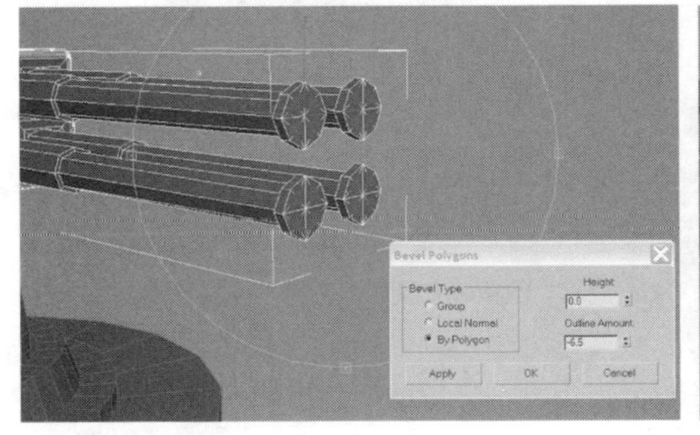

Figure 3-1096

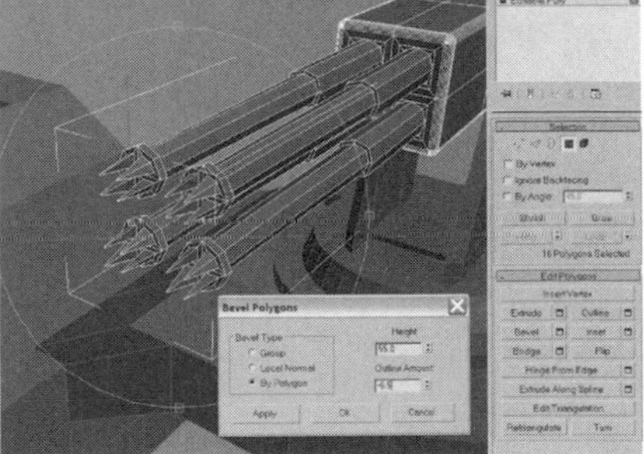

Figure 3-1097

45. Switch to the Front viewport, open the Spline panel, and create a Helix around the barrel you created with the bevels and extrusion:

Radius 1	Radius 2	Height	Turns	Bias	CW/CCW
28	25	400	50	0	CW

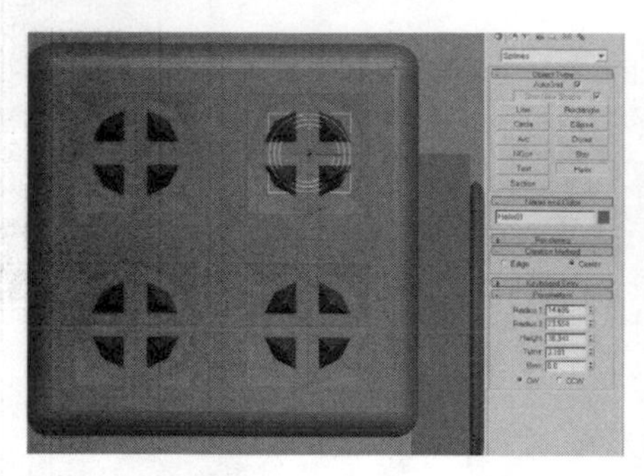

Figure 3-1098

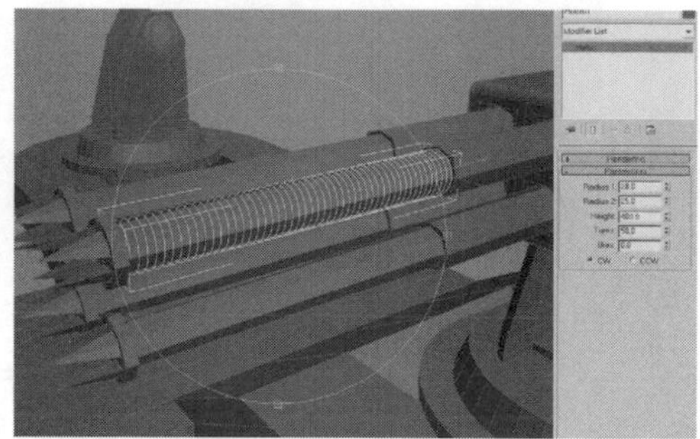

Figure 3-1099

46. Click **Enable In Viewport** and **Enable In Renderer**, and set the Thickness to **1.5** and the Sides to **12**. In the Top view, Shift-clone the helix, in the X axis, over to the other barrel. Select both helixes, switch to the front, and Shift-clone down to the bottom two barrels.

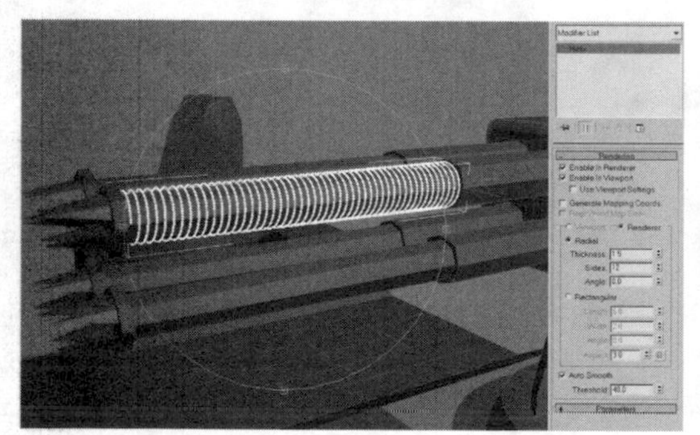

Figure 3-1100

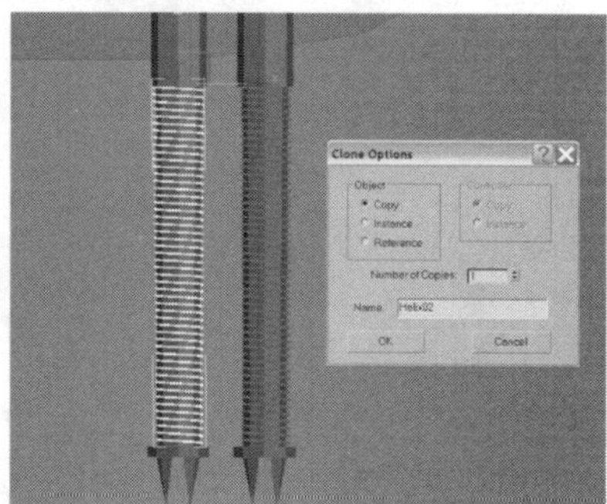

Figure 3-1101

47. Select the edges on the chamfer box as shown in Figure 3-1102 and then Extrude them by a Height of **–1.0** with a Base Width of **0.75** to create machine lines on the gun body.

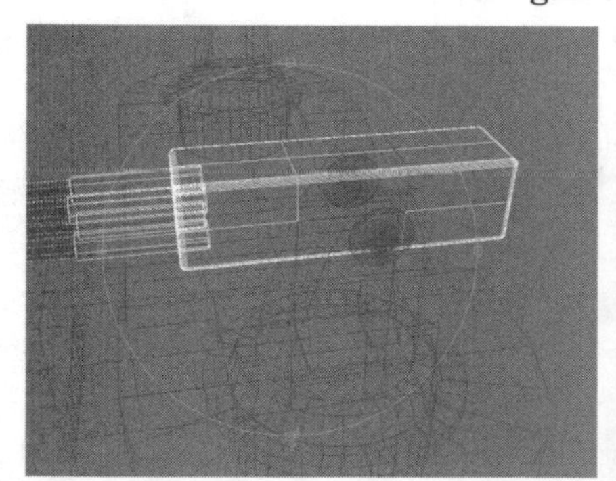

Figure 3-1102

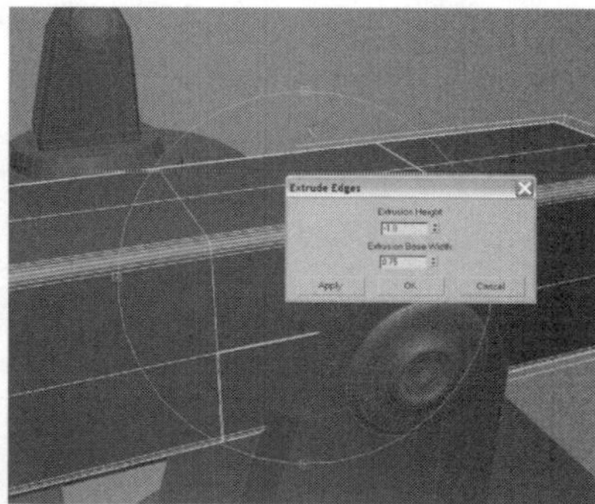

Figure 3-1103

48. Select the front polygons bounded by the machine lines and Bevel them:

Type	Height	Outline	Apply/OK
Local Normal	1	–6.5	OK

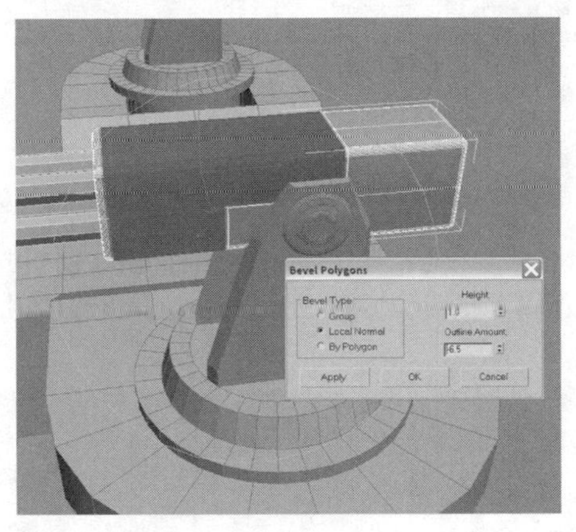

Figure 3-1104

49. Select the top front polygons and Bevel them:

Type	Height	Outline	Apply/OK
Group	0	–6.5	Apply
Local Normal	–3	0	OK

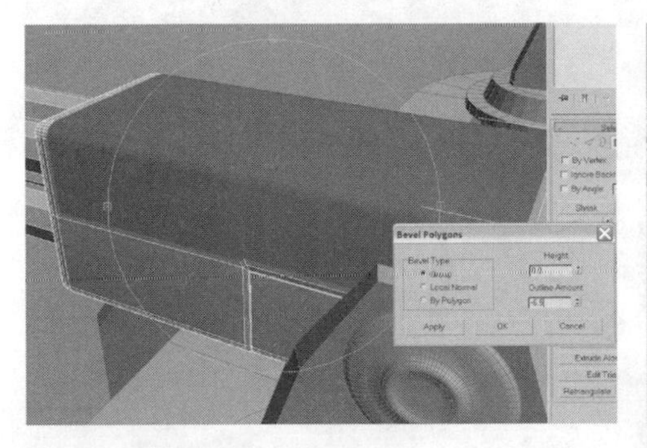

Figure 3-1105

Figure 3-1106

50. Select the bottom front polygons and Bevel them:

Type	Height	Outline	Apply/OK
Local Normal	–5	0	OK

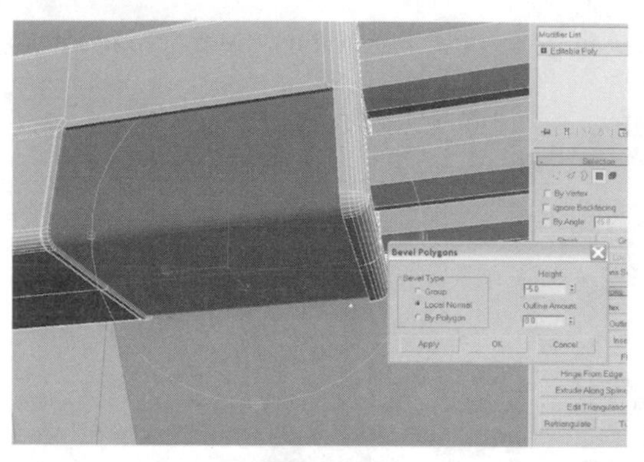

Figure 3-1107

51. Select the horizontal segments in the area you just beveled inward, Connect them with **1** Segment, and then Chamfer the edge by **45** and hit **Apply** (not OK).

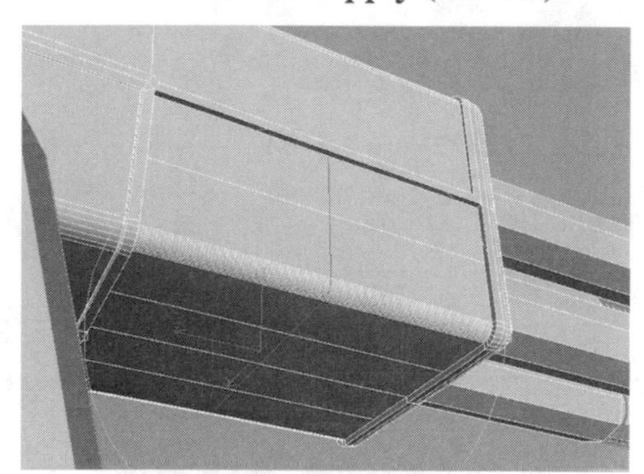

Figure 3-1108

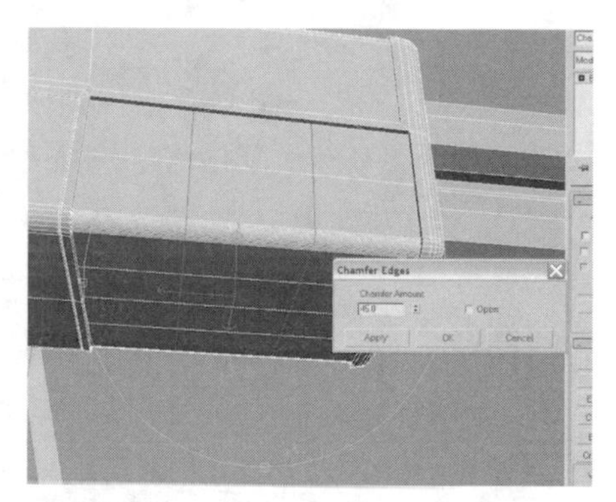

Figure 3-1109

52. Chamfer the edges by **22.262** and then by **11.353**. Now you can click **OK**.

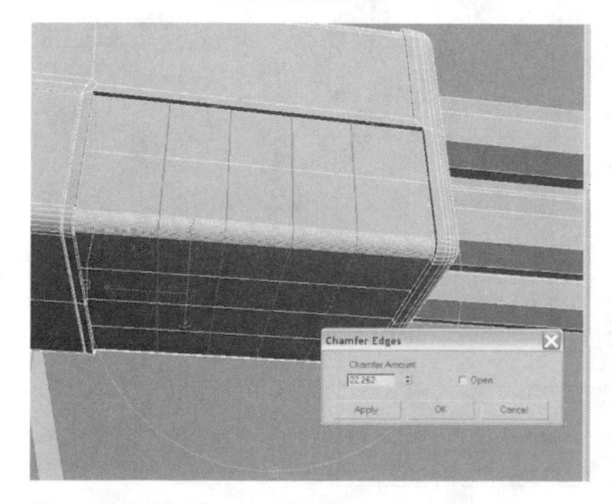

Figure 3-1110

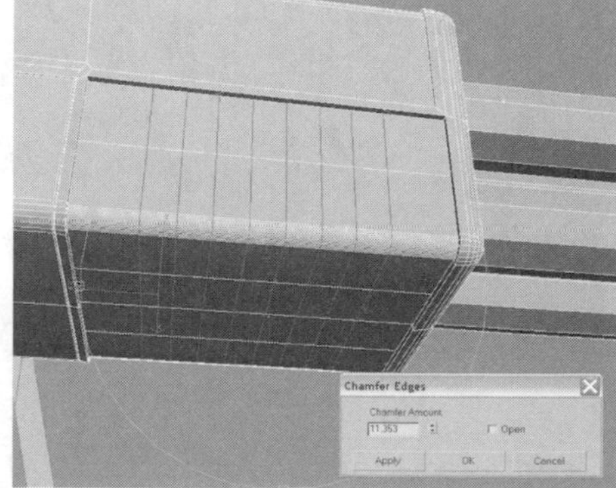

Figure 3-1111

53. Extrude the edges by **–2** with a Base Width of **1**. Select the top two middle polygons and Bevel them:

Type	Height	Outline	Apply/OK
Local Normal	0	–30	Apply
Local Normal	4	0	OK

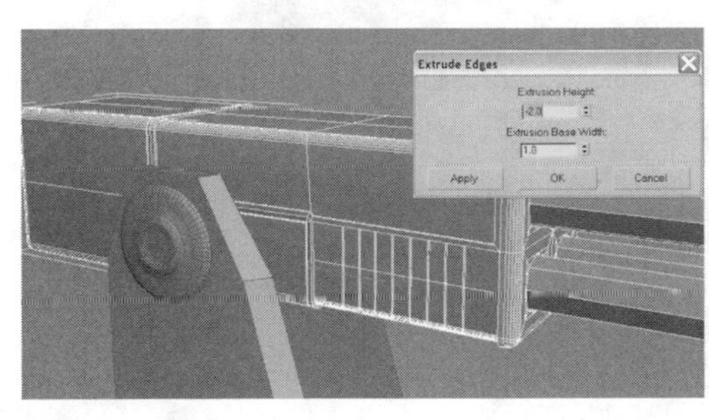

Figure 3-1112

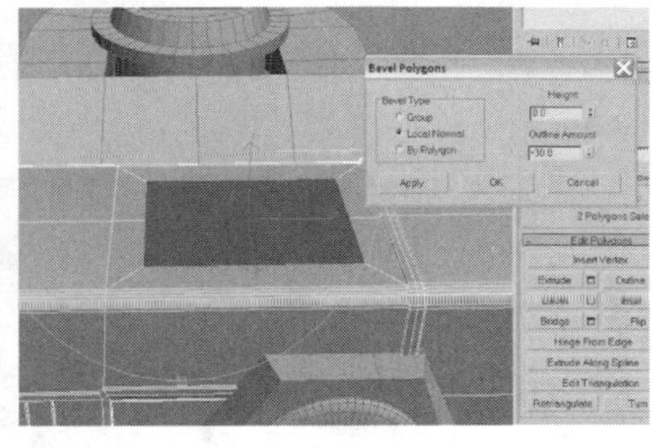

Figure 3-1113

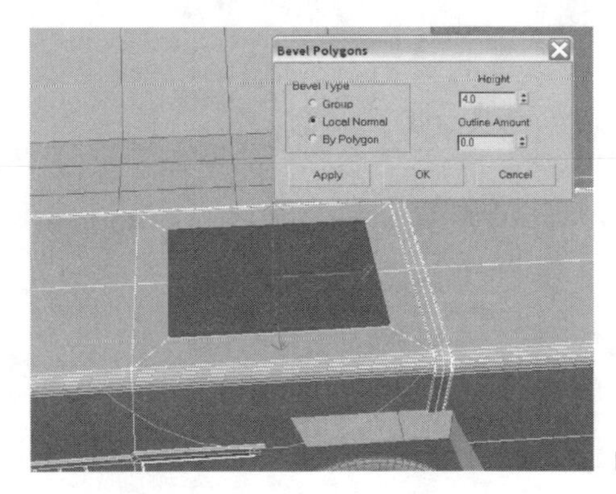

Figure 3-1114

54. Select the polygon indicated in Figure 3-1115 and click **Tessellate**. Select the opposite polygon and Bevel it:

Type	Height	Outline	Apply/OK
Local Normal	0	–9	Apply
Local Normal	40	0	OK

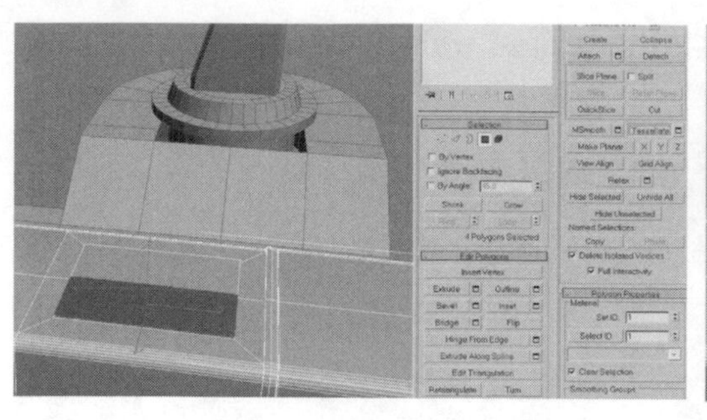

Figure 3-1115

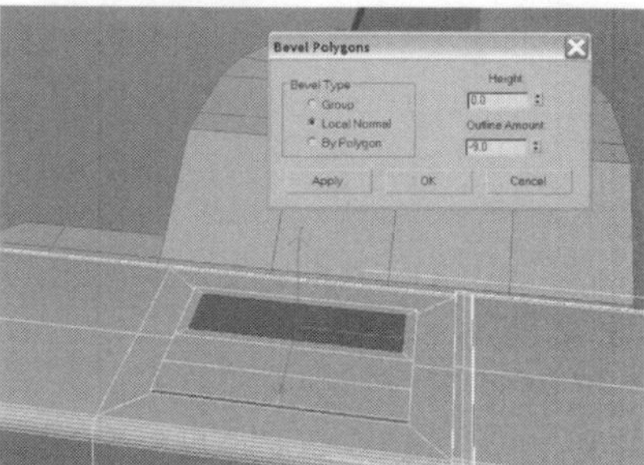

Figure 3-1116

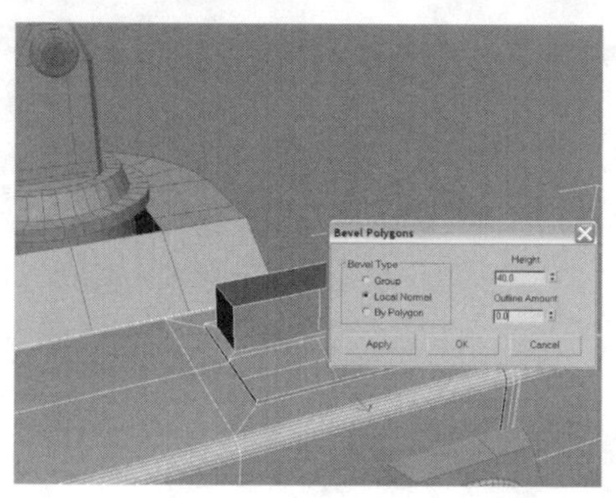

Figure 3-1117

55. Select the bottom set of polygons in the form of an L, as shown, and Bevel them:

Type	Height	Outline	Apply/OK
Local Normal	0	–10	Apply
Local Normal	14	0	OK

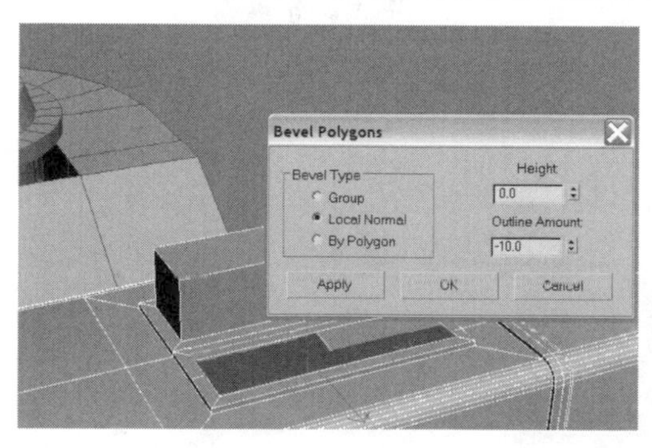

Figure 3-1118

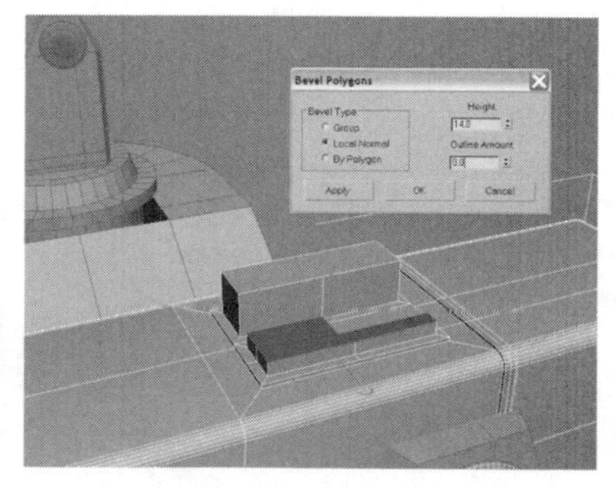

Figure 3-1119

56. Select the four vertical corners of the higher extrusion and then Connect them with **2** Segments.

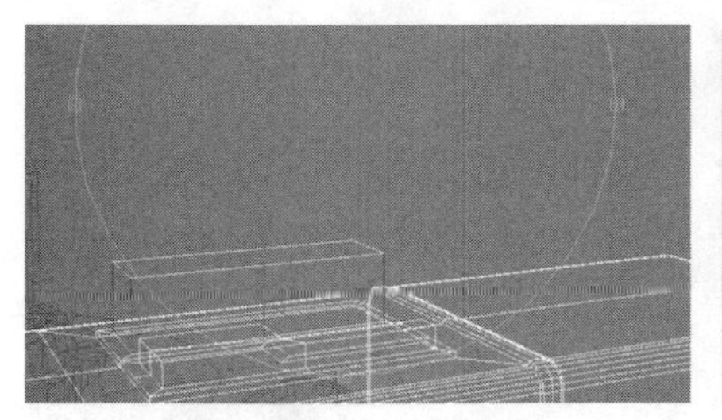

Figure 3-1120

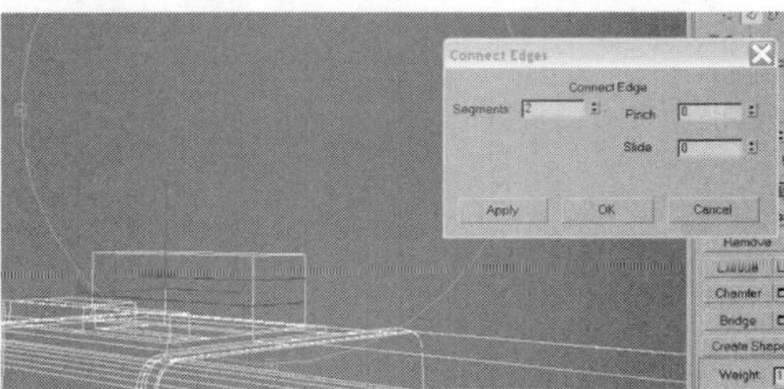

Figure 3-1121

57. Select the rear middle polygon and Extrude it by **Local Normal 12.** Non-uniform Scale the polygon down to **70** in the Y axis.

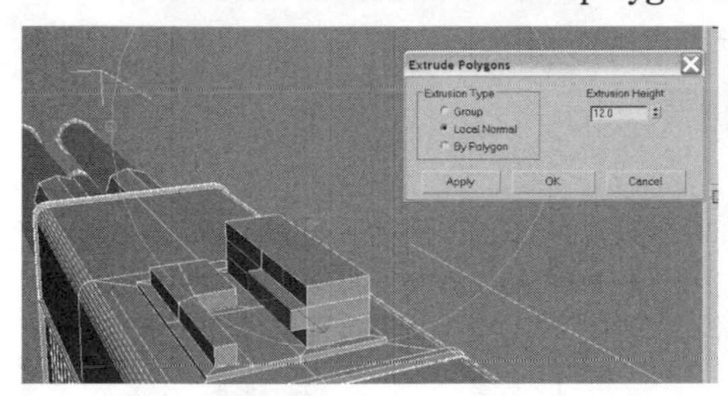

Figure 3-1122

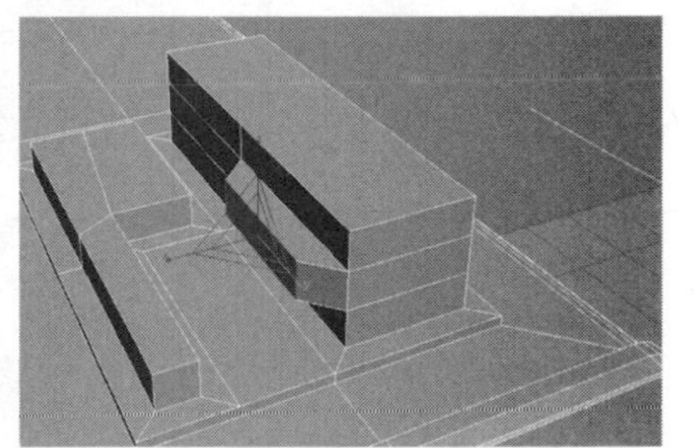

Figure 3-1123

58. Hinge From Edge an Angle of **90** degrees with **10** Segments, click **Pick Hinge**, and click the bottom edge. Bevel them:

Type	Height	Outline	Apply/OK
Local Normal	14	0	Apply

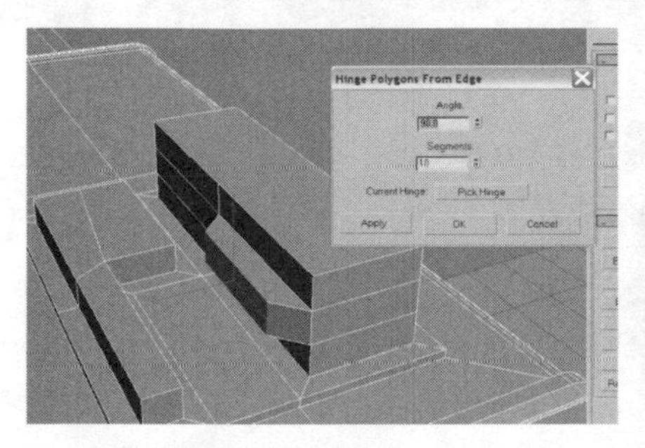

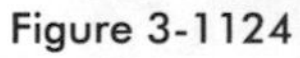

Figure 3-1124

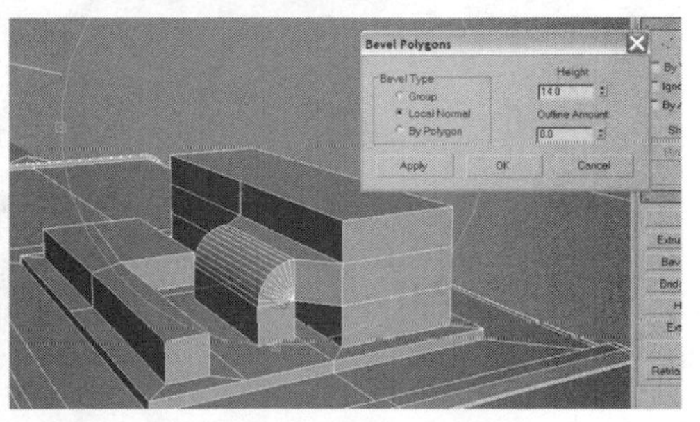

Figure 3-1125

Type	Height	Outline	Apply/OK
Local Normal	0	3.3	Apply
Local Normal	1.015	1.67	OK

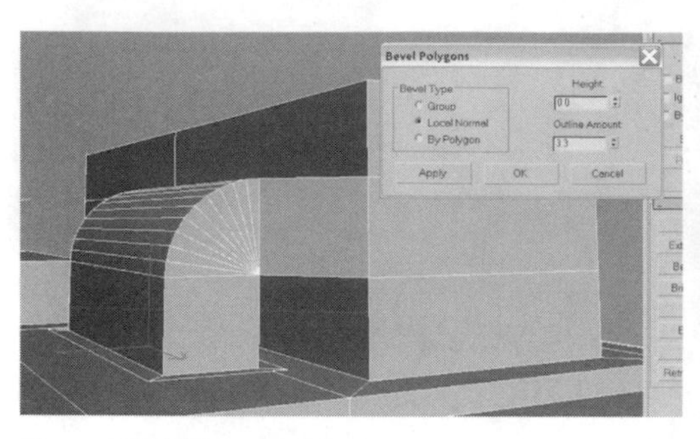

Figure 3-1126

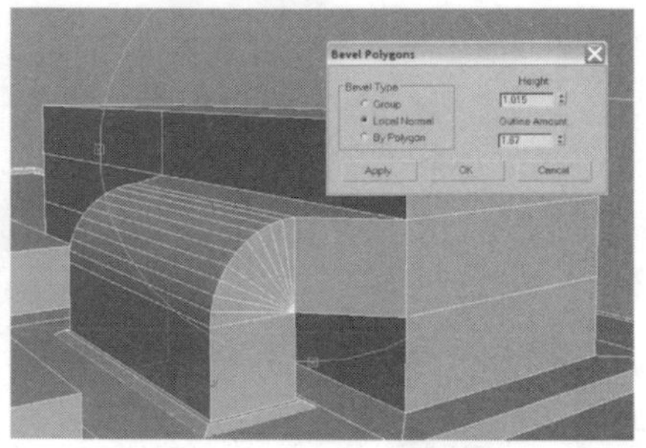

Figure 3-1127

59. Create a Tube on top of the L shape and create a clone of that tube.

Radius 1	Radius 2	Height	Height/Cap Segs	Sides	Smooth
3	5	2.8	1/1	36	Checked

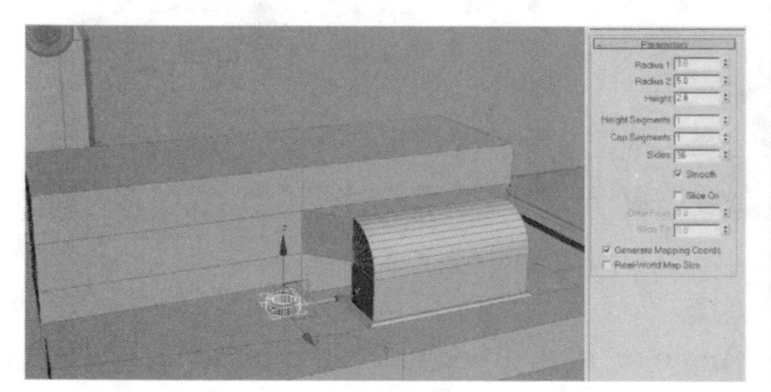

Figure 3-1128

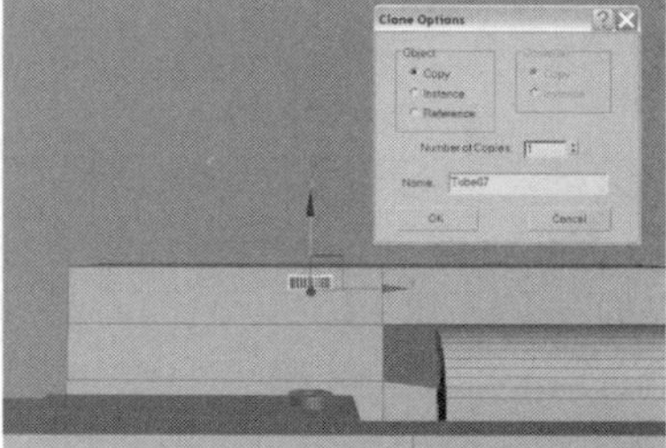

Figure 3-1129

60. Rotate the cloned tube **90** degrees in the Y axis. Move the tubes so the edges are just below the surfaces.

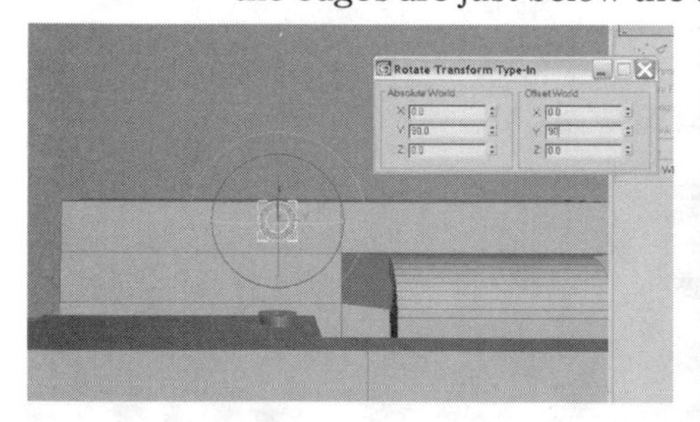

Figure 3-1130

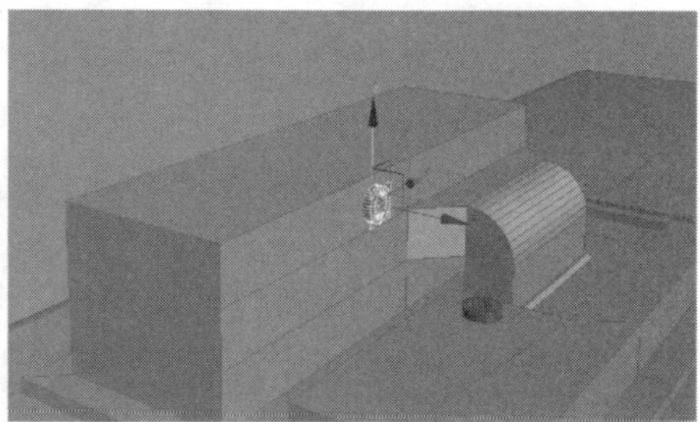

Figure 3-1131

61. Select the inside polygons and delete them. Create a three-vertex Spline between the tubes.

Figure 3-1132

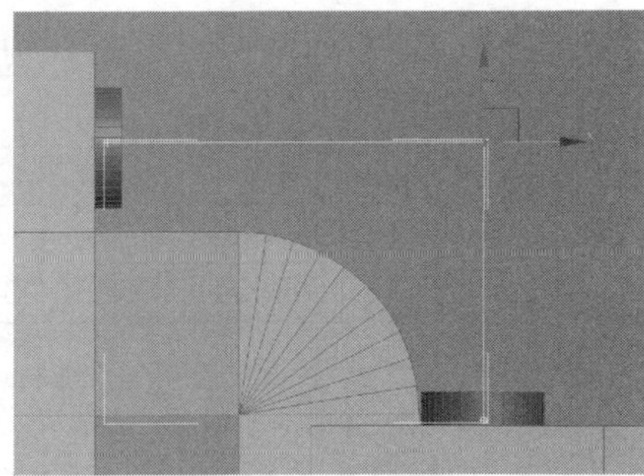

Figure 3-1133

62. Select the center vertex, right-click, and choose **Smooth.** Add a Sweep modifier to the spline's stack, choose **Use Built-In Section,** and pick **Cylinder** from the drop-down.

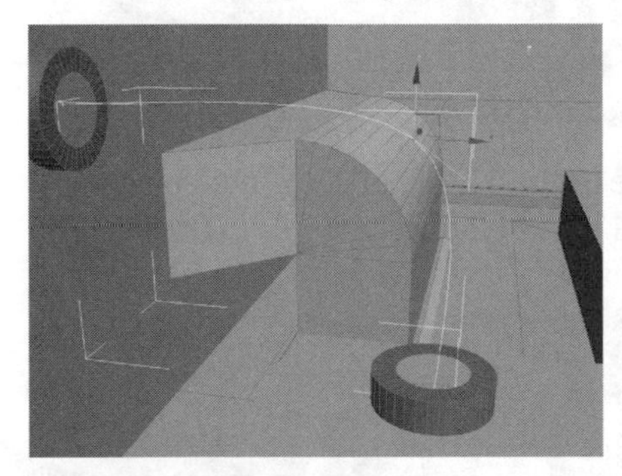

Figure 3-1134

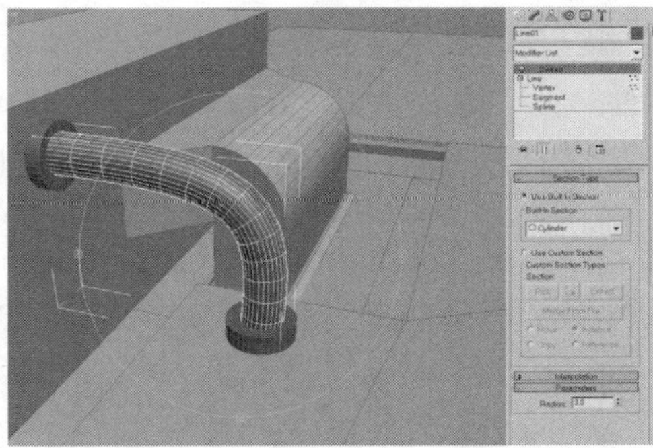

Figure 3-1135

63. Convert the spline to an Editable Polygon and Attach the tubes to it.

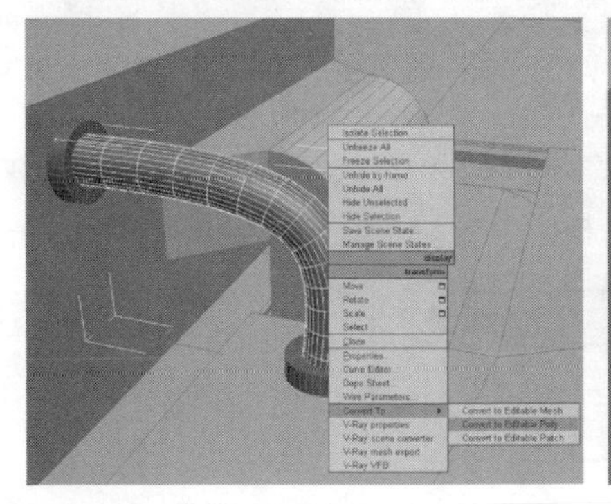

Figure 3-1136

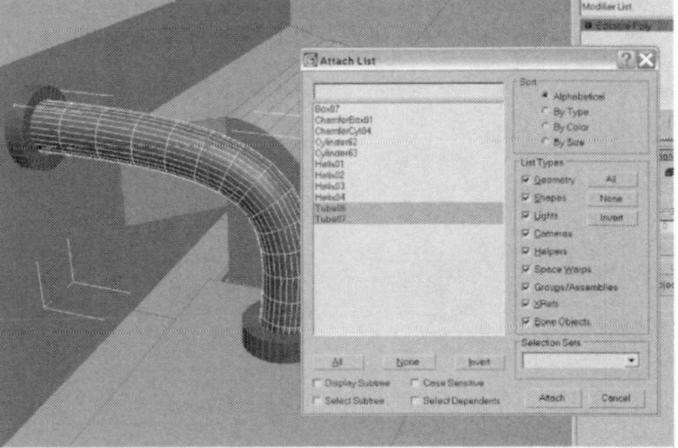

Figure 3-1137

64. Select the top two polygons on the vertical part of the box and Bevel them inward:

Type	Height	Outline	Apply/OK
Local Normal	0	–2	Apply
Local Normal	–1.6	0	OK

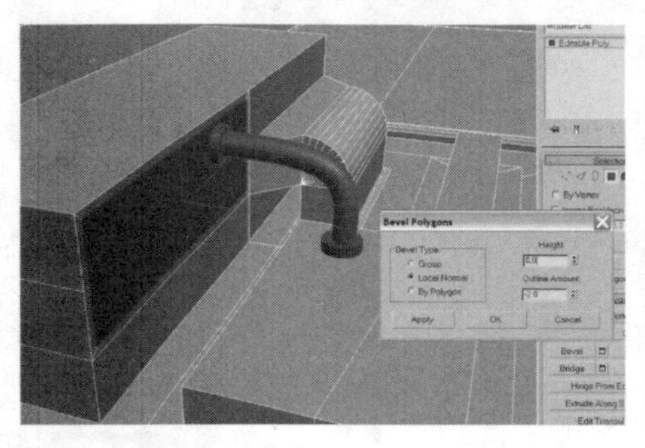

Figure 3-1138

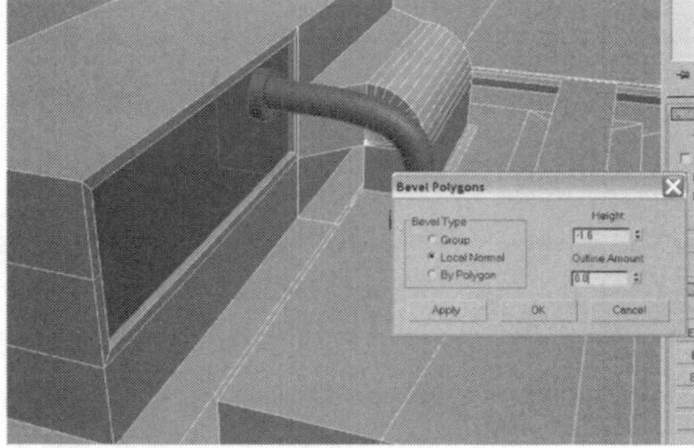

Figure 3-1139

65. Select the tube and Shift-clone in the Y axis, making four copies. Select the body and Attach the tubes (shown as Lines in the list, because they're based on splines).

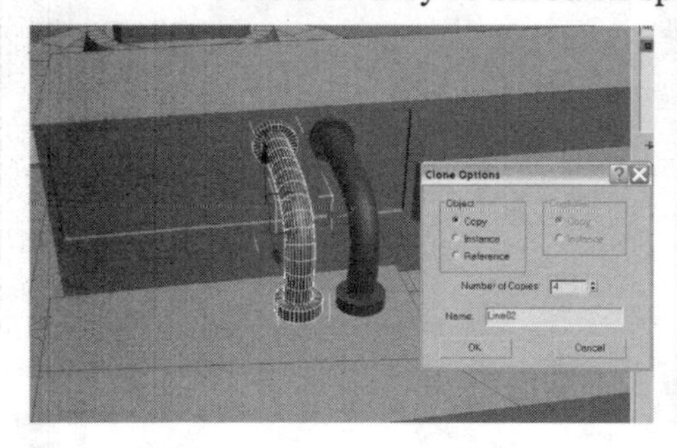

Figure 3-1140

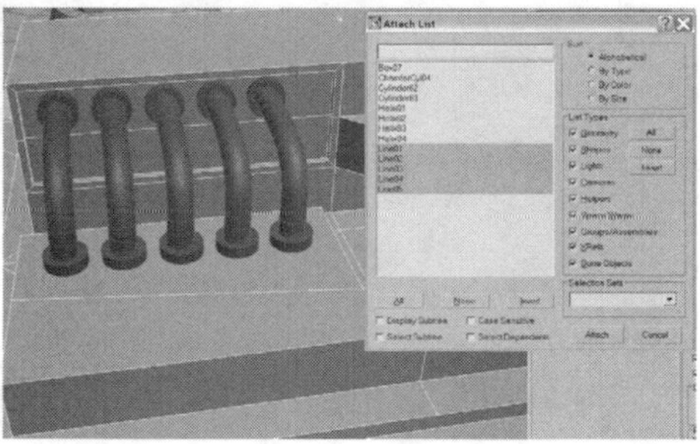

Figure 3-1141

66. Select the polygons on the rear of the box and Bevel them:

Type	Height	Outline	Apply/OK
Local Normal	0	–7	Apply
Local Normal	–7	0	OK

Day 9: Detailing the Rear Base and Adding the Turret and Upper Body

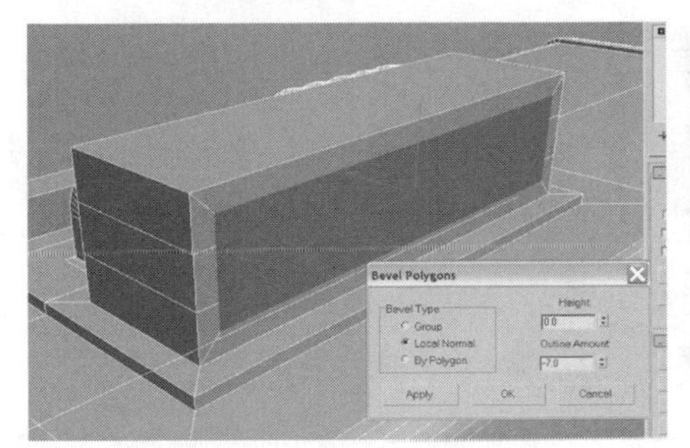

Figure 3-1142

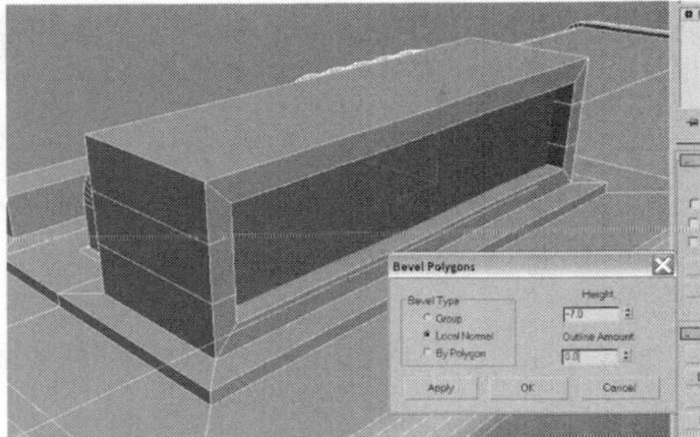

Figure 3-1143

67. Create a Gengon and convert it to an Editable Polygon, then select the back-facing polygons and delete them.

Sides	Radius	Fillet	Height	Side/Height/Fillet Segs	Smooth
6	5	0	1.429	1/1/1	Unchecked

Figure 3-1144

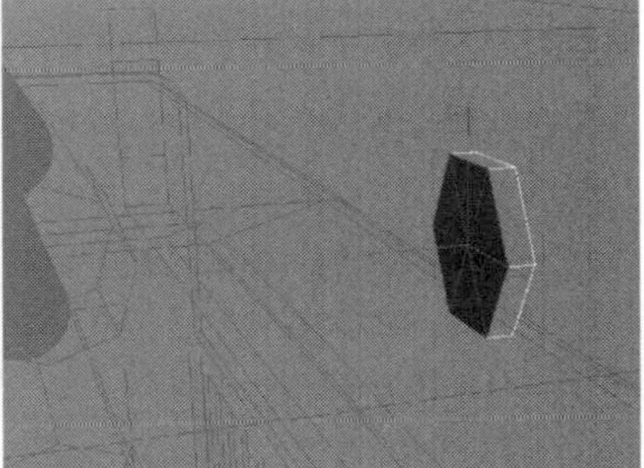

Figure 3-1145

68. Select the gengon's front polygons and Bevel them:

Type	Height	Outline	Apply/OK
Group	0	–1	Apply
Group	–0.3	0	Apply

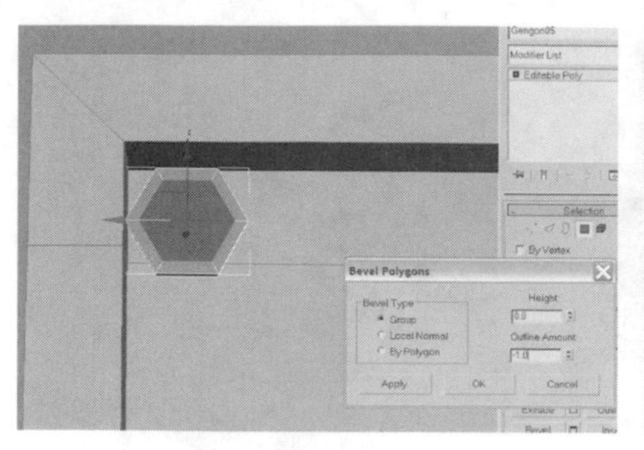

Figure 3-1146

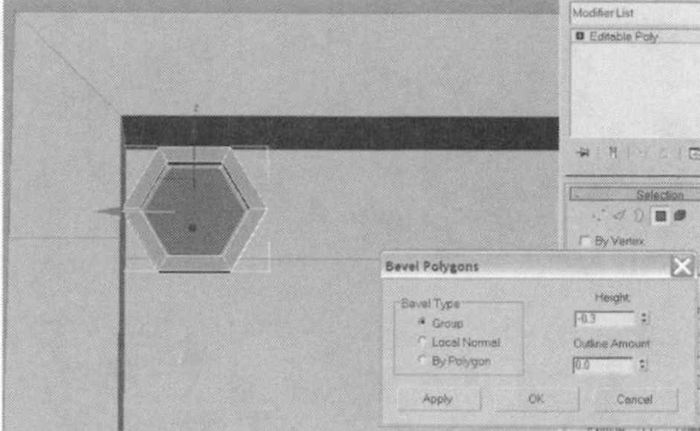

Figure 3-1147

Type	Height	Outline	Apply/OK
Group	0	–0.3	Apply
Group	1.24	0	Apply

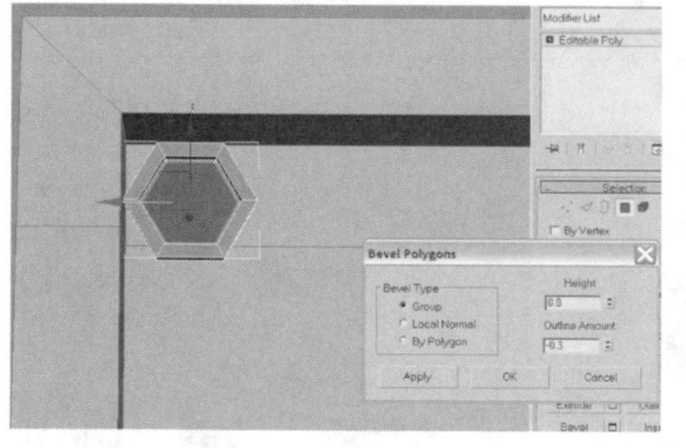

Figure 3-1148

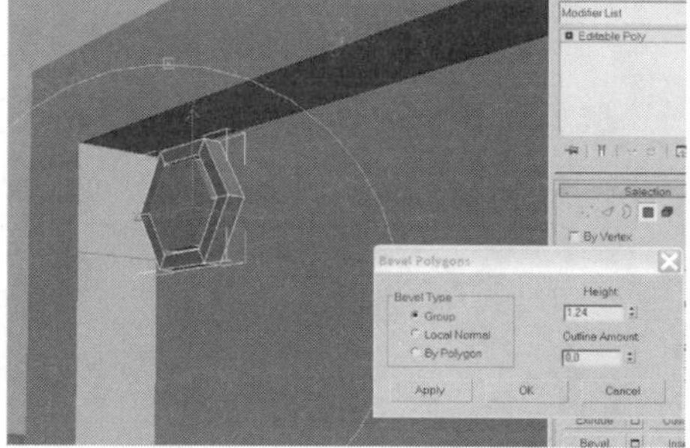

Figure 3-1149

Type	Height	Outline	Apply/OK
By Polygon	0	–0.4	Apply
By Polygon	0.5	0	OK

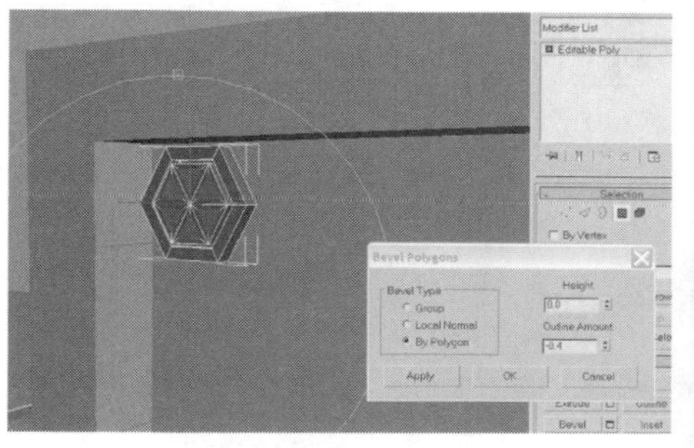

Figure 3-1150

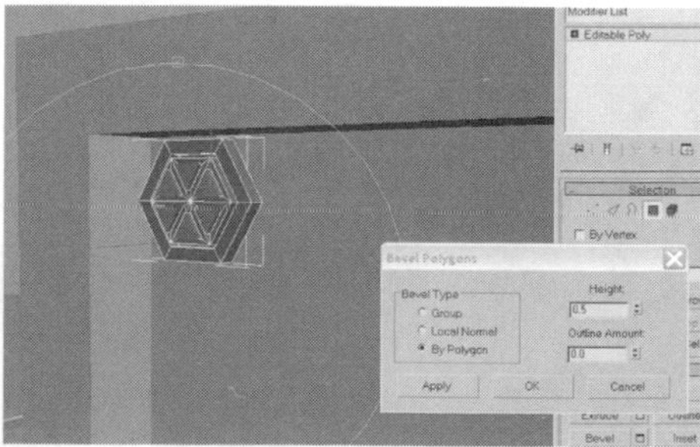

Figure 3-1151

69. Clone the gengon enough times to fill the box and arrange them as shown in Figure 3-1153, then select the body and Attach the gengons to the body.

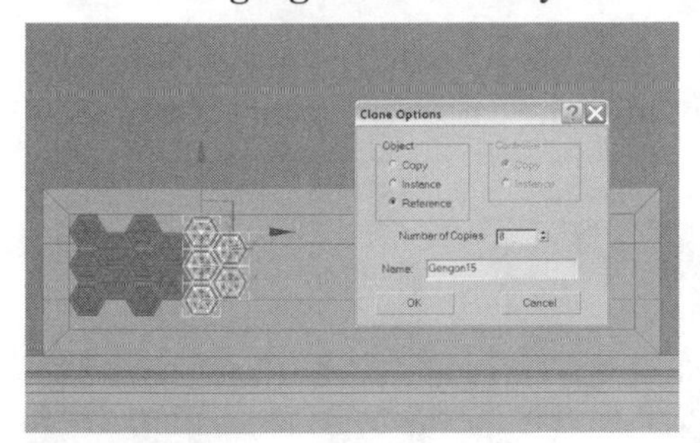

Figure 3-1152

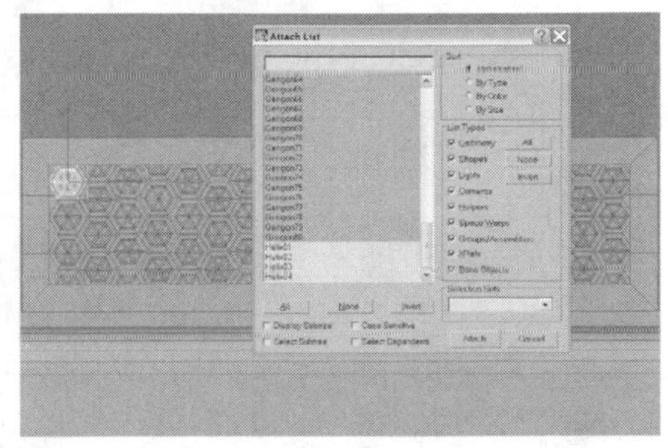

Figure 3-1153

70. Select all the objects comprising the gun, clone it, and move it to the opposite side.

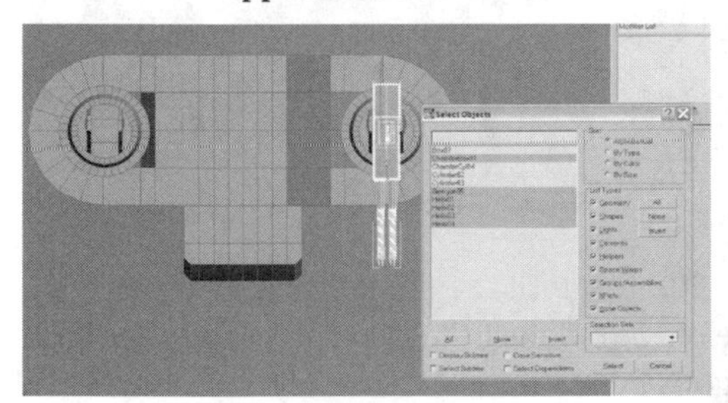

Figure 3-1154

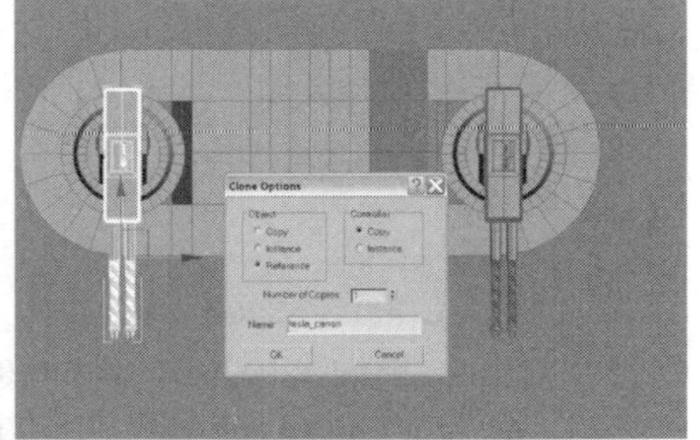

Figure 3-1155

Day 10: Detailing the Upper Body

1. Select the middle polygons of the stanchion that holds the gun mount. Bevel them and Non-uniform Scale them down to **50** in the Offset Local X axis.

Type	Height	Outline	Apply/OK
Group	0	–100	OK

Figure 3-1156

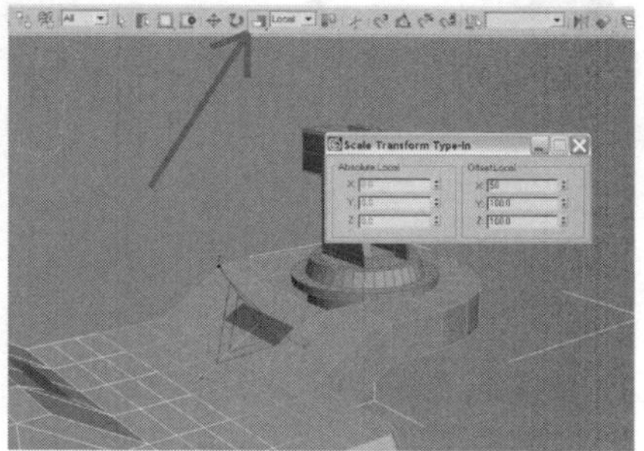

Figure 3-1157

2. Extrude the polygons by **609** (or until they meet their symmetric opposite to form a bridge shape). Select the two polygons in the middle of the three polygons beneath the extrusion you just made.

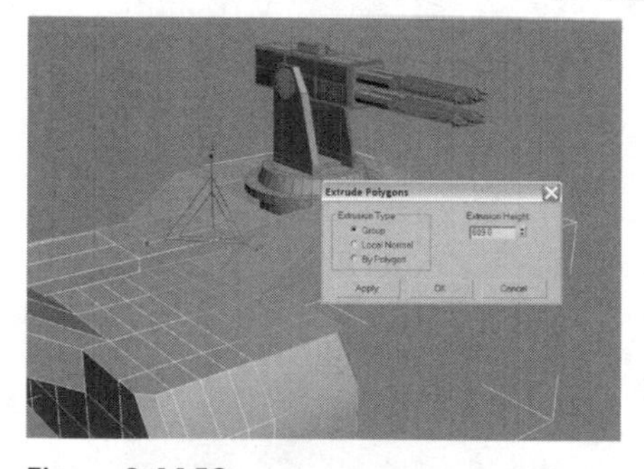

Figure 3-1158

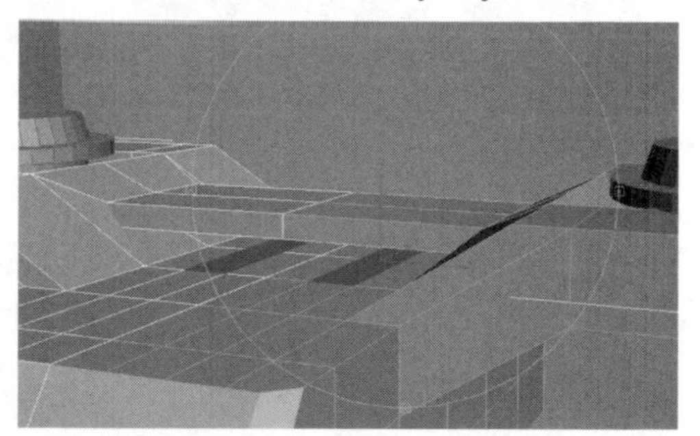

Figure 3-1159

3. Bevel the selected polygons and then Non-uniform Scale them down to **60** in the Y axis.

Type	Height	Outline	Apply/OK
Group	0	–40	OK

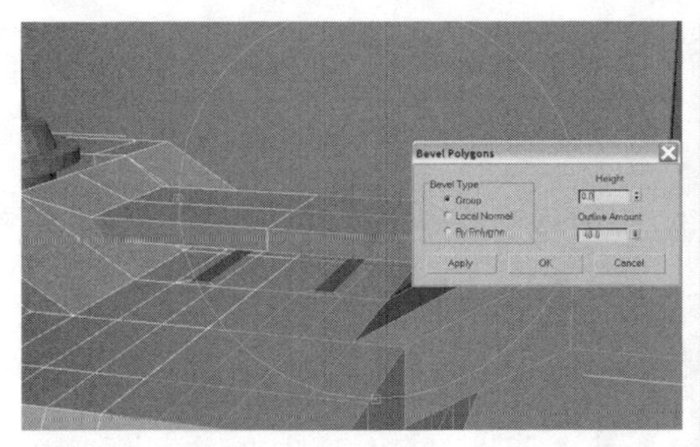

Figure 3-1160

Figure 3-1161

4. Extrude the polygons **140**. Right-click the Move tool and type **100** for the Offset Local X axis.

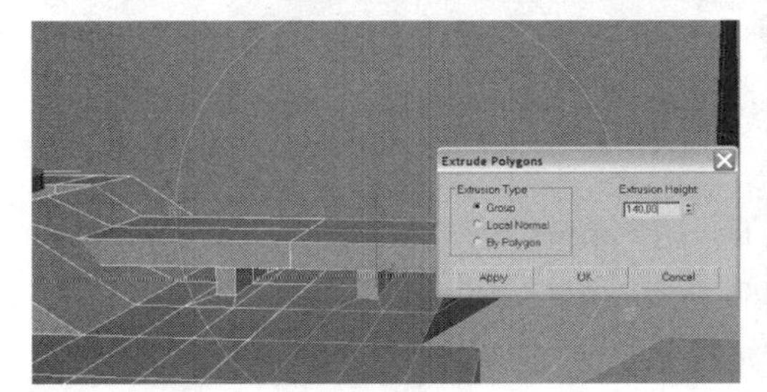

Figure 3-1162

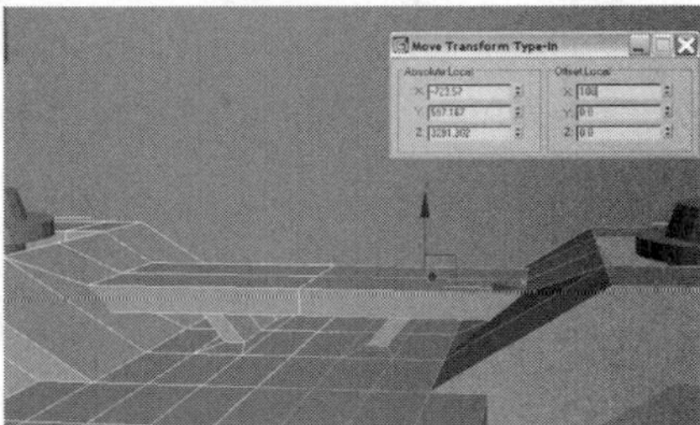

Figure 3-1163

5. Create a Box at the rear of the bridge you just made. Convert the box to an Editable Polygon, select the top polygon made by the top height segment and facing the front, and Extrude it by **223.83** so it extends halfway across the bridge.

Length	Width	Height	Length/Width/Height Segs
400	400	227.157	1/1/3

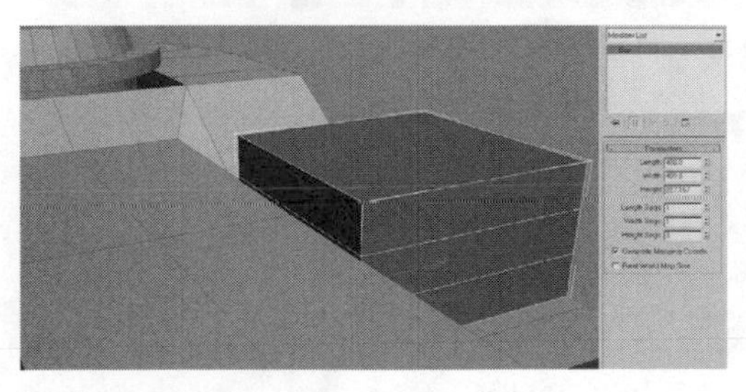

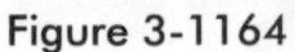

Figure 3-1164

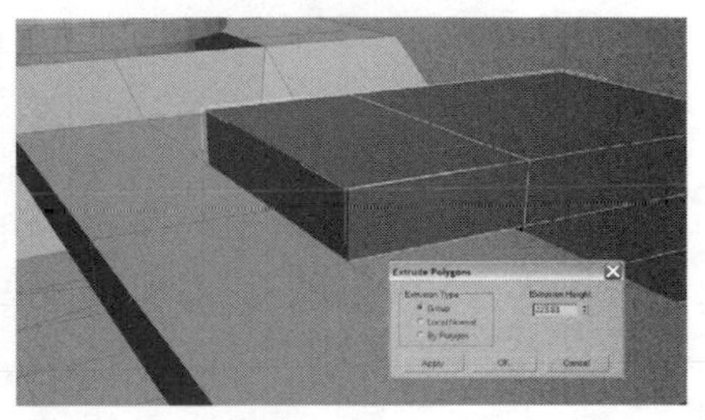

Figure 3-1165

6. Select the top edge of the extrusion and Chamfer it by **28.** Create a Cylinder at the front top corner of the extrusion over the bridge and then Clone one for the opposite side.

Radius	Height	Height/Cap Segs	Sides	Smooth
20.814	104.079	1/1	36	Checked

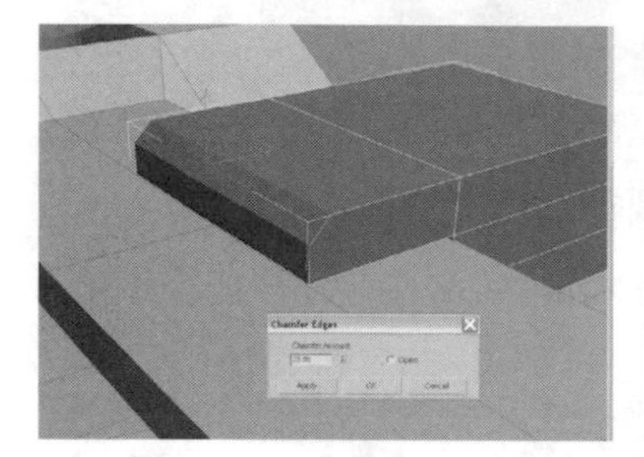

Figure 3-1166

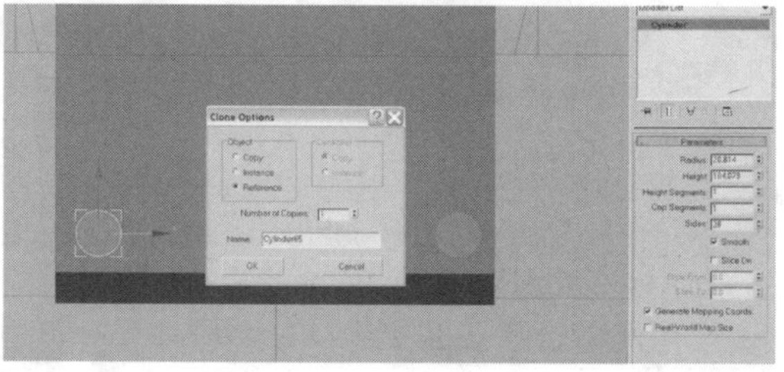

Figure 3-1167

7. Select and Link the cylinders to the box and then Select and Link the box to the body. Create a Tube on top of the box and center it over the top part of the box that does not extend over the bridge.

Radius 1	Radius 2	Height	Height/Cap Segs	Sides	Smooth
130	110	50	3/1	36	Checked

Figure 3-1168

Figure 3-1169

8. Add a Lattice modifier to the tube's stack; this will create a mesh-looking object, like an antenna tower. Add a GeoSphere to the top of the lattice tube.

Radius	Segments	Sides	Geometry
2	1	4	Struts Only from Edges

Radius	Segments	Geodesic Type	Smooth
160	4	Tetra	Checked

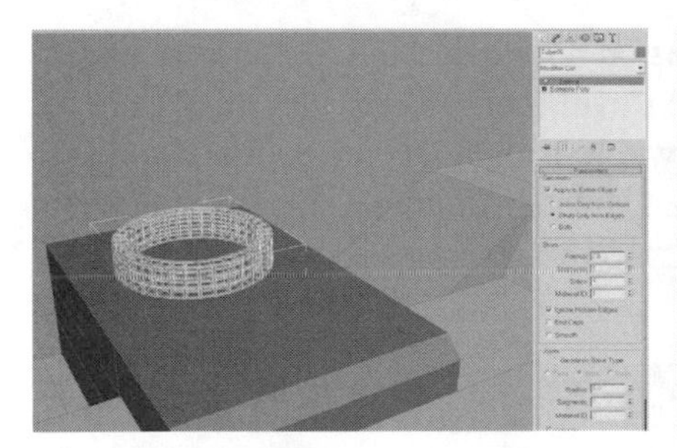

Figure 3-1170

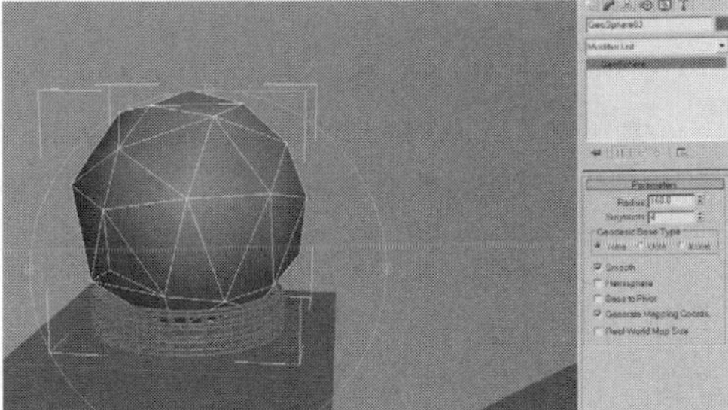

Figure 3-1171

9. Convert the geosphere to an Editable Polygon, select it, and Bevel it:

Type	Height	Outline	Apply/OK
By Polygon	0	–9	Apply
By Polygon	–7	0	Apply
By Polygon	9	0	OK

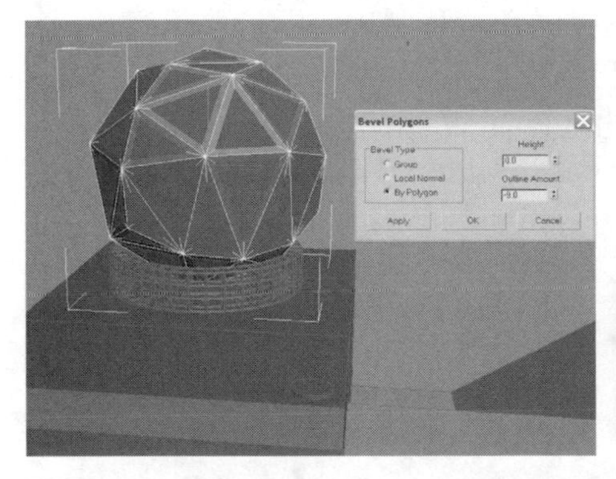

Figure 3-1172

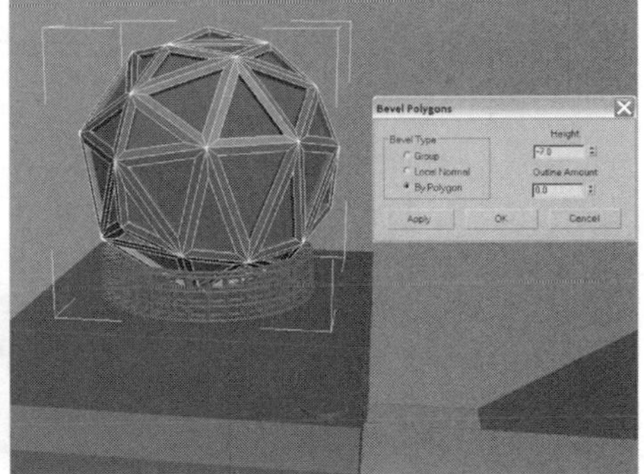

Figure 3-1173

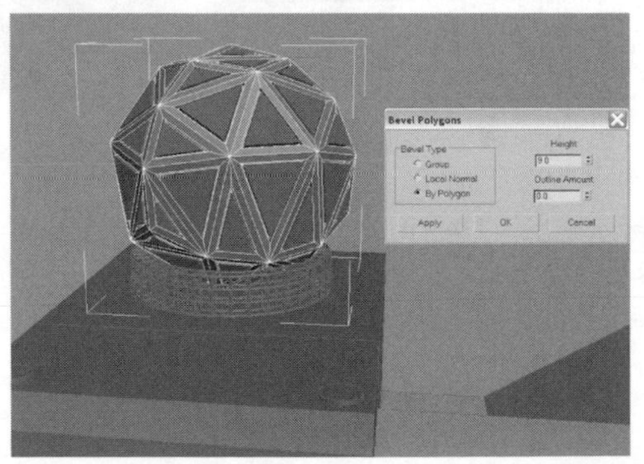

Figure 3-1174

10. Select the bottom two polygons on both sides and the middle polygon on the rear of the box, and Bevel them. Then Shift-click the Edge selection mode icon to switch from Polygon selection mode. (Note: Shift-clicking will not only switch from polygon to edge, but will select all the edges making up the polygons that are currently selected.)

Type	Height	Outline	Apply/OK
Group	0	–2	OK

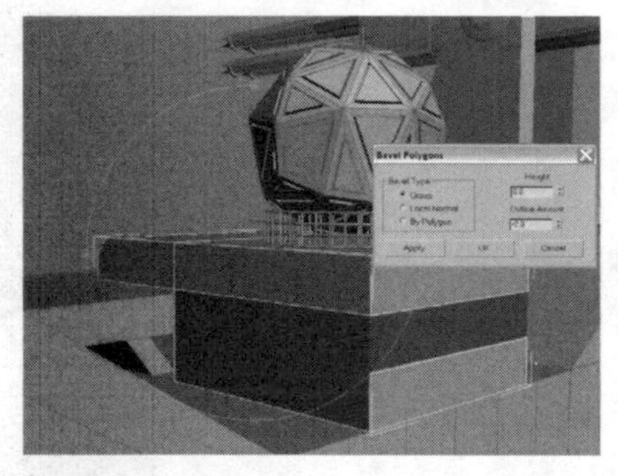

Figure 3-1175

Figure 3-1176

11. Extrude the edges by **–1** with a Base Width of **3** to create deep machine lines in the box. Switch to wireframe mode and edge-select the edges shown darkened in Figure 3-1178.

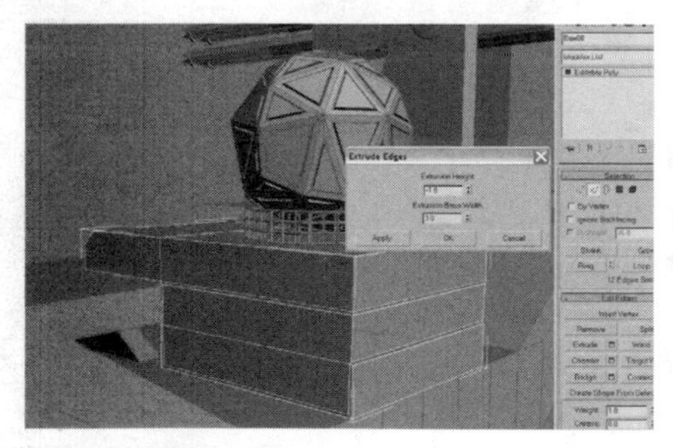

Figure 3-1177

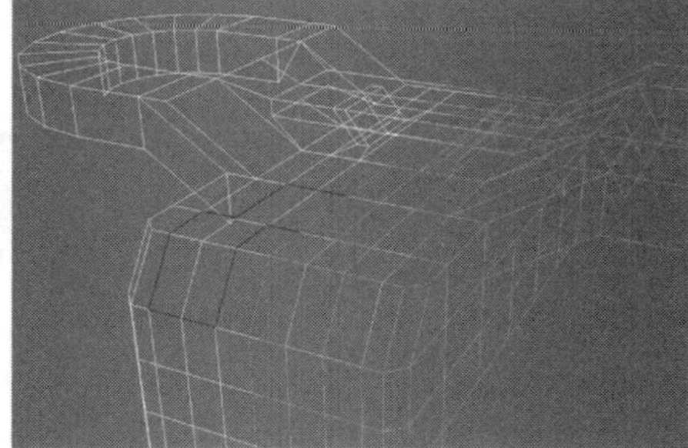

Figure 3-1178

12. Extrude the edges by **–10** with a Base Width of **3.5** to create deep machine lines in the body. Switch back and forth from wireframe to shaded as needed and select the edges shown darkened in Figure 3-1180.

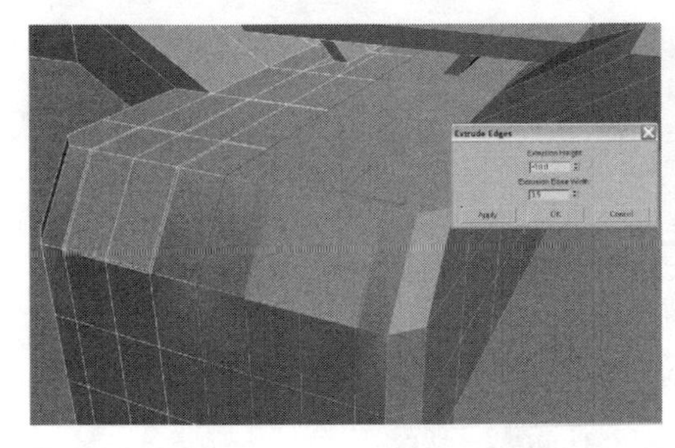

Figure 3-1179

Figure 3-1180

13. Select the edges shown in Figure 3-1181 and Extrude them by **–10** with a Base Width of **3.5** to create deep machine lines in the stanchions.

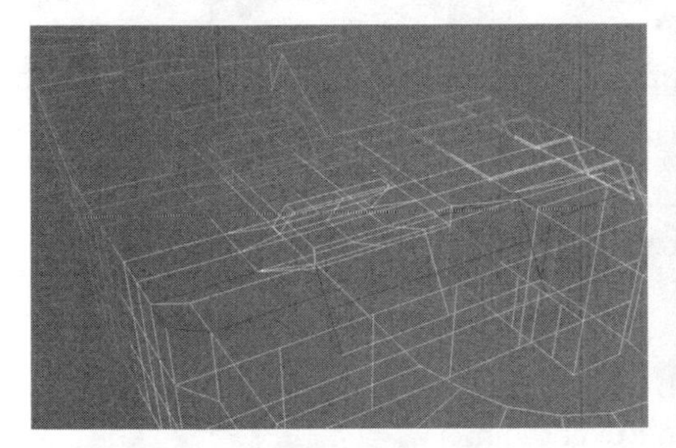

Figure 3-1181

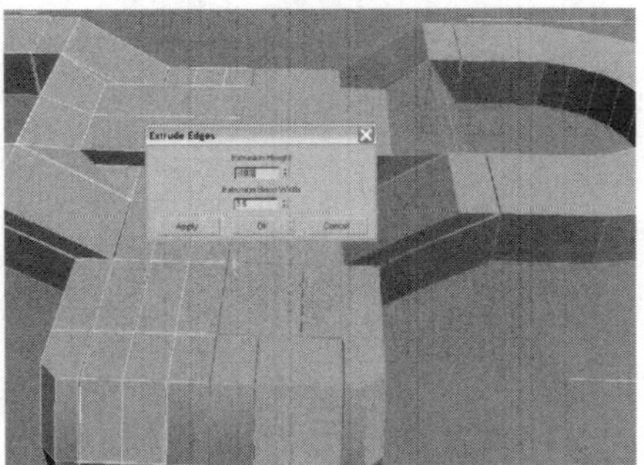

Figure 3-1182

14. Select the edges shown in Figures 3-1183 through 3-1188:

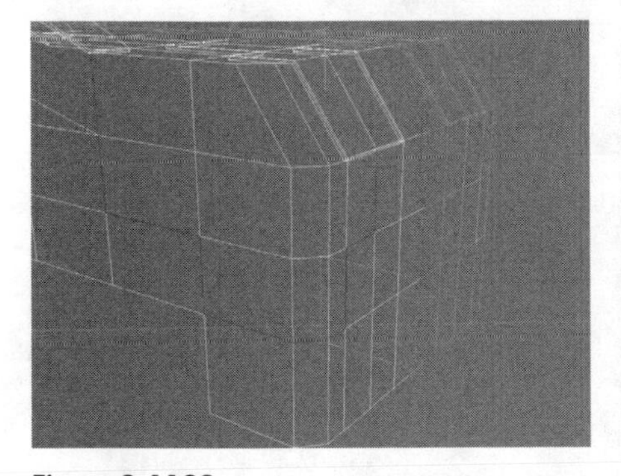

Figure 3-1183

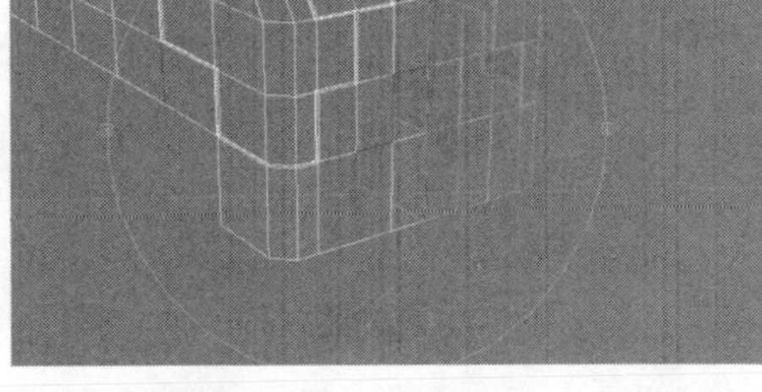

Figure 3-1184

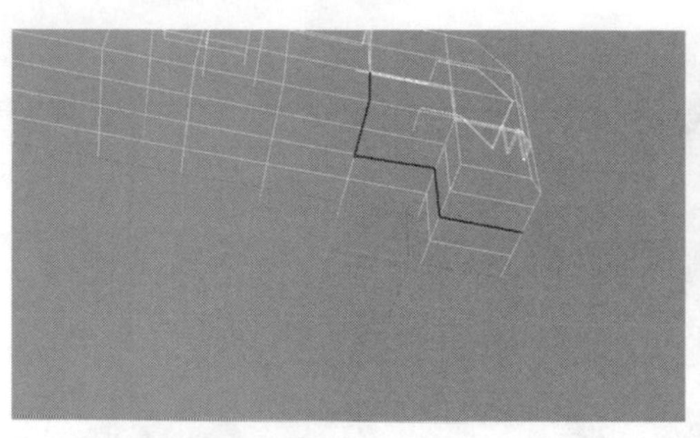

Figure 3-1185

Figure 3-1186

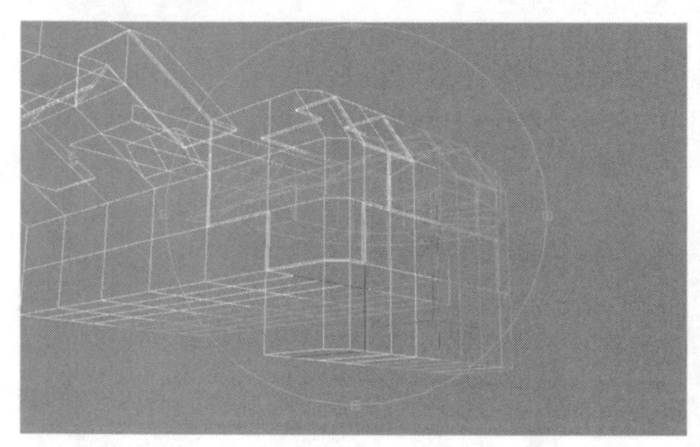

Figure 3-1187

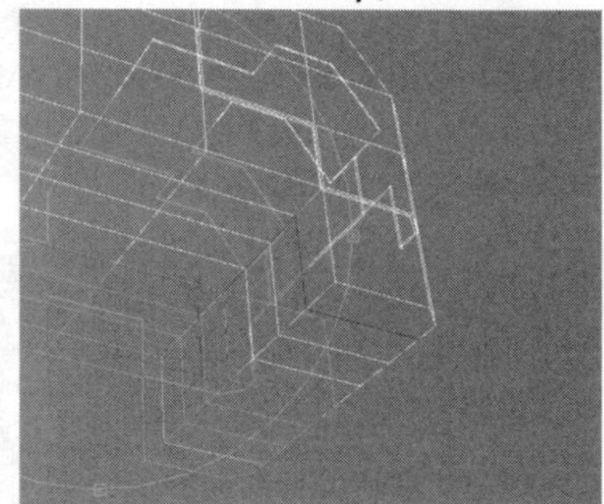

Figure 3-1188

15. Extrude the Edges by **–10** with a Base Width of **3.5**. Select the bottom front six polygons and Bevel them:

Type	Height	Outline	Apply/OK
Group	0	–20	Apply
Group	–90	0	OK

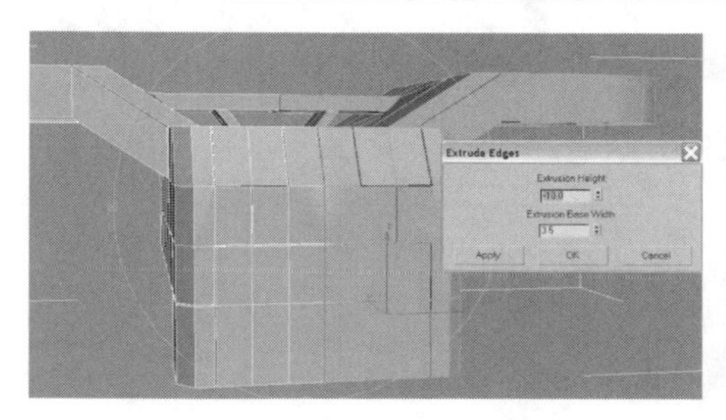

Figure 3-1189

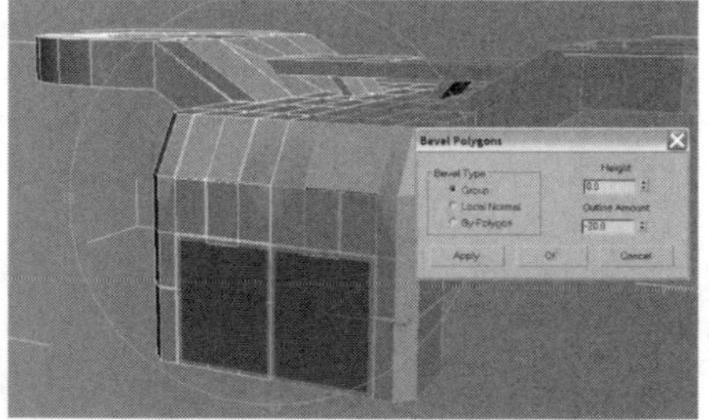

Figure 3-1190

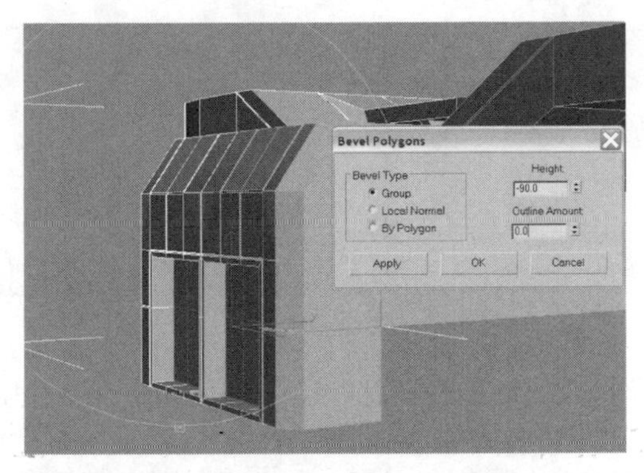

Figure 3-1191

16. Convert the body to an Editable Polygon to fuse the two halves together. Select the polygons inside the recesses and Detach them as **missle_tube template.**

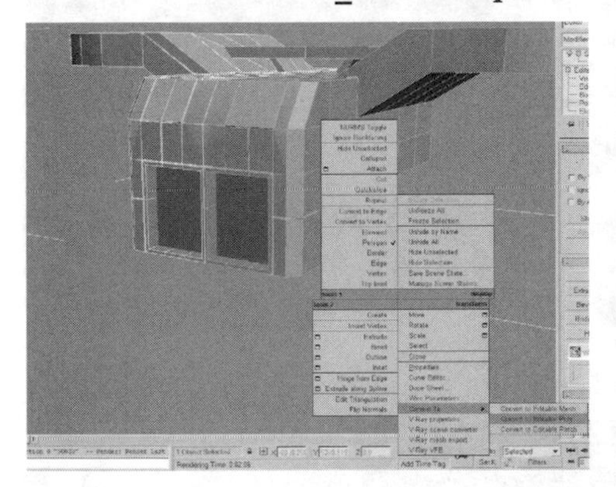

Figure 3-1192

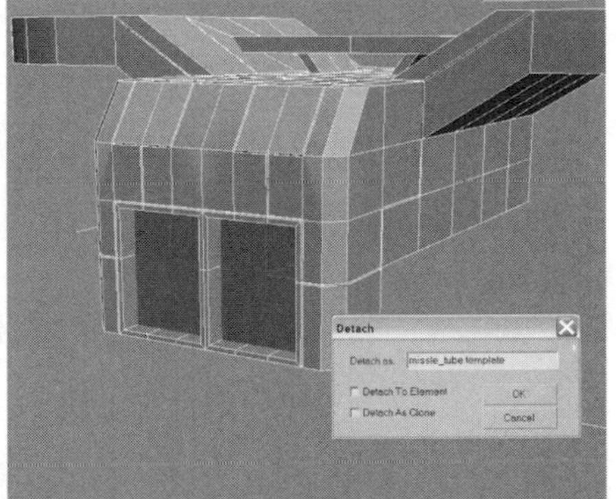

Figure 3-1193

17. Create a Tube and convert it to an Editable Polygon. Make three clones across the top of the template, select those tubes, and make five rows of clones.

Radius 1	Radius 2	Height	Height/Cap Segs	Sides	Smooth
26	20	60	3/1	36	Checked

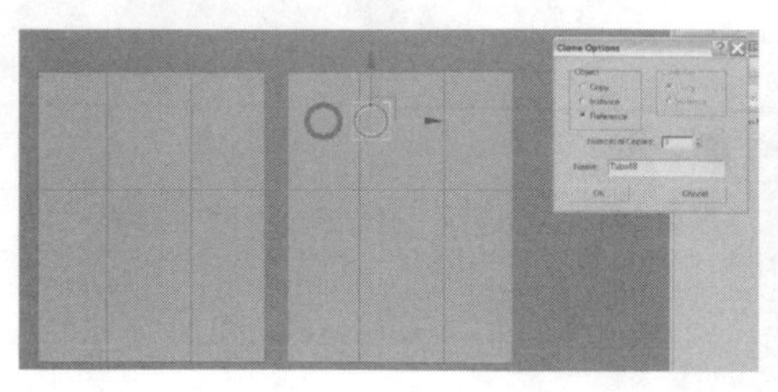

Figure 3-1194

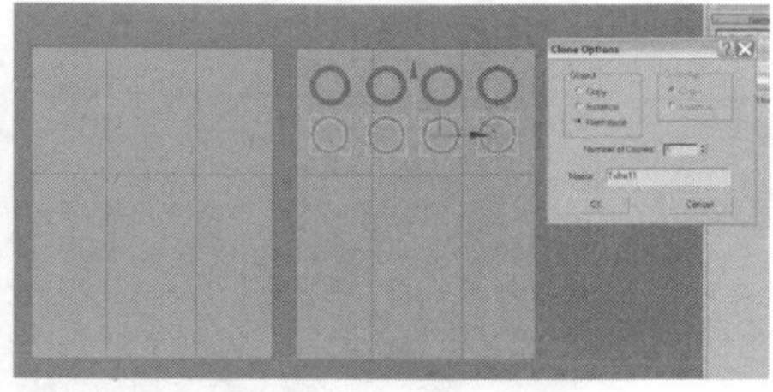

Figure 3-1195

18. Select the original tube and Attach all the clones. Select the middle five polygons on the original and on the first clone and Bridge them. Repeat this process to create the missile tubes the same way you did for the base.

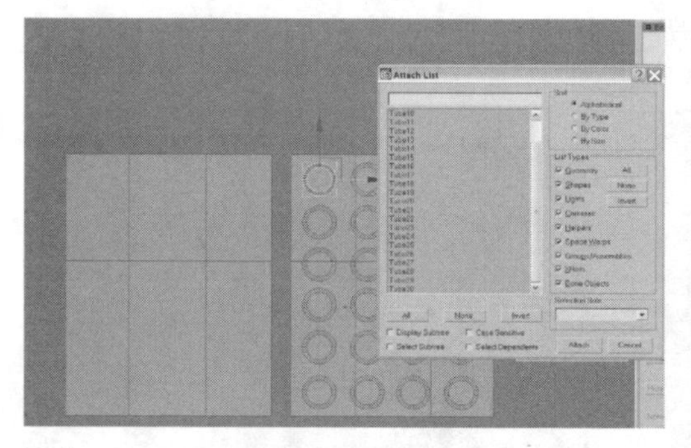

Figure 3-1196

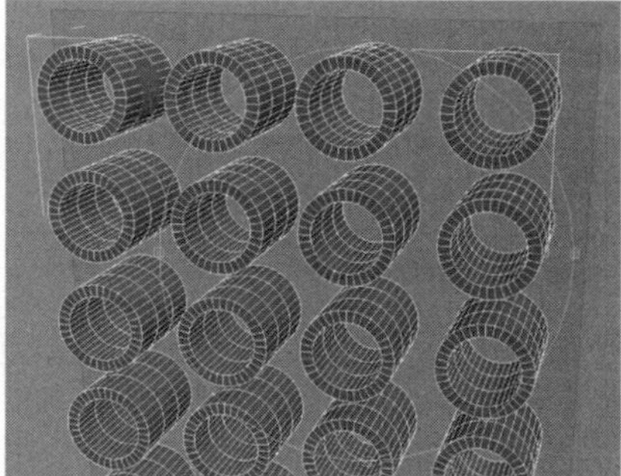

Figure 3-1197

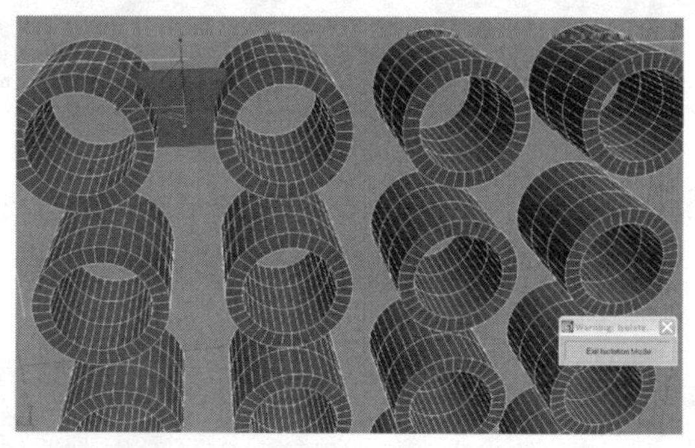

Figure 3-1198

19. Create a Cone in the first tube. Create clones of the cone and fill the tubes.

Radius 1	Radius 2	Height	Height/Cap Segs	Sides	Smooth
0.281	20	–74	3/1	36	Checked

Figure 3-1199

20. Select the caps on the undersides of the gun turrets and Bevel them:

Type	Height	Outline	Apply/OK
Group	0	–60	Apply
Group	30	0	OK

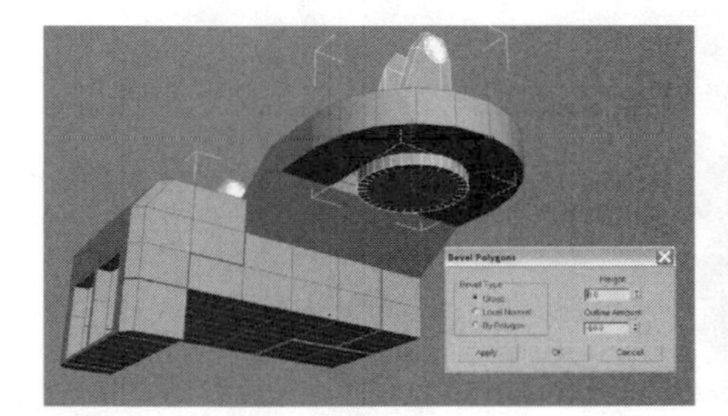

Figure 3-1200

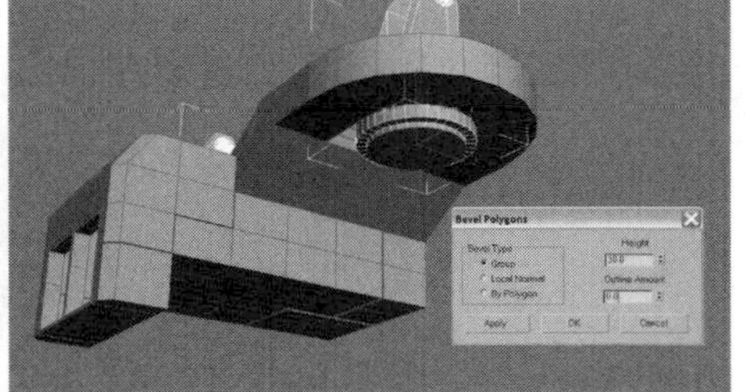

Figure 3-1201

21. Create a Pyramid on the bridge, convert it to an Editable Polygon, and delete the top.

Width	Depth	Height	Width/Depth/Height Segs
156.58	133.193	157.48	1/1/4

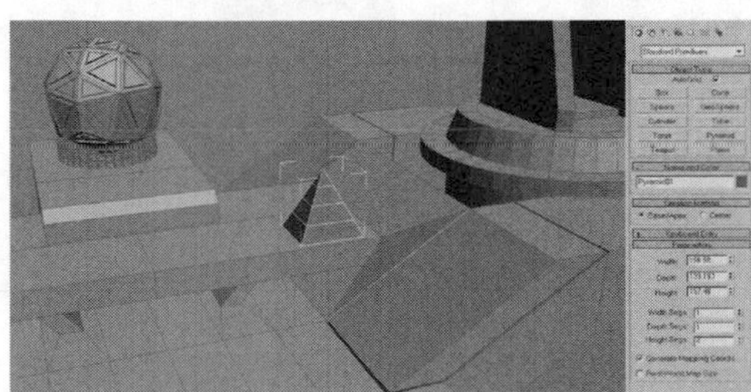

Figure 3-1202

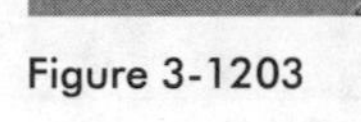

Figure 3-1203

22. Border-select the top, Cap it, and, with all the edges on the top still selected, Non-uniform Scale down to **80** in the X axis.

Figure 3-1204

Figure 3-1205

23. Select the cap and Extrude it by **–1** with the type setting of **Local Normal**, and then click **MSmooth.**

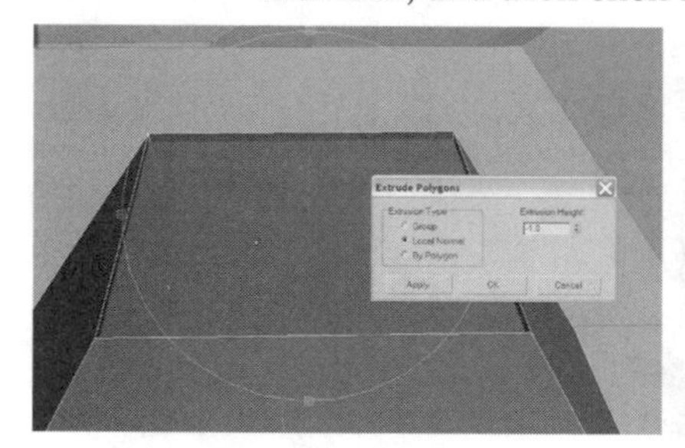

Figure 3-1206

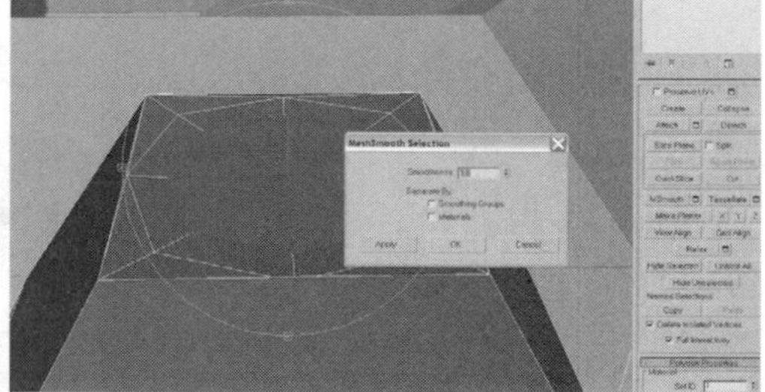

Figure 3-1207

24. Bevel the center four polygons:

Type	Height	Outline	Apply/OK
Group	–3.99	0	Apply
Group	0	–1	OK

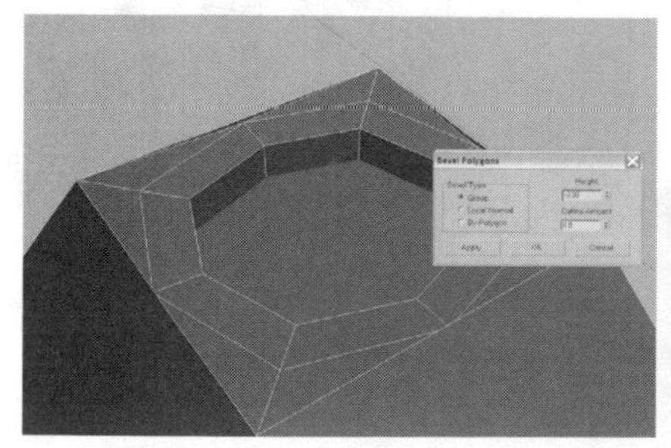

Figure 3-1208

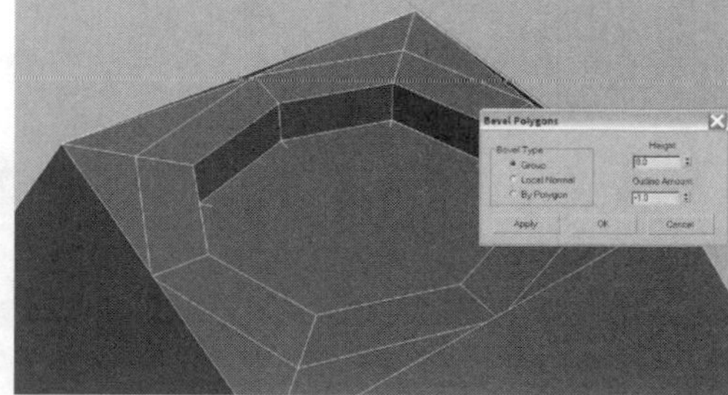

Figure 3-1209

25. Extrude by **Local Normal** by **100** and hit **Apply.** Then Extrude by **10** and hit **Apply** fifteen times. This will create a strange four-panel spade shape.

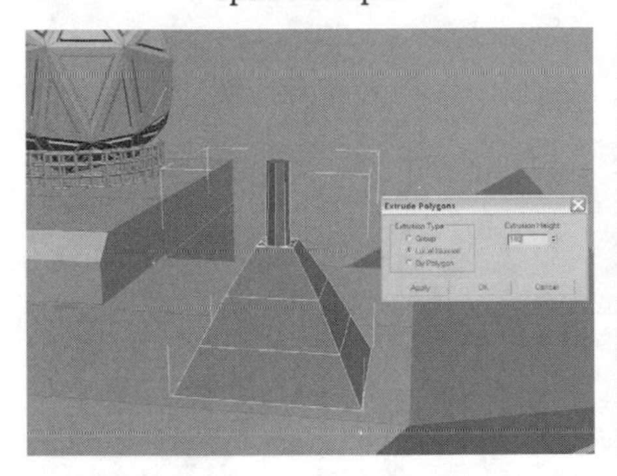
Figure 3-1210

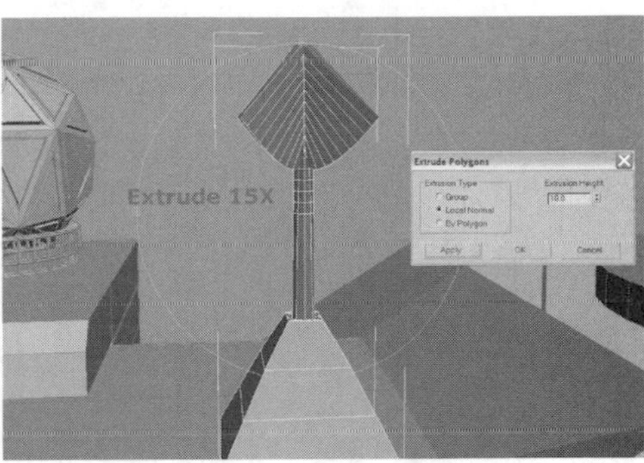

Figure 3-1211

26. Select the polygons making up the pyramid and Bevel them:

Type	Height	Outline	Apply/OK
By Polygon	0	–2	Apply
By Polygon	0	–2	Apply
By Polygon	–7	0	OK

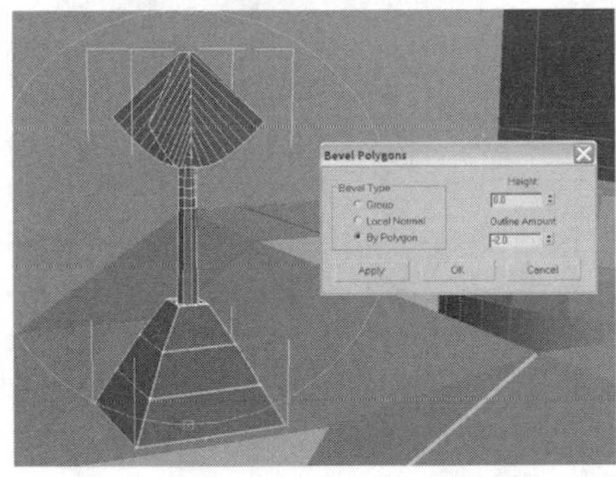
Figure 3-1212

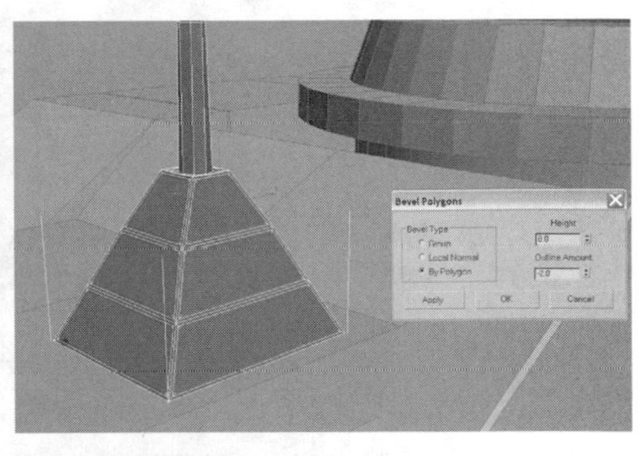
Figure 3-1213

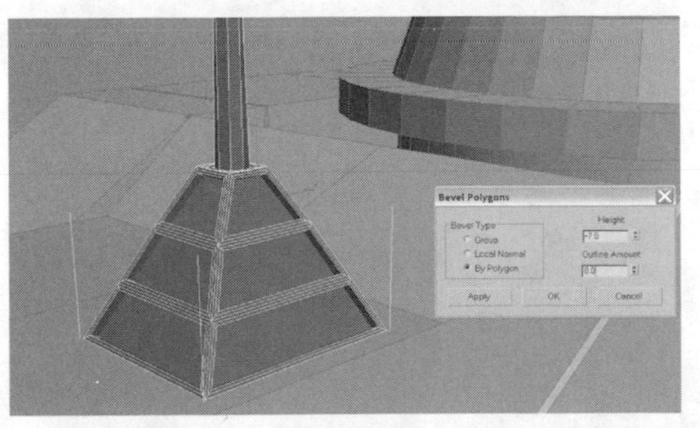
Figure 3-1214

27. Select and Detach the top and just leave it named **Object01**. With Object01 still selected, add a Lattice modifier to its stack.

Radius	Segments	Sides	Geometry
2	1	4	Both

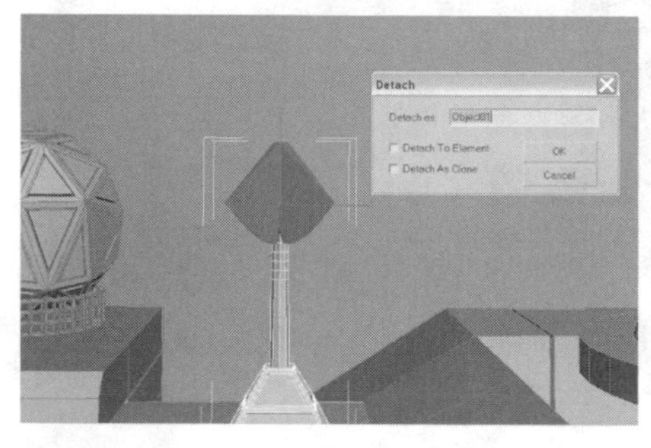

Figure 3-1215

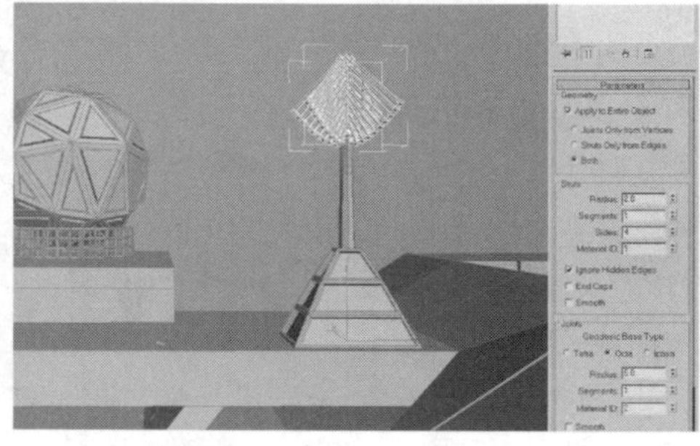

Figure 3-1216

28. Select the pyramid and Attach Object01. Loop-select the four segments on the top of the shaft.

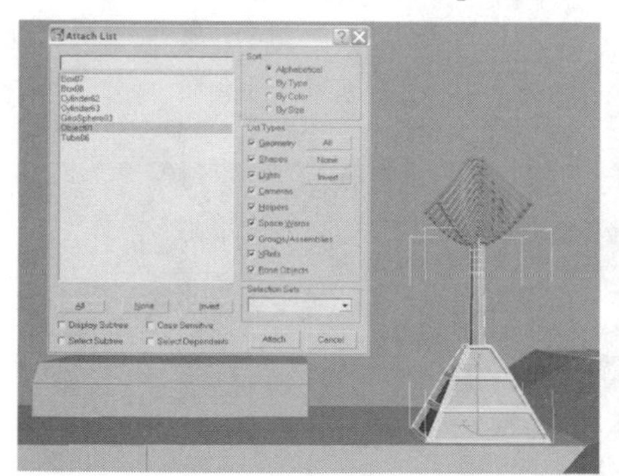

Figure 3-1217

Figure 3-1218

29. Extrude the edges by **10** with a Base Width of **3**. Clone the antenna assembly to the other side of the bridge.

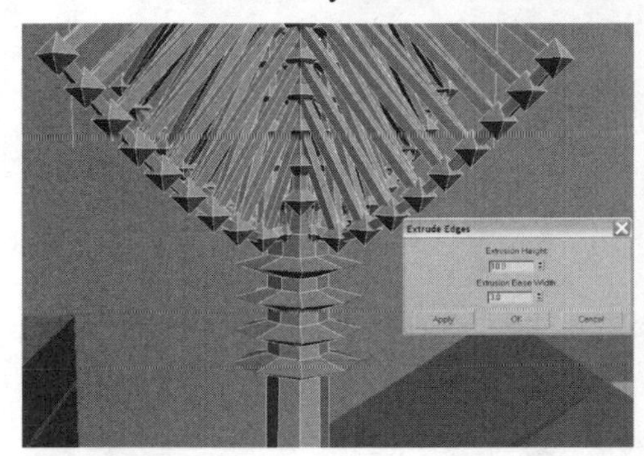

Figure 3-1219

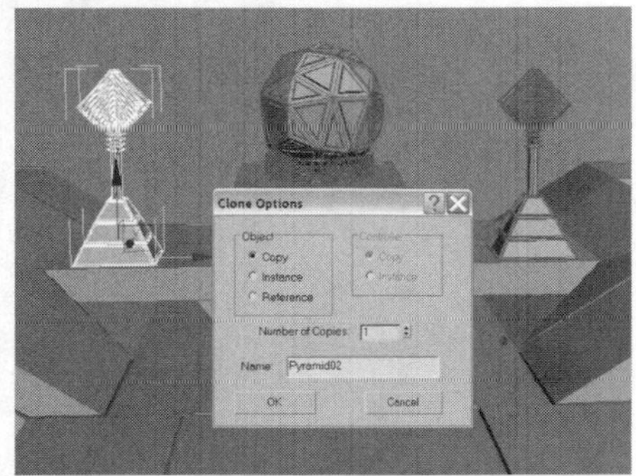

Figure 3-1220

30. Create a Spline that meanders from the base of the pyramid to the base of the geosphere. Select every vertex on the spline, right-click, and change all of them to Smooth. Switch to the Perspective view, arc rotate, and make sure the spline drapes smoothly over the edges and beneath the lattice.

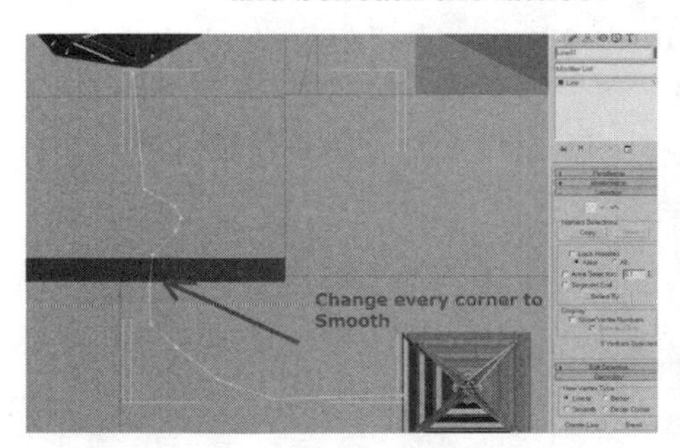

Figure 3-1221

Figure 3-1222

31. Add a Loft modifier to the spline with a Thickness of **15** and **12** Sides. Choose **Enable In Renderer** and **Enable In Viewport** and then convert it to an Editable Polygon to collapse the stack. Create another Spline connecting the other antenna to the geosphere and Loft it using the same settings.

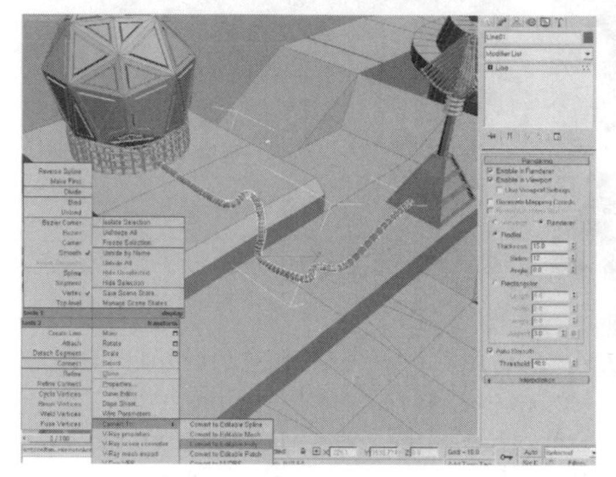
Figure 3-1223

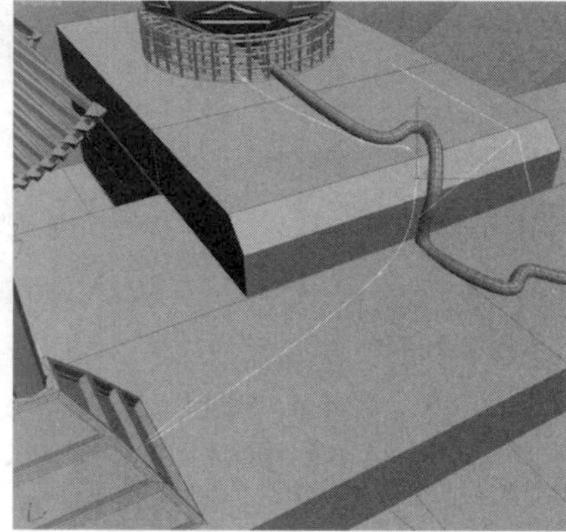
Figure 3-1224

32. Select the torso and add a Smooth modifier to its stack. Switch to the Front view and create a *closed* Spline object beneath a turret as shown in Figure 3-1226.

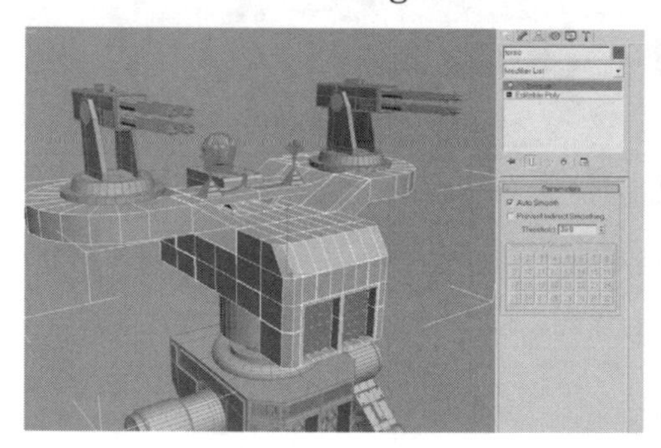
Figure 3-1225

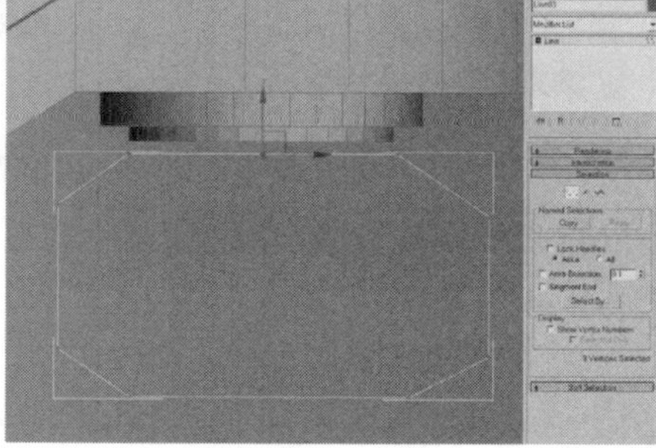
Figure 3-1226

33. Add an Edit Spline modifier to the stack and Clone the spline twice. Select the rearmost spline and Uniform Scale it down to **50** percent.

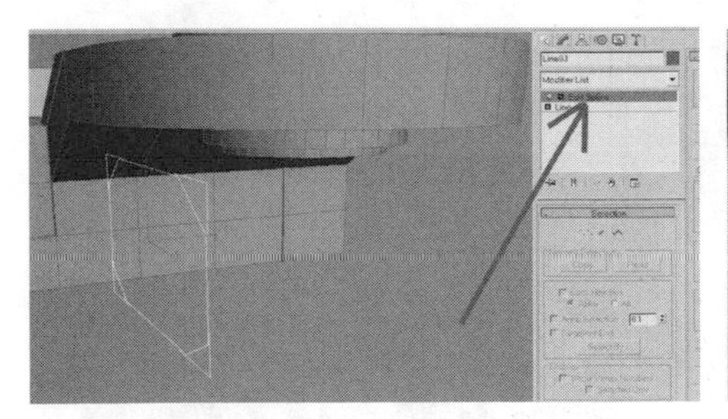

Figure 3-1227

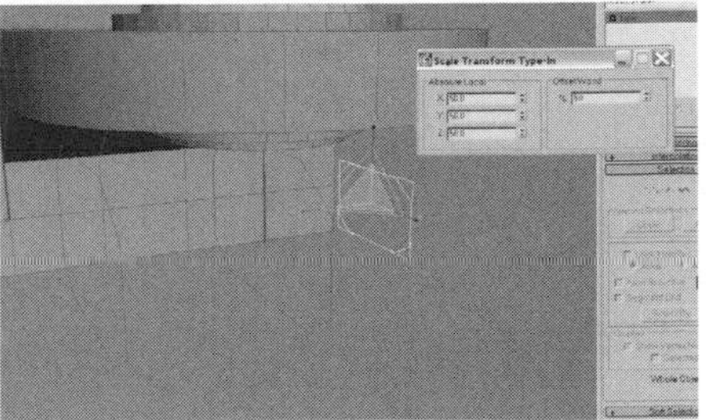

Figure 3-1228

FYI: To make the cannon nacelle, we'll use a CrossSection modifier. The CrossSection modifier requires the Edit Spline modifier be applied, the splines arranged in sequence, and the CrossSection moditier added on top.

34. Switch to the Right viewport and raise the rear spline in the Y axis, until it is centered vertically behind the middle spline. Uniform Scale the last spline to **70**.

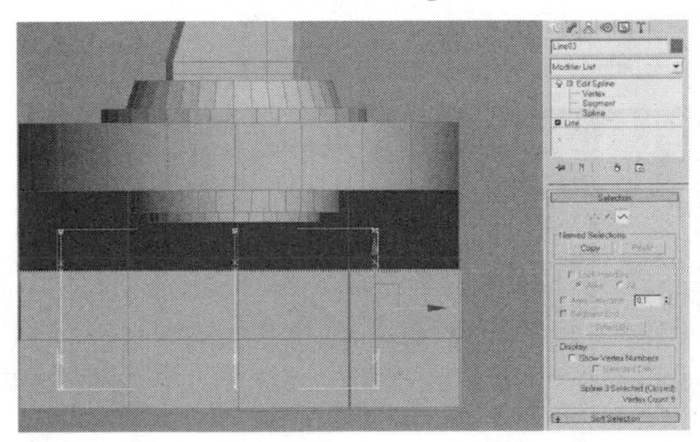

Figure 3-1229

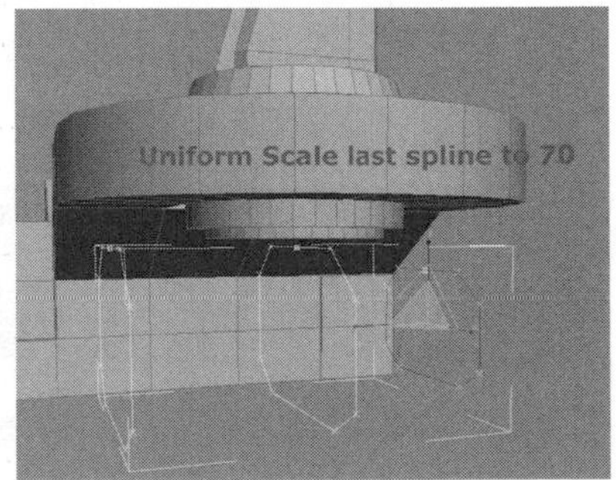

Figure 3-1230

35. Add a CrossSection modifier to the top of the stack. Add a Surface modifier to the top of the stack to "skin" it.

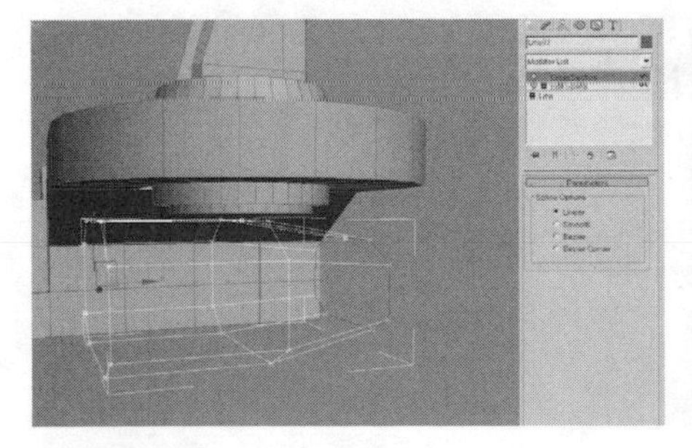

Figure 3-1231

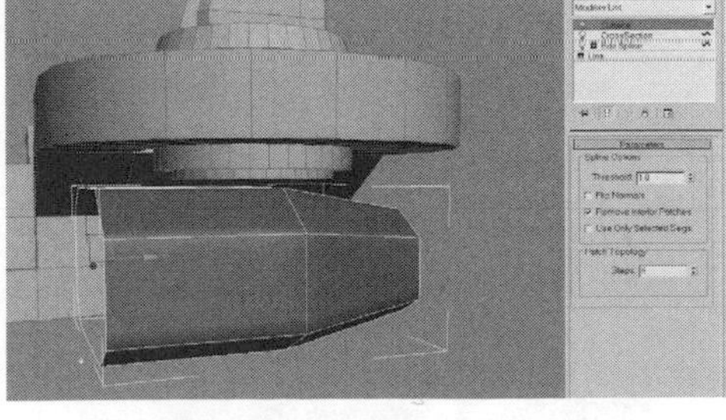

Figure 3-1232

36. Add an Edit Poly modifier to the top of the stack so we can cap the holes. Select the borders and Cap them.

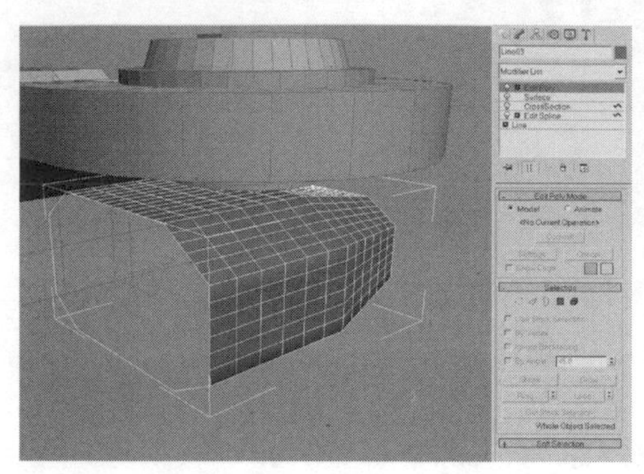

Figure 3-1233

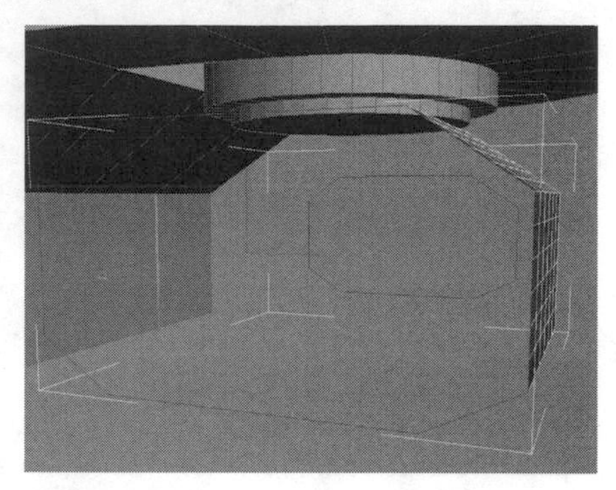

Figure 3-1234

37. Select the caps and Bevel them:

Type	Height	Outline	Apply/OK
Group	0	–20	Apply
Group	–28	0	OK

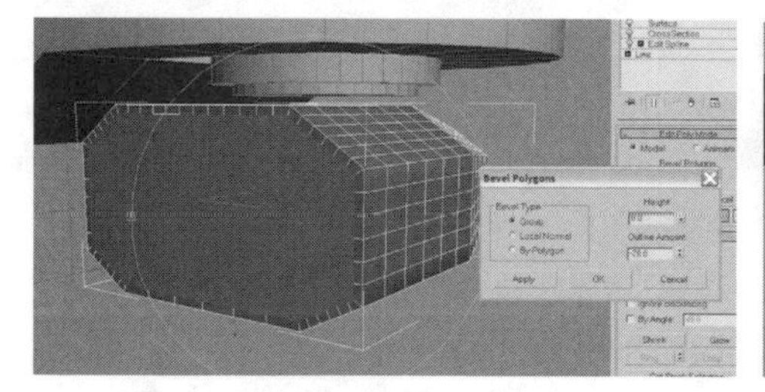

Figure 3-1235

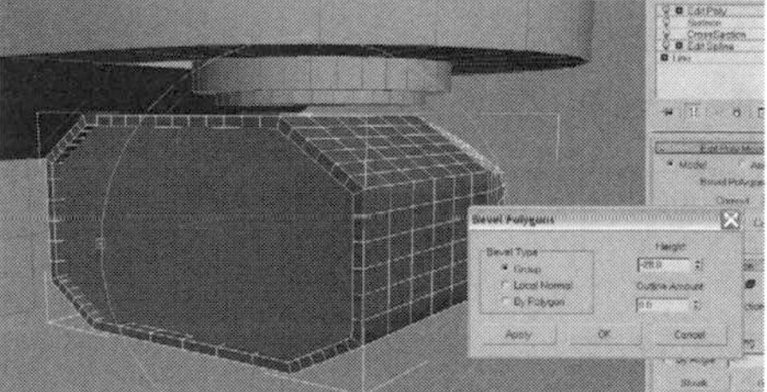

Figure 3-1236

38. Loop-select the two edges beneath the turret. Click **Create Shape** and name it **cannon_stanchions**. Uniform Scale the shapes up to **112** and set the Thickness to **95** with **4** Sides, and choose **Enable In Viewport** and **Enable In Renderer**. Select and Link the stanchions and nacelles to the turret.

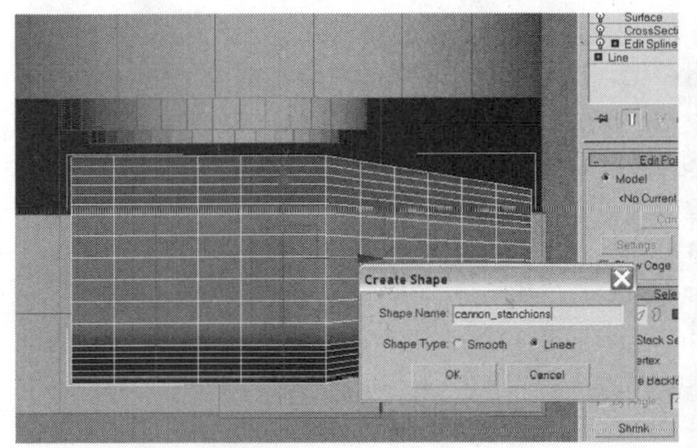

Figure 3-1237

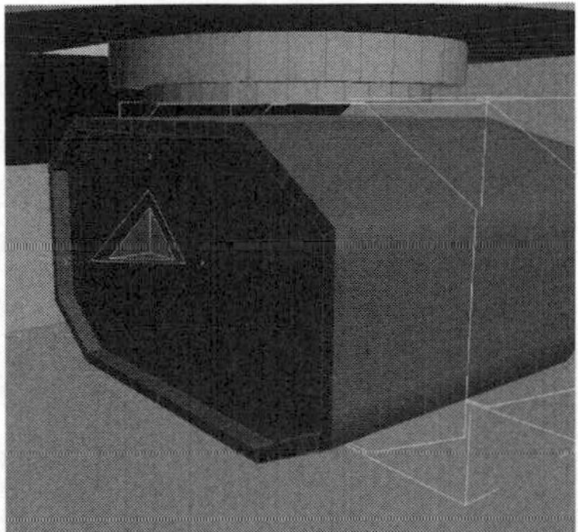

Figure 3-1238

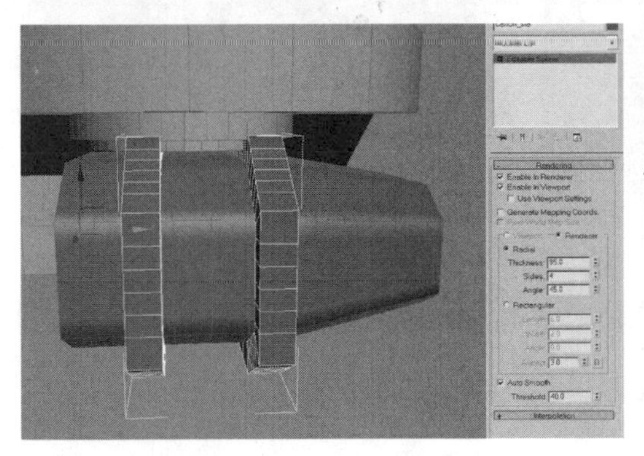

Figure 3-1239

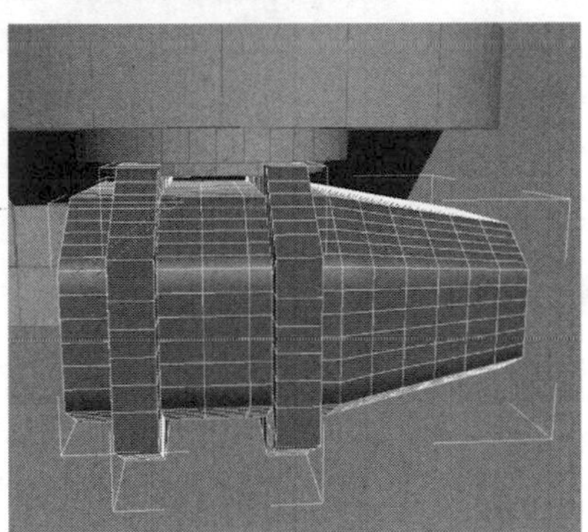

Figure 3-1240

39. To add more machine lines to the smooth sides of the cannon_stanchions, select the edges shown in Figure 3-1241. Extrude them **–5** with a Base Width of **1.2.**

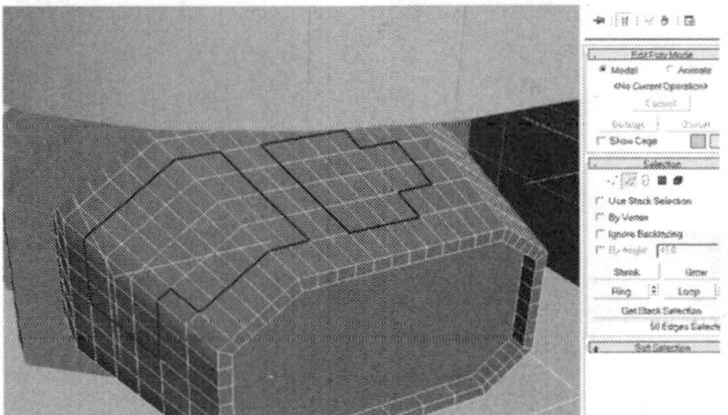

Figure 3-1241

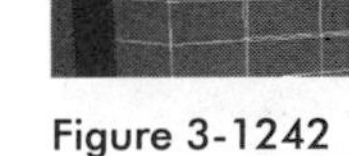

Figure 3-1242

40. Now hide everything except the right gun turret. Switch to the Right viewport and create a Spline like the one shown below. Add a Lathe modifier to the stack, set the Direction to **X**, under Align click the **Min** button, and set the output to either **NURBS** or Patch. I selected NURBS because that gives you a smooth output. (Note: Patch would give you an equally smooth output. The only real difference comes in if you want to model or edit the form, but I'm not going to so it makes little difference.) Click the Lathe modifier, click **Axis**, and move the axis cursor down in the Y axis until the cannon is the width you want.

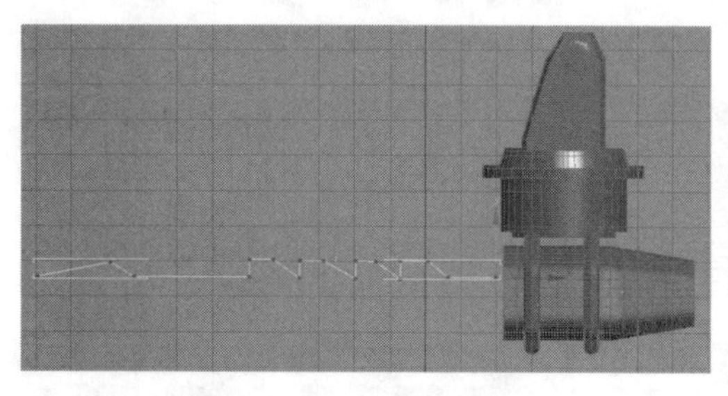

Figure 3-1243

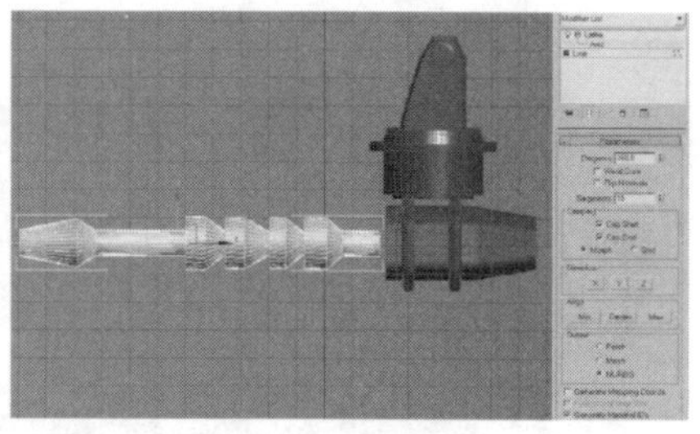

Figure 3-1244

41. Right-click the spline and choose **Convert to NURBS** to collapse the stack. Switch to the Front view and Clone to make a second cannon.

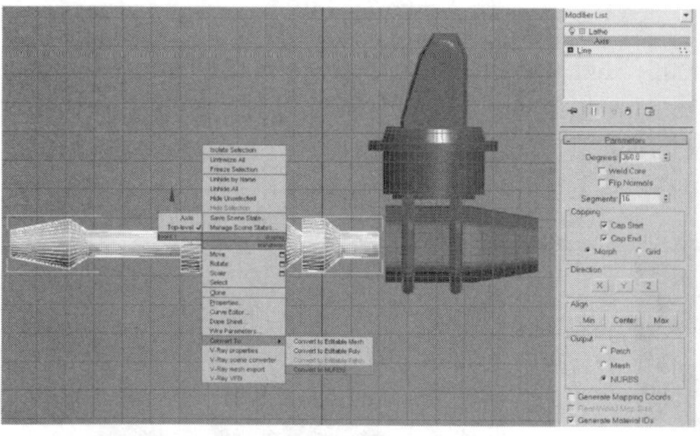

Figure 3-1245

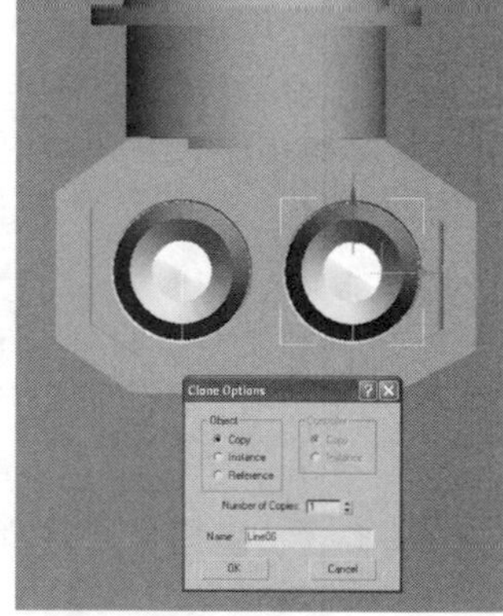

Figure 3-1246

42. Move both cannons into the nacelles. Unhide All. Select both cannons and Mirror-copy them with an Offset of **–2350** (or whatever value gets them centered on the left nacelle). Select and Link the cannons to their respective nacelles.

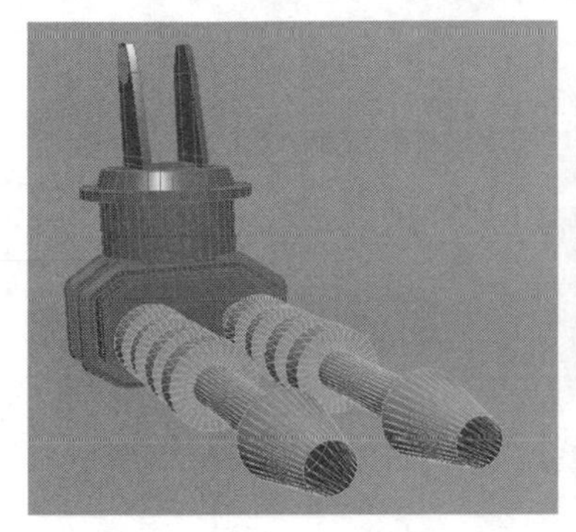

Figure 3-1247

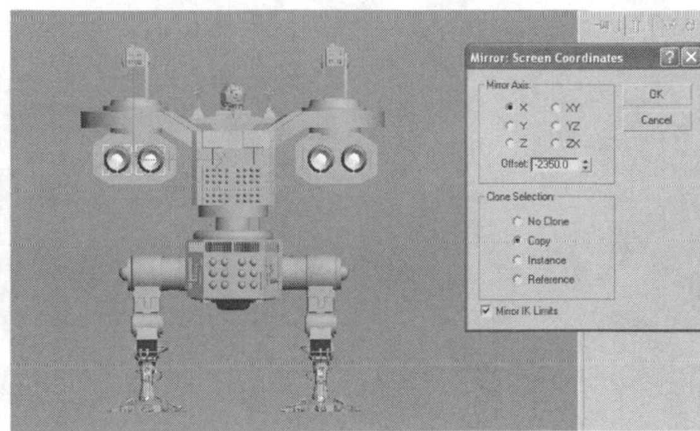

Figure 3-1248

43. Apply your materials and render.

Figure 3-1249

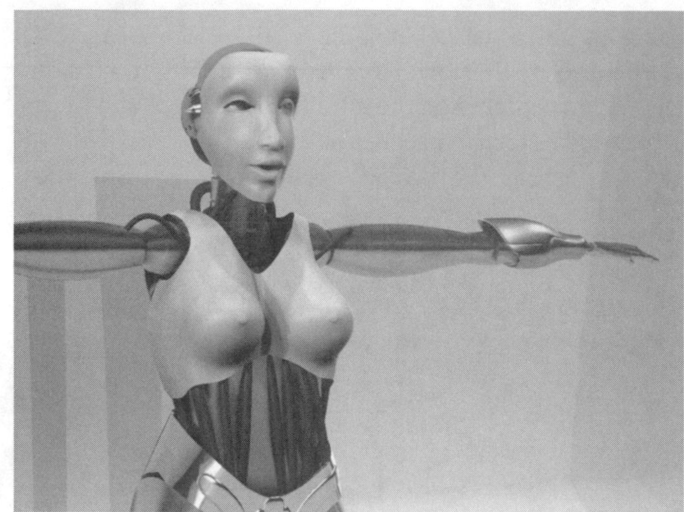

This is the android we create in Chapter 4.

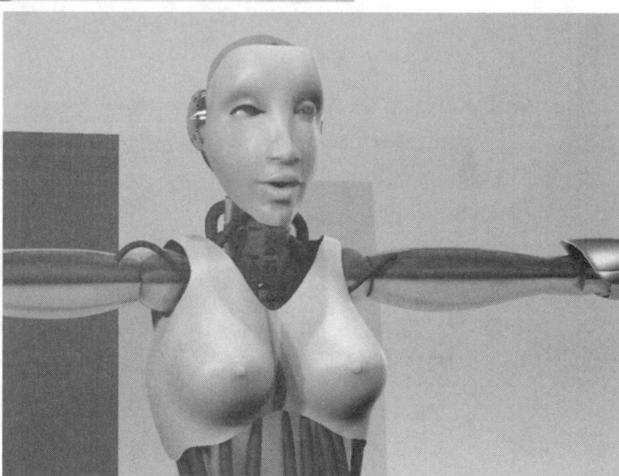

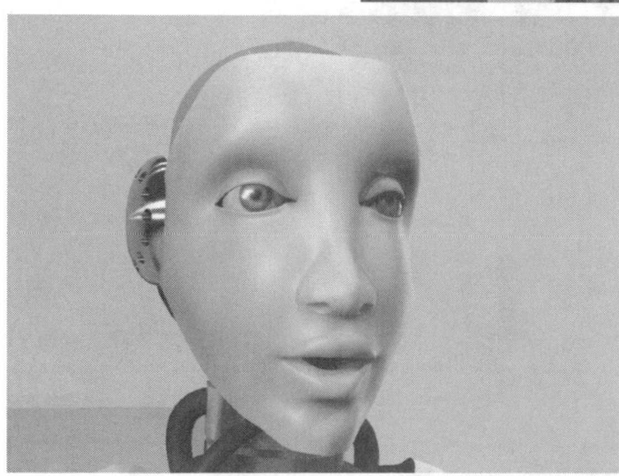

Chapter 4
Maxi the Android

I, Robot, *A.I.*, *The Terminator*, *Bicentennial Man*, *Blade Runner*, and the list goes on. Androids are a staple of science fiction books and films and have been since the origin of the term "Robot" in 1920, in Karel Capek's play *Rossum's Universal Robots*.

In this chapter, you will model a female android. But you better get a snack and get comfortable. This chapter was so big and detailed that it didn't fit into the book and had to be put on the DVD instead. And . . . rumor has it, drove an entire editorial team into rehab, but that's just a cruel and unsubstantiated rumor. ;p Nevertheless, at over 300 pages, this chapter is the size of most books, with twice the amount of learning of those "other" brands! When you've finished this chapter, you'll be highly edumacated.

So why is the chapter so long? Because I don't skip steps. There are over 1,200 full-color illustrations. Organic modeling requires more tweaking than hard surface modeling. Why? Because, like an aging supermodel, an organic model shows every bump and imperfection. So, like an aging supermodel, an organic model needs a lot of nipping and tucking.

So what can you expect in this chapter? Here's a preview.

FYI: The entire 306-page chapter is a full-color PDF file located on the companion DVD in the Chapter 4 folder and is called Chapter4_MaxiTheAndroid.pdf.

Day 1: Maxi's Head

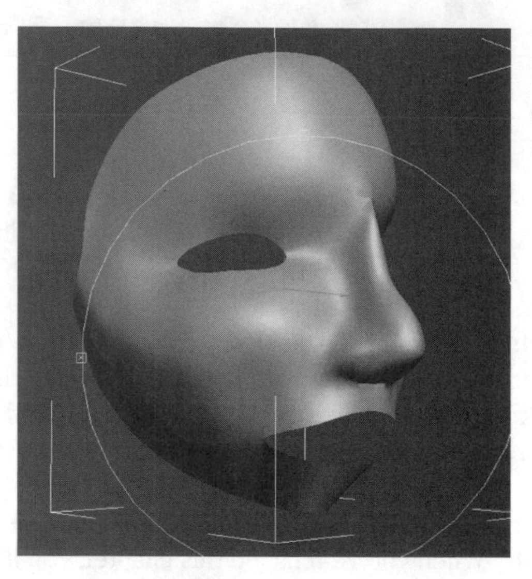

You'll set up image planes and rough out Maxi's head and face plate by extruding edges.

Day 2: Refining Maxi's Face

On the second day, you'll refine the face plate by tweaking vertices. For example, you can see in this figure that the eye sockets are too wide, there's a pinch at the bridge of the nose, and she has leech lips. That is the sort of thing you'll fix by moving subobjects such as vertices.

Day 3: Further Refining Maxi's Face

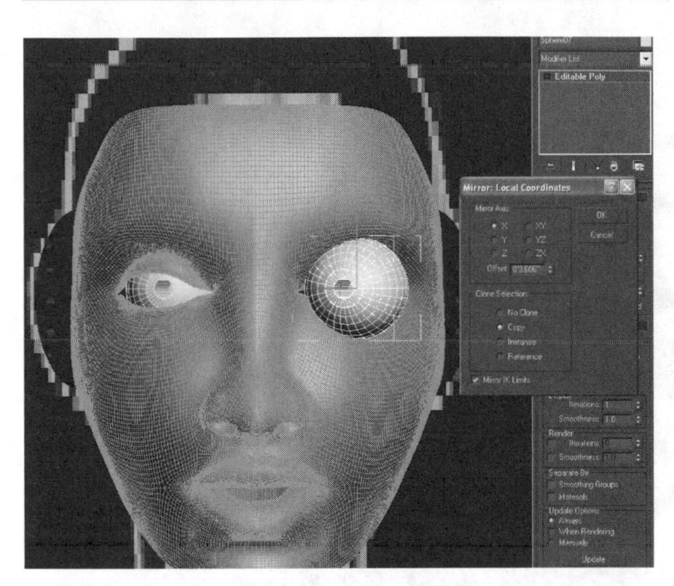

Day 3 finds us finishing up the refinements of Maxi's face plate, creating the back of Maxi's head, adding her eyes, and adding the microphones that make up Maxi's ears.

Day 4: Maxi's Chest

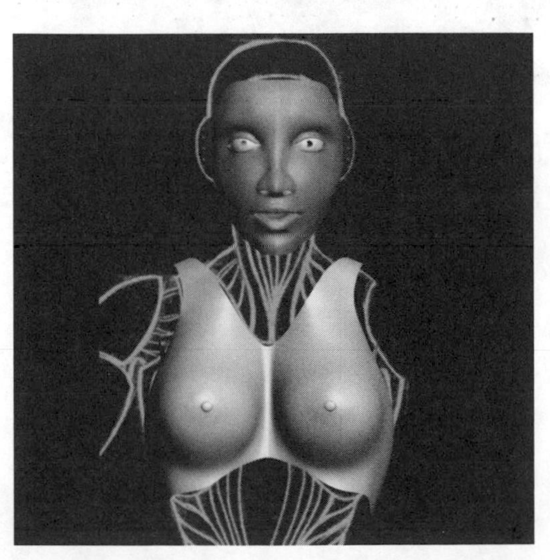

On the fourth day, we begin roughing out Maxi's torso by starting with the breastplate. Like Maxi's head, this will require us to use subobject manipulation, smoothing, and the Symmetry modifier.

Day 5: Maxi's Rear

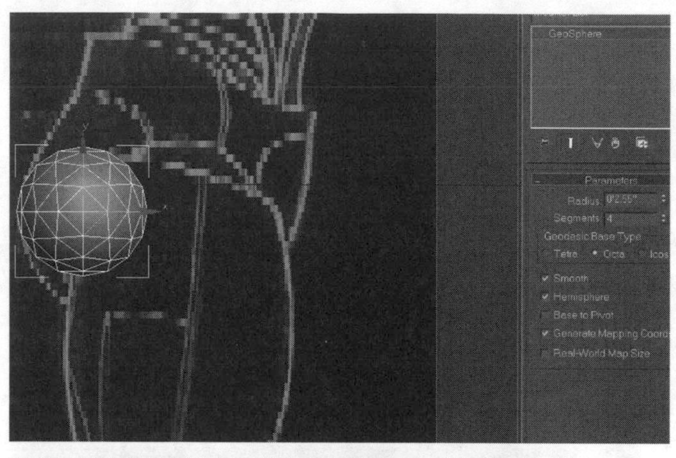

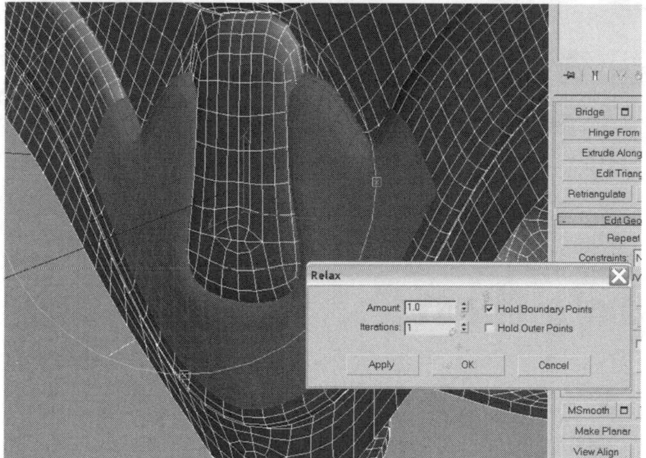

This day consists of using geospheres to create Maxi's butt and pelvic area, and introduces you to the very handy Relax modifier.

Day 6: Maxi's Legs and Feet

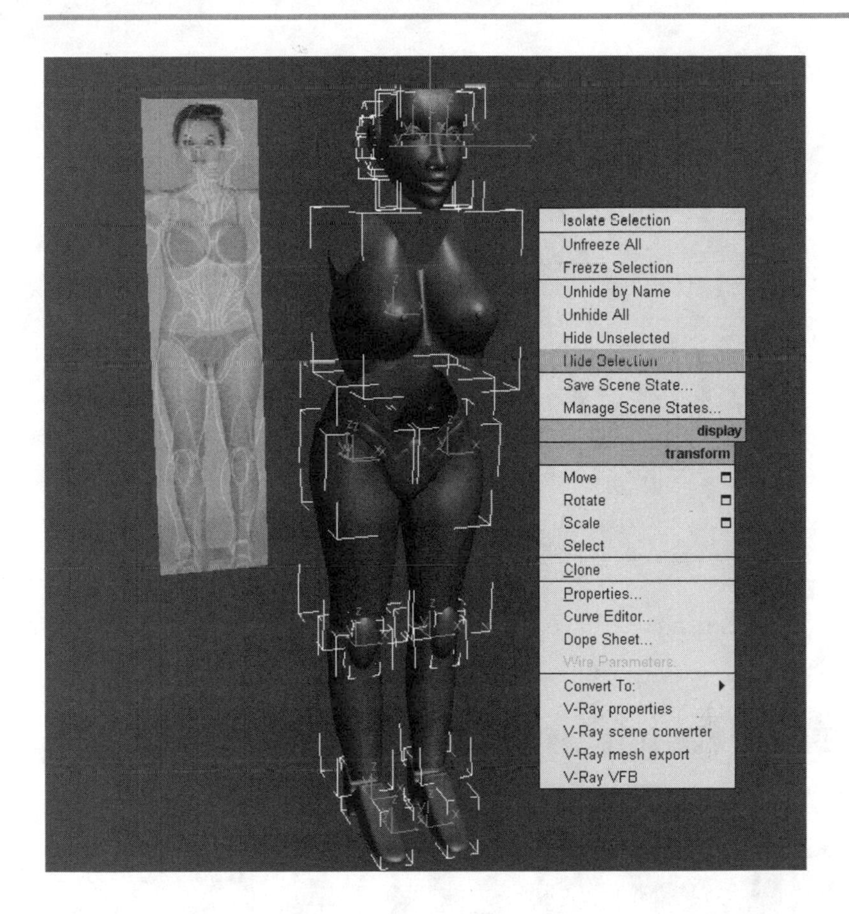

Next, we'll be putting some legs and feet on Maxi, and start to give her a more "human female" shape by using some stock photos as a reference.

Day 7: Maxi's Arms and Hands

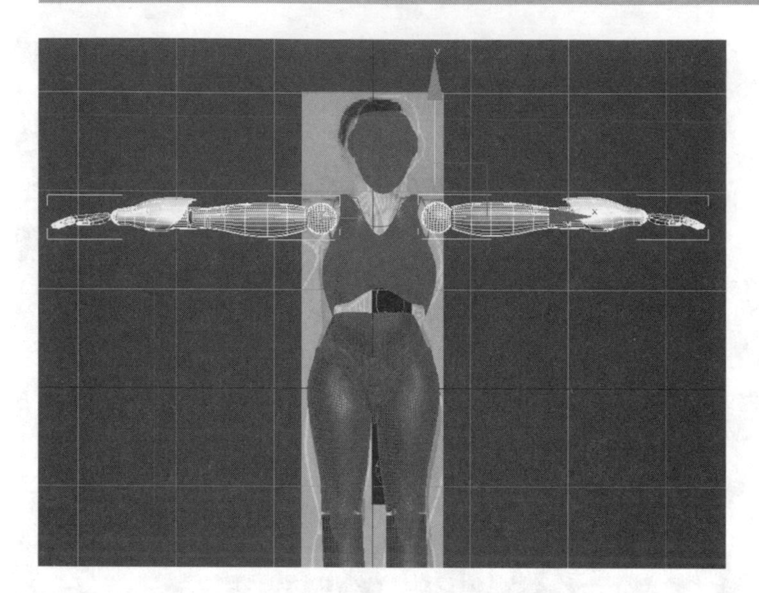

By the end of the week, you'll have modeled Maxi's hands and arms.

Day 8: Finishing the Torso

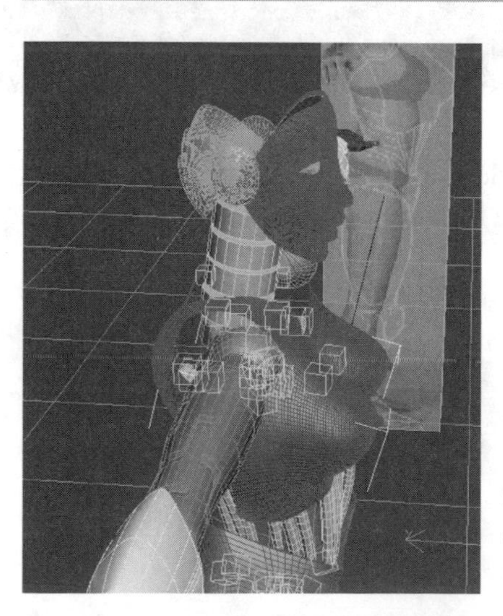

We'll wrap things up on Day 8 by giving Maxi some backbone and wiring everything together with some thick cabling and hydraulic tubing.

I hope you enjoy making Maxi as much as I enjoyed writing this chapter!

The complete text for this chapter is on the companion DVD and is called **Chapter4_MaxiTheAndroid.pdf.**

Index

About the Companion DVD

The companion DVD includes all the images in the book in full color, a PDF version of a chapter on creating an android, and video tutorials totaling 10 hours. The files are organized in the following folders:

- Chapter 4 — A PDF of Chapter 4, "Maxi the Android," and reference images used to create the android
- Images — Full-color versions of all the images in the book, compressed and organized by chapter
- Materials — Three videos showing how to create and work with materials, along with support files
- MATRIX — A tutorial from 3-d Palace demonstrating the modeling and animation of the devastating sentinel bots from the film *The Matrix*
- max script — A MAXScript file used in Chapter 3 to paint rivets on armor

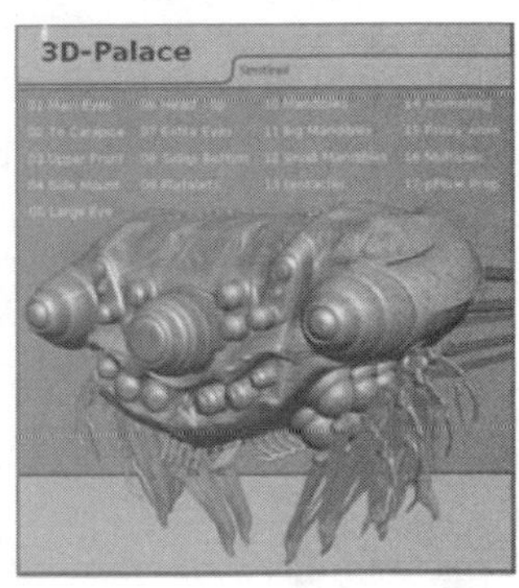

Warning: By opening the DVD package, you accept the terms and conditions of the DVD/Source Code Usage License Agreement on the following page.

Additionally, opening the DVD package makes this book nonreturnable.

DVD/Source Code Usage License Agreement

Please read the following DVD/Source Code usage license agreement before opening the DVD and using the contents therein:

1. By opening the accompanying software package, you are indicating that you have read and agree to be bound by all terms and conditions of this DVD/Source Code usage license agreement.
2. The compilation of code and utilities contained on the DVD and in the book are copyrighted and protected by both U.S. copyright law and international copyright treaties, and is owned by Wordware Publishing, Inc. Individual source code, example programs, help files, freeware, shareware, utilities, and evaluation packages, including their copyrights, are owned by the respective authors.
3. No part of the enclosed DVD or this book, including all source code, help files, shareware, freeware, utilities, example programs, or evaluation programs, may be made available on a public forum (such as a World Wide Web page, FTP site, bulletin board, or Internet news group) without the express written permission of Wordware Publishing, Inc. or the author of the respective source code, help files, shareware, freeware, utilities, example programs, or evaluation programs.
4. You may not decompile, reverse engineer, disassemble, create a derivative work, or otherwise use the enclosed programs, help files, freeware, shareware, utilities, or evaluation programs except as stated in this agreement.
5. The software, contained on the DVD and/or as source code in this book, is sold without warranty of any kind. Wordware Publishing, Inc. and the authors specifically disclaim all other warranties, express or implied, including but not limited to implied warranties of merchantability and fitness for a particular purpose with respect to defects in the disk, the program, source code, sample files, help files, freeware, shareware, utilities, and evaluation programs contained therein, and/or the techniques described in the book and implemented in the example programs. In no event shall Wordware Publishing, Inc., its dealers, its distributors, or the authors be liable or held responsible for any loss of profit or any other alleged or actual private or commercial damage, including but not limited to special, incidental, consequential, or other damages.
6. One (1) copy of the DVD or any source code therein may be created for backup purposes. The DVD and all accompanying source code, sample files, help files, freeware, shareware, utilities, and evaluation programs may be copied to your hard drive. With the exception of freeware and shareware programs, at no time can any part of the contents of this DVD reside on more than one computer at one time. The contents of the DVD can be copied to another computer, as long as the contents of the DVD contained on the original computer are deleted.
7. You may not include any part of the DVD contents, including all source code, example programs, shareware, freeware, help files, utilities, or evaluation programs in any compilation of source code, utilities, help files, example programs, freeware, shareware, or evaluation programs on any media, including but not limited to DVD, disk, or Internet distribution, without the express written permission of Wordware Publishing, Inc. or the owner of the individual source code, utilities, help files, example programs, freeware, shareware, or evaluation programs.
8. You may use the source code, techniques, and example programs in your own commercial or private applications unless otherwise noted by additional usage agreements as found on the DVD.

Warning: By opening the DVD package, you accept the terms and conditions of the DVD/Source Code Usage License Agreement.
Additionally, opening the DVD package makes this book nonreturnable.